THE BICENTENNIAL EDITION
OF THE
WORKS OF JOHN WESLEY

General Editor RICHARD P. HEITZENRATER

Textual Editor FRANK BAKER

THE WORKS OF
JOHN WESLEY

VOLUME 10

THE
METHODIST
SOCIETIES

THE MINUTES OF CONFERENCE

EDITED BY

HENRY D. RACK

ABINGDON PRESS

NASHVILLE

2011

THE WORKS OF JOHN WESLEY, VOLUME 10
THE METHODIST SOCIETIES: THE MINUTES OF CONFERENCE

Copyright © 2011 by Abingdon Press

This book is printed on acid-free paper.

Library of Congress Cataloging-in-Publication Data

The Methodist societies : the minutes of Conference / edited by Henry D. Rack.
  p. cm. — (The Bicentennial edition of the works of John Wesley ; v. 10)
  "A critical and annotated text of the whole of the surviving minutes, manuscript and printed [of the Conference of the Methodist Church of Great Britain] along with such evidence as could be found of the proceedings of Conference during the 'lost years' and of early meetings with the Calvinistic Methodists"—Pref.
  Includes bibliographical references and index.
  ISBN 978-1-4267-1190-9 (book - hardback/paper over boards : alk. paper)
  1. Methodist Church (Great Britain)—Congresses. 2. Wesley, John, 1703–1791. I. Rack, Henry D. II. Methodist Church (Great Britain). Conference.
  BX8276.M465 2011
  262'.07509033—dc22

2010042482

Unless otherwise noted, scripture quotations are taken from the Authorized Version of the Bible.

The Graeca® font used to print this work is available from Linguist's Software, Inc., P.O. Box 580, Edmonds, WA 98020-0580; telephone (206) 775-1130.

The MS Diary of Howell Harris, relating to his attendance at the Wesleyan Conferences in the 1740s, appears by permission of Llyfrgell Genedlaethol Cymru/The National Library of Wales.

11 12 13 14 15 16 17 18 19 20—10 9 8 7 6 5 4 3 2 1

MANUFACTURED IN THE UNITED STATES OF AMERICA

THE BICENTENNIAL EDITION OF
THE WORKS OF JOHN WESLEY

THIS edition of the works of John Wesley reflects the quickened interest in the heritage of Christian thought that has become evident during the last half century. A fully critical presentation of Wesley's writings had long been a desideratum in order to furnish documentary sources illustrating his contribution to both catholic and evangelical Christianity.

Several scholars, notably Professor Albert C. Outler, Professor Franz Hildebrandt, Dean Merrimon Cuninggim, and Dean Robert E. Cushman, discussed the possibility of such an edition. Under the leadership of Dean Cushman, a Board of Directors was formed in 1960 comprising the deans of four sponsoring theological schools of Methodist-related universities in the United States: Drew, Duke, Emory, and Southern Methodist. They appointed an Editorial Committee to formulate plans and enlisted an international and interdenominational team of scholars for the Wesley Works Editorial Project.

The works were divided into units of cognate material, with a separate editor (or joint editors) responsible for each unit. Dr. Frank Baker was appointed textual editor for the whole project, with responsibility for supplying each unit editor with a critically developed, accurate Wesley text. The text seeks to represent Wesley's thought in its fullest and most deliberate expression insofar as this can be determined from the available evidence. Substantive variant readings in any British edition published during Wesley's lifetime are shown in appendices to the units, preceded by a summary of the problems faced and the solutions reached in the complex task of securing and presenting Wesley's text. The aim throughout is to enable Wesley to be read with maximum ease and understanding, and with minimal intrusion by the editors.

This edition includes all Wesley's original or mainly original prose works, together with one volume devoted to his *Collection of Hymns* (1780) and another to his extensive work as editor and publisher of extracts from the writings of others. An essential feature of the project is a Bibliography outlining the historical settings of the works

v

published by Wesley and his brother Charles, sometimes jointly, sometimes separately. The Bibliography also offers full analytical data for identifying each of the two thousand editions of these 450 items that were published during the lifetime of John Wesley, and notes the location of copies. An index is supplied for each unit and a General Index for the whole edition.

The Delegates of the Oxford University Press agreed to undertake publication, but announced in June 1982 that because of severe economic problems, they would regretfully be compelled to withdraw from the enterprise with the completion in 1983 of volume 7, the *Collection of Hymns*. Abingdon Press offered its services, beginning with the publication of the first volume of the *Sermons* in 1984, the bicentennial year of the formation of American Methodism as an autonomous church. The new title now assumed, however, refers in general to the bicentennial of Wesley's total activities as author, editor, and publisher, from 1733 to 1791, especially as summarized in the first edition of his collected works in thirty-two volumes, 1771–74.

Dean Robert E. Cushman of Duke University undertook general administration and promotion of the project until 1971, when he was succeeded as President by Dean Joseph D. Quillian Jr. of Southern Methodist University, these two universities having furnished the major support and guidance for the enterprise. During the decade 1961–70, the Editorial Committee supervised the task of setting editorial principles and procedures, and general editorship was shared by Dr. Eric W. Baker, Dean William R. Cannon, and Dean Cushman. In 1969 the Directors appointed Dr. Frank Baker, early attached to the project as bibliographer and textual editor for Wesley's text, as Editor-in-Chief also. Upon Dean Quillian's retirement in 1981, he was succeeded as President of the project by Dean James E. Kirby Jr., also of Southern Methodist University. In 1986 the Directors appointed Richard P. Heitzenrater as General Editor to begin the chief editorship of the project with the *Journal and Diaries* unit. Subsequent presiding officers have been Dennis M. Campbell of Duke University, Russell E. Richey of Emory University, and William B. Lawrence of Southern Methodist University. Randy Maddox began as Associate General Editor in 2005.

Other sponsoring bodies have been successively added to the original four: Boston University School of Theology, the Conference of the Methodist Church of Great Britain, the Commission on Archives and History of The United Methodist Church, The

United Methodist Board of Higher Education and Ministry, and the World Methodist Council. For the continuing support of the sponsoring institutions, the Directors express their profound thanks. They also gratefully acknowledge the encouragement and financial support that have come from the Historical Societies and Commissions on Archives and History of many Annual Conferences, as well as the donations of the World Methodist Council, the British Methodist Church, private individuals, and foundations.

On June 9, 1976, the Wesley Works Editorial Project was incorporated in the state of North Carolina as a nonprofit corporation. In 1977, by-laws were approved governing the appointment and duties of the Directors, their Officers, and their Executive Committee.

The Board of Directors

President: William B. Lawrence, Dean of Perkins School of Theology, Southern Methodist University, Dallas, Texas

Vice President: Russell E. Richey, Candler School of Theology, Emory University, Atlanta, Georgia

Treasurer: L. Gregory Jones, Dean of the Divinity School, Duke University, Durham, North Carolina

General Editor: Richard P. Heitzenrater, the Divinity School, Duke University, Durham, North Carolina

Associate General Editor and Secretary: Randy L. Maddox, the Divinity School, Duke University, Durham, North Carolina

M. Kathryn Armistead, Editor, Abingdon Press, Nashville, Tennessee

Maxine Clarke Beach, Dean of the Theological School of Drew University, Madison, New Jersey

Dennis M. Campbell, Woodberry Forest School, Woodberry Forest, Virginia

Kenneth L. Carder, Bishop of The United Methodist Church

George H. Freeman, General Secretary of the World Methodist Council, Lake Junaluska, North Carolina

Jan Love, Dean of Candler School of Theology, Emory University, Atlanta, Georgia

Mary Ann Moman, Associate General Secretary of the Division of the Ordained Ministry, the United Methodist Board of Higher Education and Ministry, Nashville, Tennessee

Mary Elizabeth Moore, Dean of Boston University School of Theology, Boston, Massachusetts

Robert J. Williams, General Secretary of the General Commission on Archives and History of The United Methodist Church, Drew University, Madison, New Jersey

CONTENTS

PREFACE

SOME explanation of the principles and purpose in mind for this volume is necessary. It may seem odd to include a set of *Minutes* as part of Wesley's *Works*, but the imprint of his style is unmistakable in these *Minutes*. How far they represent his unchallenged and unamended opinions is a more complicated question, which will be discussed in the introduction. But in any case, the *Minutes*, it will be seen, are not simply records of decisions but include many other matters of various kinds drafted by Wesley himself.

Although Wesley distilled a quantity of material from the annual *Minutes* and published this in the form of Doctrinal, Disciplinary, and 'Large' *Minutes*, the only collected edition of these editions hitherto has been that of 1862. The Wesley Historical Society published the early manuscript Minutes many years ago. The present edition is the first to produce a critical and annotated text of the whole of the surviving *Minutes*, manuscript and printed, along with such evidence as could be found of the proceedings of Conference during the 'lost years' and of early meetings with the Calvinistic Methodists.

This task has inevitably resulted in a very bulky volume, and some omissions were unavoidable to save space. It was decided to omit the American *Minutes* partly because they were in no sense Wesley's own work and partly because they could not at present be edited up to the standard required here. The Irish *Minutes* are included in an appendix, since they are in substantial proportion also Wesley's work, though some were produced under Dr. Coke. The original design of the volume was to include brief biographies of all individuals (mainly the travelling preachers) mentioned in the records, as in other volumes in this series. But the numbers involved were too prodigal of space, and John Lenton has published a separate work[1] that catalogues all the early preachers, much improving previous lists of this kind and providing basic details of their Methodist careers. Those individuals who have been given biographical

---

[1] John Lenton, *John Wesley's Preachers* (Milton Keynes: Paternoster Press, 2009).

notes here are mainly, first, Anglican clergy and laypersons associated with Methodism or who are otherwise significant figures, and second, local preachers, unless they subsequently became itinerants (and are thus included in Lenton's work). Many of these men, however, are obscure persons of whom little is known. Third, a few itinerants, such as John Bennet, are given a note because of their significance in Wesley's life or the affairs of Methodism. The editors regret that the selection is rather arbitrary and could have legitimately been extended to more leading preachers, but space precluded doing more than indicate their significance at particular points.

The main purpose of the present volume has been not only to reproduce the *Minutes* as a formal record, but also, through the introduction and the information supplied in the notes, to convey something of the nature and role of the Conference in Methodist life and polity. This design has meant that for the period before the *Minutes* began to be published in 1765, we have not only reproduced the surviving manuscript Minutes but also collected such material as we could from other sources to show what happened on the occasions when no Minutes survive. In addition, for each year of the printed *Minutes*, 'note 1' includes collected information about the proceedings and background, which sometimes includes debates not recorded in the *Minutes*. This information comes mainly from letters and diaries of the preachers as well as from John Wesley himself. Particularly helpful on this point has been the material (some now lost) copied by Tyerman in his manuscripts in the Methodist Archives. Although a fair amount of this material is scattered in various printed volumes, some is newly published here. Thereby some sense of the Conference as a living occasion may be given that could not be gained from the *Minutes* alone. The material for the pre-1765 years for which no Minutes survive is particularly valuable in this regard. Section 7 of the introduction draws further on this material to throw some light on one of the most obscure aspects of these meetings—the extent to which they were dominated by Wesley, how far there were real debates, and how far the decisions were influenced by the preachers. Also, by sometimes ranging beyond the proceedings of the meeting itself, the introduction tries to show how the Conference related to the rest of the Methodist polity. That additional material also highlights some problems that arose in the meeting itself, which in Wesley's eyes was merely summoned to advise him but in his later years almost imperceptibly became more of a legislative and ruling body, increasingly preoccupied with what would happen after Wesley's death. At the same time, the Conference had to struggle with the problem of how to supply the place of an executive between Conferences, a role that Wesley had largely supplied in his own person.

· · · · · · · · · · · ·

This volume was originally to have been edited by Dr. John Bowmer, and I am grateful for the use of a few notes that he compiled. My greatest debt, however, is to the late Professor Frank Baker. As usual, he supplied not only a meticulous text but also numerous notes and suggestions for notes on the content of the *Minutes*, together with introductions to the MS Minutes, the Doctrinal and Disciplinary *Minutes*, the 'Large' *Minutes*, and the Irish *Minutes*. Although I take final responsibility for the finished work and the general introduction is largely by me, many of the notes originate with Professor Baker. Others were suggested by him but executed by me. Some I have abbreviated or revised, though a substantial number I have introduced myself. My hope is that this collaboration has helped us cater to more interests than might have been the case with a single editor.

Professor Baker wished to acknowledge the help of Mrs. Enid Hickingbotham in some calculations of membership losses from 1779 onwards. I would like to acknowledge the help of John Lenton in identifying some elusive preachers.

Howell Harris's MS diaries deposited in the National Library of Wales, Aberystwyth, give unique information on the proceedings during the visit to the Welsh Calvinistic Methodist Association in January 1767, the Conference of January 1768, the attempt at union in 1769, and the Conferences of August 1760 and July 1763. Professor Baker collated some published and unpublished transcription of extracts from the diaries, mainly from the work of Tom Beynon and Griffith T. Roberts. I have corrected these from the original MSS and added a few short passages. I am indebted to the Reverend J. E. Wynne Roberts, curator of the Calvinistic Methodist Archives, for permission to use and reproduce these extracts.

The admirable edition of Wesley's *Journal & Diaries* (volumes 18–24 in this series), edited by W. Reginald Ward and Richard P. Heitzenrater, has been constantly to hand and has greatly helped, especially with biographical details. I would thank Professor

Heitzenrater, in addition to the task of final copyediting, for contributing material (notably in the introduction) especially related to the features of Methodist organization during the early years of its development. And for many years, I have been served most helpfully and cheerfully by the staff of the John Rylands University Library in Manchester, both from the Methodist Archives and from their own collections. Finally, but most importantly, I must apologize to colleagues and potential readers for the long delay in producing this volume, and in this connection I am grateful to Professor Heitzenrater, as general editor of the Bicentennial Edition, for patiently bearing with me and encouraging me to continue.

H. D. R.

SIGNS, SPECIAL USAGES, ABBREVIATIONS

[ ]	Indicates editorial insertions or substitutions in the original text, or (with a query) doubtful readings.
< >	Indicates conjectural readings in manuscripts where the original text is defective.
. . .	Indicates a passage omitted by the writer from the original and so noted by Wesley, usually by a dash.
[. . .]	Indicates a passage omitted silently by Wesley from a text he was quoting, to which the present editor is drawing attention; the brackets are not used in editorial annotations and introductions.
(( ))	Encloses passages within a manuscript struck through for erasure.
[[ ]]	Encloses passages supplied by the present editors from cipher or shorthand, from an abstract or similar document in the third person, or reconstructed from secondary evidence.
a, b, c	Small superscript letters indicate footnotes supplied by Wesley.
1, 2, 3	Small superscript figures indicate footnotes supplied by the editor.
Cf.	Before a scriptural or other citation by Wesley, indicates that he was quoting with more than minimal inexactness, yet nevertheless displaying the passage as a quotation.
See	Before a scriptural citation, indicates an undoubted allusion or a quotation that was not displayed as such by Wesley, and that is more than minimally inexact.

Wesley's publications. Where a work by Wesley was first published separately, its title is italicized; where it first appeared within a different work such as a collected volume, the title appears within quotation marks. References such as '*Bibliography*, No. 3' are to the forthcoming bibliography in this edition (vols. 33–34), which has a different numbering system from Richard Green's *Wesley Bibliography*.

Book titles in Wesley's text are italicized if accurate, and given in roman type with capitals if inaccurate. If a title consists of only one generic word that forms a major part of the original title, it is italicized; but if it is inaccurate (such as 'Sermons' for a volume titled *Discourses*), it is printed in lowercase roman.

Abbreviations. In addition to many common and fairly obvious abbreviations, the following are used in the notes: *A[nswer]*, *Q[uestion]*, JW (John Wesley, 1703–91), CW (Charles Wesley), edn. (edition), SPCK (Society for Promoting Christian Knowledge), SPG (Society for the Propagation of the Gospel).

Works and institutions frequently cited are abbreviated thus:

AM	John Wesley, *Arminian Magazine* (1778–97), cont. as *Methodist Magazine* (1798–1821) and *Wesleyan Methodist Magazine* (1822–1913).
BCP	The Book of Common Prayer, London, 1662.
Bibliography	Frank Baker, *A Descriptive and Analytical Bibliography of the Publications of John and Charles Wesley* (in preparation), vols. 33–34 in this edn.
CJ	Conference Journal.
CWJ	Thomas Jackson, ed., *The Journal of the Rev. Charles Wesley, M.A.*, 2 vols., London: Wesleyan Methodist Bookroom, 1849.
DEB	*Dictionary of Evangelical Biography*, ed. D. M. Lewis, 2 vols. (Oxford, 1995).
DNB	Sir Leslie Stephen, and Sir Sidney Lee, eds., *The Dictionary of National Biography*, 22 vols., Oxford: Oxford University Press, 1921–22.
Journal (Curnock)	*The Journal of the Rev. John Wesley*, ed. Nehemiah Curnock, 8 vols., London: Epworth Press, 1909–16.
JRUL	John Rylands University Library, Manchester.
Letters (Telford)	*The Letters of the Rev. John Wesley*, ed. John Telford, 8 vols., London: Sharp, 1931.
MA	Methodist Archives, John Rylands University Library of Manchester.
MM	*Methodist Magazine* (London, 1798–1821).
OED	Sir James A. H. Murray et al., *A New English Dictionary on Historical Principles*, 11 vols., Oxford, Clarendon Press, 1884–1933.
Pawson, *Letters*	John C. Bowmer and John A. Vickers, eds., *The Letters of John Pawson*, 3 vols., Peterborough: WHMS Publications, 1994–95.
Sutcliffe, MS 'History'	Joseph Sutcliffe, 'History of Methodism', MS in 4 vols., continuously paginated, 1852, in MA.
Tyerman MSS	MS letters, diaries, and so on copied by Luke Tyerman and James Everett, three folio vols., in MA.
Tyerman, *Wesley*	Luke Tyerman, *The Life and Times of Rev. John Wesley M.A.*, 3 vols., London: Hodder and Stoughton, 1870–71.
WHS	*Proceedings of the Wesley Historical Society*, 1898–.
WMM	*Wesleyan Methodist Magazine* (1822–1913).
Works (Jackson)	*The Works of the Rev. John Wesley*, ed. Thomas Jackson, 14 vols., London: Wesleyan Conference Office, 1872.

SHORT TITLES OF OTHER WORKS OFTEN CITED

Atmore,
Methodist Memorial

Charles Atmore, *The Methodist Memorial: The Lives and Characters of the Preachers*, Bristol: Richard Edwards, 1801.

Baker,
Wesley and Church

Frank Baker, *John Wesley and the Church of England*, London: Epworth Press, 1970.

Crowther,
Portraiture

Jonathan Crowther, *A Portraiture of Methodism*, 2nd ed., London: Edwards, 1815.

Heitzenrater,
People Called Methodists

Richard P. Heitzenrater, *Wesley and the People Called Methodists*, Nashville: Abingdon Press, 1995.

Jackson, *Early
Methodist Preachers*

Thomas Jackson, ed., *The Lives of Early Methodist Preachers*, 6 vols., 4th. ed., London: Wesleyan Conference Office, 1871.

Myles,
Chronological History

William Myles, *A Chronological History of the People Called Methodists*, 4th ed., London: Conference Office, 1813.

Rack,
Reasonable Enthusiast

Henry D. Rack, *Reasonable Enthusiast: John Wesley and the Rise of Methodism*, 2nd ed., London: Epworth Press, 1992.

Seymour,
Huntingdon

A. C. H. Seymour, *The Life and Times of Selina, Countess of Huntingdon*, 2 vols., London: Painter, 1840.

1749

MINUTES

OF SOME LATE

CONVERSATIONS,

Between the REVD. M. WESLEYS,
and Others.

DUBLIN:
Printed by S. POWELL, in *Crane-lane,*
MDCCXLIX.

INTRODUCTION: THE CONFERENCE HISTORY AND *MINUTES*

THE annual Conference in eighteenth-century British Methodism, as with many features of the Wesleyan organization, did not suddenly appear at one time and place in full-blown shape. Wesley observed in 1748 that the economy of the Methodist movement in general did not follow a preconceived pattern: 'As they had not the least expectation, at first, of anything like what has since followed, so they had no previous design or plan at all; but everything arose just as the occasion offered.'[1] The Conference, likewise, evolved over the course of the decades to meet particular needs as they arose. Although it was given general purpose and guidance by Wesley's leadership intuition, the particulars of its shape and procedures came from a number of sources.

Like much of the Wesleyan movement, historical precedents helped shape many features of the Conference, and other movements provided models for structures and procedures within Methodism. Wesley's method of developing the movement entailed not only his own singleness of intention, guided by his understanding of scriptural holiness, but also his willingness to listen to other people as the voice of God's providential direction. He thus had no problem weaving many of their suggestions into the developing tapestry of holy living in the Wesleyan tradition. Throughout his life, he certainly exhibited strong leadership and was inclined to give specific directions, but at the same time he was always conferring with other people and was willing to be persuaded by Scripture that there might be a better way to do things.[2]

---

[1] Letter (Dec. 1748) to Vincent Perronet, vicar of Shoreham, published the following year as *A Plain Account of the People Called Methodists*, I.2 (9:254 in this edn.). Wesley summarizes the first formation of Methodist Societies in London with the same language: 'Thus arose, without any previous design on either side, what was afterwards called a *Society*—a very innocent name, and very common in London, for any number of people associating themselves together' (p. 256).

[2] Wesley's openness to persuasion, crucial for a full understanding of the dynamics of the Conference, is an often overlooked aspect of his leadership style, but is clearly evident in his preface to the *Sermons on Several Occasions* (§9): 'Are you persuaded you see more clearly than me? It is not unlikely that you may. Then treat me as you would desire to be treated yourself upon a change of circumstances. Point me out a better way than I have yet known. Show me it is so by plain proof of Scripture.' 1:107 in this edn.

The Conference of Methodist preachers at London in 1744 is usually considered, in retrospect, to be the first Methodist Conference as such. It is usually seen as having placed the coping-stone on the connexional structure of Methodism that had been developing at the local level over the previous few years. Sometimes improvising, but often borrowing or adapting expedients devised by others in his usual way, Wesley had created a body with a societary ethos, designed for the cultivation of conversion and Christian holiness. Some means of coordinating, if not controlling, the developing movement became a more obvious necessity.

I. Organization of Early Methodism

Even before Methodism had begun to take shape at Oxford, John Wesley's leadership became evident in the way others conferred with him concerning his understanding of the requisite pattern and activities of the Christian life. When Charles Wesley's life took a serious turn at the university in 1728, he sent a letter to his brother John, who was then serving as their father's curate at Epworth and Wroot, suggesting that he needed a 'private conference' with John to ask questions about how to proceed. He subsequently wrote to John, asking for direction in his attempts at Christian living, especially what books to read and how to keep a diary. Charles recognized that John could be an 'instrument of good' to him through his company and assistance.[3]

Within a few months, Charles sent a report home that he had begun to implement John's suggested program and had influenced another student to do the same, noting, however, that one of their mutual friends, Robert Kirkham, seemed beyond hope in this regard. Charles suggested that John might send the student, presumably William Morgan, particular suggestions, keeping Charles in the picture as well. Instead of continuing the conferencing by mail, Wesley traveled to Oxford and began meeting with them personally. Within a few weeks, the hints of a definable group began to take

---

[3] To JW, Jan. 20, 1728, and Jan. 5, 1729, *Letters*, 25:230, 236, in this edn.

shape, and within a year the discernible shape of what was to become Methodism began to be evident.

1. Oxford Methodism

In the 'first rise' of Methodism at Oxford,[4] Wesley's personal direction of a small group of friends soon began to take on a more complicated structure. Members of his small Society of a half dozen or so members soon developed groups in their own colleges, forming a secondary cluster of Societies under the one led by John. This pattern was similar to what had developed in his father Samuel's small Society in Epworth, in a fashion suggested by the Society for Promoting Christian Knowledge, of which John and Samuel were both corresponding members.[5] In both cases, the groups at the secondary level, and eventually even at a third level, received their rules and methods from the primary group.[6] If Benjamin Ingham's group at Queen's College is typical, part of the structure of the Methodist clusters that developed at the various colleges were smaller divisions, similar to the Bands that were prevalent in the later Societies.

Occasionally members from these subsidiary Societies found it necessary to consult with Wesley himself on matters of doctrine, organization, and mission.[7] Although Wesley's later reflections typify the Oxford Methodists as being of one mind and heart as faithful Church of England members,[8] contemporary evidence shows

[4] This phrase is Wesley's language, found in his treatise *A Short History of the People Called Methodists* (1781), §9, 9:430 in this edn.

[5] The SPCK, consisting of a central group of leaders in London, suggested a variety of models and methods with the design of promoting 'real holiness of heart and life.' See *Orders Belonging to a Religious Society* (London, 1724), 4, 6. For the relationship of the structures in Epworth and Oxford, see also Richard P. Heitzenrater, 'The Church of England and the Religious Societies' and 'The Oxford Methodists,' in *Mirror and Memory: Essays in Early Methodism* (Nashville: Kingswood Books, 1989), esp. 43, 82.

[6] Benjamin Ingham, *Diary of an Oxford Methodist: Benjamin Ingham, 1734–35*, ed. Richard P. Heitzenrater (Durham, N.C.: Duke University Press, 1985), 8, 9. In the SPCK model, the parish priest was the leader of the primary Society; at Oxford, John Wesley filled that role among the Methodists with his small group.

[7] See, for instance, the record of Wesley's conference with Benjamin Ingham and Michael Robson on Mar. 17, 1734, with very specific directives given for methods of proceeding in their respective groups. Ingham, *Diary*, 133–34.

[8] See *Short History of People Called Methodists*, §3, 9:427 in this edn.

that there were many differences of opinion among the members of the groups on various matters. At such private conferences, Wesley suggested certain methods of proceeding, such as the necessity of frequent Communion, the nature and use of diaries, and the importance of fasting, and responded to inquiries concerning such issues as the scope of workhouse visitations and the practice of facing east during the creed. Wesley's advice, which was mostly encouraging, in keeping with the nurturing purpose of the groups, at times distinguished between what he thought was necessary and what might be acceptable if it were useful, anticipating his later distinctions between important 'essentials' and allowable 'opinions'.[9]

These patterns of conferencing and consultation represent no unique methodology on Wesley's part in the development of Oxford Methodism, but simply exhibit his willingness to exercise conversation as a means of discerning God's will and directing people in the scripture way of salvation. It also demonstrates that Wesley's leadership derived from recognition by others that he was a person worth consulting on important religious matters.[10] He would later make the point that he did not ask to be the leader of the people called Methodists—they came to him and asked for help.[11]

As Methodism experienced the growing pains of its early years, therefore, one should not be surprised to see religious conversation become a central feature of the Wesleyan method of leadership. It was a rather natural development that, once the structures of the Conference become more set and the occasions more regularized,

[9] Ingham, *Diary*, 1–2, 9, 11, 122, 133–34, 140, 204–5. See *The Character of a Methodist* (1742), §§1–4, 9:33–35 in this edn.; Sermon 39, 'Catholic Spirit', 2:81–95 in this edn.; and *Journal* for May 29, 1745, 20:66–67 in this edn.

[10] Leadership positions can derive from several kinds of situations, such as through appointment by a hierarchical structure, through individual seizure of power within a given context, through selection within a group by election, or through common recognition of insight and imagination within a given interest group. Wesley's leadership seems to have been as much the latter as anything else.

[11] See 'Large' *Minutes* (1770), *Q.* 77 ('What power is it which you exercise over both preachers and people?'), where he describes the beginning of the revival in 1738–39, saying that 'two or three persons who desired "to flee from the wrath to come", and then seven or eight more, came to me in London, and desired me to advise and pray with them. . . . It may be observed, the desire was on *their* part, not *mine*'; cf. *Minutes* (1766), *Q.* [29].

the Minutes of their consultations should bear in the title the main characteristic of their meetings—*Conversations*.[12]

2. The Early Methodist Revival

With the beginning of the Methodist revival, coincident with the onset of field preaching in Bristol in 1739, the local Societies began to take on a more visible role within the movement. Within these Societies and following earlier precedent (including Oxford Methodism and the Moravian structures), Wesley had created 'bands' for those pursuing holiness to the point of 'perfection'; and a little later 'select bands' or 'select societies' of those to whom (he said) he might unburden his own soul. At a later stage the select Bands seem to have been of those who had received the gift of perfection; 'Penitents' were those who had fallen away from the Bands.

These groups included only a proportion of the local Methodist Society, and developing an experiment originally designed for fund-raising, Wesley organized the whole Society into 'classes' meeting regularly with lay leaders.[13] By 1744, local leaders' meetings had been organized and stewards appointed to look after 'temporal affairs' while trustees looked after the preaching-houses when they began to emerge, beginning with the Bristol New Room in 1739.

Lay preachers, who originally emerged spontaneously before being accepted by Wesley, were already becoming necessary for the economy of Methodism. Although the 1744 Conference commenced with clergy only, almost at once they resolved to allow lay helpers to attend. The cautious answer to the question, 'Are Lay Assistants allowable?' was 'Only in cases of necessity'. And the definition of their role as 'in the absence of the Minister, to feed and guide, to

---

[12] The annual (or 'penny') *Minutes* of Conference were published beginning in 1765 with the title *Minutes of some late Conversations, between the Reverend Mr. Wesley, and Others*. The 'Large' *Minutes*, containing a summary of the important doctrinal and disciplinary regulations, beginning in 1753, bore the title *Minutes of Several Conversations, between the Reverend Mr. Wesley, and Others*. See pp. 102–6.

[13] For these groups, see 9:9–15 in this edn.; see also Frank Baker, 'The People Called Methodists: Polity', in Rupert E. Davies, A. Raymond George, and E. Gordon Rupp, eds., *History of the Methodist Church in Great Britain*, 4 vols. (London, 1965–88), 1:213–25; and Henry D. Rack, *Reasonable Enthusiast: John Wesley and the Rise of Methodism*, 2nd edn. (London, 1992), 238–42.

teach and govern the flock' implied that the Wesleys still hoped to obtain the aid of more clergy than proved to be the case.[14]

Above the level of the local Society, there emerged within the next few years a grouping of several Societies in 'Circuits' or 'Rounds'. Some of these represented areas covered by independent evangelists that had been absorbed into Wesley's organization. They first appear in the Minutes in 1746 and from 1748 began to acquire a 'Quarterly Meeting' of leaders. Matters were more fluid in 1744, though the germ of the later 'stationing' process can perhaps be seen in the question (1744, §75), 'Shall we now fix where each labourer shall be (if God permits) till we meet again?' And the answer: 'Yes (which was accordingly done).' It was also argued that the best way of spreading the gospel was 'To go a little and a little farther from London, Bristol, St. Ives, Newcastle, or any other Society' (§69).

Much depended, at this early stage, on the journeyings of the Wesley brothers and on their personal supervision by occasional visits and by correspondence. Yet it seems likely, as we shall see, that the first Conference was intended to be more or less literally a forum for consultation rather than the regular and central governing and legislative body that it later became. Only in retrospect does it assume the importance that students of Methodism would now attach to it.

3. Origins of the Conference

The idea of a Conference for Wesley's clerical and lay helpers seems to have developed by force of circumstances and Wesley's will, out of certain rather different notions of a consultation between workers for revival more generally. After a rather limited attempt at a Conference in 1743 to iron out differences of opinion, at which both George Whitefield (Calvinist) and August Gottlieb Spangenberg (Moravian) failed to appear, Wesley sketched another cooperative scheme the following year in the written agenda that he prepared for another Conference: 'Can we unite any farther with Mr. Whitefield? With the Moravians? Is any conference with either advisable? When? Where? In what kind? For what ends?' (§§48–50). In the Minutes for that Conference it was asked,

[14] See Minutes (1744), §§71–72.

Can we unite any farther with the Moravians? It seems not, were it only for this reason, they will not unite with us. Can we unite any farther with Mr. Whitefield? If he make any overtures towards it. Shall we propose a conference with either? With Mr. Whitefield, if he returns to London. The Moravians absolutely decline it. Shall we send them the most material of the preceding questions, and desire their answer? This can do no hurt, and may do good. (§§89–92)

But these proposals bore no fruit.

Although the precedents and parallels for the Conference are more notable for their differences than their likenesses to the eventual Methodist pattern, there are signs that Wesley also considered seriously at this time the structures used by Count von Zinzendorf, George Whitefield, the Scottish Church, and the Quakers, perhaps desiring to learn from the organizational patterns of these bodies. The written agenda for the 1744 Conference also included the question, 'What can we adopt from C[ount] Z[inzendorf]? Mr. Whitefield? The kirk? [i.e., the established Church of Scotland] The Quakers?'[15] This was under the heading 'Discipline' and was followed by questions about lay helpers, Classes, Bands, and so on. Apparently the question was not put to the Conference itself; at least the *Minutes* do not record it.

Further attempts were made in later years and actual meetings took place with the Calvinistic Methodists in 1747 and 1749 (see the MS evidence under these years) but with little practical effect, though Howell Harris occasionally attended Wesley's Conferences as late as 1763.

Wesley also made periodic attempts to create a 'union' or some form of cooperation with Anglican evangelicals—the 1757 Conference saw a 'union' as desirable. In 1761 and 1764 some clergy did actually attend the Conference, and there seems to have been an informal meeting with some of them in the latter year. Also in 1761 and 1764 Wesley wrote letters to a number of clergy appealing for a kind of unity in basic doctrine and tolerance of differences, and he circulated them further in late 1766. These efforts had little effect, and in 1769 Wesley finally wrote these clergy off as a 'rope of sand' and turned to consolidating his own organization further.[16] Calvinism, irregularities, and perfectionism had variously caused mutual

[15] Agenda, §40. These precedents will be dealt with further in the following section.

[16] *Journal & Diaries*, 21:454–61 in this edn.; Frank Baker, *John Wesley and the Church of England* (London, 1970), 190–94.

suspicion between Wesley and other evangelicals, culminating in the open warfare with the Huntingdonians over Calvinism after the 1770 *Minutes.*

The failure of overtures of this kind, alienation from Whitefield's Calvinism and the Moravians over the previous few years, and the development of Societies controlled solely by Wesley eventually led him to confer only with those actually associated with him. No doubt in 1744, Wesley needed a Conference of his own to settle various questions of doctrine, discipline, and practice for his emerging connexion, but this also marked a decisive stage in consolidating its independence and separate existence from that of other branches of the revival despite continuing sporadic local cooperation and the tendency of individuals to shift allegiance in response to personal quests and needs. This consolidation also marked a further degree of separation from his Anglican parent church, unwilling though Wesley always was to admit the fact.

In fairness to Wesley it could be said that a separate Conference of his own preachers was forced upon him by the failure of repeated attempts between 1739 and 1744 for a wider consultation and a possible organization for cooperation. Such attempts were in a sense provoked by his alienation from the Whitefieldites and Moravians in 1739–40, which split the revival forces, though his former friends could reasonably argue that he was to blame at least as much as they were. At all events, it looks very much as though, leaving aside questions of blame for the failure to create a more comprehensive body within the wider revival, that failure made Wesley fall back on his own followers in a formal Conference.

The first attempt at a more united front was on January 5, 1739.[17] John Wesley's *Journal* reveals nothing for this date, and his diary simply notes 'Islington, George Whitefield, Hutchings, Hall, Ingham, Kinchin, and Charles'. Charles Wesley's *Journal* adds Seward to the list but merely states that 'all set upon me, but I could not agree to settle at Oxford without further direction from God.' However, Whitefield's *Journal* makes it clear that he 'Held a conference concerning things of very great importance.' Unfortunately he does not identify these matters, only that the meeting included

---

[17] I. Murray, ed., *George Whitefield's Journals* (London, 1960), 196; Thomas Jackson, ed., *The Journal of the Rev. Charles Wesley, M.A*, 2 vols. (London: Wesleyan Methodist Bookroom, 1849), 1:139, hereafter *CWJ*; *Journal & Diaries* (diary only), 19:369 in this edn.

some true ministers of Christ, despised Methodists, whom God has brought together from the East and the West, the North and the South. What we were in doubt about, after prayer, was determined by lot, and everything else was carried on with great love, meekness, and devotion. We continued in fasting and prayer till 3 o'clock, and then parted with a full conviction that God was going to do great things among us.

It seems reasonable to guess that a gathering from such a wide area must have concerned itself with some attempt at coordination and cooperation and perhaps general strategy and doctrine.

Much more specific were the concerns of a meeting on November 12, 1739, which, though it seems to have taken place by accident, produced a definite plan, though in the event it was not carried out.[18] Wesley writes that at High Wycombe

we unexpectedly found Mr. Robson and Gambold, with whom, after much prayer and consultation, we agreed: (1) to meet yearly at London, if God permit, on the eve of Ascension Day in 1740, Wednesday May 14; (2) to fix then the business to be done the ensuing year: where, when, and by whom; (3) to meet quarterly there, as many as can: viz., on the second Tuesday in July, October, and January; (4) to send a monthly account to one another of what God hath done in each of our stations; (5) to inquire whether Mr. Hall, Sympson, Rogers, Ingham, Hutchins, Kinchin, Stonehouse, Cennick, Oxlee, and Brown will join us herein; (6) to consider whether there be any others of our spiritual friends who are able and willing so to do.

Although most of these men were Anglicans and had associated earlier with Wesley and the Oxford Methodists, several of them later became Moravians at one time or another. Some of the proposals resemble those in the 1744 Minutes. However, nothing came of this scheme. The most obvious reason is that by the time the scheduled annual meeting had come around, Wesley had set up his own meeting place at the Foundery and had seceded from the Fetter Lane Society.

Meanwhile, as in some other matters such as field preaching, the Welsh Calvinistic Methodists had anticipated the English brethren, and indeed it is possible that the November 1739 gathering may reflect the Welsh experience. In September 1739, Howell Harris was

---

[18] *Letters*, 25:700 in this edn. Identified by Prof. Baker as probably a fragment of a journal-letter to James Hutton, originally printed in John Whitehead, *The Life of the Rev. John Wesley*, 2 vols. (London, 1793–96), 2:125–26. There is no reference to this in *Journal & Diaries*, and Wesley's diary for this period is lost.

considering the advisability of grouping Societies in circuits or districts and setting up monthly and bimonthly meetings to control stations. There followed on October 2, 1740, a Conference of ministers of all denominations to strengthen Welsh Methodism. He told them that he had been inspired by 'hearing of associates in Scotland and America, etc., to meet to unite, to love and strengthen each other's hands'.

The Scottish reference is to the Associate Presbytery founded by the Erskines in 1740, and from them the term 'Association' may have come for gatherings of this kind. The first Welsh Association met in January 1742 and was followed by an Anglo-Welsh one presided over by Whitefield in January 1743, though for several years there were confusions of function between Society and Association meetings. From this developed a series of Calvinistic Methodist Associations in England as well as Wales, the rough equivalent of Wesley's Conferences.[19]

This development did not perhaps bode well for any cooperating Conference between the estranged Calvinist and Arminian Methodists. In May 1742, John Cennick thought that 'all our preachers, all Mr. Wesley's and all the Moravian brethren should meet together. Who knows but we might unite? Or if not, we might consent in principles as far as we can, and love one another. At least, I think all *our* preachers should meet as the apostles did, often.'[20] Tyerman suggested that this may in fact have been the origin of a project by John Wesley the following year for a Conference of the Arminian and Calvinistic Methodists and the Moravians.

Whether or not this was so, Wesley attempted to hold a Conference in London in August 1743 'to confer with the heads of the Moravians and predestinarians'. Charles Wesley came from Cornwall, John Nelson from Yorkshire, and John Wesley from Newcastle, but the 'Moravians and predestinarians' were missing. Charles Wesley recorded that 'I heard the Moravians would not be present at the conference. Spangenberg, indeed, *said* he would, but immediately left England.'[21] Whitefield seems to have declined the

[19] M. H. Jones, *The Trevecka Letters* (Caernarvon, 1932), 257–306; Arnold A. Dallimore, *George Whitefield*, 2 vols. (London, 1970–80), 2:149–58. For the *Minutes* of the Whitefield Associations, see Edwin Welch, ed., *Two Calvinistic Methodist Chapels, 1743–1811* (Leicester: London Record Society, 1975).

[20] Luke Tyerman, *The Life and Times of John Wesley M.A.*, 3 vols. (London, 1870–71), 1:419, quoting Cennick to Mrs. Whitefield on May 6, 1742. Hereafter Tyerman, *Wesley*.

[21] *CWJ*, Aug. 12, 1743, 1:334.

invitation; James Hutton said that his (Moravian) brethren had orders not to confer at all, unless the Archbishop of Canterbury or Bishop of London were also present![22] With a view to uniting with Whitefield as far as possible, Wesley set down his views in writing on unconditional election, irresistible grace, and final perseverance.[23] On each of these key predestinarian points he made partial or apparent concessions but clearly denied double or even single predestination, though on final perseverance he seems to concede more than he would later.

Tyerman notes that this was 'the last attempt at union', though one should not forget further attempts at understanding in 1747 and 1749. Tyerman also suggests that perhaps the failure of these attempts finally suggested to Wesley the purely 'Wesleyan' Conference of 1744. Perhaps, however, some slight echo of the earlier projects may be found in the fact that, as Professor Heitzenrater has observed, there were persons invited to the Conference 'who were of a Moravian and Calvinist bent of mind', though not 'leaders of those parties' but 'persons who had committed themselves to Wesley's leadership', such as Richard Viney, a Moravian layman, and Thomas Meriton, a clergyman from the Isle of Man seeking to escape 'out of the hands of Calvin'.[24] At the end of the Conference, as was observed earlier, the possibility was indeed raised of contacting the Moravians and Whitefield, but without effect. It is probably significant that on June 24, the day before the Conference, John Wesley wrote a letter to the Moravians, setting out his criticisms of them, which he then used as a preface to Extract IV of his *Journal* for 1739–41.[25] Thus, doctrinally at least, Wesley had delineated his position in relation to his two main opponents.

4. The 1744 Conference

In the light of these repeated attempts at a 'conference' with all the main revival groups and their repeated failures, it seems

---

[22] Tyerman, *Wesley*, 1:420.

[23] *Journal & Diaries*, 19:332 in this edn., under Aug. 23, two weeks after the proposed date for a Conference but no doubt representing the basis for a possible reconciliation, and perhaps these matters were discussed by the 'Wesleyan' group that did meet.

[24] *CWJ*, 1:365; Richard P. Heitzenrater, *Wesley and the People Called Methodists* (Nashville: Abingdon Press, 1995), 142–43.

[25] *Letters*, 26:109–12 in this edn.; *Journal & Diaries*, 19:116–18 in this edn.; Heitzenrater, *People Called Methodists*, 143–44.

reasonable to conclude that Wesley had indeed finally decided that he must conduct one on his own terms, and with persons more or less actively in association with him. The general subjects for discussion were always likely to be a mixture of doctrine and evangelistic policy and strategy, and the documents cited in which Wesley had tried to define his doctrinal position in relation to Calvinists and Moravians were followed up in the 1744 Conference in much more detail on the crucial issues of justification and sanctification. But to settle this and questions of organization and discipline, he now had a much freer hand. How far he was influenced by other churches and evangelistic groups is an issue to be pursued in the next section. Though raised in the agenda and apparently omitted in the Minutes, the possibility of borrowing is always present in Wesley and he had already learned much (more than he liked to admit later) from the Moravians.

One question worth asking about the first Conference is: Precisely what kind of meeting and body was it intended to be? Was it intended to meet on a regular basis? Professor Ward commented, 'Significant as the first Conference was made to appear in later Wesleyan ecclesiology, little record of it was retained by the Wesleys themselves.'[26] On the other hand, it concluded by proposing a quarterly consultation, and though this did not happen, it was presumably felt that further meetings were needed at least for a time to clarify doctrine, discipline, and organization. Perhaps, like Wesley's publication of his *Journal*, what was started to deal with immediate problems became a habit and, in this case, a necessity. As to the nature of the meeting envisaged, the report in Wesley's *Journal* (published in 1753 when the Conference was pretty well established) speaks of days 'spent in conference', which is at least ambiguous— the act of conferring rather than a formal body is surely implied. There is no mention of the Conference as part of the Methodist polity in Wesley's *Plain Account of the People Called Methodists* (1749) or even in *A Short History of Methodism* (1765). In *A Short History of the People Called Methodists* (1781) he mentions the five days spent 'in conference' in 1744 and adds that 'the result of our consultations we set down, to be the rule of our future practice', which rather reflects the significance the body had acquired by that late date.[27]

[26] In *Journal & Diaries*, 20:34, n. 71 in this edn.
[27] See 9:39–40 in this edn.

That it was not yet regarded as the keystone of the organization in 1749 is plausible enough but that it was still not mentioned in 1765 is at least curious, yet Wesley may well have been clinging to the idea that it was merely a means of consultation to be used or disused as he thought fit and certainly to be made up only of those he chose to invite. Wesley's attitude to the nature of the Conference and his absolute control of it and of its composition were sharpened by later experience of criticisms of his autocracy and his handling of the Deed of Declaration in 1784 and will be more fully discussed later.[28] Yet his reflections then, which ignored some of the later realities, certainly reflect what he had always believed and were particularly true of the early, experimental phase. In his *Thoughts upon some Late Occurrences* (1785), after insisting that those came whom he invited, he stated that 'the term *Conference* meant not so much the conversation we had together as the persons that conferred; namely, those whom I invited to confer with me from time to time.'[29] Who was to attend and whether there was a Conference at all depended entirely on his will. Even after the body became a legal entity in 1784, Wesley asserted and exercised his right to choose who attended. Whatever the validity of this view of the body later in his life, its complete dependence on Wesley, its lack of any guarantee of regularity, and its role to advise as he thought fit seem fairly to describe its status and function at the beginning.

Moreover, some passages in the first few Conferences suggest a very private meeting for confidential discussion and in no sense a law-making body: in short, literally a 'conference'. In answer to the question (1744, §§4–5), 'How far does each of us agree to submit to the unanimous judgment of the rest?' the reply was 'In speculative things each can only submit so far as his judgment shall be convinced' and 'In every practical point so far as we can without wounding our several consciences.'

Then there was the issue of confidentiality: 'Not one word which may be here spoken of persons should be mentioned elsewhere' and 'Nothing at all [mentioned to others], unless so far as we may be convinced the glory of God requires it.' But 'from time to time' they would 'consider on each head, Is it for the glory of God that what we have now spoken should be mentioned again?'

The records of the Conference, the *Minutes*, will be considered later, but it is worth remarking that they were circulated to members

---

[28] See below, section VII, pp. 65ff.
[29] *Arminian Magazine* 8 (1785), 267–69; hereafter *AM*.

and others who might have been present, and it seems likely that more circulated than the surviving MS Minutes suggest. On the other hand, they were not published until 1765. They give little hint of debates and disagreements, and some matters were not minuted at all, as we know from other sources. But surviving preachers' diaries and letters are also often less informative in a number of cases than one might expect, especially in the early period. Wesley's *Journal* entries (and some preachers' mentions of the Conference) give the impression of all at least ending in love and harmony, which was not always the case. As to freedom to differ, John Hampson, Jun., in his *Memoirs* of Wesley, complained that this point in the early Minutes was dropped in the 'Large' *Minutes* of 1780. Though he was trying to argue that Wesley had reneged on this apparent promise of freedom to differ and that this was a sign of his autocracy, he also implied that the omission concealed that a meeting that had once been a private discussion with freedom to differ had become a ruling body bound by—what? The majority? Wesley's will?[30]

Conference as a place for 'conferring' by interested people may also be illustrated by the fact that for many years (and not just in the early years as has been supposed, following William Myles)[31] lay-people other than the preachers attended. In 1746 (§2) it is inquired, 'Who are the properest persons to be present at our conferences?' The reply was '(1) As many of the preachers as conveniently can come; (2) the most earnest and most sensible of the Band-leaders where the conference is; and (3) any pious and judicious stranger who may occasionally be in the place.' This makes the early Conferences seem more like meetings for edification and perhaps sharing of insights than legislative bodies, even allowing that Wesley in his latest years was still choosing attendees. Moreover, even in later years, a broad Methodist public was allowed in on occasion at least to hear, if not to participate in, debates sometimes on major questions such as separation from the Church. It is not even clear whether these were special 'open' sessions, though that was probably the case.[32]

---

[30] John Hampson, Jun., *Memoirs of the late Rev. John Wesley, A.M.*, 3 vols. (Sunderland, 1791), 3:3–6.

[31] *A Chronological History of the People Called Methodists*, 4th. edn. (London, 1813); hereafter Myles, *Chronological History*.

[32] See further in section III, below.

These matters are mentioned here to underline that in origin, the Conferences were essentially private, almost informal consultations rather than part of the formal Methodist machinery of government and a legislative body. That the Conference evolved into something much more like the latter was an untidy and in some ways obscure process, and Wesley's late thoughts on its nature and its relationship to himself even after 1784 tended in some ways to perpetuate the early tradition.

II. Precedents and Parallels

The discussion so far has concerned the immediate context in which the 1744 Conference took place, its possible forerunners in the evangelical community, and its original character. But it is also instructive for understanding the peculiar nature of this annual gathering to ask how the Wesleyan Conference compared and contrasted with contemporary evangelical and non-evangelical ecclesiastical leadership bodies and how far these may have influenced its character.

1. The Religious Societies

One obvious complicating factor here is that Wesley always refused to regard Methodism as a church; for him it was a 'society' or 'connexion' of Societies, and ideally an auxiliary to the Established Church and its clergy. Hence one reason for his resistance to treating his travelling preachers as ministers or ordaining them until a late date and then nearly always for America and Scotland, where he claimed Anglican writ did not run. Hence, too, his hostility to holding Methodist services at the same time as Anglican ones and encouraging Methodists to attend the latter as well. He was inconsistent, for he acknowledged 'variations' from Anglican order like lay preaching and extempore prayer, and the Methodist Societies were clearly not auxiliaries to Anglicanism because they were open to people of all churches and none. Just as important as Wesley's theory and practice is that for many Methodists, their meetings became the whole of their church life and the travelling preachers effectively their 'ministers'. Yet it could be argued that, quite apart from pragmatic necessity, seeing Methodism as a mere 'Society' helped him to feel free to borrow from non-Anglican religious traditions. Hence the agenda question in 1744 about what they might learn from a variety of sources (Whitefield, the Moravians, the Quakers, the Church of Scotland Presbyterians).[33] Even if no such borrowings were formally recorded, they may have happened, as they certainly had already from the Moravians.

Since Methodism was a religious Society rather than a church, it is natural to ask what Wesley and Methodism owed to the older Anglican religious societies that had originated in the late 1670s and were still well in evidence in the late 1730s when the new Methodist Societies emerged. There is no doubt that Wesley and many of his first converts were well acquainted with these societies and Moravian-influenced variants. There was also the rather different experience of the early Oxford Methodists, of the SPCK and SPG, and of Wesley's experiments in Georgia. How far these influenced Wesley's later Methodist Societies and how far there was real continuity are more open to debate.[34] Whitefield, Wesley, and the Moravians colonized among the older societies, made converts from them, remodeled some, and created others. This approach was above all true in London and Bristol but much less common elsewhere, though in any case such societies were more thinly scattered in other parts of England. But important new features were in the Societies founded by the evangelicals. They were open to non-Anglicans and women; they contained inner groups like the 'bands'; they had a conversionist ethos; and they gave more scope to lay leaders (though these had already displaced the clergy in some older societies). For the present question about the notion of a 'Conference' as a consultative meeting covering a wide area, it seems to be significant that there is little, if any, sign of the old societies having any links between them, other than annual charity sermons in London.

[33] Minutes (1744), §40.

[34] See above, p. 14. On Methodism and the Church of England, see Baker, *Wesley and Church*; Rack, *Reasonable Enthusiast*, 497–501, 519–23. On Methodists and Moravians, see C. W. Towlson, *Moravian and Methodist* (London, 1957). For rather different estimates of the relationship between Methodism and the old religious societies, see John Walsh, 'Religious Societies, Methodist and Evangelical, 1738–1800', *Studies in Church History* 23 (1986): 279–302; and Henry D. Rack, 'Religious Societies and the Origins of Methodism', *Journal of Ecclesiastical History* 38 (1987): 82–95.

2. The Church of England

Despite Wesley's affection for the Church of England and his adaptation of Anglican ministry, liturgy, and Articles of Religion to 'primitive' patterns for the Americans in 1784, the English Methodist connexion was conspicuously unlike the contemporary Anglican Church. In his apparently historical sketch of how he supposed forms of church government to have evolved, Wesley seems to allow for a natural process from which emerged episcopalian, presbyterian, and congregationalist forms of government.[35] None, apparently, have divine sanction, and the process looks more like the rise of Methodism than the Anglican system.

Almost everything about Methodism contradicted and cut across the existing Anglican system and seemed, if anything, to be an implicit, if not explicit, challenge to it and criticism of it. This despite claims to be supplementing its coverage and remedying its defects. For example, for more than a hundred years following 1717, the Church of England had no effective sittings of its traditional central governing bodies, the northern and southern Convocations; and their sittings had of late been riven with party strife. The membership was chosen by election by diocesan clergy, and this choice of representatives was a highly political and often contentious process.[36] In any case, the acts of Convocation were always subject to Parliament. Below this, the Church was left to the very limited activities of bishops in their dioceses—much more limited than those of their nineteenth-century successors. The effectiveness of the parish clergy mattered more, and this varied greatly. It is unnecessary to rehearse here the older criticisms of the state of the Church in this period or the more revisionist findings of recent research.[37]

---

[35] Minutes (1745), §6.

[36] Convocation was therefore not just a gathering of national representatives of the Church but an occasion for the expression of diocesan opinion. Jeremy Gregory, *Restoration, Reformation, and Reform, 1660–1828* (Oxford: Clarendon, 2000), 61.

[37] The classic attempt at partial rehabilitation was by N. H. Sykes, *Church and State in England in the Eighteenth Century* (Cambridge, 1934), but for a more recent approach, see the essays in J. Walsh, C. Haydon, and S. Taylor, eds., *The Church of England c. 1689–c. 1833* (Cambridge, 1993). For a more general survey of recent views, see K. Hylson-Smith, *The Churches in England from Elizabeth I to Elizabeth II*, 3 vols. (London, 1966–68), vol. 2: 1689–1833, which also covers other denominations; see also Jeremy Gregory and Jeffrey S. Chambers, eds., *The National Church in Local Perspective* (Woodbridge, Suffolk: Boydell Press, 2003).

What matters for the present discussion is that the size and the resources of dioceses and of parishes were inherited from earlier times. Parish boundaries were fixed, varied enormously, and often no longer related to the contemporary geography of population. This development was particularly true of growing industrial and urban areas and worsened as the eighteenth century advanced. Methodism, by contrast, was a flexible voluntary organization that could ignore traditional parish boundaries. It could meet without church buildings, build when and where it wished, and create and change groups of Societies in circuits, and it had a growing centralized system of oversight with mobile travelling preachers and a body of local ones with other lay leaders, including women.

Above all, Wesley stressed the 'connexional' nature of his Societies, which contrasted sharply with the decentralized and localized character of Anglicanism, with its rigid parish boundaries and static clergy under only limited external oversight.[38] Anglicanism was almost a clericalized Independency. This picture is increasingly true also, as the century went on, of the Evangelical clergy in the Church of England after an initial period of flexibility when a few of them acted almost like the Methodists.

3. English Dissenters

Much the same could be said, so far as local independence and lack of central oversight are concerned, of most of the old Dissenter churches, though they had further problems of their own.[39] In the early eighteenth century, the Presbyterians were the most numerous as well as the most economically and socially weighty of the Dissenters. But in terms of ecclesiastical polity they were very different from their Scottish counterparts, governed by a hierarchy of church courts crowned by the General Assembly. The experiment in 1648 of some such system in England had failed, and after the Restoration in 1660, nothing of the kind could be resurrected under persecution. The grant of limited toleration for Dissent in 1689 made no change in this respect.

[38] JW was the central point of union and the source of most decisions that were applied across the connexion, but the Church of England at this point had very little central control. See Gregory and Chambers, *National Church*, passim.

[39] The best survey of Dissent is by Michael Watts, *The Dissenters: From the Reformation to the French Revolution* (Oxford, 1978).

The only lingering trace of the older Presbyterian tradition of bodies beyond the local church was the existence of associations of ministers on a county or regional basis. But such bodies were voluntary and consultative, made up of ministers only, and any attempt at censure of local ministers and churches could not be implemented except by voluntary consent. The same was true of hybrid bodies of Presbyterians and Independents (Congregationalists) like the Cheshire Classis.[40] It is often difficult to distinguish the two traditional churches in this period since both stressed the independence of the local congregation, which is the relevant point for this discussion.

The Independents, as their usual eighteenth-century name implies, made a positive theological virtue of the notion that the 'church' exists in its local expression, independent of all others and free of control from any superior hierarchy. Unlike the Presbyterians, they were often content to hold ordinations in the local church rather than one of the Associations, and again unlike the Presbyterians, their churches were controlled by church meetings in which lay deacons and members could have a say rather than by ministers and trustees. It was only at the beginning of the next century that a new kind of county Association developed, cooperating mainly for evangelism and, eventually, the national Congregational Union. But in both cases, the tradition of localized independency curbed any drift to connexionalism on the Methodist pattern.[41]

Much the same could be said of the Baptists, who in terms of polity closely resembled them. They, too, had Associations, but Baptists were particularly sensitive to interference or suspicions of heterodoxy and some tended to eschew even voluntary consultative bodies above the local church. The General Baptists of the New Connexion, however, which had origins somewhat coloured by Methodism, had rather more sense of connexionalism.

---

[40] Alexander Gordon, ed., *The Cheshire Classis, 1690–1745* (London, 1919). For a survey of county and regional assemblies, see Geoffrey Nuttall, 'Assembly and Association in Dissent, 1689–1831', in *Studies in Church History* 7 (1971), 289–309. There is a curious foretaste of Methodism in an Anglican attack on Richard Baxter's 'Circumforaneous [*sic*] legates returning one in six or seven months out of their circuits to their Grand Master.' Baxter denied any such system, but he was involved in Association work: Geoffrey Nuttall, *Richard Baxter* (London, 1965), 74.

[41] Michael Watts, *The Dissenters: The Expansion of Evangelical Nonconformity, 1789–1859* (Oxford, 1995), 136.

It has to be said, in any case, that Wesley retained a lifelong distrust of English Dissent, though he developed a taste for some of the seventeenth-century Puritan divines, notably Richard Baxter, who was only a reluctant nonconformist and an advocate of parish ministry. What Wesley distrusted about Dissent was partly its support in some cases for Calvinism, in others for heterodoxy on the Trinity and the way of salvation (which was increasingly true of Presbyterians). Moreover, all of them in their localism and independency conflicted with his vision of a mobile, centrally directed body of preachers.

4. Scottish Presbyterians and Quakers

The Scottish Presbyterians and Quakers, however, offered a different picture, and Wesley's agenda for the 1744 Conference did, in fact, visualize consulting them and not English Dissent. Wesley's relationship with the 'Kirk' and other forms of Scottish Presbyterianism was not in the long run very happy, apart from certain individuals. The Scots were prone to be Calvinists and (Methodists thought) impervious to evangelism. Hence the eventual need for Methodist ordinations there, though Scottish Methodism had a tendency to adopt some Presbyterian habits, much to Wesley's disgust.[42] What may have engaged Wesley's attention in 1744 was the hierarchy of Church courts, which certainly was a 'connexionalism' of a sort that contrasted with most of English church life. But there is little sign of any direct influence by them on Wesley's thinking.

In the case of the Quakers, matters may be a little different. Here was a body that, despite its apparently individualist espousal of the doctrine of the inner light, had developed a local, regional, and national level of meetings for consultation and discipline, though not without resistance. It was the most 'connexional' of all English religious bodies, though this probably resulted from its small number of members and ability to make decisions according to the 'sense' of a meeting—not exactly the model, one feels, for Wesley's style of

[42] On Methodism in Scotland, see A. Skevington Wood in Davies, George, and Rupp, *History of Methodist Church*, 3:65–78; *Minutes* (1785), n. 70 (p. 564). Pawson even chose 'elders' in Scotland to Wesley's disgust: J. Telford, ed., *The Letters of the Rev. John Wesley*, 8 vols. (London, 1931), 8:35–36, hereafter *Letters* (Telford); Tyerman, *Wesley*, 3:81–82.

personalized autocracy. There was quite a scattering of Quaker converts to Methodism, though Wesley distrusted the mystical strain
in Quakers. And some evidence indicates that the idea and title of
'Quarterly Meetings,' first mentioned by Wesley in November 1739
and suggested by the Conference of 1744, was further developed
and implemented from 1748 through John Bennet and may owe
something to Bennet's interest in Quakerism.[43]

5. Moravians

The Methodist debt to the Moravians was more considerable
than to any other religious body, though Wesley probably tended to
obscure that influence in his later years. Thence came important features of the Bands, love-feasts, letter-days, and possibly watch-
nights, despite Wesley's invocations of 'primitive' precedents for
each. From the Moravians also came abortive notions of communal
experiments and no doubt the general picture of a tightly organized
community under an authoritarian head.[44]

Whitefield, too, learned from the Moravians, but did Wesley learn
from Whitefield, who, as his admirers point out, often anticipated
Wesley in his founding of Societies and other matters, notably open-
air preaching? Whitefield and his Welsh associates, as we have said,
had pioneered Associations, a possible precedent for Wesley's Conference, as well as attempts at a wider evangelical organization.
Whether Wesley actually borrowed more than the general idea from
this source is another matter. The Whitefield Connexion and its
Associations did discuss doctrine and policy and did set stations for
preachers, but Whitefield as 'Moderator' was often absent, only
guided with a lax hand, and shrank from an organization that
seemed to threaten his undenominational mission. His followers
eventually became absorbed into evangelical Independency.[45]

[43] See above, section II (3, 4) cf. pp. 29, 34, 38 above. See also John Bennet, MS Letterbook, fols. 28, 31, in MA; and Frank Baker, 'John Bennet and Early Methodist
Polity', *Proceedings of the Wesley Historical Society* 25 (1965): 1–4, hereafter *WHS*.

[44] See Towlson, *Moravian and Methodist*. For watch-nights, letter-days, and love-feasts,
see Minutes (1744), §83 and n. 228. Despite the Moravian precedent, the watch-nights
appear to have originated in Methodism among the Kingswood miners: see Rack, *Reasonable Enthusiast*, 411–12. On the 'common stock', see Minutes (1744), §62 (3) and n. 153.

[45] For the *Minutes* of the Whitefield organization, see Welch, *Two Calvinistic
Methodist Chapels*.

6. *The Huntingdon Association*

Much the same may be said of the Huntingdon Connexion up to a point, except for a small residue that has survived to the present day. The Elect Lady was certainly autocratic and rotated her preachers' appointments even more rapidly than Wesley did. Unlike Wesley, when she organized ordinations in the 1780s, she formally left the Church of England. During this later period, her adherence to Calvinism also caused a rift with Wesley. She did try to organise her Connexion as a permanent body to survive her death, complete with articles of faith and a system of 'Districts', grouping her chapels together within a national 'Association'. But very few chapels adhered to the common trust suggested.[46] All of this was much later, however, and in 1744 the Countess was more deferential to Wesley than Wesley to the Countess.

The more obvious comparison between the Wesleyan movement and the 'Association' tradition was the shared legacy of abortive attempts at cooperation among the different branches of the revival. These ventures both preceded and followed the organization of Wesley's connexion through the Conference and finally petered out in the 1760s. At a local level there were attempts to cooperate with Evangelical parish clergy like Walker of Truro or Venn of Huddersfield.[47] But these attempts at concerted efforts foundered precisely on Wesley's connexionalism as well as his distrust of the Evangelical clergy's tendencies to Calvinism and their distrust of his tendencies to Arminianism and perfectionism. There is an echo of the old Dissenting 'Associations' idea in a plan proposed by John Fletcher of Madeley for a 'Worcester Association' as a regional organization after the failure of Wesley's plan for a 'union' of evangelical clergy in 1764.[48] But Wesley's only concession to regional

[46] See A. C. H. Seymour, *The Life and Times of Selina, Countess of Huntingdon*, 2 vols. (London, 1840), 2:4–13, 436–50, 483–88, hereafter Seymour, *Huntingdon*; Edwin Welch, *Spiritual Pilgrim* (Cardiff, 1995), 190–210.

[47] For Walker, see Frank Baker, *Charles Wesley: As Revealed by his Letters* (London, 1948), 95–96; *Letters* (Telford), 3:43–47, 152–53, 192–96, 221–26; *Letters*, 26:82–88, 592–96, 606–8, 611–13 in this edn.; Tyerman, *Wesley*, 2:44–48; C. C. B. Walker, *The Early Cornish Evangelicals* (London, 1951), 88–129. For Venn, see *Letters* (Telford), 3:21–26; 4:15–18.

[48] Patrick F. Streiff, *J. W. de la Fléchère* (Frankfurt, 1984), 215–16; *Letters* (Telford), 5:4–85; F. F. Bretherton, 'A Society of Ministers of the Gospel is proposed . . . ', *WHS* 22 (1939–40): 52–57.

Conferences came in his ad hoc consultations in regional centres when faced with the problem of purging unsatisfactory preachers or of ensuring loyalty to Methodism or the Church.[49]

So whatever one may know or guess that Wesley may have borrowed at any stage from other bodies, the most striking conclusion from the preceding discussion is how unusual the Methodist organization was in its day—how little it resembled that of other churches and religious bodies. It was more 'connexional' and more centralized than any except the Quakers and Moravians in England. Unlike the Quakers, Methodism centred on one man's will; unlike the Moravians, it did not look to a foreign figure and habits beyond England. Above all, the Wesleyan movement sought to overcome what seemed to be the endemic localized nature of the greater part of English church life.

7. Civil Organization

Church life also reflected civil organization. English government in this period was heavily decentralized and very limited in scope. Parliament legislated only lightly and often focused on private bills affecting local interests; much local administration was loaded on justices of the peace, and much work was left to voluntary organizations and charity. Not only the Conference, as it developed into more of a ruling body or at least a regular vehicle for Wesley's will, but also the whole connexional network was in strong contrast with contemporary modes of government.

One should not idealize the Methodist achievement, since Wesley's constant multiplication and reiteration of rules showed how little satisfied he often was that his ideals had been achieved. Building preaching-houses created debt and diverted the Conference from evangelism to what he often called 'temporal business'. The failure to place all the houses on the Model Deed undermined the power of Wesley here and there, and undercut the Conference's attempts to control the pulpit and assert connexionalism. Methodism always exhibited an element of 'independency', in local revolts and in the larger splits of the nineteenth century.

---

[49] For these regional Conferences see below, Minutes (1751), and also Richard P. Heitzenrater, 'Purge the Preachers: The Wesleys and Quality Control', in Kenneth Newport and Ted Campbell, eds., *Charles Wesley: Life, Literature, and Legacy* (Peterborough: Epworth, 2007).

Nevertheless, the relative flexibility, the sense of connexionalism, the element of hierarchical oversight and central control, the disregard for traditional civil and ecclesiastical boundaries, and the tendency to allow organizational development to follow the logic of evangelism and pastoral care—all these characteristics contrasted in principle as well as practice with contemporary attitudes, and the germ of this approach was increasingly expressed in the annual Conference.

III. Attendance at Conference[50]

In Wesley's lifetime, the Conference was not limited to his ordained Anglican helpers or, in some cases, even to the itinerant preachers. And attendance at Conference was by Wesley's invitation, so that having been set apart as a Methodist preacher did not guarantee an invitation, even after 'members' of Conference, as such, were named in the legal changes of 1784.

The first Conference in 1744 began with only clergy present (four besides the Wesleys), but almost at once they resolved to invite some lay preachers (in this case four travelling preachers) to join them. In 1746, the Conference agenda included the question: 'Who are the properest persons to be present at our Conferences?' The answer was that they should be the travelling preachers plus 'the most earnest and most sensible of the Band leaders' and 'any pious and judicious stranger who may occasionally be in the place'.[51] This statement further underlines the argument that the early Conferences were conversations on the work of God rather than anything like a ruling body, and the meeting was therefore appropriately open to a wide range of sympathetic people.[52]

---

[50] The discussion in the following sections is confined to the English Conference. The American *Minutes* are not included in this edn. (see preface to this volume). For the Irish *Minutes* see Prof. Baker's introduction to those *Minutes* (below, Appendix B).

[51] Minutes (1746), §2. MS 'E' has the interesting variant 'at any meeting of this nature'.

[52] John S. Simon, *John Wesley and the Methodist Societies* (London, 1923), 323, thought it probable that Thomas Willis, who was present in 1746, was a Bristol layman, and that this may have suggested the question just quoted.

It is arguable that the eighteenth-century Conferences through-out Wesley's lifetime retained some marks of this early approach, especially as he controlled entry. William Myles claimed that the last two categories mentioned in 1746 were admitted only as spectators and that as the numbers of preachers increased, they could not admit even all of them, so that 'in a few years' only preachers were admitted.[53] This assertion seems to be untrue or at least overstated. That the non-preachers were admitted only as spectators is possibly, though not certainly, correct; but it is certain that, even in Wesley's last years, others were admitted only if to a kind of 'open session'.

Certainly in 1748, three stewards were present, including William Briggs, a future book steward.[54] In 1767, Whitefield, Howell Harris, and 'many stewards and local preachers' were added to the itiner-ants.[55] In 1778, Thomas Taylor recorded in his diary that on August 5, 'Today was permitted all sorts to come into the Conference, so that we had a large company.'[56] In 1781, according to a recollection many years later, 'An open Conference was held, and the most use-ful way of preaching was the subject of discussion.'[57] This comment does seem to suggest something distinct from the business sessions of the preachers and hints at a discussion intended for general edi-fication, whether or not the outsiders actually took part. On the first two days of Conference in 1785, Wesley apparently confined atten-dance to travelling preachers only, which evidently implies that oth-ers (or perhaps local preachers only?) could attend on other days, whether as spectators or otherwise.[58] In 1786, the Conference opened at 6:00 and 9:00 a.m. and 2:00 p.m. and on Friday at 1:00 'for all the Society that would attend'.[59] This again suggests an 'open session'. Wesley's *Journal* says that he allowed any of the Society into the debate on the question of separation from the Church.[60] Again, this meeting may not have been a formal session, and there is no record of such a debate in the *Minutes*, though the same is true of

[53] Myles, *Chronological History*, 45.

[54] Minutes (1748), §53.

[55] *Journal & Diaries*, 22:99 in this edn.

[56] Ibid., 23:102, n. 4 in this edn. The business consisted of discussions on preaching-houses and the call to send missions to Africa.

[57] E. Oaks to Mr. Agdon, Apr. 1829, Tyerman MSS, 3:434 in MA. On this occa-sion, several preachers gave their opinions on the matter.

[58] *Letters* (Telford), 7:282.

[59] Joseph Sutcliffe, MS 'History of Methodism', 4 vols. (1852), fol. 1123 (in MA).

[60] *Journal & Diaries*, 23:410 in this edn.

other occasions when that subject was discussed. On this occasion Wesley did append to the *Minutes* a paper on the subject.

The evidence, then, is somewhat ambiguous. Myles may have been right to say that from the first, non-preachers attended only as spectators. But to assert that they were excluded altogether 'after a few years' is clearly untrue or at most true only of formal business sessions. 'Open sessions' occurred, and on some occasions non-preachers may have spoken.

As many preachers as possible seem to have attended the Conferences, at least in the earlier years, although there were always absentees for various reasons. When Wesley's authority was challenged in the Conference of 1766, he insisted that his control sprang from the fact that people had asked for his guidance and therefore it rested with him to appoint and organize them.[61] Similarly, the preachers had originally asked permission to be his 'sons in the gospel' and so were at his disposal. The Conference began when he asked the people to *advise* him—not to *govern* him.

Also in 1766, Wesley said that after several years of inviting specific individual preachers, he gave a general permission for all itinerant preachers to attend.[62] However, keeping in mind the needs of the circuits during the meetings of Conference, in the light of this shift in approach, in 1767 Wesley restated his policy for attendance: some were *allowed* to come and others *required*.[63] Both before and after the Deed of Declaration of 1784, Wesley clearly asserted his right to control attendance, whatever the terms may have been from time to time. From or after the 1780 Conference, he apparently reverted to his earlier practice of inviting only a select number of preachers and of not allowing others to come.[64] On occasion, he certainly omitted troublemakers. Thus he wrote on July 8, 1785, 'A Conference while I live is "The preachers whom I *invite* to confer with me". . . . No contentious persons shall for the future meet in any Conference. They may *dispute* elsewhere if they please.'[65] This statement was made, incidentally, after the institution of the Deed

[61] *Minutes* (1766), *Q.* 29.

[62] Ibid., *Q.* 29 (4).

[63] *Letters* (Telford), 5:60.

[64] So Baker, *Wesley and Church*, 221, quoting the 'Large' *Minutes* (1780). Wesley's *Journal* account of the 1781 Conference (23:218 in this edn.) indicates that more than seventy persons were present 'whom I had severally invited to come and assist me with their advice'.

[65] *Letters* (Telford), 7:279.

of Declaration, which was highly contentious to some preachers. They might have supposed that at least the Legal Hundred (named in the document as the official members of Conference after Wesley's death) would have been entitled to attend, but Wesley clearly believed that as long as he lived, he did not even need to summon them—and on occasion he did omit some of them.[66] On the other hand, Wesley's letter of instructions to be read to the Conference after his death—as it was in 1791—seems to imply that the Legal Hundred should not use their power to exclude other brethren from attending the meetings of the Conference.[67]

So far as the Conference is concerned, women who were 'preaching' within Methodism were not invited to Conference because they were not formally set apart or recognized as itinerant (or even local) preachers, though some women certainly attended the 'open sessions' already described. Mary Bosanquet, perhaps the most famous of the women allowed by Wesley to preach in the Societies, had evidently considered but rejected the idea of preaching full-time, though she and other women did travel widely.[68] In any case, Wesley's attitude was equivocal, and the male itinerants were divided over the propriety and legitimacy of women preachers, on both scriptural grounds and contemporary views of female roles. The subject was hardly ever raised in the Conference, and Wesley's gradual acceptance of the practice must be sought elsewhere than in the *Minutes*. In 1748, he quoted St. Paul against female preaching to a Quaker, though in 1755 (during his appeal to the Leeds Conference against leaving the Church) he acknowledged in passing that some women had received an 'extraordinary call' in apostolic times. The 1765 Conference defended women speaking in Bands as not contrary to the Pauline veto on them speaking in church.[69] But the growth of female speaking and preaching from the 1760s onwards brought Wesley's occasional private endorsement. In 1770, Sarah

[66] Hence, perhaps, his hostility to the phrase '*life-estate*' in the Deed. *Minutes* (1785), *Q*. 21 and n. 162; and see below, pp. 92–93, 588.

[67] Letter prefaced to *Minutes* (1791).

[68] Paul W. Chilcote, *John Wesley and the Women Preachers of Early Methodism* (Metuchen, NJ, 1991), 168. This is the best survey of the phenomenon in Wesley's day. For Miss Bosanquet's powerful justification of her call, ibid., 299–300.

[69] *Letters* (Telford), 2:119; Baker, *Wesley and Church*, 333; *Minutes* (1765), *Q*. 30.

Crosby, one of the women involved, thought the question would be discussed at Conference, but there is no record of it. In 1784, the topic was apparently discussed at Conference but not recorded officially in the *Minutes*. In 1787, Sarah Mallet, a female preacher at Fakenham in Norfolk, was given authorization to preach within that circuit, under a provision that required outside preachers to obtain written permission from Wesley or his Assistant.[70]

The significance of these preachers can and has been easily under- as well as over-estimated. Nevertheless, Dr. Chilcote has identified some forty of them in Wesley's lifetime. Some evidence also exists of later Wesleyan obscuring of the fact that a significant number of Methodist holy women indulged in the practice.[71]

In nineteenth-century Great Britain, the classic Wesleyan Conference (unlike Conferences of non-Wesleyan Methodists) was notoriously confined to the travelling preachers turned ministers. This feature was one element in the repeated disruptions of that period. The Wesleyans admitted lay representatives beginning in 1878 and even then reserved some matters to a separate Ministerial Session.

In American Methodism after 1784, the Conferences of The Methodist Episcopal Church also consisted of ordained clergy for several generations.[72] The reform movement of the early nineteenth century resulted in the formation of the Methodist Protestant Church in 1830, which began to include lay representatives in Annual Conferences. About a generation or so after the split of The Methodist Episcopal Church in 1844, the two major forms of episcopal Methodism began to allow lay representation, first in 1866 in the South and six years later in the North.

---

[70] *Minutes* (1787), *Q.* 20: 'A. Let no person that is not in connexion with us preach in any of our chapels or preaching-houses without a note from Mr. Wesley, or from the Assistant of the circuit from whence he comes; which note must be renewed yearly.' Sarah received her note, authorized by Wesley, from the Assistant on the Norwich circuit, Joseph Harper. See also Chilcote, *Women Preachers*, 133–34; Zachariah Taft, *Biographical Sketches of . . . Holy Women*, 2 vols. (London, 1825–28; repr. 1992), 1:27, 84.

[71] Taft, *Holy Women*, 2:115; see also below, pp. 75–76.

[72] For a recent study, see Russell Richey, *The Methodist Conference in America: A History* (Nashville, 1996).

IV. Agenda and Business

1. Early Conferences

The planned agenda for the first Conference in 1744 has survived, apparently drawn up by Wesley at Newcastle in June 1744. He showed it to Richard Viney, who made a copy—hence its survival in Viney's diary.[73] The explicit question-and-answer format has been perpetuated in Conference agenda and *Minutes* to the present day. The specific origin of its format is not clear, but Wesley used such an approach for self-examination at Oxford, as Professor Heitzenrater has pointed out.[74] Professor Baker suggests that Wesley was conditioned to Socratic models of questioning in the college disputations at Oxford. In the case of the Conference, the 'moderator functioned as the chairman of a semi-consultative gathering whose members were led through a carefully orchestrated discussion'. It was 'an authoritative system initiated and guided by an authoritarian leader, even though in the course of its activities some debate might in fact be allowed'.[75]

W. L. Doughty has justly argued that the business of the Conference was determined in part by the exigencies of the church (that is, the connexion).[76] Questions were added to the agenda as new possibilities and precautions were needed. There were complaints in later years that 'temporal business' was overshadowing conversation of a more devotional and edifying nature.

The 1744 Conference agenda and Minutes crisply stated the design of the meeting at the outset: 'To consider before God: 1. What to teach. 2. How to teach. 3. What to do? i.e., doctrine, discipline, and practice.' Doctrine was dealt with as a very large and detailed section of the first four Conferences, up to and including 1747. Those years included widespread criticism, from within and without the evangelical camp, of Methodism's stance on the

---

[73] Simon, *Methodist Societies*, 197; and see agenda, below, n. 12.

[74] Heitzenrater, *People Called Methodists*, 146.

[75] Frank Baker, in draft comment for this edn. In his biography of JW in *DNB*, Alexander Gordon notes that the Quakers used this method but that JW apparently did not know of this.

[76] W. L. Doughty, *John Wesley: His Conferences and His Preachers* (London, 1944), 27. JW and CW occasionally refer, rather imprecisely, to the Methodist connexion as 'the church'. See Heitzenrater, 'Purge the Preachers', 491 and n. 43.

doctrines of salvation. After 1747, doctrinal questions figure only occasionally and spasmodically in the Conference discussions. The notable exceptions are the Conference *Minutes* on perfection, in the 1760s, and on Calvinism, in 1770–71. The basic principles of discussion and confidentiality had been laid out in the first two Conferences, and the significance both of this explication of procedure and of its later omission from a revised edition of the 'Large' *Minutes* has been noted.[77] The evidence is very fragmentary concerning what actually happened in the Conference: the nature of debates, the process of decision making, and the extent of Wesley's allowance for liberty to differ and freedom to discuss (implied in some of his procedural rules).

One attractive feature of the Conference, to the preachers as well as others in the locality of the meeting, was that Wesley and the leading preachers offered them a diet of preaching. The first 'circuit plan' appears in one of Wesley's notebooks, where he listed when and where the preachers were assigned during their stay in London for the period surrounding the Conference of 1754.[78] Wesley usually preached morning and evening on each day of the annual Conference. Though in 1778 his voice failed so that he had to give place to other preachers, on other occasions he claimed that he felt as fresh as ever at the end of his preaching.[79] Preachers' diaries tend to suggest that, for some at least, these sermons most merited recording, rather than debates and decisions. And some preachers complained in later years that temporal business was overshadowing devotion and edification—once again implying, through recollection, that the earlier notion of the Conference focused on spiritual matters.

Nevertheless, apart from doctrine, the main business of the earliest Conferences was to lay down the lines of discipline and procedure in the Societies, Bands, and select Bands; to spell out the duties

[77] See above, pp. 13–14.

[78] Of the two dozen or so preachers who attended the Conference, some fourteen were given preaching assignments around London during late April and into the early summer. Wesley drew up a plan that charted the who, where, and when of their daily preaching among the seven locations on the London Circuit. Heitzenrater, *People Called Methodists*, 190 and illus.; see also Colman Collection, XX ('Statuta Collegii Lincolniensis'), opp. pp. 25–43, in MA.

[79] *Journal & Diaries*, 23:102 in this edn. In 1772, Wesley said he had usually 'desired one of the brethren to preach in the morning' because he needed to talk so much during Conference. But this year he preached morning and evening and 'was no more tired than with my usual labour'. Ibid., 22:345 in this edn.

of various officers like the stewards; and to describe in detail the expected role and behaviour of the itinerants. Later Conferences continued to include additional details of discipline and behaviour, including some reiteration, refinement, and supplementation.

2. The Expanded Agenda of Later Conferences

For many years, the Conference meetings usually extended across four or five days. But in 1769, Wesley complained that 'above two days' were spent in 'temporal business'.[80] He resolved henceforth to do as much as possible of that business through 'clerks'. In 1780, however, Wesley noted in his *Journal* that the Conference had for some time been 'straitened for time', and they resolved to extend the Conference to nine or ten days in the future so that 'everything relative to the carrying on the work of God might be maturely considered'. That Conference lasted nine days, and the meetings remained about that length for subsequent years.[81]

Wesley's outline description of the course of the 1781 Conference provides a fair idea of the general order of business of the assembly at that time in its development. Its sessions began each day at six and nine o'clock in the morning and at two o'clock in the afternoon. On Tuesday and Wednesday mornings, they considered the character of the preachers. On Thursday afternoon, when separation from the Church was discussed, 'any of the Society' were admitted. On Friday and Saturday, they settled most of the 'temporal business'. On Sunday, Wesley preached three times. The Conference met again on Monday and continued on Tuesday.[82]

By that year, the agenda for the Conference had settled into a fairly fixed pattern, at least if the *Minutes* accurately reflect the order of business. First, the record listed the preachers admitted that year; then those remaining on trial, and then those admitted on trial. Next was the list of those desisting from travelling and those who had died. Then came the annual examination of preachers' characters. The stations were listed next, followed by the financial provision for

[80] *Minutes* (1769), *Q.* 20.
[81] *Journal & Diaries*, 23:182 in this edn.
[82] Ibid., 21:410–11 in this edn.; cf. Sutcliffe, MS 'History', fol. 1123, on the 1786 Conference, saying it met at 6:00 and 9:00 a.m. and 2:00 p.m. JW invited all the Society to attend at 9:00 a.m. on Friday.

wives allocated to various Societies. Then appeared the list of numbers (membership) in each circuit, the Kingswood School collection, and the names of those who received financial support at this school or elsewhere. Allowances were then listed for those supported from the Preachers' Fund (for retirement or superannuation). They named the preaching-houses built that year, frequently followed by a miscellaneous listing of current problems and regulations or advice. Finally, they fixed a date and place for the next Conference. In some years, as we have seen, there would be 'open sessions' and other business not recorded in the *Minutes*, while on other occasions a letter or statement by Wesley might be appended, probably relating to some issue raised at the Conference or currently exercising him.

Despite the intrusion of special matters, the major regular items of business were clear: admission, retirement, and deaths of preachers; examination of their characters; stations; statistics of membership; and the major funds and allocations from them. These topics contrast sharply with the long and detailed discussions of doctrine, discipline, and organization that characterized the early Conferences. The list of major items evolved gradually, but the order of the agenda tended to remain fairly stable even as new items were introduced. The patchy series of Minutes before the beginning of annual publication in 1765 fails to reveal clearly the process by which this pattern evolved, for most of the agenda appeared fixed by that date, but some of the steps are evident. In 1746, the large early circuits were first listed (§65); the preachers' stations were listed for one quarter (§67); the call, examination, and reception of preachers were outlined (§§48–50); and the first list of 'Assistants' (as all the full-time itinerants were then termed) was published (§66). The first list of local preachers was included in 1747 (§65). In 1749, the first 'Probationers' were listed (§22); the method of receiving 'Helpers' on probation and, after a year, into full connexion (and given a copy of the 'Large' *Minutes* of 1749) was described (§21, *Q*. 18 [4]); and the office of Assistant (now meaning the senior itinerant in a circuit) was also defined and men appointed to the position (§§9–10). The first extant list of preachers for a whole year appeared in 1753 (§31), and the chief local preachers were listed as half-itinerants in 1755 (§2).

In 1751, a series of regional Conferences examined the character and competence of the preachers. In 1753 (§21) came the first formal record of going over the preachers' characters one by one. In 1758 (§4) came a question on whether preachers were 'unblameable in outward conversation', which had been a recurring concern in the ill-recorded Conferences of the previous few years. One preacher remained on trial (§5). By 1765, the normal order of business appears more or less settled: What preachers are admitted this year? Who are admitted on trial? Who act as Assistants? Who are the other travelling preachers? How are they stationed? To these regular items are added that year the reports on funds, beginning with Kingswood School and the Preachers' Fund (*QQ*. 6, 7); others were added later, with sums subscribed and expended and the officers concerned.[83] The following year, 1766, they contain the full range of questions asked of preachers admitted to full connexion (*Q*. 2), and they list those 'laid aside' (*Q*. 5). In 1767, the *Minutes* listed those who 'desist from travelling' (*Q*. 5). In 1768, any objections to preachers are requested (*Q*. 6). The question about who remained on trial only became regular from 1769 (*Q*. 2). And in 1777, the *Minutes* contain a question on preachers who died during the previous year, with a short obituary on each of the deceased (*Q*. 4).

Into this growing framework, Wesley added or inserted into the agenda (not always in any apparent logical order) items of special concern at the time. Apart from miscellaneous regulations, the main topics that stand out in each decade become obvious. In the 1740s, basic doctrine and discipline had predominated. In the 1750s, the agenda increasingly included problems over separation from the Church and ordination, along with recurring campaigns of inquiry into preachers' character, competence, and loyalty. In the 1760s, the tensions over the doctrine of Christian perfection appeared. In the 1770s, the Calvinist dispute flared up and American mission expanded. In the 1780s, questions about the Church and ordination were often discussed, along with other situations, such as the American settlement, the Deed of Declaration, and other signs of preparation in anticipation of the period 'after Wesley'.

3. Temporal Business

Inevitably, as the connexion developed and the complexity of business concerns and internal crises intensified, more and more time was spent on temporal affairs. As early as 1769, people (including Wesley) complained of the time consumed by these items, and

---

[83] See section VI below.

'clerks' were appointed to do as much as possible to resolve these issues (*Q.* 20). How far this plan was actually implemented is unclear, but at all events the temporal business continued to grow. For that reason, in 1780 Wesley resolved to lengthen the Conference to nine or ten days.[84] Consequently, after Wesley's death, some preachers, in the light of this concern and the expense of the gathering of Conference, suggested a pattern comparable to the American scheme of regional and (less frequent) General Conferences.[85]

Despite the healthy diet of preaching during the Conference, complainants about the plethora of temporal business and the lack of edification probably desired explicit discussion of spiritual matters, over and above the periodic questionings that Wesley launched into the devotional and practical behaviour of the preachers. No doubt the complaints in later years depended partly on temperament, partly on nostalgia for the sacrificial dedication of the small Band of early brethren. In his later years, John Pawson was particularly prone to lament the decline of what he called 'primitive Methodism'.[86] Joseph Benson was another lamenter. He wrote to Charles Wesley in 1772:

There was so much temporal business to be transacted that there was little time for any spiritual, and therefore I had nothing to transmit worthy your notice. . . . [It was] a very tedious and unprofitable time to me. I greatly wish for my part, that it could be contrived to transact the temporal matters by the Assistants alone before the other preachers arrive; then there might be time for discussing some points of importance and material edification in faith and love. [It would then be a time of mutual spiritual advantage to all that attended, whereas] at present I can *see no end* it answers with respect to the majority at all.[87]

Benson continued to complain, though in 1778 he said that the Conference was the best he ever attended: 'Mr. Wesley has been in a sweet spirit, has preached some excellent sermons and has dealt closely and plainly with the preachers, setting two aside for misdemeanors.'[88] Evidently the 'clerks' proposed in 1769 had not helped much. And the complaints continued even after Wesley began to use

[84] *Journal & Diaries*, 23:182 in this edn.
[85] See below, section V (1), pp. 35–37.
[86] John C. Bowmer and John A. Vickers, eds., *The Letters of John Pawson*, 3 vols. (Peterborough, 1994–95), 2:16, hereafter Pawson, *Letters*; this letter was in 1794.
[87] On Aug. 26, 1772; MS PLP, 7.6, in MA.
[88] Benson to W. Churchey, Aug. 3, 1778, MS PLP, 7.7, in MA.

a selected 'Cabinet' before and during the Conference to prepare the business.[89] Pawson, one of the Cabinet, is a frequent complainant along the same lines.

Of the 1784 Conference, Pawson wrote realistically that 'our affairs are tolerably well settled, but we are grown so large a family that these require more time and are attended with far greater difficulties than they were formerly.'[90] Of the 1787 Conference, he wrote, 'We are not so spiritual at these times as I could wish. Almost the whole time is taken up with temporal things, and but little said or done that has a tendency to edification. This is a great and sore evil, under which my soul has long mourned.'[91] Similarly, he wrote to Benson in 1789 that too much time was spent on temporal things—a bad temper and spirit marked the debate; some in the Conference thought too much about money and so spent too much time on ways to raise it; and the Conference wasted too much time on such little things as points of discipline.[92] Pawson and Benson seem to have envisioned the Conference as the type of conversation on the work of God that was the model in 1744, though of course they could have had no personal memories of that time.

By the time of Wesley's last Conference in 1790, he also seems to have forgotten the earlier design of the Conference. The old man had 'in great measure become a child' and was not much use in settling Conference business. The sessions became very tedious, and this despite Mather having apparently acted, as another observer put it, like 'a kind of archdeacon'.[93]

V. Structure of the Conference

1. Timing and Place

The design for continuation of the Conference, as proposed in 1744, was to meet on a quarterly basis. This plan echoed the

---

[89] For the 'Cabinet', see below, section V (2), pp. 39–42.
[90] John Pawson, MS 'Some Account of the Life of Mr. John Pawson', fol. 26, in MA.
[91] Ibid., fol. 35.
[92] Pawson to Benson, Aug. 31, 1789, Pawson, *Letters*, 1:86.
[93] Pawson, MS 'Some Account', fol. 39; Sutcliffe, MS 'History', fols. 1193–94. For other accounts see *Minutes* (1790), n. 534.

intentions of the early gathering of Wesley associates that had met in November 1739, plans that were apparently never carried out in the earlier instance.[94] Another Conference of that sort did not gather until June 1743, and that turned out to be smaller than intended. However, the gathering the following year, in June 1744, exhibited some momentum, and Wesley proposed that they gather for quarterly sessions on November 1 at Newcastle, February 1 at Bristol, and May 1 at London, 'if God permits'.[95] The largest Methodist Societies at the time were centred in these three cities, and they would become the strategic foci for Wesley's journeys around his annual 'great triangle'. In spite of these stated plans, however, the next Conference was in Bristol on August 1, 1745, and the following one on May 12, 1746, in the same city. No explanation is given for the change of plan. At this early stage, the annual meetings did not represent a long-range plan for a formal Conference as a perpetual feature of the movement in any case. Nevertheless the annual gathering seems to emerge from the early stage over the next few years, if only by accident, usually meeting at some point between June and August, and gradually settling on the first week in August. However, these annual Conferences did not limit Wesley from calling other gatherings with a more limited agenda, whether it was to meet with other revival groups or to have regional Conferences of Methodists on particular issues.

The annual pattern has persisted to the present day, though after Wesley's death some preachers, lamenting the expense of Conference and the pressure of 'temporal concerns', suggested that something like the post-1792 American pattern of yearly regional ('Annual') Conferences and quadrennial national (General) Conferences might be used. Thus in 1797, John Pawson suggested a Conference only every two years,[96] and in 1800, Joseph Bradford lamented that they could not continue on their present foundation but could not see a way out.[97] The Legal Hundred could have amended the Deed of Declaration but had given up their right to do so. The only way to remove the evil would be to have yearly 'Provinshall [*sic*] Conferences' and a General Conference every

[94] See above, p. 9. See also Heitzenrater, *People Called Methodists*, 108–9, 112. A quarterly Conference had also been used by some Calvinistic Methodists.

[95] Minutes (1744), §96.

[96] To Charles Atmore, May 8, 1797, Pawson, *Letters*, 2:118.

[97] Bradford to Pawson, Feb. 15, 1800, Tyerman MSS, 3:81.

three, five, or seven years, which would save time and money. Similarly, in 1805 Joseph Bradford wrote on his experience of Conference, saying that he would like to change to the American model of every three, five, or seven years, [98] and it was this model—inevitable in so large a country as the United States—that Pawson possibly had in mind. Similar suggestions have sometimes surfaced in more recent times, but without official response.

As to location, no regular pattern emerged for some time. Disregarding regional and more limited meetings, the main annual assembly during the period 1744–51 was held only in London and Bristol, and not on a regular pattern. In 1752, there was a special meeting with a limited agenda in London in January, and then one in Ireland as well. But in 1753, the Conference met for the first time in Leeds. There, it was resolved that in the future, all Conferences would be held in London, Bristol, and Leeds in turn. [99]

This pattern was followed during Wesley's lifetime with the exception of 1765 and 1787, when the Conference met in Manchester. It convened there again in 1791 after Wesley's death, and thereafter the town became part of the regular rota. No explanation was given for the departures from the rule in 1765 and 1787. The Deed of Declaration (1784) rather oddly laid down as its first rule that the Conference should be held in London, Bristol, or Leeds 'except as after mentioned', adding in Rule 12 that 'the Conference shall and may appoint the place of holding the yearly assembly thereof at any other city, town, or place than London, Bristol, or Leeds, when it shall seem expedient so to do'. This statement allowed for the addition of Manchester in 1787, and other places were added in the nineteenth century—for example, Sheffield in 1805. No doubt the addition of Manchester reflected the growing importance of the town as a Methodist centre. It seems odd that Leeds rather than Newcastle figures as one of the first Conference towns. Newcastle was one of Wesley's favourite places and his original northern headquarters and had been named, predictably enough, as a place for the original plan of a quarterly assembly. Possibly Leeds was found to be more convenient as saving travelling time and expense, and Manchester may have appealed for the same reason.

[98] Bradford to James Rogers, Aug. 2, 1805, Tyerman MSS, 1:331.
[99] *Minutes* (1753), §2.

2. *Committees and Officers*

In a body implicitly taking on a legislative and even governing role in its annual meeting, committees eventually emerged as an inevitable necessity. Ad hoc committees tackled temporary problems, and permanent ones administered regularly occurring business, especially financial. It is somewhat surprising that they did not appear earlier. They seem to have been created to relieve Wesley of his temporal burdens. But how far they were due to pressure from him, or from the preachers or lay sympathizers anxious to relieve his burdens, is not obvious. The gaps in the early Minutes and limited information in the later ones make the genesis and nature of the committees less than entirely clear.

Permanent Committees. The first organized committee was, perhaps, the Committee for the Preachers' Fund, the members of which were first listed in 1767, although it appears to have existed earlier.[100] Permanent committees of this kind tended to multiply in the 1780s, partly as a result of increasing business and the need for greater efficiency, but also to provide some relief for Wesley and prepare for an orderly transition at his death. It has been suggested that while the Deed of Declaration in 1784 showed Wesley 'arranging for the continuance of Methodism after his death by establishing the Conference of preachers as the heir to his powers', he was also 'deputing that power in advance to a select number of preachers by means of committees'. [101]

The Book Committee was a case in point. Wesley appointed this himself, independently of Conference, on October 10, 1788, and its members were named in his will a few months later. They were Thomas Coke, James Creighton, and Peard Dickinson (all Anglican clergy), Thomas Rankin, George Whitefield (the Book Steward), and 'the London Assistants for the time being'. This committee also audited Wesley's accounts.[102] The basic financial aspects of book affairs had been delegated to the Book Stewards many years earlier.[103] Also, in 1790, a Building Committee was appointed for Britain, with

---

[100] *Minutes* (1767), *QQ.* 21–22. The stewards for the fund were first listed in 1765 (*Q.* 7 [3]), but fairly clearly it had existed earlier. See below, section VI on finances.

[101] Baker, 'Polity', 253.

[102] Nehemiah Curnock, ed., *Journal of the Rev. John Wesley, A.M.*, 8 vols. (London: Epworth Press, 1909–16), 7:441, hereafter *Journal* (Curnock).

[103] See below, section VI on finances.

a separate one for Ireland; and a committee was named 'for the management of our affairs in the West Indies'.[104]

Several standing committees appear shortly after Wesley's death to carry on the work that he had managed personally. The Stationing Committee was first appointed after Wesley's death in 1791 to assume the responsibility that Wesley had largely kept in his own hands.[105] Another group, in effect the first Education Committee, was also set up in 1791 to supervise the affairs of Kingswood School, another area that Wesley seems largely to have controlled.[106] Wesley's death left a large executive gap between Conferences that had to be filled also by the creation of the new District Committees in 1791.[107] Thus, by rejecting another 'King in Israel', the Conference had to create piecemeal a diffused executive in place of Wesley's one-man Band, and it clearly chose to cover the various functions through committees rather than individuals.[108] The one partial exception for a number of years was Coke's personal but inefficient handling of overseas missions—it was years before the successive committees appointed to aid (or control?) him really acted.[109]

On the matter of committees, there was a significant contrast with Anglicanism, whose bishops and parish clergy were focuses of more or less personalized authority. The 'President' and 'Chairman' in the post-Wesley Methodist tradition and practice were largely what their titles indicated, for they primarily 'presided' and 'chaired' collective bodies rather than governed in their own right. The connexion resisted schemes, such as the 'Lichfield Plan' of 1794, that called for a body of individuals ruling in episcopal fashion.[110]

Wesley's Cabinet. Of a rather different nature was the cluster of persons often called Wesley's 'Cabinet'—a term borrowed from the contemporary world of political government. This advisory body

---

[104] *Minutes* (1790), *Q.* 21.

[105] Ibid., (1791), *Q.* 32. Wesley did not always get his own way in this matter; see below, section VII.

[106] Ibid., *Q.* 35; Baker, 'Polity', 254.

[107] *Minutes* (1791), *QQ.* 8, 9. See further, section IX.

[108] This was the explicit choice expressed in the Halifax meeting in 1791, printed in Davies, George, and Rupp, *History of Methodist Church*, 4:241–42.

[109] The first committee, under Coke, was for the West Indies: *Minutes* (1790), *Q.* 21. For Coke and the committees see John A. Vickers, *Thomas Coke* (London, 1969), 271–86.

[110] See below, pp. 74, 97–98, 101–2, and *Minutes* (1791), *Q.* 8, n. 26a.

was never formally constituted or even mentioned in the *Minutes*, but is known only from scattered private references and a passage in Wesley's *Journal* in 1781. Wesley chose essentially an inner group of advisers to help him prepare business before and during the Conferences. It lacked any fixed composition, which is not surprising, since Wesley even considered the Conference attendees as simply those he chose to confer with him.[111]

The origins of this 'Cabinet' are not clear. In 1754, Charles Wesley, exasperated by what he saw as his brother's vacillations over ordination and separation from the Church of England, wrote that 'since the Melchisedechians have been taken in, I have been excluded [from] his cabinet council'.[112] This term was, no doubt, merely a highly coloured description of persons around Wesley whom Charles distrusted and not a reference to a body, however informal, connected with Conference preparation. A more likely, though still uncertain, reference comes from Thomas Taylor's diary in 1778. After recording an appeal for missions to Africa, he says, 'Afterwards *the Committee* [my italics] met and we were an hour and a half in what might have been done in five minutes'.[113] Unless this refers to an ad hoc group on the African question (which was not recorded in the *Minutes* at all), the definite article rather suggests a group for discussing general Conference business.

Much clearer (and usually taken to be the beginning of the 'Cabinet') is Wesley's statement in his published *Journal* for August 6, 1781: 'I desired Mr. Fletcher, Dr. Coke, and four more of our brethren to meet every evening [i.e., during Conference] that we might consult together on any difficulty that occurred'.[114] This development may have been provoked by particular difficulties that were expected.[115] As such, it may have been viewed only as a temporary expedient. Joseph Sutcliffe, however, seems to imply that such meetings were regular events.[116]

Wesley's diary is confusing on this matter. The diary itself is missing for nearly forty years, including the period that saw the

---

[111] This fluctuating membership of the annual Conference persisted even after its future constitution had been legally settled by the Deed of Declaration in 1784.

[112] Baker, *Charles Wesley*, 93.

[113] *Journal & Diaries*, 23:102, n. 4 in this edn.

[114] Ibid., 23:218 in this edn.

[115] For suggestions about the unspecified difficulties that seem to have led to this step, see Ward in *Journal & Diaries*, 23:218, n. 99 in this edn.

[116] Sutcliffe, MS 'History', fol. 992.

development of the Conference. But in 1783, Wesley records just before Conference, 'Dr. Coke, necessary talk for Conference', but no mention is made of a committee during it. In February 1784, he records 'The Committee' in London, which may refer to a London finance committee that we shall encounter later. There is no mention of a committee, immediately before or during the Conference. But several times in July of that year, before the Conference began, he notes 'Conference', which may be a non-specific reference to discussions of quite a different kind. This reference in February is strange, however, since John Pawson specifically says that Wesley consulted him and others in a 'select committee' on the question of ordinations for America.[117] Perhaps as yet all that was involved in such references to 'committee' was a spasmodic ad hoc consultation.

The first clear reference to the 'Cabinet', using that term, is in Wesley's diary in 1785.[118] From that time forward, Wesley mentions the meeting of such a group every year at the time of Conference, though without again using the term.[119] Notes from several contemporary observers begin to form a pattern that is revealing in this regard. Sutcliffe reports that several observers at the 1790 Conference noted Wesley's feebleness and relative inactivity, resulting in Alexander Mather taking charge at a table of leading preachers. John Valton says that Mather was Wesley's 'right-hand man' and took a leading part in the 'Select Committee' advising Wesley.[120] Rankin says that in the 1780s, most of the 'temporal business' was done by Mather and Pawson with his assistance.[121] In a letter to James Oddie, Thomas Hanby refers to some rather nasty and apparently unfounded gossip about Wesley causing 'no small stir in the Cabinet', which may or may not imply a clear-cut body.[122] A letter of Rankin to Hanby in 1789, however, has no such ambiguity: 'if I am

---

[117] For the diary references, see *Journal & Diaries*, 23:456, 477, 491, 493 in this edn.; and for Pawson's account, Tyerman MSS, 3:52, and Tyerman, *Wesley*, 3:428.

[118] Entries for July 25, 26, 27, 28; *Journal & Diaries*, 23:530 in this edn.

[119] Thus in 1786, 'Bro. Pawson, etc.', and on July 27, 'committee'; in 1787, 'committee'; in 1788, 'T. Rankin, Conf.'; in 1789, 'committee'; and in 1790, Wesley notes 'L. Conf.' ('little Conference'?) early each day. See Baker, 'Polity', 254; *Journal & Diaries*, 23:567 in this edn; *Journal* (Curnock), 7:305–7, 420, 522; 8:80–81.

[120] Thomas Jackson, ed., *Lives of the Early Methodist Preachers*, 6 vols., 4th. edn. (London, 1871), 2:219.

[121] Diary, Tyerman MSS, 2:108.

[122] Sept. 6, 1788, Tyerman MSS, 2:27; *WHS* 45 (1985): 28; Pawson, *Letters*, 1:87–88, 90.

not in the field with you and my dear brethren, I may be of some use in the Cabinet'.[123]

Rankin's comment is particularly interesting because it was written in late September and seems to refer to meetings other than during the Conference period. Thus one might ask, Just how far was Wesley really directing the connexion in his last years? Several preachers, including Hampson and Pawson, complained about Wesley's openness to misguided counselors and flatterers, though with very different people in mind, depending on their views of the direction in which Methodism should go. Etheridge, in his life of Coke, says that Wesley 'had of late years gradually devolved the administrative government of the societies to the Conference, reserving to himself a final veto on all matters'.[124] Wesley had also, 'in prospect of death, appointed that a Committee of Conference, consisting of three or of seven members, should be invested with the power that he had thus retained for his own life, a proposal that had met with the general approbation of preachers and people'. This comment seems to be an imperfect reference not to the Cabinet, but to a scheme that Wesley had suggested as far back as 1769, when he had given up hope of an evangelical union and was speculating about the future of Methodism and how to safeguard the continuance of those not leaving for the Church or Dissent.[125]

Conference Officers. Much of the business of permanent committees appears to have been overseen by individual officers, perhaps an inevitable development. There is the reference, for example, to using 'clerks' to deal with temporal business in 1769.[126] Professor Baker notes that preachers stationed in London often had connexional administrative duties to perform, but not until 1773 was a preacher given such a job without a circuit appointment.[127] Thomas Olivers was then listed as 'travels with Mr. Wesley'. Samuel Bradburn also said that he himself traveled for several years with Wesley.[128] That role, as a kind of secretary, seems to have been

---

[123] Sept. 29, 1789; quoted by Vickers in *WHS* 45 (1985): 28.
[124] J. W. Etheridge, *The Life of the Rev. Thomas Coke, D.C.L.* (London, 1860), 68.
[125] *Letters* (Telford), 5:143–45; also as a paper at the conclusion of *Minutes* (1769).
[126] *Minutes* (1769), *Q.* 20.
[127] 'Polity', 254; see *Minutes* (1773), *Q.* 7.
[128] T. W. Blanshard, *Life of Samuel Bradburn: The Methodist Demosthenes* (London, 1871), 85.

assumed for several years by Joseph Bradford, a rather enigmatic and ill-documented man who evidently knew Wesley well and exerted some influence over him.

In 1776, the list of stations was preceded by a list of what may be termed connexional officers: 'Joseph Bradford travels with Mr. Wesley. John Atlay keeps his accounts. Thomas Olivers corrects the press.' But from 1780 onwards, other officers were once more included in the regular circuit appointments.[129] In 1777, Atlay's title becomes 'the Book Steward', although he seems to have started work earlier, and as early as the 1750s, two London stewards had taken over most of the book affairs from Wesley. The Deed of Declaration of 1784 created the offices of President and Secretary, the former being filled by Wesley and the latter by Dr. Coke. John Valton had already been observed to be acting as secretary to the Conference as early as 1782,[130] and an account of the 1790 Conference notes again that 'Mr. Valton was the secretary with his small quarto ledger'.[131] Presumably he was taking the rough draft for the Conference Journal, which had been authorized by the Deed.

Although the problem of how, between Conferences, to fill the executive gap left by Wesley's death had to be dealt with at that point in 1791, suggestions had been proposed as early as 1749 for measures to tighten up and, in a measure, centralize some of the administration. These pressures were renewed in the 1760s in response to debt and other financial problems. Another recurring problem concerned preaching-house trusts that put total control of the property in the hands of local trustees, against the stipulation of the Model Deed. That document, upon which all Methodist property was to be fixed, was designed to ensure that Wesley (and after him, the Conference) would have full control of appointments and doctrine preached in the Methodist preaching-houses. But even that Deed, formalized in 1763, had flaws not remedied until the Deed of Declaration in 1784.

Worries about these local trusts also provoked ideas for centralization of control. As early as 1748, Wesley had suggested that it would be useful if the Societies could be 'more firmly and closely united together'.[132] The following November, the Conference heard

---

[129] Baker, 'Polity', 254–55.
[130] Sutcliffe, MS 'History', fol. 1014.
[131] Ibid., fol. 1193.
[132] Minutes (1748), §61.

a proposal for a 'general union', with London 'accounted the mother church' and its stewards to 'consult for the good of all the churches'.[133] The Assistants would collect information, and the London stewards would operate a clearinghouse for debt and aid. This suggestion implies that financial needs were probably the main concerns in mind, the weak Societies in effect being helped by the strong. No such centralization was carried out at that time, but the financial problems continued to increase over the years and helped to precipitate other measures for centralization.

In February 1753, Wesley records, 'A proposal was made for devolving all temporal business, books and all, entirely on the stewards, so that I might have no care upon me (in London at least) but that of the souls committed to my charge. O when shall it ever be!'[134] This change led to the local stewards nationwide becoming accountable to the two Foundery stewards in London for book money, 'who thus became the first Methodist Book Stewards'.[135] Financial needs also dictated the implementation, beginning in 1763, of an annual General Fund to help needy Societies.[136] But by 1766, the total debt was over £11,000, which led to a temporary ban on the building or acquisition of more preaching-houses unless two-thirds of the cost was raised beforehand.[137] The following year, an appeal was launched to wealthier Methodists to liquidate the debt.[138]

Though clearly provoked by financial needs, the arrangements made to organize the appeal and service the debt had unexpected consequences for Wesley. The committee of London laymen in charge of the appeal also made wide-ranging proposals about Methodist organization, in effect shifting some power from Wesley. They feared, reasonably, what would happen (at the very least, financially) after his death if nothing were done. This little-known episode recorded by Joseph Sutcliffe in his MS 'History of Methodism'[139] is an illuminating example of the importance of such lay pressure on Wesley, revealing how suspicious he could be of threats to his authority and, to be fair, to that of his preachers. Joseph Sutcliffe

---

[133] Ibid. (1749), §1.
[134] *Journal & Diaries*, 20:445 and n. 76 in this edn.
[135] See below, pp. 57–58.
[136] See *Minutes* (1763 ad fin.), first mentioned officially in the 'Large' *Minutes* (1763), §72.
[137] *Minutes* (1766), *Q*. 13.
[138] Ibid., (1767), *QQ*. 17, 18, and see below, pp. 45, 56, for details.
[139] Sutcliffe, MS 'History', fols. 675–81.

notes that in 1767, Wesley had hoped to settle the debt simply through generous friends, 'but he had done more than he intended; he himself had incorporated a permanent committee consisting of the assistant preacher for the chairman; the stewards of the chief Societies for members; and the gentlemen for auditors, with Thomas Day of Southwark, a man of business, for secretary.'[140] Sutcliffe continues: 'And though they affected not to interfere with spiritual affairs, yet they could and did interfere with the risings of all contingent cases.' Sutcliffe then quotes from the secretary's accounts an address 'To the Members of Mr. Wesley's Society', apparently written in 1792 and recounting the history of this affair.

Thomas Day says that when the London Committee was formed, he attended it from 1767 to 1792. Confronting the alarming debt, Wesley wondered what to do with his 'new and active committee' from its establishment. They were to meet quarterly to audit the accounts and once a year to read them to a general meeting of Societies, which was apparently done for twenty-six years. Later in 1767, Wesley brought funds to the committee, and apparently he and the preachers were joined in security for some of the debt. The committee, instead of paying without question, asked where the debt would fall after Wesley's death and what security the committee would have for it. Wesley had not expected such an inquiry. 'In fact Mr. Wesley found himself and all his labours and cares arraigned at the bar of his own committee.'

Wesley was displeased at the committee exceeding its powers, in his view. So in a remarkable and outspoken letter of February 6, 1768, the committee vindicated itself. Basically the members urged that, having been given the job of supervising the financial problem, it was their duty to check the arrangements, and that it was their 'prerogative and duty to speak [their] minds freely on any subject that offered'. If they had exceeded their powers by doing so, they 'did not know what they had been appointed for'.

The committee then gave eight numbered reasons to Wesley for its so-called interference. The first was 'that the uniting of the Society [which, as Sutcliffe rightly noted, means here the whole connexion] into one body is a thing very desirable, and even necessary after your decease for its existence.' This approach would be a 'great work' for Wesley and would be the only effective means to influence people to

---

[140] This appears to be the Thomas Day who joined the Foundery Society in 1756 and was an original trustee of City Road Chapel. *WHS* 7 (1910): 106–11.

pay off the debt, since that could not be effected after his death. The preaching-houses ought to be the property of the Society (connexion), 'considered as one body', and secured to it previous to the payment of the debt. This could be done only by vesting them in a 'general or united trust' selected 'from various parts of the kingdom'. Meanwhile, as things then stood, much of the debt was a kind of deposit for the building, which would be seen as a debt to the creditors. If the 'union' were to be effected, the most pressing debts might be cancelled 'by borrowing money on life annuities'.

This document was signed by eighteen men, including Thomas Day and William Briggs, Wesley's former Book Steward. Sutcliffe comments that the varying local trusts could not possibly have been reduced to a single scheme, while Wesley in his Model Deed only asserted the right of appointing preachers. Some of the objectors, Sutcliffe claimed, had attended the Fetter Lane Society with Wesley and thought the scheme there 'perfectly coincident with that of the Moravians at Fulneck'—good for a local settlement but not for the larger Methodism. How could one find men to bind themselves for millions of pounds? The life annuity idea, however, he thought excellent, as death would absolve them from the debt. But Sutcliffe also drew the moral that when a minister gathers a people, he thinks he has a right to speak to them on spiritual affairs. On the Moravian scheme, however, trustees are 'princes, patriarchs, and priests' all in one trust. For Sutcliffe, the secular and spiritual affairs of the church are 'distinct in nature and varied in operation'. No doubt this view reflected nineteenth-century Wesleyan perspectives on the ministry, but the episode also underlines the problems of the evolving, preacher-dominated Conference.

The committee's challenge probably helps to explain some subsequent proposals: in 1768, for all trust deeds to be sent to London and a 'strong box' provided for them;[141] and in 1770, for a 'general trust' to be drawn out of the whole nation.[142] In 1773, Wesley wrote to Christopher Hopper that 'we have gone a few steps further towards a general trust, but the matter goes on very slowly.'[143] Years later, John Pawson, anxious to show that the Deed of Declaration in

---

[141] *Minutes* (1768), *Q.* 15.
[142] Ibid. (1770), *Q.* 15, *A.* (3).
[143] *Letters* (Telford), 6:37.

1784 was not a plot by people like Dr. Coke, recalled that 'over forty years ago' (probably referring to this time around 1770), some preachers were uneasy about the security of the Model Deed, so they asked Wesley to remedy it. Although Wesley thought the Model Deed adequate, others were not satisfied, and John Hampson and James Oddie ('men of good judgement') pressed the case. At last Wesley yielded a little and various proposals were made: a general trust for all the Societies with trustees would be drawn from the larger ones, and all the deeds should be lodged in London. Pawson says that many were sent and then lost.[144]

According to Hampson, as late as the 1783 Conference, Coke proposed that Wesley should give absolute power to a select committee to conduct affairs after his death, and that all the trust deeds should be lodged at City Road Chapel in an iron box with Coke holding the key.[145] This last idea sounds like the 1768 proposal, but both suggestions, as reported, were no doubt coloured by Hampson's hostility to Coke. In any event, he says that large majorities rejected both.

The securing of deeds for local preaching-houses continued to cause much trouble, especially when they did not follow the template of the Model Deed. Wesley's concern was mainly to secure control of the pulpit (appointments and doctrines) to himself and, after him, to the Conference so as to preserve connexionalism against disintegration into a kind of Independency. The London men, however, had finance more in mind. The Model Deed of 1763[146] appeared to secure the control that Wesley desired, but not all houses used it as a template for their documents, and notable conflicts occurred at Birstall in 1782 and Dewsbury in 1787 as a consequence.[147] Yet even the Model Deed was not thief-proof—it did not provide guaranteed control of Methodist properties, for lack of a legal definition of the 'Yearly Conference of the People called Methodists'. Hence the need for the Deed of Declaration in 1784.

[144] Tyerman MSS, 3:65; Tyerman, *Wesley*, 3:420–21.

[145] Hampson, *Memoirs*, 3:205.

[146] See E. B. Perkins, *Methodist Preaching Houses and the Law* (London, 1952), 32–38.

[147] *Minutes* (1783), n. 949; (1788), n. 327; (1789), n. 415 and *QQ*. 19, 24.

VI. Finances

One of the most obscure aspects of eighteenth-century Methodist connexional organization is that of finance. This topic has already been touched on in the last section because of the organizational devices and committees that it provoked, as well as the unwelcome proposals that the debt committees brought to Wesley in their train. The subject is important because of the way that financial anxieties helped change the character of the Conference[148] and because it helped stimulate a desire for centralization. So far as I am aware, there has been very little discussion of the subject apart from Professor Baker's summary and Kingsley Lloyd's more detailed study of the preachers' pay and pensions.[149] On this and other financial matters it is only too clear from the *Minutes* that all aspects of Methodist finance caused recurring problems of debt and, it would seem, confusion over accounts that were never satisfactorily resolved in Wesley's lifetime. (It may be added that the *Minutes* show that the persons responsible had a disconcerting inability even to add up the lists of income and expenditure or indeed the total of membership figures correctly!)

Wesley's personal finances and sources of support are also something of a mystery, not least because for years they were often mixed up with 'connexional' ones. As a Fellow of Lincoln until his marriage, he could draw on his share of the Fellows' dues. In 1730–50 his income from this source varied between about £18 and about £80 per year, mostly about £30.[150] In 1766, Wesley, looking back to 1738, claimed that he had said then that he could live off this income with money to spare, although an examination of his financial accounts for the beginning of that decade indicates that his earnings over a five-year span ranged from £90 to £118 and his cost of living ranged from £46 to £60.[151] He lost this source of college income upon his marriage in 1751. In the 1770s, he was supposed to receive £60 per annum for his expenses from the stewards of the London Society

---

[148] As witness the complaints of Pawson and Benson discussed above, pp. 34–35.

[149] Baker, 'Polity', 251–53; A. K. Lloyd, *The Labourer's Hire* (London, 1987).

[150] V. H. H. Green, *The Young Mr. Wesley* (London, 1961), 320; and *The Commonwealth of Lincoln College* (Oxford, 1979), 327 and n. 1.

[151] From 1729 to 1733, his approximate rate of charity ranged from 4 to 15 percent. See MS Oxford Diary I and Financial Accounts, Colman Collection, in MA. Cf. *Minutes* (1766), *Q.* 29, *A.* (2).

(a longtime policy), but had trouble collecting it, and in 1775 he claimed he was still owed £30.[152] He once claimed that his literary labours had left him £500 or £600 in debt,[153] though later he said he had 'unawares grown rich' by his sales and so was able to give away upwards of £1,000 a year.[154] John had promised Charles Wesley an annuity of £100 a year on his marriage to Sally Gwynne, based on the security of the book value.[155] Samuel Bradburn claimed to know Wesley and his finances well from the old man himself.[156] In 1780–81, Wesley gave away more than £1,400 to charities, and he told Bradburn in 1787 that he never gave away less than £1,000 a year.[157] His income (said Bradburn) came from five sources. First, he had the profits of book sales, except for 10 percent taken by some preachers for eighteen years past for their sales, and Bradburn seems to imply that Wesley's charity was partly at the expense of what should have belonged to the preachers as a body.[158] Second, Wesley had about £150 per year in private subscriptions from London and Bristol. Third, he had a fixed stipend of £60 per annum from the London Society. Fourth, he received legacies almost every year. Fifth, those with whom he stayed on his travels generally gave him a few pounds.

So far as what might be called the connexional finances are concerned, following Mr. Lloyd's account and information recorded in the *Minutes*, we can trace the development of preachers' stipends, of allowances for wives and families, of the education of children, and of pensions. From the *Minutes* and other sources, the problems of debt (the General Fund), the Book Room, and annual Conference expenses can be outlined.

[152] G. J. Stevenson, *City Road Chapel* (London, 1872), 58–60.

[153] *Journal & Diaries V*, July 21, 1773, 22:384 in this edn.

[154] Tyerman, *Wesley*, 3:615–16.

[155] *Letters*, 26:346–47 in this edn.

[156] Blanshard, *Bradburn*, 85–86.

[157] This statement conflicts with his personal financial accounts, however, which indicate that his personal annual giving from 1783 to 1790 averaged about £300, about the same as was distributed by Mr. Atlay, the book steward, who left the connexion in 1788 after misappropriating funds. He may have meant that the connexional distributions, including the Preachers' Fund and the Yearly Expences, reached that annual level during the decade. Wesley, MS Diary (1782–90), in MA.

[158] This claim is somewhat suspect, since Wesley claimed publicly that the profit from the publishing enterprise went solely to the benefit of the worn-out preachers, their widows, and their children. The preachers performed the function of colporteur in the book enterprise, however, and apparently received a small commission for the sales in their Society.

1. Preachers' Stipends

As Mr. Lloyd remarks, with touching examples, poverty was the lot of many travelling preachers in the early years. For some time, they had no regular stipends, and when this money was finally granted, it was often hard to collect. Some preachers were able to live from savings, private income, or intermittent bouts at their trade (like the stonemason, John Nelson), until this double employment was forbidden. Some married a wife with a 'competence' that often figures alongside religious qualities and personal affection in the question of whether to marry. Circuit stewards were liable to regard preachers with large families as a liability to be avoided. In the days before stipends were even notionally provided, preachers merely received gifts in kind. Surviving Society accounts include items like horse hire and cobbling of boots, shirts, or even wigs.[159] Wesley admitted to Ebenezer Blackwell in 1753 that 'we have barely the first outlines of a plan with regard to temporals.'[160] Beginning in 1769, the *Minutes* stipulate that the circuit should provide the needy preachers with horses, saddles, and bridles.[161]

The Limerick Conference of 1752, however, recommended an annual clothing allowance of £8–£10 for Ireland, and later in the year the Bristol Conference recommended £12 for England plus £10 for wives and, when he was on his travels, an allowance for a preacher's children.[162] This allowance was variably paid in practice, and board was a matter for local discretion. Deficiencies were usually made up by the connexion. But as late as 1788, the *Minutes*[163] noted that many preachers had to go to friends for meals, so circuits were exhorted to provide sufficient allowances for preachers 'in general' to 'eat their meals at their own lodgings'. Some circuits obliged; some did not, even after Wesley's death. Reports from the Preachers' Friendly Society, founded in 1799, show that in 1801 the stipend was still £12, and although some circuits had raised this amount to £16,

---

[159] For example, the Manchester Society accounts, transcript in my possession (HDR).

[160] *Letters*, 26:511 in this edn.

[161] *Q.* 22.

[162] Limerick Conference Minutes (1752), §§25–27. Myles (*Chronological History*, 76) says it was fixed at £12 after this Conference with £10 for wives and allowances for children when preachers were on their travels. See Baker, 'Polity', 234, for the evidence for the obscure Bristol Conference Minutes (1752).

[163] *Q.* 23.

some had not yet reached the original figure. In 1798, 84 out of 116 circuits could not pay even that minimal amount without support from the connexion.[164]

2. Family Allowances

As to wives and families, the situation was probably even worse. Marriages of preachers were discouraged for financial reasons. Wesley, unlike most of his followers, had an equivocal attitude towards marriage and even late in life was inclined to favour celibacy where possible. He thought married preachers should attend to their work and travel as if unmarried.[165] Most of his preachers did not share his views, except that they were concerned to be sure that marriage would not hinder their itinerancy and were alert to the financial problems. Support for wives seems to have been seen as a concession rather than a right and at least partly as a connexional rather than a local responsibility.[166]

Mr. Lloyd thought that the Conference of 1749 laid down that the Assistant should inquire at the Quarterly Meeting 'what each preacher's wife will want [i.e., need] for the ensuing quarter, and let this be applied first of all out of the common stock'.[167] In fact, this appears only in the 1753 *Minutes* (§27), though Professor Baker notes the example of William Darney's wife being given an allowance as early as 1748 in the Haworth Round.[168] The 1753 provision presumably followed the Limerick and Bristol recommendation already mentioned.[169] But it had restrictive qualifications. The spousal allowance was given only when the preacher had taken counsel of the brethren before marrying, and it was to be only for those who had no other means. The 1753 Conference Minutes further ruled that even a preacher who had consulted his brethren but married 'one that has nothing' must 'return to his temporal business, and so commence a Local Preacher'.[170] In 1754, Myles, followed by

---

[164] Lloyd, *Labourer's Hire*, 14–15.

[165] *Journal & Diaries*, 20:380 in this edn. For Wesley's frequently negative views of marriage see Henry Abelove, *Evangelist of Desire* (Stanford, 1990), 49–58.

[166] Lloyd, *Labourer's Hire*, 19.

[167] Ibid., 20, n. Lloyd believed that Myles misleadingly attributed this to 1764.

[168] Davies, George, and Rupp, *History of Methodist Church*, 1:234.

[169] Limerick Conference Minutes (1752), §27; Davies, George, and Rupp, *History of Methodist Church*, 1:234.

[170] *Minutes* (1753), §§23–25; Lloyd, *Labourer's Hire*, 20.

Mr. Lloyd, suggests that five preachers who left the connexion that year would probably have remained if they had had provision for wives and children. But what we know of these cases makes it improbable: Skelton and Edwards certainly left for other reasons.[171] In any case, the recommendations for wives were liable to be honoured in the breach rather than in the observance. At all events, some historians claimed that Alexander Mather was the first married preacher to stand out successfully for a married allowance before being stationed in 1757.[172] But the real novelty of his position may be that he was married before becoming an itinerant. In this case, the London stewards promised the allowance before he would go to Epworth. Their agreement suggests a recognition of connexional rather than local responsibility, and this decision has been seen as the genesis of the Contingent Fund raised by a collection from the Societies for connexional debts and later used to help preachers' families.[173]

Then, in 1768,[174] preachers were prohibited to trade, though allowed to take a share in a ship. This move apparently was a response to complaints of the preachers giving unfair competition to local Methodists and of such work being a diversion from the preachers' gospel work. These preachers understandably complained that they traded from necessity, and Wesley promised to make up the loss. This situation was the incentive for the 1769 scheme for providing fixed allowances for wives even when their husbands' circuits could not pay it.[175] The scheme was, as Mr. Lloyd says, 'not very easy to follow, nor does Wesley's arithmetic seem entirely beyond reproach'.

The idea seems to have been for circuits currently able to support a preacher to continue also to pay the allowance even when the preacher was not married. This money, Wesley calculated, would provide a surplus to support wives and children in other circuits. In fact, there was no surplus, and the 1770 *Minutes* (*Q.* 21) ruled that children were to be provided for by the Society where the preachers were stationed. But that year a system of payments was adopted that continued until the Districts took it over from the circuits after

---

[171] See Minutes (1754), n. 3, for information about this departure.
[172] Myles, *Chronological History*, 71; Lloyd, *Labourer's Hire*, 1.
[173] Lloyd, *Labourer's Hire*, 20 and n., quoting *WHS* 8 (1911): 131.
[174] *Minutes* (1768), *Q.* 22, n. 94.
[175] Ibid., (1769), *Q.* 23.

Wesley's death. The design entailed a calculation of the number of wives to be supported and then the designation of circuits that could either pay for the whole cost of one or two wives, or otherwise contribute only half the cost of one. This arrangement often meant payment or partial payment by circuits for wives not stationed there. Perhaps, after all, this was a version of Wesley's proposal—certainly there seems no connection between the circuits and the wives they paid for elsewhere. Some circuits seem to have negotiated directly with each other. But the system remains rather unclear, and one suspects that it left some wives in need.[176]

In 1781, those wives who remained without circuit support were given allowances from the Preachers' Fund, which was financed by the preachers themselves for their retirement.[177] This bad practice was continued with some help from other sources until 1791, after which the shortfall was made up partly from the Contingent Fund and partly from local subscriptions.[178] Children's allowances were also made or proposed as early as the Limerick Conference of 1752, as we have seen.[179] Paid by the circuits, these allowances were to be fixed at £4 for each child.[180] From 1770, as already noted, children were to be supported by the Society where their fathers were stationed, but once again the connexion had to fund the deficit.

3. Education of Preachers' Children

Contrary to what is sometimes supposed, Kingswood School, started by Wesley in 1748, had not originally been founded for preachers' sons or at least not primarily for them,[181] even though it did come to cater for some of them. The Conference of 1756 instituted an annual collection for the school—the first connexional collection.[182] The 'Large' *Minutes* of 1763, in the series of questions and answers to publicize the school for Methodists generally, were particularly concerned to show the needs of preachers' children.

[176] Lloyd, *Labourer's Hire*, 21–22.
[177] *Minutes* (1781), *Q*. 10.
[178] Ibid., (1791), *Q*. 12.
[179] Davies, George, and Rupp, *History of Methodist Church*, 1:234.
[180] Lloyd, *Labourer's Hire*, 23.
[181] A. G. Ives, *Kingswood School in Wesley's Day and Since* (London, 1970), 53–57 and appendix 4.
[182] Minutes (1756), Aug. 28 and n. 969.

From 1765 to 1772, the *Minutes* record the totals of Kingswood collections, and from 1773, the names of preachers' sons supported there.

Preachers' daughters were not catered for so quickly. Some evidence indicates that at first they entered at Kingswood School with the boys or at a separate girls' school there.[183] From 1780, the Kingswood School fund also supported the education of preachers' daughters at other schools, and from 1789, some preachers' sons were also supported at other schools by the fund.[184] At the 1791 Conference after Wesley's death, a committee was formed, as already noted, for running the affairs of Kingswood School.

4. Pensions

The Preachers' Fund from 1763 was designed to provide for retired preachers.[185] John Pawson, who was present as a young preacher when the proposal was made, was amazed to find that preachers did not simply trust in God for temporal things, and he says that Wesley 'did not generally approve, thinking it mere worldly and not Christian prudence, to provide for a rainy day'.[186] The *Minutes* first record the Fund in 1765, with some rules that indicate it was intended only for those who were too worn out to preach at all.[187] For a subscription of half a guinea (10*s.* 6*d.*) for existing preachers and one guinea (£1. 1*s.*) from those joining in future, they would receive £10 per annum on superannuation (retirement) and a single payment of not more than £40 for a widow, or a single payment of not more than £10 for a child (if his or her mother had not already received the £40). A minimum premium payment of two guineas was required before any benefits could be received.

The Fund was, however, totally inadequate. By 1767, the subscriptions had reached only £54. 14*s.* 6*d.*, and the *Minutes* indicated that no benefits should be paid until the fund reached £500 and that it should not be allowed to fall below that level.[188] The rate of subscription needed to support this plan would take ten years to

---

[183] Ibid., (1773), *Q.* 10; (1774), *Q.* 12 and nn. 522–23.
[184] Ibid., (1780), *Q.* 14; (1789), *Q.* 14.
[185] Jackson, *Early Methodist Preachers*, 4:26.
[186] Ibid., 4:27.
[187] *Minutes* (1765), *Q.* 7.
[188] Ibid., (1767), *QQ.* 19, 20.

accomplish. But in 1768, with subscriptions of only £42, Wesley said that the £500 rule should be abolished as 'mere worldly prudence'.[189] By 1780, the subscriptions had risen to £87, but payments had increased to £120. 5*s*. Some of those receiving money were given more than £10 despite the rules, as had been the case for some years past—Wesley had probably disbursed according to need.[190] That same year, upwards of £700 remained in the Fund (boosted by other Methodists' gifts), and the decision was made that it should never rise above this.[191] Perhaps this surplus led to the Fund being raided, beginning in 1781, to support wives where circuits were unwilling or unable to do so. This practice continued until 1791, when the Conference resolved that the Fund should be used only for its original purpose of superannuation.[192] The subsequent history of the Fund and pressure for sounder financial arrangements for retirement do not concern us here.[193]

5. General Fund

Apart from the Kingswood School and Preachers' Funds, the other connexional fund was the General Fund (or 'Yearly Expences' or 'Contingent Fund').[194] As part of the 1749 proposals for a 'general union' of Societies with London as the 'mother church', a small fund was created 'out of which a Society under persecution or in real distress . . . might speedily be relieved'.[195] As we have seen, finance played a large part in the recurring pressures for such a connexional 'union', combined with a desire for greater unity to safeguard the connexion based on uniform and centralized trust deeds. The 1763 Conference set on foot a 'general yearly collection to which every Methodist in England is to contribute monthly', and the same year some Societies were already being helped by it. The

---

[189] Ibid., (1768), *QQ*. 17, 18.
[190] See the story of Rodda's plea for an increased grant for a widow, which suggests this; MS PLP, 92.5.3, in MA, quoted below in *Minutes* (1790), n. 534.
[191] *Minutes* (1780), *QQ*. 18, 19.
[192] Ibid., (1791), *Q*. 30. In 1795, the treasurers explained that disagreements had arisen about what seemed to be misappropriations of funds subscribed for a different purpose. Lloyd, *Labourer's Hire*, 31–32.
[193] *Labourer's Hire*, 32–38.
[194] For what follows see Baker, 'Polity', 252–53.
[195] *Minutes* (1749), §§1–4.

'Large' *Minutes* of 1763, which gave the first published account of it (§72), described the fund as intended chiefly to liquidate the heavy debts incurred by the building of preaching-houses, which amounted to about £4,000.

The fund was also used to pay debts of local preachers, to enable others to become itinerants, to send preachers on missions to new places, and to pay the cost of lawsuits to protect Methodists and their property. The Societies should send the money, said Wesley, to Leeds, Bristol, and London at the next Conference. By 1766, the total debt was £11,383 and the building of new preaching-houses was stopped, except in instances where two-thirds of the cost had been subscribed.[196] Such building was a major source of debt, and there were repeated attempts to curb it.

In 1770, Wesley banned all new building unless the proposers could defray the whole cost. In 1789, all new building was prohibited save for the exceptional case of Dewsbury, to replace the chapel lost to seceders, and a connexional subscription was raised for this.[197] During the 1790 Conference, the new Building Committee took powers to veto new buildings.[198] In 1793, however, the Conference delegated these powers to the new District Committees.

The 1766 financial crisis provoked Wesley in addition to appeal to the more affluent Methodists for subscriptions to liquidate the debt. The arrangements for receiving this money led to the confrontation about centralizing trusts.[199] During the following two years, £8,160 was collected. Various other appeals were launched, and local Methodists were urged to do the same for local debts.[200] Though the appeals dealt with existing debts, Wesley was well aware that a permanent and larger 'yearly Collection' or 'yearly Subscription' was needed to avoid recurring crises. The 'General Fund for carrying on the whole work of God' gradually improved and was able to be used for other purposes than paying building debts. In Wesley's last years, it came to be called 'The Contingent Fund'.

---

[196] Ibid., (1766), *QQ*. 12, 13.
[197] Ibid. (1770), *Q*. 14; (1789), *Q*. 19.
[198] Ibid., (1790), Addenda, *Q*. 6.
[199] See above, section V (2), pp. 43–47.
[200] *Minutes* (1770), *Q*. 15 (2).

6. Book Room

The finances connected with the Book Room were even more tangled. Although Thomas Olivers was appointed in 1776 to 'correct the press', and John Atlay was named to keep Wesley's accounts (and appointed Book Steward the following year),[201] the list of those in charge of book affairs goes farther back. The importance of the Book Room extended beyond the production of Methodist literature because it was a significant source of income for Wesley's other projects and activities and for his brother's support. In his history of the Book Room, Dr. Cumbers lists the early Book Stewards as John Wesley, 1733–53; Thomas Butts and William Briggs, 1753–59; Samuel Francks, 1759–73; John Atlay, 1773–88; and George Whitefield, 1788–1804. The Editors were John Wesley, 1733–91; Thomas Olivers ('corrector of the press'), 1776–89; and James Creighton, 1789–93.[202]

The scheme in 1753 for supervision of the debt in London seems to have been the origin of the Book Stewards as distinct from Wesley's own supervision of book affairs.[203] Wesley describes it as a scheme for 'devolving all temporal business, books and all, entirely on the Stewards, so that I might have no care upon me (in London at least) but that of the souls committed to my charge'.[204] Whatever was originally in his mind, Wesley seems to have relinquished only the book finances, at least outside London. The local Society Stewards were now to account for the book trade to the Foundery Stewards, in addition to the duties they had acquired in early years.[205]

In the previous year, Thomas Butts had told Wesley that after printers' bills were paid, the money from the sale of books 'does not amount to an hundred pounds a year'.[206] He could see no way out of this but by lessening the cost of printing by undertaking it himself, by increasing the sales of books (how, he did not know), or by giving up the copies earmarked for Charles Wesley's support to manage as he chose.

It seems that Butts was already beginning to manage the accounts for him by May 1752 when this letter was written. At all events, on

[201] See above, section V (2), p. 43.
[202] Frank Cumbers, *The Book Room* (London, 1956), 137.
[203] Ibid., 18.
[204] Feb. 8, 1753, *Journal & Diaries*, 20:445 in this edn.; and see above, p. 44.
[205] See *A Plain Account of the People Called Methodists* (1749), 9:273 in this edn.
[206] Letter to Ebenezer Blackwell, May 23, 1752, *Letters*, 26:494 in this edn.

April 20, 1753, Butts and Briggs addressed a circular to the Societies, saying that Wesley had entrusted the management of books to the Foundery Society, and to these two men in particular. They therefore urged that the Society Stewards should see themselves as stewards of the books as well as other 'temporal affairs', giving considerable detail on how they were to discharge this trust.[207] In 1759, Samuel Francks took over the job of book management until 1773 with sad results. On July 21, 1773, Wesley recorded in his *Journal* that his labour as a writer had landed him with a debt of £500 or £600.[208] Five months earlier, he had asked Thomas Ball and Alexander Mather to keep 'an exact account' of books sold on his account.[209] Ball replied that the gross value of books in February–March was £10,929. 15s. 4d.; stock in February of the previous year had been £8,833. 0s. 7d. Yet this left 'supposed to be owing in March last to printers, binders etc., £500', an odd and apparently inexact statement.[210]

Francks, the Book Steward, went insane and hanged himself.[211] Wesley inquired into the state of the accounts but said only that the confusion was less than expected.[212] On June 2, 1775, he wrote to Charles Wesley that it was strange that 'poor S. F.' (Francks) had left him £900 in debt, but stranger still that Atlay, the new Steward, had apparently paid debts amounting to £1,600 instead of £900, and Wesley was still £160 in debt.[213] Wesley seems to have thought Atlay 'cautious to an extreme'.[214] Atlay, however, broke with him over the Dewsbury Chapel affair.[215] Wesley then asked him to have an inventory made of the books for his successor, George Whitefield. Atlay replied that the stock, he thought, was worth £13,751. 18s. 5d., certainly not less, and most of the items were saleable. But Wesley claimed that two booksellers who examined the stock calculated that on October 31, 1788, the books ('errors exempted') were only worth £4,827. 10s. 3½d.[216] It may be added that Wesley found

---

[207] Tyerman, *Wesley*, 2:176–78.

[208] *Journal & Diaries*, 22:383 in this edn.

[209] Letter of Feb. 27, 1773, not 1772 as in Tyerman, *Wesley*, 3:155; see *Letters* (Telford), 6:19.

[210] Tyerman, *Wesley*, 3:155; and see *Journal & Diaries*, 22:384, n. 69 in this edn.

[211] Tyerman, *Wesley*, 3:155–56.

[212] Oct. 7, 1773, *Journal & Diaries*, 22:392 in this edn.

[213] *Letters* (Telford), 6:152.

[214] Ibid., 6:347 (in 1779).

[215] *Minutes* (1788), n. 327.

[216] Tyerman, *Wesley*, 3:559–60 quoting *AM* 13 (1790).

Thomas Olivers as editor little better than his predecessors—
Wesley frequently complained about printing errors. At the same
time, some editors, such as James Creighton, complained in the later
years that Wesley's handwriting was 'almost impossible now for anyone now to make out'.[217]

7. *Annual Conference Expenses*

The cost of the annual Conference itself was an important financial concern. The preachers were customarily lodged with local
Methodists and sympathizers. A list of thirty-six hosts and host-
esses survives for the 1765 Conference in Manchester.[218] The Societies through which the preachers passed en route to the Conference
were also expected to supply hospitality. To reduce the cost to the
Societies, the 1774 Conference stipulated that every preacher should
'pay for his house-keeping' and the Society should 'fix on the inn' for
the horses to be cared for.[219] Some old-fashioned preachers deplored
the excessively generous diet that others expected. John Pawson,
who often grumbled at this support, conceded that he provided a
good ham and half a barrel of porter, which he thought quite
enough.[220]

One source of local income, typical of contemporary churches
and chapels and indeed of later Methodism, seems to have been
largely avoided by early Methodists—pew rents. Wesley prided
himself on the 'first come and first served' basis for seating in his
preaching-houses. He took a stand on this issue as early as 1744.
Writing to Mrs. Hutton, he says that there is a 'faulty respect of persons' in all the churches he visited.[221] But at his West Street Chapel,
though there was a place kept for Lady Huntingdon, anyone could
take it after the Creed. He had doubts even about this concession
but was persuaded by his brother. At the Foundery 'we have no 5*s*.
or 2*s*. 6*d*. places'—'nor ever had, nor ever will'. It is 'first come and
first served', and the poor often had the best places. In any case, he

---

[217] Letter to his sister Ann, Aug. 22, 1789, Creighton, MS Letters, World
Methodist Library, Lake Junaluska, N.C.

[218] *WHS* 18 (1932): 130.

[219] *Minutes* (1774), *Q.* 20.

[220] On the expenses of young preachers, see Pawson, *Letters*, 2:71, 76 (1796); on
his own provisions, 2:115 (1797).

[221] *Letters*, 26:114 in this edn.

ordered 'forms', not 'pews'.[222] Elsewhere, as time went on, some pews may have been given to subscribers to the building. At City Road in 1778, however, large numbers paid for seats but were not allowed to claim pews or seats as their own. After Charles Wesley's death, apparently gates and keepers were established there.[223] In the 1790s, Macclesfield Chapel was receiving £40 per quarter from pews.[224]

These records, then, provide a window into Wesley's attitudes towards money and his manner of dealing with financial matters. Early in the movement, before he knew the eventual scope of the revival, he adopted a stance that avoided over-reliance upon people of substance. When well-heeled supporters wanted to help finance the New Room in Bristol in 1739, Wesley followed Whitefield's advice and personally borrowed the money so as to maintain control over the property and not to be reliant upon, and consequently subject to, rich people. This approach was codified in the 1780 'Large' *Minutes*, with a rule about building preaching-houses that were 'plain and decent', not ornate and expensive: 'Otherwise the necessity of raising money will make rich men necessary to us. But if so, we must be dependent upon them, yea, and governed by them. And then farewell to the Methodist discipline, if not doctrine too.'[225] Throughout the century, Wesley tried to walk a fine line between soliciting ('begging') money from the rich members of his Societies for his program of active social concern and avoiding dependence upon them for the design and direction of the movement. The other side of this approach can also be seen in his concern that everyone had a responsibility to contribute to the programs of social support—those who had the 'superfluities' of life should obviously help those who lacked the 'necessities', but even those who lacked the 'necessities' of life might help those who were experiencing the 'extremities'. Wesley's model in this regard was the widow who, in her poverty, still contributed her mite. The connexional funds presented opportunities for united action by thousands of people who might not otherwise be able to provide a noticeable level of beneficence on their own.

[222] *Letters* (Telford), 5:209 (in 1770).
[223] Stevenson, *City Road Chapel*, 77.
[224] Gail Malmgren, *Silk Town: Industry and Culture in Macclesfield, 1750–1835* (Hull, 1985), 146–47.
[225] 'Large' *Minutes* (1780), *Q*. 65 (7).

The *Minutes* also exhibit Wesley's concern that the Methodists rely upon the providence of God more than the stockpiling of resources for the future. He was never a firm believer in retirement funds (or any surplus accumulation of wealth), and his attitude may have been reflected in the connexion's difficulty getting its retirement fund up and running. His reticence in this regard may have reflected in part his attempts to deflect the criticism that he was becoming rich through the movement, its publications, the beneficent gifts, and the generosity of the people.[226] Several times, seeming to reinforce his denials of increasing riches, he complained that the publishing program was losing money; he also pointed out in his published *Journal* that the medical clinics were forced to close when the demand for services outstripped the financial support. So as not to benefit personally from any profits of the publications or the beneficence of the supporters, Wesley restricted himself to a quarterly allowance of £15 from the London Stewards, a stipend that was not dependable. His personal financial accounts also reveal that he gave away a large proportion of the money that came his way, although the actual figures he claims in this regard often included the beneficent programs of the connexion.[227] His approach in this matter seems to embody the maxim stated in his sermon on the use of money—gain all you can (be diligent and honest in gathering resources), save all you can (be frugal and wise in expending money), and give all you can (be altruistic and philanthropic as much as possible).[228] In many ways, the financial aspects of the Methodist connexion seem to be an institutional extension of this approach to finances.

[226] In the *Earnest Appeal* (1745), he countered such claims by stating that if he died with more than £10 in his pocket, people could call him a robber and a thief. *Works*, 11:88. His will in the 1780s indicates that, aside from the publication empire, which was designed to assist the connexion, he had very little to distribute to his heirs. *Journal* (Curnock), 8:342–43.

[227] See Richard P. Heitzenrater, 'Wesley and Money' (paper, Ministers Week convocation, Southern Methodist University, Dallas, Tex., 2005).

[228] This sermon was one of five Wesley published on the topic (and notable references in another dozen or so), demonstrating a continuing concern that the increasing presence of wealth among the Methodists would cause problems if they did not follow this rule diligently. See *Works*, 2:265 in this edn.

VII. The Character of the Conference: Debates and Wesley's Authority

As noted earlier, principles for the spirit of discussion, disagreement, and confidentiality were laid down at the beginning of the earliest Conferences. In 1744, it was desired (§3) that

all things may be considered as in the immediate presence of God; that we may meet with a single eye, and as little children which have everything to learn; that every point may be examined from the foundation; that every person may speak freely whatever is in his heart; and that every question proposed may be fully debated, and bolted to the bran.

There followed the question (§4): 'How far does each of us agree to submit to the unanimous judgment of the rest?' Answer: 'In speculative things each can only submit so far as his judgment shall be convinced: in every practical point so far as we can without wounding our several consciences.' Then on confidentiality (§5): 'How far should any of us mention to others what may be mentioned here?' Answer: 'Not one word which may be here spoken of persons should be mentioned elsewhere. Nothing at all, unless so far as we may be convinced the glory of God requires it. And from time to time we will consider on each head, Is it for the glory of God that what we have now spoken should be mentioned again?'

These injunctions were followed up and partly repeated in 1745. The method was to be '(1) To read and weigh at every Conference each article of those preceding. (2) To speak freely and hear calmly touching each, that we may either retract, amend, or enlarge it' (§3). The Conference should be a time of 'particular watching and self-denial', fasting and prayer (§§4–5). To ensure that everyone spoke freely, no one should be checked 'either by word or look, even though he should say what was quite wrong' (§7). In 1747, the injunctions about speculative and practical points and freedom of speech are repeated (§6), and a further assertion states that no authority can take away the right of private judgment (§7).

1. Developing Nature of the Conference

These rules seem to reflect the principles stated earlier, that the 'Conference' was intended to live up to its name as a meeting for open discussion and mutual edification, with freedom to disagree and limits on how far one was bound by what was decided. But if it began in this way, the Conference did not continue in the same spirit, perhaps because it gradually became more like a legislative body in some ways. In 1751, John Wesley said that Charles Skelton 'pleads for a kind of aristocracy and says you [Charles Wesley] and I should do nothing without the consent of all the preachers; otherwise we govern arbitrarily, to which they cannot submit'.[229]

John Hampson also made an illuminating and highly critical comment, soon after Wesley's death, on the fate of the freedom that seemed to be promised in the early *Minutes*.[230] Citing the 1744 principle of freedom of speech, Hampson said that by this promise for free debate and the rights of conscience, 'equal liberty was established as a fundamental article; and in a subsequent Conference [1752], Mr. Wesley and the preachers mutually signed an agreement not to act independently of one another.' He saw the 1744 provisions as the 'original compact' between the preachers, establishing submission to the majority (though subject to conscience) and not to Wesley individually. He went on to say that most of the rules subsequently passed were violations of that compact, culminating in the Legal Hundred and the erasure of the compact itself from the 1780 republication of the old *Minutes*.[231] In response to similar criticisms in the 1780s, Wesley claimed that he had not made such bad use of his power as to render the clauses necessary. Nevertheless, Hampson's view was, 'I had rather hold my liberties by the law, than by the power of any man.' Though he claimed there was a *nem. con.* vote[232] in 1783 to reinstate the clauses, Wesley did not do so.

Hampson's language reflects something of contemporary 'democratical' ideas of the rights of 'freeborn Englishmen'. Wesley never

---

[229] JW to CW, *Letters*, 26:475–76 in this edn. This comment seems to imply that JW felt that the 1740s provisions for free speech were not extended to voting rights for participants.

[230] Hampson, *Memoirs*, 3:203–6.

[231] He referred to the 1740s Minutes as republished at the front of successive edns. of the 'Large' *Minutes*, which section is frequently edited heavily and in 1780 omits these provisions.

[232] *Nemine contradicente*, without objection.

adhered to Lockeian notions of 'contract', either in Church or in state. Hampson was also bitterly critical of his omission from the Legal Hundred in 1784 and of what he regarded as the intrigues for power among some leading preachers. Yet he had a point. The apparently open and equal debates and freedom to differ stated in the 1740s had in practice been overshadowed by Wesley's claims that the Conference was simply made up of those he chose to summon to advise him; that by asking him to guide them, they had implicitly agreed to submit to him; and that they were free to disagree with him, but if they did, they must leave. Such accounts as we have of proceedings in Conference suggest that he used this implied autocracy in practice with only limited restraints.

To be sure, the early Conferences were gatherings for a very small body of people who needed to define their most basic beliefs and practice. Relatively free discussion and allowance for conscientious objections and simple uncertainty would have been quite natural and appropriate to what really was a process of 'conferring'. In fact, however, we do not know how prevalent free debate and disagreement existed even at this stage. Wesley also used the Conference from the beginning as a means to keep dissent or recalcitrance from appearing among the preachers.[233] As the connexion grew and became more complex, the character of the Conference was bound to change. Doctrine, as we have seen, was largely settled in the first few years (though Wesley separately modified some points later). Details of discipline and the pressure of temporal business multiplied, as we have seen. But Wesley's natural authoritarianism and his dominant position in practice are obvious, based on his social status as clergy and his position as long-lived founder of the connexion. The original implications of free debate and the rights of conscience might seem hard to reconcile with the rigid rules that emerged, largely emanating from Wesley and enforced as strongly as he could, unless one visualizes a Quaker-like consensus emerging within the body or at least submission to a majority vote, which some evidently would have preferred—even though Wesley seems never to have implied the latter in any alleged 'compact'.

Unfortunately, one problem in discerning what actually happened in the Conferences and how the decisions were made is that the process is not revealed by the *Minutes* and information from other

---

[233] The earliest Conferences were called in part to rein in some preachers who were inclined too far in the direction of Calvinism or Moravianism.

sources is tantalizingly fragmentary.[234] As we have seen, Wesley's *Journal* and other unpublished materials tend to be uninformative about Conference proceedings, though there are useful exceptions as well as a few more candid letters. The early Minutes themselves, though not published, were clearly circulated beyond the preachers who attended, and even read to Society officials, while other manuscript copies were made, even after they began to be published.[235] But the *Minutes* disclosed only agreed conclusions. Simon suggested that the confidentiality agreement explains the short and generalized remarks on the Conference in Wesley's *Journal* and the delay in publishing the annual *Minutes* until 1765.[236] In their private accounts, preachers often tend to record sermons during Conference rather than Conference business, although this may in part reflect the value they placed on the 'spiritual' side of the gathering.

The *Minutes* themselves are not only uninformative on what lay behind the decisions but, in some cases, even misleading. We know, for example, that questions were raised and discussed that did not appear in the record at all. This public record is silent on the appeal for missions in Africa in 1778,[237] and debates on separation from the Church occurred more frequently than they are included in the official record. Some of these matters might possibly have occurred in open sessions that were not part of the official business, and therefore not recorded in the *Minutes*. But in some cases they may also have been thought to be too sensitive to be recorded.

2. Wesley's Views of the Conference and Power

Wesley's attitudes towards the nature and role of the Conference are evident in his 'Thoughts upon some late Occurrences' (1785),[238] which was written in reaction to criticisms of the Deed of Declaration,

---

[234] For the character of the *Minutes*, see below, pp. 102–6.

[235] Thomas Dixon, an itinerant preacher who was admitted on trial in 1769, made a MS copy of the 'Large' *Minutes*, to which he added the annual *Minutes* for each year from 1765 through 1771. MS Dixon Minutes, Bridwell Library, Southern Methodist University, Dallas, Tex. Thanks to Page Thomas for his transcription and analysis of this material. Important variants have been noted in the appropriate places below. See also *Minutes* (1746), §70.

[236] Simon, *Methodist Societies*, 205.

[237] *Minutes* (1778), n. 719.

[238] In *The Works of the Rev. John Wesley*, ed. Thomas Jackson, 14 vols. (London: Wesleyan Conference Office, 1872), 13:248–50, hereafter cited as *Works* (Jackson).

a legal document registered in 1784 in Chancery Lane that established the Conference as a defined body. In the 'Thoughts', Wesley explains the origin of the Conference as a body created by his occasional invitation to certain groups of preachers to meet with him and advise him—not the whole body of the preachers, but those he had invited: 'The term *Conference* meant not so much the conversation we had together as the persons that conferred; namely, those whom I invited to confer with me from time to time.' It depended entirely on him (he said), not only what persons should constitute the Conference, but also whether there should even be a Conference at all. Neither preachers nor people had 'any part or lot in the matter'. Agreeing that after the Wesleys' deaths the preachers should be stationed by the Conference, the preachers in 1783 asked Wesley to 'fix the determinate meaning of the word'—hence the Deed of Declaration.

Although these comments in Wesley's 'Thoughts' reflected challenges to the Deed, they repeat a view he had frequently expressed not only about his relationship to the Conference but also over the preachers and indeed over Methodism generally. Strictly speaking, his comments did not deal specifically with the questions of freedom of debate or how the Conference was expected to reach decisions. But what we know of the proceedings in Conference does suggest that Wesley's authoritarianism extended into these areas too and that the apparently broader provisions of the early pronouncements about the terms of 'conferring' were not actually carried out.

The charge was repeatedly made by critics like Hampson and another early biographer John Whitehead (as well as by loyal colleagues like John Pawson) that Wesley was possessed by a passion for absolute power. Hampson and Pawson, like some non-Methodists such as Robert Southey, saw this desire as a weakness in Wesley. Whitehead, however, thought that Wesley exercised his power as moderately as could be expected, and that only he could exercise it—the real abuses came from preachers after his death. These views in part reflected conflicts among different parties in Methodism in the years before and after Wesley's death. A more detached observer, Alexander Knox, exonerated Wesley from the often-repeated charge of 'ambition'.[239]

[239] See Rack, *Reasonable Enthusiast*, 247–48, 538–39; Abelove, *Evangelist of Desire*, 7–18 for discussions of the sources of Wesley's authority. For Pawson's criticism, see 'Some Account', fols. 39–40, and printed in *WHS* 49 (1993): 11–12; and for Knox's defence, his 'Remarks' printed in Robert Southey, *The Life of Wesley and the Rise and Progress of Methodism*, ed. Maurice H. Fitzgerald, 2 vols. (London: Oxford University Press, 1925), 2:352–56.

Wesley had also asserted his right to control the movement and justified it on earlier occasions when, as sometimes happened, some preachers objected to his exercise of power. In 1766, he replied to criticism by a lengthy rehearsal of what his power was and how it had arisen.[240] Some preachers had said he was *'shackling free-born Englishmen'*. They wished for a *'free conference'*, that is, 'a meeting of all the preachers wherein all things shall be determined by most votes', which he allowed might happen after his death but not now. This comment, incidentally, confirms that decisions recorded in the *Minutes* were not the result of majority vote. As he said, very late in life, in reaction to desires of more democracy by the lower lay officials in Methodism, 'we are no republicans and never intend to be.'[241] Wesley's explanation of the source of his authority was that in 1738, people had asked him to advise them—hence his power to appoint and organize. Similarly, the preachers desired to serve him as 'sons in the gospel'—this request implied that they accepted his guidance on his terms. After a time, Wesley began calling some of these preachers together occasionally to give their advice on how best to carry on the work of God—they were invited to advise, not govern him. Some had complained about his power, but his response was, 'I did not seek any part of this power. It came upon me unawares. But when it was come, not daring to bury that talent, I used it to the best of my judgment.' He was not fond of it, but tried to make the best use of his talents in this regard. He only followed Providence and acted for the good of the people. He rejected requests for rule by Conference, by all the preachers, and by majority votes. The preachers were engaged to obey him, and in any case they would not submit to anyone else (which was true enough).

Again, specifically explaining his relationship to Conference, he noted in 1780 that there was no Conference at all until six years after he returned to England.[242] He had drawn up a few rules before there ever was a Conference, and people joined him under those conditions. Then he 'desired some of our preachers to meet me, in order to advise, not control, me'. They had no power at all but what he exercised through them—he chose to exercise the power that God

---

[240] *Minutes* (1766), *Q.* 29. This lengthy account was probably prepared by Wesley in advance and read to the Conference.

[241] JW to John Mason, Jan. 30, 1790 ('Charles the Martyr' day), *Letters* (Telford), 8:196.

[242] JW to Thomas Taylor, Aug. 8, 1780, *Letters* (Telford), 6:376.

had given him in this manner, 'both to avoid ostentation and gently to habituate the people to obey them when I should be taken from their head'. But until then, 'the fundamental rule of Methodism remains inviolate—as long as any Preacher joins with me, he is to be directed by me in his work.' This claim, that he was preparing the people to obey the preachers following his death, was a new and unusual note.[243]

3. Wesley's Use of Power

How Wesley actually exercised his power reveals some degree of variation from his stated attitudes, according to the time and the question at issue. In the first place, as the statements above already show, he intended to control who attended Conference,[244] but his implementation of that policy varied somewhat over the years. After several years of summoning individuals, in 1766 he gave a general permission to attend.[245] In 1767, he stated that some were *allowed* to attend and others *required* to do so.[246] From the 1780 Conference onwards, he seems to have invited a select number of preachers and did not allow the rest to come.[247] He continued to invite and exclude in the same way after the Deed of Declaration and, in 1785, said that he would have no 'contentious persons' in 'any Conference'.[248]

The Deed named one hundred preachers as the legal Conference, to take over control after Wesley's death. Wesley caused much offence by excluding some senior preachers from the list while including some junior preachers.[249] Even some of the 'Legal Hundred' were excluded on occasion during Wesley's lifetime, though the stalwart Thomas Taylor resolved to attend without being invited and apparently got away with it.[250] Yet in a letter left to be read to the

---

[243] This letter was a response to complaints about his treatment of Alexander McNab, who had resented being kept out of the Bath pulpit by Wesley's clerical associate, Rev. Edward Smyth. Tyerman, *Wesley*, 3:303; *Minutes* (1779), n. 760.

[244] The question of membership and attendance has already been discussed; see section III, above.

[245] *Minutes* (1766), *Q.* 29 (4).

[246] *Letters* (Telford), 5:6.

[247] Baker, *Wesley and Church*, 221, and see n. 60 above.

[248] *Letters* (Telford), 7:279, 282.

[249] See below, section IX (3), pp. 90–93; Rack, *Reasonable Enthusiast*, 503–4.

[250] Taylor's MS diary (1787), quoted in Tyerman, *Wesley* 3:496, and cf. *Minutes* (1787), n. 234.

Conference after his death (prefaced to the 1791 *Minutes*), Wesley urged the Hundred not to use their powers to exclude their brethren, contrary to his own practice. His concern seemed to be to retain his right to control attendance at the Conference, and indeed all his other powers, at least until he died.[251]

Control of stationing he seems to have had, though not completely at all times and in all cases, and possibly less at the very end. Hampson saw this personal control as part of Wesley's illegitimate power. When Wesley wrote in his *Journal* in 1778, 'This year, I myself (which I have seldom done) chose the preachers for Bristol',[252] he may seem to imply that some consultation was involved, either with Charles (though hardly likely at this point) or with his closest friends or Cabinet during Conference.[253] To Penelope Newman in 1782, he wrote that he had no objection to a particular stationing, 'but I do not use to determine things of this kind absolutely before Conference'.[254] This comment evidently means that stations were usually finalized during the Conference, but that he did the finalizing, though after others had made suggestions or requests. In a letter to the 'Methodist People' in 1789, he says he had often wished to transfer the task of stationing to one or more of the preachers, but none were willing to do so, and therefore he must bear the burden.[255]

In practice, Wesley occasionally met opposition, often resisting it. When Richard Rodda found that he and Samuel Bradburn were again appointed to Manchester in 1790, Rodda pleaded to have their names reversed, with Bradburn as the lead preacher ('Assistant'). But Mr. Wesley said, 'No, I will not reverse the order if you would give me fifty pounds.'[256] Yet changes could result from argument or obstinacy. Sutcliffe, describing the 1790 Conference, says that

[251] See his annoyance at the phrase 'life estate' (life interest) in the Deed and possible explanations in *Minutes* (1785), *Q.* 21, n. 90, and below, section IX (3), 92–93.

[252] Mar. 9, 1778, *Journal & Diaries*, 23:77 in this edn.

[253] Ward in *Journal & Diaries*, 23:77, n. 81 in this edn., says this entry was written long after the event and leaps ahead to the summer Conference, apparently responding to promising developments in Bristol and stationing preachers most likely to succeed there. Wesley's advisers, from whom Charles seems to have been excluded after 1754 (when he referred to them as his brother's 'cabinet council'), met irregularly and more or less informally until instituted more regularly in 1781; see above, section V (2), pp. 39–42.

[254] Mar. 9, 1778, *Letters* (Telford), 7:129.

[255] Sept. 11, 1789, *Letters* (Telford), 8:168.

[256] Rodda, MS PLP, 92.5.3 (fol. 20), in MA.

Wesley pulled out of his pocket a list of stations that no one had seen, but many changes were made to accommodate local requests and the needs of preachers' families. He was not nearly as tyrannical as some alleged but, according to Sutcliffe, 'paternal and fair'.[257]

Although this last particular instance was in extreme old age, there had been cases of resistance to his stationing much earlier. In 1770, he wrote, 'I have the credit of stationing the preachers, but many of them go where they *will* go for me.' Of John Murlin he added, 'for you know a man of fortune is master of his own notions'.[258] Thomas Rankin retired from the itinerancy because of his wife's health, and Wesley desired him to 'remain in London as long as I live'. Rankin did so, preaching as often as before and sometimes accompanying Wesley on his travels. He also assisted in the 'Cabinet'.[259] There is even a story that Adam Clarke was prevented from being stationed at Leeds because female preachers there thought his sermons were excessively learned, though as it happens he was in favour of female preachers, who were popular in that place.[260] Benson was once asked to go to Manchester but was placed at York. Wesley objected to both, so Benson was posted to Birmingham as Assistant.[261]

One would like above all to know how freely debates were allowed and whether the participants ever prevailed against Wesley's will by voting or otherwise. Or did he get his way by using a veto or perhaps simply by ignoring Conference decisions? Or did the preachers in the end allow him to have his way, even if they disagreed? There are hints that something of all these options may have occurred, though in 1766, as we have seen, Wesley seems by implication to suggest that voting was not his method, although some preachers wanted it.

As early as 1751, Charles Skelton had pleaded for 'a kind of aristocracy' and for the Wesleys to do nothing without the preachers' consent—otherwise they were governed arbitrarily, 'to which they cannot submit'. Charles Wesley had heard people complaining 'all over England' that John 'ruled with a rod of iron'.[262] Charles, too, would have liked to curb his brother's power, mainly because he

[257] Sutcliffe, MS 'History', fols. 1193–94; *WHS* 15 (1925): 57–60; *Minutes* (1790), n. 534.
[258] JW to George Merryweather, Aug. 1, 1770, *Letters* (Telford), 5:196.
[259] Tyerman MSS, 2:107–8.
[260] Chilcote, *Women Preachers*, 201.
[261] James Macdonald, *Memoirs of the Rev. Joseph Benson* (London, 1822), 169.
[262] Aug. 17, 1751, *Letters*, 26:475–76 in this edn.

feared that John would be swayed by the preachers to leave the Church.[263]

Though Wesley's *Journal* accounts of the Conference (and indeed some by the preachers too) end suspiciously often with claims that all ended in peace, unity, and love, such was evidently not always the case, at least at the outset. Debates certainly took place that could expose sharp divisions on some issues, notably on ordination and separation from the Church. Thus in 1755, the Minutes, though not published, simply record that there was a 'free and frank debate' on separation, but that all agreed to remain in the Church. But a letter of Wesley to Samuel Walker of Truro, the Evangelical clergyman, is more fully descriptive of the occasion.[264] The Conference had debated 'at large' in seven or eight long conversations whether it was *lawful* to separate. When they could not agree on this particular aspect of the matter, they debated whether it was *expedient* to do so. There were objections to the Church: its liturgy and canon law, and the doctrines and devotion of the clergy. Wesley acknowledged that he could not answer all the criticisms. Even if some debates about separation were, as was noted earlier, in the open sessions, it could not be guessed from Wesley's brief mentions of them that they were as divisive, prolonged, and critical as they obviously were in this case.

In 1774, in a passage that has often been quoted, a preacher at the Conference is reported as commenting privately that 'Mr. Wesley seemed to do all the business himself.'[265] Yet in 1775, Tyerman described the Conference as 'unexampled' for its free discussion.[266] More specifically, his source (Thomas Hanby) said that Wesley was 'not near so overbearing as he was' and that there had 'not been so free a Conference for many years nor so full a one'.[267] Perhaps the size of the body fostered debate.

If Hampson's account of the preachers' attempts to stop omissions from the 1780 edition of the 'Large' *Minutes* and two rejected proposals by Coke in 1783 can be believed, all three involved actual votes.[268] The motion on the 'Large' *Minutes*, he says, was carried

[263] Dec. 4, 1751, *Letters*, 26:479 and n. 5 in this edn.

[264] Sept. 24, 1755, *Letters*, 26:593–94 in this edn.

[265] Miss March to Miss Briggs, Tyerman MSS, 2:165, quoted in *Journal & Diaries*, 22:424, n. 68 in this edn.

[266] Tyerman, *Wesley*, 3:209.

[267] T. Hanby to J. Oddie, Aug. 5, 1775, Tyerman MSS, 1:115–16.

[268] See above, pp. 14, 47, 63, and *Minutes* (1783), n. 949.

nem. con., and Coke's motions rejected by large majorities. A later commentator, however, states that Wesley did not allow doctrine or discipline to be settled by popular vote,[269] which may well be true. Professor Baker considers that the Conference was a consultative body, yet one that implicitly expected Wesley would be guided by the majority, though not acting by majority vote in his lifetime.[270] These three statements are not easily reconcilable as they stand, but it is possible to suppose that Wesley allowed some leeway over matters other than doctrine and discipline and was rather more amenable to Conference opinion on lesser matters, on individual cases, and perhaps on temporal affairs, especially in his later years.

In the Cabinet in 1784, so Pawson recalled, the preachers were all against the American ordinations, but he perceived that Wesley's mind was made up and so it turned out.[271] Hampson says that when Wesley met opposition, he would respond by changing the subject, starting a hymn, or simply walking out.[272] No doubt this referred to personal discussion, but it may apply to his techniques in Conference as well. Hampson says that Wesley ignored the vote to keep the 'free debate' clause in the 1780 'Large' *Minutes*. In the last resort, Hampson could threaten to leave the Methodists, which he sometimes did over the separation from the Church question. But on at least two occasions, Wesley seems to have been saved from a heated confrontation and possible deadlock by impassioned appeals from Howell Harris and John Fletcher that dissolved the assembly in tears.[273] As late as 1787, Pawson claims that Wesley urged the Methodists to stay with the Church, pressing the point inside and outside the Conference with a vehemence that distressed Pawson.[274]

On matters of individual concern, Wesley could be more conciliatory. To Hopper in 1788, Wesley wrote, concerning a preacher's stationing, that he would not 'run his head' against the Conference.[275] In 1789, to William Thom on a difficult case of keeping an

---

[269] Macdonald, *Benson*, 161.

[270] Baker, *Wesley and Church*, 107.

[271] Pawson says that when Wesley made up his mind in the fall of 1784 to ordain preachers for America, he then was convinced he should ordain them for Scotland at the London Conference in 1785. Jackson, *Early Methodist Preachers*, 4:54; *Minutes* (1785), n. 70.

[272] Hampson, *Memoirs*, 3:196–97.

[273] Jackson, *Early Methodist Preachers*, 4:26 (in 1763); *Minutes* (1784), n. 1.

[274] Pawson, *Letters*, 1:45–46; *Minutes* (1787), n. 234.

[275] Aug. 27, 1785, *Letters* (Telford), 7:286.

elderly preacher, he wrote, 'surely it is not proper for me single to overcome their [the preachers'] judgment.'[276] This comment may not only reflect age and a certain mellowing, but may also be the method he had claimed some years before, of preparing the way for the preachers to inherit his authority after his death. The rise of the 'Cabinet' may also be an instance of this policy. Etheridge saw this development as a sign of Wesley's growing willingness to delegate power. Another sign is that, whereas in 1760 the preachers waited for Wesley's return from Ireland before beginning business, in 1780 Hopper presided in Wesley's absence.[277] At the very end, in Wesley's last Conference (1790), observers' accounts suggest that the old man was hardly capable of business and Alexander Mather took the lead. Yet two anecdotes suggest that even on this occasion, Wesley could rouse himself in a cross and petulant fashion over individual resistance to his proposals or opinions, though he gave way graciously if the preachers concerned either stood up to him or submitted humbly. The old Adam was not yet quite extinct in him, and some leaders seem to have humoured him, knowing he would soon be gone.[278]

These late scenes again raise the question of how far Wesley was really in direct control of the connexion in his last years. In the character sketches by Hampson, in his biography of Wesley, and in Pawson's MS autobiography, there are charges that Wesley was influenced by misguided advisers and even flatterers who, unfortunately, are not named.[279] Given differences on policy between Pawson and Hampson, no doubt they had different people in mind. Coke was often suspect in this way, but Pawson exonerated him. Mather was often seen as a key figure. Alexander Kilham saw Mather as 'Prime Minister in our Israel'. An anonymous 'Member of the Methodist Conference', in 'A Letter to the Methodist Preachers' (1795), says of Benson and Mather that 'the one struggled for universal dominion and the other for supreme power as the Lord

---

[276] Aug. 30, 1789, *Letters* (Telford), 8:162–63.

[277] Jackson, *Early Methodist Preachers*, 1:219.

[278] For the 1790 incidents, see *Minutes* (1790), n. 534.

[279] Hampson, *Memoirs*, 3:200–201. John Whitehead, who often follows Hampson, omitted this characteristic and rather emphasized Wesley's trustfulness and forgiveness even of deceivers. *Life of Rev. John Wesley*, 2:469–70, 'Some Account', fol. 40, and in *WHS* 49 (1993): 17.

Bishop of our council.'[280] These strictures certainly reflect hostility to the Church Methodists before and after Wesley's death, just as Hampson's and Whitehead's comments were on the side of the 'old Plan' or 'Mr. Wesley's Plan', which allegedly (but quite erroneously, in view of his actions) meant no Sacraments, and no services during church hours, as well as no formal separation from the Church.[281]

Wesley's authority could not be inherited by anyone else, as he came to realize. Though he thought at times of a clerical head in succession to himself, he also thought of some kind of junta of preachers. Finally he came up with a larger collective leadership embodied in the Deed of Declaration of 1784. His actions as a kind of one-man executive between Conferences left a gap at his death: hence the creation of District Committees by the 1791 Conference, though these were seen by some as far from adequate. Their perceived inadequacy led to suggestions like the Lichfield Plan in 1794 for a kind of episcopate, appealing to some of Wesley's equivocal ordinations that appeared to be for England.[282] One thing only was certain: for many reasons no one could inherit Wesley's unique authority. There would be no more 'Kings in Israel'. Not even Jabez Bunting filled that unique vacancy.

VIII. The Preachers

As we have seen, the annual Conferences consisted primarily of travelling preachers, even though others were admitted to the sessions from time to time, if with an uncertain degree of participation. Much of the Conference's time was also occupied with business relating to the preachers: their reception, discipline, stationing, and eventually, payment.

---

[280] Quoted in John C. Bowmer, *Pastors and People* (London, 1975), 24, n. 19 from Kilham's 'Martin Luther Tract', 4, and 'A Letter'.

[281] See further, below, section IX.

[282] Pawson, *Letters*, 1:164 (in 1794); and see below, section IX, for these problems.

1. Lay Preachers

Wesley very probably hoped originally that his movement would be led by a significant body of Anglican clergy who would associate with him. But lay preachers emerged as a significant feature of the Methodist movement at an early stage. This development evolved through what Dr. John Walsh has well characterized as 'the problem of the eloquent convert'—that is to say, the drift from informal testifying, through exhorting, to outright preaching. Such a progression can be seen in the often-quoted case of Thomas Maxfield (probably in 1741) and the less-remarked but earlier one of John Cennick (in 1739). Howell Harris had preceded them all in Wales.[283] As late as the 1770s, Wesley still seems to have hoped there might at least be a clergyman as head of the connexion after his death, if only because he thought (correctly) that the lay preachers would not accept one of their own number in that role. In the end, he had to settle for a collective leadership of preachers.

As early as the first Conference in 1744, one of the first acts of the Anglican clergy with whom the Conference began was to invite lay preachers to join them. Originally the lay preachers were termed indifferently 'Helpers' or 'Assistants', but from 1749 the latter term was reserved for the senior preacher among the helpers in each circuit. Part-time 'local preachers' (also laity, but non-itinerating) also increased in numbers during that period. They rarely figure in the *Minutes*, the first example being the list in 1747 of those who 'assist us in one place' as distinct from the travelling full-time preachers. They are said to have originated as 'exhorters' in Cornwall when many itinerants were pressed for the army and had to discontinue travelling as full-time preachers. The term 'exhorters' eventually designated those who informally addressed meetings rather than formally preached from a text. The distinction, however, was a fluid one, not least when it applied to the controversial case of women preachers. Given the economic and personal difficulties of many preachers, it is not surprising that they readily passed from part-time to full-time preaching and back again. There was also a category of 'half-itinerants', who were apparently committed only to limited periods of travelling, like the 'Methodist Squire', Robert Brackenbury.

[283] For these developments and what follows, see Baker, 'Polity', 230–31, 236–38, and Rack, *Reasonable Enthusiast*, 210–12, 243–44.

Female preachers began to appear from the 1760s, though they were highly controversial, since such behaviour in women seemed contrary both to the 'natural' role of women as conceived at the time and to St. Paul's often-quoted veto on them speaking in church. Wesley at first took the same view,[284] but after having to justify the work of women Class and Band leaders on the grounds that their service was not in public worship, he was finally convinced by the success of some women that they had (as he had long claimed for his male lay preachers) an 'extraordinary' call that he saw as following apostolic precedents.[285] No woman formally became an itinerant preacher in the connexion during Wesley's lifetime (though some women preachers travelled widely), and Wesley limited their leadership roles in Society meetings to 'exhorting' and prayer.[286] Wesley's rather equivocal support resulted in his claiming that 'the Methodists do not allow of women preachers' at the same time he was allowing certain women to 'preach' at Society meetings.[287] The itinerants were divided on the propriety of allowing women to 'preach', and in the generation after Wesley's death (in 1803), their activities were restricted, though not banned. The whole subject hardly ever figures in the *Minutes*, though it is known that the 1787 Conference authorized one woman, Sarah Mallet, to preach within the Norfolk Circuit.[288] Although at least forty women preached in some fashion during Wesley's lifetime,[289] so far as Conference is concerned, women figure only in the open sessions as attenders, where some of those close to Wesley took a keen interest in the proceedings and personalities, as their correspondence shows.

[284] See his first edn. (1755) of *Explanatory Notes upon the New Testament* (1 Cor. 14:34-35). His views changed on this subject in the 1760s, but he did not change his comments on this passage in subsequent editions of the *NT Notes*, though he revised many other entries.

[285] Mary Bosanquet's 1771 letter to Wesley was instrumental in convincing him of this point. Bosanquet, MS Letterbook, Special Collections Library, Duke University.

[286] Wesley's letters to Grace Walton (Sept. 8, 1761) and Sarah Crosby (Mar. 18, 1769) explain the limits that he expected, to avoid their being seen as preachers. *Letters* (Telford), 4:164, 5:130–31.

[287] Wesley advised Sarah Crosby to say, before she spoke, 'You lay me under a great difficulty. The Methodists do not allow of women Preachers: Neither do I take upon me any such character. But I will just nakedly tell you what is in my heart.' JW to Sarah Crosby, Feb. 14, 1761, *Letters* (Telford), 4:132–33.

[288] *Minutes*, n. 1.

[289] On this subject, see above, pp. 27–28, and Chilcote, *Women Preachers*.

2. The Itinerants

At the 1746 Conference (§44), the status and role of the 'Helpers' were considered to be 'Perhaps as extraordinary messengers, designed of God to provoke others to jealousy', though they should avoid the temptation to lord it over 'God's heritage' (§45). The Minutes contain a series of basic tests of gifts and grace (one set of 'historic questions') for those feeling called by the Holy Spirit to the work. Already (§50) the question of some form and solemnity for receiving them is considered but rejected so as to avoid 'stateliness' and wait on providential guidance. In 1747, the full-time itinerants were distinguished from the local preachers, and in 1749 the 'Assistant' on each circuit was defined as the senior preacher in charge.

Whatever may have been the situation earlier, in 1749 a clear procedure was laid down for receiving an itinerant 'Helper'. He was to be recommended by the Assistant in charge of his circuit; then be a probationer for a year 'on trial' and given a 'book'; then received at the next Conference and again given a 'book' (apparently an inscribed copy of the 'Large' *Minutes* of 1749). A specimen of the questions addressed to preachers being received was included in the 1766 *Minutes*.[290]

As early as 1746, the question was raised (but declined) of having some solemn form of recognition for preachers. It is not clear how far and at what time anything of this kind was used for the itinerants beyond the interrogation and the delivery of the 'Large' *Minutes*. Wesley, it should be remembered, always regarded them as laymen, not ordained ministers.[291] Two well-known incidents might suggest a quasi-ordination of the preachers distinct from Wesley's acknowledged ordinations. In 1746, Joseph Cownley was received with some ceremony at Bristol and at the Conference (or so his biographer John Gaulter evidently believed, for he contrasted it with what happened at his own reception in 1794). Cownley kneeled down, and Wesley put a New Testament in his hand and said, 'Take thou authority to preach the gospel' and gave him his benediction.[292] This event may have been an unusual gesture or a later expansion of the biographer's

---

[290] See *Q*. [2], stated as posed to one candidate, but asked of all who were to be admitted.

[291] His ordinations, which applied only to a small and select number of preachers, are another issue (considered below).

[292] Jackson, *Early Methodist Preachers*, 2:7, and see Minutes (1746), 50 n. 8.

memory, since there are no similar accounts relating this sort of rite for any other preachers. It is also hard to reconcile this recollection with Wesley's explicit rejection of the suggestion of more 'solemnity' that year and the actual mode of reception that was described in 1749, which involved presenting the itinerant with a copy of the 'Large' *Minutes* (first printed that year).[293] Though the Cownley procedure somewhat resembles the barest bones of Anglican ordination to the diaconate, when Cownley was actually ordained late in Wesley's life, he was ordained deacon and presbyter like others.

In 1790, Sutcliffe recorded what was apparently another unusual occasion, since he did not recall its being used again.[294] The candidates spoke of their experience, went forward, and 'confessed their faith'. Then Dr. Coke delivered a copy of the 'Large' *Minutes* to each, 'putting his right hand on each of our heads' in silence while Wesley looked on. Sutcliffe saw this as an 'ordination in every sense'. But these actions did not follow Wesley's procedure for his ordinations, and later commentators have generally doubted that this occasion entailed the conferring of ministerial orders.[295]

Wesley's ordinations for America and Scotland (as well as three more quite a bit later, perhaps 'in reserve' for England) do not in one sense directly concern us here. They were neither done in Conference nor recorded in the *Minutes*. Nor were those ordained listed in the *Minutes* ahead of the other itinerants, as was the case with conventional Anglican ordained clergy who assisted him in the connexion. Several other anomalies marked this controversial action. To a large extent, the whole affair was not allowed to be the business of Conference at all, for Wesley apparently discussed it only with his 'Cabinet'. He received a hostile reaction from them but carried on regardless. In 1785, he printed a statement in the *Minutes*

---

[293] As late as 1789, James Creighton (who assisted Wesley in the 1784 ordinations for America) describes Wesley's usual method of receiving preachers:

'Mr. Wesley has in some sense exercised the office of a Bishop since the first moment when he sent forth preachers and appointed them their place to labour in. He did not use the form of laying his hand on their head; but he took them by the hand and delivered them the Minutes, desiring them to preach the doctrines therein contained. Now is it not wonderful that this has not been taken notice of, at least publicly; for what is ordination if this is not?' (Letter to his sister, July 13, 1789, Creighton, MS Letters, World Methodist Library, Lake Junaluska, NC)

[294] Sutcliffe, MS 'History', fol. 1199.
[295] But see Vickers, *Coke*, 200–201.

justifying his American ordinations.[296] However, he explained neither how the ordained men related to the unordained nor how they would relate to the Conference (the Legal Hundred), which had recently been legalized in the Deed of Declaration as his successor. The significance of these ordinations and the disagreements they provoked later about 'Mr. Wesley's Plan' raised questions in connection with the Deed of Declaration itself.[297]

3. Discipline of the Preachers

The personal life of the itinerants was an early and persistent concern of Wesley. Rules, injunctions, and practical guidance for the itinerants multiplied in the *Minutes* as the years went on. The celebrated 'Rules of a Helper' in their earliest form in 1744 were a portent of much to come.[298] Three years later, Wesley asked whether the Assistants were 'exemplary in their lives? Do we inquire enough into this?' The answer: 'Perhaps not.'[299] The preachers were thereby reminded to be concerned particularly over the directions given at the previous Conference on early rising, studying, and the ordering of their day's work. In 1751, beginning at the Bristol Conference in March that year, John himself 'mentioned what I think was amiss or wanting in any of our brethren'.[300] Charles Wesley was especially concerned over some of the preachers' shortcomings and was given the task of examining the preachers in the North. This scheme entailed the calling of a succession of regional Conferences and resulted in something of a purge being carried out among the preachers. The process was not without disagreements between the Wesley brothers over the nature and extent of the discipline, and the tensions resulted not only in the necessity of third-party mediation between John and Charles, but also in the drawing up of two sets of articles of agreement between them regarding the loyalty of the

---

[296] *Minutes* (1785), *Q.* 20.

[297] See below, section 9.

[298] Minutes (1744), §73. These Rules assumed that title in the 'Large' *Minutes* (1762), but in 1744 they were called 'Rules of an Assistant', since the terminology of the early Methodist polity had not yet come to distinguish between the head preacher on a circuit (Assistant) and the other preachers (Helpers).

[299] Ibid., (1747), §67.

[300] On all this see Baker, *Wesley and Church*, 256–82; Rack, *Reasonable Enthusiast*, 230–31, 506, 510–14, 520–26.

preachers.[301] At the conclusion of the six-month cleansing, at a London Conference in January 1752, a pledge of loyalty and confidentiality in relation to each other was drawn up by the Wesleys and signed by the preachers.

In the following years, the Conference included regular inquiries regarding the adequacy and fitness of the preachers. In 1753, John Wesley, after reading over the 'Twelve Rules of an Itinerant Preacher', asked the Conference: 'Have any of you any objections to the life or doctrine of any Itinerant Preacher?'[302] The behaviour of each preacher was then considered individually, with no censures given. In 1755, the agenda included a long list of questions on how far the preachers were observing various disciplines, though no individual questioning is recorded.[303] In 1756, objections made against any itinerant or local preacher were considered.[304] In 1758, the Minutes noted objections against two preachers.[305] At London in 1759, almost the whole time was taken up with examining the preachers' lives.[306] According to Myles, the fitness of the preachers was examined from this time on at every Conference.[307] He says that Wesley punished offenders with a rebuke before the whole Conference, and then with either reversion to 'on trial' status, suspension for a year, or expulsion. The first printed annual *Minutes*, in 1765, do not include such an examination. But the following year, Wesley addressed a series of interrogations to the Conference—one preacher was left on trial 'till we know what his debts are', and two preachers were 'laid aside'.[308] The 1767 *Minutes* record that some preachers were kept on trial, and five 'desist[ed] from travelling'.[309] But from 1768 onwards, the question is asked regularly: 'Are there any objections to any of the preachers?' They are then named one by one. In the event, very few seem to have met with objections.

Discipline also included control of preachers' activities beyond their preaching and personal conduct. As early as 1747, there was a

---

[301] For details, see Heitzenrater, 'Purge the Preachers', and footnotes for 1751, below.

[302] *Minutes* (1753), §§20, 21. The document was later called 'Rules of a Helper'.

[303] Ibid. (1755), §5.

[304] *Journal & Diaries*, 21:76 in this edn.

[305] Minutes (1758), §§4–6.

[306] *Journal & Diaries*, 21:224 in this edn.

[307] Myles, *Chronological History*, 72.

[308] *Minutes* (1766), see *QQ*. 1, 2, 5.

[309] *QQ*. 2, 5.

rule against preachers promoting the singing of hymns of their own composition.[310] William Darney offended much in this respect with his doggerel, and his offence may have provoked the rule two years later that preachers were only to publish what had been 'corrected' by Wesley himself.[311] This approach was repeated, with further restrictions in some cases, in four more instances between 1761 and 1789, requiring that the preachers should publish only through the Methodist Book Concern.[312]

Apart from questions of detailed personal discipline, the Conference faced difficult problems and made repeated rules ultimately over finance, though with overtones of personal discipline that arose from the very fact of full-time service. The stipulations concerned stipends, pensions, marriage, and indulgence in trade. The history of these matters has already been outlined,[313] but the Conference additionally imposed restrictions, some by necessity, some by rule, on preachers' behaviour—for example, limiting marriage and banning 'trade' in 1768. At the same time, the development of financial support over the years, imperfect and uneven though it was, helped set preachers free to concentrate on their primary work, as did the provision of education for their children.

The question of the preachers' education was a sensitive point, in view of critics of Methodism's frequent charges that the preachers were unlettered and ignorant enthusiasts, and in the light of Charles Wesley's recurring strictures on them, which were much resented. At the first Conference, the question of a 'Seminary for labourers' was raised,[314] but the following year they recognized that it was impossible 'till God gives us a proper tutor'.[315] Meanwhile, the Minutes for both years provide a list of books that the preachers 'may' read and, in 1745, stipulate that these books are to be kept at London, Bristol, and Newcastle.[316] The list contained works not only of divinity but also of philosophy, history, poetry, and even Latin, Greek, and Hebrew, perhaps primarily with Wesley's needs in mind. In 1746, the preachers are admonished to consider themselves 'as learners rather than teachers; as young students . . . for whom

---

[310] Minutes (1747), §69, *Q*. 12 (2).
[311] Ibid. (1749), §18 (the minute reads 'revised' by Wesley).
[312] Minutes (1761), n. 6; (1765), *Q*. 24; (1781), *Q*. 25; and (1789), *Q*. 22.
[313] See above, section 6.
[314] Minutes (1744), §81.
[315] Ibid., (1745), §76.
[316] Ibid., (1744), §84; (1745), §83.

therefore a method of study is expedient in the highest degree'.[317]
There follows advice about early rising and the number of hours to
be set aside for reading. Noticeably, however, the suggested list of
books that they should read during that period consists only of
'practical divinity'. Later they were urged only to read the *Christian
Library*, which also consisted primarily of practical divinity, selected
in part through the advice of the Dissenter Philip Doddridge.[318]

In 1766, Wesley urged on the preachers the necessity of reading
all morning every day, or a minimum of five hours a day, requiring
that they peruse 'the most useful books' or 'return to [their] trade'.[319]
Admitting to critics that some of his preachers were 'unlearned',
Wesley argued that some of the Anglican clergy were little better
and that the Methodist preachers were often, at least, superior in
practical divinity.[320] A number of the preachers had had at least an
elementary education, and some much more.[321] For young people,
Wesley had high ideals in his curriculum for Kingswood School,
despite his frequent disappointments with that institution. He had
early hoped to add a higher class there for a course of 'academical
learning', though it seems to have been postponed until 1768. He
had sketched plans for this level at the outset, though they did not
appear in his *Short Account* of the school in 1749.[322] Its appearance
in the 1768 edition seems to have been stimulated by the expulsion
of Calvinistic Methodists from St. Edmund Hall, Oxford, and the
foundation of Lady Huntingdon's Trevecca College. It is doubtful
how far the scheme was carried out effectively even then.[323] In 1775,
Benson and Fletcher, as an item of their alternative plans for the
future of Methodism, proposed using the school partly for training
preachers.[324]

More realistic, perhaps, than the dream of a theological seminary,
were Wesley's occasional resumptions of his role as an Oxford tutor.

---

[317] Ibid., (1746), §§53–54.

[318] *Letters*, 26:190, n. 10 in this edn., sees Doddridge's advice as being for the
Christian Library; but the *AM* 1 (1778): 419–25, states that the suggestions were for
young students in divinity.

[319] Wesley also promised to provide the books for them if they could not afford
them. *Minutes* (1766), *Q.* 30.

[320] To Dr. Rutherforth in 1768, *Letters* (Telford), 5:359–63.

[321] Henry Bett, *The Early Methodist Preachers* (London, 1935), 38–46.

[322] Ives, *Kingswood School*, 10, 75.

[323] See Rack, *Reasonable Enthusiast*, 357–58.

[324] Ibid., 466–67; *Minutes* (1775), n. 551.

In 1770, he suggested an Oxford Methodist strategy for overcoming idleness: 'Try yourselves. Keep a diary of your employment but for a week, and then read it over. No idleness can consist with growth in grace.'[325] Sometimes his tutorial inclination came out in individual advice on reading to female correspondents or preachers, and on occasion through his collecting a group to 'read over' logic and other subjects.[326] Some preachers, predictably, responded better than others. A few, notably Adam Clarke, became considerable scholars; a number were at least serious readers and enjoyed the exercise; but some saw little use in it, at least as regards the learned languages.[327] Some were crude and only minimally educated, though Wesley could be tolerant of them if they produced spiritual results. Charles Wesley was much less so.

Recognizing the different talents of the preachers and appointing them to circuits that could best benefit from their peculiar talents rested within Wesley's authority and represented a natural matter of concern to the preachers. Stationing, like so much else in the early years, was subject to much improvisation according to local needs, the expansion of the connexion, and the number and availability of preachers. As the matter of circuit finances shows, the preachers were frequently subject to the hazards of lack of regular income, and for this and other reasons, such as personal and doctrinal disagreements and the purges in the 1750s, there was a considerable dropout rate.[328] These problems also caused men to change from full- to part-time service and back again or to function in some cases as 'half-itinerants'.[329]

The formal circuits and appointments to them emerged slowly and stabilized gradually. In 1746, when seven circuits were listed in the Minutes, changes of preachers' appointments were, at least on paper, monthly. In 1747, they became two-monthly. With the institution of quarterly circuit meetings in 1748, the length of appointment may have also coincided with the three-month pattern. But within a few years, the appointments lasted for six months and then regularly for one year. The patchy survival of the Minutes before 1765 makes it difficult to say how soon the yearly change was

---

[325] *Minutes* (1770), *Q.* 28.
[326] *Journal & Diaries*, 20:162, 263 in this edn.; Rack, *Reasonable Enthusiast*, 359–60.
[327] Jackson, *Early Methodist Preachers*, 2:191.
[328] Rack, *Reasonable Enthusiast*, 204, 334, following Tyerman, *Wesley*, 2:126–27.
[329] *Minutes* (1755), §2 and n. 954.

established, although Wesley provided a rationale in his letter to Samuel Walker in 1756: 'Were I myself to preach one whole year in one place, I should preach both myself and most of my congregation asleep.'[330] Sutcliffe says of the 1765 stations that in previous times every preacher was stationed till Christmas, and even after that date, changes could occasionally happen from necessity or preachers' desires.[331] By the time of the Deed of Declaration in 1784, the maximum stay for a preacher in a circuit was fixed at two years, with occasional exceptions for three years at most.

Inevitably, preachers did not always live up to Wesley's expectations and ideals, as the record of disciplinary cases and expulsions in the *Minutes* shows. Wesley set a very high standard, perhaps coloured too much by his exalted ideal of personal discipline as a bachelor don turned revivalist who had retained much of his old Oxford ways. Yet the record of surviving diaries and life-stories reveals a remarkable body of men who shared common ideals as well as a growing esprit de corps. And they did not lack in individuality and a sense of exercising a comprehensive ministry, which grew in Wesley's later years. Despite the fears that were freely expressed concerning the problems that they thought would follow his death and the dissensions and schisms that took place over the next half century, the Conference preserved something of that sense of a band of brothers, a committed order of preacher-ministers with a common purpose, which gave them sufficient unity to survive.

IX. The Deed of Declaration (1784) and After

The occasion for the Deed of Declaration was the continuing lack of a legal definition of the 'Yearly Conference of the People called Methodists', which the Model Deed beginning in 1763 had declared was the successor to the Wesley brothers.[332] The Model Deed was

---

[330] JW to Samuel Walker of Truro, Sept. 3, 1756, *Letters* (Telford), 3:195.

[331] Sutcliffe, MS 'History', fol. 664. For an example, see *Minutes* (1769), *Q.* 7 (16), n. 3.

[332] This legal template, adapted for local situations, secured the property of each preaching-house for the Conference.

designed, among other things, to secure control of the stationing of preachers, first to the Wesleys, then eventually to the Conference, thus to preserve the connexional system against the risk (at Wesley's death) of dissolution into a scattering of locally controlled Societies. Preaching-houses not fixed on this Model Deed could cause trouble, as the Birstall and Dewsbury Chapel cases showed even after 1784.[333]

But there was also the question that had exercised Methodist minds for years past—who or what should succeed to Wesley's authority after his death? It took a long time for Wesley himself to settle on the notion of the Conference (however defined) as his collective successor, despite the apparent implications of the Model Deed.[334]

1. Questions of Separation, Ordination, and Succession

Because of Wesley's irregularities and the dubious legality, at least in Anglican eyes, of field preaching, Society forming, and perhaps above all using lay preachers, the whole question of the status of Methodism and its relationship to the Church was controversial from the start. Wesley loudly protested that Methodism was not separating from the Church but simply a supplement to it. Methodism would never leave the Church unless it was forced out, which was not on the horizon. But the very openness of the Societies to non-Anglicans made this argument rather unconvincing, quite apart from the irregularities. Since many Methodists found that their most vital religious experiences, if not the whole of their worship, were within Methodism and not the Church's services, and some were actively hostile to the Church and clergy, they rather naturally strained at the limitations that Wesley attempted to impose upon them. His attempts to define 'separation' and to deny that Methodism was separating became increasingly threadbare. Simply to profess the Church's doctrine and to attend its worship (which many Methodists did not in any case) seemed to many an inadequate basis for claiming actual adherence to the Church. And to say that Methodists had not separated so long as the Church did not throw them out or they had not professed actual dissent[335] seemed to

---

[333] *Minutes* (1783), n. 1; (1788), n. 1; (1789), n. 1.

[334] For what follows, see Rack, *Reasonable Enthusiast*, 291-305, 464–70, 495–526; Baker, *Wesley and Church*, 216–33.

[335] 'Reasons against Separation from the Church of England' (1758), 9:332–49 in this edn.

some like a weak thread of actual connection. To many Methodists, their real 'church' and 'ministers' were the Methodist Society and its travelling preachers, and so a number of the itinerants also felt. Hence, recurring pressures for ordination, if not separation, arose within the Methodist ranks, resulting in concessions by Wesley for some places to hold Methodist services during church hours. And as some then pointed out, a few places like London and Bristol had long enjoyed the privilege of having the Sacrament administered in Methodist settings by Charles Wesley and other helpful clergy.

Charles Wesley often thought his brother dangerously wavering and too much subject to pressure by 'ambitious' preachers keen on ordination. Both brothers at first thought that Methodist ordination meant separation from the Church, though John later changed his mind on this point. Indeed, Charles had grave doubts about the quality of many preachers and at times dreamed that they might be absorbed into the parish system as Assistants to the clergy. John set his face against this development, though he also, in debates that fueled Charles's fears in the mid-1750s, ruled that ordination was not 'expedient', whether or not it was 'lawful'.[336] Yet from a very early stage John also seems to have been clear in his own mind that the work must go on, 'church or no church'.[337] He would not leave voluntarily, but if he found he had to drop his irregularities or be expelled, he would choose expulsion for the sake of the work.[338] Another ominous sign was that in spite of his reluctance to do so, John had to acquiesce in the licensing of preachers and preaching-houses on occasion to protect them under the Toleration Act, though he continued to deny that this made Methodists into Dissenters. He had become convinced as early as 1746 that he had the right to ordain in cases of necessity, though he was merely a presbyter rather than a bishop, but he abstained from doing so until the 1780s. In 1764, some Methodist preachers thought that they might obtain ordination through a person who called himself Erasmus, who had dubious Greek episcopal credentials. Some preachers took advantage of this without Wesley's permission, which created a scandal, as well as a rumour that Wesley would become a bishop through Erasmus.[339]

---

[336] See the first sentence of 'Reasons against Separation', 9:332 in this edn.; and Baker, *Wesley and Church*, chap. 10.

[337] *Letters* (Telford), 4:162.

[338] On the other hand, Charles was an Anglican first and a Methodist second. Heitzenrater, 'Purge the Preachers', 501.

[339] Baker, *Wesley and Church*, 200–201, 380–81.

But alongside this running battle over ordination and separation there was the even more practical question of the succession to Wesley and how Methodism could be perpetuated as an organization and evangelistic agency after his death. Wesley's mind seems to have been exercised on this more particularly after his efforts at a 'union' of evangelicals had finally foundered in the 1760s. Although some centralization had begun to take place with the abortive proposals in 1749, none of the decisions on finances over the years helped on the question of succession. In 1760, Wesley seems to have proposed to the Conference that after his death, the Assistants should form a 'Council' to settle matters.[340] In the 1760s, more and more preaching-houses were licensed. In 1763, Wesley's Model Deed for the preaching-houses established the succession for controlling the stationing of preachers: after the Wesley brothers, William Grimshaw of Haworth, and then 'the Yearly Conference of the People called Methodists', though Grimshaw died in 1763. Wesley's authority was challenged, as we have seen, at the 1766 Conference. In 1769, when he finally gave up all hope of an evangelical union, he speculated on the future of his Methodists. Perhaps a quarter of the preachers would take Anglican orders and some would turn Independent (Dissenters). But the rest should make 'a firm union' by all the travelling preachers meeting in London after his death, drawing up articles of agreement and dismissing those who refused them.[341] They should then choose a committee of three, five, or seven, each being Moderator in turn. They should perhaps lay a foundation for this now by articles of agreement to 'devote ourselves entirely to God, . . . to preach the old Methodist doctrines, . . . to observe and enforce the whole Methodist discipline' in the 'Large' *Minutes*.[342] This document at least made it clear what Wesley had been implying for years—that he envisaged such provisions as were necessary for his movement to continue for an indefinite period.

The Model Deed seemed to suggest a succession of clerical rule followed by control by a collective Conference of preachers. Yet Wesley seems to have been reluctant to give up the idea of a singular clerical supervisor over the preachers. Charles Wesley was not a very

[340] Ibid., 197.

[341] Wesley's will in 1789 provided a copy of the new eight-volume set of *Sermons on Several Occasions* to any faithful Methodist preacher who remained in the connexion for at least six months after Wesley's death. *Journal* (Curnock), 8:343.

[342] 'Address to the Travelling Preachers', Aug. 4, 1769; *Letters* (Telford), 5:143–45; and *Minutes* (1769), at the end.

plausible successor since from the mid-1750s he virtually ceased to itinerate and in any case was at odds with some leading preachers. According to Sutcliffe, there was a plan at the end of 1771, at a 'serious conference' held in London, for twelve preachers to be named as superintendents and stationed in the principal towns, with two clergy at their head.[343] Sutcliffe claims that this plan was Charles Wesley's idea. According to Charles, however, writing to Mark Davis, it 'was a misunderstanding to suppose that the people are to be directed by twelve lay preachers'. All that the Wesleys could do, after the brothers' deaths, was to commit the Methodists to 'the most solid and established of our preachers (be they twelve or more or less) to keep together and regulate the Society'. But Charles thought this approach would be impossible without 'a clergyman or two at the head', and hence John had approached Davis. The people, asserted Charles, would choose for themselves anyway, and the majority would prefer a clergyman to a lay preacher.[344] Davis had apparently heard that John Fletcher of Madeley would be Wesley's successor, and he wished to know if he could be Fletcher's Assistant.

In fact, John Wesley had a clerical successor in mind, and Davis, an Irish itinerant who had obtained episcopal orders, was one possibility. He was tried for a year in London but was found unsatisfactory and dismissed.[345] Wesley was much more anxious to secure Fletcher, who had great prestige among the Methodists for his saintliness. In July 1773, Wesley wrote to Fletcher, listing his qualifications for the task and concluding, 'Thou art the man!' Fletcher resisted, still feeling his call was primarily to his parish, and Wesley finally gave up the attempt to persuade him otherwise.[346]

2. The Benson-Fletcher Plan

At the 1773 Conference and again in 1774 and 1775, Wesley had to content himself with repeating the 1769 agreement to stand by the Methodist doctrines and discipline, and a number of the preachers signed a document to this effect. But some preachers were understandably worried that this was not enough, especially when, in the

---

[343] Sutcliffe, MS 'History', fols. 791–92, and cf. *Minutes* (1772), n. 381.
[344] CW to Davis, Dec. 10, 1772, quoted in Baker, *Wesley and Church*, 207–8.
[345] Ibid.
[346] *Letters* (Telford), 6:10–11.

spring of 1775, Wesley fell ill and was expected to die. Joseph Benson then proposed a plan to inquire into the character and competence of the preachers. Suitable men should be ordained by Wesley and his clerical helpers, and the rest should be either dismissed or trained at Kingswood School, if they were potentially suitable.[347]

Benson submitted his plan to Fletcher, who approved of purging the preachers but thought that the Kingswood plan was doubtful and that Wesley should try to obtain ordinations from the bishops before trying his own. Wesley apparently allowed Benson to air his plan at the Conference but without result. Fletcher then proposed a plan of his own for a 'Methodist Church of England' as a 'daughter church' to the Establishment, submitting in all that was not unscriptural, with Methodists still attending its services and Sacraments. There should be a revised liturgy ('rectified according to the purity of the gospel'), along with 'needful alterations' in the Articles and Book of Homilies. Bishops should be asked to ordain suitable preachers, accepting testimonials from Methodist sources and allowing posting in Methodist circuits. If this were refused, Wesley should ordain suitable men, make the rest deacons, and put dubious cases 'on trial' (probation). On the death of Wesley, the power of ordination would be exercised by three or five of the preachers as 'Moderators'. Kingswood School would be used for educating preachers' sons, training ministers, and caring for worn-out preachers. The revised liturgy and Articles, along with the *Minutes*, would be their guide for the Methodist preachers, and the 'general plan' would be to 'preach the doctrine of grace against the Socinians, the doctrine of justice against the Calvinists, and the doctrine of holiness against the world'.[348]

In some respects this plan anticipated what Wesley eventually decided to do for American Methodism, but as usual, he postponed decisions until events and Providence forced his hand. In 1775, he did no more than carry out yet another purge of preachers at the Conference.[349] However, as we have seen, there are signs in the 1780s that he was using a Cabinet and making more use of committees. This move can be read not only as a matter of necessity but also as preparation for the preachers to assume more authority and for the people to accept it.

[347] For this and what follows, see Baker, *Wesley and Church*, 209–12; Rack, *Reasonable Enthusiast*, 466–67; *Minutes* (1775), n. 1.
[348] *Journal* (Curnock), 8:331–34.
[349] *Journal & Diaries*, 22:459–60 in this edn.

Though Wesley perhaps never quite gave up the idea that Fletcher might act as head of the connexion as long as his friend was alive, his actions in the 1780s (even before Fletcher's death in 1785) suggest that he was increasingly fixing his hopes on a collective leadership by the preachers, in addition to developing safeguards for the succession of leadership and the control of the connexion as a connexion. Finding a clerical successor proved impossible—though Dr. Coke was a useful and faithful aide in Wesley's last years, some preachers suspected him of ambition, and Wesley had doubts about his discretion. There is no sign that he ever thought of Coke as his successor.

3. The Deed of Declaration and the Conference

The climactic year was 1784, which produced the Deed of Declaration and the scheme for ordinations in an American Methodist Church, though these developments were coloured and determined by the very different situations in the two countries.

The immediate problem that the Deed was intended to solve was that of securing the preaching-houses and their pulpits to the control of Wesley and the Conference from the whims of local trustees. Otherwise the whole connexion threatened to dissolve into local Independency. Some properties were not on the Model Deed, and nothing could be done about this except exhorting those Societies to change their legal property documents. The Deed of Declaration was directed at those Societies that were fixed on the Model Deed, and doubts about the Model Deed's security, and indeed about the general security of trust deeds, had been voiced on and off for years, as successive proposals for central custody since 1749 showed.[350] Now a lawyer contacted by Coke pointed out to Wesley that the Model Deed was indeed defective because the 'Yearly Conference of the People called Methodists' had never been legally defined. And as was shown earlier, the membership and attendance at Conference (and even the fact of one being summoned at all) had, by Wesley's own confession, been purely a matter of Wesley's will or whim.

Although the new Deed did not prevent Wesley during his lifetime from acting exactly as before (or so at least he claimed), the

---

[350] *Minutes* (1749), *Q.* 1 and n. 724; (1768), *Q.* 15 and n. 190; (1770), *Q.* 15 and n. 315; Pawson in Tyerman MSS, 3:65.

document did define the Conference for legal purposes and gave the body the legacy of all Wesley's powers. Thus it in effect also settled the succession question. Or did it? The question of the ordinations proceeded alongside and independent of the legal development of the Conference and left unclear and open to controversy, as we shall see, the exact nature of the connexion's complete power structure and organization.

The lawyer who drew up the Deed of Declaration followed Wesley's instructions to define the legal Conference as consisting of one hundred named persons with power to elect to fill vacancies in perpetuity. Within that legal framework, Wesley then had to draw up the initial list of the hundred preachers. He had apparently considered several options, including all the preachers or only a few, but he settled for the larger, though still select number, which amounted to about half of the preachers in the connexion at that time. The real trouble came when his final list included some junior preachers but omitted some seniors. Though it might be charitably supposed that he wisely mixed age and youth, the suspicion was (especially in view of his declared policy in recent years) that he took the opportunity to exclude those whom he saw as troublemakers. He tartly replied to critics who thought they should have been named, 'True, if I had thought as well of them, as they thought of themselves.'[351]

John Hampson, Sen., led the excluded preachers in an attack through a circular urging the 1784 Conference to throw out the new Deed. At the Conference, Fletcher helped to save Wesley's face by an impassioned appeal that dissolved the meeting in tears. John Pawson said that it was supposed that 'all the preachers whose names were not in the Deed were expelled the connexion.' Thus 'some of them were greatly offended, and dreadful things were to be done. But this thing blew over much better than was expected by many, and the offended brethren were seen to be offenders and were obliged to submit and ask for pardon, which was readily granted by Mr. Wesley.'[352] But several resigned, and the controversy fueled the hostile tone towards Wesley's 'ambition' and authoritarianism, which coloured biographies of him in the following decade by John Hampson, Jun., and John Whitehead.

The Deed declared that the Conference was legally made up of one hundred named preachers (the Legal Hundred) and their

[351] 'Thoughts upon some late Occurrences', in *Works* (Jackson), 13:248–52.
[352] Pawson, 'Some Account', fol. 26.

successors elected by them, and various regulations were made for the Conference's conduct.[353] It was to meet annually at London, Bristol, or Leeds, though a later clause allowed for other places to be chosen. It was to meet for a minimum of five days and a maximum of three weeks. There was to be a quorum of forty, and decisions were to be by majority vote (at last!). A President and a Secretary were to be chosen annually by the body. The Conference would settle the President's powers and could expel members absent for two years. The qualification for membership was the remarkably low period of twelve months in the itinerancy. The Conference was to have power to admit into connexion as preachers those whom it approved, and could appoint only preachers who were members of Conference to chapels, for not more than three successive years. For chapels in Ireland or outside Britain, Conference could send delegates with full powers. Rules were laid down for the possible extinction of the Conference, after which the chapels would be left to the trustees to appoint such preachers as they wished. The penultimate section then clearly states that 'nothing herein contained' in the Deed of Declaration should 'extinguish, lessen or abridge the life-estate' of the Wesleys in the chapels in which they have 'estate or interest, power or authority whatsoever'. Nothing was said in all this about Methodism's relationship to the Church or about the doctrines that Methodists should preach. Doctrinal boundaries for preaching had already been defined in the Model Deed in terms of the doctrines contained in Wesley's *Sermons* and *Explanatory Notes upon the New Testament.* As to the Church, Professor Baker very reasonably commented that to set up a legal body of this kind without either sanction from the Church or explicit subjection to it made Wesley's notion of Methodist connection to it little more than a legal fiction.[354]

The Deed seems to have made little difference to the actual functioning of the Conference during Wesley's lifetime, though he becomes listed in the *Minutes* as President, with Coke as Secretary. Wesley asserted that the Deed altered none of his existing powers and that no one would have supposed it did but for 'that improper and ambiguous word *Life-Estate*'.[355] What he meant by the term

---

[353] *Journal* (Curnock), 8:335–41, and preface to *Minutes* (1784), in this edn.

[354] Baker, *Wesley and Church*, 229–30.

[355] For further discussion of the significance of his objection to the offending words, see *Minutes* (1785), *Q*. 21, n. 92.

'*Life-Estate*' (or interest) seems never to have been explained. One explanation seems to be that the term was related to the property, meaning that those enjoying the use of Methodist property could not sell it and had interest in it only during their lifetimes. The wording of the Deed might then be taken to apply to the Wesleys' unchanged ownership of the preaching-houses for their lifetimes and so perhaps implicitly limit their powers to this. So some may have supposed (or hoped). What is certainly clear, however, is that by the explanatory terms 'interest, power or authority', Wesley intended to continue with all his powers to station and to summon or exclude those he wished to Conference as before. He believed that he still had these powers and certainly exercised them, as we have seen. He even excluded members of the Legal Hundred from attending sessions of Conference, though he occasionally let Conference have its way.

One anxiety of the preachers was that those not in the Hundred would be excluded, if not from the connexion as Pawson had described, at least from the Conference, or perhaps silenced within it. According to Henry Moore forty years later, Wesley did not intend to abolish Conference or any part of its authority, but the fruit and effect of all they do should be enjoyed by all, as Parliament develops laws but all are bound by them: 'When he [Wesley] was strong urged to put all the *temporal affairs* into the hands of those who were *only* in full connexion, which it was said might conciliate and satisfy them, he absolutely refused. He had futurity in his eye and would consent only to the Hundred being legislators.'[356] This assertion seems to be too strong, for in a letter left to be read to the Conference after his death, Wesley urged his successors (meaning the Hundred) not to assume any 'superiority' over 'your brethren' but to keep things as far as possible as in his lifetime and not to show any 'respect' for persons in making appointments.[357] Apparently neither attendance nor discussion, at least, would be restricted to the Hundred. Although there was certainly potential here for disagreement between the Hundred and the rest of the preachers (in which the former presumably must have the last word), no such showdown seems ever to have taken place.

---

[356] Letter in 1815, Henry Moore to John Pawson, Tyerman MSS, 3:111.
[357] *Minutes* (1791), opening letter.

4. Sacraments and the Wesleyan Ordinations for America and Scotland

For America the situation and the solution were, and were bound to be, very different.[358] Although Wesley provided for an independent Methodist Church there, it has not often been noted that a clause in the Deed of Declaration stated that the English Conference could send delegates with full powers to chapels in Ireland and elsewhere outside Britain. The Irish Conference was indeed presided over either by Wesley or by Coke in the former's lifetime. The first American Conference in 1773 had asked: 'Ought not the authority of Mr. Wesley and that Conference to extend to the preachers and people in America, as well as Great Britain and Ireland? *A.* Yes.'[359] This was before the separation of the colonies from Britain, but Asbury (ordained for America by Coke, though never returning to Britain) was later elected to the Legal Hundred. Professor Ward has argued that the plan was for a system of subordinate Conferences bound together at the summit with each other and the annual British Conference by travelling bishops or superintendents.[360] There is little doubt that Wesley at first had hoped to continue to control American Methodism, even after the colonies became independent. He attempted to send his choice of preachers and to set the date of American Conferences. But on the brink of separation at the Christmas Conference in 1784, the Americans made an implicit declaration of independence. They voted whether to accept Coke and Asbury as Superintendents; they set their own Conference dates and chose their own preachers; and much to Wesley's annoyance, they soon began to call their Superintendents 'bishops'. Coke travelled much in America and acted there as a Superintendent, but he had no defined position in England other than Secretary of Conference, and the Americans would not allow him to exercise English authority over them. American independence as well as distance and other practical obstacles ensured the defeat of Wesley's apparent plan for the transatlantic hierarchy.

[358] See Baker, *Wesley and Church*, chaps. 14 and 15; Rack, *Reasonable Enthusiast*, 506–18, 526.

[359] *Minutes of the Methodist Conferences, annually held in America, from 1773 to 1794* (Philadelphia: Tuckniss, 1794), *Minutes* (1773), *Q.* 1.

[360] W. R. Ward, 'The Legacy of John Wesley', in Ann Whiteman et al., eds., *Statesmen, Scholars, and Merchants* (Oxford, 1973), 323–50.

As to Wesley's controversial ordinations for America, Professor Ward has also pointed out that this was not simply an eccentric act by Wesley but has a context as one of several attempts to solve the problem of ordained ministers and bishops for the Anglican churches left stranded by the creation of the independent United States. The famous story of how Samuel Seabury obtained episcopal orders from the Scottish Episcopalians is only part of a more varied story. Some Americans even considered presbyterian ordination, as seen in the events of 1779 at Fluvanna, but were saved from it in the end. Wesley's ordinations, though irregular by orthodox Anglican standards, reflect a strand of pragmatic and latitudinarian thinking in contemporary Anglicanism, especially in the desperate American situation, oddly though it may seem to consort with his residual High Churchmanship. The complementary ordinations of Richard Whatcoat and Thomas Vasey, first as deacons and then as presbyters, fit his attempt to follow the rubrics in the BCP ordinal: if Coke's actions in America were to be 'regular', his ordinations of the preachers would, in the first instance, require the assistance of two ordained presbyters, whom Wesley was supplying.[361]

At all events Wesley, in his statement to Conference in 1784, shows that after a vain effort to get English bishops to ordain Methodist preachers for America, he turned with evident relief to what he saw as the providential freedom of Americans (or rather of himself on their behalf) to set up a version of church life in conformity to scripture and Primitive Christianity—under his supervision. Hence he saw the ordinations as part of a comprehensive plan that included revised Articles and liturgy, much as Fletcher had proposed in 1775.[362] The new church would be governed by two joint 'Superintendents', Coke and Asbury, who would ordain others on the spot. Just how this scheme emerged remains at some points obscure and controversial, mainly because of suspicions that Wesley had been pressured by the ambitious Dr. Coke, as substantiated by a letter from Coke to Wesley in which he asserts that 'the power of ordaining others should be received by me from you, by the imposition of your hands.'[363] That Coke, already as valid a presbyter as

---

[361] Thus Wesley also conscripted James Creighton (along with Coke) to assist in the ordinations of Whatcoat and Vasey.

[362] See *Minutes* (1785), *Q.* 20.

[363] Whitehead, *Life of Rev. John. Wesley*, 2:417; cf. Rack, *Reasonable Enthusiast*, 513.

Wesley, should require further ordination to empower him to ordain others has seemed to some to be illogical on Wesley's premises. But the point at issue (of which Coke was acutely aware) was how to convey Wesley's authority to America. Ordination by Wesley as superintendent gave him an authority that could not have been conveyed by episcopal ordination alone and, if Wesley's plan for subordinate Conferences is correctly interpreted, connected the Americans with their English parent.

But to return to England, Wesley's intentions for the future of Methodism there, and the significance and purpose of his ordinations, were a matter of controversy among Methodists then and have been ever since. Long before 1784, indeed as far back as the Conference of 1745,[364] Wesley had given a remarkably pragmatic account of the naturalistic development of various forms of church government. Although as late as December 1745, he had written to Westley Hall appearing to defend the necessity of bishops in the apostolic succession to ordain men to administer Sacraments, he seems in January 1746 to have been convinced by Lord King's account of the Primitive Church (and perhaps even earlier by reading Stillingfleet) that 'bishops and presbyters are (essentially) of one order' and that he as a presbyter had a right to ordain. On various occasions in the 1750s, 1760s, and 1780s, he claimed also that Stillingfleet had convinced him that apostolic succession was a 'fable' and that ordaining people would not mean separation from the Church.[365]

On the other hand, he continued to believe that ordination was necessary for administering Sacraments—a mere call to preach was insufficient. But he did not exercise his alleged right to ordain until the 1780s, keeping this power in reserve until events and Providence seemed to him to make it necessary to use it to fulfil what was always his overriding concern: to further the gospel and keep Methodism united. Despite his doubts in 1755 whether ordination meant separation, in his later years, he kept asserting that, so long as it was for the work outside England, it did not. He claimed that the Anglican Establishment no longer ruled in America by 1784 and that it did not obtain in Scotland, where the established Church was Presbyterian, so ordinations for these places did not infringe Anglican rights.[366]

[364] Minutes (1745), §56.

[365] *Letters*, 26:173–75, 572 in this edn; *Letters* (Telford), 4:150, 7:21; and see Baker, *Wesley and Church*, chap. 9.

[366] This view, however, ignored the fact that the Church of England did not recognize presbyteral ordination by Anglican clergy.

Preachers ordained for Scotland had, logically enough on Wesley's argument, to drop their ministerial status and activities when they returned to England, much to their indignation. John Pawson argued that degrading ministers in this way without moral or doctrinal cause was unprecedented in church history.[367]

The evidence suggests that Wesley acted of his own volition in ordaining, despite consultation with the Cabinet, which, according to Pawson, opposed him, though Pawson saw that Wesley's mind was made up.[368] Pawson was soon to come round to supporting ordination for England as well, having himself been ordained for Scotland. He was even ordained a 'bishop' by Coke in 1794 and was one architect of the 'Lichfield Plan' that year for a Methodist episcopal system of government.[369] Perhaps his account of the 1784 plan for ordination should be regarded with caution as his comments were made in the context of claiming that the preachers had never pressed for ordination and that the first rumblings came from Wesley in 1784. In fact, many preachers and their people had pressed for it on and off since the 1750s. But here Pawson was countering those claims, no doubt also exaggerated, by people like Hampson, Whitehead, and the Church Methodists, that the whole business was the product of the ambitions of some preachers, who pressured a perhaps senile Wesley against his better judgment.

Wesley certainly acted independently of Conference, only explaining his actions for America and Scotland after the event.[370] In May 1787, he wrote to Joshua Keighley: 'I am quite undetermined whether I shall ever ordain again. At the Conference this must be thoroughly discussed. I know not whether I have already gone too far.'[371] Doughty comments that the discussion must have been favourable, since Wesley did five more ordinations that year and others in 1788 and 1789.[372] We have no evidence of any discussion in Conference or indeed much elsewhere, and it is perhaps rash to assume that Wesley would have followed the preachers' opinions, whatever they may have been.

---

[367] Pawson, *Letters*, 1:46, 51.
[368] Tyerman MSS, 3:53.
[369] Pawson, *Letters*, 1:161, 163, 166–67.
[370] See letters read to Conference in *Minutes* (1785), *Q.* 20; (1786), after *Q.* 24.
[371] May 20, 1787, *Letters* (Telford), 7:384.
[372] Doughty, *Wesley: His Conferences*, 39.

5. *Succession and the Wesleyan Ordinations for England*

The excuses used for the American and Scottish ordinations could not be used for England, as Wesley well knew. At the 1786 Conference, the preachers argued for an ordination for a neglected place in Yorkshire but were persuaded to vote it down by John Atlay, who argued that such an action meant separation. Wesley is said to have regretted at least the Scottish ordinations, which would be quite logical on his pragmatic grounds if he thought they had not done much good. More controversially, he is alleged to have regretted the whole ordination business, saying the preachers had over-persuaded him. But other preachers said he never regretted it.[373] Those who alleged Wesley's regret probably had regrets themselves, and one of them, the Anglican clergyman James Creighton, had taken part in the first instance, while those saying Wesley did not repent were in favour of the acts. Wesley ordained even after the alleged regrets, and there is no evidence that he ceased to believe in his *right* and power to ordain, only on its advisability as a policy.

Most striking and enigmatic of all is the fact that he later ordained three men who remained in England, and one of them, Alexander Mather, allegedly as a superintendent (a quasi-bishop) as well.[374] This action led Mather and Pawson to believe that Wesley's future plans included an 'episcopal' system of rule for England and a continuation of ordinations there, presumably through Mather,[375] and this belief no doubt encouraged him, with others, to plan such a system at the notorious Lichfield meeting in 1794. Pawson had just been ordained a 'bishop' by Coke.[376] Pressure for a 'full' ministry that could administer the Sacraments and confusion about Wesley's intentions on the matter encouraged piecemeal ordinations by supporters of such views in the early 1790s after Wesley's death, until Conference stopped it. Church Methodists, as we shall see, consistently and strongly opposed all such moves away from the Church. Nevertheless, the view may be suggested that Wesley, ever the pragmatist and willing to make minimal concessions to keep restive Methodists within the connexion, may well have proceeded with the

---

[373] For the Yorkshire request, see Baker, *Charles Wesley,* 140; and for the alleged doubts on ordination, *Wesley and Church,* 282; 397, n. 88; 399, n. 17.

[374] For the evidence of this conjecture, see Baker, *Wesley and Church,* 281 and refs.

[375] Pawson, *Letters,* 1:156–57 (in 1793).

[376] Ibid., 1:164, 166–67.

three cases (including Mather, just mentioned) as preparation for the day when Methodist ordinations for England would be irresistible. These actions did not necessarily imply a complete 'episcopal' system, but merely a device for piecemeal action and a possible option for use after his death.

The questions do arise: Why was Mather considered a Superintendent if that was indeed the case and if presbyteral ordination was sufficient to give power to ordain? And what, in any case, was the relationship of the ordained men (and any possible 'episcopal' system of oversight) to the Conference as a legal governing body? As regards the Superintendent question, perhaps Wesley conveyed authority to Mather, somewhat analogous to the case of Coke, rather than a third ordination as such. But Wesley seems to have followed what he saw as the 'Primitive' (and Anglican) model of a three-fold ministry and ordination in the case of the 1784 ordination—the equivalents of deacon, priest, and bishop. In his diary, he says that he had 'ordained' Coke. And his ordinations all seem to involve ordaining men on two successive days to the first two orders. The third step, to Superintendent, as his preferred title indicates, emphasizes the practical role he envisaged for it. Whether he had it in mind to institute a succession of episcopal-style ordinations is a matter for speculation.

But it may be asked in any case whether the ordained men (clearly only a small minority of the body of preachers) were to be, so to speak, mere machines for administering Sacraments where this was necessarily unavoidable. If so, why set apart a Superintendent? Professor Ward has argued that the Superintendents were to be links between the branches of Methodism at home and abroad, but that the Americans would not allow Coke to exercise such a role. Perhaps Mather was placed in reserve to fulfil that role on the English side. He took a leading role in and out of Conference in Wesley's last years, as we have seen, and might reasonably have expected to be the first President after Wesley's death, if Coke was too controversial for the position. As it turned out, the Conference, in the anxiety to avoid 'Kings in Israel', very pointedly avoided both men until a few years later. But perhaps, as some have concluded, Wesley, if not confused or pressured by the preachers, was not clear in his own mind about the full logic of his actions, which were, as so often, primarily dictated by immediate and unavoidable necessity.

The other question is equally puzzling. It is hard to see just how the putative 'Superintendents', and indeed ordained men more generally, were supposed to relate to the Conference, unless the latter at least *were* simply a device for sacramental ministrations. Wesley certainly regarded such ministrations as not open to the preachers without ordination. There was no place provided in the Conference (through the Deed of Declaration scheme) for special officers other than the Secretary and the President (for one year only and with as-yet-undefined powers). The ordained men were not listed before the other preachers in the subsequent annual *Minutes*, as conventional ordained Anglican 'helpers' had been. The many ambiguities about the whole business, as well as ideological divisions, led to conflicts of policy after Wesley's death. Each faction claimed to follow his plan, so long as they did not reject his clinging to the Church connection. The 'Church Methodists' claimed to be following 'Mr. Wesley's Plan' or the 'Old Plan' by avoiding services in Church hours, ordinations, and Methodist Sacraments. Yet in fact Wesley had clearly not taken this hard and fast line but instead developed a more pragmatic one. At the other extreme, the Kilhamites in 1797 wanted not only independence for Methodism but also government including more lay power at all levels, as against domination by the itinerants as quasi-ministers. Men like Pawson followed Wesley's implied 'Plan' most closely—that is, to allow the Sacraments (and consequently ordain the necessary preachers) where they were demanded by 'the people', though Wesley would probably have balked at this open acknowledgment of people-power. Pawson rightly argued that 'the Old Plan' 'was really to follow the openings of Providence and to take the most effective way we can of promoting the work of God'.[377] This approach was indeed at the base of Wesley's actions. But Pawson also disliked the compromise Plan of Pacification in 1795, which had settled the sacramental question by a kind of local option, because he thought that in effect such a move granted the trustees (who had to agree by a majority) the power of veto.[378]

The question of ordination and Superintendents also involved another problem with which the Deed of Declaration (which preceded both) did not deal and on which Wesley had left no guidance.

---

[377] Ibid., 1:103, 109.

[378] Ibid., 2:31–32, 111. He preferred that 'the people' alone should decide. The Plan of Pacification depended on the stewards and leaders (as allegedly representing the members) and the trustees, each reaching a majority in favour, subject to the Conference's final decision.

This matter concerned who or what would take over Wesley's self-appointed one-man role as executive between Conferences. It is arguable that Methodism, at least in England, never did fully solve this problem because of its preference for collective leadership and fears of a second Wesley. An essential act of the 1791 Conference, in addition to the appointment of committees, was to create a new tier of government in the shape of the Districts, along with District Committees and District Committee Chairmen. They were to deal with problems arising between Conferences, and their acts were to be confirmed by the next Conference. They look more like ad hoc bodies to deal with occasional problems raised by any circuit Assistant rather than a regular ruling body, and their Chairmen were merely to preside over the called meeting—not to rule between Conferences.[379] The 1797 Conference, after the Kilhamite secession, made concessions to lay influence, including the statement that the Circuit Quarterly Meeting (and not the District Meeting) was the power 'from whence all temporary regulation during the intervals of Conference must now originally spring'. This comment seems to clarify the very limited role of the District Meetings in favour of the original two tiers of government in Wesley's day. This arrangement may be contrasted with the Primitive Methodist Connexion (formed in 1812), in which there was a degree of de-centralization from Conference to Districts, since the latter had powers of stationing and were later the location for ordinations.[380]

Pawson clearly thought the District Meetings inadequate as an executive and supervisory power between Conferences: he said it left them in a state in which they really had 'no government'.[381] For this reason, the proposals for eight regions with Superintendents or bishops in the 1794 Lichfield Plan were clearly as much concerned with supervision between Conferences as with the ordination question. The Superintendents would have actively visited circuits and dealt with problems.[382] They would not have been simply machines

---

[379] *Minutes* (1791), *QQ*. 8, 9.

[380] H. B. Kendall, *The Origin and History of the Primitive Methodist Church*, 2 vols. (London, 1906), 2:366.

[381] Pawson, *Letters*, 1:164.

[382] For the proposals, see text in Davies, George, and Rupp, *History of Methodist Church*, 4:257–59; Bowmer, *Pastors and People*, 42–45; Pawson, *Letters*, 1:166–67, who speaks of 'bishops' as he did of this further ordination by Coke (ibid., 1:161, 163), but the agreed proposals clearly speak of an order of 'Superintendents', as one would expect.

for ordination but would have been fulfilling something like Wesley's role of executive while being subject to Conference and so not violating its sovereignty or the stipulations of the Deed of Declaration. In any case, the experiment was not tried because it was seen as 'setting up unhallowed distinctions between brethren'[383]; and the fact that the Lichfield group filled most of the proposed top posts with themselves did not help. Formal ordinations were stopped altogether (except for overseas and one or two others by Coke) until the 1830s, and the travelling preachers 'in full connexion' took on sacramental ministry as the circuits accepted it. But they were full ministers in all but name.

The Deed of Declaration, then, did not solve all the problems of the succession to Wesley, and probably no scheme could have done so completely. Even the problems of trusts, which had provoked the Deed, were not fully solved by defining the 'Conference', since non–Model Deed trusts persisted and were an element in some disruptions on ordination and other matters later.[384] Nevertheless, the preachers surprised themselves by the competence and relative peaceableness with which they adjusted to Wesley's loss in 1791, even if they had many worries to come later. Despite later secessions, the main body survived.

X. The *Minutes*

Details concerning the character and sources of the various versions of the *Minutes* are placed in the Textual Editor's introductions to each category. The relationship of the annual *Minutes* to the actual proceedings and the problem of what the *Minutes* do and do not disclose of those proceedings have already been discussed. Here, for convenience, a summary account is given of the general character of each category, as well as its dating.

[383] Pawson, *Letters*, 1:164.

[384] It is an extraordinary fact that Wesley had allowed the City Road Chapel in London to be placed on a deed that did not allow full control by Conference. Perkins, *Methodist Preaching Houses*, 54–55.

1. The Annual ('Penny') Minutes of Conferences

The discussion of various points in this introduction has been overwhelmingly related to the annual *Minutes* and their manuscript predecessors, since the other versions are essentially repetitions and distillations of those primary records. Occasionally, though, the later collections may preserve material for which the pre-1765 annual record has not survived.

The form that the *Minutes* (and presumably the discussions) would take was settled from the first by the agenda and Minutes of 1744, with their question–and–answer format. This form, as suggested earlier,[385] was likely to have derived from Wesley's Oxford academic training and his mode of self-examination there.

The formal minutes of an organization frequently contain little more than decisions arrived at with little hint of debate and disagreement. This approach is broadly true of the annual *Minutes*, although other material is included from time to time. Nevertheless it has been said, with truth, that 'throughout Wesley's lifetime, his authoritative replies to his own prepared questions formed the substance of the minutes of his Conferences.'[386] He termed them 'Minutes', but they were by no means factual descriptions of what took place at each gathering or word-for-word transcriptions of group deliberations and discussions. They were prepared under his eagle eye and guaranteed by his authority. Some matters, as we have seen, were omitted or obscured and are known only from other sources. As was argued earlier, this approach may be partly due to the policy of confidentiality stated at the first Conferences (though not always subsequently observed). This policy may also have influenced the long delay before the decision was taken to publish the annual *Minutes* in 1765. However, it is also the case that portions were frequently written up in advance by Wesley for presentation as papers, which would then be entered into the record. Sometimes he discussed with his preachers marginal aspects of their task, such as episcopacy or schism,[387] which he was expected to write up fully at a later date. Occasionally, the early minutes seem to have been on corollary themes, which he developed more fully in writing after the supposed initiating event. Sometimes, however, they seem to have been

[385] See above, p. 29 and Minutes (1744), §7, n. 8.
[386] For this and the following paragraph, I follow observations by Prof. Baker.
[387] Minutes (1747), §§44–45, 51–56.

secretarial minutes in the conventional sense, submitted for the chairman's corrections, and then circulated for attendees to copy and circulate to colleagues.

The evidence is clear, however, that many documents discussed in Conference arose from Wesley's initiative and were in effect original memoranda prepared by Wesley for general approval (with an occasional emendation), after which he authorized their transmission within the Methodist preaching family. For this purpose many of the more literate preachers served him as scribes, men such as John Bennet (whose name especially was associated with the recording of the early Minutes), John Jones (whose handwriting is at times almost indistinguishable from Wesley's),[388] and Thomas Butts, who wrote in a copperplate hand.[389] It is clear that the manuscript Minutes that do survive comprise only a fraction of those originally circulated, most in several copies.[390]

The manuscript Minutes began with the first Conference in 1744, but the surviving copies are patchy in the 1750s and wholly lacking for 1759–65. Such other information as is known of the proceedings has been included in this edition under appropriate dates. From 1765 onwards, the annual *Minutes*, sometimes called the 'Penny' *Minutes* (from their small size and cost), were printed and published under the title *Minutes of Some Late Conversations between Rev. Mr. Wesley and Others.*[391]

The first Irish *Minutes* were also in manuscript, surviving for Limerick in 1752. And *Minutes* or other evidence survives for some meetings in subsequent years, but no *Minutes* and few references survive for 1765–77. In 1778, the first printed Irish *Minutes* appeared, but only from 1783 onwards in a continuous series.

Some manuscript records of early American Conferences survive, as do published annual *Minutes* beginning in 1790, and the first collection of printed *Minutes*, which included all the published versions from 1773 to 1794.[392] These *Minutes* are not included in this edition.

---

[388] See A. B. Sackett, *John Jones—First after the Wesleys? WHS* Publication No. 7 (London, 1972), 10–11; and Richard P. Heitzenrater, 'Three Tests and a Key: Identifying John Wesley's Handwriting', *Manuscripta* 33 (Summer 1981).

[389] See illustration facing 26:118 of this edn.

[390] For a recently discovered example of what looks like an unofficial copy, see Minutes (1745), n. 1.

[391] There are some variations to this title, on occasion indicating *Messrs. Charles and John Wesley*, but the first six words are invariable.

[392] See *Minutes of the Methodist Conferences*, noted on p. 94, fn. 359 above.

2. *The 'Large'* Minutes *and the MS Conference Journal*

The Doctrinal and Disciplinary *Minutes* in Great Britain were a selection of minutes from these two main areas, taken from the annual *Minutes* and published as two separate pamphlets in 1749. The Doctrinal *Minutes* contain extracts from the 1744–47 Minutes only, since basic doctrines had been settled by the latter date. That pamphlet does include, however, part of the section on discipline concerning relations with the Church taken from the 1744 Minutes. This selection of doctrinal minutes appeared with little alteration as *Minutes of Some Late Conversations* in the edition of Wesley's *Works* in 1772 and in all the subsequent editions. The Disciplinary *Minutes* are a rather different matter. Appearing originally under the same title, they contain extracts from the disciplinary material from 1744 to 1747, along with some material from the 1748 Minutes. They then turned out to be the first version of what came to be known to Methodists as the 'Large' *Minutes*, though Wesley simply calls them *Minutes of Several Conversations*,[393] with the relevant dates from 1744 on to the current date of successive editions. And thusly they appear in later editions of his *Works* under that title.

The 'Large' *Minutes*, then, were a distillation of Conference pronouncements on discipline and practice, though they also contain an introductory passage on the general character and purpose of Methodism. They went through several editions after their initial appearance as the Disciplinary *Minutes* of 1749. These editions were in 1753, 1763, 1770, 1772, 1780, and 1789, each new edition adding further selections from the later Conferences and sometimes omitting portions from earlier ones. In the nineteenth century and in later reprints of Wesley's *Works*, the 'Large' *Minutes* were printed from the 1789 edition (covering material from 1744 to 1789), collated with a copy of 1791. As even a casual reading of the collection will show, the contents are highly miscellaneous in content as well as rather haphazard in arrangement. There is no attempt in any edition (or the present edition) to rearrange the material into a systematic handbook of rules and regulations. It is certainly not simply a manual of discipline and bears the marks of the varying circumstances of the deliberations from which it was compiled, as well as the imprint of some of Wesley's pet concerns.

---

[393] This title differentiates them from the annual or 'Penny' *Minutes*, which are invariably titled *Minutes of Some Late Conversations*.

Finally, there is the manuscript Conference Journal, which was begun in 1784 in accordance with the provisions of the Deed of Declaration. This document 'was and is the legal record of Conference decisions and actions',[394] written up to be signed at the end of the proceedings. It contains some confidential matter, some material not in the printed *Minutes* (such as lists of those present and absent), and some variations from the published version.[395]

The printed annual *Minutes* continued to be produced after 1765 with a selection of administrative decisions, stations, and occasional pastoral letters. From 1779, the *Arminian Magazine* had contained a digest of the *Minutes*, including the preachers' stations.

XI. Conclusion

The development of the Methodist Conference has been traced here from the 'conversations' of the early 1740s to the mature and more formalized body defined by the Deed of Declaration in 1784. Wesley provided a more organized body for his successors, but also left them with some uncertainties and unresolved problems. The attempt to define the terms of conversation in the first few Conferences seems to consort rather uneasily with Wesley's developing authoritarian tendencies and the descriptions he gave in 1766 and 1785 of the terms on which he understood Methodism in general and the preachers in particular stood in relation to him. In fact, a certain tension of this kind is evident at all levels of the connexion. In later years, some members also were dissatisfied with the way that temporal business seemed to overshadow spiritual edification. Methodism had begun as a revival movement, and yet very early in its development, Wesley began to develop methods of pastoral care that included specific prescriptions for spiritual life, practical conduct, and personal discipline as exemplified in the various rules for the Societies, Classes, Bands, and select Bands. The increasing collection of miscellaneous injunctions in the 'Large' *Minutes*, brought

[394] Baker, *Wesley and Church*, 227.

[395] In this edn., such material or summaries of it are printed either in square brackets in the text or in footnotes.

together from the years of annual *Minutes*, also displayed the same concern for the Methodist people and more especially for the preachers.

These rules and injunctions also reflect a certain tension in Wesley's mind and spiritual history. His several accounts of how Methodism began usually hark back to the days of the Oxford Methodists and their pursuit of holiness as the main purpose of their association. The disciplines of holy living that these first Methodists used in their program of meditative piety remained a feature of the new Methodism, despite necessary adjustments when applied to a very different set of people in the movement after the late 1730s. Wesley's accounts of the rise of his movement often seem to obscure, by omission, the role of what he learned from the Moravians and his Aldersgate experience. And his early accounts tend not to highlight a great deal of the religious and emotional experiences of his followers, as recorded in their autobiographies.

A version of the Reformation concept of justification by faith is spelled out in the early Conferences, but so is Wesley's version of Christian perfection, which became more refined (as well as more central) in later years. Less obvious in these materials is any description of new birth as an emotional personal experience, which becomes characteristic of many Methodist spiritual autobiographies. In Wesley's vision, as he grew older, the experience of justification by faith came to count for less in its own right than as the door to growth in holiness through sanctification, which he felt mattered most. And he saw sanctification increasingly as both a process to be cultivated by discipline (works of piety and works of mercy) in response to God's grace and a gift that could be received in a moment through God's grace by faith. Methodism, like Wesley himself, then, held together two emphases in many aspects of the process of salvation: faith and good works, justification and sanctification, gradual development and instantaneous gift, works of piety and works of mercy, God's grace and human response. Many of Wesley's continual theological controversies and repeated attempts at doctrinal definitions were provoked by the tensions in this uneasy combination of emphases within his own and his followers' spiritual pilgrimages.

The Conferences, then, like the whole of the Methodist economy at every level, had a two-fold purpose: to spread the gospel and to consolidate its results by Wesley's system of supervision. From one point of view the Methodist system of organization was not a traditional 'church' organization at all—quite apart from Wesley's concern to deny that he was founding a church. Methodism was a means of providing opportunities for people to experience the transforming presence and power of God in their lives, leading them to Christian holiness, as the inner hierarchy of the Societies—probationary and penitential Bands, Classes, regular Bands, select Societies—clearly shows. The Conference, like the local levels of Methodist organization, often looks like a disciplinary and, as time went on, a legislative body as the early 'conversation party' atmosphere faded into memory. Indeed, some complained that too much time was spent in temporal affairs. This development was the almost inevitable effect of an increasingly large organization accumulating property and financial obligations. What greatly affected the impact of the movement as time wore on was that it was largely shaped by this meeting that occurred once a year and depended too much on one ageing executive of autocratic instincts who lacked a competent secretariat. And what made all this more distressing to many was the fact that, like Wesley, many of his preachers ideally regarded the Conference as an occasion for mutual edification and support rather than simply a business meeting.

Perhaps one can too easily judge the eighteenth-century Methodist Conference harshly or rate its character pessimistically when our main material for judging it comes from a bare record of *Minutes* of decisions laced with occasional statements of principle and illustrated with scattered personal impressions. Furthermore, Wesley's diatribes inside and outside the Conference about the defects in character and devotion of the Methodist preachers and people, especially in his later years, have to be taken with caution. The reality of the total Wesleyan movement was obviously a greater mixture of light and shade than he allowed. As for the Conference, there were open sessions and preaching services that evidently gave heart to preachers and the wider local Methodist public. At such times, participants could recapture something of the original atmosphere and intent of this curiously hybrid body. As a symbol of what Methodism had originally been—a religious Society rather than a church—to this day, what in other churches would be called a Synod or Convocation is still called a Conference, and its annual proceedings *Minutes*.

In Wesley's eyes at least, the body retained its limited status as a mere meeting for consultation, summoned as he wished and made up only of those he chose, even after it became a legal entity. Like his maintenance of the notion that he was running a mere voluntary Society in aid of the Church of England and loyal to that Church, this assumption had become a threadbare legal fiction. If the preachers humoured the old man and tended to acquiesce to his will with a mixture of affection and resignation, the fact that they adjusted fairly quickly to his loss in 1791 shows that they were able by then to manage their own affairs.

Finally, it should be asked, What picture of Methodism emerges from the Conference records? The predominant impression is of a highly organized body with elaborate rules and, from the early Conferences in particular, a theology centred on the process of salvation. It is also a picture of a body that, in intention, still related itself to the Church of England despite the signs of separation in the 1760s and 1780s. There are limited signs of splits and minor secessions and glimpses of how Wesley's tastes clashed with those of his followers.[396] There is, however, little sign of the rich charismatic and emotional side of Methodism and its taste for the supernatural, which Wesley shared and often expressed in his *Journal* and *Magazine*. The *Minutes*, in short, while supplying many details of the reality of Methodism, can provide only a faint reflection of Wesley's overall ideals for his movement.

---

[396] Such as in the matter of hymns and how they should be sung! See *Minutes* (1768), *Q.* 23 (6). Recent treatments of Methodist experience include Anne Taves, *Fits, Trances, and Visions* (Princeton, 1999), 13–118; David Hempton, *Methodism: Empire of the Spirit* (New Haven, 2005); D. B. Hindmarsh, *The Evangelical Conversion Narrative* (Oxford, 2005), 1–161; Phyllis Mack, *Heart Religion and the British Enlightenment* (Cambridge, 2008).

PART I

The Early Conferences: Manuscript Minutes, Miscellaneous References, 1744–64

INTRODUCTION

WESLEY'S calling together in 1744 of clerical and lay colleagues to 'confer' with him about the doctrine, discipline, and practice of the Methodist Societies was an occasion of far-reaching importance. This event, the culmination of several preliminary Conferences, introduced both the term and the manner of Methodist ecclesiastical polity throughout the world. Not until 1765 did the *Minutes* of these annual Conferences begin annual publication. But in 1749, Wesley began to publish selections from the preserved manuscript Minutes of Conferences in that decade. These documents contained a nucleus of the more important agreements both in doctrine and in discipline.

The opening Conferences were of great importance in resolving many theological problems that beset Wesley and his preachers, so that rarely thereafter did doctrine prompt internal dissension to any major degree. The polity (governing structure), however, was constantly developing, especially during the formative years leading to the beginning of annual publication of the *Minutes*. The records that have survived from the early Conferences, in actual Minutes of the deliberations and in various references to those Conferences (especially in Wesley's *Journal*), are all significant for their foundational information.

Fortunately, even the agenda for the first Conference is extant, along with the Minutes of those gatherings for 1744–49, 1752, 1753, 1755, and 1758, though in some cases only fragmentarily. None of these documents presently exist in Wesley's own hand; they are only copies made by others, not all of whom are identified. For this edition, all the available copies have been collated, their certain or possible writers identified by abbreviations, and the substantive variant readings noted. The texts have been styled in accordance with principles adopted for the Oxford Edition in general, spelling errors silently corrected, and abbreviations silently expanded wherever no doubt exists as to the word intended. Marginal numbering of the subsections has been added (where needed) for each major item in order to facilitate references and thus enable the reader to follow the gradual development of Methodist polity.

Although the Oxford Edition in general is designed to offer a definitive text of Wesley's *published* prose writings, and manuscript material is usually found only in footnotes or appendices, the manuscript Minutes form so essential a prerequisite to the understanding of the published *Minutes* that they are presented here as part 1 of this volume.

1. The Origins of the Manuscript Minutes

A written record of each of Wesley's early annual Conferences was certainly made at the time. No one knows, however, whether these 'official' Minutes were in the hand of Wesley or of one of his preachers who had been appointed Secretary, which was the case for Conferences some decades later. Even if a Secretary were appointed, however, Wesley, and perhaps the group as a whole, most likely would have revised these Minutes at the end of the Conference, as was done from 1784 onwards in the final reading of the Conference Journal. Individuals who were present at these events were also likely to keep their own memoranda of the discussions and decisions.

Certainly, the Minutes were regularly preserved, as indicated by a question asked at the 1747 meeting: 'Should we at every Conference read over all the Conferences we have had from the beginning?' To which the answer was, 'Only that immediately preceding; and so much of the rest as we may find needful from time to time.'[1] Just as certainly, several copies of the Minutes of each Conference were prepared (presumably in the first instance from the 'official' record), as revealed by a question in 1746: 'To whom should we give copies of our conferences?'[2] The answer was: 'Only to those who were or might have been present.'[3] Thus all members of the Conferences meeting from 1744 to 1749 were entitled to copies of the accumulated Minutes of those Conferences, in order to keep them apprised of the doctrines and discipline approved by Wesley and their

---

[1] Minutes (June 15, 1747), *Q.* 3; Disciplinary *Minutes* (1749), §4; cf. MS Minutes (1745), §§3, 6, 9.

[2] Note the plural rather than the singular in this question also, viz., the *Minutes* of *all* the preceding Conferences.

[3] Minutes (May 15, 1746), *Q.* 12 and *A.*

colleagues. In 1749, digests of these two categories of Minutes, doctrinal and disciplinary, were published and distributed to all the preachers (and some others)[4] for their information. In subsequent years, the continually developing disciplinary regulations were periodically published for them in the 'Large' *Minutes*.

The 1749 *Minutes* demonstrate clearly the form that Wesley's selection from the manuscript Minutes took in that year, as the 'Large' *Minutes* of 1753 and 1763 show for the selections from later years. Our present task is to attempt a reconstruction of the 'official' written record of each Conference as it was originally set down and presumably confirmed as the authentic Minutes of the occasion. In spite of statements to the contrary by those who have mistaken the hand of John Jones for that of Wesley—a very easy mistake to make!—no copies of the Minutes in Wesley's hand appear to have survived, though one set does have a few corrections in his hand. Indeed the first section of the 1758 Minutes may be in his hand rather than that of Jones, as may those for 1755. All we have available are one or more later copies of the Minutes of a few years—fortunately including all the years during which the doctrinal foundations of Methodism were laid—and these undated copies were made by unnamed amanuenses who may or may not have been present at the Conferences concerned.

Wesley's practice was to use many scribes in his monumental task of preserving and multiplying copies of important letters and other documents. The work of some was legible and accurate; that of others was neither, for at times he felt compelled to utilize those who could not even copy the correct spelling of many words in Wesley's originals. This method is frequently demonstrated in his correspondence[5] and is similarly seen in these copies of his Minutes. In the case of multiple copies, the further problem arises that we cannot be sure whether a scribe was copying the 'official' record or an earlier copy of it that already contained errors or revisions, thus taking us still farther away from the original. To make an absolutely accurate copy of any document demands immense concentration and alertness.

---

[4] The Doctrinal *Minutes* were apparently sent to Wesley's critic, Richard Tompson, as a summary of Methodist teaching. See July 25, 1755, *Letters*, 26:574–75 in this edn.

[5] See *Letters*, 25:44–45 in this edn., and for the making of multiple copies, p. 39.

2. The Textual Problems of the
Early Manuscript Minutes

This problem may be seen in sharp focus by studying the manuscript Minutes of the first Conference (1744). Wesley had prepared the agenda,[6] and it is probable that he also prepared the approved record of the Minutes, discarding it when the bulk of those Minutes was printed.[7] There remain four complete manuscript copies and two incomplete. One of the incomplete copies is certainly late, for the preacher who prepared it did not become an itinerant until a decade later. The other incomplete copy purports to be Wesley's reference copy and certainly contains a handful of his manuscript corrections. Two of the complete copies are in the hand of John Bennet, who was present, and the other two *may* be in the hand of Thomas Maxfield, who was also present but for whom no positive identification has been possible, because no certainly authentic sample of his handwriting has so far been discovered.

It seems quite certain that none of the other clergy present prepared the incomplete but revised copy (though in two instances this cannot readily be proved by samples of their handwriting), and it is certainly not in the hand of either Thomas Richards or John Downes, the other two lay preachers present, verified samples of whose handwriting are available.[8] After making comparisons with many other available samples of preachers' handwriting, we must concede that no positive identification of this hand can at present be made, and we therefore speak of him as scribe 'A'. Similarly, two of the other three scribes responsible for the copies of the early Minutes revised by Wesley are referred to as 'C' and 'E'. But in the case of 1747, on account of a close resemblance between an independent signature of Jonathan Reeves and the writing of that name in the document, we tentatively identify him as the third scribe—though a signature by itself is quite insufficient for a positive identification.

The errors and revisions disclosed by a careful collation of the five earlier manuscripts of the 1744 Minutes reveal clear relationships between them and a division into two categories: the earlier

---

[6] See pp. 120–22 below.

[7] The process of publishing documents commonly resulted in the discarding of the copy, probably by the printer. E.g., the only extant copy of Wesley's revised extracts of his *Journal*, published in the 1770s in the Pine edn. of his *Works*, is the extract that was omitted by Pine. See *Journal & Diaries*, 24:391 (Appendix C).

[8] In this matter of tracing handwriting it is far simpler to eliminate possibilities than to make a positive identification.

ones, which give only the 1744 Minutes, and the later ones, which form the first part of collected sets of Minutes. The latter comprise a set in four different hands, covering the Minutes of 1744–47, presently in Wesley College, Bristol, and an incomplete set of 1744–45, 1747–48, in the hand of John Bennet, preserved in the Methodist Archives, Manchester. Of the earlier group of three, the two manuscripts presumed to be in the hand of Maxfield seem to be nearer in many details to Wesley's agenda, especially in the underlining of key words. Of the Maxfield manuscripts, M^1 is demonstrably the prototext of M^2. Closely related to both these copies is Bennet[1], though he adds many individual variations. In the later group, Bennet[2] is clearly derived from B^1, but with variants that it shares with the copy by 'A'.

3. Manuscript and Published *Minutes*

None of these five early Manuscripts clearly forms the actual prototext for the others or for Wesley's 1749 published text of the 1744 Minutes. The manuscript revisions by Wesley in 'A' merely confirm his personal association with that set of early Minutes, not necessarily their value either as evidence for the original text of 1744 or as the copy-text for the printed *Minutes* of 1749. In §47, for instance, the earlier texts make it clear that the original reading was 'addition of members', which 'A' copied as 'addmition'. This apparent spelling error Wesley corrected to 'admission' by changing the 't' to 'ss', without discovering (at least at that time) that there was an error in substance. The 1749 publication reads 'addition', implying that Wesley was then using a more authentic text, either as his basic source (which appears far more likely) or at the very least as a corrective to the part of 'A' that survived. On the other hand, in §72, Wesley seems to have used an apparent error copied by 'A' to trigger a notable revision of the text, implying that the Assistant was to check the accounts of the stewards only, rather than those of stewards and leaders. Contrary to his usual practice, Wesley may well have prepared the 1749 *Minutes* for publication with the aid of more than one original source, and in addition to the later 'A' (possibly complete at that time), he used the approved official copy, which seems to have been much more similar to M^1 in most points than to any other, including the setting out of much of the material in sentences or clauses rather than paragraphs—a feature common only to M^1, M^2, B^1, and the 1749 pamphlets. This 'official' copy has since disappeared, in accordance with Wesley's normal practice of discarding a manuscript after its substance was printed.

It should be clear from the outset—a point that makes the full publication of the manuscript Minutes the more important—that in 1749, Wesley published only a selection of those early Minutes, and that the same process was involved in the publication of the later editions of the 'Large' *Minutes*. From the printed works, many decisions of topical importance only were omitted and later ones were added, while several were revised, some drastically, as in the careful rephrasing for possible general consumption of No. 3 of the Rules of an Assistant (later 'Rules of a Helper'): 'Touch no woman. Be as loving as you will, but hands off. Custom is nothing to us.' In 1749, this rule appeared in print as 'Converse sparingly and cautiously with women.'[9]

Thus, of the surviving manuscripts for 1744, M^1 is probably the nearest to forming what may be called the primary extant text of the Minutes of the first Conference, although most of the other manuscripts add minor features that probably represent Wesley's presumed original. In this instance, therefore, the edited text here presented is eclectic, although in most details it does reproduce M^1. All the major variants from the edited text are included in the footnotes for the information of those who wish to follow the basic readings of any one manuscript. Numerous purely stylistic points, however, such as the use of 'Firstly' rather than '1' by B^1, and his spelling 'eather', have been disregarded. The underlining of key words and phrases, preserved only by M^1, ^{2}, and surely stemming from the original, are incorporated, but no notes on any variants therefrom. Neither do we footnote the frequent variations from the edited text in other examples of italicizing, punctuation, capitalization, or spelling, in whatever manuscripts.

In general, the problems presented by the manuscript Minutes of the later Conferences are similar to those presented by the copies of the 1744 Minutes. They are less complex, because fewer copies are available; but they are likely to be less successful in reproducing the approved originals because for most of them we have available only one or two of the later 'collected' sets: one that is clearly incomplete, or a later printed version of which the manuscript original has disappeared, rather than a genuine original or one (like M^1)

[9] See MS Minutes (1744), §73 (3), and Disciplinary *Minutes* (1749), §73 (3).

reproducing it after a very short interval. For 1745–48, at least, it would be possible to arrive at a nearer approximation of the original by conflating the earliest manuscript with the 1749 printed edition. This prospect may be seen in particular in the frequent setting out of the matter in sentences or clauses, in which the published *Minutes* of 1749 followed the presumed prototext of M^1 for 1744, and that remained a feature of the later published *Minutes*, for which no such early manuscript witness is available. That this format was typical of Wesley's style in similar literary material may be seen from his *General Rules* of 1743 and his *Plain Account* of 1749.[10] Nevertheless it has seemed preferable here not to *assume* this oracular form where we do not find it, but simply to set out the text of the manuscript Minutes in the earliest extant form in which they actually appear. No attempt has been made to reconstruct the official prototext, for which the evidence of the 1749 *Minutes* is readily available to the reader.[11]

In any case, of course, such documents as Minutes are self-conscious selections from and rephrasings of the actual discussions, and while being grateful for the measure of early evidence of the pioneering Conferences that has survived, we must remain aware of the probable successive softening through one or more recensions of the sharp edges of the original deliberations.

F. B.

[10] See vol. 9 of this edn.

[11] See pp. 778–835 below. (The only instance where this may be attempted with some justification would be that of Bennet's copy of the 1748 Minutes, which is surely a contemporary copy.)

The London Conference of June 25–29, 1744

THE AGENDA
June 1, 1744[12]

I. [*Doctrine*]

5 [§1] What do we meet for?

[§2] To consider before God: 1. What to teach. 2. How to teach.
3. What to do? i.e., doctrine, discipline, and practice.

[§3] 1. Are we justified by faith alone? The only condition?

[§4] 2. What is implied in being justified?

10 [§5] 3. What is justifying faith? Assurance? Or— [?]

[§6] 4. What *must* go before? Repentance? Works meet for
repentance?

[§7] 5. What *must* follow? Peace, joy, love, power? In what
degree?

15 [§8] 6. Is faith seeing God? A divine ἔλεγχος?[13]

[§9] 7. Does anyone believe who has not the witness in
himself? Or, any longer than he sees, loves, obeys God?

[§10] *Must* a man come into darkness or the wilderness after he is
justified?

---

[12] On June 1, 1744, JW wrote from Newcastle to John Bennet on the problems
of theology for a preacher and continued: 'You may order your affairs so as to ride
with me to London to our Conference. Then we can clear these things up more
fully.' See *Letters* 26:108 in this edn. On that same day, apparently, Wesley invited
Richard Viney to the Conference, allowed him to copy out the written agenda that
he had already prepared, and invited him to 'set down all the objections he had
against anything in it'. In the event the group did not meet until June 25, and Viney
did not attend. From Viney's journal we present Wesley's early draft of the agenda,
with his spelling modernized and his abbreviations extended. The Viney journal is
in the Moravian Archives, London; a photocopy, MS. Eng. 965, in MA; and cf.
'Viney's Copy of Wesley's Conference Agenda' *WHS*, 14 (Pt. 8, 1924):201–3. For
the question-and-answer format, see below, Minutes (1744), §7, n. 48.

N.B. Here, as throughout the MS Minutes themselves, the paragraphs have been
numbered in square brackets to facilitate cross-reference.

[13] 'evidence or conviction'; see Heb. 11:1, and cf. *A Farther Appeal*, Pt. I, I.4,
etc., 11:106–7 in this edn.

[§11] *Will* he, unless by unfaithfulness?

[§12] *Need* a believer ever doubt or fear?

[§13] *How* is faith 'made perfect'[14] by works?

[§14] Do we think or speak high enough of justification?

[§15] Are works necessary to the continuance of faith?   5

[§16] How far shall each of us submit to the judgment of the majority? Of this whole company?

[§17] Is the *first love* the most perfect?

[§18] Is every believer a Scripture 'new creature'?[15]

[§19] What is sanctification?   10

[§20] Is not every believer 'born of God'?[16]

[§21] Can a believer fall *totally* and *finally*? How?

[§22] Is *inbred sin* taken away in this life?

[§23] How can *we know* one that is *thus saved*?

[§24] Is the second Preface true?[17]   15

[§25] You are zealous 'for the Church'? What do you mean?

[§26] What is the Church of England? How are we of it? How far to defend it?

[§27] To obey the bishops? The Injunctions? Canons?   20

II. *Discipline*

[§28] Is field preaching lawful? Expedient?

[§29] Where shall we preach?   25

[§30] Do we not undertake too much, and thereby do less than we might?

[§31] E.g. are not more sinners converted [when] *we* stay a month at Newcastle than by *us* preaching in any new place?[18]

[§32] Is it not necessary to spend more time there? At Epworth?   30
Where else? In Wales?

[§33] Should we not preach more where we have ch[urch]es? Where there is peace?

---

[14] Jas. 2:22.

[15] 2 Cor. 5:17.

[16] 1 John 5:1.

[17] I.e., the preface to *Hymns and Sacred Poems* (1740); see vol. 12 of this edn.

[18] Apparently emphasizing the importance of the leadership of ordained clergy, such as Wesley, who at the time of writing had been in Newcastle almost two weeks and was to remain one more.

[§34]   Should we not eye this more, as to the places and times of preaching?

[§35]   Should we preach *abroad* when we may preach within doors?

5   [§36]   Should we fix any more Society? Or overrun England? How? When?

[§37]   Are lay-helpers allowable? Who?

[§38]   Are our lay-helpers unblameable?

[§39]   How should each labourer spend this year?

10   [§40]   What can we adopt from C[ount] Z[inzendorf]? Mr. Whitefield? The kirk? The Quakers?

[§41]   Shall we have Helpers? Bands? Societies? Stewards?

[§42]   Band-leaders? Class-leaders? Schools?

[§43]   What shall we mend with regard to any of these?

15   [§44]   Can we have better economy in temporals?

[§45]   When shall we meet again? Who? Where?

III. *Practice*

20   [§46]   How far is it lawful to bear arms?[19] To go to law?[20]

[§47]   Cornwall?[21] Wednesbury?[22] To swear?[23]

[§48]   Can we unite any farther with Mr. Whitefield? With the Moravians?

[§49]   Is any conference with either advisable? When?

25   Where?

[§50]   In what kind? For what ends?

---

[19] Though scruples about this issue affected the 16th-century Anabaptists and later the Quakers, the source of the doubt here is probably the New Testament. See the reply in Minutes (1744), §87, *Q.* 17; (1745), §81 and n. 316. The question was the more urgent in view of the threat of Jacobite invasion (1744–45).

[20] Here the New Testament, though not quoted, would be the source of doubt. See Matt. 5:40 but esp. 1 Cor. 6:1-7, though this applied only to cases against fellow believers. The reply (Minutes [1744], §88, *Q.* 18) is noticeably cautious at least as a plaintiff. But in the face of mob violence and other attacks on Methodism, Wesley was quite prepared to fight cases. He was more successful in the higher courts than with local magistrates, who were sometimes suspected of tolerating, if not encouraging, rioters. See *Minutes* (1767), *Q.* 12, n. 156 on legal expenses and reference.

[21] The implied question is apparently, 'Shall we attempt to develop Methodism in Cornwall and Wednesbury?'—which both brothers had visited during preaching tours in 1743.

[22] Orig., 'Wensbury', the frequent spelling for Wesley as well as for Viney.

[23] I.e., to take oaths.

THE MINUTES
Monday, June 25th, 1744[24]

[§1]　The following persons being met at the Foundery:[25]
John Wesley, Charles Wesley, John Hodges,[26] Henry

[24] The 1744 MS Minutes are available in the following copies, arranged in their probable chronological order of transcription; the symbols by which they are designated are prefixed:

M[1].　In handwriting which may be that of Thomas Maxfield, labelled 'MS. 330' [?1744], 23 pp., in the MA.

M[2].　In the same handwriting as the former, labelled 'MS. 60' [?1745], 26 pp., in the MA.

B[1].　In the handwriting of John Bennet [?1746], 22 pp., at Drew University, Madison, NJ.

A.　In an unidentified hand [?1747], pp. i–xv of a notebook in the George Morley collection, Wesley College, Bristol (formerly in Headingley College, Leeds). It contains some alterations in the hand of John Wesley, and therefore the complete notebook was termed 'Wesley's' by Richard Green in Publication No. 1 of the Wesley Historical Society, 'John Bennet's Copy of the Minutes of the Conferences of 1744, 1745, 1747, and 1748; with Wesley's copy of those for 1746' (London: for the Society, 1896). The 1744 Minutes herein are incomplete, beginning on Wednesday, June 27, not Monday, June 25.

B[2].　In the handwriting of John Bennet [?1748], the first item in the notebook published by Richard Green and noted in the previous entry.

Richard Green's publication mentioned under 'A' (p. 4) also describes, as being among the Morley papers, 'a single quarto sheet, written on both sides, and containing a short extract "from a manuscript book written by John Johnson, 1751" [, which contains] a summary of the preliminary discussion on June 25th, 1744, a couple of phrases from Answer 4 of the same date, and Questions 5 and 6 with Answers from the Minutes of June 27, 1744, [which] present no variant reading'.

In his *Journal* (20:34 in this edn.), Wesley wrote, 'Monday the 25th and five following days we spent in conference with many of our brethren (come from several parts) who desire nothing but to save their own souls, and those that hear them. And surely, as long as they continue thus minded, their labour shall not be in vain in the Lord.' In his *Short History of the People Called Methodists* (1781; 9:439–40 in this edn.), he wrote, 'Monday June 25, and the five following days, we spent in Conference with our preachers, seriously considering by what means we might most effectually save our own souls and them that heard us. And the result of our consultations we set down, to be the rule of our future practice.' Though the *Journal* entry was published in 1753, it does not even then seem to reflect the importance that the Conference was acquiring. The 1781 account, referring to 'the rule of our future practice', reflects its later significance as a connexional guide for doctrine and discipline.

[25] B[2], M[1,2], 'The following persons being met at the Foundery'; B[1] has 'at Foundery', clearly in error.

[26] Rev. John Hodges (1700–77) was rector of Wenvoe, near Cardiff. Wesley first preached at his church on Oct. 18, 1741. He is said to have administered Communion every Sunday (a rarity in that century) and to have run a voluntary religious society. Late in life, he transferred his interest from Methodism to mysticism. See *Journal & Diaries*, 19:233, n. 49 in this edn.

Piers,[27] Samuel Taylor,[28] and John Meriton;[29] after some
time spent in prayer, the design of our meeting was proposed, namely, to consider:

1.[30] What to teach;

5   2. How to teach, and

3. What to do, i.e., how to regulate our doctrine, discipline, and practice.

[§2] But first it was inquired whether any of our lay brethren
should be present at this Conference.

10   And it was agreed to invite from time to time such of 'em
as we should judge[31] proper.

It was then asked, Which of 'em shall we invite today?
And the answer was:

Thomas Richards, Thomas Maxfield, John Bennet,[32] and

15   John Downes, who were accordingly brought in. Then
was read as follows:

---

[27] Rev. Henry Piers (1694–1770) was vicar of Bexley (1736–70). Son of Sir
Henry Piers, 3rd. baronet; Trinity College, Dublin, B.A., 1716; M.A., 1722.
Journal & Diaries, 19:169, n. 63 in this edn. Reputed to be a member of the Fet-
ter Lane Society, though this is open to doubt. C. J. Podmore, 'The Fetter Lane
Society—1738', *WHS* 46 (Pt. 5, 1988):138, n. 89. He helped to provide contacts
for Wesley on his tour of the North in 1743. *Letters*, 26:76, 79 in this edn.

[28] Rev. Samuel Taylor (1711–72) was vicar of Quinton (1738–72). Matriculated Merton College, Oxford, 1729; B.A. University College, 1737. Associated
with Wesley (1743–46). See *Journal & Diaries*, 19:343, n. 16 in this edn.

[29] Rev. John Meriton (1698–1753) matriculated Caius College, Cambridge, 1716; B.A.,
1720. An Englishman ordained by the bishop of Norwich in 1723, he met opposition to
evangelical preaching in the Isle of Man. Whitefield secured him for the Methodists.
Luke Tyerman, *The Life of the Rev. George Whitefield*, 2 vols., 2nd edn. (London: Hodder and Stoughton, 1890), 1:558–60; 2:39, 44. He was a regular travelling companion of
the Wesleys for some years, and though he cooled later, Charles Wesley commemorated
him with an elegy. *CWJ*, 2:303–5; see also *Journal & Diaries*, 19:208, n. 39 in this edn.

[30] B[1] alters Wesley's normal 1, 2, 3 to 'First', 'Secondly', and 'Thirdly'.

[31] B[1], M[1], 'should judge'; M[2], 'judged'; B[2], 'should think'.

[32] John Bennet (1715–59) was the son of a Presbyterian farmer in Derbyshire.
Educated at Finedon Dissenting Academy, Bennet became a justice's clerk and then
a carrier. He was converted by the influence of David Taylor, a roving evangelist formerly employed in Lady Huntingdon's family. See *Dictionary of Evangelical Biography*, ed. D. M. Lewis, 2 vols. (Oxford, 1995), hereafter *DEB*. From March 1743,
he began to preach and found a network of Societies in the northwest that were
absorbed into Wesley's connexion. He became a leading Assistant and in 1749 was
commissioned to promote the new quarterly meetings; *Minutes* (1749), §12. His
relations with Wesley became strained from 1749, partly as a result of his marriage
to Wesley's erstwhile fiancée Grace Murray, and partly through his growing

[§3] It is desired
   That all things may be considered as in the immediate
      presence of God;
   That we may meet with a single eye, and as little children
      which[33] have everything to learn;   5
   That every point may be examined from the foundation;
   That every person may speak freely whatever[34] is in his
      heart; and
   That every question proposed may be fully debated, and
      bolted to the bran.[35]   10

[§4] The first preliminary question was then proposed, namely,
   How far does each of us[36] agree to submit to the unanimous
      judgment of the rest?[37]
   It was answered, In speculative things each can only submit
      so far as his judgment shall be convinced: 15
   In every practical point so far as we can without wounding
      our several[38] consciences.

[§5] To the second preliminary question, viz., How far should
      any of us mention to others what may be mentioned here?
      it was replied,   20
   Not one word which may be here[39] spoken of persons[40]
      should be mentioned elsewhere.
   Nothing at all, unless so far as we may be convinced[41] the
      glory of God requires it.

Calvinism. In 1754, he broke with Wesley and in the same year acquired a meeting-house in Warburton, Cheshire, and was ordained as an Independent minister. He died on May 24, 1759. See H. D. Rack, 'Survival and Revival: John Bennet, Methodism, and the Old Dissent', in K. G. Robbins, ed., *Protestant Evangelicalism in Britain, Germany, and America, c. 1750–1950* (Oxford, 1990), 1–23.

[33] B[2], 'who'.

[34] M[2], 'what'.

[35] 'Bolt, boult: to sift, pass through and sieve; and fig. to examine by sifting, to search and try' (*OED*).

[36] B[1], 'do each of you'.

[37] Agenda, §16 above, reads 'judgment of the majority' rather than 'unanimous judgment of the rest'.

[38] B[2] omits 'several'.

[39] M[1, 2] omit 'here'.

[40] B[1], 'of any persons'.

[41] M[1, 2], 'unless we may be convinced . . .', to which in M[1] is appended, within commas, 'so far . . .'.

And from time to time we will[42] consider on each head, Is it for the glory of God that what we have now spoken should be mentioned again?

[§6]   About 7 o'clock we began to consider the doctrine of[43] justification, the questions relating to which were as follows, with the substance of the answers given[44] thereto.

[§7]   Q[uestion][45] 1. What is it to be justified?

A[nswer] To be pardoned and received into God's favour, and into such a state that, if we continue therein, we shall finally be[46] saved.

[§8]   Q. 2. Is faith the only[47] condition of justification?

A. Yes: For everyone who believeth not is condemned, and everyone who believes is justified.

[§9]   Q. 3. But must not repentance and works meet for repentance go before faith?

A. Without doubt, if by repentance you mean conviction of sin; and by works meet for repentance, obeying God as far as we can, forgiving our brother, leaving off from evil, doing good and using his ordinances according to the power we have received.[48]

[§10]   Q. 4. What is faith?

A. Faith, in general, is a divine supernatural *elenchos* of things not seen, i.e., of past, future, or spiritual things; it is a spiritual sight of God and the things[49] of God. Therefore repentance is a low species of faith, i.e., a supernatural sense of an offended God.

Justifying faith is a supernatural inward sight[50] of God in Christ reconciling the world to[51] himself.

---

[42] B[1], 'shall'.

[43] B[1], 'about'.

[44] B[2] omits 'given'.

[45] Alexander Gordon on JW in the *DNB* says that the question-and-answer format was used by the Quakers but that JW apparently did not know of this. R. P. Heitzenrater points out that JW had already used this method for his systems of self-examination in his Oxford period, as seen in his diaries. *People Called Methodists*, 146. It may also reflect Oxford academic practice (see introduction, section IV, above).

[46] A, B[1, 2], 'be finally'.

[47] B[2] omits 'only'.

[48] B[1], 'power received'.

[49] B[1] omits '; it is . . . things', clearly by an error of copying.

[50] B[1], 'supernatural sight'; B[2], 'supernatural inward sense, or sight'.

[51] B[1, 2], 'unto'.

First, a sinner is convinced by the Holy Ghost, Christ
loved me and gave himself for me;[52] this is that faith by
which he is justified, or pardoned, the[53] moment he
receives it. Immediately the same Spirit bears witness,
Thou art pardoned, thou hast redemption in his blood;   5
and this is saving faith, whereby the love of God is shed
abroad in his heart.

[§11] *Q.* 5. Have all true Christians this faith? May not a man be
justified and not know it?

A. That all true Christians have[54] such a faith as implies an   10
assurance of God's love, appears from Rom. 8:15, Eph.
4:32, 2 Cor. 13:5, Heb. 8:10, 1 John 4:10, and, last, 1 John
5:19.

And that no man can be justified and not know it appears
farther from the very nature of the thing,[55] for faith after   15
repentance is ease after pain, rest after toil, light after
darkness.

And from the immediate as well as distant fruits.

[§12] *Q.* 6. But may not a man go to heaven without it?

A. It does[56] not appear from Holy Writ that a man who   20
hears the gospel can (Mark 16:16), whatever a heathen
may do (Rom. 2:14).

[§13] *Q.* 7. What are the immediate fruits of justifying faith?

A. Peace, joy, love, power over all outward sin, and power to
keep down all inward sin.   25

[§14] *Q.* 8. Does anyone believe who has not the witness in himself? Or any longer than he sees, loves, obeys[57] God?

A. We apprehend not; seeing God being the very essence of
faith, love and obedience the inseparable properties of it.

---

[52] Gal. 2:20.

[53] B[1], 'that'.

[54] B[2] adds, 'this faith, even', a phrase not present in the 1749 *Minutes*. Dixon MS
Minutes read, 'such a faith as implies, an Assurance of God's love—may not . . .'.
Cf. JW's later modifications of his views of assurance, e.g., in his letter to Dr.
Rutherforth in 1768; *Letters* (Telford), 5:358f.; *AM* 9 (1786): 52ff.; and see Rack,
Reasonable Enthusiast, 393.

[55] B[2], 'of things'. This view was also modified, e.g., in favour of William Law, so
far as to allow salvation even to one denying the doctrine of justification by faith
though having the fruits of it. See Dec. 1, 1767 (first published in 1771), *Journal &
Diaries*, 22:114 in this edn.; and see Rack, *Reasonable Enthusiast*, 391–92.

[56] B[2], 'doth'.

[57] B[2], 'and obeys'.

[§15]   *Q.* 9. What sins are consistent with justifying faith?
        A. No *wilful sin.* . . . If a believer *sins wilfully*[58] he thereby
        forfeits his pardon. Neither is it possible he should have
        justifying faith again without previously *repenting.*

5 [§16]   *Q.* 10. *Must* every believer come into a state of doubt, or
        fear, or darkness? *Will* he do so unless by ignorance or
        unfaithfulness? *Does* God otherwise withdraw himself?
        A. It is certain that[59] a believer need never again come into con-
        demnation. It seems he need not come into a state of doubt,

10   or fear, or darkness; and that (ordinarily at least) he will not,
        unless by ignorance or[60] unfaithfulness. Yet it is true that the
        first joy does seldom last long, that it is commonly followed by
        doubts and fears, and that God usually permits very great
        heaviness before any large manifestation of himself.

15 [§17]   *Q.* 11. Are works necessary to the continuance of faith?
        A. Without doubt; for a man may forfeit the gift of God
        either by sins of omission or of[61] commission.

[§18]   *Q.* 12. Can faith be lost but for want of works?
        A. It cannot, but through[62] disobedience.

20 [§19]   *Q.* 13. How is faith made 'perfect by works'?[63]
        A. The more we exert our faith, the more it is increased: to
        him that *hath*, more and more is given.[64]

[§20]   *Q.* 14. St. Paul says, Abraham was not 'justified by works',
        St. James,[65] he was 'justified by works'.[66] Do they not

25   then[67] contradict each other?
        A. No.
        (1) Because they do not speak of the same justification.
        St. Paul speaks of that justification which was when
        Abraham was seventy-five years old, above twenty years

30   before Isaac was born: St. James of that justification
        which was when he offered up Isaac on the altar.

---

[58] B[1], 'wilfully sins'; B[2], 'sins'.
[59] B[1, 2] omit 'that'.
[60] B[2], 'and'.
[61] B[1, 2] omit 'of'.
[62] B[1], 'by'.
[63] Jas. 2:22. See agenda, §13.
[64] Cf. Matt. 13:12.
[65] B[1] adds 'says'.
[66] See Rom. 4:2; Jas. 2:21.
[67] B[1, 2], 'Do not they then'.

(2) Because they do not speak of the same works, St. Paul speaking of works that precede faith, St. James of works that spring from it.[68]

[§21] *Q.* 15. In what sense is Adam's sin imputed to all mankind?

A. In Adam all die, i.e.:[69]   5

(1) Our bodies then became mortal.

(2) Our souls died, i.e., were disunited from God.

(3) And hence we are all born with a sinful, devilish[70] nature, by reason whereof,

(4) We are all[71] children of wrath, liable to death eternal   10
(Rom. 5:18; Eph. 2:3).

[§22] *Q.* 16. In what sense is the righteousness of Christ[72] imputed to all mankind, or to believers?[73]

A. We do not find it affirmed expressly[74] in Scripture that God imputes the righteousness of Christ to any; although   15
we do find that faith is imputed to[75] us for righteousness.

That text, 'As by one man's disobedience all men were made sinners, so by the obedience of one all were made righteous',[76] we conceive means: By the merits of Christ all men are cleared from the guilt of Adam's actual sin.   20

We conceive farther, that through the obedience and death of Christ,

(1) The bodies of all men become immortal after the resurrection.

(2) Their souls recover a capacity of spiritual life,   25

(3) And[77] an actual seed or spark thereof.

(4) All believers become children of grace.

(5) Are reunited to God; and

(6) Made partakers of the[78] divine nature.

---

[68] B², '. . . works. St. Paul speaks of works that precede faith, St. James of works that spring from faith'.

[69] B¹ omits.

[70] B¹, 'devilish, sinful'.

[71] B², 'all are'.

[72] B¹, 'Jesus Christ'.

[73] B¹, ², 'to believers, or to all mankind'.

[74] B¹ omits 'affirmed expressly'.

[75] B², 'unto'.

[76] Rom. 5:19.

[77] B¹ omits 'And'.

[78] M², 'a'.

[§23]   *Q.* 17. Have we not then unawares[79] leaned too much towards Calvinism?

A. It seems that[80] we have.

[§24]   *Q.* 18. Have we not leaned[81] towards antinomianism?

A. We are afraid we have.

[§25]   *Q.* 19. What is antinomianism?

A. The doctrine which makes void the law through faith.

[§26]   *Q.* 20. What are the main pillars thereof?

A. (1) That Christ abolished the moral law.

(2) That therefore Christians[82] are not obliged to observe it.

(3) That one branch of Christian liberty is liberty from obeying the commandments of God.

(4) That it is bondage to do a thing because it is commanded, or forbear it[83] because it is forbidden.

(5) That a believer is not obliged to use the ordinances of God, or to do good works.

(6) That a preacher ought not to exhort to good works; not unbelievers because it is hurtful, not believers because it is[84] needless.

[§27]   *Q.* 21. What was the occasion of St. Paul's writing his Epistle to the Galatians?

A. The coming of certain men among the Galatians, who taught, Except ye be[85] circumcised, and keep the law[86] of Moses, ye[87] cannot be saved.

[§28]   *Q.* 22. What is his main design therein?[88]

A. To prove,

(1) That no man can be justified or saved by the works of the law, either moral or ritual.

(2) That every believer is justified by faith in Christ, without the works of the law.

---

[79] B[1] omits 'unawares'.

[80] B[2] omits 'that'.

[81] B[1], 'leaned too much'; B[2], 'also leaned'.

[82] B[2], 'Christians therefore'.

[83] M[2] omits 'it'.

[84] B[1] omits 'hurtful . . . is', surely by a copying error.

[85] B[1], 'Except the[y] be'.

[86] B[2], 'the whole law'.

[87] B[1], 'they'.

[88] B[1], 'herein'.

[§29] *Q*. 23. What does he mean by the works of the law?
  A. All works that do not spring from faith in Christ.

[§30] *Q*. 24. What[89] by being under the law (Chap. 3:23)?[90]
  A. Under the Mosaic dispensation.

[§31] *Q*. 25. What law has Christ abolished?
  A. The ritual law of Moses.

[§32] *Q*. 26. What is meant by liberty (Chap. 5:1)?[91]
  A. Liberty,
   (1), from that law;[92]
   (2), from sin.[93]

[§33] **On Tuesday morning, June the 26th, was considered**
  The doctrine of sanctification, with regard to which the
  questions asked and the substance of the answers given
  were as follows:

[§34] *Q*. 1. What is it to be sanctified?
  A. To be renewed in the image of God, in righteousness
  and true holiness.

[§35] *Q*. 2. Is faith the condition or[94] instrument of sanctification,
  or present salvation?
  A. It is both the condition and[95] instrument of it. When we
  begin to believe, then[96] salvation begins. And as faith
  increases, holiness increases, till we are created anew.

[§36] *Q*. 3. Is not every believer a new creature?
  A. Not in the sense of St. Paul, 2 Cor. 5:17. All old things
  are passed away in him who is so a new creature, and all
  things become new.

[§37] *Q*. 4. But has every believer a new heart?
  A. A great change is wrought in the heart or affections of
  everyone as soon as he believes; yet he is still full of sin,[97]
  so that he has not then a new heart in the full sense.

---

[89] B[1, 2], 'What is meant'.

[90] B[1, 2] omit the citation of Gal. 3:23, 'But before faith came, we were kept under the law, shut up unto the faith which should afterwards be revealed.'

[91] B[1, 2] omit the citation of Gal. 5:1, 'Stand fast therefore in the liberty wherewith Christ hath made us free. . . .'

[92] B[1], 'A liberty from the law'; B[2], 'Liberty, (1), from the law'.

[93] B[1], 'A liberty from sin'.

[94] B[1, 2], 'or the'.

[95] B[2], 'and the'.

[96] B[2], M[2] omit 'then'.

[97] B[1], 'yet much sin remains'.

[§38]   *Q.* 5. Is not every believer born of God, a temple of the
Holy Ghost?

A. In a low sense he is; but he that is in the[98] proper sense
born of God *cannot* commit sin.

5   [§39]   *Q.* 6. What is implied in being made perfect in love?

A. The loving the Lord our God with all our heart and
with all our mind, and soul, and strength[99] (Deut. 6:5,
30:6; Ezek. 36).

[§40]   *Q.* 7. Does it[100] imply that he who is thus made perfect *can-*
10   *not* commit sin?

A. St. John affirms it expressly: 'He cannot commit sin,
because he is born of God' (1 John 3:10 [i.e., 3:9]). And,
indeed how should he, seeing there is now 'none[101] occasion of stumbling in him', chap. 2:10?

15   [§41]   *Q.* 8. Does it imply that all inward sin is taken away?

A. Without doubt. Or how could he[102] be said to be saved
from all his[103] uncleannesses?

[§42]   *Q.* 9. Can we know one who[104] is thus saved? What is a reasonable proof of it?

20   *A.* We cannot, without the miraculous discernment of spirits, be infallibly certain of those who are thus saved. But
we apprehend those would be the best proofs which the
nature of the thing admits (unless they should be called to
resist unto blood):

25   If, (1), we had sufficient evidence of their unblameable
behaviour, at least from the time of their justification.
(2) If they gave[105] a distinct account of the time and manner
wherein they were saved from sin,[106] and of the circumstances
thereof, with such sound speech as could not[107] be reproved.

30   And,

---

[98] B[1], 'a'.

[99] B[2], 'The loving the Lord our God with all our mind, and soul, and strength';
B[1] omits 'and soul'.

[100] B[1, 2], 'this'.

[101] M[1, 2], 'no more'.

[102] B[1], 'could they'; M[2], 'can he'; B[2], 'should he'.

[103] B[1], 'their'.

[104] B[2], 'that'.

[105] B[2], 'give'.

[106] B[1], 'sins'.

[107] B[1], 'cannot'.

(3), If[108] upon a strict inquiry from time to time, for two or three years following, it appeared that all their tempers, and[109] words, and actions were holy and unreprovable.

[§43] *Q*. 10. How should we treat those who[110] think they have attained this?[111]

A. Exhort them to forget the things that are behind, and,[112] to watch and pray always[113] that God may search the ground of their hearts.

[§44] **Wednesday, June the 27th,[114] we began to consider points of discipline, with regard to which the questions asked and the substance of the answers given were as follows:**

[§45] *Q*. 1. What is the Church of England?

A. According to the nineteenth[115] Article, The visible Church of England is the congregation of English *believers* in which the *pure word* of God is preached, and the sacraments *duly* administered.

But the word 'Church' is sometimes taken in a looser sense for 'a congregation professing to believe'. So it is taken in the twenty-sixth Article,[116] and in the 1st, 2nd, and 3rd chapters of the Revelation.[117]

---

[108] B[2] omits 'If'.

[109] B[2] omits 'and'.

[110] B[1], 'that'.

[111] B[2] omits 'this'.

[112] B[1] omits 'to forget . . . behind, and', for which see Phil. 3:13; B[2] omits 'and'.

[113] B[1] omits 'always'.

[114] The copy made by the amanuensis 'A' begins here.

[115] Incorrectly given in A, B[1, 2], M[2] as '20th', but corrected from '20' to '19' in M[1]. Article 19 reads: 'The visible Church of Christ is a congregation of faithful men, in the which the pure Word of God is preached, and the Sacraments be duly ministered, according to Christ's ordinance, in all those things that of necessity are requisite to the same. . . .' However, this minute ignores the whole question of the status and laws of the Church of England as the established church of the land. *QQ*. 8–12 that follow show reservations on obeying the canons, and Wesley's exposition of the development of the Church in Minutes (1745), §§52–59, shows a highly pragmatic view of organization. In the 1747 Conference, a national church is seen as 'a merely political institution'; Minutes (1747), §50; see also Baker, *Wesley and Church*, 111–12; and Rack, *Reasonable Enthusiast*, 293–94.

[116] 'Of the Unworthiness of the Ministers, which hinders not the Effects of the Sacrament.' This article contains the traditional mainstream view, often challenged by revivalist and sectarian groups.

[117] B[1], M[1, 2], 'the Revelations'; B[2], 'Revelations'.

[§46] *Q.* 2. What is 'a member of the Church of England'?
       A. A believer, hearing the pure word preached, and
       partaking of the sacraments, duly administered, in this[118]
       Church.

5 [§47] *Q.* 3. What is it to be zealous for the Church?
       A. To be earnestly desirous[119] of its welfare and increase:
       Of its welfare,[120] by the confirmation of its present mem-
       bers in faith, hearing, and communicating;
       Of its increase, by the addition[121] of new members.

10 [§48] *Q.* 4. How[122] are we to defend the doctrines[123] of the
       Church?
       A. By our[124] preaching and living.

[§49] *Q.* 5. Do the 8th, 13th, 15th, 16th, 17th, 21st, 23rd, and 27th
       Articles[125] agree with Scripture?[126]

15   *A.* We will consider.

[§50] *Q.* 6. How shall we bear the most effectual testimony
       against that[127] part of the clergy who either preach or live
       contrary to the doctrine of the Church of England?
       A. Not by preaching, for they do not hear us; but rather[128]

20   by an earnest and tender address from the press.

[§51] *Q.* 7. How should[129] we behave at a false or[130] railing
       sermon?
       A. If it only[131] contain personal reflections, we may quietly
       suffer it. If it blaspheme the work and Spirit of God, it

25   may be better to go out of the[132] church. In either case, if

---

[118] B[1], 'the'.
[119] M[1,2], 'To be desirous'.
[120] A, B[2] omit 'and increase . . . welfare', obviously by an error of copying.
[121] A, 'addmition', with the 't' altered (apparently by Wesley) to 'ss'.
[122] B[1], 'How far'.
[123] B[1,2], 'doctrine'.
[124] A omits 'our'; B[1,2], 'Both by our'.
[125] '8. Of the Three Creeds'; '13. Of Works before Justification'; '15. Of Christ alone without Sin'; '16. Of Sin after Baptism'; '17. Of Predestination and Election'; '21. Of the Authority of General Councils'; '23. Of Ministering in the Congregation'; '27. Of Baptism'.
[126] A, 'with Scriptures'; B[1], 'with the Scripture'.
[127] B[1], 'the'.
[128] A, B[2] omit 'rather'.
[129] A, 'shall'.
[130] M[1,2], 'and'.
[131] M[1,2] omit 'only'.
[132] A, B[1,2] omit 'the'.

opportunity serve, it would be well to speak or write to the Minister.

[§52] *Q.* 8. How far is it our duty to obey the bishops?

A. In all things indifferent. And on this[133] ground of obeying 'em,[134] we should observe the canons, so far as we can   5
with a safe conscience.

[§53] *Q.* 9. Do we separate from the Church?

A. We conceive not. We hold communion therewith for conscience' sake, by constantly attending both the Word preached, and the Sacraments administered therein.   10

[§54] *Q.* 10. What then do they mean who say, You separate from the Church.

A. We cannot certainly tell. Perhaps they have no determinate meaning; unless by the Church they mean *themselves*, i.e., that part of the clergy who accuse us of[135] preaching   15
false doctrine. And it is sure[136] we do herein separate from *them* by maintaining the doctrine which they deny.

[§55] *Q.* 11. But do you not[137] *weaken the Church?*

A. Do not they that[138] ask this by the Church mean themselves? We do not purposely weaken any man's hands, but acciden-   20
tally we may thus far: they who come to know the truth by us will esteem such as deny it less than they did before.

But the *Church*, in the proper sense,[139] the congregation of English believers, we do not weaken at all.

[§56] *Q.* 12. Do not you entail a schism on the Church? i.e., Is it   25
not probable that your hearers after your death will be scattered into all sects and parties? Or that they will form themselves into a distinct sect?

A. (1) We are persuaded,[140] the body of our[141] hearers will even after our death remain in the Church, unless they   30
be thrust out.

---

[133] B[1], 'that'.

[134] A, B[2], 'them'.

[135] B[1], 'for'.

[136] B[1], 'it's true'.

[137] B[1], 'not you'.

[138] A, B[1,2], 'who'.

[139] A omits 'in the proper sense'.

[140] M[2] only adds 'that'.

[141] B[1] omits 'our'.

(2) We believe notwithstanding either that they will be thrust out, or that they will leaven the whole Church.

(3) We do, and will do, all we can to prevent those conse-
5   quences which are supposed likely to happen after our death.

(4) But we cannot with a good conscience neglect the present opportunity of saving souls while we live, for fear of consequences which may possibly or probably
10   happen after we are dead.

[§57]   **On Thursday, June the 28ᵗʰ**
were considered other points of discipline. The substance of the questions and answers were[142] as follows:
15 [§58]   *Q.* 1. How are the people divided who desire to be under your care?

A. Into the United Societies, the Bands, the Select Societies, and the Penitents.[143]

[§59]   *Q.* 2. How do these[144] differ from each other?
20   *A.* The United Societies (which are the largest of all) consist of awakened persons. Part of these, who are supposed to have remission of sins, are more closely united in the

---

[142] A, 'was', added over the line by Wesley.

[143] For the Rules, see vol. 9 in this edn.; Baker, 'Polity', 1:218–25. The United Societies emerged in Bristol as the seed of Wesley's connexion as he began to separate from the Moravians in 1742, and the Rules were drawn up for them in 1743. The Bands (a scheme borrowed from the Moravians) were select groups of the converts as indicated here and later were apparently those in search of perfection. The Select Society seems to have become more usually known as the Select Band and later at least, if not at this stage, consisted of those claiming perfection; see *Thoughts upon Methodism* (1781), 9:529 in this edn. It is not clear how far they continued to fulfil the function mentioned here of providing Wesley with a group for sharing his own concerns; see *Plain Account of the People Called Methodists*, 9:269 in this edn. The better-known 'Classes' were a slightly later development from a scheme originally intended to collect money but soon developed as a pastoral unit that, unlike the more select groups, included all the Society members. The penitents were those who had fallen away from the Bands, not the Society at large; see *Plain Account*, 9:268f. in this edn.

[144] M¹·², 'those'.

Bands. Those of[145] the Bands who seem to walk[146] in the light of God[147] compose the Select Societies. Those of them[148] who have made shipwreck of the faith[149] meet apart as penitents.

[§60] *Q.* 3. What are the Rules of the United Societies?[150]   5
       A. Those that follow. (Then they were read.)

[§61] *Q.* 4. What are the Rules of the Bands?
       A. They are these[151] (which were read and considered).

[§62] *Q.* 5. What are the Rules of the Select Societies?
       A. The same, and these:[152]   10

       (1) Let nothing spoken in this Society be spoken again; no, not even to the members of it.

       (2) Every member agrees absolutely to submit to his Minister in all indifferent things.

       (3) Every member, till we can have all things common,   15
       will bring once a week, *bona fide*, all he can spare towards a common stock.[153]

[§63] *Q.* 6. Are there any peculiar[154] Rules for the Penitents?
       A. Not yet.

[§64] *Q.* 7. What officers belong to these Societies?   20

---

[145] B[1, 2], 'in'.

[146] B[1], 'walk alway'.

[147] M[1], 'God's countenance'—see Ps. 89:15.

[148] A, 'em', replaced by 'them'; B[1, 2], 'them'.

[149] B[1], 'of faith'; M[2], 'of their faith'.

[150] I.e., *The Nature, Design, and General Rules of the United Societies* (1743), *Bibliography*, No. 73; see vol. 9 of this edn.

[151] M[2], 'those'. See *Rules of the Band Societies, Bibliography*, No. 81; see vol. 9 of this edn.

[152] A, B[1, 2], 'these three'.

[153] This was a plan no doubt following the 'communism' of the primitive Church (Acts 2:44-45) for a 'community of goods', though recollections of the Moravian communities may also be significant. All would live in their own houses but pool their incomes and receive what was necessary to support their families (described in Viney diary, Feb. 22, 1744, Moravian Archives, London, and copy MS Eng. 965, in MA). The plan was not implemented, though there are occasional hints of such ideals elsewhere in early Methodism. See Rack, *Reasonable Enthusiast*, 364f., and above all, John Walsh, 'John Wesley and the Community of Goods', in K. Robbins, ed., *Protestant Evangelicalism: Studies in Church History*, Subsidia 7 (Oxford, 1990), 25–50. In his *Plain Account of the Methodists* (1748, published in 1749), written to Vincent Perronet, JW repeated the Select Society rules but significantly omitted the phrase 'till we can have all things common'; 9:270 in this edn.

[154] B[2], 'particular'.

     A. The Ministers, Assistants, Stewards, Leaders of Bands, Leaders of Classes, Visitors of the Sick, Schoolmasters, Housekeepers.

[§65] *Q.* 8. What is the office of a Minister?

5   *A.* To watch over the souls whom God commits to his charge, as[155] he that must give account.[156]

[§66] *Q.* 9. What is it to be moved by the Holy Ghost to take upon yourself this office?

     A. It can mean no less than to be immediately convinced by

10   the Spirit of God that this[157] is His Will.

[§67] Q. 10. Is field preaching unlawful?

     A. We do not conceive that[158] it is contrary to any law, either of God or man. Yet (to avoid giving[159] any needless offence) we never preach *without* doors

15   when we can with any convenience[160] preach *within.* Neither would we, that. . . .[161]

[§68] *Q.* 11. Where should we endeavour to preach most?

     A. (1) Where[162] we can preach in the Church.

     (2) Where there is an open door, quiet and willing

20   hearers.

     (3) Where there is the greatest increase of souls.

[§69] *Q.* 12. What[163] is the best way of spreading the gospel?

     A. To go a little and a little farther from London, Bristol, St. Ives, Newcastle, or any other Society. So a little leaven

25   would[164] spread with more effect and less noise, and help would always be at hand.

---

[155] B[1], 'and as'.

[156] M[2], 'must account'; B[1, 2], 'must give an account'. For the reading of A, M[1] selected from *General Rules,* §7, 'let it be made known unto them who watch over that soul, as they that must give account'. This reading is also followed by Wesley in his Disciplinary *Minutes* (1749), [65].

[157] A, B[2], 'it'.

[158] B[1] omits 'that'.

[159] B[1] omits 'giving'.

[160] A, B[2], 'conveniency'.

[161] M[1] writes the closing four words with a long stroke at the end of the page, as if it were to be continued. M[2] concludes the words with a period, as if it were a complete sentence. They are absent from other copies and from the 1749 *Minutes.*

[162] B[1], 'When'.

[163] B[1], 'Which'.

[164] M[2], 'will'.

[§70]   *Q.* 13. What is the best general method in preaching?
        A. (1) To invite. (2) To convince. (3) To offer Christ.[165] And,
        lastly, to build up. And
        To do this[166] (in some measure) in every sermon.

[§71]   **Friday, June 29th, we considered:**
        Q. 1. Are Lay Assistants allowable?
        A. Only in cases of necessity.
[§72]   *Q.* 2. What is the office of our Assistants?[167]
        A. In the absence of the Minister[168] to feed and guide, to
        teach and govern the flock.
        (1) To expound every morning and evening.
        (2) To meet the United Societies,[169] the Bands, the Select
        Societies,[170] and the Penitents every week.
        (3) To visit the classes (London[171] excepted) once a
        month.
        (4) To hear and decide all differences.
        (5) To put the disorderly back on trial, and to receive on
        trial for the Bands or Society.
        (6) To see that the Stewards, the[172] Leaders,[173] School-
        masters, and Housekeepers faithfully discharge their
        several offices.

[165] B², 'Offer Christ'.
[166] B¹, 'that'.
[167] Cf. Minutes (1745), §71, called 'Assistant'; and (1746), §44, on 'Helper'. These terms are used interchangeably in the early years for the full-time travelling preachers. In *Minutes* (1749), §§5–7, the term 'Assistant' begins to be used to denote the senior and supervisory preacher in a circuit, the rest now being called 'Helpers'. The 'Assistants' are then the ancestors of those later called 'Superintendent ministers'.
[168] B¹, 'Ministers'. This evidently means in the absence of the Wesleys or their few clerical helpers and indicates surviving hopes of more such help from ordained men.
[169] A, 'Society'.
[170] A, B¹, 'Society'.
[171] A, added over the line by Wesley, '& Bristol'. This fuller revised version is incorporated in Wesley's *Plain Account of the People Called Methodists* (1749), IX.2 (3), 9:271 in this edn.; but the 1749 Disciplinary *Minutes* avoided the need for any exceptions by altering the period of visitation from monthly to quarterly.
[172] A, B¹,², 'and the'.
[173] B¹, 'Leaders of the Bands'.

(7) To meet the Stewards, and the[174] Leaders of the
Bands and Classes weekly, and overlook their accounts.[175]

[§73]   *Q.* 3. What are the Rules of an Assistant?

    A. (1) Be diligent. Never be[176] unemployed a moment. Never be
5   triflingly employed. Never while away time;[177] neither spend
        any more[178] time at any place[179] than is strictly necessary.

    (2) Be serious. Let your motto be 'Holiness to[180] the
Lord.'[181] Avoid all lightness as you would avoid hell-fire,
and laughing as you would cursing and swearing.

10   (3) Touch no woman. Be as loving as you will, but hands
off.[182] Custom is nothing to us.

    (4) Believe evil of no one. If you see it done, well; else
take heed how you credit it. Put the best construction on
everything. You know the judge is always supposed[183] to
15   be on the prisoner's side.

    (5) Speak evil of no one; else your word especially

---

[174] The reading given, apparently the original, is that of M[1,2], B[1,], B[2], 'the Stewards, the Leaders'; A, orig., 'Stewards, Leaders'. This latter reading, Wesley seems first to have altered by adding an ampersand between the two words, and then by striking out 'Stewards', and adding '& ye Stewards' above the following line to make it read: 'to meet the Leaders of the Bands and Classes, weekly, and the Stewards'.

[175] A, following up his revision earlier in the sentence, Wesley added 'to' above the line (with a caret between 'weekly' and '&'), so that it read as if only the stewards' accounts were to be checked, rather than those of stewards and of leaders; cf. *General Rules*, §3. This revised version of the passage was incorporated in Wesley's Disciplinary *Minutes* (1749), §72 (6–7).

[176] B[1], 'be never'.

[177] B[1] omits 'Never while away time'.

[178] B[1,2], 'spend no more'.

[179] A, 'at a place'.

[180] B[2], 'unto'.

[181] Isa. 23:18.

[182] B[1], 'but hold your hand off 'em'; B[2] the same, but 'hands'. A reads as the M[1,2] text, but is almost completely erased with a pattern of overlapping circles, undermining the significance of the remaining clause. In the 1749 Disciplinary *Minutes*, Wesley revises to 'Converse sparingly and cautiously with women.' The original version of the text reflects caution about customary physical courtesies to women but also the dangers of sexual license exploited by satirists and other enemies of Methodism. See, e.g., A. M. Lyles, *Methodism Mocked* (London, 1960), 69ff., 89ff.

[183] B[2], 'allowed'. A also reads 'allowed', but this Wesley has struck out and above the line has substituted what is already present in M[1], M[2], B[1], 'supposed'.

would[184] eat as doth a canker.[185] Keep your thoughts within your own[186] breast, till you come to the person concerned. (6) Tell everyone what you think wrong in him, and that plainly, and as soon as may be, else it will fester in your heart. Make all haste, therefore, to cast the fire out of your bosom.[187] 5

(7) Do nothing *as a gentleman*. You have no more to do with this[188] character than with that of a dancing-master. You are the[189] servant of all, therefore,

(8) Be ashamed of nothing but sin: not of fetching wood, if time permit,[190] or[191] drawing water; not[192] of cleaning 10 your own shoes or your neighbour's.

(9) Take no money of anyone. If they give you food when you are hungry, or clothes when you need them, it is good.[193] But not silver or gold. Let there be no pretence to say, we 'grow rich by the gospel'. 15

(10) Contract no debt without my knowledge.

(11) Be punctual; do everything exactly at the time. And in general do not *mend* our rules, but *keep* 'em, not for wrath but for conscience' sake.

(12)[194] Act in all things, not according to your own will, but 20 'as a son in the gospel'.[195] As such, it is *your part* to employ your time in that[196] manner which we direct: partly in visiting the flock from house to house (the sick in particular); partly in such a course of reading, meditation, and prayer, as we advise from time to time. Above all, if you labour 25 with us in our Lord's vineyard, it is needful you should do *that part* of the work which[197] *we* prescribe[198] at *those* times and places which we judge most for his glory.

[184] B[1], 'would especially'.
[185] 2 Tim. 2:17.
[186] B[2] omits 'own'.
[187] See Prov. 6:27.
[188] B[1], 'that'.
[189] B[1], 'a'.
[190] In B[2], 'if time permit' is given after 'drawing water'.
[191] B[1], 'or of'.
[192] A, 'nor'.
[193] B[1] omits 'it is good'.
[194] B[1] omits the whole of this paragraph.
[195] Cf. 1 Cor. 4:15; Phil. 2:22.
[196] B[2], M[2], 'the'.
[197] B[2] omits 'which'.
[198] In A, Wesley in his own hand has substituted 'direct' for 'prescribe'.

[§74]   *Q*. 4. Should all our Assistants keep journals?
      A. By all means, as well for our satisfaction as for the profit[199] of their own souls.

[§75]   *Q*. 5. Shall we now fix where each labourer shall be (if God permits)[200] till we meet again?
      A. Yes (which was accordingly done).

[§76]   *Q*. 6. What is the office of a Steward?[201]
      A.(1) To manage the[202] temporal things of the Society.
      (2) To receive the weekly contributions of the Leaders of the classes.
      (3) To expend what is needful from time to time.
      (4) To send relief[203] to the poor.
      (5) To see that the public buildings be kept clean and in good repair.[204]
      (6) To keep an exact account of receipts and expenses.
      (7) To inform the Helpers if the rules of the House, of the school, of the Bands, or[205] of the Society, be not punctually observed; and
      (8) If need be, to inform the Minister hereof.
      (9) To tell the Helpers in love, if they think anything is[206] amiss in their life and doctrine.[207]
      (10) If it be not removed, to send[208] timely notice to the Minister.
      (11) To meet his fellow Stewards weekly, in order to consult together on the preceding heads.

[§77]   *Q*. 7.[209] What are the Rules of a Steward?
      A.(1) Be frugal, save everything that can be saved honestly.
      (2) Spend no more than you receive. Contract no debt.

---

[199] In M[2], Maxfield has first written 'good' and then 'profit' above it.

[200] A, B[1], 'permit'.

[201] B[1] at this point stops numbering the questions and begins a fresh page, which is devoted solely to its heading, 'Business of a Steward, is'.

[202] B[1] omits 'the'.

[203] B[1] omits 'relief'.

[204] M[2], 'are kept clean and in repair'.

[205] B[1] omits 'or'.

[206] A, B[2] omit 'is'.

[207] A, B[1,2], 'doctrine or life'.

[208] M[1,2] omit 'to'.

[209] B[1] omits this section. Selections from both these sections (as from others) appear in Wesley's *A Plain Account of the People Called Methodists* (1749), X.2–3; 9:273 in this edn.

(3) Do nothing rashly: let every design be thoroughly weighed before you begin to execute it.

(4) Have no long accounts: pay everything within the week.

(5) Give none that ask relief either[210] an ill word or an[211] ill look. Do not hurt 'em, if you cannot help 'em.

(6) Expect no thanks from man.

(7) Remember you are a servant of the Helper, not his *master*; therefore speak to him always as such.

[§78]   *Q.* 8.[212] What is the business of the[213] Leader of a Band?
    A. It is set down in the Rules of the Bands, as the business of a Class-Leader in the Rules of the Society.[214]

[§79]   *Q.* 9.[215] What is the business of a Visitor of the sick?
    A. (1) To see every person[216] within his district thrice[217] a week.

(2) To inquire into the state of their souls, and advise 'em as occasion may require.

(3) To inquire into their disorder, and procure advice for 'em.[218]

(4) To inquire if they are in want, and relieve 'em, if it may be in kind.[219]

(5) To do anything for 'em which he can do.[220]

(6) To bring in his accounts[221] weekly to the Stewards.[222]

[§80]   *Q.* 10. What are the Rules of a Visitor?[223]

[210] B[2] omits 'either'.

[211] A, B[2] omit 'an'.

[212] B[1] omits this section.

[213] B[2], M[2], 'a'.

[214] M[2] omits 'as the business . . . Society'; A reads, 'Class-leader is in the Rules. . . .'

[215] B[1] omits the question, replacing it in the following form: 'A Visitor of the Sick is / To visit sick persons thrice a week', and so on.

[216] A, 'To visit every sick person'.

[217] M[2], 'twice'.

[218] B[1] (apparently copying from the previous entry) adds 'as occasion may require'.

[219] B[1,2] omit 'if . . . kind'; M[2] reads, 'in any kind'.

[220] B[1,2] omit 'do'.

[221] A, B[1,2], 'to bring his account weekly'.

[222] B[1], 'Steward'.

[223] B[1], 'Rules to be practised by a Visitor'.

    A.(1) Be plain and open in[224] dealing with souls.

    (2) Be mild, tender, patient.[225]

    (3) Be cleanly[226] in all you do for them.

    (4) Be not nice.

5 [§81] *Q.* 11. Can we have a Seminary for labourers?

    A. If God spare us till another Conference.

[§82] *Q.* 12. With whom should we correspond? When?

    A. Once a month, with each Assistant, and with some

    one[227] other person (at least) in each Society.

10 [§83] *Q.* 13. How shall we fix the watch-nights, letter-days, and

    love-feasts, till we meet again?

    A. At London, Bristol, and Newcastle thus:

Watch-nights	July 13	Aug. 10	Sept. 7	Oct. 12
Letter-days	July 23	Aug. 20	Sept. 17	Oct. 22
Love-feasts	July 29	Aug. 26	Sept. 23	Oct. 28[228]

15

[§84] *Q.* 14. What books may an Assistant read?

    A. Sallust, Caesar, Tully,[229] Erasmus, Castellio, Terence,

20   Virgil, Horace, Vida, Buchanan, G[reek] Test[ament],

    Epictetus, Plato, Ignatius, Ephrem Syrus, Homer, Greek

    Epigrams, Duport, Archbishop Ussher's *Sermons*, Arndt,

    Boehm, Nalson, Pascal, Francke, R. Gell, Brevint.[230]

    Our tracts.

25   Cyprian, Chrysostom.[231]

[§85] *Q.* 15. How shall we exclude formality from prayer and

    from[232] conversation?

---

[224] B[2], 'with'.

[225] A, B[2], 'patient, tender'.

[226] B[2], 'clean'.

[227] B[2], 'some'.

[228] B[2] arranges these in three columns with the dates below the events.

[229] I.e., Cicero.

[230] A, B[1,2] omit Brevint.

[231] These two authors are added, on a separate line, only in M[1,2]. Arndt is omitted from the 1745 list. Johann Arndt (1555–1621) was a Lutheran theologian and devotional writer. He is chiefly remembered for his *Vier Bücher vom Wahren Christentum* (1606), trans. as *True Christianity* by A. W. Boehm (1712) and P. C. Erb (New York, 1979). This work focuses on the work of Christ in the heart. Arndt is commonly regarded as a proto-Pietist.

[232] A, B[1,2] omit 'from'.

A.(1) By preaching frequently on this head.[233]

(2) By watching always, that we may only speak[234] what we feel.

[§86]   *Q.* 16. What shall I[235] write next? What abridge?

A. Write a farther Appeal,[236] Sermons;[237] abridge and print *Sixteen Sermons*,[238] Manual,[239] Dr. Knight's Two Discourses,[240]   5
Great Audit,[241] *The Whole Duty of Man*,[242] Edwards.[243]

[§87]   *Q.* 17. Is it lawful to bear arms?

A. We incline to think it is: (1) Because there is no command against it[244] in the New Testament; (2) Because Cornelius, a soldier, is commended there, and not mentioned   10
to have laid them down.

[§88]   *Q.* 18. Is it lawful to use the law?

[233] B[2], 'on the heads'.

[234] A, B[1, 2], 'speak only'.

[235] B[1], 'What to'; omitting 'What abridge?'

[236] Part I of Wesley's *Farther Appeal*, in succession to his *Earnest Appeal* (1743), appeared in Dec. 1744 (see vol. 11:95–202 in this edn.).

[237] Wesley did not begin his series of *Sermons on Several Occasions* until 1746; see *Bibliography*, No. 128, and vol. 1 of this edn.

[238] By Zinzendorf, viz., *Sixteen Discourses on the Redemption of Man by the Death of Christ* (London, Hutton, 1740), trans. German into English.

[239] B[2] reads 'Dr. Knight's Manual, 2 Discourses', although there does not seem to be any 'Manual' by Knight.

[240] Almost certainly James Knight, D.D. (1672–1735), minister of St. Sepulchre's, London, whose *Discourse on the Conflagration and Renovation of the World* (London, 1736) Wesley eventually published in abridged form in his own *Works* (1773), 20:290–321, using the title 'two discourses' for the two lengthy divisions of the sermon.

[241] In his *Christian Library*, vol. 30 (1753), Wesley published an extract of 'The Great Audit; with the Account of the Good Steward', from the *Contemplations Moral and Divine* (1677) of Lord Chief Justice Matthew Hale (1609–76).

[242] Wesley published an abridgement of *The Whole Duty of Man* (1657) in vol. 21 of his *Christian Library* (1753). This anonymous work from High Church circles, probably by Richard Allestree (1619–81), was designed to counter Puritan antinomian tendencies and became one of the most popular devotional works in the 18th century. JW naturally used it for his visiting work in Oxford as well as during these early years after his conversion. Most evangelicals thought it fostered salvation by works, hence Henry Venn's *Complete Duty of Man* (1763) as an explicit counter to it. But JW's preface to his abridgement implicitly defends it.

[243] Probably about May 1744, JW published an extract from the first of several works by Jonathan Edwards (1703–58), namely, *A Faithful Narrative of the Surprising Work of God in Northampton . . . in New England* (1737). In July 1744, he published an extract from Edwards's *The Distinguishing Marks of a Work of the Spirit of God* (1741); see *Bibliography*, Nos. 85, 88. It is possible, however, that the *Narrative* appeared later than May.

[244] A omits 'it'.

A. As defendant, doubtless. And perhaps as plaintiff[245] in some cases, seeing magistrates are an ordinance of God.[246]

5 [§89] **On Saturday, June the 30th**, we considered:

Q. 1. Can we unite any farther with the Moravians?

A. It seems not, were it only for this reason, they will not unite with us.

[§90] *Q.* 2. Can we unite any farther with Mr. Whitefield?

10 *A.* If he make any overtures towards it.

[§91] *Q.* 3. Shall we propose a conference with either?

A. With Mr. Whitefield, if he returns[247] to London. The Moravians absolutely decline it.

[§92] *Q.* 4. Shall we send them the most material of the preced-

15 ing questions, and desire their answer?[248]

A. This can do no hurt, and may do good.

[§93] *Q.* 5. Can we amend[249] our economy in temporal things?

A. We will consider this with the Stewards.

[§94] *Q.* 6. Have we changed in anything for the worse since we

20 began our Society?

A. It does not appear to us that we have.

[§95] *Q.* 7. Is there anything amongst us that stops the work of God?

A. Perhaps sins of omission, neglect of self-denial and

25 taking up our cross.

[§96] *Q.* 8. When and where shall those of us who can meet again?

A. If God permits, Nov. [the] 1st at Newcastle, Feb. the 1st at Bristol, May the 1st at London.[250]

---

[245] B[1], 'plaintiff'.

[246] Ezra 7:25; Titus 3:1.

[247] B[1], 'return'.

[248] B[2], 'answers'.

[249] B[1, 2], M[2], 'mend'.

[250] This entry clearly visualized a quarterly rather than annual assembly of the Conference, as also an early scheme for Conferences in 1739 stipulated three quarterly gatherings in addition to an annual one; *Letters*, 25:700 in this edn., and introduction, p. 9 above. But that schedule must quickly have been seen to be impracticable here as well as earlier. Wesley did, however, summon occasional additional Conferences on a regional basis, as will be seen. The next Conference was actually held in Bristol in Aug. 1745, as seen in the subsequent Minutes.

The Bristol Conference of August 1–3, 1745

Bristol, Thursday, August 1st, 1745[251]

[§1] The following persons being met together at the New
Room, John Wesley, Charles Wesley, John Hodges,
Thomas Richards, Samuel Larwood, Thomas Meyrick,   5
James Wheatley, Richard Moss, John Slocombe, Herbert
Jenkins,[252] Marmaduke Gwynne,[253] it was inquired:

[251] The 1745 MS Minutes are available in the following copies, arranged in the
probable chronological order of their transcription; the symbols by which they are
designated are prefixed:
   C. In an unidentified hand, pp. xvi–xxxi of the same notebook in Wesley College,
Bristol, as the 'A' copy of 1744, probably not transcribed before 1747 or even 1748.
Wesley himself made several revisions in the copy.
   B. In the handwriting of John Bennet, the second item in the notebook published by Richard Green (see p. 125 above) and in the same category as the B copy
of the 1744 Minutes, probably transcribed about 1748.
   Thus the contemporary official copy of the 1745 Minutes seems to have disappeared
and may well be reproduced more accurately (especially in its italicizing) in the published
Doctrinal and Disciplinary *Minutes* of 1749, for which see below, pp. 785–91, 811–17. The
readings of 1749 and one of these later copies will normally be preferred for the edited text
over a variant in the other, later copy. The 1749 *Minutes* also show by italics that Wesley
regarded many seemingly neutral phrases in these MS Minutes as scriptural quotations.
   In 1944, the Methodist Archives acquired a further copy of the 1745 Minutes accompanied by an incomplete cop`y in the same hand of the greater part of the first letter of
'John Smith'. The 'Smith' correspondence was printed in full by Henry Moore in his *Life
of the Rev. John Wesley*, 2 vols. (London: Kershaw, 1824–25), 2:475–576, and other MSS
of it have survived (see *Letters*, 26:145f. in this edn. for details). This suggests to the editors
that the transcriber was a sympathetic critic of Methodism who was planning an abortive
project to discuss or dispute with Wesley over Methodism. The copy of the Minutes contains many small variations from the texts used in this edn., but they do not conform to the
pattern of any one of them. Apart from a few short phrases, omissions include the second
and third resolutions in §77 and the whole of *QQ*. 9 and 10 (§§79, 80), after which *Q*. 11 is
renumbered 9. The book-list from VII to X is reduced to subject headings and the final *Q*.
14 (§84) is omitted, but the transcriber was then running out of space. It may be doubted
whether this copy has independent value as evidence of Conference proceedings, but it
confirms that several copies of the Minutes were circulating and that breaches of confidence could occur. It is also unknown how the writer obtained a copy of the 'Smith' letter.
   [252] Herbert Jenkins became a Methodist in 1743 but later joined Whitefield and
his friends, often preached for Andrew Kinsman in Plymouth, Bristol, and South
Wales, and was later apparently a Dissenting minister in Maidenstone. See *Journal
& Diaries*, 20:134, n. 95 in this edn.
   [253] Marmaduke Gwynne (c. 1694–1769) of Garth, Breconshire, was a local magistrate, a convert of Howell Harris, but also a supporter of the Wesleys and 'a pil-
lar of evangelicalism in that area'. His daughter Sarah married Charles Wesley in
1749. See *Journal & Diaries*, 19:324 n. 98 in this edn.

[§2] *Q.* 1. Should we still consider ourselves as little children, who have everything to learn?

A. Yes, so far as to have our minds always open to any farther light which God may give us.

[§3] *Q.* 2. What general method may we observe in our following conferences?

A. (1) To read and weigh at every conference each article of those preceding. (2) To speak freely and hear calmly touching each, that we may either retract, amend, or enlarge it.

[§4] *Q.* 3. Should not the time of this conference be a time of particular watching and self-denial?

A. It should.

[§5] *Q.* 4. Should we not desire all who can of the Society to join with us tomorrow in fasting and prayer?

A. We will desire them so to do.

[§6] *Q.* 5. Ought not every point[254] which shall be proposed to be examined from the foundation?

A. Without question it ought. If there was any defect herein at the last conference, let us amend it now.

[§7] *Q.* 6. How can we effectually provide that everyone may speak freely whatever is in his heart?

A. By taking care to check no one, either by word or look, even though he should say what was quite wrong.

[§8] *Q.* 7. How shall we provide that every point may be fully debated[255] and thoroughly settled?

A. Let us beware of making haste or of[256] showing any impatience, whether[257] of delay or of[258] contradiction.

[§9] About seven it was proposed to review the minutes of the last conference with regard to justification. And it was asked:[259]

[§10] *Q.* 1. How comes what is written on this subject to be so intricate and obscure? Is this obscurity from the nature of the thing itself? or from the fault or weakness of those who have generally treated of it?

---

[254] B, 'question'—1749 also reads 'point'.

[255] B omits 'debated', surely in error.

[256] B omits 'of', present in 1749.

[257] C, 'either'.

[258] C omits 'of'.

[259] B omits 'And . . . asked', present in 1749.

A. We apprehend this obscurity does not arise from the nature of the subject, but perhaps partly from hence, that the devil peculiarly labours to perplex a subject of the greatest importance, and partly from the extreme warmth of most writers who have treated of it.   5

[§11] *Q.* 2. We affirm faith is the sole condition of justification. But does not repentance go before that faith? Yea, and (supposing there be an opportunity for them) fruits or works meet for repentance?

A. Without doubt they do.   10

[§12] *Q.* 3. How then can we deny them to be conditions of justification? Is not this a mere strife[260] of words? But is it worth while to continue a dispute on the term 'condition'?

A. It seems not, though it has been generally abused. But so the abuse cease, let the use remain.   15

[§13] *Q.* 4. Shall we read over together Mr. Baxter's *Aphorisms* concerning justification?[261]

A. By all means; which were accordingly read. And it was desired that each person present would in the afternoon consult the Scriptures cited therein, and bring what   20 objections might occur the next morning.

[§14]   **Friday, August 2ⁿᵈ,**

the question was proposed:

Q. 1. Is an assurance of God's love absolutely necessary to   25 our being in his favour? Or may there possibly be some exempt cases?

A. We dare not positively say, there are not.

[§15] *Q.* 2. Is such an assurance absolutely necessary to inward and outward holiness?   30

---

[260] The word 'strife', missing from the original copy 'C', was added above the line by JW.

[261] I.e., surely JW's publication, which had just appeared, *An extract of Mr. Richard Baxter's Aphorisms of Justification*, for which see *Bibliography*, No. 99. Baxter (1615–91), Puritan divine and moderate on church government, was largely self-educated. He had a notable ministry in Kidderminster, Worcestershire, refused a bishopric at the Restoration, and was ejected for nonconformity. He was concerned about the antinomian tendencies of Calvinism; his views on justification were suspect to the stricter Calvinists, and 'Baxterianism' became a bogeyman to them throughout the 18ᵗʰ century and beyond. To the Arminian Wesley, he was naturally more attractive, and in later Conferences his system of pastoral care was also commended; see Minutes (1755), §5; (1766), *Q.* 29.

A. To inward, we apprehend it is; to outward holiness, we incline to think it is not.

[§16]   *Q.* 3. Is it indispensably necessary to final salvation? Suppose in a Papist, or a Quaker? Or, in general, among those who never heard it preached?

A. Love hopeth all things.[262] We know not how far any of these[263] may fall under the case of[264] invincible ignorance.[265]

[§17]   *Q.* 4. But what can we say of one of our own Society who dies without it, as John Warr[266] at London?

A. It may possibly be an exempt case (if the fact was really so); but we determine nothing. We leave his soul in the hands of him that made it.

[§18]   *Q.* 5. Does[267] a man believe any longer than he sees God?

A. We conceive not. But we allow there may be infinite degrees in seeing God; even as many as there are between him who sees the sun when it shines on his eyelids closed, and him who stands with his eyes wide open in the full blaze of his beams.

[§19]   *Q.* 6. Does a man believe any longer than he loves God?

A. In no wise. For neither circumcision nor uncircumcision avails without faith working by love.[268]

[§20]   *Q.* 7. Have we duly considered the case of Cornelius? Was not he in the favour of God when his prayers and alms[269] came up for a memorial before God?[270] i.e. before he believed in Christ?[271]

---

[262] 1 Cor. 13:7.

[263] B, 'those'.

[264] In C, Wesley himself added 'the case of' above the line, with a caret beneath.

[265] Cf., e.g., Thomas Aquinas, *Summa Theologica*, 1.xxvi, §2. 'An ignorance the means of overcoming or removing which are not possessed by the ignorant person himself' (*OED*). Hence, in traditional Catholic theology, such ignorance excuses the guilt of sins committed in this state.

[266] C, 'John Warr'; 1749, 'J.W.' The John Warr concerned was surely the one listed among the unmarried men at the Foundery as on trial for the Bands on Jan. 1, 1743–44, whose name is struck through, with a shorthand inscription added, 'd[ie]d'. He may be linked with the other John Warr for whom Wesley inquired in Dublin on behalf of the London banker Ebenezer Blackwell (see *Letters*, 26:283 in this edn.).

[267] B, 'How does'.

[268] See Gal. 5:6.

[269] B, 'his alms'.

[270] Acts 10:4.

[271] B, 'in him'.

A. It does seem that he was. But we speak not of those who have not heard the gospel.

[§21] *Q.* 8. But were those works of his splendid sins?[272]

A. No; nor were they done without the grace of Christ.

[§22] *Q.* 9. How then can we maintain that all works done before we have a sense of the pardoning love of God are sin? And, as such, an abomination to him?

A. The works of him who has heard the gospel and does not believe are not done as God hath willed and commanded them to be done. Therefore they are sinful. And yet we know not how to say that they are an abomination[273] to the Lord in him who feareth God, and from that principle does the best he can.

[§23] *Q.* 10. Seeing there is so much difficulty in this subject, can we deal too tenderly with them that oppose us?

A. We cannot, unless we give up any part of the truth of God.

[§24] *Q.* 11. Is a believer constrained to obey God?

A. At first he is. The love of Christ constraineth him.[274] After this he may obey, or he may not; no necessity being laid upon him.

[§25] *Q.* 12. Can faith be lost, but through disobedience?

A. It cannot. A believer first inwardly disobeys, inclines to sin with his heart. Then his intercourse with God is lost, i.e., his faith is lost, and after this he may fall into outward sin, being now weak and like[275] another man.

[§26] *Q.* 13. How can such an one recover faith?[276]

A. By repenting and doing the first works (Rev. 2:5).

[§27] *Q.* 14. Whence is it that the majority of those who[277] believe fall more or less into doubt or fear?

---

[272] Tertullian, *De carne Christi*, I: 'The virtues of the heathen, being devoid of grace, can only be looked upon as splendid sins.' But cf. also Richard Fiddes, *Practical Discourses*, II.15 (1714), on 'splendid sins', quoted in *OED* as an example of an adjective 'used by way of contrast, and qualifying nouns having an opposite or different connotation': 'Even their best actions [are] no better than splendid sins.' Cf. also Wesley's *Notes on the NT*, Acts 10:4, and Sermon 99, 'The Reward of the Righteous', I.4, in *Sermons*, 3:404 n. 31 in this edn. for further sources.

[273] B, 'are abomination'.

[274] See 2 Cor. 5:14.

[275] B, 'like unto'.

[276] B, 'How can such a man recover faith?'

[277] B, 'that'.

> *A*. Chiefly from their own ignorance or unfaithfulness;
> often from their not watching unto prayer; perhaps some-
> times from some defect or want of the power of God in
> the preaching they hear.

5 [§28]   *Q*. 15. Is there not a defect in us? Do we preach as we did at
> first?[278] Have we not changed our doctrines?

> *A*. (1) At first we preached almost wholly to unbelievers. To
> these, therefore, we spake almost continually of remis-
> sion of sins through the death of Christ and the nature
10 of faith in his blood. And so we do still, among those
> who need to be taught the first elements of the gospel of
> Christ.

> (2) But those in whom the foundation is already laid we
> exhort to go on to perfection; which we did not see so
15 clearly at first, although we occasionally spake of it from
> the beginning.

> (3) Yet we now preach, and that continually, faith in
> Christ as the Prophet, Priest, and King, at least as
> clearly, as strongly, and as fully as we did six years ago.

20 [§29]   *Q*. 16. Do we not discourage visions and dreams too much?
> As if we condemned them *toto genere*?[279]

> *A*. We do not intend to do this. We neither discourage nor
> encourage them. We learn from Acts 2:19, etc., to expect
> something of this kind in the last days. And we cannot
25 deny that saving faith is often given in dreams or visions
> of[280] the night, which faith we account neither better nor
> worse than if it came[281] by any other means.

[§30]   *Q*. 17. Do not our Assistants preach too much of the wrath
> and too little of the love of God?

30 *A*. We fear they have leaned to that extreme, and hence
> some of their hearers[282] may have lost the joy of faith.

[§31]   *Q*. 18. Need we ever preach the terror of the Lord to those
> who know they are accepted of him?

> *A*. No. It is folly so to do. For love is to them the strongest
35 of all motives.

---

[278] B, 'at the first'.

[279] 'in their whole character'.

[280] B, 'in'.

[281] B, 'come'.

[282] In C, JW added above the line (with a caret after 'some'): 'of their hearers'. It is not present in B.

[§32]   *Q*. 19. Do we ordinarily represent a justified state so great
and happy as it is?

   A. Perhaps not. A believer walking in the light is inexpressibly great and happy.

[§33]   *Q*. 20. Should we not have a care of depreciating justifica-   5
tion in order to exalt the estate of full sanctification?

   A. Undoubtedly we should beware of this, for[283] one may
insensibly slide into it.

[§34]   *Q*. 21. How shall we effectually avoid it?

   A. When we are going to speak of entire sanctification, let   10
us first describe the blessings of a justified state as
strongly as possible.

[§35]   *Q*. 22. Does not the truth of the gospel lie very near both to
Calvinism and antinomianism?

   A. Indeed it does—as it were, within a hair's breadth. So   15
that 'tis altogether foolish and sinful, because we do not
quite agree either with one or the other, to run from them
as far as ever we can.

[§36]   *Q*. 23. Wherein may we come to the very edge of
Calvinism?   20

   A. (1) In ascribing all good to the free grace of God; (2) in
denying all natural free will and all power antecedent to
grace; and (3) in excluding all merit from man, even for
what he has or does by the grace of God.

[§37]   *Q*. 24. Wherein may we come to the very edge of   25
antinomianism?

   A. (1) In exalting the merits and love of Christ; (2) in
rejoicing evermore.

[§38]   *Q*. 25. What can we do to stop the progress of
antinomianism?   30

   A. (1) Pray without ceasing that God would speak for himself. (2) Write one or two more dialogues.[284]

[§39]   *Q*. 26. Doth faith supersede (set aside the necessity of) holiness or good works?

   A. In no wise. So far from it that it implies both, as a cause   35
does its effects.

---

[283] B, 'or'.

[284] See *A Dialogue between an Antinomian and his Friend*, and *A Second Dialogue
between an Antinomian and his Friend*, both published this year, the first in June, the
second in Aug.. *Bibliography*, Nos. 102, 106, and vol. 13 of this edn.

[§40]   About ten we began to speak of sanctification, with regard
to which it was inquired:
Q. 1. When does inward sanctification begin?
A. In the moment we are justified. The seed of every virtue
5   is then instantaneously sown in the soul. From that time
the believer gradually dies to sin and grows in grace. Yet
sin remains in him, yea, the seed of all sin, till he is sanctified throughout in spirit, soul, and body.

[§41]   *Q.* 2. What will become of a heathen, a Papist, or a Church
10   of England man, if he dies without being thus sanctified?
A. He cannot see the Lord. But none who seeks it sincerely
shall or can die without it; though possibly he may not
attain it till the very article of death.

[§42]   *Q.* 3. Is it ordinarily [not] given till a little before death?
15   *A.* It is not, to those who expect it no sooner, nor probably
ask for it.

[§43]   *Q.* 4. But ought we to expect it sooner?
A. Why not? Although we grant, (1), that the generality of
believers[285] whom we have hitherto known[286] are not so
20   sanctified till near death. (2) That few of those to whom
St. Paul wrote his epistles were so at the[287] time he wrote.
(3) Nor he himself at the time of writing his former epistles. Yet this does not prove that we may not today.

[§44]   *Q.* 5. But would not one who was thus sanctified be inca-
25   pable of worldly business?
A. He would be far more capable of it than ever, as going
through all without distraction.

[§45]   *Q.* 6. Would he be capable of marriage? M[arriage] is
h[onourable] in all.[288]
30   *A.* We cannot well judge. But supposing he were not, the
number of those in that state is so small, it would produce
no inconvenience.[289]

---

[285] C, 'the believers'.

[286] The words 'whom we have hitherto known' occur only in C, written above the
line by JW.

[287] B, 'that'.

[288] JW appended this second sentence to the first. See Heb. 13:4. For his earlier
doubts on this issue, see JW to CW, Sept. 25, 1749 (a retrospect of his views on marriage), *Letters*, 26:381 in this edn.

[289] The whole of these two sentences are underlined in C, possibly by JW, as an
indication that on publication they needed special attention. In 1749 only a brief sentence was printed: 'Why should he not?' and the following two sections are omitted.

[§46]   *Q*. 7. Does the Scripture mention any living men who were
wholly sanctified?
A. Yes—St. John and all those then with the apostle, in
whose name he speaks those words (1 John 4:17): 'Herein
(or through him) is our love made perfect, that we may[290]   5
have boldness in the day of judgment, because as he is, so
are we in this world.'

[§47]   *Q*. 8. Can a justified person judge of a sanctified?
A. Not without a peculiar gift of God. For the spiritual
man is judged of no man.   10

[§48]   *Q*. 9. Should we not then beware of bearing hard on those
who think they have attained?
A. We should. And the rather, because if they are faithful to
the grace they have received, they are in no danger of perishing at last. No, not even if they remain in luminous   15
faith[291] for many months or years, perhaps till within a little time[292] of their spirits returning to God.

[§49]   *Q*. 10. In what manner should we preach entire sanctification?
A. Scarce at all to those who are not pressing forward. To
those who are, always by way of promise, always drawing   20
rather than driving.

[§50]   *Q*. 11. How should we wait for the fulfilling of this promise?
A. In universal obedience; in keeping all the commandments;
in denying ourselves, and taking up our cross daily. These
are the general means which God hath ordained for our   25
receiving his sanctifying grace. The particular are prayer,
searching the Scripture, communicating, and fasting.

[§51]   **On Saturday, Aug. 3rd,**
were considered points of discipline.   30

[§52]   *Q*. 1. Can he be a spiritual governor of the Church who is
not a believer, not a member of it?
A. It seems not; though he may be a governor in outward
things, by a power derived from the King.

[§53]   *Q*. 2. What are properly the laws of the Church of England? 35
A. The rubrics; and to those we submit as the ordinance of
man, for the Lord's sake.[293]

---

[290] In C, 'may' is added above the line, apparently in JW's hand.
[291] 1749, '*luminous faith* (as some term it)'.
[292] B, 'a little'.
[293] 1 Pet. 2:13.

[§54] *Q.* 3. But is not the will of our governors a law?

   A. No. Not of any governor, temporal or spiritual. Therefore if any bishop wills that I should not preach the
   gospel, his will is no law to me.

5 [§55] *Q.* 4. But what if he produce a law against your preaching?

   A. I am to obey God rather than man.[294]

[§56] *Q.* 5. Is Episcopal, Presbyterian, or Independent church
   government most agreeable to reason?

   A. The plain origin of church government seems to be

10   this.[295] Christ sends forth a preacher of the gospel. Some
   who hear him repent and believe the gospel. They then
   desire him to watch over them, to build them up in the
   faith, and to guide their souls in the paths of righteousness. Here then is an independent congregation, subject

15   to no pastor but their own, neither liable to be controlled
   in things spiritual by any other man or body of men
   whatsoever.

   But soon after, some from other parts who are occasionally
   present while he speaks in the name of him that sent him,

20   beseech him to come over and help them also. He complies.[296] Knowing it to be the will of God he consents,[297]
   yet not till he has conferred with the wisest and holiest of
   his congregation, and with their advice appointed one
   who has gifts and grace to watch over the flock till his

25   return.

---

[294] See Acts 5:29.

[295] Despite this highly pragmatic account of the origins of church order (which seems to allow some validity to all the main Protestant ministries and forms of order), on Dec. 27, 1745, JW wrote to Westley Hall apparently defending apostolic succession (*Letters*, 26:173–75 in this edn., but published in the 1753 *Journal*). Yet only three weeks later he recorded what appears to be a sudden conversion to pres-byteral ordination by reading Lord King's *Account of the Primitive Church* (*Journal & Diaries*, 20:112 in this edn.). His later dismissal of apostolic succession is attrib-uted to reading Bishop Stillingfleet's *Irenicon* perhaps in the early 1740s. See Baker, *Wesley and Church*, 141–49; Rack, *Reasonable Enthusiast*, 291–96. However, in the context of the preceding remarks about the authority of the Church of England and the development of Methodism at this stage, it may be that Wesley was justi-fying his own authority over the embryo connexion and his freedom to 'obey God rather than man' in relation to the Church of England. In 1746 (Minutes, §40 and n.) he concluded that congregations had a right to appoint their own pastors.

[296] 'He complies' is added in the margin of C only by JW, with a caret indicating the place of its insertion in the line.

[297] C omits 'Knowing . . . consents'.

If it please God to raise another flock in the new place,
  before he leaves them he does the same thing, appointing
  one whom God has fitted for the work to watch over these
  souls also.

In like manner, in every place where it pleases God to   5
  gather a little flock by his word, he appoints one in his
  absence to take the oversight of the rest, and to assist
  them of the ability which God giveth. These are Deacons,
  or servants of the church, and look on the[298] first pastor as
  their common father. And all these congregations regard   10
  him in the same light and esteem him still as the shepherd
  of their souls.

These congregations are not strictly independent. They
  depend on one pastor, though not on each other.

As these congregations increase, and as the Deacons grow   15
  in years and grace, they need other subordinate Deacons
  or Helpers; in respect of whom they may be called Presbyters, or Elders, as their father in the Lord may be called
  the Bishop, or Overseer of them all.

[§57] *Q.* 6. Is mutual consent absolutely necessary between the   20
  pastor and his flock?

A. No question: I cannot guide any soul unless he
  consent[299] to be guided by me. Neither can any soul force
  me to guide him, if I consent not.

[§58] *Q.* 7. Does the ceasing of this consent on either side   25
  dissolve the relation?

A. It must in the very nature[300] of things. If a man no
  longer consent to be guided by me, I am no longer his
  guide, I am free. If one will not guide me any longer, I am
  free to seek one who will.   30

[§59] *Q.* 8. But is the shepherd free to leave his sheep? Or the
  sheep to leave their shepherd?

A. Yes; if one or the others are convinced it is for the glory
  of God and the superior good of their souls.

[§60] *Q.* 9. How shall we treat those who leave us?   35

A. (1) Beware of all sharpness, or bitterness, or resentment.

---

[298] B, 'their'.
[299] B, 'consents'.
[300] B, 'the nature'.

(2) Talk with them once or twice at least. (3) If they persist in their design, consider them as dead, and name them not unless in prayer.

[§61]   *Q.* 10. Can I attend any more societies than I do? Seeing this would imply the spending less time with the rest.

A. It seems not, at least till the societies already formed are more stablished in grace.

[§62]   *Q.* 11. May we not make a trial, especially in Wales and Cornwall, of preaching without forming any societies?

A. It might be well; and by this means we may preach in every large town where a door is open.[301]

[§63]   *Q.* 12. Should we permit any serious person[302] to be present when one of our societies[303] meets?

A. At some time he may, if he particularly desire it, but not always, nor the same person frequently.

[§64]   *Q.* 13. Have we borne a sufficient witness to the truth? Particularly when attacked by the clergy?

A. Perhaps not. We have generally been content with standing on the defensive.

[§65]   *Q.* 14. May not this cowardice have hindered the work of God? And have caused us to feel less of his power?

A. Very probably it may.

[§66]   *Q.* 15. How shall we act in such cases for the time to come?

A. Not only refute, but retort the charge. Their mouths must be stopped (only in meekness and love), and the eyes of others opened.

[§67]   *Q.* 16. Is it expedient for us to converse more with the clergy?

A. Yes; wherever they are willing we should.

[§68]   *Q.* 17. With our chief opposers or persecutors?

A. It might do good: (1) When they make any overtures toward it. (2) When we can take them unawares, and converse with them alone.

[§69]   *Q.* 18. National sins call aloud for national judgments. What shall we do to prevent them?

A. The first Friday in every month, at least, speak expressly on this head and insist on the necessity of general repentance to prevent a general scourge.

---

[301] This expedient is, however, condemned in Minutes (1748), §3.

[302] B, 'persons'.

[303] B, 'our Society'.

[§70]   *Q*. 19. Should we talk of persecution before it comes?
        A. To talk or think before of any particular persecution only
        weakens our hands. And how long the general persecution
        may be deferred, God only knows.
[§71]   It was next inquired with regard to our Assistants,[304]   5
        Q. 1. Should any other rule be added to the twelve?
        A. Only this: 'You have nothing to do but to save souls.
        Therefore spend and be spent in this work. And go
        always, not only to those who want you, but to those who
        want you most.'   10
[§72]   *Q*. 2. Who are our present Assistants?
        A. Jonathan Reeves, James Wheatley, Jno. Nelson, Jno.
        Bennet, Jno. Trembath, Francis Walker,[305] Thos. Richards,
        Jno. Downes, Thos. Westell, James Jones, Samuel Lar-
        wood, Hen. Millard, Thomas Maxfield, Thos. Meyrick.   15
[§73]   *Q*. 3. What general method of spending their time may our
        Assistants have?
        A. They may spend the mornings (from six to twelve) in
        reading, writing, and prayer; from twelve to five, visit the
        sick and well; and from five to six, use private prayer.   20
[§74]   *Q*. 4. Can I travel less in order to write more?
        A. As yet it does not seem advisable.
[§75]   *Q*. 5. Should not my brother follow me step by step, and
        Mr. Meriton[306] him?
        A. As far as is possible.   25
[§76]   *Q*. 6. Can we have a Seminary for labourers yet?[307]
        A. Not till God gives us a proper tutor.
[§77]   *Q*. 7. How shall we order our correspondence at home and
        abroad?
        A. (1) Fix whom to correspond with monthly in every   30
        place. (2) Divide them between my brother and me.
        (3) Send them notice in every place.

---

[304] In the 1744 Conference, 'Assistant' is the term used for the lay preachers, who will later be called 'Helper', the 'help' and 'assistance' being in relation to Wesley and the clergy as leaders (Minutes [1744], §§71–74). By the end of the decade, 'Assistant' denotes the senior, supervising itinerant in each circuit (the 'Superintendent' of later times).

[305] B adds 'Thomas Maxfield' here instead of near the end of the list.

[306] For Meriton, see Minutes (1744), §1, n. 29.

[307] B omits 'yet'. The original Kingswood School scheme in 1748 envisaged an 'academical' course, which was revived in 1768 (see introduction, p. 82).

[§78]   *Q.* 8. Shall we keep a little stock of medicines at London,
Bristol, and Newcastle, according to the *Collection of Receipts?*[308]
A. It would be well so to do.

[§79]   *Q.* 9. Which are the watch-nights, intercession-days, and
5   love-feasts till January?

A. Watch-nights	Intercession-days[309]	Letter-days	Love-feasts
Aug. 2	Sept. 6	Aug. 13	Aug. 18
[Aug.] 28	Oct. 3	Sept. 10	Sept. 15
Sept. 27	Nov. 8	Oct. 8	Oct. 13
Nov. 1	Dec. 6	Nov. 12	Nov. 17
[Nov.] 30	Dec. 10	Dec. 15	
Dec. 27			

[§80]   *Q.* 10. What shall[310] I write next?
A. (1) *Advice to the Methodists.*[311] (2) Dialogues.[312] (3) *Appeal
to all.*[313] (4) Finish the *Farther Appeal.*[314] (5) *Sermons.*[315]

[§81]   *Q.* 11. Is it lawful to bear arms?

---

[308] This was the predecessor and foundation of Wesley's *Primitive Physick* and
had just been published under the title *A Collection of Receipts for the Use of the
Poor* (see *Bibliography*, No. 105).

[309] This was in addition to the schedule of meetings listed in Minutes (1744),
§83. It may be another adaptation from the Moravians whose settlements had an
order of intercessors, who operated on a rota over twenty-four hours and had a
weekly meeting to learn the needs of the congregation. *Journal & Diaries*, 18:256,
n. 11 in this edn. B reverses the two columns on the right.

[310] B, 'should'.

[311] *Advice to the People Called Methodists* was published later this year (see *Bibliography*, No. 108, and vol. 9 of this edn.).

[312] Probably again is intended *A Dialogue between an Antinomian and his Friend*
and its sequel (see §38 above).

[313] Wesley's *Earnest Appeal to Men of Reason and Religion* was published in 1743
(vol. 11 of this edn.); at this point, he had published Part I of the *Farther Appeal* at
the end of 1744 (title page dated 1745); this note may refer to finishing the *Farther
Appeal*, Part III.

[314] *A Farther Appeal to Men of Reason and Religion*, Part II, was published in 1745,
and he finished and published Part III that year also (see *Bibliography*, No. 96 and
vol. 11 of this edn.).

[315] JW was now discussing with his preachers in the Conferences the basic elements of the evangelical faith so that their preaching might be biblical, orthodox,
rational, and practical. He was anxious to illustrate and further unfold this faith publicly in a series of published sermons. He printed *Proposals* for a three-volume set in
Sept. 1745, though they eventually turned out to be four, to which in 1787–88 he
added a further four (see *Bibliography*, Nos. 738, etc., and vols. 1–4 of this edn.).

A. We cannot tell. We will endeavour to hear Mr. E. and K. together.[316]

[§82]   *Q.* 12. Can we unite any farther with those of the Tabernacle?[317]
A. We are ready to receive any that come, if they walk as becomes the gospel.[318]   5

[§83]   *Q.* 13. What books should we keep for our own use at London, Bristol, and Newcastle?[319]

---

[316] Though also raised at the 1744 Conference (Minutes, §87), the question had become still more urgent in view of the Jacobite invasion in 1745 and threat of French invasion. Travelling Methodists were suspect of being Jacobite agents. 'Mr. E.' may be James Erskine of Grange (1679–1754), who was Lord Justice Clerk (1710–34) and M.P. (1734–47). (Cf. correspondence with JW in Mar. 1745, *Letters*, 26:128 in this edn.) A secret Jacobite sympathiser, though also much concerned with religion in an ecumenical spirit (*Journal & Diaries*, 20:68, n. 79 in this edn.), he helped to obtain John Nelson's release from the army and attended the Conference of 1748 (Minutes, §19). 'Mr. K.' may be Abraham Kershaw, a Quaker, who accommodated the Methodists at Skircoat Green near Halifax at this time. *Journal & Diaries*, 20:114 and n. 28 in this edn. The two men would be likely to offer differing views on the use of arms. Methodists like John Haime and his friends served in the army. See his *Life* in Jackson, *Early Methodist Preachers*, 1:269–309.

[317] I.e., Whitefield's followers (cf. 1744, §§90–91).

[318] Phil. 1:27.

[319] In the 1744 Minutes (§84), Wesley had set down for his Assistants' reading a brief list of books, beginning with the classics and ending with a handful of works on practical divinity. Here, in the following year, Wesley expands that list and sets it forth in a much more elaborate and detailed form, along with the stipulation that these works were to form the nucleus for three basic libraries, one in each of his three main centres. On this occasion they were stated to be for JW's own use, but it is clear that they were also intended to stimulate the studies of his preachers. Provisions were made for the further expansion of the list by the inclusion of numbered blank spaces in several classifications. In his Disciplinary *Minutes* (1749), Wesley printed this 1745 catalogue with little change except the omission of those unfilled numbers and of Sir John Davies from the British poets, and Daniel Brevint from the 'Practical Divinity'—the original MS Minutes of 1744 had added 'Brevint', clearly referring to Daniel Brevint (1616–95), whose *Christian Sacrament and Sacrifice* (1673) Wesley abridged for *Hymns on the Lord's Supper* (1745, see *Bibliography*, No. 98 and vol. 8 of this edn.). This work was omitted in the later copies of the 1744 Minutes, however, which JW seems to have used for his 1745 expansion, so that it was also omitted from the printed list of 1749, except that in both it could then be included under the heading 'Our Tracts'. In 1744, Gell's *Works* were noted, but not in 1745, while in 1745, Fell's *Epistles* (absent from 1744) appear, but both are included in 1749: the earlier discrepancies may have been due to a copying error.
   As this list of 1745 is slightly the fuller of the two later ones, as well as the earliest in this form, it seems preferable to concentrate the footnotes documenting Wesley's standard library at this point. Specific edns. are cited when these can be determined from the short titles given, the catalogue of books held in the Kingswood School library, or extant copies of JW's personal library; cf. Randy L.

       A. Those that follow:
       I. Divinity, Practical   (1) The Bible.
                                     (2) Our Tracts.[320]
                                     (3) Abp. Ussher's.[321]
5   (4) Boehm's[322] *Sermons.*
                                     (5) Nalson's.[323]
                                     (6) Francke's *Works.*[324]
                                     (7) Pascal's *Thoughts.*[325]

Maddox, 'Kingswood School Library Holdings (ca. 1775)', *Methodist History* 41 (Oct. 2002): 342–70; 'John Wesley's Reading: Evidence in the Kingswood School Archives', *Methodist History* 41 (Apr. 2003): 49–67; 'John Wesley's Reading: Evidence in the Book Collection at Wesley's House, London', *Methodist History* 41 (July 2003): 118–33; and 'Remnants of John Wesley's Personal Library', *Methodist History* 42 (Apr. 2004): 122–28.

[320] More than five dozen of the tracts that the Wesleys had published up to this point were collected, bound together in fifteen volumes, and sold as *Tracts Publish'd by the Rev. Mr. John and Charles Wesley*, advertised as such in the back pages of the 1746 (third) edn. of *The Farther Appeal to Men of Reason and Religion.* See Frank Baker, *Union Catalog of the Publications of John and Charles Wesley* (Durham, N.C., 1966), 60 (#64B), and Heitzenrater, 'John Wesley's *A Christian Library*, Then and Now', American Theological Library Association, *Proceedings* 55 (June 2001): 133–46.

[321] James Ussher, archbishop of Canterbury (1581–1656), whose name Wesley usually (as here) spelled 'Usher'. JW frequently recommended Ussher's *Twenty Sermons preached at Oxford, before His Majesty, and Elsewhere* (London: Nathaniel Ranew, 1678).

[322] Wilhelm Boehm (1673–1722), *Several Discourses and Tracts for Promoting the Common Interest of True Christianity* (London: J. Downing, 1717). Boehm was a German chaplain to the British Court whose translations into English of Arndt's *True Christianity* and Francke's *Pietas Hallensis* and *Nicodemus* influenced Wesley, as did his sermons. Wesley's signed copy of the 1717 edn. of his *Several Discourses and Tracts* is extant.

[323] Valentine Nalson (1641–1724), *Twenty Sermons on several Subjects; most of them preached in the Cathedral of York* (London: Francis Hildyard, 1724). Extracts from this work appeared in Wesley's *AM* (1791).

[324] August Hermann Francke (1663–1727), whose *Nicodemus; or a Treatise against the Fear of Man* (London: Joseph Downing, 1706) Wesley published (see *Bibliography*, No. 15). His longer work, *Pietas Hallensis; or, A Public Demonstration of the Foot-steps of a Divine Being yet in the World. In an Historical Narration of the Orphan-House and other Charitable Institutions, at Glaucha, near Hall, in Saxony. Continued to the Beginning of the year 1702; and now done out of High-Dutch into English, with a preface bringing it down to the present time; together with a short history of pietism* (Edinburgh: J. Davidson, 1727), was also influential. Francke was one of the leaders at Halle, and it was largely through A. W. Boehm that his works became known to Wesley.

[325] Blaise Pascal (1623–62), *Thoughts upon Religion and Other Subjects*, trans. Basil Kennett (London: A. & J. Churchill, 1704), for whom see *Letters*, 25:270–71 in this edn. Wesley published an extract from this work in vol. 23 of his *Christian Library* (1753).

(8) Beveridge's *Thoughts.*[326]

[Divinity] Doctrinal   (1) Pearson on the *Creed.*[327]

(2) Fell on the *Epistles.*[328]

[(3) Dr. Gell's Works.][329]

II. Physick   (1) Drake's *Anatomy.*[330]   5

(2) Quincy's *Dispensatory.*[331]

(3) Allen's Synopsis.[332]

[326] William Beveridge (1637–1708), *Private Thoughts upon Religion; or, Necessary Directions for its Beginning and Progress upon Earth, in order to its Final Perfection in the Beatific Vision,* 2 vols. (London: R. Smith, 1709–12). Beveridge was bishop of St. Asaph, and an extract from the first part of this work, 'Upon Religion', was published in vol. 47 of Wesley's *Christian Library* (1755).

[327] John Pearson (1613–86), bishop of Chester, whose *An Exposition of the Creed* (London: Williams, 1659) Wesley uses tellingly in his *Farther Appeal to Men of Reason and Religion,* Pt. I, V.23 (11:163–66 in this edn.).

[328] John Fell (1625–86), bishop of Oxford, *A Paraphrase and Annotations upon all the Epistles of St. Paul* (London: R. Smith, 1702), though Fell probably contributed little to this work.

[329] Robert Gell (1595–1665), *Gell's Remains: Select Scriptures of the New Testament Explained,* 2 vols. (London: Nathan Brooke, 1676), to which Wesley paid tribute in his *Explanatory Notes upon the New Testament* (1755). Wesley also read his *Essay towards the Amendment of the last English Translation of the Bible* (1659). Wesley mentioned Gell in the 1744 list, and in that of 1749 (from which the entry here is inserted); it seems likely that a copying error was responsible for its omission in the surviving later copies of the 1745 list.

[330] James Drake, M.D. (1667–1707), *Anthropologia Nova; or, A New System of Anatomy,* 2 vols. (London: Smith & Walford, 1707).

[331] John Quincy, M.D. (d. 1722), *Pharmacopeia officinalis et extemporanea; or, A complete English dispensatory in four parts, containing: I. A theory of pharmacy, and the several processes therein. II. A description of the official simples, with their virtues and preparations, Galenical and chemical. III. The official compositions, according to the last alterations of the College; together with some others of uncommon efficacy, taken from the most celebrated authors. IV. Extemporaneous prescriptions, distributed into classes suitable to their intentions in cure* (London: A. Bell, W. Taylor, & J. Osborn, 1718), which went through many edns., the 14th in 1774.

[332] John Allen (1660?–1741), *Dr. Allen's Synopsis medicinae; or, A Brief and General Collection of the Whole Practice of Physick. Containing the opinions and judgments of the most celebrated authors, concerning diseases, their causes and remedies,* 2 vols. (London: Pemberton & Meadows, 1730), and in 1733 another English translation, this time by the author himself, titled *Synopsis medicinae; or, A summary View of the whole Practice of Physick.* This work was surely an important source of Wesley's *Primitive Physick,* along with Quincy's *Dispensatory* and other works.

	(4) Dr. Cheyne's Works.[333]
III. Natural Philosophy	(1) *Nature Delineated.*[334]
	(2) Miller's *Gardener's Dictionary Abridged.*[335]
IV. Astronomy	(1) Whiston's Astronom[ical]. Principles.[336]
	(2)
	(3)

5

[333] George Cheyne (1671–1743), *The Natural Method of Curing the Diseases of the Body and Disorders of the Mind Depending on the Body* (London: Strahan, 1742). His *Essay of Health and Long Life* exercised a very strong personal influence upon JW from the time that he read it in 1724, the year of its appearance, warmly welcoming its advice about simple and abstemious living. *Letters*, 25:151 in this edn. Both were reflected in JW's *Primitive Physick* (1747, *Bibliography*, No. 138, and vol. 17 of this edn.).

[334] Noël Antoine Pluche (1688–1761), *Nature Delineated: being a new translation of those universally admired philosophical conversations, entitled, Spectacle de la nature,* trans. Daniel Bellamy, 4 vols. (London: J. Hodges, 1739), reaching its 3rd edn. in 1743. This was one of the two major English translations of the famous French work; the other by Samuel Humphreys and Jean Baptist de Freval, *Spectacle de la nature; or, Nature displayed; being discourses on such particulars of natural history as were thought most proper to excite the curiosity and form the minds of youth,* appeared in four vols. in 1733 and then was extended to seven, though Pluche's eighth vol. (on man and God) does not appear to have been translated into English. Wesley seems to have known and used both translations. In the 1745 and 1749 *Minutes* he speaks of *Nature Delineated,* which also is named as one of his sources in the preface to his *Survey of the Wisdom of God in the Creation* (1763); but in a reading list published in his *AM* for 1780 (though written much earlier), he speaks of *Nature Displayed.*

[335] Philip Miller (1691–1771), *The Gardener's Dictionary; containing the methods of cultivating and improving the kitchen, fruit, and flower gardens, as also the physick garden, wilderness conservatory, and vineyard; according to the practices of the most experienced gardeners of the present age . . . and [consideration of] the particular influences of air, earth, fire, and water upon vegetation, according to the best natural philosophies,* 2 vols. (London: Rivington, 1731–39). Abridged from the original *The Gardener's and Florist's Dictionary; or, A Complete System of Horticulture,* 2 vols. (London, 1724), which was published in 1731 as a single folio vol.

[336] William Whiston (1667–1752), *Astronomical Principles of Religion, natural and revealed . . . Together with a preface, of the temper of mind necessary for the discovery of Divine truth, and the degree of evidence that ought to be expected in Divine matters,* 2 vols. (London: Senex & Taylor, 1717). JW was familiar with a number of Whiston's voluminous works and knew him personally (see *Letters,* 25:412 in this edn.).

V. History	(1) *Universal History.*[337]
VI. Poetry	(1) Spenser.[338]
	(2) Sir John Davi[e]s.[339]
	(3) Milton.
	(4) Our hymns and poems. 5
VII. Latin Prose	(1) Sallust.[340]
	(2) Caesar.[341] Cornelius Nepos.[342]
	Velleius Paterculus.[343]
	Littleton's *Dict[ionary].*[344]
	(3) Tully, *Philosophica*, and *De* 10
	Officiis.[345]

[337] Jean Le Clerc (1657–1736), the prolific French writer. Kingswood School still possesses a copy of *A Compendium of Universal History from the beginning of the World to the Reign of Emperor Charles the Great. Written originally in Latin by Monsieur Le Clerc.* Done into English (London, Gillyflower, 1609), initialled and dated by Wesley, 'JW. 1752'. See Maddox, 'Kingswood School Library Holdings (ca. 1775)', 358.

[338] I.e., Edmund Spenser's *Faerie Queene*; see *The Works of Edmund Spenser*, 6 vols. (London: Jacob Tonson, 1715). Both MS copies of the Minutes spell his name 'Spencer', but in the 1749 printed *Minutes*, JW has 'Spenser'.

[339] Sir John Davies (1569–1626), whose *Nosce Teipsum* (1599), on the immortality of the soul, was one of Wesley's favourite poems. This entry was omitted from the 1749 *Minutes*, surely by error, the list giving only '1. Spenser' and '3. Milton'.

[340] *Bellum Catilinarium, et Jugurthinium*, ed. Joseph Wasse (Oxford: Societatis Stationariorum, 1730). In 1749, Wesley published his own edn. of *Caii Sallustii Crispi Bellum Catilinarium et Jugurthinum* ('The Cataline and Jugurthine Wars') for Kingswood School (see *Bibliography*, No. 172).

[341] B omits 'Caesar'. Caius Julius Caesar, *C. Julii Caesaris quae extant omnia*, ed. John Davies (Cambridge: John Owen, 1706).

[342] *Excellentium Imperatorum Vitae*, ed. John Fell (Oxford: Sheldonian Theatre, 1697). In 1749, Wesley published his own edn. for Kingswood School (see *Bibliography*, No. 173).

[343] B, C read, 'Vell. Patera', apparently a mis-copying of 'Vell. Paterc.', but the Roman historian is clearly intended and is given in 1749 as 'Vell. Paterculus'. The reference is to his *Historiae romanae*. A copy of *C. Cornelii Taciti Opera quae extant . . . item Velleius Paterculus*, ed. Justus Lipsius (Antwerp: Balthasar Moret, 1668), is still extant in the Kingswood School Archives.

[344] Adam Littleton (1627–94), *Linguae Latinae liber dictionarius quadripartitus; A Latin Dictionary in Four Parts: I. An English-Latine, II. A Latine-classical, III. A Latine-proper, IV. A Latine-barbarous: wherein the Latine and English are adjusted, with what care might be, both as to stock of words and proprieties of speech* (London: Basset, Wright, & Chiswell, 1678).

[345] Marcus Tullius Cicero (106–43 B.C.), *M. Tullii Ciceronis philosophicorum* (Amsterdam: John Blaeu, 1649). Kingswood School library holds Wesley's annotated copy of the second vol. of this work. JW especially valued and quoted Cicero's *De Natura Deorum, De Divinatione*, and *De Officiis.*

5   (4) Cypriani *Opera*.[346]
                                     (5) Castellio's *Dialogues*.[347]
                                     (6) Erasmi *Selecta*.[348]
                                     (7) Austin's[349] *Confessions*.
                                     (8)
              Latin Verse   (1) Terence.
                                     (2) Virgil.
                                     (3)
                                     (4) Selecta Horatii, Juv[enal],
10   Pers[ius], Mart[ial].[350]
                                     (5) Vida.[351]

[346] *Sancti Caecilii Cypriani Opera*, ed. John Fell, 2 vols. (Oxford: Sheldonian Theatre, 1682). For Cyprian's *Works*, see Wesley's letter to a Roman Catholic priest (and the notes on it) in 25:428–30 in this edn.

[347] Sebastian Castellio or Castalio (1515–63), whose edn. of the *Imitatio Christi* Wesley used at Kingswood School, as well as his *Dialogorum sacrorum libri IV: De Praedestinatione, electione, libero arbitrio, fide*, of which the school library still possesses the Edinburgh edn. of 1734, with JW's MS alterations preparing it for publication in the *AM* 4–5 (1781–82).

[348] Desiderius Erasmus (1467–1536), *Colloquiorum Familiarum Opus Aureum* (1524), in many edns. Select dialogues from this work were read in Latin, turned into English, and learned by heart at Kingswood School. See *Colloquiorum, cum notis selectis variorum*, ed. Pieter Schrijver (Leiden: Samuel Luchtmans, 1729), which is in the school library.

[349] 'Austin' was familiarly used by JW (as by others) for St. Augustine of Hippo (354–430), whose *Confessions* was one of his favourite works, frequently quoted both in Latin and in English. *D. Aurelii Augustini Hippon episcopi, Libri XIII Confessionum* (Cologne: Cornelius Egmend, 1647) remains in the library at Wesley's house, London.

[350] B reads, 'Selecta Horatii, Juv., Pers., etc.' It is almost certain that this implied the *Selecta poemata Italorum qui Latine scripserunt: Curâ cujusdam anonymi anno 1684 congesta, iterum in lucem data, unà cum aliorum Italorum operibus*, ed. Alexander Pope and Francis Atterbury, 2 vols. (London: J. & P. Knapton, 1740), which appears on Bailey's Kingswood School List, No. 293. It is clearly distinct from the later selections that JW published, titled *Excerpta ex Ovidio, Virgilio, Horatio, Juvenali, Persio, et Martiali: in usum juventutis Christianae* (Bristol, 1749; see *Bibliography*, No. 174).

[351] Marcus Hieronymus Vida (1480–1566), *Marci Hieronymi Vidae, Cremonensis, Albae Episcopi, Poematum, quae haud plane disjunxit a fabula*, ed. Thomas Tristram (Oxford: Clarendon, 1722). Although the list of subscribers to that edn. contains the entry, 'John Westley, A.B., Stud. of Ch.Ch.Oxon.', this person was a colleague of Wesley who was a native of Oxford and three years older than he. 'Our' John Wesley did read Vida's *De Arte Poetica* (contained in the above work) in Dec. 1725.

(6) Casimir.[352]

(7) Buchanan.[353]

(8)

(9)

VIII. Greek Prose[354]   (1) Greek Test[ament], Hederici   5
Lexicon.[355]

(2) Plato's Select Dialogues.[356]

(3) Xenophon's *Cyropoedia.*

(4) Epictetus.

(5) Antoninus, de se ipso.[357]   10

(6) Ignatius, etc.[358]

(7) Ephraim Syrus.[359]

---

[352] Casimir Sarbiewski, or Matthias Sarbievius, or Maciej Kazimierz Sarbiewski (1595–1640), a Polish Latin poet (referred to as 'Mathias Casimir' in the 18th century), *Lyricorium Libri IV: epodon lib unus alterque epigrammatum* (Antwerp: Balthasar Moret, 1632), and published in Cambridge in 1684; his *Odes* were translated into English and published in London by 1642. Wesley's *Collection of Moral and Sacred Poems*, 3 vols. (1744), 1:212–13, includes one of his Latin epigrams translated into English by Isaac Watts.

[353] George Buchanan (1506–82), *Poemata quae extant* (Leiden: Elzevir, 1628).

[354] B, 'Verse', an obvious error.

[355] Benjamin Hedericus or Hederich (1675–1748), *Lexicon manuale Graecum* (Leipzig: Gleditsch, 1722), ed. S. Patrick (London: Knaplock, 1727; 2nd edn., 1739). From 1778 onwards the title became *Graecum lexicon Manuale*.

[356] *Platonis De rebus divinis dialogi selecti Graece & Latine*, ed. John North (Cambridge: John Hayes, 1673).

[357] The emperor Marcus Aurelius Antoninus (121–80), whose *Meditations* (*De se ipso*) have proved his best memorial, frequently published in many languages. The Kingswood School library contains an edn. of *Marci Antonini imperatoris eorum quae ad seipsum libri XII* (Glasgow: Foulis, 1744), initialed by Wesley, 'JW. 1748'. This book contains the text in alternating Latin and Greek.

[358] St. Ignatius (c. 35–c. 107), whose *Epistles* Wesley placed in vol. 1 of his *Christian Library*, 1749 (see vol. 14 of this edn.).

[359] Ephraim Syrus (c. 306–73), Syrian biblical exegete, verse writer, and controversialist; *S. Ephraim Syrus, Graece. E. codicibus manuscriptis Bodleianis* (Oxford: Sheldonian Theatre, 1709). See JW's quotation from this vol. in his *Journal*, May 21, 1761 (21:322–25 in this edn.). JW read his *Serious Exhortation to Repentance*, etc. (London: Bowyer, 1731) in Georgia, and in 1747 stated his admiration for Ephraim's picture of 'a broken and contrite heart' (*Journal & Diaries* III, 20:162 in this edn.). Outler has argued that the injection of Eastern Christian ideas of perfection as a process rather than a state influenced Wesley's distinctive view of the doctrine. A. C. Outler, *John Wesley* (New York: Oxford University Press, 1964), 9f. Ephraim Syrus and Macarius (see next n.) are major examples of this source.

	(8) Macarius,[360] Chrysost.de Sacerd[otio].[361]
Greek Verse	(1) Homer's Iliad.
	(2) *Epigrammatum Delectus.*[362]
	(3) Duport's Job, etc.[363]
	(4)
IX. Hebrew	(1) The Bible. Buxtorf.[364]

[§84] *Q.* 14. When shall we meet here again?
A. In January next, if God permit.[365]

10 The Bristol Conference of May 12–15, 1746

Monday, May 12th, 1746[366]

[360] St. Macarius of Egypt (c. 300–390), whose *Homilies* JW also included in vol. 1 of the *Christian Library*, based on the translation by John Haywood (1600?–63), published as *Primitive Morality: or, The Spiritual Homilies of St. Macarius the Egyptian* (London: Taylor, 1721). For his identity, see Outler, *John Wesley*, 9 n. 26.

[361] St. John Chrysostom (c. 347–407), *De Sacerdotio* ('On the Priesthood'), ed. Styan Thirlby (Cambridge: Edmund Jeffery, 1712).

[362] *Epigrammatum Delectus ex omnibus tum veteribus tum recentioribus Poetis; cum Dissertatione de vera Pulchritudine et adumbrata*, ed. C. Lancelot, with the closing essay on beauty by P. Nicole (Paris, 1659). From 1686 onwards, the English edns. were described as 'in usum Scholae Etonensis' ('for the use of Eton School').

[363] James Duport (1606–79), ΘΡΗΝΟΘΡΊΑΜΒΟΣ, *sive Liber Job Graeco carmine redditus*, in Greek and Latin (Cambridge, 1637), which secured fame for Duport and a secure place for the work in classical education for generations. Duport also published translations into Greek verse of Prov., Eccl., and Song (1646), and of the Pss. (1666), which are probably included in Wesley's 'etc'.

[364] John Buxtorf (1564–1629), among whose many works on the Hebrew Bible Wesley probably intends his *Lexicon Hebraicum et Chaldaicum* (Basil, 1607), of which numerous edns. were published before 1735. Also in Cornelius Bayley's list of the Kingswood School library (1789), however, are his *Thesaurus Grammaticus Linguae Sanctae Hebraeae* (1609) and his *Manuale Hebraicum et Chaldaicum* (1619), or *A Short Introduction to the Hebrew Tongue* (London: H. Moseley, 1656).

[365] This note seems to reflect a continuing intention to meet more frequently than once a year; see Minutes (1744), §96 and n. 250. In fact the next Conference was not until May 1746, and thereafter Conference becomes an annual event, though with additional and regional meetings in some years.

[366] Two MS copies of the 1746 Minutes survive, each apparently transcribed independently of the other. They are here given in the probable chronological order of transcription.

[§1] The following persons being met at the New Room in
      Bristol, John Wesley, Charles Wesley, John Hodges,
      Jonathan Reeves, Thos. Maxfield, Thos. Westell, and[367]
      Thos. Willis,[368] it was inquired:

[§2] *Q.* 1. Who are the properest persons to be present at our   5
      conferences?[369]

      A. (1) As many of the preachers as conveniently can
      come;[370] (2) the most earnest and most sensible of the
      band-leaders where the conference is; and (3) any pious
      and judicious stranger who may occasionally be[371] in the   10
      place.

D. In the MA, in an unidentified hand, somewhat rougher and less sophisti-
cated than the following E both in orthography and in expression, which leads to
the hypothesis that D is probably more faithful to a less polished original, later
revised. For instance, in §16, D has 'that', E 'who'; and in §18, D has 'of it', E
'thereof'. There are many similar variants, as well as the inclusion of brief paragraphs run together in E—for example, §§35–36, 45, 47, and so on. This document may well have been transcribed about 1746–47, omitting the outdated
§§67–68, which were retained from the original by E. A pencil note suggests that
the scribe was Thomas Maxfield, but Thomas Williams (who also was present at
the Conference) seems more likely. No indisputable MS is so far available to settle this question.

E. In an unidentified hand, found in the notebook in Wesley College, Bristol,
used by Wesley, beginning with the 'A' copy of 1744 and continuing with the 'C'
copy of 1745, though this time without numbering of the pages or any MS alterations by Wesley. It appears to incorporate several minor revisions in the text of
the original Minutes, revisions that were followed by the *Minutes* printed in 1749.
It was probably transcribed about 1747–48.

[367] D sets out the names in two columns, containing the first three (clergy) and
the last four (laymen), and omitting the 'and' found in D's paragraph form.

[368] D, 'Williams'. It is just possible that *both* men were present, for they seem to
have been two different entities, though Williams is the better known (cf. §67).
Willis was probably a Bristol layman who appears in Wesley's diary, and his presence may have suggested the need for *Q.* 1 on persons to invite. John S. Simon,
John Wesley and the Methodist Societies (London, 1923), 323. Myles, *Chronological
History*, 45, says that Band leaders and strangers were invited only as spectators
and that in a few years only preachers were permitted to attend. This appears to be
incorrect, however; see introduction, pp. 14, 25–26 above.

[369] D, '. . . present at any our conferences'; E, '. . . at any conference of this nature'.

[370] D omits 'can', E, 'come'.

[371] E, 'be occasionally'.

[§3]   *Q.* 2. Might it not be well[372] to read over one or more of our
tracts at each conference?

A. Doubtless it might; were it only to correct what is amiss,
or[373] explain what is obscure in each.

5   [§4]   *Q.* 3. Which shall we read over now?[374]

A. The New England *Narrative*, and the *Distinguishing
Marks of a Work of the Spirit of God* (which were read).[375]

[§5]   *Q.* 4. Would it not be proper to send one of these to each
bishop?[376]

10   *A.* Let them be sent as soon as possible.

Tuesday, May 13th,

[§6]   The same persons being present, it was inquired:

Q. 1. Can any unbeliever (whatsoever[377] he be in other
15   respects) challenge anything of God's justice?

A. Absolutely nothing but hell. And this is a point which
we cannot too much insist on.

[§7]   *Q.* 2. Do we empty men of their own righteousness, as we
did at first? Do we sufficiently labour, when they begin to
20   be convinced of sin, to take away all they lean on?[378]
Should we not then endeavour with all our might to over-
turn their false foundations?

A. This was at first one of our principal points, and it ought
to be so still, for till all other foundations are overturned,
25   they cannot build upon Christ.

[§8]   *Q.* 3. Did we not then purposely throw them into convic-
tions? Into strong sorrow and fear? Nay, did we not strive
to make them inconsolable? Refusing to be comforted?

A. We did, and so we should do still. For the stronger the
30   conviction, the speedier is the deliverance. And none so

---

[372] D, 'be well for us', with 'or useful' written over the line, apparently as a possible alternative for 'well'; E, 'be useful'.

[373] E, 'and'.

[374] E omits 'over'.

[375] See Minutes (1744), §86; D omits '*a Work of* '.

[376] E, '. . . send these to each of the bishops'.

[377] E, 'whatever'.

[378] E, 'upon'.

soon receive the peace of God as those who steadily refuse all other comforts.[379]

[§9] *Q.* 4. Let us consider a particular case. Was *you*, Jonathan Reeves, before you received the peace of God, convinced that, notwithstanding all you did or could do, you was in a 5 state of damnation?

A. Jonathan Reeves. I was as fully convinced of it as that I now live.[380]

[§10] *Q.* 5. Are you sure that conviction was from God?

A. Jonathan Reeves. I have[381] no doubt but it was.   10

[§11] *Q.* 6. What do you mean by a state of damnation?

A. Jonathan Reeves. A state wherein if a man dies he perishes for ever.

[§12] *Q.* 7. How did that conviction end?

A. Jonathan Reeves. I had first a strong hope that God would 15 deliver me, and this brought a degree of peace. But I had not that solid peace of God till Christ was revealed in me.

[§13] *Q.* 8. But is not such a trust in the love of God, though it be as yet without a distinct sight of God reconciled through Christ Jesus, a low degree of justifying faith?   20

A. Perhaps it is.[382] But this abides for a short time only; nor is this the proper Christian faith.

[§14] *Q.* 9. By what faith were the apostles clean before Christ died?[383]

A. By such a faith as this, by a Jewish faith, for the Holy Ghost was not then given.[384]   25

[§15] *Q.* 10. Of whom then do you understand those words (Isa. 50:10): 'Who is there among you that feareth the Lord? That obeyeth the voice of his servant, that walketh in darkness and hath no light?'

A. Of a believer under the Jewish dispensation, one in 30 whose heart God hath not yet shined to give him the light of the glorious love of God in the face of Christ Jesus.[385]

---

[379] E, 'comfort'.

[380] E, 'I was convinced of it, as fully as that I am now alive'.

[381] E, 'I can have'.

[382] D, 'Perhaps it may', with 'or is' added over 'may'.

[383] D, 'By what faith was the apostles [a blank space] before Christ died?'

[384] Cf. John 7:39.

[385] See 2 Cor. 4:6; E, 'Jesus Christ'.

[§16]   *Q.* 11. Who is a Jew inwardly?

A. A servant of God, one who sincerely obeys him out of fear. Whereas a Christian (one inwardly)[386] is a child of God, one that[387] sincerely obeys him out of love.

5 [§17]   *Q.* 12. But was you not *sincere* before Christ was revealed in you?

A. Jonathan Reeves. It seemed to me that I was in some measure.

[§18]   *Q.* 13. What is sincerity?

10   *A.* Willingness to know and do the will of God. The lowest species of it[388] seems to be faithfulness in that which is little.[389]

[§19]   *Q.* 14. Has God any regard to man's sincerity?

A. So far that no man in any estate[390] can possibly be

15   accepted[391] without it, neither indeed in any moment when[392] he is not sincere.

[§20]   *Q.* 15. But can it be conceived that God has any regard to the sincerity of an unbeliever?

A. Yes; so much that if he persevere therein, God will infal-

20   libly give him faith.

[§21]   *Q.* 16. What regard may we conceive him to have to the sincerity of a believer?

A. So much, that in every sincere believer he fulfils all the great and precious promises.

25 [§22]   *Q.* 17. Whom do you term a 'sincere believer'?

A. One that walks in the light as God is in the light.

[§23]   *Q.* 18.[393] Is sincerity the same with a 'single eye'?[394]

A. Not altogether. The latter refers to our present intention,[395] the former to our will or design.[396]

---

[386] E, omits 'one'. See Rom. 2:29.

[387] E, 'who'.

[388] E, 'thereof'.

[389] See Luke 19:17.

[390] E, 'state'.

[391] E, 'excepted'.

[392] E, 'wherein'.

[393] E, '19'.

[394] Matt. 6:22; Luke 11:34.

[395] E, 'our intention'.

[396] E, 'desires'.

[§24]   *Q.* 19. Is it not all in all?

    A. All will follow persevering sincerity. God gives every-thing with it, nothing without it.

[§25]   *Q.* 20. Are not then sincerity and faith equivalent terms?

    A. By no means. It is at least as nearly related to works as it   5
is to faith. For example, Who is sincere before he believes?
He that then does all he can: he that according to the
power he has received brings forth 'works meet for repentance'.[397] Who is sincere after he believes? He that, from a
sense of God's love, is zealous of all good works.   10

[§26]   *Q.* 21. Is not sincerity what St. Paul terms a willing mind?
ἡ προθυμία (2 Cor. 8:12).

    A. Yes, if that word be taken in a general sense, for it is a
constant disposition to use all the grace given.

[§27]   *Q.* 22. But do we not then set sincerity on a level with faith?   15

    A. No; for we allow a man may be sincere and not be
accepted, as a man[398] may be penitent and not be accepted
(not as yet), but cannot have faith and not be accepted.
The very moment he believes, he is justified.

[§28]   *Q.* 23. But do we not give up faith and put sincerity in its   20
place as the condition of our acceptance with God?

    A. We believe it is *one* condition of our acceptance, as
repentance likewise is. And we believe it a condition of
our continuing in a state of acceptance. Yet we do not put
it in the place of faith. It is by faith the merits of Christ   25
are applied to my soul; but if I am not sincere, they are
not applied.

[§29]   *Q.* 24. Is not this that 'going about to establish your own
righteousness' whereof St. Paul speaks (Rom. 10:3)?[399]

    A. St. Paul speaks there manifestly[400] of unbelievers who   30
sought to be accepted for the sake of their own righteousness. We do not seek to be accepted for the sake of our
sincerity, but through the merits of Christ alone. Indeed
so long as any man believes, he cannot go about (in St.
Paul's sense) to 'establish his own righteousness'.   35

[397] Acts 26:20.
[398] E, 'he'.
[399] Orig., 'Rom. x: 4'.
[400] E, 'St. Paul there manifestly speaks'.

[§30]   *Q.* 25. But do you consider that we are under the covenant of grace? And that the covenant of works is now
abolished?

A. All mankind were under the covenant of grace from the
very hour that the original promise was made. If by the[401]
covenant of works you mean that of[402] unsinning obedience made with Adam before the fall, no man but Adam
was ever under that covenant; for it was abolished before
Cain was born. Yet it is not so abolished but that it will
stand, in some[403] measure, even to the end of the world;
i.e., if we 'do this',[404] we shall live; if not, we shall die eternally. If we do well, we shall live with God in glory; if evil,
we shall die the second death. For every man shall be
judged in that day and shall be[405] rewarded according to
his works.[406]

[§31]   *Q.* 26. What means then, 'To him that believeth his faith is
counted for righteousness?'[407]

A. That God forgives him that is unrighteous as soon as he
believes, accepting his faith instead of perfect righteousness. But then, observe, universal righteousness follows,
though it did not precede, faith.

[§32]   *Q.* 27. But is faith thus 'counted to us for righteousness'[408]
at whatsoever time we believe?

A. Yes; in whatsoever moment we believe, all our past sins
vanish away. They are as though they had never been, and
we stand clear in the sight of God.

Tuesday, 10 o'clock,

[§33]   Mr. Taylor, of Quinton,[409] being added, it was inquired:

Q. 1. Are not the assurance of faith, the inspiration of the
Holy Ghost, and revelation of Christ in us, terms nearly
of the same import?

---

[401] E, 'that'.
[402] D omits 'of', surely a scribal error.
[403] E, 'a'.
[404] Cf. Gen. 42:18 and so on, and esp. Luke 10:28; 22:19.
[405] E omits 'shall be'.
[406] Matt. 16:27 and so on.
[407] Rom. 4:5.
[408] Ibid.
[409] See above, p. 124, §1, n. 28.

A. He that denies one of them must deny all, they are so closely connected together.

[§34] *Q.* 2. Are they ordinarily (where the pure gospel is preached) essential to our acceptance with God?[410]

A. Undoubtedly they are, and as such to be insisted on in the strongest terms.

[§35] *Q.* 3. Is not the whole dispute of salvation by faith or works[411] a mere 'strife of words'?[412]

A. In asserting salvation by faith we mean this:

(1) That pardon (salvation begun) is received by faith producing works.

(2) That holiness (salvation continued) is faith working by love.

(3) That heaven (salvation finished) is the reward of this faith.

If[413] you, who assert salvation by works, or by faith and works, mean the same thing (understanding by faith the revelation of Christ in us, by salvation, pardon, holiness, glory), we will not strive with you at all. If you do not, this is not a 'strife of words', but the very vitals—the essence of Christianity is the thing in question.

[§36] *Q.* 4. Wherein does our doctrine now differ from that we preached when at Oxford?

A. Chiefly in these two points:

(1) We then knew nothing of that[414] righteousness of faith in justification; nor

(2) Of the nature of faith itself as implying consciousness of pardon.[415]

[§37] *Q.* 5. May not some degree of the love[416] of God go before a distinct sense of justification?

A. We believe there may.[417]

---

[410] E omits 'with God'.

[411] E, 'by works'.

[412] See Minutes (1745), §12, *Q.* 3.

[413] E runs the preceding three points into one paragraph, but (like D) begins a new paragraph here.

[414] E, 'the'.

[415] E sets out the whole answer as one paragraph.

[416] E, 'of love'.

[417] E, 'it may'.

[§38]   *Q.* 6. Can any degree of sanctification or holiness?
       A. Many degrees of outward holiness may. Yea, and some of
       meekness, and several other tempers which would be
       branches[418] of Christian holiness, but that they do not
5   spring from Christian principles. For the abiding love of
       God cannot spring but from faith in a pardoning God.
       And no true Christian holiness can exist without the[419]
       love of God for its foundation.

[§39]   *Q.* 7. Is every man as soon as he believes a new creature,
10   sanctified, born again, pure in heart? Has he then a new
       heart? Does Christ dwell therein? And is he a temple of
       the Holy Ghost?
       A. All these[420] things may be affirmed of a[421] believer, in a
       low sense. Let us not therefore contradict those who
15   affirm[422] it. Why should we contend about words?

[§40]   **On Wednesday 14ᵗʰ**
       were considered points relating to Discipline.
       Q. 1. When a pastor of any[423] congregation dies, who has
20   the right of choosing another?
       A. Without all doubt, the congregation itself, whom no
       man can feed or guide without their consent.[424]

[§41]   *Q.* 2. What is the scriptural notion of an apostle?
       A. One who is sent of God to convert heathens.

25 [§42]   *Q.* 3. How many apostles were there in the[425] first church?

---

[418] D, 'would of', surely a scribal error.

[419] E, 'that'.

[420] E, 'Those'.

[421] E, 'every'.

[422] E, 'maintain'.

[423] E, 'a'.

[424] JW derived this view from a tract sent to him by Ralph Erskine of the Associate Presbytery (which had broken from the Church of Scotland). See JW's letter to Erskine, June 26, 1740, 26:16 in this edn. The tract is a remarkable piece of 'congregationalism' for JW at this date. In Jan. 1746, reading Lord King's *Inquiry* seems to have converted him to the view that 'bishops and presbyters are (essentially) of one order and that originally every Christian congregation was a church independent on all others.' *Journal & Diaries*, 20:112 in this edn.; see also Minutes (1745), §56. Yet this 'congregationalism' hardly reflects the principles and practice of JW in his treatment of Methodism, presumably because he considered it a 'society' (organised by himself) and not a 'church'.

[425] D adds an indecipherable word here.

A. A great number beside those twelve who were eminently
so called. Thus St. Paul, speaking of our Lord after his
resurrection, saith, He was seen of Cephas, then of the
twelve, after that of above five hundred brethren at once,
then of all the apostles (1 Cor. 15:[5–6]). 5

[§43] *Q.* 4. What is the New Testament notion of a prophet?
A. A builder[426] of the faithful.

[§44] *Q.* 5. In what view are we and our Helpers[427] to be considered?
A. Perhaps as extraordinary messengers, designed of God
to provoke others[428] to jealousy. 10

[§45] *Q.* 6. Do you not insensibly slide[429] into taking state upon
yourselves? Or lording it over God's heritage?
A. (1) We are not conscious to ourselves that we do.
(2) But there is a continual danger.
Therefore, (3) we cannot be too jealous lest we should. And 15
(4) we will thank anyone that shall[430] warn us against it.[431]

[§46] *Q.* 7. How shall we be more easy of access?
A. Let any speak to us after preaching, morning or evening.

[§47] *Q.* 8. How shall we try those who believe they are moved by
the Holy Ghost and called of God to preach? 20
A. Inquire (1) Do they know in whom they have believed?
Have they the love of God in their hearts? Do they desire
to[432] seek nothing but God? And are they holy in all manner of conversation?
(2) Have they *gifts* (as well as *grace*) for the work? Have 25
they (in some tolerable degree) a clear sound *understanding*? Have they a right judgment in the things of God?
Have they a just conception of *salvation by faith*? And
has God given them any degree of *utterance*? Do they
speak justly, readily, clearly? 30

---

[426] E, 'builder up'.

[427] 'Helper' here still has the same meaning as the 'Assistant' described in the
Minutes (1744), §§71–73; see also §§48 and 66 below. Though 'Assistant' is syn-
onymous with 'Helper' at this point, some will come to be 'employed more than the
rest' and will be listed as 'Assistants' for the stations. For the later distinction
between 'Assistants' and 'Helpers', see p. 809, n. 83.

[428] E, 'the others'.

[429] E, 'slide insensibly'.

[430] E, 'any who'.

[431] E sets out the answer without paragraphs.

[432] E, 'and'.

(3) Have they success? Do they not only so speak as generally either to convince or affect the hearts? But have any received remission of sins under[433] their preaching? A clear and lasting sense of the love of God?

5   As long as these three marks undeniably concur in any, we *allow* him to be called[434] to preach. These we receive as sufficient reasonable evidence that he is moved[435] by the Holy Ghost.[436]

[§48] *Q.* 9. But how shall we know, in the case of a particular per-
10   son, whether there is this evidence or no?

    A. (1) We will send one of our Helpers to hear him preach, and to talk with him on the preceding heads.

    (2) We will hear him preach, and talk with him ourselves.

15   (3) We will examine thoroughly those who think they have received remission of sins by his preaching.

    (4) We will desire him to relate or to write down the reasons[437] why he believes he is called of God to preach.

    (5) We will desire the congregation to join with us in
20   fasting and prayer, that we may judge and act according to God's will.[438]

[§49] *Q.* 10. Should we not use the same method of fasting and prayer on other occasions also?

    A. Without doubt we should use it:
25   (1) At the receiving any fellow-labourer into our Lord's vineyard;

    (2) At going ourselves, or sending any, to a new place;

    (3) Before publishing any new book.[439]

[§50] *Q.* 11. Why do we not use more form and solemnity in
30   receiving a new labourer?

    A. We purposely decline it:

    (1) Because there is something of stateliness in it, whereas we would be little and inconsiderable;

---

[433] E, 'by'.

[434] E, 'called of God'.

[435] E, 'moved thereto'.

[436] E sets out the answers without paragraphs.

[437] E, 'reason'.

[438] E, 'to the will of God'. E sets the paragraphs out as one paragraph.

[439] E, 'any book'. E introduces no paragraphing in the answer.

(2) Because we would not make haste. We desire barely
to follow Providence, as it gradually opens to us.[440]

[§51] *Q.* 12. Are there any of our Assistants whom we might
employ more than the rest? In what instances?

A. There are. We may employ Jonathan Reeves, John   5
Bennet, and John Haughton.

(1) In visiting the classes in[441] each place.

(2) In writing lists of the Society[442] and bands there. And

(3) In delivering new tickets where we cannot do it
ourselves.[443]   10

[§52] *Q.* 13. Is there any prudential help for greater watchfulness
and recollection which our Assistants might use?

A. We believe it would be an inconceivable help if they kept
a journal of every hour. The manner of doing it they may
learn in a few minutes by looking at one of our[444] journals   15
we kept at Oxford.

[§53] *Q.* 14. In what light should your Assistants consider
themselves?

A. As learners rather than teachers; as young students at
the university, for whom therefore a method of study is   20
expedient in the highest degree.

[§54] *Q.* 15. What method would you advise them to?

A. We would advise them:

(1) Always to rise at 4 o'clock in the morning.[445]

(2) From 4 to 5 in the morning, and from 5 to 6 in the   25
evening, partly to use meditation and private prayer,

---

[440] E sets out the answer as one paragraph, and omits 'to us'. For the procedures
for reception of preachers and cases of quasi-ordination of them long before JW's
ordinations beginning in 1784, see introduction, p. 77.

[441] E, 'at'.

[442] E, 'societies'.

[443] E has no paragraphing. Tickets were first given to Band members at Bristol
in 1741 as part of the process of purging the membership there (*Journal & Diaries*,
19:183–84 and n. 29 in this edn.) The first surviving tickets date from 1742 and
often have pictorial designs. From at least 1750, and probably earlier, the Band tickets are distinguished from Class tickets (first mentioned in 1749) by adding the letter 'B' to the serial letter. The quarterly tickets were distinguished by date and a
different text each quarter and from 1750 by a different serial letter. See Baker,
'Polity', 224; J. H. Verney in *WHS* 31 (1957): 2, 34, 90, with illus. At the 1765 Conference, it was suggested that a uniform pattern be adopted following a 'form' sent
from London (*Minutes, Q.* 21, n. 39).

[444] E, 'the'.

[445] E, 'at 4'. E introduces no paragraphing.

partly to read the Scripture (two or three verses, or one
or two chapters), partly some close practical book of
divinity, in particular *The Life of God in the Soul of
Man*,[446] Kempis, *Christian's Pattern*,[447] *The Pilgrim's*
5   *Progress*,[448] Mr. Law's Tracts,[449] Beveridge's *Private
Thoughts*,[450] Heylyn's *Devotional Tracts*,[451] *The Life of Mr.
Halyburton*,[452] and Monsieur De Renty.[453]
(3) From 6 in the morning (allowing one hour for break-
fast) to 12, to read in order slowly, and with much prayer,
10   Bp. Pearson on the *Creed*, Bp. Fell on the *Epistles*, Mr.
Boehm's and Mr. Nalson's *Sermons*, Mr. Pascal's
Thoughts,[454] our other tracts and poems, Milton's
Paradise Lost,[455] Cave[456] and Fleury's[457] *Primitive
Christianity*, and Mr. Echard's *Ecclesiastical History*.[458]

15 [§55] *Q.* 16. Have we in anything altered our manner of preaching for the worse since we set out?
A. Perhaps we do not preach so much concerning the blood
of atonement as we did at first.

   [§56] *Q.* 17. What inconvenience is there in speaking much of the
20   wrath and little of the love of God?

[446] By Henry Scougal (1650–78), of which JW had published an abridgement in
1744 (see *Bibliography*, No. 93).

[447] JW's extract of the *Imitatio Christi* in English was published in 1741 (see *Bibliography*, No. 45, and vol. 14 of this edn.).

[448] JW published an abridgement of Bunyan's work in 1743 (see *Bibliography*, No. 79).

[449] JW published Law's *Christian Perfection* in 1743 (*Bibliography*, No. 77), and his *Serious Call* in 1744 (*Bibliography*, No. 86).

[450] Cf. Minutes (1745), §83, I. (8).

[451] John Heylyn (1685?–1759), *Devotional Tracts concerning the Presence of God, and other Religious Subjects. Translated from the French* (London: Downing, 1724), which included Brother Lawrence's *Practice of the Presence of God*, and Fenelon's *Select Letters and Discourses.* JW spells his name 'Heylin'.

[452] JW published an extract of this work in 1739 (see *Bibliography*, No. 12).

[453] JW published an extract of this work in 1741 (see *Bibliography*, No. 43).

[454] For all these, see Minutes (1745), §83, I. Both MSS give 'Nelson', but 'Nalson' is clearly intended.

[455] Ibid., §83, VI.

[456] William Cave (1637–1713), *Primitive Christianity*, 1672, an important influence on Wesley's *General Rules*.

[457] Abbé Claude Fleury (1640–1723), *The Manners of the Ancient Christians*, of which JW published an abridgement in 1749 (see *Bibliography*, No. 157).

[458] Laurence Echard (1670?–1730), *A General Ecclesiastical History*, 1702.

A. It generally hardens them that believe not, and discourages them that do believe.[459]

[§57] *Q.* 18. What sermons do we find by experience to be attended with the greatest blessing?

A. (1) Such as are most close,[460] convincing, and practical.   5
(2) Such as have most of Christ the Priest, the atonement.
(3) Such as urge the heinousness of men's living in contempt of or ignorance of him.[461]

[§58] *Q.* 19. Should we preach in Moorfields?   10

A. It is not clear to us that we should, as we have a more convenient place which contains as many as can hear.[462]

[§59]   **Thursday, May 15th**

Q. 1. What is a sufficient call of providence to a new place,   15
suppose Edinburgh or Dublin?

A.(1)[463] An invitation from someone that is worthy, from a serious man, fearing God, who has a house to receive us.
(2) A probability of doing more good by going thither than by staying longer where we are.   20

[§60] *Q.* 2. Ought we not diligently to observe in what place[464] God is pleased to pour out his spirit more abundantly?

A. We ought, and[465] at that time to send more labourers than usual into that part of the harvest, as at this time into Yorkshire and the country round about Coleford.   25

[§61] *Q.* 3. How shall[466] we add a proper solemnity to the admission of new members into the bands or the United Society?

A.(1) Admit new members into the bands at London, Bristol, and Newcastle, only once a quarter at the general   30
love-feast.
(2) Read the names of the men to be admitted on the Wednesday, of the women on the Sunday, before.

---

[459] E omits 'believe'.
[460] D omits 'close'.
[461] E, 'men living . . . contempt or . . .', and without paragraphing.
[462] I.e., the Foundery.
[463] No division into two numbered paragraphs in E.
[464] E, 'places'.
[465] D omits 'and', probably in error.
[466] D, 'or can' added over 'shall'; E, 'can'.

(3) Admit into the Society only on the Thursday or Sunday following the quarterly visitation of the classes.

(4) Read the names of those to be admitted on the Tuesday and Thursday or Sunday evening before.

(5) The first time that anyone (on trial) meets a class, let the *Rules* of the Society be given him.

(6) And let them be publicly read on the Thursday or Sunday after every admission of new members.

(7) Then also let the names of those[467] be read who are excluded from the Society.[468]

[§62]   *Q*. 4. How shall we guard more effectually against formality in public singing?

A.(1) By the careful choice of hymns proper for the congregation.

(2) In general try by[469] choosing hymns of praise or prayer, rather than descriptive of particular states.

(3) By not singing too much together;[470] seldom a whole hymn at one time,[471] seldom more than five or six verses at once.[472]

(4) By suiting the tunes to them;[473]

(5) By stopping short often,[474] and asking the people, 'Now do you know what you said last? Did it suit your case? Did you sing it as to God with the spirit and with the understanding also?'[475]

[§63]   *Q*. 5. Should we insist more on people's going to Church? Shall we set them the example at Bristol?

A. We will make a trial of the effect of it, by going to St. James's every Wednesday and Friday.

[§64]   *Q*. 6. How shall we be more recollected[476] and more useful in conversation?

---

[467] D, 'these'.

[468] E has no new paragraphs; D none for §§4–7.

[469] D omits 'try by', apparently in error.

[470] E, 'too much'.

[471] E, 'once'.

[472] E, 'at a time'.

[473] E, 'the tune to the hymns'.

[474] E, 'By often stopping short'.

[475] 1 Cor. 14:15.

[476] D, 'collected' (i.e., 'composed', 'calm', [*OED*]).

A. (1) Plan every conversation before you begin. (2) Watch and pray during the time, that your mind be not dissipated. (3) Spend two or three minutes in every hour in prayer.[477] (4) Strictly observe morning and evening hour of retirement.

[§65] *Q.* 7. How are your circuits now divided?[478]

A. Into seven.

(1) London (which includes Surrey, Kent, Essex, Brentford, Egham, Windsor, Wycombe).

(2) Bristol (which includes Somersetshire, Portland, Wiltshire, Oxfordshire, Gloucestershire).

(3) Cornwall.

(4) Evesham (which includes Shrewsbury, Leominster, Hereford, and from Stroud to Wednesbury).

(5) Yorkshire (which includes Cheshire, Lancashire, Derbyshire, Nottinghamshire, Rutlandshire, Lincolnshire).

(6) Newcastle.

(7) Wales.

[§66] *Q.* 8. Who are our present Assistants?

A. Jonathan Reeves, John Bennet, John Haughton,[479] John Nelson, James Wheatley, John Trembath, Thomas Westell, Thomas Richards, John Down[e]s, Thomas Maxfield, Francis Walker. Perhaps Thomas Hardwick, James Jones, Samuel Larwood, William Heard, William Walker, Joseph Cownley.

[§67] *Q.* 9. How are these places to be supplied for this quarter?

A. As far as we can yet see, thus:[480]

---

[477] E, 'in solemn prayer'.

[478] This is the first list of the original (very large) circuits, also called 'Rounds'; at this stage the appointments were for one month only.

[479] Orig., 'Houghton'.

[480] D omits §§67, 68. In §67, the initials in each column are given in one line only for each place, but here these are presented in three lines in order to accommodate the extended surnames.

The names of the preachers are given by initials only, with an occasional added letter that assists identification. In the attempt to identify them, it has been assumed that a preacher was stationed in only one place each month, and that only after the preachers listed in §66 have been traced should the search be continued farther afield. Even within this 'official' list, however, problems abound, caused chiefly by the amanuensis writing a 'J', which is usually indistinguishable from a 'T', so that without an additional clue, it is frequently impossible to decide the correct name

	June	July	August
(1) London	J. W[esley]	J. W[esley]	C. W[esley]
	J. R[eeves]	To. M[axfield],	Jo. B[ennet]
		[or Meyrick?]	
	T. R[ichards]	J. R[eddall?][481]	Jo. D[ownes]
(2) Bristol	Jo. M[addern][482]	C. W[esley]	T. R[ichards?]
	T. M[axfiel]d	J. R[eeves]	J. T[rembath]
	T. W[illis][483]	T. H[ardwick?]	
(3) Cornwall	C. W[esley]	Jo. Tr[embath]	J. R. R[eeves?]
	T. M[eyric]k		F. W[alker]
	Jo. T[rembath]		
(4) Evesham	T. W[estel]l	Ja. J[ones]	Jos. Co[wnley]
	Ja. Jo[nes]	T. [or J.][484]	
		Jo.Co[wnley]	

within each of the following four groups: T. H[ardwick], J. H[aughton]; J. J[ones], J. T[rembath]; J. R[eeves], T. R[ichards], with the additional possibility of J. R[eddall] and so on; and J. W[esley], T. W[estell], J. W[heatley], with the possible addition of T. W[illis] and so on.

The fact that, in at least three instances, names seem to be included that are not found within the preceding list of preachers issues a warning that almost any name in this table is subject to query. We have placed a question mark only where the doubt is considerable; something like certainty may be claimed for all but a handful of the identifications from confirming evidence such as JW's known itinerary and the patterns that may be discerned within this stationing and that for 1747.

[481] The 1747 Minutes record T. Rawlins as preaching in one place, but more likely seems the 'Reddel' whom Charles Wesley lists among London preachers in Oct. 1747, probably identical with the 'J. Reddall' who forwarded £15 to him in 1773.

[482] 'Jo. M' (or possibly 'To. M.') was identified from an examination of every 'M' in the textual editor's comprehensive index of Wesley's preachers and confirmed by Maddern's appearance in the 1747 Minutes.

[483] 'J. W.' or 'T. W' presents major difficulties, 'possible' names including John Wesley, John Wheeler, John Whitford, John Wilkinson of Keighley, Thomas Williams, and Thomas Willis. One of the latter two, however, and possibly both, was present at the 1746 Conference (see above, §1). When Williams evangelized Ireland the following year, he seems to have been something of a maverick, so that Willis seems the more likely. Neither man nor any of the other possibles was present at or stationed by the 1747 Conference, though John Whitford and John Wheeler were listed among those who 'assist us only in one place'. It is likely that the entries for June (Bristol) and August (Newcastle) refer to the same person.

[484] In the list of regular preachers, Downes and Walker seem to be the only possibilities, whether the initial is that of a forename or a surname.

(5) Yorkshire	Jo. Ha[ughton]	J. H[aughton]	J. J[ones?]
	Jo. B[ennet]	J. B[ennet]	Jo. N[elson]
		Ja. W[heatley]	Ja. W[heatley]
(6) Newcastle	Ja. W[heatley]	Jo. N[elson]	S. L[arwood]
	Jo. N[elson]	T. W[estel]l	T. W[estell] 5
		S. L[arwood]	To. W[illis?]
(7) Wales	Mr. M[eriton]	T. R[ichards]	J. W[esley]

[§68]   *Q.* 10. Which are the intercession days, etc., next ensuing?
   A. Friday, intercession; Friday, watch-night; Sunday, love-   10
   feast; Tuesday, letter-day.

Fri.	Fri.	Sun.	Tue.
Intercession	**Watch-night**	**Love-feast**	**Letter-day**
	May 23	June 1	June 10 15
June 6	June 20	June 29	July 8
July 4	July 18	July 27	Aug. 5
Aug. 1	Aug. 22	Aug. 31	Sept. 9
Sept. 5	Sept. 19	Sept. 28	Oct. 7
Oct. 3	Oct. 17	Oct. 26	Nov. 3 [=4] 20
Nov. 7	Nov. 14	Nov. 23	Dec. 2
Dec. 5	Dec. 19	Dec. 28	Jan. 6

[§69]   *Q.* 11.[485] Can we be of any farther use to the Moravians?
   A. Perhaps by writing to the Count.[486]   25
[§70]   *Q.* 12. To whom should we give copies of our conferences?
   A. Only to those who were or might have been present.
[§71]   *Q.* 13. To whom should we read them?
   A. To the stewards and leaders of bands.
[§72]   *Q.* 14. When and[487] where shall we meet again?   30
   A. At London, next summer, if God permit.[488]

---

[485] D numbers the following questions 9–12, showing that the omission of the 'dated' sections on the preachers' stations and the special services was deliberate, not accidental.

[486] There is no evidence that anything was ever written, and in Sept., JW wrote to Benjamin Ingham defending himself against attacks on his criticisms of the Moravians in the published *Journal* for 1739–41.

[487] D, 'or'.

[488] Charles Wesley, in a MS fragment on the Conference, adds the following under the date May 16: 'One of the things agreed upon was that the preachers should attend the public worship on Wednesdays and Fridays at all opportunities' (Brown Folio Presidents, I:11, in MA).

The Bristol Conference of the Welsh Calvinistic Methodist Association, January 22, 1747

Present January 22nd, 1746/47, 10 of the clock[489]:

5   John Wesley, H. Harris, Edward Godwin, Joseph Smyth,[490] William Hogg, William Humphreys, William Vine, Thomas Scot, Thomas Adams, John Stephens, James Ingram, James Relly, Herbert Jenkins, Thomas Hardwick, Thomas Westell, John Trembath, John Haughton.[491] After prayers 'twas inquired:

10   1. How may we remove any hindrances of brotherly love which have been?

2. How may we prevent any from arising for the time to come?

'Twas agreed to go as far on each of these heads as every person can do with a clear conscience.

---

[489] Howell Harris, the lay leader of the independent Methodist movement in Wales, was anxious for fuller cooperation between the different Methodist bodies. At the Welsh Calvinistic Methodist Association held at Newcastle on Tyne on Jan. 7, 1747, it was agreed 'that Bro. Harris should speak to Mr. Wesley about some method to prevent division, till Brother Whitefield [in America] come over and some solid rules be settled for an union'. *Journal* of the Calvinistic Methodist Historical Society 49 (July 1965), hereafter *CMHS*. His overtures seem to have led to Wesley's visit (accompanied by four of his preachers) during the first day of a Quarterly Association in Bristol, Jan. 22–24, 1747. Harris recorded that

'it could be much for edification to consult to know the Lord's mind about the time and place of our next Association, and my round. Then Bro. John Wesley sent for me to ask if he should come to the Association, and he and four of his preachers came, and we settled several rules toward an union, and in prayer the Lord came down, and I had much nearness to him, and we were very happy and loving, and felt the Lord was pleased with what we did; and when I would reason I would be afraid, but when I was simple I felt the same love to them as to ourselves, and to strengthen them was to strengthen myself. Oh the sweetness of love! We sat together and did read letters from Brother Lindblom'. Harris, MS diary, vol. 125, National Library of Wales, Aberystwyth.

[490] M. H. Jones, 'An Account of an Association held at Bristol, January 22, 1746–47', *WHS* 15 (Pt. 5, 1926): 120, lists this person as 'Tobias Smith', and includes the additional variant spellings of other people on the list: Wm. Humphries, Wm. Vines, T. Scot, P. Adams, John Stevens, and Thos. Westale.

[491] Ibid. notes that the last four names are 'four of Wesley's assistants'.

(1) Tho. Prosser (an exhorter in Wales in connexion with Mr. Wesley, suspected of error). Let Bro. Haughton desire him to explain his principles, and ask him, will he be in subordination to Bro. Harris or to us?[492]

(2) Harry Lloyd (another exhorter in Wales, that went among our Societies without consulting us). Let him meet at the Glamorganshire Association in April. Let him take no step in Brecknockshire but by the joint agreement of Mr. Phillips and Bro. Tho. James.

(3) Wales in general. 'Twas feared that the consequence of Mr. Wesley's preaching at Neath would be a separation in the Society. Mr. Wesley answered, I do not design to erect any separation[493] at Neath, or in any other town in Wales where there is a Society already, but to do all that in me lies to prevent any such separation. And we all agree, wheresoever we occasionally [preach] among each other's people, we will endeavour to strengthen, not weaken, each others' hands, in particular by labouring to prevent any separation in the several Societies.[494]

(4) Plymouth. That inasmuch as a separation has been made in the west, we agreed that a brother from Mr. Wesley should now go to the west with Mr. Harris, and endeavour to heal the breach there, insisting upon the spirit of love with its fruits among the people.

(5) We agree that on each side we should be careful to defend each others' characters. When any of the contrary judgment is called to a Society, he should first consult with the brethren of the other side before he goes.[495]

---

[492] *CMHS* ends statement: 'to Mr. Westley and us'; MS 2946.

[493] Jones, 'Account of an Association', 120, reads 'Society'.

[494] *CMHS* ends here with the note: 'Matters of English interest follow.'

[495] At 3 o'clock JW and his preachers left, and the Association continued with its own domestic affairs, relating to the Whitefieldian aspects of the Methodist movement, such as *The Weekly History*, printed by John Lewis, the restrictions that John Cennick and the Moravians were placing upon Whitefield's exhorters when they sought to use Kingswood School, the settling of preachers on trial, and the itinerancies of all the superintendents and exhorters between this and the following Association. Jones, 'Account of an Association', 121.

The London Conference of June 15–18, 1747

[§1]   Monday, June 15th, 1747[496]

The following persons being met at the Foundery, John
Wesley, Charles Wesley, Westley Hall,[497] and Charles
5   Manning,[498] it was inquired:

[§2]   *Q.* 1. Which of our brethren shall we invite to be present at
this Conference?

---

[496] See June 15, 1747, *Journal & Diaries* III, 20:177 in this edn.: 'Our Conference
began, and ended on Saturday 20. The minutes of all that passed therein were some
time after transcribed and published.'

Two MS copies of the 1747 Minutes survive, as well as printed remnants of
another. They are given in the probable order of their transcription. The variants
between them are comparatively few in number, and it seems likely that the version
given in the Doctrinal and Disciplinary *Minutes* of 1749 is closer to the original
'official' copy than is true for the preceding Minutes.

Re. In a hand not identified with certainty, but probably that of one of the preachers present, Jonathan Reeves. This is the closing transcript in the notebook in Wesley College, Bristol, used by Wesley, which began with the 'A' copy of 1744,
continued with the 'C' copy of 1745, and then with the 'E' copy of 1746. If indeed
JW followed it in 1749, however, he appears to have checked with some other transcript, possibly the original.

N. In his *Methodism in Sheffield* (1823), 207–10, James Everett gives excerpts
from a MS copy lent to him by the grandson of John Nelson, by whose hand the
document was written.

B. In the handwriting of John Bennet, the third item in Bennet's notebook in
MA, probably compiled about 1748 (later published by Richard Green, see Minutes [1744], n. 24).

[497] Rev. Westley Hall (1711–76) matriculated Lincoln College, Oxford (1731),
but left without a degree. He was ordained in 1734. He was secretly engaged to
Wesley's sister Martha, later proposed to her sister Kezia, but then married Martha.
He had planned to accompany Wesley to Georgia but did not do so. In 1741 he
adopted Moravian views and founded a religious society in Salisbury in 1743. He
then turned deist and advocated polygamy and fathered illegitimate children. In
1747 he left Salisbury and later had a brief stay in the West Indies. Wesley cast him
off in a letter printed in Dec. 1747. *Journal & Diaries*, 18:238f.; 20:199–203, in this
edn.

[498] Charles Manning (c. 1715–99), scholar of Gonville and Caius College, Cambridge (1731–36), B.A. 173?; vicar of Hayes, Middlesex (1738–57), who was present at both the 1747 and the 1748 Conferences and was Wesley's lone clerical
supporter in the county. In 1749 he married two of Wesley's preachers: John Jones
to Elizabeth Mann, and Thomas Richards to Mary Davey. See *Journal & Diaries*,
20:263 n. 16 in this edn.

A. John Jones,[499] Thomas Maxfield, Jonathan Reeves, John
Nelson, John Bennet, John Downes, Thomas Crouch,[500]
Robert Swindells, and John Maddern, who were accord-
ingly brought in.

[§3]　*Q.* 2. How may the time of this Conference be made more　5
eminently a time of prayer, watching, and self-denial?

A.(1) While we are in Conference, let us have an especial
care to set God always before us.

(2) In the intermediate hours, let us visit none but the
sick, and spend all our time that remains in retirement.　10

(3) Let us then give ourselves unto prayer for one
another, and for the blessing of God on this our labour.

[§4]　*Q.* 3. Should we at every Conference read over all the Conferences we have had from the beginning?

A. Only[501] that immediately preceding, and so much of the　15
rest as we may find needful from time to time.

[§5]　*Q.* 4. In our first Conference it was agreed to examine every
point from the foundation. Have we not been some way[502]
fearful of doing this? What were we afraid of? Of overturning our first principles?　20

A. Whoever was afraid of this, it was a vain fear. For if they
are true, they will bear the strictest examination. If they
are false, the sooner they are overturned the better. Let us
all pray for a willingness to receive light; an invariable
desire to know of every doctrine whether it be of God.　25

[§6]　*Q.* 5. It was then inquired, How far does each of us agree to
submit to the unanimous judgment of the rest?

[A.] And it was answered,

In speculative things each can only submit as far as his
judgment shall be convinced.　30

In every practical point, so[503] far as we can without
wounding our several consciences.

---

[499] For Jones, see Minutes (1758), §1, n. 979.

[500] Possibly the hospitable London Methodist whose home had been the headquarters of a Society since 1739 (see *Letters*, 25:602 in this edn.). He was listed (§65
below) as one of the chief local preachers in 1747.

[501] B omits 'only'. N.B. the plural rather than the singular in the question; viz.,
the Minutes of *all* the preceding Conferences.

[502] N, 'somewhat'.

[503] B, 'as'.

[§7] *Q*. 6.[504] Can a Christian submit any farther than this to any man, or number of men, upon earth?

A. It is undeniably plain he cannot, either to Pope, Council, Bishop, or Convocation. And this is that grand principle of every man's right to private judgment, in opposition to implicit faith in man, on which Calvin, Luther, Melanchthon,[505] and all the ancient Reformers, both at home and abroad, proceeded: 'Every man must think for himself, since every man must give an account for himself to God.'

[§8] *Q*. 7. Shall each of us read over all the tracts which have been published before our next Conference? And write down every passage we do not approve, or do not fully understand?[506]

A. Everyone answered in order,[507] 'I will endeavour so to do.'

Tuesday, 16th

[§9] Mr. Bateman[508] of St. Bartholomew's, Mr. Piers, Howell Harris,[509] and Thomas Hardwick being added, it was inquired:

---

[504] B, Re, do not number this question, but give No. 7 as '*Q*. 6'. N., however, followed by 1749, has both 6 and 7.

[505] Orig., 'Melancthon'.

[506] The *Minutes* (1749), §18, enjoins no one to publish until 'we' have authorised it (see p. 235 and n. 737).

[507] B omits 'in order'.

[508] Rev. Thomas Bateman (c. 1713–61) matriculated Jesus College, Oxford (1736). Rector of St. Bartholomew the Great (1738–61) who converted during the revival in Wales, where he held a living and was one of the clergy assisting JW then. He was also at the 1748 Conference; see Seymour, *Huntingdon*, 1:62; *Journal & Diaries*, 20:175 n. 44 in this edn.

[509] See above for his Jan. 22, 1747, visit to the Association meeting. Howell Harris (1714–73) of Trevecca, Breconshire, one of the leaders of Welsh Calvinistic Methodism, was a lay evangelist who failed to obtain ordination. He founded a religious settlement in Trevecca in 1751 and later allowed Lady Huntingdon to found her college for training preachers on his estate. Harris in turn accepted invitations to be present at Wesley's Conferences in 1747 and 1748, and at length in Aug. 1749, when a Conference of the two Wesleys, Whitefield, and Harris was convened to settle the 'solid rules' for their proposed union.

Harris appears to have been present only during the opening day of the 1747 Conference and made his contribution to the discussions on Christian assurance and on sanctification, as seen in his journal:

'I went with Bro. Bateman, and they were met (five clergymen and seven or eight lay preachers), and discoursed on the assurance of faith being the essence of faith—no salvation without it. They asserted it and answered the objections to it in Scripture, but yielded [that] there was implied in it a being convinced we are lost without Christ, seeing him the only Saviour, and being made willing to receive him, and a supernatural power to come to him, to apply and receive him, and that such as have had this witness may doubt afterward, and that some are long seeking with all their hearts and without the manifestation, and shall not die without it, though they may not be able to tell others of it; and that also we can't then assure them to be in a state of damnation. . . . On sanctification I asserted that sin remained to death. . . . We agree to set the souls to press after perfection. . . . I judged I saw in the Scriptures (he having before owned that I said of owning sin did [persist] in believers—or the whole nature of sin) . . . two natures, flesh and spirit, and that the old nature is not mended (Bro. Charles here confirmed it, *"neither can it be"*), but subdued, and more and more by daily sprinkling of Christ's blood, and when 'tis all washed away, then I judged they were ripe for glory, and would go home, etc. I declared I had not these truths from Calvin, nor from any of his judgment, but had them before I knew of Mr. Gr[iffith] Jones, Bro. Rowlands, Mr. Whitefield, etc., or any Dissenting minister, etc., but they could not believe me. I also declared that I thought [about] that text, "He that is born of God cannot commit sin", and that it meant "that which is born of God", i.e. the new nature, etc.; or if it meant the man denominated from the better part, and so [he] is not said to sin because his grace sins not, etc., but his flesh, etc. He [John Wesley?] rejected this way of arguing, though Bro. Hall said there was somewhat in it, too. I think they don't wait for the instantaneous sanctification now, but the gradual one. When Bro. [Westley] Hall said that he was so passive and so filled with God that he did not sin but God ruled in him . . . I said I felt . . . such a mixture of sin in all I do and I own sin now so that if it was not for the Blood of Christ to wash me I could not live though I aim at God's glory. . . . When Bro. John said that some are so that 'tis not they that speak, but God speaks and acts, I said, the antinomians say the same; he said, they only mimicked it. . . . On coming away Bro. Charles desired (when they desired me to bring in my objection to perfection), every expression they use that hinder us, or hurts brotherly love, they'll drop them. I think they are much more moderate, and come nearer light. When Bro. John mentioned that heaven was the reward of faith, I said I could not agree to that, for though I owned there were rewards of grace to every grace, yet that heaven is the reward of Christ's obedience, and faith only the means of receiving all . . . I think they don't insist for instantaneous sanctification now but a gradual one'. Harris, MS Diary, vol. 26, cf. Tom Beynon, ed., *Howell Harris's Visits to London* (Aberystwyth: Cambrian News Press, 1960), 147–48, the transcription of his diary by Rev. Griffith T. Roberts.)

Harris also notes in his diary that he told JW that he could not 'bear any being against election and perseverance'. MS diary, vol. 127 (June 16), 150.

[§10]   *Q.* 1. Is justifying faith a divine assurance that Christ loved *me*, and gave himself for *me*?
A. We believe it is.

[§11]   *Q.* 2. What is the judgment of most of the serious Dissenters concerning this?
A. They generally allow that many believers have such an assurance, and,
That it is to be desired and prayed for by all.
But then they affirm,
That this is the highest species or degree of faith, that it is not the common privilege of believers.
Consequently they deny that this is justifying faith, or necessarily implied therein.

[§12]   *Q.* 3. And are there not strong reasons for their[510] opinion? For instance, If the true believers of old had not this assurance, then it is not necessarily[511] implied in justifying faith. But the true believers of old had not[512] this assurance.
A. David and many more of the believers of old undeniably[513] had this assurance. But even if the Jews had it not, it would not follow that this is not implied in Christian faith.

[§13]   *Q.* 4. But do you not know that the apostles themselves had it not till the Day of Pentecost?
A. The apostles themselves had not the proper Christian faith till after the Day of Pentecost.

[§14]   *Q.* 5. But were not those Christian believers in the proper sense to whom St. John wrote his first Epistle? Yet to these he says, 'These things have I written unto you that believe on the name of the Son of God that ye may know that ye have eternal life, and that ye may believe on the name of the Son of God.'[514]
A. This does not prove that they did not know they had eternal life, any more than that they did not believe. Its[515] plain meaning is, 'I have written unto you, that you may

---

[510] B, 'this'.

[511] Re, 'inexpoicly'?

[512] B omits 'not', surely in error.

[513] B, 'had undeniably'.

[514] a. [1 John] 5:13. [Footnotes beginning with a lowercase letter are Wesley's internal notes.]

[515] B, 'His'.

be the more established in the faith.' Therefore it does not
follow from hence that they had not this assurance, but
only that there are degrees therein.

[§15]   *Q.* 6. But were not the Thessalonians true believers? Yet
they had not this assurance; they had only a good hope.[516]   5

A. The text you refer to runs thus: 'Now our Lord Jesus
Christ himself, and God, even our Father, which hath
loved us, and given us everlasting consolation and good
hope through grace, comfort your hearts,[517] and stablish
you in every good word and work.' This 'good hope' does   10
not exclude, but necessarily implies, a strong assurance of
the love of God.

[§16]   *Q.* 7. But does not St. Paul say even[518] of himself, 'I know
nothing by myself, yet am I not hereby justified'?[519]

A. He does not say of himself here that he was not justified,   15
or that he did not know it, but only that, though he had a
conscience void of offence,[520] yet this did not justify him
before God. And must not every believer say the same?
This therefore is wide of the point.

[§17]   *Q.* 8. But does he not disclaim any such assurance in those   20
words, 'I was with you in weakness and in fear and in
much trembling'?[521]

A. By no means. For these words do not imply any fear
either of death or hell. They express only a deep sense of
his utter insufficiency for the great work wherein he was   25
engaged.

[§18]   *Q.* 9. However, does he not exclude Christians in general
from such an assurance, when he bids them 'work out
their salvation with fear and trembling'?[522]

A. No more than from love, which is always joined with   30
filial fear and reverential trembling.

And the same answer is applicable to all those texts which
exhort a believer to fear.

---

[516] b. 2 Thess. 2:16 [-17].
[517] Re, 'heart'.
[518] B omits 'even'.
[519] c. 1 Cor. 4:4.
[520] d. Acts 24:16.
[521] e. 1 Cor. 1:3 [i.e., 2:3].
[522] f. Phil. 2:12.

[§19] *Q.* 10. But does not matter of fact prove that justifying faith does not necessarily imply assurance? For can you believe that such a person as J. A. or E. U.,[523] who have so much integrity, zeal, and fear of God, and walk so unblameably in all things, is void of justifying faith? Can you suppose such as these to be under the wrath and under the curse of God? Especially if you add to this, that they are continually longing, striving, praying for the assurance which they have not?

A. This contains the very strength of the cause, and sometimes inclines us to think that some of these may be exempt cases. But however that be, we answer:

(1) It is dangerous to ground a general doctrine on a few particular experiments.

(2) Men may have many good tempers, and a blameless life (speaking in a loose sense), by nature and habit, with preventing grace; and yet be utterly void of faith and the love of God.

(3) 'Tis scarce possible for us to know all the circumstances relating to such persons, so as to judge certainly concerning 'em.

(4) But this we know, that [if] Christ is not revealed in them, they are not yet Christian believers.

[§20] *Q.* 11. But what becomes of them then, suppose they die in this state?

A. That is a supposition not to be made. They cannot die in this state. They must go backward or forward. If they continue to seek, they will surely find righteousness, peace, and joy in the Holy Ghost.[524] We are confirmed in this belief by the many instances we have seen of such as these finding peace at the last hour. And it is not impossible but others may even then[525] be made partakers of like precious faith, and yet go hence without giving any outward proof of the change which God hath wrought.

---

[523] J. A. is probably John Appleton, currier and local preacher of Shrewsbury, converted in Bristol (c. 1740). He appears to have been converted by the story of the fate of a clergyman who died after attacking Methodism (see *Journal & Diaries*, 19:331; 23:328 and n. 9 in this edn.). E. V. (or E. U.) has not been identified.

[524] Rom. 14:17.

[525] Re omits 'even'.

Wednesday, 17th

[§21] *Q.* 1. How much is allowed by our brethren who differ from
     us with regard to entire sanctification?

　　　A. They grant:

　　　(1) That everyone must be entirely sanctified in the arti-   5
　　　cle of death.

　　　(2) That till then a believer daily grows in grace, and
　　　comes nearer and nearer to perfection.

　　　(3) That we ought to be continually pressing after this,
　　　and to exhort all others so to do.   10

[§22] *Q.* 2. But what do we allow them?

　　　A. We grant:

　　　(1) That many of those who have died in the faith, yea,
　　　the greater part of those[526] we have known, were not
　　　sanctified throughout, not made perfect in love, till a   15
　　　little before death.

　　　(2) That the term 'sanctified' is continually applied by
　　　St. Paul to all that were justified, were true believers.

　　　(3) That by this term alone he rarely (if ever) means
　　　saved from all sin.   20

　　　(4) That consequently it is not proper to use it in this
　　　sense without adding the word wholly, entirely, or the
　　　like.

　　　(5) That the inspired writers almost continually spoke of
　　　or to those who were[527] justified, but very rarely either of   25
　　　or to those who were wholly sanctified.

　　　(6) That consequently it behooves[528] us to speak almost
　　　continually of the state of justification, but rarely,
　　　at least in full and explicit terms, concerning entire
　　　sanctification.   30

[§23] *Q.* 3. What then is the point wherein we divide?

　　　A. It is this—whether we should expect to be saved from all
　　　sin before the article of death.

[§24] *Q.* 4. Is there any clear Scripture promise of this, that God
　　　will save us from all sin?   35

　　　A. There is—Ps. 130:8, 'He shall redeem Israel from all his
　　　sins.'

---

[526] B, 'them'.

[527] B, 'are'.

[528] Orig., 'behoves'.

This is more largely expressed in the prophecy of Ezekiel: 'Then will I sprinkle clean water upon you, and ye shall be clean; from all your filthiness and from all your idols will I cleanse you. . . . I will also save you all your
5   uncleannesses.'[529] No promise can be more full and clear. And to this the Apostle plainly refers in that exhortation: 'Having these promises, let us cleanse ourselves from all filthiness of flesh and spirit, perfecting holiness in the fear of God.'[530]
10   Equally clear and express is that ancient promise: 'The Lord thy God will circumcise thy heart, and the heart of thy seed, to love the Lord thy God with all thy heart and with all thy soul.'[531]

[§25]   *Q.* 5. But does any assertion answerable to this occur in the
15   New Testament?

    A. There does, and that laid down in the plainest terms. So 1 John 3:8: 'For this purpose the Son of God was manifested, that he might destroy the works of the devil.'—the works of the devil, without any limitation or restriction.
20   But all sin is the work of the devil. Parallel to which is that assertion of St. Paul, Eph. 5:25; 27: 'Christ loved the church, and gave himself for it, that he might present it to himself a glorious church, not having spot, or wrinkle, or any such thing, but that it should be holy and without
25   blemish.' And to the same effect is his assertion in the eighth of the Romans (ver. 3, 4): 'God sent his Son that the righteousness of the law might be fulfilled in us; walking not after the flesh but after the Spirit.'

[§26]   *Q.* 6. Does the New Testament afford any farther ground
30   for expecting to be saved from all sin?

    A. Undoubtedly it does, both in those prayers and commands which are equivalent to the strongest assertions.

[§27]   *Q.* 7. What prayers do you mean?

    A. Prayers for entire sanctification: which, were there no
35   such thing, would be mere mockery[532] of God. Such in particular are, 'Deliver us from evil,' or rather, 'from the

---

[529] g. [Ezek.] 36:25, 29.
[530] h. 2 Cor. 7:1.
[531] i. Deut. 30:6.
[532] Re, 'mocking.'

evil one'.[533] Now when this is done, when we are delivered
from all evil, there can be no sin remaining. 'Neither pray
I for these alone, but for them also which shall believe on
me through their word; that they all may be one; as thou,
Father, art in me, and I in thee, that they also may be one   5
in us. . . . I in them, and thou in me, that they may be
made perfect in one.'[534]

'I bow my knees unto the God and Father of our Lord Jesus
Christ . . . , that he would grant you . . . that ye, being
rooted and grounded in love, may be able to comprehend   10
with all saints what is the breadth, and length, and depth,
and height, and to know the love of Christ, which passeth
knowledge, that ye might be filled with all the fullness of
God.'[535]

'The very God of peace sanctify you wholly; and I pray   15
God your whole spirit, soul, and body[536] be preserved
blameless unto the coming of our Lord Jesus
Christ.'[537]

[§28] *Q.* 8. What command is there to the same effect?

A. 'Be ye perfect, as your Father which is in heaven is   20
perfect.'[538]

'Thou shalt love the Lord thy God with all thy heart, and
with all thy soul, and with all thy mind.'[539]

But if the love of God fill all the heart, there can be no sin
there.   25

[§29] *Q.* 9. But how does it appear that this is to be done before
the article of death?

A. First: From the very nature of a command, which is not
given to the dead but to the living. Therefore 'Thou shalt
love the Lord thy God with all thy heart' cannot mean,   30
Thou shalt do this when thou diest, but while thou
livest.[540]

---

[533] Matt. 6:13.

[534] j. John 17:20-23. [Re omits 'also may . . . they', apparently a scribal error.]

[535] k. Eph. 3:[14], 16-19.

[536] B, 'whole body, spirit, soul'.

[537] l. 1 Thess. 5:23.

[538] m. Matt. 6:last [i.e., 5:48].

[539] n. Matt. 22:37.

[540] Re omits 'Therefore . . . livest'.

Secondly: from express texts of Scripture. 'The grace of
God that bringeth salvation hath appeared to all men,
teaching us that, having renounced (ἀρνησάμενοι)[541]
ungodliness and worldly lusts, we should live soberly,
5   righteously, and godly in this present world, looking for
the glorious appearing of our Lord Jesus Christ, who gave
himself for us, that he might redeem us from all iniquity,
and purify unto himself a peculiar people, zealous of good
works.'[542] 'He hath raised up an horn of salvation for us
10   . . . , to perform the mercy promised to our fathers . . . ,
the oath which he sware to our father Abraham, that he
would grant unto us, that we being delivered out of the
hands of our enemies should serve him without fear, in
holiness and righteousness before him, all the days of our
15   life.'[543]

[§30] *Q.* 10. Is there any example in Scripture of persons who
had attained to this?[544]

A. Yes—St. John, and all those of whom he says in his first
Epistle (4:17), 'Herein is our love made perfect, that we
20   may have confidence in the day of judgment; because as
he is, so are we in this world.'

[§31] *Q.* 11. But why are there not more examples of this kind
recorded in the New Testament?

A. It does not become us to be peremptory in this matter.
25   One reason might possibly be, because the apostles wrote
to the Church while it was in a state of infancy. Therefore
they might mention such persons the more sparingly, lest
they should give strong meat to babes.

[§32] *Q.* 12. Can you show one such example now? Where is he
30   that is thus perfect?

A. To some that make this inquiry one might answer, If I
knew one here, I would not tell *you*, for you do not
inquire out of love.[545] You are like Herod, you only seek
the young child to slay it.[546] But to the serious we answer,
35   There are numberless reasons why there should be few, if

---

[541] Re omits the Greek and leaves a space.

[542] o. Titus 2:11-14.

[543] p. Luke 1:69, etc.

[544] B, 'attained this'.

[545] B omits, 'for . . . love'.

[546] B, 'destroy'.

any, indisputable examples. What inconveniences would this bring on the person himself, set as a mark for all to shoot at! What a temptation would it be to others, not only to men who know[547] not God, but to believers themselves! How hardly would they refrain from idolizing such 5 a person! And yet how unprofitable to gainsayers! For if they hear not Moses and the prophets, Christ and his apostles, neither would they be persuaded though one rose from the dead.

[§33]   *Q.* 13. Suppose one had attained to this, would you advise   10
him to speak of it?

A. Not to them who know not God: it would only provoke them to contradict and blaspheme. Not[548] to any without some particular reason, without some particular good in view; and then they should have an especial care to avoid   15 all appearance of boasting, and to speak more loudly and convincingly by their lives than they can do by their tongues.

[§34]   *Q.* 14. Is it a sin not to believe those who say they have attained?   20

A. By no means; even though they said true, we ought not hastily to believe, but to suspend our judgment till we have farther and stronger proof.

[§35]   *Q.* 15. But are we not apt to have a secret distaste to any who say they are saved from all sin?   25

A. 'Tis very possible we may, and that on several grounds: partly from a concern for the honour of God, and the good of souls who may be hurt, yea, or turned out of the way, if these are not what they profess; partly from a kind of implicit envy at those who speak of higher attainments   30 than our own; and partly from our slowness and unreadiness of heart to believe the works[549] of God.

[§36]   *Q.* 16. Does not the harshly preaching perfection tend to bring believers into a kind of bondage and[550] slavish fear?

A. It does. Therefore we should always place it in the most   35 amiable light, so that it may excite only hope, joy, and desire.

---

[547] B, 'knew'.
[548] B, 'Nor'.
[549] Re, 'work', but 1749 has 'works'.
[550] B, 1749, 'or'.

[§37]   *Q*. 17. Why may we not continue in the joy of faith until[551]
we are made perfect?

A. Why indeed? Since holy grief does not quench this joy;
since even while we are under the cross, while we deeply
partake of the sufferings[552] of Christ, we may rejoice with
joy unspeakable.

[§38]   *Q*. 18. Do we not discourage believers from rejoicing
evermore?

A. We ought not so to do. Let them all their life long rejoice
unto God, so it be with reverence. And even if lightness
or pride should mix with their joy, let us not strike at the
joy itself (this is the gift of God), but at the lightness or
pride, that the evil may cease and the good remain.

[§39]   *Q*. 19. Ought we to be anxiously careful about perfection,
lest we should die before we have attained it?

A. In no wise. We ought to be thus careful for nothing,[553]
neither spiritual nor temporal.

[§40]   *Q*. 20. But ought we not to be troubled on account of the
sinful nature which still remains in us?

A. It is good for us to have a deep sense of this, and to be
much ashamed before the Lord. But this should only
incite us the more earnestly to turn unto Christ every
moment, and to draw light and life and strength from
him, that we may go on, conquering and to conquer. And
therefore, when a sense of our sins most abounds, the
sense of his love should much more abound.[554]

[§41]   *Q*. 21. Will our joy or trouble increase as we grow in grace?
A. Perhaps both. But without doubt our joy in the Lord
will increase as our love increases.

[§42]   *Q*. 22. Is not the teaching believers to be continually poring
upon their inbred sin the ready way to make them forget
that they are purged from their former sins?

A. We find by experience that it is; or to make them undervalue and account it a little thing. Whereas indeed
(though there are still greater gifts behind) this is inexpressibly great and glorious.

---

[551] B, 'even till'.
[552] Re, 'suffering'.
[553] q. Phil. 4:6.
[554] r. Rom. 5:20.

[§43]   About 10 (Mr. Perronet,[555] vicar of Shoreham, being added) we began to consider points of discipline.

[§44]   *Q*. 1. What is schism in the Scripture sense of the word?

A. The word only occurs twice in the New Testament: viz.; 1 Cor. 1:10, where St. Paul exhorts them, that 'there may   5
be no schisms among' them (σχίσματα is the word which we render 'divisions'); and 12:25, 'God hath mingled the body together, having given the more abundant honour to that part which lacked, that there may be no schism in the body,' i.e., in the Church, the body of Christ.   10

In both these places the word undeniably means (which consequently is the true scriptural[556] notion of *schism*) a causeless breach, rupture, or division, made among the members of Christ, among those who are the living body of Christ, and members in particular.   15

[§45]   *Q*. 2. Are not the Methodists guilty of making such a schism?

A. No more than of rebellion or murder. They do not divide themselves at all from the living body of Christ. Let any prove it if they can.

[§46]   *Q*. 3. But do not they divide themselves from the Church   20
of England?

A. No: they hold communion therewith now in the same manner as they did twenty years ago, and hope to do so until their lives' end.

[§47]   *Q*. 4. You profess to obey both the governors and rules of   25
the Church, yet in many instances you do not obey them. How is this consistent? Upon what principles do you act while you sometimes obey and sometimes not?

A. It is entirely consistent. We act at all times on one plain uniform principle: 'We will obey the rules and governors   30
of the Church whenever we can consistently with our duty to God. Whenever we cannot, we quietly[557] obey God rather than men.'

---

[555] Rev. Vincent Perronet (1693–1785), son of a naturalized Swiss Protestant; Queen's College, Oxford; B.A. (1718); vicar of Shoreham, Kent (1728–85). He was closely associated with the Wesleys from Aug. 1744 and nicknamed 'the archbishop of the Methodists'. The Wesleys consulted him on their matrimonial matters. His two sons, Charles and Edward (see below, §66), preached for the Methodists, though often causing trouble by their irregularities.

[556] B, 'spiritual'.

[557] B, 'we will quietly'.

[§48]   *Q.* 5. But why do you say you are thrust out of the
churches?[558] Has not every minister a right to dispose of
his own church?

5   *A.* He ought to have, but in fact he has not. A minister
desires I should preach in his church, but the bishop forbids him. That bishop then injures him, and thrusts me
out of that church.

[§49]   *Q.* 6. Does a church in the New Testament always mean 'a
single congregation'?

10   *A.* We believe it does. We do not recollect any instance to
the contrary.

[§50]   *Q.* 7. What instance or ground is there then[559] in the New
Testament for a national church?
A. We know none at all. We apprehend it to be a merely[560]

15   political institution.[561]

[§51]   *Q.* 8. Are the three orders of Bishops, Priests, and Deacons
plainly described in the New Testament?
A. We think they are, and believe they generally obtained in
the churches of the apostolic age.

20 [§52]   *Q.* 9. But are you assured that[562] God designed the same
plan should obtain in all churches throughout all ages?
A. We are not assured of this, because we do not know that
it is asserted in Holy Writ.

[§53]   *Q.* 10. If this plan were essential to a Christian church,

25   what must become of all the foreign Reformed Churches?
A. It would follow, they are no part[563] of the Church of
Christ—a consequence full of shocking absurdity.

[§54]   *Q.* 11. In what age was the divine right of episcopacy first
asserted in England?

---

[558] B, 'Church'.

[559] B omits 'then'.

[560] B, 'mere'.

[561] On this and the following comments on church government, see Minutes
(1744), §45 above (p. 133 and n. 115).

[562] B omits 'that'.

[563] B, 'parts'. On Anglican recognition of the real, though imperfect, validity of
non-episcopal churches' ministries even by High Churchmen, see N. H. Sykes,
Old Priest and New Presbyter (Cambridge, 1956). In modern terms they had the
'esse' but not the 'bene esse' of a church. JW, however, was certainly now allowing
more recognition to their ministries than had been the case in his Oxford and Georgia periods when he was close to the Nonjurors.

  A. About the middle of Queen Elizabeth's reign. Till then
  all the bishops and clergy in England continually allowed
  and joined in the ministrations of those who were not
  episcopally ordained.

[§55] *Q*. 12. Must there not be numberless accidental varia-   5
  tions[564] in the government of various churches?

  A. There must be in the nature of things. As God variously
  dispenses his gifts of nature, providence, and grace, both
  the offices themselves and the officers in each ought to be
  varied from time to time.   10

[§56] *Q*. 13. Why is it that there is no determinate plan of
  church-government appointed in Scripture?

  A. Without doubt, because the wisdom of God had a
  regard to this necessary variety.

[§57] *Q*. 14. Was there any thought of uniformity in the govern- 15
  ment of all churches until the time of Constantine?

  A. It is certain there was not; and would not have been
  then, had men consulted the Word of God only.

Thursday, the 18th   20

[§58] *Q*. 1. Have we not limited field preaching too much?

  A. It seems we have.

  (1) Because our calling is to save that which is lost. Now
  we cannot expect the wanderers from God to seek us: it
  is our part to go and seek them.   25

  (2) Because we are more peculiarly called, by going out
  into the highways and hedges (which none will do if we
  do not) to compel them to come in.[565]

  (3) Because that reason against it is not good, 'The
  house[566] will hold all that come.' The house may hold all 30
  that will come to the house, but not all that would come
  to[567] the field.

  (4) Because we have[568] found a greater blessing in field
  preaching than in any other preaching whatever.

---

[564] B, 'varieties'.
[565] s. Luke 14:23.
[566] Re, 'houses'.
[567] B, 'that will come into'.
[568] B, 'have always'.

[§59]   *Q.* 2. What is respect of persons, James 2:1?

    A. The regarding one person more than another, on account of some outward circumstance,[569] particularly riches.

5   [§60]   *Q.* 3. Have we not fallen into this by allowing more of our time to the rich than to the poor, by not speaking so plain and home to them, and by admitting them into the bands or Society, though they had never received remission of sins, or had met in band at all?

10   *A.* These are instances of such a respect of persons as we will endeavour to avoid for the time to come.

[§61]   *Q.* 4. Would it not be well for the minister to visit the sick on Monday, Thursday, Friday, Saturday?

    A. It seems no time could be more profitably employed,
15   either for them or us.

[§62]   *Q.* 5. How shall we keep off unworthy[570] communicants?

    A. By being exactly careful whom we admit into the Society; and second, by giving notes to none but those who come to us on the days appointed in each quarter.[571]

20   [§63]   *Q.* 6. How shall we thoroughly purge the bands?

    A. (1) In visiting the classes, meet those who are in the bands every morning before the rest, and examine them as strictly as you can both as to their heart and life.

    (2) Meet the married men and married women apart, the
25   first Wednesday and Sunday after[572] visitation; the single men and single women apart on the second Wednesday and Sunday.

[§64]   *Q.* 7. Who are our present Assistants?

    A. John Jones, Jonathan Reeves, John Haughton, Jos.
30   Cownley,[573] James Wheatley, John Nelson, John Trembath,

---

[569] B, 'circumstances'.

[570] B, 'unwary'—surely in error.

[571] This appears to be the first mention of the use of 'communicants' notes'. The implication is that members were admitted by Class tickets and non-members by these notes. These appear to have been issued quarterly on appointed days or by the minister before the service began. Rare early specimens have the letters 'IHS' in the centre surrounded by what may be rays of light. John C. Bowmer, *The Sacrament of the Lord's Supper in Early Methodism* (London, 1951), 116–17, gives examples of non-members being given notes and cites *WHS* 1 (1897): 134.

[572] B, 'after each'.

[573] B inserts Cownley after Trembath.

Robert Swindells, Thomas Richards, Samuel Larwood, Thomas Westell, Francis Walker, John Bennet, Thomas Maxfield, John Downes, Richard Moss, Edward Dunstan, Thomas Meyrick, Richard Williamson, John Maddern, Eleazer Webster; perhaps Thomas Hardwick and James Jones.   5

[§65]   *Q*. 8. Who are they[574] that assist us only in one place?[575]
A. Thomas Rawlings,[576] J. Hathway, Jas. Rogers,[577] John Slocomb,[578] Corn. Bastable, John Jane, John Whitford, David Trathen, John Jenkins, John Spargo, Anth.   10
Lyddicoat, Stephen Nichols, John Wheeler, John Osborn, Edward May,[579] John Bennet,[580] William Fenwick, Robert Blow, James Skelton, Robert Taylor,[581] John Brown,[582] Christopher Hopper, Archibald Patten, William Holmes,[583]

[574] B, 'those'.

[575] This list is important as the main piece of evidence for the host of unlettered men who served Wesley, especially during these early years, as 'local preachers'—a class known as 'exhorters' in Cornwall, where many of them served. JW appointed some for a time as full-time itinerants. They appeared in some numbers in Cornwall in 1746 as a result of the gaps left by regular preachers pressed for the army. Simon, *Methodist Societies*, 2:239; Thomas Jackson, *The Life of the Rev. Charles Wesley, M.A.*, 2 vols. (London: Mason, 1841), 1:144. In early Methodism, 'exhorting' was often distinguished from formal 'preaching' defined as taking a text and giving a formal sermon, and this helped to ease the scandal caused by the emergence of female exhorter-preachers. See *Minutes* (1770), *Q*. 26, for 'exhorters' as a separate category. There is remarkably little mention or regulation in the Conference Minutes of local preachers; see Baker, 'Polity', 237f. The majority were little known outside their own areas, and in a number of cases it has not been possible to discover anything about them or even the county where they preached. In the following notes, those becoming itinerants are catalogued in John Lenton's list (see *John Wesley's Preachers*, 453–59) and not documented here.

[576] B, 'Rawlins'.

[577] B, 'Samuel Rogers'. John Downes mentions a Rogers in London in a letter of Mar. 10, 1763, to Charles Wesley; in MA.

[578] Orig., 'Slocumb'.

[579] Possibly of St. Ives, Cornwall; *Journal & Diaries*, 21:281 in this edn.

[580] Re, 'Bennetts'. Clearly not the itinerant of that name as he appears in the Assistants list; see §64 above. In 1758, the Conference proposed as an itinerant, 'Jo. Bennets'.

[581] Probably of Burnham, Lincolnshire; letter of Richard Moss to JW, June 28, 1745, *Journal & Diaries*, 20:84f. in this edn.

[582] Probably the Northumberland farmer. *WHS* 12 (1919); 24 (1944): 132–34.

[583] Apparently of Lincolnshire (cf. Atmore, *Methodist Memorial*, 199, where the letter recounting his death might well have been dated Jan. 31, 1747–48).

William Shent,[584] Matthew Watson, Samuel Appleyard,
William Darney, Francis Scott,[585] Joseph Lee,[586] John
Eaton,[587] John Appleton,[588] John Griffiths,[589] Richard
Watts,[590] William Walker, John Gill,[591] Thomas Crouch,
5   and Henry Lloyd.

[§66] *Q.* 9. Should we admit Edward and Charles Perronet[592] into
the number of our ordinary Assistants?

A. By all means. God has given them in some low degree[593]
both grace and gifts and fruits.

10 [§67] *Q.* 10. Are our Assistants exemplary in their lives? Do we
inquire enough into this?

A. Perhaps not. We should consider each of them who is
with us as a pupil at the university, into whose behaviour
and studies we should[594] therefore make a particular
15   inquiry every day. Might we not particularly inquire: Do
you rise at 4? Do you study in the method laid down at the

---

[584] The well-known barber of Leeds. He was converted in 1742, and Charles
Wesley preached in his shop (in 1746, *CWJ*, 1:313). John Pawson says he was a
'half-itinerant' (*Letters*, 3:23 n.), but he was an Assistant in 1749 (*Minutes* [1749],
§9). He was expelled from the Society for 'falling into sin' (*Letters* [Telford],
6:333f.). He died in 1787, and according to Pawson, as a confirmed drunkard (*Letters*, 1:19).

[585] A joiner and upholsterer of Wakefield.

[586] Of Newcastle; *Journal & Diaries*, 23:383f. in this edn.

[587] Of Wednesbury (see 11:282 in this edn.).

[588] Of Shrewsbury (see §19, n. 523 above).

[589] Of West Bromwich (see 11:284 in this edn.).

[590] Of London; see Wesley to John Bennet (*Letters*, 26:395 in this edn.).

[591] Of Yorkshire, whose wife also was a preacher, according to Prof. Baker, citing
Illingworth's diary in the Special Collections at Perkins Library, Duke University;
she is not listed in Chilcote, *Women Preachers*.

[592] The sons of Vincent Perronet (see above, §43, n. 555). Charles (c. 1720–76);
the date of birth usually given as c. 1723 is incorrect according to his brother, who
said he was 56 at his death (*Letters*, 26:226, n. 1 in this edn.). He itinerated for the
Methodists but in 1754 administered the Lord's Supper without authorization
when he separated from the Wesleys. (Frank Baker, *Charles Wesley: As Revealed by
his Letters* [London, 1948], 92). He settled in Canterbury with his brother Edward.
Pawson described him as a man of deep piety and liberal education but too delicate
for the itinerancy (*Letters*, 3:27). Edward (1721–92) also itinerated but then separated along with Charles. He preached for Lady Huntingdon by c. 1771 but later
became an Independent minister in Canterbury. Pawson saw him as, in contrast
with Charles, too witty, satirical, and subject to levity (Pawson, *Letters*, 3:28).

[593] B, 'some measure'.

[594] Re has a blank space between 'behaviour and' and 'should therefore'.

last Conference? Do you read the books we advise and no
other? Do you see the necessity of regularity in study?
What are the chief temptations to irregularity? Do you
punctually observe the evening hour of retirement? Are
you exact in writing your journal? Do you fast on Friday?   5
Do you converse seriously, usefully, and closely? Do you
pray before, and have you a determinate end in, every
conversation?

[§68]   *Q.* 11. How often should our Assistants preach?

     A. Never more than twice a day, unless on a Sunday or an   10
extraordinary occasion, of which themselves are to be the
judges.

[§69]   *Q.* 12. Are there any smaller advices concerning preaching
which it may be useful for them to observe?

     A. Perhaps these that follow: 15

    (1) Be sure to begin and end precisely at the time
appointed.

    (2) Sing no hymns of your own composing.

    (3) Endeavour to be serious, weighty, and solemn in your
whole deportment before the congregation.   20

    (4) Choose the plainest text you can.

    (5) Take care not to ramble from your text, but keep close
to it, and make out what you undertake.

    (6) Always suit the subject to the audience.

    (7) Beware of allegorizing or spiritualizing too much.   25

    (8) Take care of anything awkward or affected, either in
your gesture or pronunciation.

    (9) Tell each other if you observe anything of this kind.

[§70]   *Q.* 13. Is there any part of the work of an Assistant wherein
only some of our Assistants need be employed?   30

     A. There is. Let those and those only to whom we shall
write from time to time,

    (1) Visit the classes in each place, and write new lists of
all the members.

    (2) Regulate the bands.   35

    (3) Deliver new tickets.

    (4) Keep watch-nights and love-feasts.

    (5) Take and send us up an exact account of the behaviour of the stewards, house-keepers, schoolmasters, and
leaders.   40

[§71]   *Q.* 14. How may the journeys of our Assistants be fixed for the ensuing six months?

A. So far as we can yet perceive, thus:

	July, Aug.	Sept., Oct.	Nov., Dec.
Cornwall	John Haughton	Thos. Westell[595]	John Jones
	Robert Swindells	John Trembath	John Maddern
Plymouth	Jos. Cownley	Rt. Swindells	John Trembath
Bristol	Jas. Wheatley	Jos. Cownley	Robt. Swindells
	Rd. Williams[on]	John Jones	Jonth. Reeves
	John Nelson	Eleazer Webster	Thos. Westell
Wales	Thos. Richards	John Haughton	Jon. Reeves
	John Jones	————————	————————
London	Charles Wesley	John Wesley	John Wesley
	John Jones	Thos. Richards	Jno. Haughton
	Thos. Maxfield	John Downes	Eleaz. Webster
	J. Maddern	J. Maddern	
Wednesbury	James Jones	John Bennet	John Nelson
	James Wheatley	John Nelson[596]	————————
			Francis Walker[597]
Yorkshire	Thos. Westell	John Nelson	Francis Walker
		T. Meyrick	
[Yorkshire]	John Bennet	Jas. Jones	John Bennet
	————————	Thos. Meyrick	
Newcastle	Francis Walker	Chas. Wesley	Thos. Richards
	Edwd. Dunstable	Rd. Williamson[598]	Jos. Cownley
	Eleazer Webster	Jas. Wheatley	

---

[595] No attempt is made to note the many spelling variants within and between the two surviving MSS.

[596] In Re only. B places him in Yorkshire.

[597] In Re only. B places him in Yorkshire.

[598] Re, 'Willia[a]ms'. Evidently an error for Williamson, who alone is listed above among the Assistants.

| **Lincolnshire** | Thos. Meyrick | Fras. Walker | John Bennet |
| | ————— | ————— | Jas. Wheatley |

| **Ireland** | Jonathan Reeves | | |
| | J. Trembath | | 5 |

[§72]   *Q*. 15. Which are the watch-nights (Deo Volente), [etc.], in the
ensuing months?[599]
A. They are these:

10

Intercession	Watch-nights	Letter-days	Love-feasts
July 3	July 10	July 21	July 26 M[600]
Aug. 7	Aug. 7	Aug. 18	Aug. 23 W
Sept. 4	Sept. 11	Sept. 22	Sept. 27 Genrl.
Oct. 2	Oct. 9	Oct. 20	Oct. 25 M
Nov. 6	Nov. 6	Nov. 17	Nov. 22 W
Dec. 4	Dec. 4	Dec. 15	Dec. 15 G

15

[§73]   *Q*. 16. When and where shall we meet again?
A. If God permit, the 2nd Monday in May, at Bristol.
Adieu[601]

20

The London Conference of June 2–6, 1748

Thursday, June 2, 1748[602]

---

[599] B omits the last four words.

[600] These letters, found in Re only, apparently stand for Men, Women, and General.

[601] This word is present in B only.

[602] Orig., 'Thursday, June 3, 1748', incorrectly, as also in Disciplinary *Minutes* (1749), §1. For this year, the only MS copy of the Minutes extant is that by John Bennet, the last item in his transcript of the Minutes of the early Conferences, probably prepared during that year (see p. 123 above). As a guide to any differences between this (B) and Wesley's printed *Minutes* (1749), the variants between the two are noted. They seem to indicate that not this item but a slightly different MS version was the 'official' copy of the 1748 Minutes.

[§1]   The following persons being met at the Chapel house in
       Tower Street,[603] John Wesley, Charles Wesley, William
       Felton, Charles Manning, Thomas Maxfield, John Jones,
       Thomas Meyrick, John Trembath, Edward Perronet,
5   Jonathan Reeves, and afterwards Richard Thomas Bate-
       man, John Green, and William Tucker, it was inquired:
[§2]   *Q.* 1. What is our chief business at the present Conference?
       A. Not to consider points of doctrine (the time will not
       permit), but (1) to review those parts of the Conference
10   which relate to discipline; and (2) to settle all things relat-
       ing to the school which is now to be begun at Kingswood.
[§3]   *Q.* 2. We are again pressed 'only to preach in as many places
       as we can, but not to form any societies'. Shall we follow this
       advice?
15   *A*. By no means. We have made the trial already. We have
       preached for more than a year without forming societies
       in a large tract of land from Newcastle to Berwick-upon-
       Tweed; and almost all the seed has fallen as by the way-
       side. There is scarce any fruit of it remaining.[604]
20 [§4]   *Q.* 3. But what particular inconvenience do you observe
       when people are not formed into societies?
       A. These among many others:
       (1) The preacher cannot give proper exhortations and
       instructions to those who are convinced of sin unless he
25   has opportunities of meeting them apart from the mixed,
       unawakened multitude.

---

[603] In London and not Bristol in May, as had been planned at the last Conference.
On April 16, 1748, JW wrote that the Conference must be in London this year in order
to hold a meeting of 'the stewards of all the Societies' (*Letters*, 26:310 in this edn.), but
there is no record of such a stewards' meeting, though a few stewards attended at a
later stage in this Conference (§53 and n. 703). Curiously, neither John nor Charles
Wesley mentions the Conference in his journal (*Journal & Diaries*, 20:228, n. 61 in this
edn.). Myles writes of the Conference being at Bristol on June 22, and JW was indeed
in Bristol that day. Myles says seventeen preachers were present, a figure that does not
correspond to the London meeting, though the numbers attending were twice enlarged
there during the Conference period. *Chronological History*, 65. It is possible that a
short meeting was held at Bristol, but there is no other evidence for this.
[604] Cf. Minutes (1745), §62, where the scheme was commended.

(2) They cannot watch over one another in love unless they are thus united together.

Nor, (3) can the believers build up one another and bear one another's burdens.

[§5] *Q*. 4. Ought we not to have a longer time of probation for the rich before we admit them into our Society?

A. It seems not. But neither should we have a shorter. Let either rich or poor stay three months.

[§6] *Q*. 5. How shall we more effectually avoid respect of persons?

A. (1) Let us take care to visit the poor as the rich. (2) Let us strictly examine our hearts, whether we are not more willing to preach to the rich than to the poor. (3) We will speak to the poor at the chapel as often as to the rich; to the latter on Wednesday, to the former on Friday.[605]

[§7] *Q*. 6. How often shall we permit strangers to be present at the meeting of the Society?

A. Let every other meeting of the Society, either at the Foundery, the Chapel,[606] Bristol,[607] Kingswood, Newcastle, or elsewhere, be inviolably private, no one stranger being admitted on any account or pretence whatsoever. And let public notice of this be given in every place. On the other nights we may admit them with caution.

[§8] *Q*. 7. May a relapser into gross sin, showing signs of repentance, be immediately readmitted into the Society?

A. Not till after three months. But he may be admitted on those nights when strangers are admitted.

[§9] *Q*. 8. Are we not apt, particularly in the Society, to make too long prayers?

A. It may be we are. There are several exceptions which deserve a peculiar regard. But in general we would not choose to pray above eight or ten minutes without intermission.

[§10] *Q*. 9. What can be done in order to purge and quicken the Society?

---

[605] This underlines JW's concern for the poor on an equal plane with the rich; see Rack, *Reasonable Enthusiast*, 362–63.

[606] This almost certainly means West Street Chapel, London.

[607] 1749, 'at Bristol'.

A.(1) Let us strictly examine the leaders, both with regard to their grace, their gifts, and their manner of meeting their several classes.

(2) Let the preacher meet the leaders weekly before preaching at Wapping, Snowsfields, and Deptford.[608]

[§11]   *Q.* 10. If it please God to take our present ministers away, who should succeed in their place?[609]

A. We cannot tell yet. God will make it plain whenever that time shall come.

Friday, June 3rd,[610]

[§12]   Howell Harris,[611] Samuel Larwood, James Jones, and William Shent being added, it was inquired:

---

[608] In B, this is added as a separate paragraph at the foot of the page, before the entries for Friday; in 1749, it is given as the second section of *Q.* 9.

[609] JW was suffering from fever, which may have provoked this concern for the succession. John Bennet, June 5, 1748, MS diary, in MA; *Journal & Diaries*, 20:228 in this edn.

[610] Orig. in both B and 1749, 'June 4th'.

[611] The comments of Howell Harris in his diary illuminate the proceedings. His entry for June 3 (MS diary, vol. 131) runs thus:

'This morning my dear Lord, notwithstanding all my weakness, came to me and showed me he would have me go to Mr. Wesley's Conference, where I have been invited, and so I went. I feel a deep envy [meaning 'concern'?] for the Established Church of England. . . . I found a tenaciousness in them of giving up the power of their hands, and if they would propose so to the bishops, then none but such as they would approve of who would preach, and they not till they be licensed.

'For four hours I stayed here. . . . They were settling rules for union and love (their ministers also disagreeing and having the fruits of envy as well as ours). To speak to a private person what was from one brother disclosed to another is the highest abuse of love, and to speak of it when committed as a secret is the deviation; but whether it was right to speak of it to Mr. Wesley or not was a doubt. It was agreed it should not unless it was of important occasions. I find he [John Wesley] has stewards everywhere over the preachers, to send him an account of their behaviour, and whether God is with them. He did read heads to us of an *Address to the Clergy*, where he showed the natural and acquired gracious gifts that all clergymen should have and I objected that it should be soft, as 'tis so strong a pill, and not written authoritatively, lest they object and cry, Who made him [Wesley] archbishop over us, because the prophets, apostles, and many eminent men that have been employed in the Church have not had many of those qualifications. The rules of the behaviour of the young exhorters were set also. He settled John Jones next to him and his brother, then Mr. Maxfield, and the

[§13] *Q.* 1. What can be done in order to a closer union of our
Assistants with each other?

A.(1) Let them be deeply convinced of the want there is of
it at present, and of the absolute necessity of it.

(2) Let them pray that God would give them earnestly to 5
desire it; and then that he would fulfil the desire he has
given them.

[§14] *Q.* 2. Ought not the ministers to have as much confidence
as may be in those who serve as sons in the gospel?

A. It is highly expedient they should. 10

[§15] *Q.* 3. Would it not then be well that they should be exceeding unready to believe any evil report concerning them?

A. They ought not to believe it till they have seen them, or
written to them and received an answer.

[§16] *Q.* 4. Suppose one of our Assistants should be tempted to 15
think evil of us and should mention it to another, ought
that other to mention this to us?

A. Not if it was spoken only as a temptation. And if he thinks
it a thing of moment which we ought to know, still it may
be best to wait a little, till he who was under that temptation 20
comes to town, and then let him speak it himself.

rest to look on themselves as students or pupils in the university, and their
business to save souls, and to be ready for the meanest office, wiping shoes,
etc., and not to affect the gentleman, yet to be clean, etc. To rise at 4, spend
till 5 in praying and meditation, then to preach to 6, and at 7 to breakfast,
thence to 12 reading, writing, and praying, thence to 6 to visit the flock from
house to house, and at 9 to bed. Be punctual in their time. When they told
me, when we shall be united, they would make me keep my hours, I said it
could not be; my work was not as theirs, and I could not slavishly be in subjection to man. When they brought in their objection to some of our people
in South Wales, I said the fault was alike on their part, too. I mentioned jeal-
ousies on their staying so long at Builth, and they satisfied me. I insisted on
the rule to be equal on both sides, of not going among their people as they
among ours, else an union would never come about. That I was persuaded
of my call and place and work as I was of theirs. How I thought in seeing
them stay so long in Wales, as we have above a hundred labourers of all kinds,
to take some, and to go where we are called among your people if I saw any
party arising. . . . He mentioned three qualifications of a preacher: (1) To
know salvation by faith by the remission of their sins; (2) To have sufficient
judgment, knowledge in the Scriptures, and freedom of speech; (3) That
some have been awakened and justified. He recommended books to them—
Life of God in the Soul, Thomas à Kempis, De Renty's Life, Halyburton,
some church history, etc. . . . I saw the blessing of having authority. . . .'

[§17]   *Q.* 5. What further advice can be given to our Assistants in
order to their confiding in each other?

A.(1) Let them beware how they despise each other's gifts, and
much more how they speak anything bordering thereon.

5   (2) Let them never speak slightly of each other in any kind.

(3) Let them defend one another's character in every
point to the uttermost of their power.[612]

[§18]   *Q.* 6. What Assistants do we now agree to receive into the
work?

10   *A.* Chas. Skelton (from Ireland), David Trathen, John
Whitford of Cornwall, Thomas Colbeck,[613] William
Darney, Eleazer Webster, and William Tucker.[614]

Saturday, June the 4th[615]

15 [§19]   Mr. James Erskine[616] being added, it was inquired:

---

[612] 1749 adds: '(4) Let them labour, in honour each to prefer the other to himself.' The 1749 Disciplinary *Minutes* also adds to the report of the 1748 Conference, §§19–21, some passages dealing with preachers' relationships and with popularity (see pp. 831–32 below).

[613] Of Keighley; see JW's letter, Aug. 26, 1748, *Letters*, 26:325 in this edn.

[614] 1749 adds three more questions and answers: 'How shall they avoid all approaches to jealousy and envy of each other?. . . What is popularity? . . . How can we avoid this?'

[615] Orig., 'Saturday, June the 5th'. The gist of the conversations for this Saturday session, completely dedicated to Kingswood School, was reproduced in JW, not in the 1749 *Minutes*, but as *A Short Account of the School in Kingswood, near Bristol* (see *Bibliography*, No. 162, and vol. 15 of this edn.). Howell Harris, who was present, left his own diary account for June 4:

'Conference continued. To the Foundery again to the Conference, where I heard the whole affair of the school or academy they are going to set up at Kingswood. Settling their debt. . . . £1. 10*s*. 0*d*. for each scholar, six masters, two maids. The rules of the family, viz., at 4 private prayer, reading, and singing private. At 5, public prayers. 6 breakfast. 7 to work—gather sticks or stones, or learn some trade, butter-making, shoemaking, pick silk or wool, etc. 8 to 10, English. 10 to 11, write. To 12 to work or walk, but always with their masters, 1 then dinner. Then from 2 to 5 to their books, then to 6 work. No play, and to sleep from 8 to 4 the youngest, and the rest from 9 to 4. The school to consist of seven classes before they study the sciences. After they go through Latin, Greek, Hebrew, and French and named the authors for each class. I was humbled and I learned to propose questions for Association. Knowing [?] how I had no qualifications but to be some pert but insignificant creature. . . . Afterward I was in private with the Wesleys and a few, looking over queries to be put to the Attorney General about our case.' (MS Diary, vol. 131b)

[616] James Erskine, Lord Grange (1679–1754), for whom see Minutes (1745), §81, n. 316.

[§20]   *Q*. 1. What is the design of the foundation at Kingswood?
      A. We design to train up children there, if God permit, in
      every branch of useful learning, from the very alphabet
      till they are fit as to all acquired qualifications for the work
      of the ministry.   5

[§21]   *Q*. 2. At what age do you design to take them?
      A. Ordinarily betwixt the years of six and ten.

[§22]   *Q*. 3. By what name should this foundation be called?
      A. Kingswood School.[617]

[§23]   *Q*. 4. What in particular is to be taught there?   10
      A. Reading, Writing, Arithmetic, French, Latin, Greek,
      Hebrew, Rhetoric, Geography, Chronology, History,
      Logic, Ethics, Physics, Geometry, Algebra, Music.

[§24]   *Q*. 5. How many classes do you propose to have?
      A. Seven, as far as we can now judge.   15

[§25]   *Q*. 6. What is taught in the first class?
      A. Reading, hornbook, *Instructions for Children*,[618] *Lessons
      for Children.*[619] Writing, *English Grammar*,[620] *Westminster
      Introduction to the Latin Grammar.*[621] *Praelectiones
      Pueriles*,[622] which the child translates into English.   20
      Corderii Colloquia Selecta.[623] The children translate the
      Instructions for Children into Latin and repeat
      Praelect[iones] Pueriles.

[617] For the origins and early history of the school, see Arthur G. L. Ives, *Kingswood School in Wesley's Day and Since* (London, 1970), chap. 3.

[618] Published by JW in 1745 (see *Bibliography*, No. 101).

[619] A series of extracts from the Bible, in four parts, of which JW had already published three parts, the fourth following in 1754 (see *Bibliography*, Nos. 117–20).

[620] Almost certainly JW's *Short English Grammar*, published this year (see *Bibliography*, No. 149, and vol. 15 of this edn.).

[621] [Richard Busby (1606–95)], *An English Introduction to the Latine Tongue. For the Use of the Lower Forms in Westminster School* (1659), and many other edns., with slightly varying titles. JW seems to have used this as the basis for his own *A Short Latin Grammar* (1748), which replaced the Westminster Grammar in his published *Short Account of Kingswood School* (1749; see *Bibliography*, No. 150, and vol. 15 of this edn.).

[622] An alternative title for JW's *Instructiones Pueriles*, basically a translation into Latin of his above-mentioned *Instructions for Children* (see *Bibliography*, No. 153, published 1748).

[623] *Matthurini Corderii Colloquia Selecta* (1748; see *Bibliography*, No. 151).

[§26]   *Q.* 7. What is taught in the second class?

A. The Pilgrim's Progress.[624] Kempis,[625] which they translate into English, and repeat. *Cornelius Nepos.*[626] They translate *Lessons for Children* into Latin; and so in the third class.

[§27]   *Q.* 8. What is taught in the third class?

A. Life of Haliburton.[627] St. Austin's *Confessions*, which they translate.[628] Sallust.[629] Phaedrus.[630] Buchanan, which they repeat.[631] Dilworth's *Arithmetic.*[632]

[§28]   *Q.* 9. What is taught in the fourth class?

A. Kennett's *Roman Antiquities.*[633] Castalio's *Kempis*, which they translate.[634] Caesar. Terence.[635] They translate Mr. De Renty into Latin.[636] Vida,[637] which they repeat, and make Latin verses.

[§29]   *Q.* 10. Should all the children make verses?

A. We may try them for one or two years.

[§30]   *Q.* 11. What is taught in the fifth class?

[624] JW's abridged version (1743), now in its 3rd edn. (see *Bibliography*, No. 79).

[625] JW's *Extract of the Christian's Pattern* (see *Bibliography*, No. 45, and vol. 14 of this edn.).

[626] Cf. above, p. 165, n. 342.

[627] *An Extract of the Life and Death of Mr. Thomas Haliburton* (1741 onwards; see *Bibliography*, No. 12).

[628] Cf. MS Minutes (1745), §83, VII, 7.

[629] Cf. ibid., §83, VII, 1.

[630] It is not certain which edn. of Phaedrus's *Fables* that JW prescribed for Kingswood School. In 1750 he published his own selection, *Phaedri Fabulae Selectae* (see *Bibliography*, No. 180).

[631] Cf. MS Minutes (1745), §83, VII, Verse, 7.

[632] Thomas Dilworth (d. 1780), *The Schoolmaster's Assistant; being a compendium of arithmetic*, many edns., of which the 2nd was published in 1744; the 3rd, 1748.

[633] Basil Kennett (1674–1715), *Romae Antiquae Notitia, or the Antiquities of Rome* (1696 and many edns.).

[634] Sebastian Castalio or Castellio (1515–63), *De Christo Imitando, contemnendisque Mundi Vanitatibu Libellus*, authore Thoma Kempisio, 1576, etc., which JW had abridged for his *Thomas à Kempis de Christo Imitando* (1748; see *Bibliography*, No. 154).

[635] Cf. MS Minutes (1745), §83, VII, Prose, 2, Verse, 1.

[636] *An Extract of the Life of Monsieur De Renty, a late Nobleman of France* (1741, etc.; see *Bibliography*, No. 43). Abridged from the English translation by Edward Sheldon (1658, 1684) of the French original. De Renty founded religious societies and was greatly admired by JW and other Methodists for his holy life.

[637] Cf. MS Minutes (1745), §83, VII, Verse, 5.

    A. Potter's *Greek Antiquities.*[638] Erasmus,[639] which they
translate. Velleius Paterculus.[640] Tully's Offices.[641] Virgil.[642]
They translate Mr. Haliburton into Latin. Westminster
Compendium of Greek Grammar.[643] Greek Testament. Ran-
dall's *Geography.*[644] Wall Maps.[645] Now also they learn to   5
make themes.
[§31] *Q.* 12. What is taught in the sixth class?
    A. Mr. Law's *Christian Perfection,*[646] which they translate.
Moral and Sacred Poems,[647] which they repeat.
Tusc[ulanae] Quaestiones,[648] which they translate into   10
Greek. *Horatii,* etc., *Selecta,*[649] which they repeat. Greek
Testament. Epictetus.[650] Cebetis *Tabula,*[651] which they
translate. Pythagoras.[652] Greek Epigrams,[653] which they
translate into Latin verse. Bengelii *Introductio ad*

[638] John Potter (1674–1747), *Archaelogia Graeca, or The Antiquities of Greece,* 2
vols. (Oxford, 1697–99, etc.).

[639] Cf. MS Minutes (1745), §83, VII, Prose, 6.

[640] Cf. ibid., 2.

[641] Cf. ibid., 3.

[642] Cf. ibid., VII, Verse, 2.

[643] [Richard Busby (1606–95)], *Graecae Grammaticae Compendium* (London,
1721, etc.), prepared from his large *Graecae Grammaticae Rudimenta.* The *Compendium* was a major source of JW's *Short Greek Grammar* (1765; see *Bibliography,*
No. 269, and vol. 15 of this edn.).

[644] Joseph Randall, *A System of Geography* (London: for J. Rivington, 1744). Bailey's library list for Kingswood School (1789) noted 'Gordon's *Geography'.* But the
same list notes also (as 'Salmon's *Geography') A New Geographical and Historical
Grammar* (1749), by Thomas Salmon, which he quotes in *The Doctrine of Original
Sin* (1757), I.ii.4.

[645] Orig., 'Well Mapps'.

[646] William Law, *A Practical Treatise on Christian Perfection,* JW's extract (1743;
see *Bibliography,* No. 45).

[647] *A Collection of Moral and Sacred Poems,* 3 vols. (1744; see *Bibliography,* No.
78).

[648] Cicero, *Tusculanae Disputationes.* Cf. MS Minutes (1745), §83, VII, Prose, 3.

[649] Cf. MS Minutes (1745), §83, VII, Verse, 4.

[650] Cf. ibid., VIII, Prose, 4.

[651] A Greek allegory on human life ascribed to Cebes, a pupil of Socrates, and
titled Κέβητο Θηβαίου Πίναξ; in Latin, *Cebetis Thebani Tabula.* It appeared in
many edns. throughout the 16th and 17th centuries, often in Greek and Latin
together, and occasionally in English, variously called 'The Emblem of Human
Life', 'A Picture of Human Life', and so on.

[652] Pythagoras does not appear elsewhere among the writers whom JW studied.

[653] Cf. MS Minutes (1745), §83, VIII, Verse, 2.

Chronologiam.[654] Marshall's *Chronological Tables*.[655]
Shorthand.[656]

[§32]   *Q*. 13. What is taught in the seventh class?

5
A. Mr. Law's *Serious Call*,[657] which they translate. Milton,
which they repeat. Tully, *de Natura Deorum*,[658] which they
translate. Casimir.[659] Xenophon' s *Cyrus*[660]—*translate*.
Plato's Dialogues.[661] Homer's *Iliad*[662]—repeat. Now also
they make Greek verses. And [learn] to declaim. Hebrew
Grammar.[663] Hebrew Bible. Vossii *Rhetorica*.[664]

[654] Johann Albrecht Bengel (1687–1752), *Ordo Temporum a Principio per Periodos Oeconomiae Divinae* (Stuttgart, 1741). Apparently, JW here uses a generic description of this work, which also appears in his *Short Account of the School in Kingswood* (1749), 3, in italics as if for a title. In his personal copy, however, JW struck through *Introductio ad Chronologiam* and inscribed above, 'Ordo Temporum'.

[655] Benjamin Marshall, *Tabulae Chronologicae, continentes tum sacra tum prophana maxime notatu digna, a creatione mundi usque ad Christi nativitatem (Chronological Tables, in which are contain'd not only all the chief things of sacred history from the creation of the world 'till Christ's time, but also all other the most remarkeable things of those times that are recorded in any of the antient writers now extant)*, fol. ed. (Oxford, 1713).

[656] Although JW had for a short time at Oxford used James Weston's system of shorthand (used more extensively by Benjamin Ingham; see *Diary of an Oxford Methodist: Benjamin Ingham, 1734–35*, ed. Richard P. Heitzenrater [Durham, N.C.: Duke University Press, 1985], 5 n.), and although an edn. of Aulay Macaulay' s shorthand (used by John Bennet) had been issued in 1747, it seems most likely that at Kingswood School, they were teaching orally that of John Byrom (1692–1763), presumably by some arrangement with the inventor. Byrom was part of a circle known as the Manchester Nonjurors, of whom JW's colleague John Clayton was one. The Wesley brothers used Byrom's system after the mid-1730s, although students who learned the system directly from Byrom were required to sign an agreement not to share the system, in order to protect the inventor's income. It did not become generally available until its publication in 1767.

[657] William Law, *A Serious Call to a Devout and Holy Life*, of which JW published an abridgement (1744; see *Bibliography*, No. 86).

[658] One of JW's favourite items in Cicero's philosophical works; cf. MS Minutes (1745), §83, VII, Prose, 3.

[659] Cf. ibid., VII, verse, 6.

[660] Cf. ibid., VIII, Prose, 3.

[661] Cf. ibid., 2.

[662] Cf. ibid., VIII, Verse, 1.

[663] Almost certainly the work on which JW based his *Short Hebrew Grammar* (1751; see *Bibliography*, No. 190, and vol. 15 of this edn.): *Hebraica Grammatices Rudimenta* (1717, etc.), compiled by Richard Busby for Westminster School.

[664] Gerard John Vossius (1577–1649). Of his five works on rhetoric (all in Latin, not translated into English), the one intended is almost certainly *Elementa Rhetorica oratoriis eiusdem partitionibus accommodata* (1655, etc.,) of which a 1739 edn. is in MA.

[§33] *Q.* 14. How shall the children spend one day?

    A. As far as we can discern, thus:

      4 [a.m.]. Private prayer and singing. 5. Public worship.
6. Work. Breakfast. 7. Latin, Greek, or Hebrew. 9. English. 10. Writing, Arithmetic, etc. 11. Walk or Work.   5
12 [p.m.]. Dinner. Work. 1. Latin, Greek, or Hebrew.
4. Writing, etc. 5. Private prayer and singing. 6. Walk or
Work. Supper. 7. Public prayer. 8. They go to bed, the
youngest the first.

[§34] *Q.* 15. But you leave them no time to play?   10

    A. No. He who plays when he is a child, will play when he
is a man.

[§35] *Q.* 16. How do they employ the hours of private prayer?

    A. In self-examination, partly in reading, partly in singing,
partly in prayer.   15

[§36] *Q.* 17. Do they use forms of prayer?

    A. They may use a short form (to be varied continually),
and then pray in their own words.

[§37] *Q.* 18. What work do they do?

    A. In fair days and particularly in summer they may work   20
in the garden or grounds. In rainy days they may work at
any handicraft work; and some of them will learn music.

[§38] *Q.* 19. Do they ever work alone?

    A. Never; always in the presence of a master.

[§39] *Q.* 20. What masters do you propose to have?   25

    A. For the languages: John Jones,[665] T. Richards,[666]
W. Garston.[667] For reading, writing, etc.: W. Sellon,[668]
W. Spencer,[669] Rd. Moss.[670] For French, Abra.Grou.[671]

---

[665] Jones also served JW as an itinerant preacher and continued to be very helpful after he was ordained as a clergyman; see Minutes (1758), §1, n. 979.

[666] Thomas Richards is the preacher of that name; see 25:638 n. 4 in this edn.

[667] Nothing is known of this man, though in a letter of Dec. 18, 1780, JW refers to a London Methodist as 'Sister Garston', possibly his widow. It seems doubtful whether he ever came to Kingswood. See June 22, 1751, *Journal & Diaries*, 20:392–94 in this edn.

[668] Walter Sellon (1715–92). He left in 1750 to serve Lady Huntingdon, who secured episcopal ordination for him. From his various livings he continued to support JW's Arminian teaching by five anonymous publications.

[669] Orig., 'Spenser'. An early Methodist convert who for a time had been a member of the family at the Foundery, London.

[670] Richard Moss was also one of JW's preachers.

[671] Abraham Grou was 'honest and diligent', but a figure of fun to the children. June 22, 1751, *Journal & Diaries*, 20:393, n. 6, in this edn.

[§40]   *Q.* 21. What housekeeper?
    A.

[§41]   *Q.* 22. What servants?
    A.

5   [§42]   *Q.* 23. How shall they diet?
    A. We think thus: Breakfast, milk porridge and water gruel by turns.
    Supper, bread, and butter and milk by turns.
    Dinner, Sunday: cold roast beef.

10   Monday: hash and apple dumplings.
    Tuesday: boiled mutton; broth; dumplings.
    Wednesday: vegetables.
    Thursday: boiled mutton; broth; dumplings.
    Friday: vegetables.

15   Saturday: bacon and greens; apple dumplings.

[§43]   *Q.* 24. Do they never fast?
    A. Yes (if they are in health), every Friday till three o'clock.

[§44]   *Q.* 25. What do they drink?
20   *A.* Water.

[§45]   *Q.* 26. When are they to learn French?
    A. When they have gone through the school. Qr.[672]

[§46]   *Q.* 27. Do they go to school every day?
    A. Every day except Sunday. We have no holidays,[673] so
25   called.

[§47]   *Q.* 28. How do they spend Sundays?
    A. 6. Dress; breakfast. 7 [a.m.]. Learn hymns, etc. 8. Public worship. 9. Go to church. 1. [p.m.]. Dinner, singing.
    2. Public worship. 4. Private exhortation.

30   [§48]   *Q.* 29. After they have gone through the school, what do they learn the first year?
    A. The Hebrew Bible, with Francke's *Manuductio.*[674] The Greek Testament. The Apostolic Fathers. Tertullian. Pearson on the *Creed*;[675] abridge it. Aldrich's *Logic,* and

---

[672] Probably an abbreviation for 'quaere' (query)?

[673] Orig., 'holydays'.

[674] August Hermann Francke (1663–1727), *Manuductio ad lectionem Scripturae sacrae, omnibus theologiae sacrae cultoribus commendata a Petro Allix* (London, 1706).

[675] Cf. MS Minutes (1745), §83, I, Doctrinal, 1.

Sand[erso]n, W.'s Sermons,[676] Bp. of Meaux, Introduction to History.[677] Puffendorf's *Introduction*.[678]

[§49] *Q*. 30. What the second year?

A. Marcus Antoninus.[679] Origen. Clemens Alexandrinus. St. Cyprian.[680] Pascal's Thoughts.[681] Our Tracts. Dr. Gell's Works;[682] abridge them. Universal History.[683] *Compendium of Ethics*.[684] Euclid's *Elements*.[685]

[§50] *Q*. 31. What the third year?

A. Chrysostom, *de Sacerdotio*;[686] translate it. Macarius.[687] St. Augustine. Fell on the *Epistles*.[688] Boehm's *Sermons*;[689] abridge them. Spenser's *Fairy Queen*.[690] *History of the Council of Trent*.[691] Burnet's *History of the Reformation*[692] Algebra. Physics.

[§51] *Q*. 32. What in the fourth year?

[676] Henry Aldrich (1647–1710), *Artis Logicae Compendium* (1691). JW used this work as a basis for his own *Compendium of Logic* (1750, see *Bibliography* No. 185, and vol. 15 of this edn.), adding an appendix from Bishop Robert Sanderson (1587–1663), and indicating JW's own two sermons, 'The Means of Grace' (No. 3) and 'The Nature of Enthusiasm' (No. 37) as exemplars.

[677] Jacque Benigné Bossuet (1627–1704). Apparently intended is his *Discours sur l'histoire universelle*, which was translated into English in 1686 as *Discourse on the History of the Whole World*.

[678] Samuel Puffendorf, now spelled Pufendorf (1632–94), *An Introduction to the History of the Principal Kingdoms and States of Europe, enlarged by Mr. Martiniere. Improved from the French by Joseph Sayer*, 2 vols. (London, 1748).

[679] Cf. MS Minutes (1745), §83, VIII, Prose, 5.

[680] Cf. ibid., VII, 4.

[681] Cf. ibid., I, Practical, 7.

[682] Cf. ibid., I, Doctrinal, 3.

[683] Cf. ibid., V, 1.

[684] Cf. Mar. 4, 1747, *Journal & Diaries*, 20:152 in this edn. Possibly Daniel Whitby (1638–1726), *Ethicis Compendium in usum Academicae juventutis* (1684).

[685] The most likely work intended was *Euclid's Elements of Geometry*, in one of the edns. by John Keill (1671–1721) that had revived the study of Euclid at Oxford and Cambridge, and that continued to appear in English.

[686] Cf. MS Minutes (1745), §83, VIII, 8.

[687] Cf. ibid.

[688] Cf. ibid., I, Doctrinal, 2.

[689] Cf. ibid., Practical, 4.

[690] Cf. ibid., VI, 1.

[691] Almost certainly that by Paulo Sarpi (1552–1623), which first appeared in London in 1619, and which JW studied in 1725.

[692] Gilbert Burnet (1643–1715), *History of the Reformation in England*, 3 vols. (1679, 1681, 1714).

  A. Ephrem Syrus; translate it. St. Jerome. Nalson's
  Sermons;[693] abridge them. Clarendon.[694] Rapin.[695]
  Metaphysicae Compendium.[696] Bishop of Cork.[697]

[§52] *Q.* 33. What the fifth year?
  A. St. Basil. Forbesii, *Instructiones Historico-Theologicae.*[698]
  Heylyn's Tracts.[699]

Monday, June 6th

[§53] The following persons being present at the Foundery, John
  Wesley, Charles Wesley, Charles Manning, John Jones,
  Thomas Maxfield, Jonathan Reeves, John Bennet, James
  Jones, Samuel Larwood, John Trembath, Edward Per-
  ronet, Thomas Meyrick, William Holland,[700] William
  Shent, W. Darney, Richard Moss, Howell Harris;[701] and

---

[693] Orig., 'Nelson'; cf. MS Minutes (1745), §83, I, Practical, 5.

[694] Edward Hyde, first Earl of Clarendon (1609–74), *History of the Rebellion and Civil Wars in England*, 3 vols. (Oxford, 1702–4).

[695] Paul de Rapin (1661–1725), *The History of England, as well Ecclesiastical as Civil*, trans. N. Tindal, 2 vols. fol. (1743).

[696] Probably Daniel Whitby (1638–1726), *Brevissimum Compendium Metaphysicae sec Mentem Nominalium* (Oxford, 1690), published anonymously.

[697] Peter Browne (c. 1664–1735), bishop of Cork and Ross, *The Procedure, Extent, and Limits of Human Understanding* (1728), a very important book for JW since his Oxford years; see *Letters*, 25:251 in this edn.

[698] John Forbes (1593–1648), *Instructiones Historico-Theologicae de Doctrina Christiana, et vario rerum statu, ortisque erroribus et controversiis, iam inde a temporibus apostolicis ad tempora usque seculi decime-septime priora* (Amsterdam, 1645), a celebrated work that was not translated into English.

[699] John Heylyn (1685?–1759), orig., 'Heylin', JW's usual spelling. *Devotional Tracts (concerning the Presence of God. etc) from the French* (London, 1724), containing Brother Lawrence's famous work and other mystical treatises, of which JW later published extracts in vol. 38 of his *Christian Library* and elsewhere (see *Bibliography*, No. 165).

[700] William Holland, a founding member of the Fetter Lane Society, London, and a Moravian preacher, was seeking a renewal of his early associations with JW. See JW to Holland, Feb. 6, 1748, *Letters*, 26:278 and n. 12 in this edn.

[701] Howell Harris's diary for June 6 reads thus:
  'With the lawyer. At 12 to Mr. Wesley's Conference. Mentioned that I thought that in the Church we were like to be united, and not as a party there. I saw unsurmountable difficulties in the way. (I meant his being head, ruling so, and being the eye and mouth and head, and being so dark in doctrine.) I looked on their forbidding their people to come and hear us to be a great stumbling-block to our people, and much hinders our coming nearer together than we are; and he and all denied that he ever gave such an order. I mentioned my preaching at High Wycombe among their people, and would so at

Wm. Briggs,[702] William Welch, Patrick Thompson, of
Newcastle, Stewards,[703] it was inquired:

[§54]   *Q.* 1. How may the leaders of classes be made more useful?

    A.(1) Let each of them be diligently examined concerning
his method of meeting a class. 5

(2) Let more particular directions be given on those
heads in which many of them have been wanting.

[§55]   *Q.* 2. What directions?

    A.(1) Let every leader come into the Society room as soon
as ever the sermon is ended, and there sit down and 10
commune with God in his heart till the preacher
comes.

(2) Let no leader go out till the exhortation and the
whole service is ended.

(3) Let none speak there but the preacher or the stew- 15
ards, unless in answer to a question.

(4) Let every leader then give notice by note of every sick
person and of every disorderly walker in his class.

(5) Let every leader send a note to the visitor weekly of
every sick person. 20

(6) Let the leaders near Short's Gardens meet the
preacher there every Monday night after preaching.

(7) Let the leaders converse with the preachers as frequently and as freely as possible.

(8) In meeting classes, let them diligently inquire how 25
every soul prospers. Not only how each person observes
the outward *Rules*, but how they grow in the knowledge
and love of God.

Bath, but the people feared to offend you in asking me, and he said he was free
if they desired it. In private, consulted about the letter he is to send to the
archbishops. I desired him to be as tender as possible to them. In the evening
to the Tower. Came to the Tabernacle about 11, and met the Conference, and
several letters from Bro. Whitefield. Sat together to near 2, was much
refreshed on finding that Bro. Whitefield is soon to come over.' (Beynon,
Howell Harris's Visits to London, 187–90; cf. *Bathafarn* 4 [1969]: 63–65)

[702] William Briggs (c. 1722–88), upon whom JW leaned greatly to administer
many secular affairs of the London Methodists. See Briggs to JW, Dec. 28, 1744,
Letters, 26:120 and n. 19 (see also JW's, 26:664) in this edn.

[703] Cf. JW to CW, Apr. 16, 1748: 'The Conference must be in London this year,
in order to the meeting of the stewards from all the societies.' *Letters*, 26:310 in this
edn.

[§56]   *Q.* 3. Can any further expedient be found for making these meetings lively and profitable to those who meet?

A. Let us try this: Let us observe what leaders are most blessed to those entrusted to their care; and let those meet in other classes as often as possible, and see, etc., what hinders their growth in grace.

[§57]   *Q.* 4. In the country societies one preacher has sometimes undone all which had been done by him who went before. How must this be prevented for the time to come?

A.(1) Let it be contrived as often as may be, that one should [not][704] go before another comes.

(2) When this cannot be, let him who leaves any place leave a written account of what he has done.

[§58]   *Q.* 5. How may we profit more by the work of God carried on in the distant societies?

A. Let the preacher resident in each send a circumstantial account to the minister at the Foundery:

(1) Of every remarkable conversion.

(2) Of everyone who dies in the triumph of faith.[705]

[§59]   *Q.* 6. How are our societies now divided?

A. Into nine divisions,[706] thus:

I. London, including, (1) London itself; (2) Kent and Surrey; (3) Essex; (4) Brentford; (5) Windsor; (6) Wycombe; (7) Oxford; (8) Reading; (9) Blewbury; (10) Salisbury.

II. Bristol, including, (1) Bristol itself; (2) Kingswood; (3) Bath; (4) Bearfield; (5) The Devizes; (6) Roade;[707] (7) Coleford; (8) Oakhill; (9) Shepton Mallet;[708] (10) Middlezoy;[709] (11) Beercrocombe; (12) Taunton.

III. Cornwall, including, (1) Tavistock; (2) Plymouth Dock; (3) Trewint;[710] (4) St. Ewe;[711] (5) Gwennap;

---

[704] The missing word is added in 1749.

[705] This may be the origin of such accounts in JW's *Journal* and *Arminian Magazine*.

[706] The 'divisions' at this point are equivalent to what will become known as 'circuits'; see Nov. 16, 1749, *Q.* 5, below.

[707] Orig., 'Rhoad', but 'Road' in 1749.

[708] Orig., and 1749, 'Shepton Mallard'.

[709] Orig., and 1749, 'Middlesey'.

[710] Orig., 'Truint'.

[711] Orig., 'St. Tue'.

(6) St. Agnes; (7) Illogan, etc.; (8) St. Ives; (9) The Western Societies.

IV. Ireland, including, (1) Dublin; (2) Phillipstown; (3) Tullamore; (4) Tyrrellspass;[712] (5) Ballyboy;[713] (6) Athlone.   5

V. Wales, including, (1) Cardiff; (2) Fonmon; (3) Llanmaes,[714] etc.; (4) Llantrissant.[715]

VI. Staffordshire, including, (1) Stroud; (2) Cirencester; (3) Stanley; (4) Evesham;[716] (5) Wednesbury;[717] (6) Shrewsbury; (7) Leominster.   10

VII. Cheshire, including, (1) Cheshire itself; (2) Nottingham; (3) Derbyshire; (4) Lancashire; (5) Sheffield, etc.

VIII. Yorkshire, including, (1) Leeds; (2) Birstall; (3) Keighley; (4) Acomb; (5) Sykehouse; (6) Epworth;   15
(7) Hainton; (8) Grimsby; (9) The Fens.

IX. Newcastle, including, (1) Osmotherley; (2) Newcastle itself; (3) Sunderland; (4) Biddick, (5) Burnopfield;[718] (6) Spen; (7) Swalwell; (8) Horseley; (9) Plessey; (10) Berwick-upon-Tweed.   20

[§60]   *Q.* 7. How shall we have a more exact knowledge of the state of the societies in each division?

A. [1] Let the preachers assisted by the stewards in each Society take an exact list of them every Easter. (2) Let these lists be transmitted within three weeks after Easter   25 to the persons appointed in each division to receive them. [3] Let this same person at the same time diligently inform himself of the spiritual and temporal state of each Society. [4] And let him bring these lists with him to the following Conference and give an account of all.   30

[§61]   *Q.* 8. Would it not be of use if all the societies were more firmly and closely united together?[719]

---

[712] Orig., 'Tyrrils-Pass'.
[713] Orig., 'Billiboy'.
[714] Orig., and 1749, 'Lanmais'.
[715] Orig., 'Lanission'; 1749, 'Lantrissent'.
[716] Orig., 'Eversham'.
[717] Orig., and 1749, 'Wensbury'.
[718] Orig., 'Burnep Fields'; 1749, 'Burnupfield'.
[719] This proposal was raised again and elaborated in *Minutes* (1749), §1.

A. Without doubt it would be much to the glory of God, to the ease of the minister, and to the benefit of the societies themselves both in things spiritual and temporal.

[§62]   *Q.* 9. Might not the children in every place be formed into
5   little societies?

A. Let the preacher try by meeting them apart and giving them suitable exhortations.

[§63]   *Q.* 10. How may the journeys of our Assistants be fixed for the ensuing six months?
10   *A.* So far as we can yet perceive, thus.[720]

Bristol Conference, Attempt to Unite British Methodists, August 2–3. 1749[721]

[720] Clearly the original 'official' copy of the Minutes contained a table of the stations, which was omitted from some subsequent copies, of which this by Bennet was one.

[721] This summary consists of four duodecimo pages in the Wesleys' handwriting, with the endorsement of Charles Wesley, 'Aug. 2, 1749/Vain agreement!' It is in the Elmer T. Clark Collection of the World Methodist Council, Lake Junaluska, N.C.; see Baker, *Wesley and Church*, 126–29. The background and further information, notably from Howell Harris, underline the significance of the meeting and illustrate the deep divide that marked the evangelical revival in England.

In Jan. 1747, JW attended a quarterly association of the Calvinistic Methodists at the invitation of Howell Harris, eager to secure fuller cooperation between the two major groups of the people called Methodists (see above, pp. 186–87). The discussions had been somewhat tentative, until 'Bro. Whitefield come over, and some solid rules be settled for an union', for Whitefield was their acknowledged leader, and he was in America. Harris attended JW's Conferences as a guest in 1747 and 1748, and his diary for the summer of 1748 (May 5–June 3, MS Diary, vol. 131a) reveals his concern about the possible union, ranging from eager anticipation to fear that it was impossible. On May 29, 1748, he wrote, 'I declared I thought the Lord would unite us and Bro. Wesleys when Bro. Whitefield came.' See esp. May 18, 21, 26, 28, 29; June 3, 4, 6, 9, 14; July 5, 7.

Whitefield landed at Deal on June 30, and on July 5, he wrote to the Wesleys: 'I hope I come in the spirit of love, desiring to study and pursue those things which make for peace. . . . I purpose, God willing, to be in London in a few days.' George Whitefield, *The Works of the Reverend G. W.*, ed. John Gillies, 6 vols. (London: Dilly, 1771–72), 2:146–47. He arrived in London on July 5, and Harris recorded: 'I met dear and honoured Mr. Whitefield. I opened about my conduct with Bro. Wesleys, and my burden about the Conference' (MS Diary, vol. 131b). Charles

Wesley was in London on a visit so that on July 7, the three were able to dine together and discuss the possible union. Harris then noted in his diary:

'I saw it would not do without (1) consulting the preachers in England and Wales; (2) without laying preliminaries and asking all questions freely on all sides. It seems to me that as a party it will never do, because neither of the sides can submit to either of the other [as] head—Mr. W[esley] or Mr. Whitefield; and also we should consider in the nature of the plan we go upon etc. Mr. Whitefield declared he was a sublapsarian and only held a conditional reprobation and we also [are] for a form of prayers only with liberty to pray before and after sermon; . . . that he would do nothing without consulting me, that he looked on me to him as he [CW] was to his brother. . . . Mr. Charles Wesley said he was free to commit all his societies to Mr. Whitefield, and that in a connexion, he was to be an equal with his brother, and Mr. Whitefield said he knew not who to make his executor to the Orphan House but Mr. Wesley, and that he always owned them as great men.'

CW could not speak fully for his older brother, however, and Whitefield wrote to JW (who was touring the Societies in the north of England) on Sept. l: 'My not meeting you at London has been a disappointment to me. But our Lord orders all things well. What have you thought about an union? I am afraid an external one is impracticable.' *Letters*, 26:327 in this edn. Nevertheless, he certainly hoped for peaceful understanding and something more tangible if possible. Things moved slowly in this matter, however, and there is no evidence available to trace the course of any further negotiations about union until the following year.

In July 1749, JW was reaching the end of a preaching tour in Ireland, during which he had published the consolidated Doctrinal and Disciplinary *Minutes* that incidentally would furnish a solid foundation for any future negotiations. See *Bibliography*, Nos. 169, 170, and pp. 778–835 below. He embarked for Bristol on July 20, planning to spend a week or so there. CW had his own home in Bristol, and from July 10 was briefly reunited with his wife of three months. Whitefield also had returned to Bristol from a tour in Wales on June 23 and planned another week in Bristol after a visit to London. A conference of the three friends and major Methodist leaders seemed opportune, and the place was reasonably convenient for Whitefield's second-in-command, Howell Harris. Again we are enabled to see things from Harris's point of view through his diary (vol. 136):

'July 30 . . . I had a farther proof of my heart . . . [a] messenger coming [or 'commanding'?] from Bristol from Mr. Whitefield . . . to come directly there to have a conference with Mr. Wesley in 24 hours. [Obscure words here seem to imply] 'Many things were against my going, viz., shortness of the time and places I had before me [where I was] published [to preach], weakness of my horse, having travelled now in three weeks and three days above five hundred miles . . . through twelve counties through North Wales and Glamorgan, and piles very sore, and being quite spent, felt faith to commit all to the Lord. . . . I laid the matter before the Lord to have it determined whether to go or not. . . . I was at length determined to go, giving it to him to take care to be there in the midst of us, as it was of the highest importance indeed [to settle] the terms of union among us.'

Arranging for some exhorters to supply his engagements, after two days on the road, Harris reached Bristol on Wednesday morning, Aug. 2. His diary continues:

'I went at ten to Mr. Whitefield, with whom I conferred in private. . . .

After breakfast we went to my Lady [Huntingdon]'s Room to receive the Sacrament, where the Lord came indeed to my soul. . . . After the ordinance I prayed there in company with Colonel Gumley, the Countess, Mr. Godwin, Mr. Dielin(?), Mr. and Mrs. Whitefield, Mr. Bateman, etc., about our meeting with Mr. Wesley about an union where I saw the infinite importance of the work and of the union, and of our general relation to all churches. . . . But still I felt no great hope of it, nor views how to come to it, but had much freedom to pray in the light of our afternoon conversation. . . . After conversing with Mr. Whitefield on several heads—about his going to Georgia, about Kingswood School, and our union—at four, I went with him to meet the two brothers Mr. Wesleys. . . . There after prayer, etc., we opened our hearts about the points in dispute, of a possibility of coming to terms, by confining to a practical way of preaching and keeping off the controversial way, and to adopt each other's expressions as much as possible and each to give up all we can so as to come together and to prevent the people saying of either side we have changed opinion, etc. I had freedom to be home about being so dead to all our names so to give room for God's name alone to be exalted. . . . It was agreed to draw up questions about anything weak in each other that hinders love, union, and nearness, and such rules as may be a means to keep . . . the bonds of love from being broken any more. I felt great love, joy, and freedom in my soul at our coming thus far.

'I opened my mind about justification, that we are under the law to stand by our own works till by the work of the Spirit we are made to give up ourselves wholly to the Lord Jesus on gospel terms. . . .

'Agreed about stirring up souls to live by faith on Christ. . . .

'We agreed about the degrees of superiority over the people . . . , about liberty to preach and keep private societies to build up souls, etc., to abide in the communion of the Established Church and to look upon the bishops as fathers till thrust out.

'I mentioned my fears lest he [Mr. Wesley] should ask to be head [of] a party. Mr. Whitefield mentioned his objection to his [Mr. Wesley] monopolizing the name of Methodist to himself only.

'Thursday, Aug. 3. Last night injoined [*sic*] in praying at the Countess's. I went with Brother Rowland to the Horsefair, but still the free course for fellowship in the spirit is not come down there. I was with Mr. Wesley and Mr. Whitefield again to Wesley's Room from about nine to eleven. I felt a nearer union in spirit in singing a hymn than ever before, and love to them [the Wesleys] indeed. . . . We had full freedom together, and I opened my heart about my experience . . . how I was justified and had the spirit of adoption, and how I saw election and reprobation, etc. They agreed to all, so that we settled several points towards our union. . . .

'Friday, Aug. 4. Yesterday, I went again to end our Conference with Mr. Wesley, and our hearts were indeed united in much love and freedom. . . . Settled several rules. . . . The discipline in Wales is in my hands, and so in England in his hands; agreed to lay these things before the preachers . . . and we parted lovingly and strengthened.'

Although this attempt at union fell through, Harris continued to promote union almost until his dying day. See esp. the summary of 1751–73, by M. H. Jones, *WHS* 16 (1928): 113–17.

Wedn. Aug. 2, 1749

The following persons being met together at the New Room in the Horsefair, [Bristol], George Whit[e]field, Howell Harris, John Wesley, and Charles Wesley,

It was inquired, 5

How far can we unite with each other? Either in affection? In judgment? Or in jointly carrying on the work of our common Master?

[I.] In order to remove every hindrance to the first, viz., a closer union in affection,

It was unanimously agreed, 10

(1) To believe no evil of each other till the accused has answered for himself.

(2) To speak no unkind or slighting word of each other, ((but)) and to defend one another against all that do speak so.

(3) Not willingly to speak of each other's opinions in such a man- 15 ner as to make them either odious or contemptible.

Several little objections and doubts were then proposed on both sides, and in great measure removed.

[II.] It was next considered, 'Are we agreed in judgment as to the nature and cause of justification?' 20

After some mild and friendly debate, all agreed to this:

(1) That the active as well as passive righteousness of Christ are the sole meritorious cause of our justification.

(2) That both are imputed to every believer.

(3) That by this price alone heaven is purchased for us. 25

(4) That ((God)) for the sake of these, 'all our sins in thought, word, and deed, are covered, are blotted out, shall not be remembered or mentioned against us, any more than if they had not been; that from the time we are accepted through the beloved, reconciled to God through his blood, he loves and blesses and watches over us 30 for good, even as if we had never sinned.'[722]

---

[722] See Wesley, Sermon 5, 'Justification by Faith' (1746), II.5, in *Works*, 1:189–90. in this edn. This sentiment may be compared with a statement on salvation doctrine by an English Calvinistic Methodist Association at Bristol in Mar. 1745; see E. Welch, ed., *Two Calvinistic Methodist Chapels 1743–1811* (Leicester: London Record Society, 1975), 20–22. 'That the first moment one believes, or looks to Christ, or hears his voice and opens to him, [one] receives Jesus Christ in his heart and becomes one with him. . . . That Christ alone is our compleat righteousness, holiness and sanctification. and that the very first moment we believe we stand compleatly holy and pure before the throne of God in him.' The statement guards carefully against salvation by works, though it allows for growth in knowledge and the need to 'mortify evil affections'—no doubt to guard against antinomianism.

Thurs. Aug. 3

In order to come as near each other as possible with regard to those points where we do not think alike,

[I.] It was agreed, with regard to predestination:

5   (1) Not to preach controversially either or against absolute election, irresistible grace, or final perseverance.

(2) To avoid in preaching the use of any such terms as naturally tend to revive the controversy.

(3) To confine ourselves to the very language of Scripture as far 10 as possible.

(4) To use each other's expressions, mixing them with our own, as far as we can honestly.

(5) Continually to maintain that man's whole salvation is of God, and his whole damnation of himself.

15   [II.] With regard to perfection, it was ((asked)) agreed:

(1) Not to preach controversially either for or against it.

(2) To drop the expressions 'sinless' and 'the inbeing of sin'.

(3) To exhort all to press on to perfection, in the holy law of love, by universal inward and outward conformity to the life and 20 death of Christ.

III. In order to facilitate an union in carrying on the work of God, it was agreed:

(1) Each of us to take a copy of the preceding minutes.

(2) To read these, as we find occasion, to some of our preachers.

25   (3) And to a few prudent persons of our flock.

(4) But to suffer no copy thereof to be taken, nor our own copy ever to go out of our hands.

The Newcastle Conference of November 16, 1749

30   **Thursday, November 16th, 1749**[723]

---

[723] A brief Conference held in Bristol, Aug. 2–3, was not a substitute for one of JW's regular Conferences with his preachers, and none of them seems to have been invited for the purpose of discussing the internal organization of JW's Methodist

[§1] It was inquired:

[Q.] 1. Can there be any such thing as a general union of our societies throughout England?

A. A proposal for this was made above a year ago.[724]

The substance of it is this: 5

Might not all the societies throughout England be considered as one body, firmly united together by one spirit of love and heavenly-mindedness?

Might not that in London be accounted the mother church? And the stewards of this consult for the good of   10

all the churches?

Might they not[725] answer letters from all parts, and give advice, at least in temporal affairs?[726]

[§2] But it may be asked, How can the temporal state of all the societies be known to the stewards in London?   15

I answer, Very easily, by means of the Assistants.

[§3] Let each Assistant make diligent inquiry at every Quarterly Meeting[727] concerning the temporal as well as spiritual state of each Society.

Societies. Both the doctrine and the general organization of JW's Societies had achieved maturity and formulation in his Doctrinal and Disciplinary *Minutes* published in July 1749, for which see below, pp. 778–835. Nevertheless it was clear that some annual conversations and arrangements remained necessary. JW continued to invite selected preachers to these gatherings, and MS Minutes of some of these have survived, while the permanent alterations made in Methodist organization at these gatherings were incorporated in successive edns. of the 'Large' *Minutes*, beginning in 1753.

[724] See Minutes (1748), §61. For a discussion of this and later attempts at the centralization at least of finance and the problems it caused with the London trustees, see n. 726 below and introduction, pp. 44, 48.

[725] Orig., 'Might not they not'.

[726] In the orig., 'things' is added as an alternative over 'affairs'. Nothing came of this, but in *Minutes* (1768), *Q.* 15 and n. 190, a proposal was made for all trust deeds to be lodged in London, and a 'strong box' provided for them; and in *Minutes* (1770), *Q.* 15, n. 315, for vesting all the houses in a 'general trust', including persons drawn out of the whole nation. See further, introduction, pp. 46–47.

[727] Apparently, this statement implies a gathering of the Circuit Quarterly Meeting, an institution that had been introduced the previous year. The first was at Todmorden in Yorkshire on Oct. 18, 1748, followed by another for Lancashire and Cheshire at Woodley on Oct. 20. John Bennet, Oct. 18 and 20, 1748, MS diary, in MA; see also Frank Baker, *William Grimshaw* (London, 1963), 147–50. Wesley commissioned Bennet to spread the system elsewhere (§10 and §12 below). Benjamin Ingham had had such meetings in his Societies, and it is possible that Bennet had noticed meetings with this title among the Quakers. See Bennet, MS Letterbook, fols. 29, 31, in MA; and F. Baker, *WHS* 35 (1965): 1–4.

Let him inquire particularly of each:

(1) Are you in debt?

(2) How much, and to whom?

(3) Are all in your Society poor?

(4) Are not some therein both able and willing to contribute toward the public debt?

(5) Or, to the furtherance of the gospel yearly?

(6) Or, toward a common stock?

(7) Who keeps your account? How?

And the answers he receives, let him transmit quarterly to London.

He might also put them into a regular method of keeping their accounts and transacting all their temporal affairs.

[§4] After the stewards in London are thus informed, may they not settle a regular correspondence with all the societies?

By this means we might not only be able to discharge all debts, but in a little time have a small fund, out of which a Society under persecution or in real distress, upon application made to the stewards in London, might speedily be relieved.

Being thus united together in one body, of which Christ Jesus is the head, neither the world nor the devil will be able to separate us in time or in eternity.

[§5] *Q.* 2. How may we make some advances towards this?

A. By appointing one of our Helpers in each circuit to take charge of the societies therein.

[§6] *Q.* 3. By what name may such an Helper be distinguished from the rest?

A. He may be termed an Assistant.[728]

[§7] *Q.* 4. How should an Assistant be qualified for the charge?

A. Not so much by superior gifts as by walking closely with God.

[§8] *Q.* 5. How many circuits[729] are there now?

---

[728] See above, Minutes (1745), §71 and n. 304. Hitherto the terms 'Helper' and 'Assistant' had been used interchangeably to denote Wesley's full-time lay itinerant preachers; see Minutes (1744), §72 and n. 167. The apparent association with finance here and the reference to the London stewards seem to foreshadow the scheme suggested in 1768 (see above, §1 and n. 726). The 'Assistant' is now to be the senior preacher in charge of a circuit, and the other preachers are to be termed 'Helpers'.

[729] Previously called 'divisions'; see June 6, 1748, *Q.* 6, above.

A. Nine:

I. London, including (1) London itself; (2) Kent and Surrey; (3) Essex; (4) Brentford; (5) Windsor;
(6) Wycombe; (7) Oxford; (8) Reading; (9) [Shalbourne];[730] (10) Blewbury.[731]   5

II. Bristol, including (1) Bristol itself; (2) Kingswood;
(3) Bath; (4) Bearfield; (5) Seend; (6) The Devizes;
(7) Salisbury; (8) Roade; (9) Coleford; (10) Oakhill;
(11) Shepton [Mallet]; (12) Dorsetshire; (13) Middlezoy;
(14) Beercrocombe; (15) Taunton; (16) Cullompton.[732]   10

III. Cornwall, including (1) Cornwall itself; (2) Plymouth Dock; (3) Tavistock.

IV. Ireland.

V. Wales.

VI. Staffordshire, including (1) Stroud; (2) Cirencester;   15
(3) Stanley; (4) Evesham; (5) Wednesbury;
(6) Leominster; (7) Shrewsbury; (8) Nottingham.

VII. Cheshire, including (1) Cheshire itself;
(2) Derbyshire; (3) Lancashire; (4) Sheffield.

VIII. Yorkshire and Lincolnshire.   20

IX. Newcastle, including (1) Newcastle itself; (2) the County of Durham; (3) Cumberland; (4) Northumberland; (5) Berwick.

[§9]   *Q.* 6. Who may be Assistants in these?

A. For the present, my brother or I may act as such in London; John Jones in Bristol and Cornwall; Jo. Haughton   25
and Jonathan Reeves in Ireland; Mr. Thomas[733] in Wales;
James Jones in Staffordshire; John Bennet in Cheshire;
Will. Shent in Yorkshire; John Downes in the Newcastle Circuit.   30

[§10]   *Q.* 7. What is the office of an Assistant?

---

[730] Orig., 'Shaburn', whose name was spelled in different ways at different times, and given both as in Berkshire and in Wiltshire, on whose joint boundary it lies. Now Shelbourne in Wiltshire.

[731] Orig., 'Blewberry'.

[732] Orig., 'Collumpton', as usual.

[733] Almost certainly Rev. Philip Thomas (c. 1710–81), curate to Rev. John Hodges at Wenvoe, who organized his own Methodist Societies in Llan-maes, Margam, and Neath, as well as being Mrs. Jones's chaplain for the Society at Fonmon Castle. See A. H. Williams, *John Wesley in Wales* (Cardiff: University of Wales Press, 1971), xxiii, 17, 21, 25, 58.

A. (1) To visit the classes in each place, and write new lists of the societies.[734] (2) To regulate the bands. (3) To deliver new tickets. (4) To keep watch-nights and love-feasts monthly. (5) To take in or put out of the Society or bands. (6) To hold Quarterly Meetings,[735] and therein diligently to inquire into the spiritual and temporal state of each Society. (7) To watch over the Helpers in his circuit, and see that [they] behave well, and want nothing. (8) To take care that every Society be supplied with books, and that the money for them be returned quarterly.

[§11] *Q.* 8. How shall these be apprised of what is required of them?

A. We will write to each immediately.

[§12] *Q.* 9. But some of them know not the nature of Quarterly Meetings. How shall we help them?

A. Desire John Bennet: (1) To send us up his plan. (2) To go himself as soon as may be to Newcastle and Wednesbury, and teach them the nature and method of these meetings.

[§13] *Q.* 10. What outward things should the Assistants immediately take care of?

A. Let them immediately take care: (1) That every Society provide a private room for the Helper. (2) That every Society provide a set of books for the Helper.[736] (3) Let the Assistant at London, Bristol, and Newcastle meet the married men in band, the married women, the single men, and the single women apart every quarter.

[§14] *Q.* 11. How may we have a more exact knowledge of the states of all the societies?

A. Let each Assistant take an exact list of each Society every Easter; and transmit those lists to London sometime before Whitsuntide.

[§15] *Q.* 12. How may we profit more by the work of God carried on in the distant societies?

---

[734] In the orig., 'the societies' is underlined (probably for omission rather than emphasis), and above is written 'all the members'. This was a frequent device of JW, but is probably a revision by Jones in his copy of the 'official' version of the *Minutes*.

[735] Cf. §3 and n. 727, above.

[736] See Minutes (1744), §84, and (1745), §83, for the original provision; *Minutes* (1766), *Q.* 30 for criticism of their level of reading and provision for it.

A. Let each Assistant inquire at every Quarterly Meeting, and send a circumstantial account to London:

(1) Of every remarkable conversion.

(2) Of everyone who dies in the triumph of faith.

[§16] *Q.* 13. How shall my journeying through the societies be of more use?

A. Let the Assistant of each district travel with me through all the societies therein.

[§17] *Q.* 14. How can we be assured that no Helper will disappoint a congregation?

A. Ask every one: (1) Do you see the great sin and extreme ill consequences of it? (2) Will you break a limb rather than break your word therein? (3) If you do, will you blame us for not employing you any more?

[§18] *Q.* 15. Shall we require every Helper to answer that question, Will you print nothing till we have revised it?[737]

A. By all means.

[§19] *Q.* 16. Are all our Helpers of a right spirit? Deeply serious? And full of zeal for God?

A. Let them pray more, and they will be so.

[§20] *Q.* 17. How can they be more united to each other?

A. (1) Let them speak freely to each other.

(2) When they meet let them never part without praying.

[§21] *Q.* 18. What method should we take in receiving a new Helper?[738]

A. (1) Let him be recommended to us by the Assistant to whose Society he belongs.

(2) Let him read and carefully weigh the Conferences, and see whether he can agree to them or no.

(3) Let him be received as a Probationer, by having a book given him inscribed thus:

'You think it is your duty to call sinners to repentance. Make full proof that God has called you hereto, and we shall then be glad to act in concert with you.

---

[737] This minute probably reflects problems with William Darney's use of his own doggerel hymns and poems. See also Minutes (1747), §8 on vetting pamphlets, and §69, 'sing no hymns of your own composing'; Minutes (1761), n. 1019 and later. For CW's criticism of Darney's behavior, see his account of the Leeds Conference, Sept. 1751 (below, pp. 242–44).

[738] For a possible earlier method, see Minutes (1746), §50, n. 440; introduction, p. 77.

We are. . . .'[739]

(4) Let him come to the next Conference, and after
examination, fasting, and prayer, be received as an
Helper by having a book given him inscribed thus:

5　　'So long as you freely consent and earnestly endeavour to
walk according to the following rules,[740] we shall rejoice to
go on with you hand in hand.

　　We are
　　　　Yours affectionately'

10　　　　(5) Let a new book be given at every Conference, and the
former returned.

[§22]　　　　　　　[Assistants and Helpers][741]

John Wesley, Charles Wesley, P. Thomas, John Jones, James
Jones, John Downes, John Bennet?[742] William Shent, John

15　　Haughton, Jonathan Reeves, Charles Skelton, John
Nelson, Joseph Cownley, David Trathen, R. Swindells?[743]
W. Tucker, T. Westell, F. Walker, Edward and Charles
Perronet, Thomas Maxfield, T. Meyrick, T. Richards.

---

[739] This phrase is clearly the beginning of the closing courtesies of such a note, which would be signed by JW himself. Cf. (4) below.

[740] The Disciplinary *Minutes*, superseded later by the various edns. of the 'Large' *Minutes*. For an example, see 1751, p. 239, n. 755 below.

[741] This list is a compilation of the Assistants and Helpers, though not so headed in the original, and not an indication of those who were actually present, though clearly a number of them were, almost certainly including the two Wesleys, Thomas, John, and James Jones, and John Downes, but probably not John Bennet. The query after several names surely indicates their absence and some uncertainty about their status or reliability.

[742] Although Bennet was listed as the Assistant in Cheshire (including Derbyshire, Lancashire, and Sheffield, the area where he had lived and preached from the outset), his marriage on Oct. 3 to Grace Murray had created inevitable tension with Wesley, and they were gradually drifting apart, though officially he remained an itinerant preacher in 1751 and later. It is possible that he was at this Conference or the next one, for on Aug. 10, 1750, CW wrote to him about remarks he had made 'at the last Conference', to the effect that most of the preachers were incapable of 'some improvement in humane literature'. Letter (MS MAM P6), in MA. It appears that CW was not in Bristol for the 1750 Conference, so he is presumably referring to that of 1749. By 1750, Bennet was thinking of training for the Anglican or Dissenting ministry. See Bennet to Whitefield, June 21, 1750, (Bennet, MS Letterbook, MA).

[743] Swindells was a rough diamond who frequently caused difficulties.

Probationers

C. Bastable, W. Roberts, John Whitford, Michael Fenwick, Jos. Tucker, Tho. Webb, Jo. Haime,[744] Nicholas Story, R. Higley,[745] John Trembath? James Wheatley? John Wasley? Robert Prior? Robert Gillespie? Samuel Larwood?

5

The Bristol Conference of March 8–9, [12–16?], 1750

Thur. 8 [Mar.] I desired all the preachers that were in Bristol[746] to meet me at four in the afternoon; and so every day while I was in 10 town.[747] In the evening, God rent the rocks again.[748] I wondered at the words he gave me to speak. But he doth whatsoever pleaseth him.[749]

[744] Orig., 'Hayme'.

[745] The handwriting is so distinct that it is hardly possible that this name could be other than Higley (or possibly Hagley), but no other occurrence of either name has been noted in the literature of early Methodism.

[746] In addition to JW—Charles Wesley was in London—there were probably present John Jones, who was the Assistant for Bristol and Cornwall; Christopher Hopper, who travelled with JW from Bristol to Ireland on Mar. 19; John Whitford, whom JW asked to preach for him on Sunday, Mar. 4; and among others possibly Joseph Cownley, James Wheatley, and William Baynes, a preacher serving as master at Kingswood School. John Bennet is unlikely to have been present despite the ambiguous statement in the CW letter quoted in *Minutes* (1749), §22, n. 742 above.

[747] Wesley seems to have spent Mar. 10–11 in Kingswood, and Mar. 12–19 in Bristol, after which he set out with Hopper for Ireland. There would be no Conference on Sunday (18) and probably not on Saturday (17). In any case seven days were a lengthy period for a series of business sessions, even beginning at 4:00 p.m., and it seems likely that much of the time was spent in spiritual challenge rather than discussion, so that this was one of the less formal Conferences.

[748] See 1 Kgs. 19:11, the appearance of God to Elijah.

[749] Mar. 8, 1750, *Journal & Diaries*. 20:323 in this edn.

The Bristol Conference of March 11–15, 1751[750]

Sat. [Mar.] 9, [1751]. Many of our preachers came from various parts. My spirit was bowed down among them, fearing some of them were perverted from the simplicity of the gospel. But I was revived 5 at the sight of John H[aime], John N[elson], and those who came with them in the evening, knowing they held the truth as it is in Jesus,[751] and did not hold it in unrighteousness.[752]

Mon. 11. Our Conference began, and the more we conversed, the more brotherly love increased. The same spirit we found on Tues-10 day and Wednesday. I expected to have heard many objections to our first doctrines.[753] But none appeared to have any. We seemed to be all of one mind, as well as one heart.[754]

---

[750] John Wesley, Mar. 9–15, 1751, *Journal & Diaries*, 20:379–80 in this edn. During 1749, Wesley closed the first decade of the Methodist Societies by formulating agreed standards of doctrine and discipline, and having these made readily available in printed form. During 1751, these standards were self-consciously used to test the loyalty and efficacy of the itinerant preachers upon whom Methodism depended to proclaim its message and administer its organization. It was clear that some of these men had been accepted with insufficient screening. A determined effort was therefore made to reform, restrict, or remove them. With this in mind, four distinct Conferences with the preachers were convened this year, though they differed greatly from each other in range and character. The first was this general Conference at Bristol. Unlike that of the previous March, this Conference was a full-scale meeting for preachers from different areas and stretched over five days. Although John Nelson came from Yorkshire, it seems doubtful whether many were present from the Midlands and the North, and Wesley summoned other groups in different parts of the country for a continued spiritual stocktaking. He held a brief Conference for the preachers in the Leeds area on May 15. He enrolled the aid of his brother Charles to conduct further local Conferences, one in Newcastle on Aug. 10, and another in Leeds on Sept. 11–12, both preceded by fuller local investigations than JW had felt able to carry out. Finally, the two brothers met at Shoreham, Kent, on Nov. 25, at the home of their senior clerical adviser, Rev. Vincent Perronet, in order to negotiate differences between the brothers' approaches, assess the results of their preceding itineraries and Conferences, make decisions about who should be dropped from the preaching itinerancy, and settle principles for enrolling and examining future preachers. See Richard P. Heitzenrater, 'Purge the Preachers: The Wesleys and Quality Control', in Kenneth Newport and Ted Campbell, eds., *Charles Wesley: Life, Literature, and Legacy* (Peterborough: Epworth, 2007), 488–500.

[751] See Eph. 4:21.

[752] See Rom. 1:18.

[753] As with the other Conferences, the largest part of this—the first three days—was apparently occupied with a discussion of Methodist doctrines, surely in reading through and discussing the Doctrinal *Minutes* (1749).

[754] See Acts 4:32; 2 Cor. 13:11.

Fri. 15. I mentioned whatever I thought was amiss or wanting in any of our brethren.[755] It was received in a right spirit, with much love, and serious, earnest attention. And I trust not one went from the Conference discontented, but rather blessing God for the consolation.[756]

5

[755] Wesley's *Journal* entry of Mar. 9 indicates that subjecting the preachers to more careful scrutiny and stricter discipline was one of JW's major purposes in this Conference. Almost certainly, their loyalty was tested (probably for the first time) according to the procedure agreed upon in the 1749 Conference; see *Minutes*, §18 (4). Copies of the Disciplinary *Minutes* and/or the Doctrinal *Minutes* of 1749 were apparently given not only to those who were newly accepted as JW's Helpers, but also to those who had already served loyally for several years. The giving and receiving of the *Minutes*, duly inscribed and signed, constituted their acceptance into 'full connexion'. Copies seem also to have been prepared for those of the trusted senior preachers unable to be present so that they could affirm their continued loyalty by their acceptance of these printed standards. The copy of the Doctrinal *Minutes* prepared for John Bennet (who was absent) has survived. On the verso of the title page is inscribed, apparently in the hand of Edward Perronet (the name, date, and signature being added by JW): 'To *John Bennet* / So Long as you freely consent / to & earnestly endever to ob / serve the Rules contain'd here / in I Shall rejoice to go on / with you hand in hand / *March 15.* / *1751 John Wesley*'. The inscribed copy, from which we give a *literatim* transcript, is in MA. Eventually, the presentation of a copy of its successor, the 'Large' *Minutes*, signalized a preacher's acceptance into full connexion.

[756] It is impossible to give a list of the 'many' preachers present. John Nelson and John Haime are named. That Edward Perronet was one is shown by his addition of a postscript to JW's letter of Mar. 11 to his new bride, whom JW had left in London to attend the Conference and to whom he swiftly returned for a few days before setting out on his deferred northern journey. CW was in Bristol at the time, but does not mention the Conference either in his journal or in a letter written to the absent John Bennet on Mar. 15. It seems possible that his appearances at the Conference were intermittent, for relations between him and his brother were still strained. CW, however, was deeply concerned about the welfare of the Methodist Societies, and therefore about the worthiness of the preachers who shepherded them. With this in mind, he urged Bennet's continued loyalty:

'The lessening of your affection towards my brother must not lessen your affection towards God, or his people, or his work. As to *withdrawing yourself*—stay a little and take company. *First*, let us finish the work our Lord has given us to do, and then you and I will withdraw ourselves—to paradise! Let *some* look upon us as disaffected; let others usurp authority—it alters not the case. We are called to peace, in One Body; and to *all* the members *will* we cleave.' (Bennet, MS Letterbook, MA)

The Leeds Conference of May 15, 1751

Wed. [May] 15, [1751]. We had a little Conference with about thirty preachers. I particularly inquired concerning their grace, and gifts, and fruit; and found reason to doubt of one only.[757]

---

[757] *Journal & Diaries*, 20:389 in this edn. This Conference seems to have been following up the doctrinal and disciplinary inquiries at Bristol, Mar. 11–15, when it was much more difficult for the northern preachers to be present. The disciplinary problems seemed to be serious in view of the 'poor, dead, senseless' state of the people at Epworth, where JW was informed on May 11: '(1), that some of our preachers there had diligently gleaned up and retailed all the evil they could hear of me; (2), that some of them had quite laid aside our hymns, as well as the doctrine they formerly preached; (3), that one of them had frequently spoke against our rules, and the others quite neglected them.' *Journal & Diaries*, 20:388 in this edn.

The one person who seemed clearly to be a source of harmful influence was James Wheatley, whose sexual promiscuity was bringing Methodism into disrepute. JW wrote an account of his misdemeanours and their investigation by the two brothers which led to his official suspension on June 25, 1751, at least 'till our next Conference (which I hope will be in October)'. *Journal & Diaries*, 20:394–95 in this edn.

James Wheatley (? –1775) had been an itinerant since 1742. He came under the Moravian influence, and the Wesleys complained that he absorbed antinomianism and extravagant rhetoric from them and was a bad influence on other Methodists in 1749–51. But he was also accused of immorality with women in the West country, and after being vainly urged to repent, he was expelled in 1751. *Journal & Diaries*, 20:394–96 in this edn. He then became a popular preacher in Norwich and built a 'tabernacle' there, which he offered to the Wesleys in 1754. He was finally discredited by charges of adultery, which went through the church courts (1754–59). He then became a surgeon and died in Bristol in 1775. See full account in E. J. Bellamy, *James Wheatley* (London, 1994).

JW had planned to continue his abbreviated northern journey with two months in Bristol and London, followed by a month's tour of the western Societies, and he asked Charles to tour the northern Societies on his behalf, and in particular to examine the character and usefulness of the preachers. CW set off from Bristol for this purpose on June 29, 1751, and kept his brother posted on his activities with lengthy journal letters. In this progress, he held a Conference with the preachers in the Newcastle area on Aug. 10, and a more important and inclusive one at Leeds on Sept. 11–12. Throughout this period, JW kept closely in touch with CW by letters containing comments, questions, and advice, fragments of which have survived, all relating to examination of the preachers; see July 17–Aug. 24, 1751, *Letters*, 26:470–76, which quotes CW's MS document, 'The Preachers, 1751', in MA (called 'Hints' by Frank Baker, the editor).

The Newcastle Conference of August 10, 1751

Sat. Aug. 10. Passed the day in conference with the preachers. Preached at night with a little life.[758]

The Leeds Conference of September 11–12, 1751

5

Wed. Sept. 11. Mr. Grimshaw[759] came, and soon after Mr. Milner.[760] At ten we began our Conference, at which were present J. Nelson, W. Shent, Christ. Hopper, T. Colbeck, J. Reeves, J. Bennet,[761]

---

[758] This Conference was held during a tour of the northern Societies; John had asked his brother Charles to pay particular attention to the worthiness of their preachers in view of the problems revealed earlier—cf. the Conferences of Mar. 11–15 and May 15 this year. During much of his three-month itinerary in the North, CW was ill, but at Leeds on Saturday, Aug. 3, he reported to John that he 'was enabled to ride out again, and to confer with the preachers and others', and on Monday, Aug. 5, to listen from a small adjoining room to Michael Fenwick preaching 'pure unmixed nonsense', leaving for Newcastle three days later. This meeting at Leeds on Aug. 3, like the more formal one at Newcastle a week later, was a small local Conference. Already CW was preparing for a major Conference in Leeds, which took place Sept. 11–12. The brief description of this Aug. Conference is found in CW's journal letter covering July 22–Aug. 12 (in MA), probably sent to JW.

[759] Rev. William Grimshaw (1708–63), perpetual curate of Haworth, JW's chief clerical colleague in the North, who had conducted the first Quarterly Meeting in Methodism at Todmorden Edge, Oct. 18, 1748. See Frank Baker, *William Grimshaw* (London: Epworth Press, 1963), 147–50.

[760] Rev. John Milner (c. 1710–77), vicar of Chipping, who opened his pulpit to JW, corresponded with him, and was present also at the 1753 Conference (see below, p. 259, and letter, Milner to JW, Jan. 11, 1750, 26:397–98 in this edn.).

[761] CW had written to Bennet from Newcastle on Aug. 11, pleading with him to come to this Conference:

'And pray earnestly for me, that the Lord may guide and direct me in my *most important* concern—to purge the Church, beginning with the labourers. For this end, I say again in God's name, Come and help me. On [the] 6th of Sept., I trust to see Leeds; on Wed., Sept 11, to meet in conference as many of the preachers as can be got together. Bring you all you can; and give notice everywhere I have silenced another scandalous preacher, and sent a third back to his trade. . . . Nothing is of such importance as *our* meeting at this time. Therefore let nothing but sickness or death hinder you. . . .' (Bennet, MS Letterbook, MA)

Paul Greenwood, Mich. Fenwick, Titus Knight[762] from Halifax, and
Rob. Swindells, and Matt. Watson.[763] All these I had invited, and
given them notes. Webb[764] and Trathen[765] came afterwards, but were
not admitted. Bro. Mortimer[766] also, and W. Darney,[767] who I
5   appointed to talk with before we met again in the afternoon.

Had anyone asked me the end of our Conference, I could not have
told him, only that I came to make observations, to get acquainted
with the preachers, and see if God had anything to do with us, or by
us. We began with part of an hymn, as follows:

10
    1.   Arise, thou jealous God, arise,
          Thy sifting power exert,
       Look through us with thy flaming eyes,
          And search out every heart.

15   2.   Our inmost souls thy Spirit knows,
          And let him now display
       Whom thou hast for thy glory chose,
          And purge[768] the rest away.

    3.   Th' apostles false far off remove,
20   The faithful labourers own,

---

[762] Orig., 'Tho. Knight'. Titus (d. 1792) became an Independent minister at Halifax, but at the Conferences of 1753 and 1755, he was listed as a Methodist local preacher.

[763] A local preacher of Leeds (see pp. 206, 260).

[764] Thomas Webb, a preacher of whom little is known—apparently a different man from the military officer who was important in founding Methodism in America. He had been listed as a probationer at the 1749 Conference, but was 'laid aside' on Nov. 25, 1751. See below, p. 246.

[765] David Trathen was listed in 1747 as preaching at one place, but in 1748 (§18) was received as an Assistant. He came under the influence of James Wheatley and was 'laid aside' on Nov. 25, 1751. See below, p. 246.

[766] Samuel Mortimer? See Lenton, *John Wesley's Preachers*, 457.

[767] William Darney (d. 1774) was a wandering pedlar-preacher from his conversion in the Scottish awakening in 1741 and formed his own religious societies in the West Riding of Yorkshire, which were secured for Methodism by the advocacy of Grimshaw. At the 1747 Conference he was listed as preaching in one place, but in 1748 he was received as an Assistant. He proved so uncouth and wild, however, that only Grimshaw's constant advocacy retained him in uneasy allegiance to Methodism. Cf. JW to Darney, May 25, 1754, *Letters*, 26:537 in this edn., and the following nn. 770–72 below.

[768] This hymn seems to be especially appropriate for this tour by CW, given the sentiment expressed in this stanza.

> And give *us* each himself to prove,
> And know as he is known. . . .[769]

After prayer (in which I found much of the presence of God), I
began without design to speak of the qualifications, work, and trials 5
of a preacher; and what I thought requisite in men that acted in concert. As to preliminaries and principles, we all agreed. This conversation lasted till one. I carried Mr. Grimshaw, Milner, and Bennet to
dinner at Miss N[orton]'s.

At three we met again; but first I talked to Bro. Mortimer, 10
whom I admitted, and to W. Darney, whom I rejected. His stiff-
neckedness I knew of old, and was now resolved to bend or break him.
The preachers had informed me of his obstinate behaviour toward my
patient (too patient!) brother at the last Conference; besides his scandalous begging wherever he comes, and railing at his brethren, or 15
whomsoever he is displeased with. At Epworth he got more clothes than
his horse could carry. They were ashamed to see the bags and bundles
which he carried off. I told him these things in few words, for he soon
took fire and flew out, as I expected, into such violence of behaviour
that I thought he would have beat me. I left him raging like a wild bull 20
in a net, and went to the preachers. Two hours more we spent in friendly
profitable conference. I told them my heart truly and fully concerning
the work and the workmen. We parted in the spirit of love.

At six I preached to thousands in the new room from, 'Behold he
cometh with clouds, and every eye shall see him!' We have not had 25
such a time together since I came. The same power rested on the
Society. Our souls were as a watered garden. Thanks be to God for
his unspeakable gift!

Thurs. Sept. 12. I took a delightful leave of them at five. Gave
W. Darney the hearing, at Mr. Grimshaw's desire. Mr. Milner, Hop- 30
per, Bennet, Shent were by. He denied everything, although
W. Shent proved it upon him. But I told him all past faults should
be forgotten, on condition he refrained till the spring:

1. From railing.
2. From begging.   35
3. From printing—any more of his nonsense. 'Nonsense?' quoth
he, 'nonsense? What, do you call my hymns nonsense? They are not

---

[769] See George Osborn, *Poetical Works of John and Charles Wesley* (London,
1868), 8:404–5, for all twelve stanzas. CW transferred it to his 'MS Miscellaneous
Hymns' (c. 1785), 109–11; in MA.

mine but Christ's. He *gave* them me; and Mr. John had nothing to say against them; and Mr. Grimshaw and Milner have recommended them. Here they are! What fault can you find with them?' With that he threw down his gauntlet, or book just printed, in an evil hour, his
5 fate compelling.[770] I opened it on those words:

> There's Brother-Tost, and Wrangle,
> Where Satan souls do strangle (as near as I can remember),

10 and read on till our brethren interrupted by the violence of their applause. Mr. Grimshaw and Milner were rather out of countenance, and begged pardon for having recommended such a performance. But William stood to it that it was all divine. Neither would he promise not to print his own history, which is almost ready for the press.[771]
15   After I had turned him inside out, I agreed to his preaching among us as a Probationer, upon the aforesaid conditions, and he was compelled to say he would print no more books without our imprimatur. I would not admit him to the Conference, that he might be humbled by perceiving I made a difference betwixt him and our preachers.[772]

---

[770] William Darney, *A Collection of Hymns* (Leeds: Lister, 1751). CW opened on the first hymn, pp. 9–23, titled, 'The Progress of the Gospel in divers Places of Great Britian [*sic*]', which Darney noted was 'not made so proper for singing as for reading'. It contained 104 stanzas, of which stanza 88 ran: 'There is Brother *Tost* and *Wrangle*; of late they have begun / To seek; let them never strangle, but thy work carry on.'

[771] Darney's *Collection* was published in four parts, paged continuously, part 2 beginning on p. [93]. Several hymns seem to be autobiographical, including two in part 1 (pp. 31–32, 57–61), but esp. No. 162, pp. 270–71, which he prefaces thus: 'In the Year of our Lord, 1742, after I had begun preaching (sometime when I was under great affliction both of body and mind), I began to question my call to the ministry, although I had a clear call in October before. The words were impressed upon my mind which I put in verse after, as followeth.' No other printed autobiography appears to have survived.

[772] On Sept. 16, CW had another confrontation with Darney, who 'insisted that he would sing his own hymns, and no other, seeing they were all given by inspiration, as was plain from his pouring out hundreds of them extempore'. Grimshaw was present, and he also, wrote CW, 'gave him up for the most obstinate unpersuadable man he ever saw'. As a result, CW left specific instructions with William Shent:
> 'I leave this word of notice with you for our sons in the gospel [as?] Assistants or preachers in any degree. At the desire of a very dear and faithful brother I have consented to let W. D. preach among our children as *heretofore*, although I believe his spirit is still whole and unbroken. But on these conditions I consent:
> '1. That he does not rail, or speak against anyone, much less any labourer.
> '2. That he does not beg of our people.

We passed the morning in prayer and conversation. I had hard work to keep all quiet, Mr. Grimshaw and others urging J[ohn] B[ennet] to explain his private opinions. I hardly stayed them off, resolving to avoid a rupture at this time, and to divide the confederates. J. B[ennet] indeed never had any design of setting up for himself or making a 5 party, as he solemnly assured me. Of this J. Nelson, Shent, Hopper were alike satisfied. Mr. Grimshaw many times advised me to keep fair with J. B[ennet]—'as honest-hearted a man', he called him, 'as any among us'. Trathen and Webb, I found, have complained heavily of Rob. Swindells for deserting them. Him and J. B. I have bound by 10 love, and should not fear setting them both right, especially the latter, could I but part them and Satan's messengers.

We all agreed to postpone opinions till the next General Conference; settled the affairs of the Church the best we could, and parted *friends*.

At three took horse with Mr. Grimshaw, Milner, Shent, Bennet, 15 for Birstall. . . .[773]

The Shoreham Conference of November 25, 1751

Mem. Mon. Nov. 25, 1751. At Shoreham agreed with my brother (present Mr. Perronet) to receive or reject preachers.[774]

> '3. That he does not print any more of his nonsense; and
> '4. That he does not introduce the use of his doggerel hymns in any of our societies. . . . I have promised him that in whatsoever Society of ours he uses his own verses, in that Society *he shall preach no more*'. CW. Journal letter, Aug. 13–Oct. 3, 1751, in MA.

[773] See four documents in MA, three long journal letters for the period (June 29–Oct. 3, 1751), and a collection of information relating to the examination of the preachers during this tour. CW, MS 'Preachers, 1751'.

Although the brothers corresponded during this period, marked by their different itineraries, JW and CW were not able to consult face-to-face about the implications of this northern journey until Monday, Nov. 25, 1751, during a Conference whose decisions are noted especially in CW's account of the 'purge'. See Heitzenrater, 'Purge the Preachers', 499–500.

[774] This memorandum was added by CW on a draft of his letter to Ebenezer Blackwell, Oct. 8, 1749. See *WHS* 22 (1940): 183. It was clearly prepared at the home of Rev. Vincent Perronet, the vicar of Shoreham, the elder statesmen to whom both Wesley brothers turned for advice and assistance in their personal affairs and the problems of the Methodist Societies. He had been present at the sessions of the 1747 Conference, which dealt with disciplinary questions (§§43–57 and presumably 58–73).

Monday, Nov. 25, 1751.[775]

Agreed:
To lay aside:

5

J. Wheatley[776]
Elea[zer] Webster[777]
Rob. Gillespie[778]
James Watson[779]

10   Mich. Fenwick[780]
J. Maddern[781]
D. Trathen[782]
T. Webb[783]
W. Darney[784]

---

[775] This memorandum listing the names of the preachers who were 'laid aside' appears in two copies in MA, both in the hand of CW, one (in shorthand) dated, the other undated.

[776] This confirms permanently Wheatley's suspension on June 25, 1751, at least until the next Conference; see p. 240, n. 757 above.

[777] In 1747 Webster was recognized as an Assistant, but the Minutes (1755) listed him as one of the chief local preachers.

[778] The 1749 Conference listed Gillespie (orig., 'Gilespie') as a probationer. CW wrote to Bennet on Aug. 11, 1741:

'Your last [letter] helped on the work of God for which he has sent me into his vineyard at this time; and it supplied me with more abundant proof of R. G.'s utter unworthiness to preach the gospel. I have accordingly stopped him, and shall tomorrow send him back to his proper business. A friend of ours (without God's counsel) made a preacher of a tailor. I, with God's help, shall make a tailor of him again.' (Bennet, MS Letterbook, MA)

The 'friend', of course, was John Wesley.

[779] See Lenton, *John Wesley's Preachers*, 458.

[780] Michael Fenwick remained a local preacher for some years, was apparently readmitted to a travelling status, was informed by the 1758 Conference that he should return to business, but ten years later was again travelling, and from 1772 to 1778 appeared in the stations in the printed *Minutes*, though only as 'M. F.'

[781] Orig., 'J. Madern'. Maddern did not quite disappear from view as a local preacher. In the spring of 1762 he supplied for a London itinerant (see letter, John Jones to CW, Apr. 10, 1762, MA).

[782] Orig., 'D. Trathan'. On Nov. 7, 1751, Mrs. George Whitefield wrote to Bennet from London: 'I thank you, sir, for yours by Mr. Webb. Both Mr. Webb and Trathen are here, and are by all that I can hear well approved, and as far as I have seen truly answer your account of them, and I trust if they remain steady will be blessed.' Bennet, MS Letterbook, MA. Trathen seems to have disappeared, however, from Wesley's circles.

[783] Orig., 'T. Web', for whom see previous n. and that on p. 242.

[784] Darney was reinstated from time to time and was occasionally listed in the printed stations.

With regard to the preachers we agree:[785]

1. That no one shall be permitted to preach in any of our Societies till he has been examined both as to his grace and gifts; at least by the Assistant, who, sending word to us, may by our answer admit him as a Local Preacher.[786]   5

[785] For the following document, see CW, MS 'Preachers, 1751' (cf. John Whitehead, *The Life of the Rev. John Wesley*, 2 vols. [London, 1793–96], 2:269–70, as 'from Mr. Charles Wesley's papers written in shorthand'). Whitehead adds the comment:

'Mr. John Wesley was prevailed upon with some difficulty to sign these articles. But though he did at length sign them, they produced no good effect. Mr. Wesley would not submit to any control in admitting preachers into the connexion, in appointing them to the different circuits, or in governing the societies. It appears to me that after the first difference with his brother, who disappointed his intended marriage, he made up his mind not to suffer either a superior or an equal in these respects. . . . Mr. Charles, perceiving his brother's determination, and finding that the preachers became more and more prejudiced against him, thought it most prudent to withdraw from the active situation he had hitherto held amongst them; reserving to himself, however, the right of speaking his mind freely to his brother in a friendly correspondence.'

There seems little question that although both brothers were anxious to maintain the good name and effectiveness of the Methodist Societies as a reviving influence within the Church of England, CW was more concerned about 'gifts' (and therefore removing ineffective and especially predestinarian preachers), while JW was more concerned about 'grace' (the experience of God's power and presence in their lives) in order to spread the revival. See Heitzenrater, 'Purge the Preachers', 487–90.

On Dec. 20, 1751, JW prepared a lengthy document (eventually published in his *AM* [1779]), discussing this whole problem. He controverted a letter defending the so-called gospel preachers, maintaining that such unduly emotional preaching insufficiently concerned about obedience to God's law and therefore often lax in morality did great harm to preachers and people alike: 'not only to James Wheatley himself, but to those who have learned of him, David Trathen, Thomas Webb, Robert Swindells, and John Maddern; I fear to others also, all of whom are but shadows of what they were.' See Dec. 20, 1751, esp. §25, *Letters*, 25:482–89 in this edn.; and cf. Wesley's sermons, 'The Law Established through Faith', I and II, in *Works*, 2:20–43 in this edn.

[786] The 1747 Minutes gave a long list of the preachers 'that assist us only in one place' (§65), changed in the Disciplinary *Minutes* (1749) to 'chiefly in one place' (§65). The Irish *Minutes* (1752) state that if a man cannot preach twice a day, 'he can only be a Local Preacher' (§19), and those of 1753 list the 'Local Preachers' present at the Conference (§1). This Shoreham Conference of 1751 seems to be the occasion for the first official recognition of this term, which JW used only infrequently—the first occurrence in his *Journal* is on Aug. 18, 1767 (*Journal & Diaries*, 22:99 in this edn.).

2. That such a preacher be not immediately taken from his trade, but be exhorted to follow it with all diligence.

3. That no person shall be received as a Travelling Preacher, or taken from his trade, by either of us alone, but by both conjointly, 5 giving him a note under both our hands.

4. That neither of us will re-admit a Travelling Preacher laid aside without the consent of the other.

5. That if we should ever disagree in our judgment, we will refer the matter to Mr. Perronet.

10   6. That we will endeavour to be patterns of all we expect from our preachers, particularly of zeal, diligence, and punctuality in the work; by constantly preaching and meeting the societies; by visiting yearly Ireland, Cornwall, and the north; and in general by superintending the whole work, and every branch of it, with all the strength 15 which God shall give.

We agree to the above-written, till this day the next year.

In [the] presence of Mr. Perronet.

John Wesley
Charles Wesley

20 **The London Conference of January 29, 1752**[787]

---

[787] The agreement about their preachers made by the Wesley brothers on Nov. 25, 1751, above, was followed with an attempt to disarm any criticism and to secure stronger unity among the experienced itinerants who remained faithful. A Conference with this purpose in mind was apparently planned for early March, as witness a letter from JW to John Downes, dated London, Dec. 10, 1751: 'You must needs be here (if alive), the first of March, at our Conference. None will be present but those we invite'. *Letters*, 26:481 in this edn. Matters seem to have been brought to a head, however, by the defection of John Bennet, who on Dec. 31, 1751, publicly criticized JW at Bolton, proclaiming, 'I have not been in connexion with him these three years, neither will I be any more.' See Mar. 25, 1752, *Letters*, 26:491, n. 8 in this edn. JW seems hastily to have brought the Conference forward, urged on by a letter from William Grimshaw to CW: 'These intestine divisions are dreadful. While union is preserved among us we are impregnable; . . . but being divided we become an easy prey to the common enemy, and even worry one another.' CW to Bennet, Jan. 23, 1752, Bennet, MS Letterbook, MA. A number of preachers were already serving in the London area, and JW had also invited others there for one purpose or another and now seems to have summoned more. Our only clear knowledge about this Conference, however, comes from this signed memorandum,

Janu. 29, 1752

It is agreed by us whose names are underwritten:

1. That we[788] will not listen, or willingly inquire after any ill concerning each other.

2. That if we do hear any ill of each other, we will not be forward to believe it.

3. That as soon as possible, we will communicate what we hear, by speaking or writing to the person concerned.

4. That till we have done this, we will not write or speak a syllable of it to any other person whatsoever.

5. That neither will we mention it, after we have done this, to any other person.

6. That we will not make any exception to any of these rules, unless we think ourselves absolutely obliged in conscience so to do.

> John Wesley
> Charles Wesley
> John Trembath[789]
> E. Perronet
> Jonth. Reeves[790]
> Jos. Cownley[791]
> C. Perronet
> Thos. Maxfield
> J. Downes[792]

preserved at Wesleyan University, Middletown, Conn. On Mar. 16, CW prepared an amended version, adding an agreement 'never to leave the Church of England'. This latter document contained a total of only six signatures, with that of JW in the third position, apparently an indication that this was not the fruits of a similar Conference but of CW's either circulating or taking the document around with him personally to collect signatures. See *Letters*, 25:491 in this edn. Similar preachers' covenants followed on May 8, 1754, and Aug. 30, 1756. A document expressing the same desire for unity among the preachers, dated Aug. 4, 1769, was presented by JW to the Conference of that year (see pp. 376–78 below), and this was periodically renewed at several annual Conferences from Aug. 9, 1771, onwards.

[788] Orig., 'That ((if)) we ((hear any ill of each other, we)) will not. . . .'

[789] As with others, there is no clear evidence that Trembath was in London at this time, but no evidence either that this was unlikely.

[790] In his letter to Downes, Dec. 10, 1751, JW wrote: 'Brother Reeves will be here in a day or two. But he cannot return into the north yet.' *Letters*, 26:480 in this edn.

[791] Cownley was stationed in Ireland, but on a visit to England during the winter, returning to Ireland in time for the Conference there.

[792] On Dec. 28, 1751, JW had written to Downes in Newcastle: 'I believe a journey to London will do you good. If you could borrow a horse to Leeds, you may take my mare from thence, which is in brother Shent's keeping.' *Letters*, 26:489 in this edn.

John Jones
John Nelson
Willm. Shent
John Haime

5

Memor[andum]: As many of us as are together in any place will have a conference every Monday morning.[793]

The Limerick Conference of August 14–15, 1752[794]

[793] This memorandum seems to have led to the traditional circuit staff meeting on Monday mornings.

[794] In 1751, during a series of regional Conferences in England, careful inquiry had been made into the loyalty of all the English preachers to the doctrine and discipline printed in the two collected *Minutes* of 1749, consolidated into a pact of union on Jan. 29, 1752. This inquiry was extended to Ireland later this year, by JW's summoning of the first Irish Methodist Conference. He arrived in Limerick on Aug. 13, 1752, and his *Journal* for the following two days reads: 'I spent Friday and Saturday in conference with our preachers, and the next week spake with each of the members of the society, many of whom, I now found, were rooted and grounded in love, and zealous of good works.' *Journal & Diaries*, 20:437 in this edn. Of course, JW had made arrangements well in advance, witness his letter of Aug. 8 to CW, clearly written with the assumption that CW knew all about it: 'On Friday and Saturday next is our little Conference at Limerick.' *Letters*, 26:499 in this edn.

Although this (and subsequent Irish Conferences) applied specifically to the Irish scene, it was closely tied to the English Conferences, discussing the principles already formulated within English Methodism, and in some instances initiating ideas later worked out in England (e.g., *Minutes* [1765], *QQ*. 27–38). Throughout Wesley's lifetime, British Methodism (except for the Welsh Calvinistic Methodists) was one, and JW and his preachers had travelled freely across the Irish Sea since 1747, though they usually remained in Ireland for somewhat longer periods at first than was true in an English circuit.

Two copies of the Minutes of this Conference were preserved, both probably based on an 'official' version. One was by Philip Guier (d. 1778), the German schoolmaster of Ballingrane, who was accepted as a local preacher at the Conference, and the other by Jacob Rowell (1722–83), an Englishman. Both MSS seem to have disappeared; in 1870 the Guier MS was with Luke Tyerman, the Rowell MS with John Steele of Chester (Tyerman, *Wesley*, 2:144). That by Guier was 'much dirtied and torn' when it was copied for the Irish *Arminian Magazine* in 1807, from which William Myles later copied for his *Chronological History*, 73–76, and eventually came into the possession of Luke Tyerman and is now in the Methodist

[§1] The Rev. John Wesley, Samuel Larwood, John Haughton, Joseph Cownley, John Fisher, Thomas Walsh,[795] Jacob Rowell, Thomas Kead, Robert Swindells, John Whitford, [James Morris],[796] being present, it was inquired:

[§2] *Q*. 1. What is the cause of the general decay of the societies in Ireland? Have they been taught any wrong doctrines?[797] Or has there been want of discipline among them? Or have any of our preachers behaved amiss?
A. All these causes have concurred.[798]

[§3] *Q*. 2. What wrong doctrines have been taught?[799]
A. Such as border on antinomianism and Calvinism.

[§4] *Q*. 3. How shall we guard against the former?
A. By reading and weighing Mr. Baxter's *Aphorisms on Justification*. (These were read carefully, and the Scriptures referred to be examined, and all objections considered and answered.)[800]

[§5] *Q*. 4. Are all convinced that this doctrine[801] is true and scriptural?

Historical Library at Drew University. The Rowell MS came into the hands of Anthony Steel of Barnard Castle and was first published in the 1862 Mason edn. of the *Minutes of the Methodist Conferences*, 714–17. Not only was the Guier MS physically defective and a secondary document—he himself not being present— but it was heavily edited: §§8, 12, 15, 25–29 were omitted, along with several of the stations and the numbers of the questions; two subtitles were altered, and others added; several words were misread, and others deliberately altered in order to modernize the grammar and style (as 'written' for 'wrote' in §11). In default of the actual MS, therefore, it seems wisest to reproduce the 1862 text in its entirety, but to insert from the 250 variants in Myles (noted as M) a few instances that may well represent the original text, the more important variants in Guier's original, or passages that have independent value as early interpretations.

[795] M, 'John Fenwick', omitting Walsh.

[796] The name of Morris was omitted at the beginning of both MSS, but 'James Morris' was one of the signatories at the end, §35. Probably he joined the Conference late.

[797] M reads, 'Have any wrong doctrines been preached?' and omits the following question.

[798] M, 'have been inquired into'.

[799] M prefixes this question with a subtitle, 'of Doctrine', and reads, 'What wrong doctrine has been preached?' It is clear that in the opening session of this Conference, the Doctrinal *Minutes* (1749) were studied, with emphasis on the major problems.

[800] Cf. MS Minutes (1745), §13, and Doctrinal *Minutes* (1749), §52. It seems Baxter's *Aphorisms* were studied independently at this 1752 Conference, again in JW's abridgement.

[801] M, 'this doctrine (contained in the *Aphorisms*)'.

    A. We are convinced that it is.

[§6] *Q.* 5. Why is it, then, that so many condemn this book, and that we ourselves were so[802] prejudiced against it?

    A. Because we did not understand it; and we doubt this is the case with others also.

[§7] *Q.* 6. How far do any of you believe the doctrine of absolute predestination?

    A. None of us believe it at all.

[§8] *Q.* 7. Which of you believe absolute election?

    A. Three replied: 'We believe there are some persons who are absolutely elected; but we believe likewise that Christ died for all; that God willeth not the death of any man, and that thousands are saved that are not absolutely elected. We believe, further, that those who are thus elected cannot finally fall. But we believe that other believers may fall, and that those who were once justified will perish everlastingly.'[803]

[§9] *Q.* 8. Shall we read what is said in the [record of the] Conference[804] concerning Christian perfection, and the assurance of faith?

    A. By all means. (This was done accordingly, and all present assented thereto.)

With regard to Discipline[805]

[§10] *Q.* l: Have not some of our preachers neglected some of the rules laid down in our former Conference?[806]

    A. We are resolved, by the grace of God, to keep them for the time to come.

[§11] *Q.* 2. If any Assistant[807] neglect his duty, shall the nearest preacher endeavour to supply his neglect?

---

[802] M, 'we have been'.

[803] M omits this question. JW had shared this compromise doctrine for many years but apparently rejected it as allowing too much to the Calvinists. See letters in 1725 and 1752, 25:175f.; 26:498f. in this edn.

[804] JW often used the word 'Conference' to denote not the actual gathering or its discussions, but its recorded results, in this case the Doctrinal *Minutes* (1749), and in §10 the Disciplinary *Minutes* (1749), which M (possibly not understanding this usage) altered to 'conferences'. Cf. *Minutes* (1753), §12.

[805] M, 'Of Discipline'.

[806] M, 'conferences'.

[807] M, 'Preacher'.

A. Yes; after he has[808] lovingly told him of his fault, and, secondly, wrote[809] to the next Assistant.

[§12] *Q.* 3. What shall a steward or leader do who hears any wrong doctrine preached, or sees any rules broke, either by a preacher or Assistant?

A. Immediately tell the person of his fault, betwixt him and you alone.

[§13] *Q.* 4. How shall we avoid speaking evil of each other?

A. (1) Be extremely wary of believing anything you hear before you have spoke to the party concerned.

(2) Speak to him the first time you see him.

(3) Till then, tell it to no person whatsoever.

[§14] *Q.* 5. Can we receive any as a fellow-labourer who does not agree with us both as to doctrine and discipline?

A. In no wise. 'How can two walk together, unless they be agreed?'[810]

[§15] *Q.* 6. What can be done with regard to a revolter from that agreement?

A. When a fact is proved, the Assistant should immediately send letters and disown him in all the societies.[811]

[§16] *Q.* 7. Should any set up for a preacher in any place without the approbation of an Assistant?

A. By no means. That has already been attended with ill consequences.[812]

[§17] *Q.* 8. Do we accept of James Morris, John Ellis, James Wild, Samuel Levick,[813] Samuel Hobart,[814] and Philip Guier?[815]

A. We do willingly give them the right hand of fellowship, and accept them[816] as fellow-labourers.

---

[808] M, 'has, first,'.

[809] M, 'written'.

[810] Amos 3:3.

[811] M omits this question.

[812] Orig., 'consequencies'; M, 'with great inconveniencies'.

[813] Rowell, 'George Levick'; M, 'M. Savage', apparently a misreading of the faulty original.

[814] Nothing further is known about Samuel Hobart, who seems to have remained an Irish local preacher for a short time.

[815] Rowell, 'Guyer'; M, 'Geyar'. Guier's copy of the Minutes was used by Samuel Wood and William Myles.

[816] M, 'accept of them'.

[§18]   *Q.* 9. Should the morning preaching be neglected in any
place?
A. Of the two, it is better to neglect the evening.
[§19]   *Q.* 10. How, if one be unable[817] to preach twice a day?
5   *A.* He can only be a Local Preacher.[818]
[§20]   *Q.* 11. What can one[819] do who is unable for a time?
A. He should, first[820] write immediately to the Assistant;
secondly, earnestly exhort the people to meet[821] without
him.
10   [§21]   *Q.* 12. How shall we set an example to the people of
decency in public worship?
A. (1) Let us constantly kneel during prayer; and stand
both in singing, and while the text is repeating, etc.
(2) Let us be serious and silent while service lasts, and
15   when we are coming and going away.[822]
[§22]   *Q.* 13. Shall we permit any to be present at the public meeting of the bands who have not band-tickets?
A. Certainly not. By that means we should make them
cheap, and discourage them who are admitted.[823]
20   [§23]   *Q.* 14. What if one forget his band or society ticket?
A. He may come in once; but not if he forget it two times
together.[824]
[§24]   *Q.* 15. When and where shall the Quarterly Meetings be
kept for the following year?
25   *A.* At Cork, Limerick, Coolalough,[825] and Lisburn, on the
Tuesdays after Michaelmas and Christmas, Lady Day and
Midsummer.

---

[817] M, 'But what if a preacher be unable'.

[818] In M this sentence is italicized, possibly because this was the situation of Guier
as schoolmaster at Ballingrane. Cf. *Minutes* (1753), §25.

[819] M, 'What can he'.

[820] M, 'First, he should'.

[821] M, 'exhort the people in the morning to meet'.

[822] M, '(1) Let us constantly kneel at prayer; and stand during singing, and while
the text is repeated. (2) Let us be *serious* and *silent* both while the service lasts, and
while we are coming in and going out.'

[823] M, 'Certainly no. By that means we should rather discourage those who are
admitted.'

[824] M, 'He may be permitted to come in once; but not if he forget twice together.'

[825] Rowell, 'Colylough'; M, 'Cooly-lough'.

[§25]   *Q.* 16. Is it expedient that every preacher should have a
yearly allowance for clothing?[826]
A. It might relieve some of them from much uneasiness,
and prevent many inconveniences.

[§26]   *Q.* 17. What can be allowed to each?[827]   5
A. We think £8 at least, perhaps £10 per year.

[§27]   *Q.* 18. What can we allow each of their wives for the pres-
ent year?
A. S. Edwards and her three children, £21; to S. Kead and
S. Morris, £10; to S. Fisher, ten guineas.   10

With regard to the Behaviour of the Preachers[828]

[§28]   *Q.* 1. Is there any objection to the behaviour of Thomas
Kead?[829]
A. He hath been charged with idleness and lightness; but   15
we are convinced both these charges are false.

[§29]   *Q.* 2. Have not several of the preachers spoke unkindly of
each other?
A. They have; and it has hurt the people extremely. But we
hope it will be so no more.   20

[§30]   *Q.* 3. Should we not preach more expressly[830] and strongly
on self-denial than we have hitherto done?
A. By all means; in this kingdom more especially, where it
is scarce mentioned or thought of.

[§31]   *Q.* 4. Should we not recommend fasting by preaching it?[831]   25
A. We should, both frequently and strongly.

[§32]   *Q.* 5. Ought we not to practise it ourselves?
A. Undoubtedly we ought, especially on Friday,[832] if health
permit. Nay, we ought to be patterns not barely of tem-
perance, but of abstemiousness[833] of every kind.   30

[826] See Minutes, London Conference, Aug. 1757, n. 973, and introduction, p. 50.

[827] This appears to be the beginning of the allowance system, but it took many
years to be implemented in practice. Myles (*Chronological History*, 76) says it was
fixed at £12 per annum for England after the Irish Conference of this year (see
Baker, 'Polity', 234; see also Bristol Conference, Oct. 1752, below). But see also
Mather's claim quoted below (Minutes [1757], n. 973, and introduction, pp. 50–53).

[828] M, 'of Behaviour'.

[829] He remained an itinerant and died in (?) 1761.

[830] Rowell, 'more extremely and strongly'; M, 'more expressly and more strongly'.

[831] M, 'fasting in particular?'

[832] M, 'particularly on Fridays'.

[833] M, 'abstinence'.

[§33]   *Q.* 6. What ought we to avoid next to luxury?

   A. Idleness; or it will destroy the whole work of God on the
   soul. And in order to this, let us spend one hour every
   day[834] in private prayer.[835]

5 [§34]   *Q.* 7. In what places may the Travelling Preachers labour
   for the ensuing year?

A. Joseph Cownley,	1, till Christmas at Cork.
	2, [till Lady Day in] Dublin.
	3, [till Midsummer in] Limerick.
	4, [till Michaelmas in the] North.[836]
John Fisher,	1, till Christmas at Limerick.
	2, [till Lady Day in] Cork.
	3, [till Midsummer in] Athlone Rounds.[837]
	4, [till Michaelmas in] Dublin.
Thomas Walsh,[838]	1, till Christmas at Dublin.
P[aul] G[reenwood]	2, [till Lady Day in] Limerick.
R. S[windells],	3, [till Midsummer in the] North.
	4, [till Michaelmas in] Cork.
Jacob Rowell,	1, in Wexford Circuit.
	2, — Athlone Rounds.
With J. C[ownley],[839]	3, — Limerick.
With P. G[reenwood],	4, — Wexford Circuit.
Thomas Kead,	1, in Athlone Rounds.
	2, — Wexford Circuit.
	3, — Athlone Rounds.
With J. C[ownley],	4, — North.
Robert Swindells,	1, in Athlone Rounds.
	2, — Limerick.

---

[834] M, 'let us not pass one day without spending at least one hour'.

[835] In M there follows the subtitle, 'Of Appointments'.

[836] M omits the numbers of the quarters of all the appointments printed but supplies more explicit details, such as 'till Lady-day in Dublin', etc.; these demonstrate that each quarter ended on the normal quarter-days: 1, Christmas, Dec. 25; 2, Lady Day, Mar. 25; 3, Midsummer, June 24; 4, Michaelmas, Sept. 29.

[837] M reads in each instance, 'Athlone Circuit'.

[838] M omits Walsh here, but inserts John Fenwick and his stations.

[839] M omits the initials of the preachers sharing appointments, both here and with Kead, Swindells, Greenwood, and (of course) the missing Walsh.

With T. W[alsh],	3, — North.
	4, — Athlone Rounds.
John Fenwick,	1, in North.
	2, — Athlone Rounds.
	3, — Wexford.	5
	4, — Athlone Rounds.
Paul Greenwood,	1, in Dublin.[840]
T. W[alsh],	2, — Wexford.
	3, — Dublin.
	4, — Wexford.	10
James Morris,	1, in Wexford Circuit.
	2, — Athlone Rounds.
	3, — Wexford Circuit.
	4, — Athlone Rounds.
John Edwards,	1, in Athlone Rounds.	15
	2, — North.
	3, — Cork.
	4, — Limerick.

[§35]　We, whose names are underwritten, do freely and fully con-
sent to the above-written Conference; and are resolved,　20
by the grace of God, punctually to observe the rules con-
tained therein, and in the printed Conferences, to the
utmost of our skill and power. We do likewise fully pur-
pose to labour at the times and in the places here set
down. In proof whereof we have set our hands unto this.　25
John Haughton,
Thomas Kead,
John Fisher,
Jacob Rowell,
Joseph Cownley,　30
Thomas Walsh,
James Morris,
John Whitford,
Robert Swindells,
Samuel Larwood.[841]　35
In the year of our Lord God, 1752, August the 14, 15.

---

[840] M omits Greenwood and Morris.

[841] Three men were present, but not stationed in Ireland: Haughton, Larwood,
and Whitford, each of whom was apparently stationed in England for the coming
year. These three seem to have been replaced by three from England: Edwards,
Fenwick, and Greenwood.

The Bristol Conference of October 16, 1752

This event is one of the most elusive and ill-documented of all Wesley's Conferences. He had evidently intended that a Conference should meet on March 1, 1752, but John Bennet's defection made
5 him bring it forward to January.[842] The business then was primarily, if not exclusively, to strengthen unity among the preachers. There followed the Limerick Conference of August 1752, which had a more or less normal range of business, though focused on discipline and unity and confined to Irish Methodism and its preachers. One
10 would perhaps expect that a more general English Conference would be held at some point in the year as the annual pattern was becoming established. Yet there is no evidence in Wesley's *Journal* or letters of any such meeting being held or planned. On his return to Bristol from Ireland, he records under October 14, 1752, 'I now
15 rested a week at Bristol and Kingswood, preaching only morning and evening'.[843]

It is generally believed, however, that he held a Conference at Bristol during this week's 'rest', and Professor Ward sees the week as being 'filled' by this event, as one would expect in a full-scale
20 Conference.[844] Yet this is by no means certain. The primary evidence for the Conference appears to be derived from William Myles,[845] who records 'October 16, 1752, the ninth Conference was held in Bristol. At this time, it was agreed that the preachers should receive a stipend of twelve pounds per annum, in order to provide them-
25 selves with necessities'. Hitherto the stewards had supplied the preachers' needs mainly in kind. Myles goes on to say that this took some years to implement and cites the cases in the 1760s of York (no allowance) and Norwich (a share in the meagre love-feast money). He claims that the allowance was only universally enforced by the
30 Conference of 1765.

Other references to this Conference add no more details and may well be repeating Myles.[846] Sutcliffe says it was a small Conference

---

[842] See above, London Conference, Jan. 1752, n. 787.

[843] *Journal & Diaries*, 20:441 in this edn.

[844] Ibid., n. 57.

[845] Myles, *Chronological History*, 76.

[846] See, e.g., Crowther, *Portraiture*, 57–58; George Smith, *History of Wesleyan Methodism*, 3 vols. (London, 1857–61; 5th edn., London: Longmans, Green, 1866–72), 1:258.

with Charles Wesley apparently not being present (his journal is missing for this period).[847] Though Myles does not mention the Limerick Conference, the Bristol decision was evidently a follow-up from this, with a small increase in the stipend for English conditions. It is possible that the Conference was for a single day and mainly to implement this decision concerning stipends for England.

5

The Leeds Conference of May 22–24, 1753[848]

Tuesday, May the 22nd
[§1]   John Wesley,[849] William Grimshaw, John Milner, Samuel

---

[847] MS 'History', fol. 424.

[848] There are two sources for the 1753 MS Minutes. One (which seems to have disappeared) was apparently in the hand of Jacob Rowell and was published in the 1862 edn. of the *Minutes* (1:717–20). We refer to this copy as 'Rowell'. Another is extant in the MA, in the same unidentified hand, again rough and unsophisticated, as the 'D' copy of the 1746 Minutes, which it follows as the second part of the same document. We therefore retain the same designation (D) for this document, which supplies the title, 'Minutes of a Conference held at Leeds in Yorkshire from the 22nd of June to the 25th, Anno Christ[i] 1753' (the incorrect 'June' is repeated for each day's account). There are numerous minor variations between these two sources, as well as major ones, and it is clear that neither was the 'official' original Minutes, but a copy. Yet both retain what seem to be unique phrases from the original, which is borne out by the first edn. of the 'Large' *Minutes* (1753), which is paralleled in these differences by each in turn, but much more frequently by Rowell, which we therefore treat as our major source, deserting it for D only rarely, though always giving the significant variants from the edited text.

Wesley's *Journal* briefly summarizes this Conference: 'Tue. 22. Most of our preachers met and conversed freely together, as we did, morning and afternoon, to the end of the week, when our Conference ended with the same blessing as it began, God giving us all to be not only of one heart but of one judgment.' *Journal & Diaries*, 20:459 in this edn.

[849] D lists the names of those present in two columns, in a different order, and sometimes with different spellings: John Wesley, 'Gremshaw' for Grimshaw, 'Millener' for Milner, Shent, Hitchens, 'Welch' for Walsh, Nelson, 'Joseph' Jones, Gilbert, Edward 'Paronet' for Perronet, Lowes, 'Fleam' for Haime, Fugill, 'Sheifield' for Scholefield, 'Houghton' for Haughton, 'Larrowd' for Larwood, Hopper, Fisher, James Jones, Walker, Edwards, Mitchell, 'Hamson' for Hampson, 'Mackenku' for Maskew, 'Callow' for Catlow, and 'Eroc' for Enoch Williams. D omits the name of Jacob Rowell and ends, 'all these being Travelling Preachers, besides sixteen Local Preachers', who are not named.

Larwood, John Haughton, Christopher Hopper, William
Shent, John Edwards, William Hitchens, John Fisher,
Thomas Walsh, James Jones, John Nelson, Francis
Walker, Joseph Jones, Thomas Mitchell, Nicholas
5 Gilbert, John Hampson, Edward Perronet, Jonathan
Maskew, Matthew Lowes, Jacob Rowell, John Haime,
Jonathan Catlow, William Fugill, John Turnough, James
Scholefield, Enoch Williams, Travelling Preachers—and
Thomas Colbeck, Thomas Lee,[850] Titus Knight, Ben-
10 jamin Beanland, Joseph Bradley, John Johnson,[851] Thomas
Slaton, Thomas Johnson,[852] Francis Scott,[853] William Allwood, John Thorpe, Matthew Watson,[854] William
Parker,[855] J. Coats,[856] William Greenwood,[857] John Greenwood,[858] Local Preachers—being present, it was inquired:
15 [§2] *Q.* 1. At what places, all things considered, will it be most[859]
proper to have our Conference[860] for the time to come?
A. At London, Bristol, and Leeds, by turns.[861]
[§3] *Q.* 2. What can be done in order to bear a sufficient testimony against the corruptions of the Germans?
20   *A.* It may not be improper to reprint the Letter to the
Church at Herrnhut,[862] with some additions, and a dedication to the Count.

---

[850] Later an itinerant.

[851] Later an itinerant.

[852] Later an itinerant.

[853] Cf. Minutes (1747), §65, n. 585.

[854] Cf. ibid., (1747), §65; and Newcastle (1751), n. 763.

[855] Of Bedford.

[856] Possibly the same as Alex. Coates?

[857] In Todmorden Society Accounts, 1750–52.

[858] Probably of Haworth (Todmorden Society Accounts, 1750–52).

[859] D, 'the most'.

[860] D, 'conferences'.

[861] The 1765 Conference at Manchester departed from this rule for unknown reasons, but the experiment was not repeated until after the 1784 Deed of Declaration allowed for other places.

[862] D omits 'at Herrnhut', though it seems clear that this narrowing down is intended. JW had written several such letters, including that of June 24, 1744, prefixed to Extract IV of his *Journal*, which described his pilgrimage to Herrnhut. But he apparently intended here his series of excerpts from that *Journal* extract, published in 24 pp. under the title *A Short View of the Difference between the Moravian Brethren . . . and the Reverend Mr. John and Charles Wesley.* This was first published in 1745, reprinted in 1747 and 1748 (see *Bibliography*, No. 100). It does not seem to

[§4]   *Q.* 3. Can we unite, if it be desired, with Mr. Ingham?[863]
       A. We may now behave to him with all tenderness and love,
       and unite with him when he returns to the old Methodist
       doctrine.

[§5]   *Q.* 4. Predestinarian preachers have done much hurt among   5
       us. How may this be prevented for the future?
       A. (1) Let none of them preach any more in our societies.
       (2) Let a loving and respectful letter be wrote to Mr.
       Whitefield, wherein he may be desired to advise his
       preachers not to reflect (as they have done continually,   10
       and that both with great bitterness and rudeness) either
       upon the doctrines, or discipline, or person of Mr. Wesley,
       among his own societies; to abstain himself (at least when
       he is among Mr. Wesley's people) from speaking against
       either his doctrines, rules, or preachers;[864] not to declare   15

have been reprinted separately, but only a brief excerpt in 1758, as a section of his *Preservative against unsettled Notions in Religion*, later (1773) inserted in his *Works* (Pine), vol. 20. In 1755, however, JW responded to a new challenge from the Moravians by a much fuller publication, *Queries humbly proposed to the Right Reverend and Right Honourable Count Zinzendorf* (*Bibliography*, No. 208, vol. 13 of this edn.)

[863] Benjamin Ingham (1712–72) of Ossett near Dewsbury, Yorkshire; matriculated Queen's College, Oxford, 1730; B.A., 1734; ordained 1735. An Oxford Methodist, he accompanied JW to Georgia and was converted there by the Moravians. He founded a chain of societies in Yorkshire and Lancashire but in 1742 joined them to the Moravians and then in 1754 separated from them. An attempt to unite his societies with the Wesleys in 1755 failed; see Minutes (1755), §1, n. 950. On his becoming a Sandemanian (Glasite) in 1760, only a few of his remaining societies joined him. He married a daughter of the earl of Huntingdon in 1741. See R. W. Thompson, *Benjamin Ingham and the Inghamites* (Kendal, 1958); D. F. Clark, 'Benjamin Ingham' (master's thesis, Leeds, 1971); *WHS* 38 (1972): 170–76; R. P. Heitzenrater, ed., *Diary of an Oxford Methodist; Benjamin Ingham, 1734–35* (Durham: Duke University Press, 1985).

[864] D adds '3' here, and continues: 'Not to declare war anew again as he has done by new digressions in his late printed sermon.' A copy of the letter written by JW to Whitefield is extant, beginning: 'Between forty and fifty of our preachers lately met at Leeds, all of whom, I trust, esteem you in love for your work's sake. I was desired by 'em to mention a few particulars to you in order to a still firmer union between us.' See May 28 (?), 1753, *Letters*, 25:507–8 in this edn. The sermon appears to have been the first of two on John 1:35–36 and Matt. 26:75, titled *The True Nature of beholding the Lamb of God, and Peter's Denial of his Lord, opened and explained in two Sermons* (London, 1753). See *WHS* 10 (1916): 218. In the first, Whitefield attacked JW's teaching on Christian perfection. See Luke Tyerman, *The Life of the Rev. George Whitefield*, 2 vols., 2nd edn. (London: Hodder and Stoughton, 1890), 2:296.

war anew, as he has done by a needless digression in his late sermon.

[§6]   *Q.* 5. Are none of our own preachers tainted with predestination?

A. We know of none but John Broseworth, of Fishgate.

[§7]   *Q.* 6. Does he do any hurt by his opinion?

A. Very much; for he is continually cavilling with the preachers, and disputing with them.[865]

[§8]   *Q.* 7. What can be done to prevent this?

A. (1) Let our preachers preach at his house no more.

(2) Let him preach no more in any of our societies.

[§9]   *Q.* 8. Are none of our preachers[866] tainted with antinomianism?

A. We hope not.

[§10] *Q.* 9. Shall we read over the Antinomian Dialogues?[867]

A. By all means. (Which were read; as were also[868] Mr. Baxter's *Aphorisms concerning Justification.*)

[§11] *Q.* 10. Does everyone[869] know the exact time when he was justified?

A. It is possible he[870] may not know what to call it when he experiences this; especially if he has not been accustomed to hear the scriptural doctrine concerning it. And the change then wrought in some may not be so sudden, or so observable, as it is in others. But generally, wherever the gospel is preached in a clear and a scriptural manner, more than ninety-nine in a hundred do know the exact time when they were justified.

Wednesday, May the 23rd

[§12] *Q.* 1. Shall we read over that part of the preceding Conference[871] which relates to sanctification?

---

[865] D, 'Very much. 1st, he has been continually cavilling with the preachers, and disputing with the people.'

[866] D, 'people'.

[867] *A Dialogue between an Antinomian and his Friend*, and *A Second Dialogue between an Antinomian and his Friend*, both first published in 1745 (see *Bibliography*, Nos. 102, 106, and vol. 13 of this edn.).

[868] D, 'These were read over, as was also'.

[869] D, 'every person'.

[870] D, 'a man'.

[871] Again (in both MSS) 'the Conference' is used for 'the minutes of the Conference'; cf. above, 1752, §10.

A. By all means. (Which was read and explained.)

[§13] *Q.* 2. Do we all preach strongly and closely concerning both inward and outward holiness?[872]

A. Perhaps not.[873] It would be well if we were more frequently and more largely to insist upon it in all its   5
branches.

[§14] *Q.* 3. Do we insist enough[874] upon practical religion in general? And, in particular, on relative[875] duties, using the means of grace, private prayer, self-denial, fasting, seriousness?[876]

A. It seems most of us have been wanting here. Let us take   10
care to supply the defect for[877] the time to come.

[§15] *Q.* 4. Have not some of us been led off from practical preaching by what was called[878] preaching Christ?[879]

A. It may be we have. But we find by experience the[880] most effectual way of preaching Christ is to preach him in all   15
his offices, and to declare his law as well as gospel[881] both to believers and[882] unbelievers.

[§16] *Q.* 5.[883] But if we are fully sanctified in this life, shall we then have any need of Christ?

A. Undoubtedly as much as ever: for the only[884] foundation   20
of all holiness is faith in him; a divine conviction that he died and now intercedes,[885] and a divine confidence[886] in God through him.

[§17] *Q.* 6. Do we observe any evil which has lately[887] prevailed among our societies?   25

---

[872] Cf. 'Large' *Minutes* (1753), §48.

[873] D, 'Perhaps we do not.'

[874] D omits 'enough'.

[875] D, 'And relative', omitting 'in particular, on'.

[876] D adds 'etc.' Cf. 'Large' *Minutes* (1753), §49.

[877] D, 'take care for'.

[878] D, 'what some call'.

[879] Cf. 'Large' *Minutes* (1753), §47

[880] D, 'that the'.

[881] D, 'his gospel'.

[882] D, 'as well as'.

[883] D incorrectly numbers this '*Q.* 6' and continues this incorrect series forward to §19.

[884] D omits 'only'.

[885] D, 'and intercedes for me'.

[886] D omits 'confidence', obviously in error.

[887] D, 'evils that have'.

A. Many of our members[888] have lately married with unbelievers, even such as were wholly unawakened; and this
has been attended with fatal consequences. Few of these
have gained the unbelievers, wives or husbands.[889] Gener-
5   ally they have themselves either had a grievous cross for
life, or have entirely fallen back into the world.[890]

[§18]   *Q.* 7. What can be done to put a stop to this?[891]

A. (1) Let every preacher take occasion to speak in public
of the danger of being unequally yoked together, after it
10   is openly declared.[892] (2) If any does this notwithstanding, let the Society to which he or she belongs know that
the next who acts thus grossly[893] contrary both to Scripture and reason will be expelled the Society. (3) Let an
exhortation be subjoined, showing the sinfulness of so
15   doing, and the numberless inconveniences which attend
it.[894] (4) And let it be a general rule that no Methodist[895]
marry without[896] consulting the most serious of his
brethren.

[§19]   *Q.* 8. Do not sabbath-breaking, dram-drinking, evil-
20   speaking, unprofitable conversation, lightness, and
contracting debts without sufficient care to discharge
them, prevail in many places? And what method can we
take to remove these growing evils?[897]

---

[888] D, 'people'.

[889] D, 'Few of them have gained the unbelieving wife or husband.' Cf. 'Large'
Minutes (1753), §20: 'Few of these have gained the unbelieving wife or husband'—
showing elements of each version. Some Dissenting churches, notably the Baptists
and Quakers, expelled members for marrying outside their communities, even if
believers. The concern expressed here, however, probably followed scriptural
injunctions as in 2 Cor. 6:14.

[890] D, 'General[ly] they themselves have ((gained)) had a grievous cross for life,
and some; or have . . .'.

[891] D, 'to prevent, or put a stop to this evil?'

[892] D, 'yoked with unbelievers'.

[893] D, '. . . let it be declared openly in the Society to which he belongs that the
next who acts this grossly'.

[894] D, 'inconveniences attending it'.

[895] D, 'member'.

[896] D, 'without first'.

[897] Cf. 'Large' *Minutes* (1753), §22. D, '. . . discharge the same, prevent in many
[orig., 'mank'] places the spreading of the gospel? What method shall we take to
remove this evil?'

A. (1) Let us preach expressly and strongly[898] on each of these heads. (2) Let the leaders[899] closely examine their several classes, and exhort every single person to put away the accursed thing. (3) Let the preacher[900] warn the Society in every place that none who is hereafter guilty can remain with us.[901] (4) In order to give them clearer views[902] of these and all other branches of practical religion, let every preacher recommend to every Society the reading our books preferably to[903] any other; and when any new book is sent to any place, let him give notice[904] in the public congregation.

5

10

Thursday, May the 24th

[§20]   *Q.* 1. Has any of you any objections against any of the Twelve Rules of an Itinerant Preacher?[905] (Which were read over and considered one by one.)

15

A. We have no objections against any; but are determined, by the grace of God, cheerfully to observe them.[906]

[§21]   *Q.* 2. Have any of you any objections to the life or doctrine of any Itinerant Preacher? (Whose names were then mentioned[907] one by one, and their behaviour severally considered.)[908]

20

A. We are all well[909] satisfied with each other.

[§22]   *Q.* 3. Is it expedient that John Edwards should settle at Leeds?[910]

[898] D, 'strongly and expressly'.

[899] D, 'leaders of the classes'.

[900] D, 'preachers'.

[901] D, 'that none [? one] who is guilty of those things hereafter cannot remain with us'.

[902] D, 'give as clear views'.

[903] D, 'recommend the reading of our books preferable to'.

[904] D, 'notice of it'; cf. 'Large' *Minutes* (1753), §22.1: 'let him speak of it'.

[905] D, 'objection to the Twelve Rules of the Itinerant Preachers'. See Minutes (1744), §73.

[906] D, 'We have no objection to any, but determine (by the grace of God) carefully to observe them.'

[907] D, 'Whose names was then read over'.

[908] D, 'examined', struck through, followed by 'considered'.

[909] D, 'all now well'.

[910] John Edwards (1714–85) appears to have been born in Ireland and worked there for Whitefield. Failing to gain permission to stay in Leeds, he left Methodism this year and had an Independent church built for him in Leeds. See *Journal* (Curnock), 4:67 n. 3, 95 n. 1; *DEB*, 1:345.

A. (1) He can in no wise consent to stay there always. But, (2), neither he nor we have any objections to his spending half a year in Leeds Circuit, as any other travelling preacher; and he may make a trial for the two or three

5   next months, as joint Assistant with William Shent.[911]

[§23]   *Q.* 4. What are those hardships upon the preachers which it is[912] in our power to remove?

A. One of the greatest is that which lies on the married preachers. There is no provision for their wives.

10 [§24]   *Q.* 5. Ought they not to be careful how they bring this upon themselves by marrying hand over head?[913]

A. Undoubtedly they ought. Therefore any preacher who marries without first consulting his ministers,[914] or his brethren, should not take it amiss that[915] he is then left to

15   himself to provide for her how he can.

[§25]   *Q.* 6. But if a preacher do consult them first, and still if he marry one that has nothing?

A. He must be content to return to his temporal business, and so commence a Local Preacher.[916]

20 [§26]   *Q.* 7. That the societies may the more readily assist the married preachers, ought not their wives to be as exemplary as possible?

A. Certainly they ought. In particular, they ought never to be idle, and constantly attend the morning[917] preaching.

25 [§27]   *Q.* 8. But how may they have what is needful with the least trouble?

---

[911] This appears to show that although the stations assigned at this Conference are supposedly for 'the ensuing year', in fact a quarterly or half-yearly appointment remained the norm. D reads: '(2) Neither him nor we have any objection to his spending half the year in Leeds Circuit as another travelling preacher [this apparently implies an *additional* preacher], and he may make a trial for two or three months as joint Assistant with Wm. Shent.'

[912] D, 'What are the hardships of the travelling preachers that is in our power to remove?'

[913] Cf. 'Large' *Minutes* (1753), §69.

[914] D, 'without ['the consent of J', struck through] consulting his minister'.

[915] D, 'if'.

[916] D, '*Q.* 6. But if he consult one first?'
'A. If he marries one that have nothing he must be content to return to his former business, and so become a *Local* Preacher.' Cf. 1752, §19, where the inability to preach twice a day is noted as a reason for becoming a local preacher.

[917] D underlines 'morning'.

A. (1) Let the Assistant inquire[918] what each preacher's wife wants, at every Quarterly Meeting. (2) Let those wants be supplied first of all,[919] out of the common stock. (3) Let a letter be wrote to all the societies upon this head.[920]   5

[§28]   *Q.* 9. Do the stewards behave well with regard to the preachers?
        A. Most of them do;[921] some do not.

[§29]   *Q.* 10. How may this be remedied?
        A. (1) Let the Assistant explain to the stewards in every   10
        place[922] the nature of their office. (2) Let him immediately displace those who behave amiss[923] and will not be reproved.

[§30]   *Q.* 11. How many circuits are there?
        A. Twelve: (1) London. (2) Bristol. (3) Devonshire.[924]   15
        (4) Cornwall. (5) Staffordshire. (6) Cheshire. (7) Leeds.
        (8) Haworth. (9) Lincolnshire. (10) Newcastle. (11) Wales.
        (12) Ireland.[925]

[§31]   *Q.* 12. How may these[926] be supplied the ensuing year?
        A. (1) *London*,[927] John Wesley, etc.   20
        (2) *Bristol*, William Hitchens, John Haime,[928] Paul Greenwood.
        (3) *Devonshire*, William Roberts, Peter Jaco.[929]

[918] See 'Large' *Minutes* (1753), §68. D, 'Assistant of the circuit first inquire'.

[919] D, 'Let the wives be supplied first'.

[920] D, 'Let a letter be writ to all the stewards on this head.'

[921] D, 'Some do'.

[922] D, 'Let the Assistant of the Circuit explain to the stewards.'

[923] D, 'them that do amiss'.

[924] D, 'Devon'.

[925] D lists the last five circuits differently: '(8) Newcastle. (9) Haworth. (10) Lancashire. (11) Ireland. (12) Wales'. The actual stations, however, he lists in the same order as Rowell—see below.

[926] D, 'How shall they'.

[927] Rowell, 'John Wesley, etc., *London*'.

[928] D, 'Addams, and'; in subsequent entries D also adds 'and' before the last name.

[929] D, 'Jacco', as also in the MS copies in 1755 and 1758. He signed his name this way in the preachers' agreement of May 8, 1754. By the time of the printed *Minutes* (1765), however, and thereafter, his name appeared as 'Jaco', the spelling that is here used throughout.

(4) *Cornwall,* John Fisher, Thomas Mitchell, John Turnough,[930] John Fenwick.[931]

(5) *Staffordshire,* James Jones, John Thorpe.[932]

(6) *Cheshire,* John Haughton, James Scholefield.[933]

5   (7) and (8) *Yorkshire and Haworth,* Jonathan Maskew,[934] John Whitford, Enoch Williams, Joseph Jones, William Shent, John Edwards.

(9) *Lincolnshire,* William Fugill, Thomas Johnson,[935] J. Scholefield.[936]

10   (10) *Newcastle,* Christopher Hopper, John Hampson, Jonathan Catlow, Jacob Rowell.[937]

(11) *Wales,* Francis Walker, William Darney.[938]

(12) *Ireland,* Joseph Cownley, Charles Skelton, Thomas Walsh,[939] Samuel Larwood, James Deaves,[940] Thomas

15   Kead,[941] Robert Swindells,[942] James Morris,[943] N. Gilbert.[944]

---

[930] Turnough's name was apparently pronounced, and sometimes spelled, 'Turner', as in the diary of Thomas Illingworth (Special Collections, Perkins Library, Duke University, Durham, N.C.), Sept. 19, 1756: 'I went to Keighley, John Turner preach'd; I was glad to see him, not having heard him preach of a long time.'

[931] D, 'Finick'.

[932] N.B., Thorpe is listed as a local preacher. D, 'Thros'.

[933] D, 'Jno. Houghton and Jno. Nelson'.

[934] D, 'Mackenhew'.

[935] D, 'Junson'.

[936] Rowell apparently read 'Scholefield', although his MS is not available to check. D reads 'Shiefield'. In 1755 Jones reads 'Scholfd'; Nelson 'Scholfield'. Scholefield and his wife, Susan, buried their daughter at Todmorden in Apr. 1734, when the entry in the register appears as 'Mary dr. of Jam: Schoifield', although the tombstone is inscribed 'Mary Scholefield'. See Baker, *William Grimshaw,* 320. We take the latter spelling as our norm.

[937] D, 'Christ. Hoper, Jno. Callow, Jacob Rowel, Jno. Hamson'.

[938] D, 'Francis Walker, etc.' Darney promised in Conference not to preach non-Methodist doctrines, but did not keep his promise. See May 25, 1754, *Letters,* 26:537 in this edn.

[939] D, 'Welch'.

[940] D, 'Davis'.

[941] D, 'Head'.

[942] D, 'Swindals'.

[943] D, 'Moras'.

[944] D, 'Nichs. Gilbert'. D then underlines the preceding entries and adds below: 'Jno. Callow, Wm. Fugill, Jno. Turnough, Enoc. Williams, & Thoms. Coleback, now entered on the List of Travelling Preachers.' Catlow, Fugill, Turnough, and Williams were already listed in §1 as among the itinerants present, but the point of this entry seems to be that at this Conference, they were for the first time officially accepted as itinerants. Colbeck was listed in §1 among the local preachers.

The London Conference of May 22–25, 1754[945]

Wed. [May] 22, [1754]. Our Conference began. And the spirit of peace and love was in the midst of us. Before we parted, we all willingly signed an agreement not to act independently on each other.[946]

[945] *Journal & Diaries*, 20:486 in this edn. Cf. Christopher Hopper, in Jackson, *Early Methodist Preachers*, 1:206: 'May 22, our Conference began. It was a time of love'. Thomas Mitchell (ibid., 1:252): 'From the following Conference (at which fourteen preachers were present beside Mr. Wesley and his brother), I went into Wiltshire, where Mr. Pearce of Bradford was as a father to me'. However, the *Minutes* (1753) and Thomas Olivers's account (Jackson, *Early Methodist Preachers*, 2:73) clearly show that Mitchell and Olivers were soon sent to Cornwall (on Oct. 24, 1753, according to Olivers). But more than fourteen preachers were present at that Conference, and Mitchell may be correct in his figure for 1754, confusing the 'next' Conference of 1754 with 1753 for his Cornish journey. The preachers' signed agreement at the 1754 Conference contains twenty-five names, not including Charles Wesley. The letter sent to William Darney on May 25, 1754, contains twenty-four names including CW (*Letters*, 26:537f. in this edn.). But the preaching plan for May 20–26 has fourteen names in addition to the Wesleys, though these dwindle in the following weeks as they returned to their circuits. *WMM* (1855): 223–26. The fourteen (in alphabetical order) are Joseph Cownley, James Deaves, John Edwards, John Fenwick, John Haime, Christopher Hopper, James Jones, John Jones, Thomas Mitchell, Charles Perronet, William Roberts, Jacob Rowell, Robert Swindells, Thomas Walsh, as well as the Wesleys. Of these, all except Charles Wesley and John Edwards signed the agreement. The three itinerants who remained preaching in the London area after the others had departed were James Deaves, Charles Perronet, and Thomas Walsh. The others who signed both the preachers' agreement and the condemnation of Darney were presumably present as clergy or probationers, or perhaps preachers whose likely presence was not known when JW prepared his Conference plan. James Rouquet signed the agreement; he had re-organized Kingswood School for JW and was ordained a deacon of the Church of England on Sept. 22, 1754, serving for most of his life as a clergyman in the Bristol area; see A. B. Sackett, *James Rouquet and His Part in Early Methodism* (Chester: WHS, 1972), 4–22. The itinerant preachers who signed the agreement but were not listed on JW's preaching plans were John Fenwick and John Fisher, James Jones and John Jones (one of each pair only, as either 'J. F.' or 'J. J.' signed Darney's censure); the following, who signed both: John Hampson, John Haughton, William Hitchens, Peter Jaco, Richard Lucas, Jonathan Maskew, Richard Moss, and Edward Perronet; and Thomas Maxfield, who signed only Darney's censure. Two other preachers were there as probationers, signing the agreement only, viz., Nicholas Story (listed as a probationer in 1749) and Samuel Smith (probably the same man who served in the itinerancy [1769–82] and died c. 1797).

[946] This agreement was along the same lines as that of Jan. 29, 1752 (see pp. 259–60 above). The signatures, in order, were John Wesley, John Haughton, Chr. Hopper, E. Perronet, John Jones, Jas. Rouquet, John Fenwick, Pet. Jacco [i.e., Jaco], John Hampson, John Fisher, Rich. Moss, Wm. Hitchens, Jas. Deaves, Richd. Lewcas, Thos. Mitchell, Nich. Story, Sam. Smith, James Jones, Chas. Perronet, Wm. Robert, Thos. Walsh, Rob. Swindells, Jon. Maskew, John Haime, Jos. Cownley.

So that the breach lately made has only united us more closely together than ever.[947]

The Leeds Conference of May 6, 1755[948]

[§1]   Sixty-three preachers[949] being present, it was considered at
5   large, Ought we to separate from the Established

[947] Charles Skelton had just left the itinerancy to settle in Bury St. Edmunds; Apr. 21, 1754, *Journal & Diaries,* 20:485 in this edn. He later became an Independent minister in Southwark. John Green had just walked out after being rebuked for preaching against JW; May 12, 1754, *Journal & Diaries.* 20:486 in this edn. And at this very Conference, William Darney had been declared not 'in connexion' because, contrary to his promise, he had 'preached in several of our societies a doctrine quite contrary to what we believe and preach'; May 25, 1754, *Letters,* 25:537 in this edn. Prof. Ward adds Jonathan Reeves, episcopally ordained and minister of the Magdalen Hospital; Samuel Larwood, Independent minister in Southwark; John Edwards and John Whitford, Independent ministers in Leeds and Bolton, respectively; *Journal & Diaries,* 20:486–87, n. 69 in this edn., citing *WMM* 28 (1855): 223.

[948] Two MSS are available for these Minutes, one in the handwriting of John Nelson, the other of John Jones. Although there are minor variations in the layout and spelling of the two copies, the text is almost identical. It may well be that the scholarly John Jones, a trusted confidant of JW and the others, though now not a regular itinerant, was entrusted with preparing an 'official' transcript of the Minutes. On the differences between the handwriting of Jones and JW, see R. P. Heitzenrater, "Three Tests and a Key: Identifying John Wesley's Handwriting," *Manuscripta* 33 (Summer 1981).

Both MSS are strangely headed, 'Leeds, May 22nd, 1755', but on that date JW was in Newcastle, having left Leeds with his wife on May 12. His *Journal* for May 6, 1755 (21:10 in this edn.), reads:

'Our Conference began at Leeds. The point on which we desired all the preachers to speak their minds at large was, whether we ought to separate from the Church? Whatever was advanced on one side or the other was seriously and calmly considered. And on the third day we were all fully agreed in that general conclusion that (whether it was *lawful* or not) it was no ways *expedient.'*

This date is confirmed from the correspondence of both JW and CW. The May 22 date is probably a mistaken carryover from the 1754 Conference.

[949] The presence of sixty-three preachers is almost impossible, even granting the inclusion of probationers and local preachers, and one suspects a misreading of (perhaps) 'forty-three' or (much more likely) 'twenty-three'—or some other form of error. The list given below contains thirty-four itinerants and twelve 'half-itinerants', while only forty-two preachers are listed in the whole of the stations, in addition to fifteen 'chief local preachers'. It is almost inconceivable, for instance, that all the nine men stationed in Ireland travelled to Leeds for this occasion.

Church?[950] After a free and full debate, continued for several days, it was agreed by all that we ought not.

[950] It was certainly a momentous gathering attended by more than the usual number of preachers because of the importance of its general theme. Although separation from the Church of England had been discussed earlier, the previous few months had brought matters to a head. Thomas Walsh and Charles Perronet, though laymen, had administered the Lord's Supper, JW was pondering the advisability of ordaining at least some preachers, and CW (seconded by William Grimshaw) was organizing strong opposition to such a move. See Baker, *Wesley and Church*, 162–67. CW told his wife on Apr. 30, 'All the preachers in the north are unanimous for [separation]', and William Grimshaw was coming from Haworth resolved 'to take his leave of us if we did of the Church' (MS letter in MA). They persuaded JW to greater caution, and he prepared a long paper to read to the Conference in May, titled 'Ought we to Separate from the Church of England?' See 9:567–80 of this edn. JW read this paper on Tuesday, May 6, and it was debated until Thursday, May 8, when attention turned to more routine matters.

On May 9, CW reported to his wife: 'I left the brethren in Conference but had quite enough of them first. Yet I don't repent my trouble. You will be content to wait a little for particulars. I have done with Conferences for ever. All agreed not to separate. So the wound is healed—slightly.' Baker, *Charles Wesley*, 93. See also JW's correspondence with Samuel Walker of Truro, which throws light on the preachers' objections to the Church and JW's acknowledgement that he found it difficult to answer them, particularly on the liturgy, canons, and the characters and doctrines of the clergy. *Letters*, 26:582–86, 592–96, 606–8, 611–13 in this edn.

William Batty claims that on May 6, 1745, Benjamin Ingham was asked to attend the Conference at Leeds, but the date of May 6 and location at Leeds strongly suggest that 1755 is intended. Ingham's companions, Batty and John Allen, 'who were present at this time with some view of being admitted and endeavoured to bring about a union or at least better and closer friendship', were excluded. But the providence of God prevented this union for 'wise and happy reasons'. Moravian MS 'Church History', fols. 58f., in MA. Soon after, they settled their own doctrinal standards. In 1786, JW spoke of a debate on separation in 1758 at the Leeds Conference (evidently an error for 1755) and recorded, 'After considering the whole matter calmly, we determined upon the negative. Mr. Ingham, being present, commended our determination in very strong terms, whenever the Methodists leave the Church, God will leave them' (a phrase used elsewhere by JW). JW continued:

'To prevent it we all agreed (1) to exhort all our people constantly to attend the Church and Sacraments, and (2) still to preach on Sundays, morning and evening, not in the church hours. Indeed, by taking the contrary steps, by exhorting our people not to go to church, or (which comes to the same thing) by appointing to preach in church hours, we should separate from it at once.' *Letters* (Telford), 7:332

Joseph Sutcliffe (MS 'History', 462) records further exchanges under the year 1756, but a reference to CW leaving abruptly shows it was certainly in 1755 (Baker, *Charles Wesley*, 93). Sutcliffe says that as 'Mr. Wesley's health was delicate, the Church question was mooted'. Despite local calls for the Sacrament, only Charles Perronet of the preachers called for liberty of conscience. But though the brothers

[§2]   Our present Itinerant Preachers are:
John Wesley
Charles Wesley
W. Grimshaw
5   Thomas Walsh
William Hitchens[951]
Christopher Hopper
Jacob Rowell
Robert Swindells
10   John Fenwick
Richard Moss
Nicholas Gilbert
Thomas Mitchell
James Scholefield
15   Paul Greenwood
James Deaves
Thomas Seccomb
Peter Jaco
John Nelson
20   James Massiot
James Wild
Thomas Tobias
Thomas Olivers

Wesley urged staying in the Church, they differed in that Charles required a pledge from the preacher to refuse tickets to anyone not taking their families to Church and Sacrament, John disagreed, and if he deceased, the preachers foresaw a rupture in Methodism. Titus Knight agreed with CW, whom he called 'his faithful friend', yet was the first to settle with Dissenters in Halifax (see below, p. 275). It really was trying for Methodists (continues Sutcliffe) to see some expelled from Church by the clergy; and the London Societies received the Communion from their own ministers, while they were driven off to Dissenting ministers. He notes that Valton records attending a drawing room meeting with clergy administering the Lord's Supper. (However, Valton was not yet an itinerant, and this incident appears to refer to 1765.) CW refers to preachers administering the Sacrament in a letter to Sellon, Feb. 4, 1755.

Though the issue of women preachers did not arise at this Conference (and rarely at any other), it is worthy of note that in 1748 Wesley had quoted St. Paul as authority for prohibiting such preachers against the Quaker Barclay's *Apology; Letters* (Telford), 2:119. Yet in his address on separation to the 1755 Conference, he incidentally allowed that in apostolic times women had preached under 'extraordinary inspiration' (9:573 in this edn.). This later became his justification for tolerating some women preachers who began to appear locally from the 1760s. See Chilcote, *Women Preachers*, 57, 106.

[951] Jones, 'Hichens', and 'Hitchins' in stations.

James Oddie[952]
John Johnson
John Turnough[953]
Thomas Hanby
Henry Floyd   5
Thomas Kead
John Murlin
Joseph Cownley
Thomas Lee
Thomas Johnson   10
Richard Lucas
John Hacking
Half Itin[erant]s[954] are:
William Shent
William Roberts   15
James Jones
Jonathan Maskew
James Rouquet
John Fisher
Matthew Lowes   20
John Brown
Charles Perronet
Enoch Williams
John Haim[e]
John Furz   25

[§3]   These are stationed for the ensuing year thus:
London, John Murlin, Thomas Hanby, Thomas Olivers,
    Enoch Williams.
Bristol, W. Hitchens*[955] Peter Jaco, Richard Lucas,
    John Furz.   30

---

[952] Orig. (both MSS), 'Oddey'.

[953] Jones, 'Tournough', but 'Turnough' in stations, §3.

[954] Preachers who did not itinerate full–time and in some cases financed themselves by part-time paid occupations (Baker, 'Polity', 236). Itinerants often had to have paid work on the side as well, but in 1768 (*Minutes*, *Q.* 22) this practice was forbidden. However, the famous 'Methodist Squire', Robert Brackenbury of Raithby, Lincolnshire, was an independent country gentleman and half-itinerant who travelled irregularly for Wesley. See *Minutes* (1784), *Q.* 7 'Isle of Jersey' after (72) and n. 39.

[955] The asterisk represents a cross added above the names of the preachers first listed in Bristol, Staffordshire., Cheshire, Leeds, Lincolnshire, Newcastle, and Ireland, in both MSS (and also of Swindells in Ireland in the Jones MS). It seems fairly certain that this comprises a designation of the Assistant for the circuit; cf

Cornwall, Nicholas Gilbert,[956] Paul Greenwood, Thomas
Tobias, Henry Floyd.

Staffords[hire], James Jones,* John Johnson, John Hacking.

Cheshire, Richard Moss,* Jacob Rowell.

5   *Haworth,* W. Grimshaw, John Nelson, James Scholefield.

Leeds, John Fenwick,* Thomas Lee, Thomas Johnson,
William Shent.

Lincoln, Jonathan Maskew,* Thomas Mitchell.

Newcastle, Christopher Hopper,* James Massiot,

10   Matthew Lowes, James Wild, John Turnough.

Wales, John Brown, John Wasley.[957]

Ireland, Thomas Walsh,*[958] John Deaves, Thomas
Seccomb,[959] Robert Swindells,* Joseph Cownley,
Thomas Kead, James Oddie,[960] John Fisher, Joseph

15   Tucker.

[§4] Our chief Local Preachers are:

John Jones

T. Maxfield

T. Westell

20   J. Haughton

Francis Walker

Joseph Tucker

Minutes (1758), §33. In London, one of the unlisted Wesley brothers was in charge;
in Haworth, Rev. William Grimshaw. In Wales, by analogy, it may have been Rev.
John (or James) Brown, possibly an evangelical clergyman who appears in Howell
Harris's Bristol diaries for 1762–63 as 'Mr. Brown', and who should possibly be
identified with the evangelical Rev. James Brown to whom JW wrote on Apr. 19,
1764, and visited on Aug. 13, 1776, when he met Dr. Thomas Coke, his later coad-
jutor. Coke has often been said to have been Brown's curate at Kingston on his ejec-
tion from South Petherton in 1771, but this is uncertain. John A. Vickers, *Thomas
Coke* (London, 1969), 36. But it is possible that for both Cornwall and Wales (where
the work was less carefully organised), no Assistant was appointed. The cross over
Swindells's name would probably indicate that he was to have been in England on
his third and last visit for about two years before his return to Ireland on Apr. 13,
1758, i.e., from the spring of 1756. Jackson, *Early Methodist Preachers,* 3:116.

[956] Nelson, 'Richd. Gilbert'.

[957] Both MSS have 'Wesley', but 'Wasley' is probably meant.

[958] Jones, 'Welsh'.

[959] Although his name has frequently been spelled with a final 'e', in both MSS
and in JW's letter of Sept. 28, 1760, about his death, it is spelled 'Seccomb'.

[960] Both MSS spell his name 'Oddy', but at least by 1761, JW was spelling it
'Oddie', and it always appeared thus in the printed *Minutes,* the spelling that Oddie
himself used in an extant letter of Nov. 16, 1765.

William Tucker
Thomas Colbeck
Titus Knight
John Slocomb
James Morris   5
Eleazer Webster
Michael Calender
John Bakewell
Alexander Mather
[§5]   At the close of the Conference I spoke thus: 10

It has been affirmed that none of our Itinerant Preachers
are so much alive as they were seven years ago. I fear many
are not. But if so, they are unfit for the work, which
requires much life: otherwise your labour will be tiresome
to yourself, and of little use to others. Tiresome because   15
you will no longer serve Christ and the people willingly
and cheerfully. Of little use because you will no longer
serve them diligently, doing it with your might.

I have several reasons to fear, it is so with many of you.
But let your own conscience be the judge.   20

Which of you is exemplarily alive to God, so as to carry
fire with him wherever he goes?

Which of you is a pattern of self-denial, even in little things?

Which of you drinks water? Why not?

Who rises at four? Why not?   25

Who fasts on Friday? Why not?

Who has not four meals a day?

Who goes through his work willingly and diligently?
Never, on any account, disappoints a congregation?

Who has every part of the plan at heart? Always meets   30
Society, Bands, Leaders?

Who visits in Mr. Baxter's method?[961]

Who preaches the old thundering doctrine? No faith
without light? Who constantly and zealously enforces
practical religion? Relative duties? Recommends   35
books? Kingswood School?

---

[961] On Baxter see above, Minutes (1745), §13 and n. 261. This is Richard Baxter's
Gildas Salvianus: The Reformed Pastor (1656). Wesley commended this book specifically in the 1766 *Minutes* (*Q.* 29, at n. 113) for distribution and appended an extract
outlining Baxter's 'method'.

Who is never idle?

What Assistant enforces uniformly every branch of the
   Methodist plan on the preachers and people? Visits all the
   societies quarterly?

5   Do you see that every preacher observes the Rules? Do you
   reprove, and if need be, send me word of the defaulters?

Do you send me a regular account quarterly?

Is your heart whole in the work? Do not you give way to
   unconcern, indolence, or fear of man?

10   Who will join heart and hand, according to the twelve
   Rules? Particularly the twelfth?

The Dublin Conference of April 19–23 (?), 1756[962]

In the following week, all our preachers met. I never before found
such unanimity among them. They appeared now to be not only of
15 one heart, but likewise of one mind and judgment.

The Bristol Conference of August 26–28, 1756[963]

[962] The only reference to this Conference is in JW's *Journal* for Easter Week, 1756,
the Conference itself probably meeting on Monday, Apr. 19, for two or three days.
Journal & Diaries, 21:50 in this edn. The Leeds MS Minutes (1755) show that the
preachers then in Ireland were Deaves, Seccomb, Swindells, Cownley, Kead, Oddie,
Fisher, Tucker, and Thomas Walsh, serving as Assistant; see (1755), §3. John Haughton
also seems to have been preaching in Dublin some months later; see JW's letter of June
18, 1756 to his wife: 'John Haughton is in Dublin.' *Letters* (Telford), 3:180.
   At this Conference, Mark Davis was received into the itinerancy as a young man
of twenty-two, shortly after having been made a member of the Dublin Society by
James Deaves. C. H. Crookshank, *History of Methodism in Ireland*, 3 vols. (Belfast:
Allen, 1885), 1:108.
   [963] There are two accounts of this Conference, both from JW's pen. The first
comes from his *Journal* for Aug. 26–28, 1756, but was not published until 1761.
Journal & Diaries, 21:76–77. The second is from a contemporary copy of CW's
letter of Sept. 6, 1756, to Rev. Samuel Walker, which he introduces thus: 'An Extract
of my brother's account [of the Conference] is as follows'. This extract omits details
given in the *Journal* about the Band *Rules* and Kingswood School, but gives fuller
details from the account of the debate on separation. Here JW's *Journal* is taken as
the basic text, with additions preserved by CW added within square brackets and
variants recorded in footnotes.

Thursday, [August] 26, [1756]. About fifty of us being met;[964] [both the travelling and local preachers were called over, and all objections which had been or were now made to any of them were considered. In the afternoon] the Rules[965] of the Society were read over and carefully considered one by one. But we did not find any 5 that could be spared. So we all agreed to abide by them all and to recommend them with our might. [CW, 'The phrase was altered in one or two places, and a new rule added.'][966]

We then largely considered the necessity of keeping in the Church and using the clergy with tenderness. And there was no dissenting 10 voice. God gave us all to be of one mind and one judgment.[967]

Friday 27. The Rules of the bands were read over and considered one by one; which, after some verbal alterations,[968] we all agreed to observe and enforce.

Saturday 28. The Rules of Kingswood School were read and 15 considered one by one. And we were all convinced, they were agreeable to Scripture and reason. In consequence of which it was agreed:

(1) That a short account of the design and present state of the school be read by every Assistant in every society; and

---

[964] CW wrote to Walker on Sept. 6: 'Between forty and fifty, or almost all our itinerant preachers, was present. I have talked largely with each; some of whom I had not known before so much as by name. Mr [Henry] Venn, a clergyman, was with us the whole time.' Rev. William Grimshaw was there for part of the time, urged by CW, whose effort to stave off the still-threatening separation from the Church of England had caused him to override his statement to his wife the previous year that he had 'done with Conferences for ever'. See Baker, *Wesley and Church*, 171–72, and Baker, *Charles Wesley*, 95–97. Of the lay preachers, Christopher Hopper wrote, 'In July 1756, I set out for Bristol [from Newcastle]. Our Conference began August 26th. It was a good season'. Jackson, *Early Methodist Preachers*, 1:208.

[965] *The Nature, Design, and General Rules, Bibliography*, No. 73, for which see vol. 9 of this edn.

[966] These revisions seem first to have appeared in the 7th edn. (Bristol: Pine, 1762), where the prohibition of 'going to law' was altered to 'brother going to law with brother'; see the text in 9:69–75 in this edn., and cf. the variant readings on pp. 549–50.

[967] CW's version: 'We afterwards spoke largely of keeping united to the Church, and there was no dissenting voice; but all were knit together in one mind and one judgment.' The account quoted above from Joseph Sutcliffe is ascribed by him to 1756 but fairly clearly belongs to 1755. See Minutes (1755), n. 950.

[968] *Rules of the Band Societies, Bibliography*, No. 81, for which see 9:77–79 in this edn., in the Appendix to which (p. 551) may be traced the 'verbal alterations' introduced in the text.

(2) That a subscription for it be begun in every place, and (if need be) a collection made every year.[969]

My brother and I closed the Conference by a solemn declaration of our purpose, never to separate from the Church. And all our brethren
5   concurred therein. [CW, 'My brother and I ended the Conference with a strong declaration of our resolution to live and die in the communion of the Church of England. We all unanimously agreed that whilst it is lawful or possible to continue in it, it is unlawful for us to leave it.']970

The Keighley Conference of May 21, 1757[971]

10   **Sat. 21 [May, 1757].** I had a little Conference with our preachers.

---

[969] In the 'Large' *Minutes* (1763) appeared a lengthy attempt 'to make the Methodists sensible of the excellency of Kingswood School', and mention was made of the accumulating debt, in spite of 'the yearly subscription made at London and Bristol'. It continued: 'The best means we could think of at our late Conference to supply the deficiency is, once a year to desire the assistance of all those in every place who wish well to the work of God.' At the same time it was decided that 'a collection be made for it the Sunday before or after midsummer, in every preaching-house throughout England' (§§57, 58). According to Myles (*Chronological History*, 78f.), JW explained the need of a general yearly subscription such as some Societies had already used. It was recommended to the Classes at the Christmas visitation and to be received the following March. It was to be used for the expense of building preaching-houses from 1740 to 1756; paying for preachers unable to finance themselves; supporting preachers in poor circuits; and enabling them to go to law in self-defence. JW is said to have sent a circular letter to the Societies recommending this. Myles evidently confuses this letter with the Kingswood appeal or may have ascribed it to the wrong Conference.

[970] JW's version seems to corroborate CW's view that all agreed, not simply that separation was inexpedient—which had been the position that JW contended at the 1755 Conference—but illegal. CW reported to Walker: 'My brother seems farther from a separation than ever.' The unanimity was signalized by the signing on Aug. 30 of another agreement in the same terms as that of Jan. 29, 1752, with the additional signatures of Thomas Johnson, James Jones, Peter Jaco, William Hitchens, John Johnson, John Haughton, Thomas Mitchell, William Roberts, and Richard Lucas, all of whom were presumably present, though these do not make up the complete attendance at the Conference. See *WMM* (1847): 869.

[971] The only reference to this Conference seems to be in JW's *Journal.* It seems clear that it was intended as an occasion for the encouragement of JW's preachers in the north of England rather than for any momentous decisions. Its holding at Keighley rather than at Leeds (16 miles away) was undoubtedly for the convenience of his clerical lieutenant in the North, Rev. William Grimshaw, for whom the following morning he administered Communion and in the afternoon preached in the churchyard at Haworth. See *Journal & Diaries*, 21:103.

The London Conference of August 4–11, 1757[972]

Tue. [Aug.] 2, [1757]. On his[973] expressing a desire to be present at our Conference, I invited him to it; and on Wednesday the third, in the evening, he came to the Foundery. Our Conference began the next morning, and continued till the Thursday following. From the first hour to the last there was no jarring string, but all was harmony and love.[974]

The Limerick Conference of June 21–22 (?), 1758

Wednesday, [June] 21, [1758]. Our little Conference began, at which fourteen preachers were present. We settled all things here

---

[972] Aug. 2–4, 1757, *Journal & Diaries*, 21:120 in this edn.

[973] This was John Simpson, an early follower at the Fetter Lane Society in London, who had since been ordained as a Moravian minister, but who had severed his connection with them the previous year. It seems to have been JW's practice to invite select visitors as guests. The others present included James Oddie (see letter by William Grimshaw, July 31, 1757), and Alexander Mather, who was received into the itinerancy, financial provision being made for his wife as an inducement. Mather's account is of some importance in view of what was to become a regular feature of the Methodist economy. JW had asked Mather to go with him to Ireland in 1756 and promised that his wife should be provided for in his absence, but when Mather told the London stewards that he needed 4*s.* a week to support her, and must otherwise continue in his regular work as a baker, 'they were unwilling to allow' this amount. At the 1757 Conference, however, 'it was agreed that I should travel, and that my wife should have that fixed allowance. This was the beginning of that settlement for preachers' wives which (with the addition of forty shillings a year) continues to this day'. *AM* (1780): 148–49, in an undated letter to JW (§23); see Jackson, *Early Methodist Preachers*, 2:171. But cf. above, Limerick *Minutes* (1752), §27 for proposals for an allowance. See further, introduction, pp. 50–53.

[974] In defending to Samuel Walker of Truro his continuing use of lay preachers and circuits in the parishes of evangelical clergy, JW says that at this Conference, he had asked, 'What can be done in order to a closer union with the clergy who preach the truth? . . . We all agreed that nothing would be more desirable', though he does not explain what, if anything, was proposed. Sept. 19, 1757, *Letters* (Telford), 3:224.

which we judged would be of use to the preachers or the societies, and consulted how to remove whatever might be an hindrance to the work of God.[975]

The Bristol Conference of August 12–16, 1758[976]

5

August 12th, 1758
[§1]   The following persons being met at the New Room in
Bristol:
J[ohn] W[esley]
C[harles] W[esley]
10   T[homas] M[axfiel]d[977]

---

[975] June 21, 1758, *Journal & Diaries*, 21:155. JW had met Thomas Walsh again on June 17. Walsh had recently returned from England, and died the following year in Dublin. He would be among the fourteen preachers present. Others stationed in Ireland at this time were Mark Davis, Nicholas Gilbert, Paul Greenwood, Christopher Hopper, Thomas Johnson, Thomas Kead, James Morgan, James Oddie, and William Thompson. Charges of doctrinal unorthodoxy were brought against Mark Davis, a newcomer to Methodism, but he was successfully defended by Walsh: 'Brother Davis is a wise and good man, and these objections to his phraseology will soon be done away when he becomes more acquainted with the writings of the Methodists'. Crookshank, *History of Methodism in Ireland*, 1:131; Irish *MM*, 27:517, quoted in *Journal* (Curnock), 3:275, n. 2. To make up the number to fourteen, some local preachers also must have been present.

[976] JW returned rather hurriedly from Ireland via Wales for the Conference at Bristol, while four preachers from Ireland—Nicholas Gilbert, Paul Greenwood, Christopher Hopper, and Thomas Johnson—also travelled from Ireland via Parkgate and Chester to Bristol. JW said little about it in his *Journal*: 'On the following days was our yearly Conference, begun and ended in perfect harmony.' *Journal & Diaries*, 21:161. Christopher Hopper had similar reactions: 'It was a good season. God crowned our meeting with love and unanimity.' Jackson, *Early Methodist Preachers*, 1:200.

The sole MS Minutes (in MA) appears to be mainly in the neat hand of John Jones, though the opening section may be by JW, and §§2–6 are in another hand. This is probably the 'official' record of the Conference. JW carefully distinguishes the different categories of preachers—the clergy, the lay itinerants present, the lay itinerants absent, and those newly proposed for this office. Thus we have for the first time a summary of JW's body of travelling preachers.

[977] From this listing it seems almost certain that by this time, Maxfield had been ordained by the bishop of Londonderry at the request of JW and the Countess of Huntingdon (cf. Baker, *Wesley and Church*, 185).

Fra[nci]s Okeley[978]
Jo[hn] Jones[979]
W. Roberts,[980] T. Olivers, Jo[hn] Hampson,
W. Kitchens, N. Gilbert, Al. Coats,[981]
C. Hopper, Pa[ul] Greenwood, Ja[mes] Jones,   5
Peter Jaco, T. Hanby, Lawrence Coughlan,[982]
T. Johnson, Jo[hn] Nelson, R[ichar]d Lucas,
Jam[es] Wild, Jo[hn] Murlin, Ja[mes] Morgan,
Ja[me]s Oddie, T. Seccomb, Jo[hn] Haime,
Tho. Brisco, R[ichar]d Cornish, Fr[ancis] Walker,   10
Tho. Bryant,[983] T. Colbeck, Joseph Jones,
Will Allwood,[984] Jo[hn] Turnough, W. Crabb,
John Hosmer, Jo[hn] Hacking, W. Fugill.
It was inquired:

[978] Francis Okeley was a Moravian minister of Bedford, who seemed ready to join the Methodists, and had accompanied JW during his preaching tour in Ireland. He became an enthusiast for Behmenism and had some contacts with John Byrom. Byrom, *Journal and Remains*, Chetham Society 44 (1857): 632, 642–48. He was also the founder of the 'Cambridge Methodist' group. For his career see John Walsh in P. Brooks, ed., *Christian Spirituality* (London, 1975), 252–83.

[979] JW places John Jones (1721?–85) among the clergy. He was an educated man, who graduated M.A. at Oxford (1742) and B.Med. (1745), but who for his Methodism had so far been refused ordination, even though in spirit and learning he merited the seat next to them at the Conferences that had from 1748 been accorded him by the Wesleys; see Minutes (1748), §12, n. 611. For a good biography see A. B. Sackett, *John Jones—First after the Wesleys?* (Chester: WHS, 1972); see also *Journal & Diaries*, 20:150, n. 3 in this edn. For Jones as Wesley's minute secretary, cf. Bristol Minutes (1760), n. 1014 (p. 290).

[980] Orig., 'Robarts'.

[981] Although Myles gave currency to the spelling 'Coates', his name appears as 'Coats' here, in CW's letter of Oct. 11, 1761, in JW's letter (from the *AM*) of July 7, 1761, and in Oct. 5, 1765, *Journal & Diaries*, 22:23 in this edn.

[982] Orig., 'Coghlan', as on other occasions; he himself used the spelling 'Coughlan' on the title page of his *Account of the Work of God* (1776), and JW also spells it that way in his *AM* publication of Coughlan's letter of Apr. 12, 1762.

[983] Orig., 'Briant'. JW spells his name 'Bryant' in his letter of July 5, 1764.

[984] Orig., 'Alwood'. In his own letter (May 31, 1759) and his will (Sept. 4, 1782), he signed his name 'Allwood'; see documents in possession of J. M. Groves, Hatherton, copy in MA.

[§2]   *Q.* Who are the travelling preachers that are absent?
       A. T. Walsh, Tho. Lee, Jos. Cownley, Ja. Deaves, Matth.
       Lowes, Jac. Rowell, T. Mitchell, T. Kead,[985] Hen. Floyd,
       Jo. Manners, Wm. Harry, Mark Davis, Tho. Tobias,
5   R. Swindells.

[§3]   *Q.* Who are now proposed for travelling preachers?
       A. Wm. Harwood,[986] T. Walker, John Gibbs,[987] Wm.
       Thompson, John Gilbert,[988] Roger Thomas? Philip
       Embury,[989] Fr[ancis] Gilbert,[990] Jo. Bennets?[991] Jo[hn]
10   Furz,[992] Jer[emiah] Cocker? Step[hen] Nichols?[993]
       W. Norman? And[rew] Kessel?

[§4]   *Q.* Are all our travelling preachers unblameable in outward
       conversation?
       A. We doubt W. F[ugill], N. N.,[994] and R[obert] R[oberts]
15   are not. These were afterwards examined at large. And it
       appeared that part of the complaints against them were
       groundless, and the other part removed.

[§5]   *Q.* Can we receive Saml. Meggot as a travelling preacher?
       A. Not without a farther trial.

---

[985] Orig., 'Keade'.

[986] Most of these men seem not to have come into the itinerancy, but to have remained local preachers except where otherwise indicated here. It is clear from this list that JW and his preachers were actively recruiting itinerants, but the query added after six of these names indicates that in many instances there was doubt about either their suitability or their availability. Earlier this year JW had remarked: 'No person must be allowed to preach or exhort among our people whose life is not holy and unblamable, nor any who assert anything contrary to the gospel which we have received'. JW to George Merryweather, Jan. 16, 1758, *Letters* (Telford), 4:3.

[987] Like a few others in this list, Gibbs became an itinerant for a short time (Myles, *Chronological History*, says 1758–66).

[988] John Gilbert began preaching after 1751 in and around Wrangle, Lincolnshire, and on several occasions declined JW's invitations to become an itinerant. *WMM* (1868): 481.

[989] This was Philip Embury (1728–73) a Palatine emigrant from Ballingrane, Ireland, well known later as a pioneer of Methodism in America.

[990] Francis Gilbert became an itinerant for a time; he was originally from the West Indies. For an account of him and his family's influence in Methodism, see *Minutes* (1765), *Q.* [7] (14).

[991] Cf. Minutes (1747), §65 and n. 580.

[992] Became an itinerant; autobiography in Jackson, *Early Methodist Preachers*, 5:108–34.

[993] Cf. Minutes (1747), §65 as a local preacher then.

[994] There is no known itinerant of this period with such initials. This may well be a scribal error for N. M[anners]; see §18 below and Minutes (1755), §5.

[§6] *Q.* Can we receive William Darney?

A. Not till we are fully assured that he does not rail, print, or sell wares without a licence.[995]

[§7] *Q.* Who will travel with me the ensuing year?

A. Thomas Brisco, or Joseph Jones.

[§8] *Q.* What is it best for Michael Fenwick to do?

A. Doubtless to return to his business.

[§9] *Q.* Have any of you seen any books of mine which were left behind?

A. Yes—at Sheffield, Leeds, and Dublin.

[§10] *Q.* It was agreed that every preacher should read over our Works, and bring in what remarks occurred. Who has done this?

A. None yet. We will begin without delay, and bring in our remarks at the next Conference.

[§11] *Q.* Are not many of us still wanting in seriousness?

A. We are, and have need to be particularly watchful lest we conform to the world in our manner of conversation.

[§12] *Q.* Do we all fast, or use such abstinence as our health will permit, on Friday?

A. We will, for the time to come. Neither will we accept of any invitation to breakfast abroad on that day.

[§13] *Q.* You must do one of these three things: either spend time in chit-chat; or learn Latin or Hebrew; or spend all your time and strength in saving souls. Which will *you* do?

A. The last, by the grace of God.

[§14] *Q.* Shall we drop the school at Kingswood?

A. By no means, if a fit master can be procured.

[§15] *Q.* Counterfeit franks are commonly used in Ireland. Ought any of us to use them? Can a Member of Parliament empower other persons to frank letters for them?[996]

A. By no means. It is an illegal fraud, against which therefore we must warn all our societies.

[§16] *Q.* Have the books been diligently recommended in Ireland?

A. No; nor in many parts of England.

[§17] *Q.* What can be done to promote the spreading of them?

---

[995] See above, the Leeds Conference of 1751.

[996] For the franking system and JW's use of it, see *Letters*, 25:24–25 in this edn.

A. Allow two shillings in the pound to one in every circuit
(if he desire it) for all he sells; and let the preachers be
more zealous and active in recommending them, particularly the *Preservative*.[997]

5 [§18]   *Q.* Did N. M. say, 'I want no more grace for a year and a
day'?
A. Ask himself. If he did, and will not be convinced of his
fault, let him be publicly disowned.[998]

10   **Monday, August 14th**
[§19]   We revised that part of our former Conferences which
relates to *Justification*, and all agreed that there was no
need of retracting or altering anything.

15   **Tuesday, August 15th**
[§20]   *Q.* Did you affirm that perfection excludes all infirmities,
ignorance, and mistake?[999]
A. We continually affirm just the contrary.
[§21]   *Q.* Do you say, Everyone who is not saved from all sin is in
20   a state of damnation?
A. So far from it that we will not say, anyone is in a state of
damnation that fears God and really strives to please him.
[§22]   *Q.* In what manner would you advise those who think they
have attained, to speak of their own experience?
25   *A.* With great wariness, and with the deepest humility and
self-abasement before God.
[§23]   *Q.* How should young preachers especially speak of perfection in public?
A. Not too minutely or circumstantially, but rather in gen-
30   eral and scriptural terms.
[§24]   *Q.* Have they that are perfect need of the merits of Christ?
Can they pray for forgiveness?
A. (1) Everyone may *mistake* as long as he lives. (2) A mistake in *opinion* may occasion a *mistake* in practice (as in

[997] *A Preservative against Unsettled Notions in Religion*, which JW had published
earlier this year; see *Bibliography*, No. 226.
[998] Cf. §4 above.
[999] See *Thoughts on Christian Perfection* (1765), in *Works* (Jackson), 11:402–4.
Three sections in this publication (*QQ.* 4–6) reiterated this discussion: '*Q.* 4. What
was the judgment of all our brethren who met at Bristol in August 1758 on this
head?'

Mr. de Renty).[1000] (3) Every *such mistake* is a transgression of the perfect law. (4) Therefore every such mistake, were it not for the blood of atonement, would expose to eternal damnation. (5) It follows that the most perfect have continual need of the merits of Christ, even for their actual transgressions, and may well say, for themselves as well as their brethren, 'Forgive us our trespasses.'[1001]

[§25] *Q*. What then does Christian perfection imply?

A. The loving God with all the heart, so that every evil temper is destroyed, and every thought and word and work springs from and is conducted[1002] to the[1003] end by the pure love of God and our neighbour.

Wednesday, 16th

[§26] *Q*. Ought any tickets be given to children?

A. Not to the unawakened: it makes them too cheap.

[§27] *Q*. Who should be admitted at love-feasts?

A. Only those in the bands, unless once a year.

[§28] *Q*. How can the contest between T. Richards and W. Daniel be decided?[1004]

A. Let the case be referred to W. Kitchens, B. Trezize, and Captain Berkla; and let him that will not stand to the reference be publicly disowned.

[§29] *Q*. Are our societies in general as godly, serious men as the old Puritans? Why should they not? What means can we use to effect it?

A. (1) Enforce family discipline, and diligently inquire how it is exercised in every family.

(2) Closely examine the state of every soul, not only at stated times, but in every conversation.

[§30] *Q*. Are all in our bands real believers? How shall we know? And what shall be done when we do know?

[1000] For De Renty see above, Minutes (1748), §28, n. 636.

[1001] Matt. 6:12 (BCP, Lord's Prayer).

[1002] Orig., 'condemned', an error corrected by Jones.

[1003] Query an error for 'that', 'yt' instead of the orig., 'ye'.

[1004] T. Richards was an itinerant who is later said to have been ordained by Lady Huntingdon's influence (Seymour, *Huntingdon*, 1:62, 446). The only 'Mr. Daniel' recorded by JW was in his diary in 1740–41, in London; *Journal & Diaries*, 2:430, 450 in this edn. The nature of the quarrel is not known.

A. (1) Let each Assistant take two or three sensible men with him, preachers, stewards, or leaders. (2) Let them particularly and closely examine every person that is now in the bands. (3) Let them put out two in three, if they find so many in the best of their judgment, unbelievers. (4) Let this be done at the next quarterly visitation. (5) That he may not be straitened for time, any of the local preachers may supply his place.

[§31]   *Q.* How shall we preach in the morning most profitably?
A. (1) Frequently read, often explain half a chapter.
[(2)] Sometimes read and enlarge upon select tracts in the *Christian Library.*[1005]

[§32]   *Q.* When and where may the next Conference be?
A. About the 24th of next August, at Leeds.

[§33]   [These are stationed for the ensuing year thus:][1006]
(1) *London*, John Wesley, Jo. Jones, L. Coughlan, Jos. Jones, W. Thompson, N. Gilbert, Ja. Morgan, Rd. Lucas, W. Harwood.
(2) *Bristol*, Charles Wesley.
(3) *Wiltshire*, Tho. Johnson,*[1007] Rid. Cornish, John Murlin, D[——] D[——].[1008]
(4) *Cornwall*, W. Hitchens, Jo. Hosmer, Tho. Hanby, Jo. Gibbs, W. Rodd,[1009] T. Bryant, Jo. Furz.
(5) *Staffordshire*, James Jones,* W. Fugill.

[1005] At the 1766 Conference (*Minutes, Q.* 30), it is recommended that the large Societies provide the *Christian Library* (50 vols., 1749–55) for the use of the preachers. The *Library* contained 'extracts' from a wide variety of devotional literature including the Fathers, French Quietists, and various types of Anglicans, including a considerable number of Puritans (but not contemporary Dissenters) and some Continental Protestants. The volumes were carefully edited to remove doctrines of which JW disapproved, e.g., predestination. For a classified list, see Robert C. Monk, *John Wesley: His Puritan Heritage* (London, 1966), 255–62, and see 47–61 on his methods of abridgement.

[1006] The regular *Minutes* end at the top of p. 5, with the remainder of that p. and p. 6 blank. On p. 7, reading from head to foot of the page, from the outer margin, without any introduction, follow the stationings. The introduction to them has been copied from 1755.

[1007] The cross (here shown by an asterisk) after certain names clearly denotes the Assistant, as in Minutes (1755), §3 (see n. 955).

[1008] No one among the regular itinerants had the initials 'D. D.'

[1009] Orig., 'Rob', but apparently the same as the preacher who died at Leeds in 1760, for whom see Atmore, *Methodist Memorial*, 377, and Myles, *Chronological History*, 448.

(6) *Cheshire*, Ja. Wild,* Jo. Turnough, T. Olivers.
(7) *Leeds*, Jo. Hampson,* Paul Greenwood, Jo. Nelson.
(8) *Haworth*, Ja. Oddie,* Al. Coats.
(9) *Lincolnshire*, T. Lee,* Jo. Hacking, W. Crabb.
(10) *York*, T. Mitchell,* Tho. Tobias, W. Allwood.   5
(11) *Newcastle*, C. Hopper,* Al. Mather, Jacob Rowell,
L. Coughlan.
(12) *Wales*, Fr. Walker,* W. Harry.
(13) *Ireland*, Pet. Jaco,* Jo. Johnson,* T. Seccomb, Ja.
Deaves, Jo Manners, T. Brisco, R. Swindells, T. Walsh,   10
T. Kead, M. Davis.

The London Conference of August 8–11, 1759

Wed. [Aug.] 8. Our Conference began, the time of which was almost entirely employed in examining whether the spirit and lives of our preachers were suitable to their profession. On Saturday in 15
the afternoon we concluded. Great was the unanimity and love that reigned among us. And if there were any who hoped or feared the contrary, they were happily disappointed.[1010]

At the Conference in the year 1759, perceiving some danger that a diversity of sentiments should insensibly steal in among us, we   20
again largely considered this doctrine [Christian perfection]; and soon after, I published 'Thoughts on Christian Perfection' . . . .[1011]

[1010] Aug. 8, 1759, *Journal & Diaries*, 21:224 in this edn. A leaf of JW's MS Journal has survived covering this period. It reads:
   'Wed. 8. Our Conference began, the time of which was almost entirely employed in examining the tempers and lives of our preachers. On Saturday in the afternoon, we concluded. Great were the unanimity and love that reigned throughout. Is not this another token for good? Surely while we are thus striving together for the hope of the gospel, we shall not be delivered to the will of our enemies.'

[1011] *A Plain Account of Christian Perfection* (1766), §19 (see vol. 12 of this edn.). The 'Thoughts', dated 'Bristol, Oct. 16, 1759', appeared in vol. 4 of Wesley's *Sermons* (1760). Cf. the Minutes (1758), §20ff.
   CW was in London at this time, and although his extant letters to his wife (including two dated July 30 and Aug. 13) do not mention the Conference, he was probably present in view of the general theme and the fact that William Grimshaw intended to make the journey down from Haworth for the occasion. Baker, *Grimshaw*, 157. Howell Harris also was there, at least on Friday, Aug. 10, and furnishes the information that the Conference was held in Spitalfields. *WHS* 16 (1928): 115.

Most of our preachers had very near left off preaching on practical religion. This was therefore earnestly recommended to them in the Conference at London. I am glad they followed the advice which was then given, which may be done without neglecting to
5 speak on justification.[1012]

The Limerick Conference of July 5–8, 1760

Fri. 4 [July, 1760]. I took my ease, riding in a chaise to Limerick, where on Saturday 5 ten of us met in a little Conference. By the blessing of God we were all of one mind, particularly with regard to
10 the Church. Even J[ames] D[eaves] has not now the least thought of leaving it, but attends there, be the minister good or bad. On Tuesday 8, having settled all our little affairs, we parted in much love.[1013]

The Bristol Conference of August 29–30, 1760

Thur. 28 [After landing from Ireland at Parkgate on Tuesday, Aug.
15 26, 1760, and struggling on the road against misfortunes, Wesley finally] reached Bristol before eleven.

[1012] Letter to Rev. Samuel Furly, Sept. 4, 1760, *Letters* (Telford), 4:104.
[1013] July 4, 1760, *Journal & Diaries*, 21:267 in this edn. JW undoubtedly presented to the Conference the results so far of his statistical survey, which he had written up the previous day: 'I had purposed to set out [from Birr] early in the morning; but their love constrained me to stay a day longer. So I had leisure to complete the account of the societies. At present the societies in Connaught contain little more than two hundred members; those in Ulster about two hundred and fifty; those in Leinster a thousand.' On Aug. 11 and 12, he was saddened to find a decrease in membership at Cork from 290 to 233 and wrote in his *Journal*: 'Adding to those in the other provinces about six hundred who are in Munster, the whole number [in Ireland] is a little above two thousand' (21:271 in this edn.). N.B. In this instance JW arranges his statistics according to the four great provinces into which Ireland was divided rather than into their constituent counties.

I spent the two following days with the preachers, who had been waiting for me all the week. And their love and unanimity was such as soon made me forget all my labour.[1014]

[1014] Aug. 28, 1760, *Journal & Diaries*, 21:273 in this edn. Conference evidently could not proceed in JW's absence, but in 1780, the preachers placed Hopper in the chair until JW arrived. Again the relations between Methodism and other religious bodies formed the major item in their conversations. In Feb., three preachers had administered the Lord's Supper at Norwich. In Mar., CW had reprinted as a separate publication their *Reasons against a Separation from the Church of England*. CW also aroused opposition against this separatist tendency in speech and letter while JW was in Ireland, and it seemed clear that the Bristol Conference was going to prove a stormy gathering. He invited Howell Harris to come to his support from Wales. See Baker, *Wesley and Church*, 174–79.

Howell Harris's narrative of the occasion is very full, and only a selection of his account can be given here. He arrived on Aug. 28. In his diary, he wrote,

'When I met Mr Charles Wesley, I told [him] I came six hundred miles on purpose to their Conference, and that if they went out of the Church now, the work was stopped. . . . Called at Mr Walters (the Moravian). . . . I went hence to Mr Charles Wesley, where I met him and John Jones (Mr John [Wesley] was not yet come to town). . . . We agreed about staying in the Church. . . . About three, I met the preachers with him. . . . I was glad to see them retaining their first simplicity, and if they retain their first faith and love they would be impregnable. . . . When I spoke against arms of flesh, and licensing, and taking protection from the Toleration Act, etc., they withstood me, and Mr Charles Wesley said I had stood alone.

'Bristol. Friday, 29 Aug. [1760]. Heard last night a rousing sermon from Mr Nelson on Rom. 3. This morning at six I went to Mr Ch[arle]s W[esley]s where I met [John Wesley], when I was comforted in hearing him mentioning about proposing a meeting with some of the Moravians on the point of licensing, etc. . . . I met some of their preachers—determined dissenting ministers, etc., but as they have a meek, loving, and unprejudiced spirit among them, I hope all evil will be kept out. At nine, I went with Mr Charles Wesley and John Jones to the New Room to meet all the preachers, I think above forty, where Mr. John Wesley, after singing and praying, laid before them what to do about settling the work if he should die, and . . . mentioning that the Moravians now won't have any one man, as the Count had settled as a body; so he proposed that we clergy and the Assistants (preachers that now superintend) should form a council then and settle matters, and call the preachers after his death and his brother's, and all agreed to that. In [the] meantime, that these should go now to some districts and do his work one quarter in four of the year, and perhaps divide all the labours in England to four rounds, and in Ireland to two rounds. Had a spirit . . . to see them the seed of the nation. Being asked, I spoke on my motives in coming here now, lest they should by the renewed opposition now against them by the Conventicle Act, which I read in the papers, be tempted to leave the Church. . . . That I look on preaching and administering the ordinances [as] two offices. That of exhorting I was persuaded was from the Lord, but if I meddled with the other, I look on it as the sin of Korah. Mr John We[sley] showed from the practice of the Church of England, the Kirk of Scotland, Calvinists and Lutherans and the Primitive Churches, that they all made preaching or prophesying or evangelizing and administering the ordinances two distinct offices. When they proposed to him to ordain them, he said it was not clear to him that he had a power so to do except they were wholly cut off from the Church by a public act, and also that it would be a total renouncing of the bishops and the Established Church, which he could not do, and stumbling thousands. Many spake well on the opposite side, showing they were already dissented from the Church, and by their being ordained and licensed they would remove the prejudices of [the] Dissenters, etc. If they owned they were sent to preach, why not to administer the Sacraments? . . . [Mr Wesley] read a letter from Grimshaw the minister on that head, and his answer to it that licensing the men and the houses made no further separation, and it was proposed to be debated in the evening about taking Dissenting Ministers into a Tropos as the Moravians did at Herrnhut, as the body of Methodists in England and Ireland were settled in their minds to stay in the Church. That the Dissenting ministers should be ordained and give Sacrament in Norwich, where is a congregation of Dissenters that can't have the Sacraments any other way (where I find some of the lay preachers have given the Sacrament). So we brake up after twelve. . . . Having dined with both Mr Wesleys and John Jones, at three we met at the Conference, where several things were debated. I declared that I was shocked that such laymen that had given the Sacrament did not see the great evil of it. . . . Mr J[ohn] W[esley] proposed taking some steps toward an union with the Moravians, viz., to offer a Conference, he and his brother with Mr. Gambold and Nyberg, and then for them to propose it to as many as they please, then to meet six or more on a side. . . . Mr. John and Charles Wesley spake their opinion strong of the unlawfulness of a layman administering the ordinances, and I said I could as soon murder ten thousand, and that I thought I had as good a right as any of them to it. Then it was spoken of Kingswood School. . . .

'30 Aug., Bristol. Sure the Lord has made a stand against a breach going to be made in the work by introducing licensing and even ordination, and so a total separation from the Church. Charles and I were the rough workers, and John more meekly said I could not ordain, and said if he was not ordained, he would look upon it as murder if he gave the ordinances. He struck dumb the reasoners by saying he would renounce them in a quarter of an hour, that they were the most foolish and ignorant in the whole Conference. . . .' (Harris, MS Diary, vol. 233)

During this narrative, Harris occasionally mentions 'Mr. Johannes' (the Moravian bishop, Johannes de Watteville), to whom he wrote on Oct. 9 about this Conference, esp. of the project to convene a joint Conference of Methodist and Moravian leaders to move towards closer unity. Howell Harris, *Selected Trevecka Letters*; 1747–94, ed. Gomer Morgan Roberts (Caernarvon, Wales: Calvinistic Methodist Bookroom, 1962), 79–80.

On Sept. 21, 1760, JW wrote to CW in Bristol: 'I suppose John Jones has sent you the minutes of the Conference.' See *Letters* (Telford), 4:107. This confirms the importance of Jones as JW's scribe and secretary at the later Conferences.

For further discussion of the proposal for a meeting of clergy and Assistants after JW's death and another scheme in 1772–73 that provoked CW's fears and raised the question of a possible clerical head of the connexion, see introduction, pp. 87–88 and below, *Minutes* (1772), n. 381 (p. 405).

The London Conference of
September 1–5, 1761

[Journal:] Tuesday, September 1, our Conference began, and ended on Saturday.[1015]

[Letter to Charles Wesley:] Our Conference ended, as it began, in peace and love. All found it a blessed time. . . . The Minutes John Jones can help you to, who sets out hence in two or three days. The right hand of the Lord bringeth mighty things to pass. Not the least of them is that [[my wife]][1016] cordially loves T. Maxfield.

Why should not Bath be supplied from Bristol? Order it so. I have no objection. They will by that means often have a more able preacher than they would otherwise have. If he does not linger by the way, a preacher may be at Bristol on Thursday night.

I do not at all think (to tell you a secret) that the work will ever be destroyed, Church or no Church. What has been done to present the Methodists leaving the Church you will see in the Minutes of the Conference.

I told you before, with regard to Norwich, *dixi*.[1017] I have done at the last Conference all I *can* or *dare* do. Allow me liberty of conscience, as I allow you.[1018]

[Letter to Samuel Furly:] I hope we have effectually provided against that evil disease the *scribendi cacoethes*[1019] in our preachers, as we have agreed that none shall publish anything for the time to come till he has first submitted it to the judgment of his brethren met in Conference. . . .

What all our brethren think concerning that circumstance of entire sanctification—that it is instantaneous (although a gradual growth in grace both precede and follow it)—you may see in the Minutes of the Conference, wherein it was freely debated. . . .[1020]

[1015] Sept. 1, 1761, *Journal & Diaries*, 21:341 in this edn.

[1016] In shorthand.

[1017] 'I have spoken.'

[1018] JW to CW, Sept. 8, 1761, reporting on the Conference, at which CW was not present. *Letters* (Telford), 4:161–62.

[1019] 'Itch for writing'.

[1020] JW to Rev. Samuel Furly, Sept. 8, 1761; *Letters* (Telford), 4:163.

[Letter to Matthew Lowes:] If Local Preachers who differ from us will keep their opinions to themselves, then they may preach in our societies. Otherwise, they must not. And upon this condition we are all willing to receive William Darney into connexion with
5   us.[1021]

[1021] JW to Matthew Lowes of Newcastle, Sept. 8, 1761; *Letters* (Telford), 4:163.

Thomas Maxfield also had become a centre of controversy, and at the Conference, some preachers made charges against him. In two or three years, he antagonized JW also and left Methodism. On Dec. 28, 1761, he wrote to JW, refusing to face some of his critics. JW later published a portion of this letter in his own *Journal*, parenthetically inserting a statement about his own action at the 1761 Conference: 'It is enough that I [i.e., Maxfield] was arraigned at the Conference (at which I [i.e., Wesley] earnestly defended him and silenced all his accusers). I am not convinced that it is my duty to make James Morgan, etc., my judges. If you, sir, or any one of them, have anything to say to me *alone*, I will answer as far as I see good.' *Journal & Diaries*, 21:404 in this edn.

Peter Jaco also reported his impressions of the Conference to CW:

'I have now time to inform you that our Conference relating to doctrine and discipline is finished to the satisfaction of I believe every preacher in connexion with yourself and brother. In particular, perfection. It is determined that there are no texts of Scripture which will absolutely support instantaneous perfection; that there is no state in this world which will absolutely exempt the person in it from sin, and that therefore they have need of caution, etc. These are some of the conclusions we are come to. The rest I suppose your brother will tell you soon. Whether he and the rest of the contenders on the other side of the question will abide by these concessions, time will determine.

'As my health is extremely precarious, it has been thought good by Mr. Wesley and the preachers to fix me in Canterbury and London till Christmas, and then, if Mr. Gilbert will exchange with me, I shall in the spring go to Bristol in order to make a fair trial of the Hotwell water. . . .' (Jaco MS letter to CW, Sat., Sept. 5, 1761, in MA)

A letter from John Manners to George Merryweather (Sept. 9, 1761) enlarges our knowledge of those present at the Conference and testifies to its nature: 'We had had the most satisfactory and solemn Conference that has been held for several years. It was honoured with the presence of Mr. Whitefield and other clergy several times. The Minutes you may see with Tommy Johnson, the Assistant of your circuit.' Tyerman, *Wesley*, 2:416.

The Dublin Conference of July 28–29, 1762

Dublin, July 28, 1762. . . . In two or three days I am likely to embark in order to meet our brethren at Leeds.[1022]

The Leeds Conference of August 10–[13?], 1762[1023]

5

Monday 9. I preached at Elland and Birstall in my way to Leeds, where our Conference began on Tuesday morning. And we had great reason to praise God for his gracious presence from the beginning to the end.[1024]

[1022] Letter to Ebenezer Blackwell, showing how JW's mind was moving forward from his Irish Conference to his English Conference, though neither is mentioned; July 28, 1762, *Letters* (Telford), 4:185. Neither his *Journal* nor his letters speaks about this Conference, knowledge of which comes from the diary of a Dublin stalwart, Mr. Thomas Garrett: 'July 28. Have had a good time of it since Mr. Wesley and the preachers came amongst us. 29th. Last night was a watch-night, when we had nine or ten preachers, the greatest number that I remember to have seen at one time—Messrs. J. Wesley, Manners, Kead, Swindells, Deaves, Davis, Roberts, Guilford, Lee, and Harris.' At this Conference, Thomas Rourke was received into the itinerancy (Crookshank, *History of Methodism in Ireland*, 1:165).

[1023] For Wesley's preparations for this Conference, see the previous entry, and his letter of July 30, 1762, to Rev. Samuel Furly, who was now serving as curate at Huddersfield to Rev. Henry Venn: 'Will not you meet us at Leeds on the tenth of August?' *Letters* (Telford), 4:186.

[1024] Aug. 9, 1762, *Journal & Diaries*, 21:385. Scraps of information about the Conference may be picked up from the writings of several of those present. Whether Furly actually accepted JW's invitation is not known, but other guests came from the Calvinistic circles in which he moved: the Reverends Henry Venn, Martin Madan, William Romaine, and George Whitefield, and even the Countess of Huntingdon (Seymour, *Huntingdon*, 1:281).

Methodism was growing rapidly, and this Conference seems to have marked a surge forward, witness an influx of many local preachers to serve the proliferating Societies and circuits as itinerants, the beginning, as it were, of a new generation of leaders. Three of these men left records of the Conference: George Story, a future connexional editor and publisher; Thomas Rankin, a future General Assistant of the work in America; and John Pawson, a future President of the Conference. Story wrote,

'I attended with a design of being edified by the public discourses and private conversation of the preachers. And herein I had abundant reason to be satisfied. Mr. Wesley's sermons were in a peculiar manner calculated for establishing me in what I had lately experienced. During the Conference, it appeared there wanted several more preachers as itinerants in different circuits. My friends proposed me for one, and asked if I had any objection. As I was resigned to any station Providence seemed to point out, I submitted to the judgment of my brethren. Being admitted on trial, I returned home to settle my affairs, and in the latter end of February, 1763, I went into The Dales circuit.' (Jackson, *Early Methodist Preachers*, 5:237–38)

Thomas Rankin wrote, 'I was appointed at this Conference to labour in the Sheffield circuit the ensuing year, and had for my companions John Nelson, Wm. Fugill, and James Clough. The circuit was very laborious, as the rides were long, and constant preaching. The Sheffield circuit at that time extended to Leicester on the south, and beyond Barnsley in the north.' Rankin MS journal, Garrett Theological Seminary, Evanston, Ill., with much of the detail edited out by Joseph Benson for its publication in the *MM* (1811), from which it came into Jackson, *Early Methodist Preachers*, 5:174.

John Pawson had been pressed by John Johnson, the Assistant, to attend the Conference, and without his knowledge Johnson recommended him to JW as an itinerant. Pawson wrote to JW: 'Several young men were proposed as candidates for travelling preachers, and I among the rest. When you, sir, asked me if I was willing to give myself to the work, I told you, I was conscious of my inability, but if you and the brethren thought good to make trial of me, I should deliver up myself to you. Accordingly, I was ordered for the York circuit.' Pawson's fuller account altered the last sentence to read: 'Accordingly, I was sent into the York circuit, along with Peter Jaco, John and Nicholas Manners, Richard Henderson, and James Cotty.' John Pawson, *A Short Account of the Lord's Gracious Dealings* (Leeds: Baines, 1801), 25, reprinted for the most part in *MM* (1806), and Jackson, *Early Methodist Preachers*, vol. 4 (see esp. p. 24).

Pawson also, in an aside during a lengthy obituary, reminisced about the 1762 Conference:

'At that Conference a greater number of young men set out to travel than had ever done at any former Conference, viz., Tho. Rankin, G. Story, J. Easton, W. Minethorp [orig., 'Menithorpe'], J. Shaw, J. Ellis, J. Robertshaw, J. Pawson, etc. In this love-feast ["on the Sunday after the Conference"], Mr. Hopper was led to pray in an extraordinary manner for those young men, well knowing the importance of the work in which they were engaged, and the danger and hardships they would have to endure, which so greatly affected him that he was obliged to give up, and could only (with the whole congregation) silently weep before the Lord. Mr. Nicholas Gilbert then began to pray in the same manner, but he also was so overcome by the presence of God that he was not able to proceed; and for a long time he and a vast concourse of people were all upon their knees, silently weeping at the feet of our Lord. This was a time which will never be forgotten while any are living who were then present.' *MM* (1800): 200.

M. Mitchell writing to Sarah Crosby (Sept. 21, 1762) says that Hampson was not suspended from preaching (apparently this was about a debate on the administration of the Lord's Supper). Tyerman MSS, 1:266. He believed that nine-tenths

The London Conference of July 19–23, 1763

Finding it was not expedient to leave London during the ferment which still continued by reason of Mr. M[axfield]'s separation from us, I determined not to remove from it before the Conference. This began on Tuesday, July 19, and ended on Saturday 23. And it was a 5 great blessing that we had peace among ourselves while so many were making themselves ready for battle.[1025]

of the preachers were on Hampson's side 'with regard to the remarks'. But as John Wesley was unwilling and 'some thought it would cause a division among the people', it was given up. What Whitefield said 'did not satisfy anything. . . . But Mr. Wesley and him said it was lawfull for the layman to give the Sacrament but at present not expedient, and Norwich continues as it did.' This last remark presumably means that the unauthorised administration of the Sacrament there in 1760 was continuing, contrary to what seems usually to be supposed.

[1025] July 19, 1763, *Journal & Diaries*, 21:421 in this edn. The fullest account of this Conference, including its background of devotional sessions both within and connected with its business sessions, is by Howell Harris, from whose diary some extracts may be given:

'19 July 1763. London. I went today with Mr. Peake, Mr. Charles Wesley, and Bro. Thomas . . . against four, to Mr. Wesley's Conference of about sixty preachers where they were settling their Rounds. . . . Heard Mr. John Wesley at the Foundery on perfection. . . .

'20 July. London. I mentioned today to Mr. John and Charles Wesley of setting Christ in all his character continually before the people. . . . I told him that he had reduced perfection very low, and that I was glad when he declared against lay teachers giving the ordinance at Norwich, etc. . . . I wrote this at the Foundery, where I retired whilst they were settling all their moneys of some hundreds. . . .

'21 July. London. At Mr. Baldwin [?]. Today at seven I went again to Conference, to one. . . . Dined together all at the Foundery. Met again to past five, and then I wrote four letters home and went to hear a good sermon from Mr. John Wesley. . . . I prayed for him earnestly. He published me to discourse tomorrow night at Spitalfields [orig., 'Spittle Fields'] Chapel.

'22 July. London. After twelve, being asked by Mr. Charles Wesley to discourse to the preachers, and being set by Mr. John Wesley, I told them I was glad to find the love and simplicity among them, the work going on in the spirit in which it began. I had the honour of being the first layman that went out, and I know what I had in my view, to rouse all to fly from the wrath, etc. I wanted to show I went four times to the bishop for ordination, but was rejected. . . . Of my being laid by illness several years and of my family, now 120, and of my trial and of my being in debt £300 or £400. Of the Lord sending me wool at the time when I wanted. . . . We have nothing to hope or lose, being given up wholly to the Lord—life and name; though 'tis right to make provisions for the wives of preachers, yet no preacher ought to be anxious about them, but to give them to the Lord and be as if they had no wives. . . . I was home about keeping in the old pulpit the Lord first gave them—the fields, highways, market-places, and to preach to every man you meet, even beggars. Remember, everyone is going to eternity. . . . Declared I could never call myself a preacher, but an exhorter, my gifts being so. Showed they are ambassadors for God. . . . In prayer had much freedom to cry for universal union among all. Showed of my first acquaintance with Mr. John Wesley. I saw him an honest spirit attacking the unbelief, pride, and sleep of the nation; and I loved him in that light, though I differed in some things. Dined at Mr. Ball. To Mr. Peake and to Mr. Charles Wesley, thence to Mr. Haweis, having got an interview tomorrow between him and Mr. John and Charles Wesley. Returned against six [to] the Foundery, thence to Spitalfields Chapel, where I discoursed to a large congregation indeed with great freedom on "We behold the glory of God in the face of Jesus Christ transformed, etc.". . . . It was a blessing to discourse to so many witnesses that go over the land. I find that all the preachers took it in love, especially about looking to Christ, not ourselves, and universal love. . . .

'23 July, London. To the Foundery. . . . To Mr. Charles Wesley past five. With him to meet Mr. Haweis and Mr. John Wesley at Mr. Heritage, where we had a sweet meeting indeed to near eight. . . . A motion was made to meet some of the clergy and two of the Moravian bishops for union. A meeting was settled next week with Madan, Haweis, and the two brothers—John and Charles Wesley.'

Of the preachers present, Christopher Hopper records simply: 'Our Conference began and ended in love.' Jackson, *Early Methodist Preachers*, 1:212. Thomas Rankin is a little fuller: 'My friend George Story rode with me from that circuit [Sheffield] to the Conference in London. At the Conference the Fund for the Old Preachers was first set on foot. I was appointed to labour the ensuing year in the Devonshire circuit, which took in Somerset as well as Devon. My fellow-labourers were Nicholas Manners and William Minethorp [orig., 'Menithorp']. Rankin MS journal, Garrett Theological Seminary; cf. Jackson, *Early Methodist Preachers*, 5:175.

The fullest of these accounts is by John Pawson:

'I went to the Conference in company with that amiable man, Mr. Richard Henderson. This was the first time I ever was in London, and the Conference was held in Spitalfields Chapel. We had no money matters to settle in these days; but, after the preachers' characters were examined, and they were stationed for the next year, all the time was taken up in speaking upon spiritual subjects. This was the only time I ever saw that faithful servant of God, the Welsh Apostle, Mr. Howell Harris. [Here Pawson gives details of Harris's address to the Conference on July 22.]

'At this Conference some of the preachers began to call in question the power Mr. Wesley exercised over them and the societies. Mr. Harris pleaded his cause effectually, and among other things said, "If Mr. Wesley should at any time abuse his power, who will weep for him if his own children will not!" These simple words had an astonishing effect upon the minds of the preachers; they were all in tears, on every side, and gave up the matter entirely.' [John Wesley gave a lengthy justification of his 'power' to the Conference of 1766 (*Minutes*, *Q*. 29 and n. 103).]

'At this Conference in 1763, the Preachers' Fund was first begun. It was said that several of the preachers were growing old: what then should they do for support, if they should live to be past their labour? Others of them having a family, what would become of the widow or children if the husband should die and leave them behind? Being young and unexperienced, I was utterly amazed upon hearing this. I thought that every Christian minister had an entire confidence in God respecting temporal as well as spiritual things, so as to be perfectly free from all care and concern as to what may befall either himself or family. . . . However, although Mr. Wesley did not greatly approve of what was proposed, as he always thought it worldly and not Christian prudence to provide for a rainy day, yet he consented to it, and the Fund was begun. . . .

'I had an opportunity to receive the holy Sacrament among the children of God. To see the large and deeply serious congregations that attended the chapels, the uncommon number of communicants, their devout behaviour, and the order in which the whole service was conducted, was highly pleasing to me. . . .

'As our Conferences in these days only lasted from Tuesday morning till Friday noon, my stay in London was very short; it being thought very wrong for the preachers to stay in town at all after the Conference was over. I was appointed for the Haworth circuit along with William Fugill, Paul Greenwood, and Daniel Bumstead. . . . ' (Pawson, *Short Account*, 28–30; cf. the abridged and edited version, *MM* [1806], 483–84, and Jackson, *Early Methodist Preachers*, 4:26–28).

Pawson pointed out that most of the Conference agenda in those days concerned 'spiritual subjects', by which he would surely intend what the Methodist Conference of today terms 'the work of God', as well as the avowedly devotional sessions intended for the public as well as the assembled preachers. Luke Tyerman astutely suggests that as the enlarged edn. of the 'Large' *Minutes* was published this year, it was almost certainly a concern of the Conference, and that probably many points additional to the previous 'Large' *Minutes* were approved in 1763; these he proceeds to list in detail. *Wesley*, 2:474–79. Whether *all* these additions arose in 1763 seems doubtful. It is strange at first, for instance, that the Model Deed promulgating William Grimshaw as successor to the Wesleys in charge of the Methodist Societies should be approved, for he had died Apr. 7 that year. His name was present in the document cited, which in this detail alone was outdated. Pawson stated (somewhat loosely) that 'we had no money matters to settle in these days', but there was a growing debt upon the preaching-houses, and it is indeed likely that the General Fund (first mentioned in the 1763 'Large' *Minutes*) was begun at this Conference, and that it corresponds to what Harris spoke of on July 20, when he 'retired whilst they were settling all their moneys of some hundreds'. See below for the 'Large' *Minutes* (1763), pp. 845–73.

The Bristol Conference of August 6–(10?), 1764

On Monday the 6th our Conference began. The great point I now laboured for was a good understanding with all our brethren of the clergy who are heartily engaged in propagating vital religion.[1026] **Sat. 11.** I took
5   chaise early in the morning, and at night came safe to London.[1027]

[1026] For JW's attempt to unite the evangelical clergy, see Baker, *Wesley and Church*, 180–96, esp. 190–94. Sutcliffe's MS 'History' (fol. 641) says that the clergy came to oppose, not to cooperate.

[1027] Aug. 6–11, 1764, *Journal & Diaries*. 21:485 in this edn. Very few other accounts exist. CW wrote to his wife on July 10: 'If I am in Bristol at the time of the Conference I shall be quite private.' Thomas Jackson, *The Life of the Rev. Charles Wesley, M.A.*, 2 vols. (London: Mason, 1841), 223. In fact he was present once more to defend the Church of England against the more radical preachers—see below, in Pawson's account.

Once again John Pawson's autobiography is helpful in reconstructing the occasion: 'I attended the Conference in Bristol in August 1764. Having been very much united to Mr. Bumstead the preceding year, he being appointed for Norwich, requested Mr. Wesley to let me go along with him, which was granted. . . . Twelve clergymen attended that Conference, whose principal business was to convince us that we ought not to preach in any parish where there was a gospel minister. Some of them were much more moderate than others. One of them said "If a layman was called of God to preach the gospel, then he had as good a right to do it as any clergyman whatever." Mr. Madan [orig., "Maddon"] could not agree to this, but said he would not dare to forbid such a person. Mr. C. Wesley said, if he was a settled minister in any particular parish, the preachers should not preach there. Mr. J. Hampson replied, I would preach there and never ask your leave, and should think I had as good a right so to do as you had. Mr. C. answered, "I know you are a grievous wolf, and you will tear the flock when once mine and my brother's heads are laid, if God do not give you repentance." ' (Pawson, *Short Account*, 31–32)

The closing interplay between CW and Hampson was omitted from the revision in *MM* (1806): 845, and Jackson, *Early Methodist Preachers*, 4:28–29.

CW wrote on Aug. 28, 1764, to Samuel Lloyd in London: 'We have had a Conference of the gospel clergy at Lady H[untingdon]'s. Good, I think, will come out of it. I had much conversation with your friend Mr. Jesse. Her Ladyship has invited more than an hundred to the opening of her chapel at Bath.' Holograph letter, Special Collections, Perkins Library, Duke University, Durham, N.C. It seems likely that this otherwise unknown Conference was supplementary to and later than JW's, even though it surely involved some of the same individuals. JW had suggested to Lady Huntingdon in May that 'if those of our brethren who have opportunity would be at Bristol on Thursday the 9th of August', they 'might then spend a few hours in free conversation, either separate from or conjoint with the other preachers'. *Letters* (Telford), 4:244. For his attempt at cooperation by circular letter to the clergy, see ibid., 4:235ff., and a copy to Lord Dartmouth, ibid., 4:258ff.

PART II

Printed Annual *Minutes*, 1765–83

M I N U T E S[1]

OF SOME LATE

C O N V E R S A T I O N S,

Between the Rev. Mr. W E S L E Y S,
and Others.

B R I S T O L:

Printed by WILLIAM PINE, in *Narrow-Wine-Street.*

M.DCC.LXV.

---

[1] The title page, although reproduced here from the printed original for 1765, will be omitted from subsequent items in this series of annual *Minutes*. A transcription of each title page, with historical and biographical details, will be found in *Bibliography*, No. 267 and the following entries. All the drop titles read 'Minutes, etc.' unless otherwise noted.

Annual *Minutes of some late Conversations*, 1765[2]

Manchester, August 20, 1765[3]

[2] The annual *Minutes* of the Conference, a series beginning in 1765, were almost always printed in the city where the Conference was held. Those for 1765, 1768, 1770, 1771, 1774, 1778, 1780, 1783, 1786, and 1790 were printed at Bristol, all by William Pine except 1786 and 1790. Those printed at London and Leeds have 'Conversations between the Rev. Mr. Wesley and Others' as the normal title, but the Bristol edns. usually include Charles also, either as 'Mr. Wesleys' (1765, 1768, 1777), 'Rev. Mr. John and Charles Wesley' (1780), or 'Rev. Messrs. Wesley' (1786, with a different printer). The only Bristol *Minutes* not referring to Charles are those of 1770, 1771, 1774, and (after he had died) 1790. The only occasions where the full Christian name is used are in 1780 (with 'John and Charles') and 1781 (with 'John'). For further historical and bibliographical details about the annual *Minutes* see *Bibliography*, Nos. 267–93.

[3] Wesley's *Journal* records: 'Our Conference began on Thursday 20 (August), and ended on Friday 23' (*Journal & Diaries*, 22:17 in this edn.). The location in Manchester has not been explained, for the 1753 Conference (*Minutes*, §2) had allowed for meetings only in Leeds, Bristol, and London, and other places were made possible only by the Deed of Declaration in 1784. From this Conference onwards the *Minutes* were published annually. Charles Simon (*John Wesley, the Master-Builder* [London: Epworth, 1927], 179) suggests that the Conference was in most respects considered to be a private assembly, though the 'Large' *Minutes* from 1749 had published a selection of the rulings. According to Pawson (Jackson, *Early Methodist Preachers*, 4:34), 'All the affairs of our connexion were settled in great peace and harmony'. Samuel Bardsley (MS diary, in MA; and Tyerman, *Wesley*, 2:540–41) says that 'everything was carried on with decency and order. The Rev. Mr Wesley preached every day. On Sunday evening he preached in Marsden Square'. (Wesley made a point of always preaching in the open air during Conference.) Young Bardsley found it remarkable that Wesley took him by the arm and walked through the town with him. A number of measures passed by the Irish Conference were incorporated into the English proceedings. Sutcliffe (MS 'History', fol. 644) says that a document given him by Thomas Marriott records that at a 'conference' in Jan. 1765, Wesley with some of the preachers and eight stewards agreed that six named men, 'having acted contrary to the Word of God and the duty they owe to their ministers and their brethren', could no more be received as preachers or as members of Society. The offence is not named, but this evidently refers to the Greek bishop's ordination of some preachers, which caused Wesley much embarrassment and was referred to the Manchester Conference. See *Letters* (Telford), 4:287–91, and Baker, *Wesley and Church*, 200f. and nn. 13–23.

At some point on the first day of the Conference (though the *Minutes* do not record it), Wesley read excerpts from his *Plain Account of Christian Perfection*, and apparently there were those who wished to debate the issues raised, but he would not allow it. Mark Davis wrote to Charles Wesley on Aug. 25,

Q[uestion 1]. What preachers[4] are *admitted* this year?
A[nswer]. John Mason, Peter Price, Moseley[5] Cheek,
Robert Costerdine,[6] John Whitehead, Barn. Thomas,
James Stephens, James Dempster.
Q. [2]. Who are admitted on *trial*?   5
A. Wm. Orpe,[7] Wm. Ellis, James Brownfield, Duncan
Wright, John Dillon,[8] Samuel Woodcock; James
Longbottom,[9] Joseph Pilmore,[10] Rich. Walsh, Wm.
Ashman, Richard Bourke,[11] James Rea.

'On Tuesday your Br[other] read to us his latest thoughts on Christian perfection. One [of the delegates] proposed to have seriously and calmly considered the Doctrine itself, the character of its Professors, and the
Circumstances of receiving the glorious Grace. But this your brother would
not at all permit; because first, we have not *now* all things to learn; second,
several young preachers might be unsettled and bewildered by hearing such
debates.' (Wesley Family Letters, in MA, 2:82, quoted by Stephen Gunter,
The Limits of Love Divine [Nashville: Kingswood Books, 1989], 212)

Myles (*Chronological History*, 76) says that a deputation from York appeared at
this Conference to plead against the 'large sum' of £12 for preachers' allowances
passed in 1752; Limerick Minutes (1752), §§25–26; Bristol Minutes (1752). But
they were overruled, and the allowance was 'finally and universally established',
though it still caused difficulties. See introduction, pp. 50–51.

[4] For material relating to all of Wesley's itinerant preachers, see Lenton, *John
Wesley's Preachers*.

[5] Orig., 'Mosely'; in the stations, No. 25, 'Mosly'; in 1766, 'Moses'; in 1767,
'Mosley'; in 1768, 'Moseley'.

[6] Orig. here and in stations, No. 21, 'Corstardine'. In 1766, it appears as
'Constardine'; in 1768 (once) and in 1769 as 'Consterdine'; in 1772 (once) as
'Casterdine'; but on all other occasions as 'Costerdine', which is also the signature
that he uses in his bound collection of the annual *Minutes*, 1765–92, now in Special
Collections, Perkins Library, Duke University.

[7] Orig. here and in stations, No. 12, 'Orp'; elsewhere 'Orpe', the spelling still
used by descendants of his family.

[8] Orig., 'Dilon', apparently a misprint.

[9] Orig. here and in stations, No. 17, 'Longbotham', as also in 1767 and in 1768.
In 1766 it appeared twice as 'Longbothom', and in 1769 as 'Longbottom'. Two letters by him (1768, 1769), however, are signed 'J. Longbottom'.

[10] Orig., 'Pilsmore', as twice in 1766. In 1767, it appears as 'Pilsmoor'; in 1768,
1769, 1770, 1777, 1778, 1780, 1783, and 1784, as 'Pilmoor'; in 1772, 1773, 1774,
1776, 1779, 1781, 1782, as 'Pillmore'. In the stations for 1771 the name appears as
'Pilmore', which seems to have been his own favourite spelling out of three that he
uses in his letters and journal.

[11] Orig., here and in his 1778 obituary, 'Burk', as well as once in 1777. Most entries
in the *Minutes* seem to use 'Burke' or 'Bourke' indiscriminately, with twice as many
examples of the latter. He signed the 1771 preachers' agreement as 'Bourke'. After his
death, his widow is listed as 'Burk' four times, but usually 'Burke'.

Q. [3]. Who act as *Assistants*[12] this year?

A. John Jones, James Morgan, Joseph Cownley,[13] John
Helton, Peter Jaco, James Oddie, T. Lee, T. Taylor, Alex.
Mather, John Furz, T. Johnson, George Story, John
5   Murlin, Richard Henderson, T. Hanson, Jacob Rowell,[14]
Mark Davis, W. Thompson, Robert Roberts, T. Hanby,
T. Rankin, Isaac Brown,[15] George Roe, Tho. Newall,[16]
Rich. Boardman.

Q. [4]. Who are the other *travelling preachers?*[17]
10   *A.* W. Pennington, Rich. Lucas, Wm. Darney, Daniel
Bumsted, Wm. Brammah, John Morley, John Brandon,
John Easton, James Clough, John Catermole, Tho. Tobias,
John Gibbs, John Oldham, James Cotty, Tho. Carlill, James
Glasbrook,[18] Wm. Minethorp, John Murray, John Oliver,
15   Isaac Waldron, Jos. Guilford, John Shaw, John Poole,[19] Paul
Greenwood, Tho. Brisco, John Atlay,[20] Nich. Manners, John
Nelson, Pars. Greenwood, George Hudson, Thomas
Mitchell, James Kershaw, Jer. Robertshaw, John Ellis, John
Pawson, Christop. Hopper, Matt. Lowes, Wm. Whitwell,
20   Jos. Thompson, Tho. Olivers, John Morgan, Martin Rodda,
Tho. Roorke, Samuel Levick, Tho. Westell, Richard
Blackwell, Robert Swindells, John Heslup, John Johnson.

---

[12] For the 'Assistants', responsible under Wesley for the general administration
of the circuits in which they were stationed, and usually named first, see *Minutes*
(1749), §6 and n. 728. Here and in similar sections in succeeding annual *Minutes*,
they are not listed in the numerical order of their circuits. Jones appears first, probably because he had been legitimately ordained by the bishop of London after the
fiasco of the Greek bishop affair. See above, n. 3.

[13] Orig., 'Cownly', as usually until 1771, although he signed himself 'Cownley'.

[14] Orig., 'Matt. Rowell'.

[15] Orig., here and in stations, No. 21, 'James Brown'.

[16] Orig., here and in stations, No. 31, 'Newell'; in 1769, 'Newel'; in 1773 and
once in 1774, 'Newal', but elsewhere, 'Newall'.

[17] This list of preachers (which does not complete the listing of all those
stationed) follows roughly the numerical order of the circuits in which the men are
stationed.

[18] Orig., here and in stations, No. 12, 'Glazabrook'. All other entries vary almost
indiscriminately between 'Glassbrook' and 'Glasbrook', and the latter is the spelling
he used when signing the 1771 preachers' agreement.

[19] Orig., here and in stations, No. 18, 'Pool', as also in 1771, 1777, 1778,
1785, 1786, 1789, but in all other years, 'Poole', which he used in signing the 1771
preachers' agreement.

[20] Orig., 'Alley', as also in stations, No. 21.

Q. [5]. How are these stationed this year?

A. As follows:

(1) *London*, John Jones, W. Penington, R. Lucas, W. Darney.

(2) *Sussex*, Dan. Bumsted, John Davis.[21]

(3) *Canterbury*, W. Brammah, John Morley.

(4) *Colchester*, John Brandon.

(5) *Norwich*, John Easton, James Clough.

(6) *Bedford*, John Catermole.

(7) *Oxfordshire*, Tho. Tobias.

(8) *Wilts*., Rich. Henderson, John Slocomb, Rich. Walsh, Tho. Simpson.

(9) *Bristol*, John Helton, John Gibbs.

(10) *Devon*, George Roe, John Oldham, Wm. Freemantle.

(11) *Cornwall, East*, George Story, James Cotty, Tho. Carlill.

West, John Furz, John Mason, Wm. Ellis.

(12) *Staffordshire*, T. Hanson, William Orpe,[22] James Glasbrook.

(13) *Salop*, Alex. Mather, Wm. Minethorp.

(14) *Lancashire*, James Oddie, John Oliver, John Murray, Isaac Waldron.

(15) *Derbyshire*, Robert Roberts, John Shaw, Jos. Guilford.

(16) *Sheffield*, Peter Jaco, Paul Greenwood.

(17) *Epworth*, Tho. Lee, T. Brisco, James Longbottom.

(18) *Grimsby*, Rich. Boardman, John Pool, Samuel Woodcock.

(19) *Leeds*, Tho. Hanty, John Nelson.

(20) *Birstall*,[23] John Murlin, Parson Greenwood, John Pawson.

[21] John Davis appears in the 1766 and 1767 stations in East Cornwall, and in 1768 among those who 'desisted'. 'John Davis' here, however, may be an error for 'Mark Davis', who had served in Wiltshire in 1764 and is noted as Assistant in Cork in 1766, but is not otherwise stationed in 1765, though listed as an Assistant.

[22] Orig., 'John Orp'.

[23] Orig., 'Birstal', as almost uniformly in Wesley's publications, and in his day generally. The issues of the *Minutes* printed in Leeds, however, almost all present at least one example of 'Birstall': 1769 (all), 1772 (2 of 3), 1775 (2 of 3), 1778 (all), 1781 (1 of 3), 1784 (all), 1789 (1 of 3). The London *Minutes* (1787) also have 1 of 3 instances printed 'Birstall'.

(21) *Haworth*, Isaac Brown, John Atlay, Nicholas Manners, James Stephens, Robert Costerdine.

(22) *York*, T. Johnson,[24] T. Mitchell, Geo. Hudson.

(23) *Yarm*, Jacob Rowell,[25] James Kershaw, James Brownfield.

(24) *The Dales*, T. Rankin, John Ellis, Jeremiah Robertshaw.

(25) *Newcastle*, Joseph Cownley, Christop. Hopper, Matt. Lowes, Moseley Cheek.

(26) *Edinburgh*, Tho. Taylor.

(27) *Dundee*, Wm. Whitwell.

(28) *Aberdeen*, Jos. Thompson.

(29) *Glasgow*, Tho. Olivers.

(30) *Glamorganshire*, Martin Rodda.

(31) *Pembroke*, Tho. Newall.

(32) *Dublin*, Will. Thompson, John Morgan.

(33) *Cork*, R. Swindells, S. Levick, Barn. Thomas.

(34) *Limerick*, Jam. Dempster, Tho. Rourke.[26]

(35) *Waterford*, John Dillon, T. Brisco.

(36) *Athlone*, T. Westell, John Heslop,[27] John Whitehead.

(37) *Castlebar*, R. Blackwell.

(38) *Newry*, James Rea.

(39) *Londonderry*, John Johnson.[28]

---

[24] Orig., 'Johnston'.

[25] Orig., 'Matt. Rowell'.

[26] 'Roorke' in *Q*. 4, above.

[27] 'Heslup' in *Q*. 4, above.

[28] The figures for membership begin to appear at this point starting in the 1766 *Minutes*. The following can be supplied for 1765 from Jacob Rowell's notebooks; *Methodist Recorder* (Winter Number 1905): 48–49.

Norwich	313	York	998
Bristol	1113	Devon	565
Wiltshire	976	Yarm	1060
Cornwall	2321	Barn. Castle	708
Staffs.	733	Lincs.	1300
Cheshire	447	Newcastle	1700
Lancs.	1610	Scotland	490
Derby.	706	Wales	366
Sheffield	725	London	2000
Leeds	1140	Ireland	———
Birstall	1213	Total	20,434
Haworth	———		[printed 18,484]

Q. [6]. What does the Kingswood collection amount to?
A. £100. 9s. 7d.[29]

Q. [7]. What are the Rules relating to the Preachers'
Fund?[30]

A. As to the subsistence of those who are so entirely worn   5
out that they cannot preach at all:

(1) Let every travelling preacher contribute half a guinea
yearly, at the Conference.

(2) Let this, till it can be safely placed out, be lodged in
the hands of three stewards, approved of by the majority   10
of the preachers.

(3) The present stewards are:

Samuel Franks at London.

William Hey at Leeds.

John Hosmer at Sunderland.   15

(4) Everyone, when he is received as a travelling preacher, is to pay one guinea.

(5) This fund is never to be reduced to less than an hundred pounds.

(6) Out of this are to be supplied superannuated travel-   20
ling preachers, and, when they die, their widows and
children.

(7) Every superannuated preacher shall receive at least
ten pounds a year.[31]

(8) Every widow of such a preacher shall receive, once   25
for all, a sum not exceeding forty pounds.

(9) Every child left by such a preacher shall receive, once
for all, a sum not usually exceeding ten pounds: but this
cannot be claimed by any child whose mother has
received forty pounds.   30

(10) None is entitled to anything from this fund till he
has subscribed two guineas;

(11) Nor any person from the time he ceases (unless
superannuated) to be a travelling preacher;

---

[29] Orig., 'An hundred pounds, nine shillings, and seven pence'. This collection
was first proposed at the Bristol Conference on Saturday, Aug. 28, 1756; see
Minutes (1756), (2) and n. 969. No doubt it was implemented before 1765, but
Minutes are lacking to show any results of this collection in the intervening years.

[30] For the Preachers' Fund, first noted here, see introduction, p. 54.

[31] This intention was not fully realised. See *Minutes* (1771), *Q.* 15, and later.

(12) Nor any who neglects paying his subscription for four years.

(13) But whoever is excluded shall have the money he has subscribed, returned.

5 (14) Let an exact account of all receipts and disbursements be produced at the yearly Conference by Francis Gilbert,[32] secretary.

Q. [8]. What does the yearly subscription amount to?[33]

A. £707. 18*s.*

10 *Q.* [9]. How was this disposed of?

		£	*s.*	*d.*
A.	For buildings	578	0	0
	To the preachers	53	1	0
15	For law	38	17	0
		669	18	0

This was the first distribution; but the small remainder was soon divided among the preachers who were in want, as 20 far as it would go.

[32] Francis Gilbert was the second son of Nathaniel Gilbert (c. 1697–1761), member of the Council of Antigua (1750–61). His older brother, Nathaniel, was also a high official in Antigua, and his younger brother, John, a doctor there. All three were strong Methodists, like the later generations of the influential family in general. See Frank Baker, 'The Origins of Methodism in the West Indies: The Story of the Gilbert Family', *London Quarterly Review* (Jan. 1960). In 1758, both Francis and John were proposed at the Conference as itinerant preachers, and Francis at least served as such, apparently in Bristol, though there are also clues to his being in the Wiltshire and Lancashire Circuits during the early 1760s, and a letter of Peter Jaco (Sept. 5, 1761) implies that in Jan. 1762 they might exchange places, he going to Bristol, Gilbert to Canterbury and London. Francis Gilbert's relationship to the itinerant system did not seem to be so regular as that of most itinerants, and over it all lay both his desire to return as a missionary to Antigua and his hope of being ordained. See Frank Baker, 'Francis Gilbert and Methodist Ordination', *WHS* 27 (1950): 146–48. He did return to Antigua for a time, and after his death in 1779, his widow, the former Mary Leadbetter, continued the Methodist work there.

[33] The Yearly Subscription (later known as the 'Contingent Fund') appears to be one of the oldest funds in Methodism. In the 1763 'Large' Minutes, the question was asked: 'How may we raise a General Fund?' (§72; see also *Minutes* [1763], ad fin.). It was replied: 'By a yearly subscription, to be proposed by every Assistant when he visits the classes at Christmas, and received at the Visitation following'. In later years the scheme was modified—in 1767 (*Q.* 17), collection was to begin at Easter; in 1770 (*Q.* 14), a tighter rein to be kept on building; in 1772 (*Q.* 12), collections to be taken at every preaching-house; in 1779 (*Q.* 18), every circuit was to 'bear its own burden'. See introduction, pp. 55–56.

Q. [10]. We are still overrun with debt. What can be done?

A. Let no preaching-house anywhere be begun but by the
advice of the Assistant. And let no Assistant consent
thereto without an absolute necessity.[34]

Q. [11]. Are the houses already built safe?[35]

A. Not all. Some of them are not regularly settled yet.
Several trustees for others are dead.

Q. [12]. How shall this be remedied?

A. Let a person be sent through England to survey the
deeds and supply the trustees wanting.

Q. [13]. Is anything farther advisable with regard to these
houses?

A. In all our future buildings:
  (1) Let all the windows be sashed, opening downwards.
  (2) Let there be no tub-pulpits; and (3), no backs to the
  seats.

Q. [14]. Should the men and women sit apart everywhere?[36]

A. By all means. Every preacher look to this.

---

[34] Simon suggests that one reason for the proliferation of preaching-houses was to avoid the mob (though this did not always work). *Master-Builder*, 179. New religious movements almost invariably find purpose-built meeting places to be irresistible attractions, quite apart from the need for accommodation as numbers outgrow the capacity of cottages, as was happening with Methodism.

[35] Local trusts often included people from a wider area at first but tended later to be replaced by local leaders. The recurring problem was that local trustees, unless legally restrained, were liable to try to keep control of the pulpit, whereas Wesley wished to combat this incipient congregationalism by preserving control for himself and the connexion. In 1746, he placed the Bristol, Kingswood, and Newcastle houses on a deed securing control during his lifetime to himself and those he appointed, then to Charles Wesley, and only after that to the local trustees. The 'Large' *Minutes* (1763) printed the template for a deed (Model Deed) based on the 1751 deed of the Manchester house. In this, William Grimshaw of Haworth was to succeed to the Wesleys' authority. Those preaching there were to follow the doctrines of Wesley's sermons and *Explanatory Notes upon the New Testament* and to be appointed by the yearly Conference. The Conference was only legally defined by the Deed of Declaration (1784). But deeds not on the 'model' pattern continued to cause problems. See *Minutes* (1767), *Q.* 25; (1775), *Q.* 20; (1782), *QQ.* 21–22, and introduction, pp. 43, 47, 85.

[36] Wesley may here have been following the Moravians. But segregation was not uncommon in Anglican churches in the early 17th century, so it is claimed in J. A. Peyton, ed., *Churchwardens' Presentments in Oxford Peculiars* (1928), xxxi–xxxii. As late as 1772, the poor (at least in a south Devonshire church) were seated separately by sex; J. K. Hopkins, *A Woman to Deliver Her People* (Austin, Tex., 1982), 4. So Wesley may have been perpetuating an old Anglican practice.

Q. [15]. Why is field preaching often omitted?

A. To please the stewards or society. Let it be so no more.

Q. [16]. How late may the evening preaching begin?

A. Never, but in harvest-time, later than seven.

5 *Q*. [17]. How long should a love-feast last?

A. Never above an hour and half: everyone should be at home by nine.

Q. [18]. Should the people break the cake to each other at a love-feast?[37]

10 *A*. By no means. That silly custom, invented by James Wheatley,[38] creates much confusion.

Q. [19]. Are all the preachers merciful to their beasts?

A. Perhaps not. Everyone ought, (1), never to ride hard; (2), to see with his own eyes his horse rubbed, fed, and

15 bedded.

Q. [20]. What can be done to prevent our people needlessly removing from one society to another?

A. (1) Let none remove without the advice of the Assistant. (2) Let none be received in another society without a

20 certificate from the Assistant, in these words: 'A.B., the bearer, is now a member of our society in ————. I believe *he* has a sufficient cause to remove from hence.' (3) Let notice be immediately given of this in every society.

25 *Q*. [21]. Would it not be well to have one ticket everywhere?[39]

A. It would. Send the form from London directly.

Q. [22]. Can R——— W———[40] preach among us?

A. No. We are not satisfied as to his moral character.

---

[37] This seems to confirm the claims of Joseph Nightingale that Methodists indulged in this practice. *A Portraiture of Methodism* (London, 1807), 201ff.

[38] For Wheatley see Minutes (May 1751), n. 787.

[39] For the earlier history of the tickets see Minutes (1746), §51, n. 443. The proposal for a uniform ticket with a pattern sent from London does seem to have been carried out at least from 1768, by the evidence of uniform size and printed dates, according to J. H. Verney in *WHS* 31 (1958): 34. A few variations are discernible in surviving specimens from 1765 to 1767.

[40] R——— W——— is most likely Robert Williams, who received an appointment in 1766, but initials only were used for him in 1767; see *WHS* 10 (1916): 157. The only other possibility is Robert Wilkinson, appointed to Carlisle in 1768.

Q. [23]. Can we receive R———— F————[41] or
I———— H————[42] as Itinerants?

A. Not unless we could pay their debts.

Q. [24]. Ought we to insist upon our rule that no preacher
print anything without your approbation?

A. Undoubtedly: and whoever does it for the time to come
cannot take it ill if he is excluded from our Connexion.[43]
Let everyone take this warning, and afterwards blame
none but himself.

Q. [25]. When and where shall our next Conference be?

A. At Leeds, beginning on Tuesday, August 14.

Q. [26]. What was the rise of Methodism, so called?

A. In 1729 my brother and I read the Bible; saw inward and
outward *holiness* therein, followed after it, and incited others so to do. In 1737 we saw, 'this holiness comes by *faith*'.
In 1738 we saw, 'we must be *justified* before we are sanctified'. But still *holiness* was our point, inward and outward
holiness.

God then thrust us out, utterly against our will, to raise an
holy people.

When Satan could not[44] otherwise prevent this, he threw
Calvinism in our way; and then *Antinomianism*, which
struck at the root both of inward and outward holiness.

Then many Methodists grew *rich*, and thereby *lovers* of the
present *world*.[45]

Next they married unawakened or half-awakened *wives*,
and conversed with *their relations*. Hence *worldly prudence*,

---

[41] There is no 'R. F.' among known preachers. Probably an error for Michael
Fenwick, who stopped itinerating and returned to business in 1758, but returned
to itinerating in The Dales in 1767 (though not officially stationed), and as a Helper
in Aberdeen in 1770 (see JW's letter to Storey, Oct. 26, 1770), and then to stations
as 'M. F.' in 1772.

[42] Probably John Hampson, Sen., who was stationed in Dec. 1766 at Manchester,
though a letter by Benson shows that he was negligent of the Kingswood school-
children. He was also in the Manchester Round in Dec. 1764.

[43] Orig., 'Connection'. These were two alternate spellings in Wesley's day, but normally when he spoke about the links between himself, his preachers, and his Societies,
he spoke about them being 'in connexion' with him, from which developed the continuance of this spelling for this technical use. For the rules on publishing, see *Minutes*
(1749), §18 and n. 737; (1761), n. 1019; (1781), *Q.* 25; (1789), *Q.* 22.

[44] The reading of this word follows that of the Dixon MS Minutes.

[45] See 2 Tim. 4:10.

maxims, customs, crept back upon us, producing more and
more conformity to the world.[46]

There followed gross neglect of *relative duties,* especially
education of children.

5   This is not cured by the preachers. Either they have not
light, or not *weight* enough.

But the want of these may be in some measure supplied by
publicly reading the *Sermons* everywhere, especially the
fourth volume, which supplies them with remedies suited

10   to the disease.[47]

Q. [27]. Might not some parts of the late Conference in
Dublin[48] be of some use to us?

A. They might—which therefore are subjoined.

Q. [28]. What can be done to make the people sing better?

15   *A.* (1) Teach them to sing by note, and to sing our tunes[49]
first.

(2) Take care they do not sing too slow.

(3) Exhort all that can, in every congregation, to sing.

(4) Set them right that sing wrong. Be patient herein.

20   *Q.* [29]. Have the preachers observed the rules?

A. Not exactly. For the time to come let them take care:

(1) To meet the society and the bands everywhere.

(2) To encourage all in the bands to speak freely.

(3) In Dublin, Cork, and Limerick, to meet the married

25   men and married women, the single men and single
women, apart.

(4) In all the larger societies meet the children.

[46] See Rom. 12:2.

[47] Vol. 4 of Wesley's *Sermons,* published 1760, contained not only his sermons 'On Original Sin', 'The New Birth', 'The Wilderness State', 'Heaviness through Manifold Temptations', 'Self-denial', 'The Cure of Evil-speaking', and 'The Use of Money', but 'Advice to the People called Methodists, with regard to Dress', 'The Duties of Husbands and Wives', 'Thoughts on Christian Perfection', and 'Christian Instructions: extracted from a late French author'.

[48] See July 25–26, *Journal & Diaries,* 22:14 in this edn.: 'Thursday and Friday morning I spent in a Conference with our preachers. In the afternoons I spoke to the members of the (Dublin) Society'. It seems clear that all the following questions come from this Dublin Conference, as certainly do *QQ.* 28, 29 (see section 3), and 30 (which takes up 29 [2]).

[49] This year, Wesley published the 2nd edn. (enlarged) of his *Select Hymns with Tunes Annext;* see *Bibliography,* No. 244, and vol. 7 of this edn.

(5) Use intercession on Friday, and recommend fasting, both by precept and example.

Q. [30]. But how can we encourage the women in the bands to speak, since 'it is a shame for women to speak in the church'?[a]

A. I deny, (1), that 'speaking' here means any other than speaking as a *public teacher*. This St. Paul 'suffered not', because it implied 'usurping authority over the man'.[b] Whereas no 'authority' either over man or woman is usurped by the 'speaking' now in question. I deny, (2), that the 'church' in that text means any other than the great congregation.[50]

Q. [31]. Is not family worship partly neglected, partly performed in dull, formal manner?

A. It is. Therefore strongly recommend both in public and private the having family prayer morning and evening, after reading a chapter, and that in the most lively manner. And read publicly that part of Mr. Philip Henry's *Life*, enforcing it as a pattern.[51]

Q. [32]. Are our people good economists?

A. In public and private, enlarge on economy as a branch of religion.

---

a. 1 Cor. 14:35.
b. [Cf.] 1 Tim. 2:12.

[50] Ps. 22:25, etc. This judgment appears to be the first formal comment by a Conference on female preaching. It was probably provoked by the activities of Sarah Crosby and perhaps (rather less publicly) of Mary Bosanquet in the early 1760s; see Wesley's cautious approval of Crosby in a letter of Feb. 14, 1761, and to Grace Walton on Sept. 8, 1761, quoting the Pauline injunctions as in this Conference. *Letters* (Telford), 4:133, 164, and Chilcote, *Women Preachers*, 121–28, 296–98, with a more accurate reconstruction of the letter to Walton. See also *Minutes* (1780), n. 816; (1787), n. 234 (p. 620), for other references to women preachers.

[51] Matthew Henry, *The Life of Mr. Philip Henry* (1696), of which Wesley published an abridgement in his *Christian Library* (1755), 50:7–155, which includes Philip's advice to his son Matthew to observe 'a method according to the several parts of prayer', viz., adoration, confession, petition, and thanksgiving (ibid., 153–55). In 1710, Matthew Henry published *A Method for Prayer, with Scripture Expressions Proper to be Used under Each Head*, and in the 1766 Conference (*Q.* 31 [4]), this work replaced the brief outline in Henry's *Life*, though Wesley mistakenly named Philip Henry rather than his son Matthew as the author. From the 1766 Annual *Minutes*, this recommendation was transferred into the 'Large' *Minutes* (1770).

Q. [33]. Are they guarded in their words?

A. Not sufficiently. Warn them against 'little oaths', as upon my *life*, my *faith*, my *honour*; and against *compliments*. Let them use no *unmeaning* words.

Q. [34]. Should we recommend calling each other 'Brother' and 'Sister'?[52]

A. It may be done tenderly and prudently.

Q. [35]. Do not they in general *talk* too much and *read* too little?

A. They do. Let them retrench but half the time they spend in talking, and they will have time enough to read. Speak of this everywhere. Reprove them publicly and privately for reading less useful books. Do not talk too much yourself. If you stay above an hour at any place, take out a book and read.

Q. [36]. Have they left off snuff?

A. No. Many are absolutely enslaved to it still. In order to redress this great evil:

(1) Speak to anyone who takes it in sermon-time.

(2) Let no preacher touch it on any account.

(3) Show the societies the evil of it.

Q. [37]. How shall we cure them of drinking drams?

A.(1) Let no preacher drink any, on any pretence.

(2) Strongly dissuade our people from it.

(3) Answer their presences, particularly those of curing the colic and helping digestion.

Q. [38]. Is not their religion usually too superficial?

A. It is. To remove this, preach on the most spiritual subjects. Exhort all believers to 'go on to perfection'.[53] And earnestly recommend private prayer, reading the Scriptures, and universal self-denial.

---

[52] Perhaps following Moravian practice, though the Wesley children had addressed each other in this way at Epworth. *Journal & Diaries*, 19:289 in this edn. But as the question was raised at this late date, it may be a product of popular Methodist practice.

[53] Cf. Heb. 6:1. Orig., italics. This phrase is one of Wesley's favourite exhortations, and it is uncertain whether he italicizes it because it resembles a biblical quotation or because he emphasizes it.

Annual *Minutes of some late Conversations*, 1766

Leeds, Aug. 12, etc. 1766.[54]

Q. [1]. What preachers are *admitted* this year?

A. William Orpe, William Ellis, James Brownfield, Samuel
Woodcock, James Longbottom, Joseph Pilmore, William   5
Barker, Thomas Simpson, Duncan Wright, John Dillon,[55]
James Rea: Richard Bourke remains[56] on trial, till we
know what his debts are.

Q. [2]. William Ellis, have *you* faith in Christ? Are you *going
on to perfection?* Do you expect to be *perfected in love*[57] in   10
this life? Are you groaning after it? Are you resolved to
devote yourself *wholly* to God and his
work?

Do you know the Methodist *doctrine?* Have you read the
Sermons? The *Notes* on the New Testament?   15

---

[54] JW wrote: 'Tue. 12. Our Conference began and ended on Friday evening.
An happier Conference we never had, nor a more profitable one. It was both
begun and ended in love, and with a solemn sense of the presence of God.'
Journal & Diaries, 22:56f. in this edn. In June, he had written to Charles, 'we
must have a thorough reform of the preachers. I wish you would come to Leeds
with John Jones.' *Letters* (Telford), 5:16f. In that letter he analyzed, partly in
shorthand, his sense of God and religious experience in remarkably negative
terms; see Rack, *Reasonable Enthusiast*, 546–49. Later, in July, he says that he
has set aside J. H. (John Hampson?). Then 'I will tell you a secret . . . I will not
be opposed at the Conference; for I will not dispute. I shall find them other
work. But . . . it is highly expedient *you* should be there.' *Letters* (Telford),
5:20f. Tyerman thought Charles probably did go to the Conference as the
major topics of discussion (separation from the Church, John's 'power', and
the reform of the preachers) were always of great concern to him; *Wesley*,
2:575. For the first time in Conference, a list of questions was directed at every
preacher on probation and at those being received into full connexion. A
London committee for finance was set up at this time, which met for the next
twenty-six years, though this does not appear in the *Minutes*; see Sutcliffe,
MS 'History', fol. 675. For its possible prehistory and the problems it caused,
see introduction, pp. 44–46.

[55] Orig., 'James Dillon'.

[56] Orig., 'remained'.

[57] See 1 John 2:5; 4:12.

Do you know the Methodist *Plan?*[58] Have you read the
Plain Account?[59] The *Appeals?*[60]

Do you know the *Rules* of the Society? Of the Bands? Do
you keep them?

5   Do you take no snuff, tobacco, drams? Do you constantly
attend the church and sacrament?

Have you read the *Minutes?*[61] Are you willing to conform to
them?

Have you considered the Twelve Rules of an Helper,[62] espe-
10   cially the first, tenth, and twelfth?

Will you keep them for conscience' sake?

Are you determined to employ *all* your time in the work of
God?

Will you preach every morning and evening? Endeavouring not
15   to speak too loud or too long? Not lolling with your elbows?

Have you read the 'Rules of Action and Utterance'?[63] Will you
meet the society, the bands, the Select Society,[64] the Leaders
(of bands and classes) in every place?

Will you diligently and earnestly instruct the children, and
20   visit from house to house?

Will you recommend fasting, both by precept and example?

The same questions were proposed to the rest severally,[65]
before they were admitted.

---

[58] The capital letter and italics might suggest the short title of a publication like the others mentioned. However, no such work by JW is known. It is probably best to see it as the subject of this paragraph (like '*doctrine*' in the previous one). The two works then listed would be seen as explaining the Methodist 'system'. In *Minutes* (1788), *QQ*. 24–25, the 'Methodist Plan' is clearly the Model Deed, which was published in the 'Large' *Minutes* (1763). Cf. also the concern about deeds in *Minutes* (1765), *Q*. 11.

[59] If the surmise in the last note is correct, the *Plain Account* appears to refer to *A Plain Account of the People Called Methodists* (1749), 9:253–80 in this edn., rather than the *Plain Account of Christian Perfection* (1766), which would fit more logi-cally in the preceding question on doctrine.

[60] *An Earnest Appeal to Men of Reason and Religion* and *A Farther Appeal to Men of Reason and Religion, Pts. I–III* (1743–45), see vol. 11 of this edn.

[61] I.e., the 'Large' *Minutes*.

[62] See above, Minutes (1744), §73.

[63] This title was sometimes used in Wesley's advertising also for the pamphlet first published in 1749 as *Directions concerning Pronunciation and Gesture*; see *Bibliography*, No. 161.

[64] On this group, see Minutes (1744), §58, n. 143.

[65] Meaning 'individually', 'separately'. This is the first full account of questions put to those admitted to full connexion.

Q. [3]. Who are *admitted on trial?*

A. Thomas Dancer, Simon Day, Benj. Rhodes, John Allen, Thomas Halliday, Lancelot Harrison.

Q. [4]. Who act as Assistants this year?

A. John Jones, William Pennington, Tho. Hanson, Alex. 5
Mather, Richard Henderson, Thomas Simpson, John
Furz, John Mason, William Orpe, Thomas Johnson,
P. Jaco, James Clough, Robert Roberts, T. Mitchell,
Th. Rankin, Thomas Lee, James Oddie, Is. Brown,
Richard Boardman, John Heslup, Jos. Cownley, Jacob 10
Rowell, T. Taylor, John Helton, James Morgan, M. Davis,
William Thompson, T. Brisco.

Q. [5]. What preachers are laid aside this year?

A. J———— B————[66] and J———— M————.[67]

Q. [6]. How are the preachers stationed? 15

A.(1) *London*, John Jones, John Murlin, Rich. Blackwell,
Dunc. Wright.

(2) *Sussex*, Wm. Pennington, Jo. Catermole.

(3) *Canterbury*, John Easton.

(4) *Colchester*, Tho. Tobias. 20

(5) *Norwich*, Tho. Hanson, Benj. Rhodes.

(6) *Bedfordshire*, James Glasbrook.

(7) *Oxfordshire*, William Minethorp.

(8) *Wilts.*, Alex. Mather, Tho. Dancer, Ja. Stephens, John
Oldham. 25

(9) *Bristol*, Rich. Henderson, J. Nelson.

(10) *Devon*, Tho. Simpson, James Cotty.

(11) *Cornwall, East*, J. Furz, J. Davis, Jos. Pilmore.

(12)   *West*, J. Mason, Sim. Day, W. Barker.

(13) *Staffordshire*, W. Orpe, N. Manners, J. Poole. 30

(14) *Cheshire*, T. Johnson, Parson Greenwood.

---

[66] Almost certainly John Brandon, who had been an active supporter of JW since 1755. He was appointed to Colchester in 1765 but, according to Myles, left in 1766. A dragoon, he is said to have been the first Methodist in Leicester and a leader and preacher there. He later lived in Leicester but had little or no connection with the Methodists. *Journal & Diaries*, 21:91 in this edn.; Tyerman, *Wesley*, 2:170.

[67] Almost certainly John Morley, who Myles says itinerated from 1751 but desisted in 1767. John Pawson says he was a Calvinist and a poor man at Lynn and alive very lately, i.e., in 1800. *Letters*, 3:22. A person named Morley (who may or may not be the same man) was one of Lady Huntingdon's preachers in Hull. Seymour, *Huntingdon*, 1:311.

(15) *Lancashire*, Peter Jaco, Paul Greenwood, John
Pawson, John Allen.
(16) *Derbyshire*, James Clough, Isaac Waldron, G.
Hudson.
(17) *Sheffield*, Rob. Roberts, Jos. Guilford.
(18) *Lincolnshire, East*, T. Mitchell, J. Ellis, T. Carlill.
(19)   *West*, T. Rankin, W. Brammah,
                        L. Harrison.
(20) *Leeds*, Tho. Lee, James Longbottom.
(21) *Birstall*, James Oddie, Thomas Hanby, Dan.
Bumsted, Moseley Cheek.
(22) *Haworth*, J. Brown,[68] J. Shaw, Rob. Costerdine, John
Atlay.
(23) *York*, R. Boardman, W. Whitwell,[69] J. Standring,
Sam Woodcock.
(24) *Yarm*, John Heslup, J. Kershaw, W. Darney.
(25) *The Dales*, J. Rowell, J. Robertshaw, T. Halliday.
(26) *Newcastle*, J. Cownley, Christ. Hopper, J. Oliver,
Matt. Lowes.
(27) *Dunbar*, William Ellis.
(28) *Edinburgh*, John Helton, Jos. Thompson.
(29) *Dundee*, Thomas Olivers.
(30) *Aberdeen*, Thomas Taylor.
(31) *Glasgow*, James Brownfield.
(32) *Wales*, Geo. Story, T. Newall.
(33) *Dublin*, John Morgan, John Murray.
(34) *Limerick*, Sam Levick, Barn. Thomas.
(35) *Waterford*, Rob. Swindells, T. Westell.
(36) *Cork*, Mark Davis, John Dillon.
(37) *Athlone*, Rich. Bourke, Tho. Brisco, J. Whitehead,
W. Thompson.
(38) *Castlebar*,[70] James Dempster.
(39) *North West*, John Johnson, James Morgan.
(40) *East*, James Rea, Rob. Williams.

---

[68] Apparently Isaac Brown.

[69] Orig., 'Whitewell'; 1765 and 1768 have Whitwell, as do the records of his quarterly payments in the Manchester Round for 1763–64, though one of the three
reads 'Whittwell'.

[70] Orig., 'Castlebarr', as in 1766, 1767, 1773 (1 of 2), 1774 (1 of 2), 1778 (1 of 2),
1779, 1780 (1 of 2), and 1782 (1 of 2).

Q. [7]. What number are in the Society at

London		
Sussex	197	
Canterbury		5
Colchester	141	
Norwich		
Bedford	167	
Oxfordshire		
Wilts.	941	10
Bristol	1089	
Devon		
Cornwall, East	580	
West	1655	
Staffordshire	836	15
Salop	587	
Lancashire	1742	
Derbyshire	739	
Sheffield	583	
Epworth	665	20
Grimsby	700	
Leeds	1072	
Birstall	1376	
Haworth	1536	
York	982	25
Yarm	1103	
The Dales	772	
Newcastle	1804	
Dunbar		
Edinburgh	165	30
Dundee, etc.	321	
Wales		
Ireland		

Q. [8]. What is the Kingswood collection?   35
A. £118. 13*s*. 11*d*.
Q. [9]. What can be done for Kingswood?
A. (1) Put in James Hindmarsh[71] and his wife as writing
    master and housekeeper.

---

[71] James Hindmarsh (?–1812) was originally an innkeeper in Alnwick; writing master at Kingswood School (1766–71); itinerant (1771–83), but a Swedenborgian minister from 1788. His son Robert (1759–1835) was also a Swedenborgian minister. See *DNB* and *Journal & Diaries*, 22:130 and nn. 65, 66 in this edn.

(2) Desire Mr. Price[72] to stay another year.

(3) Appoint three or five trustees.

(4) Let each Bristol preacher be an hour a week at least with the children.[73]

5

Q. [10]. What is the yearly subscription?

A. £695. 2*s.* 11*d.*

Q. [11]. What places petition for help?

		£	
A.	Aberdeen	50	granted[74]
	Edinburgh	100	
	Portarlington		
	Londonderry		
	Mountmellick	20	
	Monkwearmouth[75]	20	
	Sunderland		
	Alston[76]		
	Swaledale		
	Allendale	5	
	Barnard Castle[77]	10	
	Teesdale	4	
	Yarm	10	
	Thirsk	5	
	Stokesley[78]	10	
	Whitby	5	
	York	10	

10

15

20

25

---

[72] Peter Price was at Kingswood School (1765–68) and an itinerant (1764–68). According to John Pawson, he was, even while an itinerant, 'quite deranged' but 'now' (c. 1800) 'confined' near Bristol 'if yet alive'. Pawson, *Letters*, 3:143f.

[73] See also *Q.* 16 (5) below.

[74] The word 'granted' clearly applies to the whole list, apparently implying not only that the societies having no amounts added did not receive anything, but also that no indication of the amount originally requested is given in any instance. The order of the societies seems to be unrelated to the order of the circuits to which they belonged; they were apparently arranged in the order of their being received by Wesley.

[75] Orig., 'Monkwarem'. Several other variants appear: 'Monckw.' in 1769; 'Monckwarm.' in 1770; and 'Monkweymouth' in 1772.

[76] Orig., 'Aldstone'.

[77] Orig., 'Barnardcastle', as also in 1775; in 1770, 'Bernard-Castle'.

[78] Orig., 'Stoxley'; other variants are 'Stocksly', 1769; 'Stockesly', 1770; and 'Stokesly', 1772.

Scarborough		
Heptonstall	10	
Padiham[79]		
Bacup		
Bingley	5	5
Bradford	40	
Halifax[80]	10	
Leeds	10	
Rothwell		
Thorner		10
Horbury		
Seacroft		
Grimsby	5	
Louth[81]	5	
Sibsey[82]	10	15
Boston	10	
Sheffield	5	
Bradwell		
Rotherham	10	
Derby	20	20
Nottingham		
Burton	30	
Creech[83]		
Ashby[84]		
Stockport		25
Congleton		
Warrington		
Burslem[85]		
Macclesfield[86]		
Bolton		30

[79] Orig., 'Paddiham' as also in 1769, 1770, and 1779.

[80] Orig., 'Hallifax', as also in 1786 (3 of 5), 1786 (3 of 4), 1788 (3 of 4), and 1790 (1 of 3).

[81] Orig., 'Lowth', as also in 1770, 1776, and 1779.

[82] Orig., 'Sibrey'; in 1780, 'Sibsay'.

[83] Orig., 'Creitch'; also appears as 'Creich' (1770) and 'Critch' (1774).

[84] Orig., 'Ashly', but surely Ashby (de la Zouch).

[85] Orig., 'Borslam', as also in 1772, 1783, and 1784 (1 of 3). The name also appears as 'Boslem' in 1769, 1770, and 1783; as 'Burslam' in 1784 (1 of 3); and as 'Borslem' in 1785 (3), 1786 (3), and 1787 (3).

[86] Orig., 'Maxfield', as also in 1769, 1772 (2 of 3), 1773 (2 of 3), 1774, 1775 (3 of 4), 1776 (1 of 4), and 1777 (1 of 4). In 1770, the name is spelled 'Mackelsfield'.

Liverpool		
Chester		
Salop	4	
Birmingham	10	
Wolverhampton[87]		
Stroud		
Darlaston		
Lelant		
St. Hilary		
Crowan		
Stithian		
St. Just		
Cullompton[88]	20	
Pensford		
Bath		
Bradford		
Shepton	10	
Shaftesbury[89]	10	
Bedford		
Norwich		
Colchester	20	
Canterbury	20[a]	

Q. [12]. What is our total debt for building?

A. £11,383.[90]

Q. [13]. We shall be utterly ruined if we go on thus. How may we prevent the increase of debt?

A. (1) Let no other building be undertaken till two-thirds of the money are subscribed.

(2) We will allow nothing to any house which shall be begun after this day till the debt is reduced to three thousand pounds.

(3) Let every preacher labour with his might to increase the collection next year.

---

[a] The remainder was divided among the preachers who were in want.

[87] Orig., 'Woolverhampton'; also in 1773, as 'Woolverham'.
[88] Orig., 'Collumpton', as in 1769, 1780; in 1770, 'Columpton'.
[89] Orig., 'Shaftsbury', as also in 1769, 1772, 1773, 1778, and 1779.
[90] This was a recurring problem, as subsequent Conferences showed. See *Minutes* (1765), *Q.* 11, n. 35; (1767), *Q.* 17; and further proposals in 1770, 1789, 1790; for details, introduction, pp. 44–46.

Q. [14]. Are the houses settled according to the Plan?[91]

A. Most [of] them are. Let each Assistant take care that
the rest be so settled without delay, that at Liverpool in
particular.

And let a counsel[92] be consulted concerning the deeds, and　5
concerning endorsing new trustees.

Q. [15]. But what if the proprietors delay conveying the
houses, because they are in debt?

A. Then let them give a bond that they will convey as soon
as they are indemnified.　　　　　　　　　　　　　　　　　10

And let no classes meet in any preaching-house.

Q. [16]. (4)[93] Are the roofs of most of them well-built?

A. They need never rise above a third of the breadth.
　(5) Let a collection for the [General Fund][94] be made in
　June next in every preaching-house in England,　　　15
　Scotland, and Ireland.

Q. [17]. What is received this year for the Preachers' Fund?
A.[95]

Q. [18]. Need any rule be added relative to this?

A. Yes, let every preacher who does not bring or send his　20
money to the Conference be fined 2*s.* 6*d.*

Q. [19]. It was agreed at the last Conference that the men
and women would sit apart everywhere. Is there any
exception to this?

A. There is one. In those galleries where they have been　25
accustomed to sit together, they may do so still. But let

---

[91] I.e., the Model Deed set forth in the 'Large' *Minutes* (1763), §67; cf. *Minutes*
(1765), *Q.* 11, n. 35.

[92] Orig., 'council'.

[93] The number apparently refers back to *Q.* 13.

[94] Orig., 'school'. The number beginning this sentence seems to be in succession
to '(4)' in the previous question, and therefore presumably forms a part of the measures proposed under *Q.* 13 to 'prevent the increase of debt'. The original wording,
however, 'a collection for the school', implies that it is in succession to the '(4)'
measures to help Kingswood School (see *Q.* 9). The 'Large' *Minutes* (1763) did
indeed prescribe an annual collection for the school 'before or after Midsummer',
although it was authorized as a possibility in 1756. An annual collection for the
'General Fund' had been inaugurated in 1761. It seems possible that at this
Conference, annual collections for both funds were proposed, but that the Minutes
of these agreements are confused.

[95] No amount is given.

them sit apart everywhere below, and in all new-erected galleries.[96]

Q. [20]. It was also agreed that field preaching should not be omitted to please anyone. But who is proper to preach abroad?

A. (1) The Assistant.

(2) Any preacher whom he advises to it.

Q. [21]. We agreed, none should remove from one society to another without a certificate from the Assistant. Has this been well observed?

A. No. Let every Assistant observe it better for the time to come.

Q. [22]. When and where may our next Conference begin?

A. At London, the third Tuesday in August.

Q. [23]. How may each Assistant take a regular catalogue of the societies?

A. By writing the names of the members as they live in house-row, without regarding the classes.

Q. [24]. Should we give the *Rules* of the society to everyone when taken on trial?

A. By all means. And let every band-leader have the band *Rules*.

Q. [25]. Should we repeat or enforce the rules relating to ruffles, lace, snuff, and tobacco?

A. Enforce them vigorously, though calmly. When any person is admitted into a society, even good breeding requires him to conform to the rules of that society.

Q. [26]. When should we enforce them in Ireland and Scotland?

A. Without delay. Only show them the *reasonableness* of it in Scotland, and they will conform to anything.

Q. [27]. Have the sermons on *Wandering Thoughts,*[97] *In-being Sin,*[98] *The Lord our Righteousness,*[99] and *The Scripture Way of Salvation*[100] been carefully dispersed?

---

[96] See *Minutes* (1765), *Q.* 14, n. 36.

[97] No. 41, first published in *Sermons on Several Occasions,* vol. 3 (1750), and then separately from 1762 onwards; see *Bibliography,* No. 130.iv, and vol. 2 of this edn.

[98] No. 13, *A Discourse on Sin in Believers,* first published separately in 1763, and then collected into vol. 1 of Wesley's *Works* (1771); see *Bibliography,* No. 257, and vol. 1 of this edn.

[99] No. 20, first published separately in 1766, and then collected into vol. 2 of Wesley's *Works* (1771); see *Bibliography,* No. 295, and vol. 1 of this edn.

[100] No. 43, first published separately in 1765, and then collected into vol. 3 of Wesley's *Works* (1771); see *Bibliography,* No. 265, and vol. 2 of this edn.

A. No. Let each Assistant do it now.

And let each insist on cleanliness and decency everywhere. And give an account to his successor of the state of things in his circuit.

Let him likewise so order the preaching in his circuit that no preacher may be obliged to miss the church more than two Sundays in a month. 5

Q. [28]. Are we not then Dissenters?

A. We are irregular: (1) by calling sinners to repentance in *all places* of God's dominion; (2) by frequently using *extemporary prayer.* Yet we are not *Dissenters* in the only sense which our law acknowledges; namely, persons who believe it is sinful to attend the service of the Church; for we do attend it at all opportunities. We will not, dare not separate from the Church, for the reasons given several years ago.[101] We are not *seceders,* nor do we bear any resemblance to them. We set out upon quite opposite principles. The seceders laid the very foundation of their work in judging and condemning *others.* We laid the foundation of our work in judging and condemning ourselves. They begin everywhere with showing their hearers how fallen *the Church* and *ministers* are. We begin everywhere with showing our hearers how fallen they are *themselves.* 10

And as we are not dissenters from the Church now, so we will do nothing willingly which tends to a separation from it. Therefore let every Assistant immediately so order his circuit that no preacher may be hindered from attending the Church more than two Sundays in the month. Never make light of going to Church, either by word or deed. Remember Mr. Hook,[102] a very eminent and a zealous papist. When I asked him, 'Sir, what do you for public worship here, where you have no Romish sermon?' he answered, 'Sir, I am so fully convinced it is the duty of 15

20

25

30

---

[101] See *Reasons against a Separation from the Church of England,* first published in *A Preservative against Unsettled Notions in Religion* (1758), and then as a separate pamphlet (1760); see *Bibliography,* No. 240, and vol. 9 of this edn.

[102] Nathaniel Hooke (?–1763), Serjeant at Law, the Catholic friend who brought a priest to Pope's deathbed. His *Roman History* (1738–71) was much reprinted, and Wesley criticized it in 1771. *DNB* and *Journal & Diaries,* 22:300 in this edn. Much less likely is his son, Luke Joseph Hooke (1716–96), a Catholic divine of the Sorbonne, who seems to have resided in France and was visited there by Dr. Johnson.

every man to worship God in public that I go to Church
every Sunday. If I can't have such worship as I would, I
will have such worship as I can.'

But some may say, 'Our own service is public worship.' Yes,
in a sense—but not such as supersedes the Church service.
We never designed it should; we have an hundred times
professed the contrary. It presupposes public prayer, like
the sermons at the university. Therefore I have over and
over advised, use no *long-prayer*, either before or after sermon. Therefore I myself frequently use only a collect, and
never enlarge in prayer, unless at intercession, or on a
watch-night, or on some extraordinary occasion.

If it were designed to be instead of Church service, it
would be essentially defective. For it seldom has the four
grand parts of public prayer: deprecation, petition, intercession, and thanksgiving. Neither is it, even on the
Lord's day, concluded with the Lord's Supper.

The hour for it on that day, unless where there is some
peculiar reason for a variation, should be five in the morning, as well as five in the evening. Why should we make
God's day the shortest of the seven?

But if the people put ours in the place of the Church service, we *hurt* them that stay with us and *ruin* them that
leave us. For then they will go nowhere, but lounge the
sabbath away, without any public worship at all. I advise
therefore all the Methodists in England and Ireland who
have been brought up in the Church, constantly to attend
the service of the Church, at least every Lord's day.

Q. [29] But what power is this which *you* exercise over all
the Methodists in Great Britain and Ireland?

A. Count Z[inzendorf] loved to keep all things close. I love
to do all things openly. I will therefore tell you all I know
of the matter, taking it from the very beginning.[103]

(1) In November 1738 two or three persons who desired

---

[103] A similar challenge was apparently made at the 1763 Conference, but Howell
Harris deflected it by an emotional appeal, according to John Pawson; see Jackson,
Early Methodist Preachers; cf. *Minutes* (1763), n. 1075 (p. 296). For a discussion of
the sources of Wesley's authority, see Rack, *Reasonable Enthusiast*, 249ff.

to flee from the wrath to come,[104] and then seven or eight
more, came to me in London, and desired me to advise
and pray with them. I said, 'If you will meet on Thursday
night, I will help you as well as I can.' More and more
then desired to meet with them, till they were increased to 5
many hundreds. The case was afterwards the same at
Bristol, Kingswood, Newcastle, and many other parts of
England, Scotland, and Ireland. It may be observed, the
desire was on *their* part, not *mine*. My desire was to live
and die in retirement. But I did not see that I could refuse 10
them my help, and be guiltless before God.

Here commenced my power: namely a power to appoint
when, and where, and how they should meet; and to
remove those whose life showed that they had no desire to
flee from the wrath to come. And this power remained the 15
same whether the people meeting together were twelve,
twelve hundred, or twelve thousand.

(2) In a few days some of them said, 'Sir, we will not *sit
under you* for nothing. We will subscribe quarterly.' I said,
'I will have nothing, for I want nothing. My fellowship 20
supplies me with all, and more than I want.'[105] One
replied, 'Nay, but you want £115 to pay for the lease of
the Foundery. And likewise a large sum of money will be
wanting to put it into repair.' On this consideration I suffered them to subscribe. And when the Society met I 25
asked, 'Who will take the trouble of receiving this money,
and paying it where it is needful?' One said, 'I will do it,
and keep the account for you.' So here was the first *steward*. Afterwards I desired one or two more to help me as
stewards, and in process of time, a greater number. 30

---

[104] Matt. 3:7, and cf. Christian's impulse at the beginning of *Pilgrim's Progress*. Wesley
here more or less repeats the opening of his *Nature, Design and General Rules of the
United Societies* (1743; see 9:69 in this edn.), where he writes, however, 'the latter end
of the year 1739'. The Nov. 1738 date here presumably refers to the formation of the
Band Society, the rules of which were drawn up on Dec. 25, 1738; see 9:77 in this edn.

[105] The income from Wesley's fellowship at Lincoln College between 1738 and
1750 yielded between about £18 and £80 a year but was most often about £30.
V. H. H. Green, *The Young Mr. Wesley* (London, 1961), app. 2, and *The
Commonwealth of Lincoln College* (Oxford, 1979), 327, n. l. However, college rules
required that he subsequently lose this income upon his marriage in 1751. The
sources and scale of his finances for three decades thereafter are less clear, since
there is a gap in his extant personal financial records between 1733 and 1782.

Let it be remarked it was I myself, not the people, who
chose these stewards, and appointed to each the distinct
work wherein he was to help me, as long as I desired. And
herein I began to exercise another sort of *power*; namely,
that of appointing and removing stewards.

(3) After a time a young man came, T. Maxfield, and said
he desired to help me as a son in the gospel. Soon after
came a second, Thomas Richards, and a third, Thomas
Westell.[106] These severally desired to serve me as sons,
and to labour when and where I should direct. Observe:
these likewise desired *me*, not I *them*. But I durst not
refuse their assistance. And here commenced my *power*
to appoint each of these when, where, and how to labour.
That is, while he chose to continue with me: for each had
a power to go away when he pleased; as I had also to go
away from them, or any of them, if I saw sufficient cause.
The case continued the same when the number of
preachers increased. I had just the same power still to
appoint when, and where, and how each should help me,
and to tell any if I saw cause, 'I do not desire your help
any longer.' On these terms, and no other, we joined at
first: on these we continue joined. But they do me no
favour in being directed by me. It is true my reward is
with the Lord.[107] But at present I have nothing from it
but trouble and care, and often a burden I scarce know
how to bear.

(4) In 1744 I wrote to several clergymen, and to all who
then served me as sons in the gospel, desiring them to
meet me in London, to give me their advice concerning
the best method of carrying on the work of God. *They*
did not desire this meeting, but *I* did, knowing that 'in a
multitude of counsellors there is safety'.[108] And when
their number increased so that it was neither needful nor

---

[106] Orig., 'Westal'. These were the first preachers subject to him in his own organization. He had earlier been assisted by Joseph Humphreys, a Dissenter and associate of Whitefield who helped JW at the Foundery (1740–41). John Cennick, soon
to become a Moravian, assisted JW in Bristol after beginning to preach in 1739.
Letters, 26:46 n. 16 in this edn.; *WHS* (1908): 6:108f.; Rack, *Reasonable Enthusiast*,
201, 243f.

[107] See Wis. 5:15.

[108] Cf. Prov. 11:14; 24:6.

convenient to invite them all, for several years I wrote to
those with whom I desired to confer, and these only met
at the place appointed, till at length I gave a general permission that all who desired it might come.

Observe: I myself sent for these, of my own free choice; and   5
I sent for them to *advise*, not *govern* me. Neither did I at
any of those times divest myself of any part of that *power*
above described, which the providence of God had cast
upon me, without any design or choice of mine.

What is that power? It is a power of admitting into and   10
excluding from the societies under my care; of choosing
and removing stewards; of receiving or not receiving
Helpers; of appointing them when, where, and how to
help me; and of desiring any of them to meet me when I
see good. And as it was merely in obedience to the   15
Providence of God and for the good of the people that I at
first accepted this power, which I never sought, nay an
hundred times laboured to throw off; so it is on the same
considerations, not for profit, honour, or pleasure, that I
use it at this day.   20

(5) But several gentlemen are much offended at my having *so much power*. My answer to them is this:

I did not seek any part of this power. It came upon me
unawares. But when it was come, not daring to bury that
talent, I used it to the best of my judgment.   25

Yet I never was fond of it. I always did and do now bear it
as my burden, the burden which God lays upon me, and
therefore I dare not yet lay it down.

But if you can tell me any one, or any five men, to whom I
may transfer this burden, who *can* and *will* do just what I   30
do now, I will heartily thank both them and you.

(6) But some of our Helpers say, 'This is *shackling freeborn Englishmen*',[109] and demand a *free Conference*, that is,
a meeting of all the preachers wherein all things shall be
determined by most votes.   35

---

[109] This phrase was a political slogan of the time, a catch-phrase for radicals in
particular. After Wesley's death, it was used in a similar way by would-be Methodist
reformers, notably by those creating the Methodist New Connexion in 1797.

I answer, it is possible after my death something of this
kind may take place. But not while I live. To *me* the
preachers have engaged themselves to submit, to 'serve
me as sons in the gospel'.[110] But they are not thus engaged
to any man, or number of men, besides. To *me* the people
in general will submit. But they will not yet submit to any
other.

'Tis nonsense then to call my using *this power* 'shackling
free-born Englishmen'. None needs to submit to it unless
he will; so there is no shackling in the case. Every
preacher and every member may leave me when he
pleases. But while he chooses to stay, it is on the same
term that he joined me at first.

'But this is *arbitrary* power; this is no less than making
yourself a pope'.[111]

If by *arbitrary* power you mean a power which I exercise
singly, without any colleagues therein, this is certainly
true; but I see no hurt in it. 'Arbitrary' in this sense is a
very harmless word. If you mean *unjust, unreasonable,* or
tyrannical, then it is not true.

As to the other branch of the charge, it carries no face of
truth. The Pope affirms that every Christian must do all
he bids, and believe all he says, under pain of damnation.
I never affirmed anything that bears any, the most distant
resemblance to this. All I affirm is, 'The preachers who
choose to labour with me choose to serve me as sons in
the gospel.' And, 'The people who choose to be under my
care choose to be so on the same terms they were at first.'

Therefore all talk of this kind is highly injurious to me,
who bear this burden merely for your sakes. And it is
exceeding mischievous to the people, tending to confound
their understandings, and to fill their hearts with evil surmisings and unkind tempers toward *me*—to whom they
really owe more for taking all this load upon me, for

[110] Cf. *Q.* 29 (3, 4) above. If Wesley was not quoting himself, he may be echoing
Paul's words to Timothy as his 'son in the faith' (1 Tim. 1:2).

[111] Cf. the charge against JW as 'Pope John' by John Byrom when JW expelled
members of the Manchester Society for their 'mysticism' in 1761. Byrom, *Journal
and Remains*, Chetham Society 44 (1857): 629–31.

exercising this very *power*, for shackling myself in this
manner, than for all my preaching put together. Because
preaching twice or thrice a day is no burden to me at all;
but the care of all the preachers and all the people is a
burden indeed!   5

But all hitherto is comparatively little. I come now to speak
of greater things.

I do not depend on seeing another Conference. Therefore I
will now speak once for all, as taking my leave of you.

I cannot but know more of the state both of the Methodist   10
preachers and people than any other person, because I see
more of the preachers and more of the people, in every
part of the kingdom.

Therefore I can give you such an account both of the
preachers and the people as no other person can.   15

And you are fully assured that *I* am not prejudiced against
either the preachers or the people.

To begin with the latter. The world says, 'The Methodists
are no better than other people.' This is not true. Yet it is
nearer the truth than we are willing to imagine.   20

For, (1), personal religion, either toward God or man, is
amazingly superficial among us.

I can but touch on a few generals. How little faith is there
among us, how little communion with God! How little living in heaven, walking in eternity, deadness to every crea-   25
ture! How much love of the world, desire of pleasure, of
ease, of praise, of getting money!

How little brotherly love! What continual judging one
another! What gossiping, evil-speaking, tale-bearing!
What want of moral honesty! To instance only in a few   30
particulars:

What servants, journeymen, labourers, carpenters, brick-
layers, do as they would be done by? Which of them does
as much work as he can? Set him down for a knave that
does not.   35

Who does as he would be done by in buying and selling,
particularly in selling horses? Write him knave that
does not. And the Methodist knave is the worst of all
knaves.

(2) Family religion is shamefully wanting, and almost in
every branch.

And the Methodists in general will be little better, till we
take quite another course with them. For what avails pub-
5   lic *preaching alone*, though we could preach like angels?
I heard Dr. Lupton[112] say, 'My father, visiting one of his
parishioners, who had never missed going to church for
forty years, then lying on his death-bed, asked him,
"Thomas, where do you think your soul will go?" "Soul?
10   Soul?" said Thomas. "Yes. Do not you know what your
soul is?" "Ay, surely," said he: "Why, it is a little bone in
the back that lives longer than the rest of the body." ' So
much Thomas had learned by often hearing sermons, yea,
and exceeding good sermons, for forty years!
15   We must instruct them *from house to house*. Till this is done,
and that in good earnest, the Methodists will be little better than other people.

Can we find a better method of doing this than Mr.
Baxter's?[113] If not, let us adopt it without delay.
20   His whole tract, entitled *Gildas Salvianus*,[a] is well
worth a careful perusal. A short extract from it I have subjoined. Speaking of this visiting from house to house,
he says,[114]

---

[a] P. 351–450 [in Baxter, *Gildas Salvianus* (see below, n. 113)].

[112] William Lupton (1676–1726), of Queen's College, Oxford, who graduated
B.A. (1696), M.A. (1700), B.D. (1709), and D.D. (1712) and was elected fellow of
Lincoln College in 1698. His father, Thomas Lupton, was the rector of Bentham,
where Dr. Lupton was born. Wesley probably heard him speak in London, where
he was lecturer at St. Dunstan's in the West, as well as preacher at Lincoln's Inn
and afternoon preacher at the Temple.

[113] Richard Baxter (1615–91), the famous Presbyterian divine, whose influence on
Wesley was considerable. One of his early works was *Gildas Salvianus; the first part,
i.e. The Reformed Pastor, shewing the nature of the Pastoral Work, especially in Private
Instruction and Catechizing* (London: White for Simmons, 1656). JW had probably
inherited his love of the work from his father, who inculcated Baxter's methods of
visitation in his *Advice to a Young Clergyman*, published by JW in 1735. See
Bibliography, No. 5, and Thomas Jackson, *The Life of the Rev. Charles Wesley, M.A.*,
2 vols. (London: Mason, 1841), 2:505–7, 523.

[114] Starting on p. 351 of Baxter, *Gildas Salvianus*.

We shall find many difficulties both in ourselves and in the
people.

(1) In ourselves there is much dullness and laziness; so
that there will be much ado to get us to be faithful in the
work.

(2) We have also a base, man-pleasing temper, which
makes us let men perish, rather than lose their love; and
let them go quickly to hell, lest we should anger them.

(3) Some of us have also a foolish bashfulness. We know
not how to begin, or to speak plain. We blush to speak
for Christ, or to contradict the devil, or to save a soul.

(4) Our interest stops our mouths, and makes us unfaith-
ful in the work of Christ.

(5) But the great hindrance is, weakness of faith: so our
whole motion is weak, because the spring of it is weak.

(6) Lastly, we are unskilful in the work. How few know
how to deal with men, so as to get within them, to win
upon them, and suit all our discourse to their several
conditions and tempers; to choose the fittest subjects,
and follow them with a holy mixture of seriousness,
and terror, and love, and meekness, and evangelical
allurements!

And we have as many difficulties to grapple with in our
people.

(1) Too many of them will be unwilling to be taught, till
we conquer their perverseness by the force of reason,
and the power of love.

(2) And many are so dull, that they will shun being
taught, for fear of showing their dulness. And, indeed,
you will find it extremely hard to make them understand
the very plainest points.

(3) And it is still harder to fix things on their heart, without which all our labour is lost. If you have not, therefore, great seriousness and fervency, what good can you
expect? And when all is done, it is the Spirit of grace, he
alone, who must do the work.

(4) And when we have made some impressions upon
their hearts, if we look not after them, they will soon die
away.

But as great as this labour of private instruction is, it is
absolutely necessary. For, after all our preaching, many of

our people are almost as ignorant as if they had never
heard the Gospel. I study to speak as plain as I can; yet I
frequently meet with those who have been my hearers
many years, who know not whether Christ be God or
5   man; or, that infants have original sin. And how few are
there that know the nature of repentance, faith, and holiness! Most of them have a sort of confidence that Christ
will justify and save them, while the world has their
hearts, and they live to themselves. And I have found by
10   experience, that one of these has learned more from an
hour's close discourse, than from ten years' public
preaching.
And undoubtedly this private application is implied in
those solemn words of the Apostle: 'I charge thee before
15   God, and the Lord Jesus Christ, who shall judge the
quick and the dead at his appearing and his kingdom;
Preach the word; be instant in season, out of season;
reprove, rebuke, exhort, with all long-suffering and
doctrine.'[115]
20   This is likewise necessary to the greater glory of God, by the
fuller success of the Gospel. O brethren, if we could generally set this work on foot in all our Societies, and prosecute it
skilfully and zealously, what glory would redound to God
thereby! If the common ignorance were thus banished, and
25   our vanity and idleness turned into the study of the way of
life, and every shop and every house busied in speaking of
the word and works of God, surely God would dwell in our
habitations, and make them his delight.
And this is necessary to the welfare of our people; many of
30   whom neither believe nor repent to this day. Look round
about, and see how many of them are still in apparent danger of damnation! And how can you walk, and talk, and be
merry with such people, when you know their case?
Methinks, when you look them in the face, you should break
35   forth into tears, as the Prophet did when he looked upon
Hazael, and then set on them with the most vehement and
importunate exhortations. O then, for God's sake, and for
the sake of poor souls, bestir yourselves; and spare no pains
that may conduce to their salvation.

[115] 2 Tim. 4:1-2.

What cause have we to bleed before the Lord this day, that
have so long neglected this great and good work!—that
have been preachers[116] so many years, and have done so
little by personal instructions for the saving of men's
souls! If we had but set on this work sooner, how many 5
more might have been brought to Christ! And how much
holier and happier might we have made our Societies
before now! And why might we not have done it sooner?
There were many hindrances in the way; and so there are
still, and always will be. But the greatest hindrance was in 10
ourselves, in our dullness, and littleness of faith and love.
O that God would thoroughly humble us, and cause us to
bewail our own neglects; that we may not think it enough
to lament the sins of others, while we overlook our own!
But it is objected, (1) 'This course will take up so much 15
time, that we shall have no time to follow our
studies.'
I answer, (i) Gaining knowledge is a good thing; but saving
souls is a better. (ii) By this very thing you will gain the
most excellent knowledge of God and eternity. (iii) But 20
you will have abundant time for gaining other knowledge
too, if you spend all your mornings therein. Only sleep
not more than you need; talk not more than you need.
And never be idle, nor triflingly employed. But, (iv) if you
can do but one, either follow your studies, or instruct the 25
ignorant; let your studies alone. I would throw by all the
libraries in the world, rather than be guilty of the perdition of one soul.
It is objected, (2) 'The people will not submit to it.' If some
do not, others will gladly. And the success with them may 30
be so much, as to repay all our labour. O let us herein follow the example of St. Paul: (i) For our general business,
'serving the Lord with all humility of mind.' (ii) Our special work, 'Take heed to yourselves, and to all the flock.'
(iii) Our doctrine, 'repentance toward God, and faith in 35
our Lord Jesus Christ.' (iv) The place and manner
of teaching, 'I have taught you publicly, and from
house to house.' (v) The object, and internal manner,

---

[116] Baxter, *Gildas Salvianus*, 365: 'ministers of the gospel'.

'I ceased not to warn everyone, night and day, with tears.'
This it is that must win souls, and preserve them. (vi) His
innocency and self-denial for the advantage of the Gospel,
'I have coveted no man's silver or gold.' (vii) His patience,
'Neither count I my life dear unto myself.'

And among all our motives, these should be ever before
our eyes: (i) 'The church of God, which he hath purchased with his own blood.' (ii) 'Grievous wolves shall
enter in; yea, of your ownselves shall men arise, speaking
perverse things.' Write all this upon your hearts, and it
will do you more good than twenty years' study of lower
things.

We may, (1) Every preacher take an exact catalogue of those
in society, from one end of each town to the other.[117]
(2) Go to each house, and give, with suitable exhortation
and direction, the *Instructions for Children*.[118] (3) Be sure
to deal gently with them, and take off all discouragements
as effectually as you can. See that the children get these
by heart. Advise the grown persons to see that they
understand them. And enlarge upon and apply every sentence as closely as you can. And let your dealing with
those you begin with be so gentle, winning, and convincing, that the report of it may move others to desire your
coming. True, it is far easier to preach a good sermon,
than to instruct the ignorant in the principles of religion.
And, as much as this work is despised by some, I doubt
not but it will try the parts and spirits of us all. So
Archbishop Ussher: 'Great scholars may think it beneath
them to spend their time in teaching the first principles of
the doctrine of Christ. But they should consider, that the
laying the foundation skilfully, as it is the matter of greatest importance in the whole building, so it is the very
master-piece of the wisest builder: "According to the

[117] This paragraph begins JW's extracts from chap. 7 of Baxter's *Gildas Salvianus*, 413–52.

[118] This work replaces the original 'Catechism' of Baxter's text. For JW's *Instructions for Children* (1745), apparently part original and part borrowed, see *Bibliography*, No. 101.

grace of God which is given unto me, as a wise master-
builder, I have laid the foundation", saith the great
Apostle. And let the wisest of us all try, whenever we
please, we shall find that to lay this ground-work rightly,
to make an ignorant man understand the grounds of reli-   5
gion, will put us to the trial of all our skill.'[119]
Perhaps in doing this, it may be well,
(1) After a few loving words spoken to all in the house, to
take each person singly[120] into another room, where you
may deal closely with them, about their sin, and misery,   10
and duty. Set these home, or you lose all your labour. At
least let none be present but those who are quite familiar
with each other.
(2) Hear what the children have learned by heart.
(3) Choose some of the weightiest points, and try by far-   15
ther questions how they understand them. As, 'Do you
believe you have sin in you? that you was born in sin?
What does sin deserve? What remedy has God provided
for guilty, helpless sinners?'
(4) Often, with the question, suggest the answer. As,   20
'What is repentance? Sorrow for sin, or a conviction that
we are guilty, helpless sinners? What is faith? A divine
conviction of things not seen?'
(5) Where you perceive they do not understand the
stress of your question, you must lead them into it by   25
other questions. So I have asked some, 'How do you
think your many and great sins will be pardoned?' They
answer, 'By repenting and mending my life'; and never
mention Christ. I ask farther, 'But do you think your
amendment will make satisfaction for your past sins?'   30
They will answer, 'We hope so, or else we know not what
will.' One would think now, these had no knowledge of
Christ at all. And, indeed, some have not. But others
have, and give such answers only because they do not
understand the scope of the question. Ask them farther,   35
'Can you be saved without the death of Christ?' They

[119] Baxter cites as his source (p. 423), Ussher's 'Sermon before King James at
Wansted [*sic*], on Eph. 4:13, pp. 44–45'.
[120] Orig., 'single', representing Baxter's 'by themselves' (p. 426).

immediately say, No. And if you ask, 'What has he done or suffered for you?' they will say, 'He shed his blood for us'; and profess they trust in that for salvation. But many cannot express even what they have some conceptions of; nay, can scarce learn, when expressions are put into their mouths. With these you are to deal exceeding tenderly, lest they be discouraged.

(6) If you perceive them troubled that they cannot answer, step in yourself, and take the burden off them, answering that question yourself: and then do it thoroughly and plainly, and make a full explication of the whole business to them.

(7) Thus, when you have tried their knowledge, proceed to instruct them yourself, according to their several capacities. If a man understand the fundamentals, fall on what you perceive he most needs, either explaining further some doctrine of the Gospel, or some duty, or showing the necessity of something he neglects, as may be most edifying to him. If it be one that is grossly ignorant, give him a short recital of the Christian religion in the plainest words. And if you perceive he understands not, go over it again till he does, and, if possible, fix it in his memory.

(8) Next inquire into his state, whether convinced or unconvinced; converted or unconverted. Tell him, if need be, what conversion is. And then renew and enforce the inquiry.

(9) If you perceive he is unconverted, your next business is, to labour with all your skill and power to bring his heart to a sense of his condition. Set this home with a more earnest voice than you spoke before; for, if you get it not to the heart, you do nothing.

(10) Conclude all with a strong exhortation, which must contain two parts: (i) The duty of the heart, in order to receive Christ; and (ii) the avoiding former sins, and constantly using the outward means. And here be sure, if you can, to get their promise to forsake sin, change their company, and use means. And do this solemnly; reminding them of the presence of God, that hears their promises, and will expect the performance.

(11) Before you leave them, engage the head of each family to call all his family every Sunday, before they go to bed, and hear what they can rehearse; and so continue till they have learned all the *Instructions* perfectly. And afterwards take care that they do not forget what they 5 have learned.

(12) Speak differently according to the difference of them you have to deal with, as they are dull and obstinate, or timorous and tender. Be as plain as possible to those of weak capacities, and give them Scripture-proof 10 for all you say.[121]

Let us in every town, and wherever it is practicable, set upon this method in good earnest; and we shall soon find why *the people* are not better, viz., because *we* are not more knowing and more holy. 15

Q. [30] Why are we not more knowing?

A. Because we are idle. We forget the very first rule, 'Be diligent. Never be unemployed a moment. Never be triflingly employed. Never while away time: neither spend any more time at any place than is strictly necessary.'[122] 20

I fear there is altogether a fault in this matter; and that few of us are clear. Which of you spends as many hours a day in God's work, as you did formerly in man's work? We talk, talk—or read history, or what comes next to hand.

---

[121] JW seems to have used the first edn. of 1656, chaps. 6 and 7. Chap. 6 deals with the reasons for undertaking pastoral visitation, and chap. 7 gives 'Directions for the Right Managing this Work'. JW quotes some passages fully and fairly literally, but usually he abridges heavily, substitutes synonyms for many words, strings isolated phrases into sentences, occasionally rewrites a passage completely in his own words, and renumbers what he retains. The latter two-thirds of this lengthy section has generally been mistaken for a completely original composition by JW and was so printed in the hitherto standard edn. of the 'Large' *Minutes* (London: Nichols, 1862), 2:460–78. Thomas Jackson had indicated only the first half-page as a quotation; see *Works* (Jackson), 8:302–3. The section was taken over from the 1766 annual *Minutes* into the 'Large' *Minutes* (1770), but underwent several changes in 1780. In his characteristic manner, however, JW had selected, abridged, and rewritten Baxter so as to turn a 100-page treatise into a 7-page tract. Specific 'quotations' may be traced to the following pp., in the correct order of their appearance: 351–60, 362–63, 365, 367, 388, 390, 406–7, 410–11, 420–24, 426–28, 430–33, 436–37, 440, 442, 447–50.

[122] I.e., the first of the 'Twelve Rules of a Helper' (Assistant); see Minutes (1744), §73.

We must, absolutely must, cure this evil, or give up the
whole work.

But how? (1) Read the most useful books, and that regularly
and constantly. Steadily spend all the morning in this

5   employ, or at least five hours in twenty-four.

'But I read *only* the Bible.' Then you ought to teach others
to read only the Bible, and, by parity of reason, to *hear*
only the Bible. But if so, you need preach no more. Just so
said George Bell.[123] And what is the fruit? Why, now he

10   neither reads the Bible nor anything else.

This is rank enthusiasm. If you need no book but the Bible,
you are got above St. Paul. He wanted others too. 'Bring
the books', says he, 'but especially the parchments',[124]
those wrote on parchment.

15   'But I have no taste for reading.' Contract a taste for it by
use, or return to your trade.

'But different men have different tastes.' Therefore some
may read less than others; but none should read less than
this.

20   'But I have no books.' I will give each of you, as fast as you
will read them, books to the value of five pounds. And I
desire the Assistants will take care that all the large societies provide the *Christian Library*[125] for the use of the
preachers.

25   (2) In the afternoon follow Mr. Baxter's plan.[126] Then
you will have no time to spare, none for learning Latin,
or Greek, or Hebrew—you will have work enough

---

[123] Bell was a former corporal in the Lifeguards and converted in 1758. He
preached an extreme perfectionism, claimed gifts of healing, even to raising of the
dead, and predicted the world would end in Feb. 1763. The itinerant Thomas
Maxfield supported him, and when Bell was expelled, Maxfield led a secession from
Wesley's connexion. Bell is said to have become an 'infidel' and 'radical reformer'
in later years. See *Letters* (Telford), 4:191ff., 196f., 200–3; Robert Southey, *The Life
of Wesley and the Rise and Progress of Methodism*, ed. Maurice H. Fitzgerald, 2 vols.
(London: Oxford University Press, 1925), 2:183f.; Tyerman, *Wesley*, 2:432–41;
Journal & Diaries, 21:346 and n. 42 in this edn.

[124] 2 Tim. 4:13.

[125] See above, *Minutes* (1749), §13, enjoining every Society to provide a set of
books for the Helper. In 1758, the Conference recommended that preachers read
and enlarge on the tracts in the *Christian Library* as a way of preaching. Minutes
(1758), §31, n. 1005.

[126] I.e., for house-to-house visitation, as given above, under *Q.* 29.

for all your time. Then likewise no preacher will stay
with us who is as salt that has lost its savour.[127] For to
such this employment would be mere drudgery. And in
order to it, you will have need of all the knowledge you
can procure. 5

The sum is: go into *every house* in course, and teach *everyone* therein, young and old, if they belong to us, to be
Christians, inwardly and outwardly.

Make every particular plain to their understanding. Fix it
in their memory. Write it on their heart.[128] In order to 10
this, there must be 'line upon line',[129] precept upon precept. I remember to have heard my father asking my
mother, 'How could you have the patience to tell that
blockhead the same thing twenty times over?' She
answered, 'Why, if I had told him but nineteen times, I 15
should have lost all my labour.' What patience indeed,
what love, what knowledge is requisite for this!

Q. [31]. In what method should we instruct them?

A. Read, explain, enforce,

    (1) The *Rules* of the Society. 20
    (2) *Instructions for Children.*
    (3) The fourth volume of *Sermons.*
    (4) Philip Henry's *Method* of family prayer.[130]

Over and above: wherever there are ten children in a society, spend at least an hour with them twice a week. And 25
do this, not in a dull, dry, formal manner, but in earnest,
with your might.

'But I have no gift for this'. Gift or no gift, you are to do it,
else you are not called to be a Methodist preacher. Do it
as you can, till you can do it as you would. Pray earnestly 30
for the gift, and use the means for it, particularly studying
the children's tracts.[131]

---

[127] See Matt. 5:13.

[128] Jer. 31:33.

[129] Isa. 28:10, 13.

[130] I.e., Matthew Henry. See note above, *Minutes* (1765), *Q.* 31.

[131] These were the *Instructions for Children, Lessons for Children*, and *A Token for
Children* adapted from Fleury, Poiret, and Janeway, respectively. See Minutes
(1748), §§25, 26 and nn. 618–19.

Q. [32]. Why are not *we* more holy? Why do not *we* live in eternity? Walk with God all the day long? Why are we not all devoted to God, breathing the whole spirit of *missionaries?*

5   *A*. Because we are enthusiasts, looking for the end without using the means.

In order to be throughly convinced of this, we need only consider the first *Minutes*, pp. 12–13, and each examine himself upon each article.[132]

10   To touch only upon two or three instances:

Do *you* rise at four, or even at five when you do not preach?

Do you fast once a week, once a month? Do you know the obligation, or benefit of it?

Do you recommend the five o'clock hour for private
15   prayer? Do you observe it? Do not you find that 'any time is no time'?[133]

O let us all 'stir up the gift of God that is in us'![134] Let us no more 'sleep, as do others'.[135] But whatsoever our 'hand findeth to do' let us 'do it with our might'![136]

20   London, August 22, 1766

Annual *Minutes of some late Conversations,* 1767

London, Aug. 18, etc., 1767.[137]

---

[132] See Minutes (1746), §54; cf. below, p. 820, §54.

[133] A proverbial saying. See, e.g., W. G. Benham, *Book of Quotations*: 'Any time means no time'; James Kelly, *Complete Collection of Scottish Proverbs* (1721): 'What may be done at any time will be done at no time'. Quoted by A. C. Outler in *Sermons*, 3:2 in this edn.

[134] Cf. 2 Tim. 1:6.

[135] 1 Thess. 5:6.

[136] Cf. Eccl. 9:10.

[137] Wesley wrote: 'I met in Conference with our Assistants and a select number of preachers. To these were added, on Thursday and Friday, Mr. Whitefield, Howell Harris, and many stewards and local preachers. Love and harmony reigned from

Q. 1. What preachers are admitted this year?

A. Richard Bourke, Benjamin Rhodes, John Allen,
Alexander McNab, Lancelot Harrison, Tho. Dancer.

Q. 2. Who remain on trial?

A. Will. Fugill, Tho. Halliday, and John Smith.　　　　5

Q. 3. Ought not all those who are admitted to be present at
the Conference?

A. By all means. Let it be so for the time to come. And let
them be examined one by one, as in the last year's
Conference.　　　　10

Q. 4. Who are admitted on trial?

A. T. Janes, F. Asbury,[138] Jo. Peacock, Jo. Wittam,[139] Tho.
Cherry, Will. Hunter, Will. Harry, Tho. Ryan, and Will
Collins.

Q. 5. What preachers desist from travelling?　　　　15

A. John Morley, James Stephens,[140] Simon Day, Will
Whitwell, and James Kershaw.

Q. 6. Who act as Assistants this year?

A. Benj. Colley,[141] John Easton, Duncan Wright, W. Minethorp, James Glasbrook, Alex. Mather, John Murlin,　　　　20

the beginning to the end. But we have all need of more love and holiness, and in
order thereto, of crying continually, "Lord, increase our faith!" '. *Journal & Diaries*,
22:99 in this edn. At this Conference the norm was to be one year and never above
two, but Wesley wrote to Dr. Whitehead (Aug. 15) to allow him a second year in his
circuit 'as you desired it. . . . I have considered what you say concerning the usefulness of being present at the General Conference. And I think we may steer a
middle course. I will only require a select number to be present. But I will permit
any other travelling preacher who desires it to be present with them.' *Letters*
(Telford), 5:60. To Miss Bosanquet (Aug. 16), he wrote, 'At this Conference it will
be determined whether *all* our preachers or none shall continually *insist* upon
Christian Perfection'. Ibid., 5:61. To CW (Jan. 14, 1768), he asks whether they shall
go on preaching the doctrine or drop it. Ibid., 6:93. However, there is no record in
the *Minutes* of that doctrine being discussed at this Conference.

[138] Orig., here and in stations, No. 6, 'Ashbury'.

[139] Orig., here and in stations, No. 22, 'Whittam'; in 1769, No. 28, 'Wiltam'; in
1777, No. 3, 'Wittum'; in 1779, No. 10, 'Witham'; elsewhere, 'Wittam'.

[140] Sutcliffe, MS 'History', fol. 714, places his expulsion in 1768 for drinking
and for singing profane songs and says that at age 75 he was drowned while fleeing
a warrant for his arrest. Pawson thought he was still alive in 1800. *Letters*, 3:27.

[141] Benjamin Colley or Colly, of Tollerton, Yorkshire, was converted in 1761,
ordained, and assisted JW in London and elsewhere until his death in 1767. He
was temporarily carried away by Bell and Maxfield in 1762. See Atmore, *Methodist
Memorial*, 78–80; *Journal & Diaries*, 21:347 and n. 44 in this edn.

John Furz, Sam. Woodcock, Sam. Levick, Tho. Hanby,
Tho. Taylor, J. Pawson, Tho. Johnson, Isa. Brown,
T. Mitchell, T. Rankin, John Oliver, Daniel Bumsted,
T. Brisco, Rob. Costerdine, Richard Boardman, T. Lee,
5   Jacob Rowell, James Oddie, Geo. Hudson, W. Thompson,
John Helton, James Deaves, Richard Bourke.
Q. 7. How are the preachers stationed?
A. [1][142] *London*, Will Buckingham,[143] Benj. Colley, Peter
Jaco, Nich. Manners, Tho. Janes.
10   (2) *Sussex*, John Easton, John Allen.
(3) *Canterbury*, Duncan Wright, Alex. McNab.
(4) *Colchester*, Tho. Hanson.
(5) *Norwich*, Will. Minethorp, Benj. Rhodes.
(6) *Bedfordsh[ire]*, James Glasbrook, Fran. Asbury.
15   (7) *Oxfordshire*, Richard Henderson.
(8) *Wilts.*, Alex. Mather, John Catermole, William Orpe,
Jo. Haime.[144]
(9) *Bristol*, Jo. Murlin, Peter Price.
(10) *Devon*, Jo. Furz, James Cotty.
20   (11) *Cornw[all]*, *E[ast]*, Sam Woodcock, Jo. Magor, W. Barker.
(12) *W[est]*, Sam. Levick, Jo. Davis, Jos. Harper, Tho.
Carlill.
(13) *Staffordsh[ire]*, T. Hanby, Ro. Roberts, J. W.[145]

---

[142] The London Circuit is once more unnumbered, but this year those following are numbered successively 1–2, 4–37, 37–40. These numbers have been corrected to 2–41.

[143] Although Rev. Benjamin Colley is named above as an Assistant, he is not placed at the beginning of this list, possibly because of ill health. Instead occurs (for the first and only time) the name of Rev. William Buckingham, another clergyman who served JW for only a few years. He was a Cornishman (born c. 1728), matriculated Exeter College, Oxford, 1746; B.A., 1749. JW met him in Cornwall in 1766 and said that for fear of offending the bishop, he broke with the Methodists but still lost his curacy. He is said to have preached for Lady Huntingdon and for two years joined JW but then left Methodism. However, in 1781, he was assisting JW in London with Rev. John Richardson. See *Journal* (Curnock), 5:187 and n. 2, 6:305; *Journal & Diaries*, 22:62 and n. 75 in this edn.

[144] Orig., 'Haim', though he signed his letters with an 'e'.

[145] Occasionally JW found himself, almost of necessity, stationing preachers whom he regarded as far less than ideal, and this seems to have been his reason for indicating them in the stations by initials. Isaac Waldron is thus shown in the *Minutes* (1767–77), when he was no longer stationed, though supported by the Preachers' Fund. 'I' and 'J' being almost interchangeable in 18th-century typography, he appears as 'J. W.' except in 1769 ('Is. W.') and 1776 ('I. W.'). Cf. *WHS* 10 (1916): 154–55.

(14) *Cheshire*, Tho. Taylor, Moseley Cheek.

(15) *Lancashire*, Jo. Pawson, Jo. Whitehead, Jo. Poole, Will. Fugill.

(16) *Derbyshire*, T. Johnson, James Clough, Jo. Oldham.

(17) *Sheffield*, Isaac Brown, Jo. Shaw.   5

(18) *Lincoln, E[ast]*, T. Mitchell, Jo. Standring,[146] Lancelot Harrison.

(19)   *W[est]*, T. Rankin, Jo. Ellis, Jo. Peacock.

(20) *Leeds*, Jo. Oliver, Parson Greenwood.

(21) *Birstall*, Dan Bumsted, Jo. Nelson, Tho. Brisco,[147]   10
Tho. Westell.[148]

(22) *Haworth*, Rob. Costerdine, Jos. Guilford, John Wittam, Tho. Cherry.

(23) *York*, Rich. Boardman, Jer. Robertshaw, T. Newall, James Longbottom.   15

(24) *Yarm*, T. Lee, Jo. Heslup, Matt. Lowes.

(25) *The Dales*, Jacob Rowell, Will. Brammah, Will. Hunter.

(26) *Newcastle*, James Oddie, Jos. Cownley, Will. Ellis, Will. Darney; Christo. Hopper, super[numerary].[149]   20

(27) *Wales*, Geo. Hudson, Jos. Pilmore, Will. Harry.

(28) *Glasgow*, John Atlay.

(29) *Dunbar*, Tho. Simpson, and Jos. Thompson.

Let Jo. Atlay and Jos. Thompson change the first week in February.[150]   25

[146] Orig., 'Standering', which is also found in the accounts of the Manchester Circuit (1768) 4 out of 7 times. In his letter of Nov. 12, 1768, JW spells the name 'Standring'.

[147] Both Bumsted and Brisco are listed above as Assistants.

[148] Orig., 'Westall' in both 1766 and 1767, but elsewhere 'Westell' (and in the Preachers' Fund for 1778 and 1789, 'Westel'). In the preachers' agreement of 1771, as in an extant letter of 1763, he signed himself 'Westell'.

[149] Various abbreviations were used for this title: 'super.', as here; 'sup.', as in station No. 33 this year and No. 41 in 1773; 'supern.' or 'Supern.' in 1768 and elsewhere. In 1771, the title appears twice as 'Supernum.'. The full 'Supernumerary' appears in 1772 and from 1781 almost uniformly so. In this edn., the full word 'supernumerary' is used in all instances. In several cases a supernumerary is listed in the first (or Assistant's) position in a circuit, e.g., 1781 (24). In one case, a preacher is listed as 'invalid' (1786, No. 73, Bredin).

[150] None of the three preachers stationed in these two Scots circuits is listed as an Assistant, and the Scots circuits frequently entailed more preaching from the same pulpit and less itinerancy.

(30) *Edinburgh*, Will. Thompson, Mark Davis. This circuit includes Leith, Dalkeith, Linlithgow, and Burrowstones.[151] Each preacher is to be a fortnight in the city and in the country alternately.

5 (31) *Dundee*, Richard Blackwell.

(32) *Aberdeen*, James Brownfield. Change on Michaelmas Day, Christmas Day, Lady Day and Midsummer Day: on that day let them meet at Brechin.

(33) *Dublin*, Jo. Helton, T. Olivers,[152] (J. Johnson,
10 sup[ernumerary]).

(34) *Limerick*, Jam. Deaves, Geo. Story. Let the two former change with the latter on Feb. 1.

(35) *Waterford*, Ja. Rea.

(36) *Cork*, Richard Bourke.

15 (37) *Bandon*, Jo. Mason. Change every sixth Monday without fail.

(38) *Castlebar*, W. Penington, Rob. W[illiams].

(39) *Athlone*, Ro. Swindells, Ja. Dempster. Change Feb. 1.[153]

(40) *Augher*, Jo. Dillon, Jo. Murray, Ba[rnaba]s Thomas.
20 Change every fourth Monday.

(41) *Armagh*, Tho. Ryan, Jo. Smith, John Morgan, Tho. Halliday.

Q. 8. What number are in the society at

London	2,250
Sussex	176
Kent	147
Colchester	145
Norwich	293
Bedford	208
Oxfordshire	142
Wilts.	840
Bristol	1,064
Devon	413
Cornwall, East	558
West	1,602

25, 30, 35

---

[151] Modern name Bo'ness (in full, Borrowstrounness).

[152] Orig., 'Oliver', as also in 1772; otherwise always 'Olivers'.

[153] None of the preachers is named as an Assistant, but the tradition was that the first named should assume major responsibility.

Staffordshire	906	
Cheshire	525	
Lancashire	1,875	
Derbyshire	741	
Sheffield	591	5
Epworth	769	
Grimsby	693	
Leeds	1,120	
[Birstall][154]	1,491	
Haworth	1,366	10
York	1,000	
Yarm	825	
The Dales	833	
Newcastle	1,837	
Glasgow	64	15
Dunbar	40	
Edinburgh	150	
Dundee	40	
Aberdeen	174	
Wales	2,322	20
Ireland	2,801[155]	
In all	25,911	

Q. 9. What is the Kingswood collection?

A. £121. 9*s*.   25

Q. 10. This will by no means answer the demand. What can
be done to procure a sufficient supply?

A.(1) Let every preacher seriously consider the urgency of
the case.

(2) Let the midsummer collection be made in every   30
place, great and small.

(3) Let a subscription be set on foot at Dublin,
Newcastle, Leeds, Manchester, and Liverpool.

Q. 11. What is the yearly subscription?

A. £804. 14*s*. 8½*d*.   35

[154] Orig., 'Bristol'.

[155] In the original, the figures for Ireland came at the foot of the first of two
columns, after Derbyshire, having probably been displaced from the second column
to make even columns.

Q. 12. What part of this was paid for law?[156]

A. £134. 1*s*.

Q. 13. What, to supply the necessities of the preachers?

A. £148.

Q. [14]. What is reserved for contingent expenses?

A. £30. 13*s*. 9½*d*.

Q. 15. What remained to be divided?

A. £491. 19*s*. 11*d*.

Q. 16. How many places petition for help?

A. About seventy.

Q. 17. What can be done to enlarge this collection?

A. (1) Let every Assistant begin the subscription at Christmas, and begin the collection at Easter.

(2) Let him lay the whole case before the people, and urge them to do all they can.

Q. 18. Can we make a push toward paying the whole debt?

A. I will state the case in writing to the most substantial men in our society.[157]

Q. 19. What is received this year for the Preachers' Fund?

A. £54. 14*s*. 6*d*.

Q. 20. Need any rule be added relative to this?

A. Yes. (1) Let none have any claim on this fund till it amounts to five hundred pounds.

---

[156] For early doubts about going to law, see Agenda (1744), §46, and Minutes (1744), §88. Even physically, Methodists were not always passive resisters in the face of a mob, and JW was soon prepared to go to law to defend Methodists against physical violence or magistrates who refused to register preaching-houses or, contrary to his wishes, registered them as Dissenters. For this problem see Baker, *Wesley and Church*, 198f., 316f. JW generally had greater success by appealing to the higher courts, which were more likely to uphold the principle of religious toleration than some local magistrates. The best treatment of Methodism and the law, a somewhat obscure subject, is David Hempton, *The Religion of the People: Methodism and Popular Religion, 1750–1900* (London, 1996), chap. 8.

[157] See JW's printed circular (*Bibliography*, No. 306), which was sent throughout Methodism, inscribed with covering letters, sometimes written by JW himself, sometimes by his Assistants, with JW's signature added. *Letters* (Telford), 5:65–67. The circular was dated Nov. 30, 1767, but the campaign continued for months. The scheme was suggested by 'A. H.', a 'gentleman'. Telford (ibid., 5:65) thought this was Christopher Hopper, the itinerant, apparently on the strength of JW's jocular 'appointment' of him as his 'Lord President of the North' (ibid., 5:74). But the initials and 'gentleman' status surely rule Hopper out. He may have been from Newcastle, judging by JW's letter to Oddie on Jan. 12, 1768, saying that if the debt is paid in a year, it is 'all along of your Newcastle people' (ibid., 5:75).

(2) Let it never sink lower than this.

(3) Let a preacher's widow receive yearly a sum not exceeding ten pounds during her widowhood.[158]

(4) No money shall be returned to an excluded preacher.

Q. 21. Who are the present stewards for the Preachers' Fund?[159]

A. Jos. Cownley and John Murlin.

Q. 22. Who are the present committee?

A. Peter Jaco, Duncan Wright, Tho. Hanby, Rob. Roberts, Alex. Mather, Peter Price, Tho. Johnson, John Pawson, James Oddie, Mark Davis, Tho. Olivers, Will. Penington.

Q. 23. What is the safest way of leaving a legacy for the use of these funds?

A. To leave it absolutely to a person they can confide in; suppose to Mr. Wesley.

Q. 24. When and where may our next Conference begin?

A. At Bristol, the third Tuesday in August.

Q. 25. Are our preaching-houses settled in our form safe? Should we not have the opinion of a counsel?[160]

A. I think not: (1) because the form was drawn up by three eminent counsellors.

But (2), it is the way of every counsel to blame what another counsel has done. But you cannot at all infer that they *think* it wrong because they *say* so.

(3) If they did in reality *think it wrong*, that would not prove that it *was* so.

(4) If there *was* (which I do not believe) some defect therein, who would go to law with the body of Methodists?

---

[158] This comment is the first mention of such a provision, but it is not clear how far it was carried out. No separate fund was established for it, but widows occasionally appear as being paid from the Preachers' Fund. In *Minutes* (1774), *Q*. 16, 'M. Nelson', apparently John Nelson's widow, is so paid, but only this year (in which he died); similarly Isabel Slocomb in *Minutes* (1777), *Q*. 16, though her son was supported at Kingswood School in 1778 (*Q*. 12) for that year only. The sum 'not exceeding ten pounds' was not always adhered to, and it is probable that, like wives' allowances, it was related to need. For a rare glimpse of discussions of this matter, see the cases of Sisters Barry and Mitchell at the 1790 Conference; *Minutes* (1790), n. 534 (p. 709), from Rodda MSS. See also introduction above, p. 53.

[159] The stewards were first listed in *Minutes* (1765), *Q*. 7 (3).

[160] Orig., 'council'. For the origins of the Model Deed, see *Minutes* (1765), *Q*. 11, n. 35.

(5) And if they did, would any court in England put them out of *possession*? Especially when the intent of the deed is plain and undeniable?

Q. 26. The Wednesbury trustees are afraid lest the Conference should impose on them one preacher for many years. May not this be guarded against?

A. Yes. By inserting in the deed, 'provided that the same preacher shall not be sent, ordinarily above one, never above two years together'.[161]

Q. 27. How may the books be spread more?

A. Let every Assistant give them away prudently, and beg money of the rich to buy books for the poor.

Q. 28. How may our preaching be more extensively useful?

A. Wherever we have a large preaching-house at one end of a great town, let us preach abroad at the other end of it every Sunday morning at least, if it be fair. The want of preaching abroad, and of preaching in new places, has greatly damped the work of God.

Q. 29. What can be done to revive the work?

A. (1) Let there be a general fast in all our societies on Friday, September 18.[162]

(2) Let there be such a fast once a quarter.

(3) Let any Assistant appoint an occasional fast in his circuit.

(4) Let every preacher strongly insist upon practical religion and relative duties; but in such a manner as to keep Christ continually in view.

(5) Exhort the leaders of bands to speak to those with them in the closest manner possible.

(6) Encourage all at the public meeting of the bands to speak with all openness and simplicity.

---

[161] The 'Large' *Minutes* show that no such change was made in JW's lifetime, at least in the Model Deed, though in practice the convention seems generally to have been observed. The 1784 Deed of Declaration (clause 11) lays down a maximum of three years in a circuit.

[162] There is no sign in JW's *Journal* or letters that this was implemented, and subsequent attempts at such fasts four times a year (on varying dates) had a very patchy recorded observance; see, e.g., *Minutes* (1768), §23 (7) and n. 210. There seems to be no special significance attached to the date suggested here, and the proposed observance was a purely Methodist affair, not an official national fast that Methodists also observed.

Q. 30. How may we put a stop to smuggling?

A. (1) Speak tenderly and frequently of it in every society near the coasts.

(2) Carefully dispense the *Word to a Smuggler*.[163]

(3) Expel all who will not leave it off.

(4) Silence every local preacher[164] that defends it.

Q. 31. How may we prevent bribery at the ensuing election for Members of Parliament?[165]

A. (1) Largely show the wickedness of thus selling our country, in every society.

(2) Do the same thing in private conversation.

(3) Read everywhere the *Word to a Freeholder*,[166] and disperse it, as it were, with both hands.

But observe, a voter may suffer his expenses to be borne and not incur any blame.

Q. 32. By the absence of preachers during the Conference many places have sustained much loss.[167] How may this be prevented?

A. (1) Let not all the preachers in any circuit come to the Conference.

(2) Let those who do come set out as late as possible.

(3) Let them return as soon as possible.

(4) Let none of those who are left in the circuit go out of it during the Conference. This is the most improper time in the whole year.

---

[163] See *A Word to a Smuggler* (1767); *Bibliography*, No. 300. See Rack, *Reasonable Enthusiast*, 445, for Methodist hostility to smuggling and wrecking and their temptations (as the next question suggests).

[164] On local preachers, see Minutes (1747), §65 and n. 571.

[165] Parliament was nearing the end of its maximum seven-year term and was dissolved Mar. 12, 1768.

[166] *A Word to a Freeholder* had been first published in 1747 and reprinted in 1748. After being in abeyance for some years, two new edns. were published in 1767; see *Bibliography*, No. 139. JW advocated voting for 'one that loves God' and, failing this, those supporting the king 'who is appointed to reign over us'. This stance was implicitly anti-Jacobite and marks JW as a 'Hanoverian Tory', whatever he may have been in his youth. In later years, he came out strongly against the American Revolution and the Wilkes agitations. For JW and politics see Rack, *Reasonable Enthusiast*, 370–80, and Hempton, *Religion of the People*, chap. 4.

[167] Spiritual loss, loss of interest among members, and loss of pastoral care and evangelistic enterprise are evidently intended.

Let us all be men of *one business.* We live only for this, 'to save our own souls, and them that hear us'.[168]
London, Aug. 20, 1767.

Annual *Minutes of some late Conversations,* 1768

5   Bristol, Tuesday, Aug. 16, etc., 1768[169]
Q. 1. What preachers are *admitted* this year?
A. Thomas Janes, Francis Asbury, John Peacock, John Wittam, Thomas Cherry, William Hunter, Joseph Harper, John Smith, William Collins, Thomas Halliday, and
10   William Harry.

---

[168] Cf. 1 Tim. 4:16.

[169] Wesley records, 'Our Conference began Tuesday the 16th and ended on Friday the 19th. O what can we do for more labourers? We can only cry to "the Lord of the harvest".' *Journal & Diaries*, 22:152–53 in this edn. According to John Pawson, 'all was peace, harmony and love'. Jackson, *Early Methodist Preachers*, 4:36. Although JW lamented the lack of labourers, which was apparently influenced by shortage of money, this Conference was notable for criticism of preachers engaging in trade, which was often from financial necessity. A letter from JW to CW shows great concern about whether to continue to preach Christian perfection or drop it, and the question was asked in Conference, *Q*. 23 (8), as part of a diatribe on the neglect of fasting and a list of requirements for keeping the work in motion. June 14, 1768, *Letters* (Telford), 5:93. To Thomas Adam of Wintringham, an evangelical Anglican, JW denied that most of his preachers registered under the Toleration Act and said that several of those who did avoided being classed as Dissenters. July 19, 1768, ibid., 5:97–99. Methodists were loyal to the Church and denied they were Dissenters. This issue, too, found its place among the desiderata for the work of God, *Q*. 23 ((12)) To James Morgan, JW wrote, 'I think all you said at the Conference upon the subject of the late debate was right; and it amounted to no more than this. The general rule is, they who are in the favour of God know they are so. But there may be some few exceptions'. Sept. 3, 1768, ibid., 5:103. But he thought Morgan asserted that all penitents are in the favour of God, which is neither scriptural nor Methodist doctrine. This discussion on assurance does not appear in the *Minutes*. A Thomas Taylor (not the itinerant) in New York had written in April to appeal to Conference for help in building a preaching-house in that city and for preachers to be sent. JW argued for a financial appeal to be made but could not spare preachers. Simon, *Master-Builder*, 227–31. This subject appeared not in the Conference *Minutes* (1768) but in *Minutes* (1769), *Q*. 14, and see *Minutes* (1769), n. 223.

Q. 2. Who remains on trial?
A. None.
Q. 3. Who are admitted *on trial?*
A. John Duncan, George Shadford, Jonathan Crowle, John
Goodwin, Robert Howard, Richard Seed, Samuel 5
Bardsley, Stephen Proctor, Martin Rodda, Joseph
Garnet,[170] Robert Bell, and Christopher Watkins.
Q. 4. Who desist from travelling?
A. William Fugill and John Davis.
Q. 5. Who act as *Assistants* this year? 10
A. P. Jaco, J. Glasbrook, T. Hanson, Dun. Wright, T.
Hanby, Ben. Rhodes, N. Manners, James Cotty, John
Whitehead, John Furz,[171] Sam. Levick, T. Rankin, John
Pawson, T. Brisco, A. Mather, T. Johnson, Robert
Costerdine, John Ellis, Isaac Brown,[172] J. Oliver, C. 15
Hopper, D. Bumsted,[173] T. Mitchell, Sam. Woodcock,
Jacob Rowell, Richard Boardman, James Oddie, Joseph
Pilmore, George Hudson, William Thompson,[174] T.
Simpson, John Helton,[175] R. Bourke, G. Story, John
Dillon, John Mason, T. Taylor. 20
Q. 6. Are there any objections to any of the preachers?
A. Name them one by one: (which was done).
Q. 7. How are the preachers stationed?
A. As follows:
(1) *London*, P. Jaco, John Murlin, M. Davis. 25
(2) *Sussex*, J. Glasbrook, Richard Henderson.
(3) *Kent*, Thomas Hanson, Thomas Janes.

---

[170] Orig., 'Garnett', but 'Garnet' in stations, No. 27, for all subsequent entries until he desisted in 1773, and in the Preachers' Fund for his widow, Jane (1774–78), but 'Jane Garnett' (1779–80), and Catherine (or Katherine) Garnet (1780 onwards).

[171] Orig., 'Furze' as in stations, No. 11, and also in 1781–91 except 1788, though usually with another entry in the same *Minutes* spelling his name 'Furz', which seems to be normal, as in his letter to JW, Mar. 26, 1779. *Arminian Magazine* (1789): 332f.

[172] Orig., 'James Brown'.

[173] Orig., 'Bumpsted', as also 1770 (1 of 3); 1768, station 23 has 'Daniel Bumsted'; 1769, 'Bumpstead'; 1771, 'Bumstead', although he signs the preachers' agreement that year, 'Danl. Bumsted'.

[174] Orig., 'Thomson', as in 1779; all other references in *Minutes*, 'Thompson'.

[175] Orig., 'Hilton'—strangely enough he is not listed in the stations this year. He is also listed in 1775 and 1776 as 'Bilton', though the usual spelling of his name is 'Helton', which also seems to be his signature in the preachers' agreement (1771).

(4) *Colchester*, Francis Asbury.
(5) *Norwich*, Duncan Wright, Alex. McNab.
(6) *Bedfordshire*, T. Hanby, John Duncan.
(7) *Oxfordshire*, Benj. Rhodes, Martin Rodda.
(8) *Wilts., South*, N. Manners, William Barker.
(9) *North*, James Cotty, Jonathan Crowle.
(10) *Bristol*, John Whitehead, Will. Whitwell.
(11) *Devon*, John Furz, John Magor.
(12) *Cornwall, East*, Sam Levick, John Easton, John Goodwin.
(13) *Cornwall, West*, T. Rankin, Lanc. Harrison, George Shadford, Tho. Westell.
(14) *Staffordshire*, John Pawson, J. W.,[176] John Allen.
(15) *Cheshire*, T. Olivers, William Harry, (Stephen Proctor).
(16) *Lancashire, South*, A. Mather, J. Standring.
[(17)][177]   *North*, Tho. Brisco, J. Oldham.
(18) *Derbyshire*, Thomas Johnson, John Nelson, W. Darney.
(19) *Sheffield*, Robert Costerdine, John Wittam.
(20) *Lincoln, East*, John Ellis, John Peacock, John Poole.
(21) *Lincoln, West*, Isaac Brown,[178] John Shaw, Thomas
(22) *Leeds*, John Oliver, R. Roberts.
(23) *Birstall*, C. Hopper, T. Lee, Daniel Bumsted, P. Greenwood.
(24) *Haworth*, T. Mitchell, Joseph Guilford, William Ellis, T. Newall.
(25) *York*, Samuel Woodcock, Jer. Robertshaw, James Longbottom, Sam. Bardsley.
(26) *Yarm*, Jacob Rowell, W. Brammah, Ja. Brownfield.
(27) *The Dales*, Richard Boardman, W. Hunter, Joseph Garnet, Robert Bell.
(28) *Newcastle*, J. Cownley; James Oddie,[179] supern[umerary] Mat. Lowes, J. Thompson.

---

[176] Isaac Waldron.
[177] Lancashire North is unnumbered, and the numbers of the following circuits have therefore been corrected from 17–40 to 18–41.
[178] Orig., 'James Brown'.
[179] Oddie is listed as an Assistant, but is not given at the head of the circuit preachers, apparently because he was also listed as a 'supernumerary', not taking a full load of responsibility.

(29) *Wales*, G. Hudson, Joseph Harper, Joseph Pilmore,[180] Moseley Cheek.

(30) *Dunbar*, William Minethorp.

(31) *Edinburgh*, William Thompson.

(32) *Dundee, Perth, Aberdeen*, Thomas Cherry, Thom. Simpson,[181] Robert Howard.

(33) *Glasgow*, J. Atlay.[182]

(34) *Dublin*, T. Taylor; John Johnson, supern[umerary].

(35) *Waterford*, James Dempster.

(36) *Cork*, J. Dillon, George Story.[183]

(37) *Limerick*, Richard Bourke, J. Mason.[184]

(38) *Castlebar*, W. Collins, R. W.[185]

(39) *Athlone*, Barn. Thomas, John Murray.

(40) *Augher*, T. Halliday, [John] Smith,[186] J. Rea.

(41) *Armagh*, Christopher Watkins, Hugh Saunderson,[187] Richard Seed.[188]

Q. 8. What number are in the society? At

London	2,180
Sussex	176
Kent	230
Essex	128
Norfolk	316
Bedfordshire	170
Oxfordshire	160
Wilts.	956
Bristol	1,177
Devon	384

[180] Two of these preachers are listed as Assistants, Hudson and Pilmore.

[181] The Assistant, but not at the beginning of the list.

[182] Orig., 'Atley', as in 1765; elsewhere 'Atlay', his own signed spelling.

[183] Listed as an Assistant.

[184] Listed as an Assistant.

[185] Robert Williams? Cf. *Minutes* (1765), *Q*. 22. An Irishman who was a pioneer preacher in America from Aug. 1769; cf. Baker, *From Wesley to Asbury* (Durham, N.C., 1976), 44–49. He died in 1775; *Minutes* (1776), *Q*. 6 (55), n. 618.

[186] Orig., 'Jos.'.

[187] Orig., 'Sanderson', as in 1769, but in all succeeding years to 1777, when he desisted, 'Saunderson'.

[188] Orig., 'Steel'. This seems to be Richard Seed, who was admitted on trial this year (see *Q*. 3 above). No 'Steel' is otherwise found among JW's preachers.

	Cornwall, East	543
	West	1,495
	Staffordshire	1,994
	Cheshire	484
5	Lancashire	2,000
	Derbyshire	676
	Sheffield	600
	Epworth	871
	Grimsby	707
10	Leeds	1,088
	Birstall	1,476
	Haworth	1,356
	York	1,050
	Yarm	892
15	The Dales	890
	Newcastle	1,910
	Dunbar	40
	Edinburgh	146
	Dundee	46
20	Aberdeen	150
	Perth	24
	Glasgow	76
	Wales	250
	Ireland	2,700
25	In all	27,341[189]

  Q. 9. What is the Kingswood collection?
  A. £173.
  Q. 10. What is contributed towards the debt?
30 *A.* £5,660.
  Q. 11. What part of this was paid for law?
  A. £182.
  Q. 12. What to supply the necessities of the preachers?
  A. £26.
35 *Q.* 13. What reserved for contingent expenses?
  A. £100; so that near £5,000 were paid away.
  Q. 14. What is the whole debt remaining in England,
    Scotland, and Ireland?

---

[189] Orig., '26,341', apparently an error in addition for '27,341'. These statistics are on this occasion printed in a paragraph rather than (as here reproduced) in columns.

A. As near as we can compute, it is £7,728.

Q. 15. Would it not be proper for all the deeds relating to preaching-houses to be lodged in one place?

A. Certainly it would. Let a strong box be prepared for them in London.[190]   5

Q. 16. Many have contributed largely this year, supposing the debt would be paid off at once. Can we ask these to contribute again?

A. We cannot press them; it must be left to their own generosity.   10

Q. 17. What is received this year for the Preachers' Fund?

A. £42.

Q. 18. Is it proper that none should have any claim on this fund till it amounts to £500? And that it should never sink lower than this?[191]   15

A. By no means. This is mere worldly prudence. Let those two rules be abolished.

Q. 19. Who succeeds William Penington?[192]

---

[190] See above, *Minutes* (1749), *Q.* 1, n. 724, where the first hint of such a scheme appears, already related to concern about debt and with the use of the London stewards in mind. The debt in 1768 made the matter more urgent. In connection with this a powerful London committee of stewards was set up to receive the contributions, but its proposals seemed to Wesley to go beyond their function and infringe his prerogatives. (For their proposals see Joseph Sutcliffe, MS 'History', fols. 675–81, and introduction, pp. 45–46.) As to the trust and strong box proposals, John Pawson recalled the prehistory of the Deed of Declaration; see Tyerman MSS, 3:65, notes on Pawson's MS life of Whitehead. Tyerman also includes a comment that 'over forty years ago' some of the preachers were uneasy over whether the Model Deed did secure the chapels and asked Wesley in Conference to do something about it, but he said the Deed was sufficient. Tyerman, *Wesley*, 3:420f. This did not satisfy the preachers, especially Hampson and Oddie, 'men of good judgement'. At last JW yielded a little and several matters were proposed. There was the idea of a general trust for all the chapels with trustees from the larger societies on it. Or that all the deeds should be lodged in London. Many were (he says) and then lost. Pawson used this information to answer the charge that Dr. Coke was pressing JW into the Deed of Declaration for his own advantage, by showing that the problems the Deed was designed to solve were of long standing and that abortive attempts had been made to tackle them. His recollection is also interesting evidence for the fact that there were debates in Conference, which could effect a change of mind in JW under pressure from the preachers. See also *Minutes* (1770), *Q.* 15 and n. 315.

[191] See *Minutes* (1767), *Q.* 20 (1–2).

[192] This is apparently the preacher of this name, serving as a member of the committee for the Preachers' Fund. See ibid., *Q.* 22.

A. Thomas Taylor.

Q. 20. Where and when may our next Conference begin?

A. At Leeds, the first Tuesday in August.

Q. 21. We have very imperfect accounts of all things from
5   Ireland and Scotland.[193] How may this be remedied?

A. Let the Assistants of Dublin and Edinburgh, Thomas
Taylor and William Thompson, procure, and bring or
send to the Conference, an exact account of the societies,
the yearly subscription, the collection for Kingswood, and
10   the Preachers' Fund.

Q. 22. Should itinerant preachers follow trades?[194]

A. This is an important question. And as it is the first time
it has come before us, it will be proper to consider it thoroughly. The question is not whether they may occasionally
15   work with their hands, as St. Paul did; but whether it be
proper for them to keep shop and follow merchandise. Of
those who do at present it may be observed, they are
unquestionably upright men. They are men of considerable gifts. We see the fruit of their labour, and they have a
20   large share in the esteem and love of the people. All this
pleads on their side, and cannot but give us a prejudice in
their favour. Three of these[195] urge necessity for doing
this: one that he may help his aged father, another that he
may maintain a wife, a third that he may keep his chil-
25   dren. A fourth does not plead any necessity, but a desire of
doing more good. One answered J. O., 'If you can't help
your father without trading, and if the societies either
cannot or will not, I will allow him what you allow him
now. So this necessity is at an end.' To Ja. O. it was
30   answered, 'Your wife wants nothing yet. 'Tis not likely
she ever will. You have money beforehand. So your

[193] For this complaint, see *Minutes* (1770), *Q*. 24; (1774), *Q*. 23; (1776), *QQ*. 12,
23; (1777), *Q*. 20.

[194] Some 'half-itinerants' had supported themselves legitimately by trade, but full
itinerants often had similar needs unless they had private means; in the early years,
men like John Nelson recouped finances by periodic use of their trades. See
Heitzenrater, 'Purge the Preachers', 492. The allowances recommended in 1752 were
evidently inadequate and unreliable. As the rule on trade was tightened in 1770, JW
allowed preachers to own a share in a ship. *Minutes* (1770), *Q*. 7 and n. 289.

[195] These three men, respectively, from the evidence of their initials, seem to have
been John Oliver, James Oddie, and Robert Roberts.

necessity is not yet begun.' To R. R.: 'You do not want
now. When you do want anything for your children, you
shall have it. So here is no necessity.' As to the second
plea, doing more good, it was inquired, is it not doing evil
that good may come? Is not the thing in question both evil 5
in itself (for us), and evil in its consequences? First, is it
not (with regard to travelling preachers) evil in itself? Is it
well consistent with that Scripture, 2 Tim. 2:4, 'No man
that warreth' (takes on him the profession of a soldier, as
we eminently do) 'entangleth himself with the affairs of 10
this life'; plainly referring to the Roman law which
absolutely forbade any soldier to follow any other profession. Is it well consistent with that word, 'Give attendance
to reading, to exhortation, to teaching; meditate on those
things, give thyself wholly to them'?[a] Can we be said to 15
give ourselves wholly to these things if we follow another
profession? Does not our Church in her Office of
Ordination require every minister to do this?[196] If they do
not, the more shame for them. But this plainly shows
what both they and we ought to do. *We* indeed more par- 20
ticularly, because God has called *us* to 'provoke them to
jealousy',[197] to supply their lack of service to the sheep
that are as without shepherds,[198] and to spend and be
spent[199] therein. We above all; because every travelling
preacher solemnly professes to have nothing else to do; 25
and receives his little allowance for this very end, that he
may not need to do anything else, that he may not be
entangled in the things of this life, but may give himself
wholly to these things.[200]

Secondly, is it not evil in its consequences? Have not some 30
ill consequences appeared already? And is there not the
greatest reason to apprehend that still worse would follow? We are concerned to give no offence, either to Jew or
Gentile, or to the Church of God. But this has already

---

a. 1 Tim. 4:13, 15.

[196] BCP, from the bishop's address to the ordinand to the priesthood.
[197] Rom. 11:11.
[198] See Matt. 9:36, and so on.
[199] 2 Cor. 12:15.
[200] 2 Tim. 2:4.

offended not only many of the world, but many of our
own brethren. Many of the preachers in particular have
been much grieved. Yea, and those most who were most
alive to God. Now the beginning of offence is as when one

5   letteth out water.[201] Who can gather it up again? They are
grieved the more because they apprehend this would be
an increasing evil. For where will it stop? If one preacher
follows trade, so may twenty; so may everyone. And if any
of them trade a little, why not ever so much? Who can fix

10   how far he should go? Therefore we advise our brethren
who have been concerned herein to give up all and attend
to the one business. And we doubt not but God will recompense them an hundredfold,[202] even in this world, as
well as in the world to come.[203]

15   It is true, this can't be done on a sudden. But it may
between this and the next Conference. And even as to the
drops[204] that many sold, if their wives sell them at home,
well; but it is not proper for any preacher to hawk them
about. It has a bad appearance. It does not well suit the

20   dignity of his calling.

    Q. 23. In many places the work of God seems to stand still.
What can be done to revive and enlarge it?

    A. (1) Much good has been done by the books which have
been published, and more would be, if they were spread

25   more effectually. At present there is a grand defect
herein, almost all over Great Britain and Ireland.
Thousands of our brethren never saw or heard of the
most useful books we have printed. Many have heard of
them, but cannot have them, though they have desired it

30   over and over. Little can be done to remedy this, unless
all of you will lend an helping hand. You may do this by
recommending reading to all the people, frequently and
earnestly; not only in general, but reading this or that
tract in particular; by reading a page or two of a book in

35   the congregation, and then recommending it; by

---

[201] Prov. 17:14.

[202] See Matt. 19:29.

[203] See Eph. 1:21.

[204] Matthew Lowes, for instance, whose proprietary medicine, 'Lowes' Balsam', continued in use in the North for a century after his death. Cf. Tyerman, *Wesley*, 3:71, n. 2.

carrying round with you this or that book, suitable to the
subject of your sermon; by begging money of the rich to buy
tracts for the poor, and giving them away prudently; and by
recommending none but those which we recommend, and
selling none else, which will effectually prevent the improper 5
publications either of itinerant or local preachers.

(2) Let there be more field preaching. Without this the
work of God will hardly increase in any place.

(3) Let the preaching at five in the morning be constantly kept up, wherever you can have twenty hearers. 10
This is the glory of the Methodists. Whenever this is
dropped they will dwindle away into nothing. Rising
early is equally good for soul and body. It helps the
nerves better than a thousand medicines; and in particular preserves the sight, and prevents lowness of spirits 15
more than can well be imagined.

(4) As soon as there are four men or women believers in
any place, put them into a *band*. These need to be inquired
after continually, and the place of any that do not meet supplied. In every place where there are bands, meet them 20
constantly, and encourage them to speak without reserve.

(5) Be conscientiously exact in the whole Methodist discipline. And, that you may understand it, read over carefully the *Plain Account of the People Called Methodists*,[205]
and the several *Minutes* of the Conferences. 25

One part of our discipline has been generally neglected, namely
the changing of the stewards. This has been attended with ill
consequences. Many stewards have been ready to ride over
the preacher's head. Let every Assistant at the next Quarterly
Meeting change one steward at least in every society, if there 30
be therein any other man that can keep an account.

(6) Beware of formality in singing, or it will creep in
upon us unawares. Is it not creeping in already, by those
complex tunes which it is scarce possible to sing with
devotion? Such is 'Praise the Lord ye blessed ones'.[206] 35
Such the long quavering hallelujah annexed to the

---

[205] Published in 1749; see *Bibliography*, No. 156, and vol. 9 of this edn.

[206] This is the first line of hymn No. 33 in *Hymns for those that seek and those that
have Redemption* (1747), for which the tune originally suggested in the publication
was 'Praise the Lord, who reigns above', these words also being by Charles Wesley.

Morning Song tune,[207] which I defy any man living to
sing devoutly. The repeating the same word so often (but
especially while another repeats different words, the horrid abuse which runs through the modern church music),
as it shocks all common sense, so it necessarily brings in
dead formality, and has no more of religion in it than a
Lancashire hornpipe. Beside that, it is a flat contradiction
to our Lord's command, 'Use not vain repetitions.'[208] For
what is vain repetition, if this is not? What end of devotion does it serve? Again. Do not suffer the people to sing
too slow.[209] This naturally tends to formality, and is
brought in by those who have very strong or very weak
voices. Is it not possible that all the Methodists in the
nation should sing equally quick? Why should not the
Assistant see that they be taught to sing in every large
society? And do this in such a manner as to obviate the ill
effects which might otherwise spring therefrom?

(7) Let a fast be observed in all our societies on Friday,
September 30, and on the Friday after New Year's Day,
after Lady Day, and after Midsummer Day next.[210]

(8) Which of us 'fasts every Friday in the year'?[211] Which

---

[207] 'Morning Song', as set in Wesley's *Sacred Melody* of 1761 (p. 29, hymn No.
51, set to 'When all thy mercies'), had no 'quavering hallelujah' at the end, nor in
his *Sacred Harmony*, published 1780. These remarks are significant because they
show that rank-and-file Methodist taste was in conflict with JW's ideals. There is
also evidence that folk tunes and tunes from contemporary popular songs were used
by revivalists in this as in other periods of history. A few even crept into official
Methodist hymn-books. See Rack, *Reasonable Enthusiast*, 414–16.

[208] Matt. 6:7.

[209] Cf. Wesley's *Directions* for congregational singing (1761), of which the sixth was
'Sing in time . . . ; and take care you sing not *too slow*. This drawling way naturally
steals on all who are lazy; and it is high time to drive it out from among us, and sing
all our tunes just as quick as we did at first.' See 7:765 of this edn. (Appendix H).

[210] See also *Minutes* (1767), *Q.* 29 and n. 162. Friday, Sept. 30, 1768, was held
(*Journal & Diaries*, 22:160 in this edn.), but there are no *Journal* entries for the
first Friday in 1769, Mar. 25 (Lady Day, the Feast of the Annunciation), or June
24. A further attempt at quarterly fasts was made in *Minutes* (1777), *Q.* 26.

[211] The BCP has a 'Table of the Vigils, Fasts and Days of Abstinence' in the year.
They were generally kept in the 16th and 17th centuries, and as late as Archbishop
Sheldon (1663–77), dispensations were given from the Lenten fasts. F. L. Cross and
E. A. Livingstone, *Oxford Dictionary of the Christian Church* (Oxford: Oxford
University Press, 1993), 'Fasts'. Under Nonjuror influence, Wesley at Oxford observed
the 'station days' fasts—i.e., on Wednesday and Friday (*Letters*, 25:334 in this edn.).

of us fasts at all? Does not this show the present temper of
our minds (though not of all) soft and unnerved? How
then can we advance the work of God, though we may
preach *loud* and long enough? Here is: the root of the evil.
Hence the work of God droops; few are convinced, few   5
justified, few of our brethren sanctified. Hence more and
more doubt if we are to be sanctified at all till death—I
mean sanctified throughout, saved from all sin, perfected
in love. That we may all speak the same thing, I ask once
for all, shall we defend this perfection or give it up? You   10
all agree to defend it, meaning thereby, as we did from the
beginning, salvation from all sin, by the love of God and
our neighbour filling the heart. The Papists say, 'This
can't be attained till we have been a sufficient time in purgatory.' The Dissenters say, 'Nay it will be attained as   15
soon as the soul and body part.' The old Methodists said,
'It may be attained *before* we die: a moment after is too
late.'[212] Is it so or no? You are all agreed, we may be saved
from all sin *before death*. The substance then is settled.
But as to the circumstance, is the change instantaneous or   20
gradual? It is both one and the other. From the moment
we are justified there may be a *gradual sanctification*, or a
growing in grace, a daily advance in the knowledge and
love of God. And if sin ceased before death, there must in
the nature of the thing be an instantaneous change. There   25
must be a last moment wherein it does exist, and a first
moment wherein it does not. But should we in preaching
insist on both one and the other? Certainly we must insist
on the gradual change; and that earnestly and continually.
And are there not reasons why we should insist on the   30
instantaneous also? If there be such a blessed change
before death, should we not encourage all believers to
expect it? And the rather because constant experience
shows, the more earnestly they expect this, the more
swiftly and steadily does the gradual work of God go on   35
in their souls. The more watchful they are against all sin,
the more careful to grow in grace, the more zealous of

---

[212] Cf. Minutes (1745), §§42, 43, allow that it may be attained only just before
death but can and should be earlier. Some preachers put forward extreme views of
perfection, which JW criticized; for examples, see *Letters* (Telford), 4:10.

good works,[213] and the more punctual in their attendance
on all the ordinances of God. Whereas just the contrary
effects are observed whenever this expectation ceases.
They are 'saved by hope',[214] by this hope of a total
change saved with a gradually increasing salvation.
Destroy this hope, and that salvation stands still, or
rather decreases daily. Therefore whoever would advance
the gradual change in believers should strongly insist
upon the instantaneous.

(9) But how far from entire sanctification are we still?
The religion of the Methodists in general is not internal;
at least not deep, universal, uniform, but superficial, partial, uneven. And what pains do we take to make it otherwise? Do we visit from house to house according to the
plan laid down in the *Minutes*?[215] Have you done this?
Mr. Colley[216] begun; but he is gone to paradise. And who
has trod in his steps? What hinders? Want of time? Only
(William Penington[217] said) spend half the time in *this
visiting* which you spend in talking uselessly, and you will
have time enough. Do this, particularly in confirming
and building up believers. Then, and not till then, the
work of the Lord will prosper in your hands.[218]

(10) But what can we do for the *rising generation*? Unless
we can take care of these the present revival of religion
will be *res unius aetatis*.[219] It will last only the age of a
man. Who will *labour* herein? Let him that is zealous for
God and the souls of men begin *now*.

---

[213] Titus 2:14.
[214] Rom. 8:24.
[215] See *Minutes* (1766), *Q.* 29.
[216] Rev. Benjamin Colley. See *Minutes* (1767), *Q.* 6 and n. 141.
[217] JW's preacher of that name.
[218] Isa. 53:10.
[219] 'an event of one age only'. Cf. Sermon 94, 'On Family Religion', §3, where he speaks of this as the remark of a Roman historian, and compares Luther's state-ment that 'a revival of religion never lasts longer than one generation'. Cf. *Letters* (Telford), 6:339 (in 1779), 'seldom continues above thirty years'; also Sermon 63, 'The General Spread of the Gospel', §16. The 'Roman historian' appears to be Cicero, writing of the Roman state in *De Re Publica*, I.viii; Luther's remark comes in *Festpostille* (1525), WA, 17/2: 179, ll. 28–29; cited in Outler's notes in *Sermons*, 2:492; 3:335 in this edn.

(i) Spend an hour a week with the children in every large town, whether you like it or no.

(ii) Talk with them every time you see any at home.

(iii) Pray in earnest for them.

(iv) Diligently instruct and vehemently exhort all parents at their own houses.

(v) Preach expressly on this, particularly at midsummer when you speak of Kingswood.[220]

(11) Let every preacher read carefully over the life of Mr. Brainerd.[221] Let us be followers of him as he was of Christ, in absolute self-devotion, in total deadness to the world, and in fervent love to God and man. We want nothing but this. Then the world and the devil must fall under our feet.

(12) Lastly, (i), let us keep to the Church. Over and above all the *Reasons* that were formerly given for this,[222] we add another now from long experience: they that leave the Church leave the Methodists. The clergy cannot separate us from our brethren; the dissenting ministers can and do. Therefore carefully avoid whatever has a tendency to separate men from the Church: in particular, preaching at any hour which hinders them from going to it. Let every Assistant look to this.

(ii) Let all the servants in our preaching-houses go to church on Sunday morning at least.

(iii) Let every preacher go always on Sunday morning, and when he can in the afternoon. God will bless those who go on week-days too, as often as they have opportunity.

[220] I.e., in promoting the annual collection for the school.

[221] In 1749 Rev. Jonathan Edwards (1703–58) published the autobiography of Rev. David Brainerd (1718–47), missionary to the Native Americans in New England. It appeared in Edinburgh in 1765, and in 1768 JW published a lengthy *Extract of the Life of the late Rev. Mr. David Brainerd, Missionary to the Indians*, of which he thought so highly that it occupies almost the whole of JW's own *Works*. *Bibliography*, No. 310.

[222] I.e., 'Reasons against a Separation from the Church of England' (1758); see *Bibliography*, No. 191:13 and vol. 9 of this edn.

Annual *Minutes of some late Conversations*, 1769

Leeds, Tuesday, Aug. 1, etc., 1769.[223]

Q. 1.[224] What preachers are admitted this year?

A. George Shadford, Robert Howard, John[225] Goodwin,
5   Richard Seed, Samuel Bardsley, Stephen Proctor, Martin
Rodda, Joseph Garnet Christopher Watkins, and Francis
Wolf.

Q. 2. Who remain on trial?

A. John Duncan and Thomas Wride.

10   *Q.* 3. Who are admitted *on trial?*

A. William Pitt, William Ashman, William Whitaker,
Samuel Wells, James Hudson, Francis Wrigley, Samuel
Smith, Robert Wilkinson, Thomas Dixon, Jon. Hern,
John Bredin,[226] and John McNeese.

---

[223] Wesley reported in his *Journal* (22:197 in this edn.),
'On Monday 31, prepared all things for the ensuing Conference. Tuesday,
August 1, it began, and a more loving one we never had. On Thursday, I
mentioned the case of our brethren in New York, who had built the first
Methodist preaching house in America and were in great want of money but
more of preachers. Two of our preachers, Richard Boardman and Joseph
Pilmore, willingly offered themselves for the service, by whom we determined to send them 50 pounds in token of our brotherly love.' (See *Minutes*
[1768], n. 169, and below, *Q.* 13)

Thomas Rankin reveals that he and 'Mr Helton' were to accompany Wesley on
his travels. His 'plan and design was if, in any place which he visited there was any
particular divine influence upon the congregation or society, to leave one of us there
for a few days'. Jackson, *Early Methodist Preachers*, 5:181. To Whitehead, JW wrote,
'One for every circuit must be to Conference . . . I think that money need not be
brought; only let us have exact accounts and lists of the societies'. July 4, 1769,
Letters (Telford), 5:141. More than two days of the Conference were spent in temporal matters. This annoyed JW, who directed that in future as much as possible of
such business was to be done by secretaries before Conference met. See *Q.* 20,
below. At the conclusion of the Conference, writes JW, 'all the preachers were
melted down, while they were singing those lines for me—"Thou, who so long hast
saved me here, / A little longer save . . ."' (to Miss March, Aug. 12, 1769, *Letters*
[Telford], 5:147).

[224] Orig., '1st'.

[225] Orig., 'James'.

[226] Orig., 'Bradin', in all entries 1769–73 and 1775; and 'Breden' in 1776 and in
one entry of two in 1790. Elsewhere his name is spelled 'Bredin', including his
years as a supernumerary after JW's death. This is how he signs himself in a letter
of Aug. 13, 1782, and how JW addresses him.

Q. 4. Who desists from travelling?
A. Mark Davis,[227] John Whitehead,[228] William Whitwell, Jonathan[229] Crowle, John Peacock, and Joseph Thompson.
Q. 5. Who act as Assistants this year?
A. Peter Jaco, Thomas Rankin, John Easton, Richard   5
Henderson, Benjamin Rhodes, John Mason, John Furz,
John Helton, Samuel Levick, T. Westell, T. Hanson, James
Glasbrook, John Shaw, William Pitt, James Dempster,
Alexander Mather, Thomas Olivers, William Minethorp,
Parson Greenwood, Thomas Johnson, Isaac Brown, Daniel   10
Bumsted, Christopher Hopper, John Oliver, Thomas
Mitchell, Joseph Guilford, Robert Howard, Jac. Rowell,
Joseph Cownley, Matthew Lowes, Thomas Simpson,
Duncan Wright, John Dillon, Hugh Saunderson, Thomas
Halliday, William Harry, and William Collins.   15
Q. 6. Are there any objections to any of the preachers?
A. Name them one by one: (which was done).
Q. 7. How are the preachers stationed?
A. As follows:
   (1) *London*, John Pawson, John Allen, James Stephens.[230]   20
   (2) *Sussex*, Thomas Rankin, Thomas Janes.
   (3) *Kent*, Peter Jaco, George Shadford.
   (4) *Essex*, (John Easton)
               change every fourth week.

---

[227] Mark Davis set up a school, though serving for many years as a local preacher in London. He entered Holy Orders, and in 1772 JW sought his full-time assistance in London. *WHS* 23 (1941): 7–14. In 1791 he published *Thoughts on Dancing*, defending the practice against rigid Methodist prohibition. He died Nov. 7, 1803, age 68.

[228] John Whitehead (1740?–1804) became a linendraper in Bristol, moved to London, where he joined the Friends, took a medical degree at Leyden (1780), and became physician to the London Dispensary. He attended the Wesleys as their medical adviser, and in 1784 he returned to Methodism. He preached JW's funeral sermon and, as one of JW's literary executors, wrote his life in two vols. (1792, 1796). See further, *Journal & Diaries*, 23:340, n. 80 in this edn.

[229] Orig., 'John', as also in 1773. The 'Jonathan Crowle' who was admitted on trial in 1768, signed the preachers' agreement thus in 1771, and desisted in 1776 is apparently the same person as the 'John Crowle' who desisted in 1769 and was stationed (as 'John Crowle') in Wiltshire, North, in 1773. It was not unusual for a man to 'desist' for a year or a few months only, and to return to the itinerancy without any other mention of the hiatus, as did the following two men, John Peacock and Joseph Thompson, each of whom was stationed after a year's absence.

[230] No Assistant listed in *Q.* 5 appears in this circuit.

(5) *Norfolk*, (John Murray)

(6) *Bedfordshire*, Richard Henderson, Francis Asbury.

(7) *Oxfordshire*, Benjamin Rhodes, Richard Whatcoat.[231]

(8) *Wiltshire, South*, John Mason, Thomas Brisco.[232]

5   (9)   *North*, John Furz, James Cotty, Martin Rodda.

(10) *Bristol*, John Helton, Barnaby Thomas, Samuel Wells.

(11) *Devonshire*, Samuel Levick, Francis Wolf.

(12) *Cornwall, East*, Thomas Westell, William Ashman.

10   (13)   *West*, Thomas Hanson, John Goodwin, William Brammah, James Hudson.

(14) *Staffordshire*, Ja. Glasbrook, Ja.Clough, Jeremiah Robertshaw, Francis Wrigley.

(15) *Cheshire*, John Shaw, Richard Seed, Samuel

15   Bardsley.

(16) *Wales, East*, William Pitt,[233] William Barker.

(17)   *West*, James Dempster, William Whitaker.

(18) *Lancashire, South*, Alexander Mather, Robert Costerdine, George Story.

20   (19)   *North*, Thomas Olivers, John Morgan.

---

[231] Orig., 'Walcot'. His name also appears in the *Minutes* as 'Watcot', 1773, 1774; 'Walcott', 1770, 1771, 1772; 'Whatcot', 1773, 1774; 'Watcoat', 1775; and 'Whatcoat' once in 1773 and in 1774, and then uniformly, 1776–91. (In 1774 three different spellings are given.)

[232] Orig., 'Briscoe', as also for one entry each in 1772, 1774, 1784, 1785; for two entries each in 1787, 1788; and three in 1789, as well as in the Preachers' Fund entries for 1790–91. He himself signed a letter to CW in 1760 and the preachers' agreement of 1771 as 'Brisco', and JW used the same spelling in a letter to him, Mar. 12, 1782.

[233] William Pitt to Samuel Bardsley, Feb. 23, 1770 (in MA); from 'Newhouse old Radnor':

'The preachers in Wales were stationed after Mr Wesley came thro' it as follows: Brother Barker and Whitaker for Pembroke; I and Mr Dempster for the Glamorganshire Circuit, but while I was in the Circuit I recvd a letter from Mr Wesley to retire to Brecknock; (and he sent Martan Roda's Brother to be with Brother Dempster, but they have now changed with each other) and endeavour to open a communication with your circuit, but for some reasons I gave Mr Wesley he left it entirely to myself to act as God should direct me'.

Here it seems that JW is personally changing the stations at the end of about half a year, on the idea of two stations a year for some preachers and areas. This emphasizes the flexible nature of stationing (see introduction, pp. 83–84).

(20) *Derbyshire*, William Minethorp, Samuel Woodcock, Sam. Smith, Tho. Barnes.

(21) *Sheffield*, Parson Greenwood, James Longbottom.

(22) *Lincolnshire, East*, Thomas Johnson, John Poole, William Ellis.   5

(23)   *West*, Isaac Brown, John Ellis,[234] Joseph Garnet.

(24) *Leeds*, Daniel Bumsted, Is[aac] W[aldron].

(25) *Birstall*, Christopher Hopper, Robert Roberts.

(26) *Bradford*, John Oliver, Thomas Lee.

(27) *Haworth*, Thomas Mitchell, George Hudson,   10
Thomas Wride, David Evans.

(28) *Whitehaven*, Joseph Guilford, John Wittam.

(29) *York*, Robert Howard, Thomas Carlill,[235] N. Manners, Joseph Fothergill.[236]

(30) *Yarm*, Jacob Rowell, James Brownfield,[237] William   15
Hunter.

(31) *[The] Dales*, Matthew Lowes, Joseph Harper, James Wiltam.[238]

(32) *Newcastle*, Joseph Cownley, John Murlin, John Nelson, Thomas Hanby; James Oddie, supern[umerary].   20

(33) *Dunbar*, Thomas Simpson.

(34) *Edinburgh*, John Atlay.

(35) *Dundee, Perth*,[239] *Aberdeen*, Duncan Wright, Alexander McNab, Thomas Cherry,[240] Lancelot Harrison.   25

(36) *Glasgow*, William Thompson.

(37) *Dublin*, J. Dillon; John Johnson, supern[umerary].

(38) *Waterford*, (H. Saunderson, Jon. Hern.)

Feb. 1, let T. Taylor go to Limerick,

[234] Dixon MS Minutes have Lancelot Harrison listed here, and John Ellis in The Dales and Joseph Harper in Dundee.

[235] Orig., 'Carlisle', here and in 1772. All other references are to 'Carlill'.

[236] This is his only recorded appointment. He desisted in 1770, but was readmitted on trial in 1776. Cf. *MM* (1806), 524.

[237] Orig., 'Bromfield'. All other references are to 'Brownfield'. He desisted in 1770.

[238] This might possibly be an error for John Wittam, who is stationed in Whitehaven, a circuit in the same general area, which sprang from the Haworth Circuit. For Wittam, misspelled 'Wiltam', in No. 28, see p. 343, n. 139 above.

[239] Dixon MS Minutes insert 'Arbreath' in this list.

[240] Orig., 'Cheny'. There is no other mention of this name, which is surely an error for 'Cherry', which is the reading in Dixon MS Minutes.

    (39) *Cork*,   (Tho. Taylor, St. Proctor.   )
                        S. Proctor go to Waterford, and
    (40) *Limerick*, (Richard Bourke.   )
                        R. Bourke and H. Saunderson to Cork.
    (41) *Castlebar*, Thomas Dixon, John Bredin.[241]
    (42) *Athlone*, Thomas Newall, Christopher Watkins.[242]
    (43) *Enniskillen*,[243] George Snowden, James Rea.[244]
    (44) *Derry*, Thomas Halliday, John Smith.
    (45) *Augher*, William Harry, Robert Wilkinson.
    (46). *Armagh*, William Collins, John Duncan, John McNees.
Q. 8. What numbers are in the society?
A. They are as follow:

London	2,391
Sussex	181
Kent	252
Essex	134
Norfolk*	290
Bedfordshire	260
Oxfordshire	314
Wilts., South	200
North	814
Bristol	1,165
Devonshire	433
Cornwall, East	630
West	1,600
Staffordshire	1,090
Cheshire	575
Lancash[ire], South	1,340
North*	607
Wales	300
Derbyshire	721
Sheffield*	595[245]

[241] This preacher is not listed among the Assistants in *Q*. 5.

[242] This preacher is not listed among the Assistants in *Q*. 5.

[243] Orig., 'Iniskillin', as in 1770–72, 1773 (1 of 2), and 1778; the name appears as 'Inniskillen' in 1773 (1 of 2), 1779, 1782, 1783 (1 of 2), 1784 (1 of 2), 1786 (1 of 2), and 1788 (1 of 2); as 'Iniskillen' in 1774–77, 1780, 1783 (1 of 2), 1784 (1 of 2), 1785, 1786 (1 of 2); in 1781 once as 'Inniskilling' and once as surely 'Inniskillin'; and as 'Enniskillen' only in 1787, 1788 (1 of 2), and 1789–91.

[244] This preacher is not listed among the Assistants in *Q*. 5.

[245] Here, at the foot of the first of two columns is the total 13,892, and the second column begins 'Bro[ugh]t forward 13,892'.

Epworth	757			
Grimsby	747			
Leeds	1,156			
Birstall	859			
Bradford	732			5
Haworth	1,296			
Whitehaven	163			
York	1,130			
Yarm	1,031			
The Dales	896			10
Newcastle	1,924			
Dunbar	36			
Edinburgh	130			
Glasgow	85			
Perth	25			15
Dundee	28			
Aberdeen	150			
Arbroath*[246]	73			
Ireland	3,120			
In all	28,263			20

N.B. in the circuits marked thus * there are fewer members than there were a year ago. [In 1781 Wesley changed this principle by a note: 'N.B. The circuits marked thus * are increased this year.'] 25

Q. 9. What is the Kingswood collection?

A. £187. 13*s.* 10*d.*

Q. 10. What is contributed towards the debt?

A. £2,458. 19*s.* 7*d.*

Q. 11. How was this distributed? 30

A. As follows:

	£.	s.	d.	
Law[247]	300			
Prea[chers'] Neces[sities]	77	5	3	35

---

[246] Orig., 'Arbroth', as also once each in 1770, 1774, 1775, 1779.

[247] For JW's use of the law, see *Minutes* (1767), *Q.* 12 and n. 156. Although he probably appealed to it mainly in defence of Methodism (e.g., against mob attacks), some internal disputes may have required legal fees. They would be required for the Birstall Chapel case; see *Minutes* (1782), *Q.* 22 and n. 946; and Tyerman, *Wesley*, 3:373–82. In the Dewsbury Chapel case (1788), the rebels took over the chapel, and the Conference raised funds to build another for the connexion. *Minutes* (1788), n. 327; (1789), *Q.* 24; Tyerman, *Wesley*, 3:551–61. For enrolling the Model Deed, the Society concerned paid the legal expenses. *Minutes* (1788), *Q.* 25 (see N.B. at end).

	New York[248]	50	0	0
	London	126	7	6
	Wan[d]sworth	10	0	0
	Colchester	2	10	6
5	Norwich	71	5	9
	Bedfordshire	5	5	0
	Oxfordshire	10	0	0
	Portsmouth	20	17	0
	Bradford	20	0	0
10	Shaft[e]sbury	15	0	0
	Shepton Mallet[249]	15	0	0
	Cullompton	11	5	0
	Hil[l]farance[250]	5	0	0
	Axminster[251]	5	0	0
15	E[ast] Cornwall	61	0	0
	West	76	0	0
	Wednesbury	25	0	0
	Darlington	15	0	0
	Wolverhampton	10	0	0
20	Stroud	9	0	0
	Chester	9	0	0
	Burslem[252]	70	0	0
	Congleton	20	0	0
	Macclesfield and			
25	Stockport[253]	30	0	0
	Derby	150	0	0
	Nottingham	7	7	0
	Burton	4	8	6
	Sheffield	8	0	0
30	Rotherham	29	0	0
	Bradwell	9	0	0
	Boston	22	0	0
	Louth	20	0	0

[248] See *QQ*. 13–14 below.

[249] Orig., 'Shipton M.' and 'Shipton' in 1772, 1773. The name also appears as 'Shepton' in 1766; as 'Sheptonmallet' in 1788; and as 'Shepton-mallett' in 1791 (1 of 4).

[250] Orig., 'Hilfarance'; the name appears as 'Hilfarence' in 1770, 1772.

[251] Orig., 'Aixminster'.

[252] Orig., 'Boxlem'.

[253] Orig., 'Stopport'.

Horncastle	30	0	0	
Leeds	30	0	0	
Horbury	30	0	0	
Rothwell	12	0	0	
Seacroft	12	0	0	5
Thorner	8	16	2	
Birstall	43	10	6	
Dawgreen[254]	50	0	0	
Morley	30	0	0	
Thong[255]	104	0	0	10
Whitehaven	18	18	6	
Bingley	10	0	0	
Heptonstall	40	0	0	
Padiham	10	0	0	
Bradford	60	0	0	15
Halifax	6	1	5	
Yarm	14	14	0	
Whitby	70	0	0[256]	
R. Bell[257]	5	0	0	
Stokesley	10	0	0	20
Hutton	10	6	7	
Stockton	40	0	0	
Thirsk	20	16	6	
Monkwearmouth	94	7	11	
Edinburgh[258]	49	16	6	25
Dundee	8	0	0	
St. Daniel's[259]	21	0	0	
Ireland	300	0	0	
	£ 2,458	19	7	

[254] I.e., in Dewsbury.

[255] Cf. *Minutes* (1772), *Q.* 11. A village just south of Fulneck and east of Westgate Hill, Yorkshire.

[256] Intermediate totals are given at the feet of three columns on pp. 8–9 of orig.: after Stroud, £940. 16. 0.; after Morley, £1,565. 18. 2; and after Whitby, £1,899. 12. 1.

[257] R. Bell is probably Robert Bell, an exciseman, converted by William Grimshaw, who introduced Methodism into Carlisle in 1767. JW to Bell, Dec. 2, 1769, *Letters* (Telford), 5:163f.; *Journal* (Curnock), 5:349 n. 1; Tyerman, *Wesley*, 3:63; *WMM* (1847): 768.

[258] Orig., 'Edinbro', and in 1770, 'Edinbrough'.

[259] Orig., 'St. Daniels', as in 1770.

Q. 12. What is reserved for contingent expenses?

A. Nothing.[260]

Q. 13. We have a pressing call from our brethren at New York (who have built a preaching-house), to come over and help them.[261] Who is willing to go?

A. Richard Boardman and Joseph Pilmore.

Q. 14. What can we do further in token of our brotherly love?

A. Let us now make a collection among ourselves. This was immediately done, and out of it fifty pounds were allotted towards the payment of their debt,[262] and about twenty pounds given to our brethren for their passage.

Q. 15. What is the whole debt remaining?

A. Between five and six thousand pounds.

Q. 16. What is contributed towards the Preachers' Fund?

A. £48. 16*s.* 6*d.*

Q. 17. Who may succeed Mark Davis?[263]

A. John Helton and Christopher Hopper.

Q. 18. Who may be clerks for this,[264] and for the money collected on account of the debt?[265]

---

[260] Perhaps because of the scheme for clearing the debt? See below, *Q.* 19.

[261] For details of Thomas Taylor's letter to JW from New York, Apr. 11, 1768, appealing for help for the infant Society there, and its result, see F. Baker, *From Wesley to Asbury*, 76–83, and *Minutes* (1768), n. 169. Richard Boardman (1738–82), an itinerant since 1763, had been Assistant in The Dales circuit. He returned home in 1774 and spent most of the rest of his career in Irish circuits. Joseph Pilmore (1739–1825) was converted by JW and attended Kingswood School. He entered the itinerancy in 1765. He returned to England in 1774 and ceased travelling that year, though listed for London in 1776. He appears not to have died in the work. Wesley's brief account conceals the reticence of the preachers (see *Journal & Diaries*, 22:197 in this edn.), but Sutcliffe says that the initial appeal in the morning and again in the evening was met with silence, and JW was 'surprised and universally tried'. MS 'History', fol. 725. Only then did Boardman and Pilmore offer. Pawson says that 'several of the brethren offered to go, if I would go along with them, but I did not see that the Lord called me to leave my native country, or to lay so heavy a cross upon my affectionate and now aged parents'. Jackson, *Early Methodist Preachers*, 4:37. When JW warmly exhorted preachers to go, George Shadford felt 'my spirit stirred within me to go.' He says that he and Rankin offered to go next spring. Ibid., 6:162.

[262] Cf. the third item in the answer to *Q.* 11 above.

[263] Who had desisted at this Conference (see *Q.* 4 above). Apparently he had been in charge of the Preachers' Fund.

[264] The Preachers' Fund.

[265] I.e., the 'yearly subscription' to reduce the debt for building, or 'General Fund'; cf. 1766 (*QQ.* 10–16), 1767 (*QQ.* 11–18), 1768 (*QQ.* 10–16).

A. John Helton and Christopher Hopper.

Q. 19. What can be done to encourage our brethren in contributing to pay the remaining debt?

A. (1) Let whatever is collected in any circuit be paid away
in that circuit, as long as any debt remains therein.					5

(2) Let whatever is contributed in any single place which
is in debt, pay that as far as it will go.

(3) Whereas twelve circuits are already quite out of debt,
let the money contributed therein be always produced at
the Conference, which shall be sent wherever we judge			10
it is most wanted.

Q. 20. We have this year spent above two days in temporal
business. How may we avoid this for the time to come?

A. Let the clerks do as much of it as they can by them-
selves, and it will save us half the time.						15

Q. 21. Where and when may our next Conference begin?

A. At London, the first Tuesday in August.

Q. 22. Does it belong to each circuit to provide the preachers who need them with horses, saddles, and bridles?

A. Undoubtedly it does; for they cannot be supposed to			20
buy them out of their little allowance.

Q. 23. Many inconveniences have arisen from the present
method of providing for preachers' wives.[266] The preachers who are most wanted in several places cannot be sent
thither because they are married. And if they are sent, the		25
people look upon them with an evil eye because they cannot bear the burden of their families. How may these
inconveniences be remedied?

A. (1) Let each society contribute what it usually does now
towards maintaining the families of married preachers.			30
For instance, the London Society can assist two married
preachers. Let them contribute five pounds a quarter;
Sussex, two pounds ten shillings, for one; Salisbury
Circuit, Bradford, Bristol, Devon, Cornwall East, the
same; Cornwall West, five pounds; Staffordshire and			35
Cheshire, two pounds ten shillings; Manchester Circuit,
five pounds; Liverpool, three pounds fifteen shillings;

---

[266] For the history of the system of support, see Baker, 'Polity', 234–36, and introduction, pp. 49–55. For the first suggestion of support, see the Limerick
Conference (1752), §27.

Derbyshire, two pounds ten shillings; Sheffield, three
pounds fifteen shillings; Lincolnshire East, six pounds;
West, three pounds fifteen shillings; Leeds, five pounds;
Birstall, five pounds; Bradford, three pounds fifteen
5   shillings; Haworth, five pounds; York, five pounds; Yarm,
five pounds; The Dales, five pounds; Newcastle, seven
pounds ten shillings.

Here is provision for six and thirty wives, at two pounds
ten shillings a quarter each. At present we have only two
10   and thirty[267] in England, besides those that keep themselves. But as several of them have children, the overplus
is to be divided among them as need requires.

(2) Let the General Steward in each circuit see that the
above sum be paid at the Quarterly Meeting.
15   (3) Let each married preacher therein receive his share.
(4) If anything remains, let the Assistant send it to the
nearest circuit where there is any deficiency, till we can
procure a General Steward for this fund at London, at
Bristol, and at Leeds.
20   By this means, whether the preachers in any particular circuit are married or single, it makes no difference; so that
any preacher may be sent into any circuit without any
difficulty.

Q. 24. How shall we procure an exact account of things in
25   Scotland and Ireland?

A. Let John Atlay procure such an account in Scotland, and
John Johnson in Ireland.

Q. 25. Those who keep the books in many places have been
extremely careless. How can this be prevented for the time
30   to come?

A. Let John Helton look over the books in every place, and
where it is needful change the book-keepers.

---

35   **Friday, August 4**
Mr. W[esley] read the following paper:
My Dear Brethren,

---

[267] This shows that only about one-third of the preachers had wives (or at least
wives who travelled with them and sought help). The list of preachers for 1769 has
111 actively stationed.

1. It has long been my desire that all those ministers of our Church who believe and preach salvation by faith might cordially agree between themselves, and not hinder but help one another. After occasionally pressing this in private conversation wherever I had opportunity, I wrote down my thoughts upon the head, and sent them to each in a letter. Out of fifty or sixty to whom I wrote, only three vouchsafed me an answer.[268] So I give this up. I can do no more. They are a rope of sand;[269] and such they will continue.

2. But it is otherwise with the *travelling preachers* in our connexion. You are at present one body. You act in concert with each other and by united counsels. And now is the time to consider what can be done in order to continue this union. Indeed, as long as I live, there will be no great difficulty. I am, under God, a centre of union to all our travelling, as well as local preachers.

They all know me and my communication.[270] They all love me for my work's sake; and therefore, were it only out of regard to me, they will continue connected with each other. But by what means may this connexion be preserved when God removes me from you?

3. I take it for granted, it cannot be preserved by any means between those who have not a single eye.[271] Those who aim at anything but the glory of God and the salvation of men; who desire or seek any earthly thing, whether honour, profit, or ease, will not, cannot continue in the connexion; it will not answer their design. Some of them, perhaps a fourth of the whole number, will procure preferment in the Church. Others will turn Independents, and get separate congregations, like John Edwards[272] and Charles Skelton.[273] Lay your accounts with this, and be not surprised if some you do not suspect be of this number.

4. But what method can be taken to preserve a firm union between those who choose to remain together?

---

[268] See Apr. 19, 1764, *Journal & Diaries*, 21:454–61 in this edn.

[269] A proverbial expression possibly arising from Erasmus, *Ex arena funiculum nectis*, 'You are for making a rope of sand', and found frequently, as in *Essays*, Burton's *Anatomy of Melancholy*, Jonson's *The Devil Is an Ass*, and Butler's *Hudibras* (I.i.51–52): 'For he a rope of sand could twist / As tough as learned Sorbonist.' For the failed appeal see *Journal & Diaries*, 21:454–61 and nn. 69–95 in this edn.

[270] 2 Kgs. 9:11.

[271] Matt. 6:22.

[272] See Minutes (1753), §22, n. 910.

[273] Left in 1754; see *Minutes* (1754), n. 947. Died before 1800 ('a few years since': Pawson, *Letters*, 3:144, written c. 1800).

Perhaps you might take some such steps as these:

On notice of my death, let all the preachers in England and Ireland repair to London within six weeks.

Let them seek God by solemn fasting and prayer.

5   Let them draw up articles of agreement, to be signed by those who choose to act in concert.

Let those be dismissed who do not choose it, in the most friendly manner possible.

Let them choose, by votes, a *committee* of three, five, or seven, 10   each of whom is to be *moderator* in his turn.

Let the committee do what I do now: propose preachers to be tried, admitted, or excluded; fix the place of each preacher for the ensuing year, and the time of the next Conference.

5. Can anything be done now in order to lay a foundation for this 15   future union? Would it not be well for any that are willing to sign some articles of agreement before God calls me hence? Suppose something like these:

'We, whose names are under written, being thoroughly convinced of the necessity of a close union between those whom God is pleased 20   to use as instruments in this glorious work, in order to preserve this union between ourselves, are resolved, God being our helper,

(1) *To devote ourselves entirely to God*; denying ourselves, taking up our cross daily;[274] steadily aiming at one thing, to save our own souls and them that hear us.[275]

25   (2) To preach the *old Methodist doctrines*, and no other, contained in the *Minutes* of the Conferences.

(3) To observe and enforce the whole Methodist *Discipline*, laid down in the said *Minutes*.'[276]

The preachers then desired Mr. W[esley] to extract the most ma-
30   terial part of the *Minutes*, and send a copy to each Assistant, which he might communicate to all the preachers in his circuit, to be seriously considered.[277] Our meeting was then concluded with solemn prayer.

[274] Matt. 16:24.

[275] See above, p. 352 and pp. 424, 436 below.

[276] A draft of this 'paper' (slightly enlarged) was sent to Charles Wesley on May 12, 1769, with the note: 'Dear brother, Send me your thoughts on the foregoing articles, with as many amendments and additions as you please.' It was endorsed by Charles: 'B[rother]'s Plan of Union'. It was implemented in stages: see *Minutes* (1773), *Q.* 18; (1774), *Q.* 26; and (1775), *Q.* 26. Eventually most of the problems here envisaged were resolved by means of the Deed of Declaration, 1784, for which see below, pp. 949–56.

[277] I.e., the 'Large' *Minutes* (1770).

Annual *Minutes of some late Conversations*, 1770

London, Tuesday, Aug. 7, 1770[278]
Q. 1. What preachers are admitted this year?
A. William Pitt, William Whitaker,[279] Samuel Wells, James
Hudson, Francis Wrigley, Samuel Smith, Robert   5

---

[278] Wesley merely records that 'Tuesday 7, our Conference began and ended Friday 10'. *Journal & Diaries*, 22:243 in this edn. But apart from recording the first American appointments and severely restricting the building of new preaching-houses to save money, this Conference was notable for the notorious minute on salvation that provoked a furious Calvinistic controversy and John Fletcher's *Checks to Antinomianism*. (For this see Rack, *Reasonable Enthusiast*, 450–61 and literature there cited.) On this affair John Pawson commented, 'Wesley drew up those Minutes which afterwards gave such offence. Had they been more seriously considered in the Conference, I am persuaded they would not have been expressed in such an unguarded manner as that in which they appeared. However, the Lord brought great good out of the evil' as the controversy produced Fletcher's *Checks against Antinomianism*. Pawson points out that Walter Shirley published a circular letter and gratuitously invited 'gospel ministers' to the next Conference 'to enter their protests' against the *Minutes*, and that 'Mr Charles Wesley, who had always a very warm side towards the clergy, was greatly alarmed, as were all our principal people'. Pawson tried to explain the *Minutes* to his leaders' meeting and generally relieved them, though they thought they 'might have been expressed so as not to have given such offence'. Jackson, *Early Methodist Preachers*, 4:42–43. John Valton wrote,

'The last few days I have attended the Conference in London and found much of the gracious presence of the Lord. . . . Whitefield, previous to his embarking for America, preached at five in the morning and sat with the preachers till breakfast, and very much encouraged them to go on in their plain and humble way. He dropped several expressions of disapprobation that several preachers in connexion with him had begun to wear gowns and bands.' (Jackson, *Early Methodist Preachers*, 6:83)

To George Merryweather, JW wrote,

'I have the credit of stationing the preachers, But many of them go where they *will* for all me. For instance, I have marked down James Oddie and John Nelson for Yarm Circuit the ensuing year. Yet I am not certain that either of them will come. They can give twenty reasons for going elsewhere. Mr Murlin says he must be in London. 'Tis certain he has a mind to be there. Therefore so it must be, for you know a man of property is master of his own notions.' (Aug. 7, *Letters* [Telford], 5:196; see introduction, p. 69. for Wesley's control of stationing.)

Sarah Crosby expected the question of women preachers to be raised at this Conference, but there is no record of it in the *Minutes*. Chilcote, *Women Preachers*, 133f.

[279] Orig., 'Whittaker', as also in 1771–73 (on occasion), 1780–82. Other spellings found are 'Whiteaker', 1773, and in the 1771 preachers' agreement; and 'Whitacre', 1776, 1786–89. In view of this great divergency it seems wiser to use the normal spelling of 'Whitaker', which is that of the majority of entries, and of his obituary (1794).

Wilkinson, Thomas Dixon, Richard Whatcoat, Thomas
Wride, John Peacock, John Duncan, Joseph Thompson,
Jonathan Crowle, Jonathan Hern, William Ashman.

Q. 2. Who *remain* on trial?

5 *A.* David Evans, John Bredin, John MᶜNeese,[280] Joseph
Garnet.

Q. 3. Who are admitted on trial?

A. John MᶜEvoy,[281] Thomas Tennant,[282] Edward Slater,
Thomas Janes, James Perfect, William Linnell, John

10 Undrell, John Floyd, William Winbey,[283] Stephen
Nichols,[284] Richard Wright,[285] George Wadsworth,
Richard Rodda, Robert Swan, James Watson, George
Mowat, Michael MᶜDonald,[286] William Homer.

*Q.*4. Who desist from travelling?

15 *A.* Robert Howard, James Brownfield, Joseph Fothergill,
James Barry, and James Rea.

Q. 5. Who act as Assistants this year?

A. John Pawson, Thomas Rankin, Benjamin Rhodes,
George Shadford, John Easton, John Furz, John

20 Catermole, James Cotty, Alexander Mather, John Mason,
Samuel Wells, Thomas Hanson, James Glasbrook,
Jeremiah Robertshaw, John Shaw, Robert Costerdine,
James Dempster, William Pitt, Thomas Taylor, Parson
Greenwood, Thomas Olivers, Samuel Woodcock, Isaac

25 Brown, John Ellis, Daniel Bumsted, John Oliver,
Christopher Hopper, Richard Seed, Joseph Thompson,
Thomas Lee, Thomas Johnson, Jacob Rowell, Peter Jaco,
Duncan Wright, George Story, Thomas Simpson,

---

[280] Orig., 'Macneese', though the stations (No. 46) retain the normal 'MᶜNeese'.

[281] Orig., 'MᶜAway', while stations (No. 3) have 'M'Avoy'. In 1771–72, however, his name is given as 'MᶜEvoy'.

[282] Orig., 'Tenant', as occasionally in 1770–74, 1776–77, 1779–80, 1783, and 1789, though the bulk of entries here and elsewhere support the spelling 'Tennant'.

[283] Orig., 'Winby', but 'Winbey' in stations (No. 23) and 1771, while his signature in the 1771 preachers' agreement is 'Winbe'.

[284] There is no recorded appointment for him, and his name does not occur in the 1771 stations.

[285] Wright was not stationed in 1770, but in 1771 went to America with Asbury.

[286] Orig., here and in station No. 49, 'MᶜDaniel', which seems to be an error for 'MᶜDonald', whose name was spelled 'Macdonald' in 1771, and 'MᶜDonal' in one of two entries in 1774.

Samuel Levick, Thomas Dixon, Thomas Newall, Stephen Proctor, Richard Bourke, William Collins.[287]

Q. 6. Are there any objections to any of the preachers?

A. Name them one by one; which was done.

Q. 7. Two years ago it was agreed that itinerant preachers   5
ought not to follow trades.[288] How can we secure the observance of this?

A. It is agreed by all the brethren now met in Conference, this 9th day of August, 1770, that no preacher who will not relinquish his trade of buying and selling, or making and   10
vending pills, drops, balsams, or medicines of any kind, shall be considered as a travelling preacher any longer. And that it shall be demanded of all those preachers who have traded in cloth, hardware, pills, drops, balsams, or medicines of any kind, at the next Conference, whether   15
they have entirely left it off or not.

But observe, we do not object to a preacher's having a share in a ship.[289]

Q. 8. How are the preachers stationed this year?

A. As follows: 20

(1) *London*, John Pawson, John Murlin, Thomas Rankin, John Allen, John Helton.[290]

(2) *Sussex*, Edward Slater, Francis Wolf.[291]

(3) *Kent*, Benjamin Rhodes, John McEvoy.

(4) *Essex*,   (George Shadford.   25

(5) *Norfolk*,   (John Murray.

---

[287] Collins does not appear in the stations.

[288] See *Minutes* (1768), *Q.* 22.

[289] The exception of having a share in a ship is presumably because this would not involve preachers in taking time from preaching or competing with local tradesmen. For the problems it could cause, however, see James Oddie's experience with an unsatisfactory captain, of whom James Everett remarked that he had just as much piety as 'enabled him to play the knave'. Tyerman MSS, 2:35f. Tyerman says that in his unpublished autobiography, Matthew Lowes commented that people objected to such trading as interfering with other Methodists' business and as inconsistent with the ministry. *Wesley*, 3:71 n. 2. Lowes was obliged to leave the itinerancy partly for his refusal to give up his 'balm' and partly for health reasons. He continued to be a local preacher and supported himself by selling his 'balm'. Cf. JW to Lowes, Nov. 10, 1771, *Letters* (Telford), 5:288f.

[290] Two listed Assistants.

[291] No listed Assistants.

(6) *Bedfordshire*, John Easton, Richard Whatcoat, James Perfect.

(7) *Oxfordshire*, John Furz, John Duncan.

(8) *Wiltshire, South*, John Catermole, Francis Asbury.

(9)   *North*, James Cotty, Barnabas Thomas, John Magor.

(10) *Bristol*, Alexander Mather, Thomas Janes.

(11) *Devonshire*, John Mason, Thomas Brisco.

(12) *Cornwall, East*, Samuel Wells, William Brammah; Jonathan Crowle.

(13)   *West*, Thomas Hanson, William Ashman, James Stephens,[292] John Floyd.

(14) *Gloucestershire*,[293] James Glasbrook, Martin Rodda.

(15) *Staffordshire*, Jeremiah Robertshaw, James Clough.

(16) *Cheshire, North*, John Shaw, Joseph Guilford.

(17)   *South*, Robert Costerdine, William Linnell.

(18) *Wales, West*, Richard Rodda, William Whitaker.[294]

(19)   *East*, James Dempster, William Barker.

(20)   *North*, Richard Henderson, William Pitt,[295] John Undrell.

(21) *Lancashire, South*, Thomas Taylor, John Morgan.

(22)   *North*, Parson Greenwood, Thomas Westell.

(23) *Derbyshire*, Thomas Olivers, John Poole, William Winbey.

(24) *Sheffield*, Samuel Woodcock, Samuel Bardsley.

(25) *Lincolnshire, East*, Isaac Brown, George Mowat, Samuel Smith.

(26)   *West*, John Ellis, J. W.,[296] William Ellis.

(27) *Leeds*, Daniel Bumsted, Thomas Mitchell.

(28) *Birstall*, John Oliver, John Atlay, Robert Roberts.

(29) *Bradford*, Christopher Hopper, George Wadsworth.

(30) *Haworth*, Richard Seed, George Hudson, David Evans.

(31) *Whitehaven*, Thomas Wride, Joseph Garnet.

(32) *York*, Joseph Thompson, John Peacock.

---

[292] Orig., 'Stevens', though all other references are to 'Stephens'.

[293] Orig., 'Glocestershire', as also in 1771 (2 of 3), 1772–74, 1776 (2 of 3), 1777, 1778 (1 of 2), 1779 (2 of 3), 1780, 1783, 1786, 1790, and 1791 (1 of 2).

[294] No listed Assistant.

[295] The Assistant, though not listed first.

[296] Almost certainly Isaac Waldron, although James Watson, just admitted on trial, is not otherwise stationed.

(33) *Scarborough*, Thomas Lee, Thomas Carlill.

(34) *Yarm*, Thomas Johnson, John Nelson, William Hunter; James Oddie, supernumerary.

(35) *The Dales*, Jacob Rowell, Lancelot Harrison, Christopher Watkins.

(36) *Newcastle*, Peter Jaco, Joseph Cownley, Thomas Hanby, Matthew Lowes, Thomas Tennant.

(37) *Edinburgh*, Duncan Wright, William Thompson.

(38)[297] *Aberdeen*, George Story, Thomas Cherry, Robert Swan.

(39) *Glasgow*, Thomas Simpson, Alexander McNab.

(40) *Dublin*, Samuel Levick, John Goodwin.

(41) *Waterford*,[298] Jonathan Hern, George Snowdin.[299]

(42) *Cork*, Hugh Saunderson.

(43) *Limerick*, James Hudson.

(44) *Castlebar*, Stephen Proctor, William Horner;[300] Robert Swindells,[301] supern[umerary].

(45) *Athlone*, Richard Bourke, John Bredin.

(46) *Enniskillen*, Thomas Dixon, John McNeese.

(47) *Armagh*, Francis Wrigley, John Smith.

(48) *Derry*, Thomas Newall, Robert Wilkinson.

(49) *Tandragee*, John Wittam, Michael McDonald, Thomas Motte.

(50) *America*, Joseph Pilmore, Richard Boardman, Robert Williams, John King.[302]

Q. 9. What numbers are in the society?

A. They are as follows:

---

[297] Dixon MS Minutes insert '38. Dunbar, Jos. Harper'.

[298] No listed Assistant.

[299] Orig., 'Snowdon', as once each in 1770–76, 1779–80, 1782, 1783 (2 of 3), 1784 (all 3), and 1787. The majority of the entries in the *Minutes* until his death in 1812, however, are spelled 'Snowden'.

[300] Orig., 'Josiah Homer'. This must be an error, for William Homer is mentioned in *Q*. 3, and there is no other reference to Josiah.

[301] Orig., 'Swindell', as also in 1771 and in his own letter of May 5, 1749. In 1772 his name is spelled 'Swindalls', but in all other instances 'Swindells', which JW used in his obituary, in *Minutes* (1783), *Q*. 5.

[302] This is the first listing of America in the stations, though in 1769, *Q*. 13 noted the appeal from New York, and *Q*. 11 the gift of money to the Society there. Boardman and Pilmore went out in 1769, Williams and King being now added, though they went (about the same time) as voluntary rather than appointed preachers.

London*   2,292

N.B. In the circuits marked * there are fewer members than there
were a year ago.

Sussex	182
Kent	289
Essex*	126
Norfolk*	231
Bedfordshire	270
Oxfordshire	354
Wiltshire, South	323
North	806
Bristol	1,236
Devon	482
Cornwall, East*	602
West	1,709
Wales, West	84
East	142
North	120
Staffordshire	1,138
Cheshire*	565
Lancashire, South	1,406
North	737
Derbyshire	883
Sheffield	597
Lincolnshire, East*	717
West	760
Leeds	1,355
Birstall	965
Bradford	807
Haworth	1,333
Whitehaven	
York	1,157
Yarm	1,034
The Dales	912
Newcastle*	1,862
Dunbar*	30
Edinburgh*	62
Glasgow*	76

Perth	⎫		
Dundee	⎬ 413		
Aberdeen	⎮ "		
Arbroath	⎭		
Dublin	461		5
Waterford	164		
Cork	223		
Limerick	154		
Castlebar	388		
Athlone	256		10
Enniskillen	569		
Armagh	299		
Londonderry	60		
Tandragee	550		
			15
In all	29,181[303]		

N.B. In the circuits marked thus * there are fewer members than there were a year ago.

Q. 10. What is the Kingswood collection?
A. £218. 4*s*. 5*d*.   20
Q. 11: What is contributed towards the debt?
A. £1,958. 10*s*. 2*d*.
Q. 12. How was this distributed?
A. As follows:

	£.	s.	d.	
				25
Contingencies	100	0	0	
Law	26	0	4	
London	170	1	22	
Bow	12	10	0	
Cont[ingencies] for 1769	64	19	6	30
Printing Minut[es]	2	19	6	
Prea[chers'] Necessit[ies]	81	5	3	
Chatham	20	7	6	
Yarmouth	5	0	0	
Norwich	116	11	6	35
Salisbury	4	13	6	
Portsmouth	21	10	9	
Fareham[304]	3	3	0	
Bradford	14	12	6	

[303] Orig., '29,406'.
[304] Orig., 'Fairham'.

	Axminster	13	0	0
	Hillfarance	6	0	0
	Cullompton	4	0	0
	Redruth	10	0	0
5	St. Johns	32	15	8
	Kerley[305]	5	0	0
	Stithians	4	0	0
	Old Gwennap[306]	20	0	0
	New [Gwennap]	2	2	2
10	Stroud	20	0	0
	Wednesbury	3	2	6
	Birmingham	32	15	6
	Darlaston[307]	3	3	4
	Cradley[308]	3	11	0
15	Stourbridge[309]	13	7	6
	Wolverhampton	5	0	0
	Dudley	2	0	0
	Chester	60	8	2
	Cardiff	3	10	0
20	St. Daniel's	9	0	0
	Stockport	20	5	6
	Bolton	25	0	0
	Macclesfield	21	10	0
	New Mills[310]	12	0	0
25	Liverpool	34	0	0
	Congleton	7	0	0
	Burslem	15	0	0
	Warrington	4	0	0
	Burton	30	0	0
30	Nottingham	7	9	9
	Creech	6	1	0
	Sheffield	48	10 ·	2
	Boston	21	10	0
	Louth	14	16	0
35	Leeds	10	0	0

[305] Orig., 'Kerly'.
[306] Orig., 'Gwinnap'.
[307] Orig., 'Darliston'; in 1772, 1773, 'Darlastone'.
[308] Orig., 'Creadly'; in 1775, 'Craidley'.
[309] Orig., 'Sturbridge', as also in 1772.
[310] Orig., 'Newmill'.

Rothwell	17	15	0
Horbury	17	10	0
Armley	17	10	0
Seacroft	17	10	0
Bradford	50	6	8	5
Heptonstall	4	12	0
Rochdale	85	0	0
Mill-End[311]	1	10	6
Bacup[312]	5	10	8
Padiham	8	0	0	10
Yeadon[313]	1	10	0
Bingley	6	6	2
Whitehaven	12	12	11
York	10	0	0
Yarm	9	0	0	15
Stockton	5	12	0
Whitby	24	12	1
Hutton	4	12	6
Thirsk	30	17	9
Stokesley	10	3	0	20
Barnardcastle	30	15	7
Weardale	60	6	6
Teesdale	5	0	3
Shields	10	0	0
Monkwearmouth	19	2	6	25
Ireland, being so much collected there	163	19	0
Aberdeen	50	0	0
Arbroath	5	0	0
Dundee	56	0	0	30
Perth	5	0	0
Glasgow	12	0	0
Edinburgh	23	0	0
	£1960	12	9

[311] Orig., 'Millend'; 'Mill-End' in 1772, and in Myles, *Chronological History*, 432, who lists chapels in Mill-End, Lancashire, built 1761, 1806.

[312] Orig., 'Beacup'.

[313] Orig., 'Yeaden'.

The old debt is only reduced £1,000 this year, and the new
£700.

Q. 13. What is the whole debt remaining?

A. The old, £5,671. The new debt, £1,287.

5   *Q.* 14. We gain no ground. The debt is larger now than it
was last year. How can we prevent its farther increase?

A. By putting an absolute stop to all building for the ensuing year.[314] Let no new house be built; no addition or
alteration made in any old one, unless the proposers

10   thereof can and will defray the whole expense of it without lessening their Yearly Subscription.

Q. 15. What can be done in order to pay the old debt?

A. (1) Give a note to each Assistant, specifying the debts
toward which the money collected in each Circuit next

15   year is to be paid.

(2) Let each Assistant encourage the people in each
place, like those in Birmingham, to make a push toward
paying off their own debt.

(3) Consider the proposal of vesting all the houses in a

20   general trust,[315] consisting of persons chosen out of the
whole nation. Only beware this does not interfere with
the Yearly Subscription. Do not drop the substance by
catching at a shadow.[316]

Q. 16. What shall we do to prevent scandal, when any of

25   our members becomes a bankrupt?

A. In this case, let two of the principal members of the
Society be deputed to examine his accounts; and, if he has
not kept fair accounts, or has been concerned in that base
practice of raising money by coining notes (commonly

[314] Growing financial problems also brought this issue to the fore at the 1783
Conference, with an attempt to curb the 'needless multiplying of preaching-
houses', which was called a 'great evil'. *Minutes* (1783), *Q.* 22. See also (1776),
Q. 21.

[315] See *Minutes* (1768), *Q.* 15, n. 190, for what lay behind this proposal, which was
not implemented, at least in general. A general trust was appointed for four properties in the Wiltshire, South Circuit in 1786; see *WHS* 42 (1979): 21–24. See also
Letters (Telford), 6:37 (in 1773), and introduction, pp. 46–47.

[316] A proverbial saying going back in various forms at least two hundred years, to
Lyly and Shakespeare (see *Oxford Dictionary of English Proverbs*).

called the bill-trade),[317] let him be immediately expelled the Society.

Q. 17. What is contributed toward the Preachers' Fund?

A. £47. 5s. 3d.

Q. 18. Where and when may our next Conference begin?

A. At Bristol, the first Tuesday in August.

Q. 19. How many Preachers' wives are to be provided for?

A. Forty-three.[318]

Q. 20. By what Societies?[319]

A. As follows: The Society in London provides for S. Easton, S. Barker, and *Sussex* for S. Wolfe.[320]

Wilts, South and Bristol for S. Mathew and Janes.

Devon for S. Brisco.

Cornwall, East for S. Brammah, and half for S. Henderson.

Cornwall, West [for] S. Pitt, S. Whitaker, and half for S. Henderson.

Gloucestershire for Richard Rodda.

Staffordshire for S. Robertshaw.

Sheffield half for S. Clough.

Cheshire, North for S. Shaw.

---

[317] See *Methodist History* (Jan. 1972): 48–49, for the bill-trade, and see adjacent pages for examples of Methodist discipline over bankruptcy. Cf. *Journal & Diaries*, 21:475 in this edn., for a case of two bankrupt Methodists who were to be expelled unless it was proved not to be their own fault. Both were 'in a prosperous way till they fell into that wretched trade of bill-broking wherein no man continues long without being wholly ruined'. This refers to bills of exchange or promissory notes or accommodation notes to raise money on credit (*OED*).

[318] Thirty-six were provided for in 1769, and actually only 39 are listed below.

[319] Of the thirty-nine wives actually listed, by far the greatest number (more than two-thirds) were supported by the circuits to which their husbands were appointed this year. One might have expected that the Conference would receive reports showing which circuits had supported the preachers' wives during the year just ending, but this is clearly true in only two instances, though it is also possible in five other instances, where the preacher remained in the same circuit for a second year. In accordance with *Q.* 23 of the 1769 Conference, however, the records here illustrate the principle of the strong circuits helping the weak, for eight of the wives were supported by circuits to which their husbands were stationed neither in 1769 nor in 1770.

[320] In this context 'S' clearly means 'Sister'.

Haworth [and] Bradford, half each for S. Guilford.
Cheshire, South for S. Costerdine.
Lancashire, South for S. Taylor and S. Morgan.
    North for S. Greenwood and Westell.
5   *Derbyshire* for S. Poole.
Sheffield for S. Woodcock.
Lincolnshire, East for S. Brown and Swan.[321]
    West, [for] S. W.,[322] and Ellis.[323]
Leeds for S. Bumsted and Mitchell.
10   *Birstall,* S. Oliver and Atlay.
Bradford, S. Hopper, half for S. Guilford.
Haworth, S. Evans and Garnet.
York, S. Peacock and Carlill.
Scarborough, S. Lee.
15   *Yarm,* S. Nelson and [this space is intentionally left
    blank].
The Dales, S. Rowell, and Harrison.
Newcastle, S. Jaco, Hanby, and Lowes.
Q. 21. But some have children. How are these to be
20   provided for?
A. By the societies where they labour.
Q. 22. What poor children may be admitted now at
    Kingswood School?
A. John Poole's child, and John Peacock's.
25   *Q.* 23. But how can we secure our masters?
A. Ask each before he is received:
Do you design to stay here?
Have you any thoughts of being ordained?
Have you any design to preach?
30   *Q.* 24. How shall we procure an exact account of things in
    Scotland and Ireland?
A. Let Duncan Wright procure such an account in
    Scotland, and John Johnson in Ireland.
Q. 25. The late evening preaching in some places prevents
35   morning preaching. Is this right?
A. No. Let the evening preaching never begin later than
    seven in any place, except in harvest time.

---

[321] Robert Swan stationed in Aberdeen.
[322] Apparently Sister Waldron.
[323] Apparently Mrs. John Ellis.

Q. 26. How shall each Assistant know the exhorters[324] in his
circuit?

A. Let each give his successor a list of them.

Q. 27. How can we prevent the loss which many circuits
have sustained by want of preaching during the   5
Conference?[325]

A. Let no preacher who does not attend the Conference
leave the circuit at that time on any pretence whatever.
This is the most improper time in the whole year. Let
every Assistant see to this, and require each of these to   10
remain in the circuit till the new preachers come.

Q. 28. What can be done to revive the work of God where it
is decayed?

A. (1) We must needs visit from house to house, were it
only to avoid idleness. I am afraid we are idle still. Do   15
we not loiter away many hours in every week? Try yourselves. Keep a diary of your employment but for a week,
and then read it over. No idleness can consist with
growth in grace. Nay, without exactness in redeeming
time[326] it is impossible to retain even the life you   20
received in justification. Can we find a better method of
visiting than that set down in the *Minutes* of 1766, p. 15,
etc.[327] When will you begin?

(2) Observe what is remarked in the *Minutes* of 1768,
p. 10, etc.,[328] particularly   25
With regard to dispersing the books.
With regard to field preaching.

---

[324] These were members who gave informal addresses to groups larger than
classes and could be the raw material from which local and itinerant preachers were
recruited. They are said to have developed as a stop-gap for lay preachers when
there was a mass press-ganging of the latter in Cornwall in 1744. Jackson, *Charles
Wesley*, 1:444, quoted in G. Smith, *History of Methodism*, 2:238f.; cf. also *CWJ*,
1:419, where CW says they should speak only in the Society and not outside. The
term was also used for local preachers in Cornwall. F. Baker, 'Polity', 237 and n. 70.

[325] The necessary time taken in travel and in the Conference itself was usually a
minimum of two weeks, and might stretch to three or four.

[326] Eph. 5:16; Col. 4:5.

[327] *Minutes* (1766), *Q*. 29. According to Sutcliffe (MS 'History', fol. 743), JW
said the preachers might take a friend or a child who knew the neighbourhood when
visiting.

[328] *Minutes* (1768), *Q*. 23 (1–3), (6–8).

With regard to morning preaching, wherever you can
have twenty hearers.

With regard to singing, to fasting, and to instantaneous
deliverance from sin.

5   (3) Let a fast be observed in all our societies on Friday,
Sept. 28, and on the Friday after New Year's Day, after
Lady Day, and after Midsummer Day next.

(4) Observe what is said, p. 14,[329] with regard to the children in every large town, with regard to Mr. Brainerd,

10   regard to the Church.

(5) Let every Assistant so order the Sunday noon preaching in his circuit that no preacher may be kept from
church above two Sundays in four.

(6) Take heed to your doctrine.

15   We said in 1744, 'We have leaned too much toward
Calvinism.'[330] Wherein?

(i) With regard to *man's faithfulness.* Our Lord himself
taught to use the expression. And we ought never to be
ashamed of it. We ought steadily to assert, on his author-

20   ity, that if a man is not 'faithful in the unrighteous mammon', God will not 'give him the true riches'.[331]

(ii) With regard to working for life. This also our Lord
has expressly commanded us. 'Labour'—ἐργάζεσθε—
literally, 'work for the meat that endureth to everlasting

25   life.'[332] And in fact every believer, till he comes to glory,
works *for* as well as *from* life.

(iii) We have received it as a maxim that 'a man is to do
nothing *in order to* justification.'[333] Nothing can be more

---

[329] Ibid., *Q.* 23 (10–12).

[330] See Doctrinal *Minutes* (1744), §23, *Q.* 17. The notorious minute that follows
was the one leading to the Calvinist controversy and an attempt at reconciliation in
the Conference of 1771. When this failed, it provoked Fletcher's *Checks.* See the
first note to the present Conference and to the 1771 Conference.

[331] Cf. Luke 16:11.

[332] John 6:27.

[333] While the source of this maxim may be elusive, Wesley's interpretation of the
antinomian sentiments expressed therein represent the crux of his argument with
the Calvinists and Moravians over the years of his ministry, starting with Whitefield
and Molther in the late 1730s. Fletcher quotes this section of the minute at the
beginning of his *Checks.*

false. Whoever desire to find favour with God should
'cease from evil and learn to do well'.[334] Whoever
repents should do 'works meet for repentance'.[335] And
if this is not in *order* to find favour, what does he do
them for? 5
Review the whole affair.
(1) Who of us is *now* accepted of God?
He that now believes in Christ with a loving, obedient
heart.
(2) But who among those that never heard of Christ? 10
He that feareth God and worketh righteousness,[336]
according to the light he has.
(3) Is this the same with 'he that is sincere'?[337]
Nearly, if not quite.
(4) Is not this 'salvation by works'? 15
Not by the *merit* of works, but by works as a *condition*.
(5) What have we then been disputing about for these
thirty years?
I am afraid about words.
(6) As to *merit* itself, of which we have been so dreadfully 20
afraid: we are rewarded according to our works, yea,
because of our works. How does this differ from *for the
sake of our works*? And how differs this from *secundum
merita operum*?[338] As our works *deserve*? Can you split this
hair? I doubt, I cannot. 25
(7) The grand objection to one of the preceding proposi-
tions is drawn from matter of fact. God does in fact justify those who, by their own confession, neither feared
God nor wrought righteousness.[339] Is this an exception
to the general rule? 30
It is a doubt, God makes any exception at all. But how
are we sure that the person in question never did fear
God and work righteousness? His own saying so is not
proof: for we know how all that are convinced of sin
undervalue themselves in every respect. 35

---

[334] Cf. Isa. 1:16-17.
[335] Acts 26:20.
[336] See Acts 10:35.
[337] Cf. Minutes (1746), §19.
[338] 'According to the merits of [our] works.'
[339] 1 Pet. 2:17; Rev. 14:7; Heb. 11:23.

(8) Does not talking of a justified or a sanctified *state* tend to mislead men? Almost naturally leading them to trust in what was done in one moment? Whereas we are every hour and every moment pleasing or displeasing to God, *according to our works*—according to the whole of our inward tempers, and our outward behaviour.

5

Annual *Minutes of some late Conversations,* 1771

Bristol, Tuesday, Aug. 6, 1771[340]

[340] Though one would not guess it from the *Minutes*, this Conference was over-shadowed by the emerging Calvinist controversy following the minute on salvation in the 1770 *Minutes*. In his *Journal* (22:285f. in this edn.) Wesley wrote, 'We had more preachers than usual at the Conference in consequence of Mr Shirley's cir-cular letter. At ten on Thursday morning he came with nine or ten of his friends. We conversed freely for above two hours. And I believe they were satisfied that we were not so "dreadful heretics" as they imagined but were tolerably sound in the faith'. Benson and Fletcher had had to leave their posts in Lady Huntingdon's Trevecca College, and in Jan. 1771 the Countess had denounced the *Minutes* to Charles Wesley as 'Popery unmasked'. Jackson, *Charles Wesley,* 2:255. Walter Shirley, the Countess's chaplain, said in his circular letter that there should be a rival meeting of 'real Protestants' during the Methodist Conference and that they should go 'in a body' to that Conference and insist on a 'formal recantation' of the 1770 minute and, if this was refused, publish a protest against it. Tyerman, *Wesley,* 3:93f. Only a handful appeared, and if Wesley's account is to be trusted, the delegates were received peacefully. Tyerman (ibid., 3:100) says that Shirley produced a doc-ument that, with some changes that Shirley said were 'not very material', was signed by John Wesley and fifty-three preachers. (For a copy of this document and a list of signatures see the 'Additional Note' at the end of these 1771 *Minutes.*) Thomas Olivers refused to sign and warned that ill use would be made of their unsuspect-ing candour. He later wrote several treatises in the ensuing controversy. Jackson, *Early Methodist Preachers,* 2:87f., 90f. Seymour, in his biography of Lady Huntingdon (2:242), says that Wesley, not Shirley, drew up the document. Shirley and his friends acquiesced to it and 'candidly acknowledged their too hasty conduct in judging his (Wesley's) sentiments'. However, Fletcher had drawn up a *Vindication* of the original minute of 1770, which Wesley then published, despite Shirley's and indeed Fletcher's protests. There followed a prolonged literary battle including Fletcher's *Checks.* (See also Prof. Ward's note to *Journal & Diaries,* 22:285, n. 42 in this edn.) Pawson (Jackson, *Early Methodist Preachers,* 4:43) expected a 'warm contest with the Calvinists' at the Conference, but they were not as formidable as he had expected. They had little to say in defence of their conduct, and the dis-cussion was left in great measure to Fletcher. Wesley wrote to Lady Huntingdon that on justification by faith and the Conference minute, he had recorded only what he had taught for the last thirty years. Aug. 14, 1771, *Letters* (Telford), 5:274f.

Q. 1.What preachers are *admitted* this year?

A. John Bredin, Joseph Garnet, James Perfect, William
Linnell,[341] Richard Wright, William Winbey, John Floyd,
John Undrell, George Wadsworth, Robert Swan, James
Watson, George Mowat, Charles Boone,[342] Michael 5
McDonald, and William Horner.

Q. 2. Who remain on trial?

A. David Evans, Edward Slater, and Thomas Tennant.

Q. 3. Who are admitted on trial?

A. Joseph Benson,[343] Samuel Tooth, James Hindmarsh,[344] 10
John Watson, John Bristol, John Brettel, Thomas Tatton,
and Thomas Eden.[345]

Q. 4. Who act as Assistants this year?

A. Alexander Mather, George Shadford, John Easton,
Samuel Wells, William Pitt, Richard Bourke, John 15
Pawson, Thomas Johnson, George Hudson, Thomas
Rankin, John Furz, James Dempster, John Ellis, Robert
Costerdine, Joseph Guilford, John Shaw, Thomas Taylor,
Parson Greenwood, Thomas Olivers, Daniel Bumsted,
Benjamin Rhodes, John Peacock, Robert Roberts, John 20
Oliver, Thomas Hanson, Jeremiah Robertshaw, John
Mason, Isaac Brown, Thomas Lee, Christopher Hopper,
Jacob Rowell, Peter Jaco, Duncan Wright, George Story,
John Goodwin, James Glasbrook, Thomas Dixon,
William Collins, Francis Wrigley, Robert Wilkinson, 25
James Hudson, Thomas Wride, Alexander McNab.

Q. 5. Are there any objections to any of our preachers?

A. Examine them one by one: (which was done).

Q. 6. How are they stationed this year?

A. As follows: 30

---

[341] Orig., 'Linnel' (1 of 2 uses) and also in 1773, but on other occasions his name
is spelled 'Linnell', the spelling used by JW in his letter to Thomas Wride, Sept.
7, 1771. Letters, (Telford), 5:271.

[342] Orig., 'Boon', as uniformly in the *Minutes* until 1781, when his name began
to be spelled 'Boone', the only exceptions being in 1786 and 1787. JW also, on Oct.
5, 1790, wrote of him as 'Boon', but his obituary (1795 *Minutes*) and his biography
(*AM* [1798]) show that his family and friends honoured this change of spelling.

[343] Joseph Benson had previously taught at Kingswood School (1766–70) and in
1770 was the principal of Trevecca College.

[344] James Hindmarsh was a master at Kingswood School (1765–73).

[345] Thomas Eden was not stationed, and in 1772 he left the Methodists.

(1) *London*, J. W[esley], C. W[esley], A. Mather, Jos. Benson, John Allen, John Helton.

(2) *Kent*,[346] James Clough, John Duncan.

(3) *Sussex*,[347] Thomas Newell, Wm. Whitaker.

(4) *Norwich*, George Shadford, John Floyd,[348] John Undrell.

(5) *Bedfordshire*, John Easton, Martin Rodda, John McEvoy.

(6) *Oxfordshire*, Samuel Wells, Wm. Barker.

(7) *Wiltshire, South*, Wm. Pitt, Wm. Ashman.

(8)   *North*, Richard Bourke, Thomas Brisco, James Hindmarsh.

(9) *Bristol*, John Pawson, John Murlin.

(10) *Devon*, Thomas Johnson, Jona. Crowle.

(11) *Cornwall, East*, George Hudson, William Brammah, Richard Rodda.

(12)   *West*, Thomas Rankin, Francis Wolf, Samuel Tooth,[349] William Ellis.

(13) *Pembrokeshire*, John Furz.

(14) *Glamorganshire*,[350] John Bristol, John Brettel.

(15) *Brecon*, James Dempster, Rob. Empringham.[351]

(16) *Gloucestershire*, John Ellis,[352] James Cotty.

(17) *Staffordshire*, Rob. Costerdine, Rich. Seed.

(18) *Chester*, Joseph Guilford, Barn. Thomas.

(19) *Macclesfield*, John Shaw, Samuel Smith, Tho. Tatton.

(20) *Manchester*, Thomas Taylor, John Bredin.

(21) *Liverpool*, Parson Greenwood, Sam. Woodcock.

---

[346] No listed Assistant.

[347] No listed Assistant.

[348] Orig., 'Lloyd', though 'Floyd', as usual, in his admission into full connexion, and always elsewhere in *Minutes* except in 1775. But a copy of Byrom's *Shorthand*, 1767, was seen with 'John Floyde, Methodist Preacher' on the front cover.

[349] This is the only year in which Tooth is noted as a preacher.

[350] No listed Assistant.

[351] Robert Empringham is not listed earlier as being admitted or remaining on trial, but he is admitted into full connexion in 1773. After having a break in his service (1779–81) and being admitted on trial in 1782, he served until 1792, when he died. In 1775 his name is once spelled 'Emperingham', and in 1783, 'Empingham'.

[352] According to a note in Costerdine's copy of the *Minutes*, Ellis was 'Dead Jany. 4, 1772'.

(22) *Derbyshire*, Thomas Olivers, Samuel Bardsley, David Evans.

(23) *Lincolnshire, East*, Benjamin Rhodes, Lancelot Harrison, Thomas Tennant.

(24)   *West*, John Peacock, George Mowat, Charles Boon.   5

(25) *Sheffield*, Daniel Bumsted, Joseph Garnet, John Moulson.[353]

(26) *Leeds*, Robert Roberts, Thomas Mitchell.

(27) *Birstall*, John Oliver, John Morgan, Thomas Westell.   10

(28) *Bradford*, Thomas Hanson, John Atlay.

(29) *Haworth*, Jeremiah Robertshaw, Stephen Proctor, John Poole.

(30) *Whitehaven*, John Mason, William Linnell.

(31) *York*,[354] Isaac Brown, John Nelson.   15

(32) *Hull*, Joseph Thompson, I[saac] W[aldron], Tho. Lee.

(33) *Yarm*, Christopher Hopper, T. Carlill, Rob. Swan.

(34) *The Dales*, Jacob Rowell, Thomas Cherry,[355] Joseph Harper,[356] William Hunter.   20

(35) *Newcastle*, Peter Jaco, William Thompson, Thomas Simpson, Joseph Cownley.

(36) *Edinburgh*, Duncan Wright, Thomas Hanby, Christopher Watkins,[357] Hugh Sanderson.

(37) *Aberdeen*, George Story, Geo. Wadsworth, James   25
Watson; Thomas Cherry, supernum[erary].

(38) *Dublin*, John Goodwin, William Winbey.[358]

(39) *Waterford*,[359] William Horner.

(40) *Cork*, James Glasbrook, John Murray.

(41) *Limerick*, William Collins.   30

[353] This is the only reference to John Moulson.

[354] The original numbers of the circuits 1–30, 34–51 are here altered to 1–48.

[355] The inclusion of Thomas Cherry here is probably an error. He is listed also as the supernumerary at Aberdeen, and The Dales Circuit otherwise had only three preachers from 1769 to 1773.

[356] The Dixon MS Minutes have Joseph Harper in Aberdeen and James Watson in The Dales.

[357] Orig., 'Watkin', as 1780.

[358] William Winbey died sometime during 1771–72. Costerdine has written 'Dead' above his name in his own copy of these *Minutes*.

[359] No listed Assistant.

(42) *Athlone*, Thomas Dixon, Edward Slater, Geo. Snowden; Rob. Swindells, supernum[erary].

(43) *Castlebar*, Francis Wrigley, Jonathan Hern, Michael McDonald.

(44) *Enniskillen*, Robert Wilkinson, James Perfect, Richard Whatcoat, John Smith.

(45) *Londonderry*, James Hudson.

(46) *Armagh*, Thomas Wride, Nehem. Price.

(47) *Newry*, Alexander McNab, John Wittam, John Watson.

(48) *America*, Richard Boardman, Jos. Pilmore, Francis Asbury, Richard Wright.

Q. 7. Our brethren in America call aloud for help. Who are willing to go over and help them?

A. Five were willing. The two appointed were Francis Asbury and Richard Wright.[360]

Q. 8. What numbers are in the society?

A. They are as follows:

London	2,420
Sussex	206
Kent*	280
Norfolk	389
Bedfordshire*	284
Oxfordshire*	350
Wiltshire, South*	277
North	851
Bristol	1,271

---

[360] Pilmore and Boardman were already in America. See *Minutes* (1770), *Q*. 8.

Francis Asbury (*The Journal and Letters of Francis Asbury*, ed. Elmer T. Clark, 3 vols. [Nashville: Abingdon Press, 1958], 1:3) recorded that he had 'strong intimations' to go to America. In response to the Conference appeal he spoke his mind and offered to go. This was accepted by Wesley and others who judged he had a call. 'It was my duty to go where Conference ordered'. JW always seems to have seen overseas service as a matter for volunteers, unlike stations in Britain, though even here he was sometimes compelled to give way to individual preferences. At this Conference he allowed Samuel Bardsley to go to Derbyshire rather than a more distant place, in consideration for his mother. *Letters* (Telford), 5:271f. But others seem simply to have gone their own way; see, e.g., Wesley's complaint cited in *Minutes* (1770), n. 278. As to America, in 1770–71 JW seems to have considered making a visit, though he awaited a 'clear, pressing call'. See *Letters* (Telford), 5:183, 212, 267, 270, 273, 303.

Devonshire*	402	
Cornwall, East*[361]	570	
West	1,927	
Gloucestershire	387	
Staffordshire*	706	5
Cheshire, North	559	
South	849	
Wales, West	112	
East*	130	
North	137	10
Lancashire, South*	879	
North*	622	
Derbyshire	896	
Sheffield*	652	
Lincolnshire, E[ast]*[362]	660	15
Ditto West	806	
Leeds	1,711	
Birstall	1,111	
Bradford	831	
Haworth*	1,241	20
Whitehaven	237	
York	558	
Scarborough	596	
Yarm*	970	
The Dales*	874	25
Newcastle*[363]	1,747	
Edinburgh	137	
Aberdeen	668	
Glasgow	87	
Dublin	402	30
Waterford*	160	
Cork	260	
Limerick	168	
Castlebar	418	
Athlone	316	35
Enniskillen[364]	669	

[361] A decrease for the second consecutive year.
[362] A decrease for the second consecutive year.
[363] A decrease for the second consecutive year.
[364] Orig., 'Iniskillin'.

Armagh*	254
Derry	405
Newry	580
America	316
	———
In all	31,338[365]

N.B. In the circuits marked thus * there are fewer members than there were a year ago.

Q. 9. What is the Kingswood collection?
*A. £*230. 1*s*. 8*d*.
Q. 10. What is contributed toward the debt?[366]
*A. £*1,665. 13*s*. 8½*d*.
Q. 11. How was this distributed?
A. As follows:

	£.	*s.*	*d.*
London	159	14	1
Chatham	11	11	6
Norwich	237	16	7
Wilts., N[orth]	28	0	0
Pensford	40	0	0
Bath	40	0	0
Devonsh[ire]	19	12	6
Cornwall, W[est]	25	10	0
Stroud	21	12	9
Staffordsh[ire]	87	2	1
Chester, N[orth]	56	10	8
Chester, S[outh]	30	8	6
Lancash[ire], N[orth]	35	11	9
[Lancashire], S[outh]	53	5	8
Derbysh[ire]	35	8	7
Sheffield	30	10	6
Linc[olnshire], E[ast]	21	13	4

[365] Orig., '31,340'.

[366] On the Yearly Subscription JW wrote to CW, 'Nothing was ever yet expended out of the Yearly Subscription without being immediately set down by the Secretary. I never took a shilling out of the Fund yet'. Aug. 3, 1771, *Letters* (Telford), 5:270.

Leeds	74	0	0	
Birstall	85	11	0	
Bradford	46	8	8	
Haworth	50	0	0	
Whitehaven	5	0	0	5
Scarborough	18	3	3	
Yarm	41	4	0	
[The] Dales	57	0	0	
Newcastle	75	1	3	
Edinburgh	78	0	0	10
Aberdeen	7	0	0	
Preachers and Law	180	16	1	
Cork	10	0	0	
Derry	25	0	0	
	£1,687	12	9[367]	15

N.B. Here is more expended than received. This was supplied out of money which was borrowed.

The old debt is only reduced £1,212. 7s. 7d. this year. The
new, £272. 10s.   20

Q. 12. Still we gain little ground. What can be done to
remove this heavy burden?

A. Try a new method. (1) Let every Methodist in England,
Scotland, and Ireland give for one year a penny a week.
(2) Let those who are not poor in each society pay for those 25
that are. (3) Let any of them who are minded contribute
farther weekly, as they shall see good. (4) Let this be paid
by the leaders to the Assistant in each circuit, and let him,
(5), bring it to the ensuing Conference. If this is done, it
will both pay our whole debt and supply all contingencies. 30

Q. 13. Where and when may this begin?[368]

A. At Leeds the first Tuesday in August.

Q. 14. What is added this year to the Preachers' Fund?

A. £63. 8s. 5d.

Q. 15. What is given out of it?[369]   35

---

[367] Orig., '£1,691. 19s. 10d.' This year the distribution is mainly to circuits rather
than to individual preaching-houses, though there are exceptions, such as Chatham,
Pensford, Bath, and Stroud.

[368] I.e., 'the ensuing Conference', *A*. 12 (5).

[369] Here is introduced the practice of listing the disbursements from the
Preachers' Fund followed in later years.

	£.	s.	d.
A. To Elizabeth Standring[370]	10	0	0
Elizabeth Oldham	5	5	0
Mary Penington	5	5	0
Elizabeth Dillon	5	5	0
Samuel Levick[371]	5	5	0
Richard Lucas	5	5	0
	£36	5	0

Q. 16. What remains?
A. £27. 3s. 5d.
Q. 17. How many preachers' wives are to be provided for?
A. Forty-four. (For three are removed, and four added).[372]
Q. 18. By what societies?

S. Mather, Duncan, Clough (½)[373]	*London*
S. Whitaker	*Sussex*
S. Easton, Wolf, Crowle (½)[374]	*Cornwall, West*
S. Barker, Pitt,[375]	*Bristol*
S. Ashman (½), Cotty (½)[376]	*Devon*
S. Bourke, Brisco	*Wilts., North*
S. Brammah, Rodda	*Cornwall, East*
S. Ellis	*Gloucestershire*
S. Costerdine	*Staffordshire*
S. Guilford	*Chester*
S. Thomas, Taylor	*Manchester*
S. Shaw	*Macclesfield*
S. Greenwood, Woodcock	*Liverpool*
S. Evans	*Derbyshire*

[370] Orig., 'Standering'.

[371] Levick seems to have been ill, and on p. 3 of Costerdine's copy of the *Minutes*, he notes after John Ellis, 'Dead Jany. 4, 1772', and below, '3 preachers died, J. Ellis & Saml. Levick'.

[372] Apparently Janes, Henderson, and Lowes are removed, but Duncan, Crowle, Ashman, Cotty, Bourke, Thomas, and Hunter appear to be added.

[373] Duncan and Clough were serving the Kent Circuit.

[374] Only Wolf was serving in Cornwall. Easton was in Bedfordshire, and Crowle in Devon.

[375] Barker was in Oxfordshire; Pitt in Wiltshire.

[376] Ashman was in Wiltshire; Cotty in Gloucestershire.

S. Harrison, Westell[377]	*Grimsby*	
S. Peacock, Lee	*Epworth*	
S. Bumsted	*Sheffield*	
S. Garnet,[378] Mitchell	*Leeds*	
S. Oliver, Morgan	*Birstall*	5
S. Atlay	*Bradford*	
S. Robertshaw, Poole	*Haworth*	
S. Brown, Nelson	*York and*	
S. Waldron	*Hull*	
S. Rowell, Hunter	*The Dales*	10
S. Hopper, Carlill	*Yarm*	
S. Swan, Jaco, Hanby[379]	*Newcastle*	

[Additional Note:
The following is the clarifying statement issued by Wesley to satisfy 15
the Calvinist objections to the minute in 1770. It is in Wesley's hand.]

Bristol
August the 9th. 1771

20

Whereas the Doctrinal points in the *Minutes* of a Conference held
in London, August the 7th, 1770 have been understood to favour
justification by works: Now the Revd. John Wesley and others
assembled in Conference do declare, That we had no such meaning;
and that we abhor the doctrine of justification by works, as a most 25
perilous and abominable doctrine. And as the said *Minutes* are not
sufficiently guarded in the way they are expressed, we hereby
solemnly declare, in the sight of God, that we have no trust or confidence but in the alone merits of our Lord and Saviour Jesus Christ
for justification or salvation, either in life, death, or the day of judg- 30
ment. And that no one is a real Christian believer (and consequently
cannot be saved) who doth not good works where there is time and
opportunity, yet our works have no part in meriting or purchasing
our justification,[380] from first to last, either in whole or in part.

---

[377] Westell was serving in Birstall.
[378] Garnet was serving at Sheffield.
[379] Swan was serving at Yarm; Hanby at Edinburgh.
[380] Tyerman says that in Shirley's 'Narrative', the word 'justification' in the last
line of the statement is replaced by 'salvation'. This difference became important
in the controversy later; Wesley and Fletcher were eventually prepared to say that
'final salvation' requires 'works meet for repentance'. *Wesley*, 3:100, n. 2.

John Wesley	J. Cotty	Geoᶜ Shadford
Joˢ Cownley	John Furz	William Pitt
J. Helton	John Goodwin	Richard Bourke
Thoˢ Rankin	James Glasbrook	Jonathan Crowle
5 Jnᵒ Easton	Tho. Taylor	James Parfett
Danˡ Bumsted	Jnᵒ Oliver	Benjⁿ Rhodes
Jnᵒ Pawson	Samuel Wells	Thoˢ Hanson
Alexʳ Mather	Jos. Benson	John Murray
Joseph Thompson	Thomas Clough	Richard Seed
10 James Dempster	Martin Rodda	Richᵈ Andrews
Thoˢ Westell	John Duncan	Willᵐ Whiteaker
Barnibas Thomas	Francis Walker	Edward Slater
Joseph Guilford	Willᵐ Barker	John Poole
Thomas Potter	Richard Caddick	
15 Jasper Winscom	Christopher Watkin	
Thoˢ Twinny	Thoˢ Eden	
Jerʰ Robertshaw	Edwᵈ Bolton	
Samˡ Tooth	George Hudson	
John Magor	James Nind	
20 Mattʷ Mayer	Will. Winbe	
	Thoˢ Brisco.	

Annual *Minutes of some late Conversations*, 1772

Leeds, Tuesday, Aug. 4, 1772.[381]

[381] Wesley writes,

'On Tuesday, August 4, our Conference began. Generally during the time of Conference, as I was talking from morning to night, I had used to desire one of our brethren to preach in the morning. But having many things to say, I resolved with God's help to preach morning as well as evening. And I found no difference at all. I was no more tired than with my usual labour—that is, no more than if I had been sitting still in my study from morning to night.' *Journal & Diaries*, 22:344–45 in this edn.

Thomas Rutherford describes the effect of attending the Conference as a young itinerant. He lodged with one of the original Methodists, along with 'the venerable John Nelson'. He was greatly interested in and affected by the stories of how Methodists had suffered in the early days. He heard Wesley preach in a field from Isa. 56:8, 9, showing the nature of the work of God among the Methodists as 'quick, deep, clear, extensive and a growing work'. Rutherford found 'the deep and

Q. 1. What preachers are *admitted* this year?

A. Joseph Benson, Thomas Tatton, John Bristol, John
   Pritchard.

Q. 2. Who *remain* on trial?

A. Edward Slater, David Evans, Thomas Tennant,   5
   James Hindmarsh, John Watson, John Brettel, because
   they were not present—otherwise they might have been
   admitted.

Q. 3. Who are *admitted on trial?*

unaffected piety of the Methodists in Leeds, the sight of so many preachers: and
the accounts given in the Conference of the work throughout the connexion, greatly
strengthened me in the truth, and enlarged my view of religion'. *MM* 31(1808):
482, quoted in *Journal & Diaries*, 22:344 n. in this edn.

At this Conference, though the *Minutes* do not reveal the fact, Captain Webb
appealed for preachers for America, and Rankin and Shadford responded for the
following spring. Rankin reveals in his diary that he was at the Conference and
talked with Webb, though he notes that one had to make allowances for the fact that
Webb had 'a lively imagination and is always ready to dwell upon the marvellous'.
Tyerman MSS, 2:106.

Charles Wesley was not present. Joseph Benson wrote to him (Aug. 26, 1772,
PLP 7.6.7.12, in MA), to say that Charles 'leans on a broken reed' by depending
on him for an account of the proceedings: 'There was so much temporal business
to be transacted that there was little time for any spiritual and therefore I had nothing to transmit worth your notice, nothing but what you will see in the *Minutes.*'
He was pleased to see such 'harmony and love among the preachers' and so much
'attention' paid to 'your brother'. 'Yet it was a very tedious and unprofitable time
to me. I greatly wish for my part, that it could be contrived to transact the temporal matters by the Assistants alone, before the other preachers arrive, that there
might be time for discussing some matters of importance and material edification
in faith and love.' As it was, he could see '*no end* it answers with respect to the
majority at all'.

Joseph Sutcliffe (MS 'History', fols. 791–92) records under this year a
rumour that JW was going to America as a bishop. He followed Nathan Bangs's
History of the Methodist Episcopal Church (in America), misinterpreting a jok-
ing remark in one of JW's letters, though JW was indeed talking of an American
visit; *Letters* (Telford), 5:303. Sutcliffe then took such a trip to explain a letter
by Charles Wesley to Mark Davis (Dec. 10, 1771) describing a plan for the connexion to be directed by twelve lay preachers; see *Minutes* (1769), *Q.* 4 n. 227.
CW reassured Davis that the concern was only to keep the connexion together
after the Wesleys' deaths and that it would be necessary for them to be under
Davis's government and not vice versa. The plan was worked out at a meeting
of preachers in London and was in fact one of several abortive attempts over the
years before the 1784 Deed of Declaration to find a form of succession to the
Wesleys with or without a clerical head. See Rack, *Reasonable Enthusiast*, 464f.,
and introduction, p. 88.

A. William Eells,[382] John Roberts, William Severn, John
Broadbent, Thomas Payne, Thomas Rutherford, Robert
Dall,[383] John Watson,[384] John McBurney, Robert Davis,
and John Price.

5   *Q.* 4. Who *desist* from travelling?
A. W. P.[385] and B. T.[386]
Q. 5. Who act as *Assistants* this year?
A. Alexander Mather, John Easton, William Barker, James
Clough, Thomas Hanson, Samuel Wells, Richard Bourke,
10   George Shadford, John Pawson, John Goodwin, Robert
Wilkinson, James Dempster, Stephen Proctor, Martin
Rodda, John Furz, Francis Wolf, Thomas Brisco, John
Oliver, Samuel Woodcock, John Murlin, John Mason,
John Shaw, Benjamin Rhodes, Isaac Brown, Daniel
15   Bumsted, William Thompson, T. Taylor, John Atlay,
Thomas Johnson, Jeremiah Robertshaw, T. Rankin,
William Hunter, Joseph Thompson, James Watson,
Christopher Hopper, George Story, Duncan Wright,
Peter Jaco, James Glasbrook, William Collins, John
20   Christian, George Snowden, James Hudson, Richard
Whatcoat, and Thomas Wride.
Q. 6. Are there any objections to any of our preachers?
A. Examine them one by one: (which was done).
Q. [7]. How are they stationed this year?
25   *A.* As follows:
(1) *London*, J. W[esley], A. Mather, Thomas Olivers,
Thomas Payne.

---

[382] Orig., 'Eels'. It is extremely difficult to arrive at a 'standard' spelling for his
name. The recorded occurrences in print seem almost equally divided, with 'Eels'
in the earlier years, 'Eells' in the later—the only occurrences of 'Eells' in the
Minutes before 1782 are once in 1773, 1777, and 1778; the only occurrence of 'Eels'
after 1781 is once in 1783. The same is true in Wesley's holograph letters: those of
July 26, Sept. 18, and Oct. 16, 1774, all have 'Eels'; those of Sept. 13, 1784, and May
28, 1789, 'Eells'. On the principle that a man's mature desires about spelling his
name are probably those to be followed, and that these eventually turn up in the
writings of his contemporaries, it seems best to use 'Eells' throughout.

[383] Orig., 'John Dall', surely an error, for all other references are to 'Robert Dall',
except the stations of 1774, which speak of 'Richard Dall'.

[384] This may be John Watson, Jun.; John Watson, Sen., remained on trial in the
same year (see *Q.* 2 above).

[385] William Pitt, who was last stationed in 1771.

[386] Apparently Barnabas Thomas, who was not stationed this year, but returned
to the regular itinerancy in 1773.

(2) *Kent*, John Easton, John Undrell.

(3) *Sussex*, William Barker, John Duncan.

(4) *Norwich*, James Clough, John Pritchard, John Broadbent; T. Tennant, supernum[erary].

(5) *Bedfordshire*, Thomas Hanson, W. Ashman, John McEvoy. 5

(6) *Oxfordshire*, Samuel Wells, Wm. Brammah.

(7) *Wiltshire, South*, Richard Bourke, William Eells.

(8) *North*, James Hindmarsh, Jonat. Crowle, Tho. Newall. 10

(9) *Bristol*, John Pawson, George Hudson; John Allen, supernumerary.

(10) *Devon*, John Goodwin, James Cotty.

(11) *Cornwall, East*, Robert Wilkinson, William Ellis, John Roberts. 15

(12) *Cornwall, West*, James Dempster, Richard Rodda,[387] Joseph Bradford, Wm. Whitaker.

(13) *Pembrokeshire*, Stephen Proctor, Charles Boon.

(14) *Glamorganshire*, Martin Rodda, James Barry.[388]

(15) *Brecon*, John Furz, John Brettel. 20

(16) *Gloucestershire*, Francis Wolf, Richard Seed.

(17) *Staffordshire*, Thomas Brisco, Thomas Hanby.

(18) *Chester*, John Oliver, Robert Costerdine.

(19) *Macclesfield*,[389] Samuel Woodcock, David Evans, John Bristol. 25

(20) *Manchester*, John Murlin, Joseph Guilford.[390]

(21) *Liverpool*, John Mason, Robert Roberts.

(22) *Derbyshire*, John Shaw, Samuel Bardsley, Joseph Harper.

(23) *Lincolnshire, East*, Benjamin Rhodes, Joseph Garnet, 30 Thomas Westell.

(24) *West*, Isaac Brown, John Peacock, Robert Empringham.

(25) *Sheffield*, Daniel Bumsted, William Severn, Thomas Carlill. 35

---

[387] Orig., 'Radda'.

[388] This is the first time James Barry is mentioned in active service; see *Minutes* (1770), *Q.* 4.

[389] Orig., 'Maxfield'.

[390] Orig., 'Guildford', all other references being to 'Guilford'.

(26) *Leeds*, William Thompson, Thomas Lee, Parson Greenwood.

(27) *Birstall*, Thomas Taylor, Thomas Mitchell, John Nelson.

(28) *Bradford*, John Atlay, John Morgan.

(29) *Haworth*, Thomas Johnson, John Poole, Thomas Tatton.

(30) *Whitehaven*, Jeremiah Robertshaw, William Linnell.

(31) *York*, Thomas Rankin, J. W.[391]

(32) *Hull*, William Hunter, Lancelot Harrison, M. F.[392]

(33) *Yarm*, Joseph Thompson, John Bredin, Samuel Smith.

(34) *The Dales*, Robert Swan, James Watson, George Mowat; Thomas Cherry, supernumerary.

(35) *Newcastle*, Christopher Hopper, Jacob Rowell, Joseph Benson, Thomas Simpson.

(36) *Edinburgh*, George Story, Alexander McNab, Hugh Saunderson, George Wadsworth.

(37) *Aberdeen*, Duncan Wright, Thomas Dixon, Christopher Watkins, Thomas Rutherford, Robert Dall.

(38) *Dublin*, Peter Jaco.

(39) *Waterford*, James Glasbrook, Francis Wrigley.

(40) *Cork*, William Collins, Jonathan Hern, Robert Swindells.

(41) *Limerick*,[393] Edward Slater.

(42) *Athlone*, John Christian, James Perfect, William Horner.

(43) *Castlebar*, George Snowden, T. H.,[394] Robert Davis.

(44) *Enniskillen*,[395] James Hudson, John Watson,[396] Michael McDonald, John McBurney.[397]

(45) *Londonderry*,[398] John Floyd.

(46) *Armagh*, Richard Whatcoat, John Wittam.

(47) *Newry*, Thomas Wride, Nehemiah Price,[399] John Murray, John Price.

---

[391] Probably Isaac Waldron rather than John Watson, Jun.

[392] Michael Fenwick.

[393] No listed Assistant.

[394] Apparently Thomas Halladay, as also in 1774, 1776, 1779, and 1780.

[395] Orig., 'Iniskillin'.

[396] Apparently John Watson, Sen.

[397] Orig., 'John McCurney', clearly an error for 'McBurney'.

[398] No listed Assistant.

[399] Orig., 'Nathaniel Price', clearly an error for 'Nehemiah Price'.

(48) *America*, Francis Asbury, Richard Boardman, Joseph Pilmore, Richard Wright.

Q. 8. What numbers are in the society?

A. They are as follows:

London	2,441	
Sussex*	193	
Kent	334	
Norfolk	410	
Bedfordshire*[400]	274	10
Oxfordshire	390	
Wiltshire, South	278	
Ditto, North*	823	
Bristol*	1,249	
Devonshire	419	15
Cornwall, East	639	
Ditto, West	1,814	
Gloucestershire	391	
Staffordshire*[401]	696	
Cheshire, North	544	20
Ditto, South	975	
Wales, West	112	
Ditto, East	130	
Ditto, North	167	
Lancashire, South	907	25
Ditto, North	687	
Derbyshire	903	
Sheffield	725	
Lincolnshire, East	690	
Lincolnshire, W[est]*	716	30
Leeds	1,826	
Birstall[402]	1,155	
Bradford	849	
Haworth*[403]	1,219	
Whitehaven	256	35
York*	536	

(Line 5 appears to the right of the start of the list.)

---

[400] For the second consecutive year.

[401] For the second consecutive year.

[402] 'Birstall' here, but in the list of circuits *Q*. 7 (27), orig. lists 'Birstal'.

[403] For the second consecutive year.

Hull	608
Yarm*[404]	883
The Dales	1,003
Newcastle	1,747
Edinburgh*	245
Aberdeen	458
Dublin*[405]	347
Waterford	124
Cork*	220
Limerick	168
Castlebar	357
Athlone	326
Enniskillen[406]	937
Armagh	347
Londonderry	483
Newry*	483
America	500
In all	31,984[407]

N.B. In the circuits marked thus * there is a decrease this year.

Q. 9 What is the Kingswood collection?
A. £228. 9*s*. 10*d*.
Q. 10. What is contributed toward the debt?
A. £3,076. 7*s*. 8*d*.
Q. 11. How was it distributed?
A. As follows:

	£.	*s*.	*d*.
Law	83	19	0
Contingencies of last year	83	11	2
Ditto for the present year	99	13	4
Borrowed for Ireland	55	0	0
To relieve preachers	119	13	5
London	100	0	0

---

[404] For the second consecutive year.
[405] For the second consecutive year.
[406] Orig., 'Iniskillin'.
[407] Orig., '31,983'.

Norwich	200	0	0	
Chatham	30	15	0	
Colchester	5	0	0	
Witney[408]	9	12	3	
Newbury	2	2	0	5
Portsmouth	30	0	3	
Salisbury	8	6	6	
Fareham	5	5	0	
Bradford, W[iltshire]	7	5	8	
Shaftesbury	5	5	0	10
Shepton [Mallet]	50	0	0	
Bath	47	7	0	
Paulton	5	0	0	
Pensford	7	0	0	
Axminster	14	0	0	15
Combstock[409]	8	15	4	
Hillfarance	6	0	0	
Sidmouth	21	0	0	
Lympsham[410]	9	10	0	
Redruth	10	10	0	20
Bisveale[411]	2	10	0	
St. John's	7	7	0	
Camborne[412]	6	6	0	
Tuckingmill[413]	4	10	0	
Stroud	74	0	0	25
Worcester	70	0	0	
Darlaston	20	0	0	
Cradley	14	7	0	
Stourbridge	5	7	8	
Birmingham	12	0	0	30
Wolverhampton	10	0	0	
Chester	80	0	0	
Burslem	56	5	9	

[408] Orig., 'Whitney', as also in 1773.

[409] Culmstock in East Devon, northeast of Cullompton, close to the Somerset border. There was certainly a Society here in 1777 (see Tiverton Circuit Book, cited by Mr. R. Thorne; information courtesy of John Lenton).

[410] Orig., 'Lymsham', as also in 1773.

[411] Busveal (Gwennap Pit) in the Redruth Circuit.

[412] Orig., 'Camburn'.

[413] Orig., 'Tucking Mill', as also in 1776.

	Macclesfield	56	6	0
	Congleton	35	5	5
	Creech	10	0	0
	Brecknock	8	0	0
5	New Mills	40	0	0
	Stockport	25	0	0
	Rochdale	77	3	3
	Bury	7	0	0
	Liverpool	27	1	2
10	Warrington	10	2	0
	Bolton	28	13	5
	Derby	21	4	9
	Burton	76	0	0
	Nottingham	77	15	4
15	Ashby	12	4	0
	Bradwell[414]	5	0	0
	Sheffield	40	0	0
	Doncaster	20	0	0
	Boston	50	0	0
20	Louth	5	0	0
	Rothwell	30	0	0
	Armley	10	12	0
	Horbury[415]	40	0	0
	Seacroft	30	0	0
25	Dawgreen[416]	160	0	0
	Thong	13	0	0
	Bradford Y[orkshire]	100	18	10
	Halifax	28	7	0
	Bingley	2	10	0
30	Bacup	6	0	0
	Padiham	6	0	0
	Mill End	8	14	0
	Heptonstall	25	0	0
	Hull	130	0	0
35	Whitby	100	0	0

[414] Orig., 'Brada'.

[415] Orig., 'Horbery'.

[416] Orig., 'Daw's Green', but clearly a reference to the hamlet of Daw Green or Dawgreen in the parish of Dewsbury, where the preaching-house was subject to dispute in 1789; see *The Case of Dewsbury House*, in *Societies*, 9:512–14 in this edn.

Stockton	15	0	0	
Yarm	20	0	0	
Thirsk	8	5	6	
Stokesley	2	0	0	
Barnard Castle	10	0	0	5
Monkwearmouth	30	2	6	
Edinburgh	56	10	0	
Dunbar	46	10	0	
Greenock[417]	20	0	0	
Dublin	38	11	6	10
Cork	15	0	0	
Kilkenny	70	0	0	
Newry	6	0	0 ½	
Newcastle	10	0	0	
				15
£3,078	1	0 ½[418]		

Q. 12. What can be done toward paying the remaining
  debt?

A. (1) Let us make a trial of another method. Instead of a 20
  subscription let a collection be made at every preaching-
  house, some time in next autumn (the Kingswood collection as usual).

  (2) Let all the money collected be produced at the next
  Conference; and we will return to every house that is in 25
  debt (provided it be old debt, not otherwise) at least
  what was collected there.

Q. 13. Where and when may the next Conference begin?

A. At London, the first Tuesday in August.

Q. 14. What is contributed to the Preachers' Fund? 30

A. £83. 11*s*. 8*d*.

Q. 15. What was given out of it?

A. Thirty-eight pounds.

Q. 16. How many preachers' wives are to be provided for?

A. Forty-four. 35

Q. 17. By what societies?

A. By the following:

---

[417] Orig., 'Grenock'.
[418] Orig., '£3,076. 7[*s*.] 8[*d*]'.

	London	S. Mather, Duncan, Clough.[419]
	Sussex	S. Barker.
	Wilts., North	S. Bourke, Brisco.[420]
	Bristol	S. Barry, Christian.[421]
5	*Cornwall, East*	S. Brammah.[422]
	———, *West*	S. Whitaker, Rodda, Easton.[423]
	Gloucestershire	S. Wolf.
	Devonshire	S. Cotty (½), S. Crowle (½).[424]
	Staffordshire	S. Hanby.
10	*Chester*	S. Oliver.
	Macclesfield[425]	S. Woodcock.
	Derbyshire	S. Shaw, Evans.[426]
	Manchester	S. Costerdine, Taylor.[427]
	Liverpool	S. Roberts, Morgan.[428]
15	*Lincolnshire, East*	S. Westell, Garnet.
	———, *West*	S. Brown, Peacock.
	Sheffield	S. Bumsted.
	Leeds	S. Thompson, Lee, Greenwood.
	Birstall	S. Mitchell, Nelson.
20	*Bradford*	S. Atlay.
	Haworth	S. Robertshaw,[429] Poole.
	York	J. W.[430] ⎫
	and	⎬ S. Harrison.
	Hull	S. Hunter ⎭
25	*The Dales*	S. Swan, Empringham.[431]
	Yarm	S. Story.[432]
	Newcastle	S. Hopper, Simpson, Rowell.

[419] Duncan was stationed in Sussex; Clough at Norwich.
[420] Brisco was stationed in Staffordshire.
[421] Barry was stationed in Glamorganshire; Christian at Athlone.
[422] Brammah was stationed in Oxfordshire.
[423] Easton was stationed in Kent.
[424] Crowle was stationed in Wiltshire.
[425] Orig., 'Maxfield'.
[426] Evans was stationed at Macclesfield.
[427] Costerdine was stationed at Chester; Taylor at Birstall.
[428] Morgan was stationed at Bradford.
[429] Robertshaw was stationed at Whitehaven.
[430] John Watson, [Jun.?].
[431] Empringham was stationed in Lincolnshire.
[432] Story was stationed in Edinburgh.

Q. 18. Several Assistants were not present when their
accounts were wanted. How may this inconvenience be
prevented?

A. Let all the Assistants be present on Sunday evening
before the Conference, that they may give in their   5
accounts on Monday morning.

Annual *Minutes of some late Conversations*, 1773

London, Tuesday, Aug. 3, 1773.[433]

Q. 1. What preachers are *admitted* this year?

A. Edward Slater, David Evans, Thomas Tennant, James   10
Hindmarsh, John Brettel, William Severn, John Broadbent,
Robert Empringham, Nehemiah Price, Thomas Payne.

Q. 2. Who remain on trial?

A. Thomas Rutherford, Michael Moorhouse, Robert Dall,
John Price, John McBurney, Robert Davis, William Eells,   15
John Watson, jun.

Q. 3. Who are admitted on *trial?*

A. Richard Hunt, Joseph Bradford, James Wood, Samuel
Randal, John Wiltshaw,[434] Victory Purdy,[435] William
Percival, Ralph Mather,[436] Jasper Robinson, William   20
Dufton, Joseph Moore, John Leech.

---

[433] Wesley wrote, 'Our Conference began. I preached mornings as well as evenings. And it was all one. I found myself just as though I had preached but once a day'. *Journal & Diaries*, 22:384f. in this edn. Samuel Bardsley wrote, 'I never was at a more comfortable Conference. We had a great deal of love among us. Dear Mr. Wesley laboured hard. I had the pleasure of hearing him twelve times. He said, he had not preached so much at a Conference these twenty years, and never was more assisted'. MS letters quoted by Tyerman, *Wesley*, 3:156.

[434] Orig., 'Wiltshire'. One entry in 1775 has 'Willshaw'; one in 1790, 'Wilshaw'; but the other entries in 1775, 1788–91, like his obituary in *MM* (1818), have 'Wiltshaw'.

[435] Victory Purdy actively served only in 1773. He was posted to Wiltshire.

[436] Ralph Mather was no relation to Alexander Mather. There is no other reference to him in the *Minutes*, and his career as a preacher was short-lived. He originated in Bolton, and in 1774 JW described him as 'a devoted young man but almost driven out of his mind by Mystic Divinity'. *Journal & Diaries*, 22:397 and n. 73 in this edn. He became a Quaker and then a Swedenborgian minister and was an advocate for oppressed textile workers in Bolton; see J. F. C. Harrison, *The Second Coming* (London, 1979), 21f., 233 n. 32.

Q. 4. Who desist from travelling?

A. J. G.,[437] William Ellis, William Linnell, John Watson, Sen.

Q. 5. Who act as Assistants this year?

A. Daniel Bumsted, Alexander Mather, John Easton, James Clough, Samuel Wells, Hugh Saunderson, Richard Bourke, George Hudson, John Furz, John Goodwin, James Dempster, Robert Wilkinson, Richard Whatcoat, Richard Rodda, James Barry, John Allen, Thomas Hanby, John Oliver, Thomas Hanson, John Mason, Robert Roberts, John Shaw, Jeremiah Robertshaw, Isaac Brown, Parson Greenwood, Thomas Lee, Thomas Taylor, Thomas Johnson, Jacob Rowell, William Hunter, Benjamin Rhodes, Duncan Wright, George Story, Christopher Hopper, William Thompson, Thomas Dixon, Peter Jaco, John Murray, Francis Wrigley, James Glasbrook, John Christian, Michael Moorhouse,[438] Alexander McNab, John Pritchard.

Q. 6. Are there any objections to any of our preachers?

A. Examine them one by one: (which was done).

Q. 7. How are they stationed this year?

A. As follows:

(Thomas Olivers travels with Mr. Wesley.)

(1) *London*, Daniel Bumsted, John Atlay, John Murlin.

(2) *Kent*, Alexander Mather, Sam Smith.

(3) *Sussex*, John Easton, John Undrell.

(4) *Norwich*, James Clough, John Brettel, Richard Hunt.

(5) *Bedfordshire*, Samuel Wells, William Ashman.

(6) *Oxfordshire*, Hugh Saunderson, John Wittam.

(7) *Wiltshire, South*,[439] William Collins, Jonathan Crowle.[440]

[437] Probably Joseph Guilford, who was not listed after 1772. Joseph Garnet also is not listed after 1772, but he appears to have died, and Jane Garnet (presumably his widow) continued to be supported by the Preachers' Fund, as probably were his children, for the names Catherine (or Katherine) and Elizabeth also appear in the records of the fund up to 1790.

[438] Moorhouse was still on trial when he was listed as an Assistant.

[439] No listed Assistant.

[440] Orig., 'John', as also in *Minutes* (1769), *Q*. 4 and n. 229.

(8)   *North*,[441] George Hudson, Richard Bourke, Thomas Newall, Victory Purdy.

(9) *Bristol*, John Allen, Francis Wolf, Joseph Bradford; John Pawson, supern[umerary].

(10) *Devon*, John Goodwin, James Hindmarsh.   5

(11) *Cornwall, East*, James Dempster, Martin Rodda, George Shorter.

(12) *Cornwall, West*, Robert Wilkinson, James Cotty, Thomas Carlill, Joseph Moore.

(13) *Pembrokeshire*, Richard Whatcoat, Charles Boon.   10

(14) *Glamorgan*, Richard Rodda, W. Whitaker.

(15) *Brecon*, James Barry, Stephen Proctor.

(16) *Gloucestershire*, John Furz, William Severn.

(17) *Staffordshire*, Thomas Hanby, Joseph Harper.

(18) *Chester*, John Oliver, Thomas Brisco.   15

(19) *Macclesfield*, Thomas Hanson, Thomas Westell, Samuel Bardsley.

(20) *Manchester*, John Mason, Lancelot Harrison.

(21) *Liverpool*, Robert Roberts, John Morgan.

(22) *Derbyshire*, John Shaw, Richard Seed, Wm. Percival.   20

(23) *Lincolnshire, East*, Samuel Woodcock, John Peacock, John Wiltshaw.

(24) *Lincolnshire, West*, Jeremiah Robertshaw, David Evans, Jasper Robinson.

(25) *Sheffield*, Isaac Brown, John Leech, Wm. Dufton.   25

(26). *Leeds*, Parson Greenwood, John Nelson, J. W.[442]

(27) *Birstall*, Thomas Lee, Thomas Mitchell, John Poole.

(28) *Bradford*, Thomas Taylor, William Barker, Thomas Tennant.

(29) *Haworth*, Thomas Johnson, Edward Slater, Robert   30 Costerdine.

(30) *Whitehaven*, Jacob Rowell, George Mowat.

(31) *York*, William Hunter, Thomas Wride.

(32) *Hull*, Benjamin Rhodes, George Wadsworth, Robert Empringham.   35

(33). *Yarm*, Duncan Wright, Joseph Thompson, William Brammah.[443]

---

[441] Two listed Assistants. Was there movement between South and North circuits, and Lincolnshire, East and West?

[442] Probably Isaac Waldron.

[443] Orig., 'Bramma', though elsewhere always spelled 'Brammah'.

(34) *The Dales*, George Story, Christopher Watkins, M. F.[444]

(35) *Newcastle*, Christopher Hopper, James Hudson, Robert Swan, William Eells.

(36) *Edinburgh*, William Thompson, Joseph Benson, John Broadbent.

(37). *Aberdeen*, Thomas Dixon, Thomas Rutherford, John Bredin, Thomas Tatton, Robert Dall.

(38) *Dublin*, Peter Jaco, John Floyd.

(39) *Waterford*, John Murray, Michael McDonald.

(40). *Cork*, Francis Wrigley, John Bristol.

(41) *Limerick*,[445] Jonathan Hern;[446] Robert Swindells, sup[ernumerary].

(42) *Athlone*, James Glasbrook, George Snowden, John Price.

(43) *Castlebar*, John Christian, William Horner, John Price.

(44) *Enniskillen*, Michael Moorhouse,[447] T. H.,[448] John M'Burney.

(45) *Londonderry*, Alexander McNab, James Perfect.[449]

(46) *Armagh*,[450] Barnabas Thomas,[451] Thomas Payne, John Watson, Jun.

(47) *Newry*, John Pritchard, James Watson, Nehemiah Price.

(48) *America*,[452] Thomas Rankin, George Shadford, Francis Asbury, Richard Boardman, Richard Wright, Joseph Pilmore, Robert Williams, John King.

Q. 8. What numbers are in the society?

[444] Michael Fenwick.

[445] No listed Assistant.

[446] Orig., 'John Hern'.

[447] Orig., 'Moorhorse'; in 1776–77, 1780, and once in 1775 and 1782 the name is spelled 'Morehouse'; and once in 1775, 'Moorehouse'. All other references to the name are as 'Moorhouse'.

[448] Thomas Halliday; cf. 1772.

[449] Orig., 'Parfect'. He signed the preachers' agreement (1771) as 'James Parfett'; otherwise his name is printed as 'Perfect' (1770–85).

[450] No listed Assistant.

[451] Orig., 'Barnaby Thomas', as in 1785 (once), while in 1769 it appeared as 'Branaby'. 'Barnaby' was obviously the diminutive form of 'Barnabas'.

[452] No listed Assistant.

A. They are as follows:

London	2,442	
Sussex	223	
Kent*	311	5
Norfolk	485	
Bedfordshire	282	
Oxfordshire	442	
Wiltshire, South	340	
Ditto, North	872	10
Bristol	1,360	
Devonshire	425	
Cornwall, East*	573	
Ditto, West*[453]	1,421	
Gloucestershire	420	15
Staffordshire*[454]	631	
Cheshire, North	547	
Ditto, South	1,076	
Wales, West	141	
Ditto, East	112	20
Ditto, North*	117	
Lancashire, South	987	
Ditto, North	724	
Derbyshire	1,057	
Sheffield	910	25
Lincolnshire, East	739	
Ditto, West	650	
Leeds	1,902	
Birstall	1,185	
Bradford	900	30
Haworth*[455]	1,212	
Whitehaven	272	
York*[456]	510	
Hull	620	
Yarm*[457]	874	35

---

[453] A decrease for the second consecutive year.
[454] A decrease for the second consecutive year.
[455] A decrease for the second consecutive year.
[456] A decrease for the second consecutive year.
[457] A decrease for the second consecutive year.

	The Dales	1,053
	Newcastle*	1,716
	Edinburgh	260
	Aberdeen	470
5	Dublin	408
	Waterford	174
	Cork	230
	Limerick	170
	Castlebar	404
10	Athlone	436
	Enniskillen[458]	1,160
	Armagh	370
	Londonderry	175
	Newry	486
15	America	1,000
	In all	33,274[459]

N.B. In the circuits marked thus* there is a decrease this year.

20

Q. 9. What is the Kingswood collection?

A. £229. 16*s.* 8*d.*

Q. [10].[460] What children are admitted?

A. B[rother][461] Barry's, Greenwood's, Poole's.

25   *Q.* 11. What is contributed toward the debt?[462]

---

[458] Orig., 'Inniskillen'.

[459] Orig., '33,839'.

[460] In the orig., *Q.* 10 is left unnumbered, and those following are numbered 10–17; here renumbered 11–18.

[461] Though the Kingswood collection was begun in 1756 and the total recorded from at least 1765, this is the first time that the names of those supported are listed. From 1780 (*Minutes, QQ.* 13, 14) daughters were also supported at various schools. The mysterious Kingswood School for girls, of which very little is known, appears to have still existed in 1751 when a girl was withdrawn from it: *Letters*, 26:464, 468 and n. in this edn.; see also *Minutes* (1774), *Q.* 12 and n. 522; (1778), *Q.* 13, n. 755. A. G. Ives quotes a copy of the *Short Account of Kingswood School*, amended to provide for girls' education, and cites the case of Grimshaw's daughter, who died in 1750, as being there (*Kingswood School in Wesley's Day and Since* [London, 1970], 39–42). JW's letter of 1751 may therefore refer to both sexes being at the original school.

[462] JW was also concerned about the finances of the Book Room. Thomas Ball and Alexander Mather were appointed to make 'an exact account' in Feb. 1773 and produced a not very exact one. In July, JW complained about his debts. *Journal & Diaries*, 22:384 in this edn. He said in Oct. (ibid., 22:392 in this edn.) that the accounts were in confusion from the sudden death of the 'book-keeper'. He had committed suicide in a fit of madness. Tyerman, *Wesley*, 3:154–56, and see introduction, p. 58.

A. £2,213. 9*s*. 7*d*.
Q. 12. How was it distributed?
A. As follows:

	£.	*s*.	*d*.	
Law	184	19	2	5
Contingencies	51	0	0	
Chatham	120	0	0	
Sheerness[463]	20	0	0	
Norwich	180	0	0	10
Sarum	20	0	0	
Portsmouth	20	0	0	
Fareham	12	0	0	
Bradford [Wilts.]	34	1	3	
Shaftesbury	80	0	0	15
Shepton	96	0	0	
Frome[464]	4	0	0	
Lympsham	8	0	0	
Axminster	4	0	0	
Brecon	80	0	0	20
Stroud	30	0	0	
Worcester	30	0	0	
Darlaston	20	0	0	
Wolverhampton	40	0	0	
Chester	60	0	0	25
Macclesfield	20	0	0	
Congleton[465]	20	0	0	
Bolton[466]	34	6	0	
Liverpool	80	0	0	
Warrington	5	14	0	30
Nottingham	37	1	4	
Burton	90	0	0	
Boston	40	0	0	
Louth	20	0	0	
Rotherham	50	0	0	35
Bradwell	5	0	0	

[463] Orig., 'Sheirness'.
[464] Orig., 'Froom'; 'Froome' in 1786.
[465] Orig., 'Congelton'.
[466] Orig., 'Boulton'.

Doncaster	30	0	0
Bradford [Yorks.]	149	5	0
Halifax	15	15	0
Bingley[467]	24	0	0
Heptonstall[468]	20	0	0
Padiham	20	0	0
Hull	90	0	0
Whitby	100	0	0
Edinburgh	143	0	0
Whitehaven	20	0	0
Witney	50	0	0
Dundee	50	0	0
Greenock	20	0	0
Newbury	10	0	0
In all	£ 2,238	1	9[469]

Q. 13. What is contributed to the Preachers' Fund?
A. £81. 12*s*. 3*d*.
Q. 14. What demands are there upon it?[470]
A. The following:

	£.	s.	d.
S[ister] Oldham	7	17	6
S. Standring	10	0	0
S. Penington	5	5	0
S. Dillon[471]	5	5	0
S. Garnet	5	5	0
B[rother] Minethorp[472]	5	5	0
B. Lucas	5	5	0
	44	2	6

Q. 15. How many preachers' wives are to be provided for?
A. Forty-four (in effect).

---

[467] Orig., 'Bingly'.
[468] Orig., 'Heptonstal'.
[469] Orig., '£2,084. 11. 11.'
[470] JW had written to Hopper on Aug. 7, 1773, saying that the Preachers' Fund had lent £200 towards building the Edinburgh preaching-house: 'We have gone a few steps further towards a general trust, but the matter goes on very slowly'. *Letters* (Telford), 6:37.
[471] Orig., 'Dibbon'.
[472] Orig., 'Menithorp'.

Q. 16. By what societies?
A. By the following:

London	S[ister] Bumsted, Mather.[473]	
Sussex	S. Easton.	5
Wilts, North	S. Collins, Bourke.	
Bristol	S. Barry, Christian, Ashman (½).[474]	
Devon	S. Cotty (½), S. Crowle (½).[475]	
Cornwall, East	S. Rodda.	
———, West	S. Whitaker, Atlay, Clough (½).[476]	10
Gloucestershire	S. Wolf[477]	
Staffordshire	S. Hanby.	
Chester	S. Oliver	
Macclesfield	S. Westell.	
Derbyshire	S. Shaw, Poole.[478]	15
Manchester	S. Harrison, Taylor.[479]	
Liverpool	S. Roberts, Costerdine.[480]	
Lincolnshire, East	S. Peacock, Woodcock.	
———, West	S. Robertshaw, Empringham.[481]	
Sheffield	S. Evans.[482]	20
Leeds	S. Greenwood, S. W.,[483] Nelson.	
Birstall	S. Mitchell, Lee.	
Bradford	S. Morgan.[484]	
Haworth	S. Brown, Brisco.[485]	
York	S. Hunter	25
	S. Barker.[486]	
Hull	S. Story	

[473] Mather was serving in Kent.

[474] Barry was serving in Brecon; Christian at Castlebar, and Ashman in Bedfordshire.

[475] Cotty was serving in Cornwall; Crowle in Wiltshire.

[476] Whitaker was serving in Glamorgan; Atlay in London; Clough in Norwich.

[477] Wolf was serving in Bristol.

[478] Poole was serving at Birstall.

[479] Taylor was serving at Bradford.

[480] Costerdine was serving at Haworth.

[481] Empringham was serving at Hull.

[482] Evans was serving in Lincolnshire.

[483] 'S.W.' here apparently means Sister Waldron. See above, *Q.* 7 (26).

[484] Morgan was serving at Liverpool.

[485] Haworth did not support either of the preachers appointed. Brown was serving at Sheffield; Brisco at Chester.

[486] Why did Hull not support its own preacher, Empringham? Story was serving in The Dales; Barker at Bradford.

Yarm	S. Brammah.
The Dales	S. Rowell, Shorter.[487]
Newcastle	S. Hopper, Swan, Thompson (½).[488]

5   *Q*. 17. When and where may the next Conference begin?
A. At Bristol, the first Tuesday in August.
Q. 18. Can anything be done now, in order to lay a foundation for the future union?[489] Would it not be well for any
that are willing to sign some Articles of Agreement before
10 God calls me hence?
A. We will do it. Accordingly the following paper was written and signed.
We whose names are underwritten, being thoroughly convinced of the necessity of a close union between those
15 whom God is pleased to use as instruments in this glorious work, in order to preserve this union between ourselves, are resolved, God being our helper,
    I. *To devote ourselves entirely to God, denying* ourselves,
       taking up our cross daily,[490] steadily aiming at one
20   thing to *save our own souls and them that hear us.*[491]
    II. To preach the *old Methodist doctrines*, and no other,
        contained in the *Minutes* of the Conferences.
    III. To observe and enforce the whole *Methodist
         discipline* laid down in the said *Minutes*.[492]

[487] Rowell was serving at Whitehaven. George Shorter was serving in Cornwall, East, *Q*. 7 (11), but presumably Sister Shorter was being supported on the principle of the stronger circuits aiding the weaker. *Minutes* (1769), *Q*. 23 and n. 267; (1770), *Q*. 20 and n. 319.

[488] Thompson was serving at Edinburgh.

[489] Cf. *Minutes* (1774), *Q*. 26: 'Can anything be done in order to lay a foundation for future union?'

[490] See Luke 9:23.

[491] See 1 Tim. 4:16.

[492] See *Minutes* (1769), JW paper (5) after *Q*. 25; (1774), *Q*. 17; (1775), *Q*. 26. JW had also written to Fletcher on July 21, 1773, urging him to move to gain influence with the people and to spend a few days at the Conference, with a view to grooming him as his clerical successor. *Letters* (Telford), 6:33f. It is presumably at this Conference that John Pawson wrote in his MS life of Whitehead, 'The preachers, so far from endeavouring to persuade Mr Wesley to ordain any of them, or alter his plan at that time, much less did they think of ordaining one anointer, that it was not till ten years after that, in 1784, that ordination was first proposed' (though of course it had been debated in the 1750s). Tyerman MSS, 3:53; see also *Minutes* (1772), n. 381 (p. 405), for an earlier attempt at a succession plan with a committee under a clerical head.

Daniel Bumsted
John Atlay
John Murlin
Thomas Oliver[s]
Alexander Mather   5
Thomas Hanby
Thomas Taylor
John Oliver
William Hunter
Thomas Brisco   10
John Morgan
Samuel Woodcock
Richard Bourke
John Pawson
William Thompson   15
Joseph Thompson
John Allen
Thomas Johnson
John Nelson
Isaac Brown   20
William Eells
William Barker
Thomas Payne
James Hindmarsh
John Shaw   25
Samuel Wells
Samuel Bardsley
John Goodwin
George Hudson
John Bristol   30
David Evans
Lancelot Harrison
John Easton
James Hudson
John Pritchard   35
William Severn
Robert Wilkinson
Richard Rodda
William Brammah
James Clough   40
John Broadbent

John Mason
Thomas Tennant
William Whitaker
Joseph Harper
5   John Brettel[493]
Francis Wolf
Richard Whatcoat
Hugh Saunderson.

Annual *Minutes of some late Conversations,* 1774

10   Bristol, Tuesday, Aug. 9, 1774.[494]

[493] Orig., 'Brettell', as also in 1774 (1 of 2), 1787–91; in 1785 it appears as 'Brittel'; and in 1790 (Addenda) as 'Brittell'. His portrait in the *AM* (1784), 'aged 39', is engraved 'Brettal'. The overwhelming number of entries, however, spell his name 'Brettel'. Similar details are found for Jeremiah Brettel: 'Brettell', 1775 (1 of 3), 1778, 1784, 1785 (1 of 2), 1786, 1788 (1 of 2), 1789–91. His portrait in the *AM* (also 1784), 'aged 28', also spells the name 'Brettal'. JW's holograph letters to Jeremiah and others, however, seem uniformly to use 'Brettel'; see the originals, Aug. 3, 1778; Jan. 22, Oct. 12, 1780; June 26, 1781; Dec. 24, 1784; July 10, 1787.

[494] Wesley wrote, 'The Conference begun and ended in *love,* fully employed me on Tuesday, Wednesday and Thursday. And we observed Friday 12 a day of fasting and prayer for the success of the gospel.' *Journal & Diaries,* 22:424 in this edn. Miss March wrote, 'Our Conference is now ended. I promised myself a Jubilee, a time of holy rejoicing, but found it rather a scene of hurry and dissipation. Mr Wesley opened the Conference with a plan of great and necessary business. His preaching was chiefly to the preachers and of the searching, reproving kind. The brethren said there was much unity and concord amongst them, and one observed Mr Wesley seemed to do all the business himself. When he first came he looked worn down with care and sorrow; but left us well and lively.' Aug. 23, 1774, Tyerman MSS, 2:165. Thomas Taylor, in his MS journal, wrote,

'Aug. 9. Most of the day was taken up in temporal matters, which is dry business. Aug. 10. This morning our characters were examined and that closely. The afternoon was chiefly spent in taking in new preachers. In the evening Mr Wesley gave us but an indifferent sermon. Aug. 11. We spent this day pretty profitably in considering some things of importance, especially how to prevent levity, idleness and evil speaking. At night Mr. Wesley gave us a profitable discourse on brotherly love'. Quoted in *Journal* [(Curnock), 6:35 Sutcliffe (MS 'History', fol. 825) noted a considerable increase in membership that would have been greater if there had been more preachers in London: 'Why fight against God in adorning the City Road pulpit with a gown in the absence of the Wesleys?' (The clerical monopoly of the London pulpit by Charles Wesley and other clergy was much resented by several preachers and given as a reason for the stagnation of the London membership.)

Q. 1. What preachers are admitted this year?

A. Joseph Bradford, Samuel Randal,[495] Wm. Dufton, Joseph Moore, George Shorter.

Q. 2. Who remain on trial?

A. William Eells, Thomas Rutherford, Robert Dall, Michael Moorhouse, John Price, John McBurney,[496] John Watson, Jun., John Leech, William Dufton.[497]

Q. 3. Who are admitted on trial?

A. William Moore, Francis Smith, William Tunney, Jeremiah Brettel, John Moon, Samuel Bradburn, Thomas Corbet, William Thom, James Rogers, Arthur Kershaw, P. Mill,[498] George Guthrie, Andrew Delap, John Whitley, Robert Howard.

Q. 4. Who desist from travelling?

A. Joseph Pilmore, James Clough, John Murray, James Glasbrook.

Q. 5. Who act as Assistants this year?[499]

A. Daniel Bumsted, Alexander Mather, John Easton, George Hudson, Francis Wolf, John Goodwin, John Murlin, James Hindmarsh, Richard Rodda, John Furz, Stephen Proctor, Thomas Dixon, Charles Boon, Thomas Hanby, John Shaw, William Collins, Thomas Hanson, John Mason, Christopher Hopper, Isaac Brown, Jeremiah Robertshaw, Samuel Woodcock, John Oliver, John Pawson, Thomas Lee, Thomas Taylor, Robert Costerdine, Jacob Rowell, William Hunter, Benjamin Rhodes, James Hudson, Duncan Wright, William Thompson, Joseph Benson, Thomas Rutherford,[500] Robert Wilkinson, Joseph Thompson, Alexander McNab, John Bristol, Michael

---

[495] Orig., 'Randall', three times this year, twice in 1775, and also in 1778 and 1779. In a letter of July 23, 1780, JW spelled the name as it appears in the majority of entries in the *Minutes*—'Randal'.

[496] McBurney is not stationed in 1774, but in 1775 was 'admitted' (i.e., into full connexion).

[497] One of the two entries here and in *Q*. 1 must be incorrect, and as there is no subsequent note of his admission into full connexion, this one must be in error.

[498] Orig., 'Miln', and 'Milne' in *Q*. 7 (38). In 1776 he also once appears as 'Miln', and in 1783 and 1785 as 'Mills'. All other references are to Peter 'Mill'.

[499] This is the last annual list of Assistants.

[500] Orig., 'Rutharford'.

McDonald,[501] Barnabas Thomas, John Watson,[502] Thomas Wride, John Pritchard, Richard Boardman, James Perfect, Thomas Rankin, Francis Asbury, George Shadford.

Q. 6. Are there any objections to any of our preachers?

5   *A.* Examine them one by one (which was done).

Q. [7]. How are they stationed this year?

A. As follows:

(Joseph Bradford travels with Mr. Wesley.)[503]

(1) *London*, Daniel Bumsted, William Dufton, Arthur

10   Kershaw, John Atlay, Peter Jaco.

(2) *Kent*, Alexander Mather, Francis Smith.

(3) *Sussex*, John Easton, James Wood.

(4) *Norwich*, George Hudson, Thomas Brisco, Samuel Randal, William Moore.

15   (5) *Bedfordshire*,[504] Richard Bourke, Joseph Harper.

(6) *Oxfordshire*, Francis Wolf, Joseph Moore,[505] William Tunney.

(7) *Wilts, South*,[506] James Barry, John Undrell, Thomas Westell.

20   (8) *Wilts, North*, John Goodwin, John Moon, William Severn, William Whitaker.

(9) *Bristol*, John Murlin, Hugh Saunderson, James Cotty.

(10) *Devon*, James Hindmarsh, George Shorter.

(11) *Cornwall, East*, Richard Rodda, Thomas Newall,

25   John Brettel, I. G.[507]

(12) *Cornwall, West*, John Furz, Jonathan Crowle, Richard Wright, J. W.[508]

(13) *Pembrokeshire*, Thomas Dixon, Christopher Watkins.

30   (14) *Glamorgan*, Charles Boon, John Prickard.[509]

---

[501] Orig., 'McDonal'.

[502] Query, John Watson, Sen.? Cf. *Q.* 7 (41), (46).

[503] Thomas Olivers travelled with JW in 1773; Bradford, 1774–49.

[504] No listed Assistant.

[505] Orig., 'James Moore'.

[506] No listed Assistant.

[507] Apparently Joseph Guilford. See p. 416, n. 437.

[508] Apparently Isaac Waldron, although John Wiltshaw is not stationed this year.

[509] Orig., 'Prichard'. This is surely John Prickard, John Pritchard being listed as the Assistant at Armagh. There is no previous mention of him, but in the *Minutes* (1775), he is mentioned as 'remaining' on trial, not 'admitted on trial'. In 1775, his name appears as 'Pickard' in the stations.

(15) *Brecon*, Stephen Proctor, Richard Whatcoat.
(16) *Gloucestershire*, Thomas Hanby, Samuel Wells.
(17) *Staffordshire*, John Shaw, Edward Slater.
(18) *Chester*, William Collins, Francis Wrigley.
(19) *Macclesfield*, Thomas Hanson, John Poole, William Percival. 5
(20) *Manchester*, John Mason, Robert Roberts.
(21) *Liverpool*,[510] Christopher Hopper, Samuel Bradburn, John Morgan.
(22) *Derbyshire*, Thomas Carlill, Isaac Brown, Nicholas 10 Manners, Robert Howard.
(23) *Lincolnshire, East*, Jeremiah Robertshaw, William Thom, John Peacock.
(24) *Lincolnshire, West*, Samuel Woodcock, Jeremiah Brettel, Thomas Corbet. 15
(25) *Sheffield*, John Oliver, Thomas Mitchell, Samuel Bardsley.
(26) *Leeds*, John Pawson, John Allen, Samuel Smith.
(27) *Birstall*, Thomas Lee, Parson Greenwood, Thomas Johnson. 20
(28) *Bradford*, Thomas Taylor, William Brammah.
(29) *Haworth*, Robert Costerdine, Richard Seed, Robert Swan.
(30) *Whitehaven*, Jacob Rowell, M. F.[511]
(31) *York*, William Hunter, George Story. 25
(32) *Hull*, Benjamin Rhodes, David Evans, John Leech.
(33) *Yarm*, James Hudson, Lancelot Harrison.
(34) *Thirsk*, Duncan Wright, James Rogers.
(35) *The Dales*, Joseph Thompson, Robert Empringham, William Barker. 30
(36) *Newcastle*, William Thompson, John Broadbent, George Wadsworth, Thomas Tennant.
(37) *Edinburgh*, Joseph Benson, William Eells, John Bredin.
(38) *Dundee*, Thomas Rutherford, Peter Mill, John 35 Wittam.
(39) *Aberdeen*, Robert Wilkinson, James Watson.
(40) *Dublin*, Alexander McNab, William Horner.

[510] Orig., 'Liverpoole'.
[511] Michael Fenwick.

(41) *Waterford*, John Watson, sen., Andrew Delap.

(42) *Cork*, John Bristol, George Snowden.

(43) *Limerick*, Michael McDonald.

(44) *Athlone*, Thomas Wride, John Floyd, Jonathan
Hern.

(45) *Castlebar*, Barnabas Thomas, Michael Moorhouse,
T. H.[512]

(46) *Enniskillen*, John Watson, Jun.,[513] John Price,
George Guthrie,[514] John Christian.[515]

(47) *Londonderry*, Richard Boardman, Nehemiah Price.

(48) *Armagh*, John Pritchard, John Whitley.

(49) *Newry*, James Perfect, Thomas Payne, George
Mowat, Robert Dall.[516]

(50) *America*,[517] Thomas Rankin, Francis Asbury, George
Shadford, Robert Williams, John King, James Dempster,
Martin Rodda.

Q. 8. What numbers are in the society?

A. They are as follows:

London	2,452
Sussex*	218
Kent*[518]	306
Norfolk	525
Bedford	300
Oxfordshire	501
Wilts, South*	330
Ditto, North	892
Bristol	1,404
Devon	505
Cornwall, East	660
Ditto, West	1,482

---

[512] Apparently Thomas Halliday.

[513] If John Watson, Sen., is the Assistant listed, then Enniskillen does not have a listed Assistant.

[514] Orig., 'Guthry', as also in the 1775 stations.

[515] This was the last appointment of John Christian, though he did not officially leave until 1777.

[516] Orig., 'Richard Dall'.

[517] Three listed Assistants.

[518] A decrease for the second consecutive year.

Gloucestershire	431	
Staffordshire	733	
Cheshire North,	552	
Ditto, South	1,202	
Wales, West*	137	5
Ditto, East	120	
Ditto, North*[519]	83	
Lancashire, South	988	
Ditto, North	776	
Derbyshire	1,065	10
Sheffield	890	
Lincolnshire, East	747	
Ditto, West	686	
Leeds*	1,860	
Birstall	1,190	15
Bradford	930	
Haworth	1,213	
Whitehaven	299	
York	520	
Hull	645	20
Yarm		
	880	
Thirsk		
The Dales	1,086	
Newcastle	1,784	25
Edinburgh	287	
Aberdeen*	448	
Dublin*	310	
Waterford	204	
Cork	317	30
Limerick	178	
Castlebar	410	
Athlone*	320	
Enniskillen	937	
Armagh	500	35
Londonderry	433	
Newry	732	
America	2,204	
In all	35,672	40

[519] A decrease for the second consecutive year.

N.B. In the circuits marked thus * there is a decrease this year.

Q. 9. What is the Kingswood collection?
A. £260. 16*s.*
Q. 10. What children are admitted?
A. Charles Whatcoat, James Greenwood.[520]
Q. 11. What can be done in order to pay for the clothes of the preachers' children?[521]
A. If their parents can pay for them, in whole or in part, they should; if they cannot, all is well.
Q. 12. Can nothing be done for their daughters?[522]
A. If any of them were sent to M[iss] Owen's school (perhaps the best boarding-school for girls in Great Britain),[523] they would keep them at as small an expense as possible.
Q. 13. What is contributed for the yearly expenses?
A. £587. 12*s.* 5*d.*
Q. 14. How was it expended?
A. As follows:

	£.	*s.*	*d.*
Contingencies for 1774	73	0	0
D[itt]o at Conference	128	7	3
Chatham	10	0	0
Sheerness	5	0	0
Northampt[on]	20	0	0

[520] Sons of Richard Whatcoat and Parson Greenwood.

[521] This concern apparently does not refer to the provision of any uniform, but simply of suitable clothing.

[522] Concern for the education of girls is of significance in an age when this was regarded as unimportant, unnecessary, and a waste of time and money. Two earlier copies exist, both endorsed by Wesley, of 'Rule for Girls at Kingswood'; see vol. 14 of this edn.

[523] The formation of a school at Publow had been encouraged by Wesley. It seems to have been run by Hannah Frances Owen and was widely recognized as one of the best in England. *Journal & Diaries*, 22:348, n. 40 in this edn. Her sisters Elizabeth (who married William Pine), and Mary (who married Moseph Beardmore) may have helped in the endeavour. Frances consulted Wesley about her own possible marriage in 1779, and about 1780 the remaining family removed to London, and the school declined in spiritual quality.

Worcester	20	0	0	
Mousehole	5	0	0	
Penzance	2	0	0	
Cradley	5	0	0	
Creech	5	0	0	5
Haverfordw[est]	30	0	0	
Brecon	10	0	0	
Leicester	2	2	0	
Loughborough[524]	5	0	0	
Edinburgh	50	0	0	10
Bradford	20	10	0	
Rochdale	10	0	0	
Scarborough[525]	20	0	0	
Boston	31	1	11	
Perth	4	0	0	15
Greenock	12	0	0	
Arbroath	20	0	0	
Glasgow	10	0	0	
Reserved for the				
present year	71	9	3	20
[£] 569	10	5[526]		

Q 15. What is contributed to the Preachers' Fund?
A £65. 8*s*. 6*d*.
Q. 16. What was allowed out of it? 25
A. The following:

	£.	*s*.	*d*.	
W. Minethorp	5	5	0	
E. Standring	10	0	0	
E. Oldham	5	0	0	30
M. Penington	5	0	0	
J. Garnet	5	0	0	
M. Nelson[527]	5	0	0	
E. Dillon	2	2	0	
[£] 37	7	0[528]		35

---

[524] Orig., 'Loughbro'.
[525] Orig., 'Scarbro'.
[526] Orig., '587. 12. 5.'
[527] M. Nelson, probably the wife of John Nelson, who died in 1774. She received financial assistance this year only. 40
[528] Orig., '37. 5. 0.'

Q. 17. How many preachers' wives are to be provided for?
A. Forty-three (in effect).[529]
Q. 18. By what societies?
A. By the following

London	S[ister] Mather,[530] Jaco.
Sussex	S. Easton.
Wilts, North	S. Whitaker, Wolf.[531]
Bristol	S. Christian, S. Bourke,
	S. Cotty (½).[532]
Devon	S. Shorter.
Cornwall, E[ast]	S. Rodda.
Ditto, W[est]	S. Barry, S. Hindmarsh,[533]
	S. Crowle (½).[534]
Gloucester	S. Hanby.
Staffordsh[ire]	S. Shawl.
Chester	S. Collins.
Macclesfield	S. Poole.
Derbysh[ire]	S. Brown, S. Barker.[535]
Manchester	S. Roberts, Story.[536]
Liverpool	S. Hopper, Morgan.
Lincolnsh[ire], East	S. Robertshaw, Peacock, W. S.[537]
Ditto, W[est]	S. Woodcock, Brammah.[538]
Sheffield	S. Oliver.
Leeds	S. Greenwood, Waldron,[539]
	Westell.

[529] In fact 46 names are listed and although 3 are marked '½', presumably indicating partial support, they would then total 44½. Cf. *Minutes* (1775), *Q.* 16, where it says 42 as a total but one is marked '½'.

[530] Mather was stationed in Kent.

[531] Wolf was stationed in Oxfordshire.

[532] Christian was stationed at Enniskillen; Bourke in Bedfordshire. Who also supported Cotty? Perhaps she required only partial support.

[533] Barry was stationed in Wiltshire; Hindmarsh in Devon.

[534] Who also supported Crowle? Perhaps she required only partial support.

[535] Barker was stationed in The Dales.

[536] Story was stationed at York.

[537] Probably the wife of Samuel Smith (Leeds), and 'W' her own first name, in order to prevent confusion with the wife of Francis Smith (Kent)?

[538] Brammah was stationed at Bradford (Yorkshire).

[539] Cf. *Minutes* (1773), *Q.* 16, *Leeds*, where 'S. W.' is tentatively identified as Sister Waldron.

Birstall	S. Lee, Mitchell.[540]
Bradford	S. Taylor.
York	S. Hunter, J. Thompson (½).[541]
Hull	S. Evans.
Haworth	S. Costerdine, Swan.
Yarm	S. Harrison.
[The] Dales	S. Rowell,[542] Empringham.
Newcastle	S. Brisco, Thompson, Corbet.[543]

Q. 19. When and where may the next Conference begin?

A. At Leeds, the first Tuesday in August.

Q. 20. Are not the preachers who come to the Conference burdensome to the societies in the way?

A. Frequently. To prevent this, (1), let every preacher pay for his horse's keeping; (2), let each of those societies fix on an inn where the horses will be taken care of.

Q. 21. Do not some of the preachers neglect sending their contribution to the Preachers' Fund to the Conference?

A. They do. Each Assistant should see to bring[ing] it from the preachers in his circuit. And every Assistant should take care to attend the Conference.

Likewise it is desired that every Assistant would at Christmas take an exact account of the books that are in his circuit, and remit that and the balance to London.

Q. 22. Are not the married preachers much straitened?

A. It seems some of them are. Therefore: (1) let every preacher's wife (except at London and Bristol) have £12 a year. (2) Every circuit is to find her a lodging, coal, and candles, or to allow her fifteen pounds a year.[544]

Q. 23. We have still imperfect accounts of Scotland and Ireland.[545] How can this be remedied?

---

[540] Mitchell was stationed at Sheffield.
[541] Thompson was stationed in The Dales.
[542] Rowell was stationed at Whitehaven.
[543] Brisco was stationed in Norwich; Corbet in Lincolnshire.
[544] See also *Minutes* (1769), *Q.* 23 (*A.* 1) and n. 266 for earlier scales.
[545] Cf. *Minutes* (1768), *Q.* 21; (1777), *Q.* 20.

A. Let the General Assistant[546] of Scotland and Ireland always attend the Conference.

Q. 24. What can be done where we have no good leader?

A. Let the preacher constantly meet the society as a class.

Q. 25. Several are grieved at ——————'s[547] preaching up and down, though he has not strength regularly to supply a circuit. How can he remove this offence?

A. By following a route marked out by Mr. W[esley], and preaching where the Assistant of each circuit judges it would be most useful.

Q. [26]. Can anything be done in order to lay a foundation for future union? Would it not be well for any that are willing to sign some Articles of Agreement before God calls me hence?[548]

A. We will do it. Accordingly the following paper was written and signed:

We whose names are underwritten, being thoroughly convinced of the necessity of a close union between those whom God is pleased to use as instruments in this glorious work, in order to preserve this union between ourselves, are resolved, God being our helper,

(1) To devote ourselves entirely to God, taking up our cross daily, steadily aiming at one thing, to save ourselves, and them that hear us.

(2) To preach the old Methodist doctrines, and no other, contained in the Minutes of the Conferences.

(3) To observe and enforce the whole Methodist discipline, laid down in the said Minutes.[549]

Daniel Bumstead
William Dufton
Alexander Mather
John Easton

---

[546] The term 'General Assistant' (in the original only the 'A' is capitalized) implied one who represented all the other Assistants in an area. This was certainly technical usage in America; see American *Minutes* (1773), *Q.* 6: 'Every preacher who acts as an Assistant to send an account of the work once in six months to the General Assistant.' Both Rankin and Asbury were so designated, and from 1784 the office became that of the bishop, termed by JW the 'superintendent'.

[547] Orig. is blank. May be more than one person was intended.

[548] Cf. *Minutes* (1773), *Q.* 17.

[549] Cf. *Minutes* (1769), JW's paper (5) after *Q.* 25; (1773), *Q.* 18; (1775), *Q.* 26.

George Hudson
John Atlay
Samuel Randal
Richard Bourke
Joseph Harper   5
[Francis Wolf][550]
Joseph Moore
James Barry
John Goodwin
William Severn   10
William Whitaker
John Murlin
Hugh Saunderson
J. Cotty
Thomas Simpson   15
James Hindmarsh
George Shorter
Richard Rodda
Thomas Newall
John Brettel   20
Stephen Proctor
Richard Whatcoat
Thomas Hanby
Samuel Wells
John Shaw   25
William Collins
Robert Swindells
Francis Wrigley
Thomas Hanson
John Poole   30
John Mason
Thomas Carlill
Isaac Brown
Jeremiah Robertshaw
Thomas Mitchell   35
Samuel Bardsley
John Pawson
John Allen
Samuel Smith

---

[550] Orig., 'Thomas Woolf'.

Joseph Bradford
Thomas Lee
Parson Greenwood
Thomas Johnson
5   Thomas Taylor
William Hunter
Benjamin Rhodes
James Hudson
Dun. Wright
10   William Barker
Robert Wilkinson
Samuel Woodcock
James Dempster
Thomas Olivers
15   John Oliver
Thomas Brisco
John Morgan
William Thompson
Joseph Thompson
20   William Eells
Thomas Payne
John Bristol
David Evans
Lancelot Harrison
25   John Pritchard
William Brammah
James Clough
John Broadbent
Thomas Tennant

30 **Annual** *Minutes of some late Conversations*, **1775**

Leeds, Tuesday, August 1, 1775.[551]

---

[551] Wesley wrote in his *Journal* (22:459f. in this edn.):
'Thursday August 1 our Conference began. Having received several letters,
intimating that many of the preachers were utterly unqualified for the work,
having neither grace nor gifts sufficient for it, I read those letters to all the
Conference, and begged that every one would freely propose and enforce

Q. 1. What preachers are admitted this year?

A. James Barry, Robert Howard, Thomas Rutherford, James Rogers, James Wood, John Leech, Samuel Bradburn, William Thom, Jeremiah Brettel, William Percival, Michael Moorhouse, George Guthrie, John Watson, jun., John McBurney, Wm. Duke,[552] John Wade, 5

whatever objections he had to anyone. The objections proposed were considered at large; in two or three different cases, committees were appointed for that purpose. In consequence of this, we were all fully convinced that the charge advanced was without foundation; that God had really sent these labourers into His vineyard, and has qualified them for the work. And we were all more closely united together than we had been for many years'. (See *Q*. 5 below)

Thomas Handy wrote to James Oddie, 'We have had a very loving agreeable Conference and I think Mr Wesley is not near so overbearing as he was. We have not had so free a Conference in many years nor ever so full.' Tyerman MSS, 1:115ff. and less accurately in Tyerman, *Wesley*, 3:209.

Before the Conference, Joseph Benson had written to Fletcher suggesting a project for examining the preachers; for Wesley and others to ordain those qualified; dismissing the less qualified if defective in conduct; and placing the rest on trial or educating them at Kingswood School. In reply Fletcher approved of a purge; doubted the usefulness of Kingswood for training; and on ordination saw some good points for it but recognized that it would cut them off from the English and Scottish national churches and was a step the Wesleys could not decently take in view of their frequent professions of loyalty. JW apparently gave Benson leave to raise the plan at Conference, but if he did so, nothing was done. However, Fletcher wrote to JW on the day that the Conference began with a scheme for a 'daughter church of our holy mother'—'the Methodist Church of England'—submitting to her as far as possible. A revision should be made of the BCP and Articles, and the Archbishop of Canterbury should be asked to ordain some preachers with testimonials from the Wesleys, plus some Helpers as Deacons, while remaining subject to Conference. If the bishops refuse, the Wesleys should ordain themselves. After their deaths, a group of Methodist 'Moderators' should succeed to their authority. Confirmation should be used for admission to Communion. Candidates for orders should declare for 'the doctrine of grace against the Socinians—the doctrine of justice against the Calvinists—and the doctrine of holiness against all the world'. They should submit as far as possible to the Church of England, and Kingswood School should be used for training for orders, educating the preachers' children, and housing worn-out preachers; see the details in *Journal* (Curnock), 8:328–34. To Fletcher, JW wrote merely that they had followed his advice in examining the preachers more exactly than ever on their grace and gifts. *Letters* (Telford), 6:174. Sutcliffe says that there were twenty-two to twenty-three cases of complaint, but they were unfounded: 'When men have some favourite preacher in their eyes another though a decent man is set aside as nothing worth'. MS 'History', fol. 839.

[552] An American preacher, in common with the five who follow him.

Daniel Ruff, Edward Dromgoole,[553] Isaac Hollings, Richard Webster.

Q. 2. Who remain on trial?

A. William Tunney,[554] William Moore, William Eells, Thomas Corbet, John Moon, John Wiltshaw, John Prickard, Robert Dall.

Q. 3. Who are admitted on trial?

A. John Valton,[555] John Crook, John Dean,[556] Duncan McAllum, Peter Ferguson, Andrew Delap,[557] Hugh Brown,[558] John Beanland, Joseph Saunderson, John Roberts.

Q. 4. Who desist from travelling?

A. Nicholas Manners, Daniel Bumsted.

Q. 5.[559] Are there any objections to any of our preachers?

A. Examine them one by one.

Considerable objections being made to three of the preachers, the matter was referred to three several committees.[560]

Q. 6. How are they stationed this year?

A. (Joseph Bradford travels with Mr. Wesley)

(1) *London*, Peter Jaco, John Atlay, Thomas Ryan, John Watson,[561] John Helton.

---

[553] Orig., 'Drumgoole', as frequently. The papers for three generations of the family, however, show that the spelling was standardized as 'Dromgoole'.

[554] Orig., 'Tonney; in *Minutes* of 1777–78, 'Tunny'; but elsewhere always 'Tunney'.

[555] Orig., 'John Walton', an obvious error for 'Valton'.

[556] He could hardly be the John Dean 'admitted on trial' in 1790. Probably a mistake for Peter Dean, on trial in 1777, born in London and lived in Berwick, where he first preached. Pawson (*Letters*, 3:140), who says he married and settled in business in London, gives a lurid account of his death.

[567] Cf. *Minutes* (1774), *Q.* 3; i.e., admitted twice, perhaps in error.

[558] Orig., 'Humphrey'. There is no other mention of Humphrey Brown, so this is likely to be the Hugh Brown stationed at Enniskillen.

[559] No list of Assistants is given from this time onwards; see *Minutes* (1774), *Q.* 5, n. 499.

[560] The excluded preachers are probably the following: (1) Francis Smith, who was on trial, 1774. (2) Nicholas Manners (though he 'desists' under *Q.* 4), who returned in 1776 and probably left again in 1784. See Pawson, *Letters*, 3:78, and Tyerman, *Wesley*, 3:559. He apparently denied original sin and hence probably the question on this at the 1784 Conference (*Minutes, Q.* 20). (3) Arthur Kershaw, who was on trial, 1774; not listed in these *Minutes* for 1775 (and Crowther and Myles say he left). Another possibility is Edward Sweeney (left in 1775, according to Myles).

[561] Senior or Junior? Cf. Cork, (43).

(2) *Kent*, Charles Boon, Thomas Westell.

(3) *Sussex*, Thomas Brisco, James Wood.

(4) *Norwich*, Samuel Randal, Geo. Wadsworth, George Hudson, John Beanland.

(5) *Bedfordshire*, Richard Bourke, William Tunney, William Moore.

(6) *Oxfordshire*, Samuel Wells, John Valton, Geo. Shorter.

(7) *Wilts[hire], South*, Francis Wolf,[562] T. V.,[563] John Undrell.[564]

(8) *Wilts[hire], North*, John Goodwin, James Perfect, George Snowden, Thomas Tatton.

(9) *Bristol*, John Murlin, William Severn, William Ashman; John Floyd, supernumerary.

(10) *Devon*, James Hindmarsh, supernumerary; James Cotty, Jonathan Crowle.

(11) *Cornwall, East*, Richard Wright, John Roberts.

(12) *Cornwall, West*, Thomas Hanson, John Moon, [James][565] Watson, John Leech.

(13) *Pembrokeshire*, Samuel Bradburn, John Prickard.

(14) *Glamorganshire*, Christopher Watkins, Thomas Dixon.

(15) *Brecon*, Richard Whatcoat, John Broadbent.

(16) *Gloucestersh[ire]*, Thomas Hanby, John Furz.

(17) *Staffordshire*, Alex Mather, William Dufton.

(18) *Chester*, William Collins, Thomas Carlill.

(19) *Macclesfield*, Duncan Wright, John Poole, William Percival.

(20) *Manchester*, Robert Roberts. John Oliver.

(21) *Liverpool*, Christopher Hopper, Tho. Lee, M[ichael] F[enwick].

(22) *Derbyshire*, Isaac Brown, Edward Slater, John Peacock, John Wiltshaw.

(23) *Lincolnshire, East*, John Easton, Joseph Harper, Thomas Corbet,[566] John Wittam.

[562] Orig., 'Wolfe', as also once each in 1776 and 1777, though JW's letters to him always spell his name without a final 'e'; on one occasion (Jan. 14, 1777) as 'Wool'.

[563] I.e., Thomas Vasey. He is listed as 'T. V.' in 1775, 1776, 1777. A letter from JW shows him in Wiltshire. *Letters* (Telford), 6:171.

[564] Orig., 'Andrell'. Elsewhere always 'Undrell'—not 'Underhill'.

[565] Orig., 'Samuel', surely an error.

[566] Orig., 'Corbett', as also once in 1787; in 1783–84 he appears as 'Corbit', and in the Deed of Declaration (1784) as 'Corbitt', but elsewhere as 'Corbet'.

(24) *Lincolnshire, West*, Samuel Woodcock, Robert Howard, John Crook.

(25) *Sheffield*, Robert Costerdine, Tho. Mitchell, Richard Seed.

(26) *Leeds*, John Pawson, William Brammah, T. Tennant.

(27) *Birstall*, P. Greenwood, T. Johnson, John Morgan.

(28) *Bradford*, John Allen, J. W.,[567] Sam. Smith.

(29) *Haworth*, Thomas Taylor, Robert Swan,[568] Samuel Bardsley.

(30) *Whitehaven*, John Mason, Joseph Saunderson.[569]

(31) *York*, John Shaw, George Story.

(32) *Hull*, William Hunter, W. Barker.

(33) *Scarborough*, Benjamin Rhodes, James Hudson.

(34) *Yarm*, Jacob Rowell, Lancelot Harrison.

(35) *Thirsk*, Jeremiah Robertshaw, William Thom.

(36) *The Dales*, James Barry, Joseph Thompson, David Evans.

(37) *Newcastle*, William Thompson, Robert Empringham, Joseph Benson, Joseph Moore.

(38) *Edinburgh*, Thomas Rutherford, James Rogers, Robert Wilkinson.

(39) *Dundee*, Stephen Proctor, Francis Wrigley, Duncan McAllum.

(40) *Aberdeen*, William Eells, Peter Ferguson.

(41) *Dublin*, Alex. McNab, Barnabas Thomas.

(42) *Waterford*, John Bristol, And. Delap.

(43) *Cork*, John Watson,[570] William Horner, *change every six weeks*.

(44) *Limerick*, Nehemiah Price.

(45) *Athlone*, John Pritchard, Michael Moorhouse, Jonathan Hern, Thomas Halliday.

(46) *Sligo*, Thomas Payne, Thomas Wride.

(47) *Enniskillen*, John and Jeremiah Brettel, Hugh Brown.

---

[567] Isaac Waldron?

[568] Orig., 'Swann'; all other references in the *Minutes* being to 'Swan'.

[569] Orig., 'Sanderson', although in *Q.* 3 he appeared as 'Saunderson'. In 1776, both spellings are found, but from 1778–83, 'Sanderson' only, which from that date is replaced by 'Saunderson'.

[570] Cf. *Q.* 6 (1).

(48) *Londonderry*, Richard Boardman, Geo. Mowat, John Price.
(49) *Armagh*, John Slocomb, Robert Dall, John MᶜBurney.
(50) *Lisburn*, John Bredin, Geo. Guthrie.
(51) *America*, Thomas Rankin, Geo. Shadford, James Dempster, Martin Rodda, John King, William Duke, John Wade, Daniel Ruff, Edward Dromgoole, Isaac Hollings, Ric. Webster.

Q. 7. What numbers are in the society?
A. They are as follows:

London	2,492
Kent	312
Sussex	232
Norwich	629
Bedfordshire	412
Oxfordshire	520
Wilts, South*	315
Ditto, North*	849
Bristol	1,427
Devon	583
Cornwall, East	769
Ditto, West*	1,380
Pembrokeshire	189
Glamorganshire	120
Brecon	107
Gloucestershire	446
Staffordshire	740
Chester*	536
Macclesfield	1,238
Manchester	1,060
Liverpool	820
Derbyshire	1,120
Lancashire, East	822
Ditto, West*	683
Sheffield	1,114
Leeds	2,023
Birstall	1,250
Bradford	1,157

Haworth	1,344
Whitehaven	315
York	570
Hull	670
Yarm	640
Thirsk	530
The Dales*	862
Newcastle	1,805
Edinburgh*	260
Dundee*[571]	169
Aberdeen*[572]	240
Dublin	401
Waterford*	176
Cork	382
Limerick	185
Athlone	344
Castlebar*	327
Enniskillen	990
Londonderry	392
Armagh*	423
Newry*	617
America	3,148
	——————
In all	38,145[573]

N.B. In the circuits marked thus * there is a decrease this year.
[For South Wiltshire, this was the second consecutive
year.]

Q. 8. What is the Kingswood collection?
A. £283. 0s. 6d.
Q. [9]. What children are admitted?
A. John Greenwood,[574] Richard Rodda,[575] and Francis
Hern.[576]

---

[571] A decrease for the second consecutive year.
[572] A decrease for the second consecutive year.
[573] Orig., '38,150'.
[574] Son of Parson Greenwood.
[575] Son of Martin or Richard Rodda?
[576] Son of Jonathan Hern.

Q. 10. What can be done for the preachers' daughters?
A. Send two of them to M[iss] Owen's school.[577]
Q. 11. Which this year?
A. Paulina Taylor and Isabel Snowden.[578]
Q. 12. What is contributed for the yearly expenses?
A. £564. 9*s*. 10*d*.
Q. 13. How was it expended?
A. As follows:

	£.	*s*.	*d*.
Last year's contingencies	17	9	6
For the present year	100	0	0
Law	34	16	10
Preachers' necessities	157	12	9
Dundee	100	0	0
Arbroath	22	0	0
Aberdeen	13	4	0
Barnard Castle	16	11	5
Limerick	10	0	0
Pembroke	11	10	0
Thornhill	5	5	0
Wandsworth	10	0	0
Darlaston	10	0	0
Cradley	9	0	0
Chatham	10	0	0
Norwich	10	0	0
Sheerness	10	0	0
Macclesfield	7	0	0
Chester	10	0	0
In all	£ 564	9	6

Q. 14. What was contributed for the Preachers' Fund?
A. £ 119. 0*s*. 6*d*.
Q. 15. What was allowed out of it?
A. The following:

	£.	*s*.	*d*.
Eliz. Standring	10	0	0
John Hosmer[579]	10	0	0

[577] See *Minutes* (1774), *Q*. 12.
[578] Daughters of Thomas Taylor and George Snowden.
[579] Orig, 'Horner', almost certainly an error of transcription for the more unusual 'Hosmer', seen also in Telford's transcription of JW's letter to Christopher Hopper of May 14, 1774. Hosmer was helped from the Preachers' Fund (1775–78), and his widow in later years. See JW to Hosmer, June 7, 1761, *Letters* (Telford), 4:155 n.

Eliz. Oldham	5	5	0
Elizabeth Dillon	5	5	0
Mary Penington	5	5	0
Jane Garnet[580]	5	5	0
Wm. Minethorp	5	5	0
	£ 46	5	0

Q. 16. How many preachers' wives are to be provided for?
A. In Ireland four; in England forty-two.[581]
Q. 17. By what societies?
A. By the following:

London	S. Westell,[582] Jaco.
Sussex	S. Brisco.
Wilts, North	S. Shorter,[583] Snowden.
Bristol	S. Barker, Cotty[584] (half).
Devon	S. Hindmarsh.
Cornwall, East	S. Rodda.
Ditto, West	S. Costerdine.[585]
Gloucestershire	S. Hanby.
Staffordshire	S. Mather.
Chester	S. Collins.
Macclesfield	S. Poole.
Manchester	S. Roberts, Oliver.
Liverpool	S. Hopper, Lee.
Derbyshire	S. Brown, Peacock.
Grimsby	S. Easton,[586] Corbet.
Epworth	S. Barry, Barker.
Sheffield	S. Mitchell.
Leeds	S. Beanland, Evans.[587]
Birstall	S. Greenwood, Morgan.

[580] Orig., 'Garret'; cf. p. 353, n. 170 above.
[581] This is the first time that the preachers' wives in Ireland received financial support.
[582] Westell was stationed in Kent.
[583] Shorter was stationed in Oxfordshire.
[584] Cotty was stationed in Devon.
[585] Costerdine was stationed at Sheffield.
[586] Orig., 'Erston'.
[587] Evans was stationed in The Dales.

Bradford	S. Brammah.[588]
Haworth[589]	S. Taylor, Swan.
York	S. Story, Shaw.
Hull	S. Hunter.
Yarm	S. Rowell.
Thirsk	S. Robertshaw.
The Dales	James Thompson,
	S. Woodcock.[590]
Newcastle	W. Thompson, Empringham,
	Harrison.[591]

Q. 18. When and where may the next Conference
  begin?
A. At London, the first Tuesday in August.
Q. 19. Who are the present committee for the Preachers'
  Fund?
A. The following:
  Peter Jaco
  Christopher Hopper
  Thomas Johnson
  Alexander Mather
  John Pawson
  William Thompson
  Thomas Hanty
  John Murlin
  Robert Roberts
  Thomas Taylor
  Thomas Hanson
  Duncan Wright

Q. 20. Are not many of the trustees for the preaching-
  houses dead? And are not others out of the society?
A. Let the remaining trustees for each house meet as soon
  as possible, and endorse their deed thus (having affixed to
  it three new stamps):

---

[588] Brammah was stationed at Leeds.
[589] Orig., 'Howarth'.
[590] Woodcock was stationed in Lincolnshire.
[591] Harrison was stationed at Yarm.

We the remaining trustees for the Methodist preaching-
house in   have this day, according to the
power lodged in us by this deed, chosen and named
          to be trustees for the preaching-house
5   aforesaid, in the room of   .
Witness,   A. B., etc.[592]
Q. 21. Are not many of our classes too large?
A. Yes, Divide every one which contains above thirty
members.
10   *Q.* 22. Do we allow any to build new preaching-houses?
A. Yes, if it be proposed first at the Conference.
Q. 23. And may they go about to desire help in the neigh-
bouring circuits?
A. They may; provided first that they ask the consent of
15   each Assistant. Second, that the collection be made
between the Conference and the beginning of March.
Q. 24. Where do we allow new houses to be built this year?
A. At Oldham, Taunton, and Halifax.
Q. 25. What can be done to encourage our brethren to make
20   a push for paying off their old debt?
A. A fifth part of what is collected may be sent to the
Conference: all the rest may be kept in the circuit.
Q. 26. What preachers signed the agreement to adhere
to each other, and to the old Methodist doctrine and
25   discipline?[593]
A. The following:[594]

Peter Jaco
John Atlay
30   Charles Boon
Thomas Westell
Thomas Brisco
James Wood
Samuel Randal
35   George Wadsworth

---

[592] On the Model Deed and the problems raised by other forms of trust deed, see
Minutes (1765), *QQ.* 10–12.

[593] See above, pp. 169, 189, 229, 238, 246–50, 257, 259.

[594] This list of preachers basically follows the circuit lists, except that Bradford
is listed at the end, not at the beginning, and that the Lincolnshire and Yorkshire
preachers are mingled.

George Hudson
Richard Bourke   10
Samuel Wells
John Valton
John Goodwin   5
Francis Wolf
James Perfect
Thomas Tatton[595]
John Murlin
William Severn   10
William Ashman[596]
James Hindmarsh   20[597]
Samuel Watson[598]
Richard Rodda
William Whitaker   15
Thomas Dixon
Samuel Bradburn
John Broadbent
Thomas Hanby
Alexander Mather   20
William Dufton
William Collins   30
Thomas Carlill
Dun. Wright
John Poole   25
William Percival
Robert Roberts
John Oliver
Christopher Hopper
Thomas Lee   30
Isaac Brown
Edward Slater   40
Robert Howard
James Barry

[595] Orig., 'Falton', an obvious error.
[596] Orig., 'Ackman', an error.
[597] The numbering in tens was broken at this point (possibly because 'Hindmarsh' was a long name, and '23' (which should have been '21') was inserted after the incorrect 'Smith'.
[598] Orig., 'Samuel Smith', who also appears at the end of the list. In the stations Samuel Watson appears shortly after Hindmarsh and before Mather.

Lancelot Harrison
Thomas Mitchell
Robert Costerdine
Richard Seed
5   Parson Greenwood
Thomas Johnson
John Allen[599]
J. W.[600]   50
Robert Swan
10   Samuel Bardsley
John Mason
John Morgan
John Shaw
George Story
15   Jacob Rowell[601]
Samuel Woodcock
William Hunter
William Barker   60
Benjamin Rhodes
20   Jeremiah Robertshaw
William Thom
Joseph Thompson
Joseph Moore
David Evans
25   William Thompson
Robert Empringham
Joseph Benson
Stephen Proctor   70
Thomas Rutherford
30   James Rogers
Francis Wrigley
Thomas Olivers
James Hudson[602]
Thomas Hanson
35   John Leech
Jerem. and John Brettel

---

[599] Orig., 'Allan'.
[600] Isaac Waldron?
[601] Orig., 'James Rowall'.
[602] Orig., 'John Hudson'.

Joseph Bradford
Samuel Smith

N.B. We all deny that there is, or can be, any *merit* (properly
speaking) in man.   5

Annual *Minutes of some late Conversations*, 1776

London, Tuesday, August 6, 1776[603]

Q. 1. What preachers are admitted this year?

A. William Tunney, William Moore, Thomas Corbet, John
Mason, Joseph Pescod,[604] John Crook, John Valton.   10

Q. 2. Who remain on trial?

A. William Eells, John Prickard, Robert Dall, Hugh Brown,
Joseph Saunderson, Andrew Delap, Duncan M⋅Allum.

Q. 3. Who are admitted on trial?

---

[603] Wesley writes, 'Tue. 6. Our Conference began, and ended on Friday the 9th,
which we observed with fasting and prayer, as well for our own nation as for our
brethren in America. In several Conferences we have had great love and unity. But
in this there was over and above, such a general seriousness and solemnity of spirit
as we scarcely have had before.' *Journal & Diaries*, 23:26 in this edn. This comment
reflects the impact of the American war. No preachers were stationed for America,
and the numbers in Society there were reported at the same number as the year
before. In Mar. 1775, JW had written to the American preachers saying they should
act as peacemakers, and CW told Rankin that he was 'of neither side and both'.
Letters (Telford), 6:142f. The American Congress on July 4, 1776, had made loyalty
to the Crown a crime and forbade praying for the king. The British preachers were
naturally suspect, and JW's *Calm Address* did not help matters. By 1778, all the
British itinerants except Asbury had left America.

Thomas Taylor (journal quoted by Tyerman, *Wesley*, 3:227) says, 'Everything
was conducted in great order. A very strict scrutiny was made into every one's character; and I was glad so few were found culpable'; see *Minutes* (1775), *Q.* 5. To James
Barry in April, JW complained that The Dales Circuit was again in debt and that
the rule was that all money from the Yearly Collection was to go to Conference.
Letters (Telford), 6:215. On Aug. 9, he wrote to Penelope Newman that they had
been speaking in Conference on 'the means of preventing spiritual religion from
degenerating into formality . . . which strikes at the root of the whole work of God'.
Letters (Telford), 6:227.

[604] There is no previous mention of Joseph Pescod as on trial.

    A. Henry Robins, Thomas Hosking,[605] James Skinner, John
    Hampson,[606] James Hall, Jasper Robinson, John
    Gouldston, William Boothby, William Lumley, Joseph
    Fothergill, Peter Mill, Robert Davis, James Gaffney.

5   *Q.* 4. Who *desist* from travelling?
    A. Edward Slater, Jonathan Crowle, Samuel Woodcock,
    David Evans, James Dempster.
    Q. 5. Are there any objections to any of our preachers?
    A. Yes. It is objected that some are utterly unqualified for

10   the work, and that others do it negligently, as if they
    imagined they had nothing to do but to preach once or
    twice a day.
    In order to silence this objection forever, which has been
    repeated ten times over, the preachers were examined at

15   large, especially those concerning whom there was the
    least doubt. The result was that one was excluded for
    insufficiency, two for misbehaviour.[607] And we were thor-
    oughly satisfied that all the rest had both grace and gifts
    for the work wherein they are engaged. I hope therefore

20   we shall hear of this objection no more.
    Q. 6. How are they stationed this year?
    A. As follows:
    Joseph Bradford travels with Mr. Wesley.
    John Atlay keeps his accounts.

25   Thomas Olivers corrects the press.[608]

---

[605] Orig. 'Hoskins', spelled thus in only this instance.

[606] Apparently John Hampson, Sen., who had served as a preacher since 1751 but had been found negligent in 1765. In 1778, his son, John Hampson, Jun., was admitted on trial.

[607] The discipline exercised over the preachers perhaps comes into the open for the first time here, the fate of those dealt with under *Q.* 5 in *Minutes* (1775) being left obscure, though JW publicized the Wheatley case in 1751 in his *Journal* later (*Journal & Diaries*, 20:394–96 in this edn.). The men expelled were probably (1) William Rootes, who entered 1775 and left to become an Anglican clergyman (Myles, *Chronological History*); (2) Peter Ferguson, who entered 1774 and left 1775 (see ibid.); (3) Joseph Fothergill, who was born 1738–39 in North Shields, entered itinerancy 1769, desisted 1770 (see ibid.), local preacher and on trial in 1776 (see Crowther, *Portraiture*), died age 66.

[608] Appointments for preachers to look after accounts and publications are here published for the first time. Atlay began to keep the accounts in 1773 until 1788, and Olivers was 'corrector of the press' (1776–89). They were the precursors of the book steward and connexional editor. Frank Cumbers, *The Book Room* (London, 1956), 137. For their vicissitudes and JW's problems with book affairs, see introduction, pp. 38, 43, 57–59.

(1) *London*, Peter Jaco, supernumerary; James Hindmarsh, John Murlin, Joseph Pilmore.

(2) *Kent*, Charles Boon, William Barker.

(3) *Sussex*, Thomas Westell, Thomas Ryan, Thomas Tatton.

(4) *Norwich*, Richard Bourke, John Watson, Henry Robins.

(5) *Lynn*, Barnabas Thomas, William Tunney, William Boothby.[609]

(6) *Bedfordshire*, Samuel Randal, George Shorter, William Moore.

(7) *Oxfordshire*, John Valton, William Whitaker, John Gouldston.

(8) *Wilts., South*, Richard Rodda, James Cotty, Thomas Newall, Joseph Pescod.[610]

(9) *Wilts., North*, Samuel Wells, Thomas Brisco, John Furz, Francis Wolf.

(10) *Bristol*, John Helton, John Floyd, Hugh Saunderson.

(11) *Devon*, John Goodwin, John Undrell, George Wadsworth.[611]

(12) *Cornwall, East*, James Perfect, R[ichar]d Wright, James Watson, John Blade.

(13) *Cornwall, West*, Thomas Hanson, Richard Whatcoat, J. Poole, James Skinner.

(14) *Pembrokeshire*, James Wood, John Moon, John Broadbent.

(15) *Glamorganshire*, John Prickard, William Ashman.

(16) *Brecon*, Thomas Carlill, George Mowat.

(17) *Gloucestersh[ire]*, George Snowden, T[homas] V[asey].

(18) *Staffordshire*, Alexander Mather, John Wittam.

(19) *Macclesfield*, Duncan Wright, Tho. Hanby, James Hall.

(20) *Manchester*, Christopher Hopper, Thomas Mitchell, Jasper Robinson.

(21) *Chester*, John Mason, Robert Roberts.

---

[609] Orig., 'John Boothby'.
[610] Orig., 'John Pescod'.
[611] Orig., 'Wadsworthe', an obvious error.

(22) *Liverpool,* William Collins, John Oliver, William Percival.

(23) *Leicester,* Christopher Watkins, John Beanland.

(24) *Nottingham,* Robert Costerdine, Robert Swan, William Severn.

(25) *Grimsby,* Isaac Brown, Thomas Corbet, Nicholas Manners.

(26) *Gainsborough,* John Easton, William Thom, Joseph Harper.

(27) *Epworth,* Lancelot Harrison, Robert Howard, Richard Condy.[612]

(28) *Sheffield,* P. Greenwood, John Peacock, M[ichael] F[enwick].

(29) *Leeds,* William Thompson, Joseph Thompson, Thomas Johnson.

(30) *Birstall,* John Pawson, John Morgan, T. Tennant.

(31) *Bradford,*[613] John Allen, Thomas Lee, James Hudson.

(32) *Keighley,*[614] Thomas Taylor, Samuel Smith.

(33) *Colne,*[615] Samuel Bardsley, William Brammah.

(34) *Whitehaven,* T. Wride, Robert Empringham, Richard Seed.

(35) *York,* John Shaw, George Hudson.

(36) *Hull,* George Story, William Dufton.

(37) *Scarborough,* William Hunter, John Leech.

(38) *Yarm,* Jacob Rowell, Thomas Dixon, Michael Moorhouse.

(39) *Thirsk,* Jeremiah Robertshaw, Joseph Moore.

---

[612] Orig., 'Cundy', as in 1777–79, 1785; from 1786 onwards it appears as 'Condy'; JW's letters show him also using 'Cundy' in these early years, but 'Condy' later.

Richard Condy began active preaching in 1776, but there is no mention in this or in previous years of his being 'admitted on trial', recorded 'remaining on trial', or 'admitted'. He received recorded appointments 1776–79, and then there is no mention of him in the *Minutes* again until 1785. He is not listed as a 'desister' or being supported by the Preachers' Fund. From 1785 to 1789, he worked in Ireland, then northern England. He died in 1803[?].

[613] Orig., 'Bradforth', as in *Q.* 19, but not in *Q.* 7; also in 1777 (2 of 3), 1779–80, 1782–83, 1784 (2 of 3), 1785–91.

[614] Orig., 'Kighley', as also in 1777–90, and 1791 (4 of 5).

[615] Orig., 'Coln', as also in 1777, 1778 (2 of 3), 1779–83, 1784 (2 of 3) 1785–87, 1788 (2 of 3), 1789 (2 of 3), 1790–91.

(40) *The Dales*, John Crook, William Lumley, G[eorge] G[uthrie].

(41) *Newcastle*, Benjamin Rhodes, Jos. Benson, I[saac] W[aldron], James Barry.

(42) *Edinburgh*, Alexander McNab, T. Rutherford, James Rogers.

(43) *Dundee*, Robert Wilkinson, F. Wrigley, Joseph Saunderson.

(44) *Aberdeen*, William Eells, Stephen Proctor, Duncan McAllum.

(45) *Dublin*, J[ohn] H[ampson], John Bristol.

(46) *Waterford*, John Bredin, John Price.

(47) *Cork*, Richard Boardman, T[homas] H[alliday].

(48) *Limerick*, Samuel Bradburn.

(49) *Athlone*, John Watson, Wm. Horner, Andrew Delap.

(50) *Sligo*, T. Payne, Nehemiah Price.

(51) *Clones*, John Slocomb, John Mealy.[616]

(52) *Enniskillen*, Robert Dall, James Gaffney.

(53) *Armagh*, John and Jer. Brettel, Rob. Davis.

(54) *Londonderry*, John Pritchard, Jonathan Hern, Peter Mill, Robert Armstrong.[617]

(55) *Lisburn*, R. W.[618] John Harrison, George Brown.[619]

Q. 7. What numbers are in the society?

London*	2,425	
Kent	313	
Sussex	264	
Norwich	645	
Lynn		
Bedfordshire	450	

---

[616] Orig., 'Mayly', as 1777–78, and 'Mailey' in 1780. On all other occasions the name is spelled 'Mealy', which is also JW's spelling in his letter of Oct. 19, 1782.

[617] Orig., 'John Armstrong'.

[618] Though previously referred to as 'R. W.' in *Minutes* (1765), *Q.* 22, and (1768), *Q.* 7 (38), Robert Williams had been in America and died there in 1775 (*DEB, s. v.*), so this must be Richard Watkinson, listed by Myles (*Chronological History*) as active from 1776. His full name appears for the first time in 1778 at Dublin. There is no record of his being 'admitted on trial' or 'admitted'.

[619] America is missing from the stations this year. The membership (*Q.* 7) is given as the same as the previous year. This reflects the continuing disruption caused by the American War.

	Oxfordshire*	494
	Wilts., South	317
	Wilts., North	873
	Bristol*	1,414
5	Devon	633
	Cornwall, East	760
	Cornwall, West	1,390
	Pembrokeshire	220
	Glamorganshire	120
10	Brecon*	95
	Gloucestershire	456
	Chester*	525
	Staffordshire*	660
	Macclesfield	1,260
15	Manchester	1,118
	Liverpool	855
	Derby	1,125
	Nottingham	
	Lincolnshire, E[ast]	905
20	Lincolnshire, West	641
	Sheffield*	1,060
	Leeds	2,169
	Birstall	1,270
	Bradford	1,390
25	Keighley	1,640
	Colne	
	Whitehaven	458
	York	571
	Hull	380
30	Scarborough	410
	Yarm	745
	Thirsk	545
	The Dales*[620]	806
	Newcastle	1,908
35	Edinburgh*[621]	250
	Dundee	169
	Aberdeen	151
	Dublin	418

[620] A decrease for the second consecutive year.
[621] A decrease for the second consecutive year.

Waterford	252	
Cork*	324	
Limerick*	175	
Athlone	529	
Sligo	388	5
Clones[622]	430	
Enniskillen	442	
Londonderry	640	
Armagh	601	
Lisburn*	599	10
America	3,148	
	————	
In all	39,826[623]	

N.B. In the circuits marked thus * there is a decrease this   15
year.

Q. 8. What is the Kingswood collection?
A. £335. 0*s.* 3¾*d.*
Q. 9. What children are admitted this year?
A. William Collins,[624] John Robins,[625] John and William   20
Morgan,[626] and William Shent.[627]
Q. 10. What girls are admitted into Publow School?[628]
A. Alice Brisco,[629] and Ann Roberts.[630]
Q. 11. What is contributed for the yearly expenses?
A. £632. 12*s.* 11*d.*   25
Q. 12. What part of this was contributed in Ireland?
A. Nothing (except thirty-five shillings in Bandon). Our
brethren in Ireland said this was nothing to *them*—they
would only bear their own expenses.[631]

[622] Orig., 'Clines'.

[623] Orig., '40,071'. The American figure repeats the number for the previous year.

[624] Son of William Collins.

[625] Orig., 'Robbins'. The son of Henry Robins, whose name is also spelled 'Robbins' in 1784 (1 of 2) and 1786.

[626] Sons of John Morgan.

[627] Son of William Shent.

[628] This is Hannah Frances Owen's school; *Minutes* (1774), *Q.* 12.

[629] Daughter of Thomas Brisco.

[630] Daughter of John Roberts or Robert Roberts.

[631] For earlier complaints about 'very imperfect accounts of all things from Ireland and Scotland', see *Minutes* (1768), *Q.* 21, where the Assistants are enjoined to send exact accounts of the societies and subscriptions.

Q. 13. And do we desire any more? But this we require, if they would have any more preachers from England. We require, (1), that they bear the expenses of all English preachers going to and from Ireland, and (2), of any sickness or unavoidable distress which may befall them or their wives in that kingdom. There are properly *their* expenses; nor will we pay any part of them for the time to come unless their yearly contribution enable us so to do. The same we now adopt with regard to Scotland. Let them first contribute, then expect help from *us*.[632]

Q. 14. Is there anything else in Ireland which we complain of? *A.* There is. Part of the Leaders meet together on Sunday evening without any connection with or dependence on the Assistant. We have no such custom in the three kingdoms. It is overturning our discipline from the foundations. Either let them act under the direction of the Assistant or let them meet no more. 'Tis true, they can contribute money for the poor; but we dare not sell our discipline for money.

Q. 15. How was the yearly contribution expended? *A.* As follows:

	£.	s.	d.
Last year's contingencies	54	9	0
For the present year	100	0	0
Law	36	16	0
Preachers' necessities	144	10	6
Wandsworth	5	0	0
Chatham	5	0	0
Sheerness	5	0	0
Norwich	3	6	5
Bury	5	0	0
Holcombe	40	0	0
Axbridge	9	1	8
Exeter	3	3	0
St. John's	7	0	0
Tuckingmill	3	4	0
Kerley	1	8	0
Redruth[633]	2	0	0

---

[632] Cf. earlier reference in *Minutes* (1768), *Q.* 21.

[633] Orig., '40s. 0d.'

	£	s	d	
Worcester	12	0	0	
Dudley	16	7	6	
Chester	18	0	6	
Burslem	9	0	0	
Congleton	4	10	0	5
Macclesfield	4	10	0	
Rochdale	10	17	0	
Bolton	5	0	0	
Derby	7	5	0	
Louth	12	0	0	10
Keighley	10	12	1	
Yarm	13	3	5	
Whitby	3	14	3	
Londonderry	75	0	0	
The Dales	10	10	0	15
	£637	8	4[634]	

Q. 16. What was contributed to the Preachers' Fund?
A. £81. 17*s.* 6*d.*
Q. 17. What was allowed out of it?
A.   20

	£.	*s.*	*d.*	
John Hosmer	10	0	0	
Eliz. Standring	10	0	0	
Eliz. Oldham	5	5	0	
Jane Garnet	5	5	0	25
Wm. Minethorp	5	5	0	
Mary Penington	7	7	0	
Eliz. Dillon	5	5	0	
In all	£48	7	0	
				30

Q. 18. How many wives are to be provided for?
A. In Ireland four; in England forty-two.
Q. [19].[635] By what societies?
A. By the following:

London	S[ister] Jaco, S. Hindmarsh.	35
Sussex	S. Westell.	
Wilts. N[orth]	S. Brisco, S. Cotty, half.	

[634] Orig., '£632. 12*s.* 11*d.*'
[635] The number '19' is omitted from the original but here supplied, and the following *QQ.* 19–27 renumbered 20–28.

	Bristol	S. Bourke, S. Peacock.[636]
	Devon	S. Shorter.[637]
	Cornwall, East	S. Rodda.[638]
	Cornwall, West	S. Poole, S. Beanland.[639]
5	*Gloucestershire*	S. Snowden.
	Staffordshire	S. Mather.
	Leicestershire	S. Swan.[640]
	Nottingham	S. Costerdine.
	Chester	S. Roberts.
10	*Macclesfield*	S. Hanby.
	Manchester	S. Hopper, S. Mitchell.
	Liverpool	S. Collins, S. Oliver.
	Grimsby	S. Brown, S. Easton.[641]
	Epworth	S. Harrison, S. Corbet.[642]
15	*Sheffield*	S. Greenwood.
	Leeds	S[isters] Thompsons, S. Barker,[643]
	Birstall	S. Morgan, S. Hunter.[644]
	Bradford	S. Lee.
	York	S. Shaw, S. Story.[645]
20	*Keighley*	S. Taylor, S. Brammah.[646]
	Yarm	S. Rowell.
	Thirsk	S. Robertshaw.
	The Dales	S. Crook.
	Newcastle	S. Barry, I. W., S. Empringham[647]

25 *Q.* [20]. When and where may the next Conference begin?
A. At Bristol, the first Tuesday in August.

---

[636] Bourke was stationed at Norwich; Peacock at Sheffield.

[637] Shorter was stationed in Bedfordshire.

[638] Richard Rodda was stationed in Wiltshire, South.

[639] Beanland was stationed at Leicester.

[640] Swan was stationed at Nottingham.

[641] Easton was stationed at Gainsborough.

[642] Corbet was stationed at Grimsby.

[643] Both William Thompson and Joseph Thompson were stationed at Leeds. The plural Thompsons probably means that Leeds supported the wives of both men. Barker was stationed in Kent.

[644] Hunter was stationed at Scarborough.

[645] Story was stationed at Hull.

[646] Brammah was stationed at Colne.

[647] 'I. W' apparently intended for 'S. W.', i.e., the wife of Isaac Waldron. Empringham was stationed at Whitehaven.

Q. [21]. What houses are to be built this year?[648]

A. One at London[649] and one at Colne.

Q. [22]. Why should not all our octagon houses be built like that at Yarm,[650] all our square ones like that at Scarborough?[651] 5

A. We cannot find any better models.

Q. [23]. Our brethren at Huddersfield desire leave to collect money in the neighbouring circuits. May they do it?

A. Yes; on the terms mentioned in the late *Minutes.*[652] But it is desired that neither they, nor any other of our builders, 10 set up any Chinese paling.[653]

Q. [24]. Complaint is made that sluts[654] spoil our houses. How can we prevent this?[655]

A. Let no known slut live in any of them.

Q. [25]. People crowd into the preachers' houses as into 15 coffeehouses. Is this right?[656]

---

[648] This is the first time this question is asked, arising from a concern for the quality and cost of the houses. Myles, *Chronological History*, 427–45, supplies a list of houses and dates. See also *Minutes* (1770), *Q.* 14; (1775), *Q.* 22–23; (1783), *Q.* 22.

[649] This was the future City Road Chapel, now known as Wesley's Chapel.

[650] JW seems to have acquired the idea for this shape from Dr. Taylor's (Presbyterian) chapel in Norwich (1757). Fourteen Methodist ones were built between 1761 and 1776. JW thought the shape best for both acoustical and financial reasons. G. W. Dolbey, *The Architectural Expression of Methodism* (London, 1964), 9–115.

[651] For Scarborough, see Dolbey, *Architectural Expression*, 34. In the 'Large' *Minutes* (1780), *Q.* 65, JW gives eight directions for building preaching-houses, including the recommendation of octagons or squares 'after the design of Yarm or Scarborough'.

[652] See *Minutes* (1775), *Q.* 23.

[653] Chinese palings were a product of the fashion for 'Chinoiserie', the use of real or supposed Chinese structures and ornaments in a variety of artifacts (buildings, pottery, garden landscapes). Reticulated fretwork and lattice-work were often used for this purpose in buildings, bridges, and fences (hence 'Chinese palings', a term used as early as 1702). JW probably objected to these as unnecessary and frivolous ornament. Cf. H. Honour, *Chinoiserie* (London, 1961), 138 and illus.; *WHS* 6 (1908): 132 and 50; *WHS* (1995): 30f. with illus.

[654] The first definition in the *OED* is, 'A woman of dirty, untidy, or slovenly habits or appearance'.

[655] Cf. 'Large' *Minutes* (1780), *Q.* 69.

[656] Cf. ibid., *Q.* 70. Thomas Taylor in his journal says that circuit stewards complained of preachers' wives being 'sluts', while preachers complained that people crowded into their homes like coffee-houses. Tyerman, *Wesley*, 3:227.

A. It is utterly wrong. Let no person come into the house either on Sunday or other days, unless he wants to ask a question.

Q. [26]. Should not the Assistants come early to the
5   Conference?

A. Let them be always present on Saturday evening.[657]

Q. [27]. Calvinism has been the grand hindrance of the work of God. What makes men swallow it so greedily?

A. Because it is so pleasing to flesh and blood—the doc-
10   trine of final perseverance in particular.[658]

Q. [28]. What can be done to stop its progress?

A. (1) Let all our preachers carefully read our tracts, and Mr. Fletcher's and Sellon's.[659]

(2) Let them preach universal redemption frequently
15   and explicitly; but in love and gentleness, taking care never to return railing for railing.[660] Let the Calvinists have all this to themselves.

(3) Do not imitate them in screaming, allegorizing, call-ing themselves ordained, boasting of their learning, col-
20   lege, or 'my lady'.[661] Mildly expose these things when time serves.

(4) Visit as diligently as them, and insist on universal redemption to everyone newly convinced or converted.

---

[657] This is changed from the system established in 1772, when they were instructed to be present by Sunday evening; see *Minutes* (1772), *Q.* 18.

[658] Cf. 'Large' *Minutes* (1780), *Q.* 76. Though JW's attacks on Calvinism had occurred periodically since the early 1740s, the furious controversy of this decade had been sparked by the Conference minute of 1770 and the failed amendment of 1771; see *Minutes* (1770), *Q.* 28 (6); see also *Minutes* (1770, 1771), nn. 278, 340.

[659] JW published many anti-Calvinist writings by John Fletcher and several by Walter Sellon. Fletcher's various *Checks to Antinomianism* were the best known; see *Bibliography*, Nos. 333, 336, 516–17, 519–22, and 528. For the three of Sellon's anonymous publications already published, see *Bibliography*, Nos. 548–50.

[660] 1 Pet. 3:9.

[661] This is clearly a reference to Lady Huntingdon and her Connexion, which produced the main Calvinist protagonists against Wesley; see above, *Minutes* (1771), n. 340. The 'college' is Trevecca College (opened 1768), which had originally employed Fletcher and Joseph Benson; and the preachers there seldom had a very prolonged or academic training. For other of JW's sarcastic comments on the Countess and Calvinistic preachers, see *Letters* (Telford), 5:83f., 166. Lady Huntingdon's latest biographer gives only a brief account of the controversy and suggests an element of jealousy as well as theological disagreement over the col-lege. Edwin Welch, *Spiritual Pilgrim* (London, 1995), 120–24.

(5) Answer all their objections both in public and private with sweetness both of look and voice.

(6) Strongly advise our people 'not to hear them'.

(7) Pray constantly and earnestly that God would stop the plague![662]

5

Annual *Minutes of some late Conversations*, 1777[663]

[Bristol, August 5, 1777]

---

[662] See Num. 16:46–50, and so on.

[663] The drop-title page of the annual *Minutes* this year picks up the common reading of the title page, 'Minutes of some late Conferences' (rather than simply 'Conversations', although the actual title page keeps that term), and the place and date that have customarily headed the beginning of the *Minutes* on that page are for the first time missing.

On Aug. 1, Wesley wrote, 'I desired as many as could join together in fasting and prayer that God would restore the spirit of love and of a sound mind to the poor deluded rebels in America'. On Aug. 5: 'Our yearly Conference began. I now first inquired (as that report had been spread far and wide) of every Assistant "Have you any reason to believe, from your own observation, that the Methodists are a fallen people?"' *Journal & Diaries*, 23:64 in this edn. Prof. Ward, in his annotation of that entry (n. 16), says that this comment was provoked by charges made by John Helton, Assistant in the Bristol Circuit, who had turned Quaker and resigned from Methodism. Wesley was influenced by reading Barclay's *Apology* and alarmed at the Benson-Fletcher proposal for a 'Methodist Church of England'. George Smith, *History of Wesleyan Methodism*, 3 vols. (London, 1857–61; 5th edn., London: Longmans, Green, 1866–72), 1:411; Henry Moore, *The Life of the Rev. John Wesley*, 2 vols. (London: Kershaw, 1824–25), 2:273f.; Tyerman, *Wesley*, 3:245f. JW had in fact begun examining the preachers more strictly in response to the Benson-Fletcher plan and 'several letters' of complaint about them in 1775, and he also mentions 'the outcry raised by Mr Hilton [*sic*]'. *Letters* (Telford), 6:174, and *Minutes* (1775), n. 551, and *Q*. 5. There was a more searching inquiry in 1776; see *Minutes*, *Q*. 5. JW soon gave his reply to Helton's charges. JW's inquiries and his own comprehensive knowledge of the connexion (he claimed) showed that the Methodists were not a 'fallen people' and that this fact was shown also by their increase in numbers despite being a poor, despised people. *Journal & Diaries*, 22:64f. in this edn. Yet he wrote to Alexander Mather on Aug, 6, 1777,

'Our preachers, many of them, are fallen. They are not spiritual. They are not alive to God. They are soft, enervated, fearful of shame, toil, hardship. . . . Give me a hundred preachers who fear nothing but sin and desire nothing but God, and I care not a straw whether they be clergymen or laymen, such alone will shake the gates of hell and set up the kingdom of heaven

Q. 1: What preachers are *admitted* this year?

A. John Prickard, Thomas Hosking, Henry Robins, James Skinner.

Q. 2: Who *remains on trial?*

A. William Eells, Andrew Delap, Hugh Brown, Duncan McAllum,[664] Joseph Saunderson, Jasper Robinson, Peter Mill, Robert Davis, James Gaffney, James Hall.

Q. 3: Who are admitted on trial?

A. Joseph Taylor, Peter Dean, John Whitley,[665] W. Church, Edward Jackson, John Fenwick,[666] John Howe, Hugh Moore, J. H., Jun.[667]

Q. 4: What preachers have *died* this year?[668]

A. John Slocomb at Clones, an old labourer, worn out in the service; John Harrison, near Lisburn, a promising youth, serious, modest, and much devoted to God; William Lumley, in Hexhamshire, a blessed young man, an happy witness of the full liberty of the children of God; and William Minethorp, near Dunbar, 'an Israelite indeed, in whom was no guile'.[669]

Q. 5: Who desist from travelling?

---

upon earth.' *Letters* (Telford), 6:271f.

Thomas Taylor wrote in his journal that on Aug. 7, Fletcher appeared, emaciated and ghostlike. The assembly stood up, the apparently dying man addressed them, and all dissolved in tears. JW feared he was speaking too much and knelt by his side and prayed that he be preserved. All joined in, and Wesley exclaimed, 'He shall not die but live and declare the work of the Lord.' JW had been trying to persuade Fletcher to be his successor, and though he resisted this, he did survive for a further eight years. Taylor also said that on the Conference Sunday, the morning services at Broadmead Chapel were at 9:30 a.m., 1:00 p.m., and 5:00 in the evening. JW also preached out of doors and in Society meetings expatiated on Methodist rules. He preached for twenty minutes on the evening of the first day. See Tyerman, *Wesley*, 3:247.

[664] Orig., 'MacAllum'; in all other instances except 1791 ('McAllum'), his name is spelled 'McAllum'.

[665] Orig., 'Whiteley', although elsewhere his name is spelled 'Whitley'.

[666] John Fenwick had been one of JW's Helpers at least since 1751, though he did not receive any official appointment until he was 'admitted on trial' in 1777. From then until his death in 1787, he was appointed regularly to various circuits in the north of England.

[667] John Hampson, Jun. This reference seems to indicate that the John Hampson 'admitted on trial' in 1776 was the father. See *Minutes* (1776), *Q.* 3 and n. 606.

[668] This is the first instance of this question, which henceforth appears regularly. The characterizations of the preachers, with rare exceptions, remained brief and lacking in details of their careers during JW's lifetime.

[669] John 1:47.

A. Hugh Saunderson,[670] John Undrell, Richard Wright, John Bristol.

Q. 6: Are there any objections to any of our preachers?

A. Yes. It is objected that 'most of them are not "called of God"[671] to preach'. This deserves our serious consideration. 5

In the Large *Minutes* we ask: 'How shall we try those who think they are moved by the Holy Ghost (or called of God) to preach?'ᵃ

Q. 7: Is this method of trial sufficient? Can we find any bet- 10 ter? Weigh this matter calmly and impartially.

A. We cannot find any better method, any more scriptural, or more rational.

Q. 8: But suppose they were called once, have not many of them forfeited their calling? 15

A. Examine them one by one; and whoever has any objection or doubt concerning anyone, let him now speak without any disguise or reserve, or for ever hold his peace.[672]

Q. 9: How are they stationed this year?

A. As follows: Joseph Bradford travels with Mr. Wesley. 20 John Atlay is the Book Steward.

Thomas Olivers corrects the press.

(1) *London*, Peter Jaco, James Hindmarsh, Samuel Smith.

(2) *Kent*, Richard Bourke, Thomas Tatton. 25

(3) *Sussex*, Charles Boon, James Skinner, John Wittam.

(4) *Norwich*, Joseph Pilmore, Peter Dean, William Tunney.

(5) *Lynn*, Barn. Thomas, William Moore, Thomas Ryan.

(6) *Bedford*, Samuel Randal, William Percival, James 30 Perfect.

(7) *Oxfordshire*, James Cotty, William Severn.

(8) *Wilts. South*, Richard Rodda, James Watson.

ᵃ See pp. 36–37 [i.e., 'Large' *Minutes* (1770), *Q.* 58].

[670] Hugh Saunderson was stationed at Bristol in 1776, but Ann Chapman wrote to Charles Wesley in Aug. 1776, 'It is suspected that Mr. Helton, who was to be Assistant here, will not come, as Mr Saunderson is stationed here'. Ruth Young, *Mrs. Chapman's Portrait* (Bath, 1926), 89; for Helton, see nn. 175, 663, above.

[671] Heb. 5:4.

[672] Cf. BCP, Matrimony, opening charge.

(9)   *North*, Samuel Wells, Thomas Barker,[673] Thomas Newall.

(10) *Bristol*, John Goodwin, Thomas Carlill, John Pritchard.

(11) *Somerset*, Thomas Brisco, John Furz.

(12) *Devon*, Francis Wolf, George Wadsworth.

(13) *Cornwall, E[ast]*, Richard Whatcoat, H. Robins, Isaac Shearing,[674] James Rogers.

(14) *West*, John Mason, John Poole, George Mowat, T. V.[675]

(15) *Pembrokesh[ire]*, John Broadbent, James Hall, Thomas Hosking.

(16) *Glamorgan*, W. Ashman, W. Church.

(17) *Brecon*, James Wood, John Moon.

(18) *Gloucester*, George Snowden, John Valton.

(19) *Stafford*, Thomas Taylor, John Whitley.

(20) *Macclesfield*, John Shaw, Jasper Robinson, T. Hanby.

(21) *Manchester*, Duncan Wright, Thomas Mitchell.

(22) *Chester*, John Murlin, Robert Roberts.

(23) *Liverpool*, W. Collins, Samuel Bardsley, Nicholas Manners.

(24) *Leicester*, Christopher Watkins, Joseph Pescod, Joseph Taylor.

(25) *Nottingham*, Robert Costerdine, Tho. Corbet, John Beanland.

(26) *Grimsby*, Isaac Brown, Richard Seed, Rob. Howard.

(27) *Gainsborough*, John Easton, William Thom,[676] M[ichael] F[enwick].

(28) *Epworth*, Lancelot Harrison, John Oliver, Joseph Harper.

(29) *Sheffield*, P. Greenwood, George Shorter.

(30) *Leeds*, William Thompson, John Morgan, John Floyd.

(31) *Birstall*, John Pawson, Joseph Thompson, Thomas Johnson, T. Tennant.

---

[673] Orig., 'Baker'.

[674] Orig., 'Sharing'. In an account of his death written to JW on Feb. 7, 1778, the name is twice spelled 'Shearing'. *AM* (1789): 291.

[675] Apparently Thomas Vasey, who from independent evidence is shown to have been in Redruth this year. The initials T. V. were used for Wiltshire in *Minutes* (1775), *Q.* 6, and Vasey was certainly there then.

[676] Orig., 'Thoms', as also in 1779.

(32) *Bradford*, Christ. Hopper, Joseph Benson, T. Lee.

(33) *Keighley*, John Allen, William Brammah.

(34) *Colne*, Alexander Mather, Rich. Condy.

(35) *Whitehaven*, John Fenwick, James Barry, Thomas Rutherford, Robert Empringham. 5

(36) *York*, George Hudson, I[saac] W[aldron].[677]

(37) *Hull*, Thomas Hanson, James Hudson.

(38) *Scarborough*, William Hunter, Edward Jackson, John Peacock.

(39) *Yarm*, George Story, William Dufton, G[eorge] 10 G[uthrie].

(40) *Thirsk*, Jacob Rowell, Thomas Dixon.

(41) *The Dales*, Jer. Robertshaw, Thomas Wride, Robert Wilkinson.

(42) *Newcastle*, John Crook, John Leech, Michael 15 Moorhouse.

(43) *Alnwick*, Benjamin Rhodes, Robert Swan.

(44) *Edinburgh*, Alexander McNab,[678] Stephen Proctor.

(45) *Dundee*, William Eells, Duncan McAllum.

(46) *Aberdeen*, Francis Wrigley, Joseph Saunderson, 20 Joseph Moore.

(47) *Dublin*, John Hampson,[679] Samuel Bradburn.

(48) *Cork*, Richard Boardman, J[ohn] H[ampson].

(49) *Waterford*, Peter Mill, John Howe.

(50) *Limerick*, John Watson.[680] 25

(51) *Athlone*, Thomas Payne, Robert Armstrong, Hugh Brown, James Gaffney.

(52) *Sligo*, Andrew Delap, John Bredin.

(53) *Clones*, William Homer, Robert Davis.

(54) *Enniskillen*, John Mealy, William Boothby. 30

(55) *Armagh*, T. Halliday, George Brown, Hugh Moore.

(56) *Londonderry*, R. W.,[681] John Prickard.

(57) *Ballyshannon*,[682] Nehemiah Price, John Price.

(58) *Lisburn*, John [and] Jer. Brettel, Jonathan Hern.[683]

[677] Orig., 'J. W.'

[678] Orig., 'MacNab'.

[679] Sen.? Cf. following entry.

[680] Sen. or Jun.? One of the two seems not to have been stationed.

[681] Richard Watkinson. See *WHS* 10 (1916): 157, and *Minutes* (1776), *Q.* 6 (55), n. 678.

[682] Orig., 'Ballishannon'.

[683] There is no list of preachers for America, again reflecting war conditions.

Q. 10: What numbers are in the society?

A.	London	2,512
	Kent	258
5	Sussex	314
	Norwich	446
	Lynn	221
	Bedfordshire	503
	Oxfordshire	533
10	Wilts., South	309
	North*[684]	794
	Bristol*[685]	1,339
	Somerset	
15	Devon	637
	Cornwall, East*[686]	708
	West	1,420
	Pembrokeshire	220
	Glamorgan	149
20	Brecon	99
	Gloucestershire	484
	Staffordshire	654
	Chester*[687]	466
	Macclesfield	1,100
25	Manchester	1,152
	Liverpool	1,056
	Leicester	522
	Nottingham	773
	Grimsby	736
30	Gainsborough	471
	Epworth	500
	Sheffield*[688]	933
	Leeds	2,200
	Birstall	1,370

[684] Places marked * show a decrease in membership. A note by JW to this effect had been inserted in previous *Minutes* since 1769, and the same method of indicating this decrease is still used here.

[685] A decrease for the second consecutive year.

[686] A decrease for the second consecutive year.

[687] A decrease for the third consecutive year.

[688] A decrease for the second consecutive year.

Bradford	1,450	
Keighley	1,006	
Colne	754	
Whitehaven	671	
York	594	5
Hull	440	
Scarborough	560	
Yarm	839	
Thirsk	460	
The Dales	822	10
Newcastle	1,915	
Edinburgh*[689]	245	
Dundee*	155	
Aberdeen	273	
Dublin	458	15
Waterford	142	
Cork	345	
Limerick*	164	
Athlone*	520	
Sligo	416	20
Clones	509	
Enniskillen	487	
Londonderry	722	
Armagh*	580	
Lisburn	868	25
	————	
In all	38,274[690]	

Q. 11: What is the Kingswood collection?

A. £380. 8*s*. 2*d*.   30

Q. 12: What children are admitted this year?

A. We have no room for any more yet.

Q. 13: What girls?

A. There is no vacancy yet.

Q. 14: What is contributed for the Yearly Expenses?   35

---

[689] A decrease for the third consecutive year.

[690] Despite the war, the American figures were included in the *Minutes* of 1776 and 1778, but not of 1777, 1779, and 1780–83. The figure for 1776 repeats that for 1775; see (1776), *Q.* 7, n. 623.

A. Nothing. There is only one contribution this year, namely for the New Chapel in London.[691]

Q. 15: What was contributed to the Preachers' Fund?

A. £84. 11*s*. 6*d*.

Q. 16: What was allowed out of it?

A.

	£	*s*.
J. McBurney[692]	8	8
Eliz. Standring	10	0
John Hosmer	10	0
Eliz. Oldham	5	5
Mary Penington	7	7
Jane Garnet	5	5
Eliz. Dillon	5	5
Isab. Slocomb[693]	5	5
	£ 56	15[694]

Q. 17: How many wives are to be provided for?

A. In Ireland four, (S[isters] Watson,[695] Payne, W.,[696] and Hern),[697] in England forty-nine.

Q. 18: By what societies?

A. By the following:

London[698]	S[isters] Jaco, Hindmarsh.
Sussex	S. Boon.
Wilts, North	S. Barker, S. Wolf,[699] £6.[700]

---

[691] City Road Chapel; for the first reference to this, see *Minutes* (1776), *Q*. 21.

[692] Orig., 'McBurney', as also in 1791.

[693] See *Q*. 4 above. John Slocomb's widow, Isabel, is supported after his death.

[694] Orig., '£57. 0.'

[695] Orig. 'Watton'.

[696] Presumably Richard Watkinson's wife. See No. 56 above; he was stationed at Londonderry.

[697] This year is the first time Irish wives are named.

[698] From this year onwards (except 1779–80), the circuits in this feature are printed in roman rather than italic type.

[699] Wolf was stationed in Devon; see also Gloucestershire, below.

[700] Previously the proportion of the support has been specified (either the whole, usually understood, or 'half'); here, and in 1782–84, 1786–91, the specific amounts are noted (presumably the equivalent of a half or a quarter share), while in 1778–81, 1785, there are no exceptions noted, so the assumption is that each circuit named is fully responsible for the wives listed.

Bristol	S. Bourke, Peacock.[701]	
Devon	S. Brisco.[702]	
Cornwall, East	S. Westell.	
West	S. Poole.	
Oxford	S. Cotty, £6.	5
Gloucestershire	S. Snowden, Wolf, £6.	
Staffordshire	S. Taylor.	
Leicestershire	S. Beanland.[703]	
Nottinghamshire	S. Costerdine.	
Chester	S. Roberts.	10
Macclesfield	S. Shaw.	
Manchester	S. Mitchell, Wright.	
Liverpool	S. Collins, Oliver.[704]	
Grimsby	S. Brown.	
Gainsborough	S. Easton.	15
Epworth	S. Harrison, Corbet.[705]	
Sheffield	S. Shorter, Greenwood.	
Leeds	S. Thompson, Morgan, Floyd.	
Birstall	S. Hunter,[706] Thompson.	
Bradford	S. Hopper.	20
York	S. W[aldron], Lee.[707]	
Keighley	S. Brammah, Empringham.[708]	
Yarm[709]	S. Story.	
Thirsk	S. Rowell.	
The Dales	S. Robertshaw	25
Newcastle	S. Barry,[710] Crook.	
Alnwick	S. Swan.	

The money which was wanting was then contributed.

Q. 19: Do any of the preachers take money for wives who 30
do not want it?

---

[701] Bourke was stationed in Kent; Peacock at Scarborough.
[702] Brisco was stationed in Somerset.
[703] Beanland was stationed at Nottingham.
[704] Oliver was stationed at Epworth.
[705] Corbet was stationed at Nottingham.
[706] Hunter was stationed at Scarborough.
[707] Lee was stationed at Bradford.
[708] Empringham was stationed at Whitehaven.
[709] Orig., 'Yarmouth'.
[710] Barry was stationed at Whitehaven.

A. So it has frequently been asserted. But upon inquiry we found it an absolute slander.

Q. 20: There is a difficulty in procuring money for the preachers' wives in Ireland. How may this be removed?

A. Let each Assistant take care to send up to the General Assistant[711] in Dublin, every quarter, the money which his circuit is to pay.

Q. 21: What houses are to be built this year?

A. We have no objection to the building at Bath, at Coleorton Moor,[712] at Macclesfield, and at Newcastle–under–Lyme;[713] for which a collection may be made in the neighbouring circuits. And try if anything can be done at Birmingham.

Q. 22: Some of the late buildings have been ill-conducted.[714] How may this be remedied?

A. Let the Assistant of the circuit diligently superintend every preaching-house which shall be hereafter built.

Q. 23: What can be done for the sufferers by the fall of the gallery at Colne?[715]

A. Let a private collection be made for them in the neighbouring circuits.

Q. 24: Are not some of our preachers clownish still, and others apt to be offended?[716]

A. Great care should be taken to prevent or cure this, that the good which is in them may not be evil spoken of.[717]

Q. 25: When and where may the next Conference begin?

A. At Leeds, the first Tuesday in next August.

Q. [26]: On what days may the quarterly fasts be observed?

A. On the Friday in the Conference week, the first Friday in November, the first Friday in February, and the first Friday in May.[718]

---

[711] See *Minutes* (1768), *Q.* 21; (1774), *Q.* 23.

[712] Orig., 'Colhorton-Moor'.

[713] Orig., 'Newcastle-under-line'.

[714] The supervision at the time of building, or the raising of money for them? Apparently the former judging by the reply and perhaps *Q.* 23.

[715] An early instance of local tragedy and connexional support.

[716] This appears to mean that others are offended at the clownishness, judging by the reply.

[717] See Rom. 14:16.

[718] For earlier attempts at regular fasts see *Minutes* (1767), *Q.* 29; (1768) *Q.* 23 (7) and nn. 162, 210. These fasts were on varying dates and with little evidence of success or failure. Further fasts were appointed in 1778, 1784, 1785, and 1790.

Annual *Minutes of some late Conversations*, 1778

Leeds, Tuesday, August 4, etc., 1778[719]

Q. 1. What preachers are admitted this year?

A. Andrew Delap, Peter Mill, J. Howe, James Gaffney, Robert Davis, Hugh Moore, William Saunders,[720] Jos.   5 Taylor, Jasper Robinson, Tho. Vasey, John Whitley, Robert Armstrong, John Mealy.

[719] In August, JW wrote, 'Our Conference began; so large a number of preachers never met at a Conference before. I preached morning and evening till Thursday night, then my voice began to fail, and I desired two of our preachers to supply my place the next day. On Saturday, the Conference ended.' *Journal & Diaries*, 23:102 in this edn. Joseph Benson wrote to Walter Churchy, 'The best I was ever at. Mr Wesley has been in a sweet spirit, has preached some excellent sermons' to 'extraordinary congregations . . . and has dealt closely and plainly with the preachers, setting two aside for misdemeanors'. MS 7–6, in MA, and Tyerman, *Wesley*, 3:271. He wrote in similar terms to Charles Wesley, MS Early Methodist Letters, Aug. 8, 1778, in MA. Thomas Taylor wrote in his diary:

'August 5. Today we permitted all sorts to come into the Conference, so that we had a large company. The forenoon was occupied in speaking upon preaching-houses. In the afternoon, the sending of missionaries to Africa was considered. The call seems doubtful. Afterwards the committee met, and we were an hour and a half in what might have been done in five minutes. We are vastly tedious and have many long speeches to little purpose. August 6. This day has been employed chiefly in stationing the preachers. August 7. We were engaged in Conference till after one o'clock and then the Sacrament began, at which, I think, two thousand were present.' (Taylor, MS Diary, quoted in *Journal & Diaries*, 23:102 n. 4 in this edn.)

As to missions, thirty-five years later at the first auxiliary missionary meeting in 1813, Thomas Thompson, M.P., recalled this Conference. He said the deepest impression was made by a young man in consumption offering himself as a missionary to Africa or any other country. Thompson believed this was Duncan McAllum. If so, he must already have written to JW, who replied, refusing the offer on July 14, 1778: 'You have nothing at present to do in Africa. Convert the heathen in Scotland.' *Letters* (Telford), 6:316. The young man in Conference appears to be John Prickard, as he describes in his autobiography; see Jackson, *Early Methodist Preachers*, 4:184–86. For sources on this problem see *Journal* (Curnock), 6:206 n. 3. The call to Africa came through two young Calabar princes, who enlisted the aid of Bristol Methodists; for details see Tyerman, *Wesley*, 3:273. In the same year, John Baxter, a Chatham shipwright, left for Antigua to continue the pioneer work of the Gilberts. Ibid., 3:272f.

On stationing, JW says, 'This year, I myself (which I have seldom done) chose the preachers for Bristol.' *Journal & Diaries*, 23:77 in this edn.

[720] Orig., 'Sanders', as also in 1779 and 1780, though all other references (including the 1778 stations and his 1815 obituary) are to 'Saunders'.

Q. 2. Who *remain on trial?*

A. Duncan McAllum, James Hall, William Church, Jos. Saunderson, William Eells, John Blades,[721] Hugh Moore, Geo. Brown, E. Jackson.

5   *Q.* 3. Who are *admitted on trial?*

A. William Gill, Andrew Blair, Wm. Myles,[722] John Acutt,[723] James Burt, Thomas Warrick,[724] Daniel Jackson, John Livermore,[725] Nath. Ward, Robert Naylor, Jon. Brown, Robert Blake.[726]

10   *Q.* 4. Who desist from travelling?

A. George Guthrie, Robert Swan, Thomas Tatton, Geo. Wadsworth, Wm. Severn.

Q. 5. What preachers have died this year?

A. Thomas Hopkins, a young man, just entering on the
15   work; zealous, active and of an unblameable behaviour. And *Richard Bourke*, a man of faith and patience, made perfect through sufferings; one who joined the wisdom and calmness of age with the simplicity of childhood.

Q. 6. Are there any objections to any of our preachers?

20   *A.* Examine them one by one. This was carefully done and two were set aside.[727]

Q. 7. How are the preachers stationed this year?

---

[721] Tyerman described Blades as a 'weakminded fanatic, totally unfit for the itinerant work'. He was not appointed to a circuit but was for some years a local preacher in northern England. He left Methodism in 1784 and founded a sect of 'Bladonians', one of whom claimed a vision of destruction in 1788. Tyerman, *Wesley*, 3:536.

[722] Orig., 'Miels', elsewhere always 'Myles'.

[723] Orig., 'Accut', as also in 1779, 1781, 1785, and JW's letter of July 12, 1781. In 1789 his name appeared as 'Accutt', as also in JW's letter of Sept. 11, 1784. His portrait in the *AM* (1784), however, used the spelling 'Acutt', as did the *Minutes* (1782–84).

[724] Orig., 'Warwick', as in 1779, 1781–82, 1786, 1787 (1 of 2), and 1789. The majority, however, have 'Warrick', as do his portrait in the *AM* (1784) and JW's holograph letters for Aug. 3, 1782, Nov. 16, 1786, July 16, 1788, and Aug. 29, 1789.

[725] Orig., 'Livermoore'; once, in 1781, 'Liverman'; elsewhere 'Livermore'.

[726] Orig., 'Black', as in stations (16); elsewhere 'Blake'.

[727] Isaac Waldron is almost certainly one of them. He seems to be the I. W. or J. W. listed elsewhere in the stations; see *WHS* 10 (1916): 154; 11 (1918): 165. Pawson gives a critical report of his character and wrongly says he 'could only travel in Ireland'. *Letters*, 3:57 n. 164. The other man is probably Peter Dean; see *Minutes* (1775), *Q.* 3 and n. 556.

A. As follows:

Joseph Bradford travels with Mr. Wesley. John Atlay is the
  Book Steward. Thomas Olivers corrects the press.
  (1) *London*, John Pawson, Thomas Rankin,[728] Thomas
  Tennant, Peter Jaco, supernumerary; John Wesley,[729]   5
  Thomas Coke,[730] John Abraham.[731]
  (2) *Sussex*, Charles Boon, Benj. Rhodes, John Acutt;
  James Skinner, supernumerary.
  (3) *Kent*, James Rogers, Joseph Harper, M[ichael]
  F[enwick].   10

[728] Orig., 'Ranken' (on this occasion only).

[729] Except for 1772, where there is a reference to 'J. W.', this is the first instance of Wesley's official listing in a station in the *Minutes*. Henceforward his name continues under London until his death. JW seems here to be deliberately listing the other three ordained clergy (*not* including his brother Charles) *after* the names of his lay preachers stationed in London.

[730] Thomas Coke, LL.D. (1747–1814), was born in Brecon, the son of an apothecary; he matriculated at Jesus College, Oxford, and was ordained deacon in 1770, priest in 1772. He was curate of South Petherton in Somerset but was dismissed for his 'Methodist' behaviour in 1777. He became one of JW's chief Helpers, though it is significant that JW seems never to have proposed him as his successor. He was influential in drawing up the Deed of Declaration in 1784; he was ordained superintendent that same year and sent to America, where he ordained Asbury, both calling themselves bishops, contrary to JW's desire. Coke was an enthusiast for overseas missions and died en route for Ceylon and India. In spite of his admiration of missions, his administration of mission finance was incompetent, and latterly he had to be controlled by a committee. Despite Coke's enthusiasm and dedication, some Methodist leaders regarded him as too ambitious, hoping to be JW's successor. Wesley himself had doubts about his discretion. But some (like John Pawson) thought better of him. He was secretary of Conference in JW's later years and deputized for him in the Irish Conference, though he was often absent in America. His election as president of Conference was delayed until 1797. The most recent life is that by John Vickers, *Thomas Coke* (London, 1969).

[731] Rev. John Abraham is not listed anywhere else, either on trial or admitted, and this entry is the only recorded appointment. He graduated B.A. from Trinity College, Dublin (1768). He was converted under the influence of Rev. Edward Smyth, who also assisted JW until he settled in Manchester. Abraham preached with Smyth in Dublin (1776) and was chaplain to a chapel of ease in Londonderry but resigned to help JW at City Road (1778). He was not adapted to the itinerancy and retired to Ireland in 1779. *Letters* (Telford), 6:218; C. H. Crookshank, *Methodism in Ireland*, 3 vols. (Belfast: Allen, 1885), 1:276, 307, 397, 332. JW had offers of his return in 1781, and Abraham was in London the following year. *Letters* (Telford), 7:50, 105. But in 1783 JW said he must 'drop' him. *Letters* (Telford), 7:177. CW wrote in 1778 that he was John's 'curate' but 'almost as feeble in body as Mr. Richardson' (another clerical Helper). *CWJ*, 2:269. Myles (*Chronological History*, 299) says he left in 1783.

(4) *Norwich*, Joseph Pilmore, Barn. Thomas, Robert Naylor.[732]

(5) *Lynn*, John Moon, John Walker, Jasper Robinson.

(6) *Bedfordshire*, John Pritchard, Wm. Whitaker, Tho. Corbet.

(7) *Oxfordshire*, Tho. Carlill, Wm. Tunney.

(8) *Gloucestershire*, Thomas Brisco, Sam. Smith, John Bristol.

(9) *Wilts., South*, Richard Whatcoat, Wm. Barker, James Perfect.

(10) *Wilts., North*, Samuel Randal, Wm. Moore, Thomas Newall, Tho. Westell.

(11) *Bristol*, John Goodwin, John Valton, James Wood.

(12) *Taunton*, Francis Wolf, Henry Robins.

(13) *Tiverton*, Samuel Wells, James Burt.

(14) *Cornwall, East*, Richard Condy, John Furz, Joseph Jones, John Poole.

(15) —————— *West*, John Mason, William Ashman, Richard Rodda, James Cotty.

(16) *Glamorgan*, John Broadbent, Robert Blake.[733]

(17) *Brecon*, John Watson [Jun.], William Church.

(18) *Pembroke*, James Hall, George Mowat,[734] Joseph Pescod.

(19) *Staffordshire*, T. Mitchell, William Horner.

(20) *Macclesfield*, John Shaw, Nicholas Manners, Jeremiah Brettel.

(21) *Manchester*, Duncan Wright, Jos. Benson.

(22) *Chester*, James Barry, Robert Costerdine.

(23) *Liverpool*, Robert Roberts, Thomas Hanby, Parson Greenwood.

(24) *Leicestershire*, Thomas Dixon, Richard Seed, Michael Moorhouse.

(25) *Nottingham*, William Collins, Sam. Bardsley, William Percival.

(26) *Sheffield*, Thomas Lee, Geo. Snowden, John Fenwick.

---

[732] Orig., 'Nayler', on this occasion only.

[733] Orig. 'Black'.

[734] Orig., 'Mowatt', as also in 1789, 1790, though all other references are to 'Mowat'.

(27) *Grimsby*, John Peacock, John Norris, Will. Thom, R. Empringham.

(28) *Gainsborough*, Lan. Harrison, Joseph Taylor.

(29) *Epworth*, Geo. Shadford, Martin Rodda, George Shorter.

(30) *Leeds*, John Easton, John Floyd, Ja. Hindmarsh.   5

(31) *Birstall*, Thomas Taylor, John Oliver, W. Brammah, Rob. Howard.

(32) *Bradford*, Christ. Hopper, Tho. Johnson, John Murlin.

(33) *Keighley*, John Allen, Geo. Hudson.

(34) *Colne*, Alex. Mather, Tho. Vasey.   10

(35) *Whitehaven*, Rob. Wilkinson, Stephen Proctor.

(36) *Isle of Man*, John Crook, Robert Dall.

(37) *York*, Thomas Hanson, John Morgan.

(38) *Hull*, Christ. Watkins, J. Beanland.

(39) *Scarborough*, Isaac Brown, John Wittam, William Saunders. 15

(40) *Thirsk*, William Hunter, John Whitley.

(41) *Yarm*, George Story, Edward Jackson, Thomas Wride.

(42) *The Dales*, Jer. Robertshaw, John Leech, Jon. Brown.

(43) *Newcastle*, William Thompson, Jac. Rowell, Joseph Thompson, Wm. Eells.   20

(44) *Edinburgh*, Francis Wrigley, Joseph Moore.

(45) *Dundee*, Alex. McNab, William Dufton.

(46) *Aberdeen*, Jos. Saunderson, J. Watson, Sen., Duncan McAllum.[735]

[735] Again, there are no listings for America, and the Irish stations are omitted for this year.

The following list of Irish stations for 1778 is taken from the first published Irish *Minutes*, see below.

Dublin, R. Watkinson, W. Eells. (Eells was also appointed to Newcastle, and Crookshank adds: 'At [the] subsequent meeting of [the] Conference Mr. Eells was appointed to Newcastle and Mr. Rutherford to Dublin.')

Waterford, T. Halliday, R. Armstrong.

Cork, J. Hampson, Sen., S. Bradburn.

Limerick, A. Delap, J. Bredin.

Castlebar, N. Price, W. Myles.

Athlone, T. Payne, R. Boardman.

Sligo, R. Lindsay, H. Moore.

Clones, W. Boothby, J. Hern.

Enniskillen, J. Price, G. Brown.

Lisleen, J. Mealy, J. Howe, W. McCornock.

Armagh, P. Mill, A. Blair, W. Gill.

Londonderry, John Brettel, J. Gaffney.

Belfast, T. Rutherford.

Lisburn, J. Prickard, J. Hampson, Jun.

Q. 8: How many wives are to be provided for?
A. Forty-four.
Q. 9: By what societies?

5	*A.* London	S. Jaco, Harper[736]
	Sussex	S. Boon
	Gloucestershire	S. Brisco
	Bristol	S. Barker, Westell[737]
	Devon	S. Wolf
10	Cornwall, East	S. Poole
	Cornwall, West	S. Rodda
	Staffordshire	S. Mitchell
	Macclesfield	S. Shaw, Crook[738]
	Manchester	S. Wright, Costerdine[739]
15	Chester	S. Barry
	Liverpool	S. Roberts, Greenwood
	Leicestershire	S. Thom[740]
	Nottingham	S. Collins
	Sheffield	S. Lee, Snowden
20	Grimsby	S. Peacock
	Gainsborough	S. Harrison
	Epworth	S. Shorter
	Leeds	S. Easton, Floyd, Hindmarsh
	Birstall	S. Taylor, Brammah
25	Bradford	S. Hopper
	Keighley	S. Oliver[741]
	Colne	S. Mather
	York	S. Morgan
	Hull	S. Beanland
30	Halifax[742]	S. Wilkinson[743]
	Thirsk	S. Hunter

[736] Joseph Harper was stationed in Kent.
[737] Barker and Westell were stationed in Wiltshire.
[738] Crook was stationed in the Isle of Man.
[739] Costerdine was stationed at Chester.
[740] Thom was stationed at Grimsby.
[741] Oliver was stationed at Birstall.
[742] Halifax is not listed as a circuit in 1778 stations or in any previous *Minutes*. The only mention of this town is in the lists of monetary distributions. This inclusion of Halifax occurs also in the listing of wives in 1779, 1785, 1786, but it is not until 1787 onwards that Halifax is included in the list of stations for preachers.
[743] Wilkinson was stationed at Whitehaven.

Yarm	S. Story	
The Dales	S. Robertshaw	
Newcastle	S. Thompsons,[744] Rowell	
Oxfordshire		
	S. Corbet	5
Bedfordshire		

Q. 10: What numbers are in the society?

A. London	2,559	10
Sussex	340	
Kent	259	
Norwich	484	
Lynn	238	
Bedfordshire	550	15
Oxfordshire	547	
Gloucestershire	529	
Wilts., South*[745]	301	
North*	727	
Bristol*[746]	1,330	20
Taunton		
	693	
Tiverton		
Cornwall, East	718	
West	1,430	25
Glamorganshire*	138	
Brecon	117	
Pembrokeshire	242	
Staffordshire	690	
Macclesfield	1,160	30
Manchester	1,250	
Chester	510	
Liverpool	1,095	
Leicestershire	626	

[744] Wives of William and Joseph Thompson. See also *Minutes* (1776), *Q.* 16, *Leeds*.

[745] N.B. In the circuits marked thus* there is a decrease this year. This usual explanatory note is omitted from the printed text this year, though the asterisks denoting such decreases are present.

[746] A decrease for the third consecutive year.

	Nottingham*	739
	Sheffield*[747]	795
	Grimsby	733
	Gainsborough	502
5	Epworth	510
	Leeds	2,337
	Birstall	1,751
	Bradford	1,522
	Keighley	1,104
10	Colne	770
	Whitehaven ⎫	
	⎬	933
	Isle of Man ⎭	
15	Hull	500
	Scarborough[748]	565
	Thirsk	573
	Yarm	880
	The Dales	825
20	Newcastle*	1,887
	Edinburgh*[749]	161
	Dundee*[750]	142
	Aberdeen	311
	Dublin	462
25	Cork*	325
	Waterford	170
	Limerick	257
	Castlebar ⎫	
	⎬	526
30	Athlone ⎭	
	Sligo	402
	Clones	461
	Enniskillen	511
	Lisleen ⎫	
35	⎬	582
	Armagh ⎭	

[747] A decrease for the third consecutive year.
[748] Orig., 'Scarbrough'.
[749] A decrease for the fourth consecutive year.
[750] A decrease for the second consecutive year.

Londonderry	708	
Belfast ⎤		
⎟	932	
Lisburn ⎦		
America	6,968	5

In all   47,057[751]

Q. 11: What is the Kingswood collection?
A. £366. 14*s*. 11*d*.   10
Q. 12: What children are admitted this year?
A. John Slocomb, John Bourke, Ja. Mitchell,[752] Jos.
  Pinder,[753] Corn. Peacock.[754]
Q. 13: What girls?
A. Ann Easton, Sarah Brown.[755]   15
Q. 14: Ought all the money that is contributed anywhere to
  be produced at the Conference?
A. Undoubtedly. Nothing should be stopped, on any reason
  or pretense whatsoever.
Q. 15: What is contributed for the yearly expenses?   20
A. £366, 14*s*. 11*d*.
Q. 16: How was this distributed?

A.	Preachers' necessities	£227	12	10	
	Law	15	12	0	25
	Contingencies	85	10	0	
	London	161	18	0	
	Londonderry	75	0	0	
	Dublin	10	0	0	
	Newcastle	21	0	0	30

[751] Orig., '44, 859'.

[752] Sons of Isabel Slocomb and Lucia Bourke, both of whose husbands had died. James Mitchell, the son of Thomas Mitchell.

[753] There is no preacher of this name, and the presumption must be that this was an ordinary layman's son. The only Pindar [*sic*] in Wesley's *Journal* was a contemporary of JW at Oxford. See *Journal & Diaries*, 22:421 and n. 58 in this edn.

[754] Cornelius Peacock, son of John Peacock.

[755] Daughters of John Easton and of Isaac Brown or George Brown. Not likely to be the daughter of Hugh Brown, who left in 1777, or Jonathan Brown, who was admitted on trial in 1778. For the question of girls at Kingswood School, see *Minutes* (1773), *Q*. 10 and n. 461; *Q*. 13 here seems to imply attendance of girls at Kingswood.

	£	s	d
Shaftesbury	10	0	0
Macclesfield	10	0	0
Bodmin	5	0	0
	£ 621	17	10

Q. 17: What is contributed for the Preachers' Fund?
A. £99. 8*s*. 6*d*.
Q. 18: What was allowed out of it?

	£.	s.
To E. Standring	10	0
John McBurney	8	8
John Hosmer	10	0
Mary Penington	7	7
Lucia Bourke[756]	14	14
Eliz. Oldham	5	5
Jane Garnet	5	5
Eliz. Garnet[757]	5	5
Is. Slocomb	5	5
I. Waldron	20	0
T. Westell	*13*	*3*
	£ 104	12

Q. 19: Is it not advisable for us to visit all the jails[758] we can?
A. By all means. There cannot be a greater charity.
Q. 20: What houses are to be built this year?
A. At Addingham, Padiham, Pannall, Davyhulme,[759] Frome, Macclesfield.
Q. 21: Many trustees are dead. What is to be done?
A (1) Let each Assistant inquire before Christmas trustees are wanting in his circuit.
(2) Let him write me word when they think proper to supply the want.

---

[756] Lucia Bourke, widow of Richard Bourke, received support from the fund, 1778–95.

[757] Joseph Garnet, the only preacher of that name, appears to have died c. 1775. Jane Garnet (his widow?) appears in the Preachers' Fund (1775–79); Catherine Garnett (1780–90, 1795–96); Mrs. Garnet, widow, (1797–98); but Elizabeth Garnet only in 1778. Two of these may be dependent daughters.

[758] Orig., 'gaols'.

[759] Orig., 'Davyholme'.

Q. 22: Some trustees may abuse their power after my death. What can be done now to prevent this?

A. It seems we need take no thought for the morrow. God will provide when need shall be.

Q. 23: Why do so many of our preachers fall into nervous 5 disorders?

A. Because they do not sufficiently observe Dr. Cadogan's rules—to avoid indolence and intemperance.

They do indeed use exercise. But many of them do not use enough; not near so much as they did before they were 10 preachers. And sometimes they sit still a whole day. This can never consist with health. They are not intemperate in the vulgar sense—they are neither drunkards nor gluttons. But they take more food than nature requires, particularly in the evening. 15

Q. 24: What advice would you give to those that are nervous?

A. Advice is made for them that will take it. But who are they? One in ten, or twenty?

Then I advise: 20
   (1) Touch no dram, tea, tobacco, or snuff.
   (2) Eat very light, if any, supper.
   (3) Breakfast on nettle or orange-peel tea.
   (4) Lie down before ten; rise before six.
   (5) Every day use as much exercise as you can bear—or, 25
   (6) Murder yourself by inches.

Q. 25: When and where may the next Conference begin?

A. At London, the first Tuesday in next August.

Q. 26: On what days may the quarterly fasts be observed?

A. Next Friday, the first Friday in November, the first 30 Friday in February, and the first in May.

Annual *Minutes of some late Conversations,* 1779[760]

London, Tuesday, August 3, 1779

Q. 1: What preachers are admitted this year?

A. Edward Jackson, Joseph Saunderson, William Eells,
5   John Norris, James Hall, Daniel Jackson, Robert Naylor.
David Evans and George Wadsworth were *re-admitted.*[761]

Q. 2: Who remain on trial?

A. Duncan McAllum, William Church, Hugh Moore,[762] George
Brown, William Gill, Andrew Blair, William Myles, Thomas
10   Warrick, John Acutt, Jonath. Brown, and Robert Blake.

Q. 3. Who are *admitted on trial?*

A. Henry Moore,[763] Thomas Barber, Thomas Davis, John
Booth, Samuel Mitchell, James Christie, George Button,
William Simpson, George Wawne,[764] Alexander Suter,
15   William Warrener.[765]

---

[760] The title page on this occasion reads: 'Minutes of some late Conversations, &c. / at London / Tuesday, August 3d., 1779 / Printed by R. Hawes, (No. 40), the Corner of *Dorset-Street*, Spitalfields. 1779'.

Wesley wrote, 'Tuesday, August 3, our Conference began, which continued and ended in peace and love'. *Journal & Diaries*, 23:142 in this edn. He preached at the Foundery for the last time as the City Road Chapel was soon to be opened. A major concern was the decline of membership in several circuits (see *QQ.* 11, 12, and the reasons given). Behind the evil-speaking against those in authority, there no doubt lay the national divisions over the American war. So far as London was concerned, where CW had recently moved from Bristol, some leading preachers resented CW's tendency to monopolize the pulpit and to criticize the lay itinerants, which made his reputation equivocal for some of them long afterwards. Pawson was outspoken about this issue, and some blamed CW's uneven preaching for the lack of growth of Methodism in London. See Tyerman, *Wesley*, 3:297–301; Tyerman MSS, 3:49–51. In 1779–80, a similar dispute blew up over Rev. Edward Smyth keeping the itinerant Alexander McNab out of the Bath pulpit, and the Wesley brothers differed in their handling of this matter at the personal level, though the affair provoked JW into another rehearsal of the grounds of his authority over the preachers. Tyerman, *Wesley*, 3:303–12, and cf. *Minutes* (1766), *Q.* 29. Earlier in the year, Thomas Maxfield, separated from the connexion since the Bell affair in the early 1760s, asked to return. The Wesleys agreed not to receive him unless he acknowledged his faults. Nothing came of this. Tyerman, *Wesley*, 3–296.

[761] See *Minutes* (1776), *Q.* 4; (1778), *Q.* 4.

[762] Orig., 'Moor', as also in 1781 (1 of 2), 1785–87.

[763] Orig., 'Moor', as also in 1783 (1 of 2 and wife), 1789 (1 of 2).

[764] Orig., 'Vaughan'.

[765] Orig., 'Warren' (twice). The name also appears as 'Warrenner' in 1786 (Wilmington, N.C.), 1790 (1 of 2 in Antigua), and in 1791 (St. Christopher's).

Q. 4: Who desist from *travelling*?

A. William Whitaker, disabled by the stone, Joseph Moore, Robert Empringham, and John Whitley.

Q. 5: What preachers have died this year?

A. George Shorter, an Israelite indeed,[766] a lively, zealous, active man; a witness of full salvation, and an earnest exhorter of all believers to aspire after it. And James Gaffney, a young man of considerable abilities, wise above his years. He was snatched away by a galloping consumption; but was fully delivered from the fear of death, and was unspeakably happy, though in violent pain, till his spirit returned to God.

Q. 6: Are there any objections to any of our preachers?

A. Examine them one by one.

Q. 7: How are the preachers *stationed* this year?

A. As follows:

Joseph Bradford travels with Mr Wesley.

John Atlay is the Book Steward.

Thomas Olivers corrects the press.

(1) *London*, J[ohn] Wesley], T. Coke, John Pawson, Thomas Rankin, John Murlin.

(2) *Sussex*, Samuel Wells, Joseph Harper, Alexander Suter.

(3) *Kent*, Parson Greenwood, Francis Wrigley, James Perfect.

(4) *Norwich*, George Shadford, Samuel Bardsley, John Acutt.

(5) *Lynn*, John Pritchard, John Moon, James Skinner.

(6) *Bedfordshire*, Charles Boone, William Barker.

(7) *Oxfordshire*, George Story, Thomas Newall.

(8) *Northamptonshire*, Wm. Eells, Thomas Corbet.

(9) *Gloucestershire*, John Goodwin, James Wood, John Broadbent.

(10) *Wiltshire, South*, John Wittam, Richard Seed.

(11) *Wiltshire, North*, Samuel Randal, Francis Wolf, Henry Robins, Thomas Tennant.

(12) *Bristol*, Alexander McNab, John Valton, John Bristol.

(13) *Taunton*, John Mason, Michael Moorhouse.

(14) *Tiverton*, Thomas Carlill, Wm. Ashman.

---

[766] John 1:47.

(15) *Cornwall, East,* Richard Condy, Wm. Tunney, Robert Blake, John Poole.

(16) *Cornwall, West,* Tho. Hanson, G. Wadsworth, Richard Rodda, Wm. Simpson.

5   (17) *Glamorgan,* William Church, James Cotty.

(18) *Brecon,* J. Watson, Jun., Robert Swan.

(19) *Pembroke,* William Moore, John Booth, Zach. Yewdall.[767]

(20) *Staffordshire,* T. Mitchell, Robert Costerdine.

10   (21) *Macclesfield,* John and Jeremiah Brettel, Robert Howard.[768]

(22) *Manchester,* Joseph Benson, George Snowden.

(23) *Chester,* James Barry, William Homer.

(24) *Liverpool,* Robert Roberts, John Leech, Thomas

15   Hanby.

(25) *Leicester,* Thomas Dixon, John Furz, Jos. Pescod.

(26) *Nottingham,* William Collins, John Walker, Geo. Wawne.

(27) *Sheffield,* Thomas Lee, William Brammah.

20   (28) *Grimsby,* John Peacock, Daniel Jackson, George Button.

(29) *Gainsborough,* Lancelot Harrison, Wm. Warrener, Thomas Warrick.

(30) *Epworth,* Nicholas Manners, John Norris, Joseph

25   Taylor.

---

[767] Zachariah Yewdall. His Christian name appears as 'Zach.' (1779–81, 1784), 'Zachariah' (1782, 1787, 1788), 'Zachary' (1783). In more than twenty letters (1779–89), JW addressed him as 'Zachary'. In 1785, 1786, 1789–91, however, he appears as 'Zechariah', which is also used in his autobiography; see *AM* (1795). It seems clear that the pronunciation was 'Zach.', but that he spelled it differently for a year or two before JW's death. During JW's lifetime at least, however, it seems more appropriate to use 'Zachariah Yewdall'. His surname also appears variously: 'Yewdal' (1779–82), 'Udal' (1783), 'Udall' (1784–86), and in his portrait in *AM* (1787). The consensus, however, including JW's letters to him and his autobiography, seems to be 'Yewdall'. Written evidence of his own preference is lacking, but in the Deed of Declaration (1784) his name is spelled 'Zachariah Udall'.

[768] Orig., 'Hayward', as also in 1781–82, 1784, 1786; 'Heywood' in 1780; in the 1790 Conference Journal, he appears as 'Hayworth'; and in his obituary (1804) as 'Heyward'. JW's holograph letter of Dec. 24, 1769, spells his name, 'Howard'. The sequence in the stations makes it quite clear that the two basic spellings, 'Howard' and 'Hayward', refer to the same man, about whose name there arose similar phonetic problems as in the pronunciation of the Yorkshire town 'Haworth' as 'Howarth'.

(31) *Leeds*, John Easton, John Allen, James Rogers.
(32) *Birstall*, Thomas Taylor, John Floyd, John Oliver.
(33) *Bradford*, Alexander Mather, Tho. Johnson, Thomas Brisco.
(34) *Keighley*, James Hindmarsh, Geo. Hudson. 5
(35) *Colne*, Christopher Hopper, W. Percival
(36) *Whitehaven*, Jeremy Robertshaw, Tho. Vasey.
(37) *Isle of Man*, John Crook, Martin Rodda.
(38) *York*, John Fenwick, John Morgan.
(39) *Hull*, Isaac Brown, John Beanland. 10
(40) *Scarborough*, Christopher Watkins, James Watson, Thomas Wride.
(41) *Thirsk*, William Hunter, Jonath. Brown.
(42) *Yarm*, Duncan Wright, Edw. Jackson, William Saunders. 15
(43) *The Dales*, Jacob Rowell,[769] Robert Wilkinson, Thomas Richy.[770]
(44) *Newcastle*, William Thompson, John Watson, Sen., Stephen Proctor, Wm. Thom.
(45) *Edinburgh*, Joseph Pilmore, Barnabas Thomas, 20
Benjamin Rhodes.
(46) *Dundee*, George Mowat, Robert Naylor.
(47) *Aberdeen*, Joseph Saunderson, Wm. Dutton.
(48) *Inverness*, Duncan McAllum, Jasper Robinson.
(49) *Dublin*, Richard Watkinson, James Hall. 25
(50) *Cork*, Samuel Bradburn, John Bredin.
(51) *Waterford*, Hugh Moore, William Gill.
            Let these change once in two months.
(52) *Limerick*, Thomas Payne, Rd. Boardman.
(53) *Castlebar*, Robert Armstrong, T[homas] H[alliday]. 30
(54) *Athlone*, J[ohn] H[ampson], Sen., John H[ampson], Jun., Nehemiah Price.

---

[769] In 1765, he was named as 'Matt. Rowell'; in 1773, his wife appeared as 'Rowel'; in 1775, his name on the list of signatures at the end appeared as 'Rowall'; and in the stations here (orig.) it is also misspelled 'Rowel'. All other references, however, are to 'Rowell'.

[770] There is no other mention of Thomas Richy in the *Minutes*. He seems to be identifiable as Thomas Readshaw of Hexham. He was in The Dales Circuit in 1779 but 'without any particular acceptability' and returned to his own neighbourhood. Anthony Steele, *A History of Methodism in Barnard Castle and the Principal Places in The Dales Circuit* (London: Vickers, 1857), 141 (information from John Lenton).

(55) *Sligo*, John Price, Thomas Barber.

(56) *Clones*, Robert Lindsay,[771] John McBurney.

(57) *Enniskillen*, John Mealy, Wm. McCornock.[772]

(58) *Armagh*, Peter Mill, Jonathan Hern,[773] T. Davis.

(59) *Lisleen*, George Brown, Samuel Mitchell.

(60) *Londonderry*, Tho. Rutherford, Henry Moore, Andrew Blair.

(61) *Belfast*, John Prickard, James Christie.

(62) *Lisburn*, William Boothby, Robert Davis, William Myles.

Q. 8: How many wives are to be provided for?

A. Forty-three.

Q. 9: By what societies?

A. London	S. Boone, S. Story.[774]
Sussex	S. Harper.
Gloucestershire	S. Goodwin.
Bristol	S. Wilkinson, S. Evans.[775]
Wilts., North	S. Swan.[776]
Devon	S. Wolf.[777]
Cornwall, East	S. Poole.
West	S. Rodda.
Staffordshire	S. Mitchell.
Macclesfield	S. Costerdine.[778]

[771] Orig., 'Lindsey'. An Irishman, he originally served in America on trial, but then was stationed in Ireland (1778–84). In 1784, he married without his wife's parents' permission and against the Conference rule. Unfortunately, he had been named that year to the Legal Hundred, so it appears that an example had to be made of him. The *Minutes* (1784) note him as 'desisted', but the CJ shows he was expelled and Francis Asbury elected in his place. From 1785, he served again in Ireland at first on trial, but in 1788 he again 'desisted' (according to the CJ he was expelled). See W. W. Sweet, *Religion on the American Frontier,* vol. 4, *The Methodists* (Chicago, 1946), 130–32, 135–36.

[772] Orig., 'McCordock', as also in 1780; his name appears as 'Wm. McCormuck' in 1781, and as 'John McCornock' in 1782; in 1787 he is distinguished as 'W. McCornock, Sen.'

[773] Orig., 'John'.

[774] George Story was stationed in Oxfordshire; Charles Boone in Bedfordshire.

[775] David Evans was stationed in Wiltshire, South. See n. 777 below, Wolf.

[776] Robert Swan was stationed at Brecon.

[777] Francis Wolf was stationed in Wiltshire, North.

[778] Robert Costerdine was stationed in Staffordshire.

Manchester	S. Snowden, and S. Oliver.[779]	
Chester	S. Barry.	
Liverpool	S. Roberts, S. Greenwood.[780]	
Leicestershire	S. Corbet.[781]	
Nottinghamshire	S. Collins.	5
Sheffield	S. Lee, S. Brammah.	
Grimsby	S. Peacock.	
Gainsborough	S. Harrison.	
Epworth	S. Robertshaw.[782]	
Leeds	S. Easton, S. Rogers, S. Floyd.[783]	10
Birstall	S. Taylor, S. Shaw.	
Bradford	S. Mather.	
Keighley	S. Hindmarsh, S. Crook.[784]	
Colne	S. Hopper.	
York	S. Morgan.	15
Scarborough	S. Brown.[785]	
Halifax	S. Brisco.[786]	
Thirsk	S. Hunter.	
Yarm	S. Wright.	
The Dales	S. Rowell.	20
Newcastle	S. Thompson, S. Thom,[787]	
	S. Watson.	
Oxfordshire		
	S. Barker.	
Bedfordshire		25

Q. 10: What numbers are in the societies?

A. London[788]   2,436*

---

[779] John Oliver was stationed at Birstall.

[780] Parson Greenwood was stationed in Kent.

[781] Thomas Corbet was stationed in Northamptonshire.

[782] Jeremiah Robertshaw was stationed at Whitehaven.

[783] John Floyd was stationed at Birstall.

[784] John Crook was stationed in the Isle of Man.

[785] Isaac Brown was stationed at Hull.

[786] Thomas Brisco was stationed at Bradford.

[787] Orig., 'Thorn'.

[788] The membership numbers marked thus * indicate a decrease from the previous year. The usual explanatory note (see *Minutes* [1769], *Q.* 8, N.B. at end) is omitted from the printed text for the third successive year, though the asterisks denoting such decreases are present.

	Sussex	321*
	Kent	330
	Norwich	497
	Lynn	187
5	Bedfordshire	494*
	Oxfordshire	523*
	Gloucestershire	496*
	Wilts., South	307
	———— North	843
10	Bristol	1,505
	Taunton	209*
	Tiverton	355*
	Cornwall, East	718
	———— West	1,412*
15	Glamorgan	152
	Brecon	140
	Pembrokeshire	239*
	Staffordshire	713
	Macclesfield	1,236
20	Manchester	1,307
	Chester	550
	Liverpool	1,031*
	Leicestershire	632
	Nottingham	780
25	Sheffield	843
	Grimsby	837
	Gainsborough	480*
	Epworth	630
	Leeds	2,222*
30	Birstall	2,323
	Bradford	1,541
	Keighley	1,260
	Colne	790
	Whitehaven	302
35	Isle of Man	1,051
	York	653*
	Hull	681
	Scarborough	670
	Thirsk	600
40	Yarm	900
	The Dales	828

Newcastle	1,890	
Edinburgh	193	
Dundee[789]	121*	
Aberdeen	27[6]*[790]	
Inverness	42	5
Dublin	562	
Cork[791]	239*	
Waterford*	300*	
Limerick	355	
Castlebar	182*	10
Athlone	230*	
Sligo	489	
Clones	615	
Enniskillen	560	
Lisleen	638	15
Armagh	811	
Londonderry	150*	
Belfast	334*	
Lisburn	475	
	———	20
	42,486[792]	

N.B. America is omitted.[793]

Q. 11: How can we account for the decrease in so many cir- 25
cuits this year?[794]

A. It may be owing partly to want of preaching abroad and
of trying new places; partly to prejudice against the king
and 'speaking evil of dignities';[795] but chiefly to the

---

[789] A decrease for the third consecutive year.

[790] The omission of the '6' has been supplied from the 1862 edn. It is omitted in
the original printed *Minutes.*

[791] A decrease for the second consecutive year.

[792] Orig., '42,507'.

[793] See *Minutes* (1777), *Q.* 10, n. 690, to total of membership.

[794] Twenty circuits are recorded as reduced in numbers, 12 out of 60 in 1778, 10
out of 58 in 1777, 14 out of 55 in 1776, and 13 out of 51 in 1775. Twenty out of 62
are recorded as reduced in 1779. Such details are not recorded in 1780 but have
been supplied in this edn. from a comparison of the respective figures: 7 out of 64.
In 1781 there was a large increase in such circuits: 33 out of 63; 37 out of 66 in
1782; 31 out of 69 in 1783; and 53 out of 74 in 1784.

[795] Cf. 2 Pet. 2:10; Jude 8. As noted earlier, these divisions probably resulted in
large part from national divisions over the American war. Not all Methodists shared
Wesley's loyalist Toryism; see Rack, *Reasonable Enthusiast,* 378f.

increase of *worldly mindedness* and *conformity to the world*.[796]

Q. 12: How can we stop this *evil-speaking*?

A. Suffer none that speak evil of those in authority, or that prophesy evil to the nation, to preach with us. Let every Assistant take care of this.

Q. 13: What is the Kingswood collection?

A. £368. 18*s*.

Q. 14: What children are admitted this year?

A. George Snowden, John Barry,[797] Charles Margate.[798]

Q. 15: What is contributed for the yearly expenses?

A. £473. 6*s*. 2*d*.

Q. 16: How was this distributed?

A.	£.	*s.*	*d.*
For the preachers' necessities	235	3	2
Law	28	15	0
Contingencies for the present year	100	0	0
To Grimsby	5	5	0
To Louth	10	0	0
To Londonderry	10	0	0
To Colne	30	0	0
To Padiham	20	0	0
To Newlyn[799]	10	0	0
To Shaftesbury	10	0	0
To Arbroath	10	0	0
To Exeter	3	3	0
To Neston[800]	1	0	0
	[£473	6*s*.	2*d*.][801]

---

[796] See Rom. 12:2.

[797] Sons of George Snowden and James Barry.

[798] Possibly the son of Samuel Meggot, who died in 1764. In 1784, £5 was allowed out of the Preachers' Fund to 'S[ister] Meggit'.

[799] Orig., 'Newlin'.

[800] No previous mention; it could be in Cheshire or Wiltshire. Although the list seems not to be in a strictly geographical order, its placing next to Exeter may suggest the south rather than the north.

[801] The total amount of money is omitted from the original.

Q. 17. Exceeding little has been contributed this year. How may this be altered?

A. Let every Assistant: (1) Read publicly the article in the *Minutes*. (2) Ask every person at the Christmas visitation, 'What will you subscribe?' (3) Receive it at the next 5 visitation.

Q. 18. But whatever is subscribed will not answer the numberless demands. What can be done to lessen these?

A. (1st) Let every circuit bear its own burden, and not *lean* upon the Conference (2) Tell everyone expressly, 'We do 10 not make a subscription for paying debts.' (3) Let all the Assistants in Ireland do the same as those in England.[802]

Q. 19. When should casual collections be made?[803]

A. Between the Conference and January the first.

Q. 20. Should not the *Plans*[804] be brought in yearly? 15

A. Certainly—the Plan of *every circuit*.

Q. 21. What is contributed for the Preachers' Fund?

A. £106. 8*s.* 2*d.*

Q. 22. What is allowed out of it?

A.	£.	*s.*	20
To Isaac Waldron	18	0	
Eliz. Standring	10	0	
T. Westell	12	0	
Lucia Bourke[805]	10	0	
W. Whitaker[806]	10	0	25
Eliz. Oldham	5	5	
Eliz. Dillon	5	5	

[802] For problems with Irish subscriptions, see *Minutes* (1768), *Q.* 21 and n. 193; (1776), *Q.* 12.

[803] Collections not assigned to a particular cause, e.g., the Preachers' Fund and Kingswood Fund.

[804] Circuit preaching plans seem originally to have had the local preachers mainly in mind, though JW produced plans for the London Circuit in 1754 mainly for itinerants. Pawson says he was placed on the Leeds Circuit as a local preacher in 1761, and in 1776, JW urged the Assistant of The Dales Circuit to fix a regular plan for the local preachers. MS circuit plans survive for Leeds for 1776–77, and JW was probably responsible for the first printed circuit plans (for London) in the 1780s. This example was slowly followed, first by the larger urban and then the rural circuits. Most covered three months at a time. Baker, 'Polity', 238 and refs.

[805] 'Lucy', 1786, 1791.

[806] See above, *Q.* 4, and *Minutes* (1769), *Q.* 3. This is the first year Whitaker was supported by the Preachers' Fund, and this support continued until his death in 1794.

Jane Garnet	5	5
Mary Penington	5	5
Eliz. Shorter[807]	7	7
	[£88.	7s.][808]

5

Q. 23: What houses are to be built this year?

A. At Huntingdon, High Wycombe,[809] Plymouth, Plymouth Dock, Salop, Nottingham, Sheffield, Hunslet,[810] Greetland,[811] Mirfield.

10   We do not judge it proper that an house should be built at South Shields.[812]

Q. 24: Has each Assistant inquired what trustees were wanting for any house in his circuit? And considered who are proper persons to supply the want?[813]

15   *A.* No. But let it be done this year.

Q. 25: Should an Assistant take into the society any whom his predecessor has put out?

A. Not without first consulting him.

Q. 26: Preachers hasten home to their wives after preach-

20   ing. Ought this to be done?

A. Never, till they have met the society.

Q. 27: What can be done to revive the work in Scotland?[814]

A. (1) Preach abroad as much as possible.

        (2) Try every town and village.

25   (3) Visit every member of every society at home.

---

[807] Elizabeth Shorter, now a widow, was supported 1779–86; see *Minutes* (1773), *Q.* 7 (Cornwall), and above, *Q.* 5.

[808] The total amount expended is omitted from the original.

[809] Orig., 'High Wycomb'.

[810] Orig., 'Hunsleet'.

[811] Orig., 'Greatland'.

[812] However, South Shields had erected one by 1789 (Myles, *Chronological History*, says in 1785); see the list, *Minutes* (1785), *Q.* 19, n. 149. Pawson says that North and South Shields and Alnwick had refused to settle on the 'Conference Plan' (i.e., Model Deed), hence perhaps the refusal of permission here at Conference? Pawson, *Letters*, 1:80.

[813] See *Minutes* (1778), *Q.* 21.

[814] There seems to have been a tendency in Scotland to approximate to Presbyterian ways, on which JW made many complaints. He particularly objected to the habit of concentrating on town societies and reluctance to 'preach abroad'. See *Letters* (Telford), 6:42, 52, 77, 107.

(4) Let the preachers at Dundee and Arbroath never stay at one place more than a week at a time.

(5) Let each of them once a quarter visit Perth and Dunkeld, and the intermediate villages.[815]

Annual *Minutes of some late Conversations*, 1780[816] 5

Bristol, Tuesday, August 1, 1780

[815] One major question is not included in these *Minutes* (1779), viz., 'When and where may the next Conference begin?' Other examples of this omission are 1780, 1783, and 1786.

[816] The title page reads, *Minutes of some late Conversations between the Rev. Mr. John and Charles Wesley and others, begun at Bristol, Tuesday, August 1, 1780.* Wesley wrote, 'Friday August 1, our Conference began. We have been always hitherto straitened for time. It was now resolved, for the future we allow nine or ten days for each Conference that everything relative to the carrying on of the work of God may be maturely considered.' On Friday, he preached in the open air, much of the congregation having never heard this kind of preaching before. On Sunday, 'We had the largest number of communicants that had ever met in the New Room, and the largest congregation at five that had ever met near King Square. Wednesday 9, we concluded the Conference in much peace and love.' *Journal & Diaries* 23:182 in this edn. Prof. Ward comments that it is probable that the 'insistence of the "Large" *Minutes* that Methodism was a movement within the Church of England occasioned some demur (Simon, *Last Phase*, 162), for Charles Wesley detected "the working of principles unfavourable to that strict churchmanship which he believed to be essential", and left Conference (he said for the last time), writing verses of protest'. Ibid., n. 9. Sutcliffe recorded that CW said that if he was at Bristol at the time of the Conference, he would 'keep regularly present' and did so, but would not allow his name in the *Minutes* that year. MS 'History', fols. 994f. But in fact his name appeared on the stations for the first time; see *Q.* 7 (1), and n. 823. On Aug. 5, JW wrote to Miss Bosanquet, 'Hitherto we have had a blessed Conference. The case of the Church we shall consider by and by; and I believe we shall agree that none who leave the Church shall remain with us.' *Letters* (Telford), 7:29, and Tyerman, *Wesley*, 3:329f. On Aug. 10, he wrote to Bishop Lowth asking for the ordination of ministers for America (without success). *Letters* (Telford), 7:30. John Pawson recalled that a friendly dispute was held between 'the preachers and the clergy who labour with us, respecting our dissenting from the Church of England, and I think that it fully appeared that the preachers were better attached to the church than the clergy, and neither had, nor desired, to dissent from it'. MS 'Some Account of the Life of Mr. John Pawson', fol. 14, in MA. However, there was tension in the background over the McNab affair, which in some minds at least was linked with the question of the future of the connexion and succession to JW; see *Minutes* (1779), n. 760. Christopher Hopper wrote to Miss Crosby on Apr. 6, 1780 (MS PLP55, in MA) that they must not give way to McNab. He is 'a stranger to our former discipline. If we are to make a scheme of Independency he must not be President of the Congress. But I think the old man [Wesley] must reign his days and

Q. 1. What preachers are *admitted* this year?
A. William Church, George Button, William Warrener, Robert Blake.
Q. 2. Who remain on trial?
5   *A.* Nathanael Ward, George Dice,[817] Robert Bridge,[818] Jonathan Brown, John Booth, Alexander Suter, Zach. Yewdall, George Wawne, Duncan McAllum, Hugh Moore, George Brown, Andrew Blair, William Myles, Henry Moore, Thomas Barber, Samuel Mitchell, William
10   Simpson, Edward Jackson.
Q. 3. Who are admitted on trial?
A. John Cricket, Joseph Cole, William Green, T. Shaw, Jon. Coussins,[819] John Livermore, Robert Hopkins, Samuel Hodgson, Joshua Keighley,[820] Andrew Inglis,[821] and Henry
15   Foster.

how we are to be governed after I cannot tell. I leave it to one who cannot err.' Dr. Coke had charged Joseph Benson with being suspect on the doctrine of the person of Christ, but JW would not allow this to be decided in Conference, and a committee of preachers was appointed to consider the charge. The committee unanimously acquitted Benson of Arianism, and Coke offered to acknowledge his fault before Conference. On Aug. 3 the committee reported, and the two men shook hands. James Macdonald, *Memoirs of the Rev. Joseph Benson* (London, 1822), 105. Tyerman (*Wesley*, 3:334) says that Benson was influenced by Watts's *Glory of Christ.* John Wesley Etheridge says that Coke charged Bradburn with the same offence. *The Life of the Rev. Thomas Coke* (London: J. Mason, 1860), 64–67.

A notable innovation at this Conference was that at some point JW was absent, and Christopher Hopper records, 'Our brethren made me President. . . . A poor helpless worm! Superintendent! President! Great words! I doubt I have not grace to bear them.' Jackson, *Early Methodist Preachers*, 1:219.

[817] Orig., 'Edward Dice', and in 1781 (1 of 2) 'Edward Price'; otherwise always 'George Dice'.

[818] Orig., 'Robert Briggs', as in 1781, but elsewhere 'Bridge'.

[819] Orig., 'Cosins'. His name is spelled no fewer than eight ways in the *Minutes*: 'Cosins', 1780, 1781, 1782; 'Cousens', 1783 (1 of 2); 'Cozins', 1783 (1 of 2); 'Cussins', 1784 (1 of 2); 'Cousins', 1784 (1 of 2), 1785 (2 of 3); 'Coussins', 1785 (1 of 2), 1789 (2 of 4), 1790 (2); 'Cussens', 1786 (2), 1787 (2), 1788 (2), 1789 (2 of 4); 'Coussens', 1791 (2). In his letters, JW spelled the name 'Cussens', 'Cussins', 'Coussens', and 'Coussins'—the latter two in one letter of Feb. 25, 1785. His portrait in the *AM* (1786), however, and the lengthy obituary in the *MM* (1806) use the spelling 'Coussins'.

[820] Orig., 'Kighley'—also often used in the original for the spelling of the town in the printed *Minutes*. The only printed example of the spelling 'Keighley' is in 1785 and in the Deed of Declaration; it is invariably 'Kighley' in JW's 18th century journals. In his letter of May 20, 1787, however, JW addressed him as 'The Revd. Mr. Keighley'.

[821] Orig., 'English'.

Q. 4. Who desist from travelling?

A. Thomas Newall, George Hudson, Thomas Wride, William Barker, and John Beanland for want of health.

N.B. As we admit no one as a travelling preacher unless we judge him to have grace, gifts, and fruit, so we cannot   5 receive anyone as such any longer than he retains those qualifications.

Q. 5. What preachers have died this year?

A. Samuel Wells, a sensible, honest, upright man, who put forth all his strength in every part of his work. He was   10 particularly zealous in observing discipline and in exhorting believers to go on to perfection. And William Brammah, who, having had much weakness and pain, finished his course with joy.

Q. 6. Are there any objections to any of our preachers?   15

A. They were examined.

Q. 7. How are the preachers stationed this year?

A. As follows:[822]

(1) *London*, John Wesley, Charles Wesley,[823] Thomas Coke, Richard Boardman, Joseph Bradford, John Atlay.   20

(2) *Sussex*, Francis Wrigley, William Ashman.

(3) *Kent*, Richard Whatcoat, Thomas Mitchell.

(4) *Colchester*, Peter Mill, James Perfect.

(5) *Norwich*, James Wood, John Moon, Jonathan Coussins.   25

(6) *Lynn*, Charles Boone, Robert Hopkins.

(7) *Bedford*, Thomas Vasey, John Norris.

(8) *Northampton*, William Eells, Joshua Keighley.

(9) *Oxfordshire*, George Story, John Acutt.

(10) *Gloucestershire*, John Goodwin, George Wawne,   30 Joseph Cole.

(11) *Salisbury*,[824] William Tunney, John Poole, John Walker, William Green.

---

[822] There is no separate listing this year of those who travelled with JW, the Book Steward, or the corrector of the press.

[823] CW is mentioned in the stations for the first time in 1780. This is also the first time that his name—like that of John—was specifically mentioned on the title page. From then onwards until his death in 1788, he was listed in the London Circuit.

[824] The Wiltshire Circuits, South and North, are listed for the first time as *Salisbury* and *Bradford [-on-Avon]*.

(12) *Bradford [-upon-Avon]*, John Mason, Richard Rodda, Alex. Suter, John Wittam.

(13) *Bristol*, John Pawson, Thomas Rankin, Thomas Tennant.

(14) *Taunton*, John Pritchard, James Skinner.

(15) *Tiverton*, Nicholas Manners, Thomas Shawl.

(16) *Cornwall, East*, Jeremiah Brettel, Martin Rodda, Simon Day, Henry Foster.

(17) *Cornwall, West*, Thomas Hanson, John Booth, Francis Wolf, Stephen Proctor.

(18) *Glamorgansh[ire]*, William Homer, Zach. Yewdall.

(19) *Brecon*, John Prickard, Henry Robins.

(20) *Pembrokesh[ire]*, Samuel Randal, William Moore, William Church.

(21) *Staffordsh[ire]*, John Broadbent, Robert Swan.

(22) *Macclesfield*, Robert Roberts, Robert Costerdine, Thomas Corbet.

(23) *Manchester*, John Valton, George Snowden.

(24) *Chester*, William Boothby, Jon. Hern.

(25) *Liverpool*, John Easton, Thomas Hanby, Richard Seed.

(26) *Leicester*, James Barry, John Brettel, M. Moorhouse; J. Furz, supernumerary.

(27) *Nottingham*, John Hampson, Sen., Joseph Pescod, David Evans.

(28) *Sheffield*, James Rogers, Alexander McNab, Samuel Bardsley.

(29) *Grimsby*, George Shadford, Robert Wilkinson, Robert Howard, William Warrener.

(30) *Gainsboro[ugh]*, Isaac Brown, Jeremiah Robertshaw, George Button.

(31) *Epworth*, Joseph Harper, Thomas Warrick, John Oliver.

(32) *Leeds*, John Allen, John Murlin, Joseph Benson.

(33) *Birstall*, Thomas Lee, John Floyd, John Shaw.

(34) *Huddersfield*, Parson Greenwood, Tho. Johnson.

(35) *Bradford*, Alex. Mather, James Hindmarsh, John Fenwick.

(36) *Keighley*, Samuel Bradburn, Wm. Simpson.

(37) *Colne*, Christopher Hopper, Tho. Longley.

(38) *Whitehaven*, William Thom, Joseph Thompson.

(39) *Isle of Man*, John Crook, Thomas Readshaw.

(40) *York*, Thomas Taylor, Joseph Taylor, Samuel Hodgson.

(41) *Hull*, Lancelot Harrison, Wm. Percival.

(42) *Scarborough*, Thomas Dixon, John Peacock, James Watson.

(43) *Thirsk*, Christopher Watkins, John Leech.[825]

(44) *Yarm*, Duncan Wright, Daniel Jackson, Jon. Brown; Jacob Rowell, supernumerary.

(45) *The Dales*, Edward Jackson, William Saunders, John Morgan.

(46) *Newcastle*, William Hunter, William Collins, Benjamin Rhodes, Thomas Brisco.

(47) *Edinburgh*, William Thompson, John Watson, Sen., Duncan McAllum.

(48) *Dundee*, Jasper Robinson, Wm. Dufton.

(49) *Aberdeen*, Joseph Saunderson, John Hampson, Jun.

(50) *Inverness*, John Watson, Jun., Geo. Mowat.

(51) *Dublin*, Joseph Pilmore, Barnabas Thomas.

(52) *Cork*, Richard Watkinson, Wm. Myles.

(53) *Waterford*, Thomas Payne, Thomas Barber.

(54) *Limerick*, John Livermore, Robert Naylor.

(55) *Castlebar*, Robert Lindsay, Samuel Mitchell.

(56) *Athlone*, Nehemiah Price, T[homas] H[alliday], John Bredin.

(57) *Sligo*, Andrew Blair, James Jordan, William West.

(58) *Clones*, John Price, William McCornock, Robert Bridge.

(59) *Enniskillen*, George Brown, Robert Davis, Edward Evans.

(60) *Charlemont*,[826] Henry Moore, Robert Blake, Nathanael Ward.

(61) *Lisleen*, Hugh Moore, Robert Armstrong, John Cricket.

(62) *Londonderry*, Thomas Rutherford, Tho. Davis.

(63) *Belfast*, John Mealy, George Dice.

(64) *Lisburn*, Tho. Carlill, James Hall.

Q. 8. How many *wives* are to be provided for?

---

[825] Orig., 'Leach'.

[826] Orig., 'Charlemount', as almost uniformly in the *Minutes*.

A. Fifty-two.

Q. 9. By what societies?

	A. By *London,*	S[isters] Bradford, Wood.[827]
5	*J[ohn] W[esley],*	
	and	S. Poole, Hindmarsh, Naylor.[828]
	T[homas] C[oke][829]	
	Sussex	S. Mitchell.[830]
10	*Gloucestershire*	S. Goodwin.
	Bristol	S. Boone, Story, Church.[831]
	North Wilts.	S. Rodda.
	Cornwall, East	S. Day.
	West	S. Booth, Green.[832]
15	*Devon*	S. Corbet.[833]
	Birmingham	S. Swan.
	Macclesfield	S. Roberts, Costerdine.
	Manchester	S. Snowden, Oliver.[834]
	Chester	S. Hern.
20	*Liverpool*	S. Easton, Thom.[835]
	Leicester	S. Barry.
	Nottingham	S. Evans.
	Sheffield	S. Rogers, W. Thompson.[836]
	Grimsby	S. Wilkinson.
25	*Gainsborough*	S. Robertshaw.
	Epworth	S. Harper.
	Leeds	S. Greenwood, Longley, Jos. Thompson.[837]

[827] Wood was stationed at Norwich.

[828] Poole was stationed at Salisbury; Hindmarsh at Bradford (Yorkshire); Naylor at Limerick.

[829] This is the first time any individuals are named as supporting preachers' wives.

[830] Mitchell was stationed in Kent.

[831] Boone was stationed at Lynn; Story in Oxfordshire; and Church in Pembrokeshire.

[832] Green was stationed at Salisbury.

[833] Corbet was stationed at Macclesfield.

[834] Oliver was stationed at Epworth.

[835] Thom was stationed at Whitehaven.

[836] William Thompson was stationed at Edinburgh. 'W' is added here to make clear that Joseph Thompson's wife was not the one supported by Sheffield.

[837] Parson Greenwood was stationed at Huddersfield; Thomas Longley was stationed at Colne; Joseph Thompson was stationed at Whitehaven.

Birstall	S. Floyd, Shaw.
Bradford	S. Mather, Brisco.[838]
Keighley	S. Bradburn, Brown.[839]
Colne	S. Hopper.
York	S. Taylor, Rowell.[840]
Hull	S. Harrison.
Scarborough	S. Peacock.
Thirsk	S. Leech.
Yarm	S. Wright.
The Dales	S. Morgan.
Newcastle	S. Watson,[841] Collins, Hunter.
Isle of Man	S. Crook.

5

10

Q. 10. What numbers are in the societies?[842]

15

A. (1)[843] In London	2,498
(2) Sussex[844]	288
(3) Kent	253
(4) Norwich	555
(5) Lynn	
	372
(6) Colchester	
(7) Bedfordshire[845]	244
(8) Northampton	217
(9) Oxfordshire[846]	445
(10) Gloucestershire	626
(11) Salisbury	331
(12) Bradford	925
(13) Bristol	1,492

20

25

---

[838] Brisco was stationed at Newcastle.

[839] Brown was stationed at Gainsborough.

[840] Rowell was stationed at Yarm.

[841] Watson [Sen.] was stationed at Edinburgh and in the previous year had been stationed in Newcastle.

[842] There are no asterisks indicating decreased membership in some circuits, as in previous *Minutes*. The editor has supplied these details, however.

[843] For the first time the societies are numbered, but this does not become a general practice.

[844] A decrease for the second consecutive year.

[845] A decrease for the second consecutive year.

[846] A decrease for the second consecutive year.

(14) Taunton ⎫
                              517
(15) Tiverton ⎭ [847]
(16) Cornwall, East   637
(17)   West[848]   1,334
(18) Glamorgan   168
(19) Brecon   135
(20) Pembrokeshire[849] 196
(21) Birmingham   681
(22) Macclesfield   1,380
(23) Manchester   1,323
(24) Chester   507
(25) Liverpool[850]   1,023
(26) Leicester   633
(27) Nottingham   700
(28) Sheffield   823
(29) Grimsby   748
(30) Gainsborough   507
(31) Epworth   659
(32) Leeds   2,330
(33) Birstall ⎫
                          2,340
(34) Huddersfield ⎭
(35) Bradford   1,754
(36) Keighley   1,360
(37) Colne   951
(38) Whitehaven   305
(39) Isle of Man   1,486
(40) York   720
(41) Hull   696
(42) Scarborough   665
(43) Thirsk   626
(44) Yarm   940
(45) [The] Dales   832
(46) Newcastle   1,944
(47) Edinburgh   208
(48) Dundee   127

---

[847] A decrease for the second consecutive year.
[848] A decrease for the second consecutive year.
[849] A decrease for the second consecutive year.
[850] A decrease for the second consecutive year.

(49) Aberdeen	
	220
(50) Inverness	
(51) Dublin	527
(52) Waterford	177
(53) Cork	243
(54) Limerick	283
(55) Castlebar	197
(56) Athlone	315
(57) Sligo	694
(58) Clones	615
(59) Enniskillen	569
(60) Lisleen	651
(61) Charlemont	782
(62) Londonderry	166
(63) Belfast	415
(64) Lisburn	475
In all	43,830

Q. 11. What is the Kingswood collection?

A. £402. 1*s*. 9*d*.

Q. 12. What boys are received there this year?

A. Thomas Warrick, James Hanby, and Thomas Harrison.[851]

Q. 13. What girls are removed from school?[852]

A. E. Taylor, ——— Brisco, and Mary Payne.[853]

Q. 14. Should any others be admitted?

A. Not yet. Instead of this, give P. Taylor, A. Brisco, M. Roberts, and H. Barry six pounds each;[854] and consider how to dispose of Mary Payne.

---

[851] The sons of Thomas Warrick, Thomas Hanby, and Lancelot Harrison.

[852] For the first suggestions of supporting the girls' education and first payments, see *Minutes* (1774), *Q.* 12, and (1775), *Q.* 10. Miss Owen's school, which JW had commended in 1774 for Methodist use, had been 'removed' from Publow by Sept. 1781, but that Miss Bishop, one of JW's favoured correspondents, had by then set up a school in Keynsham, near Bath. In his *Journal*, Sept. 29, 1781, he commented that 'it is worthy to be called a *Christian school*. It is what the school at Publow was.' *Journal & Diaries*, 23:224 and n. 32 in this edn.

[853] Daughters of Thomas or Joseph Taylor, Thomas Brisco, and Thomas Payne.

[854] These are presumably the mothers of the daughters just named plus the wives of Robert Roberts and James Barry for their daughters.

Q. 15. What was contributed for the yearly expenses?
A. £629. 1*s*. 9*d*.
Q. 16. How was this exceeded?

	£.	s.	d.
A. Thus: This year's contingencies	100	0	0
Last year's deficiencies[855]	16	2	6
Preachers' necessities	270	18	3
Law	4	0	0
Edinburgh	102	18	0
Arbroath	10	0	0
Dunbar	10	0	0
Sheffield	12	18	6
Greenock	5	0	0
Sibsey[856]	10	0	0
Bolton	15	0	0
Huntingdon	20	0	0
Wolverhampton	10	0	0
Worcester	10	0	0
Melton	2	0	0
Donington[857]	10	0	0
Taunton	5	0	0
Cullompton	5	0	0
Carmarthen	5	0	0
Chatham	5	0	0
	£628	17	3[858]

Q. 17. What was contributed to the Preachers' Fund?
A. Eighty-seven pounds.
Q. 18. What was allowed out of it?

A. To Isaac Waldron	20	0	0
Thomas Westell	18	0	0
John Shaw[859]	14	0	0

[855] Deficiencies have not previously been listed.

[856] Orig., 'Sibsay'.

[857] Orig., 'Donnington'.

[858] Orig., '£629. 1. 9.'

[859] Why did Shaw receive support while still actively preaching? See *Q*. 7 (33) above, *Birstall*. He did not receive any money from the Preachers' Fund in 1781. This may have been a case of irregularly raiding the fund for lack of money elsewhere to support preachers not receiving a full allowance from their circuits. Cf. *Minutes* (1769), *Q*. 23. Frank Baker, in 'Polity', says that this dangerous expedient was begun in 1781; see *Minutes* (1781), *Q*. 10; and (1791), *Q*. 12, when it ended.

William Whitaker	12	0	0	
Elizabeth Standring	10	0	0	
Mary Penington	10	0	0	
Alice Brammah[860]	10	0	0	
Lucia Bourke	5	5	0	5
Elizabeth Dillon	5	5	0	
Elizabeth Oldham	5	5	0	
Elizabeth Shorter	5	5	0	
Catherine Garnet	5	5	0	
In all	£120	5	0[861]	10

Q. 19. What remains in the Preachers' Fund?

A. Upwards of seven hundred pounds; and never desire it should rise higher.

Q. 20. What houses are to be built this year? 15

A. At Davarel,[862] Cowbridge,[863] Lane End,[864] Birmingham, Delph,[865] and Retford.[866]

Q. 21. What business have we remaining?

A. The main business for which we met: to revise and enforce the 'Large' *Minutes* of the Conference.[867] 20

[*Q*]. 22. Where and when may we meet again?

[*A*]. At Leeds, on the first Tuesday in August.

---

[860] The widow of William Brammah; see *Q*. 5 above.

[861] Orig., '£119. 5. 0.'

[862] Probably Longbridge Deverill in Wiltshire.

[863] Either in Glamorgan or Somerset. The *Journal* entries are regularly for visits to the Glamorgan town, though as late as 1788 the preaching at least was in the town hall, and there is no mention of a chapel. *Journal* (Curnock), 7:431.

[864] *Journal & Diaries*, 23:300, n. 94 in this edn., identifies this place as 'a market town with Longton, and a chapelry in the parish of Stoke-on-Trent, 4 miles south-east from Newcastle-under-Lyme'.

[865] Orig., 'Delf'.

[866] Orig., 'Redford'.

[867] The 'revision' was presumably carried out between the 1780 and 1781 Conferences, as on the latter occasion the unfinished business was to 'enforce' the 'Large' *Minutes*; see *Minutes* (1781), *Q*. 28.

Annual *Minutes of some late Conversations*, 1781

Leeds, Tuesday, August 7, etc., 1781[868]

[868] Wesley wrote,
'Mon. 6. I desired Mr. Fletcher, Dr Coke, and four more of our brethren, to meet every evening that we might consult together on any difficulty that occurred. On Tuesday our Conference began, at which were present about 70 preachers whom I had severally invited to come and assist me with their advice in carrying on the work of God. Wed. 8. I desired Mr. Fletcher to preach. I do not wonder he should be so popular, not only because he preaches with all his might, but because the power of God attends both his preaching, and prayer. On Monday and Tuesday, we finished the remaining business of the Conference and ended it with solemn prayer and thanksgiving.' (*Journal & Diaries*, 23:218 in this edn.)
Though the *Minutes* do not explain the difficulties that produced what was to be termed Wesley's 'Cabinet', Thomas Taylor recorded in his diary that 'I feel much concerned respecting several things; but how to have them remedied I cannot tell. Many things are exceedingly wrong, but where to turn to attempt amendment I know not'. Quoted in Tyerman, *Wesley*, 3:361. John Valton wrote, 'The former part of the Conference seemed to me more serious than the latter but upon the whole a good time.' Aug. 6, 1781, MS diary, in MA. Among the problems (not all revealed in the *Minutes*) were the cost of preachers and their wives; conflicts with the Anglican clergy; and William Hey's criticisms; perhaps also the doctrinal dispute between Coke and Benson (see *Minutes* [1780], n. 816). A letter from Joseph Pescod says that Fletcher preached on 2 Pet. 1:4 and that the Lord's Supper was administered by JW, Fletcher, and nine other clergy. JW preached in the afternoon on Heb. 8:10, 12. *WMM* (1829): 528, quoted in *Journal* (Curnock), 6:330 n. 1. Dr. Hey did not get his way and left the Conference; see Tyerman, *Wesley*, 3:363; John Pearson, *Life of William Hey* (London, 1822), 2:93–100. Sutcliffe says he meant to damage Methodism, but with the appearance of religious principle. So he read a paper in Conference asking for the withdrawal of preachers where there was a good Church minister. MS 'History', fol. 448; cf. the complaints of Walker of Truro in the mid-1750s. In reply, the Venn experiment was quoted; see *Letters* (Telford), 3:221–26; 4:215–18. It is claimed that Hey was trying to enter the Leeds Corporation, but his Methodism was against him. Leslie Church, *More about the Early Methodist People* (London, 1949), 39f.
A writer reminiscing in 1829 about a Conference in Leeds (which must be 1781) says that Fletcher, David Simpson (of Macclesfield), and other clergy were present: 'An Open Conference was held and the most useful way of preaching was the subject of discussion. Several preachers gave their opinions. At length one of the preachers asked Mr Wesley if a young man had a good memory and heard a good sermon and could believe it, would there be any harm if he should retail it to any distant place. "No brother", said Mr Hopper, "if you take plenty of salt with it." ' Some preachers alluded to Billy Brammah, and 'one person after another got up in the gallery and blessed God for Billy Brammah for under him they were brought to God. This continued until the whole place was in a flame for the name of Billy Brammah was like throwing fire among the people.' E. Oakes to Mr. Agar, in

Q. 1. What preachers are admitted this year?

A. John Booth, Zach. Yewdall, Duncan McAllum, William
Simpson, Jonathan Coussins, William Green, Samuel
Hodgson, Joshua Keighley, Jon. Brown, George Gibbon,
Andrew Inglis, Nath. Ward, Thomas Shaw, and Tho. 5
Longley.

Q. 2. Who *remain on trial?*

A. Edw. Price, Robert Bridge, Alex. Suter, Hugh Moore,
George Brown, Andrew Blair, William Myles,
Henry Moore, Thomas Barber, Samuel Mitchell, 10
John Cricket, Joseph Cole,[869] John Livermore,[870] and
Henry Foster.

Q. 3. Who are admitted on trial?

A. Tho. Ellis, Charles Atmore. T. Cooper, James Wray, Phil.
Hardcastle, John Ingham, William Graham, T. Tattershall, 15
and Christ. Peacock.

Q. 4. Who desist from travelling?

A. Martin Rodda, William Tunney.

Q. 5. What preachers have died this year?

A. George Wawne,[871] a young man zealous for God, and of 20
an unblameable behaviour. And Robert Wilkinson, an
Israelite indeed,[872] a man of faith and prayer, who, having
been a pattern of all good works, died in the full triumph
of faith.

Q. 6. Are there any objections to any of our preachers? 25

A. Let them be examined one by one.

Q. 7. How are the preachers stationed this year?

A. As follows:

(1) *London*, John Wesley, Charles Wesley, John

Tyerman MSS, 3:434. Wesley says that William Dodwell of Welby and John Pugh
of Rauceby were other clergy present. *Letters* (Telford), 7:137.

Though not recorded in the *Minutes*, a letter by JW makes it clear that the debates
at this Conference included the problem of attending church when the minister
preached false doctrine. The decision was that those bred to it should attend
Church but should quietly leave if the minister preached 'the Absolute Decrees' or
'railed' against Christian perfection. *Letters* (Telford), 7:98f., and cf. 7:91–93, 107f.
See statement appended to *Minutes* (1786).

[869] Orig., 'Joshua Cole'.
[870] Orig., 'Liverman'.
[871] See *Minutes* (1779), *Q.* 3.
[872] John 1:47.

Fletcher,[873] Thomas Coke, John Atlay; Joseph Bradford, supernumerary.

(2) *Sussex*, Wm. Ashman, Tho. Cooper.

(3) *Kent*, Thomas Rankin, James Hindmarsh.

5 (4) *Colchester*, Tho. Carlill, John Ingham.

(5) *Norwich*, James Wood, William Homer, John Acutt, Rob. Hopkins.

(6) *Lynn*, John Prickard, Geo. Button.

(7) *Bedford*, Thomas Vasey, Robert Swan.

10 (8) *Northampton*, Rich. Whatcoat, Mich. Moorhouse.

(9) *Oxfordshire*, Rich. Rodda, Tho. Warrick.

(10) *Gloucester*, Geo. Story, Joseph Cole, John Walker.

(11) *Sarum*, Francis Wrigley, Tho. Shaw, Jonathan Coussins, John Poole.

15 (12) *Bradford*, John Mason, James Perfect, Geo. Gibbon, W. Green.

(13) *Bristol*, John Pawson, John Murlin, William Moore.

(14) *Taunton*, John Pritchard, Charles Boone.

(15) *Tiverton*, John Moon, Alexander Suter.

20 (16) *Cornwall, East,* Tho. Payne, John Wittam, Wm. Saunders, Geo. Wadsworth.

(17) ——— *West*, Christ. Watkins, Nich. Manners, Fran. Wolf, Simon Day.

---

[873] Rev. John William Fletcher (Jean Guillaume de la Fléchère, 1729–85) was born in Nyon, Switzerland. He came to England and in 1752 became tutor to the family of Thomas Hill of Tern Hall, Shropshire. He was converted by the Methodists and ordained into the Church of England, and on Mar. 13, 1757, he offered his services to JW at West Street Chapel, London. See *Journal & Diaries*, 21:88 and n. 33 in this edn. He became vicar of Madeley, Shropshire, in 1760 and made a lasting impression as a man of devout and holy life. In 1768, he was appointed head of Lady Huntingdon's Trevecca College but resigned in 1771 over the Calvinist controversy; see *Minutes* (1771), n. 340. His *Checks to Antinomianism* series was the main contribution on the Methodist side to the debate. JW wished to groom Fletcher as his successor, but though he aided JW from time to time and on occasion helped to quell opposition to him in Conference by emotional appeals, Fletcher resisted leaving his parish for various reasons, no doubt wisely, in view of his precarious health. The inclusion of his name for the London Circuit was surely merely a gesture, though he was included again in the 1785 *Minutes*' list of attendees and n. 71 to *Q*. 1 in the CJ. His wife, Mary Bosanquet, was a celebrated female preacher and, after his death, continued to preach and apparently dominated the parish and its clergy. In 1775, Fletcher had proposed a plan for a 'Methodist Church of England'; see *Minutes* (1775), n. 351. The best life of him is by Patrick P. Streiff, *Jean Guillaume de la Fléchère, 1729–85* (Bern, 1984), in German.

(18) *Glamorgan*, Steph. Proctor, Wm. Church.
(19) *Pembroke*, Sam. Randal, Tho. Tennant, James Hall.
(20) *Brecon*, Henry Robins, Nath. Ward.
(21) *Staffordshire*, John Broadbent, John Goodwin,
Thomas Hanby.   5
(22) *Macclesfield*, Robert Roberts, John Hampson, Jun.,
John Leech; Rich. Seed, supernumerary.
(23) *Manchester*, John Valton, John Allen, Alex. McNab.
(24) *Chester*, Wm. Boothby, supernumerary; Jonathan
Hern, W. Simpson.   10
(25) *Liverpool*, John Easton, Jeremiah Brettel, William Eells.
(26) *Leicester*, Jos. Harper, Robert Costerdine, Dav.
Evans; John Furz, supernumerary.
(27) *Nottingham*, John Hampson, Sen., John Brettel,
James Skinner.   15
(28) *Sheffield*, James Rogers, Wm. Percival, Jos. Taylor.
(29) *Grimsby*, Geo. Shadford, Tho. Corbet, Jos. Pescod,
Cha. Atmore.
(30) *Gainsborough*, Jer. Robertshaw, W. Warrener, P.
Hardcastle.   20
(31) *Epworth*, James Barry, John Norris, Tho. Tattershall.
(32) *Leeds*, Alex. Mather, Christ. Hopper, Joseph Benson.
(33) *Birstall*, Tho. Brisco, John Shaw, Tho. Longley.
(34) *Huddersfield*, Geo. Snowden, Tho. Lee.
(35) *Bradford*, Samuel Bradburn, John Floyd, John Oliver. 25
(36) *Keighley*, Isaac Brown, Robert Howard.
(37) *Colne*, Tho. Hanson, Tho. Readshaw, Parson
Greenwood.
(38) *Whitehaven*, Tho. Dixon, John Booth.
(39) *Isle of Man*, Daniel Jackson, Jon. Brown.   30
(40) *York*, Tho. Taylor, Tho. Johnson, Joshua Keighley.
(41) *Hull*, Lancelot Harrison, Wm. Dufton, Samuel
Hodgson.
(42) *Scarborough*, John Fenwick, John Peacock, Christ.
Peacock.   35
(43) *Thirsk*, Joseph Thompson, John Beanland, James
Wray.[874]

[874] Orig., 'Ray'; as also 1782–87, 1791. In (*Q.* 3) above, he appears as 'James Wray',
as in JW's letter of Feb. 27, 1789, and his obituary in the *AM* (1793). The CJ for
1790 misspells his first name, 'John Wray'.

(44) *Yarm*, Wm. Collins, James Watson, Benjamin Rhodes.

(45) *The Dales*, Wm. Thom, John Morgan, Jasper Robinson.

(46) *Newcastle*, Duncan Wright, Wm. Hunter, Edw. Jackson.

(47) *Edinburgh*, Wm. Thompson, Jos. Saunderson, Duncan McAllum.

(48) *Dundee*, Barn. Thomas.

(49) *Aberdeen*, Peter Mill, Samuel Bardsley, Andrew Inglis.

(50) *Dublin*, Jos. Pilmore, John Crook.

(51) *Waterford*, Rob. Lindsay, Zach. Yewdall.

(52) *Cork*, Rich. Watkinson, N. Price.

(53) *Limerick*, John Cricket, Rich. Boardman.

(54) *Castlebar*, Thomas Barber, Rob. Naylor.

(55) *Athlone*, John Price, Geo. Mowat, John Watson, Sen.

(56) *Sligo*, And. Blair, Tho. Davis, John Mealy, John Miller, George Dice: change once in three months.

(57) *Clones*, Samuel Mitchell, Rob. Blake, Edward Evans.

(58) *Enniskillen*, John Livermore, Rob. Armstrong, Rob. Bridge.

(59) *Charlemont*, Hen. Foster, Wm. McCornock, Robert Davis.

(60) *Lisleen*, George Brown, Jam. Jordan, William Graham.

(61) *Londonderry*, Hugh Moore, Wm. West.

(62) *Belfast*, Wm. Myles, John Watson, Jun.

(63) *Lisburn*, Tho. Rutherford, Hen. Moore.

Q. 8. How many wives are to be provided for?

A. Forty-eight.

Q. 9. By what societies?

A. London	S. Bradford, Wood[875]
Sussex	S. Hindmarsh[876]
Gloucestershire	S. Story
Bristol	S. Church,[877] Moore

---

[875] Wood was stationed at Norwich.

[876] Hindmarsh was stationed in Kent.

[877] Church was stationed in Glamorgan.

Bradford	S. Poole[878]	
Cornwall, East	S. Payne	
Cornwall, West	S. Day, Swan[879]	
Devon	S. Boone[880]	
Birmingham	S. Goodwin	5
Macclesfield	S. Roberts, Costerdine[881]	
Manchester	S. Longley, Oliver[882]	
Chester	S. Hern.	
Liverpool	S. Rutherford,[883] Easton	
Leicester	S. Evans	10
Nottingham	S. Harper[884]	
Sheffield	S. Rogers, Thompson[885]	
Grimsby	S. Corbet	
Gainsborough[886]	S. Robertshaw	
Epworth	S. Barry	15
Leeds	S. Mather, Moore,[887] Hopper	
Birstall	S. Brisco, Snowden[888]	
Bradford	S. Bradburn, Floyd	
Keighley	S. Brown, Shaw[889]	
Colne	S. Greenwood	20
York	S. Taylor	
Hull	S. Harrison	
Scarborough	S. Peacock[890]	
Thirsk	S. Thompson	
Yarm	S. Collins	25
Newcastle	S. Wright, Hunter, Watson.	

[878] Poole was stationed at Sarum.

[879] Swan was stationed at Bedford.

[880] Boone was stationed at Taunton.

[881] Costerdine was stationed at Leicester.

[882] Longley was stationed at Birstall; Oliver at Bradford (Yorkshire).

[883] Rutherford was stationed at Lisburn.

[884] Harper was stationed at Leicester.

[885] William Thompson was stationed at Edinburgh; Joseph Thompson at Thirsk. Thirsk lists support for S. Thompson also, so perhaps it is more logical to suppose Sheffield supported William Thompson's wife.

[886] Orig., 'Gainsborugh'.

[887] Which 'Moore' was this? Henry was at Lisburn; Hugh at Londonderry; William at Bristol.

[888] Snowden was stationed at Huddersfield.

[889] Shaw was stationed at Birstall.

[890] Both John and Christopher Peacock were stationed at Scarborough.

Q. 10. Three wives are still unprovided for. What shall we do for them?

A. Supply them from the Preachers' Fund.[891]

Q. 11. What numbers are in the societies?

A. (1) In London* 2,511
    (2) Sussex 187
    (3) Kent 213
    (4) Colchester 151
    (5) Norwich 582
    (6) Lynn 161
    (7) Bedford* 274
    (8) Northampton* 251
    (9) Oxfordshire 442
    (10) Gloucestershire* 667
    (11) Sarum* 346
    (12) Bradford 889
    (13) Bristol 1,444
    (14) Taunton* 204
    (15) Tiverton 397
    (16) Cornwall, East 613
    (17) —— West* 1,538
    (18) Glamorgansh[ire]* 163
    (19) Pembroke 181
    (20) Brecon 110
    (21) Birmingham* 803
    (22) Macclesfield 1,326
    (23) Manchester* 1,426
    (24) Chester* 515
    (25) Liverpool 927
    (26) Leicester* 660
    (27) Nottingham* 767
    (28) Sheffield* 920
    (29) Grimsby* 880
    (30) Gainsborough* 580

[891] See below, *Q*. 18, where several wives are listed. For the system hitherto and still implemented for most of the wives, see *Minutes* (1769), *Q*. 23, and n. 266. For JW's appeal for support for the Preachers' Fund for superannuation, see *Letters* (Telford), 7:79. As to children, he had written a little earlier that 'To allow money for the keeping of children is not the business of Conference but of the circuits'. Ibid., 7:76. 'So it is expressly appointed in the Minutes'; see (1770), *Q*. 21.

(31) Epworth*	702	
(32) Leeds*	2,480	
(33) Birstall	1,431	
(34) Huddersfield	795	
(35) Bradford*	1,830	5
(36) Keighley	1,201	
(37) Colne*	958	
(38) Whitehaven	290	
(39) Isle of Man	1,597	
(40) York*	767	10
(41) Hull*	709	
(42) Scarborough*	670	
(43) Thirsk*	650	
(44) Yarm	970	
(45) The Dales	821	15
(46) Newcastle	1,786	
(47) Edinburgh	191	
(48) Dundee	112	
(49) Aberdeen		
	198	20
(50) Inverness		
(51) Dublin*	546	
(52) Cork*	246	
(53) Waterford*	252	
(54) Limerick	212	25
(55) Castlebar*	206	
(56) Athlone	258	
(57) Sligo*	910	
(58) Clones*	627	
(59) Enniskillen	569	30
(60) Charlemont	680	
(61) Lisleen	646	
(62) Londonderry*	172	
(63) Belfast	393	
(64) Lisburn	458	35

In all	44,461[892]	

[892] Orig., '44,417'.

N.B. The circuits marked thus * are increased this year. [In previous years except for 1780, where no changes were recorded, the asterisk denoted the circuits showing a *decrease.*]

Q. 12. What is the Kingswood collection?
A. £440. 1*s.* 1*d.*
Q. 13. What boys are received there this year?
A. Tho. Brisco, James Poole, David Evans, Joseph Collins, James Rowell, James Barry.[893]
Q. 14. What shall we allow to those parents whose children cannot be received?
A. Allow Harriet[894] Barry, Mary Roberts, Hannah Peacock, Jane Thompson, Eliz. Brown, and Eliz. Easton, six pounds each. And let each Assistant diligently inquire how this is expended, and give an account of it at the yearly conference.
Q. 15. Can anyone recommend a writing master for Kingswood School?
A. John Inwood[895] is every way qualified for the place.
Q. 16. What can be done to lessen the burden which lies on those societies where the conference is held?
A. Let every preacher pay for his own horse.
Q. 17. What was contributed to the Preachers' Fund?
A. £207. 13*s.* 8*d.*
Q. 18. What was allowed out of it?

A.	£.	*s.*
To Thomas Westell	30	0
Isaac Waldron	20	0
Jacob Rowell	15	0
Sarah Hosmer	10	0
William Whitaker	12	0
John Furz	12	0
Elizabeth Standring	12	0

[893] Sons of Thomas Brisco, John Poole, David Evans (? rather than Edward Evans), William Collins, Jacob Rowell, James Barry.

[894] Orig., 'Harriot'.

[895] He is not otherwise known and is not in the list of masters in A. H. L. Hastling, W. Addington Willis, and W. P. Workman, *The History of Kingswood School* (London: C. H. Kelly, 1898).

Mary Penington	10	0	
Jane Wilkinson	20	0	
Alice Brammah	10	0	
Lucia Bourke	10	0	
Elizabeth Dillon	5	5	5
Elizabeth Oldham	5	5	
Elizabeth Shorter	10	0	
Kath. Garnet[896]	5	5	
S[ister] Beanland	12	0	
S. Thom	12	0	10
S. Booth	12	0	
S. Eells	12	0	
S. Boothby	6	0	
Money advanced last year	15	15	15
£.	256	10	

Q. 19. What houses are to be built this year?

A. Nottingham, Beverley, Stockport, Ashton.

Q. 20. If bankrupts ever are able, is it not their duty to pay their whole debt?

A. Doubtless it is. If they do not, they ought not to continue in our society.[897]

Q. 21. Ought we not to exhort all dying persons to be then, at least, merciful after their power?

A. We ought, without any regard to the reflections which will be cast upon us on that account.

Q. 22. Does the rule for giving each wife £15 a year take place with regard to them that live at home?

A. It was never intended so to do.

Q. 23. We have neither money nor houses for any more wives. What can we do?

A. (1) We must admit no more married preachers, unless in defect of single preachers. (2) The societies that have not houses must hire lodgings for the preacher's wife.

Q. 24. Can we erect a school for preachers' children in Yorkshire?[898]

---

[896] Orig., 'Katherine' until 1783, but 'Catherine', 1780, 1784–90.

[897] For the discipline on bankruptcy, see *Minutes* (1770), *Q.* 16, n. 317.

[898] This would, of course, serve those in the north of England as Kingswood did in the south, but nothing came of the proposal, at least in JW's lifetime. Woodhouse Grove School (opened 1812) finally filled the gap.

A. Probably we may. Let our brethren think of a place and a master, and send me word.

Q. 25: Have not our preachers printed anything without my consent and correction?

A. Several of them have (not at all to the honour of the Methodists), both in verse and prose. This has, (1), brought a great reproach; (2), much hindered the spreading of more profitable books. Therefore we all agree, (3), that no preacher print or reprint anything for the time to come till it is corrected by Mr. W[esley]. And, (4), that the profits thereof shall go into the common stock.[899]

Q. 26. What shall be done with the remaining copies of the *Notes on the Old Testament*?[900]

A. Let them be sold weekly at 3*d.* a number.

Q. 27. How shall we prevent the waste of books?

A. Let every Assistant, before he leaves his circuit, deliver an exact catalogue to Mr. Atlay.[901]

Q. 28. What business have we remaining?

A. The main business for which we met, to enforce the 'Large' *Minutes* of the Conference.[902]

Q. 29. When and where may we meet again?

A. On the first Tuesday in August at London.

ADDENDA.[903]

Q. 30. Has that rule which occurs in the 'Large' *Minutes, Q.* (10) been observed, 'At every other meeting of the society let no stranger be admitted; and let them show

---

[899] See *Minutes* (1749), §18 (*Q.* 15), n. 737, for the beginnings of this rule; also (1761), n. 1019; (1765), *Q.* 24, for the existing rule. The disposal of the profits is a fresh rule. Tyerman gives as an example of offending literature, *The Methodist: Attempted in Plain Metre*, by James Kershaw; see *Wesley*, 3:362.

[900] JW published the *Explanatory Notes upon the Old Testament* in 1765–66, issuing them in weekly numbers (see *Bibliography*, No. 294).

[901] The book steward.

[902] See *Minutes* (1780), *Q.* 21: where to 'revise and enforce' the 'Large' *Minutes* was left as unfinished business. As this year they were simply to be 'enforced'; it is to be presumed that the 1780 version had been completed since the 1780 Conference.

[903] This printed Addenda is found in one copy only of the *Minutes* (1781), formerly preserved at Richmond College, now in MA.

their tickets before they come in'?[904] Has it been observed in the Birstall circuit?[905]

A. Hardly at all. Let the preacher, stewards, and leaders see this observed for the time to come.

Q. 31. Have the weekly and quarterly contribution[s] been duly made in all our societies?

A. In many it has been shamefully neglected. To remedy this:

(1) Let every Assistant remind every society that this was our original Rule: every member contributes one penny weekly (unless he is in extreme poverty), and one shilling quarterly. Explain the reasonableness of this.

(2) Let every leader receive the weekly contribution from each person in his class.

(3) Let the Assistant ask every person at changing his ticket, Can you afford to observe our rule? And receive what he is able to give.

Q. 32. The Scripture says, 'If any man that is called a brother be a fornicator, or covetous, [. . .] with such an one no not to eat.' And 'put away from among yourselves that wicked person.'[906] This is an express command, and it is of unspeakable importance. These *money-lovers* are the pest of every Christian society. They have been the main cause of destroying every revival of religion. They will destroy *us* if we do not put them away. But how shall we know them without the miraculous discernment of spirits?

A. (1) By their own confession. Tell anyone alone, with all tenderness: 'I am to give an account of your soul to God. Enable me to do it with joy. I am afraid you are covetous. Answer me a few questions, in order to remove that fear.'

(2) By their fruits. For instance; a man not worth a shilling enters our society. Yet he freely gives a penny a week. Five years after, he is worth scores of pounds. He gives a penny a week still. I must think this man covetous unless he assures me he bestows his charity some

[904] See 'Large' *Minutes* (1780), *Q*. 10.
[905] Apparently some complaint had been made about the laxness at Birstall.
[906] 1 Cor. 5:11, 13.

other way. For everyone is covetous whose beneficence does not increase in the same proportion as his substance.

Q. 33. In the 'Large' *Minutes, Q.* 25, it is asked, 'What is the office of an Helper?' It is answered, 'to preach morning and evening.' Therefore none who does not can perform this office.

'But he cannot.' Perhaps so. Then he cannot undertake this office.

'I did this for many years. But I cannot do it any longer.' Then you can no longer undertake this office. But you may be a supernumerary, as John Furz and Richard Seed are.

Q. 34. Should we insist on that rule, 'Sing no hymns of your own composing'?[a]

A. Undoubtedly; and let those who will not promise this be excluded at the next conference.

Q. 35. It was agreed last year that all the preachers should join as one man to prevent people's talking before and after sermon. Has this been done?

A. Hardly at all. People talk just as they did before. Nay, the preachers themselves seem to have quite forgotten it. One and another speaks to *me*, even in the pulpit.

Q. 36. But what be done now?

A. (1) Let the preacher desire every person to go silent away. (2) Let no preacher speak one word in the house. (3) Let each preacher do this over and over, till the point is gained.

Annual *Minutes of some late Conversations,* 1782

London, Tuesday, August 6, 1782[907]

---

[a] P. 25 [i.e., in 'Large' *Minutes* (1780), *Q.* 37 (9)]

[907] JW writes,
'Friday August 2, we observed as a day of fasting and prayer for a blessing on the ensuing Conference. And I believe God clothed his work with power in an uncommon manner throughout the week. So that were it only on this account,

Q. 1. What preachers are *admitted* this year?

A. James Wray, John Ingham, Thomas Tattershall, George
Brown, Andrew Blair, John Livermore, William Myles,
Henry Moore, Thomas Barber, Samuel Mitchell, Henry
Foster, Thomas Davis, Robert Bridge.   5

Q. 2. Who *remain* on trial?

A. Alexander Suter, Jos. Cole. John Cricket, Thomas Ellis,
Thomas Cooper, Charles Atmore, Robert Hopkins, Philip
Hardcastle, George Dice, Hugh Moore, James Jordan,
Christopher Peacock, William West, William McCornock, 10
John Miller, Joseph Algar.

Q. 3. Who are *admitted* on trial?

A. Robert Scot, William Hoskins, Edward Rippon, John
Barber, James Christie, Thomas Bartholomew, John

the preachers who came from all parts found their labour was not in vain. Tue.
13. Being obliged to leave London a little sooner than I intended, I concluded
the Conference today and desired all of our brethren to observe it as a day of
solemn thanksgiving.' (*Journal & Diaries*, 23:248–49 in this edn.)

Having extended the Conference of 1780 and found the cost of 1781 a burden
upon the hosts, JW cut the meetings short this year. The main concern this time was
'the radicalism generated by the American war and the settlement of the chapel
trusts' (the Birstall case, *Q.* 22). *Journal & Diaries*, 23:248 n. 47 in this edn.

On July 12, 1782, JW wrote to Mrs. Fletcher, 'It seems to have been the will
of God for many years that I should have none to share *my proper labour*. My
brother never did. Thomas Walsh began to do it; so did John Jones. But one died
and one fainted. Dr Coke promises fair; at present I have none like-minded.
When a lot is cast, I have no more to say.' *Letters* (Telford), 7:128. To Penelope
Newman on July 12, he wrote that he did not yet see any reason why Jonathan
Coussins should not labour next year in Gloucester Circuit (and he did): 'But I
do not use to determine things of that kind absolutely before Conference.' Ibid.,
7:129. To Ann Bolton on Aug. 3, he wrote that he divided Nottingham into two
circuits and stationed Mr. Warwick in the Derby part of it (though he actually
appeared in the stations for Leicestershire). Ibid., 7:134. Two clergymen,
William Dodwell of Welby and John Pugh of Rauceby, were again attenders at
this Conference, as in 1781. Ibid., 7:136–37; Tyerman, *Wesley*, 3:383. Dodwell
left legacies to the Wesleyan Methodist Missionary Society and British and
Foreign Bible Society on his death in 1829; see Tyerman, *Wesley*, 3:356. At this
Conference, Dr. Coke raised the question of the future Deed of Declaration to
define the Conference legally; see *Minutes* (1784), p. 545 below. Samuel
Bradburn said that the Conference was more pleasant than usual in several
respects, but that there was great uneasiness over temporal concerns, presumably referring to the business under *QQ.* 8–19. Thomas W. Blanshard, *The Life
of Samuel Bradburn* (London, 1870), 90. John Valton says that the Conference
ended in 'mutual love'. Aug. 13, 1782, MS diary. He was appointed Secretary of
the Conference. Sutcliffe, MS 'History', fol. 1014.

Glascock, Samuel Botts, George Holder,[908] James Bogie,
John Ogylvie, John Kerr,[909] Gustavus Armstrong, Thomas
Wride, Robert Empringham.

Q. 4. Who *desist* from travelling?

5 *A*. James Skinner, Francis Wolf, John Floyd, Robert
Hayward[910]—these without blame; Stephen Proctor, John
Walker.[911]

Q. 5. What preachers have *died* this year?

A. John Norris, a lover and a witness of Christian perfec-
10 tion, who died as he lived, full of faith and of the Holy
Ghost. And

John Morgan, a plain, rough man who after various trials
and a long, painful illness, joyfully committed his soul, his
wife, and his eight little children to his merciful and faith-
15 ful Creator.

Q. 6. Are there any objections to any of our preachers?

A. Let them be examined one by one.

Q. 7. How are the preachers stationed this year?

A. As follows:

20 (1) *London*, John Wesley, Charles Wesley, Thomas Coke,
John Murlin, Thomas Lee, John Broadbent, John
Prickard, John Atlay.

(2) *Sussex*, James Wood, William Homer.

---

[908] Orig., 'Halder', as also in *Q*. 7 (45). In 1789, his name is spelled 'Holden' (1 of 4), but on all other occasions 'Holder'.

[909] Orig., 'Carr', as also in *Q*. 7 (62). In 1783 and 1785 it appears as 'Karr', but elsewhere as 'Kerr'.

[910] Orig., 'Howard'.

[911] The construction leaves it slightly ambiguous as to who are 'without blame': the first four or the last two? The original semicolon rather than a colon, however, together with what is known of the subsequent history of the six men, makes it almost certain that the last two were considered blameworthy. Skinner had to retire through ill health; see Jackson, *Lives of the Early Methodist Preachers*, 6:268. Wolf remained a local Methodist official in Redruth and died in 1807. *MM* (1808): 583–85. Floyd set up as an apothecary in Halifax and later in Leeds and officiated in an Episcopal chapel and occasionally for the Methodists, though Pawson said he was 'never any credit to us'. Atmore, *Methodist Memorial*, 142–44; Pawson, *Letters*, 3:52 and n. 136. Hayward is a problem because, despite retiring this year, he may be the same as Robert Howard who appears on the stations in 1768–70 and again from 1783 and was not a supernumerary until 1792. Hayward died in 1803. Proctor is merely recorded as 'left' by Myles. JW reluctantly gave Walker a guinea in May 1782: 'But I have nothing more to do with him'; perhaps he was in financial trouble. *Letters* (Telford), 7:124.

(3) *Kent*, Wm. Ashman, John Glascock.

(4) *Colchester*, Geo. Gibbon, Rob. Hopkins.

(5) *Norwich*, James Hindmarsh, T. Cooper, Joshua Keighley, Rob Scot.

(6) *Lynn*, Richard Whatcoat, J. Ingham.   5

(7) *Bedford*, Joseph Harper, Robert Empringham.

(8) *Northampton*, Joseph Pescod, James Walker.

(9) *Oxfordshire*, Richard Rodda, Joseph Cole.

(10) *Gloucester*, George Story, John Brettel, Jonathan Coussins.   10

(11) *Sarum*, John Mason, William Moore, Wm. Hoskins, Nathanael Ward.

(12) *Bradford*, Francis Wrigley, John Poole, Edward Rippon, Joseph Algar.

(13) *Bristol*, Tho. Rankin, Charles Boone, Thomas   15
Payne.

(14) *Taunton*, Christopher Watkins, William Church; John Furz, supernumerary.

(15) *Tiverton*, John Moon, John Acutt.

(16) *Cornwall, East*, William Green, Thomas Shaw, Geo.   20
Wadsworth, A. Suter.

(17) ——— *West*, Joseph Taylor, James Hall, William Saunders, Simon Day.

(18) *Glamorgan*, John Wittam, Henry Robins.

(19) *Pembroke*, Tho. Tennant, Sam. Hodgson; Richard   25
Seed, supernumerary.

(20) *Brecon*, John Leech, James Perfect.

(21) *Birmingham*, John Easton, Thomas Hanby, Samuel Randal.

(22) *Macclesfield*, James Rogers, Christopher Peacock,   30
William Myles, William Simpson.

(23) *Manchester*, John Allen, Jonathan Hern, Jeremiah Brettel.

(24) *Chester*, John Fenwick, John Goodwin, John Oliver.

(25) *Liverpool*, Parson Greenwood, Robert Costerdine,   35
George Button.

(26) *Leicestershire*, Joseph Bradford, Thomas Warrick, Jeremiah Robertshaw.

(27) *Nottingham*, Geo. Snowden, Joseph Pilmore.

(28) *Derby*, John Hampson, Jun., Thomas Longley.   40

(29) *Sheffield*, Thomas Taylor, Wm. Percival, John Booth.

(30) *Grimsby*, Thomas Carlill, James Wray, Sam. Botts, Thomas Wride.

(31) *Gainsborough*, Thomas Corbet, James Barry, Thomas Bartholomew.

(32) *Epworth*, Geo. Shadford, Barnabas Thomas, John Beanland.

(33) *Leeds*, Alexander Mather, Rob. Roberts, John Shawl.

(34) *Birstall*, John Valton, Christopher Hopper, Thomas Brisco.

(35) *Huddersfield*, John Hampson, sen., Philip Hardcastle.

(36) *Bradford*, Samuel Bradburn, T. Mitchell, Joseph Benson.

(37) *Keighley*, Isaac Brown, William Hunter.

(38) *Colne*, Tho. Hanson, Thomas Johnson, David Evans.

(39) *Whitehaven*, Wm. Boothby, James Watson.

(40) *Isle of Man*, Jasper Robinson, Jon. Brown, Thomas Tattershall.

(41) *York*, John Pawson, Wm. Thompson, Thomas Readshaw.

(42) *Hull*, Jos. Thompson, Nicholas Manners, Edward Jackson.

(43) *Scarborough*, William Dufton, Lancelot Harrison, Charles Atmore.

(44) *Thirsk*, Benj. Rhodes, Michael Moorhouse, William Thom.

(45) *Yarm*, William Collins, William Eells, George Holder.

(46) *[The] Dales*, John Peacock, Robert Swan, Thomas Vasey.

(47) *Sunderland*, Duncan Wright, Thomas Dixon.

(48) *Newcastle*, Duncan McAllum, Alexander McNab, Thomas Ellis, John Pritchard.

(49) *Edinburgh*, Joseph Saunderson, Samuel Bardsley, James Bogie.

(50) *Dundee*, Peter Mill, John Ogylvie.

(51) *Aberdeen*, Andrew Inglis, Hugh Moore, William Warrener.

(52) *Dublin*, Thomas Rutherford, Andrew Blair.

(53) *Waterford*, Nehemiah Price, Tho. Davis.

(54) *Cork*, Zachariah Yewdall, Richard Boardman.

(55) *Limerick*, Richard Watkinson, Robert Blake.

(56) *Castlebar*, John Price, George Mowat.

(57) *Athlone*, Daniel Jackson, Gustavus Armstrong.

(58) *Sligo*, George Brown, Robert Armstrong.

(59) *Ballyconnell*, Samuel Mitchell, Robert Davis, James Christie.

(60) *Clones*, John Watson, Sen., George Dice, John Mealy.

(61) *Enniskillen*, Robert Naylor, William West.

(62) *Charlemont*, Thomas Barber, John Livermore, John Kerr.

(63) *Lisleen*, Robert Lindsay, John Miller, William McCornock.

(64) *Londonderry*, Henry Moore, John Cricket.

(65) *Belfast*, Henry Foster, Robert Bridge.

(66) *Lisburn*, John Crook, James Jordan.

Q. 8. How many wives are to be provided for?

A. Sixty-four.

Q. 9. What part of these are provided for by the societies with whom their husbands labour?[912]

A.

(1) London	S. Lee, Hindmarsh[913]	
(2) Gloucestershire	S. Story	
(3) Bradford	S. Poole	
(4) Bristol	S. Boone, Payne, Moore[914]	
(5) Devon	S. Church[915]	
(6) Cornwall, East	S. Green, Wadsworth	
(7) Cornwall, West	S. Rodda,[916] Harper[917]	

---

[912] The phrasing of this question is completely different from that in previous *Minutes* and implies a system of support by the preacher's present circuit that does not uniformly seem to have been the case. In virtually all cases (except Moore and Rodda), there is no correspondence between the supporting circuit this year and the previous year or the preacher's birthplace circuit.

[913] Hindmarsh was stationed at Norwich.

[914] Wm. Moore was stationed at Sarum.

[915] Church was stationed at Taunton.

[916] Richard Rodda was stationed in Oxfordshire.

[917] Joseph Harper was stationed in Sussex.

	(8) Birmingham	S. Easton
	(9) Macclesfield	S. Rogers, Wood[918]
	(10) Manchester	S. Hern, Goodwin[919]
	(11) Chester	S. Crook[920]
5	(12) Liverpool	S. Greenwood, Costerdine
	(13) Leicester	S. Bradford
	(14) Nottingham	S. Snowden
	(15) Sheffield	S. Taylor, Booth
	(16) Grimsby	S. Robertshaw,[921] Boothby[922]
10	(17) Gainsborough	S. Barry
	(18) Epworth	S. Corbet,[923] S. Wride £6.[924]
	(19) Leeds	S. Mather, Shaw, Roberts
	(20) Huddersfield	S. Hampson
	(21) Birstall	S. Brisco, Hopper
15	(22) Bradford	S. Bradburn, Mitchell
	(23) Keighley	S. Brown
	(24) Colne	S. Evans
	(25) York	S. W[illiam] Thompson, Thom[925]
	(26) Hull	S. Jos. Thompson
20	(27) Scarborough	S. Harrison
	(28) Thirsk	S. Moorhouse
	(29) Yarm	S. Collins
	(30) [The] Dales	S. Peacock
	(31) Sunderland	S. Wright, Swan[926]
25	(32) Newcastle	S. Ellis

Q. 10. How are the other eleven provided for, viz. S. Beanland,[927] Day,[928] Hunter,[929] Empringham,[930] Longley,[931]

---

[918] James Wood was stationed in Sussex.
[919] Goodwin was stationed at Chester.
[920] Crook was stationed at Lisburn.
[921] Robertshaw was stationed in Leicestershire.
[922] Boothby was stationed at Whitehaven.
[923] Corbet was stationed at Gainsborough.
[924] Wride was stationed at Grimsby.
[925] Wm. Thom was stationed at Thirsk.
[926] Swan was stationed in The Dales.
[927] Beanland was stationed at Epworth.
[928] Day was stationed in Cornwall, West.
[929] Wm. Hunter, Sen., was stationed at Keighley.
[930] Empringham was stationed at Bedford.
[931] Longley was stationed at Derby.

H. Moore,[932] Mill,[933] Mowat,[934] Watson,[935] Naylor,[936] S. Eells?[937]

A. Out of the Preachers' Fund.

Q. 11. What numbers are in the societies?

A. London*	2,515	
Sussex*	214	
Kent	209	
Colchester*	190	
Norwich*	590	10
Lynn	156	
Bedfordshire*	300	
Northamptonshire	246	
Oxfordshire	440	
Gloucestershire	505	15
Sarum*	373	
Bradford*	891	
Bristol*	1,457	
Taunton	200	
Tiverton*[938]	400	20
Cornwall, East*	756	
———— West*	1,813	
Glamorganshire	163	
Pembrokeshire	177	
Brecon*	118	25
Birmingham*	925	
Macclesfield	1,325	
Manchester*	1,500	
Chester*	532	
Liverpool*	952	30
Leicestershire*	697	
Nottingham ⎫		
⎬	710	
Derby ⎭		

---

[932] H[enry] Moore was stationed at Londonderry.

[933] Mill was stationed at Dundee.

[934] Mowat was stationed at Castlebar.

[935] John Watson, [Sen.], was stationed at Clones.

[936] Naylor was stationed at Enniskillen.

[937] Eells was stationed at Yarm.

[938] Tiverton also increased its membership, though no asterisk is printed in the original. Costerdine supplied this in MS in his own copy, however.

	Sheffield*	1,060
	Grimsby*	882
	Gainsborough*	648
	Epworth*	740
5	Leeds	2,383
	Birstall*	1,448
	Huddersfield	749
	Bradford	1,800
	Keighley	1,160
10	Colne*	986
	Whitehaven*	310
	Isle of Man*	1,683
	York*	810
	Hull	680
15	Scarborough	642
	Thirsk*	698
	Yarm	889
	The Dales	810
	Sunderland ⎫	
20	⎬	2,020
	Newcastle* ⎭	
	Edinburgh	187
	Dundee	62
	Aberdeen*	210
25	Dublin*	550
	Waterford	208
	Cork*	383
	Limerick	197
	Castlebar	205
30	Athlone*	273
	Sligo* ⎫	
	⎬	1,098
	Ballyconnell* ⎭	
	Clones*	728
35	Enniskillen	556
	Charlemont*	702
	Lisleen*	654
	Londonderry*	180
	Belfast	354

Lisburn 424

45,723[939]

N.B. The Circuits marked thus * are increased this year.

Q. 12. What is the Kingswood collection? 5

A. £457. 4*s*. 6*d*.

Q. 13. What boys are received this year?

A. Joshua Collins, John Mitchell, James Morgan.

Q. 14. Are the children at Amesbury used well?[940]

A. Far from it. Therefore remove them at Michaelmas. 10

Q. 15. What can we allow the female children?

A. Allow Elizabeth Roberts, Hannah Peacock, Jane
Thompson, Elizabeth Brown, Elizabeth Easton, and Ann
Snowden six pounds each.

Q. 16. What was contributed to the Preachers' Fund? 15

A. £252. 3*s*.

Q. 17. What was allowed out of it?

	£.	*s*.	*d*.	
A. To Thomas Westell	30	0	0	
Ann Morgan	30	0	0	20
Jacob Rowell	20	0	0	
William Whitaker	20	0	0	
Jane Wilkinson	20	0	0	
Lucia Bourke	15	0	0	
John Furz	12	0	0	25
John Bredin	12	0	0	
Thomas Halliday	12	0	0	
Elizabeth Standring	12	0	0	
S[isters] Beanland and Eells	24	0	0	
S. Day	12	0	0	30
S. Hunter and Empringham	24	0	0	
S. Longley and Mill	24	0	0	
S. Hen. Moore and Watson	24	0	0	
S. Naylor and Mowat	24	0	0	
Mary Penington	10	0	0	35
Alice Brammah	10	0	0	

[939] Orig., '46,331'.

[940] JW's *Journal* and diaries during this period occasionally use 'Amesbury' to refer to 'Almondsbury'; see *Journal & Diaries*, 23:107–8, 150, 459 (and cf. 287), and so on, in this edn.

Elizabeth Shorter	10	0	0
Katharine Garnet	5	5	0
Elizabeth Oldham	5	5	0
Elizabeth Dillon	5	5	0
Tabitha Norris	5	5	0
Sarah Hosmer	10	0	0
In all	£376	0	0

Q. 18. What was contributed for the yearly expenses?

A. £661. 14*s.* 2½*d.*

Q. 19. How was this expended?

A. Arrears of last year	£142	16	6
This year's contingencies	100	0	0
Law	12	0	0
Preachers' necessities	406	17	8½
	£661	14	2½

Q. 20. What houses are to be built this year?

A. Nottingham, Hinckley,[941] Penshaw,[942] Carlisle.

Q. 21. Several of our preaching-houses are awkwardly settled. How shall this be prevented for the time to come?

A. (1) Let none collect for any house but the itinerant preachers.

(2) Let none collect for any house unless the undertakers or managers of the building first give a written promise to the Assistant,

[i] To conform to the 3rd, 4th, 5th, 6th, and 8th articles of Answer 65 (pp. 44–45) in the 'Large' *Minutes* of the Conference;[943]

[ii] To settle the house, without meddling with lawyers, in the form set down, pp. 42–43 of the *Minutes*;[944] and

[941] Orig., 'Hinkley'.

[942] Orig., 'Painsher'.

[943] I.e., 'Large' *Minutes* (1780). Orig., '63', probably from confusion with the form for the Model Deed, which is contained in *Q.* 63 of those *Minutes*; see (ii) below.

[944] I.e., 'Large' *Minutes* (1780), *Q.* 63.

[iii] To engage that the men and women shall sit apart, both above and below.[945]

Q. 22. What can be done with regard to the preaching-house at Birstall?

A. If the trustees still refuse to settle it on the Methodist 5
Plan,

(1) Let a plain state of the case be drawn up.[946]

(2) Let a collection be made throughout all England in order to purchase ground, and to build another preaching-house as near the present as may be. 10

Q. 23. Several members of our societies who make a conscience of sabbath-breaking have been much distressed, barbers in particular. What can be done to relieve them?

A. (1) Let no members of our society have their hair 15
dressed on Sunday.

(2) Let all our members that possibly can employ those barbers.

Q. 24. Is it well for our preachers to powder their hair, or to wear artificial curls? 20

A. To abstain from both is the more excellent way.[947]

Q. 25. Ought any person to be continued as a member of our society in Ireland who learns or performs the military exercise as a volunteer on the Lord's Day?[948]

---

[945] Cf. *Minutes* (1765), *Q*. 14 and n. 36.

[946] See *The Case of Birstal House, Bibliography*, No. 430, in vol. 9 of this edn.; and Tyerman, *Wesley*, 3:373–83 for an account of the affair and correspondence. The issue was whether local trustees or JW and then the Conference after him should control the appointment of preachers. Even the Model Deed (where it was used, as was not the case in Birstall) was not a complete safeguard and hence the Deed of Declaration of 1784. See also *Minutes* (1765), *Q*. 11 and n. 35.

[947] 1 Cor. 12:31. JW seems always to have worn his own hair and eschewed wigs, judging by his portraits; and judging by his recommendations, one must presume that the curled ends of his hair were natural. The portraits of CW and of many itinerants in the *AM* clearly show them wearing wigs, and they appear as an item in 18th-century circuit accounts for preachers. Powdering (with flour if all else failed!) was customary but to be eschewed by self-denying Methodists as unnecessary expenditure.

[948] Though JW was evidently not hostile to the Volunteer (militia) movement as such, at this time in Ireland there was an element of constitutional reform agitation, influenced by the American example, among the Irish Volunteers.

A. No, certainly. Let him be excluded.

N.B. Meeting on the parade in order to attend divine service is not to be considered as an infringement of this rule.
Nor shall the above minute refer to anything which it may
5   be necessary for them to do in case of an actual invasion.

Q. 26. Ought any person to be excluded our society who,
after proper admonition, will on the Lord's day continue
a spectator of the exercise of the volunteers?

A. Certainly they ought.

10   *Q*. 27. When and where may we meet again?

A. On the last Tuesday in July, at Bristol.

Annual *Minutes of some late Conversations*, 1783

Bristol, Tuesday, July 29, 1783[949]

[949] JW confided to Miss Ritchie that he expected 'a good deal of difficulty at this
Conference'; *Letters* (Telford), 7:184. In his *Journal* (23:286 in this edn.), he wrote,
'Tues. 29 July. Our Conference began, at which two important points were
considered, first, the case of Birstall House, and secondly, the state of
Kingswood School. With regard to the former, our brethren earnestly
desired, that I would go to Birstall myself, believing this would be the most
effectual way of bringing the trustees to reason. With regard to the latter,
we all agreed that either the school should cease or the rules of it be particularly observed; particularly that the children shall never play and that a
master should be always present with them.'
The Birstall case was not so easily resolved, but Kingswood School survived
despite JW's frequent, almost despairing criticisms. Though Birstall was not mentioned in the *Minutes*, there is little doubt that it influenced the resolution to send
Coke throughout the English societies to persuade them to settle all the preaching-
houses on the Model Deed; see *Q*. 24. The concern about Kingswood School may
have been influenced by Adam Clarke's unsatisfactory experiences there. *Journal &
Diaries*, 23:286, n. 36 in this edn.; Ives, *Kingswood School*, 91–95; Adam Clarke, *An
Account of the . . . Life of Adam Clarke*, ed. J. B. B. Clarke, 3 vols. (London: T. S.
Clarke, 1833), 1:159–69. The Birstall problem also initiated the process by which
the 1784 Deed of Declaration emerged. In a letter by the preachers responding to
the Deed in July 1785, they recalled that at the 1783 Conference, they resolved,
'without a dissentient voice, to draw up a Deed which should give a legal specification of the phrase, "The Conference of the People called Methodists", and that the
mode of doing it was entirely left to his [Wesley's] judgment and discretion'. *Minutes*
(1785), after *Q*. 24. Sutcliffe recalled that JW said ' "in his laconic manner" that I
want nothing but the right of stationing preachers'. MS 'History', fols. 1037–38.

Q. 1. What preachers are admitted this year?

A. Joseph Cole, John Barber, Joseph Algar, Thomas Wride, John Kerr, William West, James Christie, William McCornock, Adam Clarke.[950]

Q. 2. Who *remain* on trial?

A. Alexander Suter, Thomas Cooper, Thomas Ellis, Charles Atmore, Christopher Peacock, Rob. Hopkins, Robert Scot, John Cricket, Gustavus Armstrong, George Dice, John Miller.

Q. 3. Who are *admitted* on trial?

A. John Cowmeadow, Lawrence Kane, William Wilson, James Thom, Jos. Jerom, Charles Bond, Samuel Edwards, George Holder, Edward Burbeck, John King, John Crosby.

Q. 4. Who *desist* from travelling?

A. James Hindmarsh, David Evans, Thomas Readshaw.

Q. 5. What preachers have *died* this year?

A. Richard Boardman, a pious, good-natured, sensible man, greatly beloved of all that knew him. He was one of the two first that freely offered themselves to the service of

From Aug. 5, for the next three weeks, JW suffered from 'a most impetuous flux'. He had, suffered an earlier bout in March, at which time he told Miss Roe that 'one of our sisters' had dreamed twice of seeing his funeral. Miss Roe predicted his recovery and then ascribed that recovery to the time that some of his preachers were praying for him. *Letters* (Telford), 7:171–72. Pawson reveals that the renewed attack during Conference forced the preachers to do much of the business without him. Jackson, *Early Methodist Preachers*, 4:50. In his MS autobiography, Pawson says, 'Indeed we all expected that he would die, but the Lord raised him up again in answer to the many prayers offered up for him.' Pawson, MS 'Some Account', fol. 15. This episode no doubt sharpened concern over future control of the connexion.

John Hampson, Jun., claims that at this Conference, Coke tried to pass a minute agreeing to JW giving absolute power to a select committee to conduct the affairs of the Society after his death; and another to lodge the deeds of the preaching-houses in a safe at City Road with Coke holding the key. But large majorities rejected both motions. John Hampson, *Memoirs of the Late Rev. John Wesley*, 3 vols. (Sunderland: Graham, 1791), 3:206–7; see also introduction, pp. 47, 63, above.

Alexander Mather wrote to Mr. Marriott (Aug. 3), 'It has pleased God to favour us with much unanimity and concord at the Conference. As also with a considerable degree of his presence. And I hope those things which has threatened our peace will be quite removed'. Tyerman MSS, 1:175. At this Conference, David Lloyd, vicar of Llanbister, attended and offered himself for the itinerancy but was refused for health reasons. His wife was a Methodist and his house open to them. He built a chapel on his estate for them. Tyerman, *Wesley*, 402–3.

[950] Orig., 'Clark', as also in 1785, 1786, 1789; in 1784 the name was spelled 'Clcrk', but normally he used and continued to use the spelling 'Clarke'.

our brethren in America. He died of an apoplectic fit, and
preached the night before his death. It seems he might
have been eminently useful, but good is the will of the
Lord.[951]

5   *Robert Swindells* had been with us above forty years. He was
an Israelite indeed.[952] In all those years I never knew him
to speak a word which he did not mean; and he always
spoke the truth in love: I believe no one ever heard him
speak an unkind word. He went through exqu[is]ite pain

10   (by the stone) for many years; but he was not weary. He
was still
        Patient in bearing ill, and doing well.[953]
One thing he had almost peculiar to himself; he had no
enemy! So remarkably was that word fulfilled, 'Blessed are

15   the merciful; for they shall obtain mercy.'[954]
James Barry was for many years a faithful labourer in our
Lord's vineyard. And as he laboured much, so he suffered
much; but with unwearied patience.
In his death he suffered nothing, stealing quietly away in a

20   kind of lethargy.
Thomas Payne was a bold soldier of Jesus Christ. His temper was uncommonly vehement; but before he went hence
all that vehemence was gone, and the lion was become a
lamb. He went away in the full triumph of faith, praising

25   God with his latest breath.
Robert Naylor, a zealous, active young man, was caught
away by a fever in the strength of his years. But it was in a
good hour; for he returned to him whom his soul loved, in
the full assurance of faith.

30   A fall from his horse, which was at first thought of little
consequence, occasioned the death of *John Livermore*; a
plain, honest man, much devoted to God, and determined
to live and die in the best of services.
Q. 6. Are there any objections to any of our preachers?

35   *A.* They were examined one by one.

---

[951] See 2 Kgs. 20:9.
[952] John 1:47.
[953] One of JW's favourite quotations, from his older brother Samuel's poem, 'The
Battle of the Sexes; A Poem', stanza 35; see *Poems on Several Occasions* (London:
Say, 1736), 38.
[954] Matt. 5:7.

Q. 7. How are the preachers stationed this year?
A. As follows:

(1) *London*, John Wesley, Charles Wesley, Tho. Coke, Tho. Lee, Tho. Tennant, John Atlay, J. Prickard; Tho. Rankin, supernumerary.

(2) *Sussex*, Joshua Keighley, William Homer; Henry Robins, supernumerary.

(3) *Kent*, James Wood, John Acutt, William Wilson.

(4) *Colchester*, John Booth, Thomas Cooper.

(5) *Norwich*, Rich. Whatcoat, Jos. Thompson, Wm. Adamson, Adam Clarke.

(6) *Lynn*, Jer. Brettel, John Ingham, Jon. Parkin.

(7) *Bedford*, Jos. Pescod, Mich. Moorhouse.

(8) *Northampton*, Christop. Watkins, John Barber.

(9) *Oxfordshire*, J. Broadbent, Sim. Day, J. Cole.

(10) *Gloucestershire*, Jonathan Coussins, John Brettel, Robert Empringham.

(11) *Sarum*, John Mason, George Story, Jos. Jerom.

(12) *Bradford*, John Pritchard, Francis Wrigley, John Poole, Geo. Wadsworth.

(13) *Bristol*, George Shadford, John Hampson, [Sen.], William Green.

(14) *Devon*, William Ashman, Nath. Ward, Charles Bond; John Furz, supernumerary.

(15) *Plymouth*, John Moon, James Hall.

(16) *Cornwall, East*, James Thom, Joseph Algar, John Cowmeadow.

(17) ———, *West*, Jos. Taylor, William Moore, John Wittam, William Holmes.

(18) *Glamorgan*, John Watson, jun., Wm. Hoskins.

(19) *Pembroke*, James Perfect, Wm. Church, Sam. Hodgson.

(20) *Brecon*, John Leech, William Saunders.

(21) *Birmingham*, Richard Rodda, Charles Boone.

(22) *Burslem*, John Fenwick, Thomas Hanty.

(23) *Macclesfield*, James Rogers, Samuel Bardsley.

(24) *Manchester*, John Murlin, Jon. Hern, Wm. Percival.

(25) *Chester*, Duncan Wright, John Goodwin, George Gibbon.

(26) *Liverpool*, P. Greenwood, William Eells, Zachary Yewdall, Thomas Vasey.

(27) *Leicester*, Jos. Bradford, Samuel Randal, Jer. Robertshaw.

(28) *Nottingham*, Wm. Myles, John Hampson, jun.; Geo. Snowden, supernumerary.

(29) *Derby*, Thomas Longley, Sam. Edwards.

(30) *Sheffield*, Thomas Taylor, Thomas Johnson, William Simpson.

(31) *Grimsby*, Thomas Carlill, Robert Scot, Samuel Bolls, Jos. Harper.

(32) *Gainsborough*, Thomas Corbet, Thomas Wride, James Wray.

(33) *Epworth*, John Beanland, Peter Mill, Philip Hardcastle.

(34) *Leeds*, Wm. Thompson, Rob. Roberts, Samuel Bradburn.

(35) *Birstall*, John Valton, John Allen, Isaac Brown.

(36) *Huddersfield*, Thomas Hanson, John Shaw.

(37) *Bradford*, Alexander Mather, Jos. Benson, Wm. Dufton.

(38) *Keighley*, Benj. Rhodes, Thomas Mitchell.

(39) *Colne*, John Easton, Rob. Costerdine, Thomas Warrick.

(40) *Whitehaven*, Thomas Ellis, Hugh Moore.

(41) *Isle of Man*, Jasper Robinson, George Button, Edward Burbeck.

(42) *York*, John Pawson, Thomas Simpson, Charles Atmore.

(43) *Scarborough*, Lanc. Harrison, Robert Howard,[955] Thomas Shaw.

(44) *Hull*, Edward Jackson, Barn. Thomas, Rob. Johnson.

(45) *Thirsk*, Robert Swan, John Crosby, James Watson.

(46) *Yarm*, Thomas Brisco, Christ. Peacock.

(47) *Whitby*, William Thom, Rob. Hopkins.

(48) *The Dales*, John Peacock, Matthew Lumb,[956] John King.

(49) *Sunderland*, William Collins, George Holder.

[955] See *Minutes* (1782), *Q*. 4, n. 910 as possibly Hayward.

[956] Orig. 'Lum', as also *Minutes* (1784–87); 'Lumm' in the CJ. In a printed letter of his (July 6, 1835), as well as the holograph covering note, he spells his name 'Lumb'.

(50) *Newcastle*, Thomas Dixon, Christo. Hopper, William Boothby.

(51) *Berwick*, William Hunter, James Bogie.

(52) *Edinburgh*, Jos. Pilmore, Andrew Inglis.

(53) *Dundee*, Jos. Saunderson, Wm. Warrener.

(54) *Aberdeen*, Duncan McAllum, Alex. Suter, Tho. Bartholomew, J. Ogylvie.

(55) *Dublin*, Tho. Rutherford, Dan. Jackson.

(56) *Waterford*, Thomas Davis, John Price.

(57) *Cork*, Henry Moore, Andrew Blair, Lawrence Kane.

(58) *Limerick*, Rich. Watkinson, Wm. West.

(59) *Castlebar*, George Dice, John Mealy.

(60) *Athlone*, Nehemiah Price, Robert Blake, Tho. Halliday, supernumerary.

(61) *Sligo*, Rob. Lindsay, Gusta. Armstrong.

(62) *Ballyconnell*, Robert Armstrong, John Kerr.

(63) *Clones*, George Brown, John Cricket, William McCornock.

(64) *Enniskillen*, James Jordan, John Miller.

(65) *Charlemont*, Thomas Barber, James Christie, James Rennick.

(66) *Lisleen*, Sam. Mitchell, Tho. Hetherington, Joseph Armstrong.

(67) *Londonderry*, John Watson, T. Tattershall.

(68) *Belfast*, Henry Foster, George Mowat, Robert Bridge.

(69) *Lisburn*, John Crook, Jonathan Brown.

Q. 8. How many wives are to be provided for?

A. Sixty-six.

Q. 9. How many of these are to be provided for by the societies?

A. Fifty-two: namely,

(1) London	S[isters] Lee, Wood.[957]	
(2) Gloucestershire	S. Coussins.	
(3) Bradford	S. Poole.	
(4) Bristol	S. Green, Hampson, Day.[958]	
(5) Devonshire	S. Church.[959]	

[957] Wood was stationed in Kent.
[958] Day was stationed in Oxfordshire.
[959] Church was stationed in Pembroke.

(6) Plymouth	S. Moon.
(7) Cornwall, West	S. Ellis, Moore.[960]
(8) Birmingham	S. Rodda.
(9) Macclesfield	S. Rogers.
(10) Burslem	S. Boone.[961]
(11) Manchester	S. Hern, Wright.[962]
(12) Chester	S. Goodwin.
(13) Liverpool	S. Greenwood, Eells.
(14) Leicester	S. Bradford.
(15) Nottingham	S. Myles.
(16) Sheffield	S. Taylor, Wm. Simpson.
(17) Grimsby	S. Harper, Mill.[963]
(18) Gainsborough	S. Corbett, Longley.[964]
(19) Epworth	S. Beanland, Wride.[965]
(20) Leeds	S. Bradburn, Roberts, Inglis.[966]
(21) Huddersfield	S. Shaw.
(22) Birstall	S. Robertshaw,[967] Brown.
(23) Bradford	S. Mather, Story.[968]
(24) Keighley	S. Mitchell.
(25) Colne	S. Easton.
(26) York	S. T. Simpson.
(27) Hull	S. Costerdine.[969]
(28) Scarborough	S. Thom.[970]
(29) Thirsk	S. Swan.
(30) Yarm	S. Brisco.
(31) [The] Dales	S. Peacock.
(32) Newcastle	S. Boothby.
(33) Sunderland	S. Collins, Warrick.[971]

[960] Ellis and Hugh Moore were stationed in Whitehaven; William Moore in West Cornwall.

[961] Boone was stationed in Birmingham.

[962] Wright was stationed in Chester.

[963] Mill was stationed in Epworth.

[964] Longley was stationed in Derby.

[965] Wride was stationed in Gainsborough.

[966] Inglis was stationed at Edinburgh.

[967] Robertshaw was stationed at Leicester.

[968] Story was stationed at Sarum.

[969] Costerdine was stationed at Colne.

[970] William Thom was stationed at Whitby.

[971] Warrick was stationed at Colne.

(34) Ireland   S. Rutherford, H[enry] Moore,
                      Price, Watkinson.

Q. 10. How are the other fourteen to be provided for? viz.,
  S. Booth,[972] G. Brown,[973] Crook,[974] Empringham,[975]   5
  Hunter,[976] Joyce,[977] Kane,[978] Moorhouse,[979] Mowat,[980]
  Pritchard £6.,[981] Snowden,[982] Jos. Thompson,[983] James
  Watson,[984] John Watson.[985]
A. Out of the Preachers' Fund.
Q. 11. What numbers are in the societies?   10

A. London*   2,617
    Sussex*   216
    Kent   198
    Colchester*   170   15
    Norwich   547
    Lynn   127
    Bedford*   330
    Northampton   229
    Oxfordshire*   480   20
    Gloucester   460
    Sarum*   386
    Bradford [on Avon]*   893
    Bristol*   1,481
    Taunton*   206   25
    Tiverton   347
    Plymouth   266

[972] Booth was stationed at Colchester.
[973] Geo. Brown was stationed at Clones.
[974] Crook was stationed at Lisburn.
[975] Empringham was stationed in Gloucestershire.
[976] Wm. Hunter, [Sen.], was stationed at Berwick.
[977] Joyce does not appear in the English stations this year, though the Irish *Minutes* show him in Ballyconnell.
[978] Kane was stationed at Cork.
[979] Moorhouse was stationed at Bedford.
[980] Mowat was stationed at Belfast.
[981] Pritchard was stationed at Bradford [N. Wiltshire].
[982] Snowden [supernumerary] was stationed at Nottingham.
[983] Jos. Thompson was stationed at Norwich.
[984] James Watson was stationed at Thirsk.
[985] John Watson, [Sen.], was stationed at Londonderry.

	Cornwall, East	496
	———, West*	2,047
	Glamorgan*	173
	Pembroke*	181
5	Brecon*	133
	Birmingham	753
	Macclesfield*	1,380
	Manchester*	1,600
	Chester	497
10	Liverpool*	965
	Leicestershire*	713
	Nottingham*	573
	Derby*	345
	Sheffield*	1,166
15	Grimsby*	923
	Gainsborough*	658
	Epworth	706
	Leeds	2,356
	Birstall*	1,773
20	Huddersfield*	781
	Bradford	1,709
	Keighley	1,045
	Colne*	1,003
	Whitehaven	275
25	Isle of Man*	1,758
	York*	817
	Hull*	696
	Scarborough	615
	Thirsk	632
30	Yarm	875
	[The] Dales	802
	Sunderland	1,000
	Newcastle	1,020
	Edinburgh	173
35	Dundee*	103
	Aberdeen*	247
	Dublin	495
	Waterford	208
	Cork	370
40	Limerick*	218
	Castlebar	195

Athlone*	282	
Sligo	303	
Ballyconnell	670	
Clones	673	
Enniskillen	476	5
Charlemont	669	
Lisleen	590	
Londonderry	164	
Belfast	331	
Lisburn	409	10
In all	45,995[986]	

N.B. The circuits marked thus * are increased this year.

Q. 12. What is the Kingswood collection? 15

A. £464. 6*s.* 1½ *d.*

Q. 13. What boys are received this year?

A. Isaac Barry, Michael Harrison, Samuel Roberts, Isaac Brown, David Poole.

Q. 14. What can we allow the daughters of the preachers? 20

A. Mary Ann Collins, Elizabeth Roberts, Jane Thompson, Ann Snowden, Sarah Barry, £6 each.

Q. 15. Can any improvement be made in the management of Kingswood School?

A. My design in building the house at Kingswood was to 25 have therein a Christian family, every member whereof (children excepted) should be alive to God, and a pattern of all holiness.

Here it was that I proposed to educate a few children according to the accuracy of the Christian model. And 30 almost as soon as we began God gave us a token for good, four of the children receiving a clear sense of pardon.

But at present the school does not in any wise answer the design of its institution, either with regard to religion or learning. 35

The children are not religious: they have not the power, and hardly the form of religion. Neither do they improve in learning better than at other schools, no, nor yet so well.

---

[986] Orig. '45,955'.

Insomuch that some of our friends have been obliged to remove their children to other schools.

And no wonder that they improve so little either in religion or learning, for the rules of the school are not observed at all.

All in the house ought to rise, take their three meals, and go to bed at a fixed hour. But they do not.

The children ought never to be alone, but always in the presence of a master. This is totally neglected, in consequence of which they run up and down the wood, and mix, yea, fight with the colliers' children.

They ought never to play: but they do, every day, yea, in the school.

Three maids are sufficient; now there are four, and but one (at most) truly pious.

How may these evils be remedied, and the school reduced to its original plan? It must be mended, or ended, for no school is better than the present school.

Can any be a master that does not rise at five, observe *all* the rules, and see that others observe them?

There should be three masters, and an usher, chiefly to be with the children out of school.

The head master should have nothing to do with temporal things.

Q. 16. But how can Mr. Simpson[987] be provided for?

A. He desires to be an itinerant preacher.

Q. 17. What is contributed to the Preachers' Fund?

A. £244. 10*s*.

Q. 18. What is allowed out of it?

	£.	s.	d.
A. To Thomas Westell	30	0	0
Jacob Rowell	20	0	0
William Whitaker	20	0	0
Ann Morgan	30	0	0

---

[987] Thomas Simpson, M.A., was an itinerant (1765–72); headmaster of Kingswood School (1772?–83); and his wife, the housekeeper. Dismissed by the 1783 Conference due to corruption in the school, he wished to return to the itinerancy and was appointed to York but did not go and was replaced by Edward Jackson as 'it was necessary'. He opened a school at Keynsham near Bath, where his son eventually became vicar. He left in 1784 and died before 1833; see Tyerman, *Wesley*, 3:397–99; *MM* (1808): 440–41; (1833): 122–24; (1845): 11.

Jane Wilkinson	20	0	0
Lucia Bourke	10	0	0
Elizabeth Standring	12	0	0
Mary Penington	10	0	0
Alice Brammah	12	0	0	5
Elizabeth Shorter[988]	10	0	0
Kath. Garnet	5	5	0
Elizabeth Dillon	7	17	6
Tabitha Norris	5	5	0
Margaret Payne	12	0	0	10
Sarah Barry	24	0	0
Sarah Naylor	12	0	0
Fourteen wives	162	0	0
	£402	7	4[989]

15

Q. 19. What is contributed for the yearly expenses?
A. £716. 14*s*. 3*d*.
Q. 20. How was this expended?

	£.	*s*.	*d*.	
A. Arrears of last year and contingencies	84	1	0	20
This year's contingencies	100	0	0	
Law	21	1	0	
Preachers' necessities	511	12	3	
In all	£716	14	3	25

Q. 21. What houses are to be built this year?
A. None that are not already begun.
Q. 22. Has not the needless multiplying of preaching-houses been a great evil?[990]   30
A. So it appears.
Q. 23. How may this be prevented?
A. By permitting none for the future to beg for any house, except in the circuit wherein it stands.
   Q. 24. What can be done to get all our preaching-houses   35
   settled on the Conference Plan?

---

[988] Orig., 'Sharter'. George Shorter had died in 1770.
[989] Orig., '£444. 7*s*. 6*d*.'
[990] For the first signs of questions on new preaching-houses, see *Minutes* (1770), *Q*. 14; (1776), *Q*. 21; and for renewed permission to build after a halt of a year, *Minutes* (1785), *Q*. 19.

A. Let Dr. Coke[991] visit the societies throughout England, as far as is necessary for the accomplishment of this design; and let the respective Assistants give him all the support in their power.

5   *Q*. 25. When and where may our next conference be?

A. In Leeds, the last Tuesday in next July.

---

[991] For Coke, see above, *Minutes* (1778), *Q*. 7 (1), n. 730.

PART III

Annual Conference *Minutes*
and Conference Journal,
1784–91

INTRODUCTION

THE Conference and its records from this year onwards were marked by two new and important developments, namely, (1) the beginning in 1784 of the manuscript Conference Journal, and (2) a formal legal basis and constitution laid down by the Deed of Declaration of 1784.[1] These changes altered the nature of the records kept by the Conference and therefore affect the way this material is considered in this volume.

1. The Conference Records

With the beginning of the manuscript Conference Journal, a much fuller and more authoritative record of the transactions of the annual Conference exists. Information is now available at three distinct levels:

(a) The final and legally binding authoritative signed record of the Conference, maintained in large manuscript journal volumes annually to the present time. This account was apparently written up in a fair hand on the basis of notes and lists so as to be signed at the end of the proceedings. It contains much confidential material that has never been made available to the general public.

(b) The printed *Minutes* of the Conference, a selection of the major administrative decisions, including the stationing of the preachers, a number of decisions relating to the Methodist procedure at all levels, and occasional pastoral letters to the Methodist people.

(c) A digest of these printed *Minutes*, published annually in the *Arminian Magazine* and its successors from 1779 onwards, of which the main feature was the appointments to new stations.

A summary of the additional material in the Conference Journal will be furnished either in the footnotes or occasionally (as in the opening attendance lists and the answer to Q 5, below) within square brackets in the main text.

[1] The text of the Deed of Declaration is in Appendix A in the present volume.

After the recital of the Deed of Declaration, which set up the Conference as a legal entity, the folio volumes (referred to herein as CJ) contain the officially inscribed and signed *Minutes* of the successive Conferences, beginning with those for 1784, which comprise pages 1–23.

2. Background to the Conference of 1784 and the Deed of Declaration

In his *Journal*, Wesley wrote,

Tuesday 27, our Conference began, at which four of our brethren, after long debate (in which Mr Fletcher took much pains), acknowledged their fault, and all that was past was forgotten. Thursday 29, being the public Thanksgiving day [for the conclusion of the peace with America], as there was not room for us in the old church, I read prayers, as well as preached, at our Room. . . . Having five clergymen to assist me, we administered the Lord's Supper, as was supposed, to sixteen or seventeen hundred persons. Sunday, August 1, we were fifteen clergymen at the old church. Tuesday 3. Our Conference concluded, in much love, to the great disappointment of all.[2]

The five clergy assisting were Coke, Fletcher, Cornelius Bayley (who taught at Kingswood School and was later an Anglican clergyman in Manchester), David Simpson (an evangelical clergyman from Macclesfield), and Dillon (who was stationed in London).[3] Wesley's sarcastic closing remark refers to the controversy over the Deed of Declaration.

This Deed was Wesley's response (assisted by Coke and a lawyer) to the request made at the 1783 Conference for a watertight definition of the Conference that would remedy that weak point in the Model Deed.[4] Despite suspicions of intrigue by Coke, the really controversial provision of one hundred named persons as the legal Conference (Legal Hundred)—controversial because it did not include all the preachers and excluded some senior preachers in favour of younger ones—appears to be solely Wesley's work. It may be surmised that he either sensibly mixed old and young or took the

---

[2] *Journal & Diaries*, 23:324 in this edn.
[3] Ibid., 23:325 and n. 6, in this edn.
[4] See *Minutes* (1783), n. 949.

opportunity to exclude troublemakers (which he certainly did on occasion in his invitations to Conference).[5] The Deed, issued in February 1784, provoked a published *Appeal* on behalf of the excluded by John Hampson, Sen.

John Pawson, though anxious to exonerate Coke from intrigue, fairly pointed out that the problem of the undefined Conference had troubled preachers even before Coke joined the Methodists.[6] Pawson said Wesley alone named the Hundred 'whether by design or otherwise I cannot pretend to say'. But older and respected preachers who had been left out viewed it as a lack of confidence and affection. Many trustees were also alarmed, since they thought of the chapels as their own property.[7] In his published autobiography, Pawson emphasized that the sole purpose of the Deed was to remedy the long-standing weakness of the Model Deed, but he conceded that Wesley acted 'without due consideration, not foreseeing the consequences which would follow'.[8]

In the Conference (though not recorded in the *Minutes*), there was evidently much tension. Joseph Benson recorded that on the morning of July 27, the Deed and *Appeal* were considered. Wesley then once again, as on other occasions, traced his 'power' from its first rise and showed that the Conference was for those he asked to meet with him. He insisted that he had the right to nominate the members and fix their number. The *Appeal*, he said, represented him as unjust, oppressive, and tyrannical, which he denied. He claimed that the authors of the *Appeal* 'had betrayed him and hurt the minds of many. He therefore required that they should acknowledge their fault and be sorry for it, or he would have no further connection with them.' Two acknowledged their fault and submitted. Macdonald, in publishing this account from Benson's diary (now lost), commented 'on the propriety of his [Wesley] using the power he claimed as to which we think he was entitled, even men of sense and piety will think differently'. He added that it did not appear that Wesley ever allowed any part of doctrine or discipline to be decided by popular vote.[9] The conclusion of the episode was more dramatic

---

[5] See introduction, pp. 26, 68, 91.

[6] The worries about trusts had been raised several times with abortive suggestions to solve them: *Minutes* (1749), §1; (1768), *Q*. 15 and n. 190; (1770), *Q*. 15 and n. 315.

[7] Tyerman MSS, 3:65–67.

[8] Jackson, *Early Methodist Preachers*, 4:52.

[9] James Macdonald, *Memoirs of the Rev. Joseph Benson* (London: Blanshard, 1822), 159–61.

than this account suggests. Christopher Hopper says that there was 'war' for many days but that 'dear Mr. Fletcher's intervention gained his point at last'.[10] One famous account of the scene comes from Atmore's recollections:

> Never . . . shall I forget with what ardour and earnestness Mr. Fletcher expostu-lated, even on his knees, both with Mr. Wesley and the preachers. To the former he exclaimed, 'My father! my father! they have offended, but they are your children'. To the latter he exclaimed, 'My brethren! my brethren! he is your father' and then, portraying the work in which they were unitedly engaged, fell again on his knees and with much fervour and devotion engaged in prayer. The Conference was bathed in tears, many sobbed aloud.

However, Joseph Algar, as a very young preacher, was a chief speaker, and 'it was before this stripling that Fletcher dropped on his knees and begged him not to dissolve the societies but to let love bind the whole. Algar replied, "Yes, Sir, love shall bind, but it should not blind us." '[11] Tyerman says that five preachers retired as a result of the dispute: the two Hampsons, Pilmore, Eells, and Atlay.[12] In fact, Eells and Atlay continued in the stations (were they the two penitents after Wesley's diatribe?), but they left over the Dewsbury chapel case.[13] One reason for disquiet even among those not excluded from the Legal Hundred was that, as Pawson said,

> By the Deed it was supposed that all those preachers whose names were not in the deed were expelled the Conference and accordingly some of them were greatly offended, and dreadful things were to be done. But this thing blew over much bet-ter than was expected by many, and the offended brethren were found to be offend-ers and were obliged to retreat and ask for parole, which was readily granted by Mr. Wesley.[14]

But James Oddie and Robert Oastler petitioned the Hundred to give them an assurance that the preachers not named in that body would be treated equally under the Deed when it came into force after Wesley's death.[15] Wesley, who continued to invite and exclude attendance at Conference much as before seems to have shared this

---

[10] Jackson, *Early Methodist Preachers*, 1:220.
[11] *WMM* 68 (1845): 14–15; and *Journal & Diaries*, 23:324, n. 3 in this edn.
[12] *Wesley*, 3:425.
[13] See *Minutes* (1788), n. 327.
[14] Pawson, MS 'Some Account of the Life of Mr. John Pawson', fol. 26, in MA.
[15] Tyerman MSS, 2:29f.

view and left a letter with Joseph Bradford to be read to the Conference after his death, begging them to treat all the brethren equally. Bradford complied with the request, and the letter was printed as a preface to the *Minutes* (1791).[16]

3. The Question of Ordinations for America

Although the new arrangements for America and Wesley's controversial ordinations did not figure in the Conference *Minutes* until 1785, he was already considering plans to send preachers abroad. To James Barry on July 3, 1784, he wrote,

We purpose to consider fully at the Conference what we can do to help our brethren abroad; not only those that are settled in the southern provinces of America, but those in Nova Scotia and Newfoundland. Indeed, it is an invariable rule with me not to require any one to go over to America—nay, I scruple even to advise them to it. I shall only propose it at the Conference, and then, of them that freely offer themselves, we shall select such as we believe will most adorn the gospel.[17]

But possibly as early as October 1783, he was considering a plan for a church government and ordination for America.[18] He then supplied them with ordained ministry, as well as Articles of Religion and a prayer-book, revised and reduced from the Anglican ones. Although there was no mention of all this in the *Minutes* (1784), John Etheridge (seventy-five years later) claims that 'the measure was laid before the Conference. Mr. Fletcher took part in the deliberations and fully concurred in the affirmative resolution then confirmed.'[19] Pawson's picture of a meeting of the 'Cabinet', at least about the ordination, seems more plausible. He says (having denied that the preachers had pressed for an ordination in the 1770s) that it was first proposed in 1784 by Wesley:

[16] Tyerman, *Wesley*, 3:417. See further, introduction, pp. 13, 26–27, 66.

[17] *Letters* (Telford), 7:225.

[18] For this and what followed, see Baker, *Wesley and Church*, 262–70; Rack, *Reasonable Enthusiast*, 508–16; W. R. Ward, 'The Legacy of John Wesley', in *Statesmen, Scholars and Merchants*, ed. Anne Whiteman, et al. (Oxford: Clarendon, 1973), 323–50; and for JW's account, *Minutes* (1785), *Q.* 20.

[19] John Etheridge, *The Life of the Rev. Thomas Coke* (London, 1860), 102. This Conference was Fletcher's last before his death in 1785.

I was a member of the select committee and was present when it was proposed. I believe never were the preachers more astonished than when this was mentioned, and to a man they opposed it and freely expressed their disapprobation and accordingly nothing of the kind took place at this time. But I plainly saw it would be done as it was quite clear to me that Mr. Wesley's mind was fixed in that particular; and accordingly an ordination took place soon after at Bristol by Mr. Wesley, Dr. Coke, and Mr. Creighton.[20]

An almost equally controversial subject seems to have been raised at this Conference—the question of female preaching. Several preachers told Wesley that they were against it, though some were in favour. Wesley spoke for them in particular cases. Thomas Mitchell, 'a reasonable man', said, 'I know not what you would do with the good women, for all the fish they catch they put in our net.'[21]

[20] Tyerman MSS, 3:52.
[21] Zachariah Taft, *Biographical Sketches of . . . Holy Women* (London, 1825; repr. 1992), 1:27.

Annual *Minutes of some late Conversations*, 1784

Leeds, Tuesday, July 27, etc. 1784.
[Conference Journal: 'The Minutes or Journals of the Conference of
the People called Methodists, begun at Leeds in the County of York
on Tuesday, the 27 day of July, in the year 1784, and continued by   5
various adjournments to Tuesday, the 3d day of August following,
inclusive.'

[Present
[The Revd. John Wesley, President[22]
[Revd. Thomas Coke, Secretary   10

(There are seventy-four names in three columns. N.B. Here as
elsewhere obvious spelling errors, such as 'Ducan' Wright and
Francis 'Wrighley', are corrected silently.)
[John Allen, Charles Atmore, John Barber, Samuel Bardsley,
Joseph Benson, John Booth, Samuel Bradburn, Joseph Bradford,   15
Thomas Brisco, Jeremiah Brettel, John Broadbent, Isaac Brown,
Thomas Carlill, William Collins, Robert Costerdine, Thomas
Corbet, Jonathan Coussins, Thomas Dixon, William Dutton, John
Easton, John Fenwick, Henry Foster, John Goodwin, William
Green, Parson Greenwood, Thomas Hanby, Thomas Hanson,   20
Joseph Harper, Lancelot Harrison, Christopher Hopper, Robert
Hopkins, William Hunter, Edward Jackson, Joshua Keighley, John
Leech, Thomas Longley, Duncan McAllum, John Mason,
Alexander Mather, John Moon, Henry Moore, John Murlin,
William Myles, John Pawson, Christopher Peacock, John Peacock,   25
Joseph Pescod, Thomas Rankin, James Wray, Robert Roberts,
Jeremiah Robertshaw, Jasper Robinson, Richard Rodda, James
Rogers, Benjamin Rhodes, Thomas Rutherford, Robert Scot, John
Shaw, George Shadford, William Simpson, Joseph Taylor, Thomas
Taylor, William Thom, Barnabas Thomas, William Thompson,   30
Zachariah Yewdall, John Valton, Thomas Vasey, William Warrener,
Christopher Watkins, Richard Whatcoat, James Wood, Duncan
Wright, Francis Wrigley.

---

[22] JW is now designated as President and Thomas Coke as Secretary, in accordance with the Deed of Declaration.

[Absent

(There are twenty-four names in three columns.)

[Charles Wesley, Thomas Barber, Andrew Blair, William Boothby, John Brettel, George Brown, George Button, Joseph Cole, Thomas
5 Cooper, James Creighton, John Crook, James Hall, William Hoskins, Daniel Jackson, Robert Lindsay, Jonathan Parkin, William Percival, Nehemiah Price, William Saunders, Joseph Saunderson, George Story, Thomas Tennant, James Thom, Richard Watkinson.

[For the absence of all of whom a dispensation is passed.

10   [*Question 1ˢᵗ*. Who are in full connexion with the Conference?

(There are fifty-four names in three columns. N.B. 'John Bo' is inserted in error at the beginning.)

[*Answer*: William Adamson, Joseph Algar, William Ashman, John Atlay, John Beanland, James Bogie, Charles Bond, Charles Boone,
15 Samuel Botts, William Church, Adam Clarke, John Crosby, Simon Day, Richard Dillon, Samuel Edwards, William Eells, Thomas Ellis, Robert Empringham, George Gibbon, John Hampson, Sen., John Hampson, Jun., Philip Hardcastle, Jonathan Hern, Samuel Hodgson, George Holder, William Holmes, William Horner, Robert
20 Howard, John Ingham, Andrew Inglis, Robert Johnson, Thomas Johnson, John King, Thomas Lee, Matthew Lumb, Peter Mill, Michael Moorhouse, William Moore, James Perfect, Joseph Pilmore, John Poole, John Pritchard, Thomas Shaw, George Snowden, Robert Swan, Joseph Thompson, George Wadsworth,
25 Nathanael Ward, Thomas Warrick, James Watson, John Watson, Jun., John Wittam, Thomas Wride, George Whitfield.

(Other questions continue in the same form as in the earlier and current *Minutes*, usually with different numbers, and with the names often in a different order. Thus '*Question 2ⁿᵈ*. Which of those were
30 admitted at this conference?' becomes '*Q*. 1' in the *Minutes*. In most instances, however, the basic contents remain the same; any exceptions are noted.)

Minutes

Q. 1. What preachers are admitted this year?
35   *A*. Thomas Ellis, Charles Atmore, Christ. Peacock, Robert Scot, Robert Hopkins, Samuel Botts, George Holder,

Samuel Edwards, Robert Johnson, Phil. Hardcastle, James
Bogie, John King, John Crosby, Matthew Lumb, Charles
Bond, Lawrence Kane, James Jordan, Matthias Joyce,
John Cricket, Thomas Hetherington, Gust. Armstrong,
Jos. Armstrong, James Rennick, George Dice, John   5
Miller.[23]

Q. 2. Who *remain on trial*?

A. John Cowmeadow, Jos. Jerom, Edward Burbeck, Alex.
Suter, Thomas Bartholomew, John Ogylvie, William
Adamson.   10

Q. 3. Who are *admitted on trial*?[24]

A. William Palmer, Charles Kyte, Benjamin Pearce, Joseph
Entwisle,[25] Melville Horne,[26] Vince Sellor,[27] John
McKersey,[28] and Richard Cornish.[29]

Q. 4. Who *desist* from travelling?[30]   15

A. Robert Blake, Robert Lindsay, Henry Robins, ———,
Joseph Saunderson, Tho. Simpson.

Q. 5. Who have died this year?

[23] CJ adds George Whitfield, but does not include Charles Atmore, Christopher
Peacock, or Robert Scot.

[24] Cornish does not appear in CJ: Timothy Crowther (as 'Crowder') is added—
see *Minutes* (1785) and CJ.

[25] Orig., 'William Entwistle'; 'William' is an error for 'Joseph'. Although the
Minutes (1784–91) uniformly spell the name 'Entwistle', in his own extant letters
and publications, he dropped the 't', as did his son Joseph, also an itinerant.

[26] Orig., 'Horn'.

[27] Orig., 'Seller'. His name is struck through in CJ.

[28] Orig., 'Mucklesey'; his name is variously spelled in the *Minutes*: 'Muckarsy',
1785 (2), 1786 (1), 1787 (2), 1788 (2); 'Muckersy' and 'Muckersey', 1789;
'McKersie' and 'McKersie', 1790.

[29] Orig., 'John Cornish' (2) in 1784; 'Richard' elsewhere.

[30] CJ lists only Blake and Robins, the list being limited to 'those who are in
connexion with Conference'. The name of 'Robert Lindsay' is inserted in reply
to *Q.* 6, 'Is any member of the Conference expelled?' CJ continues, under *Q.* 7,
'Who is elected a member of the conference [i.e., of the Legal Hundred] in his
place?' The answer is 'Francis Astbury [*sic*], General Assistant of America'. There
follows: '*Q.* 8: Is any member of the conference laid aside because he has desisted
from travelling?' The answer is, 'Joseph Saunderson'. In *Q.* and *A.* 9, the member elected to replace Saunderson is 'Robt. Carr Brackenbury Esqr. of Raithby in
the County of Lincoln'. On Robert Lindsay, see also *Minutes* (1779), *Q.* 7 (56) and
n. 771. On Brackenbury, see below, as posted to 'Isle of Jersey', in *Minutes* (1784),
Q. 7 (72) and n. 39.

A. John Prickard, a man thoroughly devoted to God, and an eminent pattern of [all] holiness: and *Jacob Rowell*, a faithful old soldier, fairly worn out in his Master's service.

Q. 6. Are there any objections to any of our preachers?

5   *A.* They were examined, one by one.[31]

Q. 7. How are the preachers stationed this year?

A. As follows:

(1) *London*, John Wesley, Charles Wesley, James Creighton, Ric. Dillon, Henry Moore, Tho. Tennant,[32]

10   Thomas Rankin, and John Atlay, supernumeraries.

(2) *Sussex*, Henry Foster, Will. Adamson.

(3) *Kent*, James Wood, William Horner,[33] Zach. Yewdall.[34]

(4) *Colchester*, William Boothby, Tho. Cooper.

15   (5) *Norwich*, Jon. Coussins, George Button, William Palmer, Jos. Jerom.

(6) *Lynn*, John Barber, John McKersey.

(7) *Bedford*, Jos. Pescod, John Ingham.

(8) *Northampton*, Jos. Harper, Joseph Entwisle.[35]

20   (9) *Oxford*, Samuel Hodgson, Simon Day.

(10) *Gloucester*, Joseph Taylor, John Poole, Barnabas Thomas.

(11) *Sarum*, John Moon, George Story, George Wadsworth.

25   (12) *Bradford*, Chris. Watkins, John Pritchard, M. Moorhouse, John Wittam.

(13) *Bristol*, Samuel Bradburn, Thomas Lee, James Hall.

(14) *Devon*, John Mason, William Ashman, Rob. Empringham, Ch. Kyte.

30   (15) *Plymouth*, Phil. Hardcastle, Wm. Moore.

---

[31] In CJ this, marked *Q.* 11, is followed by *Q.* 12, 'How many wives are to be provided for?' This and the answer 'seventy-three' are then struck through as an error of placing, to appear later as *Q.* 13 after the stations—a clear indication that the CJ was a fair copy compiled from various memoranda.

[32] CJ here adds but erases the name of Zachariah Udall (*sic*), evidently in error, for his station was in the Kent Circuit.

[33] CJ strikes through Horner's name; there is also a dotted underline, perhaps implying that Horner's status was under discussion.

[34] 'Udall', in CJ.

[35] Orig.,'Will Entwistle'.

(16) *Cornwall, East*, Francis Wrigley, Wm. Church, Adam Clarke.[36]

(17) ———, *West*, Wm. Green, John Acutt, Jos. Algar, J. Cowmeadow, Richard Cornish.[37]

(18) *Pembroke*, Jos. Keighley, William Holmes, Benjamin Pearce.

(19) *Glamorgan*, Will. Saunders, James Perfect.

(20) *Brecon*, Joseph Cole, William Hoskins.

(21) *Birmingham*, Rich. Rodda, Tho. Warrick.

(22) *Burslem*, R. Costerdine, Tho. Hanby.

(23) *Macclesfield*, Jos. Bradford, Wm. Percival.

(24) *Manchester*, John Pawson, John Murlin, John Goodwin.

(25) *Chester*, Duncan Wright, Thomas Corbet, Edward Jackson.

(26) *Liverpool*, Jon. Hern, John Fenwick, Melville Horne.

(27) *Bolton*, Chris. Hopper, William Eells.

(28) *Leicester*, William Myles, John [i.e., Jonathan] Parkin, Samuel Edwards.

(29) *Nottingham*, Charles Boone, Sam. Bardsley.

(30) *Derby*, John Brettel, Nath. Ward.

(31) *Sheffield*, Joseph Benson, Benj. Rhodes, George Gibbon.

(32) *Grimsby*, Wm. Dufton, James Watson, Robert Scot, John Watson, Jun., James Christie, supern[umerary].

(33) *Epworth*, Tho. Longley, Tho. Wride, Lancelot Harrison.

(34) *Gainsborough*, Thomas Carlill, Peter Mill, Samuel Botts.

(35) *Leeds*, Wm. Thompson, Tho. Brisco, Thomas Rutherford.

(36) *Birstall*, John Broadbent, John Allen, Robert Roberts, T. Johnson, supern[umerary].

---

[36] In CJ 'Jonathan Crowder' is added, then struck through.

[37] Orig.,'J. Cornish'. In CJ 'Richd. Cornish' is added by Thomas Coke. He was born in Wiltshire in 1758, served successively in West Cornwall, St. Austell, St. Ives, Brecon, and Salisbury, and in 1789 remained on trial, but with no station. According to Myles (*Chronological History*), he died in 1796.

(37) *Huddersfield*, Thomas Hanson, Isaac Brown.
(38) *Bradford*, John Valton, Thomas Taylor, John Shaw.
(39) *Keighley*, Parson Greenwood, John Booth.
(40) *Colne*, John Easton, Thomas Dixon, Charles Atmore.
(41) *Whitehaven*, Jasper Robinson, Jos. Thompson.
(42) *Isle of Man*, James Thom, James Bogie, Edward Burbeck.
(43) *York*, Alex. Mather, Joseph Pilmore, Robert Hopkins.
(44) *Hull*, Jer. Robertshaw, Wm. Thom, George Holder.
(45) *Scarborough*, Wm. Simpson, Charles Bond, John King.
(46) *Whitby*, John Peacock, James Wray.
(47) *Thirsk*, Robert Swan, Rob. Howard, Thomas Shaw.
(48) *Yarm*, G. Shadford, J. Hampson, Sen.
(49) *The Dales*, Thomas Ellis, John Ogylvie, James MᶜCaddin.
(50) *Sunderland*, W. Collins, J. Hampson, Jun.
(51) *Newcastle*, Jer. Brettel, George Snowden, John Beanland.
(52) *Berwick*, Wm. Hunter, Wm. Warrener.
(53) *Edinburgh*, Rich. Watkinson, Andr. Inglis.
(54) *Dundee*, Alex. Suter, Th. Bartholomew.
(55) *Aberdeen*, Duncan M'Allum, John Crosby.
(56) *Inverness*, Robert Johnson, Matthew Lumb.
(57) *Dublin*, James Rogers, Andrew Blair.
(58) *Waterford*, T. Tattershall, James Wilson.
(59) *Cork*, Christ. Peacock, Tho. Davis. ⎫ Let these
(60) *Bandon*, Daniel Jackson, Lawr. Kane. ⎭ change every quarter.
(61) *Limerick*, John Leech, John Watson, Sen.
(62) *Castlebar*, James Jordan, John Kerr, Thomas Halliday, supern[umerary].
(63) *Athlone*, Matthias Joyce, John Cricket.
(64) *Sligo*, Robert Bridge, John Clarke.[38]
(65) *Ballyconnell*, Robert Armstrong, Wm. West, James MᶜDonald.

---

[38] Orig., 'Clark', as also in the Irish *Minutes*, and in 1785–86.

(66) *Clones*, Nehem. Price, George Mowat, T. Hetherington, S. Mitchell, supernumerary.

(67) *Enniskillen*, Tho. Barber, Gust. Armstrong.

(68) *Charlemont*, John Crook, John Mealy, Walter Griffith.

(69) *Lisleen*, Jos. Armstrong, James Rennick.

(70) *Londonderry*, Jonathan Brown, George Dice, William McCornock.

(71) *Belfast*, John Price, John Miller.

(72) *Lisburn*, George Brown, Wm. Hammet.

Isle of Jersey, Robert Carr Brackenbury.[39]

America, Thomas Coke, Rich. Whatcoat, Thomas Vasey.[40]

Q. 8. How many wives are to be provided for?

A. Seventy.

Q. 9. How many of these are to be provided for by the societies?

A. Fifty-three, namely,

(1) London	S. Moore,[41] Wood.[42]
(2) Gloucestershire	S. Poole.
(3) Bradford	S. Moorhouse.
(4) Bristol	S. Bradburn, Moon,[43] Lee.
(5) Devon	S. Church.[44]
(6) Plymouth	S. W. Moore.
(7) Cornwall, West	S. Green, Coussins.[45]
(8) Birmingham	S. Rodda.
(9) Burslem	S. Costerdine.
(10) Macclesfield	S. Bradford.

---

[39] Robert Carr Brackenbury (1752–1818) of Raithby Hall (the 'Methodist squire') was a rarity: a Methodist magistrate who built a chapel at the Hall for Methodist use (still existing over the old horse stalls). He often travelled for JW, so was in effect a 'half-itinerant'; see *Minutes* (1755), §2 and n. 954. Indeed from 1784 to 1790, JW appointed him 'as Assistant in the Channel Islands without the formality of admitting him by Conference'. Ward in *Journal & Diaries* 23:23, n. 99, in this edn. with refs.

[40] Asbury's name as JW's potential candidate for superintendent ('bishop') is not inserted either in CJ or in *Minutes*.

[41] Henry Moore was in London.

[42] James Wood was in Kent.

[43] John Moon was in Sarum.

[44] William Church was in Cornwall, East.

[45] Jonathan Coussins was in Norwich.

(11) Manchester	S. Goodwin, Day,[46] Warrick.[47]
(12) Chester	S. Wright.
(13) Liverpool	S. Hern.
(14) Bolton	S. Hopper.
(15) Leicester	S. Myles.
(16) Nottingham	S. Boone, Horner.[48]
(17) Sheffield	S. Gibbon, Harper.[49]
(18) Grimsby	S. Peacock,[50] (Ja.) Watson.
(19) Gainsborough	S. Corbet,[51] Mill.
(20) Epworth	S. Longley, McAllum.[52] £6
(21) Leeds	S. Brisco, Rutherford, Inglis.[53]
(22) Huddersfield	S. (Is.) Brown.
(23) Birstall	S. Roberts, Robertshaw.[54]
(24) Bradford	S. Taylor, Shaw.
(25) Keighley	S. Booth.
(26) Colne	S. Easton.
(27) York	S. Mather.
(28) Hull	S. Thom.
(29) Thirsk	S. Swan.
(30) Yarm	S. Hampson.
(31) The Dales	S. Ellis.
(32) Sunderland	S. Collins, Hunter.[55]
(33) Newcastle	S. Snowden.
Ireland	S. Price,[56] Blair,[57] Watson, Sen.,[58] Crook.[59]

Q. 10. How are the other seventeen, viz. S. (Jos.) Thompson, Pescod,[60] Empringham, Story, Simpson,

---

[46] Simon Day was in Oxford.
[47] Thomas Warrick was in Birmingham.
[48] Wm. Horner was in Kent. His name is here struck through in CJ.
[49] Joseph Harper was in Northampton.
[50] John Peacock was in Whitby.
[51] Thomas Corbet was in Chester.
[52] Duncan McAllum was in Aberdeen.
[53] Andrew Inglis was in Edinburgh.
[54] Jeremiah Robertshaw was in Hull.
[55] William Hunter was in Berwick.
[56] John Price was in Belfast.
[57] Andrew Blair was in Dublin.
[58] John Watson, Sen., was in Limerick.
[59] John Crook was in Charlemont.
[60] 'Pescod' here struck through in CJ.

Wride, Beanland, Boothby, Kane, Watkinson, West, (Geo.) Brown, Rennick, £6 Mowat, Bridge, Greenwood, and Joyce, to be provided for?

A. Out of the Preachers' Fund.

Q. 11. What numbers are in the society?

A. As follows:

London+[61]	2,680[62]
Sussex+	255
Kent+	235
Colchester+	253
Norwich	482
Lynn+	140
Bedford	263
Northampton+	267
Oxfordshire+	495
Gloucestershire+	580
Sarum	385
Bradford+	916
Bristol+	1,549
Devon+	681
Plymouth	222
Cornwall, East+	650
West+	2,393
Glamorgan	151
Pembroke	176
Brecon	127
Birmingham+	770
Burslem+	694
Macclesfield+	800
Manchester+	1,757
Chester+	630

[61] Neither the symbols '+' nor the note concerning the symbol are not present in CJ.

[62] These statistics do not follow the numbered ordering of the circuits as given in the stations, Nos. 1–5, 6–10 being at the head of the two columns beginning the list both in the printed *Minutes* (where p. 8 ends) and in CJ, where column 1 continues 11–31 and column 2 continues 42–64, though this list also shows other displacements of the original ordering of the stations. There is even a hint here that the CJ somehow followed the printed *Minutes*, which could hardly be true. These peculiarities cannot be explained at present.

Liverpool+	1,020
Leicester+	795
Nottingham	562
Derby+	369
Sheffield+	1,200
Grimsby+	971
Gainsborough	612
Epworth+	744
Leeds+	2,480
Birstall+	2,024
Huddersfield+	825
Bradford+	1,850
Keighley+	1,050[63]
Colne+	1,044
Whitehaven	269
Isle of Man+	2,121
York+	851
Scarborough	595
Hull+	808
Thirsk+	641
Yarm+	505
Whitby+	442
The Dales+	808
Sunderland+	1,100
Newcastle	970
Berwick	52
Edinburgh+	126
Dundee+	104
Aberdeen+	251
Dublin+	582
Waterford+	209
Cork+	633
Limerick+	270
Castlebar+	259
Athlone	272
Sligo+	308[64]
Ballyconnell+	672
Clones	627

[63] This is altered in CJ to 1,150, which leads to the altered total of 64,255.
[64] '305' in *Minutes*; '308' in CJ.

Enniskillen+	562	
Charlemont+	684	
Lisleen	452	
Londonderry+	171	
Belfast	287	5
Lisburn+	441	
America+	14,988	
	64,155[65]	

N.B. The circuits marked thus + [instead of the previous   10
'*'] are increased this year.

Q. 12. What is the Kingswood collection?
A. £507. 12s.
Q. 13. What boys are admitted this year?   15
A. John Goodwin, Jon. Hern, John Leech.
Q. 14. What can we allow the daughters of the preachers?
A. Eliz. Rodda, Eliz. Corbet, Jane Thompson, Eliz. Roberts
   (for her 2nd year), Ann Snowden (for her 2nd year), Mary
   Ann Collins (for her 2nd year), £6 each.   20
Q. 15. What is contributed to the Preachers' Fund?
A. £370. 7s.
Q. 16. What is allowed out of it?
A. To

	£.	s.	25
Tho. Westell	30	0	
S. Rowell	10	0	
Wm. Whitaker	20	0	
Ann Morgan	24	0	
Jane Wilkinson	20	0	30
Lucia Bourke	10	0	
Eliz. Standring	12	0	
Mary Penington	10	0	
Alice Brammah	12	0	
Eliz. Shorter	10	0	35
Cath. Garnet	10	0	
Elizabeth Dillon	5	0	

[65] CJ, '64,255'. The reason for the altered total seems to be CJ's inserted alteration of Keighley's '1,050' to '1,150'. But should be 64,157 and 64,257, respectively.

Tabitha Norris	5	0
Margaret Payne	12	0
Sarah Barry	24	0
Sarah Naylor	12	0
Eliz. Oldham	12	0
S. Meggott	5	0
S. Hosmer	10	0
Tho. Mitchell	30	0
Tho. Johnson	12	0
John Furz	12	0
Jam. Christie	12	0
Henry Robins	12	0
Tho. Halliday	12	0
Sam Mitchell	12	0
John Bredin	12	0
17 Wives	198	0
[£]	565	0[66]

Q. 17.   What is contributed for the yearly expenses?

A. £ 803. 0*s*. 2*d*.

Q. 18. How was this expended?

	£.	s.	d.
A. Arrears of last year and contingencies	281	19	6
This year's contingencies	100	0	0
Law	10	5	0
Preachers' necessities	410	15	8
[£]	803	0	2

Q. 19. Is not the time of trial for preachers too short?

A. It is—for the time to come, let them be on trial four years.

Q. 20. Some who once preached with us deny original sin. What is to be done in this case?

A. No preacher who denies original sin can preach among us; and we advise our brethren not to hear him.[67]

---

[66] CJ lists only 21 individuals together with the 17 wives, but Coke inserted a further 6, all being numbered in accordance with this printed listing. He does not include, however, No. 26, Sam Mitchell.

[67] Nicholas Manners was probably a case in point; see *Minutes* (1775), *Q.* 5 and n. 560.

Q. 21. Many of our brethren have been exceedingly hurt by
frequenting feasts or wakes on Sundays. What do you
advise in this case?

A. Let none of our brethren make any wake[68] or feast, neither go to any on Sunday, but bear a public testimony 5
against them.

Q. 22. Is the making candles for our own use, without paying duty for them, contrary to law?

A. Certainly it is. It is a species of smuggling, not to be
practised by any honest man. 10

N.B. No preacher is to leave his circuit till the Monday
sevennight before the conference, except the Cornish
preachers when the conference is at Leeds, and the
Scotch preachers when the conference is at Bristol.

Let the four quarterly fasts be duly observed, in August, 15
November, February, and May.[69]

Q. 23. When and where is the next conference to begin?

A. At London, on the last Tuesday in July, 1785.

[John Wesley
Thomas Coke, Secretary] 20

Annual *Minutes of some late Conversations,* 1785

London, Tuesday, July 26, 1785[70]

---

[68] Feasts and sports originally connected with the day of the patron saint of the parish
church, especially in northern England (elsewhere generally termed a 'feast'). Moralists
often condemned them for their disorder and drunkenness. Methodist preaching was
sometimes deliberately timed to coincide with and counter these celebrations.

[69] Cf. for earlier recommendations and datings for these, *Minutes* (1777), *Q*. 26.

[70] CJ for 1785 occupies pp. 25–37. A new feature is the listing of the overseas
preachers and their stations, brought over by Thomas Coke. JW writes,

'The rest of the week [July 18–23] I was fully employed in writing for the
magazine [*AM*] and preparing for the Conference. Sunday 24, I preached at
West Street, morning and afternoon, when both the largeness and earnest-
ness of the congregation gave me a comfortable hope of a blessing at the
ensuing Conference. Tuesday 26, our Conference began, at which about seventy preachers were present whom I had invited by name. One consequence
of this was that we had no contention or altercation at all, but everything
proposed was calmly considered and determined as we judged would be
most for the glory of God. Monday August 1. Having, with a few select
friends, weighed the matter thoroughly, I yielded to their judgment and set

apart three of our well-tried preachers, John Pawson, Thomas Handy and Joseph Taylor, to minister in Scotland. And I trust God will bless their ministrations and show that he has sent them. Wednesday 3, our peaceful Conference ended, the God of power having presided over all our consultations.' (*Journal & Diaries*, 23:371–72, in this edn.)

In letters at this time JW underlined his control over invitations as before the Deed of Declaration. To Thomas Wride on July 7, 1785, he writes,

'I desire you to come to the Conference. A Conference while I live is the preachers whom I *invite* to confer with me. . . . Many years ago, one informed me at London "The Stewards have discovered that they are not your Stewards but the people's, and are to direct not to be directed by you". The next Sunday I let them drop, and named seven other stewards. No contentious person shall for the future meet in Conference. . . . They may *dispute* elsewhere if they please.' (*Letters* [Telford], 7:279)

He writes similarly to Mrs. Christian on July 17, adding that the first two days of Conference only travelling preachers are present. Ibid., 7:281. But the limitations on his influence show when he wrote in Aug. to Christopher Hopper that an unnamed person could at the utmost be allowed to preach as a local preacher, 'for I will not run my head against all the Conference by reversing what they have determined'. Ibid.,7:286.

At this Conference, the American scheme was published and justified; *Q.* 20 below, and see Introductory Note to *Minutes* (1784). In a retrospective justification in a letter to Henry Brooke on June 14, 1786, JW writes that 'the case of our brethren in N. America was considered, wholly cut off both from the English Church and State. In so peculiar a case I believed it my duty to take an extraordinary step in order to send them all the help I could. Some asked why not here (in England). "Because it is not the same case. They separate from nobody. They had no Church" alas "no King". We have both.' *Letters* (Telford), 7:333.

But as the CJ acknowledged in 1785, he ordained for Scotland. Pawson wrote (Jackson, *Early Methodist Preachers*, 4:54), 'I found, to my great surprise, that Mr. Wesley had come to a determination to ordain ministers for Scotland', and 'I am well assured that this was a matter fully determined upon by Mr Wesley himself, from the time that he ordained ministers for America', the decision being purely his own. In his MS life of Dr. Whitehead (Tyerman MSS, 3:53), he says that Hopper, Mather, and Thompson had originally been proposed for Scotland, 'but as none of them had any previous knowledge of this, they could not go at such short notice and refused'. Pawson and the others finally chosen were taken by surprise and only reluctantly accepted under pressure from JW and Coke: 'Mr Wesley was so displeased with Hopper for refusing that he said in great wrath "As the Lord liveth, if you do not accept of it now, you never shall have the imprint of my hand on your head while I live."' Pawson then recounts that JW ordained Mather as a bishop and Rankin and Moore, none of these being for Scotland. In his MS autobiography (MS 'Some Account', fol. 28), Pawson says that he 'heartily approved' this, 'believing it would prove an introduction to the same thing in England, which is greatly desired both by the preachers and the people'. But JW hesitated to do this openly, on the grounds that unlike the case with America and Scotland, he would be conflicting with the Church of England. On returning to England, those ordained for Scotland were required to cease to act as ordained ministers, much to Pawson's indignation. He regarded this as against all church precedent. Pawson to Atmore,

[The Minutes or Journals of the Conference of the people called *Methodists*, begun in London on Tuesday, the 26th day of July, in the year of our Lord 1785, and continued by various adjournments to Wednesday the third day of August following inclusive.

5

[Present
[The Revd. John Wesley, President,
[Revd. Thomas Coke, Secretary.
(There are fifty-four names in three columns.)
[John Barber, Samuel Bardsley, William Boothby, Samuel 10 Bradburn, Joseph Bradford, Jeremiah Brettel, John Broadbent, Isaac Brown, George Button, Thomas Carlill, Joseph Cole, William Collins, Jonathan Coussins, James Creighton, William Dufton, John Easton, John Fenwick, Henry Foster, William Green, Parson Greenwood, James Hall, Thomas Hanby, Joseph Harper, 15 Christopher Hopper, Joshua Keighley, Thomas Longley, Alexander Mather, John Moon, Henry Moore, John Murlin, William Myles, John Pawson, John Peacock, Joseph Pescod, Thomas Rankin, Jeremiah Robertshaw, Jasper Robinson, Richard Rodda, Benjamin Rhodes, William Saunders, George Shadford, William Simpson, 20 Thomas Taylor, Joseph Taylor, Thomas Tennant, Barnabas Thomas, William Thompson, Zachariah Yewdall, John Valton, William Warrener, Christopher Watkins, James Wood, Duncan Wright, Francis Wrigley.

[Absent   25
(There are forty-four names in three columns.)
Charles Wesley, John Allen, Francis Asbury, Charles Atmore, Thomas Barber, Joseph Benson, Andrew Blair, John Booth, Robt. Carr Brackenbury, John Brettel, Thomas Brisco, George Brown, Thomas Cooper, Robert Costerdine, Thomas Corbet, John Crook, 30 Thomas Dixon, John Goodwin, Thomas Hanson, Lancelot Harrison, Robert Hopkins, William Hoskins, William Hunter,

---

Aug. 8, Oct. 20, 1787, *Letters*, 1:46, 51. Hanby persisted in Communion in Nottingham and was condemned by JW. Tyerman, *Wesley*, 3:574–76. There are frequent references to these tensions in Pawson's letters in 1788–89, and he thought that 'the good old man' (Wesley) was so pestered by 'High Church' preachers that 'he does not know what to do'. Pawson to Atmore, June 2, 1786, *Letters*, 1:42. The whole debate over ordination, sacraments, their implications for separation, and what was 'Mr. Wesley's Plan' dragged on for several years after his death. Pawson was an advocate of Methodist sacraments where the local Society wished for them; the 'High Church' Methodists were against them.

Daniel Jackson, Edward Jackson, John Leech, Duncan McAllum.
John Mason, Jonathan Parkin, Christopher Peacock, William
Percival, Nehemiah Price, James Wray, Robert Roberts, James
Rogers, Thomas Rutherford, Robert Scot, John Shaw, George Story,
5   James Thom, William Thom, Thomas Vasey, Richard Watkinson,
Richard Whatcoat.

[For the absence of all of whom a dispensation is passed.
[*Question 1st.* Who are in full connexion with the Conference?
[*Answer.* (There are forty names in three columns, p. 26)
10   [William Adamson, Joseph Algar, William Ashman, John Atlay,
John Beanland, James Bogie, Charles Bond, Charles Boone, Samuel
Botts, William Church, Adam Clarke, John Crosby, Simon Day,
Samuel Edwards, William Eells, Thomas Ellis, Rob. Empringham,
George Gibbon, Philip Hardcastle, Jonathan Hern, Samuel
15   Hodgson, George Holder, William Holmes, William Homer, Robert
Howard, John Ingham, Andrew Inglis, Robert Johnson, Thomas
Johnson, John King, Thomas Lee, Matthew Lumb, Peter Mill,
Michael Moorhouse, John Poole, Thomas Shaw, George Snowden,
Robert Swan, Joseph Thompson, George Wadsworth.
20   (On p. 27 the list is continued with the addition of Fletcher's
name and with a further eighty-three names in three columns. Many
of them are British, that of Walter Griffith appearing twice. The
remainder are mostly Americans, first of the Elders, then of the
Helpers, listed in the order of their stations.)
25   [John Fletcher,[71] Thomas Warrick, James Watson, John Watson,
Sen., John Watson, Jun., John Wittam, Thomas Wride, George
Whitfield, John Pritchard, Walter Griffith, John Clark, Hugh
Moore, Beverly Allen, John Tunnell, Henry Willis, Reuben Ellis,
Richard Ivy, Lemuel Green, Michael Ellis, Thomas Curtis, Joseph
30   Cromwell, Samuel Dudley, Jesse Lee, John Cooper, Adam Cloud,
James Jordan, Daniel Jackson, Matthias Joyce, Nelson Reed, Enoch

---

[71] Fletcher was consulted before the preparation of the Deed of Declaration in
1784, but his name was not included among the other clergy in the Legal
Hundred—the two Wesleys, Coke, and Creighton. JW now had little hope that
Fletcher would leave his parish, but JW wished to list him among the preachers in
connexion with the Methodist Conference. This was implemented by an after-
thought in adding his name to the preachers' stations in 1785 as 'Assistant' for the
Chester Circuit. Fletcher died shortly after the 1785 Conference. For Fletcher's
plan for a 'Methodist Church of England', see *Minutes* (1775), n. 551; and for a
biographical note, *Minutes* (1781), *Q.* 7 (1), n. 873. In the latter year he was notionally stationed in London.

Matson, James O'Kelly, Thomas Foster, Ignatius Pigman, Caleb
Boyer, William Gill, Thomas Chew, John Hagerty, Freeborn
Garrettson, James Cromwell, John Baxter, Jeremiah Lambert,
Woolman Hickson, Richard Swift, John Baldwin, Philip Bruce, John
Paup, William Ringold, George Moore, William Thomas, Joseph 5
Wyatt, Henry Ogburn, Ira Ellis, Robert Cloud, William McCornock,
Thomas Davis, John Mealy, Thomas Humphries, Edward Morris,
Henry Jones, James Hinton, William Partridge, Thomas Anderson,
John Dickins, William Glendenning, John Easter, Edward
Dromgoole, James Haw, John Major, William Damaron, Thomas 10
Bowen, James Kenny, Peter Moriarty, John Fidler, Joseph Everett,
Jonathan Forrest, Thomas Haskins, Philip Cox, William Cannan,
James White, William Phoebus, John McClaskey, Walter Griffith,
Lawrence Kane, Thomas Halliday.]

Minutes 15

Q. 1. What preachers are *admitted* this year?
A. William Adamson.[72]—*Ireland*,[73] Walter Griffith, John
    Clarke, Hugh Moore—*America*, Jesse Lee, James Hinton,
    Thomas Anderson, Thomas Bumphries, Richard Swift,
    William Damaron, Thomas Bowen, William Phoebus,[74] 20
    William Ringold, Lemuel Green.
Q. 2. Who remain on trial?
A. Alexander Suter, Thomas Bartholomew, Joseph Jerom,
    Edward Burbeck, John Ogylvie, Melville Home, William
    Palmer, Charles Kyte, Benjamin Pearce,[75] Timothy 25
    Crowther, Jonathan Crowther, John McKersey, William
    Butterfield, Richard Cornish.—*Ireland*, James Wilson,
    James McDonald, William Hammet,—*America*, David

---

[72] Although Adamson was admitted into full connexion and stationed in York,
his name is not included in CJ here, but appears among those already in full
connexion.

[73] CJ omits 'Ireland'.

[74] Orig., 'Phebus', as sometimes elsewhere.

[75] Orig., 'Pearse', as in 1786, and once in 1787; his name is incorrectly given in
stations (18) as 'Robert Pearse', 'Benjamin' in CJ.

Jefferson, Isaac Smith, John Smith, Elijah Ellis, John
Robertson, William Jessop, James Riggin, Wilson Lee,
Simon Pile,[76] Thomas Jackson, Samuel Breeze, Matthew
Greentree, Thomas Ware, James Thomas.

5   *Q*. 3. Who are admitted on trial?

A. John Phillips, Thomas Jones, James Ridall,[77] John
Gaulter,[78] Peter Walker, William Fish,[79] John Smith,
Charles Bland, John Ramshaw, William Hunter, Jun.,
William Blagborne,[80] Robert Gamble,[81] Alexander

10   Kilham, Joseph Entwisle, Jun., John Robotham,[82] William
Thoresby,[83]—*Ireland*, John Dinnen, Robert Lindsay,
Andrew Coleman, Thomas Verner,—*America*, Mark
Whitaker, Henry Bingham, George Noseworthy, Stephen
Johnson, Thomas Williamson, John Freeman, Michael

15   Gilbert, Joshua Hartley, Jeremiah Maston, Hope Hull,
Ezekiel Cooper, Hezekiah Bonham,[84] Stephen Dickins,[85]
Levin Ross, Shores Bright, Eleazor Hatheway,
Robert Sparks, William Steens, John Street, Garret
Thompson, Robert Ayres, Jacob Brush, Moses Hurley,

20   Robert Cann.[86]

Q. 4. Who desist from travelling [of those who are in connexion with the conference]?

[76] In the American *Minutes* (1784–91), his name is spelled 'Pyle' only in 1789.

[77] Orig.,'Ridel', as also in 1786 (1). His name appeared in various forms: 'Ridell', 1786 (1), 1789 (3), 1791; 'Ridale', 1788, 1789 (1); 'Riding', 1791. At his death in 1822 he spelled it 'Ridall'.

[78] Orig., 'Gwaltier'; his name was spelled 'Gualtier' in 1785 (1), 1786 (1), 1788 (2), 1789 (2), 1790 (2), and 1791 (1). The anglicized form 'Gaulter' (misspelled as 'Gualter' in 1787) first appeared in 1789 and continued until his death in 1839, aged 74.

[79] Orig., 'Fisher' (1 of 2).

[80] Orig., 'Blagborn' (1 of 2); in 1789, 'Blackburne' (1 of 4).

[81] Here, as in stations, the name is spelled 'Gambold'.

[82] Orig., 'Roebotham' (1 of 2).

[83] Orig., 'Thirsby' (also in CJ); 1789, 'Theorsbee' (1 of 4).

[84] Orig., 'Bonum'. Bonham was a former Baptist who joined Strawbridge's first Society at Sam's Creek, Maryland, to whom Asbury gave a licence to exhort on Nov. 22, 1772.

[85] In 1786 his name was spelled 'Dicken' and 'Dickens'; in 1787 (when he was both accepted into full connexion and disappeared), 'Deakins'.

[86] Orig., 'Can' (and once also in 1786).

A. Thomas Cooper, William Moore,[87] John Acutt, Nathanael Ward, John Hampson, Sen. and Jun.,[88] John Fenwick,[89] James Perfect.[90]

Q. 5. Who have *died* this year?

A. Thomas Mitchell, an old soldier of Jesus Christ.   5

Q. 6. Are there any objections to any of our preachers?

A. They were examined one by one.

Q. 7. How are the preachers stationed this year?

A. As follows:

(1) *London*, John Wesley, Charles Wesley, Thomas Coke,   10
James Creighton, Henry Moore, Benjamin Rhodes,
George Whitfield; Thomas Rankin and John Atlay,
supernumeraries.

(2) *Sussex*, William Boothby, J. Phillips.

(3) *Kent*, George Shadford, W. Homer, Zachariah   15
Yewdall.

(4) *Colchester*, Joseph Algar, Thomas Shaw.

(5) *Norwich*, Thomas Wride,[91] T. Jones, J. McKersey.

(6) *Yarmouth*, Samuel Hodgson, Geo. Button.

(7) *Lynn*, William Palmer, Charles Bland.   20

(8) *Bedfordshire*, William Ashman, John Ingham, John
Watson, Jun., supernumerary.

---

[87] CJ omits Moore from this list, but gives his name in answer to *Q.* 8: 'Is any member of the conference laid aside because he desists from travelling?' Against JW's wishes, Cooper married a woman whose mother built him a chapel in Manningtree, Essex; he also formed his own Society in Harwich, Essex. Unhappy away from the Methodists, however, he was reinstated in 1787, though not as a member of the Legal Hundred. CJ adds *Q.* 9: 'Who is elected a member of the conference in his stead?' and names Thomas Merrick.

[88] John Hampson, Sen. (d. 1795), was raised as a Unitarian at Chowbent, Lancashire. He became an itinerant by 1751, as did his son John Hampson, Jun. (1753–1819) from 1777. Both men were offended at being omitted from the Legal Hundred in the Deed of Declaration and left Methodism. The father became a Dissenting minister and schoolmaster near Tunbridge Wells. The son entered St. Edmund Hall, Oxford, and became curate and then rector of St. John's, Sunderland. He published the controversial but illuminating *Memoirs of the late Rev. John Wesley*, 3 vols. (Sunderland, 1791). See *Journal & Diaries* 20:451–52 and n. 7, in this edn., for refs.

[89] CJ adds *Q.* 6: 'Is any member of the conference expelled?' and answers: 'John Fenwick, for the sin of drunkenness'. *Q.* 7 adds Thomas Lee in his stead.

[90] CJ adds *Q.* 10: 'Is any preacher in full connexion with the conference expelled?' and answers: 'James Perfect, for lewdness, pride and want of sense.'

[91] CJ here adds Button, which is then struck through; this was possibly an error in transcription, for he was stationed in the following circuit, Yarmouth.

(9) *Northampton*, Joseph Harper, Jon. Parkin.

(10) *Oxfordshire*, Jonathan Coussins, Barnaby[92] Thomas.

(11) *Gloucester*, James Hall, William Church, John Robotham.

(12) *Sarum*, John Moon, John Wittam, Robert Empringham.

(13) *Bradford*, Christopher Watkins, Simon Day, Charles Kyte, Timothy Crowther.

(14) *Bristol*, Samuel Bradburn, John Murlin, Jeremiah Brettel.

(15) *Taunton*, John Pritchard, John Poole.[93]

(16) *Devon*, George Wadsworth, Michael Moorhouse.

(17) *Plymouth*, John Mason, Adam Clarke, J. King.[94]

(18) *St. Austell*,[95] William Myles, Richard Cornish, Benjamin Pearce.

(19) *Redruth*, Francis Wrigley, Charles Bond, Joseph Jerom.

(20) *St. Ives*, William Green, Peter Walker, Robert Gamble.

(21) *Pembroke*, Joshua Keighley, Joseph Cole, William Hoskins.

(22) *Glamorgan*, William Saunders, W. Holmes.[96]

(23) *Brecon*, William Warrener, J. Cricket.

(24) *Birmingham*, Andrew Blair, George Story, Robert Costerdine; John Brettel, supernumerary.

(25) *Burslem*, Thomas Warrick, S. Edwards.

(26) *Macclesfield*, Joseph Bradford, T. Dixon.

(27) *Manchester*, William Thompson, Thomas Lee, William Eells; John Furz, supernumerary.

(28) *Chester*, John Fletcher,[97] Richard Rodda, Melville Horne, James Wray.

---

[92] This colloquial form is also used in 1769, 1772; in CJ it appears as 'Barnabas'.

[93] In CJ, 'John Pool, James Ridel', with the latter struck through and 'John Pritchard' inserted before Poole. Ridall was stationed in No. 53, Yarm.

[94] In CJ, John King replaces William Thoresby ('Thirsby'), who received no station.

[95] Here, as throughout JW's lifetime, the spelling was 'St. Austle'.

[96] In CJ, the names are given in reverse order, with '2' and '1' added above them, confirming the assumption that in general the first named (in this case Saunders) was to be regarded as JW's 'Assistant', or man in charge of the circuit.

[97] CJ here inserts, above the line, 'John Fletcher'.

(29) *Liverpool*, Jonathan Hern, William Percival, George Gibbon.

(30) *Bolton*, Christopher Hopper, Jasper Robinson.

(31) *Colne*,[98] Charles Atmore, Edward Jackson, Robert Howard.   5

(32) *Leicester*, John Easton, Thomas Corbet, Joseph Pescod.

(33) *Nottingham*, Charles Boone, James Bogie.

(34) *Derby*, Thomas Tattershall, J. Booth.

(35) *Sheffield*, Joseph Benson, Robert Hopkins, John Barber.   10

(36) *Grimsby*, William Dufton, G. Holder, Lancelot Harrison, Alexander Kilham.

(37) *Gainsborough*, Thomas Carlill, Robert Scot, Samuel Botts.

(38) *Epworth*, Thomas Longley, James Watson, W.   15
Butterfield.[99]

(39) *Leeds*, Thomas Taylor, Thomas Rutherford, Duncan Wright.

(40) *Birstall*, John Broadbent, J. Goodwin.

(41) *Dewsbury*, Robert Roberts, Tho. Tennant.   20

(42) *Huddersfield*, Isaac Brown, Wm. Hunter, Jun.

(43) *Halifax*, John Allen, Thomas Johnson.

(44) *Bradford*, John Valton, supernumerary, John Shaw, Henry Foster.

(45) *Keighley*, Parson Greenwood, Joseph Entwisle.   25

(46) *Whitehaven*, Alex Suter, Jos. Thompson.

(47) *Isle of Man*, James Thom, John Ogylvie, John Gaulter, John Smith.

(48) *York*, Alex. Mather, Jer. Robertshaw, William Adamson.

(49) *Hull*, Peter Mill, Wm. Thom, Wm. Fish.   30

(50) *Scarborough*, Wm. Collins, Samuel Bardsley, Jonathan Crowther.[100]

(51) *Whitby*, John Peacock, John Ramshaw.[101]

---

[98] In CJ, the list first read, 'Thomas Tattershall, Edward Jackson, Jonathan Crowther'. Tattershall and Crowther were struck through, and replaced by Atmore and Howard. For Tattershall and Crowther, see circuits 34 and 13. (In the latter, 'Bradford', Crowther was added as an extra, after a period.)

[99] In CJ, Butterfield was inserted to replace John Ramshaw, who was stationed at Whitby, No. 51.

[100] Crowther ('Crowder') replaced Robert Howard in CJ.

[101] Ramshaw replaced John Smith.

(52) *Thirsk*, Philip Hardcastle, Tho. Brisco, J. Crosby.[102]

(53) *Yarm*, Robert Swan, James Ridall.[103]

(54) *The Dales*, Thomas Ellis, George Mowat, Edward Burbeck.

(55) *Sunderland*, James Wood, John Beanland.

(56) *Newcastle*, George Snowden, William Simpson, Andrew Inglis.

(57) *Berwick*, Wm. Hunter, Wm. Blagborne.

(58) *Edinburgh*, John Pawson, Rob. Johnson.

(59) *Dundee*, Tho. Hanty, Duncan McAllum.

(60) *Aberdeen*, J. Taylor, R. Watkinson. (61) *Inverness*, T. Bartholomew, M. Lumb ⎱ These two are to change twice a quarter with Brother Bartholomew and Lumb.[104]

(62) *Dublin*, James Rogers, Christ. Peacock.

(63) *Waterford*, James Jordan, Wm. McCornock, Walter Griffith.

(64) *Cork*, Daniel Jackson, Geo. Brown, John Dinnen.

(65) *Limerick*, Thomas Davis, Law. Kane.

(66) *Castlebar*, John Leech, J. Watson, Sen.

(67) *Athlone*, Matthias Joyce, John Mealy, John Wilson, Thomas Halliday, supernumerary.

(68) *Sligo*, George Dice, And. Coleman.

(69) *Ballyconnell*, Rob. Bridge, Gustavus Armstrong, Thomas Verner.

(70) *Clones*, Nehemiah Price, John Clarke, James Rennick.

(71) *Enniskillen*, Thomas Barber, Tho. Hetherington, Samuel Mitchell.

(72) *Charlemont*, John Crook, John Miller, J. McDonald.

(73) *Lisleen*, Jos. Armstrong, Rich. Cundy.

(74) *Londonderry*, Jon. Brown, Wm. West, Wm. Hammet.

(75) *Belfast*, Rob. Armstrong, R. Lindsay.

(76) *Lisburn*, John Kerr, Hugh Moore, John Price.

---

[102] In CJ, Crosby ('Crosbie') replaced Matthew Lumb.

[103] In CJ, Ridall ('Ridel') replaced John King.

[104] In CJ, Lumb replaced John Crosby; CJ omits the note about the interchange of preachers between Aberdeen and Inverness Circuits.

A M E R I C A

Superintendents. Tho. Coke, Francis Asbury.

	Elders	
(77) *Georgia,*	B[everly] Allen	5
(78) *Charleston,* (79) *George Town,* Wool[man] Hickson	J[ohn] Tunnell	
(80) *Broad River,* (81) *Yadkin,*[105] H. Gingham, Tho. Williamson (82) *Holstein,* Rich. Swift, M. Gilbert	H[enry] Willis	10 15
(83) *Wilmington,* John Baldwin (84) *New River,* Philip Bruce (85) *Tar River,* Tho. Humphries, Isaac Smith (86) *Roanoke,*[107] Edward Morris, M. Whitaker (87) *New Hope,* Henry Jones	R[euben] Ellis[106]	20 25

[105] Orig., 'Yeadkin'.

[106] The American *Minutes* do not always correspond in their records with what Thomas Coke brought over for JW's British *Minutes*, and must remain their own primary authority. In the American *Minutes*, for instance, the circuits are not numbered, and Guilford is shown under the oversight of Reuben Ellis as elder, while in the British *Minutes* it is shown under that of Richard Ivy and is numbered 90. Similarly the American 'Guilford' appears in Britain as 'Guildford', and the American 'Ivy' as 'Ivey'. In general our spellings here follow a system of standard American spellings based on the massive files prepared by Rev. Edwin Schell for the United Methodist Historical Society of the Baltimore Conference, compiled over many years, and known as 'Ministerial Records'. We are very grateful to Mr. Schell for his kindness in making these records available to us. To note all the many such variations in stationing and variant spellings would be far too complex for our purposes, and therefore in general they are regretfully ignored.

[107] Orig., 'Roan-Oak', as regularly in JW's day.

(88) *Caswell,*
Elijah Ellis
(89) *Salisbury,*
Joshua Hartley,
5   H. Hull   R[ichard] Ivy[108]
(90) *Guilford,*[109]
J. Smith,
Stephen Johnson
(91) *Halifax,*
10   James Hinton,
       G. Noseworthy

(92) *Camden,*[110]
William Partridge,
15   William Steens
(93) *Portsmouth,*
T. Anderson,   N[elson] Reed
John Street
(94) *Williamsburg,*[111]
20   Jer. Maston

(95) *Bertie,*[112]
John Dickins,
D. Jefferson
25   (96) *Sussex,*
W. Glendenning,[113]
J. Easter   Enoch Matson[114]
(97) *Brunswick,*
Edw. Dromgoole,[115]
30   James Haw
(98) *Mecklenburg,*[116]
John Major,
John Robertson

---

[108] Orig., 'Ivey'; he always appears in the American *Minutes* as 'Ivy'.
[109] Orig., 'Guildford'.
[110] Orig., 'Cambden'.
[111] Orig., 'Williamsburgh'.
[112] Orig., 'Bartie'.
[113] Orig., 'Glendinning', as often.
[114] Orig., 'Mattson'; normally 'Matson' in American *Minutes*.
[115] 'Drumgoole' as often, in CJ and American *Minutes*.
[116] Orig., 'Mecklenburgh'.

(99) *Amelia*,
William Damaron,
John Freeman
(100) *Bedford*,
T. Bowen,   5
J. Kenny   James O'Kelly
(101) *Orange*,
T. Jackson,
H. Bonum,
S. Dickins   10
(102) *Hanover*,

(103) *Redstone*,
Peter Moriarty,   15
J. Fidler, W. Lee
(104) *Alleghany*,[117]
L. Green, J. Paup,
W. Jessop   T[homas] Foster
(105) *Berkley*,[118]   20
Eleazor Hatheway
(106) *Fairfax*,
Simon Pyle

                                                             25
(107) *Lancaster*,
J. Everett, L. Ross
(108) *St. Mary's*   I[gnatius] Pigman
(109) *Calvert*,
Michael Ellis   30

(110) *Frederick*,
William Ringold,
S. Breeze   R[ichard] Whatcoat   35
(111) *Baltimore*,
Jon. Forrest,
F. Poythress

---

[117] Orig., 'Allegany'.
[118] Orig., 'Berclay'.

(112) *Kent,*
Thomas Curtis,
G. Moore
(113) *Talbot,*
5   Thomas Haskins,
 J. Cromwell   C[aleb] Boyer
(114) *Dorset,*
W. Thomas,
G. Thompson
10   (115) *Northampton,*
Philip Cox,
M. Hurley

(116) *Dover,*
15   Samuel Dudley,
J. Wyatt
(117) *Caroline,*
William Cannon,
J. Lee, S. Bright   W[illiam] Gill
20   (118) *Somerset,*
Henry Ogburn
(119) *Annamessex,*
James White, R. Cann

25   (120) *Little York,*
John Cooper
(121) *Philadelphia,*
Ira Ellis,
James Thomas,   T[homas] Vasey
30   Robert Ayres
(122) *Juniata,*
James Riggin

(123) *West Jersey,*
35   Wm. Phoebus,
T. Ware, R. Sparks
(124) *East Jersey,*
Adam Cloud,
M. Greentree   T[homas] Chew
40   (125) *Trenton,* Rob.
Cloud, John McClaskey,
J. Brush

(126) *New York*		
(127) *Long Island*,	}	J[ohn] Hagerty[119]
Ezekiel Cooper		

(128) *Nova Scotia*		F[reeborn] Garrettson	5
(129) *Newfoundland*,	}		
John McGeary		James Cromwell	

		J[ohn] Baxter	
(130) *Antigua*	}		10
		Jer[emiah] Lambert	

Q. 8. How many wives are to be provided for?
A. Sixty-nine.
Q. 9. How many of these are to be provided for by the   15
  circuits?
A. Fifty-two: namely,

(1) London	S. Moore, Boothby.[120]	
(2) Gloucestershire	S. Church.	
(3) Bradford	S. Empringham.[121]	20
(4) Bristol	S. Bradburn, Moon,[122] Day.[123]	
(5) Devonshire and		
Taunton	S. Moorhouse.	
(6) St. Austell	S. Poole.[124]	
(7) Redruth	S. Story.[125]	25
(8) St. Ives	S. Green.	
(9) Birmingham	S. Blair.	
(10) Burslem	S. Warrick.	
(11) Macclesfield	S. Bradford.	
(12) Manchester	S. Goodwin,[126] Lee, Corbet.[127]	30
(13) Chester	S. Rodda.	
(14) Liverpool	S. Hern.	

---

[119] Orig., 'Haggerty'.
[120] William Boothby was stationed in Sussex.
[121] Robert Empringham was stationed in Sarum.
[122] John Moon also was stationed in Sarum.
[123] Simon Day was stationed in Bradford.
[124] John Poole was stationed in Taunton.
[125] George Story was stationed in Birmingham.
[126] John Goodwin was stationed in Birstall.
[127] Thomas Corbet was stationed in Leicester.

5	(15) Bolton	S. Hopper.
	(16) Colne	S. Swan.[128]
	(17) Leicester	S. Easton.
	(18) Nottingham	S. Boone.
	(19) Sheffield	S. Peacock,[129] Mowat.[130]
	(20) Grimsby	S. Jam[es] Watson.[131]
	(21) Horncastle[132]	S. Inglis.[133]
	(22) Gainsborough	S. Scot, Thom.[134]
	(23) Epworth	S. Longley.
10	(24) Leeds	S. Taylor, Rutherford, Wright.
	(25) Birstall	S. Jos. Thompson.[135]
	(26) Dewsbury	S. Roberts.
	(27) Huddersfield	S. Is. Brown.
	(28) Bradford	S. Shaw.
15	(29) Halifax	S. Robertshaw.[136]
	(30) Keighley	S. Greenwood.
	(31) York	S. Mather.
	(32) Hull	S. Mill.[137]
	(33) Scarborough	S. Collins.
20	(34) Thirsk	S. Brisco.
	(35) Yarm	S. Simpson.[138]
	(36) [The] Dales	S. Ellis.
	(37) Sunderland	S. Wood, Beanland.
	(38) Newcastle	S. Snowden.
25	(39) Ireland.	S. Brown, Dinnen, Kane, Watson.[139]

[128] Robert Swan was stationed in Yarm.

[129] John Peacock was stationed in Whitby.

[130] George Mowat was stationed in The Dales.

[131] James Watson, Jun., was stationed in Epworth.

[132] Horncastle was separated from Grimsby Circuit in 1786 for the purpose of stationing, but the division was clearly in mind even in 1785.

[133] Andrew Inglis was stationed in Newcastle.

[134] William Thom was stationed in Hull.

[135] Joseph Thompson was stationed in Whitehaven.

[136] Jeremiah Robertshaw was stationed in York.

[137] Orig., 'Mills'; Peter Mill, then stationed in Hull, was referred to as 'Mills' in 1783 and this year.

[138] William Simpson was stationed in Newcastle.

[139] These four Irish preachers were stationed thus: George Brown and John Dinnen in Cork, Lawrence Kane in Limerick, and James Watson, Sen., in Castlebar.

Q. 10. How are the other seventeen to be provided for?
A. Eight out of the yearly collection, viz. S. Harper,
Coussins, Watkinson, Joyce, Bridge, Crook, Condy,
Lindsay.[140] And nine out of the Preachers' Fund, viz.
S. Wride, McAllum, Myles, Butterfield, Price, West,   5
Rennick, Booth, (Tho.) Shaw,[141] £6.
Q. 11. What numbers are in the societies?[142]
A. As follows:

London	2,437[143]	
Sussex	240	10
Kent	322	
Colchester	209	
Norwich	617	
Lynn	202	
Bedford	336	15
Huddersfield	788	
Bradford	1,088	
Halifax	974	
Keighley	1,080	
Colne	1,240	20
Whitehaven	232	
Isle of Man	2,422	
Northampton	331	
Oxfordshire	500	
Gloucester	584	25
Sarum	380	
Bradford	1,156	
Bristol	1,531	

[140] Joseph Harper was in Northampton, Jonathan Coussins in Oxfordshire, Richard Watkinson in Aberdeen and Inverness, Matthias Joyce in Athlone, Robert Bridge in Ballyconnell, John Crook in Charlemont, Richard Condy ('Cundy') in Lisleen, and Robert Lindsay in Belfast.

[141] Thomas Wride was in Norwich, Duncan McAllum in Dundee, William Myles in St. Austell, William Butterfield in Epworth, John Price in Lisburn, William West in Londonderry, James Rennick in Clones, John Booth in Derby, and Thomas Shaw in Colchester.

[142] The feature of indicating the circuits with increases is dropped from this year onwards, perhaps because the inclusion of American statistics would make this almost impossible as well as extremely cumbersome.

[143] Again (as in 1784) there is a strange disparity in the ordering of the circuits, apparently linked with the careless copying of columns of figures broken between two pages.

	Taunton	614
	Tiverton	
	Plymouth	282
5	Cornwall, East	757
	West	2,578
	Glamorgan	197
	Brecon	133
	Birmingham	900
10	Burslem	715
	Macclesfield	912
	Manchester	2,064
	Chester	670
	Liverpool	587
15	Leicestershire	710
	Nottingham	596
	Derby	324
	Sheffield	1,300
	Grimsby	959
20	Gainsborough	682
	Epworth	691
	Leeds	2,500
	Birstall	2,001
	York	872
25	Hull	884
	Scarborough	651
	Thirsk	648
	Yarm	506
	Whitby	530
30	The Dales	805
	Sunderland	1,050
	Newcastle	1,020
	Berwick	73
	Edinburgh	134
35	Dundee	110
	Aberdeen	290
	Dublin	700
	Waterford	300
	Cork	720
40	Limerick	250
	Castlebar	293

Athlone	400	
Sligo	311	
Ballyconnell	698	
Clones	710	
Enniskillen	651	5
Charlemont	943	
Lisleen	574	
Londonderry	444	
Belfast	303	
Lisburn	520	10

A M E R I C A[144]

Charleston	13	} South	
Broad River	110	Carolina	
Roanoke	468		15
Tar River	425		
New River	588		
Wilmington	55		
New Hope	150		
Caswell	191	North Carolina	20
Salisbury	457		
P[ee] D[ee]	20		
Yadkin	338		
Guilford	413		
Bertie	575[145]		25
Halifax	371		
Holstein	173		
Orange, { Whites	383		30
Orange, { Blacks	40		
Bedford	321		
Mecklenburg	372		

[144] N.B. No membership figures are available in the American *Minutes* for 1785, and these differ from those for 1784.

[145] Orig., '57*b*'; CJ, '575'.

	Brunswick	Whites	408	
		Blacks	47	
	Amelia		265	
5	Sussex		524	
	Nansemond	Whites	202	
		Blacks		
	Portsmouth		180	Virginia
10	Camden		334	
	Williamsburg	Whites	180	
		Blacks	5	
	Hanover		20	
15	Redstone		115	
	Alleghany	Whites	267	
		Blacks	7	
	Berkley	Whites	143	
20		Blacks	11	
	Fairfax	Whites	231	
		Blacks	14	
25	Northampton	Whites	133	
		Blacks	2	
30	Calvert	Whites	175	
		Blacks	100	
	Frederick	Whites	500	
		Blacks	37	
35	Baltimore	Whites	635	
		Blacks	131	

Kent	Whites	505		
	Blacks	328	Maryland	
Talbot	Whites	648		5
	Blacks	286		
Dorset	Whites	600		
	Blacks	135		
Somerset	Whites	260		10
	Blacks	40		
Annamessex		258		
Caroline		800		
				15
Dover	Whites	740	Delaware	
	Blacks	169		
Little York	Whites	100		20
	Blacks	1		
Juniata		10	Pennsylvania	
Philadelphia	Whites	400		25
	Blacks	11		
West Jersey	Whites	473		
	Blacks	8		30
Trenton	Whites	278	New Jersey	
	Blacks	7		
East Jersey	Whites	258		35
	Blacks	9		

New York	Whites	94	
	Blacks	12	New York
Long Island		46	
Nova Scotia		300	
Antigua	Whites	8	
	Blacks	1,100	
In all		70,466[146]	

Q. 12. What is the Kingswood collection?
A. £649. 16*s.* 9*d.*
Q. 13. What children are admitted this year?
A. John Rodda and William Thom.
N.B. We will receive none for the time to come under nine
years old.
Q. 14. What can we allow the daughters of the preachers?
A. Mary Rodda, £6; the second year, Ann Watkinson, and
Ann Roberts.
N.B. We allow nothing to a girl under ten years old.
Q. 15. What is contributed to the Preachers' Fund?
A. £471. 12. 1.
Q. 16. What is allowed out of it?

A. To Thomas Westell	£30	0	0
William Whitaker	20	0	0
James Christie	10	0	0
John Bredin	12	0	0
Thomas Halliday	12	0	0
Matthew Lowes	5	15	6
Ann Morgan	12	0	0
Jane Wilkinson	20	0	0
Lucia Bourke	10	0	0
Elizabeth Standring	12	0	0
Mary Penington	10	0	0
Alice Brammah	12	0	0
Elizabeth Shorter	10	0	0
Catherine Garnet	12	0	0
Elizabeth Dillon	5	0	0
Tabitha Norris	5	0	0
Margaret Payne	12	0	0

[146] Orig., '71,277'.

Sarah Barry	20	0	0
Sarah Naylor	10	0	0
Elizabeth Oldham	12	0	0
Sarah Rowell	6	0	0
Sarah Hosmer	10	0	0
Sarah Jaco	5	5	0
Nine Wives	102	0	0
In all	[£] 423	0	6
	12[147]		
	[£] 411	0	6

Q. 17. What is contributed for the yearly expenses?
A. £899. 14*s.* 4*d.*
Q. 18. How was this expended?

A. Arrears of last year	£75	8	0
Law	65	8	3
Towards the contingencies of the current year	100	0	0
Preachers' necessities[148]	562	18	1
Eight Wives	96	0	0
In all	[£]899	14	4

Q. 19. What houses are to be built this year?[149]
A. One at Winchelsea, Sheerness, Margate,

[147] The actual sum of the amounts is £399. 0. 6, not £423. 0. 6, as given in CJ. The sum of £411. 0. 6, given in *Minutes*, is apparently derived from the CJ total, less £12 for some undisclosed purpose.

[148] CJ, 'Present necessities', surely an error, though corrected in the printed *Minutes*.

[149] JW was greatly concerned from the outset about the building of his preaching-houses, and especially about safeguarding their legal status. He also sought to regulate the numbers built and the debts incurred as a result. Related themes were constantly discussed at the annual Conference. In order to exercise careful control, from 1776 a question had been added to the Conference agenda: 'What houses are to be built this year?' (*Q.* 21 and n. 648). The number agreed had ranged from 2 to 10, but in 1783 a halt was made to granting permission for any new buildings, and this was continued during the epochal year of 1784. In 1785 no fewer than 25 were allowed, and the number continued high: 17 in 1786, 22 in 1787, and 21 in 1788. The misappropriation by the trustees of the Dewsbury house caused another halt, except for the replacement of that building, and a determined effort to secure all Methodist buildings upon the Methodist standard trust deed template ('Model Deed'). In 1813, William Myles published a list of 1,540 Methodist preaching-houses, with the dates of their building, prepared on his own initiative but with the assistance of his colleagues. *Chronological History*, 427–45. Although this list is slightly incomplete and minimally incorrect in some details, it underlines the proliferation of these buildings during the last decade of JW's life and the following twenty years.

Winchester, Ditcheat,[150] Wellington,[151]
Camelford, Birmingham, Chesterton, Bullock
Smithy,[152] Failsworth, Colne, Haslingden,[153]
Bramley, Gainsborough, Hatfield, Holbeck,[154]
5   Wichfield,[155] Carlisle, Easingwold,[156] Selty, Market
Weighton,[157] Redcar, South Shields, North Biddick.
Q. 20. What is the state of our societies in North America?
A. It may best appear from the following letter.[158]

Bristol, Sept. 10, 1784
10   To Dr. Coke, Mr. Asbury, and our Brethren in North America.

1. By a very uncommon train of Providences many of the
provinces of North America are totally disjoined from their mother
country, and erected into independent States. The English government has no authority over them, either civil or ecclesiastical, any
15   more than over the states of Holland. A civil authority is exercised
over them, partly by the Congress, partly by the Provincial
Assemblies. But no one either exercises or claims any ecclesiastical
authority at all. In this peculiar situation some thousands of the
inhabitants of these States desire my advice; and in compliance with
20   their desire, I have drawn up a little sketch.

2. Lord King's account of the primitive church convinced me
many years ago that Bishops and Presbyters are the same Order, and
consequently have the same right to ordain. For many years I have
been importuned from time to time to exercise this right, by ordain-
25   ing part of our travelling preachers. I have still refused, not only for
peace' sake; but because I was determined as little as possible to violate the established order of the national Church to which I belonged.

[150] Orig., 'Dutchitt'.

[151] Orig., 'Wallington'.

[152] A village on the outskirts of Stockport.

[153] Orig., 'Haslington'. [154] Orig., 'Holdbeck'.

[155] Cf. John Valton's autobiography, in Jackson, *Early Methodist Preachers*, 6:118,
for Oct. 1785: 'In opening the new chapel at Wichfield, halfway between Bradford
and Halifax, we had a very serious alarm by the breaking of an old bench.' Myles
gives 'Witchfield, 1794'. Later known as Shelf.

[156] Orig., 'Easingwood'.

[157] Orig., 'Market-Weeton'.

[158] JW's footnote: 'If anyone is minded to dispute concerning diocesan episcopacy, he may dispute. But I have better work.' (Neither the question nor the answering letter appears in CJ.)

3. But the case is widely different between England and North America. Here there are bishops who have a legal jurisdiction. In America there are none, neither any parish ministers. So that for some hundred miles together there is none either to baptize or to administer the Lord's Supper. Here therefore my scruples are at an 5 end; and I conceive myself at full liberty, as I violate no order and invade no man's right by appointing and sending labourers into the harvest.

4. I have accordingly appointed Dr. Coke and Mr. Francis Asbury to be joint *Superintendents* over our brethren in North America: as 10 also Richard Whatcoat and Thomas Vasey,[159] to act as *Elders* among them, by baptizing and administering the Lord's Supper. And I have prepared a liturgy little differing from that of the Church of England[160] (I think, the best constituted national Church in the world), which I advise all the travelling preachers to use, on the 15 Lord's Day, in all the congregations, reading the Litany only on Wednesdays and Fridays, and praying extempore on all other days.[161] I also advise the Elders to administer the Supper of the Lord on every Lord's Day.

5. If anyone will point out a more rational and scriptural way of 20 feeding and guiding those poor sheep in the wilderness, I will gladly embrace it. At present I cannot see any better method than that I have taken.

6. It has indeed been proposed, to desire the English bishops to ordain part of our preachers for America. But to this I object, (1) I 25 desired the Bishop of London to ordain only one, but could not prevail. (2) If they consented, we know the slowness of their proceedings; but the matter admits of no delay. (3) If they would ordain them *now*, they would likewise expect to govern them. And how grievously would this entangle us. (4) As our American brethren are now 30

[159] Whatcoat and Vasey also were sent to perform the important function of assisting Coke in the ordination of Asbury, since the ordinal in the BCP required the assistance of two ordained priests.

[160] On this, see *WHS* 23 (1945): 124–33; 29 (1953): 12–20; 32 (1960): 97v101; J. C. Bowmer, *The Lord's Supper in Early Methodism* (London, 1951), 206–15; Baker, *Wesley and Church*, chap. 14; Rack, *Reasonable Enthusiast*, 509–10.

[161] The BCP requirement of daily reading of Morning and Evening Prayer was observed only in a small number of 18th-century churches. Prayers on Wednesday and Friday and saints' days were more common. The Lord's Supper was commonly celebrated quarterly in villages and monthly in some town churches. A weekly Eucharist was uncommon except in cathedrals and some London churches influenced by the religious societies and among Nonjurors.

totally disentangled both from the state and from the English hierarchy, we dare not entangle them again, either with the one or the
other. They are now at full liberty simply to follow the Scriptures
and the primitive church. And we judge it best that they should
5 stand fast in that liberty wherewith God has so strangely made them
free.

JOHN WESLEY

Q. 21. When and where is our next conference to begin?
10   *A.* At Bristol, the last Tuesday in July 1786.

Whatever preacher has been a year on trial, may subscribe to
the Preachers' Fund.

No power which I ever enjoyed is given up by the Declarative
Deed. No such thing could have been supposed had it not
15   been for that improper and ambiguous word *Life-Estate*.[162]
This also has given the grand occasion of offence to them that
sought occasion.

Let the four quarterly fasts be duly observed, in August,
November, February, and May.[163]

---

[162] The meaning of this complaint seems to have eluded commentators who are
indeed silent about it. The contexts of matters before and after it give no clues, as
they are on different and disparate subjects. 'Life estate' in a secular property context would normally mean that the person granted the property has the use of it
only for his or her lifetime and therefore could not alienate it to anyone else. JW
might then be complaining that some were claiming that he no longer had power
to alter or dispose of Methodist property as he could do before the Deed was
enrolled. However, his main concern was not with control of property as such but
with his 'power', and it may well be that what he had in mind was the ability to
control the proceedings of Conference and the fate of Methodism; and in the light
of the Birstall and Dewsbury cases, the power of stationing preachers, which safe-
guarded connexionalism and would be inherited by the Conference after his death.
As has been seen, he was also very insistent on his right to invite those he chose to
Conference, apparently regardless of the Legal Hundred. His appeal (printed as a
preface to the *Minutes* of 1791)—that the Deed should not be allowed to disadvan-
tage the rest of the brethren—had the implication that it should not define who
attended Conference, which would be left to Conference itself to decide as JW's
corporate successor. It may be that 'the grand occasion of offence' was that some
had supposed that a 'life interest' did in some way limit JW's authority to mere
possession of the chapels. They were then annoyed to find that (at least in his view)
it did not. Whatever the precise applications he had in mind, the main point is clear:
JW believed that he had precisely the same authority in all respects as he had before
the Deed was enrolled. See also introduction, pp. 92–93.

[163] Neither this nor the preceding paragraph is to be found in CJ.

Q. 22. Is it proper to sell any books on the Lord's Day?
A. By no means. Neither to talk of worldly things, more
than is strictly needful.
Q. 23. Is it lawful to employ a hairdresser on Sunday?
A. We are all fully persuaded it is not. 5
Q. 24. Is it right to send our children to a dancing school?
A. It is entirely wrong. Neither do we think it right for any
that keep boarding-schools to admit a dancing-master into
their house.
[The former election of Rob. Carr Brackenbury, Esqr. as a 10
member of the Conference is confirmed.

> John Wesley
> Thomas Coke][164]

London, July 30, 1785. 15
We whose names are underwritten do declare that Mr. Wesley
was desired at the last Bristol conference, without a dissentient voice,
to draw up a Deed which should give a legal specification of the
phrase, 'The Conference of the People called Methodists', and that
the mode of doing it was entirely left to his judgment and discretion. 20
And we do also declare, That we do approve of the *substance* and
design of the Deed which Mr. Wesley has accordingly executed and
enrolled.

> Thomas Coke
> Thomas Hanby 25
> John Pawson
> John Murlin
> Thomas Taylor
> John Broadbent
> George Shadford 30
> Samuel Bradburn
> Francis Wrigley
> Duncan Wright
> William Thompson
> John Valton 35
> Alexander Mather
> Thomas Rankin

---

[164] This sentence was added to CJ in the handwriting of Thomas Coke, and subscribed are the actual signatures of Wesley and Coke. The passage following is not
found in CJ.

Richard Rodda
Thomas Wride
Joseph Cole
Joseph Taylor
5   James Wood
Benjamin Rhodes
Charles Boone
John Barber
Joshua Keighley
10   Joseph Harper
William Collins
Thomas Tennant
William Ashman
Simon Day
15   Thomas Warrick
William Myles
Isaac Brown
Joseph Pescod
John Peacock
20   John Moon
Christopher Watkins
William Green
John Easton
George Whitfield
25   Parson Greenwood

London, July 30, 1785

We whose names are underwritten, but who were not present at
the last Bristol conference, do declare our approbation of the sub-
30   stance and design of the deed which Mr. Wesley has lately executed
and enrolled for the purpose of giving a legal specification of the
phrase, 'The Conference of the People called Methodists'.

James Creighton
Christ. Hopper
35   Jeremiah Brettel
Jonathan Hern
William Boothby
Samuel Hodgson
William Saunders
40   Jonathan Coussins
Thomas Carlill

William Adamson
Thomas Ellis
George Button
Robert Swan
William Warrener   5
William Simpson
James Hall
Joseph Bradford
Thomas Longley
Robert Johnson   10
Samuel Bardsley
Melville Horne
Joseph Agar
Charles Rogers Bond
John Furz   15
Jeremiah Robertshaw
Barnabas Thomas
Jasper Robinson
Henry Moore
John Cricket   20
Henry Foster

Annual *Minutes of some late Conversations*, 1786

Bristol, July 25, 1786[165]

[165] CJ for 1786 occupies pp. 38–47 of the original volume. Here and elsewhere, the alphabetical listings have been reproduced in the original order, though in many instances the spellings themselves have been altered in accordance with the 'standard' spellings adopted and annotated for this edn. of Wesley's *Works*. Occasionally the anomalies in the order in CJ arise from these changes in spelling: thus among those absent, James Wray appears among the Rs, which would be justified by its frequent spelling as 'Ray'; however, only the last of the six names beginning with R (Thomas Rutherford) appears in its true alphabetical position. Similarly in the list of those in full connexion, James O'Kelly consistently appears among the Ks rather than the Os. Another problem is that although names beginning with M^c, Mc, or Mac in this edn. uniformly follow the general rule of being listed alphabetically as if they were spelled 'Mac', CJ instead arranges them by the first letter after their prefix—just as it does in the case of O'Kelly.

JW wrote,

'Tue. 25. Our Conference began. About eighty preachers attended. We met every day at six and nine in the morning, and at two in the afternoon. On Tuesday and Wednesday morning the characters of the preachers were considered, whether already admitted or not. On Thursday in the afternoon, we permitted any of the society to be present and weighed what was said about separating from the church. But we all determined to continue therein, without one dissenting voice. And I doubt not but this determination will stand, at least till I am removed to a better world. On Friday and Saturday, most of our temporal business was settled. Sunday 30, I preached in the room morning and evening, and in the afternoon at Kingswood, where there is rather an increase than a decrease in the work of God. Mon. 31 the Conference met again, and concluded on Tuesday morning. Great had been the expectations of many that we should have warm debates. But by the mercy of God, we had none at all. Everything was transacted with great calmness, and we parted as we met, in peace and love.' (*Journal and Diaries*, 23:410–11 in this edn.)

JW's diary shows that he ordained Joshua Keighley, William Warrener, and William Hammet; and on the next day ordained again. *Journal and Diaries*, 23:567–68 in this edn. As no names are given for the latter occasion, it seems that he ordained the same men on successive days as Deacon and Elder or Presbyter. John S. Simon in *WHS* 9 (1914): 145. About this time Charles Atmore was ordained, and it is just possible that Edward Burbank, who was appointed to the Inverness Circuit with Keighley, was also ordained for Scotland. For the problems this caused, see *Minutes* (1785), n. 70.

John Valton's view of the Conference was more sombre than Wesley's: 'It was (I thought) the most uncomfortable Conference that I have been at. I thought that we were less serious and governable than I had ever observed.' 'Excerpts from John Valton's MS. Journal', *WHS* 8 (Pt. 3, Sept. 1911): 67. This may have been over relations with the Church of England, for JW's *Journal* entry, the letter appended to the *Minutes*, and directions on Church attendance underline the prominence of this issue, as does other evidence. JW wrote to CW on Apr. 1, 1786:

'Eight or ten preachers it is probable (but I have not met with one yet) will say something about leaving the Church before the Conference ends. It is not unlikely many will be driven out of it where there are Calvinist ministers. . . . *They* will ordain no one without my full and free consent. It is not true that they have done it already'. (*Letters* [Telford], 7:326)

Tyerman (*Wesley*, 3:478–79) says this was the last Conference at which Charles Wesley was present. In a letter to the Moravian Benjamin Latrobe, CW states that those of a Dissenter spirit will leave after the Wesleys' deaths: 'An old Baptist minister, forty years ago, told me he looked on the Methodists as a seminary for the Dissenters. . . . The bishops might, if they pleased, save the largest and soundest part of them back into the Church, "perhaps to leaven the whole lump" as Archbishop Secker said to me'. Thomas Jackson, *The Life of the Rev. Charles Wesley, M.A.*, 2 vols. (London: Mason, 1841), 2:402.

Pawson says (Tyerman MSS, 3:61) that this was the last Conference attended by Dr. Whitehead, who was 'wonderfully afraid lest we separate from the Church. Coke at this time thought our public services ought to be held in Church hours in large towns and freely spoke "in a public conference" on this as necessary because nearly all the awakened clergy were Calvinists. On hearing this Charles Wesley

[The Minutes or Journals of the Conference of the people called Methodists, begun in Bristol on Tuesday the 25th day of July, in the year of our Lord 1786, and continued by various adjournments to the 1st day of August following inclusive.

5

[Present
[The Revd. John Wesley, President.
[The Revd. Thomas Coke, Secretary.
(There are fifty-four names in three columns.)
[John] Allen, Charles Atmore, John Barber, Samuel Bardsley,   10

loudly said, "No"—the only word he spoke at this Conference. Mather confirmed what Coke said, "which we all knew to be the case." ' In his MS autobiography ('Some Account', fol. 32) Pawson wrote,

'It was generally expected that something effective would have been done at this Conference respecting our separation from the Church of England, which it was thought by many of the preachers and people also, would be much to the glory of God. But this happy time is yet to come. Mr. Charles Wesley did everything in his power to prevent it, and human policy yet prevails too much amongst us, which ought to have no place in the Church of God. However five of the preachers were ordained and the prayers of the Church were ordered to be read in a good many places, so that we gain a little ground towards that which is exceedingly desired by many, and strongly opposed by others.'

Sutcliffe (MS 'History', 1123) says that as the Scots began to refuse baptism to the Methodists unless they became regular members of the Presbyterian Church, it was necessary to ordain more preachers.

On July 23, 1786, CW wrote to JW that he was too hasty in ordaining and that Lord Mansfield had told him 'ordination is separation'. Frank Baker, *Charles Wesley: As Revealed by His Letters* (London, 1948), 140. Six days later, CW wrote to his wife,

'The Dissenting party made a bold push for a separation, strongly urging my brother to ordain a preacher for a desolate place in Yorkshire. John Atlay made a noble stand against them and fairly conquered them all, with the Doctor (Coke) at their head. Pawson and those of his leaven could have torn him in pieces, believing him all their own and the most zealous Republican. He proved that ordination was separation. My brother thanked him. All agree to let my brother and me remain in the old ship, till we get to land.' (Ibid.)

On other matters, JW wrote to Kitty Warren, 'Every year I have many applications for the continuance of profitable preachers more than two years in a circuit. . . . But I dare not comply'. June 8, 1786, *Letters* (Telford), 7:330. Finally, though not discussed at Conference, it was significant for the future of Methodism that earlier in the year, Coke had finally obtained JW's support for raising a subscription for overseas missions (after failing to float a Society for the purpose in 1784). In Mar. 1786 he issued an address to this end, supported by JW. Tyerman, *Wesley*, 3:484–85.

Charles Boone, John Booth, William Boothby, Andrew Blair, Robert
Carr Brackenbury, Samuel Bradburn, Joseph Bradford, Jeremiah
Brettel, Thomas Brisco, John Broadbent, Isaac Brown, Thomas
Carlill, William Collins, Jonathan Coussins, James Creighton,
5   William Dutton, John Easton, John Goodwin, Parson Greenwood,
William Green, James Hall, Lancelot Harrison, Christopher
Hopper, Joseph Harper, Joshua Keighley, Thomas Lee, Thomas
Longley, John Mason, John Moon, Alexander Mather, Henry
Moore, John Murlin, William Myles, John Pawson, John Peacock,
10   Thomas Rankin, Richard Rodda, Robert Roberts, George Shadford,
William Saunders, James Thom, Thomas Taylor, William
Thompson, John Valton, William Warrener, Thomas Warrick,
Christopher Watkins, Charles Wesley, James Wood, Francis Wrigley

15   [Absent
(There are forty-four names in three columns.)
[Duncan McAllum, Francis Asbury, Thomas Barber, Joseph
Benson, John Brettel, George Brown, George Button, Joseph Cole,
Thomas Corbet, Robert Costerdine, John Crook, Thomas Dixon,
20   Henry Foster, William Hoskins, Thomas Hanby, Thomas Hanson,
Robert Hopkins, William Hunter, Edward Jackson, Daniel Jackson,
John Leech, Jonathan Parkin, Joseph Pescod, Nehemiah Price,
William Percival, Jeremiah Robertshaw, James Rogers, James Wray,
Benjamin Rhodes, Jasper Robinson, Thomas Rutherford, John
25   Shaw, Robert Scot, William Simpson, George Story, Thomas
Tennant, William Thom, Joseph Taylor, Barnabas Thomas,
Zachariah Yewdall, Thomas Vasey, Richard Watkinson, Richard
Whatcoat, Duncan Wright.

30   [For the absence of all of whom a dispensation is passed.
[*Question 1st*. Who are in full connexion with the Conference?
[*Answer*. (There are one hundred and twenty-eight names in
three columns, pp. 39–40, combining in one alphabetical list both
British and American preachers. There are also four names that are
35   struck through: 'Edward Dromgoole' and 'James Hinton' because
they had 'located', 'John Funnell' because his name correctly
appeared later as 'Tunnell', and 'William Ringold', an American
preacher who had also located in 1786. Against seven names an X
appears in the left margin, for varied reasons, which if known will be
40   noted. John Fidler is listed twice.)

[Joseph Algar, Beverly Allen, Thomas Anderson, William Ashman, John Atlay, John Baldwin, John Baxter, John Beanland, James Bogie, Charles Bond, Charles Boone, ˣSamuel Botts, ˣCaleb Boyer, Thomas Bowen, Philip Bruce, William Cannan, Thomas Chew, James Christie, John Clarke, Adam Clarke, John MᶜClaskey, Adam Cloud, 5 Robert Cloud, John Cooper, William MᶜCornock, Philip Cox, John Cricket, James Cromwell, Joseph Cromwell, John Crosby, Thomas Curtis, William Damaron, Simon Day, Thomas Davis, John Dickins, ((Edward Dromgoole)), Samuel Dudley, John Easter, Samuel Edwards, William Eells, Thomas Ellis, Reuben Ellis, Michael Ellis, 10 Ira Ellis, Robert Empringham, Joseph Everett, ˣJohn Fenwick, John Fidler, Jonathan Forrest, Thomas Foster, ((John Funnell)), George Gibbon, Freeborn Garrettson, William Gill, Lemuel Green, Walter Griffith, ˣJohn Hagerty, ˣThomas Haskins, James Haw, Woolman Hickson, ((James Hinton)), Jonathan Hern, Samuel Hodgson, 15 George Holder, William Holmes, William Horner, Robert Howard, William Hoskins, Thomas Humphries, Daniel Jackson, Joseph Jerom, Andrew Inglis, Robert Johnson, Thomas Johnson, ˣHenry Jones, Thomas Jackson, Henry Jones, William Jessop, James Jordan, Matthias Joyce, Richard Ivy, Lawrence Kane, ˣJames Kenny, James 20 O'Kelly, John King, Jeremiah Lambert, Jesse Lee, Matthew Lumb, John Major, Enoch Matson, John Mealy, Peter Mill, George Moore, Hugh Moore, Edward Morris, Peter Moriarty, George Mowat, Henry Ogburn, William Partridge, John Paup, William Phoebus, Ignatius Pigman, John Fidler, Wilson Lee, Elijah Ellis, John Poole, 25 John Pritchard, Nelson Reed, ((William Ringold)), Joseph Saunderson, Thomas Shaw, George Snowden, Alexander Suter, Robert Swan, Richard Swift, James Thom, William Thomas, Joseph Thompson, John Tunnell, George Wadsworth, James Watson, John Watson, ˣGeorge Whitfield, James White, John Wittam, Thomas 30 Wride, Joseph Wyatt, James Riggin, John Robertson, John Smith, Isaac Smith, Thomas Ware]

Minutes

Q. 1. What preachers are *admitted* this year?

A. In *Great Britain*: Alexander Suter, Joseph Jerom, James 35
 Thom, William Hoskins. In *Ireland*, William Hammet,

James McDonald. In *America*, Isaac Smith, John Smith,
Elijah Ellis, John Robertson, Thomas Jackson, Henry
Jones, William Jessop, James Riggin, Wilson Lee, Tho.
Ware, John Fidler.

5   *Q.* 2. Who *remain on trial?*

A. In *Great Britain*, Thomas Bartholomew, Edward
Burbeck, John Ogylvie, William Palmer, Charles Kyte,
Benjamin Pearce, Timothy Crowther, Jonathan Crowther,
John McKersey, William Butterfield, Richard Cornish,
10   William Holmes, James Ridall, Peter Walker, Charles
Bland, Robert Gamble, John Smith, Alexander Kilham,
William Fish, John Ramshaw, William Hunter, Jun.,
William Blagborne, Henry Robins.[166] In *Ireland*, John
Dinnen, Thomas Verner. In *America*, M. Whitaker, H.
15   Bingham, S. Johnson, Thomas Williamson, J. Hartley, H.
Hull, William Steens, J. Maston, E. Cooper, L. Ross,
Robert Sparks, J. Brush, Robert Ayres, G. Thompson, J.
Paup, J. McClaskey, Robert Cann, S. Dickins, S. Pyle.

Q. 3. Who are *admitted on trial?*

20   *A.* In *Great Britain*, James Gore, John Reynolds, Richard
Phillips, Wm. Bramwell, James Byron,[167] John Townsend,
Geo. Baldwin, Theoph. Lessey, Tho. Jones, James Evans,
William Stephens, Thomas Roberts, William Heath,
Thomas Smith, William Thoresby, John Robotham,
25   James Williams, George Highfield, John Barrett,[168] John
Tregortha,[169] John Atkins, John Beaumont, Thomas Gill,
Jonathan Edmondson,[170] Duncan Kay, Richard Thoresby,

[166] CJ omits Robins. He had desisted in 1784, remained unlisted and without a
station in 1785, but in the 1786 CJ, he was added at the end of circuit No. 54
(Thirsk) in Coke's hand, and so printed in the *Minutes*—but was never stationed
again.

[167] Orig., 'Byrom', as also once in 1787, and also in CJ (1791). James McKee
Byron (1760–1827) was an Irishman who, after travelling briefly with JW in Ireland,
was sent to Norwich in Nov. 1785, possibly to take the place of Thomas Jones, who
apparently was unable to take up his appointment there. Byron had been taken out
from Thirsk, where apparently Robins was sent as a substitute.

[168] John Barrett (1756–1841), whose name was originally spelled 'Barret' in the
Minutes (and CJ) from 1786 to 1790, although 'Barrett' appeared once in 1787 as
well as in 1791; in 1789 one spelling was 'Barritt'.

[169] In CJ his name appeared as 'William Tregortha', but Coke replaced 'William'
by 'John'.

[170] Orig., 'Edmonson', once, as in CJ (1790).

Abraham Moseley, John de Quêteville,[171] Michael Griffiths.[172] In *Ireland*, Samuel Bates, Tho. Owens, David Gordon, Francis Frazier, Thomas Seaward,[173] John Harper, John Gillis, Samuel Moorhead, John Grace, William Cowen.[174] In *America*, Sihon Smith, J. Mason, R.   5
Johnson Miller, M. Moore, Charles Hardy, Daniel Asbury, Caleb Maxey,[175] John Steward, H. Vanover, T. Burns, Micaiah Tracy, Elijah Lumsdon, Newman Spain, J. Lurton, William Hudson, John Jarrell, William Hervey, Benjamin Ogden,[176] J. Simmons, Moses Hurley, J.   10
Merrick, S. Talbot, L. Matthews, M. Laird.[177]

Q. 4. Who desist from travelling?[178]

[171] Orig., 'John de Queataville', and usually 'de Quedville' or 'de Quedeville'. De Quêteville (1761–1843) was born in Jersey and became the French-speaking patriarch of Methodism in the Channel Islands, translating many Methodist writings into French, and for thirty-four years editing the *Magazin Methodiste*. His name does not appear in CJ this year.

[172] CJ adds Thomas Broadbent (c. 1763–1845) as admitted on trial. The omission from *Minutes* was apparently simply an oversight, for both CJ and *Minutes* record his stationing in Yarm (No. 55). CJ also adds Joseph Sutcliffe and Robert Dall.

[173] Orig., 'Seward'; named 'Seaward' in CJ, in circuit No. 70, and in his 1787 obituary.

[174] CJ adds 'Daniel Graham', who was not admitted until 1788. Little is known of him except his four years in the Irish itinerancy and his death as an ardent missionary in Barbados (1793).

[175] Orig., 'Maxcy', apparently a misspelling from the misleading handwriting in CJ. The American *Minutes* have 'Maxey'.

[176] Orig., 'Ogdon', in CJ and *Minutes*, but 'Ogden' throughout American *Minutes*.

[177] In CJ and *Minutes* his name appears as 'Lard'; in American *Minutes* as 'Leard' (as usual 1786–92). His signature in 1829, however, was 'Mica Laird'.

[178] CJ, *Q*. 12: 'What Preachers that have been in connexion with the Conference have desisted from travelling the last year?'

'*A*. Philip Hardcastle, William Adamson.'

CJ, *Q*. 13: 'What Preachers that have been in connexion with the Conference have been expelled?'

'*A*. John Ingham, for drunkenness. Michael Moorhouse, for malice and obstinacy. William Church for lewdness. George Dice for adultery; and Thomas Halliday for habitual drunkenness.'

No details are given about the four American preachers who desisted.

CJ, *Q*. 7 asks, 'Is any member of the Conference dropped on account of his not being able to travel?' with the answer, 'Thomas Hanson'. To *Q*. 8: 'Who is elected a Member of the Conference in his place?' the reply is, 'Charles Boone, stationed for the ensuing year in Liverpool' (the latter word written by Coke's hand over the erased 'Birmingham').

CJ, *Q*. 9 asks, 'Is any Member of the Conference dropped for withdrawing himself from the general work?' And the answer is given, 'John Brettel'. He was replaced by 'George Snowden, stationed at this Conference for Leeds'.

A. In *Great Britain*, Philip Hardcastle, William
Adamson,—John Ingham, William Church, Michael
Moorhouse. In *Ireland*,—George Dice, Thomas Halliday.
In *America*, James Hinton, Edward Dromgoole, William
5   Glendenning, William Ringold.
Q. 5. Who has *died* this year?
A. John Fletcher, a pattern of all holiness, scarce to be par-
alleled in any century;[179] and Christopher Peacock,[180]
young in years, but old in grace; a pattern of all holiness,
10   full of faith and love, and zeal for God.
Q. 6. Are there any objections to any of our preachers?
A. They were examined one by one.
Q. 7. How are the preachers *stationed* this year?
A. As follows:
15   John Broadbent travels with Mr. Wesley.[181]
          (1) *London*, John Wesley, Charles Wesley, James
          Creighton, Sam. Bradburn,[182] Benjamin Rhodes,
          Jeremiah Brettel:—Tho. Rankin, John Atlay, and George
          Whitfield, supernumeraries.
20   (2) *Sussex*, William Boothby, John Reynolds, James
          Byron.
          (3) *Kent*, George Shadford, Tho. Wride, William
          Bramwell, James Gore.
          (4) *Colchester*, Joseph Algar, Charles Bland.
25   (5) *Norwich*, Jas. Robinson, R. Empringham,[183] Tho.
          Shaw, Abraham Moseley, Robert Gamble.
          (6) *Lynn*, William Palmer, John McKersey, John Gaulter.
          (7) *Bedford*, Barnabas Thomas, Wm. Homer.

[179] In CJ the protocol is followed of dealing with members of the Legal Hundred
first, so that the death of Peacock is recorded in *QQ.* 5 and 6, of Fletcher in *Q.* 11,
in the form 'Has any Preacher who was in connexion with the Conference died this
year?' The answer was in the same form as in the *Minutes*.

[180] Orig., 'Jn. Peacock', as in the CJ list of members, though the CJ obituary gives
his correct name and adds a closing clause, 'whom he eminently glorified in life
and in death'. CJ continues (in *Q.* 6) to appoint in his place, 'Jonathan Herne, stationed at this Conference for Nottingham'.

[181] This statement is not present in CJ.

[182] Thomas Blanshard says Bradburn was in London to assist JW in temporal
affairs. *The Life of Samuel Bradburn* (London: Stock, 1870), 115.

[183] CJ (in Coke's hand) shows the addition immediately after Jasper Robinson of
John Cricket, whose name is then stricken through and replaced by Robert
Empringham.

(8) *Northampton*, Joseph Pescod, Michael Griffiths.

(9) *Oxfordshire*, Joseph Harper, Samuel Edwards,[184] John Robotham.

(10) *Gloucestershire*, James Hall, Robert Hopkins, William Stephens.

(11) *Sarum*, Wm. Ashman, Wm. Butterfield, Charles Kyte.

(12) *Bradford*, John Mason, Simon Day, Wm. Hoskins, John King.

(13) *Bristol*, John Valton, Christopher Watkins, John Pritchard, Thomas Tennant.

(14) *Taunton*, George Wadsworth, John Poole.

(15) *Tiverton*, Joseph Jerom, Peter Walker.

(16) *Plymouth*, William Myles, Charles Bond, Timothy Crowther.

(17) *St. Austell*, John Moon, John Cricket,[185] John Townsend.

(18) *Redruth*, Francis Wrigley, Jonathan Coussins, Joseph Sutcliffe.

(19) *St. Ives*, George Button, Richard Cornish, Theophilus Lessey.

(20) *Pembroke*, Joseph Cole, John Tiegortha, James Evans.

(21) *Glamorgan*, William Holmes, George Baldwin.

(22) *Brecon*, William Saunders, Tho. Jones.

(23) *Birmingham*, Andrew Blair, John Murlin, Duncan Wright:—John Brettel, supernumerary.

(24) *Burslem*, Thomas Warrick, Tho. Corbet.

(25) *Macclesfield*, George Story, Wm. Thoresby.

(26) *Manchester*, William Thompson, William Eells, Thomas Smith.

(27) *Stockport*, Robert Roberts, Duncan Kay.

(28) *Chester*, Richard Rodda, Thomas Brisco, John Beaumont.

(29) *Liverpool*, Charles Boone, Christ. Hopper, James Williams.

(30) *Bolton*, Jeremiah Robertshaw, Thomas Lee.

---

[184] CJ orders the names Edwards, Harper, then adding '2' and '1' over them, to reverse the order, surely to show Harper as Assistant.

[185] CJ, 'John Cricket' added by Coke over 'Robert Empringham'.

(31) *Colne*, Edward Jackson, Samuel Bardsley, James Ridall.

(32) *Leicester*, John Easton, Robert Howard, Thomas Gill.

(33) *Nottingham*, Jonathan Hern, James Bogie, William Heath.

(34) *Derby*, Thomas Carlill, Robert Scot.

(35) *Sheffield*, Alexander Mather, George Gibbon, Thomas Tattershall.

(36) *Grimsby*, Lancelot Harrison, James Wray.

(37) *Horncastle*, Thomas Longley, John Barrett, Richard Thoresby.

(38) *Gainsborough*, William Dutton, George Mowat, Thomas Ellis, Alexander Kilham.

(39) *Epworth*, James Watson, John Fenwick, Jonathan Edmondson.

(40) *Leeds*, Thomas Taylor, John Shaw, George Snowden.

(41) *Birstall*, John Goodwin, John Wittam.

(42) *Dewsbury*, Parson Greenwood, Jonathan Parkin.

(43) *Huddersfield*, John Booth, John Crosby.

(44) *Halifax*, John Allen, Alexander Suter.

(45) *Bradford*, William Collins, Samuel Hodgson,[186] Thomas Johnson, supernumerary.

(46) *Keighley*, Joseph Bradford, John Beanland.

(47) *Whitehaven*, John Peacock, James Christie.[187]

(48) *Isle of Man*, John Crook, John Ogylvie, Jonathan Crowther, John Ramshaw.

(49) *York*, Thomas Rutherford, Samuel Botts, George Highfield.

(50) *Pocklington*, Robert Swan, George Holder.

(51) *Hull*, Joseph Benson, John Barber.

(52) *Scarborough*, Peter Mill, Robert Costerdine, William Fish.

(53) *Whitby*, Isaac Brown, Thomas Dixon.

(54) *Thirsk*, William Simpson, William Hunter, Jun., Henry Robins.[188]

[186] In CJ, 'Samuel Hodgson' replaces an erased 'John Beanland', and in No. 46, 'John Beanland' replaces an erased 'Samuel Hodgson'.

[187] In CJ, 'James Christie' replaces an erased 'John Smith'.

[188] In CJ, Coke has added 'Henry Robbins' at the end.

(55) *Yarm*, Joseph Thompson, Tho. Broadbent.

(56) *The Dales*, James Thom, John Atkins, J. Smith.[189]

(57) *Sunderland*, James Wood, Wm. Thom.

(58) *Newcastle*, Andrew Inglis, Joseph Saunderson, William Percival.   5

(59) *Berwick*, William Hunter, Sen., Zachariah Yewdall, Matthew Lumb.

(60) *Edinburgh*, John Pawson, Charles Atmore.

(61) *Ayr*, Duncan McAllum.

(62) *Dundee*, Thomas Hanby, Robert Johnson, William   10 Blagborne.

(63) *Aberdeen*, Joseph Taylor, Richard Watkinson.

(64) *Inverness*, Joshua Keighley, Thomas Bartholomew, Edward Burbeck.

(65) *Jersey*, Rob. Carr Brackenbury, Adam Clarke.   15

(66) *Guernsey*, John de Quêteville.

(67) *Dublin*, James Rogers, Henry Moore.

(68) *Waterford*, George Brown, David Gordon.

(69) *Cork*, Jonath. Brown, Matthias Joyce, John Dinnen.

(70) *Limerick*, Daniel Jackson, Thomas Seaward.   20

(71) *Castlebar*, Nehemiah Price, Wm. McCornock.

(72) *Athlone*, Lawrence Kane, John Miller, John Mealy, supernumerary.

(73) *Longford*, Thomas Davis, James McDonald, John Bredin, invalid.[190]   25

(74) *Sligo*, James Jordan, Francis Frazier.

(75) *Ballyconnell*, Joseph Armstrong, James Rennick, Thomas Owens.

(76) *Clones*, William Green,[191] Thomas Hetherington, John Harper.   30

(77) *Enniskillen*, Samuel Mitchell, Thomas Verner, John Gillis.

(78) *Ballyshannon*, Thomas Barber,[192] Rich. Condy.

---

[189] In CJ, 'John Smith' replaces an erased 'James Christie'.

[190] This is the first appearance of this term in the stations. Bredin had been supported by the Preachers' Fund in 1782 and 1784, and was to be supported by it 1786–87 and 1791–96, though he was apparently able to play an active, if irregular, role in circuit activities.

[191] In CJ, a blank had been left for a still undecided name, which Coke filled in later.

[192] Orig., 'Barbor', in *Minutes*, Irish *Minutes*, and CJ, a change that had also appeared in 1784, and was again the case from 1788 to 1791. Some confusion about the spelling continued until his death in 1825, however. In *WMM* (1826), among the recent deaths (p. 68), he appeared as 'The Rev. Thomas Barbor', but in the official obituary (p. 645) as 'Thomas Barber'.

(79) *Omagh*, John Price, Samuel Moorhead.
(80) *Charlemont*, Hugh Moore, Gustavus Armstrong.
(81) *Newry*, John Kerr, Robert Bridge.
(82) *Londonderry*, John Leech, Thomas Roberts.
(83) *Coleraine*, Walter Griffith,[193] Wm. West, Wm. Cowen.
(84) *Belfast*, Robert Armstrong, John Howe, John Grace.
(85) *Lisburn*, Robert Lindsay, Samuel Bates, Benjamin Pearce.[194]

A M E R I C A.

Superintendents, Thomas Coke, Francis Asbury.

	Elders
[86] Georgia, Tho. Humphries, J. Major [87] *Broad River*, S. Johnson	J[ames] Foster
[88] *Charleston*, J. Smith	Hen. Willis
[89] *Santee*, Richard Swift [90] *Pee Dee*, J. Maston, H. Hull	Bev. Allen
[91] *Salisbury*, Tho. Williamson, H. Bingham [92] *Yadkin*, R. J. Miller, J. Mason [93] *Holstein*, M. Whitaker, M. Moore	Reub. Ellis

[193] In CJ, a blank was left at the beginning for the Assistant, which was later filled in by Coke as 'Thomas Roberts'. The change to Griffith was presumably made subsequently. Roberts had only been admitted on trial this year, and the *Minutes* show him as stationed as the second man in Londonderry (No. 82), a simple exchange, for Griffith is shown in CJ in that position. Griffith, however, had been admitted into full connexion the previous year.

[194] In CJ, a gap had been left in the first place for an Assistant to be appointed, which Coke had later filled in as 'Benjamin Pearse', adding a '3' over his name, however, to show his position in the circuit, with a '2' over the name of Bates, so that Lindsay moved up to the first position.

[94] *Guilford*, J. Baldwin
[95] *Halifax*, E. Morris,
C. Hardy   J[ames] O'Kelly
[96] *Mecklenburg*, J. Easter,
H. Jones   5

[97] *New Hope*, W.
Partridge
[98] *Tar River*, T. Anderson,
M. Tracy   Rich. Ivy   10
[99] *Roanoke*, T. Bowen,
W. Steens
[100] *Caswell*, S. Smith

[101] *Bertie*, T. Jackson, J.   15
Freeman
[102] *Camden* and *Banks*,
J. Robertson, John   Phil. Bruce
Steward
[103] *Portsmouth*, T. Burns   20

[104] *Brunswick*, P. Cox,
J. Gibbons, H. Merritt
[105] *Sussex*, S. Pyle,
L. Matthews   F[rancis] Poythress
[106] *Amelia*, E. Ellis,   25
D. Asbury

[107] *Williamsb[urg]*,
Levin Ross   30
[108] *Orange*, William
Damaron, E. Lumsdon
[109] *Bedford*,
W. Cannan,   Tho. Chew
H. Vanover, N. Spain   35
[110] *Hanover*, Ananias
Hudson

[111] *Alleghany*, G. Thompson, A. Edwards, M. Laird
[112] *Redstone*, J. Smith, R. Ayres, S. Dickins
} Enoch Matson

[113] *Westmoreland*, L. Green, J. Paup
[114] *Fairfax*, R. Owings, J. Fidler
[115] *Berkley*, W. Watters, W. Hervey
} Nelson Reed

[116] *Kent*, J. Lee, S. Talbot
[117] *Talbot*, J. White, W. Lee
[118] *Dover*, Ira Ellis, George Moore[195]
} R[ichard] Whatcoat

[119] *Caroline*, W. Jessop, M. Hurley, J. Jarrell
[120] *Dorset*, S. Dudley, J. Everett
} J[ohn] Hagerty

[121] *Somerset*, J. Riggin, J. Merrick
[122] *Annamessex*, W. Thomas
[123] *Northampton*, T. Curtis
} Tho. Foster

[124] *Philadelphia*, H. Ogburn, P. Moriarty
[125] *Little York*
} Matthew Greentree
[126] *Juniata*
} Caleb Boyer

---

[195] Orig., 'I Moore', in CJ and *Minutes*, but apparently the same George Moore who served 1780–81, 1784–92.

[127] *Trenton*, R. Sparks,
R. Cann
[128] *West Jersey*, J.
Brush, J. Simmons, J. Lurton   T[homas] Vasey

5

[129] *East Jersey*, J.
M°Claskey, E. Cooper
[130] *Newark*, Robert Cloud
[131] *New York*, J. Dickins   J[ohn] Tunnell
[132] *Long Island*,
Thomas Ware   10

[133] *Baltimore*,
W. Hickson, A. Cloud
[134] *Frederick*, M. Ellis,   Wm. Gill   15
J. Cromwell   Ign. Pigman
[135] *Calvert*,
Jonathan Forrest

[136] *Kentucky*, B. Ogden   James Haw   20

[137] *Newbern*,
[138] *New River*, J. Hartley,   Lee Roy Cole
C. Maxey
[139] *Wilmington*,   25

[140] *Antigua*,   J[ohn] Baxter

                                      Wm. Warrener
                                                        30
[141] *Nova Scotia*, W. Black,   F[reeborn] Garrettson[196]
J. Mann   J[ames] Cromwell
[142] *Newfoundland*,   John Clarke
John M°Geary   W[illiam] Hammet

---

[196] In CJ, station 127 for Nova Scotia was inserted among the New England circuits, and beneath it, Coke added ' & Newfoundland, John McGeary' and as Elders
'John Clark, William Hammet'. In the printed *Minutes*, as may be seen, both were
transferred to the end of the listing, making one station for the West Indies and
two for British North America.

Q. [8]. How many wives are to be provided for?
A. Seventy-five.
Q. [9]. How many of these are to be provided for by
   the circuits?[197]
A. Fifty-seven: namely,

(1) London,	S. Brethel, Boothby.[198]
(2) Gloucestershire,	S. Hall.
(3) Bradford,	S. Green.[199]
(4) Bristol,	S. Hopkins[200] £6; Dixon[201] £6; Day,[202] Algar.[203]
(5) Devon and Taunton,	S. Poole.
(6) Plymouth,	S. Myles.
(7) St. Austell,	S. Moon. £6
(8) Redruth,	S. Wride.[204]
(9) St. Ives,	S. Shaw (Thomas).[205]
(10) Birmingham,	S. Blair, Wright.
(11) Burslem	S. Warrick.
(12) Macclesfield,	S. Story.
(13) Stockport,	S. Roberts.
(14) Manchester,	S. Coussins,[206] Corbet.[207]
(15) Chester,	S. Rodda.
(16) Liverpool,	S. Boone, Hopper.
(17) Bolton,	S. Robertshaw.
(18) Colne,	S. Lee,[208] Harper.[209]
(19) Leicester,	S. Easton.
(20) Nottingham,	S. Hern.

[197] CJ frames the question differently: *Q.* 18. 'How many of these are to be provided for by the Circuits?' giving the reply, 'Fifty-seven'; no details are furnished.
[198] William Boothby was stationed in Sussex.
[199] William Green was stationed in Clones.
[200] Robert Hopkins was stationed in Gloucestershire.
[201] Thomas Dixon was stationed in Whitby.
[202] Simon Day was stationed in Bradford, Wiltshire.
[203] Joseph Algar was stationed in Colchester.
[204] Thomas Wride was stationed in Kent.
[205] Thomas Shaw was stationed in Norwich.
[206] Jonathan Coussins was stationed in Redruth.
[207] Thomas Corbet was stationed in Burslem.
[208] Thomas Lee was stationed in Bolton.
[209] Joseph Harper was stationed in Oxfordshire.

(21) Sheffield,	S. Mather, Gibbon, Brisco.[210]
(22) Grimsby,	S. Butterfield.[211]
(23) Gainsborough,	S. Ellis, Mowat.
(24) Epworth,	S. Longley.[212]
(25) Leeds,	S. Taylor, Shaw, Snowden.
(26) Birstall,	S. Goodwin.
(27) Dewsbury,	S. Greenwood.
(28) Huddersfield,	S. Booth.
(29) Bradford,	S. Collins.
(30) Halifax,	S. Crosby.[213]
(31) Keighley,	S. Bradford.
(32) York,	S. Rutherford.
(33) Hull,	S. Swan.[214]
(34) Scarborough,	S. Mill.
(35) Yarm,	S. Thompson (Jos.).
(36) The Dales,	S. Watson.[215]
(37) Sunderland,	S. Wood, Thom.
(38) Newcastle,	S. Inglis.
(39) Ireland,	S. Jackson, Price, Brown (Geo.), Joyce, Dinnen.[216]

Q. [10]. How are the other eighteen to be provided for? namely: S. Williams, Scot, Beanland, Peacock, Crook, Costerdine, Brown (Isaac), Simpson, Percival, Hunter, Sen., Watkinson, McAllum, Atkins, Moon £6., Moore, Kane, Rennick, West, Condy.[217]

[210] Thomas Brisco was stationed in Chester.

[211] William Butterfield was stationed in Sarum.

[212] Thomas Longley was stationed in Horncastle.

[213] John Crosby was stationed in Huddersfield.

[214] Robert Swan was stationed in Pocklington.

[215] James Watson was stationed in Epworth.

[216] Daniel Jackson was stationed in Limerick, John Price in Omagh, George Brown in Waterford; Matthias Joyce and John Dinnen were stationed in Cork.

[217] These preachers were stationed thus: James Williams, Liverpool; Robert Scot, Derby; John Beanland, Keighley; John Peacock, Whitehaven; John Crook, Isle of Man; Robert Costerdine, Scarborough; Isaac Brown, Whitby; William Simpson, Thirsk; William Percival, Newcastle; William Hunter, Sen., Berwick; Richard Watkinson, Aberdeen; Duncan McAllum, Ayr; John Atkins, The Dales; William Moon, St. Austell; Henry Moore, Dublin; Lawrence Kane, Athlone; James Rennick, Ballyconnell; William West, Coleraine; Richard Condy, Ballyshannon.

A. Partly out of the Yearly Collection and partly out of the Preachers' Fund.[218]

N.B. The money for them all, except the five last, will be lodged in the hands of Mr. Atlay: the money for the five last, in the hands of Mr. James Rogers.[219]

Q. 11. What numbers are in the societies?[220]

A. As follows:

(1) London	2,517
(2) Sussex	217
(3) Kent	400
(4) Colchester	184
(5) Norwich	600
(6) Lynn	237
(7) Bedford	264
(8) Northampton	350
(9) Oxfordshire	500
(10) Gloucester	647
(11) Sarum	430
(12) Bradford	1,193
(13) Bristol	1,600
(14) Taunton	180
(15) Devon	442
(16) Plymouth	483
(17) St. Austel	816
(18) Redruth	1,404
(19) St. Ives	1,292
(20) Pembroke	186
(21) Glamorgan	209
(22) Brecon	100
(23) Birmingham	1,010
(24) Burslem	780
(25) Macclesfield	922
(26) Manchester	2,460
(27) Chester	700

[218] CJ reads: 'Partly by the Contingent Fund, partly by the yearly collection', the latter phrase being altered by Coke to 'Preachers' Fund'.

[219] This is the first time such an arrangement is mentioned.

[220] By way of answer CJ reads: 'In Great Britain, Ireland, and America, 79,600', but gives no details.

(28) Liverpool	655	
(29) Bolton	650	
(30) Colne	1,500	
(31) Leicester	674	
(32) Nottingham	700	5
(33) Derby	366	
(34) Sheffield	1,550	
(35) Grimsby	480	
(36) Horncastle	582	
(37) Gainsborough	745	10
(38) Epworth	644	
(39) Leeds	2,384	
(40) Birstall	1,043	
(41) Dewsbury	925	
(42) Huddersfield	800	15
(43) Halifax	1,000	
(44) Bradford	1,146	
(45) Keighley	1,100	
(46) Whitehaven	227	
(47) Isle of Man	2,433	20
(48) York	890	
(49) Hull	900	
(50) Scarborough	700	
(51) Whitby	536	
(52) Thirsk	667	25
(53) Yarm	512	
(54) The Dales	805	
(55) Sunderland	1,076	
(56) Newcastle	1,063	
(57) Berwick	80	30
(58) Edinburgh	219	
(59) Dundee	134	
(60) Aberdeen	324	
(61) Jersey	136	
(62) Guernsey	42	35
(63) Dublin	900	
(64) Waterford	300	
(65) Cork	800	
(66) Limerick	266	
(67) Castlebar	303	40
(68) Athlone	600	

(69) Sligo	391
(70) Ballyconnell	636
(71) Clones	929
[73][221] Enniskillen	1,400
[74] Charlemont	1,200
[75] Lisleen	950
[76] Londonderry	700
[77] Belfast	420
[78] Lisburn	550
Total in Europe	58,156[222]

A M E R I C A

Portsmouth,	Whites	330
	Blacks	26
Sussex,	Whites	416
	Blacks	72
Brunswick,	Whites	305
	Blacks	59
Amelia,	Whites	382
	Blacks	30
Mecklenburg,	Whites	392
	Blacks	37
Bedford,	Whites	524
	Blacks	16
Orange,	Whites	374
	Blacks	75
Williamsburg,	Whites	167
	Blacks	11
Alleghany,	Whites	350
	Blacks	18
Berkley,	Whites	140
	Blacks	26

[221] No. 72 is missing. The numbered circuits in Ireland are 67–85 with Coleraine No. 83. CJ does not give or number the Society memberships, but here they are numbered 63–71, 73–78, i.e., supposedly statistics for fifteen Societies in sixteen circuits. However, it seems almost certain that the statistics were for the circuits themselves. Coleraine was a new circuit, and it may be that the membership there was incorporated in that of Londonderry, from which it seems to have been formed.

[222] Orig., '58,150'.

Redstone,		523	
Fairfax,		260	
Lancaster,		174	
Frederick,	Whites	390	
	Blacks	32	5
Calvert,	Whites	295	
	Blacks	316	
Baltimore,	Whites	655	
	Blacks	111	
Little York,		136	10
Kent,		1,013	
Talbot,	Whites	632	
	Blacks	332	
Dorset,		719	
Somerset,		220	15
Annamessex,	Whites	317	
	Blacks	33	
Northampton,	Whites	151	
	Blacks	9	
Caroline,	Whites	657	20
	Blacks	243	
Dover,	Whites	690	
	Blacks	158	
Philadelphia,		498	
Georgia,		78	25
Charleston,	Whites	35	
	Blacks	23	
Santee,		75	
Pee Dee,	Whites	285	
	Blacks	10	30
Broad River,		200	
Salisbury,	Whites	327	
	Blacks	10	
Yadkin,	Whites	426	
	Blacks	11	35
Holstein,		250	
Guilford,	Whites	400	
	Blacks	10	
Halifax,	Whites	324	
	Blacks	14	40

	New Hope,	Whites	192
		Blacks	3
	Tar River,	Whites	607
		Blacks	42
5	New River,	Whites	500
		Blacks	72
	Roanoke,		474
	Caswell,		153
	Bertie,	Whites	405
10		Blacks	58
	Camden and Banks,		257
	West Jersey,		492
	Trenton,		352
	East Jersey,		365
15	New York,	Whites	178
		Blacks	25
	Long Island,	Whites	146
		Blacks	8
	Newark,		50
20	Nova Scotia,		510
	Newfoundland,		100
	Antigua,	Whites	10
		Blacks	<u>1,559</u>

	Total in America,	21,350[223]
25	Total in Europe,	58,156
	Total in Europe and America,	79,506[224]

Q. 12. What is the Kingswood collection?
A. £685. 7*s*. 10*d*.
30   *Q*. 13. What children are admitted this year?[225]
A. ———— Morgan, Samuel Barry, Lawrence Kane.
Q. 14. What can we allow the daughters of the preachers?
A. Hannah Roberts, £6, the second year. Ann Watkinson,
£6, the second year.
35   *Q*. 15. What is contributed to the Preachers' Fund?
A. £365. 8*s*. 2*d*.[226]
Q. 16. What is allowed out of it?[227]

---

[223] Orig., '21,450'.
[224] Orig., '79,600'.
[225] *QQ*. 13–14 are not present in CJ.
[226] CJ adds, 'besides the contributions of the Preachers'.
[227] CJ answers, '£337. 5. 0.', with no details.

A. Thomas Westell	£30	0	
William Whitaker	20	0	
John Bredin	12	0	
Matthew Lowes	5	5	
Thomas Hanson	12	0	5
John Furz	12	0	
Henry Foster	12	0	
John Watson, Jun.	12	0	
John Mealy	12	0	
Ann Morgan	24	0	10
Lucy Bourke	12	0	
Mary Penington	20	0	
Elizabeth Shorter	10	0	
Catherine Garnet	12	0	
Elizabeth Dillon	5	0	15
Tabitha Norris	5	0	
Margaret Payne	12	0	
Sarah Barry	24	0	
Sarah Naylor	10	0	
Elizabeth Oldham	12	0	20
Sarah Hosmer	10	0	
Sarah Mitchell	24	0	
In all,	£307	5	

Q. 17. What is contributed for the yearly expenses?   25
A. £917. 13*s*. 8*d*.[228]
Q. 18. How was it expended?

A. Last year's contingencies	£167	5	6	
Present year's contingencies	100	0	0	30
Law	84	8	0	
Sending out preachers in Great Britain and Ireland	25	15	0	
Preachers' necessities	540	5	2	
In all,	£917	13	8	35

Q. 19. What houses are to be built this year?[229]

---

[228] CJ answers, '£917. 14. 6.' and continues:
Q. 24: 'How was this expended?
'*A*. In contingencies for the past year.
'In contingencies for the present year.
'In law, and in providing for the Preachers' deficiencies'.
[229] *QQ*. 19–23 are omitted from CJ.

A. One at Gloucester, Frome, Trowbridge, St. Austell, Probus, Wolverhampton, Alnwick, Glasgow, Kinsale, Castlebar, Aughrim, Cloughagady, Ballynamallard, Killydart, Armagh, Dungannon, and Portaferry.

Q. 20. Does the *General Deed* require any alteration in the mode of settling our preaching-houses?

A. None, except the insertion of the phrase, 'The Conference of the People called Methodists, as established by a Deed Poll of the said J. Wesley, under his Hand and Seal, bearing date the 28th day of February, in the year 1784, and enrolled in his Majesty's High Court of Chancery, and no others', instead of the phrase, 'The Conference of the People called Methodists, in London, Bristol, or Leeds, and no others'.

Q. 21. Is there any further direction to be given, to secure the proper settlement of our preaching-houses?

A. Let no Assistant make, or suffer to be made, in his respective circuit, a collection for any preaching-house, till every step be previously taken to secure it on the Conference Plan, by a trust deed, a bond, or sufficient Articles of Agreement.

Q. 22. Directions are given in the Minutes concerning the windows, etc. of preaching-houses: Have those directions been observed?

A. In some places they have; in others, not at all, particularly with regard to the windows, doors, pews, and the dividing of the men from the women.

Q. 23. Shall we insist on the observance of these directions for the time to come, or no?

A. We will permit none to collect for any future building, unless security be first given to observe the Rules laid down in the Large *Minutes*.

Q. 24. When and where is the next Conference to be held?

A. At Manchester, on the last Tuesday in next July.[230] And all succeeding Conferences are to be held in the following order, viz.——1st in London; 2ndly, in Leeds; 3rdly, in Bristol; 4thly, in Manchester.

Aug. 30, 1785.

---

[230] CJ ends at this point, with the actual signatures of John Wesley and Thomas Coke. The closing sentence in *Q*. 24 and the three appended letters are not present.

Of Separation from the Church.

1. Ever since I returned from America, it has been warmly affirmed, "You separate from the Church." I would consider how far, and in what sense, this assertion is true.

2. Whether you mean by that term the building so called, or the 5 congregation, it is plain I do not separate from either; for wherever I am, I go to the Church, and join with the congregation.

3. Yet it is true that I have in some respects varied, though not from the doctrines, yet from the discipline of the Church of England; although not willingly, but by constraint. For instance: 10 Above forty years ago I began 'preaching in the fields'; and that for two reasons—first, I was not suffered to preach in the Churches: secondly, no parish church in London or Westminster could contain the congregation.

4. About the same time several persons who were desirous to save 15 their souls, prayed me to meet them apart from the great congregation. These little companies (*Societies* they were called) gradually spread through the three kingdoms. And in many places they built houses in which they met, and wherein I and my brethren preached. For a few young men, one after another, desired to serve me as 'sons 20 in the gospel'.

5. Some time after, Mr. Deleznot,[231] a clergyman, desired me to 'officiate at his chapel' in Wapping. There I read prayers, and preached, and administered the Lord's Supper, to a part of the society. The rest communicated either at St. Paul's or at their several 25 parish churches. Meantime, I endeavoured to watch over all their souls, as one that 'was to give an account'; and to assign to each of my fellow-labourers the part wherein I judged he might be most useful.

---

[231] Cf. Aug. 2, 1741, *Journal & Diaries*, 19:208 n. 38 in this edn., where it is noted that J. L. Deleznot in 1734–35 ministered at a Huguenot chapel in Swanfield. 'Mr' was changed to 'Dr' in the 1774 edn. In the *Short History* (9:433 in this edn.) JW said it was Sunday, Sept. 13, 1741, supported by his *Journal* of that date (no diary for this date). The diary for Aug. 2 has 'Wapping', but not Deleznot—a Huguenot. This was an important predecessor to JW's use of West Street. For Deleznot see further in Baker, *Wesley and Church*, 85, 363.

This document contains many of the thoughts found in JW's letter to CW on Aug. 19, 1785; see *Letters* (Telford), 7:284–85.

6. When these were multiplied I gave them an invitation to meet me together in my house at London, that we might consider in what manner we could most effectually 'save our own souls', and 'them that heard us'. This we called a 'Conference' (meaning thereby *the*
5 *persons*, not *the conversation*, they had). At first I desired all the preachers to meet me; but afterwards only a select number.

7. Some years after, we were strongly importuned by our brethren in America, to 'come over and help them'. Several preachers willingly offered themselves for the service; and several went from time
10 to time. God blessed their labours in an uncommon manner. Many sinners were converted to God; and many societies formed, under the same *Rules* as were observed in England; insomuch that at present the American societies contain more than eighteen thousand members.

15 8. But since the late Revolution in North America, these have been in great distress. The clergy having no sustenance, either from England or from the American States, have been obliged almost universally to leave the country, and seek their food elsewhere. Hence those who had been members of the Church had none either to
20 administer the Lord's Supper, or to baptize their children. They applied to England over and over: but it was to no purpose. Judging this to be a case of real necessity, I took a step which for peace and quietness I had refrained from taking for many years: I exercised that power which I am fully persuaded the Great Shepherd and
25 Bishop of the Church has given me. I appointed three of our labourers to go and help them, by not only preaching the Word of God, but likewise administering the Lord's Supper and baptizing their children, throughout that vast tract of land, a thousand miles long and some hundreds broad.

30 [9.] These are the steps which, not of choice but of necessity, I have slowly and deliberately taken. If anyone is pleased to call this 'separating from the Church', he may. But the law of England does not call it so; nor can anyone properly be said so to do, unless out of conscience he refuses to join in the service, and partake of the
35 Sacraments administered therein.

JOHN WESLEY

Camelford,
August 30, 1785

40 After Dr. Coke's return from America, many of our friends begged I would consider the case of Scotland, where we had been labouring so

many years and had seen so little fruit of our labours. Multitudes indeed have set out well, but they were soon turned out of the way— chiefly by their ministers either disputing against the truth, or refusing to admit them to the Lord's Supper, yea, or to baptize their children, unless they would promise to have no fellowship with the 5 Methodists. Many who did so soon lost all they had gained, and became more the children of hell than before. To prevent this, I at length consented to take the same step with regard to Scotland which I had done with regard to America. But this is not a separation from the Church at all. Not from the Church of Scotland, for we were never connected 10 therewith, any further than we are now; not from the Church of England, for this is not concerned in the steps which are taken in Scotland. Whatever then is done either in America or Scotland is no separation from the Church of England. I have no thought of this: I have many objections against it. It is a totally different case. But for all 15 this, is it not possible there may be such a separation after you are dead? Undoubtedly it is. But what I said at our first Conference, above forty years ago, I say still: 'I dare not omit doing what good I can while I live, for fear of evils that may follow when I am dead.'[232]

20

Bristol, July 22, 1786.

Perhaps there is one part of what I wrote some time since which requires a little further explanation. In what cases do we allow of service in Church hours? I answer:

1. When the minister is a notoriously wicked man.   25

2. When he preaches Arian or any equally pernicious doctrine.

3. When there are not Churches in the town sufficient to contain half the people; and

---

[232] JW is referring in this letter to his ordinations for Scotland. In accordance with the principles declared here, he insisted that when the preachers returned to England, they were to cease wearing gowns and bands and administering Sacraments. For the criticism this aroused from Pawson, and Thomas Hanby's refusal to obey, see *Minutes* (1785), n. 70. Creighton, who assisted in Coke's ordination for America, later claimed that JW had repented of the Scottish and indeed all the ordinations, though he may simply have regretted the Scottish ones as they did not lead to much success. See Baker, *Wesley and Church*, 282, 397 n. 88, 399 n. 117. JW continued to ordain after this alleged admission, including three men apparently in reserve for England. See Pawson's claims: *Minutes* (1785), n. 70. and introduction, p. 97; see doubts also to Joshua Keighley, May 20, 1787, *Letters* (Telford), 7:384.

4. When there is no Church at all within two or three miles. And we advise everyone who preaches in the Church hours to read the Psalms and Lessons with part of the Church Prayers; because we apprehend this will endear the Church service to our brethren, who
5 probably would be prejudiced against it, if they heard none but extemporary prayer.[233]

A few little advices I would add to the preachers.

I advise the Assistants:

1. To re-establish morning preaching, in all large towns, at least.
10 2. To exert themselves in restoring the Bands.

3. And the Select Societies.

4. Change both a general and particular steward in each circuit:
     I advise all the preachers.

1. Always to conclude the service in about an hour.
15 2. Never scream.

3. Never lean upon or beat the Bible.

4. Wherever you preach, meet the Society.

5. Do not, without the utmost necessity, go home at night.

6. Never take part against the Assistant.
20 7. Never preach a funeral sermon but for an eminently holy person; nor then, without consulting the Assistant. Preach none for hire; beware of panegyric, particularly in London.

8. Have Love-feasts in more places.

9. Introduce no new tunes. See that none sing too slow, and the
25 women sing their parts. Exhort all to sing, and all to stand at singing, as well as to kneel at prayers.

10. Let none repeat the last line, unless the preacher does.

11. Inform the Leaders that Every Assistant is to change both the Stewards and Leaders when he sees good. And that no Leader has
30 power to put any person either into or out of the Society.

JOHN WESLEY

Aug. 1, 1786

---

[233] On the recurring problem of attending church services and holding Methodist worship in Church hours, see *Minutes* (1781), n. 868 in the reply to Hey's charges; and Baker, *Wesley and Church,* 286–303.

Annual *Minutes of some late Conversations*, 1787

Manchester, July 31, 1787[234]

[234] CJ for 1787 occupies pp. 48–57 of the original volume, and follows the general lines of earlier years, including the ordering of names referred to in 1786.

In his *Journal*, JW says nothing about the Conference even taking place. The diary records July 28 in Manchester (where the Conference was held, for the second time) 'on business'. He met 'the Committee' (evidently the 'Cabinet', see introduction, p. 39) on several days between July 28 and Aug. 4; and the Conference on July 31 to Aug. 4. On Aug. 3 he 'ordained 4' and 'ordained D. McAllum etc.' on Aug. 4 (evidently once again as deacon and elder). The others ordained were Alexander Souter, Joseph Wray, and an unknown. Simon in *WHS* 9 (1914): 145. This was despite doubts expressed to Joshua Keighley (May 20 in *Letters* [Telford], 7:384) about ordaining again and whether he had already 'gone too far'. This, he said, must be 'thoroughly discussed at the Conference'. He did ordain again, and there is no reference in the *Minutes* or any other source to such a discussion. See also *Minutes* (1786), n. 232. Tyerman notes (*Wesley*, 3:496) that the preachers were invited individually on no very obvious criteria. Thomas Taylor writes (MS diary quoted in Tyerman, 3:496) that 'Mr Wesley has sent a special summons to each preacher whom he wishes to attend Conference, and has apparently forbidden everyone else to go. I am unbidden and think I am ill-used. . . . Besides, I am a member of the legal Conference. I'll resolve to go, let consequences be what they may'. He went, but with little satisfaction; he spent much of the time trying to supersede the hymn-book published by Robert Spence. For which, see Tyerman, *Wesley*, 3:539.

Though there was no reference to separation in the *Minutes*, the subject seems to have dominated JW's mind and was often mentioned in his correspondence and the writings of others.

Pawson wrote to Atmore that there were 'very many preachers and abundance of people' at the Conference; 'I think more than ever I saw at a Conference before. . . . Almost the whole time was taken up with temporal affairs'. JW was in great haste as he and Coke were to go to the Channel Isles:

'Mr. W. seems more determined to abide in the Church than ever. He talked about it, and about it again in the public Conference, in the Society, etc., and in such a hot, fiery spirit as I did not like to see. He talked of fighting with a flail, etc., and of putting all out of the Society who do not go to the Church.

'We are to be just as, and what we were, in every respect before we came to Scotland. No sacraments, no gowns, no nothing at all, of any kind or sort whatsoever. With entreaty I got him to ordain Mr. McAllum and Souter. Two more were ordained also, one for the West Indies and one for Nova Scotia. . . . Charles Wesley the Sunday before the Conference spoke in the society in London to this effect. "I told you 40 years ago that from among yourselves grievous wolves would arise who would rend and tear the flock. You now see my words fulfilled. These self-created bishops and self-made priests are the very men. But I charge you all in the presence of God, never

[The Minutes or Journals of the Conference of the People called
Methodists, begun in Manchester on Tuesday the 31ˢᵗ day of July in
the year of our Lord 1787, and continued by various adjournments
to the 4ᵗʰ day of August following, inclusive.

5

Present
The Revd. John Wesley, President
The Revd. Thomas Coke, Secretary
(There are seventy-one names in four columns.)[235]

10 [John Allen, John Barber, Samuel Bardsley, Joseph Benson,
Andrew Blair, John Booth, William Boothby, Charles Boone,
Samuel Bradburn, Joseph Bradford, R. C. Brackenbury, Thomas
Brisco, John Broadbent, Isaac Brown, George Button, Thomas
Carlill, Joseph Cole, William Collins, Robt. Costerdine, James
15 Creighton, John Crook, ((Thos. Dixon)), William Dufton, John
Easton, John Goodwin, William Green, Parson Greenwood,
James Hall, Thomas Hanby, Joseph Harper, Lanct. Harrison,
Jonathan Hern, Robert Hopkins, Christopher Hopper, William
Hunter, Edward Jackson, Daniel Jackson, Thomas Longley,
20 John Mason, Alexr. Mather, Duncan McAllum, John Moon,
Wm. Myles, Jonathan Parkin, John Pawson, John Peacock,
Willm. Percival, Joseph Pescod, Thos. Rankin, James Wray, Ben.
Rhodes, Rich. Rodda, Robert Roberts, Jerem. Robertshaw,
James Rogers, Thos. Rutherford, ((Joseph Saunderson)), Will.
25 Saunders, Robert Scot, Will. Simpson, George Shadford, John
Shaw, George Story, Thos. Taylor, Barns. Thomas, James Thom,
Willm. Thompson, John Valton, James Wood, Duncan Wright,
Frans. Wrigley

receive the sacrament of any of them, etc." ' (Aug. 8, 1787, Pawson, *Letters*,
1:45–46)

In his MS autobiography ('Some Account', fol. 35) Pawson says that all their
affairs were 'peaceably settled' but that 'we are not so spiritual at these times as I
could wish. Almost the whole time is taken up with temporal things and but very
little said or done which has a tendency to edify. This is a very great evil under
which my soul has long mourned'. Benson often complained similarly. James
Macdonald, *Memoirs of the Rev. Joseph Benson* (London: Blanshard, 1822), 185.

At this Conference a note was given to allow Sarah Mallet to be a female preacher
within a circuit in East Anglia. Taft, *Holy Women*, 1:84.

[235] Two of the original names, 'Thos. Dixon' and 'Joseph Saunderson', were
later struck through. That of Wm. Myles was added in another hand above the
line.

Absent
(There are twenty-seven names in four columns.)
[Francis Asbury, Charles Atmore, Thomas Barber, Jerem. Brettel,
George Brown, Thomas Corbet, Jonathn. Coussins, Thos. Dixon,
William Hoskins, Joshua Keighley, John Leech, Henry Moore, John 5
Murlin, Nehh. Price, Jasper Robinson, Joseph Taylor, Thos.
Tennant, Willm. Thom, Zach. Yewdall, Willm. Warrener, Thos.
Warrick, Chrisr. Watkins, Rich. Watkinson, Rich. Whatcoat, Charles
Wesley, Thomas Vasey, George Snowden
                                                                    10

[For the absence of all of whom a dispensation is passed.
[*Question* 1st. Who are in full connexion with the Conference?
[*Answer*. (There are one hundred and thirty-six names in four
columns, most of which are in roughly alphabetical order, with a
group of nine added at the end. Two names are struck through: 15
Daniel Jackson and Jeremiah Lambert. John Fidler is again listed
twice.)
Jos. Algar, Beverly Allen, Thos. Anderson, Will. Ashman, John Atlay,
John Baldwin, John Baxter, John Beanland, James Bogie, Charles
Bond, Samuel Botts, Thomas Bowen, Thos. Bartholomew, Hen. 20
Bingham, Philip Bruce, Robert Cann, Will. Cannan, Thos. Chew,
Jas. Christie, John Clarke, Adam Clarke, John McClaskey, Ezek.
Cooper, John Cooper, Adam Cloud, Robert Cloud, Will.
McCornock, Philip Cox, John Cricket, James Cromwell, Joseph
Cromwell, John Crosby, Thos. Curtis, Will. Damaron, Simon Day, 25
Thos. Davis, John Dickins, Stephen Dickins, Samuel Dudley, John
Easter, Sam. Edwards, Willm. Eells, Thos. Ellis, Reuben Ellis,
Michael Ellis, Ira Ellis, Rob. Empringham, Jos. Everett, John Fidler,
Jonn. Forrest, Thos. Foster, George Gibbon, Freeborn Garrettson,
Willm. Gill, Lemuel Green, Walter Griffith, John Hagerty, James 30
Haw, Woolman Hickson, Samuel Hodgson, Geo. Holder, Will.
Holmes, Robert Howard, Willm. Horner, Will. Hoskins, Hope Hull,
Thos. Humphries, ((Daniel Jackson)), Joseph Jerom, Andrew Inglis,
Robert Johnson, Thos. Johnson, Stephen Johnson, Thos. Jackson,
Henry Jones, Will. Jessop, James Jordan, Matthias Joyce, Richd. Ivy, 35
Lawrence Kane, James O'Kelly, John King, ((Jerem. Lambert)),
Jesse Lee, Mathw. Lumb, John Major, Jerem. Maston, Enoch
Matson, John Mealy, Peter Mill, Geo. Moore, Edward Morris, Peter
Moriarty, Geo. Mowat, Henry Ogburn, John Ogylvie, William
Partridge, John Paup, William Phoebus, Ignatius Pigman, John 40
Fidler, Wilson Lee, Elijah Ellis, John Poole, John Pritchard, Simon

Pile, William Palmer, Nelson Reed, Joseph Saunderson, Thos. Shaw,
Robert Sparks, Alexander Suter, Robert Swan, Richard Swift, Levin
Ross, James Thom, William Thomas, Joseph Thompson, John
Tunnell, George Wadsworth, James Watson, John Watson, James
5   White, Thos. Williamson, John Wittam, Thomas Wride, Joseph
Wyatt, James Riggin, John Robertson, John Smith, Isaac Smith,
Robert Ayres, Jacob Brush, Garret Thompson, Thomas Ware, Mark
Whitaker.].

Minutes

10   *Q.* 1. What preachers are *admitted* this year?[236]
          A. In *Great Britain*, T. Bartholomew, John Ogylvie, William
          Palmer, Jonathan Parkin, William Holmes.—In *America*,
          Robert Ayres, Henry Bingham, Jacob Brush, Robert
          Cann, Ezekiel Cooper, Stephen Dickins, Hope Hull,
15   Thomas Williamson, Stephen Johnson, Jeremiah Maston,
          John McClaskey, John Paup, Simon Pile, Levin Ross,
          Robert Sparks, Garret Thompson, Mark Whitaker.
          Q. 2. Who *remain* on trial?
          A. In *Great Britain*, Edward Burbeck, Charles Kyte,
20   Benjamin Pearce, Timothy Crowther, Jon. Crowther, John
          McKersey, William Butterfield, Richard Cornish, James
          Ridall, Charles Bland, Robert Gamble, John Smith,
          Alexander Kilham, William Fish, William Hunter, Jun.,
          William Blagborne, James Gore, John Reynolds, William
25   Bramwell, James Byron, John Townsend,[237] G. Baldwin,
          Theophilus Lessey, Thomas Jones, J. Evans, William
          Stephens, Thomas Roberts, T. Smith, William
          Thoresby,[238] George Highfield, John Barrett, John
          Tregortha, John Atkins, John Beaumont,[239] Jonathan
30   Edmondson, Joseph Sutcliffe, Duncan Kay, Abraham
          Moseley, John de Quêteville, John Gaulter, William
          Franklin, Stephen Kessall.[240]

[236] CJ, 'Which of these were admitted this year?'—showing that 'admitted'
implied 'admitted into full connexion'. CJ omits John Paup.
[237] Orig., 'Townshend' (twice), as also in 1788, 1789, and 1790.
[238] CJ adds 'John Robotham', which is then struck through.
[239] CJ adds 'Thos. Gill', which is then struck through.
[240] CJ omits 'Franklin' and 'Kessall'.

In *Ireland*, Benjamin Pearce, John Dinnen, Thomas Verner, Samuel Bates, Thomas Owens, David Gordon, Francis Frazier, John Harper, Thomas Roberts, John Gillis, Samuel Moorhead, John Grace.

In *America*, Sihon Smith, John Mason, Mark Moore,   5
Charles Hardy, John Simmons, Lastley Matthews, M. Laird, Henry Merritt, Daniel Asbury, Henry Vanover, Terence Burns, Micaiah Tracey, Jacob Lurton, John Jarrell, Benjamin Ogden, John Merrick,[241] S. Quinton Talbot, Aquila Edwards, John Simmons.   10

Q. 3. Who are *admitted* on trial?

A. In *Great Britain*, Samuel Gates, John Stamp,[242] George Phillips, John Holmes, John Woodrow, John Sandoe, Thomas Cooper, R. Reece, Michael Marshall, Joseph Cross, Robert Harrison, William Joughin,[243] Joseph   15
Entwisle, Francis Truscott, Thomas Crossley, David Barrowclough, John Saunders, William Collins, Jun., Robert Dall.

In *Ireland*, John Burnet, Andrew Jefferys,[244] John Black, William Johnson, George Henderson, John Darragh,   20
Francis Armstrong, William M\`Cornock, Thomas Hewett, John Malcomson,[245] Thomas Kerr, John West, Hugh Pue.[246]

In *America*, Edward West, James Conner, William Bradbury, Jeremiah Minter,[247] D. Lockett, Lemuel Andrews,   25
Matthew Harris, Lewis Grigg, Barnabas M\`Henry, Benjamin Carter, Isaac Lowe,[248] Nathaniel Moore, David Haggard, Jeremiah Abel, Thomas Weatherford,[249] Thomas Davis, L. Chastain,[250] Francis Spry, Cornelius Cook, T. Morrell, Christopher Spry, Nathaniel Mills, R. Pearson,   30

---

[241] Orig., 'Marrick'.

[242] CJ omits 'John Stamp'.

[243] Myles (probably in error) gives his name as 'Youglin'.

[244] Orig., 'Jeffers' (2), 'Jeffreys' once in 1789.

[245] Orig., 'Melcomson' (1) and in 1788 (2). From 1789 to 1791 the name appears as 'Melcombson', but in his obituary (1828) and his obituary of his sister (*WMM* [1827]: 797–802) he spells his name 'Malcomson'.

[246] Orig., 'Pugh' (twice); but in 1788 and his obituary (1789), 'Pue'.

[247] Orig., 'Mintor'.

[248] Orig., 'Low'.

[249] Orig., 'Wetherford'.

[250] Orig., 'Chasteen'.

Charles Conaway,[251] James Wilson, John Todd, J.
Milburn,[252] B. Riggin,[253] George Callahan,[254] David
Coombes, Dan. Coombes, T. Haymond,[255] B. Roberts,
Aaron Hutchinson, Elijah Phelps.

5   *Q*. 4. Who have died this year?[256]

A. *Thomas Lee*, a faithful brother, and a good old soldier of
Jesus Christ. *Henry Foster*, an excellent young man,
wholly devoted to God. *John Cowmeadow*, a pious young
man, unblameable in spirit and conversation.[257] *John*

10   *Fenwick*, who died, I believe, in peace. *Thomas Seaward*, a
pious, zealous, blameless, useful young man.[258]

Q. 5. Are there any objections to any of our preachers?

A. They were examined one by one.

Q. 6. How are the preachers stationed this year?

15   *A*. As follows:

(1) *London*, John Wesley, Charles Wesley, Thomas Coke,
James Creighton, Peard Dickinson, Samuel Bradburn;
Thomas Rankin and John Atlay, supernumeraries—
Joseph Bradford travels with Mr. Wesley.

20   (2) *Sussex*, John Reynolds, Robert Empringham,
Abraham Moseley.

(3) *Kent*, Joseph Algar, James Byron, W. Butterfield, J.
Holmes.

(4) *Colchester*, John Poole, Samuel Gates, John Woodrow.

25   (5) *Norwich*, Jasper Robinson, Joseph Harper, John
Cricket, Charles Bland, John Roberts.[259]

---

[251] In the American *Minutes* the name is spelled 'Conaway', but the English spelling was usually (as in orig. here) 'Connoway'.

[252] Orig., 'Milburne'.

[253] Orig., 'Reggin'.

[254] Orig., 'Callaughan'.

[255] Orig., 'Hayman'.

[256] CJ, 'Has any Member of Conference' (struck through) with 'Who have' (added above) 'died this last year?' The first two names only are given. The following three are added in the hand of Coke to *Q*. 5 in CJ, 'Has any Preacher who was in connexion with the Conference died this year?'

[257] CJ, to *Q*. 6, 'Who are elected members of the Conference in their place?' the answer is given: 'William Ashman and William Palmer'.

[258] CJ adds *QQ*. 7, 9, 10, in each case with the answer 'No'.

[259] The name of Roberts is added in the hand of Coke, and a following surname (?Flogg, possibly 'Floyd' intended) is struck through.

(6) *Lynn*, John Gaulter, William Bramwell, George Phillips.

(7) *Bedford*, Barnabas Thomas, T. Broadbent; J. Watson, supernumerary.

(8) *Northampton*, William Homer, W. Hoskins.

(9) *Oxfordshire*, Joseph Pescod, J. Entwisle, R. Reece; J. Murlin, supernumerary.

(10) *Gloucestershire*, Christopher Watkins, M. Marshall, R. Hopkins, J. Beaumont.

(11) *Sarum*, William Ashman,[260] J. Pritchard, W. Hunter, Jun.

(12) *Isle of Wight*, Thomas Warrick.[261]

(13) *Bradford*, John Furz, supernumerary, J. Mason, J. Easton, G. Wadsworth,[262] C. Kyte.

(14) *Bristol*, John Valton, supernumerary, J. Broadbent, B. Rhodes, J. Brettel.

(15) *Taunton*, William Green, C. Bond.

(16) *Tiverton*, George Button, J. McKersey.

(17) *Plymouth*, Lawrence Kane, S. Bardslcy, J. Cole.

(18) *St. Austell*, John Moon, James Evans, J. Sandoe.

(19) *Redruth*, George Shadford, W. Palmer, J. Gore.

(20) *St. Ives*, Jonathan Coussins, T. Lessey, J. Sutcliffe.

(21) *Pembroke*, William Dufton, Simon Day, S. Kessall.[263]

(22) *Glamorganshire*, George Baldwin, T. Jones.

(23) *Brecon*, William Holmes, R. Cornish.

(24) *Birmingham*, Daniel Jackson, T. Tennant, T. Cooper, J. Brettel.

(25) *Burslem*, Richard Rodda, T. Corbet, J. Tregortha.

(26) *Macclesfield*, George Story, T. Smith.

(27) *Manchester*, Thomas Taylor, E. Jackson, J. Beanland.

(28) *Stockport*, Robert Roberts, T. Carlill.

(29) *Chester*, Andrew Blair, William Eells, J. Ridall.

(30) *Wolverhampton*, Melville Home, supernumerary; J. Leech, W. Saunders.

---

[260] In CJ, Coke adds 'John Beaumont' over 'Ashman'.

[261] In CJ, 'George Hayter' was added, but is struck through.

[262] CJ, 'Charles' (struck through) 'George Wadsworth'.

[263] In CJ, 'Stephen Kessall' is added by Coke above 'Francis Truscott', which is struck through.

(31) *Liverpool,* Charles Boone, T. Brisco, R. Armstrong.[264]

(32) *Bolton,* Duncan Wright, C. Hopper.

(33) *Colne,* James Hall, S. Edwards.

(34) *Blackburn,*[265] Francis Wrigley, E. Burbeck.

(35) *Leicester,* William Boothby, T. Ellis, J. Jerom.

(36) *Nottingham,* Jonathan Hern, Rob. Scot, G. Highfield.

(37) *Derby,* George Gibbon, T. Crowther, T. Wood.[266]

(38) *Sheffield,* Alexander Mather, T. Hanty, J. Bogie.

(39) *Grimsby,* Thomas Longley, W. Fish.

(40) *Horncastle,* James Watson, J. Townsend, Jon. Edmondson.[267]

(41) *Gainsborough,* Launcelot Harrison, J. Barrett, T. Crossley.

(42) *Epworth,* Tho. Tattershall, G. Mowat, Rob. Howard.

(43) *Leeds,* John Pawson, G. Snowden, J. Shaw, supernumerary.[268]

(44) *Wakefield,* John Allen, S. Hodgson.

(45) *Birstall,* William Thompson, William Thoresby.

(46) *Dewsbury,* Parson Greenwood, W. Percival.

(47) *Huddersfield,* John Booth, R. Costerdine.

(48) *Halifax,* John Goodwin, Jon. Parkin.

(49) *Bradford,* William Collins, Jer. Robertshaw, T. Johnson, supernumerary.[269]

(50) *Keighley,* William Blagborne, T. Dixon, T. Shaw.[270]

(51) *Whitehaven,* John Peacock, J. Wittam.

(52) *Isle of Man,* John Crook, John Smith, D. Barrowclough.[271]

---

[264] In CJ, 'Robs. Armstrong' is added above the line by Coke, who also struck out the original 'Thomas Owens'. He then wrote over that name, 'John' and 'Willm. Collins, Junr.'

[265] In CJ, Blackburn ('Blackborne') in the hand of Coke, replaces the original 'Preston'.

[266] In CJ, Coke adds 'Thos. Wood'.

[267] In CJ, Coke adds the third name.

[268] In CJ, 'supernumerary' is added by Coke.

[269] In CJ, 'supernumerary' is added by Coke.

[270] In CJ, the last name, 'John Atkin[s]', is struck through—he was eventually stationed in Scarborough—and Coke added 'Thos. Dixon' in the second place.

[271] In CJ, 'James Christie' in the second place was struck through (transferred to 58), and Coke added 'David Barrowclough' at the end.

(53) *York*, Thomas Rutherford, J. Barber, W. Franklin.[272]

(54) *Pocklington*, Robert Swan, J. Cross.

(55) *Hull*, Joseph Benson, Tho. Bartholomew.

(56) *Scarborough*, Peter Mill, Alex. Kilham, J. Atkins.[273]

(57) *Whitby*, Isaac Brown, G. Holder.[274]   5

(58) *Thirsk*, John King, John Ogylvie, J. Christie.[275]

(59) *Yarm*, William Simpson, D. Kay.

(60) *The Dales*, James Thom, J. Saunders, J. Stamp; J. Thompson, supernumerary.

(61) *Sunderland*, William Hunter, A. Inglis, J. Crosby.   10

(62) *Newcastle*, James Wood, W. Thom, T. Wride.

(63) *Berwick*, Joseph Taylor, Matt. Lumb, R. Gamble.

(64) *Musselburgh*, Zachariah Yewdall.

(65) *Edinburgh*, Charles Atmore, J. Keighley.

(66) *Ayr and Greenock*, Alex Suter, W. Joughin.   15

(67) *Dumfries*, Robert Dall.

(68) *Dundee*, Richard Watkinson, S. Botts.

(69) *Aberdeen*, Robert Johnson, Joseph Saunderson.

(70) *Everness*, Duncan McAllum, J. Crowthcr, R. Harrison.   20

(71) *Jersey*, Robert Carr Brackenbury, A. Clarke.

(72) *Guernsey and Alderney*, John de Quêteville, Wm. Stephens.

(73) *Dublin*, Henry Moore, W. Myles.

(74) *Waterford*, David Gordon, A. Jefferys.   25

(75) *Cork*, James Rogers, M. Joyce.

(76) *Bandon*, Richard Condy, B. Pearce.

(77) *Limerick*, Jonathan Brown, J. Dinnen.

(78) *Castlebar*, George Brown, W. McCornock, Sen., W. McCornock, Jun.   30

(79) *Athlone*, Walter Griffith, J. Miller.

(80) *Longford*, William West, J. West.

---

[272] In CJ, Coke erased 'George Holder' (transferred to 57), and added 'William Franklin'.

[273] In CJ, Coke erased 'Thos. Dixon' from the second position and added 'John Atkins' at the end.

[274] In CJ, Coke erased 'Thomas Gill' in the second position, added 'Hugh L,——', erased that, and added 'George Holder'. (The only two itinerants with the forename Hugh at this time were Moore and Pue, both in Ireland.)

[275] In CJ, Coke replaced 'David Barrowclough' in the second place by 'James Christie' at the end.

(81) *Sligo*, Francis Frazier, W. Johnson.
(82) *Ballyconnell*, Joseph Armstrong, J. Rennick, J. Grace.
(83) *Clones*, Hugh Moore,[276] John Black, H. Pue.
(84) *Lisbellaw*, Samuel Mitchell, Tho. Verner, J. Gillis.
(85) *Enniskillen*, George Henderson, T. Kerr.
(86) *Ballyshannon*, Thomas Barber, J. Darragh.
(87) *Lisleen*, Robert Bridge, J. Malcomson.
(88) *Omagh*, John Price, T. Hewett.
(89) *Charlemont*, Samuel Bates, J. Collins.[277]
(90) *Londonderry*, Thomas Davis, J. McDonald.
(91) *Coleraine*, Thomas Roberts, N. Price, G. Armstrong.
(92) *Belfast*, John Howe, T. Owens.[278]
(93) *Lisburn*, Robert Lindsay, J. Burnet,[279] F. Armstrong.
(94) *Newry*, John Kerr, T. Hetherington, S. Moorhead.

A M E R I C A.

The United States.
Superintendents. Tho. Coke, Francis Asbury.   ELDERS

(95) *Burke*, John Major, M. Harris.   R[ichard]
(96) *Augusta*, T. Humphries, M. Park.   Ivy.
(97) *Broad River*, J. Mason, T. Davis.

(98) *Edisto*, E. West.   B[everly]
(99) *Charleston*, L. Green.   Allen.

(100) *Cainhoy*[280] *and Santee*, I. Smith.   R[euben]
(101) *Pee Dee*, H. Bingham, L. Andrews,   Ellis.
H. Leadbetter.

---

[276] In CJ, Coke erased the original 'Robert Armstrong' and inserted 'Hugh Moor[e]'.

[277] In CJ, Coke erased 'Hugh Moore' from the first position and added 'John Collins' at the end.

[278] In CJ, Coke erased 'James Jordan' from the second position and added 'Thomas Owens'.

[279] Orig. here 'Burnett'.

[280] Orig., 'Cainboy'.

(102) *Yadkin*, W. Partridge, B. McHenry, J. Conner.
(103) *Salisbury*, M. Moore.

[no name given]

(104) *Guilford*, J. Minter.   5
(105) *Halifax*, D. Asbury, J. Abel.   F[rancis]
(106) *New Hope*. J. Baldwin.   Poythress.
(107) *Caswell*, T. Burns.

(108) *Bladen*, D. Coombes.   10
(109) *New River*, E. Morris, H. Ogburn.
(110) *Tar River*, T. Bowen, T. Weatherford.
(111) *Roanoke*, T. Anderson, B. Carter.   J[ames]
(112) *Mecklenburg*, R. Swift, C. Hardy.   O'Kelly.
(113) *Brunswick*, J. Easter, H. Jones.   15
(114) *Sussex*, P. Cox, L. Grigg.
(115) *Amelia*, H. Hull, M. Whitaker.

(116) *Portsmouth*, T. Jackson, D. Jefferson.
(117) *Camden*, S. Smith.   P[hilip]   20
(118) *Banks*, D. Haggard.   Bruce.
(119) *Bertie*, H. Merritt, L. Chastain.

(120) *Bedford*, J. Paup, W. Bradbury.
(121) *Greenbrier*, J. Smith.   25
(122) *Orange*, I. Lowe, D. Lockett.   Lee Roy Cole.
(123) *Hanover*, H. Vanover.
(124) *Williamsburg*, S. Johnson.

(125) *Holstein*, J. Maston, Nath. Moore.   30
(126) *Nolachuckie*, T. Ware, M. Tracy.   J[ohn] Tunnell.
(127) *New River*, E. Morris, H. Ogburn.

(128) *Kentucky*, T. Williamson,
   W. Lee.   J[ames] Haw.   35
(129) *Cumberland*, B. Ogden.

(130) *Redstone*, W. Phoebus,
   J. Wilson, E. Phelps.   Jos.
(131) *Clarksburg*, R. Cann, R. Pearson.   Cromwell.   40
(132) *Ohio*, J. Conaway, G. Callahan.

(133) *Alleghany*, John Simmons,
J. Todd.
(134) *Bath*, R. Ayres, M. Laird.
(135) *Berkley*, L. Matthews,
5   J. Lurton.

R[ichard]
Whatcoat,
E[noch]
Matson,
Invalid.[281]

(136) *Fairfax*, M. Ellis,
A. Hutchinson.
(137) *Lancaster*, W. Cannan,
10   E. Ellis.

[Caleb Boyer,
Invalid.][282]

(138) *Frederick*, J. Forrest,
B. Riggin, B. Roberts.
(139) *Calvert*, J. Riggin.
15   (140) *Baltimore*, J. Lee.

N[elson] Reed.
J[ohn] Hagerty,
I[gnatius]
Pigman.

(141) *Kent*, I. Ellis, J. Merrick.
(142) *Talbot*, J. Cooper.
(143) *Dover*, A. Cloud, J. Brush.
20   (144) *Caroline*, J. White,
G. Thompson, F. Spry.

T[homas]
Chew,
J[ames]
Cromwell.

(145) *Dorset*, T. Curtis.
(146) *Somerset*, L. Ross, C. Spry.
25   (147) *Annamessex*, J. Everett,[283]
M. Greentree.
(148) *Northampton*, R. Sparks.

F[reeborn]
Garrettson.

(149) *Philadelphia*, S. Dudley,
30   W. Thomas.
(150) *Little York, Juniata*,
D. Coombes.

W[illiam] Gill.

[281] Orig., 'Maston'. Matson 'located' in 1788.
[282] The American *Minutes* have 'Caleb Boyer, Elder'; CJ has 'Caleb Boyer, Invalid', struck through; the British *Minutes* leave a blank.
[283] Orig., in CJ and *Minutes*, 'Evritt', but in American *Minutes*, 'Everett', as generally.

(151) *Eliza. Town*, R. Cloud,
T. Morrell.
(152) *West Jersey*, Rob. Cann,
J. McClaskey, J. Milburn.
(153) *Trenton*, Ezek Cooper, N. Mills.
(154) *East Jersey*, S. Pile, C. Cook.
(155) *New York*, [John Dickins,
Henry Willis]²⁸⁴
(156) *New Rochelle*, S. Talbot.
(157) *Long Island*, P. Moriarty.

J[ohn] Dickins, 5
H[enry] Willis.

10

The British Dominions.

(158) *Nova Scotia*, Wm. Jessop,
W. Black, J. Mann,
James Mann.

J[ames] Wray. 15

(159) *Newfoundland*,
J. McGeary.
(160) *Antigua*

W[illiam] Warrener,
J[ohn] Clarke.²⁸⁵ 20

(161) *St. Vincents*

J[ohn] Baxter.

(162) *St. Christophers*

W[illiam] Hammet. 25

Under the Government of Holland?

(163) *St. Eustatius*.

J. Harper.²⁸⁶

30

Q. 7. How many wives are to be provided for?
A. Seventy-nine.²⁸⁷
Q. 8. How many of these are to be provided for by the
circuits?

---

²⁸⁴ These names are supplied from the American *Minutes* and represent some of
the changes made after Coke sailed from Philadelphia on May 27, 1787.

²⁸⁵ Up to this period John Clarke's name appeared in both CJ and *Minutes* without the 'e', which henceforth became normal. Similarly Adam Clarke's name frequently appeared without his normal 'e'.

²⁸⁶ In CJ, 'John Harper' is added by Coke.

²⁸⁷ In CJ, 'eight' is altered to 'nine'.

A. Sixty-three: namely,[288]

(1)	London	S. Bradburn, Empringham.[289]
(2)	Gloucestershire	S. Hopkins.
(3)	Bradford	S. Easton.
(4)	Bristol	S. Rhodes, Brettel, Poole.[290]
(5)	Tiverton and Taunton	S. Green.
(6)	Plymouth	S. Kane.
(7)	St. Austell	S. Moon. £6
(8)	Redruth	S. Algar, Moon.[291] £6
(9)	St. Ives	S. Coussins.
(10)	Birmingham	S. (D) Jackson, Butterfield.[292]
(11)	Burslem	S. Rodda.
(12)	Macclesfield	S. Story.
(13)	Stockport	S. Roberts.
(14)	Manchester	S. Taylor, Beanland.
(15)	Chester	S. Blair.
(16)	Liverpool	S. Boone, Brisco.
(17)	Bolton	S. Wright.
(18)	Colne	S. Hall, Hopper. £6
(19)	Blackburn	S. Hopper. £6[293]
(20)	Leicester	S. Boothby.
(21)	Nottingham	S. Hern.
(22)	Sheffield	S. Mather, Gibbon,[294] Scot.[295]
(23)	Grimsby	S. Longley.
(24)	Gainsborough	S. Watson,[296] S. Ellis.[297]
(25)	Epworth	S. Mowat.

---

[288] In CJ, apparently 'sixty-four' first, then erased and altered to 'sixty-five'. For the first two circuits their three wives for support are listed, then erased, and the CJ moves on to 'Quest. 15. How are the others to be provided for?' (*Q.* 9 in the *Minutes.*) The answer is partly added in the hand of Coke, but omits 'sixteen', 'Atkins £6', and '(J.) Collins'.

[289] Robt. Empringham was stationed in Sussex.

[290] John Poole was stationed in Colchester.

[291] John Moon was stationed in St. Austell.

[292] Wm. Butterfield was stationed in Kent.

[293] Christopher Hopper's wife was being supported by two contiguous circuits; he was stationed in Bolton.

[294] George Gibbon was stationed in Derby.

[295] Robert Scot was stationed in Nottingham.

[296] James Watson was in his fourth year in the Lincolnshire area.

[297] Thomas Ellis was stationed in Leicester.

(26) Leeds	S. Snowden, Shaw, Costerdine.[298]
(27) Wakefield	S. Percival.[299]
(28) Birstall	S. Horner.[300]
(29) Dewsbury	S. Greenwood.
(30) Huddersfield	S. Booth.
(31) Bradford	S. (W.) Collins.
(32) Halifax	S. Goodwin.
(33) Keighley	S. Crosby.[301]
(34) York	S. Rutherford.
(35) Pocklington	S. Swan.
(36) Hull	S. Robertshaw.[302]
(37) Scarborough	S. Mill.
(38) Yarm	S Simpson.
(39) Whitby	S. (Is.) Brown.
(40) Thirsk	S. (T.) Shaw.[303]
(41) The Dales	S. Thom.[304]
(42) Sunderland	S. Inglis, Ogylvie.[305]
(43) Newcastle	S. Wood.
(44) Edinburgh	S. Atmore.
(45) Ireland	S. Moore, Myles,
	Joyce, Hetherington,
	(G.) Brown, Griffith, Price.[306]

Q. 9. How are the other sixteen to be provided for: namely, S. Harper, Warrick, Corbet, Peacock, Crook, Dixon, £6;

[298] John Shaw was a supernumerary in Leeds; Robert Costerdine was stationed in Huddersfield.

[299] Wm. Percival was stationed in Dewsbury.

[300] Wm. Horner was stationed in Northampton.

[301] John Crosby was stationed in Sunderland.

[302] Jeremiah Robertshaw was stationed in Bradford (Yorkshire).

[303] Thomas Shaw was stationed in Keighley.

[304] James Thom was stationed in The Dales Circuit, and his wife was supported for 1788 to 1791, so that presumably she is intended. On the other hand, his brother William's wife had been receiving support (1778–86) and continued to do so (1788–91), so that he (although stationed in Newcastle) may well be intended here.

[305] John Ogylvie was stationed in Thirsk.

[306] These preachers were stationed thus: Henry Moore, Dublin; Wm. Myles, Dublin; Matthias Joyce, Cork; Thomas Hetherington, Newry; George Brown, Castlebar; Walter Griffith, Athlone; John Price (who is probably intended) was stationed in Omagh.

Atkins £6; Dall, Watkinson, Johnson £6; Hunter, McAllum, Condy, Rennick, Dinnen, (J.) Collins?[307]

A. Partly out of the yearly collection, and partly out of the Preachers' Fund.

N.B. The money for them all, except the four last, will be lodged in the hands of Mr. Atlay; the money for the four last in the hands of Mr. Henry Moore.

Q. 10. What numbers are in the societies?

A. As follows:

London	2,600
Sussex	222
Kent	450
Colchester	334
Norwich	576
Lynn	247
Bedford	252
Northampton	370
Oxfordshire	560
Gloucestershire	707
Sarum	593
Bradford	1,199
Bristol	1,864
Taunton	205
Tiverton	426
Plymouth	660
St. Austell	820
Redruth	1,620
St. Ives	1,287
Pembroke	182
Glamorganshire	219
Brecon	96
Birmingham	1,343
Burslem	1,064

[307] These preachers were stationed thus: Joseph Harper, Norwich; Thomas Warrick, Isle of Wight; Thomas Corbet, Burslem; John Peacock, Whitehaven; John Crook, Isle of Man; Thomas Dixon, Keighley; John Atkins, Scarborough; Robert Dall, Dumfries; Richard Watkinson, Dundee; Thomas Johnson, Bradford (Yorkshire), supernumerary; Wm. Hunter, Sen., Sunderland; Duncan McAllum, Inverness; Richard Condy, Bandon; James Rennick, Ballyconnell; John Dinnen, Limerick; J. Collins, Charlemont.

Macclesfield	972	
Manchester	1,852	
Stockport	880	
Chester	840	
Liverpool	752	5
Bolton	869	
Colne	1,850	
Leicester	700	
Nottingham	800	
Derby	397	10
Sheffield	1,600	
Grimsby	530	
Horncastle	629	
Gainsborough	777	
Epworth	636	15
Leeds	2,470	
Birstall	900	
Dewsbury	808	
Huddersfield	945	
Hull	580	20
Scarborough	630	
Whitby	547	
Thirsk	640	
Halifax	128[x308]	
Bradford	1,128[x]	25
Keighley	1,240[x]	
Whitehaven	247[x]	
Isle of Man	2,116[x]	
York	910[x]	
Pocklington	680[x]	30
Jersey	200[x]	
Yarm	455	
The Dales	950	
Sunderland	1,100	
Newcastle	1,093	35
Berwick	100	
Edinburgh	261	

[308] The nine circuits and totals marked with a superscript 'x' were omitted from the original draft of CJ and added at the end (on p. 57) by Coke. The membership of other circuits was completely omitted from both CJ and *Minutes*.

	Ayre	55
	Dundee	125
	Aberdeen	243
	Inverness	144
5	Guernsey and Alderney	100[x]
	Dublin	1,137
	Waterford	320
	Cork	820
	Limerick	240
10	Castlebar	351
	Athlone	356
	Longford	340
	Sligo	288
	Ballyconnell	700
15	Clones	887
	Enniskillen	1,450
	Charlemont	680
	Ballyshannon	800
	Omagh	413
20	Londonderry	236
	Coleraine	446
	Belfast	425
	Lisburn	600
	Newry	824[309]
25		
	Total in Europe	62,088[310]

A M E R I C A.

The British Dominions.

	Nova Scotia	600
30	Newfoundland	100
	Antigua, { Whites	43
	{ Blacks	1,957

[309] In CJ there were no circuit details given for Ireland, simply the total, 'Ireland, 11,313'.

[310] Orig., '62,087'.

St. Vincent's,	{ Whites	9
———— [311]	{ Blacks	31
St. Kitt's,[312]	{ Whites	50
————	{ Blacks	100

5

Under the Dutch Government.

| St. Eustatius, | { Whites | 2 |
| ———— | { Blacks | 60 |

In the United States,	25,347	10
Total in America,	28,299	
Total in Europe and America[313]	90,386	

Q. 11. What is the Kingswood Collection?

A. £739. 0s. 11d.[314]   15

Q. 12. What children are admitted this year?

A. Benjamin Rogers, Lawrence Kane, Wesley Hern, William Hern.[315]

Q. 13. What can we allow the daughters of the preachers out of the Kingswood Collection?   20

A. Mary Rodda, £6 the second year; Margaret Story, £6 the first year; Sarah Harrison, £6 the first year,——N.B. John Brown is allowed £6.[316]

Q. 14. What is contributed to the Preachers' Fund?

A. £458. 13s. 0d.   25

Q. 15. What is allowed out of it?

A. To Thomas Westell,	£30	0	0
William Whitaker	20	0	0
John Bredin (for the				30
present year)	15	0	0

[311] CJ has 'Catechumens' before 'Blacks'.

[312] CJ, 'St. Christopher's', and reverses the order to Blacks, Whites.

[313] In CJ this is in the hand of Coke, as also his addition of 'Ireland' to 'Total in Great Britain'. There are many erasures in the arithmetic, and the total should apparently be 91,296.

[314] In CJ, Coke adds: '11s. more recd. & a Guinea & a half', i.e., a total supplement of £2. 2s. 6d. In CJ, the answer to '*Q*. 11: What is the Kingswood Collection?' is '£736. 18s. 5d.' The two sums together amount to the answer to *Q*. 11 in the *Minutes*.

[315] Orig., 'Herne' (twice).

[316] *QQ*. 12–13 do not appear in CJ.

	Matthew Lowes	5	0	0
	Thomas Hanson	12	0	0
	John Furz	12	0	0
	John Watson	12	0	0
5	John Mealy	12	0	0
	Ann Morgan	24	0	0
	Lucy Bourke	12	0	0
	Mary Penington	15	0	0
	Sarah Shorter	10	0	0
10	Catherine Garnet	12	0	0
	Elizabeth Dillon	10	0	0
	Tabitha Norris	12	0	0
	Margaret Payne	12	0	0
	Sarah Barry	24	0	0
15	Sarah Naylor	10	0	0
	Elizabeth Oldham[317]	15	0	0
	Sarah Hosmer	10	0	0
	Elizabeth Jaco	12	0	0
	Mary Lee	10	0	0
20	Sarah Evans (a gift)	10	0	0
	In all,	£340	5	0[318]

Q. 16. What is contributed for the yearly expenses?
A. £1,035. 16*s.* 1*d.*

25   *Q.* 17. How was it expended?

	A. Last year's deficiencies	£60	0	0
	This year's contingencies	100	0	0
30	For the deficiencies of the preachers and their families in Ireland	243	7	6
	For the deficiencies of the preachers and their families in Scotland	173	16	9
35	For the deficiencies of the preachers, etc. in Wales	57	15	6
	For the deficiencies of the preachers and their families in England	446	12	11

[317] Orig., 'Holdham'.

[318] CJ, '£337. 5. 0.' with no details of the expenditure; the *Minutes* total is correct.

Law	22	3	6
In all,	£1,103	16	2[319]

Q. 18. What houses are to be built this year?

A. One at Rye, Stourport, Godshill, Winterbourne, Neath,   5
Dudley, Altrincham,[320] Mosley,[321] Salford, Leigh, Burnley,
Preston, Sheephead, Ackworth, Pontefract,[322]
Kettleshang,[323] Lofthouse, Howden, Tullamore, Carlow,
Moat, and Tandaragee.

Q. 19. Are there any directions to be given concerning   10
Kingswood School?

A. Let the number of boarders be reduced as soon as possible to ten; and the number of preachers' sons be raised to
thirty.[324]

Q. 20. Are there any directions to be given concerning   15
preachers to whom we are strangers?

A. Let no person that is not in connexion with us preach in
any of our chapels or preaching-houses without a note
from Mr. Wesley, or from the Assistant of the circuit from
whence he comes; which note must be renewed yearly.   20

Q. 21. Many of our people who have been travelling on
business have crowded into the preachers' dwelling-
houses, and taken up their lodgings there, to the great
inconvenience of the preachers and their families, and
expense of the respective societies. What can be done to   25
remedy this evil?

A. Let none of our friends that travel on business expect to
be entertained in the preachers' houses.

[319] The total is, in fact, £1,103. 16. 2; CJ reads '£1035. 16. 1.' CJ gives no details,
but summarizes the answer thus:
 'In contingencies for the past year.
 'In contingencies for the present year.
 'In law, and in providing for the preachers' deficiencies.'
[320] Orig., 'Akdringham'.
[321] Mossley, Lancashire.
[322] Orig., 'Pomfret'.
[323] Kettlesham, Yorkshire.
[324] Kingswood School was originally designed for sons of lay supporters of
Methodism and not primarily for sons of itinerants. The new provision marks a
shift in favour of sons of itinerants, and later the school was kept exclusively for
them despite attempts in the 19th century to reopen it to laymen's sons; such
attempts in the 20th century were successful.

Q. 22. What can be done to prevent the heavy burdens and
expenses which are needlessly thrown on the Conference?
A. Those circuits that do not provide for their preachers
(except Scotland, Ireland and Wales, and a few small
5   circuits in England) shall have no more preachers sent to
them for the time to come than they will provide for.
Q. 23. Are there any directions to be given concerning
singing?
A. Let no anthems be introduced into our chapels or
10   preaching-houses for the time to come, because they
cannot be properly called Joint-Worship.[325]
Q. 24. When and where shall our next Conference be
held?
A. In London, on the last Tuesday in July, 1788.[326]
15   [*Q.* 25]. [Who are the two new Stewards of the Preachers'
Fund, who are to act jointly with John Pawson?
A. Alexander Mather and Thos. Rankin.]

John Wesley

Annual *Minutes of some late Conversations*, 1788

20   London, Tuesday, July 29, 1788.[327]
[The Minutes or Journals of the Conference of the People called
Methodists, begun in London on Tuesday the twenty-ninth day of
July in the year of our Lord, 1788, and continued by various
adjournments to the 6th day of August following inclusive.

[325] *QQ.* 18–23 are not present in CJ.
[326] *Q.* and *A.* 24 are in the hand of Coke, as also is the closing *Q.* 23 added to CJ.
[327] CJ for 1788 occupies pp. 58–64 and is mainly in an unknown hand, with additional notes by Coke.
JW wrote,
'Mon. 21. I retired to Highbury-Place, and spent the residue of the week in
answering letters, revising papers, and preparing for the Conference. Sun.
27. . . . I preached at the New Chapel every morning during the Conference;
which continued nine days, beginning on Tuesday July 29th; and ending on
Wednesday August 6. And we found the time little enough, being obliged to
pass over many things very briefly which deserved a fuller consideration.
. . . Monday 4. . . . One of the most important points considered at this
Conference, was that of leaving the Church. The sum of a long conversation

was (1) that, in the course of fifty years, we had neither premeditately nor willingly varied from it in one article either of doctrine or discipline; (2) that we were not yet conscious of varying from it in any point of doctrine; (3) that we have in a course of years, out of necessity, not choice, slowly and warily varied in some points of discipline, by preaching in the fields, by extemporary prayer, by employing lay preachers, by forming and regulating societies, and by holding yearly Conferences. But we did none of these things till we were convinced we could no longer omit them at the peril of our souls. Wed. 6. Our Conference ended as it began, in great peace. We kept this day as a fast, meeting at five, nine, and one, for prayer; and concluding the day with a solemn watch-night.' *Journal & Diaries*, 24:103–4.

The diary reveals the ordination on successive days (as Deacon and Presbyter) of six preachers, followed by that of Alexander Mather, the first ordained for England. It seems that Mather was ordained Superintendent also, so he and others later claimed, with a view to continuing the succession. Baker, *Wesley and Church*, 281 and refs.; Pawson, *Letters*, 1:156–57 in 1793. There are also almost daily references to Thomas Rankin, who was a supernumerary in London, close to JW, and also ordained by him for England in Feb. 1789.

John Valton in his journal writes, 'This day our Conference ended. I think we moved very slowly in our work, but what made full amends for this was the love and gentleness which seemed to prevail through the whole.' *WHS* 8 (1912): 101, 102. JW and three other clergy administered Communion.

Though not mentioned in the *Minutes*, the Dewsbury chapel dispute was already under way and no doubt reflected in *Q*. 25, which recited the 'Conference Plan', i.e., the Model Deed. For the dispute and the need to build a new chapel when the trustees held on to the old one, see also *Minutes* (1789), n. 415 and *QQ*. 19, 24. On July 30, 1788, JW wrote to the trustees,

'The question between us is, "By whom shall the preachers sent from time to time to Dewsbury be judged?" You say, "By the trustees". I say, "By their peers—the preachers met in Conference". You say, "Give up this and we will receive them". I say, "I cannot, I dare not, give up this". Therefore, if you will not receive them on these terms, you renounce connection with, Your affectionate brother, John Wesley.' (*Letters* [Telford], 8:77)

Atlay and Eells then supported the trustees in a secession. Pawson's attempt to make peace failed. *Letters*, 1:67; and see Tyerman, *Wesley*, 3:552–600. Francis Wrigley wrote to JW on July 11, 1788, saying, 'Are we not making rich men needful to us by building preaching houses?' and he thought preachers were undermining the itinerancy by staying too long in the larger places. MS Box 'Letters to JW', in MA. JW was inclined to agree. *Letters* (Telford), 8:72.

In his diary, Charles Atmore wrote, 'Mr. Charles Wesley having died the 28th March preceding, it was expected by many that a separation from the Church would immediately take place. Mr. Wesley reacted with great caution. He told us [at the Conference] he was not John skipping like a flea but John creeping like the louse'. Quoted by Tyerman, Tyerman MS biography of Atmore, in MA.

After this Conference, JW appointed a committee for auditing his accounts 'and superintending the business of the Book-Room, which, I doubt not, will be managed in a very different manner from what it has been hitherto.' *Journal & Diaries*, 24:112, and see introduction, p. 38.

[Present
[The Revd. John Wesley, President.
[The Revd. Thos. Coke, Secretary.
(There are sixty-one names in three columns,
5   the twenty-fifth, Atmore, at the head of the second.)
[John Allen, William Ashman, Samuel Bardsley, Andrew Blair,
John Booth, William Boothby, Samuel Bradburn, Joseph Bradford,
R. Carr Brackenbury, Thomas Brisco, John Broadbent, Isaac Brown,
George Button, Joseph Cole, William Collins, Jonathan Coussins,
10 James Creighton, Thomas Dixon, William Dufton, John Goodwin,
Parson Greenwood, James Hall, Thomas Hanby, Joseph Harper,
Charles Atmore, Lant. Harrison, Jonn. Hern, Robert Hopkins,
William Hunter, Daniel Jackson, John Leech, Thos. Longley, John
Mason, Alexr. Mather, John Moon, Henry Moore, John Murlin,
15 John Peacock, John Pawson, Joseph Pescod, Thomas Rankin, Jasper
Robinson, Benj. Rhodes, Richard Rodda, Robert Roberts, Thos.
Rutherford, George Shadford, William Simpson, George Story,
Thos. Taylor, Joseph Taylor, James Thom, Barnabas Thomas,
Thomas Tennant, William Thompson, John Valton, Thomas Vasey,
20 Thomas Warrick, Chrisr. Watkins, James Wood, Francis Wrigley.

[Absent
[There are thirty-five names in four columns,
Robertshaw being struck through, surely because of his death.]
25   John Barber, Thomas Barber, Joseph Benson, Charles Boone, Jer.
Brettel, George Brown, Thomas Carlill, Thomas Corbet, Rob.
Costerdine, Francis Asbury, John Crook, John Easton, William
Green, George Snowden, Christr. Hopper, William Hoskins,
Edward Jackson, Duncan McAllum, William Myles, William
30 Palmer, Jonathan Parkin, William Percival, Neh. Price, James Wray,
James Rogers, ((Jerem. Robertshaw)), William Saunders, Robert
Scot, John Shaw, Will. Thom, Zach. Yewdall, Will. Warrener, Rich:
Watkinson, Rich. Whatcoat, Duncan Wright.

35   [For the absence of all of whom a dispensation is passed.
[*Quest: 1ˢᵗ*. Who are in full connexion with the Conference?
(There are one hundred and twenty-nine names in four columns,
pp. 58–59, combining in one alphabetical list both British and
American preachers, reading first down four columns of four on p.
40 58, then down four columns of twenty-four names each on p. 59,
then reading across four rows of four, from Will. Thomas to Geo.

Wadsworth in row 25, and finishing with Mark Whitaker as the sole name in row 29. John Fidler again appears twice.)

[*Ans.* Jos. Algar, Beverly Allen, Thos. Anderson, John Atlay, Robert Ayres, John Baldwin, John Baxter, John Beanland, James Bogie, Charles Bond, Samuel Botts, Thomas Bowen, Thos. 5 Bartholomew, Henry Bingham, Philip Bruce, Jacob Brush, Will. Butterfield, Robert Cann, William Cannan, Thomas Chew, James Christie, John Clarke, Adam Clarke, John McClaskey, Ezek. Cooper, John Cooper, Adam Cloud, Robert Cloud, Thos. Cooper, Will. McCornock, Philip Cox, John Cricket, James Cromwell, Jos. 10 Cromwell, John Crosby, Thomas Curtis, Robert Dall, Will. Damaron, Simon Day, Thomas Davis, John Dickins, Stephen Dickins, Samuel Dudley, John Easter, Will. Eells, Thomas Ellis, Reuben Ellis, Michael Ellis, Ira Ellis, Rob. Empringham, Jos. Everett, John Fidler, Jon Forrest, George Gibbon, Freeborn 15 Garrettson, Will. Gill, Lemuel Green, Walter Griffith, John Hagerty, James Haw, Woolman Hickson, Samuel Hodgson, George Holder, William Holmes, Robert Howard, William Horner, William Hoskins, Hope Hull, Thos. Humphries, Joseph Jerom, Andrew Inglis, Robert Johnson, Thomas Johnson, Stephen Johnson, Thos. 20 Jackson, Henry Jones, Will. Jessop, Matthias Joyce, Richard Ivy, Lawrence Kane, James O'Kelly, John King, Charles Kyte, Jesse Lee, Matthew Lumb, Jerem. Maston, Enoch Matson, Peter Mill, Edward Morris, Peter Moriarty, Geo. Mowat, Henry Ogburn, John Ogylvie, Will. Partridge, John Paup, Will. Phoebus, Ignatius Pigman, John 25 Fidler, Wilson Lee, Elijah Ellis, John Poole, John Pritchard, Simon Pile, Nelson Reed, Jos. Saunderson, Thomas Shaw, Robert Sparks, Alexander Suter, Robert Swan, Richard Swift, Levin Ross, James Thom, Will. Thomas, Joseph Thompson, John Tunnell, Geo. Wadsworth, James Watson, John Watson, James White, Thos. 30 Williamson, John Wittam, Tho Wride, Joseph Wyatt, James Riggin, John Smith, Isaac Smith, Garret Thompson, Thos. Ware, Mark Whitaker.

Minutes

Q. 1. What preachers are admitted this year?   35
A. Charles Kyte, William Butterfield, Thomas Cooper, Robert Dall, Benjamin Pearce.[328]

---

[328] Pearce's name added in CJ by Coke.

Q. 2. Who remain on trial?

A. Timothy Crowther, Jonathan Crowther, John McKersey,
Richard Cornish, James Ridall, Charles Bland, Robert
Gamble, John Smith, Alexander Kilham, William Fish,
5   William Hunter, Jun., William Blagborne, James Gore,
John Reynolds, William Bramwell, James Byron, John
Townsend, George Baldwin, Theophilus Lessey,[329]
Thomas Jones, James Evans, William Stephens, Thomas
Roberts, William Thoresby, George Highfield, John
10   Barrett, John Tregortha, John Atkins, Jonathan
Edmondson, Joseph Sutcliffe, Duncan Kay, Abraham
Moseley, John de Quêteville, John Gaulter, Thomas
Wood, William Heath, Samuel Gates, John Stamp,
George Phillips, John Holmes, John Woodrow, John
15   Sandoe, Richard Reece, Michael Marshall, Joseph Cross,
Robert Harrison, Joseph Entwisle, Francis Truscott,[330]
David Barrowclough, John Dinnen, Thomas Verner,
Samuel Bates, Thomas Owens, David Gordon, Francis
Frazier, John Gillis, Samuel Moorhead, John Grace,
20   Andrew Jefferys, John Black, William Johnson, John
Darragh, Francis Armstrong, William McCornock, Jun.,
Thomas Hewett, John Malcomson, Thomas Kerr, John
West, Hugh Pue.[331]

N.B. All those who have travelled four years are to be
25   present at the next Conference.

Q. 3. Who are *admitted on trial?*

A. Richard Phillips, Thomas Rogerson, Thomas Wyment,
John Wiltshaw, George Lowe, Thomas Allen, Henry
Taylor, John Hickling,[332] Charles Tunnycliffe,[333] John
30   Furnace, Thomas Kelk, Thomas Dobson, Richard

---

[329] Orig., 'Lessy', as also in 1791 (2).

[330] Orig., 'Truscot', as also in 1789.

[331] CJ lists these preachers in exactly the same order, but includes and then strikes out 'Thomas & Smith' and 'John Beaumont', listed as the opening names (though in reverse order) of the five who desisted.

[332] From 1789 to 1791 the *Minutes* gave his name as 'Hicklin', but it appeared as 'Hickling' in 1788, and from his admittance into full connexion in 1792 until his death at age 92 in 1858, when he had gained some repute as the oldest preacher called into the work by Wesley. *WHS* 26 (Pt. 1, 1947): 16.

[333] Orig., and occasionally 1789–91, 'Tunycliffe'; at his death in 1828 his name appears as 'Tunnicliffe'.

Burdsall,[334] Richard Seed, Jasper Winscom,[335] John
Stephens, James Lyons, James McMullen, Alexander
Moore, Matthew Stewart, Thomas Elliott,[336] Frederick
Hamilton, Andrew Hamilton, Robert Smith,
Nebuchadnezzar Lee, John Stephenson, William   5
Hamilton, Daniel Graham, John Riles,[337] Mark Willis.[338]
Q. 4. Who have died this year?
A. 1. *Jeremiah Robertshaw*, who was a good soldier of Jesus
Christ, fairly worn out in his Master's service. He was a
pattern of patience for many years, labouring under   10
sharp and almost continual pain, of meekness and gen-
tleness to all men, and of simplicity and godly sincerity.
2. *Joshua Keighley*, who was a young man deeply
devoted to God, and greatly beloved by all that knew
him. He was   15

> About the marriage state to prove;
> But death had swifter wings than love.[339]

3. *Edward Burbeck*, who from a child was eminent for
uprightness, industry, and the fear of God. He was qualified for eminent service in his Lord's vineyard, but was 20
taken just in the dawn of his usefulness.
4. *John Roberts*, who for many years was clearly convinced that God had called him to preach the gospel.
But he delayed from time to time, till at length conscience prevailed over all other considerations.   25

It was almost too late; for after labouring a few
months, he fell into a lingering illness. For some weeks
he was in utter darkness; then God scattered the clouds,
and gave him to die in peace.
5. Mr. *Charles Wesley*, who after spending fourscore   30
years with much sorrow and pain, quietly retired into
Abraham's bosom. He had no disease; but after a gradual decay of some months

---

[334] Orig., 'Birdsall' (2).

[335] Orig., 'Wynscombe', as also 1789–91, with an alternative 'Winscomb' in 1790, and 'Winscom' in 1789, as well as in his personal signature in 1771 and 1791.

[336] Orig., 'Elliot' (1), as also 1789 (1), and 1791 (2).

[337] Orig., 1788, 1790–91, 'Ryle'; 1789, 'Ryles'.

[338] Added in CJ by Coke.

[339] Samuel Wesley, Jun., *Poems* (1736), 8.

The weary wheels of life stood still at last.[340]

His least praise was, his talent for poetry; although
Dr. Watts did not scruple to say, that 'that single poem
"Wrestling Jacob", was worth all the verses he himself
had written.'[341]

6. *John Mealy*, worn out in the service of his Master: he
suffered much in his last illness, and died triumphant in
the Lord.

7. *John Burnet*, a very pious, devoted, useful young man:
he continued through a long illness in a very triumphant
state of mind, and departed this life in extraordinary
triumph.[342]

Q. 5. Are there any objections to any of our preachers?

A. They were examined one by one.

Q. 6. Who have desisted from travelling?

A. John Beaumont, Thomas Smith, Robert Lindsay, James
Jordan, Robert Armstrong.

Q. 7. How are the preachers stationed this year?

A. As follows:

(1) *London*, John Wesley, Thomas Coke, James
Creighton, Peard Dickinson,[343] Henry Moore, Samuel
Bradburn;[344] Thomas Rankin, John Atlay, Alexander
Suter, supernumeraries—Joseph Bradford travels with
Mr. Wesley.

(2) *Sussex*, Timothy Crowther, J. Holmes, Thomas Jones.

[340] Cf. Dryden, *Oedipus*, Act iv. Scene 1: 'The wheels of weary life at last stood still'.

[341] This poem first appeared in *Hymns and Sacred Poems* (1742), 115–18.

[342] CJ adds here:

Q. 6: Who are elected Members of the Conference in the room of the above named Mr. Charles Wesley, Jeremiah Robertshaw, and Joseph Keighley, deceased?

A. Peard Dickinson, Joseph Cownley ['Cownley' added by the hand of Coke], and Alexander Suter.

Q. 7: Is any Preacher expelled who has been in connexion with the Conference?

A. James Jordan, Robert Lindsay, Robert Armstrong. [The latter two are added in the hand of Coke. One and a half names, also added in his hand, 'Thos. Smith, John', are struck through, See CJ above, and *Minutes*, *Q*. 6.]

[343] Orig., 'Dickenson', as also in 1789 and 1791.

[344] In CJ, Bradburn replaces Charles Boone—in Coke's hand.

(3) *Kent*, John Pritchard, William Butterfield, Charles Kyte,[345] James Byron; Barnabas Thomas, supernumerary.

(4) *Colchester*, Joseph Harper, Thomas Broadbent, Thomas Rogerson.

(5) *Norwich*, John Poole, Richard Reece, Thomas Kelk. 5

(6) *Yarmouth*, Thomas Tattershall, J. Woodrow.

(7) *Lynn*, John Reynolds, W. Green, John Cricket.

(8) *Bedford*, Robert Empringham, Thomas Ellis.[346]

(9) *Northampton*, William Horner, Thomas Wyment.

(10) *Oxfordshire*, Joseph Pescod, Charles Bland, 10
Abraham Moseley; John Murlin, supernumerary.

(11) *Gloucestershire*, Robert Hopkins, Michael Marshall.

(12) *Worcestershire*, Christopher Watkins, Thomas Wood.[347]

(13) *Sarum*, William Thom, W. Holmes, Richard 15
Cornish, J. Winscom, Thomas Allen.[348]

(14) *Isle of Jersey*, Robert Carr Brackenbury, Adam Clarke.

(15) *Isles of Guernsey and Alderney*, John Bredin, John de Quêteville. 20

(16) *Bradford*, John Easton, Joseph Algar, William Hoskins, William Hunter, Jun.; John Furz, supernumerary.

(17) *Bristol*, John Broadbent,[349] T. Tennant, Thomas Warrick; John Valton, supernumerary. 25

(18) *Taunton*, Jonathan Coussins, William Heath.

(19) *Tiverton*, William Ashman, J. McKersey.

(20) *Bideford*, Richard Drew, John Sandoe.

(21) *Plymouth*, Lawrence Kane, G. Wadsworth, Thomas Cooper. 30

(22) *St. Austell*, John Mason, Theophilus Lessey, William Fish.[350]

[345] CJ inserts and strikes through 'Sam¹. Gates', and Coke inserts 'James Byron' after Kyte.

[346] CJ adds 'John Watson, supernumerary', which is later struck through.

[347] In CJ, Coke replaces John Brettel with Wood.

[348] CJ reverses the order of Winscom and Allen.

[349] In CJ, Coke has replaced Richard Rodda in the first position by John Broadbent.

[350] In CJ, Coke replaced Benjamin Leggatt by William Fish.

(23) *Redruth*, Benjamin Rhodes, Samuel Bardsley, Richard Phillips.

(24) *St. Ives*, George Shadford, J. Gore, Joseph Sutcliffe, S. Gates.[351]

(25) *Pembroke*, William Palmer, C. Bond, Francis Truscott.

(26) *Glamorganshire*, William Stephens, George Button.

(27) *Brecon*, George Baldwin, William Church.

(28) *Birmingham*, Andrew Blair, Jeremiah Brettel, John Moon.

(29) *Wolverhampton*, Melville Home, supernumerary; John Leech, John Brettel.[352]

(30) *Burslem*, Richard Rodda,[353] T. Shaw, Thomas Dobson.

(31) *Macclesfield*, John Allen, John Tregortha, George Highfield.

(32) *Stockport*, Thomas Rutherford, William Dufton.[354]

(33) *Manchester*, Thomas Taylor, George Snowden, James Hall.[355]

(34) *Bolton*, Parson Greenwood, Christopher Hopper.

(35) *Chester*, Robert Roberts, Geo. Lowe;[356] Thomas Brisco, supernumerary.

(36) *Wirral*,[357] John Hickling.

(37) *Liverpool*, Daniel Jackson,[358] Hen. Taylor.

(38) *Blackburn*, George Story, William Bramwell.

(39) *Colne*, Charles Atmore, J. Ridall.

(40) *Leicester*, James Watson, Simon Day, Richard Seed; John Watson,[359] supernumerary.

(41) *Nottingham*, Joseph Taylor, T. Hanby, Joseph Jerom.

---

[351] In CJ, Coke changed James Byron to James Gore, and added Samuel Gates.

[352] In CJ, Coke replaced Simon Day by John Brettel.

[353] In CJ, Coke replaced Robert Roberts by Richard Rodda.

[354] In CJ, Coke replaced Boothby by Dufton.

[355] In CJ, Coke replaced Samuel Bradburn in the second position by James Hall.

[356] In CJ, Coke replaced James Hall and William Eells by Robert Roberts and George Lowe.

[357] Orig., 'Worrell'.

[358] In CJ, 'Thomas Vasey' appeared as the second of three names, having been listed as present among the Legal Hundred at the Conference. Bishop White re-ordained him in America, however, and it seems that he accepted an English curacy for a time, but returned to the Methodist stations in 1789.

[359] In CJ, Coke replaced Robert Scot and Thomas Wood by James Watson and Simon Day, and added John Watson.

(42) *Derby*, George Gibbon, T. Corbet, Robert Costerdine.

(43) *Sheffield*, Edward Jackson, A. Inglis, John Beanland.

(44) *Grimsby*, Thomas Longley, George Phillips.

(45) *Horncastle*, Thomas Carlill, Robert Scot, Benjamin Leggatt.[360]

(46) *Gainsborough*, Lancelot Harrison, George Mowat, James Evans.

(47) *Epworth*, Robert Swan, James Christie, John Atkins.

(48) *Leeds*, John Pawson, John Peacock, William Collins.

(49) *Wakefield*, Alexander Mather, Jonathan Parkin.

(50) *Huddersfield*, Francis Wrigley, William Boothby.[361]

(51) *Birstall*, William Thompson, Jos. Entwisle, William Thoresby.[362]

(52) *Bradford*, John Booth, Samuel Hodgson; Thomas Johnson, supernumerary.

(53) *Halifax*, John Goodwin, John Shaw.

(54) *Keighley*, James Wood, Thomas Bartholomew, William Blagborne; Robert Howard, supernumerary.

(55) *Whitehaven*, Thomas Wride, John Wiltshaw.

(56) *Isle of Man*, George Holder, John Smith, John Wittam.[363]

(57) *York*, Jonathan Hern, John Gaulter, Richard Burdsall.

(58) *Pocklington*, Jasper Robinson, William Percival, Thomas Dunn.[364]

(59) *Hull*, Joseph Benson, Jonathan Edmondson.

(60) *Scarborough*, Thomas Dixon, Isaac Brown, Alexander Kilham.

(61) *Whitby*, James Thom, J. Townsend.[365]

(62) *Thirsk*, John King, Duncan Kay, John Crosby.

(63) *Yarm*, William Simpson, Charles Tunnycliffe.[366]

---

[360] In CJ, Coke removed James Watson from the first position, thus promoting Carlill, and entered Scot and Leggatt to replace William Fish.

[361] In CJ, Coke replaced John Ogylvie by William Boothby.

[362] In CJ, Entwisle and Thoresby have their positions reversed.

[363] In CJ, Holder appears at the end, but is marked with a plus sign.

[364] In CJ, Coke replaced John Townsend by Dunn.

[365] In CJ, Coke replaced George Lowe by Townsend.

[366] In CJ, Coke replaced John Barrett by 'Tunnycliffe'.

(64) *The Dales*, William Saunders, Thomas Gill, Mark Willis.[367]

(65) *Sunderland*, William Hunter, Duncan Wright, John Ogylvie.[368]

(66) *Newcastle*, Peter Mill, Joseph Thompson, John Stamp.[369]

(67) *Berwick*, James Bogie, Zachariah Yewdall, John Furnace.

(68) *Dalkeith*, Jonathan Crowther.

(69) *Edinburgh*, Joseph Cownley, John Barber.

(70) *Ayr and Dumfries*, Joseph Cole, Robert Dall.

(71) *Dundee*, Richard Watkinson, Samuel Botts; Joseph Saunderson, supernumerary.

(72) *Aberdeen*, Robert Johnson, J. Cross.[370]

(73) *Inverness*, Duncan McAllum, John Barrett,[371] Robert Harrison.

(74) *Dublin*, Charles Boone,[372] W. Myles.

(75) *Wexford*, Hugh Moore, Thomas Verner.

(76) *Waterford*, Richard Condy, Francis Frazier.

(77) *Cork*, James Rogers, T. Roberts.

(78) *Bandon*, John Kerr, Robert Bridge.

(79) *Limerick*, Jonathan Brown, Andrew Jefferys.

(80) *Birr*, Thomas Davis, Gustavus Armstrong.

(81) *Castlebar*, James McDonald, Thomas Kerr.

(82) *Athlone*, John Dinnen, William Wilson.

(83) *Longford*, Thomas Barber, John Malcomson.

(84) *Sligo*, David Gordon, T. Hewett.

(85) *Ballyconnell*, George Brown, John Miller, Francis Armstrong; John Price, supernumerary.

(86) *Clones*, Joseph Armstrong, Samuel Moorhead,[373] Alex. Moore.

---

[367] In CJ, Coke replaced John Stamp by Willis.

[368] In CJ, Coke replaced Thomas Dunn by Ogylvie.

[369] In CJ, Coke replaced Charles Tunnycliffe by Stamp.

[370] In CJ, Coke replaced Duncan McAllum in the first position with Joseph Cross in the second.

[371] In CJ, Coke replaced William Dutton and Joseph Cross by McAllum and Barrett.

[372] In CJ, Coke entered Boone in the blank left in the first position.

[373] Orig., 'Moorehead', on this one occasion only.

(87) *Brookborough*, William McCornock, Jun., William Hamilton.

(88) *Enniskillen*, John Black, Daniel Graham.

(89) *Ballyshannon*, James Rennick, Andrew Hamilton.

(90) *Killybeggs*, John Stephenson, Thomas Elliott.   5

(91) *Lisleen*, Matthew Stewart, Nebuchadnezzar Lee.

(92) *Omagh*, Samuel Bates, James McMullen.[374]

(93) *Charlemont*, John Crook, David Barrowclough.

(94) *Londonderry*, William West, John West.

(95) *Coleraine*, Matthias Joyce, William Johnson, John   10
Stephens; John Howe, supernumerary.

(96) *Belfast*, Samuel Mitchell, John Darragh.

(97) *Lisburn*, Thomas Hetherington, John Gillis,
Frederick[375] Hamilton; Hugh Pue, supernumerary.

(98) *Newry*, Walter Griffith, John Grace.   15

(99) *Tandragee*, Nehemiah Price, James Lyons, Robert
Smith.[376]

A M E R I C A.

The British Dominions in America.

	ELDER.	20
(100) *Newfoundland*, John McGeary		
(101) *Nova Scotia*, William Jessop, William Black	J[ames] Wray.	
John Mann, James Mann.		25
(102) *Antigua*,	W[m] Warrener.	
	J[ohn] Harper.	30
(103) *St. Vincents*,	J[ohn] Baxter	
	J[ohn] Clarke.	

---

[374] Orig., 'McMullin' here and in 1791 stations.

[375] Orig., 'Frederic'.

[376] CJ moves from this point to *Q*. 10 (*Q*. 11 in *Minutes*), 'What numbers are in the Societies?'

(104) *St. Christophers,*
Under the Government
    of Holland   W[m.] Hammet.
(105) *St. Eustatius.*

5

The United States of America.

Superintendents, Tho. Coke, Francis Asbury.

N.B. The last Conference in America for the present year has not yet been held, so that we are not able to insert the exact stations of
10 the preachers in the United States.[377]

[377] The eighth American Conference of 1788 was held in New York, Sept. 30– Oct. 4; see Asbury, *Journal,* ed. Elmer T. Clark (London: Epworth Press, 1958), 2:580. The American stations for 1788 as they eventually appeared in the American *Minutes* are given here; the numbers following upon the listings above are added editorially.

Q. 11. *How are the Preachers stationed?*
Ans.

Richard Ivy, *Elder*

[106] *Burke*	Moses Park, Bennet Maxey
[107] *Richmond*	Matthew Harris
[108] *Washington*	Hope Hull, James Conner, Reuben Ellis, *Elder*
[109] *Seleuda*	Lemuel Andrews
[110] *Broad River*	William Partridge
[111] *Edisto*	Henry Bingham, William Gassaway
[112] *Charleston*	Ira Ellis
[113] *Santee*	John Smith, Hardy Herbert
[114] *Waxhaw* (orig., 'Waxsaws')	Michael Burdge
[115] *Pee Dee*	Thomas Humphries, Mark Moore

John Tunnell, *Elder*

[116] *Tar River*	Henry Merritt, William Moss, Daniel Lockett
[117] *Bladen*	Thomas Hardy
[118] *New River*	Thomas Anderson, James Parks
[119] *Roanoke*	Charles Hardy, William Heath, Michael Smith
[120] *Caswell*	Isaac Lowe
[121] *New Hope*	Henry Ogburn, John Ellis, Nathaniel Moore
[122] *Guilford*	Jeremiah Abel, James Conner
[123] *Salisbury*	John Baldwin, Doily Baird
[124] *Yadkin*	Sihon Smith, Micaijah Tracy
[125] *Halifax*	Edward West, Josiah Askew

Edward Morris, *Elder*

[126] *Holstein*   Jeremiah Maston, Joseph Doddridge
[127] *French Broad*   Daniel Asbury
[128] *New River*   Thomas Ware, Jesse Richardson
[129] *Greenbrier*   Richard Swift, Benjamin Carter

James O'Kelly, *Elder*

[130] *Anson*   David Haggard
[131] *Bertie*   James Meachem, Archer Davis
[132] *Camden*   Henry Birchett, J. Difnal
[133] *Portsmouth*   John Barker
[134] *Sussex*   John Easter, Lewis Grigg, Benjamin Barnes
[135] *Brunswick*   John Paup, Benjamin Ogden
[136] *Amelia*   Jeremiah Minter, Salathiel Weeks
[137] *Mecklenburg*   Philip Cox, William McKendree
[138] *Buckingham*   Joseph Dawson
[139] *Bedford*   Joshua Hartley, Isaac Lunsford
[140] *Amherst*   John Ford
[141] *Orange*   Thomas Weatherford, Samuel Davis
[142] *Hanover*   Richard Pope
[143] *Williamsburg*   Lee Roy Cole

Philip Bruce, *Elder*

[144] *Gloucester*   Stephen Johnson, Aquila Sugg
[145] *Lancaster*   Thomas Bowen, John Chalmers
[146] *Fairfax*   Amos G. Thompson, James Thomas
[147] *Berkley*   Robert Ayres, Elisha Phelps
[148] *Alleghany*   Michael Leard, Lewis Chastain

Philip Bruce, *Elder*

[149] *Rockingham*   William Phoebus, James Riggin

Nelson Reed, *Elder*

[150] *Bath*   James Wilson, John Rowen
[151] *Frederick*   Eliphalet Reed, Griffith Callahan
[152] *Montgomery*   Robert Green, John Allen
[153] *Calvert*   Jonathan Forrest, Valentine Cook
[154] *Little York*   John Hill
[155] *Baltimore*   Ezekiel Cooper, Francis Spry
[156] *Huntingdon*   Samuel Breeze, Daniel Coombes
[157] *Annapolis*   John Hagerty
[158] *Harford*   John Cooper, George Hagerty

Richard Whatcoat, *Elder*

[159] *Cecil*   John Smith, George Wells
[160] *Kent*   William Gill, William Thomas
[161] *Talbot*   Thomas Foster, John Jarrell, Lenox Martin

Q. 8. How many wives are to be provided for?
A. Ninety-one.
Q. 9. How many of these are to be provided for by the circuits?

[162] *Dorchester*	Robert Sparks, William Jessop
[163] *Annamessex*	Christopher Fry
[164] *Somerset*	James White, Emory Prior
[165] *Northampton*	Jacob Brush, Levin Ross
[166] *Caroline*	Joseph Everett, Matthew Greentree, Benjamin Roberts
[167] *Dover*	George Moore, Benton Riggin
[168] *Clarksburg*	John Simmons, George Callahan
[169] *Redstone*	Jacob Lurton, Lastley Matthews
[170] *Ohio*	Richard Pearson, John Todd
[171] *Pittsburgh*	Charles Conaway
[172] *Philadelphia*	Lemuel Green
[173] *Chester*	Robert Cann, John Milburn
[174] *Bristol*	William Dougherty

James O. Cromwell, *Elder*

[175] *Salem*	Joseph Cromwell, Nathaniel B. Mills, John Cooper
[176] *Trenton*	John Merrick, Thomas Morrell, Jethro Johnson
[177] *Elizabeth Town*	John MᶜClaskey, Simon Pile
[178] *Flanders*	Jesse Lee, Aaron Hutchinson, John Lee

Henry Willis, *Elder*

[179] *New York*	John Dickins
[180] *Long Island*	Robert Cloud

Freeborn Garrettson, *Elder*

[181] *New Rochelle*	Peter Moriarty, Albert Van Nostrand
[182] *Dutchess*	Cornelius Cook, Andrew Harpending
[183] *Shoreham*	Darius Dunham
[184] *New City*	Samuel Q. Talbot, David Kendall
[185] *Cambridge*	Lemuel Smith
[186] *Lake Champlain*	Samuel Wigton

Francis Poythress, James Haw, *Elders*

[187] *Lexington,*	Thomas Williamson, Peter Massey, Benjamin Snelling
[188] *Danville*	Wilson Lee
[189] *Cumberland*	David Coombes, Barnabas MᶜHenry

A. Seventy-eight: as follows, viz.

(1) London,	S. Moore, Bradburn, Crowther, Empringham.[378]
(2) Sussex, £3.[379]	
(3) Norwich, £3.	5
(4) Yarmouth, £3.	
(5) Lynn, £3.	
(6) Oxfordshire, £6.	
(7) Gloucestershire,	S. Hopkins, £6.
(8) Worcestershire,	S. Hopkins, £6.[380]	10
(9) Sarum and Portsmouth,	S. (Wm.) Thom.
(10) Bradford,	S. Easton, and £6.
(11) Bristol,	S. Broadbent, Warrick, Algar, J. Shaw.[381]	15
(12) Tiverton and Taunton,	S. Coussins.
(13) Plymouth,	S. Kane, and £6.
(14) St. Austell,	S. Church.[382]
(15) Redruth,	S. Rhodes, and £6.	20
(16) St. Ives,	S. Horner.[383]
(17) Birmingham,	S. Blair, Brettel, Story.[384]
(18) Burslem,	S. Rodda, and £6.
(19) Macclesfield,	S. Pritchard, and £6.[385]
(20) Stockport,	S. Rutherford, and £6.	25
(21) Manchester,	S. (Tho.) Taylor, Snowden, Roberts.[386]
(22) Chester,	S. Hall, and £6.[387]
(23) Liverpool,	S. (D.) Jackson, Brisco,[388] (H.) Taylor.	30

[378] Timothy Crowther was stationed in Sussex; Robert Empringham in Bedford.

[379] This seems to be the full-scale beginnings of a clear assessment upon all circuits. However, the Preachers' Fund continued to be raided until 1791; see the appeal in JW's letter prefacing the *Minutes* (1791) and introduction, p. 55.

[380] Robert Hopkins was stationed in Gloucestershire.

[381] Joseph Algar was stationed in Bradford [Wiltshire]; John Shaw in Halifax.

[382] William Church was stationed in Brecon.

[383] William Horner was stationed in Northampton.

[384] George Story was stationed in Blackburn.

[385] John Pritchard was stationed in Kent.

[386] Robert Roberts was stationed in Chester.

[387] James Hall was stationed in Manchester.

[388] Thomas Brisco was stationed in Chester.

(24) Bolton,	S. Greenwood.
(25) Colne,	S. Atmore, Bramwell.[389]
(26) Leicester,	S. Scot.[390]
(27) Nottingham,	S. (Jos.) Taylor, Atkins.[391]
(28) Derby,	S. Gibbon.
(29) Sheffield,	S. Inglis, Hopper, Moon.[392]
(30) Grimsby,	S. Longley.
(31) Horncastle,	£6.
(32) Gainsborough,	S. Watson,[393]
(32) [*sic*] Epworth,	S. Swan.
(33) Leeds,	S. Collins, Peacock, (T.) Shaw.
(34) Wakefield,	S. Mather, Ogylvie.[394]
(35) Birstall,	S. Butterfield.[395]
(36) Huddersfield,	S. Boothby.
(37) Bradford,	S. Booth.
(38) Halifax,	S. Goodwin.
(39) Keighley,	S. Wood, and £3.
(40) York,	S. Hern, and £3.
(41) Pocklington,	S. Percival.
(42) Hull,	S. Mowat.[396]
(43) Scarborough,	S. (Is.) Brown, and £3.
(44) Yarm,	S. Simpson, and £6.
(45) Whitby,	S. (Jam.) Thom.
(46) The Dales,	S. Gill, and £3.
(47) Sunderland,	S. Hunter, Dunn, and £6.[397]
(48) Newcastle,	S. Mill, and £6.
(49) Edinburgh,	S. Watkinson.[398]
(50) Ireland,	S. Boone, Myles, West, Dinnen, (G.) Brown, Stewart, Rennick, Joyce.[399]

[389] William Bramwell was stationed in Blackburn.
[390] Robert Scot was stationed in Horncastle.
[391] John Atkins was stationed in Epworth.
[392] John Moon was stationed in Birmingham.
[393] James Watson was stationed in Leicester.
[394] John Ogylvie was stationed in Sunderland.
[395] William Butterfield was stationed in Kent.
[396] George Mowat was stationed in Gainsborough.
[397] Thomas Dunn was stationed in Pocklington.
[398] Richard Watkinson was stationed in Dundee.
[399] Charles Boone and William Myles were stationed in Dublin, William West in Londonderry, John Dinnen in Athlone, George Brown in Ballyconnell, Matthew Stewart in Lisleen, James Rennick in Ballyshannon, and Matthias Joyce in Coleraine.

Q. 10. How are the other twelve to be provided for?

A. By the Preachers' Fund. N.B. The money for all those wives whose names are not inserted in the *Minutes* will be lodged in the hands of Mr. Atlay.

Q. 11. What numbers are in the societies?   5

A. As follows:

London	2,800	
Sussex	251	
Kent	530	10
Colchester	280	
Norwich	460	
Lynn	290	
Bedford	250	
Northampton	358	15
Oxfordshire	620	
Gloucestershire	381	
Worcestershire	339	
Sarum	464	
Isle of Wight	87	20
Bradford	1,365	
Bristol	2,040	
Taunton	246	
Tiverton	444	
Plymouth	745	25
St. Austell	818	
Redruth	1,776	
St. Ives	1,231	
Pembroke	183	
Glamorgan	215	30
Brecon	150	
Birmingham	1,300	
Burslem	1,250	
Macclesfield	972	
Manchester	1,950	35
Stockport	846	
Chester	600	
Wolverhampton	493	
Liverpool	792	
Bolton	1,100	40
Colne	993	

	Blackburn	878
	Leicester	606
	Nottingham	810
	Derby	640
5	Sheffield	1,620
	Grimsby	557
	Horncastle	600
	Gainsborough	660
	Epworth	650
10	Leeds	2,058
	Wakefield	670
	Birstall	903
	Dewsbury	768
	Huddersfield	910
15	Halifax	1,100
	Bradford	1,040
	Keighley	1,317
	Whitehaven	221
	Isle of Man	2,262
20	York	990
	Pocklington	690
	Hull	647
	Scarborough	644
	Whitby	525
25	Thirsk	647
	Yarm	506
	The Dales	982
	Sunderland	1,160
	Newcastle	1,100
30	Berwick	111
	Edinburgh and Dalkeith[400]	330
	Ayr and Dumfries[401]	45
	Dundee	129
	Aberdeen	249
35	Inverness	165
	Jersey	248
	Guernsey and Alderney[402]	105

[400] CJ, 'Edinburgh and Musselburgh'.
[401] CJ, 'Dumfries and Ayr'.
[402] CJ, 'Guernsey'.

Dublin	1,150	
Waterford	350	
Cork	550	
Bandon	280	
Limerick	244	5
Castlebar	344	
Athlone	396	
Longford	331	
Sligo	330	
Ballyconnell	750	10
Clones	1,268	
Brookeborough	648	
Enniskillen	655	
Ballyshannon	500	
Killybeggs	300	15
Lisleen	327	
Omagh	310	
Charlemont	838	
Londonderry	221	
Coleraine	491	20
Belfast	373	
Lisburn	611	
Newry	946	
In all	66,375[403]	25

A M E R I C A.

The *British* Dominions in *America.*

Newfoundland		200	
Nova Scotia,	Whites	302	
	Blacks	200	30
Antigua,	Whites &		
	Mulattoes	60	
	Blacks	2,670	
St. Christopher's,	Whites	25	
	Coloured People	375	35
St. Vincent's,	Whites	12	
	Blacks	149	
In all,		3,993	

[403] Orig., in both CJ and *Minutes*, '65,375', which should in fact be 66,375.

Under the Government of *Holland.*

St. Eustatius,	⌈ Whites	2
	⌊ Blacks	140
In all,		142

In the United States of *America.*

Burke,			82	⌉ GEORGIA.
Richmond,	⌠	Whites	345	
	⌡	Blacks	22	
Washington,	⌠	Whites	707	
	⌡	Blacks	71	⌋
Charleston,	⌠	Whites	50	⌉
	⌡	Blacks	65	
Edisto,	⌠	Whites	340	
	⌡	Blacks	25	
Cainhoy,	⌠	Whites	36	
	⌡	Blacks	24	SOUTH CAROLINA.
Santee,	⌠	Whites	225	
	⌡	Blacks	20	
Pee Dee,	⌠	Whites	885	
	⌡	Blacks	50	
Broad River,	⌠	Whites	460	
	⌡	Blacks	29	
Seleuda,[404]	⌠	Whites	230	
	⌡	Blacks	11	⌋
Salisbury,[a]	⌠	Whites	391	⌉
	⌡	Blacks	24	
Yadkin,	⌠	Whites	517	
	⌡	Blacks	20	
Holstein,	⌠	Whites	449	
	⌡	Blacks	1	

---

[a] The remaining numbers are taken from the return of last year, the Conference at Baltimore for the present year having not yet been held; it began Sept. 9 (Lee) or 10 (Asbury); but we have sufficient reason to believe that many thousands have been added to the societies in Virginia and the States that lie north of it.

[404] Orig., 'Selaida'.

Guilford,	{ Whites	409	
	Blacks	15	
New Hope,	{ Whites	291	
	Blacks	30	
Tar River,	{ Whites	680	5
	Blacks	50	
Roanoke,	{ Whites	419	
	Blacks	129	
Caswell,	{ Whites	207	
	Blacks	6	10
Bertie,	{ Whites	386	
	Blacks	50	
Camden and Banks,	{ Whites	370	
	Blacks	34	
New River,	{ Whites	495	15
	Blacks	80	
Bladen		30	

NORTH CAROLINA.

Halifax,	{ Whites	403	
	Blacks	23	20
Mecklenburg,	{ Whites	828	
	Blacks	76	
Portsmouth,	{ Whites	391	
	Blacks	57	
Brunswick,	{ Whites	407	25
	Blacks	59	
Sussex,	{ Whites	496	
	Blacks	93	
Amelia,	{ Whites	573	
	Blacks	51	30
Williamsburg,	{ Whites	217	
	Blacks	5	
Orange,	{ Whites	337	
	Blacks	34	
Amherst,	{ Whites	100	35
	Blacks	7	
Bedford,	———	252	
Buckingham,	{ Whites	87	
	Blacks	10	
Kentucky,		90	40
Alleghany,		736	

VIRGINIA.

		Whites	203	
	Berkley,	Blacks	26	
	Redstone,	———	756	
	Fairfax,	———	270	
5	Lancaster,	Whites	400	
		Blacks	155	
	Northampton,	Whites	178	
		Blacks	22	
	Greenbrier,	———	100	
10				

		Whites	445	
	Frederick,	Blacks	55	
	Calvert,	Whites	443	
		Blacks	550	
15	Baltimore,	Whites	756	
		Blacks	196	
	Kent,	Whites	607	
		Blacks	604	
	Talbot,	Whites	1,077	MARYLAND.
20		Blacks	524	
	Dorset,	Whites	594	
		Blacks	135	
	Somerset,	Whites	223	
		Blacks	56	
25	Annamessex,	Whites	343	
		Blacks	43	
	Caroline,	Whites	616	
		Blacks	268	

30				
	Dover,	Whites	654	DELAWARE.
		Blacks	209	

35	Philadelphia,		513	PENNSYLVANIA.
	Little York, Juniata		136	

West Jersey,	{	Whites	557		
	{	Blacks	8		
Trenton,			372		
East Jersey,			465	NEW JERSEY.	
Elizabeth Town,			240		5

New York,	{	Whites	235		
	{	Blacks	40		
Long Island,	{	Whites	160	NEW YORK.	
	{	Blacks	7		10

In all,	27,333	
Total in *Europe*,	65,375	
Total in *America*,	31,468	15
Total in *Europe* and		
America,	96,843[405]	

Q. 12. What is the Kingswood collection?[406]

A. £781. 16*s*. 7*d*.   20

Q. 13. What children are admitted this year?

A. Joseph Rogers, Edward Price, Lancelot Harrison.

Q. 14. What children are sent to Rainham School?[407]

A. Joseph Harper.

Q. 15. What can we allow the daughters of the preachers   25
out of the Kingswood collection?

A. Frances Longley, £6 the first year; Jane Allen, £6 the
first year; Catherine Thompson, £6 the first year.———
—N.B. John Brown is allowed £6 the second year.

Q. 16. What is contributed to the Preachers' Fund?   30

A. £420. 12*s*. 0*d*.

Q. 17. What is allowed out of it?

A. To Thomas Westell	£30	0	0	
William Whitaker	20	0	0	35

---

[405] CJ does not include the American statistics, except for the addition by Coke
of 27,333 and 96,843. With the correction of the European figures to 66,375, the
total becomes 97,843.

[406] First proposed in Minutes (1756), n. 969, though first recorded in *Minutes*
(1765), *Q*. 6 and n. 29.

[407] Orig., 'Raynham'.

Thomas Hanson	12	0	0
Robert Howard	12	0	0
John Furz	12	0	0
John Price	12	0	0
John Watson	12	0	0
William Church	12	0	0
Ann Morgan	24	0	0
Lucy Bourke	15	0	0
Mary Penington	12	0	0
Sarah Shorter	10	0	0
Catherine Garnet	12	0	0
Elizabeth Dillon	10	0	0
Tabitha Norris	12	0	0
Margaret Payne	12	0	0
Sarah Barry	24	0	0
Sarah Naylor	10	0	0
Elizabeth Oldham	15	0	0
Sarah Hosmer	10	0	0
Sarah Mitchell	20	0	0
Elizabeth Jaco	12	0	0
S. Robertshaw	12	0	0
S. Rowell	10	0	0
Thomas Johnson	6	0	0
Twelve wives	144	0	0
In all,	£492	0	0

Q. 18. What is contributed for the Yearly Expenses?
A. £1,203. 7s. 1d.
Q. 19. How was it expended?

A. Last year's deficiencies	£ 56	5	10
This year's contingencies	100	0	0
For the deficiencies of the preachers and their families in Ireland	214	8	7
For the deficiencies of the preachers and their families in Scotland	151	9	0
For the deficiencies of the preachers, etc. in Wales	68	0	6
For the deficiencies of the preachers and their families in England	469	4	0

Law	37	4	2
Houses,	106	15	0
In all,	[£] 1,203	7	1

Q. 20. What houses are to be built this year?

A. Brompton,[408] St. Stephens, Penryn, Penzance, Birmingham, Oldham, Tunstall,[409] Madeley Bank, Liverpool, Owston, Whitby, Kelso, Dumfries, Dalkeith, Dundee, Wexford, Ross, Bandon, Ballinrobe, Richhill, Brookeborough, and Dublin house to be enlarged.

Q. 21. What further directions may be given concerning the Prayers of the Church of England?

A. The Assistants shall have a discretionary power to read the Prayer Book in the preaching-houses on Sunday mornings, where they think it expedient, if the generality of the society acquiesce with it, on condition that Divine Service never be performed in the church-hours on the Sundays, when the Sacrament is administered in the parish church where the preaching-house is situated, and the people be strenuously exhorted to attend the Sacrament in the parish church on those Sundays.[410]

Q. 22. Are any directions to be given concerning the weekly and quarterly collections in the circuits?

A. Let every Assistant be particularly careful to enforce the weekly collection of a penny from each member of our society in the class-meetings, and the quarterly collection of a shilling from each member that can afford to pay it at the quarterly visitation.

Q. 23. Many of our preachers have been obliged to go from the house of one friend to another for all their meals, to the great loss of their time and to the injury of the work of God. What can be done to prevent this evil in future?

---

[408] Orig., 'Brumpton'.

[409] Orig., 'Turnstead'.

[410] Added in CJ, in Coke's hand, as *Q.* 11. See also JW's report, Aug. 4, 1788, *Journal & Diaries*, 24:104; see n. 327 above. James Oddie commented on the question of forms of prayer and extempore prayer that at the Conference it was 'concluded in favour of having a form of prayer in public worship. . . . Leave was given to all congregations the majority of whome desired it to introduce it immediately', and he added arguments in favour of it. Tyerman MSS, 1:96.

A. Let every circuit provide a sufficient allowance for the preachers, that they may in general eat their meals at their own lodgings.

Q. 24. What can be further done to secure our preaching-houses to the connexion?

A. Let no house be built, on any consideration, till the ground be first settled on the Conference Plan.

Q. 25. What is the Conference Plan?[411]

A. Though it has been printed in many editions of the large *Minutes*, yet at the desire of the Conference, it is inserted here:

This Indenture made ————— ————— between *Benjamin Heap* of ————, in the County of ————, on the one part, and *Thomas Philips*, Hatter, etc. on the other part, WITNESSETH, That in consideration of five shillings, lawful money of Great Britain, by the said *T. P.* etc. to the said *B. H.* truly paid, before the sealing and delivering hereof (the receipt whereof the said *B. H.* doth hereby acknowledge) and for divers other considerations him thereunto moving; the said *B. H.* hath granted, bargained and sold, and by these Presents doth bargain and sell, unto the said *T. P.* etc. their heirs and assigns for ever, all that lately erected house or tenement, with the yard thereunto adjoining, situate ———— in ———— aforesaid, now in the tenure or occupation of ————, together with all the ways, drains and privileges to the said premises appertaining, and all the profits thereof, with all the right, title and interest in law and equity: TO HAVE AND TO HOLD, the said house, yard and other premises, to the said *T. P.* etc. their heirs and assigns for ever. NEVER-THELESS upon special trust and confidence, and to the intent that they and the survivors of them, and the Trustees for the time being, do and shall permit *John Wesley*, of the City Road, London, Clerk, and such other persons as he shall from time to time appoint, and at all times, during his natural life, and no other persons, to

---

[411] As the reply shows, the term 'Plan' here clearly refers to the Model Deed. The first use of the term in this sense may have been in *Minutes* (1766), *Q*. 2.

have and enjoy the free use and benefit of the said premises; that the said *John Wesley*, and such other persons as
he appoints, may therein preach and expound God's holy
Word. And after his decease, upon farther trust and confidence, and to the intent that the said *T. P.* etc., or the   5
major part of them, or the survivors of them and the
major part of the Trustees of the said premises for the
time being, shall from time to time, and at all times for
ever, permit such persons as shall be appointed at the
yearly Conference of the people called *Methodists*, as   10
established by a Deed Poll of the said *John Wesley* under
his hand and seal, bearing date the 28th day of February in
the year 1784, and enrolled in his Majesty's High Court
of Chancery, and no others, to have and to enjoy the said
premises, for the purposes aforesaid: provided always, that 15
the said persons preach no other doctrine than is contained in Mr. Wesley's *Notes upon the New Testament*, and
four volumes of sermons: and upon farther trust and confidence, that as often as any of these Trustees, or the
Trustees for the time being, shall die, or cease to be a   20
member of the society commonly called Methodists, the
rest of the said Trustees, or of the Trustees for the time
being, as soon as conveniently may be, shall and may
choose another Trustee or Trustees, in order to keep up
the number of ——— Trustees for ever. In witness   25
whereof the said *B. H.* hath hereunto set his hand and
seal, the day and year above written.'412

In this form the proprietors of the house are to make it
over, to five, seven, or nine Trustees.

But observe, (1) Every deed must be enrolled within six 30
months after its execution, the persons in whose names
the premises have been bought acknowledging their execution of the deed before a Master in Chancery, and the
Master in Chancery inserting on the margin of the deed
the following words, or words to this purport: 'A. B. of   35
the Parish of _____ in the County of _____ (and C. D.
etc., if the premises have been purchased in the names of

412 This is basically the form inserted in the 'Large' *Minutes* of 1780 with alterations made possible by the enrollment in Chancery of the Deed Poll of 1784 (see
below, p. 930).

two or more) did appear before me, this _____ day of
_____ in the year of _____, and did acknowledge that he
did sign, seal, and deliver this Indenture as his own act
and deed: and prays that the same may be enrolled in his
Majesty's High Court of Chancery.

E. F. Master Extraordinary
in Chancery.'

N.B. Almost every eminent attorney in the country is a
Master Extraordinary in Chancery. If the deed be then
sent to Mr. Clulow, No. 10, Chancery Lane, London,
it will be carefully enrolled, and returned to the
country according to directions, the society to which the
preaching-house belongs paying the expenses of the
enrollment, etc.

(2) If the preaching-house is in debt, a clause may be
inserted empowering the Trustees to mortgage the
premises.

Q. 26. Is it necessary to make any alteration in the economy
of Kingswood School?

A. Let the number of the preachers' sons be raised to forty,
and the number of boarders be reduced to ten, as soon as
possible.

Q. 27. The general collections for preaching-houses are
become a great grievance both to the preachers and people. What method can be taken to remedy this evil?

A. Let no collection be made for preaching-houses after
this year, except in the circuits in which they shall respectively be built.

Q. 28. Who are the missionaries appointed this Year for the
West Indies?

A. William McCornock Sen., Benjamin Pearce, Matthew
Lumb, Robert Gamble, Thomas Owens.

Q. 29. When and where is our next Conference to
be held?

A. In Leeds, on the last Tuesday in July, 1789.[413]

John Wesley [signed]
Thomas Coke [signed]

---

[413] ('*Q*. 12') in Coke's hand in CJ.

To our Societies in England and Ireland [414]

Fifty years ago and for several years following, all our preachers were single men, when in process of time a few of them married. Those with whom they laboured maintained both them and their wives, there being then no set- 5 tled allowance either for the one or the other. But above thirty years ago it was found most convenient to fix a stated allowance for both, and this was found by the circuits where they were stationed; till one year some of the circuits complained of poverty. Dr. Coke and I supplied 10 what was wanting. The next year, the number of wives increasing, three or four of them were supplied out of the Continent Fund. This was a bad precedent, for more and more wives were thrown upon this Fund, till it was likely to be swallowed up thereby. We could think of no way to 15 prevent this but to consider the state of our societies in England and Ireland, and to beg the members of each circuit to give us that assistance, which they can easily do without hurting their families.

Within these fifty years, the substance of the Metho- 20 dists is increased in proportion to their numbers. Therefore if you are not straitened in your own bowels, this will be no grievance, but you will cheerfully give food and raiment to those, who give up all their time, and strength, and labour to your service. 25

JOHN WESLEY

London, Aug. 2, 1788

Annual *Minutes of some late Conversations*, 1789

Leeds, Tuesday, July 28, 1789[415]

---

[414] JW prepared this pastoral letter during the Conference, apparently on Saturday, Aug. 2, after the only sessions that day, 6:00–8:00 a.m. and 9:00–12:00 noon. The Conference actually finished on Wednesday, Aug. 6, a day of prayer-meetings and a watch-night service. *Journal & Diaries*, 24:104 in this edn.

[415] CJ for 1789 occupies pp. 65–70. The opening page is mostly in the hand of the secretary, Thomas Coke, who is succeeded by another scribe at the foot of p. 65 onwards.

JW wrote to Henry Moore on July 14, 1789, that he expected 'to see Brother Rankin, Whitfield and you at the Conference, . . . We shall have some points of deep importance to consider'. *Letters* (Telford), 8:153. The Dewsbury affair may have been in mind but also the perennial question of separation from the Church. In the same letter, he complained of the 'vile misrepresentation' of Coke that had 'set all Ireland in a flame'. This was over rumours of JW leaving the Church because of the Dublin Society being allowed to have services in Church hours; see *Letters* (Telford), 8:139–43, 146–47; Tyerman, *Wesley*, 3:152f. In his *Journal*, he records, 'Tues. 21. I hid myself in Otley, and prepared for the Conference'. Then,

'Tues. 28. The Conference began. About a hundred preachers were present, and never was our Master more eminently present with us. The case of separation from the Church was largely considered, and we were all unanimous against it. Aug. 1, Sat. We considered the case of Dewsbury house, which the self-elected trustees have robbed us of. The point they contended for was this—that they should have a right of rejecting any preachers they disapproved of. But this, we saw, would destroy itinerancy. So they chose J[ohn] A[tlay] for a preacher, who adopted W[illiam] E[ells] for his curate. Nothing remained but to build another preaching-house, toward which we subscribed two hundred and six pounds on the spot. Sun. 2. Knowing the church would not contain half of our congregation added to its own, we began at our room at half an hour past nine. After preaching, with the assistance of three other clergymen, I administered the Sacrament to fifteen or sixteen hundred persons, I hope, all desirous to be inward Christians. Tue. 4. Having before preached to the people at large, I now spoke directly to the preachers on "If any man speak, let him speak as the oracles of God"; and, I am persuaded, God applied his word to many of their hearts.' (*Journal & Diaries*, 24:148–49 in this edition.)

John Pawson (MS 'Some Account', fol. 38) says that many preachers were present. At the request of his wife, he entertained JW, 'who is now a feeble old man, nearly worn out in the service of a good Master. . . . This was attended with a good deal of trouble and expence.' All their affairs, he says, were 'settled in peace and love. . . . Those who are not quite satisfied respecting the Church were willing to submit for the sake of peace, and patiently to wait for better days.' John Valton says that Wesley preached, and 'I perceive with pain of mind that he is almost too weak to preach so as to be heard'. MS diary, July 16, 1789, in MA. Zechariah Yewdall supposed that 150 preachers were present. There were 3,000 to 4,000 to hear every night and 1,500 to 2,000 at five in the morning: 'Great peace and unanimity seemed to reign among us. Our aged Father preached but was much assisted in the business as he begins to fail, though he preaches every morning and evening.' July 27, 1789, MS diary, in MA. Tyerman says that 'what may be called the *Conference sermon* was preached by a local preacher, perhaps the only instance of the kind in Methodist history'. *Wesley*, 3:586. This was James Hamilton, M.D., who attacked the drift to separation from the Church as fatal to Methodism.

Thomas Hanby continued to stand out for his 'ministerial' rights; see *Minutes* (1785), n. 70. To James Oddie, he wrote on Aug. 5, 1789, 'My connexion hung in suspense for many days, and even to the last there was nothing certain as I durst not come into a promise to forbear or give up my ministerial function which was the cause of my not answering yours. However, matters are at last assured. The people of Nottingham are to have the ordinances, and I retain my authority and am

[The Minutes or Journals of the Conference of the People called Methodists, begun in Leeds on Tuesday the twenty-eighth day of July in the year 1789, and continued by various adjournments to the 5th day of August following.

[Present   5

[The Revd. John Wesley, President

[Thomas Coke, Secretary

(There are sixty-eight names in three columns,

wholly in the hand of Coke.)[416]

[John Allen, John Barber, Samuel Bardsley, Joseph Benson, 10 Andrew Blair, John Booth, William Boothby, Samuel Bradburn, Joseph Bradford, Thomas Brisco, John Broadbent, Isaac Brown, Thomas Carlill, Joseph Cole, William Collins, Robert Costerdine, Jonathan Coussins, Thomas Dixon, William Dutton, John Easton, John Goodwin, Parson Greenwood, Thomas Hanby, Joseph Harper, 15 Charles Atmore, Lancelot Harrison, Jonathan Hern, Robert Hopkins, Christopher Hopper, William Hunter, Edward Jackson, Daniel Jackson, John Leech, Thomas Longley, John Mason, Alexander Mather, Henry Moore, William Myles, John Peacock, William Palmer, John Pawson, Jonathan Parkin, Joseph Pescod, 20

appointed for Bolton.' Tyerman MSS, 1:92. He wrote again to Oddie, Sept. 12, 1789, saying that he was uneasy at the Conference on the subscription for Dewsbury chapel. He wished to know the truth of things from Oddie and wished him to 'ask Mr Atley whether he was ever told by a certain person that he helped Mr W. from his horse drunk? This latter circumstance occasioned much altercation at the Conference. Mr W. is highly prejudiced'. Ibid., 1:95. (Pawson indignantly rejected this charge and one on sexual impropriety, which one suspects had been circulated by JW's enemies during the Dewsbury case; Pawson, *Letters*, 1:87.)

JW wrote to Thomas Tattersall in Apr. and Dec. 1790 that he no longer had anything to do with buildings; he had passed the business to a building committee. Letter not in Telford; printed in T. Byrth, ed., *Sermons of the Rev. Mr Tattersall* (London and Liverpool, 1848), xxxix, xl; cf. his relinquishing of book affairs, *Journal & Diaries*, 24:112. in 1788.

On stationing, it is said that the local women preachers stopped Adam Clarke's appointment to Leeds or Halifax because they did not think much of his preaching! Paul W. Chilcote, *John Wesley and the Women Preachers of Early Methodism* (Metuchen, N.J., 1991), 201.

[416] The second name originally to appear was that of William Ashman, which is then struck through because he was absent, the name of John Barber being inserted over it. Again the name of Charles Atmore—and again out of order—heads the second column.

William Percival, Thomas Rankin, Jasper Robinson, Richard Rodda, Robert Roberts, Thomas Rutherford, William Saunders, George Shadford, John Shaw, William Simpson, George Snowden, George Story, Alexander Suter, Thomas Taylor, Joseph Taylor, James Thom,
5　William Thom, William Thompson, John Valton, Thomas Vasey, Christopher Watkins, James Wood, Duncan Wright, Francis Wrigley, Zachariah Yewdall.

[Absent
10　　　　(There are twenty-eight names in two columns.)
[William Ashman, R. Carr Brackenbury, Geo. Button, Jas. Creighton, Jas. Hall, Thos. Barber, Charles Boone, Jer. Brettel, Geo. Brown, William Hoskins, Jno. Moon, Jno. Murlin, Benj. Rhodes, Frans. Asbury, Jno. Crook, Willm. Green, Duncan McAllum,
15　Thos. Tennant, Thos. Warrick,[417] Peard Dickinson, Joseph Cownley, Nehemiah Price, James Wray, James Rogers, Robert Scot, William Warrener, Richard Watkinson, Richard Whatcoat.

[For the absence of all of whom a dispensation is passed.]
20　[*Question* 1st. Who are in full connexion with the Conference?
[*Answer.* (There are fifty names in four columns, of which three are struck through, Adam Clarke, William Horner, and Alexander Suter.)[418]
[Joseph Algar, Jno. Baxter, Jno. Beanland, Jas. Bogie, Saml. Botts,
25　Thos. Bartholomew, Willm. Butterfield, Jas. Christie, Jno. Clarke, ((Adam Clarke)), Thos. Cooper, Willm. McCornock, Sen., Jno. Cricket, Jno. Crosby, Robt. Dall, Simn. Day, Thos. Davis, Jas. Watson, Jno. Wittam, Jno. Smith, Mark Whitaker, Robt. Empringham, Geo. Gibbon, Walter Griffith, Saml. Hodgson, Geo.
30　Holder, Willm. Holmes, Joseph Thompson, Jno. Watson, Thos. Wride, ((Willm. Horner)), Jos[eph] Jerom, Andw. Inglis, Robt. Johnson, Thos. Johnson, Mathias Joyce, Lawrence Kane, Jno. King, Chas. Kyte, Matthew Lumb, Peter Mill, Geo. Mowat, Jno. Ogylvie, Jno. Poole, Jno. Pritchard, Thos. Shaw, ((Alexander Suter)), Robt.
35　Swan, James Thom, Geo. Wadsworth.]

[417] The following are in the hand of Coke: Hoskins, Dickinson, Cownley, Price, Wray, Rogers, Scot, Warrener, Watkinson, Whatcoat.
[418] Clarke and Horner had been made members of the Legal Hundred this year; Suter in 1777.

Minutes

Q. 1. What preachers are *admitted* this year?[419]
A. In *Great Britain,* Timothy Crowther, Jonathan
Crowther, James Ridall, Charles Bland, John Smith,
Alexander Kilham, William Hunter, Jun., William   5
Blagborne, John Reynolds, James Byron, George
Highfield, John Barrett, John Atkins, William Bramwell,
and John Gaulter. In *Ireland,* Thomas Verner, and John
Dinnen. In *Jersey,* John de Quêteville.
In *British America,* Robert Gamble and Thomas Owens. In   10
the United States, Matthew Harris, James Conner, Michael
Burdge, Lemuel Andrews, Daniel Lockett, Barnabas
McHenry,[420] Micaijah Tracy, Benjamin Carter, Edward
West, David Haggard, Jeremiah Abel, Isaac Lowe,
Jeremiah Minter, Thomas Weatherford, Joshua Hartley,   15
John Barker, Lewis Chatstain, George Hagerty, John Hill,
James Wilson, Benton Riggin, Benj. Roberts, John Jarrell,
Christopher Spry, John Milburn, Nathaniel[421] Mills, Aaron
Hutchinson, Andrew Harpending, and John Bloodgood.

[419] In 1789, apparently for the first and only time, JW and Coke between them seem to have decided to issue two edns. of the annual *Minutes,* one geared (as usual) to the transatlantic community, and one also to the British alone. It would not be surprising, of course, if eventually there turned up a similar British–only edn. of at least 1790. In 1773, Thomas Rankin had conducted the first American Conference, and from that time the annual American *Minutes* were circulated in manuscript and seem to have been published only occasionally, and not regularly. Similarly in 1778, JW published a supplementary set of Irish *Minutes,* and from 1783 these were published annually, with the responsibility carried mainly by Thomas Coke. It was against such a background, apparently, that this 1789 experiment was made. The printer, title page, and format were the same for each of these two edns., which were probably prepared in the following order:
  (A) Leeds, 1789, 12 mo., (*1*) [*2*] (3), 4–32, A–B⁶ C⁴—the edn. for America.
  (B) Leeds, 1789, 12 mo., (*1*) [*2*] (3), 4–21 [22–24], A–B⁶—the British edn.
  The B edn. was apparently formed by simply omitting the major American details, after the American edn. had been printed, distributing the unneeded type, moving the remaining lines forward, and supplying new pages and new catchwords for the resultant pages. See Station No. 34, n. 454; but cf. n. 455, the correcting of an error in A; cf. also n. 459 (No. 67). The numbered questions remained basically the same. Here we print, of course, the fuller American edn. and note the omissions for the British edn. In this instance, B omits 'In British America . . . Bloodgood'.
  In CJ, the names are in four columns, reading across the rows, with the countries not named, and omitting all the preachers listed after 'the *United States*'.

[420] Orig., 'McKendree'.
[421] Orig., 'Nathanael'.

Q. 2. Who *remain* on trial?[422]

A. In *Great Britain,* John McKersey, Richard Cornish,
William Fish, James Gore, John Townsend, George
Baldwin, Theophilus Lessey, Thomas Jones, James Evans,
5   William Stephens,[423] Thomas Roberts, William Thoresby,
John Tregortha, Jonathan Edmondson, Joseph Sutcliffe,
Duncan Kay, Abraham Moseley, Thomas Wood, William
Heath, Samuel Gates, John Stamp, John Woodrow, John
Sandoe, Richard Reece, Michael Marshall, Joseph Cross,
10   Robert Harrison, Joseph Entwisle, Francis Truscott,
Richard Drew, Thomas Gill, Thomas Rogerson, Thomas
Wyment, John Wiltshaw, George Lowe, Henry Taylor,
John Hickling, Charles Tunnycliffe, John Furnace,
Thomas Kelk, Thomas Dobson, Richard Seed, and Jasper
15   Winscom.
In *Ireland,*[424] John Stephens, James Lyons, James
McMullen, Alexander Moore, John Riles, Mark Willis,
Samuel Bates, David Gordon, Thomas Roberts, John
Gillis, Samuel Moorhead, John Grace, Andrew Jefferys,
20   John Black, William Johnson, John Darragh, Francis
Armstrong, William McCornock, Jun., Thomas Hewett,
John Malcomson, Thomas Kerr, John West, James Lyons,
James McMullen, Alexander Moore, Matthew Stewart,
Thomas Elliott, Andrew Hamilton, Robert Smith,
25   Nebuchadnezzar Lee, William Hamilton, John
Stephenson, Daniel Graham, Michael Murphy, William
Wilson, and David Barrowclough.[425]
In *British America,* William Brazier, William Meredith,
John Lynn, and George Skerritt. In *The United States,*
30   Bennet Maxey, William Gassaway, Hardy Herbert, James
Parks, Doily Baird, John McGee, William Moss, Joseph
Doddridge, Jesse Richardson, John Ellis, Richard Pope,

[422] Again the four columns in CJ are to be read across.

[423] In CJ, 'Stevens'.

[424] CJ does not have 'In *Ireland*'. The list does not match that in the Irish *Minutes*, which begins with Samuel Bates. Of the six preceding names, Lyons, McMullen, and Moore appear again later in the list, John Stephens had died in June 10, Riles was stationed in Grimsby, and Willis in the Isle of Man.

[425] CJ adds, in Coke's hand, 'John Beaumont, Thomas Broadbent'. Both CJ and B omit 'In *British America* . . . Nostrand'.

Archer Davis,[426] Benjamin Barnes,[427] Henry Birchett,[428]
Salathiel Weeks, Aquila Suggs, James Meachem,[429] Peter
Massey, Julius Conner, William Heath, Stephen Davis,[430]
John Fore, William McKendree, Lewis Dawson, Isaac
Lunsford, Thomas Hardy, John Chalmers, Thornton   5
Fleming,[431] George Wells, James Thomas, Benjamin
Snelling, John Rowen, Eliphalet Reed, Griffith Callahan,
John Allen, Robert Green, Valentine Cook, Daniel
Coombes,[432] Aquila Edwards, Lenox Martin, William
Dougherty,[433] John Cooper, Jethro Johnson, Emory   10
Prior,[434] John Lee, Lemuel Smith, David Kendall,[435]
Darius Dunham, Samuel Wigton, Albert Van Nostrand.
Q. 3. Who are *admitted* on trial?
A. In *Great Britain*, William Jenkins, William Cox, William
Saunderson, Henry Saunders, Robert Lomas, John   15
Ramshaw, Miles Martindale,[436] Thomas Hutton, William
Smith, John Kershaw, John Nelson, John Denton, Robert
Crowther, Robert Smith, and Jonathan Thompson.[437]
In *Ireland*, William Brandon, George Donovan, Samuel
Wood,[438] Thomas Ridgeway,[439] James McQuigg, Thomas   20
Patterson, Andrew Hamilton, Jun., James Irwin, Thomas
Werrill,[440] and Robert McCay.[441]

[426] Orig., 'Davies'.
[427] Orig., 'Barns'.
[428] Orig., 'Birchet'.
[429] Orig., 'Mechem'.
[430] Orig., 'Davies'.
[431] Orig., 'Flemming'.
[432] Orig., 'Combs'.
[433] Orig., 'Dougharty'.
[434] Orig., 'Emory Prior'.
[435] Orig., 'Candall', as in American *Minutes* (1788, 1791); his ministry (1788–95) completely dovetails together under the two spellings.
[436] Orig., 'Myles Martendale', but he used the changed spelling for his many publications from 1789 onwards.
[437] The copy at Queens College, Melbourne, contains MS annotations, presumably by James Anderson, adding his own name here (p. 5), and after Station 71, Inverness (p. 9), where he inserts: 'Campbletown James Anderson'. On p. 19, at the end of the July 29 list, he adds, 'Joseph Benson, total 116'.
[438] Orig., 'Woods'.
[439] Orig., 1789–90, 'Ridgway'; 1791, 'Ridgley'.
[440] Orig., 'Worrell', as also in Station 93.
[441] Myles gives 'McKay', but CJ and Irish *Minutes* also have 'McCay'. CJ, B, omit 'In *the States . . .* Losee.'

In *the States of America*, Wheeler Grissom, John Andrew, John Crawford, Lemuel Moore,[442] John Russell, William McDowell, Jonathan Jackson, Philip Matthews, Henry Leadbetter, Jonathan Bird, John Robinson, Myles Green,
5   Jesse Nicholson, William Spencer, Rice Haggard, Daniel Southall, John Lindsey, Wyatt[443] Andrews, Christopher Mooring, Stephen Brooks, John Hutt, Benjamin Brown, William McLenahan,[444] Nicholas Sebrell, Pemberton Smith, Thomas Carroll, Daniel Fidler, John Childs,
10   Joshua Wells, Thomas Workman, Jeremiah Cosden,[445] William Jackson, Joseph Benson, Walter Fountain, William Ratcliffe, James Campbell, William Ward, Anthony Banning, Richard Swain, Sylvester Hutchinson, Benjamin Abbott, John Crawford, and William Losee.
15   *Q*. 4. Who have *died* this year?
A. In *Great Britain, Thomas Corbet*, a plain, honest, pious, useful man. He endured much in his last illness, manifested great fortitude, and died in the full triumph of faith.[446]
20   In *Ireland, Hugh Pue*, a zealous, pious young man, who suffered much in his illness, but died happy in God. *Francis Frazier*, a good young man, and a good preacher. And *John Stephens*, who being little more than a child in years, was a man both in knowledge and piety, and went hence in
25   the full triumph of faith.
In[447] *the States of America, Henry Bingham*, a native of Virginia, four years a labourer in the vineyard, serious, faithful, zealous, humble, and teachable, and during part of the last year more than commonly successful; fervent in
30   exhortation during his sickness, and resigned in death.

---

[442] Orig., 'Moor', which is the American spelling.

[443] Orig., 'Wyat'.

[444] Orig., 'McLennahan'.

[445] Orig., 'Causden'.

[446] CJ adds: '*Quest*. 6. Who are elected members of the Conference instead of Thos. Corbet and Barnabas Thomas, who are dead?'

'*A*. William Horner, Adam Clarke.'

Thomas had become a supernumerary in the Kent Circuit (1788) and then quietly resigned from the Conference (1789). He died in 1793. See Atmore's *Memorials* and *WHS* 31 (1957): 10.

[447] CJ, B omit the whole of this paragraph.

William Gill, a native of Delaware, an elder in the
Church, and a labourer in it for about twelve years,
blameless in life, of quick and solid parts, sound in the
faith, clear in his judgment, meek in his spirit, resigned
and solemnly happy in his death. *John Cooper*, fifteen   5
years in the work, quiet, inoffensive and blameless; a son
of affliction, subject to dejection, sorrow and suffering;
often in want, but too modest to complain till observed
and relieved by his friends. He died in peace. *James
White*, a native of Maryland, about eight years in the   10
work, a simple-hearted man and a lively preacher, afflicted
yet active and labourious, soft and kind in his affections,
patient in suffering, well received and much esteemed,
successful in the work of God, resigned in his death.
Francis Spry, a pious man, skilful and lively in his preach- 15
ing, sound in judgment, holy in his life, placid in his
mind, of unshaken confidence and patience in his death;
four years a labourer in the vineyard.

Q. 5. Are there any objections to any of our preachers?
A. They were examined one by one.[448]   20

Q. 6. Who have desisted from travelling?
A. In *Great Britain*, William Hoskins, George Phillips, and
John Holmes.[449] In *Ireland*, John Howe. In *the States of
America*, Robert Ayres.[450]

Q. 7. How are the preachers stationed this year?   25
A. As follows:—

(1) *London*, John Wesley, James Creighton, Peard
Dickinson, Henry Moore, John Broadbent; Thomas
Rankin, supernumerary; George Whitfield, Book
Steward; Joseph Bradford travels with Mr. Wesley.   30
(2) Sussex, Timothy Crowther, John Woodrow, William
Cox.
(3) *Kent*, John Pritchard, Thomas Jones, Charles Kyte,
Thomas Wyment.

---

[448] CJ omits this question.

[449] Cf. n. 446 above for Barnabas Thomas. CJ adds 'John Atlay' (who had mis-
appropriated Book Room funds), 'Charles Bond' (who was reinstated in 1790), and
William (corrected to Thomas) Ellis. Most of *QQ.* 6 and 7 were in the hand of Coke.

CJ adds *Q.* 8: 'Who have desisted from travelling who were in connexion?' and
the other scribe recites the names of Hoskins, Phillips, Bond, Holmes, and Howe.

[450] CJ, B omit this sentence.

(4) *Colchester*, Joseph Harper, Jonathan Crowther, Robert Miller.

(5) *Norwich*, Thomas Tattershall, Thomas Broadbent, Thomas Rogerson, William Green, Thomas Hutton.

(6) *Lynn*, John Reynolds, John Hickling, Thomas Kelk.

(7) *Bedford*, William Jenkins, John Ramshaw.

(8) *Northampton*, George Gibbon, James Byron.

(9) *Oxfordshire*, William Horner, John Cricket, Richard Reece; John Murlin, supernumerary.

(10) *Gloucestershire*, George Baldwin, Simon Day.

(11) *Worcestershire*, John Leech, Lawrence Kane.

(12) *Sarum*, William Thom, Theophilus Lessey, Michael Marshall.

(13) *Isle of Wight*, Jasper Winscom, Henry Saunders.

(14) *Isles of Jersey, Guernsey, and Alderney*, Robert Carr Brackenbury, John de Quêteville, John Bredin, William Stephens, William Dieuaide.

(15) *Bradford*, Joseph Sutcliffe, Robert Empringham; John Furz, supernumerary.

(16) *Bristol*, Adam Clarke, George Wadsworth, Samuel Hodgson; John Valton, James Gore, supernumeraries.

(17) *Shepton Mallet*, John Easton, Joseph Algar.

(18) *Taunton*, Jonathan Coussins, Christopher Watkins.

(19) *Tiverton*, Richard Drew, John Poole.

(20) *Bideford*, Samuel Bardsley.[451]

(21) *Plymouth*, Thomas Warrick, William Dufton,[452] Charles Bland.

(22) *St. Austell*, John Mason, William Ashman, Benjamin Leggatt.

(23) *Redruth*, Benjamin Rhodes, William Holmes, John McGeary.[453]

---

[451] In CJ, Coke adds 'Michael Fenwick', who had been dropped in 1778, and whose name JW apparently still did not wish to record in the *Minutes*.

[452] In CJ, Coke inserts 'Jasper Robinson' (unsuccessfully) in place of Dufton.

[453] John McGeary emigrated from Ireland to America, and in the spring of 1782 was appointed to the Somerset Circuit in Maryland, under Freeborn Garrettson. In 1783 he was received into full connexion and stationed in West Jersey. The following year he served as Assistant in Frederick Circuit. After these appointments, he returned to England and was welcomed by JW in Oct. 1784. JW first sent him as a special Assistant to Joseph Taylor in Gloucester. When JW wrote to Taylor on Apr. 7, 1785, McGeary added a note, signed 'Jno. McGeary', the name by which

(24) *St. Ives*, Alexander Suter, Joseph Pescod, Thomas Dobson, John Sandoe.

(25) *Pembroke*, William Palmer, James Hall, William Heath.

(26) *Glamorganshire*, George Button, William Fish.

(27) *Brecon*, Joseph Jerom, William Church, John McKersey.

(28) *Birmingham*, Joseph Benson, George Snowden, William Thoresby, John Smith.

(29) *Wolverhampton*, Melville Home, supernumerary; Thomas Cooper, Jeremiah Brettel.

(30) *Burslem*, Robert Roberts, John Brettel, Abraham Moseley, John Beaumont.

(31) *Macclesfield*, John Allen, Samuel Gates, Robert Lomas.

(32) *Stockport*, Daniel Jackson, Thomas Tennant.

(33) *Manchester*, Richard Rodda, Christopher Hopper, Samuel Bradburn, William Hunter, Jun.

(34) *Bolton*, Thomas Hanty, William Smith.[454]

(35) *Chester*, Parson Greenwood, Francis Truscott, John Denton.[455]

(36) *Liverpool*, William Myles, Henry Taylor, John Tregortha.

(37) *Blackburn*, George Story, George Lowe.

(38) *Colne*, William Collins, William Bramwell.

at the following Conference JW appointed him to Newfoundland, where he stayed until 1791, with a brief interlude (1788–90) in England. He returned to Newfoundland in time to welcome William Black on Aug. 11, 1791, and to accompany Black on his brief but invigorating tour. His own frustrating ministry there, however, was taken over by a substitute, and he returned to England, was stationed by the 1792 Conference, but desisted from the itinerancy the following year.

His name was variously spelled: in America, 'Magary'; in Newfoundland, 'Magery'; in England, 'McGeary'; though his personal choice seems to have been 'McGeary'—which was the uniform usage for the Thomas McGeary who was the headmaster of Kingswood School (1783–94). Apparently this latter McGeary signed the manifesto at the end of the 1789 *Minutes* and made his guinea contribution to the preaching-house cause.

[454] CJ and B read 'John Wiltshaw', replaced in A by 'William Smith'—which seems to reverse the order of publication of A and B suggested above.

[455] CJ and B add 'T. Brisco, supernumerary', as in 1788, apparently the correcting of an error in A.

(39) *Leicester*, Wm. Butterfield, Miles Martindale, James Christie; John Watson, supernumerary.

(40) *Nottingham*, Joseph Taylor, Thomas Vasey, John Moon.

(41) *Derby*, James Watson, Robert Costerdine, Richard Seed, John Atkins.

(42) *Sheffield*, Andrew Inglis, Lancelot Harrison, Thomas Bartholomew.

(43) *Grimsby*, William Saunders, Robert Scot, John Riles.

(44) *Horncastle*, Thomas Carlill, George Mowat, James Evans, John Kershaw.

(45) *Gainsborough*, Thomas Longley, Thomas Wood, Robert Howard.

(46) *Epworth*, Robert Swan, William Boothby, William Saunderson.

(47) *Leeds*, Andrew Blair, John Goodwin, Isaac Brown.

(48) *Wakefield*, Alexander Mather, George Highfield.

(49) *Huddersfield*, Francis Wrigley, Jonathan Parkin.[456]

(50) *Birstall*, John Pawson, Joseph Entwisle, James Ridall; Thomas Johnson, supernumerary.

(51) *Bradford*, George Shadford, John Booth.

(52) *Halifax*, William Thompson, John Shaw.

(53) *Keighley*, James Wood, John Peacock,[457] John Beanland.

(54) *Whitehaven*, John Crosby, John Barrett.

(55) *Isle of Man*, George Holder, Jonathan Brown, Mark Willis.

(56) *York*, Edward Jackson, Joseph Thompson, Jonathan Edmondson.

(57) *Pocklington*, Thomas Dixon, William Percival, Alexander Kilham.

(58) *Hull*, Thos. Taylor, Wm. Simpson.

(59) *Scarborough*, Duncan Kay, Jonathan Hern, Thomas Dunn.

(60) *Whitty*, Jas. Thom, Wm. Blagborne.

---

[456] In CJ, Coke replaces Parkin (unsuccessfully) with 'John Peacock', who remained in No. 53 (Keighley) despite Coke's suggestion in CJ there that Peacock should be replaced by Parkin.

[457] See n. 456.

(61) *Thirsk*, Jasper Robinson,[458] Tho. Shaw, Charles Tunnycliffe.

(62) *Yarm*, Robert Hopkins, John King.

(63) *The Dales*, Thomas Gill, Thomas Wride, John Wittam.

(64) *Sunderland*, Duncan Wright, John Gaulter, John Stamp.

(65) *Newcastle*, Charles Atmore, John Ogylvie.

(66) *Alnwick*, William Hunter, William Stephenson, John Furnace.

(67) *Edinburgh*, Joseph Cole, Robert Dall;[459] Joseph Cownley, supernumerary.[460]

(68) *Glasgow*, Richard Watkinson, James Bogie, Zachariah Yewdall.

(69) *Dundee*, Robert Johnson, Peter Mill.

(70) *Aberdeen*, Duncan M\cAllum, Robert Harrison.

(71) *Inverness*, John Barber, Samuel Botts, Joseph Cross, Jonathan Thompson.[461]

(72) *Dublin*, Thomas Rutherford, Charles Boone.

(73) *Wicklow*, John Gillis.

(74) *Wexford*, Thomas Kerr, Robert Smith.

(75) *Waterford*, Robert Bridge, John West.

(76) *Cork*, John Kerr, Thomas Roberts.

(77) *Bandon*, James Rogers, Gustavus Armstrong.

(78) *Limerick*, Richard Condy, Andrew Jefferys, J. M\cQuigg.

(79) *Birr*, William West, John Darragh.

(80) *Castlebar*, Hugh Moore, Thomas Verner.

(81) *Athlone*, John Dinnen, Thomas Davis.

(82) *Longford*, Thomas Barber, John Miller.

(83) *Sligo*, John Black, Michael Murphy.

(84) *Ballyconnell*, George Brown, Alexander Moore, John Stephenson, John Price, supernumerary.

---

[458] In CJ, Coke replaces Robinson unsuccessfully with William Dufton, who remained in Plymouth, No. 21 (n. 452).

[459] CJ adds 'Jno. Nelson', as does B; Coke replaces this in CJ with 'John Townsend', who is not, however, stationed in either A or B.

[460] In CJ, Coke changes this to No. 68 (Glasgow).

[461] Anderson's copy of B adds in MS: 'Campbletown, James Anderson'; see n. 437 above. B (not present in CJ or A) adds a separate line: 'Thomas McGeary, Head Master of Kingswood School.' John McGeary was stationed in Redruth, No. 23.

(85) *Cavan*,[462] Joseph Armstrong, Jas. Irwin.

(86) *Clones*, Matthew Stewart, William Wilson, Thomas Ridgeway.

(87) *Brookeborough*, William M{c}Cornock, James Lyons, Andrew Hamilton, Sen.

(88) *Enniskillen*, Thomas Hetherington, Robert M{c}Cay.

(89) *Ballyshannon*, Samuel Moorhead, Wm. Hamilton, Francis Armstrong.

(90) *Lisleen*, James Rennick, Thomas Elliott, Andrew Hamilton, Jun.

(91) *Omagh*, Samuel Bates, Nebuchadnezzar Lee.

(92) *Charlemont*, John Crook, Jas. M{c}Mullen.

(93) *Londonderry*, John Grace, Thomas Werrill.

(94) *Coleraine*, David Gordon, Thomas Patterson, Samuel Wood.

(95) *Belfast*, Samuel Mitchell, Nehemiah Price, William Brandon.

(96) *Lisburn*, Matthias Joyce, William Johnson.

(97) *Downpatrick*, John Malcomson, Daniel Graham.

(98) *Tandragee*, David Barrowclough, Thomas Hewett, George Donovan.

(99) *Newry*, Walter Griffith, James M{c}Donald.

A M E R I C A.[463]

The West Indies
Superintendent—Thomas Coke

(100) *Antigua*, William Warrener, George Skerritt.

(101) *Tobago*, William Meredith.

(102) *Barbados*, Benjamin Pearce.

(103) *Grenada*, Thomas Owens.

(104) *St. Vincent's,* John Baxter, Robert Gamble, John Clarke.

(105) *Dominica*, John Lynn.

(106) *Montserrat*, John M{c}Vean.

(107) *Nevis,*

(108) *St. Christopher's,*   Wm. M{c}Cornock,

(109) *St. Eustatius,*   John Harper.

---

[462] Orig., in both A and B, 'Cavon'.

[463] CJ, B omit pp. 13–17 of A, dealing with the American Stations 100–[210].

(110) *Tortola*, William Brazier.
(111) *Santa Cruz*, Matthew Lumb.
(112) *Jamaica*, William Hammet.

Nova Scotia and Newfoundland   5

(113) *Halifax,*   James Wray, John
          Mann,   William Black,
(114) *Liverpool,*   James Mann, Elders;   Presiding
(115) *Cumberland,*   Thomas Whitehead,   Elder.
    etc.   Preacher.   10

The UNITED STATES

Bishops—Thomas Coke and Francis Asbury
(116)[464] *Washington*, Moses Park,   15
   Elder, Wyatt Andrews.   Richard Ivy,
(117) *Richmond,* Matthew Harris,   Presiding Elder.
   Wheeler Grissom.
(118) *Burke*, Hope Hull, Elder,   Beverly Allen,
   Bennet Maxey.   Elder.   20
(119) *Augusta*, James Conner.

(120) *Cherokee*, John Andrew,
   Philip Matthews.
(121) *Seleuda*, John Crawford.   25
(122) *Broad River*, Michael
   Burdge, William McDowell.
(123) *Bush River*, William Gassaway.
(124) *Santee*, Mark Moore,   Reuben Ellis,
   John Russell.   Presiding   30
(125) *Edisto*, Isaac Smith,   Elder.
   Lemuel Andrews.
(126) *Charleston,*
(127) *Great Pee Dee*, Aquila   Ira Ellis,
   Sugg, Hardy Herbert.   Elder.   35
(128) *Little Pee Dee*, Thomas
   Humphries, Lemuel Moore.
(129) *Anson*, John Ellis,
   Jonathan Jackson.

---

[464] B numbers the British Americas' Stations 100–115, and the United States Stations 100–196, the latter being changed here to [116]–[210]. The American *Minutes* do not number the stations and show many variants.

(130) *Bladen*,
(131) *New Hope*, Thomas Anderson, Doily Baird.
(132) *East New River*, Jeremiah Maston, Daniel Lockett.
(133) *Tar River*, Charles Hardy, Micaiah Tracy, Myles Smith.
(134) *Pamlico*, James Parks.[465]
(135) *Roanoke*, Henry Merritt, Edward West, Jonathan Bird.
(136) *Caswell*, Thomas Ware, Henry Leadbetter.
(137) *Guilford*, Isaac Lowe, Benj. Carter.
(138) *Salisbury*, Sihon Smith, Julius Conner, Josiah Askew.
(139) *Yadkin*, Daniel Asbury, John McGee.

Edward Morris, Presiding Elder.

(140) *Holstein*, John Baldwin, Mark Whitaker.
(141) *West New River*, Jeremiah Abel, Joseph Doddridge.
(142) *Greenbrier*, James Riggin, Jesse Richardson.
(143) *Bottetourt*, Henry Ogburn.

John Tunnell,[466] Presiding Elder.

(144) *Halifax*, David Haggard, William Moss, William Heath.
(145) *Mecklenburg*, John Paup.
(146) *Bedford*, Richard Pope.
(147) *Cumberland*, John Barker, William McKendree.
(148) *Amelia*, John Easter, Eld. John Fore.

---

[465] Orig., 'Park'.
[466] Orig., 'Tunnel'.

(149) *Brunswick*, Jer. Minter,
M. Green.

(150) *Sussex*, Stephen
Johnson, Stephen Davis,
John Lindsey.

(151) *Greensville*,[467]
James Meachem.

(152) *Bertie*, H. Birchett,
Jesse Nicholson.

(153) *Camden*, Rice Haggard,
Daniel Southall.

(154) *Portsmouth*, Archer Davis,
Lewis Dawson.

(155) *Williamsburg*, John
Robertson, William Spencer.

(156) *Hanover*, Thomas
Weatherford, Christopher
Mooring.

(157) *Orange*, Thomas Hardy,
Salathiel Weeks, Benjamin
Barnes.

James O'Kelly,
Presiding
Elder.

5

10

15

20

(158) *Rockingham*, Samuel
Breeze.

(159) *Alleghany*, Ja. Thomas,
John Hutt.

(160) *Berkley*, Thorn. Fleming,
B. Brown.

(161) *Fairfax*, Thomas Bowen,
John Chalmers, Benjamin
Snelling.

(162) *Lancaster*, Garret
Thompson, Isaac Lunsford.

(163) *Gloucester*, Lewis
Chastain, Valentine Cook,
Thomas Scott,[468] Philip
Cox, Elder and Book
Steward.

Philip
Bruce,
Presiding
Elder.

25

30

35

[467] Orig., 'Grenville'.
[468] Orig., 'Scot', but 'Scott' in American *Minutes*.

(164) *Calvert*, Lenox Martin, Rob. Green.

(165) *Annapolis*, Ezekiel Cooper.

(166) *Baltimore*, John Hagerty, Elder.

(167) *Fell's Point*, Thomas Foster, Elder.

(168) *Montgomery*, James Wilson, John Childs.

(169) *Frederick*, John Hill.

(170) *Bath*, Geo. Hagerty, Josh. Wells.

(171) *Huntingdon*, Michael Laird, Thomas Workman.

(172) *Little York*, Jonathan Forrest, Elder.

(173) *Hartford*, John Allen, John Rowen.

(174) *Baltimore Circuit*, Benton Riggin.

Nelson Reed, Presiding Elder.

(175) *Cecil*, George Moore, Benj. Roberts.

(176) *Kent*, Matthew Greentree, Walter Fountain.

(177) *Talbot*, John Smith, John Milburn.[469]

(178) *Dorset*, John Jarrell, Ant. Banning.

(179) *Annamessex*, William Ward.

(180) *Somerset*, Eliphalet Reed, Griffith Callahan.[470]

Richard Whatcoat, Presiding Elder.

(181) *Northampton*, Christopher Spry, Jeremiah Causden.

(182) *Caroline*, Rcb. Sparks, Jos. Benson.

(183) *Milford*, Thomas Jackson, William Ratcliffe.[471]

(184) *Dover Cir.*, W. Thomas, Levin Ross.

Joseph Everett, Elder.

---

[469] Orig., 'Milbourn'.
[470] Orig., 'Griffin Callahan'.
[471] Orig., 'Ratcliff', but in American *Minutes*, 'Ratcliffe'.

(185) *Dover and Duck Creek*,
Jacob Brush.

(186) *Wilmington*, William Jessop.   5
(187) *Chester*, Wm. Dougherty,
James Campbell.   Henry
(188) *Philadelphia*, John Dickins,   Willis,
Elder and Book Steward.   Presiding
(189) *Bristol*, Robert Cann.   Elder.   10
(190) *Clarksburg*, Jacob Lurton,
Lastley Matthews.
(191) *Redstone*, J. Simmons,   Lemuel
Nic. Sebrell.[472]   Green,
(192) *Pittsburgh*,[473] Charles   Presiding   15
Conaway, Pemberton Smith.   Elder.
(193) *Ohio*, Rich. Pearson,
Tho. Carroll.[474]

                                                            20

(194) *Salem*, Simon Pile,
Jethro Johnson, Sylvester
Hutchinson.
(195) *Trenton*, Joseph
Cromwell, Elder,   James   25
Richard Swain.   Oliver
(196) *Burlington*, John   Cromwell,
McClaskey, William Jackson.   Presiding
(197) *Flanders*, Aaron   Elder.
Hutchinson, Daniel Coombes.   30
(198) *Elizabeth Town*, John
Merrick, John Cooper.
(199) *Newburg*, Nathaniel Mills,
Andrew Harpending.

---

[472] Orig., 'Sebrel'.
[473] Orig., 'Pitsburg'.
[474] Orig., 'Carrol'.

(200) *New York*, Robert Cloud,
Elder, John Merrick, William
Phoebus, each for four months.
(201) *Long Island*, William
5   Phoebus, John Lee.
(202) *New Rochelle*, Peter
Moriarty, Lemuel Smith.
(203) *Dutchess*, Samuel Talbot,
Benjamin Abbot.
10   (204) *Columbia*, John
Bloodgood, Samuel Wigton.
(205) *Cambridge*, Darius
Dunham.
(206) *Lake Champlain*,[475]
15   David Kendall, William
Losee.
(207) *Coeyman's Patent*,[476]
John Crawford.
(208) *Stanford*, Jesse Lee,
20   Albert[477] Van Nostrand.
(209) *Schenectady*,[478] Lemuel
Smith, Cornelius Cook.

Thomas
Morrell,
Elder.

Freeborn
Garrettson,
Presiding
Elder.

(210) *Lexington*, James Haw,
25   Elder, Wilson Lee,
Stephen Brooks.
(211) *Danville*,[479] Barnabas
McHenry, Peter Massey.
(212) *Cumberland*, Thomas
30   Williamson, Joshua Hartley

Francis
Poythress,
Presiding
Elder.

Q. 8.[480] How many wives are to be provided for?
A. Ninety-eight.
Q. 9. How many of these are to be provided for by the
35   circuits?

---

[475] Orig., 'Lake Champlaine'.
[476] Orig., 'Coeman's Patent'.
[477] Orig., 'Andrew'.
[478] Orig., 'Shenectada'.
[479] Orig., 'Dansville'.
[480] CJ omits *QQ*. 8–9.

A. Seventy-eight, as follows, viz.

(1) London,	S. Moore, Broadbent, Crowther,[481] Ramshaw.[482]	
(2) Kent,	S. Pritchard.	
(3) Norwich,	S. Green.	5
(4) Lynn,	£6.	
(5) Oxfordshire,	£6.	
(6) Gloucestershire,	S. Day, £6.	
(7) Worcestershire,	S. Day,[483] £6.	
(8) Sarum,	S. Thom.	10
(9) Bradford,	S. Empringham.	
(10) Bristol,	S. Clarke, Hodgson, Easton,[484] Poole.[485]	
(11) Shepton Mallet,	£6.	
(12) Tiverton and Taunton,	S. Coussins.	15
(13) Plymouth,	S. Warrick, Stephens.[486]	
(14) St. Austell,	S. Church.[487]	
(15) Redruth,	S. Rhodes, and £6.	
(16) St. Ives,	S. Kane.[488]	20
(17) Birmingham,	S. Snowden, Simpson.[489]	
(18) Wolverhampton,	S. Brettel.	
(19) Burslem,	S. Roberts, Beaumont.	
(20) Macclesfield,	S. T. Shaw,[490] and £6.	
(21) Stockport,	S. D. Jackson, and £6.	25
(22) Manchester,	S. Rodda, Hopper, Bradburn.	
(23) Bolton,	S. Story.[491]	
(24) Chester,	S. Greenwood, and £6.	
(25) Liverpool,	S. Myles, H. Taylor, Beanland.[492]	
(26) Blackburn,	S. Bramwell, £6.	30

[481] Timothy Crowther was stationed in Sussex.
[482] John Ramshaw was stationed in Bedford.
[483] Simon Day was stationed in Gloucestershire.
[484] John Easton was stationed in Shepton Mallet.
[485] John Poole was stationed in Tiverton.
[486] Wm. Stephens was stationed in the Channel Isles, No. 14.
[487] Wm. Church was stationed in Brecon.
[488] Lawrence Kane was stationed in Worcestershire.
[489] Wm. Simpson was stationed in Hull.
[490] Thomas Shaw was stationed in Thirsk.
[491] Geo. Story was stationed in Blackburn.
[492] John Beanland was stationed in Keighley.

(27) Colne,	S. Collins, and to S. Bramwell,[493] £6.
(28) Leicester,	S. Butterfield, and to S. Moon[494] £6.
(29) Nottingham,	S. Jos. Taylor, and to S. Moon, £6.
(30) Derby,	S. Watson.
(31) Sheffield,	S. Inglis, Costerdine,[495] Boothby.[496]
(32) Grimsby,	S. Scot.
(33) Horncastle,	£6.
(34) Gainsborough,	S. Longley.
(35) Epworth,	S. Swan.
(36) Leeds,	S. Blair, Goodwin, Brown.
(37) Wakefield,	S. Mather, Dunn.[497]
(38) Huddersfield,	S. Parkin.
(39) Birstall,	S. Peacock.[498]
(40) Bradford,	S. Booth.
(41) Halifax,	S. Jn. Shaw.
(42) Keighley,	S. Wood.
(43) Isle of Man,	S. Holder.
(44) York,	S. Jos. Thompson, and £3.
(45) Pocklington,	S. Percival.
(46) Hull,	S. Tho. Taylor.
(47) Scarborough,	S. Hern.
(48) Whitby,	S. James Thom.
(49) Yarm,	S. Hopkins.
(50) The Dales,	S. Gill, and £6.
(51) Sunderland,	S. Hunter,[499] Gaulter, and to S. Ogylvie,[500] £6.
(52) Newcastle,	S. Atmore, and to S. Ogylvie, £6.
(53) Edinburgh,	S. Watkinson,[501] £6.

---

[493] Wm. Bramwell was stationed in Colne, which shared his wife's expenses with Blackburn.

[494] John Moon was stationed in Nottingham, which shared his wife's expenses with Leicester.

[495] Robert Costerdine was stationed in Derby.

[496] Wm. Boothby was stationed in Epworth.

[497] Thomas Dunn was stationed in Scarborough.

[498] John Peacock was stationed in Keighley.

[499] Wm. Hunter, Sen., was stationed in Alnwick.

[500] John Ogylvie was stationed in Newcastle, which shared his wife's expenses with Sunderland.

[501] Richard Watkinson was stationed in Glasgow, which shared his wife's expenses with Edinburgh.

| (54) Glasgow | S. Watkinson, £6. |
| (55) Ireland, | S. Rutherford, Boone, West, Dinnen, G. Brown, Stewart, Rennick, McDonald, Griffith,[502] and £8. | 5 |

Q. 10. How are the other twenty wives to be provided for?
A. Fifteen, viz. S. Mill, McAllum, Harper, Horner, Gibbon, Lessey, Mowat, R. Johnson, Dall, Condy, Crook, Price, Hetherington, Joyce, and J. Armstrong,[503] out of the 10
Preachers' Fund; and the remaining five, viz. S. Kyte, Stephenson, Atkins, Crosby, and T. Shaw,[504] by the money collected in various circuits for the wives, which money will be lodged in the hands of Mr. Whitfield, London.
Q. 11. What numbers are in the Societies? 15
A. As follows:

London	2,680	
Sussex	268	
Kent	611	20
Colchester	290	
Norwich		
	730	
Yarmouth		
Lynn	350	25
Bedford	237	
Northampton	370	
Oxfordshire	650	
Gloucestershire	381	

[502] These preachers were stationed thus: Thomas Rutherford and Charles Boone, Dublin; Wm. West, Birr; John Dinnen, Athlone; George Brown, Ballyconnell; Matthew Stewart, Clones; James Rennick, Lisleen; James McDonald and Walter Griffith, Newry.

[503] These preachers were stationed thus: Peter Mill, Dundee; Duncan McAllum, Aberdeen; Joseph Harper, Colchester; Wm. Horner, Oxfordshire; George Gibbon, Northampton; Theophilus Lessey, Sarum; George Mowat, Horncastle; Robert Johnson, Dundee; Robert Dall, Edinburgh; Richard Condy, Limerick, John Crook, Charlemont; John Price, Ballyconnell; Thomas Hetherington, Enniskillen; Matthias Joyce, Lisburn; Joseph Armstrong, Cavan.

[504] These preachers were stationed thus: Charles Kyte, Kent; William Stephenson, Alnwick; John Atkins, Derby; John Crosby, Whitehaven; Thomas Shaw, Thirsk.

	Worcestershire	235
	Sarum	636
	Isle of Jersey	294
	Isles of Guernsey, etc.	105
5	Bradford	1,290
	Bristol	2,203
	Taunton	275
	Tiverton	420
	Bideford	83
10	Plymouth	805
	Redruth	1,800
	St. Ives	1,379
	Pembroke	163
	Glamorganshire	273
15	Brecon	202
	Birmingham	1,260
	Wolverhampton	548
	Burslem	1,280
	Macclesfield	1,060
20	Stockport	827
	Manchester	2,050
	Bolton	1,080
	Chester	
		599
25	Wirral	
	Liverpool	900
	Blackburn	880
	Colne	960
	Leicester	622
30	Nottingham	840
	Derby	742
	Sheffield	1,670
	Grimsby	609
	Horncastle	640
35	Gainsborough	720
	Epworth	670
	Leeds	2,140
	Wakefield	689
	Huddersfield	866
40	Birstall	1,403
	Bradford	1,075

Halifax	1,100	
Keighley	1,330	
Whitehaven	240	
Isle of Man	2,569	
York	886	5
Pocklington	800	
Hull	684	
Scarborough	660	
Whitby	611	
Thirsk	660	10
Yarm	522	
The Dales	1,060	
Sunderland	1,240	
Newcastle	1,000	
Berwick		15
	142	
Dalkeith		
Edinburgh	348	
Ayr and Dumfries	80	
Dundee	137	20
Aberdeen	261	
Inverness	220	
Dublin	1,000	
Wexford	221	
Waterford	246	25
Cork	600	
Bandon	220	
Limerick	350	
Birr	150	
Castlebar	200	30
Athlone	540	
Longford	400	
Sligo	300	
Ballyconnell	880	
Clones	1,268	35
Brookeborough	757	
Enniskillen	520	
Ballyshannon	570	
Killybeggs	480	
Lisleen	500	40
Omagh	330	

Charlemont		1,100
Londonderry		288
Coleraine		640
Belfast		450
Lisburn		800
Tanderagee		810
Newry		390[505]

In all	70,305[506]

A M E R I C A[507]

The British Dominions

Nova Scotia and	⎰	Whites	600
Newfoundland,	⎱	Blacks	200
Antigua,	⎧	Whites and	
	⎨	Mulattoes	70
	⎩	Blacks	2,730
Barbados,	⎰	Whites	10
	⎱	Blacks	93
St. Vincent's,	⎰	Whites	16
	⎱	Blacks	140
Dominica,		Coloured People	24
Nevis,		Coloured People	98
St. Christopher's	⎧	Whites and	
	⎨	Mulattoes	280
	⎩	Blacks	500
Tortola		Coloured People	400

The Dutch Dominions

St. Eustatius,	⎰	Whites	3
	⎱	Blacks	153

[505] The Irish statistics, Dublin to Newry, are omitted from B.

[506] Really 70,205. B omits the Irish statistics, Dublin to Newry, though the same sum of 70,305 is given for 'Europe'. The same Irish figures are given in the Irish *Minutes*, with a sum of 14,010.

[507] The statistics of the British Dominions and the United States are not included in B.

The United States

Washington	{ Whites	900	
	Blacks	148	
Richmond	{ Whites	545	GEORGIA.
	Blacks	30	5
Burke	Whites	297	
Augusta,	Whites	87	
Cherokee,	{ Whites	78	
	Blacks	10	10
Seleuda,	{ Whites	231	
	Blacks	11	
Broad River,	{ Whites	411	
	Blacks	18	
Edisto,	{ Whites	340	15
	Blacks	251	
Charleston,	{ Whites	52	
	Blacks	69	SOUTH CAROLINA.
Cainhoy	{ Whites	27	
	Blacks	12	20
Santee,	{ Whites	420	
	Blacks	63	
Anson,	{ Whites	561	
	Blacks	23	
Great Pee Dee,	{ Whites	369	25
	Blacks	39	
Little Pee Dee,	{ Whites	598	
	Blacks	20	
Tar River,	{ Whites	878	
	Blacks	131	30
Bladen,	Whites	34	
East New River,	{ Whites	730	
	Blacks	420	
Roanoke,	{ Whites	758	
	Blacks	321	35
Caswell	{ Whites	351	
	Blacks	43	
New Hope,	{ Whites	527	
	Blacks	31	
Guilford,	{ Whites	410	40
	Blacks	22	

Salisbury,	{	Whites	480
		Blacks	27
Yadkin	{	Whites	345
		Blacks	7
Bertie,	{	Whites	510
		Blacks	20
Camden,	{	Whites	424
		Blacks	85
Cumberland,		Whites	225

NORTH CAROLINA.

Holstein,	{	Whites	411
		Blacks	9
West New River,	{	Whites	299
		Blacks	6
Greenbrier,	{	Whites	222
		Blacks	5
Bottetourt,		Whites	40
Halifax,	{	Whites	470
		Blacks	54
Portsmouth,	{	Whites	480
		Blacks	473
Sussex,	{	Whites	1,300
		Blacks	508
Brunswick,	{	Whites	1,182
		Blacks	318
Amelia	{	Whites	754
		Blacks	154
Mecklenburg,	{	Whites	692
		Blacks	98
Cumberland,	{	Whites	394
		Blacks	10
Bedford,	{	Whites	221
		Blacks	20
Orange,	{	Whites	616
		Blacks	71
Hanover,	{	Whites	497
		Blacks	183
Williamsburg,	{	Whites	274
		Blacks	50

VIRGINIA.

Line numbers in margin: 5, 10, 15, 20, 25, 30, 35

Gloucester,	Whites	657	
	Blacks	62	
Lancaster,	Whites	630	
	Blacks	244	
Fairfax,	Whites	474	5
	Blacks	76	
Berkley,	Whites	325	
	Blacks	36	
Alleghany,	Whites	499	
	Blacks	21	10
Rockingham,	Whites	79	
	Blacks	5	
Northampton,	Whites	360	
	Blacks	84	
Lexington,	Whites	402	15
	Blacks	21	
Danville,	Whites	410	
	Blacks	30	
Bath,	Whites	400	20
	Blacks	34	
Frederick,	Whites	322	
	Blacks	56	
Montgomery,	Whites	648	
	Blacks	103	25
Annapolis,	Whites	128	
	Blacks	141	
Calvert,	Whites	943	
	Blacks	909	
Baltimore,	Whites	719	30
	Blacks	218	
Hertford,	Whites	451	
	Blacks	110	
Cecil,	Whites	257	
	Blacks	252	35
Kent,	Whites	616	
	Blacks	637	
Talbot,	Whites	1,006	
	Blacks	608	
Dorset,	Whites	685	40
	Blacks	347	

MARYLAND.

	Annamessex,	{	Whites	135
			Blacks	10
	Somerset,	{	Whites	400
			Blacks	48
5	Caroline,	{	Whites	705
			Blacks	229

	Dover,	{	Whites	509	
			Blacks	227	
10	Chester,	{	Whites	228	
			Blacks	18	
	Wilmington,	{	Whites	43	DELAWARE AND PENNSYLVANIA.
			Blacks	19	
	Bristol,	{	Whites	51	
15			Blacks	2	
	Little York,		Whites	151	
	Philadel.	{	Whites	256	
			Blacks	17	
	Huntingdon,	{	Whites	185	
20			Blacks	4	
	Redstone,		Whites	290	

	Salem,	{	Whites	680	
			Blacks	24	
25	Trenton,	{	Whites	527	
			Blacks	5	NEW JERSEY.
			Indians	3	
	Eliz. Town,	{	Whites	216	
			Blacks	13	
30	Flanders,	{	Whites	281	
			Blacks	2	

	New York,	{	Whites	290	
			Blacks	70	
35	Long Island,	{	Whites	215	
			Blacks	9	
	New Rochelle,	{	Whites	725	
			Blacks	6	
	Dutchess,	{	Whites	200	
40			Blacks	3	

Columbia,	{	Whites	60		
	{	Blacks	1		
Cambridge,		Whites	154	NEW YORK.	
Coeyman's Patent,		Whites	10		
Newburg,	{	Whites	257		5
	{	Blacks	4		

Total	43,265	
Total in America	48,582	10
Total in Europe	70,305	

Total in Europe and America,	118,887[508]	

15

Q. 12.[509] What is the Kingswood collection?

A. £822. 5*s.* 5*d.*

Q. 13. What children are admitted this year?

A. Martin Rodda, Benjamin Peacock, James Wood, James
Kane, Joseph Harper, Peter Morgan.   20

Q. 14. What can we allow the sons and daughters of the
preachers out of the Kingswood collection?

---

[508] *Q.* 10 in CJ (all in Coke's hand) reads simply: 'What are the numbers in our
societies?'

A. In England and Scotland	56,295
In Ireland	14,010
In the West Indies	4,622
In the States of America	43,265
In Nova Scotia and Newfoundland	800
In all	118,992
Total in Europe	70,305
Total in America	48,687

But the correct figures appear to be:

England and Scotland	56,195
Ireland	14,010
West Indies	4,517
States of America	43,865
Nova Scotia and Newfoundland	800

Total	119,387
Total in Europe	70,205
Total in America	49,182

[509] *QQ.* 12–24 are basically the same in both A and B; all are absent from CJ.

A. Joseph Goodwin, £6; John Brown, £6; Thomas
Rutherford, £6; John Thom, £6; Francis Longley, £6 the
second year; Jane Allen, £6 the second year; Catherine
Thompson, £6 the second year; Sarah Roberts, £6 the
first year; Elizabeth Dall, £6 the first year; Mary Ann
Brisco, £6 the first year.

Q. 15. What is contributed towards the Preachers' Fund?

A. £455. 2*s.* 9*d.*

Q. 16. What is allowed out of it?

A. To Thomas Westell	£30	0	0
William Whitaker	20	0	0
Matthew Lowes	5	0	0
Thomas Hanson	12	0	0
John Furz	12	0	0
John Watson	12	0	0
Ann Morgan	24	0	0
S. Robertshaw	12	0	0
Lucy Bourke	15	0	0
Mary Penington	12	0	0
Sarah Shorter	12	0	0
Catherine Garnet	12	0	0
Elizabeth Dillon	12	0	0
Sarah Barry	24	0	0
Sarah Naylor	10	0	0
S. Hosmer	10	0	0
Sarah Mitchell	20	0	0
Elizabeth Jaco	12	0	0
John Price	12	0	0
S. Corbet	24	0	0
Thomas Johnson	6	0	0
Fifteen wives	180	0	0
In all	£488	0	0

Q. 17. What is contributed for the Yearly Expenses?

A. £1,125. 15*s.* 10*d.*

Q. 18. How was it expended?

A. Last year's deficiencies	£263	16	4
This year's contingencies	100	0	0
For the deficiencies of the preachers and their families in Ireland	118	1	8

For the deficiencies of the preachers and their families in Scotland	£106	0	0	
For the deficiencies of the preachers etc. in Wales	46	14	0	5
For the deficiencies of the preachers and their families in England	297	8	4	
Law	171	15	6	
Houses (several of the sums granted under this Article have been long due)	122	0	0	10
In all,	£1,225	15	10	15

Q. 19. What directions are to be given concerning the building of preaching-houses?

A. We do not permit any preaching-house to be built this year, except one at Dewsbury,[510] and those which have   20 already been begun or set on foot.

Q. 20. Are there any directions to be given to the preachers?

A. 1. Let the Rules of the Society be read in every society once a quarter.

2. No person shall be admitted into the love-feasts with-   25 out a society-ticket, or a note from the Assistant.

3. Every watch-night shall continue till midnight.

4. The money collected at the love-feasts shall be most conscientiously given to the poor.

5. It is advised that no preacher go out to supper, or be   30 from home after nine at night.

Q. 21. We are frequently reproached with the dress of our preachers' children: how ought they to dress?

A. Exactly according to the Rules of the Bands.

Q. 22. Are there any directions to be given concerning the   35 books?

A. No books are to be published without Mr. Wesley's sanction; and sold by his book-keeper.[511]

---

[510] See *Q.* 24 and n. 512.

[511] See *Minutes* (1749), §18; (1761), n. 1019; (1765), *Q.* 24; (1781), *Q.* 25 and n. 899 for previous rulings on this. The restriction to publishing through Wesley's press is new.

Q. 23. Are there any directions to be given concerning Scotland?

A. Only one preacher is to come in future to the Conference from Scotland, except those who are to be
5   admitted into full connexion.

Q. 24. What directions are to be given concerning the building of a new preaching-house at Dewsbury?[512]

A. Let every Assistant make a private and public collection in his circuit for the purpose as soon as possible.

10   *Q.* 25. When and where is our next Conference to be held?

A. In Bristol, on the last Tuesday in July 1790.[513]

L E E D S, JULY 29, 1789.

WHEREAS it has been affirmed, That many of our itinerant preachers disapprove of settling the preaching-houses upon the
15 Methodist Plan: We whose names are underwritten do hereby certify, That we entirely approve of the settling all our preaching-houses on the said Plan.

John Wesley	John Valton
20 Thomas Coke | Richard Rodda |
Alexander Mather | D. Wright |
John Pawson | Francis Wrigley |
Joseph Bradford | Thomas Johnson |
William Thompson | Peter Mill |
25 John Easton | John Pritchard |
George Story | Thomas Rutherford |
Thomas Rankin | Daniel Jackson |
Christopher Hopper | Joseph Taylor |
Thomas Wride | H. Moore |
30 John Mason | Charles Atmore |

[512] See above, n. 415 in these *Minutes*, and n. 327 in *Minutes* (1788). See also the list of preachers declaring agreement with the Model Deed followed by a subscription list for building the new house, at the end of these *Minutes*.

[513] CJ closes in Coke's hand:

'*Q.* 11. When and where shall our next Conference be held?

'*A.* In Bristol, the last Tuesday in July 1790.

John Wesley

Thomas Coke'.

John Peacock
John Gaulter
Robert Dall
Joseph Cole
William Myles
Andrew Inglis
George Highfield
Jonathan Edmondson
William Thom
John Crosby
James Thom
Charles Bland
William Saunders[514]
Thomas Carlill
William Boothby
P. Greenwood
John Booth
Samuel Bradburn
John Atkins
William Thoresby[515]
Thomas McGeary[516]
Robert Swan
James Watson
John King
John Goodwin
Lawrence Kane
George Snowden
John Broadbent
Robert Roberts
Zachariah Yewdall
Robert Hopkins
George Gibbon
Thomas Cooper

Jonathan Coussins
William Simpson
John Shaw
Joseph Benson
Thomas Taylor — 5
Andrew Blair
William Collins
James Wood
Thomas Dixon
Henry Taylor — 10
Thomas Vasey
W. Dufton
Thomas Brisco[517]
William Blagborne
John Beaumont — 15
Isaac Brown
William Horner
George Holder[518]
Alexander Kilham
Lancelot Harrison — 20
Thomas Longley
Thomas Shaw
Samuel Bardsley
William Palmer
John Reynolds — 25
Thomas Tattershall
John Smith
Thomas Gill
John Stamp
John Leech — 30
Thomas Bartholomew
Joseph Entwisle
William Stephenson[519]

[514] Orig., 'Saunder'. N.B. These names were in their origin probably signed, but the evidentiary value of the printed product of this and the following document must be in doubt.

[515] Orig., 'Theorsbee'.

[516] See n. 453.

[517] Orig., 'Briscoe'.

[518] Orig., 'Holden'.

[519] Orig., 'Stevenson'.

Richard Drew	Duncan Kay
James Ridall	Thomas Dunn
Jonathan Crowther	William Hunter
William Bramwell	Robert Costerdine
5 Jonathan Parkin	Joseph Pescod
Christopher Watkins	John Barrett[521]
John Allen	Jasper Robinson
Joseph Harper	Thomas Dobson
James Byron	George Baldwin
10 Edward Jackson	Samuel Hodgson
William Hunter	W. Percival
Timothy Crowther	Simon Day[522]
William Stephens[520]	

15   *Subscribed towards a new preaching-house at*
                         D E W S B U R Y[523]

		£.	s.	d.
	John Wesley	50	0	0
	Thomas Coke	50	0	0
20	Thomas Rankin	5	5	0
	Wm. Thompson	3	3	0
	Henry Moore[524]	1	1	0
	Joseph Bradford	1	1	0
	Geo. Whitfield	1	1	0
25	John Robinson, Burslem	5	5	0
	Tim Crowther	0	10	6
	Thomas Taylor	1	1	0
	Joseph Harper	0	5	0
	Thos. Tattershall[525]	0	10	6
30	John Reynolds	0	10	6
	R. Empringham	0	2	6

---

[520] Orig., 'Stevens'.
[521] Orig., 'Barritt'.
[522] James Anderson (see n. 437 above) adds 'Joseph Benson, total 116'.
[523] See above, *Q.* 24 and n. 512.
[524] Orig., 'Moor'.
[525] Orig., 'Tattershal'.

William Horner	0	10	6	
Joseph Pescod	0	10	6	
Charles Bland	0	10	6	
Robert Hopkins	1	1	0	
Christ. Watkins	1	1	0	5
William Thom	0	5	0	
William Holmes	0	10	6	
John Easton	0	10	6	
Wm. Hunter, Jun.	0	10	6	
John Broadbent	1	1	0	10
Thomas McGeary	1	1	0	
Thomas Tennant	1	1	0	
Thomas Warrick[526]	0	10	6	
John Valton	10	10	0	
Jonathan Coussins	0	10	6	15
Richard Drew	0	10	6	
Lawrence Kane	1	1	0	
John Mason	0	10	6	
Thomas Cooper	1	1	0	
Samuel Bardsley	0	10	6	20
William Fish	0	10	6	
George Shadford	1	1	0	
William Palmer	0	10	6	
William Stephens	0	5	0	
Andrew Blair	0	10	6	25
John Leech	1	1	0	
Richard Rodda	1	1	0	
Thomas Shaw	0	10	6	
Thomas Dobson	0	10	6	
John Allen	1	1	0	30
George Highfield	1	1	0	
Thos. Rutherford	0	5	0	
William Dufton	0	10	6	
George Snowden	0	10	6	
Parson Greenwood	0	5	0	35
Robert Roberts	0	10	6	
Thomas Brisco[527]	0	10	6	
Daniel Jackson	0	10	6	
Henry Taylor	0	10	6	
George Story	0	10	6	40

[526] Orig., 'Warwick'.
[527] Orig., 'Briscoe'.

	Thomas Vasey	1	1	0
	Charles Atmore	1	1	0
	James Ridall[528]	0	5	0
	James Watson	0	10	6
5	Joseph Taylor	1	1	0
	Thomas Hanby	0	10	6
	George Gibbon[529]	1	1	0
	Robert Costerdine	0	10	6
	Edward Jackson	1	1	0
10	Andrew Inglis	0	5	0
	Thomas Longley	0	5	0
	Thomas Carlill	1	1	0
	Launc. Harrison	1	1	0
	Robert Swan	0	5	0
15	James Christie	0	10	6
	John Atkins	0	10	6
	John Pawson	5	5	0
	John Peacock	0	10	6
	William Collins	0	10	6
20	Alexander Mather	1	1	0
	Jonathan Parkin	0	10	6
	Francis Wrigley	1	1	0
	William Bramwell	0	10	6
	William Boothby	1	1	0
25	Joseph Entwisle	0	10	6
	William Thoresby	0	10	6
	John Booth	0	10	6
	Thomas Johnson	1	1	0
	John Goodwin	0	10	6
30	John Shaw	1	1	0
	James Wood	0	10	6
	T. Bartholomew	0	10	6
	W. Blagborne[530]	2	2	0
	Thomas Wride	1	1	0
35	George Holder	0	10	6
	John Smith	0	10	6
	John Gaulter[531]	0	5	0
	W. Stephenson	0	10	6

[528] Orig., 'Ridell'.
[529] Orig., 'Gibbons'.
[530] Orig., 'Blackburne'.
[531] Orig., 'Gualtier'.

Jasper Robinson	0	10	6
William Percival	0	5	0
Thomas Dunn	0	5	0
Jon. Edmondson	0	5	0
Thomas Dixon	0	10	6
Isaac Brown	0	5	0
Alexander Kilham	1	1	0
James Thom	1	1	0
John King	0	10	6
Duncan Kay	0	5	0
John Crosby	1	1	0
William Simpson	0	5	0
William Saunders	0	5	0
Thomas Gill	0	5	0
William Hunter	1	1	0
Duncan Wright	1	1	0
Peter Mill	0	10	6
John Stamp	1	1	0
Zach. Yewdall	1	1	0
Jon. Crowther	0	10	6
John Barber	0	10	6
Joseph Cole	1	1	0
Robert Dall	0	5	0
John Barrett[532]	1	1	0
William Myles	1	1	0
James Byron	0	10	6
John Beaumont	0	5	0
Marm. Pawson	1	1	0
Simon Day	0	5	0
George Baldwin	0	10	6
Samuel Bradburn	1	1	0
R. Empringham	0	2	6
John Pritchard	1	1	0
£206	6	0[533]	

Marginal numbers: 5, 10, 15, 20, 25, 30

[532] Orig., 'Barret'.
[533] The sum seems to be incorrect and should be £208. 8s. 0d.

Annual *Minutes of some late Conversations,* 1790

Bristol, Tuesday, July 27, 1790.[534]
[The Minutes or Journals of the Conference of the People called
Methodists, begun in Bristol on Tuesday, July 27th, 1790, and con-
5 tinued by various adjournments to the 4th day of August following.

[534] CJ for 1790 occupies pp. 71–76 and is mainly in an unknown hand, with some
insertions in the hand of Thomas Coke.

JW's *Journal* is missing for the period of the Conference. The diary shows that
he stayed with Valton, attended by Rankin 'in order to be retired that he might prepare his papers for the Conference'. Valton, July 20, 1790, MS diary; *Journal &*
Diaries, 24:323. There are, however, more surviving individual and detailed recollections than usual, very possibly because this turned out to be the last Conference
before JW's death.

John Pawson wrote, 'This was the last Conference that Mr. Wesley attended, he
was now nearly worn out, and his faculties evidently much impaired, especially his
memory'. Jackson, *Early Methodist Preachers*, 4:58. In his MS autobiography
('Some Account', fol. 39) he says that JW 'was in a great measure become a child
through old age and although he preached many times, yet in reality he was not
much use in settling the business of Conference. By reason of his old age and many
infirmities, our business became very tedious and we could but get very slowly forward', though they got through peacefully in the end.

Atmore says that 'Mr. Wesley appeared very feeble; his eyesight had failed so
much that he could not see to give out the hymns; yet his voice was strong and his
spirit remarkably lively and the powers of his mind and his love towards his fellow-
creatures were as bright and as ardent as ever'. Tyerman, *Wesley*, 3:618 quoting
MM (1845): 123.

Sutcliffe has a lengthy account including the mode of receiving into full
connexion:

'Mr. Wesley, amidst his sons, looked fresh and lively, and likely to run out his
course for years to come. . . . But he himself, having other views, had prepared a book of *Minutes . . . from the years 1744 to 1789* [the "Large" *Minutes*]
and a copy was given to each of the new preachers. . . . A long table being
placed across the chapel, which had no pews, Mr. Wesley sat in a chair at
the head of the table, and about twenty remarkable men on the benches, ten
on each side, distinguished by bushy or cauliflower wigs, aged men that had
borne heat and burden of the day. Mr. Mather, as a sort of archdeacon, a
man of clear head and commanding voice, conducted the whole business of
the Conference. Mr. Valton was the secretary, with his small quarto ledger.
The rest of the preachers were distributed on the benches, the more aged sitting nearer to the long table.'

When stations were mentioned,

'Mr. Wesley put his hand into his pocket and pulled out the manuscript order
of the stations, which it is believed no one had seen since he transcribed it

in Newcastle on his way to the Conference. While proceeding, very many changes were made for mutual accommodation in regard to the prayers of the people for personal and family reasons, Mr. Wesley rarely interfering, except when he had promised a certain station.'

Sutcliffe thought him fair here and not tyrannical as often claimed. But he did 'colour up a little and stamped with his foot' when a point of discipline had been neglected, saying he would expel the preacher. Robert Roberts then protested this was too severe, and JW 'patted him on the head with a smile'.

Sutcliffe was impressed with the close of the Conference when the young men spoke of their experience and call to preach and confessed their faith: 'After this, Dr. Coke came . . . with the "Large" *Minutes* on his left arm and delivered a copy to each, putting his right hand on each of their heads. This was an ordination in every view', though he did not recollect it being done at other Conferences, but he was told it was done at the Scottish ordinations. 'Mr. Wesley took no part' in all this, but 'his presence sanctioned the whole'. The Sacrament followed. MS 'History', fols. 1193–94; also in *WHS* 15 (1925): 57–60, and Davies, George, and Rupp, *History of Methodist Church*, 4:231–34.

Richard Rodda wrote, 'This was the last Conference Mr. Wesley held. In this Conference while I was pleading the case of Sr. Barry, a preacher's widow and desiring that 4 pounds might be added to her sallery [*sic*], which was 20. Mr. Wesley was offended with me and told me that if I did not sit down he would leave the place.' After the session, Wesley said, 'Dicky, I ask your pardon, I spoke too warmly.' Rodda said, 'Sir, I ask yours.' Later, however, he argued Sr. Barry's case again, and this time Wesley praised him for his case, his friendship to 'the dead and the living', and his honesty, and granted the increase. July 1790, MS diary, in MA.

Miss Ritchie wrote to the wife of Peard Dickinson, one of JW's clerical helpers, that 'Mr. Wesley has very openly and fully declared his sentiments respecting the impropriety of a separation from the Church; and the preachers, in general, have agreed to abide by the old plan'. Preachers' dress had been 'largely debated, and what is verging towards worldly conformity is to be laid aside. We all lament dress as a growing evil among the Methodists'. Wesley at breakfast 'among a very few select friends' said he had a few things to complain of including the ruffles on Dickinson's shirts. She had tried to soften matters but now begged Mrs. Dickinson never to let her husband wear a ruffled shirt again to avoid grieving JW. Tyerman, *Wesley*, 3:621.

Pawson wrote to Atmore on May 19 about a proposed 'Scotch Conference' but had heard nothing of it and 'could not see what good end' it 'was to answer'. Pawson, *Letters*, 1:90. After the Conference on Sept. 14, he wrote that 'they have made a Minute on account of our coming away from Conference', which he was sorry to see. Ibid., 1:92 (see last item in Addenda, below, on preachers leaving services early). On *Q*. 21, Rule 1 for Building Committee—'All preaching-houses are to be settled on the Methodist' (Addenda, below)—he continues, 'You may depend upon it that I will never be concerned in the settlement of any house whatsoever upon that Plan while I live.'

Thomas Hanby continued to be obstinate over administering Communion; see *Minutes* (1788), n. 327; (1789), n. 415. He writes that he will not give it up and does not know what will happen to him at the Conference; to Oddie, Jan. 2, 1790, Tyerman MSS, 2:32. In fact, he survived.

[Present

[The Revd. John Wesley, President

[Thos. Coke, Secretary

(There are fifty-seven names in three columns.)

5   [John Allen, Charles Atmore, Samuel Bardsley, Joseph Benson, Andrew Blair, Saml. Bradburn, Joseph Bradford, Tho. Brisco, John Broadbent, Geo. Button, Jeremiah Brettel, Tho. Carlill, Joseph Cole, Wm. Collins, Jonn. Coussins, Adam Clarke, Thos. Dixon, John Easton, John Goodwin, Parson Greenwood, Thomas Hanby, Joseph

10   Harper, Robt. Hopkins, Wm. Hunter, Wm. Homer, Edwd. Jackson, Daniel Jackson, John Leech, Thos. Longley, John Murlin, John Mason, Alexr. Mather, Henry Moore, Wm. Myles, Wm. Palmer, John Pawson, Benj. Rhodes, Tho. Rankin, Richd. Rodda, Robt. Roberts, Wm. Saunders, Geo. Shadford, Geo. Story, Alexr. Suter,

15   James Rogers, Tho. Taylor, Joseph Taylor, James Thom, Wm. Thom, Wm. Thompson, Tho. Tennant, John Valton, Christr. Watkins, Francis Wrigley, James Wood, Duncan Wright, Thos. Warrick.

[Absent

20   (There are thirty-one names in three columns, of whom

William Simpson is entered and struck through,

undoubtedly because he superannuated.)

[Robt. Carr Brackenbury, John Barber, John Booth, Jonathn. Brown, Rob. Costerdine, Wm. Dutton, Lancelot Harrison, John

25   Parkin, Joseph Pescod, James Hall, Peard Dickinson, Wm. Percival, Jasper Robinson, Thos. Rutherford, John Shaw, ((Wm. Simpson)), Geo. Snowden, Tho. Vasey, Zach. Yewdall, Ja. Creighton, Joseph Cownley, Tho. Barber, Charles Boone, Geo. Brown, John Moon, Francs. Asbury, John Crook, Duncan McAllum, James Wray, Richd.

30   Watkinson, Richd. Whatcoat.

[For the absence of whom a Dispensation is granted.

[*Question* 1st. Who are in full connexion with the Conference?

[*Answer*. (There are forty-one names in four columns, of whom

35   James Christie and James Thom are struck through.)

[Joseph Algar, John Baxter, John Beanland, James Bogie, Saml. Botts, Tho. Bartholomew, Wm. Butterfield, ((James Christie)), Tho. Cooper, John Cricket, John Crosby, Robert Dall, Simon Day, Tho. Davis, James Watson, John Watson, John Smith, Robt.

40   Empringham, Geo. Gibbon, Walter Griffith, Samuel Hodgson, Geo. Holder, Wm. Holmes, Joseph Thompson, Thos. Wride, Joseph

Jerom, Andrew Inglis, Robt. Johnson, Thos. Johnson, Matthias Joyce, Lawrence Kane, John King, Charles Kyte, Matthew Lumb, Peter Mill, John Ogylvie, John Pritchard, Thos. Shaw, Robt. Swan, ((James Thom)), Geo. Wadsworth.]

Minutes 5

Q. 1. What preachers are admitted this year?[535]

A. George Baldwin, William Heath, Duncan Kay, Abraham Moseley, Joseph Sutcliffe, William Thoresby, James Evans, Thomas Roberts, John McKersey, William Fish, Thomas Jones, Thomas Gill, Theophilus Lessey, John 10 Townsend, Samuel Bates, David Gordon, John Gillis, Samuel Moorhead, and John Grace.[536]

[*Question* 2d. Who are dropped from being Members of the Conference [?]

[*Answer* 1st. Our dear and much respected Brother, 15 Christopher Hopper, who is superannuated.

[2. Wm. Boothby, who is also superannuated.

[3. Wm. Green, who has left us.

[4. Wm. Hoskins, who has also left us.

[5. Wm. Ashman, for impropriety of conduct. 20

[6. Jonathan Hern, for impropriety of conduct.

[7. John Peacock, for ditto.

[8. Robert Scot, who has been expelled for too great familiarity with women.

[9. Nehemiah Price, for ditto. 25

[10. William Simpson, who is superannuated.[537]

[*Question* 3. Who have been chosen in their place?

[*Answer*. Thos. Tattershall, Geo. Highfield, John Crosby, Thos. Mitchell, Wm. Stephens, John Brown, Geo. Holder, Joseph Armstrong, ((and James (Thom)')), 30 Samuel Botts, and Thomas Bartholomew.[538]

---

[535] CJ, 'And the following persons who are admitted this year'.
[536] In CJ, Grace appears after Gill.
[537] Added by Coke.
[538] The last two in the hand of Coke.

[*Question* 4. Who have desisted from travelling that were in
full connexion with the Conference?

[*Answer*. Wm. Church for improper behaviour towards
women.

5   (Almost erased: 'He was before expelled in 1786 for
lewdness.')]

Q. 2. Who remain on trial?

A. Thomas Broadbent, William Stephens, Jonathan
Edmondson, Thomas Wood, Samuel Gates, John Stamp,
10   John Woodrow, John Sandoe, Richard Reece, Michael
Marshall, Joseph Entwisle, Francis Truscott, Richard
Drew, Thomas Rogerson, Thomas Wyment, John
Wiltshaw, George Lowe, Henry Taylor, John Hickling,
Charles Tunnycliffe, John Furnace, Thomas Kelk,
15   Thomas Dobson, Jasper Winscom, William Jenkins,
William Cox, William Saunderson, Henry Saunders,
Robert Lomas, John Ramshaw, Miles Martindale,
Thomas Hutton, John Kershaw, John Nelson, John
Denton, Robert Crowther, Robert Smith, John Grant,
20   John Beaumont, Robert Miller, William Stephenson,
Mark Willis, John Riles, James Anderson, William
Johnson, John Darragh, Francis Armstrong, William
McCornock, Thomas Hewett, John Malcomson, Thomas
Kerr, James Lyons, James McMullen, Alexander Moore,
25   Matthew Stewart, Thomas Elliott, Andrew Hamilton,
Robert Smith, and William Hamilton.[539]

Q. 3. Who are *admitted* on trial?

A. Owen Davies,[540] Edward Gibbons, George Sargent, John
Braithwaite, Thomas Simmonite,[541] Joseph Burgess,

---

[539] CJ seems to arrange these names haphazardly. The scribe who prepared the
text for the printed *Minutes* used a peculiar system for transcribing the names from
their four columns (reading from left to right) and followed these in turn with each
of the eight successive rows of four and the last row of three. The same fifty-nine
names are present in each list, though the spelling varies. Here, as usual, we have
standardized the spelling. N.B. A further fourteen names should have been added
from the Irish *Minutes*, but were apparently overlooked. This would have made the
total seventy-three.

[540] Orig., 'Davis' (twice in 1790).

[541] From 1790 to 1792, these names were spelled Sargant, Braithwayte, and
Simeonite, but eventually were standardized to those used in the text.

William Ainsworth, Richard Elliott, George Sykes, James
Lawton, Thomas Tretheway,[542] John Pipe, Samuel Taylor,
William Shelmerdine, John Dean, John Boyle, Thomas
Harrison, John Doncaster, Booth Newton, John
Saunderson, John Simpson, Thomas Greaves, and John   5
Grant.[543]

Q. 4. Who has died this year?[544]

A. *James Gore*. He was a young man of good understanding, great sweetness of temper, and eminent piety. And
his end was glorious. He poured out his blood and his   10
soul together.[a]

Q. 5. Are there any objections to any of our preachers?

A. They were examined one by one.

Q. 6. Who have desisted from travelling?

A. Robert Scot,[545] William Church.[546]   15

Q. 7. How are the preachers stationed this year?

A. As follows:

(1) *London*, John Wesley, Thomas Coke, James
Creighton, Peard Dickinson, James Rogers, John
Broadbent, Duncan Wright; Thomas Rankin, super-   20
numerary:—George Whitfield, Book Steward. Joseph
Bradford travels with Mr. Wesley.

(2) *Sussex*, Charles Kyte, Thomas Rogerson, Robert
Miller.

(3) *Chatham,,* John Pritchard, Thomas Greaves.   25

(4) *Canterbury*, Charles Boone, William Cox, John Pipe.

(5) *Colchester*, William Ashman, Robert Crowther; Mark
Willis, supernumerary.

---

[a] He died vomiting blood.

[542] Orig., 'Trethewey' (1790–92).

[543] Again the amanuensis transcribing from the haphazardly arranged list for the
Minutes does not arrange them alphabetically, but presents first the three first names
in each column, followed by the names as they were written across in the remaining three rows. Again the ten names given in the Irish *Minutes* are omitted.

[544] Also Jonathan Thompson, who was omitted here; see Addenda below (p. 27 of
original).

[545] See CJ, *Q*. 2 (8).

[546] See CJ, *Q*. 4. In answer to this question, the Irish *Minutes* (1790) list the names
of Hugh Moore, Nehemiah Price, Robert Bridge, John West, Nebuchadnezzar Lee,
Andrew Jefferys.

(6) *Norwich*, John Reynolds, John Hickling, Thomas Jones, James Lawton.

(7) *Diss*, Thomas Carlill, William Shelmerdine.

(8) *Lynn*, Thomas Tattershall, Joseph Harper, Thomas Simmonite.

(9) *Bury*, Thomas Broadbent, Joseph Jerom.

(10) *Bedford*, William Jenkins, Owen Davies, Edward Gibbons.

(11) *Northampton*, John Leech, James Byron, William Saunders.

(12) *Oxfordshire*, William Homer, Joseph Sutcliffe, Jasper Winscom; John Murlin, supernumerary.

(13) *Gloucestershire*, John Mason, Simon Day.

(14) *Worcestershire*, William Palmer, Lawrence Kane.

(15) *Sarum*, William Holmes, Joseph Algar.

(16) *Portsmouth*, John Easton, William Stephens, Henry Saunders.

(17) *Isle of Jersey*, John Bredin, John de Quêteville.

(18) *Isle of Guernsey, etc.*, William Dieuaide, Thomas Kelk.

(19) *Bradford*, George Snowden, William Thoresby, Michael Marshall; John Furz, supernumerary.

(20) *Bristol*, Henry Moore, Alexander Suter, Thomas Roberts; John Valton, supernumerary. Thomas McGeary, Headmaster of Kingswood School.

(21) *Shepton Mallet*, Jonathan Coussins, George Wadsworth, Thomas Wyment.

(22) *Taunton*, Christopher Watkins, Joseph Pescod.[547]

(23) *Tiverton*, Richard Drew, Theophilus Lessey.

(24) *Bideford*, Samuel Bardsley, Thomas Wride.

(25) *Plymouth*, Thomas Warrick, John Smith, Abraham Moseley.

(26) *St. Austell*, Benjamin Rhodes, Charles Bland, John Boyle.

(27) *Redruth*, Timothy Crowther, Jonathan Crowther, Thomas Dobson.

(28) *St. Ives*, Richard Watkinson, Robert Empringham, Benjamin Legatt, Thomas Tretheway.

---

[547] Pescod and Lessey were listed in CJ in 22 and 23, respectively, but later Coke transposed their names in CJ.

(29) *Pembroke*, John McKersey, James Hall.

(30) *Glamorgan*, George Button, William Heath, John Dean.

(31) *Brecon*, William Fish, John Cricket.

(32) *Birmingham*, Joseph Benson, George Gibbon, George Baldwin, Francis Truscott.

(33) *Wolverhampton*, Jeremiah Brettel, Robert Lomas: Melville Home, supernumerary.

(34) *Burslem*, Robert Roberts, Thomas Cooper, Samuel Gates, Charles Tunnycliffe.

(35) *Macclesfield*, Andrew Inglis, George Shadford, William Dufton.

(36) *Stockport*, Daniel Jackson, Thomas Hutton.

(37) *Manchester*, Richard Rodda, Samuel Bradburn, Thomas Tennant, Charles Bond.

(38) *Bolton*, Thomas Hanby, James Ridall.[548]

(39) *Chester*, Parson Greenwood, Richard Seed, John Wiltshaw.

(40) *Liverpool*, William Myles, John Beaumont, John Denton, Joseph Burgess.

(41) *Blackburn*, James Wood,[549] John Nelson.

(42) *Colne*, Thomas Longley, William Bramwell, William Hainsworth.

(43) *Leicester*, William Butterfield, Robert Costerdine, Thomas Dunn.

(44) *Nottingham*, John Moon, Miles Martindale, Richard Elliott.

(45) *Derby*, Joseph Taylor, William Hunter, Jun., John Sandoe, George Sykes.

(46) *Sheffield*, Francis Wrigley, Lancelot Harrison, Henry Taylor.

(47) *Grimsby*, Jasper Robinson, John Peacock, James Evans.

(48) *Horncastle*, John King, George Mowat, John Riles, George Sargent.

(49) *Gainsborough*, William Collins, Thomas Wood, William Saunderson; Robert Carr Brackenbury, supernumerary.

---

[548] In both CJ and *Minutes*, this appears as 'Riding'.

[549] In CJ, 'Thom' is changed to 'Wood' by Coke.

(50) *Epworth*, Isaac Brown, Thomas Shaw, John Ramshaw.
(51) *Leeds*, James Thom, John Goodwin, Samuel Hodgson.
(52) *Wakefield*, Alexander Mather, supernumerary; George Highfield, Richard Reece.
(53) *Huddersfield*, George Story, Robert Smith.
(54) *Birstall*, John Pawson, William Percival, Samuel Taylor; Thomas Johnson, supernumerary.
(55) *Bradford*, John Allen, Jonathan Edmondson.
(56) *Halifax*, William Thompson, Joseph Entwisle.
(57) *Keighley*, John Booth, John Grant.
(58) *Otley*, Jonathan Parkin, John Atkins.
(59) *Whitehaven*, John Crosby, John Kershaw.
(60) *Isle of Man*, Jonathan Brown, John Barrett, William Franklin.
(61) *York*, Edward Jackson, Robert Howard,[550] Thomas Bartholomew.
(62) *Pocklington*, William Thom, Thomas Gill, Duncan Kay.
(63) *Hull*, Thomas Taylor, John Shaw.
(64) *Scarborough*, Robert Swan, John Beanland, John Simpson.
(65) *Whitby*, Thomas Dixon, Alexander Kilham.
(66) *Thirsk*, James Watson, George Lowe, William Stephenson.
(67) *Yarm*, Robert Hopkins, Booth Newton.
(68) *[The] Dales*, George Holder, Jonathan Hern, John Wittam; William Blagborne, supernumerary.
(69) *Sunderland*, John Gaulter, Joseph Thompson, John Furnace.
(70) *Newcastle*, Charles Atmore, John Brettel; Joseph Cownley, supernumerary.
(71) *Allnwick*, John Stamp, John Ogylvie.
(72) *Edinburgh*, Joseph Cole, Thomas Vasey, Zachariah Yewdall.[551]
(73) *Glasgow*, William Hunter,[552] James Bogie, John Braithwaite.

---

[550] In CJ, 'Haworth', with a caret and 'y' after 'a'.
[551] In CJ, 'Udale'.
[552] CJ adds 'Sen.'

(74) *Campbeltown*,[553] Robert Harrison.
(75) *Dumfries*, Samuel Botts.
(76) *Kelso*, Robert Dall.
(77) *Dundee*, Robert Johnson, Peter Mill, John
Doncaster.   5
(78) *Aberdeen*, Duncan McAllum, John Townsend.
(79) *Inverness*, John Barber, Thomas Harrison, James
Anderson, John Saunderson.
(80) *Dublin*, Adam Clarke, Thomas Rutherford.
(81) *Wicklow*, Thomas Kerr, John Hurley.   10
(82) *Carlow*, Thomas Barber, John Gillis.[554]
(83) *Waterford*, Walter Griffith, John Woodrow.[555]
(84) *Cork*, Andrew Blair, John Kerr.
(85) *Bandon*, William West, James Lyons, Jun., Andrew
Hamilton, Jun.   15
(86) *Limerick*, Matthias Joyce, James McQuigg.
(87) *Kerry*, Charles Graham.
(88) *Birr*, David Gordon, James Hurley.
(89) *Castlebar*, John Darragh, Tho. Patterson.
(90) *Athlone*, Richard Condy, James Irwin.[556]   20
(91) *Longford*, Thomas Davis, John Miller.
(92) *Sligo*, James Rennick, Daniel Graham.
(93) *Ballyconnell*, Matthew Stewart, William Wilson,
William Ferguson; John Price, supernumerary.
(94) *Cavan*, Samuel Moorhead, William Hamilton,   25
Thomas Ridgeway.
(95) *Clones*, William McCornock, Thomas Hewett,
William Brandon.
(96) *Brookeborough*, William Johnson, Thomas Elliott,
Thomas Brown; Andrew Hamilton, Sen., supernumerary.   30
(97) *Enniskillen*, Joseph Armstrong, George Donovan.
(98) *Ballyshannon*, Robert Smith, John Graham,
Archibald Murdock.
(99) *Lisleen*, George Brown, Alexander Moore.
(100) *Omagh*, Michael Murphy, John Stephenson.   35

[553] Orig., 'Cambleton'.
[554] Orig., in *Minutes*, but not in *Q.* 1 or in CJ, 'Gilles'.
[555] Woodrow and Lyons were listed in CJ in No. 83 and No. 85, respectively, but later Coke transposed their names in CJ.
[556] In CJ, 'Erwin'.

(101) *Charlemont*, John Dinnen, John Malcomson; Samuel Bates, supernumerary.
(102) *Londonderry*, David Barrowclough, William Smith.
(103) *Coleraine*, John Grace, James McMullen.
(104) *Belfast*, Thomas Hetherington, Thomas Verner.
(105) *Lisburn*, Samuel Mitchell, Gustavus Armstrong.
(106) *Downpatrick*, Francis Armstrong, Thomas Ryan.
(107) *Tandragee*, John Crook, John Cross, Samuel Steel.
(108) *Newry*, James McDonald, Samuel Wood.

A M E R I C A.

The West Indies

(109) *Antigua*, William Warrener, John Harper.
(110) *Barbados*, Benjamin Pearce.
(111) *St. Vincent's*, John Baxter, Matthew Lumb.
(112) *St. Christopher*, Robert Gamble, George Skerritt.
(113) *Nevis*, Thomas Owens.
(114) *Tortola*, William Brazier, John McVean.
(115) *Jamaica*, William Hammet.
New Missionaries, James Lyons, Thomas Werrill.

Nova Scotia and Newfoundland

(113) *Halifax*, James Wray, John Mann,
(117) *Liverpool*, James Mann, Elders; Thomas Whitehead,
(118) *Cumberland*, Preacher.
(119) *Newfoundland*, John McGeary.

William Black, Presiding Elder.

The U N I T E D   S T A T E S[557]

Superintendents—Thomas Coke and Francis Asbury.

---

[557] The United States stations appear not in CJ, but in the *Minutes* themselves.

(120) *Washington*, Moses Park,
Elder, Wyatt Andrews.   Richard Ivy,
(121) *Richmond*, Matthew Harris,   Presiding
Wheeler Grisson.   Elder.
(122) *Burke*, Hope Hull,   5
Bennet Maxey.   Beverley[558]
(123) *Augusta*, James Conner.   Allen, Elder.

(124) *Cherokee*, John Andrew,
Philip Matthews   10
(125) *Seleuda*, John Crawford.
(126) *Broad River*, Mich. Burdge,   Reuben
William McDowell.   Ellis,
(127) *Bush River*, William Gassaway.   Presiding Elder.
(128) *Santee*, Mark Moore, John   15
Russell.
(129) *Edisto*, Isaac Smith, Lemuel
Andrews.
(130) *Charleston*,[559]   Ira
(131) *Great Pee Dee*, Aquila Suggs,   Ellis,   20
Hardy Herbert.   Elder.
(132) *Little Pee Dee*, Thomas
Humphries, Lemuel Moore.
(133) *Anson*, John Ellis, Jonathan
Jackson   25

(134) *Bladen*,[560]
(135) *New Hope*, Thomas Anderson,
Doily Baird.
(136) *East New River*, Jeremiah   Edward   30
Maston, Daniel Lockett   Morris,
(137) *Tar River*, Charles Hardy,   Presiding
Micaiah Tracy, Miles Smith.   Elder.
(138) *Pamlico*, James Parks.
(139) *Roanoke*, Henry Merritt,   35
Edward West, Jonathan Bird.

---

[558] All American *Minutes* read 'Beverly'.

[559] Left blank. When eventually the American *Minutes* appeared, there were many changes, including Isaac Smith being stationed in Charleston, and two different preachers in Edisto.

[560] Bladen remained vacant in the American *Minutes*.

(140) *Caswell*, Thomas Ware,
  Henry Leadbetter.
(141) *Guilford*, Isaac Lowe,
  Benjamin Carter.
(142) *Salisbury*, Sihon Smith, Julius
  Conner, Josiah Askew.
(143) *Yadkin*, Daniel Asbury,
  John McGee.

(144) *Holstein*, John Baldwin,
  Mark Whitaker.
(145) *West New River*, Jeremiah Abel,
  Joseph Doddridge
(146) *Greenbrier*, James Riggin,
  Jesse Richardson.
(147) *Bottetourt*, Henry Ogburn.

> John
> Tunnell,
> Presiding
> Elder.

(148) *Halifax*, David Haggard,
  William Moss, William Heath.
(149) *Mecklenburg*, John Paup.
(150) *Bedford*, Richard Pope.
(151) *Cumberland*, John Barker,
  William McKendree.
(152) *Amelia*, John Easter, Elder,
  John Fore.
(153) *Brunswick*, Jer. Minter,
  M. Green.
(154) *Sussex*, Stephen Johnson,
  Stephen Davis, John Lindsey.
(155) *Greenville*,[561] James Meachem.
(156) *Bertie*, H. Birchett, J. Nicholson.
(157) *Camden*, Rice Haggard, Daniel
  Southall.
(158) *Portsmouth*, Archer Davis,
  Lewis Dawson.
(159) *Williamsburg*, John Robertson,
  William Spencer.
(160) *Hanover*, Thomas Weatherford
  Christopher Mooring.
(161) *Orange*, Tho. Hardy, Salathiel
  Weeks, Benjamin Barnes.

> James O'Kelly,
> Presiding Elder

[561] Orig., 'Grenville'.

(162) *Rockingham*, Samuel Breeze.
(163) *Alleghany*, Ja. Thomas,
  J. Hutt.
(164) *Berkley*, T. Fleming, B. Brown.   Philip
(165) *Fairfax*, Thomas Bowen, John   Bruce,   5
  Chalmers, Benjamin Snelling.   Presiding
(166) *Lancaster*, Garret Thompson,   Elder.
  Isaac Lunsford.
(167) *Gloucester*, Lewis Chastain,
  Valentine Cook, Thomas Scot,   10
  Philip Cox, Elder, and
  Book Steward.

(168) *Calvert*, L. Martin, R. Green.
(169) *Annapolis*, Ezekiel Cooper.   15
(170) *Baltimore*, John Hagerty,
  Elder.
(171) *Fell's Point*, Tho. Foster,
  Elder.
(172) *Montgomery*, James Wilson,   20
  John Childs.   Nelson
(173) *Frederick*, John Hill.   Reed,
(174) *Bath*, Geo. Hagerty, Josh.   Presiding
  Wells.   Elder.
(175) *Huntingdon*, Michael Laird,   25
  Thomas Workman.
(176) *Little York*, Jon. Forrest,
  Elder.
(177) *Hartford*, J. Allen, J. Rowen.
(178) *Baltimore Circuit*, Bent.   30
  Riggin.

(179) *Cecil*, Geo. Moore, Ben.
  Roberts.
(180) *Kent*, Matthew Greentree,   35
  Walter Fountain.   Richard
(181) *Talbot*, J. Smith, J. Milburn.   Whatcoat,
(182) *Dorset*, J. Jarrell, A. Banning.   Presiding
(183) *Annamessex*, William Ward.   Elder.
(184) *Somerset*, Eliph. Reed,   40
  Griffith Callahan.

(185) *Northampton*, Christ. Spry,
Jeremiah Causden.
(186) *Carolina*, R. Sparks,
J. Benson.
5   (187) *Milford*, Tho. Jackson,
William Ratcliffe.
(188) *Dover Cir.*, W. Thomas,
L. Ross.
(189) *Dover and Duck Creek*,
10 J. Brush.

Joseph
Everett,
Elder.

(190) *Wilmington*, William
Jessop.
(191) *Chester*, Wm. Dougherty,
15 James Campbell.
(192) *Philadelphia*, J. Dickins,
Elder and Book Steward.
(193) *Bristol*, Robert Cann.
(194) *Clarksburg*, Jacob Lurton,
20 Lastley Matthews.
(195) *Redstone*, J. Simmons,
N. Sebrell.
(196) *Pittsburgh*, Charles
Conaway, Pemberton Smith.
25 (197) *Ohio*, R. Pearson,
Tho. Carroll.

Henry
Willis,
Presiding
Elder.

Lemuel
Green,
Presiding
Elder.

(198) *Salem*, Sim. Pile, J. Johnson,
Sylvester Hutchinson.
30 (199) *Trenton*, Joseph Cromwell,
Elder, Richard Swain.
(200) *Burlington*, John McClaskey,
William Jackson.
(201) *Flanders*, Aaron Hutchinson,
35 Daniel Coombes.
(202) *Elizabeth Town*, John Merrick,
John Cooper.
(203) *Newburg*, Nathaniel Mills,
Andrew Harpending.

James
Oliver
Cromwell,
Presiding
Elder.

(204) *New York*, Rob. Cloud, Elder,
John Merrick, W. Phoebus,
each for four months.   Thomas
(205) *Long Island*, William Phoebus,   Morrell,
John Lee.   Elder.   5
(206) *New Rochelle*, Peter Moriarty,
Lemuel Smith.
(207) *Dutchess*, Samuel Talbot,
Benjamin Abbott.
(208) *Columbia*, J. Bloodgood,   10
Sam. Wigton.
(209) *Cambridge*, Darius Dunham.   Freeborn
(210) *Lake Champlain*, David Kendall,   Garrettson,
William Losee.   Presiding
(211) *Coeyman's Patent*, J. Crawford.   Elder.   15
(212) *Stanford*, Jesse Lee,
Albert Van Nostrand.
(213) *Schenectady*, Lemuel Smith,
Cornelius Cook.

                                                          20
(214) *Lexington*, James Haw, Elder,
Wilson Lee, Steph. Brooks.   Francis
(215) *Danville*, Barn. McHenry,   Poythress,
Peter Massey.   Presiding
(216) *Cumberland*, Tho. Williamson,   Elder.   25
Joshua Hartley.

Q. 8.[562] How many wives are to be provided for?
A. Ninety-eight.
Q. 9. How many of these are to be provided for by the   30
circuits?
A. Eighty-two, as follows, viz.

(1) London,	S. Broadbent, Kyte, Davis, Boone.[563]
(2) Sussex,	£3
(3) Chatham,	S. Pritchard.[564] 35
(4) Canterbury,	

---

[562] *QQ.* 8–10 are not present in CJ.

[563] Charles Kyte was stationed in Sussex, Owen Davis in Bedford, and Charles Boone in Canterbury.

[564] John Pritchard was stationed in Chatham.

(5) Norwich,	S. Reynolds.	
(6) Lynn,	S. Tattershall.	
(7) Oxfordshire,	£6	
(8) Gloucestershire,	} S. Day.	
(9) Worcestershire,		
(10) Portsmouth,	S. Easton.	
(11) Bradford,	S. Snowden.	
(12) Bristol,	S. Moore, Kane, Stephens,[565] Poole.	
(13) Shepton Mallet,	S. Coussins.	
(14) Taunton,	} S. Empringham.	
(15) Tiverton,		
(16) Plymouth	S. Warrick, Horner.[566]	
(17) St. Austell,	S. Rhodes.	
(18) Redruth,	S. Tim. Crowther, and £6.	
(19) St. Ives.	S. Watkinson.	
(20) Birmingham,	S. Benson, Gibbon.	
(21) Wolverhampton,	S. Brettel.	
(22) Burslem,	S. Roberts.	
(23) Macclesfield,	S. Inglis, and £6.	
(24) Stockport,	S. Jackson.	
(25) Manchester,	S. Rodda, Bradburn, Shelmerdine.[567]	
(26) Bolton,	S. Ridall.	
(27) Chester,	S. Greenwood.	
(28) Liverpool,	S. Beaumont, Harper,[568] Lessey.[569]	
(29) Blackburn,	S. (Jam.) Thom.	
(30) Colne,	S. Longley, and £6.	
(31) Leicester,	S. Butterfield, £6.	
(32) Nottingham,	S. Moon, and £6.	
(33) Derby,	S. Taylor.	
(34) Sheffield,	S. (Hen.) Taylor, Ramshaw,[570] Costerdine.[571]	

[565] Wm. Stephens was stationed in Portsmouth.
[566] Wm. Horner was stationed in Oxfordshire.
[567] Wm. Shelmerdine was stationed in Diss.
[568] Joseph Harper was stationed in Lynn.
[569] Theophilus Lessey was stationed in Tiverton.
[570] John Ramshaw was stationed in Epworth.
[571] Robert Costerdine was stationed in Leicester.

(35) Grimsby,	S. Peacock.
(36) Horncastle,	£6.
(37) Gainsborough,	S. Collins.
(38) Epworth,	S. Brown.
(39) Leeds,	S. Wood,[572] Goodwin, Hodgson. 5
(40) Wakefield,	S. Dunn,[573] Tunnycliffe.[574]
(41) Huddersfield,	S. Story.
(42) Birstall,	S. Percival.
(43) Bradford,	S. Bramwell.[575]
(44) Halifax,	S. Mowat.[576] 10
(45) Keighley,	
(46) Otley,	S. Booth.
(47) Isle of Man,	S. (Jon.) Brown.
(48) York,	S. Gill.[577]
(49) Pocklington,	S. (Will.) Thom. 15
(50) Hull,	S. (Tho.) Taylor.
(51) Scarborough,	S. Swan.
(52) Whitby,	S. Beanland.[578]
(53) Yarm,	S. Hopkins.
(54) [The] Dales,	S. Holder, and £6. 20
(55) Sunderland,	S. Gaulter, [Joseph] Thompson, Hunter.[579]
(56) Newcastle,	S. Atmore, (John) Brettel.
(57) Edinburgh,	
(58) Glasgow,	S. Bogie.[580] 25
(59) Ireland,	S. Clarke, Blair, Rutherford, Griffith, West, Joyce, Graham, Dinnen, Condy, Rennick, Stewart; and Stephenson, £6.[581]

[572] James Wood was stationed in Blackburn.
[573] Thomas Dunn was stationed in Leicester.
[574] Charles Tunnycliffe was stationed in Burslem.
[575] Wm. Bramwell was stationed in Colne.
[576] Geo. Mowat was stationed in Horncastle.
[577] Thomas Gill was stationed in Pocklington.
[578] John Beanland was stationed in Scarborough.
[579] Wm. Hunter was stationed in Glasgow.
[580] James Bogie was stationed in Glasgow.
[581] These preachers were stationed thus: Adam Clarke in Dublin; Andrew Blair in Cork; Thomas Rutherford in Dublin; Walter Griffith in Waterford; Wm. West in Bandon; Matthias Joyce in Limerick; Charles Graham (1750–1824), 'the Apostle of Kerry', in Kerry; John Dinnen in Charlemont; Richard Condy in Athlone; James Rennick in Sligo; Matthew Stewart in Ballyconnell; and John Stephenson in Omagh.

N.B. S. Parkin, Martindale, Atkins, and Ogylvie,[582] are to
receive their salaries from the money that is to be collected in the circuits above mentioned, which money is to
be lodged in the hands of Mr. Whitfield.

5   *Q.* 10. How are the other twelve wives, viz. S. Dall,
Johnson, Mill, McAllum, (Jam.) Watson, Price,
Armstrong, Brown, Smith, Hetherington, Crook, and
McDonald, to be provided for?[583]
A. Out of the Preachers' Fund. N.B. The money will be

10   lodged in Mr. Whitfield's hands.
Q. 11. What numbers are in the societies?
A. As follows:

London	2,740
Sussex	249
Kent	570
Colchester	300
Norwich	900
Lynn	385
Bedford	376
Northampton	406
Oxfordshire	636
Colcestershire	354
Worcestershire	339
Sarum	556
Isle of Wight	150
Isles of Jersey, Guernsey, and Alderney	498
Bradford	730
Shepton Mallet	880
Bristol	1,841
Taunton	226
Tiverton	380
Bideford	140

---

[582] Jonathan Parkin and John Atkins were stationed in Otley; Miles Martindale
in Leicester; and John Ogylvie in Alnwick.

[583] These preachers were stationed thus: Robert Dall in Kelso; Thomas Johnson
in Birstall; Peter Mill in Dundee; Peter McAllum in Aberdeen; James Watson in
Thirsk; John Price in Ballyconnell; Joseph Armstrong in Enniskillen; George
Brown in Lisleen; Robert Smith in Ballyshannon (N.B. Smith discovered by suc-
cession of stations, Enniskillen, Ballyshannon, Lisleen.); Thomas Hetherington in
Belfast; John Crook in Tandragee; and James McDonald in Newry.

Plymouth	804	
St. Austell	762	
Redruth	1,840	
St. Ives	1,391	
Pembroke	159	5
Glamorganshire	240	
Brecon	167	
Birmingham	1,400	
Wolverhampton	559	
Burslem	1,400	10
Macclesfield	1,090	
Stockport	830	
Manchester	2,060	
Bolton	1,152	
Chester	604	15
Liverpool	1,020	
Blackburn	930	
Colne	976	
Leicester	775	
Nottingham	910	20
Derby	736	
Sheffield	1,690	
Grimsby	584	
Horncastle	643	
Gainsborough	585	25
Epworth	697	
Leeds	2,157	
Wakefield	706	
Huddersfield	846	
Birstall	1,266	30
Bradford	1,085	
Halifax	1,111	
Keighley	1,480	
Whitehaven	302	
Isle of Man	2,580	35
York	880	
Pocklington	830	
Hull	665	
Scarborough	652	
Whitby	582	40
Thirsk	674	

	Yarm	525
	The Dales	989
	Sunderland	1,300
	Newcastle	700
5	Alnwick	290
	Edinburgh	204
	Glasgow	300
	Dundee	132
	Aberdeen	260
10	Inverness	190
	Dublin	1,040
	Wicklow	117
	Wexford	260
	Waterford	186
15	Cork	660
	Bandon	250
	Limerick	330
	Birr	240
	Castlebar	155
20	Athlone	560
	Longford	450
	Sligo	371
	Ballyconnell	875
	Cavan	580
25	Clones	800
	Brookeborough	800
	Enniskillen	530
	Ballyshannon	838
	Lisleen	520
30	Omagh	290
	Charlemont	1,023
	Londonderry	300
	Coleraine	440
	Belfast	560
35	Lisburn	380
	Downpatrick	340
	Tandragee	856
	Newry	355
40	Total	71,568[584]

[584] CJ does not record these membership details, but agrees with the total, 71,568, for which see below. But the British total is really 71,472.

A M E R I C A.

The British Dominions[585]

Nova Scotia and	⎰ Whites	600	
Newfoundland	⎱ Blacks	200	
Antigua	⎰ Whites and Mulattoes	70	5
	⎱ Blacks	2,180	
Barbados[586]	⎰ Whites	10	
	⎱ Blacks	47	
St. Vincent's	⎰ Whites	13	
	⎱ Blacks	350	10
Nevis	Coloured people	200	
St. Christopher's	⎰ Whites and Mulattoes	280	
	⎱ Blacks	500	
Tortola	Coloured people	900	
			15
Total		5,350	

The United States

Washington	⎰ Whites	900		
	⎱ Blacks	148		
Richmond	⎰ Whites	545		20
	⎱ Blacks	30	GEORGIA.	
Burke	⎰ Whites	297		
	⎱ Blacks	4		
Augusta	Whites	87		
				25
Cherokee	⎰ Whites	78		
	⎱ Blacks	10		
Seleuda	⎰ Whites	231		
	⎱ Blacks	11		
Broad River	⎰ Whites	411	SOUTH CAROLINA.	30
	⎱ Blacks	18		
Edisto	⎰ Whites	340		
	⎱ Blacks	25		
Charleston	⎰ Whites	52		
	⎱ Blacks	69		35

[585] This year there is no 'Dutch Dominions', i.e., St. Eustatius.
[586] Orig., 'Barbadoes', as frequently.

	Cainhoy	Whites	27
		Blacks	12
	Santee	Whites	420
		Blacks	63
5	Anson	Whites	561
		Blacks	23
	Great Pee Dee	Whites	369
		Blacks	39
	Little Pee Dee	Whites	598
10		Blacks	20
	Tar River	Whites	878
		Blacks	131
	Bladen	Whites	34
15	East New River	Whites	730
		Blacks	420
	Roanoke	Whites	758
		Blacks	321
	Caswell	Whites	351
20		Blacks	43
	New Hope	Whites	527
		Blacks	31
	Guilford	Whites	410
		Blacks	22
25	Salisbury	Whites	480
		Blacks	27
	Yadkin	Whites	345
		Blacks	7
	Bertie	Whites	510
30		Blacks	20
	Camden	Whites	424
		Blacks	85
	Cumberland	Whites	225
35	Holstein	Whites	411
		Blacks	9
	West New River	Whites	299
		Blacks	6
	Greenbrier	Whites	222
40		Blacks	5
	Bottetourt	Whites	40

NORTH CAROLINA.

Halifax	{	Whites	470	
		Blacks	54	
Portsmouth	{	Whites	480	
		Blacks	473	
Sussex	{	Whites	1,300	5
		Blacks	508	
Brunswick	{	Whites	1,182	
		Blacks	318	
Amelia	{	Whites	754	
		Blacks	154	10
Mecklenburg	{	Whites	692	
		Blacks	98	
Cumberland	{	Whites	394	
		Blacks	10	
Bedford	{	Whites	221	15
		Blacks	20	
Orange	{	Whites	616	
		Blacks	71	
Hanover	{	Whites	497	
		Blacks	183	20
Williamsburg	{	Whites	274	
		Blacks	50	
Gloucester	{	Whites	657	
		Blacks	62	
Lancaster	{	Whites	630	25
		Blacks	244	
Fairfax	{	Whites	474	
		Blacks	76	
Berkley	{	Whites	325	
		Blacks	36	30
Alleghany	{	Whites	499	
		Blacks	21	
Rockingham	{	Whites	79	
		Blacks		
Northampton	{	Whites	360	35
		Blacks	84	
Lexington	{	Whites	402	
		Blacks	21	
Danville	{	Whites	410	
		Blacks	30	40

VIRGINIA.

	Bath	Whites	400
		Blacks	34
	Frederick	Whites	344
		Blacks	56
5	Montgomery	Whites	648
		Blacks	103
	Annapolis	Whites	128
		Blacks	141
	Calvert	Whites	943
10		Blacks	909
	Baltimore	Whites	719
		Blacks	218
	Hertford	Whites	451
		Blacks	110
15	Cecil	Whites	257
		Blacks	252
	Kent	Whites	616
		Blacks	637
	Talbot	Whites	1,006
20		Blacks	608
	Dorset	Whites	685
		Blacks	347
	Annamessex	Whites	135
		Blacks	10
25	Somerset	Whites	400
		Blacks	48
	Caroline	Whites	705
		Blacks	229

MARYLAND.

30	Dover	Whites	509
		Blacks	227
	Chester	Whites	228
		Blacks	18
	Wilmington	Whites	43
35		Blacks	19
	Bristol	Whites	51
		Blacks	2
	Little York	Whites	151
	Philadelphia	Whites	256
40		Blacks	17
	Huntingdon	Whites	185
		Blacks	4
	Redstone	Whites	290

DELAWARE AND PENNSYLVANIA.

Salem	Whites	680	
	Blacks	24	
Trenton	Whites	527	
	Blacks	5	NEW JERSEY.
	Indians	3	5
Eliz. Town	Whites	216	
	Blacks	13	
Flanders	Whites	281	
	Blacks	2	
			10
New York	Whites	290	
	Blacks	70	
Long Island	Whites	215	
	Blacks	9	
New Rochelle	Whites	725	15
	Blacks	6	
Dutchess	Whites	200	NEW YORK.
	Blacks	3	
Columbia	Whites	60	
	Blacks	1	20
Cambridge	Whites	154	
Coeyman's Patent[587]	Whites	10	
Newburg	Whites	257	
	Blacks	4	
			25

Total	43,265	
Total in America,	48,615[588]	
Total in Europe,	71,568	30
Total in Europe and America,	120,183[589]	

Q. 12.[590] What is the Kingswood collection?
A. £907. 8*s.* 11*d.*   35

---

[587] Orig., 'Coeman's Patent'.

[588] I.e., including the 5,350 in 'The British Dominions'.

[589] The totals are also in CJ, in the hand of Coke: '*Q.* 10. What numbers are in the Societies? *A.* In Europe, 71,568; In America, 48,615; In all, 120,183.'

[590] CJ does not include *QQ.* 12–21.

Q. 13. What children are admitted this year?

A. Joseph Goodwin, Joseph Hanby, Thomas Leech, Edmond Barry, Joseph Empringham, and William Dieuaide.

Q. 14. What can we allow the sons and daughters of the preachers out of the Kingswood collection?

A. John Brown, once for all, £12; William Thompson, £6; Thomas Rutherford, the second year, £6; John Thom, £6, second year; Maria Bradburn, the first year, £6; Mary Goodwin, £6, the first year; Sarah Roberts, £6, the second year; Elizabeth Dall, £6, the second year; Mary Ann Brisco,[591] £6, the second year; Mary Joyce, £6, the first year; Joseph Benson, £6, the first year; Sarah Longley, £6, the first year; Ann Allen, £6, the first year.

Q. 15. What is contributed towards the Preachers' Fund?

A. £695. 8*s*. 7*d*.

Q. 16. What is allowed out of it?

A. To Thomas Westell	£35	0	0
William Whitaker	20	0	0
Matthew Lowes	5	5	0
Thomas Hanson	12	0	0
John Furz	12	0	0
Ann Morgan	24	0	0
S. Robertshaw	12	0	0
Lucy Bourke	12	0	0
Mary Penington	12	0	0
Sarah Shorter	12	0	0
Catherine Garnet	12	0	0
Elizabeth Dillon	12	0	0
Sarah Barry[592]	24	0	0
Sarah Naylor	10	0	0
S. Hosmer	10	0	0
Sarah Mitchell	20	0	0
Elizabeth Jaco	12	0	0
John Price	12	0	0
S. Corbet	12	0	0
Thomas Johnson	6	6	0
Samuel Bates	12	0	0

[591] Orig., 'Briscoe'.
[592] See n. 534, above, for her case being debated.

Christopher Hopper	20	0	0	
John Poole	35	0	0	
James Christie	12	0	0	
William Boothby	24	0	0	
Ditto.	20	0	0	5
Thomas Brisco	30	0	0	
12 wives	144	0	0	
In all,	£583	11*s.*	0*d.*	

Q. 17. What is contributed for the yearly expenses?   10
A. £1,225. 15*s.* 10*d.*
Q. 18. How was it expended?

A. Last year's deficiencies	£52	13	11	
Present year's contingencies	100	0	0	15
Law	72	3	0	
Ireland	248	18	0	
Scotland	200	0	0	
Wales, Isles of Guernsey, etc.	78	0	0	
In all England	473	4	11	20
	£1,225	15*s.*	10*d.*[593]	

Q. 19. Are any directions to be given concerning
   collections?
A. No collections shall be made in future for the building   25
   or repairing of preaching-houses, except in the circuits
   where they are respectively built or repaired.
Q. 20. Are any directions to be given concerning the
   Conference?
A. No preachers shall in future attend the Conference,   30
   whose circuits, in which they respectively labour, will not
   provide for their travelling expenses—the preachers who
   labour in Scotland and Wales excepted.
Q. 21. At what times shall the quarterly fasts be held?
A. On the first Friday in August, November, February, and   35
   May.
[Special Committees]
The committee for the management of our affairs in the
   West Indies:

---

[593] Total of this is £1,224. 19*s.* 10*d.* and not £1,225. 15*s.* 10*d.*

Thomas Coke, Alexander Mather, Thomas Rankin,
James Rogers, Henry Moore, Adam Clarke, John Baxter,
William Warrener, Matthew Lumb.
The Building Committee for Great Britain:
5   Alexander Mather, John Pawson, Thomas Rankin,
William Thompson, William Jenkins,[594] and the London
Assistant.
[The Building Committee] for Ireland:
Andrew Blair, Adam Clarke, Thomas Rutherford,
10   Thomas Mitchell.
Rules to be observed by the Building Committee.
1st. All preaching-houses are to be settled on the
Methodist Plan.
2nd. All preaching-houses are to be built in future on the
15   same plan as the London or Bath chapel.[595]
Q. 22. When and where shall our next Conference be held?
A. At Manchester, on the last Tuesday in July, 1791.[596]

20   A D D E N D A,
Taken out of former Minutes
Q. 1. What is subscribed will not answer the demands:
What can be done to lessen these?
A. 1. Let every circuit bear its own burden. 2. Tell everyone
25   expressly, 'We do not make a subscription for paying
debts.' 3. Let all the Assistants declare this in every
place.[597]
Q. 2. Has each Assistant inquired, what trustees are wanting in every place?
30   *A.* No. Let it be done in every preaching-house.[598]
Q. 3. Should any Assistant take into the society any whom
his predecessor has put out?

---

[594] William Jenkins (c. 1763–1844) had had some architectural training, and after
ill health caused his retirement from the active ministry in 1810, he set up as an
architect specializing in Methodist chapels; see Howard Colvin, *A Biographical
Dictionary of English Architects, 1600–1840* (London: John Murray, 1954).
[595] See also Addenda, below.
[596] CJ, '*Q.* 11'.
[597] Cf. 1779, *Q.* 18.
[598] Cf. 1779, *Q.* 24.

A. Not without consulting him.[599]

Q. 4. Preachers hasten home to their families after preaching in the evening. Ought this to be done?

A. Never, till they have met the society.[600]

Q. 5. Ought we not to exhort all dying persons to be then, at least, merciful after their power?

A. We ought, without any regard to the reflections which will be cast upon us on that account.[601]

Q. 6. What can be done to prevent the heavy burdens and expenses, which are needlessly thrown on the Conference?

A. Those circuits that do not provide for their preachers and their children (except Scotland, Ireland and Wales) shall have no more preachers sent to them, for the time to come, than they will provide for.[602]

The following preachers, who had not the opportunity of subscribing at the last Conference towards the building of Dewsbury preaching-house, desire to have their names added to the list, as follows:

Benjamin Rhodes	1	1	0
Charles Bond	1	1	0
James Hall	1	1	0
John Murlin	1	1	0
James Christie	0	10	6
John Nelson	0	10	6
John McKersey	0	10	6
James Rogers	1	1	0
John Bredin	0	5	0
Joseph Jerom	0	5	0
Joseph Algar	1	1	0
Thomas Brisco	0	10	6
Joseph Benson	1	1	0
John Brettel	0	10	6
Adam Clarke	0	10	6

Omitted under the 4th question:

Jonathan Thompson, who died in Scotland in the course of the last year; a young man full of faith and the Holy

---

[599] 1779, *Q.* 25.
[600] 1779, *Q.* 26.
[601] 1781, *Q.* 21.
[602] 1787, *Q.* 22.

Ghost, an ornament and honour to our society in
Scotland. His great zeal for God, and the salvation of
souls, united with the fervour and imprudence of youth,
led him to excessive labour in the work of his great
5   Master, which proved the cause of his death.[603]

Further directions concerning the Building Committee.
1. Everything relative to the building or repairing of
preaching-houses is to be referred to them.
10   2. No house shall be undertaken without the consent of
the majority of them; and not a stone laid till the house is
settled after the Methodist form, verbatim. N.B. No
lawyer is to alter one line, neither need any be employed.
3. No building is to be undertaken till an estimate of the
15   expense is made, and two-thirds of the money raised, or
subscribed.
4. Every preaching-house equal to or less than the Bath
house is to be built in the same form without and within.
5. Every house larger than the Bath house is to be built on
20   the plan of the New Chapel in London, both within and
without.

N.B.[604] 1. No preacher shall preach three times the same
day to the same congregation.
25   2. No preacher shall preach oftener than twice on a
weekday, or oftener than three times on the Lord's day.
3. No preacher shall in future leave the Conference
before the conclusion of it, without consent publicly
obtained in the Conference.
30   [John Wesley[605]
                              Thomas Coke]

---

[603] Another omission from *Q.* 4 was the obituary of John Black, given only in the
Irish *Minutes* (1790).

[604] The following memoranda are also inserted in the hand of Coke at the end of
CJ, just before the closing signatures. JW had proposed that no preacher should
preach more than three times a day, and several preachers objected. He argued that
such 'excessive labour' would lose preachers. When they cited his own case, he said
his 'life and strength had been under an especial providence'. He secretly altered
the minute for the press by adding 'to the same congregation'. Tyerman, *Wesley*,
3:619–20, quoting *Life of Clarke*, 1:277.

[605] JW's last signature in CJ is very frail and disjointed, written in three separate
portions, the topmost being 'sley'.

M I N U T E S [606]

OF SEVERAL

CONVERSATIONS

BETWEEN THE

PREACHERS

LATE IN

CONNECTION

WITH THE

Rev. Mr. WESLEY

❦()❦

LONDON:

Printed by G. Paramore, North-Green, Worship-Street;
And fold by G. Whitfield, at the Chapel, City-Road; and at
all the Methodist Preaching-Houfes in Town and Country, 1791.

[Price TWO-PENCE.]

[606]The title of the annual *Minutes* changes this year from '*some late Conversations*' to '*Several Conversations*', wording that was more commonly used for the titles of the various edns. of the 'Large' *Minutes*, which are still distinguishable by the notation of cumulative dates in the title: '*from 1744 to . . .*'.

Annual *Minutes of Several Conversations, 1791*

A Copy of a Letter from the
REV. JOHN WESLEY, to the Conference.

Chester, April 7th, 1785.[607]

5   To the Methodist Conference.
My dear Brethren,
    Some of our travelling preachers have expressed a fear that after
my decease you would exclude them either from preaching in connexion with you, or from some other privileges which they now
10 enjoy. I know no other way to prevent any such inconvenience than
to leave these my last words with you.

---

[607] JW died on Mar. 2, 1791, so that the Conference beginning in July 1791 was
no longer presided over by him, and it introduced several new features into the
Methodist organization, notably the District system (*Q.* 8). Nevertheless in most
respects it was clearly a continuation of his organizing instrument, fulfilled many
of his preliminary arrangements, and was overshadowed by his presence. It seems
fitting, therefore, that these 1791 *Minutes* should take their place along with those
that preceded them. In 1785, JW had prepared for such an occasion, whenever it
might happen. And the surviving preachers prefixed to the regular *Minutes* his message to them and their remarks upon it.
    Considerable agitation among the preachers followed JW's death, with printed res-
olutions and much correspondence, so that it was clear that some modifications in
their traditional procedure were called for and especially that they were not prepared
to elect from among themselves another 'King in Israel'. Hopper wrote to Benson
(Apr. 11, 1791, PLP 55, MA), 'We think our Conference deed and Mr. Wesley's will
are incompatible. . . . Many among us aspire too high but the pride of man must come
down.' Bradburn's biographer T. W. Blanshard commented that some preachers
seemed a little jealous of Coke and Mather, who had almost ruled the connexion in
JW's name for some time previous to his death and had received ordination from him
so that some feared they might claim his authority on these grounds. *Life of Samuel
Bradburn: The Methodist Demosthenes* (London, 1871), 137. The election of William
Thompson as first President after JW suggests a pointed snub to such a possibility.
    Various unofficial regional meetings made proposals for the future; the most
influential was one at Halifax that issued a circular dated Mar. 30 and signed by
Thompson, Pawson, Robert Roberts, John Allen, Richard Rodda, Samuel
Bradburn, Thomas Tennant, Thomas Hanby, and Hopper. They rejected a 'King
in Israel' as incompatible with the Deed of Declaration. Instead they should use
committees. The Legal Hundred should have vacancies filled by seniority;
Presidents should be for one year only; committees should manage affairs of
'Districts' between Conferences and appoint their own 'Presidents' for a year. See
Davies, George, and Rupp, *History of Methodist Church*, 4:241–42, for details.
Henry Moore wrote to Benson (May 19 or 24, MS PLP 77–1, MA) reporting the

findings of a committee in Bristol that agreed with much of the advice given in similar meetings in Leeds and Manchester as well as Halifax, and following Leeds in suggesting Thompson as President. Richard Rodda, after the Halifax meeting, joined a meeting of numerous 'respectable preachers' at Manchester, the vast majority of whom agreed with 'us', which was a good preparation for the Conference. They seem to have been worried about the claims of the executors to JW's will that might have clashed with Conference authority over some matters. Rodda MSS 92–5–3, p. 22, in MA. This did indeed happen. See Richard P. Heitzenrater, *"Faithful unto Death": Last Years and Legacy of John Wesley* (Dallas: Bridwell Library, 1991). Despite the weight of these meetings, there were dissidents. A meeting of Cornish 'delegates' at Redruth on June 14 wished for amendments to 'our discipline', which included Classes choosing their own leaders and Societies choosing their stewards and having a majority vote for admitting and expelling members. Stewards along with preachers should judge delinquent preachers; all preachers should have an equal vote in Conference; and the District scheme proposed at Halifax was opposed. This foreshadowed the 'democratic' revolt against control by the itinerants that split Wesleyanism periodically from 1797. For details see Davies, George, and Rupp, *History of Methodist Church*, 4:243–44.

We can only guess who took the chair at the opening of the Conference. It is entirely possible, however, that the veteran Christopher Hopper, who had superannuated the previous year and thus was no longer a member of the Legal Hundred (though present), was called upon by the preachers to preside at the opening, for in 1780 they had done so during JW's absence. In his autobiography, however, Hopper merely states, 'Above two hundred preachers attended. Our new mode of government was settled with great unanimity. For such a body of men to agree in one, we must say, "is the Lord's doing, and marvellous in our eyes" '. Jackson, *Early Methodist Preachers*, 219, 223. The first public action of the Conference seems to have been to elect by ballot (only the members of the Legal Hundred voting) a new President and Secretary. Coke was deliberately passed over in favour of William Thompson as President, but continued as Secretary. See Jonathan Crowther, *The Portraiture of Methodism*, 2nd edn. (London: Edwards, 1815), 131, 290; cf. Myles, *Chronological History*, 196–97.

Thomas Dixon described the scene: the preachers 'came together as children who had lost their father. The chair in which Mr. Wesley formerly sat at was hung with black as was also the table at which we sat, and everything about us bore the appearance of sorrow and mourning'. Thompson 'filled the chair beyond anything I expected. He proved himself a wise, calm, dispassionate and prudent man in every part of the business of the Conference'. MS autobiography in Tyerman MSS, 2:301. But the future rebel Alexander Kilham struck a more discordant note. Bradburn, he said (approvingly), criticized the clergy. There were warm altercations, and the Conference lacked order and seriousness becoming ministers in Christ. There was a warmth he did not approve. There were absurd arguments in favour of adhering to the Church, but Thomas Taylor 'behaved a man of God' and he and some others 'defended the truth'. Kilham, *Life of Mr Alexander Kilham* (Nottingham, 1799), 50–58.

For this pivotal year the CJ occupies pp. 77–91, the opening items of business being in the following order:

I beseech you by the mercies of God that you never avail yourselves of the Deed of Declaration to assume any superiority over
your brethren; but let all things go on among those itinerants who
choose to remain together exactly in the same manner as when I was
5 with you, so far as circumstances will permit.

In particular I beseech you, if ever[608] you loved me, and if you now
love God and your brethren, to have no respect of persons in stationing the preachers, in choosing children for Kingswood School, in dis-
posing of the yearly contribution and the Preachers' Fund, or any
10 other public money. But do all things with a single eye, as I have done
from the beginning. Go on thus, doing all things without prejudice or
partiality, and God will be with you even to the end.

JOHN WESLEY

15

N.B. The Conference have unanimously resolved, that all the
preachers who are in full connexion with them shall enjoy every
privilege that the members of the Conference enjoy, agreeably to the
above-written letter of our venerable deceased Father in the Gospel.
20 It may be expected that the Conference make some observations on
the death of Mr. Wesley; but they find themselves utterly inadequate
to express their ideas and feelings on this awful and affecting event.

Their souls do truly mourn for their great loss; and they trust
they shall give the most substantial proofs of their veneration for
25 the memory of their most esteemed Father and Friend, by endeavouring with great humility and diffidence to follow and imitate him
in doctrine, discipline, and life.

[The Minutes or Journals of the Conference of the People called
Methodists begun in Manchester on Tuesday, July 26th, 1791, and con-
30 tinued by various adjournments to the 9th day of August following.

Attendance: the Legal Hundred.
Preachers in full connexion.
Q. 2. Members chosen in room of Wesley and Wright.
Copy of Wesley's letter of 1785.
Resolution of Conference thereon.
Q. 3. Who remain on trial?
N.B. The 1784 Deed of Declaration (see below, Appendix A), stated:
'6th. Immediately after all the vacancies occasioned by death or absence are filled
up by the election of new members as aforesaid, the Conference shall choose a
President and Secretary of their assembly out of themselves. . . .'

[608] The text of CJ; *Minutes* have 'if you ever'.

Present
William Thompson, President
Thomas Coke, Secretary
(There are eighty-six names in three columns, two of which are
crossed out, and five have '+' before their names.)   5
[John Allen, Joseph Armstrong, Charles Atmore, John Barber,
+Thomas Barber, Samuel Bardsley, Thomas Bartholomew, Joseph
Benson, Andrew Blair, Charles Boone,[609] John Booth, ((Samuel
Botts)), Robt. Carr Brackenbury, Samuel Bradburn, Joseph
Bradford, Jeremiah Brettel, +Thomas Brisco, John Broadbent, 10
Jonathan Brown, Isaac Brown, George Button, Adam Clarke,
William Collins, Joseph Cole, Robert Costerdine, Jonathan
Coussins, Joseph Cownley, James Creighton, John Crook, John
Crosby, Peard Dickinson, Thomas Dixon, William Dufton, John
Easton, John Goodwin, Parson Greenwood, James Hall, Thomas 15
Hanby, Joseph Harper, Lancelot Harrison, George Highfield,
George Holder, Robert Hopkins, William Homer, William Hunter,
Daniel Jackson, Edward Jackson, John Leech, Thomas Longley,
Duncan McAllum, John Mason, Alexander Mather, +Samuel
Mitchell, John Moon, Henry Moore, +John Murlin, William Myles, 20
William Palmer, Jonathan Parkin, John Pawson, Joseph Pescod,
+Thomas Rankin, Benjamin Rhodes, Robert Roberts, Jasper
Robinson, Richard Rodda, James Rogers, Thomas Rutherford,
William Saunders, George Shadford, William Simpson, George
Snowden, George Story, Alexander Suter, Thomas Tattershall, 25
Joseph Taylor, Thomas Taylor, Thomas Tennant, James Thom,
William Thom, John Valton, Richard Watkinson, Thomas Warrick,
((William Warrener)), James Wood, Francis Wrigley.

[Absent   30
(There are twelve names in three columns, two having '+' before
their names and the last two in the handwriting of Coke.)
[+Francis Asbury, George Brown, Thomas Carlill, William
Percival, James Wray, John Shaw, Thomas Vasey, Christopher
Watkins, +Richard Whatcoat, Zachariah Yewdall, Samuel Botts, 35
William Warrener.]
[For the absence of whom a dispensation is passed.
[*Question* 1. Who are in full connexion with the Conference?

[609] Orig., 'Bain'.

[*Answer.* (There are seventy-four names in three columns; six names are crossed out, and the last fourteen added by Coke; William Blagborne was added twice.)

[Christopher Hopper, Joseph Algar, John Baxter, John Beanland,
5 James Bogie, ((Samuel Botts)), ((Thomas Bartholomew)), William Butterfield, Thomas Cooper, John Cricket, John Crosby (crossed out), Robert Dall, Simon Day, ((Thomas Davis)), Thomas Broadbent, William Stephens, Jonathan Edmondson, Thomas Wood, Samuel Gates, John Stamp, John Woodrow, James Watson,
10 John Watson, John Smith, Robt. Empringham, George Gibbon, Walter Griffith, Samuel Hodgson, ((George Holder)), William Holmes, Joseph Thompson, Joseph Jerom, Andrew Inglis, Robert Johnson, John Sandoe, Richard Reece, Joseph Entwisle, Francis Truscott, John Beaumont, Thomas Dunn, Thomas Kerr,[610] Thomas
15 Johnson, Lawrence Kane, John King, Charles Kyte, Matthew Lumb, Peter Mill, John Ogylvie, John Pritchard, Thomas Shaw, ((Robert Swan)), George Wadsworth, Matthias Joyce, John Darragh, William McCornock, William Johnson, John Malcomson, Davis Barrowclough, Francis Armstrong, Thomas Hewett, John
20 McKersey, Thos. Jones, William Thoresby, Wm. Fish, Willm. Heath, Thomas Gill, Thos. Wood, William Bramwell, Thomas Roberts, William Blagborne (named twice), John Wittam, John Townsend, Timothy Crowther, Jonathan Crowther.

[*Question* 2d. Who have been chosen Members of the Conference
25 in the room of the Revd. John Wesley and Duncan Wright?
[*Answer.* Robert Hayward and William Ashman.[611]

Minutes

Manchester, Tuesday, 26th of July, 1791.
*Q.*1. What preachers are admitted this year?[612]
30   *A.* Thomas Broadbent, William Stephens, Jonathan
Edmondson, Thomas Wood, Samuel Gates, John Stamp,

---

[610] Orig., 'Carr'.

[611] This line in Coke's handwriting.

[612] Strangely, CJ this year completely omits this question, yet it appears in the printed *Minutes*.

John Woodrow, John Sandoe, Richard Reece, Joseph
Entwisle, Francis Truscott, John Beaumont, Thomas
Dunn, Thomas Kerr, John Darragh, William McCornock,
William Johnson, John Malcomson, David Barrowclough,
Francis Armstrong, and Thomas Hewett.   5
N.B. The Irish preachers in this Minute are admitted to all
    the privileges of travelling preachers in full connexion,
    but must be received in form at the next Irish Conference.
Q. 2. Who remain on trial?[613]
A. Thomas Rogerson, John Wiltshaw, George Lowe, Henry 10
    Taylor, John Hickling, Charles Tunnycliffe, John Furnace,
    Thomas Kelk, Thomas Dobson, Jasper Winscom,
    William Jenkins, William Cox, William Saunderson,
    Henry Saunders, Robert Lomas, John Ramshaw, Miles
    Martindale, Thomas Hutton, John Kershaw, John Nelson, 15
    John Denton, Robert Crowther, Robert Smith, John
    Grant, Robert Miller, William Stephenson, Mark Willis,
    John Riles, James Anderson, James Lyons, James
    McMullen, Alexander Moore, Matthew Stewart, Thomas
    Elliott, Andrew Hamilton, Sen., Robert Smith, William 20
    Hamilton, Daniel Graham, Michael Murphy, William
    Wilson, George Donovan, Samuel Wood,[614] Thomas
    Ridgeway, James McQuigg, Thomas Patterson, Andrew
    Hamilton, Jun., James Irwin, John Stephenson, John
    Cross, Charles Graham, John Hurley, Samuel Steel,[615] 25
    William Smith, William Ferguson, Owen Davies, Edward
    Gibbons, George Sargent, John Braithwaite, Thomas
    Simmonite, Joseph Burgess, William Hainsworth,
    Richard Elliott, George Sykes, James Lawton, Thomas
    Tretheway, John Pipe, Samuel Taylor, William   30
    Shelmerdine, John Dean, John Boyle, Thomas Harrison,
    John Doncaster, Booth Newton, Robert Swan, John
    Saunderson, John Simpson, Thomas Greaves, Robert
    Harrison, Thomas Brown, John Graham, Archibald

[613] The names are not arranged according to any obvious plan, clearly not alphabetical or in any rational order of circuits but apparently haphazard.

[614] Orig., 'James', corrected in CJ by Coke to 'Samuel'; from the fact that the
printed *Minutes* do not follow Coke's correction, it appears that Coke entered this
later.

[615] Samuel Steel (once spelled 'Steele' in 1791) was not listed among those admitted on trial in 1790, but was stationed in Circuit 107, Tandragee.

Murdock, William Aver, William Denton, Isaac Lilly,
Thomas Black, William Franklin, James Bell, Blakeley
Dowling,[616] and Joseph Cross.[617]

Q. 3. Who are *admitted on trial?* [618]

5   *A*. Thomas Robinson, Henry Mahy, William Mahy, James
Jay, and Michael Emmett.[619]

Q. 4. Who have died this year?

A. Duncan Wright, an old, faithful labourer in the vineyard
of the Lord. Gravity and steadiness were two eminent
10   parts of his character. After an useful life spent in the
service of his divine Master, he gave indubitable proofs in
his last illness that he was going to rest from his labours in
Abraham's bosom.

And Robert Gamble, who died in the Island of St. Vincent
15   the West Indies. He laboured for some years as a travelling
preacher in England, but spent the last three years of his
life in the conversion of the poor, despised negroes. Last
February he was seized with a putrid fever, and after a
sickness of sixteen days entered into glory in the triumph
20   of faith.

Q. 5. Are there any objections to any of our preachers?

A. They were examined one by one.

Q. 6. Who have desisted from travelling?

A. Thomas Wyment and Thomas Ryan; Jonathan Hern,
25   Thomas Verner, and William Brandon.[620]

Q. 7. How are the preachers stationed this year?

---

[616] Dowling was apparently accepted as an itinerant in 1790, but remained unstationed, and the 1792 *Minutes* list him as having travelled one year only. Although noted in CJ as 'Blakely', the 1791 *Minutes* use the spelling 'Blakeley'.

[617] In error Coke adds in CJ: '& / Benjamin Leggatt / Samuel Steele'. Leggatt (whose name is spelled 'Leggat' in the *Minutes* [1789–91], but 'Leggatt' in his biography and obituaries) is an anomaly; JW appointed him to supply the Epworth and Gainsborough Circuits in 1787; he was stationed in the *Minutes* from 1788 onwards, but he was never listed as either on trial or in full connexion until this year. Steel had already been listed as remaining on trial.

[618] In CJ, Coke adds William Denton and Henry Mahy to its original list of Robinson, 'William Mahay', Jay, and 'Emmet', as against five named in *Minutes*.

[619] Orig., 'Emmet'.

[620] In CJ, Coke inserts comments in each instance: Wyment, 'for marrying contrary to our rule'; Ryan, 'through infirmity'; Hern 'for drunkenness'; Verner, 'for fornication'; Brandon, 'for trifling'.

A. As follows:

(1) *London*, Thomas Coke, James Creighton, Peard Dickinson, James Rogers, Joseph Bradford, Richard Rodda; Thomas Rankin, supernumerary:—George Whitfield, Book Steward.   5

(2) *Sussex*, Charles Kyte, Robert Crowther, John Poole.

(3) *Rochester*, Thomas Warrick, John Pipe.

(4) *Canterbury*, Charles Boone, Thomas Rogerson, William Cox.

(5) *Colchester*, William Ashman, Joseph Jerom, William   10
Aver.

(6) *Norwich*, John Reynolds, Thomas Simmonite, John Wiltshaw, Isaac Lilly.

(7) *Diss*, William Shelmerdine, James Lawton.

(8) *Bury*, John Hickling, Mark Willis.   15

(9) *Lynn*, William Jenkins, Owen Davies.

(10) *Wells*, Thomas Broadbent, Jasper Winscom.

(11) *Bedford*, Thomas Tattershall, John Wittam, Ed. Gibbons, Wm. Denton.[621]

(12) *Northampton*, John Leech, Joseph Harper.   20

(13) *Oxfordshire*, George Baldwin, William Stephens, Thomas Jones; John Murlin, supernumerary.

(14) *Gloucestershire*, John Mason, Lawrence Kane.

(15) *Worcestershire*, Jeremiah Brettel, Francis Truscott.

(16) *Sarum*, Joseph Algar, Thomas Fearnley.   25

(17) *Portsmouth*, John Easton, Michael Marshall, Thomas Dobson.

(18) *Isle of Jersey*, Joseph Sutcliffe, William Dieuaide.

(19) *Isle of Guernsey*, Henry Saunders, John de Quêteville.   30

(20) *Isle of Alderney*, Henry Mahy.

To change every two months

(20) **France*, William Mahy.[622]

---

[621] In CJ, Coke added the last two names.

[622] In CJ, the presentation of this new station with the same number as the previous one apparently denotes that France was an offshoot of the work in the Channel Isles, which was indeed the case. Mahy had ventured into France as a Local Preacher from Guernsey in 1790, raised several Societies during a ministry of more than eighteen years, and died ill and impoverished in Dec. 1813.

(21) *Bath*, John Broadbent, James Hall, George Button; John Furz, supernumerary.[623]

(22) *Bristol*, Henry Moore, Thomas Rutherford, Thomas Tennant, Thomas Roberts, John Valton, supernumerary. Thomas McGeary, Headmaster of Kingswood School.

(23) *Shepton Mallet*, Jonathan Coussins, William Saunders.

(24) *Taunton*, Charles Bland, James Jay, Christ. Watkins.

(25) *Tiverton*, Theophilus Lessey, George Wadsworth.

(26) *Bideford*, Robert Empringham.

(27) *Plymouth*, William Homer, William Thoresby, Thomas Kelk.

(28) *St. Austell*, Benjamin Rhodes, Samuel Bardsley, Thomas Tretheway.

(29) *Redruth*, Timothy Crowther, Abraham Moseley, John Boyle.

(30) *Penzance*, Richard Watkinson, Jonathan Crowther, John Smith, James Byron.

(31) *Pembroke*, Thomas Hutton, William Fish, Benjamin Leggatt.[624]

(32) *Glamorgan*, William Hainsworth, John Cricket, Robert Miller.

(33) *Brecon*, John Dean, William Heath.

(34) *Birmingham*, Samuel Bradburn, George Gibbon, Thomas Bartholomew, Samuel Taylor.

(35) *Coventry*, William Palmer, who is to change quarterly with the single preachers of the Birmingham circuit.[625]

(36) *Wolverhampton*, Alexander Suter, Simon Day; Melville Horne, supernumerary.

(37) *Burslem*, Andrew Inglis, Thomas Cooper, Richard Seed, John Nelson.

(38) *Macclesfield*, John Goodwin, John Denton, John Furnace; George Shadford, supernumerary.

(39) *Stockport*, William Myles, Samuel Gates.

(40) *Manchester*, Joseph Benson, Adam Clarke.

---

[623] In CJ (by Coke), 'John Valton and [John Furz, supernumerar]ies'; 'John Valton, supernumerary' is struck from No. 22, Bristol.

[624] Coke in CJ strikes out Hutton and adds 'Stephen Wilson' at end.

[625] In CJ, Coke replaces Palmer by 'Charles Bond' (an exchange).

(41) *Oldham*, Thomas Hanby, Robert Costerdine.

(42) *Bolton*, Robert Roberts, Robert Lomas.

(43) *Chester*, Parson Greenwood, James Thom, George Lowe.

(44) *Liverpool*, Thomas Taylor, Joseph Burgess.   5
    (44) **Warrington*, George Snowden, ((Charles Bond)), William Palmer.[626]

(45) *Blackburn*, Henry Taylor, James Evans.

(46) *Colne*, Thomas Longley, Charles Tunnycliffe, William Saunderson.   10

(47) *Leicester*, John Moon, Miles Martindale, John Sandoe, William Hunter, Jun.

(48) *Nottingham*, Thomas Carlill, William Butterfield, John Beaumont, Thomas Wood.

(49) *Derby*, Joseph Taylor, Joseph Pescod, Thomas   15
Dunn, Tho. Greaves.

(50) *Sheffield*, Francis Wrigley, Daniel Jackson, George Highfield.

(51) *Grimsby*, Jasper Robinson, George Mowat, George Sargent.   20

(52) *Horncastle*, John King, John Ramshaw, John Riles, Jonathan Edmondson; Robert Carr Brackenbury, supernumerary.

(53) *Gainsborough*, William Collins, John Peacock, John Simpson.   25

(54) *Epworth*, Isaac Brown, Thomas Shaw, John Atkins.

(55) *Leeds*, James Wood, Lancelot Harrison, William Percival.

(56) *Wakefield*, William Thompson, Richard Reece.

(57) *Huddersfield*, George Story, Richard Elliott.   30

(58) *Birstall*, Edward Jackson, John Kershaw; Thomas Johnson, supernumerary.	The single preachers
(59) *Dewsbury*, William Bramwell, George Sykes; Jonathan Parkin, supernumerary.	to change every quarter.

35

[626] As in the case of France above, No. 20, CJ indents and duplicates the number and adds an asterisk, apparently as an indication that Warrington forms a branch or offshoot of the Liverpool Circuit, though in this case the asterisk is added after the number. In CJ, Coke inserts 'William Palmer' after the erased 'Charles Bond'.

(60) *Bradford*, John Allen, John Grant.
(61) *Halifax*, John Pawson, Joseph Entwisle.
(62) *Keighley*, John Booth, James Ridall.
(63) *Otley*, William Dufton, William Simpson.
(64) *Whitehaven*, John Crosby, Jonathan Brown.
(65) *Isle of Man*, John Ogylvie, John Barrett, William Franklin.
(66) *York*, Sam. Hodgson, John Beanland, William Blagborne.
(67) *Pocklington*, Wm. Thom, Robert Howard.
(68) *Hull*, Alexander Mather, John Shaw.
(69) *Bridlington*, John Braithwaite, Booth Newton.
(70) *Scarborough*, George Holder, James Watson, Thomas Robinson.
(71) *Whitby*, Rob. Hopkins, Duncan Kay.
(72) *Thirsk*, Thomas Dixon, Thomas Gill, Robert Smith.
(73) *Yarm*, William Hunter, Sen., John Stamp.
(74) *Barnard* Castle, John Brettel, Wm. Stephenson.
(75) *Hexham*, Peter Mill, John McKersey.
(76) *Sunderland*, John Pritchard, Zachariah Yewdall, Joseph Thompson.
(77) *Newcastle*, John Gaulter, Alex. Kilham; Jo. Cownley.
(78) *Alnwick*, Charles Atmore, Michael Emmett.

S C O T L A N D

(79) *Edinburgh*, Joseph Cole, Samuel Botts, John Saunderson.
(80) *Glasgow*, Robert Johnson, John Barber,[627] Robert Harrison.
(81) *Dumfries*, Joseph Cross.
(82) *Kelso*, Robert Swan.
(83) *Dundee*, James Bogie, Robert Dall, Thomas Harrison; Joseph Saunderson, supernumerary.
(84) *Aberdeen*, Thomas Vasey, John Townsend.
(85) *Inverness*, Duncan McAllum, James Anderson, John Doncaster.

[627] In CJ, Coke replaces John Barber with Joseph Cross, and in No. 81 replaces Cross with Barber.

IRELAND

(86) *Dublin*, Andrew Blair, Walter Griffith; Matthias Joyce, supernumerary.

(87) *Wicklow*, David Gordon,[628] James Lyons.

(88) *Carlow*, Thomas Davis, John Miller.   5

(89) *Waterford*, John Darragh, Tho. Ridgeway.

(90) *Cork*, David Barrowclough, John Woodrow.

(91) *Bandon*, William McCornock, William West, James McQuigg.

(92) *Limerick*, Samuel Wood,[629] Andrew Hamilton, Jun.,   10
Charles Graham.

(93) *Birr*, Thomas Kerr, Thomas Patterson, James Hurley.

(94) *Castlebar*, Samuel Moorhead, William Wilson.

(95) *Athlone*, Richard Condy, William Johnson.   15

(96) *Longford*, James McMullen, Thomas Black.

(97) *Sligo*, Francis Armstrong, Blakely Dowling.

(98) *Ballyconnell*, Matthew Stewart, Daniel Graham, Joseph Hennin.

(99) *Cavan*, John Malcomson, Michael Murphy, Thomas   20
Brown.

(100) *Clones*, Robert Smith, Andrew Hamilton, Sen., William Hamilton.

(101) *Brookeborough*, James Rennick, Thomas Elliott, William Ferguson.   25

(102) *Enniskillen*, Joseph Armstrong, George Donovan.

(103) *Ballyshannon*, Thomas Hewett, John Hurley, John Cross.

(104) *Lisleen*, Archibald Murdock, John Graham.

(105) *Omagh*, Alexander Moore, John Fury.   30

(106) *Charlemont*, John Dinnen, Gustavus Armstrong; Samuel Bates, supernumerary.

(107) *Londonderry*, John Kerr, Samuel Mitchell.

(108) *Coleraine*, William Smith, John Gillis, John Stephenson.   35

---

[628] In CJ, Coke replaces Gordon with 'James Wood', altered to 'Samuel Wood'; James Wood was stationed in No. 55, Leeds; Gordon was inserted in No. 92, Limerick, where the entry 'James Wood' was an error for Samuel Wood.

[629] Orig., 'James', in error.

(109) *Belfast*, James McDonald, James Irwin.
(110) *Lisburn*, John Grace, James Bell.
(111) *Downpatrick*, Thomas Barber, Thomas Hetherington.
5   (112) *Tandragee*, George Brown, William Armstrong, John McFarland.
(113) *Newry*, John Crook, Samuel Steel.

A M E R I C A.

The British Dominions
10   Nova Scotia and New Brunswick

Halifax, William Jessop, John Mann, Elders.	
Liverpool, Thomas Whitehead.	William
Shelbourne, William Early.	Black,
Newport, John Cooper.	Presiding
Cumberland, Benjamin Fisler.[630]	Elder
River, St. John, John Ragan,[631]	
Annapolis, James Boyd.[632]	

                    Newfoundland
20   *Carbonear*,[633] John McGeary.

The West Indies
Antigua, John Baxter, Benjamin Pearce.
Barbados, Matthew Lumb.
St. Vincent's. James Wray, James Lyons.
25   *Grenada*, Thomas Owens.
Nevis, John McVean.
St. Christopher's, William Warrener, and a preacher from the continent of America; George Skerritt, supernumerary.

---

[630] Orig., 'Fizler'.
[631] Orig., 'Regan'.
[632] Orig., 'Boid'.
[633] Orig., 'Carboniere'.

Tortola, John Harper, and a preacher from the continent.
Jamaica, William Brazier, Thomas Werrill.

N.B. As we have not received the Minutes of the
  Conferences of the United States for the present year, on   5
  account of the sudden departure of Dr. Coke from
  America in consequence of Mr. Wesley's death, we are not
  able to insert the stations of the preachers of those States
  in their usual places.
                                                                10
Q. 8. What regulations are necessary for the preservation of
  our whole economy as the Rev. Mr. Wesley left it?
A. Let the three Kingdoms be divided into Districts:[634]
  England into eighteen Districts,[635] Scotland into two, and
  Ireland into five,[636] as follows: 15
(1) London, Sussex, Colchester, Rochester, Canterbury,
  Bedford, Oxford.
(2) Norwich, Diss, Lynn, Bury, Wells.
(3) Nottingham, Derby, Leicester, Northampton.
(4) Sarum, Portsmouth.   20
(5) Jersey, Guernsey, Alderney.
(6) Redruth, St. Austell, Penzance.
(7) Plymouth, Bideford, Tiverton.
(8) Bristol, Taunton, Shepton Mallet, Bath, Gloucester.
(9) Pembroke, Glamorgan, Brecon.   25
(10) Birmingham, Worcester, Wolverhampton.
(11) Manchester, Stockport, Oldham, Bolton, Liverpool,
  Blackburn.[637]

[634] This was the major organizational innovation of the Methodism system as left by JW. He had acted as his own executive between Conferences, and his death therefore left a gap that the District organization was designed to fill. The wording does not suggest a regular meeting or a permanent presiding preacher but a temporary chairman of an ad hoc meeting summoned as need arose rather than the 'Chairman of the District' as understood by later Methodism. However, *Q.* 31 suggests that at least an annual meeting was required for settling financial accounts in the District. Pawson later complained that the system left them without real government: 'We have no executive government at all between Conference and Conference'. To Atmore, Feb. 18, 1794, *Letters*, 1:164. This was one reason for his support of the notorious Lichfield Plan (1794), which provided such an executive and not simply an episcopal 'order'. (See Pawson's account of this affair, to Atmore, Apr. 8, 1794, ibid., 1:166–67; and introduction, pp. 74, 101. For the initial account of organization and functions of the District Committee, see *Q.* 9 below.)

[635] Actually nineteen Districts.

[636] In CJ, Coke changes to '6'—the actual number.

[637] CJ, 'Blagborne'.

(12) Chester, Macclesfield, Burslem.
(13) Halifax, Colne, Keighley, Bradford, Huddersfield.
(14) Leeds, Sheffield, Wakefield, Birstall, Dewsbury, Otley.
(15) York, Hull, Pocklington, Bridlington, Scarborough.
(16) Grimsby, Horncastle, Epworth, Gainsborough.
(17) Whitby, Yarm, Thirsk, Barnard Castle.
(18) Whitehaven, Isle of Man.
(19) Newcastle, Sunderland, Hexham, Alnwick.
(20) Edinburgh, Glasgow, Dumfries, Kelso.
(21) Aberdeen, Dundee, Inverness.
(22) Dublin, Wicklow, Carlow, Longford.
(23) Cork, Bandon, Limerick, Waterford.
(24) Athlone, Birr, Castlebar, Sligo.
(25) Clones, Cavan, Ballyconnell, Enniskillen,
    Brookeborough.
(26) Londonderry, Coleraine, Lisleen, Ballyshannon,
    Omagh.
(27) Charlemont, Tandragee, Newry, Downpatrick,
    Lisburn, Belfast.

Q. 9.[638] What directions are necessary concerning the management of the Districts?

A. The Assistant of a Circuit shall have authority to summon the preachers of his District who are in full connexion, on any critical case which, according to the best of his judgment, merits such an interference. And the said preachers, or as many of them as can attend, shall assemble at the place and time appointed by the Assistant aforesaid, and shall form a committee for the purpose of determining concerning the business on which they are called. They shall choose a Chairman for the occasion; and their decision shall be final till the meeting of the next Conference, when the Chairman of the committee shall lay the minutes of their proceedings before the Conference. Provided nevertheless, that nothing shall be done by any committee contrary to the resolutions of the Conference.

---

[638] This question is numbered '8' in error, without any correction for succeeding numbers. We have made the necessary corrections, 9–38, without the use of square brackets.

Q. 10. How many wives are to be provided for?[639]

A. One hundred and nine.

Q. 11. How many of these are to be provided for by the circuits?

A. Eighty-three, as follows, viz.:   5

(1) London,	S. Rodda, Boone,[640] Poole, Kyte.[641]
(2) Sussex,	£3.
(3) Rochester,	S. Warrick.[642]
(4) Canterbury,	
(5) Norwich,	S. Reynolds. 10
(6) Lynn,	S. Davies.
(7) Northampton,	S. Harper.
(8) Oxfordshire,	£6.
(9) Portsmouth,	S. Easton.
(10) Isle of Jersey,	£3. 15
(11) Bath,	S. Broadbent.
(12) Bristol,	S. Moore, Rutherford, Kane.[643]
(13) Shepton Mallet,	S. Coussins.
(14) Taunton,	S. Lessey.[644]
(15) Tiverton,	20
(16) Plymouth,	S. Homer, Bland.[645]
(17) St. Austell,	S. Rhodes.
(18) Redruth,	S. (Tim.) Crowther, and £6.
(19) Penzance,	S. Watkinson.
(20) Birmingham,	S. Bradburn, Gibbon. 25
(21) Wolverhampton,	S. Day.
(22) Burslem,	S. Inglis.
(23) Macclesfield,	S. Goodwin, and £6.
(24) Stockport,	S. Myles, Empringham.
(25) Manchester,	S. Clarke, Ashman, Tattershall. 30
(26) Oldham,	S. Costerdine.
(27) Bolton,	S. Roberts.
(28) Chester,	S. Greenwood.
(29) Liverpool,	S. (Tho.) Taylor.

[639] *QQ.* 10–13 are not included in CJ.

[640] Charles Boone was stationed in Canterbury.

[641] Charles Kyte was stationed in Sussex.

[642] Thomas Warrick was stationed in Rochester.

[643] Lawrence Kane was stationed in Gloucestershire.

[644] Theophilus Lessey was stationed in Tiverton.

[645] Charles Bland was stationed in Taunton.

	(29)* Warrington,	S. Snowden.
	(30) Blackburn,	S. (Hen.) Taylor.
	(31) Colne,	S. Longley, and £6.
	(32) Leicester,	S. Moon.
5	(33) Nottingham,	S. Butterfield, and £6.
	(34) Derby,	S (Jos.) Taylor.
	(35) Sheffield,	S. Jackson, Pescod,[646] Dunn.[647]
	(36) Grimsby,	S. Mowat.
	(37) Horncastle,	£6
10	(38) Gainsborough,	S. Collins.
	(39) Epworth,	S. (Is.) Brown.
	(40) Leeds,	S. Wood, Percival, Ramshaw.[648]
	(41) Wakefield,	S. (Wm.) Thompson, (Jam.) Thom.[649]
15	(42) Huddersfield,	S. Story.
	(43) Birstall,	S. Beanland.[650]
	(44) Bradford,	S. Bramwell.[651]
	(45) Halifax,	S. Beaumont.[652]
	(46) Keighley,	S. Booth.
20	(47) Isle of Man,	S. Ogylvie.
	(48) York,	S. Hodgson.
	(49) Pocklington,	S. (Wm.) Thom.
	(50) Hull,	S. Shaw, Peacock.[653]
	(51) Scarborough,	S. Holder.
25	(52) Whitby,	S. Hopkins.
	(53) Yarm,	S. Hunter.
	(54) Hexham,	S. Mill.
	(55) Sunderland,	S. Pritchard, (Jos.) Thompson.
	(56) Newcastle,	S. Gaulter, Atmore.[654]
30	(57) Edinburgh, (58) Glasgow,	} S. Botts.[655]

---

[646] Joseph Pescod was stationed in Derby.
[647] Thomas Dunn was stationed in Derby.
[648] John Ramshaw was stationed in Horncastle.
[649] James Thom was stationed in Chester.
[650] John Beanland was stationed in York.
[651] Wm. Bramwell was stationed in Dewsbury and Birstall.
[652] John Beaumont was stationed in Nottingham.
[653] John Peacock was stationed in Gainsborough.
[654] Charles Atmore was stationed in Alnwick.
[655] Samuel Botts was stationed in Edinburgh.

(59) Ireland,   S. Blair, Griffith, Hetherington,
West, Graham, Condy, Rennick,
Stewart, Armstrong, Dinnen,
Smith, McDonald.⁶⁵⁶

5

Q. 12. How are the other twenty six wives, viz., S.
Martindale, Atkins,⁶⁵⁷ £6, Simpson, Ridall, Dufton, £6,
Crosby, (Jon.) Brown, Franklin £6, Watson, Gill, (John)
Brettel, (Jer.) Brettel, (Wm.) Stephenson, Tunnycliffe,
Stephens, Cross, Swan, Joyce,⁶⁵⁸ Dall, Townsend,
McAllum, Grace, (Geo.) Brown, Crook, Woodrow, and
(John) Stephenson, £3. 16*s*. 0*d*., to be provided for?⁶⁵⁹

10

A. Partly by the small subscriptions raised in the circuits,
and partly by the Contingent Fund.⁶⁶⁰

N.B. The money for the twenty-six wives above mentioned
will be lodged in the hands of Mr. Whitfield.

15

Q. 13. What are the subscriptions of the circuits in Ireland
towards the support of the wives?

A. As follows:

20

Dublin	£30	0	0
Wicklow	0	10	6

---

⁶⁵⁶ These preachers were stationed thus: Andrew Blair and Walter Griffith in Dublin; Thomas Hetherington in Downpatrick; William West in Bandon; Daniel Graham in Ballyconnell; Richard Condy in Athlone; James Rennick in Brookeborough; Matthew Stewart in Ballyconnell; Joseph Armstrong in Enniskillen; John Dinnen in Charlemont; William Smith in Coleraine; and James McDonald in Belfast.

⁶⁵⁷ Orig., 'Atkinson'.

⁶⁵⁸ Orig., 'Boyce'.

⁶⁵⁹ These preachers were stationed thus: Miles Martindale in Leicester; John Atkins in Epworth, William Simpson in Otley; James Ridall in Keighley; William Dufton in Otley; John Crosby in Whitehaven; Jon. Brown in Whitehaven; William Franklin in the Isle of Man; James Watson in Scarborough; Thomas Gill in Thirsk; (John) Brettel in Barnard Castle; Jer. Brettel in Worcestershire; Wm. Stephenson in Barnard Castle; Charles Tunnycliffe in Colne; William Stephens in Oxfordshire; Joseph Cross in Dumfries; Robt. Swan in Kelso; Matthias Joyce in Dublin (supernumerary); Robt. Dall in Dundee; John Townsend in Aberdeen; Duncan McAllum in Inverness; John Grace in Lisburn; Geo. Brown in Tandragee; John Crook in Newry; John Woodrow in Cork; and (John) Stephenson in Coleraine.

⁶⁶⁰ This finally ended the dubious system of making up the deficit by raiding the Preachers' Fund. See *Minutes* (1780), *Q.* 18 and n. 859; (1781), *Q.* 10 and n. 891.

	Carlow	2	10	6
	Waterford	3	13	6
	Cork	16	0	0
	Bandon	1	10	0
5	Limerick	5	10	0
	Birr	4	0	0
	Castlebar	2	0	0
	Athlone	7	0	0
	Longford	8	0	0
10	Sligo	1	10	0
	Ballyconnell	2	10	0
	Clones	6	0	0
	Cavan	6	0	0
	Brookeborough	4	0	0
15	Enniskillen	3	10	0
	Ballyshannon	1	10	0
	Lisleen	1	10	0
	Omagh	1	10	0
	Charlemont	5	10	0
20	Londonderry	3	0	0
	Coleraine	5	10	0
	Belfast	6	10	0
	Lisburn	8	0	0
	Downpatrick	1	10	0
25	Tandragee	5	0	0
	Newry	2	10	0
		£146	4	0

Q. 14. What numbers are in the society?[661]

30   *A.* As follows:

	London	2,950
	Sussex	260
	Chatham	280
35	Canterbury	295
	Colchester	145
	Norwich	580

[661] As on some other occasions, there was some disruption of blocks of statistics dealing with Society membership, with some jumbled ordering within the columns. The listing has been reordered here so that they may be found to approximate the order of the circuits (as with other years) while still maintaining the correct tabulation of the membership.

Diss	310	
Bury	160	
Lynn	370	
Bedford	500	
Northampton	470	5
Oxfordshire	700	
Gloucestershire	316	
Worcestershire	288	
Sarum	238	
Portsmouth	430	10
Isle of Jersey	316	
Isle of Guernsey	222	
Bradford	952	
Bristol	1,562	
Shepton Mallet	950	15
Taunton	234	
Tiverton	406	
Bideford	150	
Plymouth	816	
St. Austell	950	20
Redruth	1,705	
St. Ives	1,537	
Pembroke	168	
Glamorgan	250	
Brecon	116	25
Nottingham	1,000	
Derby	785	
Sheffield	1, 690	
Grimsby	583	
Horncastle	638	30
Gainsborough	700	
Epworth	710	
Leeds	2,080	
Wakefield	730	
Huddersfield	780	35
Birstall	1,230	
Bradford	1,095	
Halifax	1,115	
Keighley	900	
Otley	560	40
Whitehaven	282	
Isle of Man	2,500	

	York	874
	Pocklington	834
	Scarborough	621
	Whitby	545
5	Thirsk	629
	Yarm	554
	Hull	664
	Birmingham	1,600
	Wolverhampton	612
10	Burslem	1,434
	Macclesfield	1,140
	Stockport	655
	Manchester	2,090
	Bolton	1,160
15	Chester	614
	Liverpool	1,050
	Blackburn	955
	Colne	1,020
	Leicester	768
20	The Dales	986
	Sunderland	1,250
	Newcastle	780
	Alnwick	300
	Edinburgh	205
25	Glasgow	218
	Campbeltown[662]	16
	Dumfries	44
	Kelso	31
	Dundee	157
30	Aberdeen	286
	Inverness	222
	Dublin	970
	Wicklow	200
	Carlow	293
35	Waterford	230
	Cork	450
	Bandon	240
	Limerick	350
	Birr	280
40	Castlebar	184

[662] Orig., 'Cambleton'.

Athlone	499	
Longford	440	
Sligo	320	
Ballyconnell	764	
Clones	670	5
Cavan	1,006	
Brookeborough	760	
Enniskillen	400	
Ballyshannon	745	
Lisleen	357	10
Omagh	430	
Charlemont	1,112	
Londonderry	268	
Coleraine	412	
Belfast	450	15
Lisburn	500	
Downpatrick	412	
Tandragee	858	
Newry	458	
Kerry	100	20

$$\overline{72,476}$$

A M E R I C A

The British Dominions

Nova Scotia	Whites	530	25
	Blacks	200	
Newfoundland	Whites	150	
Antigua	Whites	36	
	Mulattoes	105	
	Blacks	2,113	30
Barbados	Whites	30	
	Coloured People	30	
St. Vincent's	Whites	13	
	Coloured People	450	
Nevis	Whites	6	35
	Coloured People	394	
St. Christopher	Whites and		
	Mulattoes	280	
	Blacks	1,120	

Tortola	{	Whites	18
	{	Coloured People	900[a]
Jamaica	{	Whites and	
	{	Mulattoes	40
	{	Blacks	110

Total—	6,525
The United States	57,621
Total in America	64,146
Total in Europe	72,476
Total in Europe and America	136,622[663]

Q. 15. What is the Kingswood collection?

A. £1,035. 11. 9.[664]

Q. 16. What children are admitted this year?

A. James McBurney, 11 years old; William Rutherford,
9 years old; John Wiltshaw, 9 years old; Samuel Wood,
8 years old; Andrew Inglis, near 8 years old; and Richard
Summers for one year.

Q. 17. What can we allow for the education of the preachers' children that cannot be admitted into Kingswood
School?

A. £108[665]

Q. 18. What is contributed towards the Preachers' Fund?

A. £730. 10. 8.[666]

---

[a]The return of the last Conference in the West Indies was 1,800; but the work has been of such short continuance, and the increase so rapid, that only half the number is set down.

[663] CJ gives only a summary of the membership statistics, thus:

In Europe	72,476
British America	6,521
States of America	57,625
	136,622 Total

[664] Coke inserts same total in CJ, erasing previous figure of £967. 0. 9.

[665] In CJ, Coke's original '£108' is altered to '£168'.

[666] CJ has same total, Coke erasing previous '£549. 14. 9.'

Q. 19. What is allowed out of it?

A. To Thomas Westell	£35	0	0	
William Whitaker	20	0	0	
Matthew Lowes	10	0	0[667]	5
Thomas Hanson	12	0	0	
John Furz	12	0	0	
Ann Morgan	24	0	0[668]	
S. Robertshaw	12	0	0	
Lucy Bourke	15	0	0	10
Mary Penington	12	0	0	
Elizabeth Dillon	12	0	0	
Sarah Naylor	10	0	0	
Sarah Barry	24	0	0	
S. Hosmer	10	0	0	15
Sarah Mitchell	20	0	0	
Elizabeth Jaco	12	0	0	
John Price[669]	30	0	0	
S. Corbet	12	0	0	
Thomas Johnson	6	6	0	20
Samuel Bates	12	0	0	
Christopher Hopper	24	0	0	
James Christie	12	0	0	
William Boothby	24	0	0	
Thomas Brisco	24	0	0	25
John Watson	12	0	0	
Thomas Wride				
for the past year	22	10	0	
–ditto– for this year	20	0	0	
Thomas Olivers	24	0	0	30
George Shadford	12	0	0	
S. Wright	8	8	0	
John Bredin	£12	0	0	
In all,	£495	14	0[670]	

[667] In CJ, '£10. 10. 0.'

[668] In CJ, Coke here inserts: 'Sarah Barry £24. 0. 0.', which was omitted from its position lower down.

[669] In CJ, 'John Pipe'.

[670] CJ has total '£466. 2. 0.' (£496. 2. 0.?) The total on p. 421 is '£495. 4. 0.', but if one regards Matthew Lowes (No. 58) as really having 10 guineas, then the printed total is '£495. 14. 0.'

Q. 20. What is contributed for the yearly expenses?
A. £1,338. 8. 1.[671]
Q. 21. How was it expended?

A. Deficiencies of last

year's contingencies	£35	7	6
Law	87	8	1
Deficiencies of the salaries of the preachers	372	18	3
Deficiencies of the salaries of the wives of the preachers	223	5	6
Deficiencies in the allowance made for the children	206	0	0
Sick families	44	5	0
Rent for houses, etc.	104	3	0
Travelling expenses this *extraordinary year*	167	8	0
Various contingencies for the three Kingdoms	97	12	9
	£1,338	8	1[672]

Q. 22. Who is appointed to hold the Conference in Dublin on the first Friday of next July?
A. Thomas Coke.[673]
Q. 23. Are there any directions necessary concerning the preceding Minute?[674]
A. No letters of complaint, or on circuit business, shall be written to England on account of this appointment. The Committees of the Districts shall determine all appeals whatsoever during the intervals of the Conference; and therefore all applications on society business during the said intervals which cannot be determined by the Assistants of the circuits shall be made to the Committees only.

---

[671] In CJ, this total replaces '£1,227. 17. 8.'

[672] CJ includes only the first amount, has a different order, omits law and travelling expenses, and adds 'sick single Preachers'.

[673] In CJ, orig., 'Doctor Coke'; he himself has stricken 'Doctor' and inserted 'Thomas'.

[674] In CJ, 'concerning the above appointment?'

Q. 24. Whereas we have been disappointed by married preachers coming out to travel in expectation of being themselves able to maintain their wives independently of the connexion, who very soon became entirely dependent, how shall this be prevented in future?   5

A. [(1)] Let no preacher be received on this plan unless he can bring in writing such an account of his income, signed by the Assistant, as shall satisfy the Conference.

(2) If any person shall propose to keep a preacher's wife or children, he shall give a bond to the Conference for   10 the sum he is to allow.

[*Q*. 21st. Who have ceased from being members of the Conference?[675]

A. Francis Asbury, Thomas Barber, Thomas Brisco, Samuel Mitchell, John Murlin, Thomas Rankin, and Richard   15 Whatcoat.

[*Q*. 22d. Who have been elected in their places?

[*A*. John Pritchard, James Watson, Samuel Hodgson, Andrew Inglis, George Gibbon, Thomas Davis, and John Kerr.

[We the Underwritten, being appointed by the Will of the   20 late Revd. John Wesley as a Committee to preach in, and appoint Preachers for the New Chapel in the City Road, London, and also the Methodist Chapel in King's Street in Bath, do engage that we will use all the rights and privileges given us by Mr. Wesley in the present instance in   25 entire subservience to the Conference.

> Willm. Thompson
> Thomas Coke
> Jas. Creighton
> Alexr. Mather   30
> Henry Moore
> Jno. Valton
> Jos. Bradford

[675] On p. 87 of CJ appear the following entries in the hand of Thomas Coke—official legal business that was apparently deferred at the opening session because of the stresses of meeting without JW's presence. They replace the first draft of the answer to *Q*. 21, which was struck through. This read: 'John Murlin, Thomas Rankin, Joseph Cownley, George Shadford, and John Valton, our very respectable brethren; and Thomas Barber and Thomas Mitchell for misdemeanours.' The discrepancies will be noted: to the second list the two chief American leaders were added, Asbury and Whatcoat; Cownley, Shadford, and Valton, each of whom had suffered intermittent health failures, were retained; Thomas Brisco was added as retired; and Thomas Mitchell was corrected to Samuel.

Andw. Blair
Wm. Myles
James Rogers
Peard Dickinson][676]

5   *Q.* 25. Is it necessary to enter into any engagements in respect to our future plan of economy?

A. We engage to follow strictly the plan which Mr. Wesley left us at his death.[677]

Q. 26. Are any directions necessary concerning the station-
10   ing of the preachers?

A. No preacher shall be stationed for any circuit above two years successively, unless God has been pleased to use him as the instrument of a remarkable revival.

Q. 27. Are any directions necessary concerning the dis-
15   bursement[678] of the yearly collection?

[676] These are actual signatures of the eleven men on CJ, p. 88. These houses were clearly not settled on the 'Conference Plan', and such chapels could still trouble the Conference and oppose its will. This was notably the case with the New Room in Bristol, which virtually went into schism in 1794 in opposition to Methodist sacraments. See A. W. Harrison, *The Separation of Methodism from the Church of England* (London, 1945), 50–53; D. Hempton, *Methodism and Politics in British Society, 1750–1850* (London, 1984), 62–65.

[677] CJ, 'left at his death'. Though the term 'Methodist Plan' seems often to have been used to refer to the Model Deed as securing JW's and the Conference's stationing of preachers as against local trustees (see, e.g., the declaration at the end of the 1789 *Minutes*), the use of the term here refers to disputes over attitudes to services in Church hours, Methodist ordinations and sacraments, and in general separation from the Church of England. The 'Church Methodists' constantly spoke as if JW's 'Plan' was to avoid all these moves; and their more extreme opponents in effect wished for Methodism to move into open separation and, in the case of men like Kilham, to assert also a more 'democratic' form of government in Methodism. JW in fact had never set his face against moves that might lead to separation, though he frequently denied he had separated and urged adherence to the Church even when he 'varied' from its rules. He certainly allowed services in church hours in some cases as well as ordaining for America and Scotland (where he claimed Anglican jurisdiction did not apply). His three ordinations for England suggested to some a contingency plan for that country as well. John Pawson in any case was undoubtedly right to state that 'Mr. Wesley's Plan' was not that alleged by the Church Methodists but to follow Providence by piecemeal concessions to pressure as need arose (*Letters*, 2:158, 162), and Pawson broadly followed this line, though allowing more to the local will of the people than JW might have countenanced. JW's concern (and Pawson's) was primarily to further the work and maintain the unity of Methodism.

[678] CJ, 'disbursements'.

A. It shall be disbursed in the following manner, as far as
the money will extend, viz.:

(1st) The demands of the connexion in Scotland, as far as
they are approved by the Conference, shall be disbursed.

(2nd) The demands of Ireland.[679]   5

(3rd) Those of Wales.

(4th) Those of France.

(5th) Those of the poor circuits in England.

Lastly. The demands of all the remaining circuits,
according to the judgment of the Conference.   10

Q. 28. A great expense is incurred by letters to the preachers.[680] What directions are necessary on this subject?

A. (1) Let the preachers return all circular letters to the
persons respectively from whom they are sent.

(2) Let the postage of all letters sent to the Conference   15
on public business, be paid by the stewards of the societies from which they are sent. But the postage of the
private letters sent to the preachers during the sitting of
the Conference, shall be paid by the Conference.

Q. 29. When and where shall the next Conference be held?   20

A. In London, on the last Tuesday in July 1792.

A list of the preachers that were received on trial at this
Conference, but were not immediately wanted:

(1) Richard Pattison,[681] of the Oxford Circuit.

(2) John Ashall, of the Manchester Circuit.   25

(3) Francis Thorsbey, of the Stockport Circuit.

(4) John Kingston, of the London Circuit.

(5) George Deverell, of the Shepton Mallet Circuit.

(6) Roger Crane, of the Blackburn Circuit.

(7) Stephen Wilson, of the Sunderland Circuit.   30

(8) Paul Wilson, of the Manchester Circuit.

(9) James Buckley, of the Manchester Circuit.

(10) Robert Harper, of the Keighley Circuit.

(11) John Foster, of The Dales Circuit.

(12) Alexander Cummins, of the Liverpool Circuit.   35

(13) John Ward, of the Sheffield Circuit.

---

[679] CJ reverses the order of (1st) and (2nd).

[680] Although a few letters were prepaid, the usual system throughout JW's lifetime was for the recipient to bear the cost. See *Letters*, 25:21–22 in this edn.

[681] Orig., 'Patterson'.

(14) Henry Anderson, of the Pocklington Circuit.[682]

Q. 30. Are any directions necessary concerning the management of the Preachers' Fund?

A. No money that has been or shall be subscribed
5   to that fund shall be applied on any account to the
discharge of contingencies,[683] or to any other purposes
whatsoever, except those which the rules of the fund
direct.

Q. 31. Are any directions necessary concerning the
10   disbursement of the yearly collection?

A. Let the District Committees settle the temporal
accounts of their respective districts annually, either on
the Saturday before the Conference or at such time as is
most convenient.

15   *Q*. 32. What directions are necessary concerning the forming of committees to draw up plans for stationing of the
preachers in Great Britain and Ireland?

A. (1) The Committee of every District in England and
Scotland shall elect one of their body to form a commit-
20   tee to draw up a plan for the stationing of the preachers
in Great Britain; which committee shall meet at the
place where the Conference is held, three days in the
week preceding the Conference, in order to draw up the
above-mentioned plan.[684]

25   (2) The Committee of every District in Ireland shall
send one of their body to meet the delegate two days
before the Irish Conference for the same purpose.

Q. 33. Have we not made too great advances towards conformity to the world?

30   *A*. We fear we have.

Q. 34. How shall we prevent this?

---

[682] Coke adds in CJ: 'Andrew Jeffreys of the Limerick Circuit'.

[683] CJ, 'of the contingencies'.

[684] This is the origin of the Stationing Committee, still extant. Its creation was necessary because JW himself had in effect fulfilled its functions, though he quite often had to accede to local and individual pressures and could not always enforce his will (see introduction, p. 69).

A. (1) Those school-masters and school-mistresses who
receive dancing masters into their schools, and those
parents who employ dancing masters for their children,
shall be no longer members of our society.[685]

(2) Let every Assistant read the thoughts on dress once a   5
year in all his societies.[686]

Q. 35. What directions are necessary concerning Kingswood School?

[*A*]. (1) The following persons shall be appointed as a committee to superintend the *School* for the ensuing year,   10
viz.: Henry Moore, Thomas McGeary, John Valton,
and Thomas Roberts and John Ewer of Bristol.[687]

(2) The preachers' children that cannot be admitted
into the School, and are allowed £12 per ann. for their
education, shall not receive the usual salary of £4   15
either from the circuit or from the yearly collection.

(3) The assistants of the School, and the servants of the
house, shall be under the control of the master, and
accountable to him for their conduct.

Q. 36. What preachers were received on trial in Ireland?   20

A. Thomas Black, William Armstrong, John MᶜFarland,
James Bell, John Fury, Blakely Dowling, and Joseph
Hennin.

N. B. Andrew Jefferys is in reserve.

---

[685] Hostility to dancing became an evangelical shibboleth, though some into the
early 19th century were less censorious than others. JW wrote to Miss Bishop about
dancing at her school. She had excluded it and so had trouble with some parents.
JW said God had decided the question, showing his approval 'by sending those
children to you again. If dancing be not evil in itself, yet it leads young women to
numberless evils'. *Letters* (Telford), 7:227–28. If asked whether one can be saved
when one plays cards or dances, 'I answer, "Possibly you may be saved though you
dance and play at cards. But I could not". . . . So much and no more I advise our
preachers to speak.' Ibid., 8:12. Adam Clarke put the Methodist case that if harmless in itself, it led to mixed company and conformity to the world. *AM* (1792):
15:264–72.

[686] 'Thoughts upon Dress' in *Works*, vol. 11 (replying to strictures on his remarks
in *AM* 11 [1788] regarding dressing according to one's social status). He is very
censorious on dress in some of his late sermons; see e.g., Sermons 87 and 88, 3:227,
247 in this edn.

[687] Here again a new committee was necessary to take over the school's overall
supervision that JW had undertaken personally. It may be seen as the origin of the
later Methodist Education Committee.

Q. 37. Whom does the Conference appoint as their delegate for the West Indies, etc.?

A. Thomas Coke.

Q. 38. Who are the committee for examining accounts, letters, missionaries that are to be sent to the Islands?

A. The President, Alexander Mather, John Pawson, Thomas Taylor, Henry Moore, Samuel Bradburn, James Rogers, Richard Rodda, and Joseph Bradford.

WILLIAM THOMPSON, President

THOMAS COKE, Secretary

(The CJ does not contain *QQ* 32–36, but continues, all in the hand of Coke, on pp. 90–91, with its own signed additions after *Q*. 31, i.e., *Q*. 29 of CJ:)

[1. George Whitfield is to pay all the legacies, etc., due on Mr. Wesley's will to the executors, in such way as the Conference shall direct, if the executors consent to sell the stock for such a sum of money as shall be sufficient to enable them to discharge every obligation lying on them on account of Mr. Wesley's will.

[2. If the executors will not consent to sell the stock within the time prescribed by the Conference, the preachers, on information sent them by Mr. George Whitfield, shall send all the stock of books remaining in their hands to such place as the executors shall appoint, together with all the money for books remaining in their hands.

[3. The circuits shall be regularly supplied with the Magazines and hymn-books, as all events as far as possible.

[4. The trustees shall convey all their right to Mr. Wesley's stock by any legal instrument the Conference shall approve of.

[5. The printing-presses, types, etc. are to be conveyed to the Conference by Thomas Rankin and George Whitfield.

[*Question* 30th. What regulations is it necessary to make in respect to the President of the Conference?

[*A*. 1. Everything to be debated by the Conference is to be introduced by the President.

[2. The President is to preserve order, and restore it whenever necessary; and for that purpose shall have full support from the Conference if any continue refractory.

[3. The President is to bring the debates of the Conference to a conclusion, or shall appeal to the Conference for that purpose whenever he sees it proper.

[4. The same person shall not be chosen President for two years successively.   5

[Q. 31st. Who is chosen Delegate for the West Indies?

[A. Thomas Coke.

[Q. 32nd. Who are the Committee for examining the accounts, letters, missionaries to be sent out to the West Indies, etc.?   10

[A. The President, Alexander Mather, Henry Moore, John Pawson, Thomas Taylor, Samuel Bradburn, James Rogers, Richard Rodda, and Joseph Bradford.

[The Trustees of the Preachers' Fund are to be allowed a salary of one guinea each annually.   15

[The Committee in London, who are to determine what shall be printed in the Magazines, and who are in all other respects to regulate the books for the present year, are: Thomas Coke, John Whitehead, James Creighton, Peard Dickinson, and Richard Rodda.   20

[The persons who are desired by the Conference to assist the Committee in London in furnishing materials for the Magazines are the President, Alexander Mather, John Pawson, Joseph Benson, Samuel Bradburn, Joseph Cownley, Thomas Taylor, Henry Moore, Adam Clarke,   25
Andrew Blair, John Crook, Matthias Joyce, George Story, James Wood, Joseph Cole, Joseph Taylor, Duncan McAllum, and Benjamin Rhodes.

[N.B. The Committee in London may advance the price of drawing or engraving the prints if they judge it necessary. 30

[The Committee in London are also appointed to judge for the ensuing year concerning the propriety or impropriety of printing any books or pamphlets for the use of the Bookroom.

[The Book Steward in Dublin shall be allowed £20 annually for his trouble and for the expences he incurs in man- 35
aging the books for the Kingdom of Ireland, besides the usual commission money for books sold in Dublin.

[The London Committee shall audit the accounts of the Bookroom once a month.

Willm. Thompson   40
Thomas Coke

PART IV

The *Minutes* Codified:
The Doctrinal and
Disciplinary *Minutes*

INTRODUCTION

In 1749, Methodism was coming of age, and Wesley (along with his colleagues, clerical and lay) had begun to ponder its basic theology, its ecclesiastical polity, and its administrative policy.[1] During the years 1744–48, the basic doctrines and polity of the Methodist movement had been discussed in the annual Conferences between John Wesley and his invited colleagues. Doctrinal issues had occupied their attention for part of eight days during the Conferences of 1744–47, and matters of organization and practice had been on the agenda of the Conference on thirteen days from 1744–48. Manuscript Minutes of their deliberations were preserved and copied (in slightly differing forms) by several of his preachers, as we have already seen.[2]

By 1749, it seemed to Wesley that something like a consensus was beginning to emerge about most problems, and that the time had come to prepare publications consolidating the results. Thus it would become clear what Methodism stood for and how it worked. In the middle of this period, the preachers had asked him to produce a collection of sermons that would provide doctrinal assistance, which he began publishing with the first volume of *Sermons on Several Occasions* in 1746. At the 1748 Conference, he had made the suggestion, 'Would it not be of use if all the societies were more firmly and closely united together?'[3] This idea surely prompted Wesley to prepare a printed prospectus for such a firm union, probably with very little assistance. No copy in his handwriting of any of the original manuscript Minutes, or the 1749 attempt to summarize them, has survived. These edited selections from the preceding manuscript Minutes, however, seem to have been a deliberate, though rudimentary, formulation of a doctrinal outline and an ecclesiastical framework for Methodism.

Most likely, Wesley had in mind the presentation of such a printed summary to his preachers meeting in Conference in 1749, and perhaps also to the smaller group meeting earlier to discuss a closer

---

[1] Baker, *Wesley and the Church*, 106–9.
[2] 'The Textual Problems of the Early Manuscript Minutes', pp. 116–17 above.
[3] Minutes (1748), §61.

union with George Whitefield and Howell Harris. Both gatherings took place in August 1749. At some point, Wesley decided to produce two separate pamphlets, the first dealing with doctrinal issues, the second with discipline (organization and practices). Rough drafts may well have been prepared in England, but there can be little doubt that the final touches to them were made while Wesley was in Ireland from April to July 1749.

Wesley may have given the two manuscripts to Samuel Powell, the Dublin printer, in April and collected the printed copies in July, but in those days it would have proved quite possible to finish off the whole task during his last two weeks in Dublin, July 5 to July 20. The titles and imprints of both pamphlets were exactly the same: *Minutes of some late Conversations between the Revd. M. Wesleys and others* (Dublin: Printed by S. Powell in Crane-lane, 1749). As was the usual practice, the printer seems to have discarded the manuscripts, once the items were printed.

In the agenda that Wesley had prepared for his 1744 Conference, he had listed their primary concerns as *doctrine, discipline*, and *practice*. Whether the 1749 *Minutes* were prepared and delivered to the printer in that order must be largely conjectured. But there can be no question that such was their logical order in Wesley's mind, and therefore we order them thus. Traditionally these pamphlets have been distinguished as the Doctrinal *Minutes* and the Disciplinary *Minutes*, though neither description appears in the title.

As selections of major policy minutes from previous Conferences, they were, in fact, the first set of 'Large' *Minutes*. The Doctrinal *Minutes* contain excerpts from discussions of theological matters during eight of the sessions of the Conferences between 1744 and 1747, and the Disciplinary *Minutes* include selections concerning polity and procedures decided during thirteen of the sessions between 1744 and 1748. This division of issues and shifting of attention toward matters of polity and discipline was symptomatic of what was to come. (1) The doctrinal issues faded from the later Conference agendas and found their way into other venues and publications after 1749, such as sermons, Bible commentaries, and treatises. Within a few years, the doctrinal standards of the movement, providing the doctrinal boundaries for Wesley's lay preachers, were defined by the Model Deed included in the 1763 'Large' *Minutes* in terms of Wesley's *Sermons and Explanatory Notes upon the New*

Testament.[4] (2) The disciplinary concerns of organization and practice, however, became the continuing focus of the Conference agendas; these matters were revised and expanded in the annual and selected ('Large') *Minutes* of later years.

Wesley reproduced both the Doctrinal and Disciplinary *Minutes* in his collected *Works*, vol. 15 (Bristol: Pine, 1772). There was hardly any change in the doctrinal reprint of the 1749 edition, except for a few minor errors, later corrected in his printed and manuscript errata. One feature, characteristic of that edition of his *Works*, was the addition of a number of asterisks to paragraphs that he considered especially instructive or uplifting. The disciplinary *Minutes*, however, did not follow the 1749 edition, by then long outdated. Instead, it presented a revision of the 1770 edition and took its own place as the fourth of the revised editions that succeeded the 1749 Disciplinary *Minutes* and have carried the informal moniker 'great' or 'Large' *Minutes* because of their increased importance (if not size), though those terms never appeared in their title.[5]

It would have been possible to reconstruct the 1749 Doctrinal and Disciplinary *Minutes* by means of a chart of cross-references back to the corresponding sections of the manuscript Minutes of 1744 to 1748. It seems far preferable, however, to present in their entirety these two printed units of collected *Minutes* published by Wesley. Since they are arranged under the dates of the various Conference sessions, their relationship to the manuscript originals upon which they were based has been indicated by inserting in the left margins the same section numbers that were used in the corresponding manuscript Minutes for that date. Ellipses and brief footnotes also indicate changes made by Wesley in these later selections. In general, the footnotes relating to the substance of the original text are not duplicated, and the main burden of footnoting here has been to depict the textual alterations in 1749, such as the omission of characters and words from the manuscript documents of 1744–48.

---

[4] Nevertheless, when Thomas Dixon joined the Conference 'on trial' in 1769 and began keeping handwritten copies of the annual minutes in a little leather-bound paperbook, he entered the 1749 Doctrinal *Minutes* as the opening item in his book, followed then by the 1763 'Large' *Minutes* (the most recent version of the Disciplinary *Minutes*) before starting to incorporate the annual *Minutes*, beginning with.those of 1767. Wesley did essentially the same thing in his *Works* (vol. 15) in the 1772: put together the 1749 Doctrinal *Minutes* and a slightly revised version of the most recent Disciplinary *Minutes*, the 1770 'Large' *Minutes.*

[5] Wesley himself did use these terms, however. See below, p. 836.

1. The Doctrinal *Minutes*, 1749

[§1]   **Conversation the First**

Monday, 25th of June, 1744.

The following persons being at the Foundery, John Wesley,
5   Charles Wesley, John Hodges, rector of Wenvo, Henry
Piers, vicar of Bexley, Samuel Taylor, vicar of Quinton,
and John Meriton. After some time spent in prayer, the
design of our meeting was proposed, namely to consider:
10   (1) What to teach,
(2) How to teach, and
(3) What to do, how to regulate our doctrine, discipline,
and practice.[6]

[§6]   We began with considering the doctrine of justification: the
15   questions relating to [which], with the substance of the
answers given thereto, were as follows:[7]

[§7]   *Q.* 1. What is [it] to be justified?
A. To be pardoned, and received into God's favour, into
such a state that if we continue therein, we shall be
20   finally saved.

[§8]   *Q.* 2. Is faith the [only] condition of justification?
A. Yes; for everyone, who believeth not is condemned; and
everyone who believes is justified:

[§9]   *Q.* 3. But must not repentance and works meet for repen-
25   tance go before this faith?
A. Without doubt—if by repentance you mean conviction
of sin; and by works meet for repentance, obeying God
as far as we can, forgiving our brother, leaving off from
evil, doing good, and using his ordinances according to
30   the power we have received.

[§10]   *Q.* 4. What is faith?

---

[6] Omitted are §§2–5 of the original, dealing with the composition and organization of the Conference.

[7] 1744: 'About 7 o'clock, we began to consider the doctrine of justification, the
questions relating to which were as follows, with the substance of the answers given
thereto.'

A. Faith in general is, a divine supernatural *elenchos* of things not seen; i.e., of past, future, or spiritual things: it is a spiritual sight of God and the things of God. [. . .]

First a sinner is convinced by the Holy Ghost, 'Christ loved me and gave himself for me,'—this is that faith by which he is justified or pardoned the moment he receives it. Immediately the same spirit bears witness, 'Thou art pardoned, thou hast redemption in his blood'—and this is saving faith, whereby the love of God is shed abroad in his heart.   10

[§11] *Q.* 5. Have all [true] Christians this faith? May not a man be justified and not know it?

A. That all true Christians have such a faith as implies an assurance of God's love, appears from Rom. 8:15, Eph. 4:32, 2 Cor. 13:5, Heb. 8:10, 1 John 4:10, 5:19. And that no man can be justified and not know it appears farther from the [very] nature of the thing. For faith after repentance is ease after pain, rest after toil, light after darkness. It appears also from the immediate, as well as distant fruits thereof.   20

[§12] *Q.* 6. But may not a man go to heaven without it?

A. It does not appear from Holy Writ that a man who hears the gospel can (Mark 16:16), whatever a heathen may do (Rom. 2:14).

[§13] *Q.* 7. What are the immediate fruits of justifying faith?   25

A. Peace, joy, love, power over all outward sin, and power to keep down [all] inward sin.

[§14] *Q.* 8. Does anyone believe who has not the witness in himself, or any longer than he sees, loves, obeys God?

A. We apprehend not; *seeing* God being the very essence of   30 faith; love and obedience the inseparable properties of it.

[§15] *Q.* 9. What sins are consistent with justifying faith?

A. No *wilful* sin. If a believer *wilfully* sins, he casts away his faith.[8] Neither is it possible he should have *justifying faith*   35 again without previously *repenting*.

[§16] *Q.* 10. *Must* every believer come into a state of doubt or fear or darkness? Will he do so, unless by ignorance or unfaithfulness? Does God otherwise withdraw himself?

---

[8] 1744: 'he therefore *forfeits his pardon*'.

A. It is certain a believer *need* never again come into condemnation. It seems he need not come into a state of
doubt or fear or darkness; and that (ordinarily at least) he
will not, unless by ignorance or unfaithfulness. Yet it is
true that the first joy does seldom last long; that it is
commonly followed by doubts and fears; and that God
frequently permits [very] great heaviness before any large
manifestation of himself.

[§17]   Q. 11. Are works necessary to the continuance of faith?
A. Without doubt; for a man may forfeit the free gift of
God, either by sins of omission or commission.

[§18]   Q. 12. Can faith be lost, but for want of works?
A. It cannot but through disobedience.

[§19]   Q. 13. How is faith made 'perfect by works'?
A. The more we exert our faith, the more it is increased. To
him that hath, shall be given.[9]

[§20]   Q. 14. St. Paul says, Abraham was not 'justified by works',
St. James, he was 'justified by works'. Do they not contradict each other?
A. No: (1) Because they do not speak of the same justification. St. Paul speaks of that justification which was when
Abraham was seventy-five years old, above twenty
before Isaac was born; St. James of that justification
which was when he offered up Isaac on the altar.
(2) Because they do not speak of the same works, St.
Paul speaking of works that precede faith, St. James of
works that spring from it.

[§21]   Q. 15. In what sense is Adam's sin imputed to all mankind?
A. In Adam all die, i.e., (1) Our bodies then became mortal.
(2) Our souls died, i.e., were disunited from God; and
hence, (3) We are all born with a sinful, devilish nature; by
reason whereof, (4) We are [all] children of wrath, liable to
death eternal (Rom. 5:18; Eph. 2:3).

[§22]   Q. 16. In what sense is the righteousness of Christ imputed
to all mankind, or to believers?
A. We do not find it expressly affirmed in Scripture that
God imputes the righteousness of Christ to any; although
we do find that faith is imputed to us for righteousness.

---

[9] 1744: 'to him that *hath*, more and more is given'.

That text, 'As by one man's disobedience all men were made sinners, so by the obedience of one, all were made righteous,' we conceive means: by the merits of Christ, all men are cleared from the guilt of Adam's actual sin.

We conceive farther, that through the obedience and death of Christ, (1) The bodies of all men become immortal after the resurrection; (2) Their souls receive[10] a capacity of spiritual life; and, (3) an actual spark or seed thereof. (4) All believers become children of grace, [5] Are reconciled[11] to God, and [6][12] made partakers of the divine nature.

[§23] *Q.* 17. Have we not then unawares leaned too much towards Calvinism?

A. We are afraid we have.[13]

[§24] *Q.* 18. Have we not also leaned towards antinomianism?

A. We are afraid we have.

[§25] *Q.* 19. What is antinomianism?

A. The doctrine which makes void the law through faith.

[§26] *Q.* 20. What are the main pillars thereof?[14]

A. (1) That Christ abolished the moral law.

(2) That therefore Christians are not obliged to observe it.

(3) That one branch of Christian liberty, is liberty from obeying the commandments of God.

(4) That it is bondage to do a thing because it is commanded, or forbear it because it is forbidden.

(5) That a believer is not *obliged* to use the ordinances of God, or to do good works.

(6) That a preacher ought not to exhort to good works; not unbelievers, because it is hurtful; not believers because it is needless.

[§27] *Q.* 21. What was the occasion of St. Paul's writing his Epistle to the Galatians?

---

[10] 1744: 'recover'.

[11] 1744: 'reunited'.

[12] 1744: '(5)'.

[13] 1744: 'It seems that we have.'

[14] 1744: 'thereof'; 1749, 1772 (*Works*), in error: 'hereof'.

A. The coming of certain men amongst the Galatians, who taught, 'Except ye be circumcised and keep the law of Moses, ye cannot be saved.'

[§28]   *Q.* 22. What is his main design therein?

A. To prove, (1) That no man can be justified or saved by the works of the law, either moral or ritual. (2) That every believer is justified by faith in Christ, without the works of the law.

[§29]   *Q.* 23. What does he mean by 'the works of the law' (Gal. 2:16, etc.)?

A. All works which do not spring from faith in Christ.

[§30]   *Q.* 24. What by being 'under the law' (Gal. 3:23)?

A. Under the Mosaic dispensation.

[§31]   *Q.* 25. What law has Christ abolished?

A. The ritual law of Moses.

[§32]   *Q.* 26. What is meant by *liberty* (Gal. 5:l)?

A. Liberty, (1), from the law;[15] (2), from sin.

[§33]   ***On Tuesday morning, June 26, [1744] was considered,***
   The doctrine of sanctification, with regard to which the questions asked and the substance of the answers given were as follows:

[§34]   *Q.* 1. What is it to be sanctified?

A. To be renewed in the image of God in righteousness and true holiness.[16]

[§35]   *Q.* 2. Is faith the condition or the instrument of sanctification?[17]

A. It is both the condition and instrument of it. When we begin to believe, then sanctification[18] begins. And as faith increases, holiness increases, till we are created anew.[19]

[§39]   *Q.* 3. What is implied in being a *perfect Christian?*[20]

---

[15] 1744, 1770: 'that law'.

[16] Indicated as a quotation from Eph. 4:24 in the extract from these Doctrinal *Minutes* in *A Plain Account of Christian Perfection*, §17.

[17] 1744 adds: 'or present salvation'.

[18] 1744: 'salvation'.

[19] 1744 adds: '*Q.* 36. Is not every believer a new creature?', '*Q.* 37 "But has every believer a new heart?"' ', and '*Q.* 38 Is not every believer born of God, a temple of the Holy Ghost?'.

[20] 1744: 'in being made perfect in love'.

A. The loving the Lord our God with all our heart,[21] and
with all our mind, and soul and strength (Deut. 6:5, 30:6;
Ezek. 36:25–29).[22]

[§41] *Q.* 4. [8] Does this imply that all inward sin is taken away?
A. Without doubt. Or how could he[23] be said to be saved   5
'from all his uncleannesses?' (ver. 29).

[§42] *Q.* 5. [9] Can we know one who is thus saved? What is a
reasonable proof of it?
A. We cannot, without the miraculous discernment of spirits, be infallibly certain of those who are thus saved. But   10
we apprehend, these would be the best proofs which the
nature of the thing admits:[24] (1) If we had sufficient evidence of their unblameable behaviour, at least from the
time of their justification.[25] (2) If they gave a distinct
account of the time and manner wherein they were saved   15
from sin, and of the circumstances thereof, with such
sound speech as could not be reproved. And (3) If upon a
strict inquiry[26] from time to time, for two or three years
following, it appeared that all their tempers and words
and actions were holy and unreprovable.   20

[§43] *Q.* 6. [10] How should we treat those who think they have
attained this?
A. Exhort them to forget the things that are behind, and to
watch and pray always, that God may search the ground
of their hearts.   25

[§44]   *Wednesday, June 27 [1744].*
We began to consider points of discipline, with regard to
which the questions asked and the substance of the
answers given were as follows:

[§45] *Q.* 1. What is the Church of England?   30

---

[21] 1749: 'hearts'.

[22] 1744: '*Q.* 7. Does it imply that he who is thus made perfect *cannot* commit sin?
'*A.* St. John affirms it expressly: "He cannot commit sin, because he is born of
God" (1 John 3:10 [i.e., 3:9]). And, indeed, how should he, seeing there is now
"none occasion of stumbling in him", chap. 2:10?'

[23] 1772 (*Works*): 'we'.

[24] 1744 adds 'unless they should be called to resist unto blood'.

[25] 1772 (*Works*): 'their unblameable behavior, preceding'.

[26] 1772 (*Works*) inserts: 'afterwards', and omits 'for . . . following'.

A. According to the nineteenth[27] Article, the visible church of England is the congregation of English *believers* in which the *pure word* of God preached, and the sacraments duly administered.

5   (But the word 'Church' is sometimes taken in a looser sense for 'a congregation professing to believe'. So it is taken in the twenty-sixth Article, and in the 1st, 2nd, and 3rd chapters of the Revelation.)

[§46] *Q*. 2. What[28] is a member of the Church of England?

10   *A*. A believer, hearing the *pure word* of God preached, and partaking of the sacraments duly administered, in that Church.

[§47] *Q*. 3. What is it to be zealous for the Church?

    A. To be earnestly desirous of its welfare and increase: of its

15   welfare, by the confirmation of its present members in faith, hearing, and communicating; and of its increase, by the addition of new members.

[§48] *Q*. 4. How are we to defend the doctrine[s] of the Church?

    A. Both by our preaching and living. [. . .][29]

20 [§51] *Q*. 5. How should we behave at a false, or railing sermon?

    A. If it only contain personal reflections, we may quietly suffer it. If it blaspheme the work and Spirit of God, it may be better to go out of the church. In either case, if opportunity serve, it would be well to speak or write to the Minister.

25 [§52] *Q*. 6. [8] How far is it our duty to obey the bishops?

    A. In all things indifferent. And on this ground of obeying them, we should observe the canons, so far as we can with a safe conscience.

[§53] *Q*. 7. Do we separate from the Church?

30   *A*. We conceive not: we hold communion therewith, for conscience' sake, by constantly attending both the Word preached and the Sacraments administered therein.

[§54] *Q*. 8. What then do they mean who say, 'You separate from the Church'?

---

[27] 1749, 1772 (in error): 'twentieth'.

[28] 1772 (*Works*): 'Who'.

[29] 1744 adds:

    Q. [49]. 'Do the 8th, 13th, 15th, 16th, 17th, 21st, 23rd, and 27th Articles agree with Scripture?'

    Q. [50] 'How shall we bear the most effectual testimony against that part of the clergy who either preach or live contrary to the doctrine of the Church of England?'

A. We cannot certainly tell. Perhaps they have no determinate meaning; unless by the Church they mean *themselves*, i.e., that part of the clergy who accuse us of preaching false doctrine. And it is sure we do herein separate from them, by maintaining that which they deny. 5

[§55]   *Q.* 9. But do you not weaken the Church?

A. Do not they who ask this, by the 'Church' mean *themselves*? We do not purposely weaken any man's hands, but accidentally we may, thus far: they who come to know the truth by us will esteem such as deny it less than they did before. 10

But the Church, in the proper sense, the congregation of English believers, we do not weaken at all.

[§56]   *Q.* 10. Do you not entail a schism on the Church? I.e., Is it not probable that your hearers after your death will be scattered into all sects and parties? Or that they will form 15 themselves into a distinct sect?

A. (1) We are persuaded, the body of our hearers will even after our death remain in the Church, unless they be thrust out.

(2) We believe notwithstanding either that they will be 20 thrust out, or that they will leaven the whole Church.

(3) We do, and will do, all we can, to prevent those consequences which are supposed likely to happen after our death.

(4) But we cannot with a good conscience neglect the 25 present opportunity of saving souls while we live, for fear of consequences which may possibly or probably happen, after we are dead.

Conversation the Second

Bristol, Thursday, August 1, 1745.   30

The following persons being met together at the New Room,[30] John Wesley, Charles Wesley, John Hodges, Thomas Richards, Samuel Larwood, Thomas Meyrick,

---

[30] 1772 (*Works*) adds: 'in Bristol'.

James Wheatley,[31] Richard Moss, John Slocomb, Herbert Jenkins, and Marmaduke Gwynne. [. . .][32]

[§9]   [About seven] it was proposed to review the Minutes of the last Conference with regard to justification. And it was asked:

5   *Q.* 1. How comes what is written on this subject to be so intricate and obscure? Is this obscurity from the nature of the thing itself? Or from the fault or weakness of those who have generally treated of it?

A. We apprehend this obscurity does not arise from the

10   nature of the subject, but perhaps partly from hence, that the devil peculiarly labours to perplex a subject of the greatest importance, and partly from the extreme warmth of most writers who have treated of it.

[§11]   *Q.* 2. We affirm faith in Christ is the sole condition of justi-

15   fication. But does not repentance go before that faith? Yea, and (supposing there be opportunity for them) fruits or works meet for repentance?

A. Without doubt they do.

[§12]   *Q.* 3. How then can we deny them to be *conditions* of

20   justification? Is not this a mere strife of words? But is it worthwhile to continue a dispute on the term 'condition'?

A. It seems not, though it has been grievously abused. But so let the use remain.

[§13]   *Q.* 4. Shall we read over together Mr. Baxter's *Aphorisms*

25   concerning justification?

A. By all means; which were accordingly read. And it was desired that each person present would in the afternoon consult the Scriptures cited therein, and bring what objections might occur the next morning.

30 [§14]   *Friday, August 2, [1745].*

The question was proposed:

Q. 1. Is an assurance[33] of God's pardoning love[34] absolutely necessary to our being in his favour? Or may there possi-

bly[35] be some exempt cases?

---

[31] 1772 omits Wheatley, who was expelled in 1751.

[32] 1749 omits §§2–8, dealing with the debating rules of the Conference.

[33] 1772 (*Works*): 'a sense'.

[34] 1745: 'God's love'.

[35] 1772 (*Works*) omits: 'possibly'.

   A. We dare not positively[36] say, there are not.

[§15] *Q.* 2. Is such an assurance absolutely necessary[37] to inward
   and outward holiness?

   A. To inward, we apprehend it is; to outward holiness, we
   incline to think it is not.[38]   5

[§16] *Q.* 3. Is it indispensably necessary to final salvation?
   Suppose in a Papist? Or a Quaker? Or, in general, among
   those who never heard it preached?

   A. Love hopeth all things. We know not how far any of
   these may fall under the case of invincible ignorance. 10

[§17] *Q.* 4. But what can we say of one of our own Society who
   dies without it, as J[ohn] W[arr] at London?

   A. It may possibly be[39] an exempt case (if the fact was really
   so). But we determine nothing. We leave his soul in the
   hands of him that made it.   15

[§18] *Q.* 5. Does a man believe any longer than he sees a reconciled God?[40]

   A. We conceive not. But we allow there may be infinite
   degrees in seeing God; even as many as there are between
   him who sees the sun when it shines on his eyelids closed, 20
   and him who stands with his eyes wide open in the full
   blaze of his beams.

[§19] *Q.* 6. Does a man believe any longer than he loves God?

   A. In no wise. For neither circumcision [n]or uncircumcision avails, without faith working by love.   25

[§20] *Q.* 7. Have we duly considered the case of Cornelius? Was
   not he in the favour of God, 'when his prayers and alms
   came up for a memorial before God'? i.e., before he
   believed in Christ?

   A. It does seem that he was, in some degree.[41] But we speak 30
   not of those who have not heard the gospel.

[§21] *Q.* 8. But were those works of his *splendid sins*?

   A. No; nor were they 'done without the grace of'
   Christ.

---

[36] 1772 (*Works*): 'not say'.
[37] 1772 (*Works*): 'Is it necessary'.
[38] 1772 (*Works*): 'We incline to think, it is.'
[39] 1772 (*Works*): 'It may be'.
[40] 1745: 'sees God?'
[41] 1745: 'that he was'.

[§22]   *[42]*Q*. 9. How then can we maintain that all works done
before we have a sense of the pardoning love of God, are
sin? And, as such, an abomination to him?

A. The works of him who has heard the gospel, and does
5   not believe, are not done as God hath 'willed and commanded them to be done'. [Therefore they are sinful.]
And yet we know not how to say that they are an abomination to the Lord in him who feareth God, and from that
principle, does the best he can.

10 [§23]   *Q*. 10. Seeing there is so much difficulty in this subject, can
we deal too tenderly with them that oppose us?

A. We cannot, unless we were to give up any part of the
truth of God.

[§24]   *Q*. 11. Is a believer *constrained* to obey God?
15   *A*. At first he often is.[43] The love of Christ constraineth
him. After this, he *may* obey, or he may not; no constraint[44] being laid upon him.

[§25]   *Q*. 12. Can faith be lost but through disobedience?

A. It cannot. A believer first inwardly disobeys, inclines to
20   sin with his heart. Then his intercourse with God is cut
off,[45] i.e., his faith is lost. And after this he may fall into
outward sin, being now weak and like another man.

[§26]   *Q*. 13. How can such an one recover faith?

A. By repenting and doing the first works (Rev. 2:5).

25 [§27]   *Q*. 14. Whence is it that so great a majority of those who
believe fall more or less into doubt or fear?

A. Chiefly from their own ignorance or unfaithfulness;
often from their not watching unto prayer; perhaps sometimes from some defect or want of the power of God in
30   the preaching they hear.

[§28]   *Q*. 15. Is there not a defect in us? Do we preach as we did at
first? Have we not changed our doctrines?

A. (1) At first we preached almost wholly to unbelievers. To
those therefore we spake almost continually of

---

[42] 1772 (*Works*) adds here and elsewhere an asterisk denoting the special importance of a section to JW. Cf. also 45:25, 36, 49, and 46:19, 25, 27, 30, and 35 below.

[43] 1745: 'At first he is.'

[44] 1745: 'necessity'.

[45] 1745: 'is lost'.

remission of sins through the death of Christ, and the
nature of faith in his blood. And so we do still, among
those who need to be taught the first elements of the
gospel of Christ.

(2) But those in whom the foundation is already laid we 5
exhort to go on to perfection; which we did not see so
clearly at first; although we occasionally spoke of it from
the beginning.

(3) Yet we now preach, and that continually, faith in
Christ, as the Prophet, Priest and King, at least, as 10
clearly, as strongly, and as fully, as we did six years ago.

[§29] *Q*. 16. Do we not discourage visions and dreams too much?
As if we condemned them *toto genere*?

A. We do not intend to do this. We neither discourage nor
encourage them. We learn from Acts 2:19, etc. to expect 15
something of this kind 'in the last days'. And we cannot
deny that saving faith is often given in dreams or visions
of the night: which faith we account neither better nor
worse than if it came by any other means.

[§30] *Q*. 17. Do not some of our Assistants preach too much of 20
the wrath and too little of the love of God?

A. We fear they have leaned to that extreme; and hence
some of their hearers may have lost the joy of faith.

[§31] *Q*. 18. Need we ever preach the terrors[46] of the Lord to
those who know they are accepted of him? 25

A. No; it is folly so to do. For love is to them the strongest
of all motives.

[§32] *Q*. 19. Do we ordinarily represent a justified state so great
and happy as it is?

A. Perhaps not. A believer, walking in the light, is inex- 30
pressibly great and happy.

[§33] *Q*. 20. Should we not have a care of depreciating justification in order to exalt the state of full sanctification?

A. Undoubtedly we should beware of this, for one may
insensibly slide into it. 35

[§34] *Q*. 21. How shall we effectually avoid it?

A. When we are going to speak of entire sanctification, let
us first describe the blessings of a justified state as
strongly as possible.

---

[46] 1745: 'terror'.

[§35]   *Q*. 22. Does not the truth of the gospel lie very near both to
          Calvinism and antinomianism?
          A. Indeed it does—as it were, within a hair's breadth. So
          that 'tis altogether foolish and sinful, because we do not
5   quite agree either with one or the other, to run from them
          as far as ever we can.
[§36]   *Q*. 23. Wherein may we come to the very edge of Calvinism?
          A. [1] In ascribing all good to the free grace of God; (2) in
          denying all natural free will, and all power antecedent to
10   grace; and (3) in excluding all merit from man, even for
          what he has or does by the grace of God.
[§37]   *Q*. 24. Wherein may we come to the edge of antinomianism?
          A. (1) In exalting the merits and love of Christ. (2) In
          rejoicing evermore. [. . .][47]
15 [§39] *Q*. 25. Does faith supersede (set aside the necessity of) holi-
          ness or good works?
          A. In no wise. So far from it that it implies both, as a cause
          does its effects.

20 [§40] *About ten we began to speak of sanctification, with
          regard to which it was inquired:*
          Q. 1. When does inward sanctification begin?
          A. In the moment we are justified. The seed of every virtue
          is then sown in the soul. From that time the believer grad-
25   ually dies to sin, and grows in grace. Yet sin remains in
          him, yea, the seed of all sin, till he is sanctified throughout
          in spirit, soul, and body.
[§41]   *Q*. 2. What will become of a heathen, a Papist, a Church of
          England man, if he dies without being thus sanctified?
30   *A*. He cannot see the Lord. But none who seeks it sincerely
          shall or can die without it; though possibly he may not
          attain it 'till the very article of death'?
[§42]   *Q*. 3. Is it ordinarily [not] given till a little before death?
          A. It is not, to those that expect it no sooner, nor conse-
35   quently ask for it, at least, not in faith.[48]
[§43]   *Q*. 4. But ought we to expect it sooner?
          A. Why not? For although we grant, (1), that the generality
          of believers whom we have hitherto known were not so

[47] 1745, §38, *Q*. 25. 'What can we do to stop the progress of antinomianism?'
[48] 1745: 'nor probably ask for it'.

sanctified till near death; (2), that few of those to whom
St. Paul wrote his epistles were so at the time he wrote;
(3), nor he himself at the time of writing his former epistles. Yet this does not prove that we may not today.

[§44]   *Q.* 5. But would not one who was thus sanctified be incapable of worldly business?

    A. He would be far more capable of it than ever, as going
through all without distraction.

[§45]   *Q.* 6. Would he be capable of marriage?[49]

    A. Why should he not?[50]

[§48]   *Q.* 7. Should we not[51] beware of bearing hard on those who
think they have attained?

    A. We should. And the rather, because if they are faithful to
the grace they have received, they are in no danger of perishing at last. No, not even if they remain in *luminous faith*
(as some term it)[52] for many months or years, perhaps will
within a little time of their spirits returning to God.

[§49]   **Q.* 8. In what manner should we preach entire sanctification?

    A. Scarce at all to those who are not pressing forward. To
those who are, always by way of promise, always drawing
rather than driving.

[§50]   *Q.* 9. How should we wait for the fulfilling of this
promise?

    A. In universal obedience; in keeping all the command-
ments, in denying ourselves, and taking up our cross daily.
These are the general means which God hath ordained for
our receiving his sanctifying grace. The particular are,
prayer, searching the Scripture, communicating, and
fasting.

---

[49] JW omits the phrase that he had added in 1745, 'Marriage is honourable in all'.
[50] JW also omits *QQ.* 7–8 of 1745, on examples of sanctification.
[51] 1745 adds 'then'.
[52] 1749 adds the italics and the parenthetic phrase.

Conversation the Third

Tuesday, May 13, 1746

The following persons being met at the New Room in
Bristol, John Wesley, Charles Wesley, John Hodges,
5   Jonathan Reeves, Thomas Maxfield, Thomas Westell, and
Thomas Willis, it was inquired: . . .[53]

[§6] *Q.* 1. Can an unbeliever (whatever[54] he be in other respects)
challenge anything of God's justice?
A. Absolutely nothing but hell. And this is a point which
10   we cannot too much insist on.

[§7] *Q.* 2. Do we empty men of their own righteousness, as we
did at first? Do we sufficiently labour, when they begin to
be convinced of sin, to take away all they lean upon?
Should we not then endeavour with all our might to over-
15   turn their false foundations?
A. This was at first one of our principal points. And it
ought to be so still, for till all other foundations are overturned, they cannot build upon Christ.

[§8] *Q.* 3. Did we not *then* purposely throw them into convic-
20   tions? Into strong sorrow and fear? Nay, did we not
strive to make them inconsolable? Refusing to be
comforted?
A. We did. And so we should do still. For the stronger the
conviction, the speedier is the deliverance. And none so
25   soon receive the peace of God as those who steadily refuse
all other comfort[s].

[§9] *Q.* 4. Let us consider a particular case. Was you, Jonathan
Reeves, before you received the peace of God, convinced
that notwithstanding all you did, or could do, you was in a
30   state of damnation?
J[onathan] R[eeves]. I was convinced of it as fully as that I
am now alive.

[§10] *Q.* 5. Are you sure that conviction was from God?
35   *J.R.* I can have, no doubt but it was.

---

[53] The original 1746 document shows that the Conference actually began on
Monday, May 12, and that §§2–5 dealt with some of JW's pamphlets.
[54] 1746: 'Can any unbelievers (whatsoever . . .)'.

[§11] *Q*. 6. What do you mean by a state of damnation?

J.R. A state wherein if a man dies he perisheth for ever.

[§12] *Q*. 7. How did that conviction end?

J.R. I had first a strong hope that God *would* deliver me,
and this brought a degree of peace. But I had not that   5
solid peace of God till Christ was revealed in me.

[§13] *Q*. 8. But is not such a trust in the love of God, though it be
as yet without a distinct sight of God reconciled[55] through
Christ Jesus, a low degree of justifying faith?

A. It is an earnest of it.[56] But this abides for a short time   10
only; nor is this the proper Christian faith.

[§14] *Q*. 9. By what faith were the apostles clean before Christ
died?

A. By such a faith as this; by a Jewish faith. For 'the Holy
Ghost was not then given'.   15

[§15] *Q*. 10. Of whom then do you understand those words (Isa.
50:10.): 'Who is there among you that feareth the Lord?
That obeyeth the voice of his servant, that walketh in
darkness, and hath no light?'

A. Of a believer under the Jewish dispensation, one in   20
whose heart God hath not yet shined, to give him the light
of the glorious love of God in the face of Jesus Christ.

[§16] *Q*. 11. Who is a Jew (inwardly)?

A. A *servant* of God; one who sincerely obeys him out of
fear. Whereas a Christian (inwardly) is a *child* of God, one   25
who sincerely obeys him out of love.

[§17] But was not you sincere before Christ was revealed in you?

J[onathan] R[eeves]. It seemed to me that I was in some
measure.

[§18] *Q*. 12. What is sincerity?   30

A. Willingness to know and do the whole will of God. The
lowest species thereof seems to be 'faithfulness in that
which is little'.

[§19] **Q*. 13. Has God any regard to man's sincerity?

A. So far, that no man in any state can possibly please God[57]   35
without it, neither indeed in any moment wherein he is
not sincere.

[55] 1772 (*Works*): 'reconciled to me'.

[56] 1746: 'Perhaps it is'.

[57] 1746: 'possibly be accepted'.

[§20] *Q*. 14. But can it be conceived that God has any regard to the sincerity of an unbeliever?

A. Yes, so much that if he persevere therein, God will infallibly give him faith.

5 [§21] *Q*. 15. What regard may we conceive him to have to the sincerity of a believer?

A. So much, that in every sincere believer he fulfils all the great and precious promises.

[§22] *Q*. 16. Whom do you term a 'sincere believer'?

10 *A*. One that walks in the light, as God is in the light.

[§23] *Q*. 17. Is sincerity the same with a 'single eye'?

A. Not altogether. The latter refers to our [present] intention, the former to our will or desires.[58]

[§24] *Q*. 18. Is it not all in all?

15 *A*. All will follow persevering sincerity. God gives everything with it, nothing without it.

[§25] **Q*. 19. Are not then sincerity and faith equivalent terms?

A. By no means. It is at least as nearly related to works as it is to faith. For example, who is sincere before he believes?

20 He that then does all he can: he that according to the power he has received brings forth 'fruits[59] meet for repentance'. Who is sincere after he believes? He that, from a sense of God's love, is zealous of all good works.

[§26] *Q*. 20. Is not sincerity what St. Paul terms a willing mind?

25 ἡ προθυμία? (2 Cor. 8:12).

A. Yes, if that word be taken in a general sense, for it is a constant disposition to use all the grace given.

[§27] **Q*. 21. But do we not then set sincerity on a level with faith?

A. No. For we allow a man may be sincere, and not be justi-

30 fied, as he may be penitent, and not be justified: (not as yet), but he cannot have faith, and not be justified.[60] The very moment he believes he is justified.

[§28] *Q*. 22. But do we not give up faith, and put sincerity in its place, as the condition of our acceptance with God?

35 *A*. We believe it is one condition of our acceptance, as repentance likewise is. And we believe it a condition of our continuing in a state of acceptance. Yet we do not put

---

[58] 1746: 'design'.

[59] 1746: 'works'.

[60] In 1746, the three previous uses of 'justified' appear as 'accepted'.

it in the place of faith. It is by faith the merits of Christ
are applied to my soul. But if I am not sincere, they are
not applied.

[§29] *Q.* 23. Is not this that 'going about to establish your own
righteousness' whereof St. Paul speaks, (Rom. 10:[3])?

A. St. Paul there manifestly speaks of unbelievers, who
sought to be accepted for the sake of their own righteousness. We do not seek to be accepted for the sake of our
sincerity; but through the merits of Christ alone. Indeed,
so long as any man believes, he cannot go about (in St.
Paul's sense) to 'establish his own righteousness'.

[§30] **Q.* 24. But do you consider that we are under the covenant
of grace? And that the covenant of works is now
abolished?

A. All mankind were under the covenant of grace from the
very hour that the original promise was made. If by the
covenant of works you mean that of unsinning obedience
made with Adam before the fall, no man but Adam was
ever under that covenant; for it was abolished before Cain
was born. Yet it is not so abolished but that it will stand,
in a measure, even to the end of the world; i.e., If we 'do
this', we shall live; if not, we shall die eternally: if we do
well, we shall live with God in glory; if evil, we shall die
the second death. For every man shall be judged in that
day, and [shall be] rewarded 'according to his works'.

[§31] *Q.* 25. What means then, 'To him that believeth his faith is
counted for righteousness'?

A. That God forgives him that is unrighteous as soon as he
believes, accepting his faith instead of perfect righteousness. But then, observe, universal righteousness follows, though it did not precede faith.

[§32] *Q.* [27][61] But is faith thus 'counted to us for righteousness'
at whatsoever time we believe?

A. Yes. In whatsoever moment we believe, all our past sins
vanish away. They are as though they had never been, and
we stand clear in the sight of God.

[61] Orig., '26'.

[§33]   *Tuesday, [May 13, 1746] 10 o'clock.*
          Mr. Taylor of Quinton, and T. Glascot[62] being added, it was
          inquired:
          Q. 1. Are not the assurance of faith, the inspiration of the
5   Holy Ghost, and the revelation of Christ in us, terms
              nearly of the same import?
          A. He that denies one of them, must deny all, they are so
              closely connected together.
[§34]   *Q.* 2. Are they ordinarily, where the pure gospel is
10   preached, essential to our acceptance [with God]?
          A. Undoubtedly they are, and as such to be insisted on, in
              the strongest terms.
[§35]   *Q.* 3. Is not the whole dispute of salvation by faith, or by
              works, a mere 'strife of words'?
15   *A.* In asserting salvation by faith, we mean this: (1) That
              pardon (salvation begun) is received by faith, producing
              works. (2) That holiness (salvation continued) is faith
              working by love. (3) That heaven (salvation finished) is the
              reward of this faith.
20   If you, who assert salvation by works, or by faith and
              works, mean the same thing (understanding by faith the
              revelation of Christ in us, by salvation, pardon, holiness,
              glory), we will not strive with you at all. If you do not, this
              is not a 'strife of words', but the very vitals—the essence
25   of Christianity is the thing in question.
[§36]   *Q.* 4. Wherein does our doctrine now differ from that we
              preached when at Oxford?
          A. Chiefly in these, two points: (1) We then knew nothing
              of that righteousness of faith in justification; nor (2) Of
30   the nature of faith itself as implying consciousness of
              pardon.
[§37]   *Q.* 5. May not some degree of the love of God go before a
              distinct sense of justification?
          A. We believe it may.
35 [§38] *Q.* 6. Can any degree of sanctification or holiness?
          A. Many degrees of outward holiness may. Yea, and some
              degree of meekness, and several other tempers which
              would be branches of Christian holiness, but that they do

---

[62] 1749 adds (followed by 1772) 'and T. Glascot'—one of Wesley's lay preachers.

not spring from Christian principles. For the abiding love
of God cannot spring but from faith in a pardoning God.
And no true Christian holiness can exist without that love
of God for its foundation.

[§39] *Q.* 7. Is every man, as soon as he believes, a new creature,   5
sanctified, [born again], pure in heart? Has he then a new
heart? Does Christ dwell therein? And is he a temple of
the Holy Ghost?

A. All these things may be affirmed of every believer, in a
true sense.[63] Let us not therefore contradict those who   10
maintain[64] it. Why should we contend about words?

Conversation the Fourth

Tuesday, June 16, 1747.

The following being met at the Foundery, John Wesley,   15
Charles Wesley,[65] and Charles Manning, vicar of Hayes,
Richard Thomas Bateman, rector of St. Bartholomew's
the Great, Henry Piers, Howell Harris, and Thomas
Hardwick,[66] it was inquired. [. . .][67]

[§10] *Q.* 1. Is justifying faith a divine assurance that Christ loved   20
me and gave himself for *me*?

A. We believe it is.

[§11] *Q.* 2. What is the judgment of most of the serious
Dissenters concerning this?

A. They generally allow that many believers have such an   25
assurance, and

That it is to be desired and prayed for by all.

But then they affirm,

---

[63] 1746: 'a low sense'.

[64] 1746: 'affirm'.

[65] 1747 inserts here: 'Westley Hall', JW's brother-in-law and former pupil, who
became a renegade Anglican priest.

[66] The 1747 Conference actually began on June 15, and these last four were added
on the 16th.

[67] §§2–9 dealt with the inclusion of nine laymen, and Conference procedure.

That this is the highest species or degree of faith,

That it is not the common privilege of believers.

Consequently they deny that this is justifying faith, or necessarily implied therein.

[§12]   *Q.* 3. And are there not strong reasons for their opinion? For instance, if the true believers of old had not this assurance, then it is not necessarily implied in justifying faith.

But the true believers of old had not this assurance.

A. David, and many more of the believers of old, undeniably had this assurance. But even if the *Jews* had it not, it would not follow that this is not implied in *Christian* faith.

[§13]   *Q.* 4. But do you not know that the Apostles themselves had it not till after the[68] day of Pentecost?

A. The Apostles themselves had not the proper Christian faith till after the day of Pentecost.

[§14]   *Q.* 5. But were not those Christian believers, in the proper sense, to whom St. John wrote his first Epistle? Yet to these he says (5:13), 'These, things have I written unto you that believe on the name of the Son of God, that ye may know that ye have eternal life, and that ye may believe on the name of the Son of God.'

A. This does not prove that they did not know they had eternal life, any more than that they did not believe. His plain meaning is, 'I have only written unto you, that you may be the more established in the faith.' Therefore it does not follow from hence that they had not this assurance, but only that there are degrees therein.

[§15]   *Q.* 6. But were not the Thessalonians true believers? Yet they had not this assurance; they had only a 'good hope' (2 Thess. 2:16).

A. The text you refer to runs thus: 'Now our Lord Jesus Christ himself, and God, even our Father, which hath loved us, and given us everlasting consolation and good hope through grace, comfort your hearts, and establish you in every good word and work.' This 'good hope' does not exclude, but necessarily implies, a strong assurance of the love of God.

[68] 1747: 'till the'.

[§16] *Q*. 7. But does not St. Paul say even of himself (1 Cor. 4:4),
'I know nothing by myself, yet am I not hereby justified'?
A. He does not say of himself here, that he was not justified, or that he did not know it, but only that though he
had a conscience void of offence, yet this did not justify 5
him before God. And must not every believer say the
same? This therefore is wide of the point.

[§17] *Q*. 8. But does he not disclaim any such assurance in those
words (1 Cor. 1:3), 'I was with you in weakness and in
fear, and in much trembling'? 10
A. By no means. For these words do not imply any fear
either of death or hell. They express only a deep sense of
his utter insufficiency for the great work wherein he was
engaged.

[§18] *Q*. 9. However, does he not exclude Christians in general 15
from such an assurance, when he bids them 'work out'
their 'salvation with fear and trembling' (Phil. 2:12)?
A. No more than from love, which is always joined with filial fear and reverential trembling.
    And the same answer is applicable to all those texts 20
which exhort a believer to fear.

[§19] *Q*. 10. But does not matter of fact prove, that justifying
faith does not necessarily imply assurance? For can you
believe that such a person as J. A. or E. [U.],[69] who have so
much integrity, zeal, and fear of God, and walk so 25
unblameably in all things, is void of justifying faith? Can
you suppose such as these to be under the wrath and
under the curse of God? Especially if you add to this, that
they are continually longing, striving, praying for the
assurance which they have not? 30
A. This contains the very strength of the cause and sometimes inclines[70] us to think that some of these may be
exempt cases. But however that be, we answer:
    (1) It is dangerous to ground a general doctrine on a
    few particular experiments. 35
    (2) Men may have many good tempers, and a blameless life
    (speaking in a loose sense), by nature and habit, with pre-
    venting grace; and yet not have faith and the love of God.

---

[69] Orig., 1747 and 1772 (*Works*): 'E. V.'
[70] 1772 (*Works*): 'and inclines'.

(3) 'Tis scarce possible for us to know all the circumstances relating to such persons, so as to judge certainly
concerning them.

(4) But this we know, if Christ is not revealed in them,
they are not yet Christian believers.

[§20] *Q.* 11. But what will become of them then, suppose they
die in this state?

A. That is a supposition not to be made.

They cannot die in this state. They must go backward
or forward. If they continue to seek, they will surely find
righteousness, and peace, and joy in the Holy Ghost. We
are confirmed in this belief by the many instances we have
seen, of such as these finding peace at the last hour. And it
is not impossible but others may then be made partakers
of like precious faith, and yet go hence without giving any
outward proof of the change which God hath wrought.

Conversation the Fifth

Wednesday, [June 17 [1747].

[§21] *Q.* 1. How much is allowed by our brethren who differ from
us with regard to entire sanctification?

A. They grant, (1) That everyone must be entirely sanctified in the article of death; (2) That till then, a believer
daily grows in grace, comes nearer and nearer to perfection; (3) That we ought to be continually pressing after
this, and to exhort all others so to do.

[§22] *Q.* 2. What do we allow them?

A. We grant, (1) That many of those who have died in the
faith, yea, the greater part of those we have known,
were not sanctified throughout, not made perfect in
love, till a little before death.

(2) That the term 'sanctified' is continually applied by
St. Paul to all that were justified, were true believers.

(3) That by this term alone he rarely (if ever) means
saved from all sin.

(4) That consequently it is not proper to use it in this
sense without adding the word, 'wholly', 'entirely', or
the like.

(5) That the inspired writers almost continually speak[71]
of or to those who were[72] justified; but very rarely,   5
either of or to those who were wholly sanctified.

(6) That consequently it behoves us to speak in public[73]
almost continually of the state of justification; but more
rarely, as least[74] in full and explicit terms, concerning
entire sanctification.   10

[§23]   *Q*. 3. What then is the point wherein we divide?
        A. It is this—whether we should expect to be saved from all
        sin before the article of death.

[§24]   *Q*. 4. Is there any clear Scripture *promise* of this? That God
        will save us from *all* sin?   15
        A. There is (Psalm 130:8), 'He shall redeem Israel from *all*
        his sins.'

        This is more largely expressed in the prophecy of
        Ezekiel: 'Then will I sprinkle clean water upon you, and
        you shall be clean; from all your filthiness and from all   20
        your idols will I cleanse you. [. . .] I will also save you
        from all your uncleannesses.' (Chap. 36:25, 29) No prom-
        ise can be more [full and] clear. And to this the Apostle
        plainly refers in that exhortation, 'Having these promises,
        let us cleanse ourselves from all filthiness of flesh and   25
        spirit, perfecting holiness in the fear of God.' (2 Cor. 7:1)
        Equally clear and express is that ancient promise, 'The
        Lord thy God will circumcise thine heart and the heart of
        thy seed, to love the Lord thy God with all thy heart and
        with all thy soul.' (Deut. 30:6)   30

[§25]   *Q*. 5. But does any *assertion* answerable to this occur in the
        New Testament?
        A. There does, and that laid down in the plainest terms. So
        [1] St. John 3:8: 'For this purpose the Son of God was
        manifested, that he might destroy the works of the   35

---

[71] 1747: 'spoke'.

[72] 1772 (*Works*): 'are'.

[73] 1747 does not contain 'in public', but this 1749 addition was followed in 1772
(*Works*).

[74] 1747: 'but rarely, at least'; 1772 (*Works*) omits 'at least'.

devil'—the works of the devil, without any limitation or
restriction. But all sin is the work of the devil. Parallel to
which is that assertion of St. Paul (Eph. 5:25, 27): 'Christ
loved the church, and gave himself for it, . . . that he
might present it to himself a glorious church, not having
spot or wrinkle or any such thing, but that it should be
holy and without blemish.'

And to the same effect is his assertion in the 8th of the
Romans, (ver. 3, 4), 'God sent his Son . . .' that the 'righteousness of the law might be fulfilled in us, walking not
after the flesh but after the spirit.'

[§26]   *Q.* 6. Does the New Testament afford any farther ground
for expecting to be saved from all sin?

A. Undoubtedly it does, both in those prayers and com-
mands which are equivalent to the strongest assertions.

[§27]   *Q.* 7. What prayers do you mean?

A. Prayers for entire sanctification; which, were there no
such thing, would be mere mockery of God. Such in particular, are, (1) 'Deliver us from evil', or rather, 'from the
evil one'. Now when this is done, when we are delivered
from all evil, there can be no sin remaining. (2) 'Neither
pray I for these alone, but for them also which shall
believe on me through their word; that they all may be
one, as thou, Father, art in me, and I in thee, that they also
may be one in us. [. . .] I in them, and thou in me, that
they may be made perfect in one' (John 17:20, 21, 23).
(3) 'I bow my knees unto the God and Father of our Lord
Jesus Christ . . . that he would grant you . . . that ye, being
rooted and grounded in love, may be able to comprehend
with all saints, what is the breadth and length [and
depth]⁷⁵ and height, and to know the love of Christ, which
passeth knowledge, that ye might be filled with all the
fullness of God' (Eph. 3:14, 16–19). (4) 'The very God of
peace sanctify you wholly; and I pray God, your whole
spirit, soul, and body, be preserved blameless unto the
coming of our Lord Jesus Christ' (1 Thess. 5:23).

[§28]   *Q.* 8. What command is there to the same effect?

A. (1) 'Be ye perfect, as your Father which is in heaven is
perfect' (Matt. 6:ult.).

---

⁷⁵ 1772 omits 'and depth', which is restored in the errata and in JW's MS notes.

(2) 'Thou shalt love the Lord thy God with all thy heart,
and with all thy soul, and with all thy mind' (Matt.
22:37). But if the love of God fill all the heart, there can
be no sin there.

[§29] *Q.* 9. But how does it appear that this is to be done before   5
the article of death?

A. First, from the very nature of a command, which is not
given to the dead, but to the living.

Therefore, 'Thou shalt love God with all thy heart', cannot mean, Thou shalt do this when thou diest, but while   10
thou livest.

Secondly, from express texts of Scripture:
(1) 'The grace of God that bringeth salvation hath
appeared to all men, teaching us, that having renounced
(ἀπειπάμενοι) ungodliness and worldly lusts, we   15
should live soberly, righteously, and godly in this present
world; looking for . . . the glorious appearing of our Lord
Jesus Christ; who gave himself for us, that he might
redeem us from "*all*" iniquity; and purify unto himself a
peculiar people, zealous of good works'   20
(Tit. 2:11-14).
(2) 'He hath raised up an horn of salvation for us . . . , to
perform the mercy promised to our fathers; the oath
which he sware to our father Abraham, that he would
grant unto us, that we being delivered out of the hands   25
of our enemies, should serve him without fear, in holiness and righteousness before him, all the days of our
life' (Luke 1:69, etc.).

[§30] *Q.* 10. Is there any example in Scripture of persons who
had attained to this?   30

A. Yes, St. John, and all those of whom he says in his First
Epistle (4:17), 'Herein is our love made perfect, that we
may have confidence in the day of judgment, because as
he is, so are we in this world.'

[§31] *Q.* 11. But why are there not more examples of this kind   35
recorded in the New Testament?

A. It does not become us to be peremptory in this matter.
One reason might possibly be because the apostles wrote
to the church, while it was in a state of infancy. Therefore
they might mention such persons the more sparingly,   40
least they should give strong meat to babes.

[§32] *Q.* 12. Can you show one such example now? Where is he
that is thus perfect?

A. To some who make this inquiry one might answer, If I
knew one here, I would not tell *you,* for you do not
inquire out of love. You are like Herod, you only seek the
young child to slay it.

But more directly[76] we answer, There are numberless
reasons why there should be few (if any indisputable)
examples. What inconveniences would this bring on the
person himself, set as a mark for all to shoot at! What a
temptation would it be to others, not only to men who
knew not God, but to believers themselves! How hardly
would they refrain from idolizing such a person! And yet,
how unprofitable to gainsayers! For if they hear not Moses
and the prophets, Christ and his apostles, neither would
they be persuaded though one rose from the dead.

[§33] *Q.* 13. Suppose one had attained to this, would you advise
him to speak of it?

A. Not to them who know not God. It would only provoke
them to contradict and blaspheme. Nor to any without some
particular reason, without some particular good in view.
And then they should have an especial care to avoid all
appearance of boasting, and to speak more loudly and convincingly by their lives than they can do by their tongues.[77]

[§34] *Q.* 14. Is it a sin not to believe those who say they have
attained?

A. By no means, even though they said true. We ought not
hastily to believe, but to suspend our judgment till we
have full and strong proof.

[§35] *Q.* 15. But are we not apt to have a secret distaste to any
who say they are saved from all sin?

A. 'Tis very possible we may; and that on several grounds:
partly from a concern for the honour of God, and the
good of souls who may be hurt, yea, or turned out of the
way, if these are not what they profess; partly from a kind
of implicit envy at those who speak of higher attainments
than our own; and partly from our slowness and unreadiness of heart to believe the works of God.

---

[76] 1747: 'But to the serious'.
[77] 1772 (*Works*) omits 'and to speak . . . tongues'.

[§36]   *Q*. 16. Does not the harshly preaching perfection tend to
bring believers into a kind of bondage or[78] slavish fear?
A. It does. Therefore we should always place it in the most
amiable light, so that it may excite only hope, joy, and
desire.   5

[§37]   *Q*. 17. Why may we not continue in the joy of faith even till
we are made perfect?
A. Why indeed? Since holy grief does not quench this joy;
since even while we are under the cross, while we deeply
partake of the sufferings of Christ, we may rejoice with   10
joy unspeakable.

[§38]   *Q*. 18. Do we not discourage believers from rejoicing evermore?
A. We ought not so to do. Let them all their life long rejoice
unto God, so it be with reverence. And even if lightness   15
or pride should mix with their joy, let us not strike at the
joy itself (this is the gift of God), but at that lightness or
pride, that the evil may cease and the good remain.

[§39]   *Q*. 19. Ought we to be anxiously careful about perfection,   20
lest we should die before we have attained?
A. In no wise. We ought to be thus *careful for nothing*,
neither spiritual nor temporal.

[§40]   *Q*. 20. But ought we not to be *troubled* on account of the
sinful nature, which still remains in us?   25
A. It is good for us to have a deep sense of this, and to be
much ashamed before the Lord. But this should only
incite us the more earnestly to turn unto Christ every
moment, and to draw light, and life, and strength from
him, that we may go on, conquering and to conquer. And   30
therefore, when the sense of our sin most abounds, the
sense of his love should much more abound.

[§41]   *Q*. 21. Will our joy or our trouble increase as we grow in
grace?
A. Perhaps both. But without doubt our joy in the Lord   35
will increase as our love increases.

[§42]   *Q*. 22. Is not the teaching believers to be continually poring
upon their inbred sin the ready way to make them forget
that they were purged from their former sins?

---

[78] 1747: 'and'.

A. We find by experience, it is; or to make them undervalue, and account it a little thing. Whereas indeed (though there are still greater gifts behind) this is inexpressibly great and glorious.

2. The Disciplinary *Minutes*, 1749[79]

Monday, 25th of June, 1744

[§1]   First, it was inquired:

[§2]   Whether any of our lay brethren should be present at the
Conference.

And it was agreed to invite, from time to time, such of them as we should judge proper.

It was then asked, Which of them shall we invite today? And the answer was, Thomas Richards, Thomas Maxfield, John Bennet, and John Downes; who were accordingly brought in.

[§3]   *Then was read as follow[s]:*

It is desired that all things be considered as in the immediate presence of God;

That we may meet with a single eye, and as little children who have everything to learn;

That every point may be examined from the foundation;

That every person may speak freely what is in his heart; and

That every question proposed may be fully debated, and 'bolted to the bran'.

---

[79] Details of the preparation of JW's companion *Minutes* of 1749 in two pamphlets are given at the beginning of the preceding section. The Doctrinal *Minutes* remained almost static through 1772 (*Works*) and later, but the Disciplinary *Minutes* were subject to constant growth and development for forty years—and indeed long after JW's death. Yet it seems desirable to present the latter first as it appeared in 1749 as a separate entity, incorporating segments of the early manuscript Minutes. The editorial principles governing this pamphlet are the same as those set forth above for the Doctrinal *Minutes*.

The later revisions will be seen below in a separate series of documents, the 'Large' *Minutes*, which in effect were a gradually expanding and rearranged version of the 1749 Disciplinary *Minutes*.

[§4]   The first preliminary question was then proposed, namely,

How far does each of us agree to submit to the unanimous judgment of the rest?

It was answered, In speculative things, each can only   5
submit so far as his judgment shall be convinced.

In every practical point, so far as we can, without wounding our several consciences.

[§5]   To the second preliminary question, viz., How far should any of us mention to others what may be mentioned here?   10
it was replied,

Not one word which may be here spoken of persons should be mentioned elsewhere.

Nothing at all, unless so far as we may be convinced, the glory of God requires it.   15

And from time to time we will consider on each head, Is it for the glory of God that what we have now spoken, should be mentioned again?

[§57]   **On Thursday, June 28 [1744]**   20
Were considered other points of discipline. The substance of the questions and answers, were as follows:

[§58]   *Q.* 1. How are the people divided who desire to be under your care?

A. Into the united societies, the bands, the select societies,   25
and the penitents.

[§59]   *Q.* 2. How do these differ from each other?

A. The united societies (which are the largest of all) consist of awakened persons. Part of these, who are supposed to have remission of sins, are, more closely united in the   30
bands. Those of the bands who seem to walk in the light of God compose the select societies. Those of them who are for the present fallen from grace[80] meet apart as penitents.

[§60]   *Q.* 3. What are the rules of the united societies?
A. Those that follow. (Then they were read.)   35

[§61]   *Q.* 4. What are the rules of the bands?
A. They are these. (Which were read and considered.)

[§62]   *Q.* 5. What are the rules of the select societies?
A. The same, and these three:

---

[80] 1744: 'who have made shipwreck of the faith'.

(1) Let nothing spoken in this Society be spoken again; no, not even to the members of it.

(2) Every member agrees absolutely to submit to his Minister in all indifferent things.

(3) Every member, till we can have all things common, will bring once a week, *bona fide*, all he can spare toward a common stock.

[§63]   *Q.* 6. Are there any peculiar rules for the penitents?
A. Not yet.

[§64]   *Q.* 7. What officers belong to these societies?
A. The Ministers, Assistants, stewards, leaders of bands, leaders of classes, visitors of the sick, schoolmasters, housekeepers.

[§65]   *Q.* 8. What is the office of a Minister?
A. To watch over the souls whom God commits to his charge, as he that must give account.

[§66]   *Q.* 9. What is it to be moved by the Holy Ghost to take upon yourself this office?
A. It can mean no less than to be immediately convinced by the Spirit of God that this is his will.

[§67]   *Q.* 10. Is field preaching unlawful?
A. We do not conceive that it is contrary to any law, either of God or man. Yet (to avoid giving any needless offence) we never preach *without* doors when we can with conveniency preach *within*.

[§68]   *Q.* 11. Where should we endeavor to preach most?
A. (1) Where we can preach in the church.
(2) Where there is an open door, quiet and willing hearers.
(3) Where there is the greatest increase of souls.

[§69]   *Q.* 12. What is the best way of spreading the gospel?
A. To go a little and little farther from London, Bristol, St. Ives, Newcastle, or any other Society. So a little leaven would spread with more effect and less noise, and help would always be at hand.

[§70]   *Q.* 13. What is the best general method in preaching?
A. (1) To invite. (2) To convince. (3) To offer Christ. Lastly, to build up, and to do this (in some measure) in every sermon.

[§71]   *Friday, June 29 [1744],*
We considered:
Q. 1. Are lay Assistants allowable?
A. Only in cases of necessity.

[§72] [*Q.*] 2. What is the office of our Assistants?   5
A. In the absence of the Minister to feed and guide, to
teach and govern the flock.

(1) To expound every morning and evening.
(2) To meet the united societies, the bands, the select
societies and the penitents, every week.   10
(3) To visit the classes once a quarter.[81]
(4) To hear and decide all differences.
(5) To put the disorderly back on trial, and to receive on
trial for the bands or Society.
(6) To see that the stewards, the leaders, schoolmasters   15
and housekeepers faithfully discharge their several
offices.
(7) To meet the leaders of the bands and classes weekly,
and the stewards,[82] and to overlook their accounts.

[§73] *Q.* 3. What are the rules of an Assistant?[83]   20
A. (1) Be diligent. Never be unemployed a moment. Never
be triflingly employed. Never while away time; neither
spend any more time at any place than is strictly necessary.
(2) Be serious. Let your motto be 'holiness to the Lord.' 25
Avoid all lightness as you would avoid hell-fire, and
laughing as you would cursing and swearing.
(3) Converse sparingly and cautiously with women.[84]
(4) Take no step toward marriage without first acquainting us.[85]   30
(5) Believe evil of no one. If you see it done, well. Else
take heed how you credit it. Put the best construction

---

[81] 1744: '(London excepted) once a month'.

[82] 1744 begins, 'To meet the Stewards'.

[83] By 1749, the term 'Assistant', as primary preacher in a circuit, was beginning
to be differentiated from 'Helper', the rest of the preachers. See Minutes (1744),
§72, n. 167.

[84] 1744: 'Touch no woman', etc., as MS Minutes.

[85] This rule is not present in 1744. As a result of this insertion, the rules following are numbered one greater than in 1744.

on everything. You know the judge is always supposed to
be on the prisoner's side.

(6) Speak evil of no one; else *your* word especially
would eat as doth a canker. Keep your thoughts within
your own breast till you come to the person concerned.

(7) Tell everyone what you think wrong in him, and that
plainly, and as soon as may be. Else it will fester in your
heart. Make all haste to cast the fire out of your bosom.

(8) Do nothing *as a gentleman*. You have no more to do
with this character than with that of a dancing-
master. You are the servants of all. Therefore

(9) Be ashamed of nothing but sin: not of fetching
wood, if time permit, or drawing water; not of cleaning
your own shoes or your neighbour's.

(10) Take no money of anyone. If they give you food
when you are hungry, or clothes when you need them, it
is good. But not silver or gold. Let there be no pretence
to say we grow rich by the gospel.

(11) Contract no debts without our knowledge.[86]

(12) Be punctual; do everything exactly at the time.
And in general do not mend our rules, but keep them;
not for wrath, but for conscience' sake.

(13) Act in all things, not according to your own will,
but 'as a son in the gospel'. As such, it is your part to
employ your time in that manner which we direct:
partly in visiting the flock from house to house (the sick
in particular); partly in such course of reading, meditation, and prayer, as we advise from time to time. Above
all, if you labour with us in our Lord's vineyard, it is
needful you should do *that* part of the work which *we*
direct,[87] at *those* times and *places* which we judge most
for *his* glory.

[§74]   *Q.* 4. Should our Assistants[88] keep journals?

A. By all means, as well for our satisfaction as for the profit
of their own souls.[89]

---

[86] 1744: 'no debt without my knowledge'.

[87] 1744: 'prescribe'.

[88] 1744: 'all our Assistants'.

[89] In 1744, §75 deals with stationing 'each labourer'; §§76–77 with the office and
rules of the stewards; §§78–80 with the business of Band leaders, visitors of the
sick; §81 speaks of 'a Seminary for labourers'.

[§82]   *Q.* 5. With whom should we correspond? When?

  A. Once a month, with each Assistant, and with some one other person (at least) in each Society.[90]

[§85]   *Q.* 6. How shall we exclude formality from prayer and conversation?

  A. (1) By preaching frequently on that head.

   (2) By watching always, that we may speak only what we feel.[91]

[§87]   *Q.* 7. Is it lawful to bear arms?

  A. We incline to think it is: (1) Because there is no command against it in the New Testament. (2) Because Cornelius, a soldier, is commended there, and not mentioned to have laid them down.

[§88]   *Q.* 8. Is it lawful to use the law?

  A. As defendant doubtless. And perhaps as plaintiff in some cases, seeing magistrates are an ordinance of God.

[§1]   *Bristol, Thursday, Aug. 1, 1745,*
     It was inquired:

[§2]   *Q.* 1. Should we still consider ourselves as little children, who have everything to learn?

  A. Yes, so far as to have our minds always open to any farther light which God may give us.

[§3]   *Q.* 2. What general method may we observe in our following Conferences?

  A. First, to read and weigh at every Conference each article of those preceding. Secondly, to speak freely and calmly hear touching each, that we may either retract, amend, or enlarge it.

[§4]   *Q.* 3. Should not the time of this Conference be a time of particular watching and self-denial?

  A. It should.

[§5]   *Q.* 4. Should we not desire all who can of the Society to join with us tomorrow in fasting and prayer?

  A. We will desire them so to do.

[§6]   *Q.* 5. Ought not every point which shall be proposed to be examined from the foundation?

---

[90] In 1744, §§83–84 deal with special meetings and with the Assistants' reading.
[91] In 1744, §86 deals with JW's future publications.

A. Without question it ought. If there was any defect
herein at the last Conference, let us amend it now.

[§7]   *Q.* 6. How can we effectually provide that everyone may
speak freely whatever is in his heart?

5   *A.* By taking care to check no one, either by word or look,
even though he should say what is quite wrong.

[§8]   *Q.* 7. How shall we provide that every point may be fully
debated, and thoroughly settled?

A. Let us beware of making haste; or of showing or

10   indulging any impatience, whether of delay, or of
contradiction.[92]

[§51]   *On Saturday, August 3 [1745],*
were considered points of discipline.

15   [§52]   *Q.* 1. Can he be a spiritual governor of the Church who is
not a believer, not a member of it?

A. It seems not; though he may be a governor in outward
things, by a power derived from the King.

[§53]   *Q.* 2. What are properly the laws of the Church of England?

20   *A.* The rubrics; and to those we submit as the ordinance of
man, for the Lord's sake.

[§54]   *Q.* 3. But is not the will of our governors a law?

A. No; not of any governor, temporal or spiritual. Therefore if any bishop wills that I should not preach the

25   gospel, his will is no law to me.

[§55]   *Q.* 4. But what if he produce a law against your preaching?

A. I am to obey God rather than man.

[§56]   *Q.* 5. Is Episcopal, Presbyterian, or Independent church
government most agreeable to reason?

30   *A.* The plain origin of church government seems to be this.
Christ sends forth a preacher of the gospel. Some
who hear him repent and believe the gospel. They
then desire him to *watch over* them, to *build* them
up in the faith, and to *guide* their souls in the paths of

35   righteousness.

---

[92] The remainder of Aug. 1 and the whole of Aug. 2, 1745, were devoted to discussions of doctrine; see above, pp. 148–55, 786–91.

Here then is an *independent* congregation, subject to no pastor but their own, neither liable to be controlled in things spiritual by any other man or body of men whatsoever.

But soon after, some from other parts who are occa- 5
sionally present while he speaks in the name of him that sent him, beseech him to come over to help them also. Knowing it to be the will of God, he consents. Yet not till he has conferred with the wisest and holiest of his con-gregation, and with their advice *appointed* one or more 10
who has gifts and grace to watch over the flock till his return.

If it please God to raise another flock in the new place, before he leaves them he does the same thing, *appointing* one whom, God has fitted for the work to watch over 15
these souls also. In like manner, in every place where it pleases God to gather a little flock by his word, he *appoints* one in his absence to take the oversight of the rest, and to assist them of the ability which God giveth. These are *deacons*, or servants of the church, and look on 20
the first pastor as their common father. And all these con-gregations regard him in the same light, and esteem him still as the shepherd of their souls.

These congregations are not absolutely *independent*. They depend on one pastor, though not on each other. 25

As these congregations increase, and as their *deacons* grow in years and grace, they need other subordinate Deacons or Helpers; in respect of whom they may be called *Presbyters*, or Elders, as their father in the Lord may be called the *Bishop*, or Overseer of them all. 30

[§57]   *Q*. 6. Is mutual consent absolutely necessary between the pastor and his flock?

A. No question: I cannot guide any soul unless he consent to be guided by me. Neither can any soul force me to guide him if I consent not. 35

[§58]   *Q*. 7. Does the ceasing of this consent on either side dis-solve that relation?

A. It must in the very nature of things. If a man no longer consent to be guided by me, I am no longer his guide, I am free. If one will not guide me any longer, I am free to 40
seek one who will.

[§59] *Q.* 8. But is the shepherd free to leave his sheep, or the sheep to leave their shepherd?

A. Yes; if one or the others are convinced, it is for the glory of God, and the superior good of their souls.

[§60] *Q.* 9. How shall we treat those who leave us?

A. (1) Beware of all sharpness, or bitterness, or resentment. (2) Talk with them once or twice at least. (3) If they persist in their design, consider them as *dead*. And name them not, unless in prayer.

[§61] *Q.* 10. Can I attend any more societies than I do? Seeing this would imply the spending less time with the rest?

A. It seems not, at least till the societies already founded are more established in grace.

[§62] *Q.* 11. May we not make a trial, especially in Wales and Cornwall, of preaching without settling any societies?

A. It might be well; and by this means we may preach in every large town where a door is open.

[§63] *Q.* 12. Should we permit any serious person to be present when one of our societies meets?

A. At some time we may,[93] if he particularly desire it; but not always, nor the same person frequently.

[§64] *Q.* 13. Have we borne a sufficient witness to the truth? Particularly when attacked by the clergy?

A. Perhaps not. We have generally been content with standing on the defensive.

[§65] *Q.* 14. May not this cowardice have hindered the work of God? And have caused us to feel less of his power?

A. Very probably it may.

[§66] *Q.* 15. How shall we act in such cases for the time to come?

A. Not only refute, but retort the charge. Their mouths must be stopped (only in meekness and love), and the eyes of others opened.

[§67] *Q.* 16. Is it expedient for us to converse more with the clergy?

A. Yes; wherever they are willing we should.

[§68] *Q.* 17. With our chief opposers or persecutors?

A. It might do good: (1) When they make any overtures toward it. (2) When we can take them unawares, and converse with them alone.

---

[93] 1745: 'he may'.

[§69]   *Q*. 18. National sins call aloud for national judgments.
        What shall we do to prevent them?
        A. The first Friday in every month, at least, speak expressly
        on this head, and insist on the necessity of a general
        repentance to prevent a general scourge.   5

[§70]   *Q*. 19. Should we talk of persecution before it comes?
        A. To talk or think before of any particular persecution only
        weakens our hands. And how long the general persecution
        may be deferred, God only knows.

[§71]   It was next inquired with regard to our Assistants,   10
        Q. 1. Should any other rule be added to the twelve?
        A. Only this: 'You have nothing to do but to save souls.
        Therefore spend and be spent in this work. And go always, not
        only to those who want you, but to those who want you most.'

[§72]   *Q*. 2. Who are our present Assistants?   15
        A. Jonathan Reeves, James Wheatley, John Nelson, John Bennet,
        John Trembath, Francis Walker, Thomas Richards, John
        Downes, Thomas Westell, James Jones, Samuel Larwood,
        Henry Millard, Thomas Maxfield, Thomas Meyrick.

[§73]   *Q*. 3. What general method of spending their time may our   20
        Assistants have?
        A. They may spend the mornings (from six to twelve) in
        reading, writing, and prayer; from twelve to five, visit the
        sick and well; and from five to six, use private prayer.

[§74]   *Q*. 4. Can I travel less in order to write more?   25
        A. As yet it does not seem advisable.[94]

[§77]   *Q*. 5. How shall we order our correspondence at home and
        abroad?
        A. (1) Fix whom to correspond with monthly in every
        place. (2) Divide them between my brother and me.   30
        (3) Send them notice in every place.[95]

[§83]   *Q*. 6. What books should we keep for our own use at
        London, Bristol, and Newcastle?
        A. Those that follow:[96]

---

[94] 1745, §75, on CW and John Meriton following JW 'step by step'; §76, on a
'Seminary for labourers'.

[95] 1745: §78, keeping a stock of medicines at Methodist headquarters; §79, special days; §80, JW's publishing plans; §81, bearing arms; §82, uniting with the
Tabernacle Society.

[96] For details on most of these books, see the corresponding section in the 1745
Minutes.

I. Divinity, Practical.   1. The Bible.

        2. Our tracts.

        3. Boehm's Sermons.

        4. Nalson's Sermons.

        5. Francke's *Works.*

        6. Pascal's *Thoughts.*

        7. Heylyn's tracts.[97]

        8. Bishop Beveridge's *Private Thoughts.*

Doctrinal.   1. Bishop Pearson on the Creed.

        2. Bishop Fell on the Epistles.

        3. Dr. Gell's Works.

II. Physic.   1. Drake's *Anatomy.*

        2. Quincy's *Dispensatory.*

        3. Allen's Synopsis.

        4. Dr. Cheyne's Works:

III. Natural Philosophy.   1. *Nature Delineated.*

        2. Miller's *Gardener's*

          Dictionary Abridged.

IV. Astronomy.   1. Whiston's Astronomical

          Principles.

V. History.   1. *Universal History.*

VI. Poetry.   1. Spenser.

        [2. Sir John Davies.]

        3. Milton.

VII. Latin Prose. 1. Sallust.

        2. Caesar.[98] Corn[elius] Nep[os], Vell[eius]

        Paterculus. Littleton's *Dictionary.*

        3. Tullii, *Philosophica* and *De Officiis.*

        4. Cypriani *Opera.*

        5. Castellio's *Dialogues.*

        6. Erasmi *Selecta.*

        7. Austin's *Confessions.*

---

[97] *Devotional Tracts concerning the Presence of God, and other Religious Subjects* (London: Downing, 1724), anonymously edited by John Heylyn (1685?–1757)— spelled 'Heylin' by JW—used by JW in vol. 38 of his *Christian Library.*

[98] B omitted Caesar in Minutes (1745), §83, and numbered the following three items as '2'; these *Minutes* follow the 1745 text above, but insert a superfluous '3' at this point.

Verse.   1. Terence.
    2. Virgil.
    3. *Selecta* Horatii, Juv[enal], Pers[eius], Mart[ial].
    4. Vida.
    5. Casimir.   5
    6. Buchanan.
VIII. Greek Prose. 1. Greek Test[ament], Hederici
         Lexicon.
    2. Plato's Select Dialogues.
    3. Xenophon's *Cyropoedia.*   10
    4. Epictetus.
    5. Antoninus de se ipso.
    6. Ignatius, etc.
    7. Ephraim Syrus.
    8. Macarius, Chrysost[om] *De Sacerd[otio]* 15
Greek Verse.   1. Homer's *Iliad.*
    2. *Epigrammatum Delectus.*
    3. Duport's Job, etc.
Hebrew. 1. The Bible. Buxtorf.   20

[§1] *Monday, May 12, 1746, it was inquired:*
[§2] *Q.* 1. Who are the properest persons to be present at any
   Conference of this nature?
   A. First, as many of the preachers as conveniently can; 25
   [2] the most earnest and most sensible of the bandleaders
   where the Conference is; and (3) any pious injudicious
   stranger who may be occasionally in the place.
[§3] *Q.* 2. Might it not be useful to read over one or more of our
   tracts at each Conference?   30
   A. Doubtless it might, were it only to correct what is amiss,
   and explain what is obscure in each.

[§39]   ***On Wednesday [May] 14 [1746],*** 35
    Were considered points relating to discipline.
[§40] *Q.* 1. When the pastor of a congregation dies, who has the
   right of choosing another?
   A. Without all doubt, the congregation itself, whom none
   can feed or guide without their own consent. 40

[§41]   *Q.* 2. What is this scriptural notion of an apostle?
        A. One who is sent of God to convert heathens.

[§42]   *Q.* 3. How many apostles were there in the first church?
        A. A great number, besides those 12 who were eminently so
        called. Thus St. Paul, speaking of our Lord after his res-
        urrection, saith, 'He was seen of Cephas, then of the 12;
        after that of above 500 brethren at once; then of all the
        apostles.' (1 Cor. 15:7 [i.e., 5-7]).

[§43]   *Q.* 4. What is the New Testament notion of a prophet?
        A. A builder up of the faithful.

[§44]   *Q.* 5. In what view are we and our Helpers to be
        considered?
        A. Perhaps as *extraordinary* messengers, designed of
        God to provoke the others to jealousy.

[§45]   *Q.* 6. Do you not slide insensibly into taking state upon
        yourselves? Or lording it over God's heritage?
        A. (1) We are not conscious to ourselves that we do,
        (2) but there is a continual danger. Therefore, (3) we can-
        not be too jealous, lest we should, and (4) we will thank
        any who warned us against it.

[§46]   *Q.* 7. How shall we be more easy of access?
        A. Let any speak to us after preaching, morning or evening.

[§47]   *Q.* 8. How shall we try those who believe they are moved by
        the Holy Ghost and called of God to preach?
        A. Inquire (1) Do they know in whom they have believed?
        Have they the love of God in their hearts? Do they
        deserve and see nothing but God? And are they holy in all
        manner of conversation?
        (2) Have they *gifts* (as well as *grace*) for the work? Have
        they (in some tolerable degree) a clear, sound *under-
        standing*? Have they any right judgment in the things of
        God? Have they a just conception of *salvation by faith*?
        And has God given them any degree of *utterance*? Do
        they speak justly, readily, clearly?
        (3) Have they success? Do they not only so speak as
        generally either to convince or affect the hearers? But
        have any received remission of sins either preaching? A
        clear and lasting sense of the love of God?
        As long as these three marks undeniably concur in any,
        we allow him to be called of God to preach.

These we received as sufficient, reasonable evidence
that he is moved thereto by the Holy Ghost.

[§48]   *Q.* 9. But how shall we know, in the case of a particular person, whether there is this evidence or no?

A. (1) We will send one of our Helpers to hear him preach,   5
and to talk with him on the preceding heads.
(2) We will hear him preach, and talk with him ourselves.
(3) We will examine thoroughly those who think they have
received remission of sins by his preaching. (4) We will
desire him to relate or to write down the reasons why he   10
believes he is called of God to preach. (5) We will desire
the congregation to join with us in fasting and prayer, that
we may judge and act according to the will of God.

[§49]   *Q.* 10. Should we not use the same method of fasting and
prayer on other occasions also?   15

A. Without doubt we should use it: (1) At the receiving any
fellow-labourer in our Lord's vineyard. (2) At going ourselves, or sending any, to a new place. (3) Before publishing any book.   20

[§50]   *Q.* 11. Why do we not use more form and solemnity in the
receiving of a new labourer?

A. We purposely decline: (1) Because there is something of
stateliness in it. (2) Because we would not make haste. We
desire barely to follow Providence, as it gradually opens.[99]   25

[§51]   *Q.* 12. Are there any of our Assistants whom we might
employ more than the rest? In what instances?

A. There are. We may employ some (1) in visiting classes at
each place; (2) in writing lists of the societies and bands
there; (3) in delivering new tickets, where we cannot do it   30
ourselves; (4) in holding love-feasts, where needful.[100]

[§52]   *Q.* 13. Is there any Prudential help for greater watchfulness
and recollection which our Assistants might use?

A. We believe it would be an inconceivable help if they kept
a journal of every hour. The manner of doing it they may   35
learn in a few minutes, by looking at one of the journals
we kept at Oxford.

---

[99] 1746: 'opens to us'.
[100] This fourth point is not present in 1746.

[§53]   *Q*. 14. In what light should your Assistants consider themselves?

A. As learners rather than teachers; as young students at
the university, for whom therefore a method of study is
expedient in the highest degree.

[§54]   *Q*. 15. What method would you advise them to?

A. We would advise them: (1) Always to rise at 4.

(2) From 4–5 in the morning, and from 5 to 6 in the
evening, partly to use meditation and private prayer;
partly to read the Scripture (two to three verses, or one or
two chapters), partly some close, practical book of divinity. In particular, *The Life of God in the Soul of Man*,
Kempis, *The Pilgrim's Progress*, Mr. Law's Tracts,
Bishop Beveridge's *Private Thoughts*, Heylyn's
Devotional Tracts, The Life of Mr. Halyburton, and
M[onsieur] De Renty. (3) From 6 in the morning (allow-
ing one hour for breakfast) to 12, to read in order, slowly,
and with much prayer, Bishop Pearson on the *Creed*,
Bishop Fell on the *Epistles*, Mr. Boehm's and Mr.
Nalson's Sermons, Mr. Pascal's *Thoughts*, our other
tracts and poems, Milton's *Paradise Lost*, Cave and
Fleury's *Primitive Christianity*, and Mr. Echard's
Ecclesiastical History.

[§55]   *Q*. 16. Have we in anything altered our manner of preaching for the worse since we set out?

A. Perhaps we do not preach so much concerning the blood
of atonement as we did at first.

[§56]   *Q*. 17. What inconvenience is there in speaking much of the
wrath, and little of the love of God?

A. It generally hardens them that believe not, and discourages them that do.

[§57]   *Q*. 18. What sermons do we find my experience to be
attended with the greatest blessing?

A. (1) Such as are most close, convincing, particular;
(2) Such as have most of Christ the Priest, the atonement;
(3) Such as urge the heinousness of men's living in and
contempt or ignorance of him.[101]

---

[101] 1746, §58, on preaching in Moorfields.

Thursday, May, 15 [1746].

[§59] *Q*. 1. What is a sufficient call of Providence to a new place?
Supposed to Edinburgh or Dublin?

A. (1) An invitation from someone that is worthy; from a
serious man, fearing God, who has a house to receive us.   5
(2) A probability of doing more good by going thither
than by staying longer where we are.

[§60] *Q*. 2. Ought we not diligently to observe in what place God
is pleased to pour out his Spirit more abundantly?

A. We ought, and at that time to send more labourers than   10
usual into that part of the harvest, as, at this time, into
Yorkshire and the country round Coleford.

[§61] *Q*. 3. How can we add a proper solemnity to the admission
of new members into the bands or the United Society?

A. (1) Admit new members into the bands at London,   15
Bristol, and Newcastle, only once a quarter, at the general
love-feast. (2) Read the names of the men to be admitted
under Wednesday; other women on the Sunday before.
(3) Admit into the Society only on this Thursday or
Sunday following the quarterly visitation of the classes.   20
(4) Read the names of those to be admitted on the
Tuesday and Thursday or Sunday evening before. (5) The
first time that anyone (on trial) meets a class, let the *Rules*
of the Society be given him. (6) And let them be publicly
read of the Thursday or Sunday after every admission of   25
new members. (7) Then also let the names of those be
read who are excluded from the Society.

[§62] *Q*. 4. How shall we guard more effectually against formality
and public singing?

A. (1) By the careful choice of hymns proper for the con-   30
gregation. (2) In general, by choosing hymns of praise or
prayer, rather than descriptive of particular states. (3) By
not singing too much; seldom a whole hymn at once, seldom more than five or six verses at a time. (4) By suiting
the tunes to the hymns. (5) By often stopping short and   35
asking the people, 'Now! Do you know what you said last?
Did it suit your case? Did you sing it as to God? With the
spirit and with the understanding also?'

[§63] *Q*. 5. Should we insist more on people's going to church?
Shall we set them the example at Bristol?   40

A. We will make a trial of the effects of it by going to St. James's every Wednesday and Friday.

[§64] *Q.* 6. How shall we be more recollected and more useful in conversation?

A. (1) Plan every conversation before you begin. (2) Watch and pray during the time, that your mind be not dissipated. (3) Spend two or three minutes every hour in solemn prayer. (4) Strictly observe the morning and evening hour of retirement.

[§65] *Q.* 7. How are your circuits now divided?

A. Into seven. (1) London (which includes Surrey, Kent, Essex, Brentford, Egham, Windsor, Wycombe). (2) Bristol (which includes Somersetshire, Portland, Wilts[hire], Oxfordshire, Gloucestershire). (3) Cornwall. (4) Evesham (which includes Shrewsbury, Leominster, Hereford, and from Stroud to Wednesbury). (5) Yorkshire (which includes Cheshire, Lancashire, Derbyshire, Nottinghamshire, Rutlandshire, and Lincolnshire). (6) Newcastle. (7) Wales.

[§66] *Q.* 8. Who are our present Assistants?

A. Jonathan Reeves, John Bennet, John Haughton, John Nelson, James Wheatley, John Trembath, Thomas Westell, Thomas Richards, John Downes, Thomas Meyrick, Thomas Maxfield, Francis Walker; perhaps James Jones, Samuel Larwood, Joseph Cownley.[102]

[§69] *Q.* 9. Can we be of any further use to the Moravians?

A. Perhaps by writing to the Count.

[§70] *Q.* 10. To whom should we give copies of our Conferences?

A. Only to those who were or might have been present.

[§71] *Q.* 11. To whom should we read them?

A. To the stewards and leaders of bands, the Sunday and Thursday following the Conference.[103]

[§1]   *Monday, June 15th, 1747.*

[§2] *Q.* 1. Which of our brethren shall we invite to be present at this Conference?

---

[102] Adding to 1746, Meyrick, and omitting Hardwick, Heard, Walker; §§67–68 added details of a quarter's supplies and of special days.

[103] Details of the time of reading were not present in 1746.

A. John Jones, Thomas Maxfield, Jonathan Reeves, John Nelson, John Bennet, John Downes, Thomas Crouch, Robert Swindells, and John Maddern; who were accordingly brought in.

[§3] *Q.* 2. How may the time of this Conference be made more eminently a time of prayer, watching, and self-denial?

A. (1) While we are in Conference, let us have an especial care to set God always before us.

(2) In the intermediate powers, let us visit none but the sick, and spend all our time that remains in retirement.

(3) Let us then give ourselves under prayer for one another, and for the blessing of God upon this our labour.

[§4] *Q.* 3. Should we every Conference read over all the Conferences[104] we have had from the beginning?

A. Only that immediately preceding, and so much of the rest as we may find needful from time to time.

[§5] *Q.* 4. In our first Conference, it was agreed to examine every point from the foundation. Have we not been some way fearful of doing this? What were we afraid of? Of overturning our first principles?

A. Whoever was afraid of this, it was a vain fear. For if they are true, they will bear the strictest examination. If they are false, the sooner they are overturned the better. Let us all pray for a willingness to receive the light; an invariable desire to know of every doctrine whether it be of God.

[§6] *Q.* 5. It was then inquired, How far does each of us agree to submit to the unanimous judgment of the rest?

And it was answered, In speculative things, each can only submit so far as his judgment shall be convinced. In every practical point, so far as we can without wounding our several consciences.[105]

[§7] *Q.* 6. Can a Christian submit any farther than this to any man, or number of men, upon earth?

A. It is undeniably plain he cannot, either to Pope, Council, Bishop, or convocation. In this is that grand principle of every man's right to private judgment, in

---

[104] I.e., Conference *Minutes.*
[105] This entry duplicates 1744, §4.

opposition to implicit faith in man, on which Calvin,
Luther, Melanchthon on, and all the ancient reformers,
both at home and abroad, proceeded: 'Every man must
think for himself, since every man must give an account
5   for himself to God.'

[§8]   *Q.* 7. Shall each of us read over all the tracts which have
been published before our next Conference? And write
down every passage we do not approve, or do not fully
understand?
10   *A.* Everyone answered, in order, 'I will endeavor so to do.'

[§43]   ***About 10 (Mr. Peronnet, vicar of Shoreham, being
added), we began to consider points of discipline.***
Q. 1. What is schism, in the Scripture sense of the word?
15   *A.* The word occurs only twice in the New Testament, viz.,
1 Cor. 1:10, where St. Paul exhorts them that 'there may
be no schisms among them' (σχίσματα is the word
which we render 'divisions'); and 12:15, 'God hath mingled the body together, having given the more abundant
20   honour to that part which lacked; that there may be no
schism in the body'; i.e., in the Church, the body of
Christ.
In both these places, the word undeniably means (which
consequently is the true scriptural notion of schism) a
25   causeless breach, rupture, or division made among the
members of Christ; among those who are the living body
of Christ, and members in particular.

[§45]   *Q.* 2. Are not the Methodists guilty of making such a
schism?
30   *A.* No more than of rebellion or murder. They do not
divide themselves at all from the living body of Christ.
Let any prove it if they can.

[§46]   *Q.* 3. But do they not divide themselves from the Church
of England?
35   *A.* No. They hold communion therewith now in the same
manner they did twenty years ago, and hope to do so to
their lives' end.

[§47]   *Q.* 4. You profess to obey both the governors and the rules
of the Church, yet in many instances you do not obey
40   them. How is this consistent? Upon what principle do you
act when you sometimes obey and sometimes not?

A. It is entirely consistent. We act at all times on one, plain, uniform principle: 'We will quietly obey God rather than man.'

[§48] *Q.* 5. But why do you say you are thrust out of the churches? Has not every minister a right to dispose of his own church?

A. He ought to have, but in fact he has not. A minister desires I should preach in his church. But the Bishop forbids him. That Bishop then injures him, and thrusts me out of that church.

[§49] *Q.* 6. Does a church in the New Testament always mean 'a single congregation'?

A. We believe it does. We do not recollect any instance to the contrary.

[§50] *Q.* 7. What instance or ground is there then in the New Testament for a *national* church?

A. We know none at all. We apprehend it to be a merely political institution.

[§51] *Q.* 8. Are the three orders of bishops, priests, and deacons plainly described in the New Testament?

A. We think they are, and believe they generally obtained in the churches of the apostolic age.

[§52] *Q.* 9. But are you assured that God designed the same plan should obtain in all churches, throughout all ages?

A. We are not assured of this, because we do not know that it is asserted in Holy Writ.

[§53] *Q.* 10. If this plan were essential to a Christian church, what must become of all the foreign Reformed Churches?

A. It would follow, they are no parts of the Church of Christ! A consequence full of shocking absurdity!

[§54] *Q.* 11. In what age was the divine right of episcopacy first asserted in England?

A. About the middle of Queen Elizabeth's reign. Till then, all the bishops and clergy in England continually allowed and joined in the ministrations of those who were not episcopally ordained.

[§55] *Q.* 12. Must there not be numberless accidental varieties in the government of various churches?

A. There must, in the nature of things. For as God variously dispenses his gifts of nature, providence, and grace,

both the offices themselves and the officers in each ought
to be varied from time to time.

[§56]   *Q.* 13. Why is it that there is no determinate plan of church
government appointed in Scripture?

A. Without doubt, because the wisdom of God had a
regard to this necessary variety.

[§57]   *Q.* 14. Was there any thought of uniformity in the government of all churches until the time of Constantine?

A. It is certain there was not; and would not have been
then, had men consulted the Word of God only.

[§58]   ### Thursday, June 18 [1747].

Q. 1. Have we not limited field preaching too much?

A. It seems we have. (1) Because our calling is to save that
which is lost. Now we cannot expect the wanderers from
God to seek us. It is our part to go and see them.

(2) Because we are more peculiarly called, by going out
into the highways and hedges (which none will do, if we
do not), to compel them to come in.

(3) Because that reason against it is not good, 'The
house will hold all that come.' The house may hold all
that will come to the house, but not all that would come
to the field.

(4) Because we have always found a greater blessing in
field preaching than in any other preaching whatever.

[§59]   *Q.* 2. What is 'respect of persons'? (James 2:1)

A. The regarding one person more than another, on
account of some outward circumstances, particularly
riches.

[§60]   *Q.* 3. Have we not fallen into this by allowing more of our
time to the rich than to the poor? By not speaking so plain
and home to them? And by admitting them into the
Society, or even the bands, though they had never
received remission of sins, and had met in no band at all?

A. These are instances of such a respect of persons as we
will endeavour to avoid for the time to come.

[§61]   *Q.* 4. Would it not be well for the minister to visit the sick
on Monday, Thursday, Friday, and Saturday?

A. It seems no time could be more profitably employed,
either for them or us.

[§62] *Q.* 5. How shall we keep off unworthy communicants?

A. (1) By being exactly careful whom we admit into the Society; and,

(2) By giving notes to none but those who come to us on the days appointed in each quarter.   5

[§63] *Q.* 6. How shall we thoroughly purge the bands?

A. (1) In visiting the classes, meet those who are in the bands every morning before the rest; and examine them as strictly as you can, both as to their heart and life.

(2) Meet the married men and married women apart, the first Wednesday and Sunday after each visitation; the single men and single women apart, on the second Wednesday and Sunday.   10

[§64] *Q.* 7. Who are our present Assistants?   15

A. John Jones, Jonathan Reeves, John Haughton, Jos. Cownley, James Wheatley, John Nelson, John Trembath, Robert Swindells, Thomas Richards, Samuel Larwood, Thomas Westell, Francis Walker, John Bennet, Thomas Maxfield, John Downes, Richard Moss, Edward Dunston,   20
Thomas Meyrick, Richard Williamson, John Maddern; perhaps James Jones, and Eleaz[er] Webster.[106]

[§65] *Q.* 8. Who are there that assist us chiefly in one place?

A. Thomas Rawlings, J. Hathaway, James Rogers, John Slocomb, Corn. Bastable, John Jane, John Whitford,   25
David Trathen, John Jenkins, John Spargo, Ant. Lyddicoat, Steph. Nichols, John Wheeler, John Osborne, Edw. May, John Bennet, William Fenwick, Robert Blow, James Skelton, Robert Taylor, John Brown, Christopher Hopper, Archibald Patten, William Holmes, William   30
Shent, Matthew Watson, Samuel Appleyard, William Darney, Francis Scott, Joseph Lee, John Eaton, John Appleton, John Griffiths, Richard Watts, William Walker, John Gill, Thomas Crouch, Henry Lloyd.[107]

[§67] *Q.* 9. Are our Assistants exemplary in their lives?   35

A. Perhaps not. We should consider each of them who is with us as a pupil at the University, into whose behavior and studies we should therefore make a particular inquiry every day.

---

[106] For details, see 1747, §64.
[107] Local preachers; for details, see 1747, §65.

[§68]   Might we not particularly inquire: Do you rise at four? Do
you study in the method laid down at the last Conference?
Do you read the books we advise and no other? Do you
see the necessity of regularity and study? What are your
chief temptations to irregularity? Do you punctually
observe the evening hour of retirement? Are you exact in
writing your journal? Do you fast on Friday? Do you converse seriously, usefully, and closely? Do you pray before,
and have you a determinate end in, every conversation?

[§69]   *Q.* 10. How often should our Assistants preach?
        A. Never more than twice a day, unless on a Sunday or an
extraordinary occasion, of which themselves are to be the
judges.

[§70]   *Q.* 11. Are there any smaller advices concerning preaching
which it may be useful for them to observe?
        A. Perhaps these that follow:
        (1) Be sure to begin and end precisely at the time
        appointed.
        (2) Sing no hymns of your own composing.
        (3) Endeavour to be serious, weighty, and solemn in
        your whole deportment before the congregation.
        (4) Choose the plainest texts you can.
        (5) Take care not to ramble from your text, but to keep
        close to it, and make out what you undertake.
        (6) Always suit your subject to your audience.
        (7) Beware of allegorizing or spiritualizing too much.
        (8) Take care of anything awkward or affected, either in
        your gesture or pronunciation.
        (9) Tell each other if you observe anything of this kind.

[§71]   *Q.* 12. Is there any part of the work of an Assistant wherein
only some of our Assistants need to be employed?
        A. There is. Let those, and those only, to whom we shall
write from time to time: (1) Visit the classes in each place,
and write new lists of all the members. (2) Regulate the
bands. (3) Deliver new tickets. (4) Keep watch-nights and
love-feasts. (5) Take and send to us an exact account of the
behaviour of the stewards, housekeepers, schoolmasters,
and leaders.

[§1]   **Thursday, June 2, 1748.**[108]

The following persons being met at the Chapel House in
Tower Street, London, John Wesley, Charles Wesley,
William Felton, Charles Manning, Thomas Maxfield,
John Jones, Thomas Meyrick, John Trembath, Edward   5
Perronet, Jonathan Reeves, and afterwards Richard
Thomas Bateman, John Green, and William Tucker; it
was re-enquired,

[§2] *Q.* 1. What is our chief business at the present Conference?
A. Not to consider points of doctrine (the time will not   10
permit), but (1), to review those parts of the former
Conferences which relate to discipline; and (2), to settle
all things relating to the school which is now to be begun
at Kingswood.
                                                                   15
[§3] *Q.* 2. We are again pressed 'only to preach in as many places
as we can, but not to form any societies'. Shall we follow
this advice?
A. By no means. We have made the trial already. We have
preached for more than a year without forming societies   20
in a large tract of land from Newcastle to Berwick-upon-
Tweed, and almost all the seed has fallen by the wayside.
There is scarce any fruit of it remaining.

[§4] *Q.* 3. But what particular inconveniencies do you observe
when people are not formed into societies?   25
A. These, among many others:
(1) The preacher cannot give proper exhortations and
instructions to those who are convinced of sin unless he
has opportunities of meeting them apart from the
mixed, unawakened multitude.   30
(2) They cannot watch over one another in love unless
they are thus united together. Nor
(3) Can the believers build up one another and bear one
another's burdens.

[§5] *Q.* 4. Ought we not to have a larger time of probation for   35
the rich, before we admit them into our Society?
A. It seems not. But neither should we have a shorter. Let
either rich or poor stay three months.

[§6] *Q.* 5. How may we more effectually avoid respect of persons?

---

[108] Orig., 'Thursday, June 3', incorrectly.

A. (1) Let us take care to visit the poor as much as the rich. (2) Let us strictly examine our hearts, whether we are not more willing to preach to the rich than to the poor. (3) We will apply to the poor at the Chapel as often as to the rich; to the latter chiefly on Wednesday, to the former on Friday.

[§7] *Q.* 6. How often shall we permit strangers to be present at the meeting of the Society?

A. Let every other meeting of the Society, either at the Foundery, the Chapel, at Bristol, Kingswood, Newcastle, or elsewhere be inviolably kept private, no one stranger being admitted on any account or pretence whatsoever. And let public notice of this be given in every place. On the other nights we may admit them with caution.

[§8] *Q.* 7. May a relapser into gross sin, showing signs of repentance, be immediately readmitted into the Society?

A. Not till after three months. But he may be admitted on those nights wherein strangers are admitted.

[§9] *Q.* 8. Are we not apt, particularly in the Society, to make too long prayers?

A. It may be we are. There are several exceptions which deserve a particular regard. But in general we would not choose to pray above eight or ten minutes without intermission.

[§10] *Q.* 9. What can be done in order to purge and quicken the Society?

A. [1] Let us strictly examine the leaders, both with regard to their grace, their gifts, and their manner of meeting their several classes. (2) Let the preacher meet the leaders weekly before preaching at Wapping, Snowsfields, and Deptford.

[§11] *Q.* 10. If it please God to take our present ministers away, who should succeed in their place?

A. We cannot tell yet. God will make it plain whenever the time shall come.

[§12] *Friday, June [3, 1748].*[109]
Howell Harris, Samuel Larwood, James Jones, and William Shent being added, it was inquired:

---

[109] Orig., 'Friday. June 4.'

[§13]   *Q.* 1. What can be done in order to a closer union of our
          Assistants with each other?
          A. [1] Let them be deeply convinced of the want there is of
          it at present, and of the absolute necessity of it.
          (2) Let them pray that God would give them earnestly   5
          to desire it; and then that he would fulfil the desire he
          hath given.

[§14]   *Q.* 2. Ought not the ministers to have as much confidence
          as may be in those who serve it as Sons in the Gospel?
          A. It is highly expedient they should.   10

[§15]   *Q.* 3. Would it not then be well that they should be exceed-
          ing unready to be leaving any evil report con-
          cerning them?
          A. They ought not to believe it till they have seen them, or
          written to them and received an answer.   15

[§16]   *Q.* 4. Suppose one of our Assistants should be tempted to
          think evil of us, and should mention it to another; ought
          that other to mention this to us?
          A. Not if it was spoken only as a temptation. And if he
          thinks it a thing of moment, which we ought to know, still 20
          it may be best to wait a little, till he who was under that
          temptation comes to town, and then let him speak it
          himself.

[§17]   *Q.* 5. What farther advice can be given to our Assistants, in
          order to their confiding in each other?   25
          A. (1) Let them beware how they despise each other's gifts,
          and much more how they speak anything bordering
          thereon.
          (2) Let them never speak slightly of each other in any
          kind; and   30
          (3) Let them defend one another's character in every
          point to the outermost of their power.
          (4) Let them labour, in honour each to prefer the other
          to himself.[110]

[§18]   *Q.* 6. What Assistants do we now agree to receive into the 35
          work?
          A. Charles Skelton (from Ireland), David Trathen, and
          John Whitford of Cornwall, Thomas Colbeck, William

---

[110] This fourth point was not present in 1748.

Darney, and El[eazer] Webster of Yorkshire, and William Tucker.[111]

[§19]   *Q*. 7. How shall they avoid all approaches to jealousy and envy of each other?

A. Let each examine his own heart, 'Am I glad that another has greater success than me?' Do I pray that he may be more blessed than myself?

[§20]   *Q*. 8. What is popularity?

A. In cautioning you against it, we mean thereby gaining a greater degree of esteem or love from the people than it is for the glory of God.

[§21]   *Q*. 9. How can we avoid this?

A. (1) Earnestly pray for a piercing sense of the danger and sinfulness of it.

(2) Take care how you ingratiate your self too much with any people.

(3) Or how you do it at all, by slackness of discipline.

(4) Or by any method which another cannot follow.

(5) Warn the people against esteeming or loving you too much.

(6) Converse sparingly with those who are fond of you.

[§53]   *Monday, June 6 [1748]*.

The following persons being present at the Foundery: John Wesley, Charles Wesley, Charles Manning, John Jones, Thomas Maxfield, Jonathan Reeves, John Bennet, James Jones, Samuel Larwood, John Trembath, Edward Perronet, Thomas Meyrick, William Holland, William Shent, William Darney, Richard Moss, Howell Harris; with William Briggs, William Welch, Patrick Thompson (of Newcastle), stewards, it was inquired:

[§54]   *Q*. 1. How may the leaders of classes be made more useful?

A. (1) Let each of them be diligently examined concerning his method of meeting a class.

(2) Let more particular directions be given on those heads in which many of them have been wanting.

[§55]   *Q*. 2. What directions?

---

[111] §§19–21 (as given here) were not present in the original 1748 Minutes, where §§19–52, for Saturday, June 4, were devoted to Kingswood School.

A. (1) Let every leader coming into the Society room as soon as ever service[112] is ended, and there sit down and commune with God in his heart to the preacher comes in.

(2) Let no leader go out till the exhortation and the whole service are ended.   5

(3) Let none speak there but the preacher or the stewards, unless in answer to a question.

(4) Let every leader there give in a note of every sick person and of every disorderly walker in his class.

(5) Let every leader send a note to the visitor weekly of   10 every sick person.

(6) Let the leaders near Short's Gardens meet the preacher there every Monday night after preaching.

(7) Let the leaders converse with all the preachers as frequently and as freely as possible.   15

(8) In making classes, let them diligently inquire how every soul prospers. Not only how each person observes the outward *Rules*, but how they grow in the knowledge and love of God.

[§56] *Q.* 3. Can any farther expedient be found for making these   20 meetings lively and profitable to those who meet?

A. Let us try this. Let us observe, what leaders are most blessed to those entrusted to their care; and let these meet in other classes as often as possible, and see what hinders their growth in grace.   25

[§57] *Q.* 4. In the country societies, one preacher has sometimes done all which had been done by him who went before. How shall this be prevented for the time to come?

A. (1) Let it be contrived as often as may be that one should not go before another comes.   30

(2) When this cannot be, let him who leaves anyplace leave a written account of what he has done.

[§58] *Q.* 5. How may we profit more by the work of God carried on in the distant societies?

A. Let the preachers resident in each send a circumstantial   35 account to the minister at the Foundery.

First, of every remarkable conversion.

Secondly, of everyone who dies in the triumph of faith.

[§59] *Q.* 6. How are our societies divided?

---

[112] 1748: 'the sermon'.

A. Into nine divisions, thus:

 I. London, including, (1) London itself; (2) Kent and Surrey; (3) Essex; (4) Brentford; (5) Windsor; (6) Wycombe; (7) Oxford; (8) Reading; (9) Blewbury; (10) Salisbury.

 II. Bristol, including, (1) Bristol itself; (2) Kingswood; (3) Bath; (4) Bearfield; (5) The Devizes; (6) Road; (7) Coleford; (8) Oakhill; (9) Shepton Mall[et]; (10) Middle[zoy]; (11) Beercrocombe; (12) Taunton; (13) Cullompton.

 III. Cornwall, including, (1) Tavistock; (2) Plymouth Dock; (3) Trewint; (4) St. [Ewe]; (5) Gwennap; (6) St. Agnes; (7) Illogan, etc.; (8) St. Ives; (9) The Western Societies.

 IV. Ireland, including, (1) Dublin; (2) Tullamore; (3) Tyrrellspass; (4) Athlone.

 V. Wales, including, (1) Cardiff; (2) Fonmon; (3) [Llanmaes, etc.]; (4) Llantrissant.

 VI. Staffordshire, including, (1) Stroud; (2) Cirencester; (3) Stanley; (4) Evesham; (5) Wednesbury; (6) Shrewsbury; (7) Leominster.

 VII. Cheshire, including, (1) Cheshire itself; (2) Nottingham; (3) Derbyshire; (4) Lancashire; (5) Sheffield.

 VIII. Yorkshire, including, (1) Leeds; (2) Birstall; (3) Keighley; (4) Acomb; (5) Sykehouse; (6) Epworth; (7) Hainton; (8) Grimsby; (9) The Fens.

 IX. Newcastle, including, (1) Osmotherley; (2) Newcastle itself; (3) Sunderland; (4) Biddick; (5) Burnopfield; (6) Spen; (7) Swalwell; (8) Horseley; (9) Plessey; (10) Berwick-upon-Tweed.

[§60] *Q.* 7. How shall we have a more exact knowledge of the states of the societies in each division?

 A. [1] Let the preacher assisted by the steward in each Society, take an exact list of them every Easter.

 (2) Let those lists be transmitted, within three weeks after Easter, to the person appointed in each division to receive them.

 (3) Let this person at the same time diligently inform himself of the spiritual and temporal state of each Society; and

(4) Let him bring those lists with him to the following
Conference, and give an account of all.

[§61] *Q.* 8. Would it not be of use if all the societies were more
firmly and closely united together?

A. Without doubt it would be much to the glory of God, to   5
the ease of the ministers, and to the benefit of the societies
themselves, both in things spiritual and temporal.

[§62] *Q.* 9. Might not the children in every place be formed into
a little Society?

A. Let the preachers try by meeting them apart, and giving   10
them suitable exhortations.

THE REVISED DISCIPLINARY *MINUTES*, 1753–89, INTRODUCTION

The summary of organizational principles that began with the publication of the Disciplinary *Minutes* in 1749 continued to appear periodically to summarize the major policies, both old and new, over the years. Wesley recognized the necessity of consolidating Methodist organization and practice and the important role played by these publications, produced at different stages in its history: 1749, 1753, 1763, 1770, 1772 (in his *Works*), 1780, and 1789. Throughout Wesley's lifetime, these new editions, continuations of the Disciplinary *Minutes*, bore a similar title, *Minutes of Several Conversations between the Reverend Mr. John and Charles Wesley and others*, where the differential was the adjective 'several' instead of 'some late' (found on the annual *Minutes*). To this title was added, from 1780 onwards in the summary collections, the limiting years, 'from the year 1744 to the year 1780'—or '1789'.

To these successive summary editions of collected policies on organization and practice has traditionally been prefixed the description 'Large'. This word was never used in any official printed title, but Wesley had given it currency in his correspondence. Writing to his preachers about Methodist procedure, he realized that they must know to which species of *Minutes* he was referring. Thus he wrote to Zachariah Yewdall in 1782: 'Undoubtedly you are to act as Assistant; and if you carefully read the great Minutes of the Conference and keep close to them in every point, assuredly you will see the fruit of your labour.' In 1784 he wrote to John Baxendale about the 'large Minutes of the Conference'—he rarely underlined the titles of books to indicate italics, and his use of underlining here indicates emphasis of both words—'large' was simply a generic adjective, not an integral part of the official title. In writing to Charles Atmore in 1785, however, he capitalized 'Large' and did the same in 1787 in a letter to Joseph Benson.[113] Wesley therefore established a precedent for 'Large' *Minutes* as a traditional usage that recognizes both the significance of the descriptor and the accuracy of the published title.

[113] *Letters* (Telford), 7:145, 210, 296, 375.

The administration of the Methodist Societies was constantly being developed to face new difficulties and new opportunities. Wesley quickly realized that he must constantly update his handbook of discipline. The original 1749 Disciplinary *Minutes* had been divided into sections that were headed by dates in the 1740s on which those decisions (listed by Question and Anwer) had been made in Conference. In 1753, when that work was slightly revised and somewhat enlarged into a new edition of Disciplinary *Minutes*, the Questions and Answers were reorganized into a more rational arrangement, but the work retained until 1780 many of the dates as useless and confusing headings, since the entries were no longer arranged according to date.[114]

As the new editions appeared, they included more than just the collected major policy statements on organization or practice from the annual Conferences. Other memoranda comprised about half the total amount of the new material that gradually accumulated— and was occasionally discarded—in the pages of the six revised editions. These included papers that Wesley had prepared and delivered to the Conference on various themes, ideas that he had broached briefly to the members and then written up privately, even a huge extract on pastoral visitation (including material adapted from Richard Baxter's *Gildas Salvianus*), which occupied six and a half closely printed pages in the 1770 'Large' *Minutes*.[115] These six volumes, indeed, are so miscellaneous in their contents that they are exceedingly difficult to handle responsibly: various kinds of original material by Wesley are all but buried there, including interesting *obiter dicta*.

There has been one valiant attempt to publish the six revised editions after 1749 in parallel columns, covering pages 444–675 of vol. I of *Minutes of the Methodist Conferences*, published by the Wesleyan Conference Office, London, in 1862. This method inevitably entailed hundreds of blank columns, and in spite of many cross-references the reader has difficulty visualizing the outline of any one edition in its entirety. Nor can one easily (or successfully?) trace the changes from one edition to another in every piece of legislation or exhortation. That edition contains many duplications of material, sometimes with very minor variants, sometimes with none at all

---

[114] For the titles and other details of the six edns., see the Stemma below, p. 843.

[115] This material was also included in the subsequent editions of the 'Large' *Minutes* in Wesley's lifetime.

except a few printers' errors. After pondering and discussing the most practicable methods of displaying this material to the best advantage, the editors have decided first to analyse the demonstrable history of Wesley's composition of this little known *magnum opus*, and then present the last six editions in three pairs of documents.

THE REVISED *MINUTES*

The first edition of 1749 had included the discussions seriatum as they took in the various Conferences between 1744 and 1749.[116] The edition of 1753 (**A**)—though the date is not absolutely certain, no date having been provided on the publication—contains about one-third of the Questions and Answers from the 1749 Disciplinary *Minutes* (in half the number of pages—sixteen), adds some material from the intervening four years, and rearranges all the material.[117] The topics include various areas of Conference procedure, the formation of Societies; Class leaders, membership, Methodist behavior, and Wesley's preachers and their testing, training, reception, duties, and circuits.

The next edition (**B**, in 1763) follows basically the same order as 1753, and contains about one-third more material, taking the size back to thirty pages. There are a handful of omissions and a few minor changes. One minor addition was the question about God's design in Methodism. Four additions accounted for most of the added material. One was a subdivided memorandum on the means of grace (see §40.1 and following), appended to the question on watching over the preaching Helpers.[118] Another (§57) was a moving and lengthy appeal for Kingswood School, which Wesley instructed his Assistants—in the technical sense, that is, as circuit superintendents—to read annually in every Society. The third (§67) was a section on building, into which Wesley inserted the full text of his Model Deed. And the last was a seven–part plan (§72) to form a General Fund to liquidate building debts and recruit preachers, with a detailed scheme for raising the money.

---

[116] See discussion in the introduction to that material, above.

[117] Especially from the Conferences in November 1749 (about a half dozen) and May 1753 (nearly a dozen, including the last four, listed under 1749).

[118] (In the A edition, these had been termed, apparently in a generic nontechnical sense, 'Assistants'.)

When Wesley turned sixty, in 1763, he began to enlist his preachers to help him in reviewing his many publications, having in mind a collected edition of his *Works*.[119] Throughout the latter half of this decade, he continued to produce new documents to this end. The developments leading up to the publication of first annual *Minutes* (1765) have an important role in the development of the subsequent *'Large' Minutes*. After the 1766 Conference, Wesley wrote down several matters while they were fresh in his mind, and while there remained on hand a few preachers for possible reference. When he returned to London, he prepared some additional documents on themes that had probably been touched on in their conversations, but that only he could develop adequately and only at leisure. He prepared one under the title, 'Are we not Dissenters?' (C42), and another replying to some preachers' critical murmurings about the unchecked power that he exercised over people and preachers (C77). He also wrote a pastoral letter to the Methodist people (C17.1) that contained a lengthy extract on pastoral visitation from Richard Baxter (C17.2–12). This material swelled the 1766 *Minutes* from seven to twenty-four pages. In 1769, he also wrote a paper (read to the Conference in August) on the future of Methodism after his death, ending with a challenge to the preachers present to devote themselves altogether to God, to 'preach the old Methodist doctrines, contained in the *Minutes* of the Conferences', and 'to observe and enforce the whole Methodist discipline, laid down in the said *Minutes*'. All these major new documents eventually found their way into the 1770 'Large' *Minutes*, along with other memoranda prepared during the intervening years. The printed annual *Minutes* in 1769 closed with the following statement: 'The preachers then desired Mr. W. to extract the most material part of the *Minutes*, and send a copy to each Assistant, which he might communicate to all the preachers in his circuit, to be seriously considered.' Thus it was the preachers themselves who pushed Wesley into preparing in 1770 yet another revision of the 'Large' *Minutes* (**C**).

A major feature of the 1770 'Large' *Minutes* was a revision of the format. Wesley had long placed importance on the 'honest art' of logical reasoning, and his reordering of the literary units of the 1763 edition for that of 1770 exhibit in some detail the principles entailed. Almost nothing remained in the same relative position in 1770—sixteen questions were omitted and the retained material was largely

---

[119] Launched in 1771; see Dec. 1, 1763, *Journal & Diaries*, 21:439 in this edn.

rearranged. And so many diverse and lengthy documents were added that the net result was to double the thirty pages of 1763 to sixty in 1770. Among the documents that Wesley incorporated was a statement 'Take heed to your doctrine', which claimed that the Arminian-Calvinist disputes for thirty years had been mainly *'about words'*—a claim that only helped to perpetuate the controversy, which dragged on for years.

Much of the logic behind the realignment of old units and the disposition of new units can readily be recognized, such as the taking over of 'Are we not Dissenters?' from the 1766 *Minutes* to follow two passages on attending the Church, which had been transferred from a section on miscellaneous advice to Assistants. Many of his allocations remain puzzling, however, and his 'cut and paste' approach to the material, which still included some 1740s entries, resulted in such terms as 'Helper' (or preacher in general) being confused with 'Assistant', the latter being used in most post-1749 documents to designate 'that preacher in each circuit who is appointed from time to time to take charge of the Societies and the other preachers therein'.

The 1772 edition of the 'Large' *Minutes* (D) was published as part of his collected *Works* in the preconceived ordering of vol. 15. This volume incorporated also other major publications dealing with the history of Methodism. Only three minor revisions were made in the 1770 text, which were in the composition of the Preachers' Fund Committee (61.14), the numbering of the circuits (63.1), and the 1771 decision to change the annual subscription to the General Fund to a weekly one (74.7). By 1772, then, there are two pairs of revised editions: (1) the first revision (A) as a basis for its fuller successor (B), with a similar format, and (2) the third revision (C), much fuller in size and then reproduced in the collected *Works* (D).

A similar pairing—probably felicitous from the point of view of the scholar—took place with the fifth and sixth revisions. In 1780, Wesley produced what might be called the definitive edition of the 'Large' *Minutes* (E), which became the foundation for American Methodism,[120] formulated when British Methodism had not only matured in polity but also grown immensely in size. The fifty-two-page revision was somewhat smaller than that of 1770, with its sixty pages, mainly because there was so little new text, though there was

---

[120] See Robert E. Cushman, *John Wesley's Experimental Divinity: Studies in Methodist Doctrinal Standards* (Nashville: Kingswood Books, 1989), 157–62.

much revision and rearrangement of older material and much abridgement of routine details. One major new provision made by the 1780 Conference, written into *Q*. 2 of the 1780 'Large' *Minutes*, extended the four-day Conference to nine days, so that there was more opportunity to move from administrative routine into lengthy conversations on 'the work of God'.[121] The 1789 'Large' *Minutes* (F) were largely an echo of 1780, almost (as that of 1772 was to 1770). Though it is noteworthy that Wesley tends to tighten the screws of his discipline against those preachers who showed any slackness, or undue ambition, or lack of loyalty to the Church of England.

Despite their diversity, there was continuity in the seven editions from 1749 to 1789. Each revision entailed some changes from its predecessor, but the major changes after the rearrangements of 1753 were undoubtedly between the successive pairs, **AB** (1753–63), **CD** (1770–72), and **EF** (1780–89). Each, and especially each pair, served and reflected its own period, while at the same time introducing distinctive steps in a complex development. Each pair presented a contemporary selection of representative documents in a slightly different order, the actual contents changing with each edition, but especially between the pairs. Some items were continued throughout most of the series, some were dropped at an early stage, and other new ones were added for varying periods, sometimes for no apparent reason. Many of the documents can be shown to be extracts from specific manuscript or annual or Irish *Minutes*, but many are the original compositions of Wesley himself, appearing nowhere else.

The cumulative effect is to show the development of Wesley's views about the Methodist Societies and their organization over some forty years. The individual entries, however, relate to some hundreds of themes specific to some particular time and place. Because so many of the extracts come from identifiable passages in the *Minutes* already presented, few footnotes are included, but editorial notes that do appear in the text are always enclosed within square brackets. The general index to the volume will incorporate references to persons, places, and subjects within these 'Large' *Minutes*.

In reproducing the text, the best method of displaying this material seemed to be in the chronological order of the appearance of each of its pairs of revised editions, **AB, CD,** and **EF.** The 1753 document is set out in full and then the new material from 1763 is inserted into it. The order of the 1763 'Large' *Minutes* supercedes

---

[121] Examples of this approach are seen in *QQ*. 55–58.

that of 1753—though it should be noted that neither of these two editions actually numbers its basic questions, as do the following four. The whole numbers of the entries represent numbers assigned to the successive questions either by the editor (**A–B**) or by Wesley (**C–F**); the subsidiary numbers after decimal points are sometimes added arbitrarily by the editor or follow Wesley's own sub-sections. In a similar manner, the new material (only) in the 1770 document is printed in *its* order, linking with it the few 1772 revisions. Last, the new 1780 material is presented in its own order, interweaving with it the few 1789 revisions. Throughout, cross-references to earlier passages are incorporated in the appropriate order. Important variants are noted, but not printers' errors or merely stylistic differences.

For all the substantive material, new and old, in all three pairs of editions, we offer an 'Analytical Summary; Disciplinary *Minutes*, 1749–89'. It identifies some 140 textual units by an individual title and the specific number in the editions where they first appear. Immediately after each title appears its source in this volume where this is known. Here the last two digits indicate the year and the reference point in that year, which is not the number of Wesley's original question—for he often incorporated a separate sequence of numbers for each day of a Conference—but the marginal numbers added in this edition of the *Minutes* within square brackets, which bypass Wesley's confusing numbering. The last column indicates the various editions of the 'Large' *Minutes* and the number of the question incorporating that unit within each edition. The dates of many actual *sources* of the units differ greatly from the dates and positions of their placing in the 'Large' *Minutes*.

To identify the many categories of Wesley's printed sources used in this volume, the following brief codes are used: **AM**, American *Minutes*; **AN**, Annual *Minutes*; **DI**, Disciplinary *Minutes*; **DO**, Doctrinal *Minutes*; **IM**, Irish *Minutes*; and **LA**, 'Large' *Minutes*. The distinctive year may readily be identified by its last two digits, 44, 49, 53, and so on.

F. B.

The Editions of John Wesley's
Disciplinary *Minutes*: A Stemma

See *Bibliography*, Nos. 200–202, 334.15, 203–204.

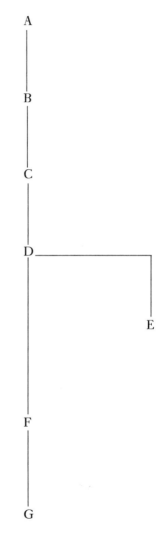

A. *Minutes of Some Late Conversations, Between the Revd Mr. Wesleys, and Others.* Dublin: S. Powell, 1749.

B. *Minutes of Several Conversations Between the Reverend Mr. John and Charles Wesley, and Others.* [London, n.p., 1753]

C. *Minutes of Several Conversations Between the Rev. Mr. John and Charles Wesley, and Others.* London, 1763.

D. *Minutes of Several Conversations Between the Reverend Messieurs John and Charles Wesley, and Others.* London, 1770.

E. *Minutes or Several Conversations, Between the Reverend Messieurs John and Charles Wesley, and Others.* [Works, vol. 15 (Bristol: Pine, 1772), pp. 277–358]

F. *Minutes of Several Conversations Between The Reverend Mr. John and Charles Wesley, and Others. From the Year 1744, to the year 1780.* [London: J. Paramore, 1780]

G. *Minutes of Several Conversations Between The Rev. Mr. Wesley, and Others. From the Year 1744, to the Year 1789.* London: For the Author. 1789.

1. The 'Large' *Minutes*, A and B (1753, 1763)[122]

MINUTES OF SEVERAL CONVERSATIONS
between the Reverend Mr. John and
Charles Wesley, and Others.

5   June 25, 1744.[123]

[§0.1] It is desired that all things be considered as in the immediate presence of God.

[§0.2] That we may meet with a single eye, and as little children who have everything to learn.

10   That every point which is proposed may be examined to the foundation.

[§0.3] That every person may speak freely whatever is in his heart, and

[§0.4] That every question which may arise should be thoroughly

15   debated and settled.

[§0.5] *Q.* Need we be fearful of doing this? What are we afraid of? Of overturning our first principles?]

A. If they are false, the sooner they are overturned the better. If they are true, they will bear the strictest examina-

20   tion. [CD add 'Meantime'] Let us all pray for a willingness to receive light, to know of every doctrine whether it be of God.

---

[122] The basic text here, in regular roman type, is that of the 'Large' *Minutes*, edn. **A** (undated, but c.1753, which is a revision of the first edition, the Disciplinary *Minutes* of 1749). Into that text are inserted (in **bold** type) revisions and additions from edn. **B** (1763). The reference numbers in the left margin are not present in the original, but are based on the succession of *Q.* and *A.* given in the text of **A** (1753). The numbering of the insertions from **B** (1763) is subsidiary and indicated by decimals. It would be impracticable to import into this **A/B** numbering pattern the much more detailed and varied numbering schemes of editions **C/D** (1770/1772) and **E/F** (1780/1789), which will stand on their own in succeeding sections. Comparisons among the six revised editions can be seen in the right-hand column of the analysis at the end of this section.

[123] The inserted dates are vestigial remnants from JW's published *Minutes* of 1749, and are irrelevant to most of the text that follows them, even those sections that are from 1749 (see analysis at end of this section).

[§1] *Q.* How may the time of this conference be made more
eminently a time of watching unto prayer?
A. 1. While we are conversing, let us have an especial care
to set God always before us.
2. In the intermediate hours let us visit none but the   5
sick, and spend all the time that remains in retirement.
3. Let us then give ourselves to prayer for one another,
and for a blessing upon this our labour.

[§2] *Q.* How far does each of us agree to submit to the judgment
of the majority?   10
A. In[124] speculative things, each can only submit so far as
his judgment shall be convinced.
In every practical point, each will submit so far as he can
without wounding his conscience.

[§3] *Q.* Can a Christian submit any farther than this to any man   15
or number of men upon earth?
A. It is undeniable [orig., 'undeniably'; CD, 'plain'] he cannot; either to Council, Bishop, or Convocation. And this is
that grand principle of private judgment, on which all the
Reformers proceeded: 'Every man must judge for himself;   20
because every man must give an account for himself to
God.'

June 28, etc.[125]
[B, 1763]   25
[§4] ***Q.* What may we reasonably believe to be God's
design in raising up the preachers called
'Methodists'?**
***A.* To reform the nation, and in particular the
Church, to spread scriptural holiness over the land.**   30
[A, 1753]
[§5] *Q.* Is it advisable only to preach in as many places as we
can, without forming any societies?
A. By no means. We have made the trial in various places,
and that for a considerable time. And all the seed has fallen   35
as by the way-side. There is scarce any fruit of it remaining.

---

[124] Dixon MS adds 'all'.

[125] The inserted dates are vestigial remnants from JW's published *Minutes* of
1749, and are irrelevant to most of the text that follows them, even those sections
that are from 1749 (see note at §59 and the analysis at the end of this section).

[§6]   *Q.* But what particular inconveniences do you observe
when societies are not formed?

A. These among many others: 1. The preacher cannot give
proper instructions and exhortations to them that are

5   convinced of sin. 2. They cannot watch over one another
in love. Nor 3, can the believers bear one another's burdens, and build up each other in faith and holiness.

[§7]   *Q.* Where should we endeavour to preach most?

A. 1. Where we [**B, 1763, adds '(clergymen)'**] can preach

10   in a Church. 2. Where there is the greatest number of
quiet and willing hearers. 3. Where there is most fruit.

[§8]   *Q.* Is field preaching then unlawful?

A. We conceive not. We do not know that it is contrary to
any law, either of God or man.

15 [§9]   *Q.* Have we not used it too sparingly?

A. It seems we have. 1. Because our call is, to save that
which is lost. Now we cannot expect such to seek us.
Therefore we should go and seek them. 2. Because we are
particularly called, by going into the highways and hedges

20   (which none else will) to compel them to come in. 3. Because that reason against it is not good, 'The house will
hold all that come.' The house may hold all that come to
the house, but not all that *would come* to the field.

25   **[B, 1763]**

[§9.1] **The greatest hindrances to this you are to expect
from the rich, or cowardly, or lazy Methodists. But
regard them not, neither stewards, leaders, nor people. Whenever the weather will permit, go out in**

30   **God's name into the most public places, and call all
to 'repent and believe the gospel'. Every Assistant at
least, in every circuit, should endeavour to preach
abroad every Sunday. Especially in the old societies,
lest they settle upon their lees.**

35   **[A, 1753]**

[§10]   *Q.* Ought we not diligently to observe in what places
God is pleased at any time to pour out his Spirit more
abundantly?

A. We ought, and at that time to send more labourers than

40   usual into that part of the harvest.

[§11]   *Q.* What is a sufficient call to a new place?

A. 1. An invitation from a serious man, fearing God, who
has an house to receive us. 2. A probability of doing more
good by going thither than by staying longer where we
are.

[§12] *Q*. How often shall we permit strangers to be present at the   5
meeting of the Society?

A. Let every other meeting of the Society, in every place,
be strictly private; no one stranger being admitted on any
account or pretence whatsoever. On the other nights we
may admit them with cautions, but not the same persons   10

[§12.1] above twice or thrice. [**B, 1763**] **In order to this, see
that all in every place show their tickets before they
come in. If the stewards and leaders are not exact
and impartial herein, employ others which have
more resolution.**   15

[A, 1753]

[§13] *Q*. May a relapser into gross sin, confessing his fault, be readmitted into the Society?

A. Not as a member, till after three months; but he may be
permitted to stay as a stranger.   20

[§14] *Q*. How may the leaders of classes be made more useful?

A. 1. Let each of them be diligently examined concerning
his method of meeting a class.

[§14.1] 2. Let us recommend to all the following Directions.

(1) Let each leader carefully inquire how every soul in   25
his class prospers. Not only how each person observes
the outward rules, but how he grows in the knowledge
and love of God.

(2) Let the leaders converse with all the preachers as
frequently and as freely as possible.   30

(3) Let every leader come into the room on Tuesday,
as soon as the service is ended, and then sit down, and
commune with God in his heart till the preacher
comes in.

(4) ['3'] Let no leader go out till the preacher goes.   35

(5) ['4'] Let none speak there but the preacher or the
stewards, unless in answer to a question.

(6) ['5'] Let every leader bring a note of every sick
person in his class.

(7) ['6'] Let every leader send the same note to the   40
visitor of the sick weekly.

[§15]   *Q.* Can anything further be done to make the meetings of
the classes lively and profitable?

[§15.1]*A.* 1. Let the leaders frequently meet each other's classes.

[§15.2]   2. Let us observe which leaders are most blest to those
5   under their care.

And let these meet in other classes as often as possible, and
see what hinders their growth in grace.

[§16]   *Q.* How can we further assist those [**B, 1763,** 'these'] under
your care?

10 [§16.1]*A.* 1. By examining them more closely at the General
Meeting of the classes.

[§16.2]   2. By then meeting these [**B, 1763,** 'those'] who are in
bands every morning before the rest: and examining
them both ['**as**', **supplied in B, 1763**] to their inward
15   state and their observance of the *Rules.*

[§16.3]   3. By meeting the married men and married women
apart, the first Wednesday and Sunday after every
Visitation: the single men and single women apart on
the second Wednesday and Sunday.

20 [§16.4]   4. By examining and instructing them at their own
houses, at times set apart for that purpose.

[**B, 1763**]

[§16.5]   **This has never been effectually done yet; though
25   Tho. Walsh took some steps therein. Who will take
up that cross? It will be of great use to others, and a
blessing to his own soul.**

**Do all you can herein, if not all you would. In-
quire in each house, Have you family prayer? Do
30   you read the Scripture in your family? Have you a
fixed time for private prayer? Examine each as to
his growth in grace, and discharge of relative
duties.**

[A, 1753]

35 [§17]   *Q.* How shall we prevent improper persons from insinuat-
ing themselves into the Society?

1. Give tickets to none till they are recommended by a
leader with whom they have met three months on a trial.

2. Give notes to none but those who are recommended
40   by a leader with whom they have met three or four
times.

3. Give them the *Rules* the first time they meet.

[§18] *Q.* How can we add a proper solemnity to the admission of new members?

A. 1. In all large towns, admit new members into the bands only at the Quarterly Love-feast following the Visitation. 5
2. Read the names of the men to be admitted to the men bands, of the women to the women bands, the week before. 3. Admit into the Society only on the Sunday following the Quarterly Visitation. 4. Read the names of those to be admitted on the Sunday evening before. 10
5. Then also let the names of those be read who are excluded from the Society.

[B, 1763]

[§18.1]*Q.* **Should we insist everywhere on the Band Rules? Particularly that relating to ruffles?** 15

A. **By all means. This is no time to give any encouragement to superfluity of apparel. Therefore give no band-tickets to any in England or Ireland till they have left them off.**

In order to this, 1. Read in every Society the 20
thoughts concerning dress. 2. In visiting the classes be very mild, but very strict. 3. Allow no exempt case, not even of a married woman: better one suffer than many.

To encourage meeting in band. 1. In every large 25
Society have a love-feast quarterly for the bands only. 2. Never fail to meet them apart from the Society, once a week. 3. Exhort all believers to embrace the advantage. 4. Give a band-ticket to none till they have met a quarter on trial. 30

[A, 1753]

[§19] *Q.* Might not the children in every place be formed in to a little Society?

[*A.*] Let the preachers try, by meeting them together, and giving them suitable exhortations. 35

[B, 1763]

[§19.1][1.] **At each meeting we may first set them a lesson in the 'Instructions' or 'Tokens for Children'.**
2. Hear them repeat it. 3. Explain it to them in an easy, familiar manner. 4. Often ask, 'What have I 40
been saying?' And strive to fasten it on their hearts.

[A, 1753]

[§20]   *Q.* Do we observe any evil which has lately prevailed among
our societies?

A. Many of our members have lately married with unbelievers, even such as were wholly unawakened. And this
has been attended with fatal consequences. Few of these
have gained the unbelieving wife or husband. Generally
they have themselves either had an heavy cross for life, or
have entirely fallen back into the world.

[§21]   *Q.* What can be done to put a stop to this?

A. 1. Let every preacher take occasion publicly to enforce
the Apostle's caution, 'Be ye not unequally yoked with
unbelievers.'

2. Let it be openly declared in every place that he who
acts contrary to this will be expelled the Society.

3. When any such is expelled, let an exhortation be subjoined, dissuading others from following that bad example.

[§21.1]   4. And let all be advised [B, 1763, 'exhorted'] to take no
step in so weighty a matter without first advising with
the most serious of his brethren.

[B, 1763]

[§21.2]*Q.* **Ought any woman to marry without the consent
of her parents?**

A. **In general she ought not. Yet there may be an
exception. For if, 1, a woman be under a necessity of
marrying; if, 2, her parents absolutely refuse to let
her marry any Christian: then she may, nay ought
to marry without their consent. Yet even then a
Methodist preacher ought not to marry her.**

[A, 1753]

[§22]   *Q.* Doth [B, 1763, 'Do'] not sabbath-breaking, dram-
drinking, evil-speaking, unprofitable conversation, lightness, gaiety, or expensiveness of apparel, and contracting
debts without sufficient care to discharge them, still prevail in several places? What method can we take to remove
these evils?

[§22.1]*A.* 1. Let us preach expressly and strongly on each of these
heads. [B, 1763, adds, '**2. Read the sermon upon
evil-speaking in every society.' and adjusts the
numbering of the next three items.**] 2. Let the leaders

closely examine and exhort every person to put away the accursed thing. 3. Let the preachers warn the society in every place that none who is hereafter guilty can remain with us. 4. In order to give them clearer views of the evil of these things, let every preacher recommend to every   5
society, and that frequently and earnestly, the reading the books we have published preferable to any other. And when any new book is sent to any place, let him speak of it in the public congregation.

[B, 1763]   10

[§22.2]   **6. Extirpate smuggling, buying or selling uncustomed goods, out of every Society, particularly in
Cornwall, and in all seaport towns. Let no person
remain with us which will not totally abstain from
every kind and degree of it. 7. Extirpate bribery,**   15
**receiving anything, directly or indirectly, for voting
in any election. Show no respect of persons herein,
but expel all who touch the accursed thing. Let this
be particularly observed at Grimsby and St. Ives.**
[A, 1753]   20
June 29, etc.[126]

[§23]   *Q.* What is the office of a Christian Minister?
        A. To watch over souls, as he that must give an account.

[§24]   *Q.* What does St. James mean by respect of persons?   25
        A. The regarding one person more than another on account
        of some outward circumstances, particularly riches.

[§25]   *Q.* Have we not fallen into this, 1. By spending more of our
        time with the rich than with the poor? 2. By not speaking
        so plain and home to them? And 3. By suffering them to   30
        be present at the Love-feasts?
        A. These are palpable instances of respect of persons. We
        will endeavour to avoid them for the time to come.

[§26]   *Q.* Would it not be well for the Minister in town to visit the
        sick on Monday, Thursday, Friday, and Saturday? **[B,**   35
        **1763, alters to read 'Would it not be well for every
        preacher in town to visit the sick constantly?']**

---

[126] The inserted dates are vestigial remnants from JW's published *Minutes* of 1749, and are irrelevant to most of the text that follows them, even those sections that are from 1749 (see analysis at end of this section).

A. No time could be employed more profitably, either for them or us.

[§27] *Q.* Do we not slide insensibly into taking state up on ourselves? Or lording it over God's heritage?

A. We hope not. But there is continual danger. Therefore we cannot be too jealous lest we should. And we will thank any who warn us against it.

[B, 1763, substitutes for the previous question the following:]

[§27.1][*Q.* **How may we be most useful herein?**

[*A.* **1. Examine carefully what state the sick is in.**

2. Instruct, reprove, or exhort accordingly.]

[A, 1753]

[§28] *Q.* How shall we be more easy of access?

A. Speak to any that desire it every day after preaching, morning and evening.

[B, 1763, omits the following two questions and answers:]

[§29] *Q.* Have we borne a sufficient testimony to the truth? Particularly when attacked by the clergy?

A. Perhaps not. We have generally been content with standing on the defensive.

[§30] *Q.* How shall we act in this case for the time to come?

A. Not only refute, but retort the charge. Their mouths must be stopped (only in meekness and love) and the eyes of others opened.

[§31] *Q.* Is it expedient for us to converse more with the clergy?

A. When any of them desire it.

[§32] *Q.* With our chief opposers and persecutors?

A. It may do good, 1. When they make any overtures toward it. 2. When any of them will converse with us in private.

[§33] *Q.* National sins call aloud for national judgments. What can we do to prevent them?

A. The first week in every month (at least) speak expressly on this head, and insist on the necessity of a general repentance, to prevent a general visitation.

[§34] *Q.* Should we talk of persecution before it comes?

A. To talk or think before of any particular persecution only weakens our hands. And how long the general persecution may be deferred, God only knows.

[§35] *Q.* In what view may we and our helpers be considered?
    A. Perhaps as extraordinary messengers, designed by God
    to provoke others to jealousy.
[§36] *Q.* What is the office of an helper?
    A. In the absence of a Minister to feed and guide the flock. 5
    In particular,
        1. To expound every morning and evening.
        2. To meet the United Society, the Bands, the Select
        Society, and the Penitents every week.
        3. To receive On Trial for the Society and the Bands, 10
        and to put the disorderly back On Trial.
        4. To meet the leaders of the bands and classes weekly,
        and the stewards, and to overlook their accounts.
                    [B, 1763]
[§36.1] **Let every preacher be particularly exact in the morn-** 15
    ing preaching, and meeting the leaders.
                    [A, 1753]
[§37] *Q.* What are the Rules of an Helper?
    A. 1. Be diligent. Never be unemployed a moment. Never be
    triflingly employed. Never while away time; neither spend 20
    any more time at any place than is strictly necessary.
        2. Be serious. Let your motto be, Holiness to the Lord.
    Avoid all lightness, jesting, and foolish talking.
        3. Converse sparingly and cautiously with women, par-
    ticularly with young women in private. 25
        4. Take no step toward marriage without acquainting us
    with your design, **[B, 1763, omits the following:]** as
    soon as you conveniently can.
        5. Believe evil of no one. Unless you see it done, take
    heed how you credit it. Put the best construction on 30
    everything. You know the Judge is always supposed to be
    on the prisoner's side.
        6. Speak evil of no one. Else *your* word especially would
    eat as doth a canker. Keep your thoughts within your
    own breast till you come to the person concerned. 35
        7. Tell everyone what you think wrong in him, and that
    plainly, and as soon as may be, else it will fester in your
    heart. Make all haste to cast the fire out of your bosom.
        8. Don't affect the gentleman. You have no more to do
    with this character than with that of a dancing-master. A 40
    preacher of the gospel is the servant of all.

9. Be ashamed of nothing but sin: not of fetching wood (if time permit) or drawing water; not of cleaning your own shoes, or your neighbour's.

10. Be punctual. Do everything exactly at the time. And in general, do not *mend* our *Rules*, but keep them; not for wrath, but for conscience' sake.

11. You have nothing to do but to save souls. Therefore spend and be spent in this work. And go always, not only to those who want you, but to those who want you most.

12. Act in all things, not according to your own will, but as a son in the gospel. As such it is your part to employ your time in the manner which we direct: partly in preaching, and visiting the flock from house to house; partly in reading, meditation, and prayer. Above all, if you labour with us in our Lord's vineyard, it is needful you should do *that part* of the work which we advise, at those *times* and places which we judge most for his glory.

[§38]   *Q.* What general method of employing our time would you advise us to?

A. We advise you, 1. As often as possible to rise at four.

2. From four to five in the morning, and from five to six in the evening, to meditate and pray, partly to read the Scriptures, [**B, 1763, reads 'to meditate, pray, and read, partly the Scriptures, with the *Notes* on the New Testament, partly Kempis and the *Instructions for Children*, and . . .'**], and partly the closely practical parts of the *Christian Library*. 3. From six in the morning till twelve (allowing an hour for breakfast) to read in order, with much prayer, Bishop Pearson on the Creed, Mr. Boehm's and Nalson's sermons, the remaining parts of the *Christian Library*, our other tracts and poems, *Paradise Lost*, and Professor Franck's works.

[§39]   *Q.* How may we be more useful in conversation?

1. Fix the end of each conversation before you begin. 2. Watch and pray during the time. 3. Spend two or three minutes every hour in earnest prayer. 4. Strictly observe the morning and evening hour of retirement.

[B, 1763]

[§39.1] 5. Rarely spend above an hour at a time in conversing with anyone. 6. Earnestly recommend the five
o'clock hour to all.

5

[A, 1753]

[§40] *Q*. Do we sufficiently watch over our Helpers?
    A. We might consider those that are with us as our pupils,
in to whose behaviour and studies we should therefore
make a particular inquiry every day.

10

    Should we not particularly ask each, Do you walk close
with God? Have you now fellowship with the Father and
the Son? At what hour do you rise? Do you punctually
observe the morning and evening hour of retirement? Do
you spend the day in the manner which we advise? Do

15

you read the books we advise, and no other? Do you fast
as often as your health will permit? Do you converse seriously, usefully, and closely? Do you pray before, and have
you a determinate end in, every conversation?

[B, 1763]

20

[§40.1] To be more particular:
    **Do you use all the means of grace yourself, and
enforce the use of them on all persons?
They are either Instituted or Prudential.**

I. The Instituted are,

25

    **1. Prayer: private, family, public; consisting
of deprecation, petition, intercession,
thanksgiving.**

      **Do you use each of these constantly (at set
times) and fervently?**

30

      **Do you use private prayer every morning and
evening? If you are your own master, at five in
the evening, and the hour before or after morning preaching?**

      Do you forecast wherever you are, how to secure

35

      these hours?

      Do you avow it everywhere?

      Are you resolute herein?

      **Do you ask everywhere, 1. Have you family
prayer? 2. Do you retire at five 'clock?**

40

[§40.2]   2. Searching the Scripture, by
(1) Reading: *constantly*, some part of everyday,
and at all vacant hours; *regularly*, all the New
Testament (at least) and the *Lessons for Children*
in order; *carefully*, with the *Notes, seriously, delib-*
erately, with much prayer preceding, accompanying, and following; *fruitfully*, immediately
practising what you learn there?
    What other books do you read? Is it wise to
read any till you have read our tracts, and the
Christian Library?
    Do you give the morning to reading, writing,
and prayer?
(2) Meditating. At set times? How? by Bishop
Hall's or Mr. Baxter's rule? How long?
(3) Hearing. Constantly? Every morning?
Humbly? Uncritically, devoutly? Carefully?
With prayer before, at, after? Fruitfully?
Immediately putting in practice? Have you a
New Testament always in your pocket?
(See that the *Notes* are in every Society. Explain
them to the congregation.)

[§40.3]   3. The Lord's Supper. Do you use this
At every opportunity? With due preparation? i.e.
with solemn prayer? with careful self-examination?
With deep repentance suited thereto? With
earnest and deliberate self-devotion?
    Do you in communicating discern the Lord's
Body?
    Do you afterward retire, not formally, but in
earnest?

[§40.4]   4. Fasting. God led us to this at Oxford. And he led
all of you to it when you first set out.
How often do you fast now? Every Friday? In
what degree?
I purpose generally to eat only vegetables on
Friday, and take only toast and water in the
morning.

[§40.5]   5. Christian Conference.
Are we convinced how important and how difficult it is to order our conversation right?

Is it always *in grace*? Seasoned with salt? Meet to
minister grace to the hearers?

Do we not converse too long at a time? Is not an
hour at a time commonly enough?

Would it not be well to plan our conversation   5
beforehand? To pray before and after it?

[§40.6] II. Prudential means we may use either as Common
Christians, as Methodists, as Preachers, or as
Assistants.

  1. As common Christians. What particular rules   10
  have you, for avoiding evil, doing good? Growing
  in grace? What arts of holy living?

  2. As Methodists. Do you never miss any meeting
  of the society? Neither your class or band?

  3. As Preachers. Do you meet every society weekly?   15
  Also the leaders? And bands, if any?

  Do you visit the sick? And the well? Instructing
  masters and parents? And in all relative duties?

  4. As Assistants. Do you fill up and regulate the
  bands wherever you come? Diligently inquire into   20
  the state of the books, and do all you can to propa-
  gate them? Keep watch-nights once a month? And
  love-feasts? With one twice a year for all the society?

  Do you visit every society once a quarter, and reg-   25
  ulate all things therein?

  Do you take a regular catalogue of your societies
  at least once a year?

  Do you write me an account of all the defects of
  the common preachers which you cannot yourself   30
  cure?

[§40.7] [III.] These means may be used without fruit. But
there are some means which cannot. Namely,
watching, denying ourselves, taking up our cross,
exercise of the presence of God.   35

  1. Do we steadily watch against the world, the
  devil, ourselves? The besetting sin?

  2. Do you deny yourselves every useless pleasure
  of sense? Imagination? Honour? Are you temperate in all things? To take one instance, in food?   40

Do you use only that *kind* and that *degree* which is
best both for the body and soul? Do you see the
necessity of this?
Do you eat no flesh suppers? No late suppers?
These naturally tend to destroy bodily health.
Do you eat only three meals a day? If four, are you
not an excellent pattern to the flock?
Do you take no more food than is necessary at
each meal? You may know if you do by a load at
your stomach; by drowsiness, or heaviness; and in
a while by weak or bad nerves.
Do you use only that *kind* and that *degree* of drink
which is best both for your body and soul?
Do *you* drink water? Why not? Did you ever? Why
did you leave it off? If not for health, when will
you begin again? Today?
How often do you drink wine or ale? Every day? Do
you *want* or *waste* it?
3. Wherein do you 'take up your cross' daily? Do
you cheerfully 'bear your cross' (whatever is grievous to nature) as a gift of God, and labour to profit
thereby?
4. Do you endeavour to set God always before you?
To see his eye continually fixed upon you? Never
can you use these means but a blessing will ensue.
And the more you use them, the more will you
grow in grace, and in the knowledge of our Lord
Jesus Christ.

[A, 1753]

[§41]   *Q.* What can be done in order to a closer union of our
Helpers with each other?
A. 1. Let them be deeply convinced of the want there is of
it at present, and the absolute necessity of it.
2. Let them pray for an earnest desire of union.
3. Let them speak freely to each other.
4. When they meet, let them never part without prayer.
5. Let them beware how they despise each other's gifts.
6. Let them never speak slightingly of each other in any
kind.

7. Let them defend one another's character in everything, to the utmost of their power, and

8. Let them labour in honour, each to prefer the other before himself.

[§42] *Q*. How shall we avoid popularity? We mean such esteem or love from the people as is not for the glory of God?

A. 1. Earnestly pray for a piercing sense of the danger there is, and the sinfulness of it.

2. Take care how you ingratiate yourself with any people by slackness of discipline;

3. Or by any method which another preacher cannot follow.

4. Warn the people among whom you are most of esteeming or loving you too much.

5. Converse sparingly with those who are particularly fond of you.

[§43] *Q*. How often should our Helpers preach?

A. Not more than twice a day, unless on a Sunday or some extraordinary occasion.

[§44] *Q*. Which is the best general method of preaching?

A. 1. To invite. 2. To convince. 3. To offer Christ. 4. To build up: and to do this in some measure in every sermon.

[§45] *Q*. Are there any smaller advices relating to preaching which might be of use to us?

A. Perhaps these: 1. Be sure to begin and end precisely at the time appointed.

2. Endeavour to be serious, weighty, and solemn in your whole deportment before the congregation.

3. Always suit your subject to the audience.

4. Choose the plainest texts you can.

5. Take care not to ramble from your text, but keep close to it, and make out from it what you take in hand.

6. Beware of allegorizing or spiritualizing too much.

7. Take care of anything awkward or affected, either in your phrase, gesture, or pronunciation.

8. Tell each other if you observe anything of this kind.

9. Sing no hymns of your own composing.

10. Without a pressing reason, do not pray above eight or ten minutes (at most) without intermission.

[B, 1763]

[§45.1] **11. It would be well for every young preacher frequently to exhort, without taking any text. And for
everyone, young or old, frequently to read and
enlarge upon a portion of the *Notes*.**

[A, 1753]

[§46] *Q.* What sermons do we find by experience to be attended
with the greatest blessing?
A. 1. Such as are most close, convincing, searching.
2. Such as have most of Christ. 3. Such as urge the
heinousness of men's living in contempt or ignorance
of him.

[§47] *Q.* But have not some of us been led off from practical
preaching by (what was called) *preaching Christ*?
A. Indeed we have. The most effectual way of preaching
Christ is to preach him in all his offices, and to declare his
law as well as his gospel, both to believers and unbelievers.

[§48] *Q.* Do we now all preach strongly and closely concerning
both inward and outward holiness?
A. It would be well if we were more frequently and more
largely to insist upon it in all its branches.

[§49] *Q.* Do we insist enough upon practical religion in general?
And in particular on relative duties? Using the means of
grace? Private prayer? Self-denial? Fasting? Seriousness?
A. It seems most of us have been wanting here. Let us take
care to supply this defect for the future.

[§50] *Q.* How shall we be assured that no preacher will ever disappoint a congregation?
A. Ask every one, 1. Do you see the great sin and fatal consequences of it? 2. Will you break a limb rather than wilfully break your word herein? 3. If you do, can you blame
us for not employing you any more?

[§51] *Q.* How shall we guard against formality in public worship?
Particularly in singing?
A. 1. By preaching frequently on that head. 2. By taking
care to speak only what we feel. 3. By choosing such
hymns as are proper for the congregation, generally hymns
of prayer or praise rather than descriptive of particular
states. 4. By not singing too much at once—seldom more
than five or six verses. 5. By suiting the tune to the nature
of the hymn. 6. By often stopping short and asking the

people, 'Now! Do you know what you said last? Did you
speak no more than you felt? Did you sing it as unto the
Lord; with the spirit and with the understanding also?'
[B, 1763]

[§51.1]*Q.* **What can be done to make the people sing true?** 5
    A. **1. Learn to sing true yourselves. 2. Recommend
the Tunes everywhere. 3. If a preacher cannot sing
himself let him choose two or three persons in every
place to pitch the tune for him.**

[§51.2]*Q.* **What is it best to take just after preaching?** 10
    A. **Lemonade, candied orange peel, or a little soft,
warm ale. But egg and wine is downright poison.
And so are late suppers.**
[A, 1753]
May 24, 1746, etc.[127] 15

[§52]   *Q.* How shall we try those who think they are moved by the
    Holy Ghost, and called of God to preach?
    A. Inquire, 1. Do they know God as a pardoning God?
    Have they the love of God abiding in them? Do they
    desire and seek nothing but God? And are they holy in 20
    all manner of conversation?
    2. Have they *gifts* (as well as *grace*) for the work? Have
    they (in some tolerable degree) a clear, sound under-
    standing? Have they a right judgment in the things of
    God? Have they a just conception of salvation by faith? 25
    And has God given them any degree of utterance? Do
    they speak justly, readily, clearly?
    3. Have they fruit? Are any truly convinced of sin and
    converted to God by their preaching?
    As long as these three marks concur in any, we believe 30
    he is called of God to preach.
    These we receive as a sufficient proof that he is moved
    thereto by the Holy Ghost.

[§53]   *Q.* But how shall we know whether they concur or no in any
    particular person? 35
    [*A.*] 1. If he is near us, we will talk with him on the pre-
    ceding heads, and then hear him preach.

---

[127] The inserted dates are vestigial remnants from JW's published *Minutes* of
1749, and are irrelevant to most of the text that follows them, even those sections
that are from 1749 (see analysis at end of this section).

2. We will desire him to write down or relate the reasons why he thinks he is called of God thereto.

3. We will examine those who seem to have been convinced of sin or converted to God by his preaching.

4. If he is at a distance, we will desire one of the neighbouring preachers to do this; and to inquire what is the judgment of the society in that place concerning him?

[§54] *Q.* What method may we use in receiving a new Helper?

A. A proper time for doing this is at a Conference, after solemn fasting and prayer.

We may then receive him as a probationer, by giving him a book inscribed thus:

'To A.B.

'You think it your duty to call sinners to repentance. Make full proof hereof, and we shall be glad to receive you as a fellow-labourer.'

[B, 1763 adds]

[§54.1]**'Observe. You are not to ramble up and down, but to go where the Assistant directs, and there only.'**

[A, 1753]

[§54.2]Let him then read and carefully weigh what is contained therein, and see whether he can agree to it or no.

If he can, let him come to the next Conference, where after examination, fasting, and prayer, he may be received into Full Connexion with us, by giving him a book [**B, 1763,** reads 'the *Minutes*'] inscribed thus:

'So long as you freely consent to, and earnestly endeavour to walk by, these rules, we shall rejoice to acknowledge you as a fellow-labourer.'

[B, 1763, omits the following *Q.* and *A.*]

[§55] *Q.* Why do you not use more form and solemnity in admitting a new labourer?

A. Because we would not make haste. We desire barely to follow Providence as it gradually opens.

[B, 1763]

[§56] **Q. What can we do to prevent unqualified persons from preaching or exhorting?**

A. 1. Let none exhort in any of our societies without a note of recommendation from the Assistant.

2. Let every exhorter see that this be renewed yearly.

3. Let every Assistant rigorously insist upon this.

[§57] *Q.* What can be done to make the Methodists sensible
of the excellency of Kingswood School?

A. 1. Let every Assistant read the following account
of it yearly in every Society. 2. Let every preacher
earnestly exhort all parents that are able to send   5
their children thither, and be at the pains to answer
all their objections, and refute all the lies they have
heard about it.

1. The wisdom and love of God have now thrust
out a large number of labourers into his harvest,   10
men who desire nothing on earth but to promote
the glory of God, to save their own souls, and them
that hear them. And those to whom they minister
spiritual things, willingly minister to them carnal
things; so that they have food to eat and raiment   15
to put on, and content therewith.

2. A competent provision is likewise made for the
wives of married preachers. These also lack nothing, having a weekly allowance, over and above,
for their little children; so that neither they nor   20
their husbands need be careful about many
things, but may wait upon the Lord without distraction.

3. Yet one considerable difficulty lies on those who
have boys, when they grow too big to be under   25
their mother's direction. Having no father to govern and instruct them, they are exposed to a thousand temptations. To remedy this, we have a
school on purpose for them, wherein they have all
the instruction they are capable of, together with   30
all things needful for the body, clothes only
excepted. And it may be, if God prosper this
labour of love, they will have these too shortly.

4. In whatever view we look upon this, it is one of
the noblest charities that can be conceived. How   35
reasonable is the institution! Is it fit that the children of those who leave wife, home, and all that is
dear, to save souls from death, should want what is
needful either for soul or body? Ought not we to
supply what the parent cannot, because of his   40
labours in the gospel? How excellent are the

effects of this institution! The preacher eased of
this weight can the more cheerfully go on in his
labour. And perhaps many of these children may
hereafter fill up the place of those that shall rest

5   from their labours.
5. It is not strange, therefore, considering the excel-
lence of this design, that Satan should have taken
much pains to defeat it: particularly by lies of every
kind, which were plentifully invented and handed

10   about for several years, even by some of our preachers. But truth now prevails, and its adversaries are
put to silence. It is well known that the children
want nothing; that they scarce know what sickness
means; that they are well instructed in whatever

15   they are capable of learning; that they are carefully
and tenderly governed; and that the behaviour of
all in the house, elder and younger, is as becometh
the gospel of Christ.
6. But the expense of such an undertaking is very

20   large: so that although we have at present but thirteen or fourteen poor children, we are continually
running behind, notwithstanding the yearly subscription made at London and Bristol.
The best means we could think of at our late

25   Conference to supply the deficiency is once a year
to desire the assistance of all those in every place
who wish well to the work of God, all who long to
see sinners converted to God, and the Kingdom of
Christ set up in all the earth.

30   7. All of you who are thus minded have an opportunity now of showing your love to the gospel.
Now promote, as far as in you lies, one of the
noblest charities in the world. Now forward, as you
are able, one of the most excellent designs that

35   ever was set on foot in this kingdom. Do what you
can to comfort the parents who give up their all for
you, and to give their children cause to bless you.
You will be no poorer for what you do on such an
occasion. God is a good pay-master. And you know,

40   in doing this, you lend unto the Lord. In due time
he shall pay you again.

[§58] *Q.* But how can we keep it out of debt, which never
was done yet?

A. Let a collection be made for it the Sunday before
or after midsummer, in every preaching-house
throughout England.   5

[A, 1753]

[§59]   November 16, etc., 1749[128]

Q. Can there be any such thing as a general union of our
societies throughout England?

A. A proposal for this was made some time since. The sub-   10
stance of it is this:

'May not all the societies in England be considered as one
body, united by one Spirit?

'May not that in London, the Mother Church, consult for
the good of all the Churches?   15

'May not the stewards of this answer letters from all parts,
and give advice, at least in temporals?'

[§60] *Q.* But how can the state of all the societies be known to the
stewards in London?

A. Very easily, by means of the Assistant.   20

[§61] *Q.* Who is the Assistant?

A. That preacher in each circuit who is appointed from
time to time to take charge of the societies and the other
preachers therein.

[§62] *Q.* How should an Assistant be qualified for this charge?   25

A. By walking closely with God, and having his work
greatly at heart.

[§62.1][**B, 1763, adds**]**; by understanding and loving discipline, ours in particular, and by loving the Church
of England, and resolving not to separate from it.**   30

[A, 1753]

[§63] *Q.* What is the business of an Assistant?

A. 1. To see that the other preachers in his circuit behave
well, and want nothing. 2. To visit the classes quarterly in
each place; to regulate bands, [**B, 1763, omits 'to'**] and   35
deliver new tickets. 3. To keep watch-nights and love-
feasts. 4. To take in or put out of the bands or society.

---

[128] This inserted date, seemingly similar to those above, is also the date of a
Conference, but of the questions that follow in edn. A, only §§50–54 are from 1749.
Two previous §§, 50 and 54, are also from 1749; see analysis at end of this section.

5. To hold Quarterly Meetings, and therein diligently to inquire both into the spiritual and temporal state of each society. 6. To take care that every society be duly supplied with books, and that the money for them be constantly returned. 7. To send from every Quarterly Meeting a circumstantial account to London, (1) Of every remarkable conversion; (2) Of everyone who dies in the triumph of faith. 8. To take exact lists of his societies every Easter, and transmit them to London before Whitsuntide [**for the last clause, B, 1763, reads 'and bring them to the next Conference'**]. 9. To meet the married men, the married women, the single men, and the single women in the large societies once a quarter. 10. To see that every society have a private room, and a set of the *Library* for the Helper, and 11. To travel with me [**B, 1763, adds 'if required'**] once a year, through the societies in his circuit.

[§64] *Q.* How many circuits are there now?
A. Twelve. (1) London, (2) Bristol, (3) Wiltshire, (4) Cornwall, (5) Staffordshire, (6) Cheshire, (7) Leeds, (8) Haworth, (9) Lincolnshire, (10) Newcastle, (11) Wales, (12) Ireland.

[§64.1][**B, 1763, '*A.* Twenty in England, seven in Ireland, two in Scotland, and two in Wales.**

(1) London, (2) Sussex, (3) Norwich, (4) Bedford, (5) Wilts., (6) Bristol, (7) Devonshire, (8) Cornwall, (9) Staffordshire, (10) Cheshire, (11) Whitehaven, (12) Lincolnshire, (13) Sheffield, (14) Leeds, (15) Birstal, (16) Haworth, (17) York, (18) Yarm, (19) The Dales, (20) Newcastle.
(1) Dublin, (2) Waterford, (3) Cork, (4) Limerick, (5) Castlebar, (6) Athlone, (7) The North.
(1) Edinburgh, (2) Aberdeen.
(1), (2) Wales.']

[B, 1763]

[§65] *Q.* **But has the office of an Assistant been thoroughly executed?**
A. **No; not by one Assistant out of three. For instance, every Assistant ought, 1. To 'see that the other preachers behave well'. But who has sent me word**

whether they did or no? 2. 'To visit the classes, regulate the bands, and deliver tickets quarterly'. How few have done this! 3. Love-feasts for the bands have been neglected. 4. Nor have persons been regularly taken in and put out of the bands. 5. I fear many of 5 the Quarterly Meetings are formal, not spiritual. 6. The societies are not half supplied with books, not even with Kempis, 'Instructions for Children', and *Primitive Physic*, which ought to be in every house. And why should not each of you do like Wm. 10 Penington, carry books with you through every round? Exert yourselves in this. Be not ashamed. Be not weary. Leave no stone unturned. And let none print anything of his own till it has been approved by the Conference. 7. How few accounts have I had 15 either of remarkable deaths or remarkable conversions! 8. How few exact lists have we received of the societies! Take more time and more pains in preparing them. 9. Who of you has met the married and single men and women once a quarter, even in 20 the largest societies? 10. You have not provided a private room everywhere for the preacher; nor a bed to himself; neither the *Library*, for want of which some still read trash. Till this can be done, let there be immediately in every place at least the *Notes* and 25 the tract on *Original Sin*.

[§66] *Q.* Is there any other advice which you would give the Assistants?

A. [1] Yes. In every place exhort those who were brought up in the Church constantly to attend its 30 service. And in visiting the classes, ask everyone, 'Do *you* go to Church as often as ever you did?' Set the example yourself. And immediately alter every Plan that interferes therewith.

[§66.1] Is there not a cause for this? Are we not unawares, 35 by little and little, tending to a separation from the Church? O remove every tendency thereto with all diligence. 1. Let all our preachers go to Church. 2. Let all our people go constantly. 3. Receive the Sacrament at every opportunity. 4. Warn all against 40 niceness in hearing, a great and prevailing evil.

5. Warn them likewise against despising the prayers of the Church. 6. Against calling our Society 'a Church', or 'the Church'. 7. Against calling our preachers 'ministers', our houses 'meeting-houses' (call them plain preaching-houses). [8.][129] Do not license them as such. The proper form of a petition to the Judges is, 'A.B. desires to have his house in C. licensed for public worship.' [9.] Do not license yourself till you are constrained; and then not as a 'Dissenter', but as a Methodist preacher. It is time enough when you are prosecuted to take the oaths: thereby you are licensed.

[§67] *Q.* What do you advise with regard to public buildings?

A. [1.] Let none be undertaken without the consent of the Assistant. 2. Build, if possible, in the form of Rotherham House. 3. Settle it in the following form: This Indenture made _____ between B. Heap of Manchester, in the County of   on the one part, and Tho. Philips, Hatter, etc. on the other part, WITNESSETH, that in consideration of five shillings, lawful money of Great Britain, by the said T.P., etc. to the said B.H. truly paid, before the sealing and delivery hereof (the receipt whereof the said B.H. doth hereby acknowledge) and for divers other considerations him thereunto moving, the said B.H. hath granted, bargained, and sold; and by these presents doth grant, bargain, and sell unto the said T.P., etc., their heirs and assigns for ever, All that lately erected house or tenement, with the yard thereunto adjoining, situated near the upper end of Market-street Lane in Manchester aforesaid, now in the tenure or occupancy of T. Woolfinden; together with all the ways, drains, walls and privileges to the said premises, or any part thereof appertaining, as the same were purchased of S. Hope, of Manchester aforesaid, bricklayer, before the said house or tenement was built; and all the profits thereof, and all the right, title and interest in law and equity.

---

[129] Orig. misnumbers the last two items in this list.

TO HAVE AND TO HOLD the said house or tenement, yard and other premises, to the said T.P., etc.,
their heirs and assigns for ever: NEVERTHELESS
upon special trust and confidence, and to the intent,
that they and the survivors of them, and the   5
trustees for the time being, do and shall permit
John Wesley, late of Lincoln College, Oxford, Clerk,
and such other persons as he shall from time to
time appoint, and at all times during his natural
life, and no other persons, to have and enjoy the free 10
use and benefit of the said premises; that the said
J.W. and such other persons as he appoints may
therein preach and expound God's holy Word; and
after his decease, upon farther trust and confidence,
and to the intent that the said trustees and the sur-   15
vivors of them, and the trustees for the time being,
do and shall permit Charles Wesley, late of Christ
Church College, Oxford, Clerk, and such other persons as he shall from time to time appoint, during
his life, and no others, to have and enjoy the said   20
premises for the purposes aforesaid; and after his
decease, upon farther trust and confidence, and to
the intent that the said trustees and the survivors of
them, and the trustees for the time being, do and
shall permit Wm. Grimshaw, Clerk, and such other   25
persons as he shall from time to time appoint, during his life, and no others, to have and enjoy the
said premises for the purposes aforesaid; and after
the decease of the survivor of the said J.W., C.W.,
and W.G. Then upon farther trust and confidence,   30
and to the intent that the said T.P., etc., or the
major part of them, or the survivors of them, and
the major part of the trustees of the said premises
for the time being, shall from time to time, and at
all times, for ever thereafter, permit such persons   35
as shall be appointed at the Yearly Conference of
the People called Methodists, in London, Bristol or
Leeds, and no others, to have and enjoy the said
premises for the purposes aforesaid; *Provided*
always that the said persons preach no other doctrine 40
than is contained in Mr. W.'s Notes upon the New

Testament *and four Vol[ume]s of Sermons; Provided also that they preach in the said house evenings in every week, and at five o'clock on each morning following.* And upon farther trust and confidence that as often as any of these trustees, or of the trustees for the time being shall die, *or cease to be a member of the Society commonly called Methodists*, the rest of the said trustees, or of the trustees for the time being, as soon as conveniently may be, shall and may choose another trustee or trustees in order to keep up the number of nine trustees for ever. In witness whereof the said B.H. hath hereunto set his hand and seal, the day and year first above written.

In this form the first proprietors of the house are to make it over to trustees.

One thing more should be done without delay.

Let the vacancies everywhere be filled up with new trustees. We know not what danger may ensue from delay.

[A, 1753]

[§68]   *Q.* How may the married preachers be provided for?
A. 1. Let the Assistant inquire at the Quarterly Meeting what each preacher's wife will want for the ensuing quarter. 2. Let this be supplied first of all out of the common stock.

[§69]   *Q.* But what if a preacher marries hand over head?
A. Then he must provide for himself.

[§70]   *Q.* The predestinarian preachers have done much hurt among us. How may we prevent this for the future?
A. Let none of them preach any more in any of our societies.

[§71]   *Q.* Mr. Ingham seems to desire a reunion. Can we unite with him?
A. Yes, as soon as he returns to the old Methodist doctrine. Meantime let us behave with all tenderness and love.

FINIS [end of A]

[B, 1763, adds:]

[§72]   *Q.* How may we raise a General Fund?
A. By a yearly subscription, to be proposed by every Assistant when he visits the classes at Christmas, and received at the Visitation following.

To this end he may then read and enlarge upon the
following hints in every Society.

'1. Within these twelve or fifteen years several of
our brethren in various parts, having no room which
would contain the congregation, by the advice of the 5
preachers have built houses for preaching capable of
containing the usual number of hearers. But this
has necessarily involved them in large debts. Their
debts at Halifax, for instance, amounted two or
three years ago to two hundred pounds, that at 10
Leeds to more than three hundred pounds, that at
Manchester to three hundred and fifty pounds, that
at Liverpool to four hundred pounds. So that the
whole debt contracted by building was, I apprehend,
little short of four thousand pounds. This the soci- 15
eties to whom those houses belong are by no means
able to pay. But the whole body of Methodists joining together can do it without inconvenience. Only
let them cheerfully exert on so pressing an occasion
the ability which God hath given them. 20

'2. But there is a greater difficulty than this. Where
there are houses there are not preachers. Though
the harvest is plenteous, the labourers are few. And
what can we do for a supply? We cannot purchase
them for money. We cannot hire or make them. God 25
alone can do this. And he has in some measure done
it already. In several parts of England there are
local preachers, who have both gifts and graces
equal to those of most itinerants. "Why then do
they not travel?" They are willing so to do. But they 30
are afraid of bringing a scandal upon the gospel,
because they have contracted debts, which, though
very small, they are not yet able to pay. So they are
bound hand and foot. But shall we suffer this? Shall
we not set them at liberty? We cannot buy a 35
preacher for ten thousand pounds—but we may
release one for ten or twelve. Can any money be better bestowed? Let us in the name of God send these
labourers into his harvest! Men who desire only to
give their bodies, souls, time, all, for Him that was 40
given for us.

'3. But still how shall we send them into those parts where they are most of all wanted? Suppose the north-west of Ireland, and the north of Scotland? Many are willing to hear, but not to bear the expense. Nor can it as yet be expected of them. Stay till the Word of God has touched their hearts, and then they will gladly provide for them that preach it. Does it not lie upon us, in the mean time, to supply their lack of service? To raise a General Fund out of which from [time] to time that expense may be defrayed? By this means those who willingly offer themselves may travel through every part, whether there are societies or not, and stay wherever there is a call, without being burdensome to any. Thus may the gospel, in the life and power thereof, be spread from sea to sea. Which of you will not rejoice to throw in your mite to promote this glorious work?

'4. It is true, when want of money to defray the expense is removed, another hindrance will often arise. Satan will stir up his trusty servants, to fight lest his kingdom be destroyed. But is there no way to quell riotous mobs, even when magistrates will not do their duty? There is one, and only one way. Move the King's Bench for an information against them. This is a way which has never failed us yet. No, not in a single instance. The only objection is the expense. A suit in the King's Bench usually costs fifty or sixty pounds. But if we all join hand and heart together, cannot we make this easy too? Cannot we raise a common stock which shall suffice for this as well as for the preceding purposes? By the blessing of God we can. And who would not gladly contribute toward it?

'5. Let then every member of our Society in England, once a year, set his shoulder to the work; contributing more or less as God has prospered him, at the Lady Day Visitation of the classes. Let none be excluded from giving something, be it a penny, a halfpenny, a farthing. Remember the widow's two mites! And let those who are able to

give shillings, crowns, and pounds, do it willingly.
The money contributed will be brought to Leeds,
Bristol, or London, at the ensuing Conference. Two-
thirds of it at least will be allotted for those public
debts which call the loudest. The rest will be partly   5
employed in setting at liberty such local preachers
as are tied down by small debts; partly reserved for
propagating the gospel where there are none to bear
the expenses of the preacher.

'6. Men and brethren, help! Was there ever a call like   10
this, since you first heard the gospel-sound? Help to
relieve your companions in the Kingdom of Jesus,
who are pressed above measure. Bear ye one
another's burdens, and so fulfil the law of Christ.
Help to send forth able, willing labourers into your   15
Lord's harvest: so shall ye be assistant in saving souls
from death, and hiding a multitude of sins. Help to
spread the gospel of your salvation into the remotest
corners of the kingdom, till the knowledge of our
Lord shall cover the land, as the waters cover the sea.   20
Help to deliver the poor out of the hand of the
oppressor, to procure them the blessings which we
enjoy: so shall it appear to ourselves, and all men,
that we are indeed one body, united by one Spirit; so
shall the baptized heathens be yet again constrained   25
to say, "See how these Christians love one another."'

The money received is to be brought by the
Assistants to the next Conference, and delivered to
the General Stewards.

[§72.1]   The General Stewards at London are Sam. Franks,   30
Rich. Kemp, Wm. Evans. At   Bristol, Tho. Lewis,
John Spragg. At Leeds, James Roads, Rich.
Watkinson. These are to pay to each Assistant what
is allotted for his circuit, and keep an exact account
of receipts and disbursements.   35

[§73]   *Q.* How may provision be made for old or worn-out
preachers?

[*A.*] As to their employ, they may be Supernumerary Preachers, or Assistants, in those circuits
wherein there is most need. As to their subsistence,   40

1. Let every travelling preacher contribute ten shillings yearly, at the Conference.

2. Let this be lodged in the hands of three stewards, approved by the majority of the preachers.

3. Out of this, let what is needful be allowed yearly; first for the old or sickly preachers, and their families (if they have any), then for the widows and children of those that are dead.

[§74] *Q.* If God should call you away, what would be the most probable means of preventing the people from being scattered?

A. Let all the Assistants for the time being immediately go up to London and consult, what steps are fittest to be taken. And God will then make the way plain before them.

FINIS

2. The 'Large' *Minutes*, C and D (1770, 1772)

Text of C (1770), and D (1772), compared
with A (1753) and B (1763)[130]

MINUTES OF SEVERAL CONVERSATIONS
between the Reverend Messieurs John and
Charles Wesley, and Others.

[§0.1–4] [As AB, 1753/1763, Conference preamble.]

[§0.5] [CD retains from AB the sentence after 'meantime': 'Let us all pray for a willingness to receive light, to know of every doctrine whether it be of God.']

---

[130] Comments are made within square brackets, with excerpts within quotation marks; complete new text from C, 1770, is given with the original *Q.* or *A.* numbers, and without brackets or quotation marks; there are only three batches of new text in **D, 1772**, namely Nos. 61.14, 63.1, and 74.7, which are given in **bold** type, with the original *Q.* or *A.* numbers. The assumption is that the *Q.* number given is that of both 1770 and 1772 unless some other number is indicated.

[§1]   [CD as AB, 1753/1763, Confer in presence of God.]

[§2]   [CD as AB, 1753/1763, Confer accepting majority judgment.]

[§3]   [CD as AB, Respecting private judgment, but 'to Bishop, Convocation, or General Council' and 'account of himself'.]

[§4]   *[131][CD as B, God's design in Methodism, but 'and to spread' in C (not in D).]

[§5]   *Q.* 5. What was the rise of Methodism, so called?

A. In 1729 two young men, reading the Bible, saw they could not be saved without holiness, followed after it, and incited others so to do. In 1737 they saw, holiness comes by faith. They saw likewise that men are justified before they are sanctified: but still holiness was their point.

God then thrust them out, utterly against their will, to raise an holy people. When Satan could no otherwise hinder this, he threw *Calvinism* in the way; and then *Antinomianism*, which strikes directly at the root of all holiness.

Then many of the *Methodists* growing *rich*, became lovers of the present world. Next they married unawakened or half awakened wives, and conversed with their relations. Hence worldly *prudence, maxims, customs*, crept back upon them, producing more and more *conformity to the world*.

Hence followed gross neglect of *relative duties*, especially *education* of children. And this is not easily cured by the preachers. Either they have not *light*, or not *weight* enough. But the want of both may in some measure be supplied by publicly reading the *Sermons* everywhere, particularly the fourth volume.

[§6]   [CD6 as AB5, Preach without forming societies?]

[§7]   [CD7 as AB6, Inconvenience of not having societies.]

[§8]   [CD8 as B7, Where preach most?]

[§9]   [CD9 as AB8, Is field preaching unlawful?]

[§10] [CD10 as AB9, Has field preaching been used too sparingly?]

---

[131] 1772 (*Works*) adds here and elsewhere an asterisk denoting the special importance of a section to JW. Cf. also 31, 33, 44, 60, and 77.

[§10.1][CD10.1 as B9.1, Overcoming hindrances to field preaching, altering 'Every Assistant . . . their lees' to 'every
Sunday in particular; especially in the old societies, lest
they settle upon their lees'.
5 [§11]   [CD11 as AB10, Observe where Holy Spirit works most.]
[§12]   [CD12 as AB11, A sufficient call to a new place.]
[§13]   [CD13 as AB12, Permitting the presence of strangers in
society.]
[§13.1][CD13.1 as B12.1, Members must show their class-tickets.]
10 [§14]   [CD14 as AB13, Re-admitting relapsers.]
[§15.1][CD15.1 as AB14.1, Making class-leaders more useful.]
[§15.2][C15.2 as AB14.2, Directions for class-leaders, but D15.2
omits directions 5 and 7.]
[§16]   [CD16 as AB15, Making class-meetings more profitable,
15   but omit the closing sentence.]
[§16.3]D, 1772, adds '3. Frequently making new leaders.'
[§17]   [CD17 as AB16.1–4, Examining and instructing members,
revised thus:]
Q. 17. How can we farther assist those under our care?
20   *A*. 1. By closely examining them at each Visitation.
2. By meeting the married men and women together on
the first Sunday after the Visitation, the single men and
women apart on the two following.
3. By instructing them at their own houses.
25   [B16, 16.5, Visitation of homes by Thomas Walsh and *QQ*.
for family visitation are omitted from CD.]
[§17.1]What unspeakable need is there of this! The world says,
'The Methodists are no better than other people.' This is
not true. Yet it is nearer the truth than we are willing to
30   imagine.
For (1) personal religion, either toward God or man, is
amazingly superficial among us.
I can but just touch on a few generals. How little faith is
there among us! How little communion with God! How
35   little living in heaven, walking in eternity, deadness to
every creature! How much love of the world, desire of
pleasure, of ease, of praise, of getting money!
How little brotherly love! What continual judging one
another! What gossiping, evil-speaking, tale-bearing!
40   What want of moral honesty! To instance only in a few
particulars:

What servants, journeymen, labourers, carpenters, brick-layers, do as they would be done by? Which of them does as much work as he can? Set him down for a knave that does not.

Who does as he would be done by in buying and selling, particularly in selling horses? Write him knave that does not. And the Methodist knave is the worst of all knaves.

(2) Family religion is shamefully wanting, and almost in every branch. And the Methodists in general will be little better till we take quite another course with them. For what avails public preaching alone, though we could preach like angels!

I heard Dr. Lupton say:[132] My father, visiting one of his parishioners, who had never missed going to church for forty years, then lying on his death-bed, asked him, 'Thomas, where do you think your soul will go?' 'Soul? Soul?' said Thomas. 'Yes. Do not you know what your soul is?' 'Aye, surely,' said he. 'Why, it is a little bone in the back, that lives longer than the rest of the body.' So much Thomas had learned by often hearing sermons, yea, and exceeding good sermons, for forty years!

We must instruct them 'from house to house'. Till this is done, and that in good earnest, the Methodists will be little better than other people.

[§17.2] Can we find a better method of doing this than Mr. Baxter's? If not, let us adopt it without delay. His whole tract, entitled, Gildas Salvianus, is well worth a careful perusal. A short extract from it I have subjoined. Speaking of this visiting from house to house, he says, page 351:[133]

'We shall find many difficulties both in ourselves and in the people.

'1. In ourselves there is much dullness and laziness, so that there will be much ado to get us to be faithful in the work.

'2. We have also a base man-pleasing temper, which makes us let men perish rather than lose their love, and let them go quietly to hell lest we should anger them.

---

[132] See annual *Minutes* (1766), *Q.* 29.
[133] See ibid.

'3. Some of have also a foolish bashfulness. We know not
how to begin, or to speak plain. We blush to speak for
Christ, or to contradict the devil, or to save a soul.

'4. Our interest stops our mouths, and makes us unfaith-
ful in the work of Christ.

'5. But the greatest hindrance is, weakness of faith; so
our whole motion is weak, because the spring of it is
weak.

'6. Lastly, we are unskilful in the work. How few know
how to deal with men so as to get within them, to win
upon them, and suit all our discourse to their several conditions and tempers; to choose the fittest subjects, and
follow them with an holy mixture of seriousness, and terror, and love, and meekness, and evangelical allurements.'

[§17.3]'And we have as many difficulties to grapple with in our
people.

'1. Too many of them will be unwilling to be taught till
we conquer their perverseness by the force of reason and
the power of love.

'2. And many are so dull that they will shun being
taught, for fear of showing their dullness. And indeed you
find it extremely hard to make them understand the very
plainest points.

'3. And it is still harder to fix things on their heart, without which all our labour is lost. If you have not therefore
great seriousness and fervency, what good can you expect?
And when all is done, it is the Spirit of grace, he alone,
who must do the work.

'4. And when we have made some impressions upon
their hearts, if we look not after them, they will soon die
away.

[§17.4]'But as great as this labour of private instruction is, it is
absolutely necessary. For after all our preaching, many of
our people are almost as ignorant as if they had never
heard the gospel. I study to speak as plain as I can, yet I
frequently meet with those who have been my hearers for
many years, who know not whether Christ be God or
man; or that infants have any original sin. And how few
are there that know the nature of repentance, faith, and
holiness! Most of them have a sort of confidence that
Christ will justify and save them, while the world has

their hearts, and they live to themselves. And I have
found by experience that one of these has learned more
from an hour's close discourse than from ten years'
public preaching.

'And undoubtedly this private application is implied in   5
those solemn words of the Apostle: "I charge thee before
God and the Lord Jesus Christ, who shall judge the quick
and the dead at his appearing, preach the Word, be instant
in season, out of season; reprove, rebuke, exhort, with all
long-suffering and doctrine."   10

'This is likewise necessary to the greater glory of God,
by the fuller success of the gospel. O brethren, if we could
generally set this work on foot in all our societies, and
prosecute it skilfully and zealously, what glory would
redound to God thereby! If the common ignorance were   15
thus banished, and our vanity and idleness turned into the
study of the way of life, and every shop and every house
busied in speaking of the word and works of God, surely
God would dwell in our habitations, and make them his
delight.   20

'And this is necessary to the welfare of our people, many
of whom neither believe nor repent to this day. Look
round about, and see how many of them are still in apparent danger of damnation! And how can you walk, and talk,
and be merry with such people, when you know their   25
case? Methinks when you look them in the face, you
should break forth into tears, as the prophet did when he
looked upon Hazael, and then set on them with the most
vehement and importunate exhortations. O then for
God's sake, and for the sake of poor souls, bestir your-   30
selves, and spare no pains that may conduce to their
salvation!

'What cause have we to bleed before the Lord this day,
that have so long neglected this great and good work!
That have been preachers so many years, and have done   35
so little by personal instructions for the saving of men's
souls! If we had but set on this work sooner, how many
more might have been brought to Christ! And how much
holier and happier might we have made our societies
before now! And why might we not have done it sooner!   40

'There were many hindrances in the way. And so there are still, and always will be. But the greatest hindrance was in ourselves, in our dullness and littleness of faith and love. O that God would thoroughly humble us, and cause us to bewail our own neglects; that we may not think it enough to lament the sins of others while we overlook our own!

[§17.5]   'But it is objected, I. "This course will take up so much time that we shall have no time to follow our studies."

'I answer, 1. Gaining knowledge is a good thing; but saving souls is better. 2. By this very thing you will gain the most excellent knowledge of God and eternity. 3. But you will have abundant time for gaining other knowledge too, if you spend all your mornings therein. Only sleep not more than you need; and never be idle, nor triflingly employed. But, 4. If you can do but one, either follow your studies or instruct the ignorant, let your studies alone; I would throw by all the libraries in the world, rather than be guilty of the perdition of one soul.

'It is objected, II. "The people will not submit to it." If some do not, others will gladly. And the success with them may be so much as to repay all our labour. O let us herein follow the example of St. Paul. 1. For our general business, "Serving the Lord with all humility of mind." 2. Our special work, "Take heed to yourselves, and to all the flock." 3. Our doctrine, "Repentance toward God, and faith in our Lord Jesus Christ." 4. The place and manner of teaching, "I have taught you publicly, and from house to house." 5. The object and internal manner, "I ceased not to warn everyone, night and day, with tears." This it is that must win souls and preserve them. 6. His innocency and self-denial for the advantage of the gospel, "I have coveted no man's silver or gold." 7. His patience, "Neither count I my life dear unto myself."

'And among all our motives, these should be ever before our eyes: 1. "The Church of God, which he hath purchased with his own blood." 2. "Grievous wolves shall enter in; yea, of your own selves shall men arise, speaking perverse things." Write all this upon your hearts, and it will do you more good than twenty years' study of lower things.

[§17.6][N.B. Wesley continues to rewrite Baxter, from chap. VII of
    his work.]

    'We may, 1. Every preacher take an exact catalogue of
those in Society, from one end of each town to the other.
2. Go to each house, and give, with suitable exhortation
and direction, the *Instructions for Children.* 3. Be sure to
deal gently with them, and take off all discouragements as
effectually as you can. See that the children get these by
heart. Advise the grown persons to see that they understand them. And enlarge upon and apply every sentence
as closely as you can. And let your dealing with those you
begin with be so gentle, winning and convincing, that the
report of it may move others to desire your coming. True,
it is far easier to preach a good sermon than to instruct
the ignorant in the principles of religion. And as much as
this work is despised by some, I doubt not but it will try
the parts and spirits of us all. So Archbishop Ussher:
"Great scholars may think it beneath them to spend their
time in teaching the first principles of the doctrine of
Christ. But they should consider that the laying the foundation skilfully, as it is the matter of greatest importance
in the whole building, so it is the masterpiece of the wisest
builder: 'According to the grace of God which is given
unto me, as a wise master-builder, I have laid the foundation,' saith the great Apostle. And let the wisest of us all
try whenever we please, we shall find that to lay this
ground rightly, to make an 'ignorant man understand the
grounds of religion, will put us to the trial of all our
skill'."

[§17.7]'Perhaps in doing this, it may be well, 1. After a few loving
words spoken to all in the house, to take each person
singly into another room, where you may deal closely with
them, about their sin and misery and duty. Set these
home, or you lose all your labour. At least let none be
present but those who are quite familiar with each other.

    '2. Hear what the children have learned by heart.

    '3. Choose some of the weightiest points, and try by far-
ther questions how they understand them. As, "Do you
believe you have sin in you? That you was born in sin?
What does sin deserve? What remedy has God provided
for guilty, helpless sinners?"

'4. Often with the question, suggest the answer. As, "What is repentance?" Sorrow for sin, or a conviction that we are guilty, helpless sinners? "What is faith?" A divine conviction of things not seen?

'5. Where you perceive they do not understand the stress of your question, you must lead them into it by other questions. So I have asked some, "How do you think your many and great sins will be pardoned?" They answer, "By repenting and mending my life", and never mention Christ. I ask farther, "But do you think your amendment will make satisfaction for your past sins?" They will answer, "We hope so, or else we know not what will." One would think now, these had no knowledge of Christ at all. And indeed some have not. But others have, and give such answers only because they do not understand the scope of the question. Ask them farther, "Can you be saved without the death of Christ?" They immediately say, "No." And if you ask, "What has he done or suffered for you?" they will say, "He shed his blood for us," and profess they "trust in that for salvation." But many cannot express even what they have some conception of, nay, can scarce learn when expressions are put into their mouths. With these you are to deal exceeding tenderly, lest they be discouraged.

'6. If you perceive them troubled that they cannot answer, step in yourself, and take the burden off them, answering that question yourself; and then do it thoroughly and plainly, and make a full explication of the whole business to them.

'7. Thus, when you have tried their knowledge, proceed to instruct them yourself, according to their several capacities. If a man understand the fundamentals, fall on what you perceive he most needs, either explaining further some doctrine of the gospel, or some duty, or showing the necessity of something he neglects, as may be most edifying to him. If it be one that is grossly ignorant, give him a short recital of the Christian religion in the plainest words. And if you perceive he understands not, go over it again till he does, and if possible fix it in his memory.

'8. Next, inquire into his state, whether convinced, or unconvinced, converted or unconverted. Tell him, if need be, what conversion is. And then renew and enforce the inquiry.

'9. If you perceive he is unconverted, your next business is to labour with all your skill and power to bring his heart to a sense of his condition. Set this home with a more earnest voice than you spoke before—for if you get not to the heart, you do nothing.

'10. Conclude all with a strong exhortation, which should contain two parts: 1. The duty of the heart, in order to receive Christ. 2. The avoiding former sins, and constantly using the outward means. And here be sure, if you can, to get their promise to forsake sin, change their company, and use means. And do this solemnly; reminding them of the presence of God, that hears their promises, and will expect the performance.

'11. Before you leave them, engage the head of each family to call his family every Sunday, before they go to bed, and hear what they can rehearse, and so continue till they have learned the *Instructions* perfectly. And afterwards take care that they do not forget what they had learned.

'12. Speak differently, according to the difference of them you have to deal with, as they are dull and obstinate, or timorous and tender. Be as plain as possible to those of weak capacities, and give them Scripture proof for all you say.' [The end of Wesley's revision of Baxter.]

[§18]   [CD18 as AB17, Protecting Societies against the unworthy.]

[§19]   [CD19 as AB18, Solemnizing admission of members.]

[§20]   [CD20 as B18.1, Insisting on Band Rules.]

[§21]   *Q.* 21. Have those in Band left off snuff and drams?
A. No. Many are still enslaved to one or the other. In order to redress this, 1. Let no preacher touch either on any account. 2. Strongly dissuade our people from them. 3. Answer their pretences, particularly those of curing the colic, or helping digestion.
[CD omit A19, Children's societies, and B19.1, Children's reading.]

[§22]   [CD22 as AB20, Marriage with unbelievers.]

[§23]   [CD23 as AB21, Preventing marriage with unbelievers, following 'exhorted' in 21.1.]

[§24]   [CD24 as B21.2, A woman marrying without consent of
        parents.]

[§25]   [CD25 as AB22, Unsuitable and immoral conduct, with
        alterations in B.]

5 [§25.6][After B22.2, Extirpate smuggling, CD add:]
        And after admonishing him, silence every Local Preacher
        who speaks in defence of it. Speak tenderly, but earnestly
        and frequently of it in every society near the coasts. And
        read to them and disperse diligently among them the
10   Word to a Smuggler.

[§25.7][After B22.3, 'Extirpate bribery', CD add:]
        Largely show in every Society the wickedness of thus sell-
        ing our country. Do the same thing in private conversa-
        tion. And read everywhere the Word to a Freeholder, and
15   disperse it with both hands: and in public and private
        enlarge on the economy as a branch of religion.

[§26]   *Q*. 26. What shall we do to prevent scandal when any of our
        members become bankrupt?
        A. Let two of the principal members of the Society be
20   deputed to examine his accounts. And if he has not kept
        fair accounts, or has been concerned in that base practice
        of raising money by coining notes (commonly called the
        bill-trade), let him be immediately expelled the Society.

[§27]   [CD27 as AB24, Office of a Minister.]
25   [CD here omit from AB *QQ*. 24, Respect of persons; 25,
        Favouring the rich; 26, Visiting the sick in town;
        27, Taking state upon ourselves; 28, Being more easy of
        access; 29, Testifying to the truth; 30, Retorting charges;
        31, Conversing with the clergy; 32, Conversing with
30   opposers; 33, Preventing national sins; 34, Talking of
        persecution.]

[§28]   [CD28 as AB35, Function of a Helper.]

[§29]   [CD29 as A36, B36.1, Office of a Helper.]

[§30]   [CD30 as AB37, Rules of a Helper, including the revision
35   of B in 37.4.]

[§31]   *[134][CD31, similar to AB38, but somewhat abridged, with
        no reference to the *Christian Library*, *Paradise Lost*, or
        Franck's works.]

---

[134] 1772 (*Works*) adds here and elsewhere an asterisk denoting the special importance of a section to JW.

[CD here omit from AB *QQ*. 39 (Being more useful in
conversation) and the very lengthy 40 (Watching over the
Helpers, including their use of the means of grace, instituted, prudential, and watching and denying ourselves);
also omitted are 41 (securing Union between the Helpers) 5
and 42 (How to avoid popularity). These are included
later as Nos. 44–46.]

[§32] *Q*. 32. Should our Helpers follow trades?[135]

    A. This is an important question; therefore it will be proper
to consider it thoroughly. The question is not whether 10
they may occasionally work with their hands, as St. Paul
did, but whether it be proper for them to keep shop and
follow merchandise. Of those who do so at present it may
be observed, they are unquestionably upright men. They
are men of considerable gifts. We see the fruit of their 15
labour, and they have a large share in the esteem and love
of the people. All this pleads on their side, and cannot but
give us a prejudice in their favour. Three of these urge
necessity for doing this: one that he may help his aged
father; another that he may maintain his wife; a third that 20
he may keep his children; a fourth does not plead any
necessity, but a desire of doing more good. One answered
J.O.: 'If you cannot help your father without trading, and
if the societies either cannot or will not, I will allow him
what you allow him now. So this necessity is at an end.' To 25
Ja.O. it was answered: 'Your wife wants nothing yet. It is
not likely she ever will. You have money beforehand. So
your necessity is not yet begun.' To R.R. 'You do not want
now. When you do want anything for your children, you
shall have it. So here is not necessity.' 30

    As to the second plea, doing more good, it was inquired,
is it not doing evil that good may come? Is not the
thing in question both evil in itself (for us) and evil in its
consequences? *First*, is it not (with regard to travelling
preachers) evil in itself? Is it well consistent with that 35
Scripture, 2 Tim. 2:4, 'No man that warreth' (takes on
him the profession of a soldier, as we eminently do),
'entangleth himself with the affairs of this life,' plainly
referring to the Roman law, which absolutely forbade any

---

[135] See *Minutes* (1768), *Q*. 22.

soldier to follow any other profession. Is it well consistent with that word, 'Give attendance to reading, to
exhortation, to teaching: meditate on these things, give
thyself wholly to them' (1 Tim.4:13, 15)? Can we be said
to give ourselves wholly to these things if we follow
another profession? Does not our Church, in her office
of ordination, require every minister to do this? If they
do not, the more shame for them. But this plainly shows
what both they and we ought to do. We indeed more particularly, because God has called us to 'provoke them to
jealousy', to supply their lack of service to the sheep that
are as yet without shepherds, and to spend and be spent
therein. We above all, because every travelling preacher
solemnly professes to have nothing else to do, and
receives his little allowance for this very end, that he
may not need to do anything else, that he may not be
entangled in the things of this life, but may give himself
wholly to these things.

Secondly, Is it not evil in its consequences? Have not
some ill consequences appeared already? And is there not
the greatest reason to apprehend that still worse would
follow? We are concerned to give no offence, either to Jew
or Gentile, or to the Church of God. But this has already
offended, not only many of the world, but many of our
own brethren. Many of the preachers in particular have
been much grieved; yea, and those most who were most
alive to God. Now the beginning of offence 'is as when
one letteth out water'—who can gather it up again? They
are grieved the more because they apprehend this would
be an increasing evil. For where will it stop? If one
preacher follows trade, so may twenty—so may everyone.
And if any of them trade a little, why not ever so much?
Who can fix how far he should go? Therefore we advise
our brethren who have been concerned herein to give up
all, and attend to the one business. And we doubt not but
God will recompense them an hundred fold, even in this
world, as well as in the world to come.

It is true, this cannot be done on a sudden. But it may
between this and the next conference. And even as to the
drops that many sold, if their wives sell them at home,
well: but it is not proper for any preacher to hawk them

about. It has a bad appearance. It does not well suit the
dignity of his calling.

Two years after it was agreed by all our brethren that no
preacher who will not relinquish his trade of buying and
selling, or of making and vending pills, drops, balsams, or   5
medicines of any kind, shall be considered as a travelling
preacher any longer, and that it shall be demanded of all
those preachers who have traded in cloth, hardware, pills,
drops, balsams, or medicines of any kind, at the next conference, whether they have entirely left it off or not.   10

[§33] *[136]*Q. 33. Why is it that the people under our care are no
better?

A. Other reasons may concur, but the chief is, because we
are not more *knowing* and more holy.

[§34] *Q.* 34. But why are we not more *knowing*?   15

A. Because we are idle. We forget the very first rule, 'Be
diligent. Never be unemployed a moment. Never be triflingly employed. Never while away time. Neither spend
any more time at any place than is strictly necessary.'

I fear there is altogether a fault in this matter, and that   20
few of us are clear. Which of you spends as many hours a
day in *God's work* as you did formerly in *man's work*? We
talk, talk—or read history, or what comes next to hand.

We must, absolutely must, cure this evil, or give up the
whole work.   25

[§34.1]But how? 1. Read the *most useful books*, and that regularly
and constantly. Steadily spend all the morning in this
employ, or at least five hours in twenty-four.

'But I read only the Bible.' Then you ought to teach
others to read only the Bible, and by parity of reason, to   30
hear only the Bible. But if so, you need preach no more.
Just so said George Bell. And what is the fruit? Why, now
he neither reads the Bible nor anything else.

This is rank enthusiasm. If you need no book but the
Bible, you are got above St. Paul. He wanted others too.   35
'Bring the books', says he, 'but especially the parch-
ments'—those wrote on parchment.

---

[136] 1772 (*Works*) adds here and elsewhere an asterisk denoting the special importance of a section to JW.

'But I have *no taste* for reading.' Contract a taste for it by use, or return to your trade.

'But different men have different tastes.' Therefore some may read less than others, but none should read less than this.

'But I have no books.' I will give each of you, as fast as you will read them, books up to the value of five pounds. And I desire the assistants will take care that all the large Societies provide *The Christian Library* for the use of the preachers. [**D, 1772, adds, '. . .** *Library,* **or at least the** *Notes* **on the New Testament, for the use. . .'.**]

[§34.2]2. In the afternoon follow Mr. Baxter's plan. Then you will have no time to spare—none for learning Latin, or Greek, or Hebrew. You will have work enough for all your time. Then likewise no preacher will stay with us who is as salt that has lost its savour. For to such this employment would be mere drudgery. And in order to it, you will have need of all the knowledge you can procure.

The sum is. Go into *every house* in course, and teach *everyone* therein, young or old, if they belong to us, to be Christians, inwardly and outwardly.

Make every particular plain to their understanding. Fix it in their memory.

Write it on their heart. In order to this, there must be 'line upon line, precept upon precept'. I remember to have heard my father asking my mother, 'How could you have the patience to tell that blockhead the same thing twenty times over?' She answered, 'Why, if I had told him but nineteen times, I should have lost all my labour.' What patience indeed, what love, what knowledge is requisite for this?

[§34.3][CD both read '*Q.* 34' here, an incorrect duplication, which is therefore altered to '34.3'.]

Q. 34[.3]. In what method should we instruct them?

A. Read, explain, enforce.

1. The *Rules* of the Society.
2. *Instructions for Children.*
3. The fourth volume of *Sermons.*
4. Philip Henry's *Method of Family Prayer.*

Over and above: Where there are ten children in a Society, spend at least an hour with them twice a week.

And do this, not in a dull, dry, formal manner, but in earnest, with your might.

'But I have no gift for this.' Gift or no gift, you are to do it, else you are not called to be a Methodist preacher. Do it as you can, till you can do it as you would. Pray 5 earnestly for the gift, and use the means for it, particularly studying the children's tracts.

[§35]   *Q*. 35. Why are not we more holy? Why do not *we* live in eternity? Walk with God all the day long? Why are we not all devoted to God? Breathing the whole spirit of 10 *missionaries*?

A. Because we are enthusiasts, looking for the end without using the means.

In order to be thoroughly convinced of this, we need only consider the first *Minutes*, pp. 12, 13,[137] and each 15 examine himself upon each article.

To touch only upon two or three instances:

Do you rise at four? Or even at five, when you do not preach?

Do you fast once a week? Once a month? Do you know 20 the obligation or benefit of it?

Do you recommend the five o'clock hour for private prayer? Do you observe it? Do not you find that *any time* is *no time*.

O let us all 'stir up the gift of God that is in us'! Let us 25 no more 'sleep, as do others'; but whatsoever our 'hand findeth to do', let us 'do it with our might!'

[§36]   [CD36 as AB61, The Assistant defined.]

[§37]   [CD37 as A62, B62.1, How is the Assistant qualified?]

[§38]   [CD38 as B63, The business of the Assistant.] 30

[§39]   *Q*. 39. Ought we to insist upon our rule that no preacher print anything without your approbation?

A. Undoubtedly. And whoever does it for the time to come, cannot take it ill if he is excluded from our Connexion. Let everyone take this warning, and afterwards blame 35 none but himself.

[§40]   [CD40 as B65, Shortcomings of Assistants, with the omission of the closing clause of section 6, which had been taken over by *Q*. 39.]

---

[137] He is referring to the '*Large*' *Minutes* (1763), *Q*. 40.

[§41] [CD41 prefixes new matter to B66:]

Q. 41. Are there any other advices which you would give the Assistants?

A. Several. 1. Take a regular catalogue of your societies as they live, in house-row. 2. Leave your successor a particular account of the state of the circuit. 3. See that every band-leader have the Rules of them. 4. Vigorously but calmly enforce the Rules concerning ruffles, drams, snuff, and tobacco. When any person is admitted into a society, even good breeding requires him to conform to the rules of that society. The same you should enforce in Scotland as England. The Scots will hear reason as well as the English. 5. As soon as there are four men or women believers in any place, put them into a band. 6. Everywhere insist on decency and cleanliness. Tell them cleanliness is next to godliness. 7. Suffer no love-feast to last above an hour and [a] half; let not one duty interfere with another, and stop all breaking the cake with one another. That silly custom was introduced by James Wheatley, and creates much confusion. And 9.[138] Inform all the people from time to time that none should remove from one Society to another without a sufficient reason; and that those who desire to remove are to acquaint you with their reasons, and to have a certificate in these words (else they will not be received in other Societies): 'A.B. the bearer is a member of our society in M———; I believe he has a sufficient cause for removing.'

[§41.10] [CD41.10 takes over B66, Encourage attendance at Church, adding at end:] 'So that every preacher may attend the Church at least two Sundays out of four.'

[§41.11] [CD41.11 takes over B66, Precautions against separation from Church, but in number 5 opens, 'Warn them also . . .' instead of 'likewise'; in number 8 'petition to the Judges' becomes 'petition to the Judge or Justice', and number 9 ends '. . . oaths. And by so doing you are licensed.']

[§42] *Q.* 42. But are we not Dissenters?

A. We are irregular, (1) By calling sinners to repentance in all places of God's dominion. (2) By frequently using

---

[138] Orig. omits '8'.

extemporary prayer. Yet we are not Dissenters in the only sense which our law acknowledges, namely persons who believe it is sinful to attend the service of the Church. For we do attend it at all opportunities. We will not, dare not separate from the Church, for the reasons given several years ago. We are not Seceders, nor do we bear any resemblance to them. We set out upon quite opposite principles. The Seceders laid the very foundation of their work in judging and condemning *others.* We laid the foundation of our work in judging and condemning ourselves. They begin everywhere with showing their hearers how fallen the Church and Ministers are. We begin everywhere with showing our hearers how fallen they are *themselves.*

.And as we are not Dissenters from the Church now, so we will do nothing willingly which tends to a separation from it. Therefore let every Assistant immediately so order his circuit that no preacher may be hindered from attending the Church more than two Sundays in the month. Never make light of going to Church, either by word or deed. Remember Mr. Hook, a very eminent and zealous Papist. When I asked him, 'Sir, what do you for public worship here, where you have no Romish service?'[139] He answered, 'Sir, I am so fully convinced, it is the duty of every man to worship God in public, that I go to Church every Sunday. If I cannot have such worship as I would, I will have such worship as I can.'

But some may say, 'Our own service is public worship.' Yes, in a sense. But not such as supersedes the Church service. We never designed it should. We have an hundred times professed the contrary. It presupposed Public Prayer, like the sermons at the university. Therefore I have over and over advised, 'Use no long prayer, either before or after sermon.' Therefore I myself frequently use only a collect, and never enlarge in prayer, unless at intercession, or on a watch-night, or on some extraordinary occasion.

If it were designed to be instead of Church service it would be essentially defective. For it seldom has the four

---

[139] Orig., 'Sermon' in 1770; this was corrected in the errata to the *Works,* 1772, both in the printed errata and in manuscript in Wesley's own copy, to 'service'.

grand parts of Public Prayer, deprecation, petition, intercession and thanksgiving. Neither is it, even on the Lord's
day, concluded with the Lord's Supper.

5   The hour for it on that day, unless where there is some
peculiar reason for a variation, should be five in the morning as well as in the evening. Why should we make God's
day the shortest of the seven?

But if the people put ours in the room of the Church
service, we hurt them that stay with us, and ruin them
10   that leave us. For then they will go nowhere, but lounge
the sabbath away, without any public worship at all.

I advise therefore all the Methodists in England and
Ireland who have been brought up in the Church, constantly to attend the service of the Church, at least every
15   Lord's day.

[§43]   *Q.* 43. Are all our preachers merciful to their beasts?
A. Perhaps not. Everyone ought not only to ride moderately, but also to see with his own eyes his horse rubbed,
20   fed and bedded.

[§44]   *[140]*[CD44 as AB40, Watching over the Helpers.]
[§44.1][CD44.1 as B40.1, The Helpers' use of the means of grace.]
[§44.2][CD44.2 as B40.2, Searching the Scripture.]
[§44.3][CD44.3 as B40.3, The Lord's Supper.]
25   [§44.4][CD44.4 as B40.4, Fasting.]
[§44.5][CD44.5 as B40.5, Christian conference.]
[§44.6][CD44.6 as B40.6, Prudential means for Methodists, etc.]
[§44.7][CD44.7 as B40.7, Watching, denying ourselves.]
[§45]   [CD45 as AB41, Closer union between Helpers.]
30   [§46]   [CD46 as AB42, How to avoid popularity.]
[§47]   [CD47 as AB43, How often should Helpers preach?]
[§48]   [CD48 as AB44, Best method of preaching.]
[§49]   [CD49 as AB45 and B45.1, Other advice to preachers.]
[§50]   [CD50 as AB46, Most useful sermons.]
35   [§51]   [CD51 as B47, 'Preaching Christ'.]
[§52]   [CD52 as AB48, Preaching on holiness.]
[§53]   [CD53 as AB49, Insisting on practical religion.]
[§54]   [CD54 as AB50, Preachers disappointing congregations.]

---

[140] 1772 (*Works*) adds here and elsewhere an asterisk denoting the special importance of a section to JW.

[§55]   [CD55 as AB51 (though C—not D—fails to number section 3, though giving it, Against formality in worship.]

[§56]   [CD56 as B51.1, Helping people to 'sing true'.]

[§57]   [CD57 as B51.2, omitting closing phrase, about late suppers being 'poison', Relaxants after preaching.]   5

[§58]   [CD58 as AB52, Testing those called to preach.]

[§59]   [CD59 as AB53, Verifying the evidence.]

[§60]   [CD60 as AB54, Receiving a new Helper.]

[After the opening *Q.* and *A.* CD60.1 adds:]

[§60.1] Every person to be admitted is then to be present, and each   10
of them may be asked, *[141]'A.B., Have you faith in Christ?
Are you "going on to perfection"? Do you expect to be
"perfected in love" in this life? Are you groaning after it?
Are you resolved to devote yourself wholly to God and his
work? Do you know the Methodist plan? Have you read   15
the *Plain Account?* The *Appeals?* Do you know the *Rules* of
the Society? Of the Bands? Do you keep them? Do you
take no snuff? Tobacco? Drams? Do you constantly attend
the Church and Sacrament? Have you read the *Minutes?*
Are you willing to conform to them? Have you considered   20
the Twelve Rules of a Helper? Especially the first, tenth,
and twelfth? Will you keep them for conscience' sake? Are
you determined to employ all your time in the work of
God? Will you preach every morning and evening?
Endeavouring not to speak too long (an hour in the whole)   25
or too loud? Not lolling with your elbows? Have you read
the *Rules of Action and Utterance?* Will you meet the
Society, the Bands, the Select Society and the Leaders in
every place? Will you diligently and earnestly instruct the
children, and visit from house to house? Will you recom-   30
mend fasting, both by precept and example?'

[§60.2] [CD60.2 is as AB54, the last phrase amended to read thus:
'we are then to receive him as a probationer by giving him
the Minutes of the Conference inscribed thus, To A.B. . . .
fellow-labourer', followed by B54 and AB54.2, again   35
replacing 'a book' with 'the Minutes of the Conference'.
There follows a revision of B55;

---

[141] 1772 (*Works*) adds here and elsewhere an asterisk denoting the special importance of a section to JW.

'Meantime let none exhort in any of our societies without a note of permission from the Assistant. Let every
exhorter take care to have this renewal yearly. And let
every Assistant rigorously insist upon it.'

5 [§61] [CD61 is based partly on B73, Provision for worn-out
preachers, with so many revisions that it seems preferable
to repeat them verbatim.]

Q. 61. How can we provide for worn-out preachers?

A. Those that can preach a little may be supernumerary
10   preachers where there is most need. As for those who cannot preach at all,

1. Let every travelling preacher contribute *half a guinea*
yearly at the Conference.

2. Let everyone when first received as a travelling
15   preacher pay one guinea.

3. Let this be lodged in the hands of the stewards
approved by the majority of the preachers.

4. The present stewards are Joseph Cownl[e]y and John
Murlin.

20   5. Out of this let provision be made, first for the worn-
out preachers, then for the widows and children of those
that are dead.

6. Every worn-out preacher shall receive at least *ten
pounds* a year.

25   7. Every widow of a preacher shall receive yearly during
her widowhood (if she wants it) a sum not exceeding *ten
pounds*.

8. Every child left by a preacher shall receive once for all
a sum not usually exceeding *ten pounds*.

30   9. But none is entitled to anything from this fund till he
has subscribed *two guineas*.

10. Nor any person from the time he ceases (unless
worn-out) to be a travelling preacher.

11. Nor any who neglects paying his subscription for
35   four years together.

12. Let every preacher who does not bring or send his
subscription to the Conference be fined *two shillings and
sixpence*.

13. This fund is never to be reduced to less than an *hun-
40   dred pounds*.

14. Let a committee be chosen to see these rules duly executed. The present committee are,

Peter Jaco	John Pawson
Duncan Wright	James Oddie
Thomas Hanby	Thomas Olivers
Robert Roberts	John Helton
Alexander Mather	Christopher Hopper
Thomas Johnson	

[D, 1772]

[§61.14] **[D61.14 alters the composition of the committee, inserting between Pawson and Hopper in the second column Daniel Bumstead, Thomas Olivers, and John Helton.]**

[C, 1770]

15. Let an exact account of all receipts and disbursements be produced at the Conference.

[§62] *Q.* 62. How may the wives of the travelling preachers be provided for?

A. If a preacher marries hand over head, he must provide for himself. [Cf. A69] As to the rest, we cannot but observe many inconveniences have arisen from the present method of providing for the wives of the preachers. Those who are most proper for several places cannot be sent thither because they are married. And if they are sent, the people look upon them with an evil eye because they are burdened by their families. In order to remedy these inconveniences, let it be considered, 1. What each circuit can contribute. 2. How many wives are to be provided for. (Their children are provided for where they are.) 3. By what circuits? By this means, whether the preachers in any particular circuit are married or single, it makes no difference: so that any preacher may be sent to any circuit, without any difficulty.

[§63] *Q.* 63. How many circuits are there now? [Cf. A64, B64.1.]

A. Three and thirty in England, ten in Ireland, three in Wales, two in Scotland, and two in America.

[D, 1772]

[§63.1]*A.* **Four and thirty in England, ten in Ireland, three in Wales, two in Scotland, and three in America.**

[C, 1770]

[§64] *Q.* 64. Are our preaching-houses safe?

A. Not all; for some of them are not settled on trustees. Several of the trustees for others are dead.

[§65]   *Q.* 65. What then is to be done?

A. 1. Let the surviving trustees choose others without delay. 2. Let those who have debts on any of the houses give a bond to settle them as soon as their debt is paid.

[§66]   *Q.* 66. In what form may an house be settled?

A. In the following:

[CD66 then copies the Indenture given in B67 (1763), the first publication of a Model Deed, whose history goes back to properties in Bristol and Newcastle (1746) and in Manchester in 1751.[142] The major difference in the 1770 and 1772 versions is that the name of William Grimshaw of Haworth disappears as the one to succeed John Wesley in the supervision of Methodist property after the death of himself and his brother Charles. Grimshaw died in 1763.]

[§67]   *Q.* 67. But is this form a safe one? Should we not have the opinion of a counsel upon it?

A. I think this would be throwing money away. 1. Because this form was drawn up by three eminent counsellors. But, 2. It is the way of almost every lawyer to blame what another has done. Therefore you cannot at all infer that they think a thing wrong because they say so. 3. If they did in reality think it wrong, this would not prove it was so. 4. If there was (which I do not believe) some defect therein, who would go to law with the body of Methodists? 5. And if they did, would any court in England put them out of *possession?* Especially when the *intent* of the deed was plain and undeniable.

[68]   *Q.* 68. Is anything further advisable with regard to building?

A. 1. Build all preaching-houses, if the ground will admit, in the octagon form. It is best for the voice, and on many accounts more commodious than any other. 2. Let the roof rise only one third of the breadth: this is the true proportion. 3. Have enough[143] windows and doors; and let

---

[142] E. Benson Perkins, *Methodist Preaching Houses and the Law* (London: Epworth Press, 1952), 31–40.

[143] Orig., 'enow'.

all the windows be sashed, opening downward. 4. Let
there be no tub-pulpit, but a square projection, with a
long seat behind. 5. Let there be no backs to the seats,
which should have aisles[144] on each side, and be parted in
the middle by a rail running all along, to divide the men   5
from the women.

[§69]   *Q.* 69. Is there any exception to the rule, 'Let the men and
women sit apart?'
A. In those galleries where they have always sat together,
they may do so still. But let them sit apart everywhere   10
below, and in all new-erected galleries.

[§70]   [CD70 from B57 (1763), Excellency of Kingswood School,
repeated without any updating of such references as those
in number 6 to the setting up of an annual collection at
'our late Conference'. At the 1756 Conference it was   15
agreed that a subscription list to support the school
should be opened 'in every place', and '(if need be) a collection made every year'. The clues to the making of such
a decision at any intervening Conferences before that of
1763, however, are so far lacking, but see *Q.* 71 below.]   20

[§71]   [CD71 repeats B58, An annual Kingswood collection,
adding Scotland and Ireland.]

[§72]   [CD72 from B72, Raising a General Fund, repeated with
no updating, but omitting the closing reference to the
General Stewards, and the added paragraph referring to   25
their functions.]

[§73]   *Q.* 73. But notwithstanding all that has been contributed
and paid, we are still six thousand nine hundred and fifty-
eight pounds in debt. So that we gain no ground. What
can be done? How can we prevent the increase of debt?   30
A. By putting an absolute stop to all building for the ensuing year. Let no new house be built, no addition or alteration be made in any old one, unless the proposers thereof
can and will defray the whole expense of it.

[§74]   *Q.* 74. What can be done in order to pay the old debt?   35
A. 1. Give a note to each Assistant, specifying the debts
toward which the money collected in each circuit next
year is to be paid.

---

[144] Orig., 'isles'.

2. Let each Assistant encourage the people in each place, like those in Birmingham, to make a push toward paying off their own debt.

3. Let whatever is contributed in any circuit be paid away in that circuit so long as any debt remains therein.

4. Let whatever is contributed in any single place which is in debt, pay that as far as it will go.

5. Let whatever is contributed in the circuits which are out of debt be produced at the Conference.

6. Let us try whether any part of it may be paid off by annuities.

[D, 1772]

[§74.7][**Omits C74.3, 5, and 6, and adds:] But even this method being found ineffectual, it was agreed at the Conference in 1771 to change the yearly subscription into a weekly one. [A holograph footnote by John Wesley in his own copy of his *Works* (1772), 15:340, adds: 'By this means the pressing debts are now paid.']**

[C, 1770]

[§75]   *Q.* 75. What is the safest way of leaving a legacy for any charitable purpose?

A. To leave it absolutely to a person they can confide in.

[§76]   *Q.* 76. What is the method wherein we usually proceed in our conferences?

A. We inquire,

1. What Preachers are *admitted*?
   What remain on trial?
   Who are *admitted* on trial? and
   Who *desist* from travelling?

2. Who act as *Assistants* this year?

3. Are there any objections to any of the preachers? (who are named one by one.)

4. How are the preachers stationed this year?

5. What numbers are in the Society?

6. What is the Kingswood Collection?

7. What is contributed toward the debt?

8. How was this expended?

9. What is contributed toward the Preachers' Fund?

10. What demands are there upon it?

11. How many preachers' wives are to be provided for?

12. By what societies?

13. Where and when may our next Conference begin?

[§77]   *[145]*Q*. 77. What power is it which you exercise over both
preachers and people?   5

A. Count Zinzendorf loved to keep all things close. I love to
do all things openly. I will therefore tell you all I know of
the matter, taking it from the very beginning.

1. In November 1738 two or three persons who desired
'to flee from the wrath to come', and then seven or eight   10
more, came to me in London, and desired me to advise
and pray with them. I said, 'If you will meet me[146] on
Thursday night I will help you as well as I can.' More and
more then desired to meet with them, till they were
increased to many hundreds. The case was afterwards   15
the same at Bristol, Kingswood, Newcastle, and many
other parts of England, Scotland, and Ireland. It may be
observed the desire was on *their* part, not *mine*. My desire
was to live and die in retirement. But I did not see that I
could refuse them my help, and be guiltless before God.   20

Here commenced my power, namely a power to appoint
when, and *where*, and *how* they should meet; and to
remove those whose lives showed that they had no desire
to 'flee from the wrath to come'. And this power remained
the same whether the people meeting together were   25
twelve, twelve hundred, or twelve thousand.

2. In a few days some of them said, 'Sir, we will not *sit
under you* for nothing. We will subscribe quarterly.' I said,
'I will have nothing, for I want nothing. My fellowship
supplies me with all, and more than I want.' One replied,   30
'Nay, but you want one hundred and fifteen pounds to pay
for the lease of the Foundery. And likewise a large sum of
money will be wanting to put it into repair.' On this consideration I suffered them to subscribe. And when the
Society met, I asked, 'Who will take the trouble of *receiv-*   35
ing this money, and *paying* it where it is needful?' One

---

[145] 1772 (*Works*) adds here and elsewhere an asterisk denoting the special importance of a section to JW.

[146] The word 'me' was added in holograph in JW's copy of his *Works* (1772),
15:341.

said, 'I will do it, and keep the account for you.' So here
was the first *steward*. Afterwards I desired one or two
more to help me as stewards, and in process of time a
greater number.

Let it be remarked, it was I *myself*, not the people, who
chose these stewards and appointed to each the distinct
work wherein he was to help me, as long as I desired. And
herein I began to exercise another sort of *power*, that of
appointing and removing stewards.

3. After a time a young man came, T. Maxfield, and said
he desired to help me as a Son in the Gospel. Soon after
came a second, Thomas Richards, and a third, Thomas
Westell.[147] These severally desired to serve me as sons,
and to labour when and where I should direct. *Observe.*
These likewise desired *me*, not I *them*. But I durst not
refuse their assistance. And here commenced my *power* to
appoint each of these *when*, *where*, and *how* to labour—
that is, while he chose to continue with me. For each had a
power to go away when he pleased, as I had also to go
away from them, or any of them, if I saw sufficient cause.
The case continued the same when the number of preachers increased. I had just the same power still, to appoint
when, and *where*, and *how* each should help me, and to tell
any, if I saw cause, 'I do not desire your help any longer.'
On these terms, and no other, we joined at first: on these
we continue joined. But they do me no favour in being
directed by me. It is true, 'My reward is with the Lord.'
But at present I have nothing from it but trouble and care,
and often a burden I scarce know how to bear.

4. In 1744 I wrote to several clergymen, and to all those
who then served me as Sons in the Gospel, desiring them
to meet me in London, to give me their advice concerning
the best method of carrying on the Work of God. *They*
did not desire this meeting, but I did, knowing that 'in a
multitude of counsellors there is safety'. And when their
number increased, so that it was neither needful nor convenient to invite them all, for several years I wrote to
those with whom I desired to confer, and these only met

---

[147] Orig., 'Westal'.

at the place appointed; till at length I gave a general permission that all who desired it might come.

Observe. I myself sent for these of my own free choice;
and I sent for them to *advise*, not *govern* me. Neither did I
at any of those times divest myself of any part of that　　5
power above described, which the Providence of God had
cast upon me, without any design or choice of mine.

What is that power? It is a power of *admitting into* and
excluding from the Societies under my care. Of choosing
and removing *stewards*, of receiving or not receiving　　10
Helpers, of appointing them *when*, *where*, and *how* to help
me; and of desiring any of them to meet me when I see
good. And as it was merely in obedience to the Providence
of God, and for the good of the people, that I at first
accepted this power, which I never sought, nay an hun-　　15
dred times laboured to throw off, so it is on the same considerations, not for profit, honour, or pleasure, that I use
it at this day.

5. But several gentlemen are much offended at my having *so much power*. My answer to them is this.　　20

I did not seek any part of this power: it came upon me
unawares. But when it was come, not daring to bury that
talent, I used it to the best of my judgment.

Yet I never was fond of it. I always did, and do now bear
it as my burden; the burden which God lays upon me, and　　25
therefore I dare not yet lay it down.

But if you can tell me any one, or any five men, to whom
I may transfer this burden, who *can* and *will* do
just what I do now, I will heartily thank both them and
you.　　30

6. But some of our Helpers say, 'This is shackling freeborn Englishmen'; and demand a *free Conference*; that is, a
meeting of all the preachers, wherein all things shall be
determined by most votes.

I answer: It is possible after my death something of this　　35
kind may take place. But not while I live. To *me* the
preachers have engaged themselves to submit, to serve me
as 'sons in the gospel'. But they are not thus engaged to
any man or number of men besides. To *me* the people in
general will submit. But they will not yet submit to any　　40
other.

It is nonsense then to call my using *this power* 'shackling freeborn Englishmen'. None needs to submit to it unless he *will*; so there is no shackling in the case. Every preacher and every member may leave me when he pleases. But while he chooses to stay, it is on the same terms that he joined me at first.

'But this is *arbitrary power*; this is no less than *making yourself a Pope.*'

If by *arbitrary power* you mean a power which I exercise *single*, without any colleagues therein, this is certainly true: but I see no hurt in it. *Arbitrary* in this sense is a very harmless word. If you mean *unjust, unreasonable*, or *tyrannical*, then it is not true.

As to the other branch of the charge, it carries no face of truth. The Pope affirms that every Christian must do all he bids, and believe all he says, under pain of damnation. I never affirmed anything that bears any the most distant resemblance to this. All I affirm is, 'The preachers who choose to labour with me choose to serve me as Sons in the Gospel.' And 'the people who choose to be under my care choose to be so on the same terms they were at first'.

Therefore all talk of this kind is highly injurious to *me*, who bear this burden merely for *your* sakes. And it is exceeding mischievous to the people, tending to confound their understandings, and to fill their hearts with evil surmisings and unkind tempers towards me, to whom they really owe more for taking all this load upon me, for exercising this very *power*, for shackling myself in this manner, than for all my preaching put together. Because preaching twice or thrice a day is no burden to me at all: but the care of all the preachers and all the people is a burden indeed!

[§78] *Q.* 78. What can be done in order to the future union of the Methodists? [Cf. AB59.]

A. On Friday, August 4, 1769, Mr. Wesley read in the Conference the following paper.

1. It has long been my desire that all those Ministers of our Church who believe and preach salvation by faith might cordially agree between themselves, and not hinder but help one another. After occasionally pressing this in private conversation wherever I had opportunity, I wrote

down my thoughts upon this head, and sent them to each
in a letter. Out of fifty or sixty to whom I wrote, only *three*
vouchsafed me an answer. So I give this up. I can do no
more. They are a rope of sand, and such they will continue.

2. But it is otherwise with the *Travelling Preachers* in our   5
Connexion:[148] you are at present one body. You act in concert with each other, and by united counsels. And now is
the time to consider what can be done in order to continue this union. Indeed, as long as I live there will be no
great difficulty—I am, under God, a centre of union to all   10
our *travelling* as well as *local* preachers.

They all know me and my communication. They all love
me for my work's sake; and therefore, were it only out of
regard to me, they will continue connected with each
other. But by what means may this Connexion[149] be pre-   15
served, when God removes me from you?

3. I take it for granted, it cannot be preserved, by any
means, between those who have not a single eye. Those
who aim at anything but the glory of God and the salvation of men; who desire or seek any earthly thing, whether   20
honour, profit, or ease, will not, cannot continue in the
Connexion[150]—it will not answer their design. Some of
them, perhaps a *fourth* of the whole number, will procure
preference in the Church. Others will turn Independents,
and get separate congregations, like John Edwards and   25
Charles Skelton. Lay your accounts with this, and be not
surprised if some you do not suspect be of this number.

4. But what method can be taken to preserve a firm
union between those who choose to remain together?

Perhaps you might take some such steps as these: 30

On notice of my death, let all the preachers in England
and Ireland repair to London within six weeks.

Let them seek God by solemn fasting and prayer.

Let them draw up Articles of Agreement, to be signed by
those who choose to act in concert.   35

Let those be dismissed who do not choose it, in the most
friendly manner possible.

---

[148] Orig., 'Connection'.
[149] Orig., 'Connection'.
[150] Orig., 'Connection'.

Let them choose, by votes, a *Committee* of three, five, or seven, each of whom is to be *Moderator* in his turn.

Let the Committee do what I do now: propose *preachers* to be *tried, admitted,* or *excluded.* Fix the place for each preacher for the ensuing year, and time of the next Conference.

5. Can anything be done now in order to lay a foundation for this future union? Would it not be well, for any that are willing, to sign some Articles of Agreement before God calls me hence? Something like these:

'We, whose names are underwritten, being thoroughly convinced of the necessity of a close union between those whom God is pleased to use as instruments in this glorious work, in order to preserve this union between ourselves, are resolved, God being our helper,

'I. To devote ourselves entirely to God; denying ourselves, taking up our cross daily, steadily aiming at one thing, to save our own souls, and them that hear us.

'II. To preach the old Methodist Doctrines, and no other, contained in the Minutes of the Conferences.

'III. To observe and enforce the whole Methodist Discipline, laid down in the said Minutes.'

[§79] *Q.* 79. What can be done in order to revive the Work of God where it is decayed?

A. 1. See that no circuit be at any time without preachers. Therefore let no preacher who does not attend the Conference leave the circuit at that time on any pretence whatever. This is the most improper time in the whole year. Let every Assistant see to this, and require each of these to remain in the circuit till the new preachers come.

Let not all the preachers in any circuit come to the Conference.

Let those who do come set out as late as possible, and return as soon as possible.

2. Be more diligent in field preaching. The want of preaching abroad, and of preaching in new places, has greatly damped the Work of God.

3. Wherever we have a large preaching-house at one end of a great town, let us preach abroad at the other end of it, every Sunday morning at least.

4. Be more diligent in morning preaching wherever you can have twenty hearers.

5. Be more active in dispersing the books, particularly the Sermon on the *Good Steward*, on *In-being Sin*, the *Repentance of Believers*, and the *Scripture Way of Salvation*. Every Assistant may give away small tracts. And he may beg money of the rich to buy books for the poor.

6. Let every preacher strongly insist upon practical religion and relative duties, but in such a manner as to keep Christ continually in view.

7. Exhort the leaders of bands to speak to those with them in the closest manner possible.

8. Encourage all at the public meeting of the bands to speak with all openness and simplicity.

9. Let a fast be observed in all our Societies on the last Friday in September, and on the Friday after New Year's Day, after Lady-Day, and after Midsummer Day.

10. Wherever you can, use intercession on Friday, and recommend fasting both by precept and example.

11. Be conscientiously exact in the whole Methodist discipline. And that you may understand it, read over carefully the *Plain Account of the People called Methodists*, and the several *Minutes of the Conferences*.

12. Beware of *formality* in singing, or it will creep in upon us unawares. Is it not creeping in already, by those complex tunes which it is scarce possible to sing with devotion? Such is 'Praise ye the Lord, ye blessed ones', such the long quavering Hallelujah annexed to the Morning Song tune, which I defy any man living to sing devoutly. The repeating the same word so often (but especially while another repeats different words, the horrid abuse which runs through the modern Church music), as it shocks all common sense, so it necessarily brings in dead formality, and has no more of religion in it than a Lancashire hornpipe. Besides that it is a flat contradiction to our Lord's command, 'Use not vain repetitions.' For what is vain repetition if this is not? What end of devotion does it serve? Again, Do not suffer the people to sing too slow. This naturally tends to formality, and is brought in by those who have very strong or very weak voices. Is it

not possible that all the Methodists in the nation should
sing equally quick? Why should not the Assistant see that
they be taught to sing in every large society? And do this
in such a manner as to obviate the ill effects which might
5   otherwise spring therefrom?

13. Which of us 'fasts every Friday in the year?' Which of
us fasts at all? Does not this show the present temper of our
minds (though not of all), soft and unnerved? How then
can we advance the Work of God, though we may preach
10   loud and long enough! Here is the root of the evil. Hence
the Work of God droops; few are convinced, few justified,
few of our brethren sanctified! Hence more and more
doubt if we are to be sanctified at all till death—I mean
sanctified throughout, saved from all sin, perfected in love.
15   That we 'may all speak the same thing', I ask once for all,
Shall we defend this perfection or give it up? You all agree
to defend it; meaning thereby, as we did from the beginning, salvation from all sin, by the love of God and our
neighbour filling the heart. The Papists say, 'This cannot be
20   attained till we have been a sufficient time in Purgatory.'
The Dissenters say, 'Nay, it will be attained as soon as the
soul and body part.' The Old Methodists said, 'It may be
attained before we die—a moment after is too late.' Is it so
or no? You are all agreed, we may be saved from all sin
25   before death. The substance then is settled. But as to the
circumstance, is the change instantaneous or gradual? It is
both one and the other. From the moment we are justified
there may be a *gradual* sanctification or a growing in grace,
a *daily* advance in the knowledge and love of God. And if
30   sin cease before death, there must in the nature of the thing
be an instantaneous change. There must be a last moment
wherein it does exist, and a first moment wherein it does
not. But should we in preaching insist on both one and the
other? Certainly we must insist on the *gradual change*, and
35   that earnestly and continually. And are there not reasons
why we should insist on the *instantaneous* also? If there be
such a blessed change before death, should we not encourage all believers to expect it? And the rather because constant experience shows, the more earnestly they expect this,
40   the more swiftly and steadily does the gradual work of God
go on in their souls. The more watchful they are against all

sin, the more careful to grow in grace, the more zealous of good works, and the more punctual in their attendance on all the ordinances of God. Whereas just the contrary effects are observed whenever this expectation ceases. They are 'saved by hope', by this hope of a total change saved with a gradually increasing salvation. Destroy this hope, and that salvation stands still, or rather decreases daily. Therefore whoever would advance the gradual change in believers should strongly insist upon the *instantaneous*. 5

14. But how far from entire sanctification are we still? The religion of the Methodists in general is not internal, at least, not deep, universal, uniform; but superficial, partial, uneven. And what pains do we take to make it otherwise? Do we visit from house to house, according to the Plan laid down in the Minutes? Have you done this? Mr. Colley began. But he is gone to paradise. And who has trod in his steps? What hinders? Want of time? Only (as William Penington said) spend half the time in this visiting which you spend in talking uselessly, and you will have time enough. Do this, particularly in confirming and building up believers. Then and not till then, the work of the Lord will prosper in your hands. 10 15 20

15. But what can we do for the *rising generation*? Unless we can take care of these, the present revival of religion will be *res unius aetatis*—it will last only the age of a man. Who will *labour* herein? Let him that is zealous for God and the souls of men begin *now*. 25

'(1) Spend an hour a week with the children in every large town, whether you like it or no.

'(2) Talk with them every time you see any at home. 30

'(3) Pray in earnest for them.

'(4) Diligently instruct and vehemently exhort all parents, at their own home.

'(5) Preach expressly on education, particularly at Midsummer, when you speak of Kingswood.' 35

16. Let every preacher read carefully over the Life of Mr. Brainerd. Let us 'be followers of him, as he was of Christ', in absolute self-devotion, in total deadness to the world and in fervent love to God and man. We want nothing but this. Then the world and the devil must fall under our feet. 40

17. (1) Let us keep to the Church. Over and above all the reasons that were formerly given for this, we add another now from long experience. They that leave the Church leave the Methodists. The clergy cannot separate us from our brethren, the dissenting ministers can and do. Therefore carefully avoid whatever has a tendency to separate men from the Church. In particular preaching at any hour which hinders them from going to it. Let every Assistant look to this.

(2) Let all the servants in our preaching-houses go to Church on Sunday morning at least.

(3) Let every preacher go always on Sunday morning, and when he can in the afternoon. God will bless those who go on weekdays too, as often as they have opportunity.

18. Take heed to your doctrine.

We said in 1744, 'We have leaned too much toward Calvinism.' Wherein?

(1) With regard to man's faithfulness. Our Lord himself taught us to use the expression. And we ought never to be ashamed of it. We ought steadily to assert, on his authority, that if a man is not 'faithful in the unrighteous mammon', God will not 'give him the true riches'.

(2) With regard to working for life. This also our Lord has expressly commanded us. 'Labour'—ἐργάζεσθε—work for the meat that endureth to everlasting life.' And in fact every believer, till he comes to glory, works *for* as well as *from* life.

(3) We have received it as a maxim that 'a man is to do nothing *in order to* justification': nothing can be more false. Whoever desires to find favour with God should 'cease from evil, and learn to do well'. Whoever repents should do 'works meet for repentance'. And if this is not *in order* to find favour, what does he do them for?

Review the whole affair.

(1) Who of us is *now* accepted of God?

He that now believes in Christ, with a loving obedient heart.

(2) But who among those that never heard of Christ?

He 'that feareth God, and worketh righteousness', according to the light he has.

(3) Is this the same with, 'He that is sincere?'
Nearly, if not quite.
(4) Is not this 'salvation by works'?
Not by the *merit* of works, but *by* works as a *condition*.
(5) What have we then been disputing about for these
thirty years?
I am afraid, *about words.*
(6) As to *merit* itself, of which we have been so dreadfully
afraid, we are rewarded 'according to our works', yea,
'because of our works'. How does this differ from 'for the
sake of our works'? And how differs this from *secundum
merita operum?*—as our works *deserve?* Can you split this
hair? I doubt I cannot.
(7) The grand objection to one of the preceding proposi-
tions is drawn from matter of fact. God does in fact justify those who by their own confession neither feared God
nor wrought righteousness. Is this an exception to the
general rule?
It is a doubt whether God makes any exception at all.
But how are we sure that the persons in question never
did fear God and work righteousness? His own saying so
is not proof: for we know how all that are convinced of sin
undervalue themselves in every respect.
(8) Does not talking of a *justified* or a *sanctified state* tend
to mislead men? Almost naturally leading them to trust in
what was done in one moment? Whereas we are every
hour and every moment pleasing or displeasing to God
according to our works? According to the whole of our
inward tempers, and our outward behaviour.
19. Lastly, We must needs visit from house to house,
were it only to avoid idleness. I am afraid we are idle still.
Do we not loiter away many hours in every week? Try
yourselves. Keep a diary of your employment but for a
week, and then read it over. No idleness can consist with
growth in grace. Nay, without exactness in *redeeming
time* it is impossible to retain even the life you received in
justification.

3. The 'Large' *Minutes*, E and F (1780, 1789)

Text of E (1780) and F (1789) compared with AB
(1753, 1763) and CD (1770, 1772).[151]

MINUTES OF SEVERAL CONVERSATIONS
5   *between the Reverend Mr. John and*
Charles Wesley, and others,
From the year 1744, to the Year 1780.

[Two sentences from A, 1753, Conference preamble:]
[§0.1, 3] It is desired that all things be considered as in the imme-
10   diate presence of God. That every person speak freely
whatever is in his heart.
Q. 1. How may we best improve the time of this conference? [This is followed by CD *A*.1, *A*.2. abridged to 'In
the intermediate house let us redeem all the time we can
15   for private exercises', and *A*.3.]
[§2]   *Q.* 2. Have our conferences been as useful as they might
have been?
A. No; we have been continually straitened for time.
Hence scarce anything has been searched to the bottom.
20   To remedy this, let every conference last nine days, concluding on Wednesday in the second week. [See JW's
Journal, Aug. 1, 1780.]
[§3]   [EF as C4, God's design in Methodism.]
[§4]   [EF as CD5, The rise of Methodism.]
25 [§5]   [EF as CD6, Preach without forming societies?]
[§6]   [EF as CD8, Where preach most? but omitting *A*. 1.]
[§7]   [EF as CD9, Is field preaching unlawful?]
[§8]   [EF as CD10, Has field preaching been used too
sparingly?]

---

[151] Comments are made within square brackets, with excerpts within quotation
marks; complete new text from E, 1780, is given with the original *Q.* and *A.* numbers, and without brackets or quotation marks. Any new text from F, **1789**, is supplied in **bold** type. It is assumed that the comments include both edns. unless
exceptions are noted.

[§8.1] [EF add passage, Stewards oppose field preaching.]
    The stewards will frequently oppose this, lest they lose
      their usual collection. But this is not a sufficient reason
      against it. Shall we barter souls for money?

[§9] [EF as CD11, Observe where Holy Spirit works most.]   5

[§9.1] [EF add, A reserve of preachers.]
    But whence shall we have them? 1. So far as we can afford
      it, we will keep a reserve of preachers at Kingswood.
      2. Let an exact list be kept of those who are proposed for
      trial, but not accepted.   10
    [EF drop D12, 'What is a sufficient call to a new place?']

[§10] [EF abridge D13.]
    Q. 10. How often shall we permit strangers to be present at
      the meeting of the society?
    A. At every other meeting of the society in every place, let   15
      no stranger be admitted. At other times they may, but the
      same person not above twice or thrice. In order to this,
      see that all in every place show their tickets before they
      come in. If the stewards and leaders are not exact herein,
      employ others that have more resolution.   20
    [EF drop D14, 'May a relapser . . . be re-admitted . . . ?']

[§11] [EF revise and abridge D15:]
    Q. 11. How may the leaders of classes be made more
      useful?
    A. 1. Let each of them be diligently examined concerning   25
      his method of meeting a class.
      Let this be done with all possible exactness at the next
      quarterly visitation. And in order to this, allow sufficient
      time for the visiting of each society.
      2. Let each leader carefully inquire how every soul in his   30
      class prospers. Not only how each person observes the
      outward rules, but how he grows in the knowledge and
      love of God.
      3. Let the leaders converse with the Assistant frequently
      and freely.   35

[§12] *Q.* 12. [enlarged] Can anything further be done in order to
    make the meetings of the classes lively and profitable?
    A. 1. Change improper leaders.
      2. Let the leaders frequently meet each other's
      classes.   40

3. Let us observe which leaders are the most useful. And
let these meet the other classes as often as possible.
4. See that all the leaders be not only men of sound
judgment, but men truly devoted to God.

5   [§13]   [EF as D17, 'How can we further assist those under our
care?' but omitting A1, and adding to the former A2, 'all
the large societies', which is further extended in **F, 'this
has been much neglected'**. EF continue '2. By instructing them at their own houses . . .', the end changed to
10   'willing to believe'.]

[§13.1][EF as D17, 'For 1. personal religion . . . getting money,'
but F has '**NB. For 1**' at beginning and omits 'of praise'
near end. EF repeat 'How little brotherly love . . . two
particulars', omit 'What servants . . . that does not', and
15   repeat 'Who does . . . knaves' and 'Family religion . . .
angels?' The episode of Dr. Lupton and the soul is omitted, but the closing challenge of D17.1 is repeated and
enlarged:]

We must, yea every travelling preacher must, instruct
20   them *from house to house.* Till this is done, and that in
good earnest, the Methodists will be little better than
other people.

Our religion is not deep, universal, uniform, but superficial, partial, uneven. It will be so till we spend half as
25   much time in *this visiting* as we now do in talking
uselessly.

[§13.2][EF13.2 continue with the lengthy extract of Baxter's
Gildas Salvianus from CD17.2, omitting '4. Our interest
stops our mouths . . . Christ', and with the following
30   paragraphs renumbered, to close with '5. . . . meekness.']

[§13.3][EF13.3 continue as CD17.3, 'And we have many difficulties to grapple with in our people,' with the four listed
difficulties.]

[§13.4][EF13.4 continue as CD17.4, omitting the first sentence of
35   para. 3, and opening para. 4 'And this is absolutely necessary', and an abridged para. 6 closes 'But the greatest hindrance was in ourselves, in our littleness of faith and
love.']

[§13.5][EF13.5 continues as CD17.5, with many small revisions,
40   such as 'the loss of one soul' for 'the perdition of one
soul'.]

[§13.6][EF13.6 continues as CD17.6, heavily abridged.]

[§13.7][EF13.7 continues Baxter, on questioning children, CD17.7, again abridged.]

[§14] [EF14 as CD18, Excluding 'improper persons' from society. To 'Give them the *Rules* the first time they meet' **F** adds '**See that this be never neglected.**']   5

[§15] [EF15 abridges and revises CD19, Solemnizing admission of members.]

Q. 15. When shall we admit new members?

A. In large towns, admit them into the bands at the quarterly love-feast following the visitation; into the society on the Sunday following the visitation. Then also read the names of them that are excluded.   10

[§16] [EF16 revises the opening question of CD20, extends the first paragraph, and adds a sting to the tail of the second.]   15

Q. 16. Should we insist on the band rules? Particularly with regard to dress?

A. By all means. This is no time to give any encouragement to superfluity of apparel. Therefore give no band-tickets to any till they have left off superfluous ornaments. In order to this, 1. Let every Assistant read the thoughts upon dress at least once a year, in every large society. 2. In visiting the classes, be very mild, but very strict. 3. Allow no exempt case, not even of a married woman. Better one suffer than many. 4. Give no ticket to any that wear calashes, high-heads, or enormous bonnets. . . .   20   25

Observe! You give none a band-ticket *before* he meets, but *after* he has met!

[§17] [EF17 as 21, Band-members leaving off snuff and drams, but omitting from the end, 'or aiding digestion'.]   30

[§18] [EF18 revise CD22, Marriage with unbelievers.]

A. Many of our members have married with unbelievers, yea, with unawakened persons. This has had fatal effects. They had either a cross for life, or turned back to perdition.   35

[§19] [EF19 as CD23, with some revision of paras. 2 and 3.]

2. Let him ['the preacher'] openly declare, whoever does this will be expelled the society. 3. When any such is expelled, let a suitable exhortation be subjoined.

[§20] [EF20 as CD24, A woman marrying without consent.]   40

[§21]   [EF21 as CD25, Unsuitable and immoral conduct, but *QQ*.
and *AA*. altered in some details:]

    Q. 21. Do not sabbath-breaking, dram-drinking, evil-
speaking, unprofitable conversation, lightness, expensiveness or gaiety of apparel, and contracting debts without
due care to discharge them, still prevail in several places?
How may these evils be remedied?

    [The general recommendation of Wesley's social publi-
cations is dropped, and the condemnation of smuggling
and bribery in paras. 5 and 6 is revised.]

    5. Extirpate smuggling, buying or selling uncustomed
goods, out of every society. Let none remain with us who
will not totally abstain from every kind and degree of it, in
every society near the coasts. And read to them, and diligently disperse among them, the *Word to a Smuggler*.

    6. Extirpate bribery, receiving anything, directly or indi-
rectly, for voting in any election. Show no respect of persons herein, but expel all that touch the accursed thing.
Largely show, both in public and private, the wickedness
of thus selling our country. And everywhere read the *Word
to a Freeholder*, and disperse it with both hands.

[§22]   [EF22 follow CD26, Methodist bankrupts, revises the
answer:]

    A. Let the Assistant talk with him at large. And if he has
not kept fair accounts, or has been concerned in the base
practice of raising money by *coining notes* (commonly
called the *bill-trade*) let him be expelled immediately.

[§23]   [EF23 as CD27.]

[§24]   [EF24 as CD23, but with added note to 'extraordinary
messengers'.]

    Q. 24. In what view may we and our helpers be
considered?

    A. Perhaps as extraordinary messengers (i.e. out of the
ordinary way) designed (1) To provoke the regular
Ministers to jealousy. (2) To supply their lack of service
toward those who are perishing for want of knowledge.

[§24.1]   [F, 1789, adds:] **But how hard is it to abide here! Who
does not wish to be a little higher? Suppose, to be
ordained!**

[§25]   [EF25 as CD29, Office of a Helper, revised.]
 Q. 25. What is the office of an helper?
 A. In the absence of a Minister, to feed and guide the flock:
  in particular,

   1. To preach morning and evening. (But he is never to 5
  begin later in the evening than seven o'clock, unless in
  particular cases.)

   2. To meet the society and the bands weekly.

   3. To meet the leaders weekly.

  Let every preacher be particularly exact in this, and in 10
  the morning preaching. If he has twenty hearers, let him
  preach. If not, let him sing and pray.

  N.B. We are fully determined never to drop the morning
  preaching; and to continue preaching at five wherever it is
  practicable, particularly in London and Bristol. 15

[§26]   [EF26 as CD30, Rules of a Helper, with some variants. No.
 3 omits 'in private' after 'young women'. No. 4, 'consulting with your brethren' (about marriage) rather than 'first
 acquainting us with your design'. To no. 11 a long note is
 added:] 20

  Observe. It is not your business to preach so many times,
 and to take care of this or that society, but to save as many
 souls as you can; to bring as many sinners as you possibly
 can to repentance, and with all your power to build them
 up in that holiness without which they cannot see the 25
 Lord. And remember! A Methodist preacher is to mind
 every point, great and small, in the Methodist Discipline!
 Therefore you will need all the sense you have—and to
 have all your wits about you!

[§27]   [EF27 as CD77,'What *power* is this which you exercise over 30
 both the preachers and the societies?' CD have 'both
 preachers and people'. In general the substance of the
 paper read before the Conference is the same, but there is
 slight re-arrangement in the content and numbering of
 the sections. The two penultimate paragraphs are changed 35
 in the focus, arbitrary power being dropped in favour of
 making himself a Pope, which he answers thus:]

  'But this is *making yourself a Pope*.' This carries no face
 of truth. The Pope affirms, that every Christian must do
 all he bids, and believe all he says, under pain of damna- 40
 tion. I never affirmed anything that bears any, the most

distant resemblance to this. All I affirm is, 'The preachers who choose to labour with me choose to serve me as Sons in the Gospel. And the people who choose to be under my care choose to be so on the same terms they were at first.'

5 [§28] *Q.* 28. What reasons can be assigned why so many of our preachers contract nervous disorders?

A. The chief reason, on Dr. Cadogan's principles, is either indolence or intemperance. 1. Indolence. Several of them use too little *exercise*, far less than when they wrought at

10   their trade. And this will naturally pave the way for many, especially nervous disorders. 2. Intemperance (though not in the vulgar sense). They take more *food* than they did when they laboured more. And let any man of reflection judge how long this will consist with health. Or they

15   use more *sleep* than when they laboured more. And this alone will destroy the firmness of the nerves. If then our preachers would avoid nervous disorders, let them (1) Take as little meat, drink, and sleep as nature will bear; and (2) Use full as much exercise daily as they did before

20   they were preachers.

[§29]   [EF29 as CD31, Method of employing time, with omission of Pearson, Boehm, and Nalson at end, closing, 'to read in order, with much prayer, the *Christian Library* and the other books which we have published in prose and

25   verse'.]

F, 1789

[§29.1]and then those which we recommended in our Rules of Kingswood School.

[§30]   [EF30 use CD32, Should our Helpers follow trades, in

30   greatly abridged form.]

A. The question is not, whether they may occasionally work with their hands, as St. Paul did, but whether it be proper for them to keep shop or follow merchandise. After long consideration it was agreed by all our brethren that

35   no preacher who will not relinquish his trade of buying and selling (though it were only pills, drops, or balsam), shall be considered as a travelling preacher any longer.

[§31]   [EF31 as CD33.]

[§32]   [EF32 as CD34, but with some changes after 'Contract a

40   taste for [reading] or return to your trade.' The following paragraph is omitted; the following paragraph ends 'that

all the large societies provide our *Works* for the use of the preachers'. The passages on Baxter's plan omit Wesley's reminiscence of his mother's patience in teaching her children, 'I remember . . . my labour.']

[§33] [EF33 uses CD34.1–4, then adds other segments:] 5

[§33.1]We must needs do this, were it only to avoid idleness. Do we not loiter away many hours in every week? Each try himself: no idleness can consist with growth in grace. Nay, without exactness in *redeeming time*, you cannot retain the grace you received in justification. 10

[Wesley then adds, 'But what shall we do for the *rising generation*?' closing with the five numbered advices on children's education; see CD79.15. He continues:]

[§33.2]'But I have no gift for this.' Gift or no gift, you are to do it; else you are not called to be a Methodist preacher. Do it 15 as you can, till you can do it as you would. Pray earnestly for the gift, and use the means for it. Particularly study the *Instructions* and *Lessons for Children*.

[§34] [EF34 as CD35, 'Why are we not more holy?' with minor variants: 'Chiefly because' instead of 'Because'; 'Who of 20 you rises' for 'Do you rise'; slightly expanding the section on prayer: 'Or any other fixed time? Do not you find my experience that *any time* is *no time*?' And moving the altered section on fasting to the end, with an enlargement:] 25

[§34.1]Do you know the obligation and the benefit of fasting? How often do you practice it?

The neglect of this alone is sufficient to account for our feebleness and faintness of spirit. We are continually grieving the Holy Spirit of God, by the habitual neglect 30 of a plain duty! Let us amend from this hour.

[§35] *Q.* 35. But how can I fast, since it hurts my health?

A. There are several degrees of fasting which cannot hurt your health. I will instance in one. Let you and I every Friday (beginning on the next) avow this duty throughout 35 the nation, by touching no tea, coffee, or chocolate *in the morning*, but (if we want it) half a pint of milk or water-gruel. Let us dine on potatoes, and (if we need it) eat three or four ounces of flesh in the evening. At other times let us eat no flesh–suppers. These exceedingly tend to 40 breed nervous disorders.

[§36]   [EF36 as CD48, Best general method of preaching.]
[§37]   [EF37 uses CD49, with so many changes that it seems best
to give it complete.]

Q. 37. Are there any smaller advices relative to preaching
which might be of use to us?

A. Perhaps these, 1. Be sure never to disappoint a congregation, unless in case of life or death.

2. Begin and end precisely at the time appointed.

3. Let your whole deportment before the congregation
be serious, weighty, and solemn.

4. Always suit your subject to your audience.

5. Choose the plainest texts you can.

6. Take care not to ramble, but keep to your text, and
make out what you take in hand.

7. Be sparing in allegorizing or spiritualizing.

8. Take care of anything awkward or affected, either in
your gesture, phrase, or pronunciation.

9. Sing no hymns of your own composing.

10. Print nothing without my approbation.

11. Do not usually pray above eight or ten minutes (at
most) without intermission.

12. Frequently read and enlarge upon a portion of the
Notes. And let young preachers often *exhort*, without taking a text.

13. In repeating the Lord's Prayer, remember to say h*a*l-
lowed, not h*o*llowed, trespass against *us, Amen.*

14. Repeat this prayer aloud after the Minister, as often as
he repeats it.

15. Repeat after him aloud every confession, and both the
doxologies in the Communion Service.

16. Always kneel during Public Prayer.

17. Everywhere avail yourself of the Great Festivals, by
preaching on the occasion, and singing the hymns, which
you should take care to have in readiness.

18. Avoid quaint words, however in fashion, as *object,
originate, very, high,* etc.

19. Avoid the fashionable impropriety of leaving out the u
in many words, as honor, vigor, etc. This is mere childish
affectation.

20. Beware of clownishness. Be courteous to all.

21. Be merciful to your beast. Not only ride moderately, but see, with your own eyes, that your horse be rubbed, fed, and bedded.

[§38] [EF38 is as CD51, with a closing change: 'to preach him in all his offices, and to declare his *love* as well as his *gospel*, both to believers and unbelievers. Let us strongly insist upon inward and outward holiness in all its branches'.]

[§39] [EF39 is based on CD55, with omissions from the opening section, which is here given in full, and a large added section.]

Q. 39. How shall we guard against *formality* in public worship? Particularly in *singing*?

A. 1. By preaching frequently on the head. 2. By taking care to speak only what we feel. 3. By choosing such hymns as are proper for the congregation. 4. By not singing too much at once; seldom more than five or six verses. 5. By suiting the tune to the words. 6. By often stopping short and asking the people, 'Now! Do you know what you said last? Did you speak no more than you felt?'

[§39.1]Is not this formality creeping in already, by those complex tunes which it is scarce possible to sing with devotion? Such is, 'Praise the Lord, ye blessed ones.' Such the long quavering Hallelujah annexed to the Morning Song tune, which I defy any man living to sing devoutly. The repeating the same words so often (but especially while another repeats different words, the horrid abuse which runs through the modern church music), as it shocks all common sense, so it necessarily brings in dead formality, and has no more of religion in it than a Lancashire hornpipe. Besides, it is a flat contradiction to our Lord's command, 'Use not vain repetitions.' For what is vain repetition if this is not? What end of devotion does it serve?

[§39.2]7. Do not suffer the people to sing too slow. This naturally tends to formality, and is brought in by them who have either very strong or very weak voices. 8. In every large society let them learn to sing; and let them always learn our own tunes first. 9. Let the women constantly sing their parts alone. Let no man sing with them, unless he understands the notes, and sings the bass, as it is pricked down in the book. 10. Introduce no new tunes till they are perfect in the old. 11. Let no organs be placed anywhere till proposed in Conference. 12. Recommend our tune-book everywhere; and if you cannot sing yourself, choose a person or two in each place to pitch the tune for you.

5   13. Exhort everyone in the congregation to sing, not one in ten only. 14. If a preacher be present, let no singer give out the words. 15. When they would teach a tune to the congregation, they must sing only the tenor.

[§39.3]After preaching, take a little lemonade, mild ale, or candied
10   orange-peel. All spirituous liquors, at that time especially, are deadly poison. [Cf. CD57.]

[§40]   [EF40 as CD36, Who is the Assistant?]

[§41]   [EF41 as CD37, 'How should the Assistant be qualified for his charge?' N.B., not 'this charge'.]

15

F, 1789

[§41.1]**Let this be well observed. I fear, when the Metho-dists leave the Church, God will leave them. But if they are thrust out of it, they will be guiltless.**

20 [§42]   [EF42 as CD38, The business of an Assistant, revised, reversing '3. To keep watch-nights and love-feasts' and '4. To take in or put out of the Society or the bands.' Adding library notes, '6. To take care that every Society be duly supplied with books: particularly with Kempis,
25   *Instructions for Children*, and the *Primitive Physic*, which ought to be in every house', but omitting 'and that the money for them be constantly returned', [F42 also adds, **'O, why is not this regarded?'**], and 10, requiring a pri-vate library for each society. Revises 8: '**To take exact
30   lists of his societies every quarter, and send them up to London.**' Omitting 11, travelling with Wesley, but adding '**10. To overlook the accounts of all the stewards.**'

[§43]   [EF43 is as CD40, but heavily abridged.]
35   *Q.* 43. Has the office of an Assistant been well executed? *A.* No, not by half the Assistants. 1. Who has sent me word whether the other preachers behave well or ill? 2. Who has visited all the classes, and regulated the bands quarterly? 3. Love-feasts *for the bands* have been ne-
40   glected. Neither have persons been duly taken in and put out of the bands. 4. The societies are not half supplied

with books; not even with those above mentioned. O
exert yourselves in this! Be not weary! Leave no stone
unturned! 5. How few accounts have I had, either of
remarkable deaths, or remarkable conversions? 6. How
few exact lists of the societies? 7. How few have met the   5
married and single persons once a quarter?

[§44]   [EF44 as CD41, but greatly revised. The passage in 4 about
good breeding demanding obedience to the rules about
'ruffles, drams, snuff, and tobacco' is replaced by, 'Give
no band-ticket to any man or woman who does not prom-   10
ise to leave them off.' The later advices are revised and
rearranged, thus:]
     6. Suffer no love-feast to last above an hour and an
half—and instantly stop all breaking the cake with one
another. 7. Warn all from time to time that none are to   15
remove from one society to another without a certificate
from the Assistant, in these words (else he will not be
received in other societies): 'A.B. the bearer is a member
of our society in C. I believe he has sufficient cause for
removing.' 8. Everywhere recommend decency and clean-   20
liness. Cleanliness is next to godliness. 9. Exhort all that
were brought up in the Church to continue therein. Set
the example yourself; and immediately change every plan
that would hinder their being at Church at least two
Sundays in four. Carefully avoid whatever has a tendency   25
to separate men from the Church, in particular preaching
at any hour which hinders them from going to it. And let
all the servants in our preaching-houses go to Church
once on Sunday at least.

[§44.1][EF44, from B66.1, via CD41.11, does little more than   30
minor revising.]
     Is there not a cause? Are we not unawares by little and
little sliding into a separation from the Church? O use
every means to prevent this! 1. Exhort all our people to
keep close to the Church and Sacrament. 2. Warn them all   35
against niceness in hearing, a prevailing evil! 3. Warn
them also against despising the Prayers of the Church.
4. Against calling our society 'the Church'. 5. Against calling our preachers, 'Ministers', our houses 'Meeting-
houses': call them plain 'preaching-houses' or chapels.   40
6. Do not license them as 'Dissenters'. The proper paper

to be sent in at the Assizes, Sessions, or Bishop's Court is
this: 'A.B. desired to have his house in C. licensed for
public worship.' Do not license yourself till you are
constrained; and then not as a 'Dissenter', but as a
5   'Methodist'. It is time enough when you are prosecuted
to take the oaths. And by so doing you are licensed.

[§45]   [EF45 is based on CD42, but slightly revised and greatly
abridged.]
Q. 45. But are we not *Dissenters*?
10   *A*. No. Although we call sinners to repentance *in all places*
of God's dominion; and although we frequently use
extemporary prayer, and unite together in a *religious*
society, yet we are not Dissenters in the only sense which
our law acknowledges, namely those who renounce the
15   service of the Church. . . . [F adds:] **What they do in
America, or what their Minutes say on this subject,
is nothing to us. We will keep in the good old way.
. . . If the people put ours in the room of the Church
Service, we** *hurt* **them that stay with us, and** *ruin*
20   **them that leave us. For then they will go nowhere,
but lounge the Sabbath away, without any public
worship at all.**

[§46]   *Q*. 46. Nay, but is it not our duty to separate from the
Church, considering the wickedness both of the clergy
25   and the people?
A. We conceive not, 1. Because both the priests and the
people were full as wicked in the Jewish Church. And yet
it was not the duty of the holy Israelites to separate from
them. 2. Neither did our Lord command his disciples to
30   separate from them. He rather commanded the contrary.
3. Hence it is clear, *that* could not be the meaning of St.
Paul's words, 'Come out from among them, and be ye
separate.'

[§47]   *Q*. 47. But what reasons are there why we should not sepa-
35   rate from the Church?
A. Among others, those which were printed above twenty
years ago, entitled, 'Reasons against a Separation from the
Church of England.'

F, 1789

40 [§47.1]**We allow two exceptions, 1. If the parish Minister
be a notoriously wicked man. 2. If he preach**

Socinianism, Arianism, or any other essentially false doctrine.

[§48]   [EF48 as CD44, Do we sufficiently watch over our helpers? With much abridgement, reducing it to a summary of its original appearance in B, 1763. In AB40, CD44, para. 2, the first six sentences of EF close with 'Do you converse seriously, usefully, and closely.' B40.1 reads, 'Do you use each of these?' but EF lacks 'constantly (at set times) and fervantly'. B40.1 reads, 'Do you use private prayer' but EF lacks 'If you are your own master', and 'Do you ask everywhere . . . at five o'clock?' There is also a careful abridging of later passages:]

[§48.2] 2. Searching the Scriptures: by (1) Reading; *constantly,* some part of every day; *regularly,* all the Bible, in order; *carefully,* with the *Notes; seriously,* with prayer before and after; *fruitfully,* immediately practicing what you learn there? (2) Meditating: at set times? By any rule? [B–D, 'Meditating: at set times? How? By Bishop Hall's, or Mr. Baxter's rule? How long?'] (3) Hearing: Every morning? Carefully? With prayer before, at, after? Immediately putting in practice? Have you a New Testament always about you?

[§48.3] 3. The Lord's Supper. Do you use this at every opportunity? With solemn prayer before? With earnest and deliberate self-devotion.

[§48.4] 4. Fasting. How do you fast every Friday?

[§48.5] 5. Christian conference. Are you convinced how important and how difficult it is to 'order your conversation right'? Is it always 'in grace'? 'Seasoned with salt'? Meet to 'minister grace to the hearers'? Do not you converse too long at a time? Is not an hour commonly enough? Would it not be well always to have a determinate end in view? And to pray before and after it?

[§48.6] II. *Prudential* means we may use either as common Christians, as Methodists, as Preachers, or as Assistants.

1. As common Christians: What particular *rules* have *you* in order to grow in grace? What *arts* of holy living?

2. As Methodists, do you never miss your class or band?

3. As Preachers, do you meet every society? Also, the leaders and bands if any?

4. As Assistants, have you thoroughly considered your office? And do you make a conscience of executing every part of it?

[§48.7] These means may be used without fruit. But there are some means which cannot; namely, watching, denying ourselves, taking up our cross, exercise of the presence of God.

1. Do you steadily watch against the world? The devil? Yourselves? Your besetting sin?

2. Do you deny yourself every useless pleasure of sense? Imagination? Honour? Are you temperate in all things? Instance in food. Do you use only that *kind* and that *degree* which is best both for your body and soul? Do you see the necessity of this?

3. Do you eat no flesh-suppers? No late suppers?

4. Do you eat no more at each meal than is necessary? Are you not heavy or drowsy after dinner?

5. Do you use only that kind and that degree of drink which is best both for your body and soul?

6. Do you drink water? Why not? Did you ever? Why did you leave it off? If not for health, when will you begin again? Today?

7. How often do you drink wine or ale? Every day? Do you *want* [i.e., need] *it*?

8. Wherein do you 'take up your cross daily'? Do you cheerfully 'bear your cross' (whatever is grievous to nature) as a gift of God, and labour to profit thereby?

9. Do you endeavour to set God always before you? To see his eye continually fixed upon you? Never can you use these means but a blessing will ensue. And the more you use them the more will you grow in grace.

[§49] [EF49 as CD45, A closer union between the Helpers.]

[§50] [EF50 as CD58, Testing those called to preach.]

[§51] [EF51 as CD60, Receiving a new Helper, abridged. The latter one-third of 60.1 is reduced to the following: 'Will you preach every morning and evening, endeavouring not to speak too long or too loud? Will you diligently instruct the children in every place? Will you visit from house to house? Will you recommend fasting, both by precept and example?']

[E adds] Are you in debt? [To this **F** adds] **Are you
engaged to marry? (N.B. A preacher who marries
while on trial is thereby set aside.**

[In 60.2 the observation about 'rambling up and down' is
omitted, but a new one is added:]   5

Observe! Taking *on trial* is entirely different from *admitting* a preacher. One on trial may be either admitted or
rejected, without doing him any wrong. Otherwise it
would be no trial at all. Let every Assistant explain this to
them that are on trial.   10

At the next conference, if recommended by the
Assistant, he may be received into full connexion, by giving him the *Minutes* inscribed thus:

'As long as you freely consent to, and earnestly endeavour to walk by these Rules, we shall rejoice to acknowl-   15
edge you as a fellow-labourer.'

Meantime let none exhort in any of our societies without
a note of permission from the Assistant. Let every
exhorter take care to have this renewed yearly. And let
every Assistant insist upon it.   20

[§52] [EF52 is based on CD76, the Conference Agenda, with
some alterations: 'Who *remain on trial*?' The question
'Who act as *Assistants* this year?' is omitted. After 'What is
the Kingswood Collection?' come:]

6. What boys are received this year?   25

7. What girls are assisted?

8. What is contributed for the contingent expenses?

9. How was this expended?

10. What is contributed toward the fund for superannu-
ated and supernumerary preachers?   30

11. What demands are there upon it?

12. How many preachers' wives are to be provided for?
By what societies?

13. Where and when may our next conference begin?

[§53] *Q.* 53. How can we provide for superannuated and supernu-   35
merary preachers?

A. Those who can preach four or five times a week are
supernumerary preachers. As for those who cannot,

1. Let every travelling preacher contribute half a guinea
yearly at the conference.   40

2. Let everyone when first admitted as a travelling preacher pay a guinea.

3. Let this be lodged in the hands of the stewards.

4. The present stewards are John Murlin and John Pawson.

5. Out of this let provision be made first for the worn-out preachers, and then for the widows and children of those that are dead.

6. Every worn-out preacher shall receive, if he wants it, at least ten pounds a year.

7. Every widow of a preacher shall receive yearly (if she wants it) during her widowhood, a sum not usually exceeding ten pounds.

[EF53 continues largely with the text of CD61, omitting no. 10, and adding at the end: '15. Let every Assistant bring to the conference the contribution of every preacher in his circuit.' The committee named in E (1780) was Christopher Hopper, Robert Roberts, Thomas Coke, Thomas Hanby, John Allen, Thomas Lee, Duncan Wright, Thomas Taylor, William Thompson, and Thomas Rankin, and in F (1789), the same, except that Henry Moore replaces Thomas Lee, and Andrew Blair is added at the end of the list.]

[§54]   [EF54 replaces CD62, 'How may the wives of the Travelling Preachers be provided for?']

Q. 54. Are not many of the preachers' wives still straitened for the necessaries of life?

A. Some certainly have been. To prevent this for the time to come,

1. Let every circuit either provide each with a lodging, coals and candles, or allow her fifteen pounds a year.

2. Let the Assistant take this money at the Quarterly Meeting, before anything else be paid out of it.

[§54.1][F adds to no. 2:] **Fail not to do this.**

[§55]   *Q.* 55. How can we account for the decrease of the work of God in some circuits, both this year and the last?

A. It may be owing either, 1. To the want of zeal and exactness in the *Assistant*, occasioning want of discipline throughout. Or 2. To want of life and diligence in *the preachers*. Or 3. To our people's losing the life of God, and sinking into the spirit of the world.

It may be owing farther, to the want of more field-
preaching, and of trying more new places.

[§55.1][In E only] And now in particular, to their senseless *prejudice* against the King, and *speaking evil of dignities*. To stop
this flame, let none preach with us who speak evil of our   5
governors, or prophesy evil to the nation. Let every
Assistant take care of this.

[§56]   *Q*. 56. [E only] But are all our Assistants themselves clear
of this?

A. Who can testify the contrary? No one.   10

[§57]   *Q*. 57. What can be done in order to revive the work of God
where it is decayed?

[EF57 is based on CD79, with some additional matter, here
given.]

A. 1. Let every preacher read carefully over the *Life of*   15
David Brainerd. Let us be 'followers of him, as he was of
Christ', in absolute self-devotion, in total deadness to
the world, and in fervent love to God and man. Let us
but secure this point, and the world and the devil must
fall under our feet.   20

2. Let both Assistants and preachers be conscientiously
exact in the whole Methodist discipline.

3. See that no circuit [as CD79.1].

4. Wherever you can appoint prayer-meetings, and particularly on Friday.   25

5. Let a fast be observed in all our societies on the last
Friday in September, and on the Friday after New Year's
day, after Lady day, and after Midsummer day.

6. Be more active in dispersing the books, particularly
the Sermon on *The Good Steward*, on Indwelling Sin,   30
The Repentance of Believers, and *The Scripture Way of*
Salvation. Every Assistant may give away small tracts.
And he may beg money of the rich to buy books for the
poor.

[EF57 (7) in fact has its roots in CD79 (13–14), though   35
greatly disguised.]

7. Strongly and explicitly exhort all believers to 'go on
to perfection'. That we may 'all speak the same thing',
I ask once for all, Shall we defend this perfection, or
give it up? You all agree to defend it, meaning thereby   40
(as we did from the beginning), salvation from all sin,

by the love of God and man filling our heart. The
papists say, 'This cannot be attained till we have been
refined by the fire of purgatory.' The Calvinists say,
'Nay, it will be attained as soon as the soul and body
part.' The Old Methodists say, 'It may be attained *before*
we die—a moment after is too late.' Is it so or no? You
are all agreed, we may be saved from all sin *before death*.
The substance then is settled. But, as to the circumstance, is the change gradual or instantaneous? It is both
the one and the other. From the moment we are justified
there may be a gradual sanctification, a growing in
grace, a daily advance in the knowledge and love of God.
And if sin cease before death there must, in the nature
of things, be an instantaneous change. There must be a
last moment wherein it does exist, and a first moment
wherein it does not. 'But should we in preaching insist
both on one and the other?' Certainly we must insist on
the *gradual change*, and that earnestly and continually.
And are there not reasons why we should insist on the
instantaneous also? If there be such a blessed change
before death, should we not encourage all believers to
expect it? And the rather, because constant experience
shows, the more earnestly they expect this, the more
swiftly and steadily does the gradual work of God go on
in their soul: the more watchful they are against all sin;
the more careful to grow in grace, the more zealous of
good works, and the more punctual in their attendance
on all the ordinances of God. (Whereas just the contrary
effects are observed whenever this expectation ceases.)
They are *saved by hope*, by this hope of a total change,
with a gradually-increasing salvation. Destroy this hope,
and that salvation stands still, or rather decreases daily.
Therefore whoever would advance the gradual change
in believers should strongly insist on the instantaneous.

[§58] *Q.* 58. What can be done to increase the work of God in
Scotland?

A. 1. Preach abroad as much as possible.

2. Try every town and village.

3. Visit every member of the society at home.

[§58.1][F, 1789, omits nos. 4 and 5.]

4. Let the preachers at Dundee and Arbroath not stay at either place more than a week at a time.

5. Let each of them once a quarter visit Perth, Dunkeld, and the intermediate villages.

[§59]   [E59 takes over the paper read in Conference on Aug. 4, 1769, on the future union of the Methodists, which reappeared in CD78, though the spelling in 2 and 3 is 'Connexion' rather than 'Connection' as in the orig. of 1770 and 1772. This section is reprinted in EF almost verbatim, though the last paragraph of 4 begins 'Let this Committee propose Preachers. . . .']

[§60]   *Q.* 60. How many circuits are there now? [Cf. CD63, 63.1.]
A. Of America we have no late account. There are six and forty circuits in England, four in Scotland, and fourteen in Ireland.

[F, 1789]

[§60.1]*Q.* **58. How many circuits are there now?**
A. **Of America we have no late account. There are sixty-four circuits in England, Wales, and the Isle of Man; six in Scotland, and twenty-eight in Ireland.**

[E, 1780]

[§61]   [E61, F59, repeat the *Q.* and *A.* of CD64, Are our preaching-houses safe?]

[§62]   *Q.* 62. What then is to be done?
[E62, F60, give a somewhat more detailed answer than that in CD65.]
A. 1. Let those who have debts on any of the houses give a bond to settle them as soon as they are indemnified.

2. Let the surviving trustees choose others without delay, by endorsing their deed thus:

'We the remaining trustees of the Methodist Preaching-house in _____, do according to the power vested in us by this deed, choose _____ to be trustees of the said house in the place of _____

'Witness our hands _____.'

N.B. The deed must have three new stamps, and must be enrolled in Chancery within six months.

[§63] *Q.* 63. In what form may an house be settled?

A. In the following, which was drawn by three of the most eminent lawyers in London. Whoever therefore objects to it only betrays his own ignorance.

[E63, F61, then continue with the same basic Indenture as that given in CD66, except that the original building is not identified (by the omission of 'Market-street lane, in Manchester'). In F (1789), the name of Charles Wesley, as successor to John, was omitted, he having died in 1788, and the regulatory body after the death of John Wesley was noted as the Conference itself, in accordance with the 1784 Deed of Declaration: '**The major part of the trustees of the said premises for the time being, shall from time to time, and at all times for ever, permit such persons as shall be appointed at the yearly Conference of the People called Methodists, in London, Bristol, Leeds, Manchester, or else-where, specified by name in a Deed enrolled in Chancery, under the hand and seal of the said John Wesley, and bearing date the 28th day of February 1784, and no others, to have and to enjoy the said premises, for the purposes aforesaid.**']

[§64] [E64, F62 repeat CD67, Is this form safe?]

[§65] [E65, F63, continue the opening Advices with regard to building of CD68, but greatly enlarged.]

Q. 65. Is anything farther advisable with regard to building?

A. 1. Build all preaching-houses, where the ground will permit, in the Octagon form. It is best for the voice, and on many accounts more commodious than any other.

2. Why should not any Octagon House be built after the model of Yarm? Any Square House after the model of Bath or Scarborough? Can we find any better model?

3. Let the roof rise only one-third of its breadth—this is the true proportion. 4. Have doors and windows enough; and let all the windows be sashes, opening downward.

5. Let there be no Chinese Paling, and no tub-pulpit, but a square projection with a long seat behind. 6. Let there be no pews and no backs to the seats, which should have aisles on each side, and be parted in the middle by a rail running all along, to divide the men from the women, just

as at Bath. 7. Let all preaching-houses be built plain and
decent, but not more expensively than is absolutely
unavoidable. Otherwise the necessity of raising money
will make rich men necessary to us. But if so, we must be
dependent upon them, yea, and governed by them. And   5
then farewell to the Methodist discipline, if not doctrine
too. 8. Wherever a preaching-house is built, see that lodgings for the preachers be built also.

[§66] [E66, F64 reprint CD69, Men and women sit apart.]
[§67] *Q*. 67. But how can we secure their sitting apart here?   10
    A. I must do it myself. If I come into any new house and
    see the men and women together, I will immediately go
    out. I hereby give public notice of this. Pray let it be
    observed.
[§68] [E68, F66] *Q*. 68. But there is a worse indecency than this   15
    creeping in amongst us, Talking in the preaching-houses
    before and after service. How shall this be cured?
    A. Let all the preachers join as one man, and the very next
    Sunday they preach in any place, enlarge on the impropri-
    ety of talking before or after service, and strongly exhort   20
    them to do it no more. In three months, if we are in
    earnest, this vile practice will be banished out of every
    Methodist congregation. Let none stop till he has carried
    his point.

[F, 1789]   25

[§68.1] **Q. 67. Is there not another shocking indecency fre-
    quently practised by filthy men against the wall of a
    preaching-house—enough to make any modest
    woman blush!**
    **A. There is. But I beg anyone who sees another do   30
    this will give him a hearty clap on the back.**

[E, 1780]

[§69] *Q*. 69 [F, *Q*. 68]. Complaint has been made that sluts spoil
    our houses. How may we prevent this?
    A. Let none that has spoiled one ever live in another. But   35
    what a shame is this! A preacher's wife should be a pattern
    of cleanliness, in her person, clothes and habitation. Let
    nothing slatternly be seen about her: no rags, no dirt, no
    litter. And she should be a pattern of industry: always at
    work, either for herself, her husband, or the poor. I am   40
    not willing any should live in the Orphan House at

Newcastle, or any preaching-house, who does not conform to this rule.

[§70] *Q*. 70 [F, *Q*. 69]. It has been complained also that people
crowd into preaching-houses, as into coffee-houses, without any invitation. Is this right?

A. It is utterly wrong. Stop it at once. Let no person come
into the preacher's house unless he wants to ask a question.

[§71] *Q*. 71 [F, *Q*. 70]. May any new preaching-houses be built?

A. Not unless, 1. They are proposed at the Conference. No,
nor 2. Unless two-thirds of the expense be subscribed. And if any collection be made for them, it must
be made between the Conference and the beginning of
February.

[§72] [E72, F71 repeating CD70, The excellency of Kingswood
School. The preamble is different:]

A. Let every Assistant read the following account of it
yearly in every congregation.

[EF omit the following passage in para. 6: 'but thirteen or
fourteen poor children . . . subscription made at London
and Bristol'.]

[§73] [E73, F72 remain as CD71, The Kingswood Collection,
but 'for this school' instead of 'for it'.]

[§74] [EF74, based on CD72, but much abridged after the new
title and old preamble:]

Q. 74. How may we raise a General Fund for carrying on
the whole Work of God?

A. 1. Within these thirty years several of our brethren in
various parts, having no room which would contain the
congregation, by the advice of the preachers have built
houses for preaching capable of containing the usual
number of hearers. But this has necessarily involved them
in large debts. This the societies to whom those houses
belong are by no means able to pay. But the whole body of
Methodists joining together can do it without inconvenience. Only let them cheerfully exert on so pressing an
occasion the ability which God hath given them.

[F, 1789, omits the foregoing paragraph.]

2. But how shall we send labourers into those
parts where they are most of all wanted? Suppose the

north-west of Ireland and the north of Scotland? Many
are willing to hear, but not to bear the expense. Nor can it
as yet be expected of them. Stay till the word of God has
touched their hearts, and then they will gladly provide for
them that preach it. Does it not lie upon *us*, in the mean 5
time, to supply their lack of service? To raise a General
Fund out of which from time to time that expense may be
defrayed? By this means, those who willingly offer themselves may travel through every part, whether there are
societies or not, and stay wherever there is a call, without 10
being burdensome to any. Thus may the gospel, in the life
and power thereof, be spread from sea to sea. Which of
you will not rejoice to throw in your mite to promote this
glorious work?

Besides these, in carrying on so large a work through the 15
three kingdoms, there are calls for money in various ways,
and we must frequently be at considerable expense, or the
work must be at a full stop. Many too are the occasional
distresses of our preachers or their families, which require
an immediate supply. Otherwise their hands would hang 20
down, if they were not constrained to depart from the
work.

3. Let then every member of our society, once a year, set
his shoulder to the work, contributing more or less as
God hath prospered him, at the Lady-Day visitation of 25
the classes. Let none be excluded from giving something,
be it a penny, a half-penny, a farthing. Remember the
widow's two mites! And let those who are able to give
shillings, crowns, and pounds, do it willingly. The money
contributed will be brought to Leeds, Bristol, or London, 30
at the ensuing Conference.

4. Men and brethren, help! Was there ever a call like *this*,
since you first heard the gospel-sound? Help to relieve
your companions in the kingdom of Jesus, who are
pressed above measure. 'Bear ye one another's burdens, 35
and so fulfil the law of Christ.' Help to send forth able,
willing labourers into your Lord's harvest: so shall ye be
assistant in saving souls from death and hiding a multitude of sins. Help to spread the gospel of your salvation
into the remotest corners of the kingdom, till 'the knowl- 40
edge of our Lord shall cover the land, as the waters cover

the sea'. So shall it appear to ourselves, and all men, that we are indeed one body, united by one Spirit; so shall the baptized heathens be yet again constrained to say, 'See how these Christians love one another.'

In this, may not even the Romanists provoke us to jealousy? They have a General Fund at Rome, and another at Paris, which bears all the expenses of their missionaries throughout all the world.

[§75]   *Q.* 75. What is the direct antidote to Methodism (the doctrine of heart-holiness)?

A. Calvinism. All the devices of Satan for these forty years have done far less toward stopping this work of God than that single doctrine. It strikes at the root of salvation from sin previous to glory, putting the matter on quite another issue.

[§76]   *Q.* 76. But wherein lie the charms of this doctrine? What makes men swallow it so greedily?

A. 1. It seems to magnify Christ—although in reality it supposes him to have died in vain. For the absolutely elect must have been saved without him; and the non-elect cannot be saved by him.

2. It is highly pleasing to flesh and blood, Final Perseverance in particular.

[§77]   *Q.* 77. What can be done to guard against it?

A. 1. Let all our preachers carefully read over ours and Mr. Fletcher's tracts.

2. Let them frequently and explicitly preach the truth, though not in a controversial way. But let them take care to do it in love and gentleness—not in bitterness, not returning railing for railing. Let Mr. R[owland] and R[ichard] H[ill] and their associates have all this to themselves.

3. Do not imitate them in screaming, allegorizing, boasting. Rather mildly expose these things when time serves.

4. Imitate them in this. They readily seize upon anyone that is newly convinced or converted. Be diligent to prevent them, and to guard those tender minds against the predestinarian poison.

5. Answer all their objections as occasion offers, both in public and private. But take care to do this with all possible sweetness both of look and of accent.

6. Very frequently, both in public and private, advise our people not to hear them.   5

7. Make it a matter of constant and earnest prayer, that God would stop the plague.

[§78]   [EF78 is based on CD79 (18), 'Take heed to your doctrine', with only minor changes.]

4. Analytical Summary: Disciplinary *Minutes*, 1749–89

The 1749 Doctrinal and Disciplinary *Minutes* are arranged chronologically by annual Conference meeting and do not need to be included in the following chart, since the origin of each item is clearly indicated by the dated headings for each section. The 1753 Disciplinary *Minutes*, however, drastically revises the 1749 edition by rearranging the Questions more topically than chronologically, and the next three editions generally follow that ordering. Even though that material contains sections headed by dates, those dates (even though they are also included in the following three editions) have very little bearing whatsoever on the date or source of the Questions and Answers contained in that particular section. The reshuffling of the material out of chronological order can be seen in the first of the following charts by noticing the way the dates of the 'Source' shift as one proceeds through the publication. Even §§64.68–71, which constitute nearly half of an added section at the end dated 'November 19, 1749', are from 1753, and two items from 1749 precede that heading.

The following charts indicate the sources and relationships of the material in the six revisions of the Disciplinary *Minutes*, as seen in their three main correlated groupings between 1753 and 1789.

A/B, 1753/1763

Section	Subject	Source	Editions and Questions
0.1–4	Conference preamble: the presence of God	44:3	A–F
0.5	Conference: fear of over-turning principles	47:5	A–D
1	Conference: time of watching unto prayer	47:3	A–D
2	Conference: accepting majority judgment	44:4	A–D
3	Principle of private judgment	47:7	AB4, CD3
4	God's design in Methodism	1763:cf. 65:26	B4, CD4, EF3
5	Preach without forming societies?	48:3:cf. 45:62	A5, BCD6, EF5
6	Inconvenience of no societies	48:4	A6, BCD7
7	Where should we preach most?	44:68	A7, BCD8, EF6
8	Is field preaching unlawful?	44:67	A8, BCD9, EF7
9	Have we used it too sparingly?	47:58	A9 BCD10, EF8
9.1	Hindrances to field preaching	1763?:cf. 65:15	BCD10, EF8
10	Where does God work most abundantly?	46:60	A10, BCD11, EF9
11	A sufficient call to a new place	46:59	A11, BCD12
12	When may strangers attend society?	48:7	A12, BCD13, EF10
12.1	Showing tickets	1763?	BCD13, EF10

Section	Subject	Source	Editions and Questions
22.1	Read sermon on evil-speaking	1763?	BCD25, EF21
22.2	Extirpate smuggling	1763?	BCD25, EF21
22.3	Extirpate bribery	1763?	BCD25, EF21
23	The office of a Christian minister	44d:8	A23, B26, CD27, EF23
24	Respect of persons	47:59	A24, B27
25	Favouring the rich	47:60	A25, B28
26	Visiting the sick	47:61	A26, B29
27	Do we take 'state up on ourselves'?	46:45	A27
27.1	Method of sick-visiting	1763?	B30
28	How shall we be more easy of access?	46:46	A28, B31
29	Bearing testimony against the clergy	45:64	A29
30	Bearing testimony for the future	45:66	A30
31	Conversing with the clergy	45:67	A31, B32
32	Conversing with opposers	45:68	A32, B33
33	National sins and our witness	45:69	A33, B34
34	Talking of persecution before it comes	45:70	A34, B35
35	Wesley's helpers 'extra-ordinary messengers'	46:44	A35, B36, CD28, EF24
36	The office of a helper	44:72	A36, B37, CD29, EF25
36.1	Be exact in morning preaching; meet leaders	1763?	B37, CD29, EF25
37	The rules of a helper	44e:2	A37, B38, CD30, EF26

Section	Subject	Source	Editions and Questions
51.1	Helping people to 'sing true'	1763?	B53, CD56
51.2	A relaxant after preaching	1763?	B54, CD57
52	Testing those called to preach	46:47	A52, B55, CD58, EF50
53	Verifying the evidence	46:48	A53, B56, CD59
54	Receiving a new helper	49:21	A54, B57, CD60, EF51
54.1	Go where Assistant directs	1763?	B57, CD60
54.2	Approach to Full Connexion	49:21	A54, B57, CD60, EF51
55	Admit with more solemnity?	46:50	A55
56	Exhorter's note of recommendation	1763?	B58, CD60, EF51
57	The excellency of Kingswood School	1763?	B59, CD70, E72, F71
58	A Collection for Kingswood School	1763?	B60, CD71, E73, F72
59	A general union of the societies?	49:1	A59, B61
60	Through agency of the London stewards	49:2	A60, B62
61	Who is the Assistant?	49:5–6	A61, B63, CD36, EF40
62	The qualifications of an Assistant	49:7	A62, B64, CD37, EF41

C/D, 1770/1772

Section	Subject	Source	Editions and Questions
5	The rise of Methodism	65:26	CD5, EF4
16.3	Making new class leaders	1772?	D16
17	Closely examine members at each Visitation	1770?	CD17
17.1–7	Methodists no better than others?	66:29	CD17, EF13
21	Band members forsaking snuff and drams	65:36, 37	CD21, EF17
25.6	Extirpate smuggling, addition	67:30	CD26, EF22
25.7	Extirpate bribery, addition	67:31	CD26, EF22
26	Methodist bankrupts	70:16	CD26, EF22
32	Should our helpers follow trades?	68:22	CD32
33	Why are our people no better?	66:29	CD33, EF31
34.1–2	Why are we not more knowing?	66:30	CD34, EF32
34.3	How should we instruct children?	66.31	CD34, EF33
35	Why are we not more holy?	66:32	CD35, EF34
39	No preacher prints without approval	65:24	CD39
41	Miscellaneous advice to Assistants	66:21, 23–25, 27	CD41, EF44
42	Are we not Dissenters?	66:28	CD42, EF45
43	Being merciful to our horses	65:19	CD43
60.1	Receiving a new Helper, addition	66:32	CD60, EF51
61	Providing for worn-out preachers, add	65:7	CD61, EF53
62	Providing for preachers' wives: add	69:23	CD62, EF55

63.1	How many circuits?	1772?	CD63, E60, F58
64	Are preaching-houses safe? (rev'd)	65:11	CD64, E61, F59
65	Surviving trustees choose new trust	67:25	CD65, E62, F60
66	Revised Model Deed	1770	CD66, E64, F62
67	Is the form a safe one?	67:25	CD67, E64, F62
68	More advice on building, octagons	Cf. *Journal* 7/27/44	CD68
69	Men and women sit apart, enforced	65:14; 66:19	CD69, E66, F64
73	Increasing debt: stop building	70:14	CD73
74	Liquidating old debt	69:19; 70:15	CD74
74.7	Yearly subscription becomes weekly	1771	D74
75	Legacies	67:23	CD75
76	Conference procedure (1–13)	1770	CD76, EF52
77	Wesley's power (1–6) [Cf. 1763, p. 147b]	66:29	CD77, EF27
78	Future union of Methodists (1–4) [Cf. 84]	69:close	CD78, E59
79	Reviving the work of God (1–11 of 19)	67:29, 32 68:23; 70:27	CD79
79.12	Formality in singing	68:23.6	CD79:12
79.13	Fasting every Friday	68:23.8	CD79.13
79.14	Building up believers	68:23.14	CD79:14
79.15	The rising generation	68:23.10	CD79:15
79.16	Read Brainerd's *Life*	68:23.11	CD79:16
79.17	Keep to the Church	68:23.12	CD79:17
79.18	Take heed to your doctrine	70:28.6	CD79:18
79.19	Visitation re-emphasized	70:28.1	CD79:19

E/F, 1780/1789

Section	Subject	Source	Editions and Questions
1	Improving time of Conference: variant	1780	EF1
2	Nine-day Conference	*Journal*, 8/1/80	EF2
8.1	Field preaching hindered for finances	1780?	EF8
9.1	A reserve of preachers	1780?	EF9
12	Improve class meetings, addition	1780?	EF12
15	When shall we admit new members? (rev'd)	1780?	EF15
16	Band rules and dress, addition	1780?	EF16
18	Marriage with unbelievers (rev'd)	1780?	EF18
19	Defaulters will be expelled	1780?	EF19
21	Smuggling, bribery, bankruptcy (rev'd)	1780?	EF21
24	Helpers, extraordinary messengers (rev'd)	1780?	EF24
24.1	Do preachers seek improved status?	1789?	F24
25	Never drop early morning preaching	1780?	EF25
26	Rule 11 for Helper, varied	1780?	EF26
27	Wesley's power (rev'd)	1780?	EF27
28	Preachers contract nervous disorders	78:25	EF28
30	Helpers trading (abridged comment)	1780?	EF30
35	Fasting hurts my health	1780?	EF35
37	Advices on preaching (rev'd) (1–21)	1780?	EF37
39	Guarding against formality (rev'd) (1–14)	1780?	EF39
41.1	Methodists leave Church, leave God	1789?	F41
43	Assessment of Assistants, heavily abridged	1780?	EF43

Section	Subject	Source	Editions and Questions
75	Calvinism the direct antidote to Methodism	76:27, 28	EF75
76	Calvinism seems to magnify Christ	1780?	EF76
77	Guarding against Calvinism	1780?	EF77

Appendices

APPENDIX A

THE DEED OF DECLARATION, 1784[1]

To all to whom these presents shall come, John Wesley, late of Lincoln College, *Oxford*, but now of the *City Road*, London, Clerk, sendeth greeting:

Whereas divers buildings commonly called Chapels, with a messuage and dwelling-house, or other appurtenances to each of the same belonging, situate in various parts of *Great Britain*, have been given and conveyed from time to time by the said *John Wesley* to certain persons and their heirs in each of the said gifts and conveyances named; which are enrolled in his Majesty's High Court of Chancery, upon the acknowledgement of the said *John Wesley* (pursuant to the Act of Parliament in that case made and provided); upon trust, that the trustees in the said several deeds respectively named and the survivors of them and their heirs and assigns, and the trustees for the time being to be elected as in the said deeds is appointed, should permit and suffer the said John Wesley and such other person and persons as he should for that purpose from time to time nominate and appoint, at all times during his life at his will and pleasure to have and enjoy the free use and benefit of the said premises, that he the said John Wesley and such person and persons as he should nominate and appoint, might therein preach and expound God's Holy Word: And upon further trust that the said respective trustees and the survivors of them, and their heirs and assigns, and the trustees for the time being, should permit and suffer Charles Wesley, brother of the said John Wesley, and such other person and persons, as the said Charles Wesley should for that purpose from time to time nominate and appoint, in like manner during his life— To have, use, and enjoy the said premises respectively for the like purposes as aforesaid: and after the decease of the survivor of them

[1] This text is taken from a contemporary certified copy of the Deed, which was also printed in London in 1784. A very small number of errors and variations in spelling have been silently corrected in accordance with the principles of this edn.

the said John Wesley and Charles Wesley, then upon further trust, that the said respective trustees and the survivors of them and their heirs and assigns, and the trustees for the time being for ever, should permit and suffer such person and persons and for such time and times as should be appointed at the *Yearly Conference of the People called Methodists in London, Bristol, or Leeds*, and no others, to have and enjoy the said premises for the purposes aforesaid: And whereas divers persons have in like manner given or conveyed many Chapels, with messuages and dwelling-houses or other appurtenances to the same belonging, situate in various parts of Great Britain, and also in Ireland, to certain trustees, in each of the said gifts and conveyances respectively named upon the like trusts, and for the same uses and purposes as aforesaid (except only that in some of the said gifts and conveyances, no life estate or other interest is therein or thereby given and reserved to the said Charles Wesley). And whereas, for rendering effectual the trusts created by the said several gifts or conveyances, and that no doubt or litigation may arise with respect unto the same, or the interpretation and true meaning thereof, it has been thought expedient by the said John Wesley, on behalf of himself as donor of the several Chapels, with the messuages, dwelling-houses, or appurtenances before-mentioned, as of the donors of the said other Chapels, with the messuages, dwelling-houses, or appurtenances to the same belonging given or conveyed to the like uses and trusts, to explain the words *Yearly Conference of the People called Methodists*, contained in all the said trust deeds, and to declare *what persons* are members of the said Conference, and how the *succession* and *identity* thereof is to be continued: *Now therefore these presents witness* that for accomplishing the aforesaid purposes, the said John Wesley doth hereby declare, that the Conference of the People called Methodists, in London, Bristol, or Leeds, ever since there hath been any Yearly Conference of the said People called Methodists in any of the said places, hath always heretofore consisted of the preachers and expounders of God's Holy Word, commonly called Methodist Preachers, in connection with, and under the care of the said John Wesley, whom he hath thought expedient year after year to summon to meet him, in one or other of the said places, of London, Bristol, or Leeds, to advise with them for the promotion of the Gospel of Christ, to appoint the said persons so summoned, and the other preachers and expounders of God's Holy Word, also in connection with, and under the care of the said John Wesley, not summoned to the said Yearly Conference, to the use and enjoyment of the said

Chapels and premises so given and conveyed upon trust for the said John Wesley, and such other person and persons as he should appoint during his life as aforesaid, and for the expulsion of unworthy and admission of new persons under his care and into his connection to be preachers and expounders as aforesaid, and also of other persons upon trial for the like purposes; the names of all which persons so summoned by the said John Wesley, the persons appointed with the Chapels and premises to which they were so appointed, together with the duration of such appointments, and of those expelled or admitted into connection or upon trial, with all other matters transacted and done at the said Yearly Conference, have year by year been printed and published under the title of *Minutes* of Conference. *And these presents further witness*, and the said John Wesley doth hereby avouch and further declare, that the several persons hereinafter named, to wit, the said *John Wesley, and Charles Wesley, Thomas Coke*, of the City of London, Doctor of Civil Law, *James Creighton*, of the same place, Clerk, *Thomas Tennant*, of the same place, *Thomas Rankin*, of the same place, *Joshua Keighley* of Sevenoaks in the county of Kent, *James Wood* of Rochester in the said county of Kent, *John Booth* of Colchester, *Thomas Cooper* of the same place, *Richard Whatcoat* of Norwich, *Jeremiah Brettel* of Lynn in the county of Norfolk, *Jonathan Parkin* of the same place, *Joseph Pescod* of Bedford, *Christopher Watkins* of Northampton, *John Barber* of the same place, *John Broadbent* of Oxford, *Joseph Cole* of the same place, *Jonathan Coussins* of the City of Gloucester, *John Brettel* of the same place, *John Mason* of Salisbury, *George Story* of the same place, *Francis Wrigley* of St Austell, in the county of Cornwall, *William Green* of the city of Bristol, *John Moon* of Plymouth Dock, *James Hall* of the same place, *James Thom* of St Austell aforesaid, *Joseph Taylor* of Redruth, in the said county of Cornwall, *William Hoskins* of Cardiff, Glamorganshire, *John Leech* of Brecon, *William Saunders* of the same place, *Richard Rodda* of Birmingham, *John Fenwick* of Burslem, Staffordshire, *Thomas Hanby* of the same place, *James Rogers* of Macclesfield, *Samuel Bardsley* of the same place, *John Murlin* of Manchester, *William Percival* of the same place, *Duncan Wright* of the city of Chester, *John Goodwin* of the same place, *Parson Greenwood* of Liverpool, *Zachariah Yewdall* of the same place, *Thomas Vasey* of the same place, *Joseph Bradford* of Leicester, *Jeremiah Robertshaw* of the same place, *William Myles* of Nottingham, *Thomas Longley* of Derby, *Thomas Taylor* of Sheffield, *William Simpson* of the same place,

Thomas Carlill of Grimsby in the county of Lincoln, *Robert Scott* of the same place, *Joseph Harper* of the same place, *Thomas Corbett* of Gainsborough in the said county of Lincoln, *James Ray* of the same place, *William Thompson* of Leeds in the county of York, *Robert Roberts* of the same place, *Samuel Bradburn* of the same place, *John Valton* of Birstall in the said county, *John Allen* of the same place, *Isaac Brown* of the same place, *Thomas Hanson* of Huddersfield in the said county, *John Shaw* of the same place, *Alexander Mather* of Bradford in the said county, *Joseph Benson* of Halifax in the said county, *William Dufton* of the same place, *Benjamin Rhodes* of Keighley in the said county, *John Easton* of Colne in the county of Lancaster, *Robert Costerdine* of the same place, *Jasper Robinson* of the Isle of Man, *George Button* of the same place, *John Pawson* of the city of York, *Edward Jackson* of Hull, *Charles Atmore* of the said city of York, *Launcelot Harrison* of Scarborough, *George Shadford* of Hull aforesaid, *Barnabas Thomas* of the same place, *Thomas Briscoe* of Yarm in the said county of York, *Christopher Peacock* of the same place, *William Thom* of Whitby in the said county of York, *Robert Hopkins* of the same place, *John Peacock* of Barnard Castle, *William Collins* of Sunderland, *Thomas Dixon* of Newcastle upon Tyne, *Christopher Hopper* of the same place, *William Boothby* of the same place, *William Hunter* of Berwick upon Tweed, *Joseph Saunderson* of Dundee, Scotland, *William Warrener* of the same place, *Duncan McAllum* of Aberdeen, Scotland, *Thomas Rutherford* of the city of Dublin in the Kingdom of Ireland, *Daniel Jackson* of the same place, *Henry Moore* of the city of Cork, Ireland, *Andrew Blair* of the same place, *Richard Watkinson* of Limerick, Ireland, *Nehemiah Price* of Athlone, Ireland, *Robert Lindsey* of Sligo, Ireland, *George Brown* of Clones, Ireland, *Thomas Barber* of Charlemont, Ireland, *Henry Foster* of Belfast, Ireland, and *John Crook* of Lisburn, Ireland, Gentlemen, being preachers and expounders of God's Holy Word, under the care and in connection with the said John Wesley, have been, and now are, and do, on the day of the date hereof constitute the *members of the said Conference*, according to the true intent and meaning of the said several gifts and conveyances wherein the words 'Conference of the People called Methodists' arc mentioned and contained. And that the said several persons before-named, and their successors for ever, to be chosen as herein after mentioned, are and shall for ever be construed, taken and be the *Conference of the People called Methodists*. Nevertheless upon the terms and subject to the regulations hereinafter prescribed, that is to say,

First, That the members of the said Conference and their successors for the time being for ever, shall assemble once in every year, at London, Bristol, or Leeds (except as after mentioned) for the purposes aforesaid; and the time and place of holding every subsequent Conference shall be appointed at the preceding one, save that the next Conference after the date hereof, shall be holden in Leeds in Yorkshire, the last Tuesday in July next.

Second. The act of the majority in number of the Conference assembled as aforesaid, shall be had, taken, and be the act of the whole Conference to all intents, purposes and constructions whatsoever.

Third. That after the Conference shall be assembled as aforesaid, they shall first proceed to fill up all the vacancies occasioned by death or absence as after mentioned.

Fourth. No act of the Conference assembled as aforesaid, shall be taken or be the act of the Conference, until forty of the members thereof are assembled, unless reduced under that number by death since the prior Conference or absence as after mentioned; nor until all the vacancies occasioned by death or absence shall be filled up by the election of new members of the Conference, so as to make up the number one hundred, unless there be not a sufficient number of persons objects of such election: and during the assembly of the Conference there shall always be forty members present at the doing of any act, save as aforesaid, or otherwise such act shall be void.

Fifth. The duration of the Yearly Assembly of the Conference, shall be not less than five days, nor more than three weeks, and be concluded by the appointment of the Conference, if under twenty-one days; or otherwise the conclusion thereof shall follow of course at the end of the said twenty-one days; the whole of all of which said time of the assembly of the Conference shall be had, taken, considered, and be the Yearly Conference of the People called Methodists, and all acts of the Conference during such yearly assembly thereof, shall be the acts of the Conference and none others.

Sixth. Immediately after all the vacancies occasioned by death or absence are filled up by the election of new members as aforesaid, the Conference shall choose a President and Secretary of their assembly out of themselves, who shall continue until the election of another President or Secretary in the next, or other subsequent Conference; and the said President shall have the privilege and power of two members in all acts of the Conference during his presidency, and such other powers, privileges and authorities, as the Conference shall from time to time see fit to entrust into his hands.

Seventh. Any member of the Conference absenting himself from the yearly assembly thereof for two years successively without the consent or dispensation of the Conference, and be not present on the first day of the third yearly assembly thereof at the time and place appointed for the holding of the same, shall cease to be a member of the Conference from and after the said first day of the said third yearly assembly thereof, to all intents and purposes, as though he was naturally dead. But the Conference shall and may dispense with, or consent to, the absence of any member from any of the said yearly assemblies, for any cause which the Conference may see fit or necessary, and such member whose absence shall be so dispensed with, or consented to, by the Conference shall not by such absence cease to be a member thereof.

Eighth. The Conference shall and may expel and put out from being a member thereof, or from being in connection therewith, or from being upon trial, any person member of the Conference, admitted into connection, or upon trial, for any cause which to the Conference may seem fit or necessary; and every member of the Conference so expelled and put out, shall cease to be a member thereof to all intents and purposes, as though he was naturally dead. And the Conference immediately after the expulsion of any member thereof as aforesaid, shall elect another person to be a member of the Conference in the stead of such member so expelled.

Ninth. The Conference shall and may admit into connection with them, or upon trial, any person or persons whom they shall approve, to be preachers and expounders of God's Holy Word, under the care and direction of the Conference, the name of every such person or persons so admitted into connection or upon trial as aforesaid, with the time and degrees of the admission, being entered in the Journals or *Minutes* of the Conference.

Tenth. No person shall be elected a member of the Conference who hath not been admitted in connection with the Conference as a preacher and expounder of God's Holy Word, as aforesaid, for twelve months.

Eleventh. The Conference shall not nor may nominate or appoint any person to the use and enjoyment, or to preach and expound God's Holy Word in, any of the Chapels and premises so given or conveyed, or which may be given or conveyed upon the trusts aforesaid, who is not either a member of the Conference or admitted into connection with the same, or upon trial as aforesaid, nor appoint any person for more than three years successively to the use and enjoyment of any Chapels and premises already given, or to be given or conveyed upon the trusts aforesaid, except ordained ministers of the Church of England.

Twelfth. That the Conference shall and may appoint the place of holding the yearly assembly thereof at any other city, town, or place than London, Bristol, or Leeds, when it shall seem expedient so to do.

Thirteenth. And for the convenience of the Chapels and premises already or which may hereafter be given or conveyed upon the trusts aforesaid, situate in Ireland or other parts out of the Kingdom of Great Britain, the Conference shall and may, when and as often as it shall seem expedient, but not otherwise, appoint and delegate any member or members of the Conference with all or any of the powers, privileges and advantages herein before contained or vested in the Conference; and all and every the acts, admissions, expulsions, and appointments whatsoever of such member or members of the Conference so appointed and delegated as aforesaid, the same being put into writing, and signed by such delegate or delegates, and entered in the Journals or *Minutes* of the Conference and subscribed as after mentioned, shall be deemed, taken and be, the acts, admissions, expulsions, and appointments of the Conference, to all intents, constructions, and purposes whatsoever from the respective times, when the same shall be done by such delegate or delegates; notwithstanding any thing herein contained to the contrary.

Fourteenth. All resolutions and orders touching elections, admissions, expulsions, consents, dispensations, delegations, or appointments and acts whatsoever of the Conference shall be entered and written in the Journals or *Minutes* of the Conference which shall be kept for that purpose, publicly read, and then subscribed by the President and Secretary thereof for the time being, during the time such Conference shall be assembled; and when so entered and subscribed, shall be had, taken, received, and be the acts of the Conference, and such entry and subscription as aforesaid shall be had, taken, received, and be evidence of all and every such acts of the said Conference and of their said delegates without the aid of any other proof; and whatever shall not be so entered and subscribed as aforesaid, shall not be had, taken, received, or be the act of the Conference: and the said President and Secretary are hereby required and obliged to enter and subscribe as aforesaid every act whatever of the Conference.

Lastly. Whenever the said Conference shall be reduced under the number of forty members, and continue so reduced for three yearly assemblies thereof successively, or whenever the members thereof shall decline or neglect to meet together annually for the purposes aforesaid, during the space of three years, that then, and in either of the said events, the Conference of the People called Methodists shall be extinguished, and all the aforesaid powers, privileges, and advantages shall cease, and the said Chapels and premises, and all other Chapels and premises which now are or hereafter may be settled, given or conveyed, upon the trusts aforesaid, shall vest in the trustees for the time being of the said Chapels and premises respectively, and their successors for ever: upon trust that they, and the survivors of them, and the trustees for the time being, do, shall, and may appoint such person and persons to preach and expound God's Holy Word therein, and to have the use and enjoyment thereof, for such time, and in such manner as to them shall seem proper.

Provided always that nothing herein contained shall extend or be construed to extend, to extinguish, lessen or abridge the life-estate of the said John Wesley, and Charles Wesley, or either of them, of and in any of the said Chapels and premises, or any other Chapels and premises, wherein they the said John Wesley, and Charles Wesley, or either of them now have, or may have any estate or interest, power or authority whatsoever. *In witness whereof the said John Wesley hath hereunto set his hand and seal, the Twenty-eighth Day of February, in the Twenty-fourth Year of the Reign of our Sovereign Lord George the Third, by the Grace of God of Great Britain, France, and Ireland, King, Defender of the Faith, and so forth, and in the Year of our Lord, One Thousand Seven Hundred and Eighty-four.*

JOHN (Seal) WESLEY

Sealed and Delivered (being first duly
Stamped) in the Presence of
WILLIAM CLULOW, *Quality Court, Chancery Lane, London.*
RICHARD YOUNG, Clerk to the said William Clulow.

APPENDIX B

MINUTES OF THE METHODIST CONFERENCES IN IRELAND

INTRODUCTION

In introducing the MS Minutes of the first Methodist Conference conducted in Ireland, Wesley in 1752 hints about subsequent Irish Conferences during his lifetime, demonstrating the substantial unity of British Methodism in the British Isles. In 1864, the Irish Conference sought to secure and publish details of the somewhat sporadic occurrence and records of the Irish Methodist Conferences. We are able to enlarge a little on their published work for the period 1752–91. In the earlier pages, we have presented all the information that seems to remain of the other early Irish Conferences: Limerick, 1752; Dublin, 1756; Limerick, 1758 and 1760; and Dublin, 1762. On July 25–26, 1765, Wesley had held a preliminary Conference in Dublin, which was just prior to the English annual Conference in Manchester, August 1765, the first to have its *Minutes* published (as the beginning of the regular annual series).[1] During the following years, Conferences were held in Ireland just prior to the English Conference, and their stationing of preachers was usually confirmed at the English Conference and printed in their *Minutes*.

Eventually, English preachers (in later years, Coke) were nominated at the English Conference to accompany Wesley to Ireland the following year and preside over the Irish Conference, always held in Dublin. Occasionally, special addenda dealing with Ireland, in addition to the stations, were published in the English *Minutes*. In 1778, the first separately printed Irish *Minutes* appeared. From 1783, they were published annually in Dublin. In speaking of these below, we do not usually duplicate matter appearing in the English *Minutes*, except for reproducing in their entirety the *printed* Irish *Minutes* for 1778 and 1783–90.

---

[1] See Part II, above.

Minutes and Miscellaneous References

1765 CONFERENCE

'Wed. 24 [July]. I rode, in the hottest day I have felt this year, to Dublin. Thursday and Friday morning I spent in a Conference with
5 our preachers. In the afternoons, I spoke to the members of the Society. I left four hundred and forty, and find above five hundred— more than ever they were since my first landing in the kingdom.'[2]

1766

Wesley did not visit Ireland in 1766.[3]

1767 CONFERENCE

10

[Dublin, July 23]. 'On Wednesday and Thursday, we had our lit- tle Conference at Dublin. Friday we observed as a day of fasting and prayer, and concluded it with the most solemn watch-night that I ever remember in this kingdom.'[4]

1768

15

Wesley did not visit Ireland in 1768.[5]

---

[2] July 24, 1765, *Journal & Diaries*, 22:14 in this edn. For the minutes of this Conference, see English *Minutes* (1765), *QQ.* 5 (32–39), 27–38. These were reprinted in *Minutes* of the *Methodist Conferences in Ireland* (Dublin: Religious & General Book Co. Limited, 1864), 1:7–9.

[3] For the Irish stations, see English *Minutes* (1766), *Q.* 6 (33–40).

[4] July 22, 1767, *Journal & Diaries*, 22:95 in this edn. For the stations, see *Minutes* (1767), *Q.* 7 (33–41), and for membership, *Q.* 8, 'Ireland, 2,801'.

[5] For Irish stations and membership see *Minutes* (1768), *QQ.* 7 (34–41) and 8, 'Ireland, 2,700'.

1769 CONFERENCE

[Dublin, July 19]. 'On Wednesday and Thursday, we had our little Conference, at which most of the preachers in the kingdom were present. We agreed to set apart Friday the 21st for a day of fasting and prayer. At every meeting, particularly the last, our Lord 5 refreshed us in an uncommon manner.'[6]

1770

Wesley did not visit Ireland in 1770.[7]

1771 CONFERENCE

[Dublin, July 18.] 'On Thursday and Friday, we had our little 10 Conference—a solemn and useful meeting.'[8]

1772

Wesley did not visit Ireland in 1772.[9]

1773 CONFERENCE[10]

'Friday [June] 25 I went on to Dublin. I left three hundred and 15 seventy-eight members in the society, and found four hundred and twelve, many of whom were truly alive to God.'[11]

---

[6] July 19, 1769, *Journal & Diaries*, 22:96 in this edn. 'This Conference is memorable for the decided measures adopted by Mr. Wesley in thoroughly organizing the itinerant system.' C. H. Crookshank, *History of Methodism in Ireland*, 3 vols. (Belfast: Allen, 1885), 1:229. For the Irish stations and membership, see *Minutes* (1769), *QQ.* 7 (37–46) and 8, 'Ireland, 3,120'.

[7] For Irish stations and membership, see *Minutes* (1770), *QQ.* 8 (40–49) and 9, separate membership of ten circuits, with a total of 3,124.

[8] July 18, 1771, *Journal & Diaries*, 22:284 in this edn. For the Irish stations and membership, see *Minutes* (1771), *QQ.* 6 (38–47) and 8, ten separate circuits, with a total of 3,632.

[9] For the Irish stations and membership, see *Minutes* (1772), *QQ.* 7 (38–47) and 8, ten separate circuits, with a total of 3,792.

[10] Wesley made his biennial visit to Ireland and spent June 25 to July 5 in Dublin.

[11] June 25, 1773, *Journal & Diaries*, 22:379 in this edn. For the Irish stations and membership, see *Minutes* (1773), *QQ.* 7 (38–47) and 8, ten circuits, with a total of 4,013.

'Wednesday and Thursday, June 30 and July 1, our Conference [was] held. We had a solemn time, and all things seemed to be in order.'[12]

1774

5   Wesley did not visit Ireland in 1774.[13]

1775 CONFERENCE[14]

A 'very smart Conference was held, which concluded in peace and love'.[15]

1776

10   Wesley did not visit Ireland in 1776.[16]

1777

Wesley did not make his regular biennial visit to Ireland this year, though he did pay a hurried visit in October to deal with a controversial emergency.[17]

15   Dublin, Tuesday, July 7, 1778

---

[12] Although JW does not mention the Conference in his *Journal*, he did hold one, and his companion, Hugh Saunderson, described it thus. *Journal & Diaries*, 22:379, n. 50 in this edn.

[13] For the Irish stations and membership, see *Minutes* (1774), *QQ.* 7 (40–49) and 8, the circuits with a total of 4,341.

[14] During his visit to Ireland this year, JW was desperately ill in June but was able to conduct a Conference in July, probably on Wednesday and Thursday, July 19 and 20.

[15] Jonathan Hern's unpublished diary, quoted in *Journal & Diaries*, 22:458, n. 16 in this edn. For the Irish stations and membership, see *Minutes* (1775), *QQ.* 6 (41–50) and 7, ten circuits, total 4,237.

[16] For the Irish stations and membership, see *Minutes* (1776), *QQ.* 6 (45–55) and 7, eleven circuits, total 4,798.

[17] For the Irish stations and membership, see *Minutes* (1777), *QQ.* 9 (47–58) and 10, eleven circuits, total 5,211.

1778 *Minutes*[18]

Q. 1. What preachers are *admitted* this year?

A. Andrew Delap, Peter Mill, James Gaffney, John Howe,[19] John Mealy, John Hampson, Jun., Robert Davis, Robert Armstrong.[20]

Q. 2. Who remain on *trial?*

A. Hugh Moore, George Brown, and John Price.[21]

Q. 3. Who are *admitted on trial?*

A. William Myles,[22] Andrew Blair, and William Gill.

Q. 4. Are there any objections to any of our preachers?

A. Examine them one by one; which was done, and the objections made to all of them but one were clearly and plainly answered.

Q. 5. How are they stationed this[23] year?

A. As follows:

   1. *Dublin*, R. W[atkinson], William Eells.[24]

   2. *Waterford*, T. H[alliday], Robert Armstrong.

   3. *Cork*, J. H[ampson, sen.], S. Bradburn, change monthly.

   4. *Limerick*, Andrew Delap, and John Bredin.[25]

---

[18] 'Tue. 7. Our little Conference began, at which about twenty preachers were present. On Wednesday we heard one of our friends at large upon the "Duty of *leaving the Church*"; but, after a full discussion of the point, we all remained firm in our judgment that it is our duty *not to leave the Church*, wherein God has blessed and does bless us still.' July 7, 1778, *Journal & Diaries*, 23:98 in this edn. The advocate for leaving the Church was Edward Smyth, an Anglican minister who had turned to Methodism after expulsion from the Church of England in northern Ireland. The unique copy of these poorly printed *Minutes* with no title page (and with many spelling errors) was preserved by Samuel Bradburn, stationed in Cork, and is now in MA.

[19] Orig., 'How', as also in the stations.

[20] Seven of these appear also (in different order) among the thirteen listed in the English *Minutes*, in which John Hampson, Jun., does not appear, though he is similarly stationed in Lisburn.

[21] John Price does not reappear in the English *Minutes*, though he is similarly listed as stationed in Enniskillen.

[22] Orig., 'Miles', as also in the stations.

[23] Orig., 'the'.

[24] At the English Conference, Eells was appointed to Newcastle and Rutherford to Dublin.

[25] Orig., 'Breedin'.

5. *Castlebar*, Nehemiah Price, William Myles.
6. *Athlone*, T. Payne, Richard Boardman.
7. *Sligo*, Robert Lindsay,[26] Hugh Moore.[27]
8. *Clones*, William Boothby, Jonathan Hern.[28]
9. *Enniskillen*, John Price, George Brown.
10. *Lisleen*, John Mealy, John Howe, William McCornock.[29]
11. *Armagh*, Peter Mill, Andrew Blair, William Gill.
12. *Londonderry*, John Brettel,[30] James Gaffney.
13. *Belfast*, Thomas Rutherford, Robert Davis.
14. *Lisburn*, John Prickard, John H[ampson], Jun.[31]

Q. 6. What members are there in the society?

A.
Dublin,	460
Waterford,	172
Cork,	325
Limerick,	257
Athlone,	526
Sligo,	402
Clones,	461
Enniskillen,	511
Lisleen and Londonderry,	708
Armagh,	586
Lisburn,	932
	5,340[32]

Q. 7. What is the Kingswood collection?
A. £15. 5s. 5½d.
Q. 8. What is contributed toward[s][33] the new Chapel in London?

---

[26] Orig., 'Lindsey'.
[27] Orig., 'Moor'.
[28] Orig., 'Johnothan Heron'.
[29] Orig., 'McCordock'.
[30] Orig., 'Brethel'.
[31] Orig., 'H——'.
[32] Orig., '5,323'; there are slight differences from the figures in the *Minutes* (1778).
[33] Orig., 'to toward'.

A. £91. 14*s*. 6*d*.

Q. 9. How many wives are to be provided for?

A. Four, S. W[atkinson], Payne, Hern, and Bradburn.

Q. 10. By what Societies?

A. S. W[atkinson] by Dublin; S. Bradburn by Cork £4, Limerick £3, Derry £1, and Coleraine £2; S. Payne, Athlone £6, Castlebar £2, Enniskillen £1, and Belfast £1; S. Hern, Clones £4, Armagh £1, Lisburn £5.

Q. 11. What is contributed to the Preachers' Fund?

A. Fourteen pound[s] fourteen shillings.

Q. 12. How may we remove the difficulty which the married preachers have found in procuring this?

A. At every Quarterly Meeting, let each Assistant set aside the money first, and transmit it as soon as possible to the preacher to whom it belongs.

Q. 13. As the whole yearly contribution is reserved for London, how shall we supply the present wants of the preachers and their wives?

A. We will desire the English Conference to allow seven guineas and a half for the preachers, and ten guineas for their wives.

Q. 14. On what days may the Quarterly Fasts be observed?

A. Next Friday, and the first Friday in November, February, and May.

Q. 15. Can any of the circuits be altered for the better?

A. Yes, the Athlone and the Lisburn Circuits may each be divided into two.

Q. 16. When shall the Quarterly Meeting in the Athlone Circuit be held?

A. Twice a year (if he chooses it), at Mr. Handy's,[34] and twice a year at Athlone.

Q. 17. Who may be General Stewards for the ensuing year?

A. Waterford Circuit,   John Fitzhenry.
    Limerick,   Alexander Palmer.
    Castlebar,   James Richardson.
    Athlone,   Andrew M᷄Hutchin.

---

[34] Samuel Handy and his brother Jonathan are said to be the sons of a Cromwellian lieutenant. JW held the Quarterly Meeting in this country place rather than a town because of Handy's hospitality. Crookshank, *History of Methodism in Ireland*, 1:22–24; see *Journal & Diaries*, 20:217, n. 16 in this edn.

Sligo,	Thomas Price.
Clones,	John Armstrong.
Enniskillen,	Henry Wood.
Lisleen,	John Nelson.
Londonderry,	John McGaghan.
Armagh,	Samuel Bates.
Belfast	
	John Johnson
Lisburn	

Q. 18. If anything is deficient in their accounts, are the
stewards to make it good?

A. There is no doubt of it. This is an universal rule.

Q. 19. The Cork steward is deficient in his accounts several
pounds. Is he to make that good?

A. He is obliged thereto, both in law and conscience.

Q. 20. Should not all preachers recommend cleanliness
everywhere?

A. Yes, with all possible correctness.

Q. 21. Are there any other little advices which you would
give the preachers?

A. I advise you: (1) In repeating the Lord's Prayer, remember to say '*ha*llowed', not 'hollowed'.—In '*that trespass
against us*', say, that trespass against *us*. Always repeat the
Amen. (2) At church repeat the prayer after the minister as
often as he repeats it. (3) Repeat all the confessions after
him, as well as both the doxologies in the communion
service. (4) Always *kneel* during public prayer, and *stand* at
the text. (5) Learn of Englishmen how to pronounce the
English vowels, *a* as in *face*, *e* as in *me*, *i* as in *high*.
(6) Avail yourselves of the great festivals by preaching on
the occasion; and singing our hymns, which we should
take care to have in readiness.

Q. 22. Not a fourth part of the books which might have
been sold have yet been sold in Ireland. What can be done
to remedy this?

A. 1. Let the Assistant in every circuit take charge of the
books.

2. Let each Assistant, as soon as he comes into his circuit, see what books are there, and take them into his
own hands.

3. Let him immediately write for what is wanting.

4. Let him procure as many subscribers to the Magazine as he can; and see that the subscribers be duly supplied.

Q. 23. Is it not our duty to separate from the Church, considering the wickedness both of the clergy and of the people?

A. We conceive not: (1) Because both the priests and the people were full as wicked in the Jewish Church, and yet God never commanded the holy Israelites to separate from them. (2) Neither did our Lord command his disciples to separate from them—if he did not command just the contrary. (3) Because from hence it is clear that this would not be the meaning of those words [used][35] by St. Paul, 'Come out from among them, and be ye separate.'[36]

Q. 24. Are all things done to edifying[37] among us? Is the singing to edification?

A. It does not fully answer the end proposed, teaching the congregation. This would be far better answered if the singers would observe the rules which were given them three years ago.[38]

Q. 25. What reasons can be assigned why so many of our preachers contract nervous disorders?

A. I answer on Dr. Cadogan's principles; the chief reason is either indolence or intemperance. Several of them use too little exercise, far less than when they wrought at their trades; and this cannot long consist with health. It will pave the way for many, especially renew our disorders. Several of them, instead of taking less, take more food than they did when they laboured more; and let any man of reason judge how long this will consist with health. Several use more sleep than when they laboured more, and this itself is enough to destroy the firmness of the nerves.

If then our preachers would escape nervous disorders, let them, (1) Take as little meat, drink, and sleep as nature

---

[35] Orig., 'asked'.

[36] 2 Cor. 6:17.

[37] 1 Cor. 14:26.

[38] Lacking the Irish *Minutes* for the relevant year, and the English *Minutes* (1775) are silent on the matter, it is not possible to say exactly what JW had in mind. But in *Minutes* (1768), *Q.* 23 (6), after criticizing faults in singing, JW had suggested that the Assistants in the larger Societies might give instruction.

will bear, and (2) Use full as much exercise as they did before they were received.

Q. 26. Are we sufficiently serious, holy, devoted to God?

A. By no means. We have need to take shame to ourselves. We are dwarfs in grace. Let us look at David Brainerd, and be followers of him as he was of Christ.

Q. 27. Have we a right view of our work?

A. Perhaps not. It is not to take care of this or that society, or to preach so many times: but to save as many souls as we can, to bring as many sinners as we can to repentance, and with all our power to build them up in that holiness without which they cannot see the Lord.[39]

1779

Wesley did not visit Ireland in 1779.[40]

1780

Wesley did not visit Ireland in 1780.[41]

1781

Wesley planned to, but did not, visit Ireland in 1781.[42]

---

[39] See Heb. 12:14.

[40] Nor apparently did Thomas Coke, though he was already being groomed to take over this as well as many other tasks from JW. JW remained in constant touch by correspondence, however, with his Assistants in Ireland, and some examples remain of his Irish concerns, including a letter to Bradburn (July 10), about Methodist prayer for the national emergency, and one to John Bredin (July 24), about the stationing of the Irish preachers. See *Letters* (Telford), 6:348–49. For the Irish stations and membership, see *Minutes* (1779), *QQ.* 7 (49–62) and 10, fourteen circuits, total 5,940.

[41] Wesley had planned on visiting Ireland in the spring of 1780, but on the advice of his friends he did not go. For the Irish stations and membership, see the *Minutes* (1780), *QQ.* 7 (51–64) and 10, fourteen circuits, total 6,109.

[42] On Apr. 12, 1781, JW embarked with three preachers for Dublin, but was driven back by a severe storm, and again abandoned his Irish visit, going instead to Wales and the Isle of Man. See Apr. 9–June 13, *Journal & Diaries*, 23:198–210 in this edn. Cf. his letter from Whitehaven to his niece Sally (May 28, 1781): 'Here I am, waiting for a passage to the Isle of Man. Which way I shall steer from thence I know not. But I believe Providence will direct me either to the North of Ireland or to Newcastle upon Tyne.' *Letters* (Telford), 7:65.

1782 CONFERENCE

Again in the spring of 1782 Wesley planned a visit to Ireland for a Conference,[43] but again his visit was put off.[44] This time, however, he sent the now seasoned Thomas Coke as his deputy in Ireland to hold the Conference. It was a great occasion for William Myles, 5 whose autobiography notes, 'In June 1782, Dr. Coke was appointed to hold a Conference in Ireland; accordingly we all met in Dublin, and I was admitted into full connexion, after having travelled five years.'[45] There had not been a Conference in Ireland during the space of four years. Myles records a brief account of the proceedings 10 of this Conference: 'Among other things, the Doctor read the *Minutes*, and enforced on the preachers the necessity of maintaining them, which they engaged to do; and it was agreed that thenceforward a yearly Conference should be held in Dublin.'[46]

1783 *Minutes*[47]   15

Dublin, Tuesday, April 29, 1783

Q. 1. What preachers are admitted this year?

[43] On Apr. 6, JW wrote to John Bredin, 'It is probable I shall be able to hold a little Conference in Dublin before the middle of July'; and on May 1 to Zachariah Yewdall, 'If nothing unforeseen prevent, I shall be at Dublin the beginning of July.' *Letters* (Telford), 7:118, 122.

[44] R. Lee Cole suggested that this was a precaution urged on him because of his controversy with Father O'Leary. *A History of Methodism in Dublin* (Dublin, 1932), 66. But it seems to have been mainly owing to the pressure of his work in England, for he wrote on June 16 to Jonathan Hern in Chester:

'I have made all the haste from the North of Scotland which I reasonably could. But still my time falls short. I shall not be able to reach York before the 27th instant. And I shall then have all the Midland societies to visit; so that I cannot get any time for Ireland this summer. For before I have well done my business in the country the Conference will call me to London.' (*Letters* [Telford], 7:126)

[45] *AM* 20 (1797): 263. John Beecham's memoir of Myles adds, apparently on reliable authority, that he 'received the usual mark of acknowledgement, the large *Minutes* with a suitable inscription, and signed by the Doctor's own hand'. *Methodist Magazine and Quarterly Review*, new series 13 (1831): 365.

[46] *WMM* (1831): 293. For the Irish stations and membership, see the *Minutes* (1782), *QQ.* 7 (52–66) and 11, fifteen circuits, in all 6,512.

[47] Drop title, *Minutes of some late Conversations between the Rev. Mr. Wesley and others.* June 1783 would bring JW's eightieth birthday, and he decided that he should try to spend it in Ireland, as the climax of a visit of three or four

A. James Christie, John Kerr,[48] William McCornock.[49]

Q. 2. Who remain on trial?

A. John Cricket, George Dice, James Jordan, John Miller, and Gustavus Armstrong.

Q. 3. Who are *admitted on trial?*

A. Matthias Joyce, James Rennick,[50] and Thomas Hetherington.

Q. 4. Who desist from *travelling?*

A. Robert Davis.

Q. 5. What preachers have *died* this year?

A. Richard Boardman, a pious, sensible man, greatly beloved of all that knew him. He died of an apoplectic fit, and preached the night before his death; and *Robert Naylor*, a plain, honest man, devoted to God, and owned of him wherever he laboured.

Q. 6. Are there any objections to any of our preachers?

A. Let them be examined one by one.

Q. 7. How are they stationed?

A. As follows:

1. *Dublin*, Thomas Rutherford, Daniel Jackson.
2. *Waterford*, Thomas Davis, John Price.
3. *Cork*, Henry Moore, Andrew Blair, Zach. Yewdall.
4. *Limerick*, Richard Watkinson, W. West.
5. *Castlebar*, George Dice, John Mealy.
6. *Athlone*, Nehemiah Price, Robert Blake; Thomas Halliday, supernumerary.
7. *Sligo*, Robert Lindsay, Geo. Mowat.

months. See Mar. 16, 1783, *Journal & Diaries*, 23:264–65 in this edn. Cf. letter to his brother Charles, Apr. 4, 1783, *Letters* (Telford), 7:173. Once more, illness altered his plans, but he improved sufficiently to spend at least a few weeks in Ireland, and summoned an early Conference, beginning on Apr. 29. This was the first of the new series of Irish *Minutes* to be published, though still without a title page. He entered in his *Journal* for that day: 'Our little Conference began, and continued till Friday, May 2. All was peace and love, and I trust the same spirit will spread through the nation.' See Apr. 29, 1783, *Journal & Diaries*, 23:267 in this edn. To his brother Charles he wrote on the closing day: 'We had an exceeding *happy Conference*, which concluded this morning. I wish all our English preachers were of the same spirit with the Irish, among whom is no jarring string. I never saw such simplicity and teachableness run through a body of preachers before.' *Letters* (Telford), 7:177.

[48] Orig., 'Karr'.

[49] Orig., 'McCornack'.

[50] Orig., 'Renneck'.

8. *Ballyconnell*, Robert Armstrong, Matthias Joyce, and John Kerr.

9. *Clones*, George Brown, Wm. McCornock, John Cricket.

10. *Enniskillen*, James Jordan, John Miller. 5

11. *Charlemont*, Thomas Barber, James Christie, and James Rennick.

12. *Lisleen*, Samuel Mitchell, Thomas Hetherington.

13. *Londonderry*, John Watson, Thomas Tattershall.

14. *Belfast*, Henry Foster, Gustavus Armstrong, and 10 Robert Bridge.

15. *Lisburn*, John Crook, Jonathan Brown.

Q. 8. How many preachers' wives are to be provided for?

A. Ten: six out of the Preachers' Fund, and four in Ireland.

Q. 9. What does each Circuit contribute to these? 15

	£.	s.	d.
A. Dublin,	10.	0.	0
Cork,	5.	0.	0.
Limerick,	3.	0.	0.
Castlebar,	2.	0.	0.	20
Athlone,	6.	0.	0.
Ballyconnell,	1.	0.	0.
Clones,	4.	0.	0.
Enniskillen,	1.	0.	0.
Charlemont,	1.	10.	0.	25
Londonderry, ⎤	1.	0.	0.
Coleraine, ⎦	2.	0.	0.
Belfast,	2.	0.	0.
Lisburn,	4.	0.	0.[51]

30

Q. 10. What was contributed to the Preachers' Fund?

A. Fifteen pounds, four shillings and six pence.

Q. 11. What further can be done to stop the extravagant use of snuff and tobacco?

A. Let none who use either be received either as travelling 35 or local preachers.

Q. 12. When may this Conference meet again?

A. On the first Tuesday in July, 1784.

---

[51] The total is £42. 10*s*. 0*d*.

N.B. Let all the Assistants take care to be in Dublin the Saturday before.[52]

1784 *Minutes*[53]

Dublin, Tuesday, July 6, 1784

5   *Q.* 1. What preachers are *admitted* this year?

A. John Cricket, Gustavus Armstrong, George Dice, John Miller, Lawrence Kane, James Rennick, James Jordan, Thomas Hetherington, Joseph Armstrong, and Matthias Joyce.

10   *Q.* 2. Who *remain* on trial?

A. None.

Q. 3. Who are *admitted on trial?*

---

[52] It is noteworthy that these printed *Minutes* are far shorter than those for 1778. The stations are given and remained almost the same at the Bristol Conference, except that Lawrence Kane replaced Zachariah Yewdall in Cork, Gustavus Armstrong replaced George Mowat in Sligo, Matthias Joyce was removed from Ballyconnell, Joseph Armstrong was added to Lisleen, and George Mowat replaced Gustavus Armstrong in Belfast. Among the major items that were omitted were the figures for membership, which were given in the English *Minutes* (1784), *Q.* 11, sixteen circuits, with a total of 6,409.

[53] This is the first copy of the Irish *Minutes* to be published with a complete title page: '*Minutes of some late Conversations between the Rev. Thomas Coke, L.L.D. and others.* Dublin: Printed in the Year 1784.' JW made no attempt to visit Ireland during the epochal year of 1784. He arranged that Dr. Coke should carry out this task on his behalf and conduct the Conference in Dublin at its pre-arranged time, beginning on the first Tuesday in July. In preparing his Deed of Declaration defining the Methodist Conference, JW had made sure that Ireland was integrated with Great Britain, naming among the 'Legal Hundred' eleven preachers stationed in Ireland and three other Irishmen stationed in England. Lee Cole, *Methodism in Dublin*, 67. Coke took copies of the Deed with him to Ireland in order to explain the whole situation to the preachers. J. W. Etheridge, *The Life of the Rev. Thomas Coke, D.C.L.* (London: Mason, 1860), 71. Afterwards, JW wrote happily to the leading layman in Dublin, Arthur Keene (on July 23, 1784): 'The Irish preachers have shown both their understanding and their uprightness. I am glad they and you are satisfied with the Declaration.' *Letters* (Telford), 7:226. Coke handled the Conference well and published its *Minutes* worthily. Henceforth Ireland, its preachers, and its annual Conference remained his undisputed territory, although JW continued to maintain his own concern with Irish Methodism and his correspondence with her leaders, and continued to visit her biennially into his eighties, in 1783, 1785, 1787, and 1789.

A. John Clark, Walter Griffith, William Hammet, James Wilson, James McDonald.[54]

Q. 4. Who *desist from travelling?*

A. Robert Blake.

Q. 5. Are there any objections to any of our preachers?

A. They were examined one by one.

Q. 6. How are the preachers stationed this year?

A. As follows:

1. *Dublin*, James Rogers, Andrew Blair.
2. *Waterford*, Thomas Tattershall, James Wilson.
3. *Cork*, A preacher from England,[55] Thomas Davis. ⎫ Let these
4. *Bandon*, Daniel Jackson, Lawrence Kane. ⎬ change every Quarter.
5. *Limerick*, John Leech, John Watson.
6. *Castlebar*, James Jordan, John Kerr; Thomas Halliday, supernumerary.
7. *Athlone*, Matthias Joyce, John Cricket.
8. *Sligo*, Robert Bridge, John Clarke.
9. *Ballyconnell*, Robert Armstrong, William West, James McDonald.
10. *Clones*, Nehemiah Price, George Mowat, Thomas Hetherington; Samuel Mitchell, supernumerary.
11. *Enniskillen*, Thomas Barber, Gustavus Armstrong.
12. *Charlemont*, John Crook, John Mealy, Walter Griffith.
13. *Lisleen*, Joseph Armstrong, James Rennick.
14. *Londonderry*, Jonathan Brown, George Dice, Wm. McCornock.
15. *Belfast*, John Price, John Miller.
16. *Lisburn*, George Brown, William Hammet.

Q. 7. What shall we do with Robert Lindsay?

A. We refer his case to Mr. Wesley; and in the meantime we suspend him.

Q. 8. How many preachers' wives are to be provided for?

A. Ten: Sister Price, Blair, Kane, Brown, Watson, Mowat, Bridge, Joyce, Crook, and Rennick, £6.

---

[54] Orig., 'McDonnel'. None of these five names is inserted in *Q.* 3 of the English *Minutes*.

[55] Christopher Peacock was added in the English *Minutes*.

Q. 9. What does each Circuit contribute to these?

	£.	s.	d.
A. Dublin,	13	0.	0.
Cork,	4.	0.	0.
Bandon,	1.	0.	0.
Limerick,	4.	0.	0.
Castlebar,	2.	0.	0.
Athlone,	6.	0.	0.
Sligo,	1.	0.	0.
Ballyconnell,	1.	0.	0.
Clones,	5.	0.	0.
Enniskillen,	1.	0.	0.
Charlemont,	1.	10.	0.
Londonderry, ⎫	1.	0.	0.
Coleraine, ⎭	2.	0.	0.
Belfast	2.	0.	0.
Lisburn	4.	0.	0.[56]

Q. 10. What numbers are in the Societies?

A. *Dublin,	582
*Waterford,	209
*Cork,	633
*Limerick,	270
*Castlebar,	259
Athlone,	272
*Sligo,	306
*Ballyconnell,	672
Clones,	627
*Enniskillen,	562
*Charlemont,	684
Lisleen,	452
*Londonderry,	171
Belfast,	287
*Lisburn,	441
	―――――
	6,427

*N.B. The Circuits marked thus * are increased this year.*
Q. 11. What is the Kingswood collection?
A. £20. 9. 3.

[56] Total £48. 10*s*. 0*d*.

Q. 12. What is contributed to the Preachers' Fund?
A. £45. 6. 0.
Q. 13. What is contributed for the yearly expenses?
A. £43. 5. 9½.
Q. 14. What shall we do with those who wilfully and
repeatedly neglect to meet their class?
A. 1. Let the Assistant or one of his Helpers personally
visit them, wherever it is practicable, and explain to
them the consequence if they continue to neglect, viz.
expulsion.
2. If they do not amend, let the Assistant exclude them
in the society, informing it that they are laid aside for a
breach of our rules of discipline, and not for immoral
conduct.
Q. 15. Is it right in a Methodist preacher to wear powder in
his hair as part of his dress?
A. It is not right. Let it be so no more.
Q. 16. What further can be done to stop the excessive use
of tobacco in snuff, or by smoking or chewing the same?
A. Let every preacher engage with an audible voice, in the
presence of God and his brethren, that he will not snuff,
smoke, or chew tobacco.
Q. 17. Is it not right that the Assistant, and not the steward,
should receive the quarterly subscriptions at the visitation
of the classes?
A. Certainly it is. This has ever been the practice in almost
every part of England, and in many parts of Ireland. And
therefore let every Assistant look to it, and ask every person who can afford it for his subscription at every quarter's visitation, when he delivers the tickets; and in due
time let him deliver the whole into the hands of the stewards for carrying on the work of God in the circuit.
Q. 18. What can be done to enforce morning preaching?
A. Let every preacher with an audible voice engage, in the
presence of God and his brethren, that he will, to the
utmost of his power, preach every morning where he can
have a congregation, and, as far as practicable, at five
o'clock.
      Whereas a Deed Poll has been lately enrolled in his
Majesty's High Court of Chancery in London by the Rev.
John Wesley, for the specification and establishment of the

Conference of the People called Methodists; and whereas
an anonymous *Appeal*[57] has been circulated among the
societies, with the design of depreciating and destroying
the force of the said Deed; We the Preachers in
5   Conference assembled do testify that we do approve of
the said Deed, do prefer it to the former plan of government set forth in the large *Minutes* of Conference, and are
willing to submit to its regulations, and to support it; and
that we also do condemn the said anonymous *Appeal* as
10   false and inflammatory. Let the next Conference be held
in Dublin on the first Friday in next July.

1785 *Minutes*[58]

Dublin, Friday, July 1st, 1785
Q. 1. What preachers are *admitted* this year?
15   *A.* Walter Griffith, John Clarke, and Hugh Moore.
Q. 2. Who *remain on trial?*
A. James Wilson, James MᶜDonald, and William Hammet.
Q. 3. Who are *admitted on trial?*
A. John Dinnen, Robert Lindsay, Andrew Coleman, and
20   Tho. Verner. None have died or desisted from travelling
this year.

---

[57] This document was the attack by John Hampson on the Deed of Declaration, appealing for objectors to attend Conference and rescind it. See English *Minutes* (1784).

[58] The title page runs, '*Minutes of some late Conversations between the Rev. John Wesley, M.A. and others.* Dublin: Printed in the Year 1785.' Once again JW was present and in control, having embarked for Ireland on Apr. 10 and remained until July 10. In his *Journal* he summarized the beginning and end of the Conference thus:

'July 1, Friday. Most of our travelling preachers met to confer together on the things of God. We began and ended in much peace and love; being all resolved not to "do the work of the Lord so lightly". . . . Wed. 6. We con-cluded our Conference. I remember few such Conferences, either in England or Ireland, so perfectly unanimous were all the preachers, and so determined to give themselves up to God.' (*Journal & Diaries*, 23:369–70 in this edn.) Coke was not present, being on his way back from his first visit to America, though he arrived in time to present the American stations and statistics to the English Conference.

Q. 4. Are there any objections to any of our preachers?
A. They were examined one by one.
Q. 5. How are they stationed this year?
A. As follows:

1. *Dublin*, James Rogers, Christopher Peacock. 5
2. *Waterford*, James Jordan, Wm. McCornock, Walter Griffith.
3. *Cork*, Daniel Jackson, G. Brown, John Dinnen.
4. *Limerick*, Thomas Davis, Lawrence Kane.
5. *Castlebar,* John Leech, John Watson, sen. 10
6. *Athlone*, Matthias Joyce, John Mealy, J. Wilson; T. Halliday, supernumerary.
7. *Sligo*, G. Dice, Andrew Coleman.
8. *Ballyconnell*, Robert Bridge, Gustavus Armstrong, T. Verner. 15
9. *Clones*, Nehemiah Price, J. Clarke, James Rennick.
10. *Enniskillen*, Thomas Barber, Thomas Hetherington, Samuel Mitchell.
11. *Charlemont*, John Crook, John Miller, James McDonald. 20
12. *Lisleen*, Joseph Armstrong, Richard Condy.
13. *Londonderry*, Jonathan Brown, William West, William Hammet.
14. *Belfast*, Robert Armstrong, Robert Lindsay.
15. *Lisburn*, John Kerr, Hugh Moore, John Price. 25

Q. 6. How many preachers' wives are there?
A. Twelve.
Q. 7. How many of these are provided for by the circuits?
A. Four: Sister George Brown, Dinnen, Kane, and Watson.
Q. 8. How are the rest provided for? 30
A. By the Preachers' Fund.
Q. 9. What does each circuit contribute for the wives?

	£.	s.	d.
A. Dublin,	12.	0.	0.
Cork and Bandon,	5.	0.	0.	35
Limerick,	3.	0.	0.
Castlebar,	2.	0.	0.
Athlone,	6.	0.	0.
Sligo,	1.	0.	0.
Ballyconnell,	1.	0.	0.	40
Clones,	5.	0.	0.

Enniskillen,	1.	0.	0.
Charlemont,	2.	0.	0.
Londonderry,	1.	0.	0.
Coleraine,	2.	0.	0.
Belfast,	2.	0.	0.
Lisburn,	5.	0.	0.[59]

N.B. This is English money.

Q. 10. What numbers are in the societies?

A.
Dublin,	700
Waterford,	300
Cork,	720
Limerick,	250
Castlebar,	293
Athlone,	400
Sligo,	311
Ballyconnell,	698
Clones,	710
Enniskillen,	651
Charlemont,	943
Lisleen,	574
Londonderry,	444
Belfast,	303
Lisburn,	520
	7,817

Q. 11. What is contributed to the Preachers' Fund?

A. £49. 9. 0.

Q. 12. What is allowed out of it?

A.
To Mary Penington,	£10.	0s.	0d.
John Bredin,	12.	0.	0.
Thomas Halliday,	12.	0.	0.
Preachers' wives,	15.	9.	0.
	15.	9.	0.

Q. 13. What is contributed to the yearly collection?

A. £58. 13. 10.

Q. 14. How was this expended?

[59] Total £47. 0s. 0d.

A. In supplying the deficiencies and wants of our preachers, as far as it would go.

Q. 15. What is the Kingswood collection?

A. £38. 11. 3.

Q. 16. There have been great losses in Ireland through mis- 5
management of the Books. How may this be remedied?

A. (1) Let the books in every circuit be kept locked up in a
box, chest, or book-press.

(2) Let none ever be lent.

(3) If the preachers read any, let him take care they be 10
not dirtied.

(4) Let none be sold on trust; in particular, let everyone
pay for the magazines when he takes them.

(5) Let every Assistant deliver a list of the subscribers to
his successor, and an inventory of the books, and let him 15
bring a copy of it to the Conference.

(6) When an Assistant wants any books, let him send
word to Mr. Rogers, a week beforehand, 'I will order a
carman to call upon you for such and such books.'

(7) The books may frequently be sent with the goods of 20
some of our friends, which will save much expense.

(8) Let every Assistant leave his circuit clear when he
comes to the Conference.

Q. 17. How may the Assistants be more useful?

A. 1. By earnestly enforcing all our rules, particularly those 25
of the bands.

2. By exerting themselves as to the magazines, the weekly
contribution, and the quarterly and yearly collection.

3. By informing all the stewards of two universal
Methodist rules, the one, that a married preacher is to 30
have eighteen-pence a week for each child, the other,
that every circuit is to bear the expense of their preachers to and from the Conference. Also by informing them
that the stipend of each preacher is £12 English
yearly. 35

4. By renewing the notes of the Local Preachers
yearly.

5. By preaching in every large town at five in the morning during Summer.

Q. [18]. What houses are allowed to be built?

A. Those at Waterford, Londonderry, and Prosperous.

Q. 19. When shall the next Conference be held?

A. The first Friday in next July.

5   F I N I S

1786 *Minutes*[60]

                                    Dublin, Friday, July 7th, 1786.

Q. 1. What preachers are *admitted* this year?

A. William Hammet, James McDonald.

10   *Q.* 2. Who *remain on trial?*

A. John Dinnen, Thomas Verner.

Q. 3. Who are *admitted on trial?*

A. Samuel Bates, Thomas Owens, David Gordon, Francis
      Frazier, Thomas Seaward, John Harper, John Gillis,
15   Samuel Moorhead, John Grace, William Cowen, Daniel
      Graham.

Q. 4. Who have *died* this year?

A. Christopher Peacock, a precious, devoted labourer,
      highly favoured of God and man; and Andrew Coleman, a
20   sensible, promising youth, likely, if he had lived, to have
      been a burning and a shining light.

Q. 5. Are there any objections to any of our preachers?

A. They were examined one by one.

Q. 6. Who were laid aside?

25   *A.* George Dice, Thomas Halliday.

Q. 7. How are the preachers stationed this year?

A. As follows:

      1. *Dublin*, James Rogers, Joshua Keighley.[61]

---

[60] The title page runs, '*Minutes of some late Conversations between The Rev. Thomas Coke, L.L.D. and others.* Dublin: Printed in the Year 1786.' Once again, Dr. Coke was completely in charge of the Irish Conference, and JW had not visited Ireland this year.

[61] At the subsequent Conference in Bristol, Henry Moore requested that he should be stationed in Dublin in place of Joshua Keighley. Crookshank, *History of Methodism in Ireland*, 1:421.

2. *Waterford*, George Brown, David Gordon.
3. *Cork*, Jonathan Brown, Matthias Joyce, John Dinnen.
4. *Limerick*, Daniel Jackson, Thomas Seaward.
5. *Castlebar*, Nehemiah Price, William McCornock.
6. *Athlone*, Lawrence Kane, John Miller; John Mealy, supernumerary.
7. *Longford*, Thomas Davis, James McDonald, John Bredin, invalid.
8. *Sligo*, James Jordan, Francis Frazier.
9. *Ballyconnell*, Joseph Armstrong, James Rennick, Thomas Owens.
10. *Clones*, A preacher from England,[62] Thomas Hetherington, John Harper.
11. *Enniskillen*, Samuel Mitchell, Thomas Verner, John Gillis.
12. *Ballyshannon*, Thomas Barber, Richard Condy.
13. *Omagh*, John Price, Samuel Moorhead.
14. *Charlemont*, Hugh Moore, Gustavus Armstrong.
15. *Newry*, John Kerr, Robert Bridge.
16. *Londonderry*, John Leech, Walter Griffith.
17. *Coleraine*, A preacher from England,[63] William West, William Cowen.
18. *Belfast*, Robert Armstrong, John Howe, John Grace.
19. *Lisburn*, A preacher from England,[64] Robert Lindsay, Samuel Bates.
Q. 8. How many preachers' wives are there?
A. Nine.
Q. 9. How many of these are provided for by the circuits?
A. Five; Sister Jackson, Price, George Brown, Joyce, and Dinnen.
Q. 10. How are the rest provided for?
A. By the English Conference.
Q. 11. What does each circuit contribute for the wives?

	£.	s.	d.
A. Dublin,	14.	0.	0.
Waterford,	2.	0.	0.
Cork and Bandon,	6.	0.	0.

---

[62] William Green was added in the English *Minutes*.
[63] Walter Griffith was inserted in the English *Minutes*.
[64] Benjamin Pearce was added in the English *Minutes* but in the third place.

Limerick,		3.	0.	0.
Castlebar,		2.	0.	0.
Athlone,		2.	0.	0.
Longford,		6.	0.	0.
Sligo,		1.	0.	0.
Ballyconnell,		1.	0.	0.
Clones,		6.	0.	0.
Enniskillen,		2.	0.	0.
Newtown Stewart,		1.	0.	0.
Ballyshannon,		1.	0.	0.
Charlemont,		1.	10.	0.
Newry,		1.	10.	0.
Londonderry,		1.	0.	0.
Coleraine,		2.	0.	0.
Belfast,		2.	0.	0.
Lisburn,		5.	0.	0.
In all		£60.	0*s*.	0*d*.

N. B. This is English money.

Q. 12. What numbers are in the societies?

A.
Dublin,	900
Waterford,	300
Cork,	800
Limerick,	266
Castlebar,	303
Athlone,	600
Sligo,	391
Ballyconnell,	636
Clones,	929
Enniskillen,	1,400
Charlemont,	1,200
Lisleen,	950
Londonderry,	700
Belfast,	420
Lisburn,	550
In all,	10,345

Q. 13. What is contributed to the Preachers' Fund?

A. £53. 6. 10.

Q. 14. What is contributed to the yearly collection?

A. £67. 0. 0.

Q. 15. How was this expended?

A. In supplying the wants and deficiencies of the preachers, as far as it would go.

Q. 16. What is the Kingswood collection?

A. £38. 11. 3.

Q. 17. What is the collection for the Foreign Missions?

A. £20. 5. 6.

Q. 18. What houses are allowed to be built?

A. Kinsale, Castlebar, Aughrim, Cloghagaddy,[65] Ballynamallard, Killydart, Armagh, Dungannon, and Portaferry.

Q. 19. Does the *General Deed* require any alteration in the mode of settling our preaching-houses?

A. None, except the insertion of the phrase, 'the Conference of the People called Methodists, as established by a Deed Poll of the said John Wesley, under his hand and seal, bearing date the 28th day of February, in the year 1784, and enrolled in his Majesty's High Court of Chancery in London, and no others', instead of the phrase, 'the Conference of the People called Methodists in London, Bristol, or Leeds, and no others'.

Q. 20. Are there any directions to be given concerning the appointment of stewards?

A. The Conference entreat Mr. Wesley by himself or his delegate to appoint the general steward of every circuit, and all the stewards of the particular societies, annually in the course of his visitation.

Q. 21. What can be done in order still further to carry on the present glorious revival of the work of God?

A. (1) Let the preachers fervently urge the leaders, and even the private believers, to go into the houses of the ungodly, and wherever they are suffered, to pray earnestly with them and for them, and the world will be set on fire.

(2) Let the preachers meet the classes in the country places, as often as the circumstances of things will admit of it.

---

[65] Orig., 'Cloughagady'.

(3) Let the Assistants in planning the duties of the
Lord's day consider only the numbers of the congregations and the societies, and not be anywise influenced by
the preaching-houses; rather than which let the
preaching-houses be given to the bats and to the moles.[66]

Q. 22.[67] Some preachers have been brought into difficulties
by raising money for preaching-houses on their own notes
of hand. What can be done to prevent this in future?

A. Let no travelling preacher become a surety on any such
occasion.

Q. 23. We fear that mistakes have been sometimes made in
the annual returns of the numbers of our societies. How
shall these be prevented?

A. Let the Assistants return only the members to whom
they have given society tickets, and not those who are only
on trial.

Q. 24. Preachers who have been expelled for their evil conduct have notwithstanding been suffered without the consent of Mr. Wesley or the Conference to preach in our
circuits. How shall this great evil be remedied?

A. Let every Assistant, as he would not incur the displeas-
ure of the Conference, oppose to the utmost every such
instance. And let him withdraw the preaching from the
house of any member of our society who after warning
given, will permit any person under the sentence of
expulsion to preach under his roof.

Q. 25. What further direction can be given to secure the
proper settlement of our preaching-houses?

A. Let no Assistant make, or suffer to be made, in his
respective circuit, a collection for any preaching-house till
every step be previously taken to secure it on the
Conference plan by a trust deed, a bond, or sufficient articles of agreement.

Q. 26. Is it lawful to send, deliver, or carry home work or
goods on the sabbath day?

---

[66] Cf. Isa. 2:20.

[67] Orig., '24', followed by *QQ*. 25–30. It is possible that there were two intervening *QQ*. 23 and 24, which were omitted by accident or design. It seems more likely,
however, that '24' was an uncorrected misprint. Here we alter to 22–28.

A. It is not lawful: it is contrary to the laws of God, and therefore must not be suffered in our societies.

Q. 27. Out of what fund are the carriage of the goods of the preachers, their letters on the business of the circuits, and the shoeing of their horses to be discharged?

A. The general stewards are to defray these expenses out of the public funds of their respective circuits, as far as they are able. Whereas various letters, some anonymous entitled *Free Thoughts*,[68] etc., and others signed 'Michael Moorhouse',[69] have been circulated with great diligence, to the great disturbance of our societies, we do unanimously bear this public testimony of our disapprobation of these proceedings, and esteem the authors of them as enemies to our Connection, and disturbers of the peace of Zion, and of that spiritual union which is so necessary for the preservation and increase of the work of God.

Q. 28. When shall the next Conference be held?

A. The first Friday in next July.

FINIS

1787 *Minutes*[70]

Dublin, July 6th, 1787.

Q. 1. What preachers are *admitted* this year?

A. None.

---

[68] This pamphlet is by 'A Layman of the Methodist Society', *Free Thoughts concerning a Separation of the People called Methodists from the Church of England, addressed to the Preachers of the Methodist connection* (London, 1785).

[69] Moorehouse had been an itinerant for twelve years until leaving this year. In 1785 and 1786, he published pamphlets airing his personal grievances and criticizing what he alleged was the favouring of some preachers more than others. See Tyerman, *Wesley*, 3:467–68.

[70] The title page runs, '*Minutes of some late Conversations between the Rev. John Wesley, M.A., and others.* Dublin: Printed by B. Dugdale, No. 150, Capel Street, 1787.' Again, Wesley spent three months itinerating through the Irish Societies before conducting the Irish Conference early in July. Meantime, Coke spent a similar period in America, summoning and conducting a general Conference in May, and pushing JW's nominations so untactfully as to arouse the Americans'

Q. 2. Who *remain on trial*?

A. Benjamin Pearce, John Dinnen, Thomas Verner, Samuel
Bates, Thomas Owens, David Gordon, Francis Frazier,
John Harper, Thomas Roberts, John Gillis, Samuel
Moorhead, John Grace.

Q. 3. Who are *admitted on trial*?

A. John Burnet,[71] Andrew Jefferys,[72] John Black, William
Johnson, George Henderson, John Darragh, Francis
Armstrong, William McCornock, Thomas Hewett, John
Malcomson,[73] Thomas Kerr, John West, Hugh Pue.[74]

Q. 4. Who has *died* this year?

A. Thomas Seaward, a pious, zealous, blameless, useful
young man.

Q. 5. Are there any objections to any of our preachers?

A. They were examined one by one.

Q. 6. How are the preachers *stationed* this year?

A. As follows:

1. *Dublin*, Henry Moore, William Myles.
2. *Waterford*, David Gordon, Andrew Jefferys.
3. *Cork*, James Rogers, Matthias Joyce.
4. *Bandon*, Richard Condy, Benjamin Pearce.
5. *Limerick*, Jonathan Brown, John Dinnen.
6. *Castlebar*, George Brown, William McCornock, Sen.,
   William McCornock, Jun.
7. *Athlone*, Walter Griffith, John Miller.

independent ire, so that they removed JW's name from their own *Minutes* that year.
It seemed that in their zeal to secure the unity of Methodism, JW and Coke were
striving to carve up the world between them. Coke left Philadelphia on May 27,
arriving in Dublin (after a twenty-nine-day crossing) on June 26. JW summoned the
neighbouring preachers to meet Coke on Saturday, June 29, to 'consider the state
of our brethren in *America*, who have been terribly frightened at their own shadow,
as if the *English* preachers were just going to enslave them'. Coke joined JW at the
regular Conference, July 6–10, about which JW reported: 'We had no jarring string,
but all, from the beginning to the end, was love and harmony.' June 26, 30, July 5,
Journal & Diaries, 24:40, 42 in this edn. Coke also stayed on in Dublin, and after
the Conference, JW hired the complete accommodation of the *Prince of Wales*
packet to take himself, Coke, and a large Methodist company across to the English
Conference in Manchester at the end of July. Ibid., 24:43.

[71] Orig., 'Burnett', (2).

[72] Orig., 'Jeffers', (2).

[73] Orig., 'Melcombson', (2).

[74] Orig., 'Pugh', (2).

8. *Longford*, William West, John West.
9. *Sligo*, Francis Frazier, William Johnson.
10. *Ballyconnell*, Joseph Armstrong, James Rennick, John Grace.
11. *Clones*, Robert Armstrong,[75] John Black, Hugh Pue.
12. *Lisbellaw*, Samuel Mitchell, Thomas Verner, John Gillis.
13. *Enniskillen*, George Henderson, Thomas Kerr.
14. *Ballyshannon*, Thomas Barber,[76] John Darragh.
15. *Lisleen*, Robert Bridge, John Malcomson.
16. *Omagh*, John Price, Thomas Hewett.[77]
17. *Charlemont*, Hugh Moore, Samuel Bates.[78]
18. *Londonderry*, Thomas Davis,[79] James McDonald.
19. *Coleraine*, Thomas Roberts, Nehemiah Price, Gustavus Armstrong.
20. *Belfast*, John Howe, James Jordan.[80]
21. *Lisburn*, Robert Lindsay, John Burnet, Francis Armstrong.
22. *Newry*, John Kerr, Thomas Hetherington, Samuel Moorhead.

Q. 7. How many wives are to be provided for?
A. Ten.
Q. 8. How are these to be provided for?
A. Sister Moore, Myles, Joyce, Hetherington, Brown, Griffith, and Price in Ireland; Sister Condy, Rennick, and Dinnen from England.
Q. 9. In what proportion do the circuits in Ireland provide for the wives?
A. As follows:

	English.		
Dublin,	£24.	0s.	0d.
Waterford,	3.	0.	0.
Cork,	12.	0.	0.
Bandon,	1.	0.	0.
Limerick,	3.	0.	0.

[75] Replaced at the Manchester Conference by Hugh Moore.
[76] Orig., 'Barbor'.
[77] Orig., 'Hewet'.
[78] At the Manchester Conference, Hugh Moore (orig., 'Moor') was removed to Clones and was replaced by J. Collins (after Bates).
[79] Orig., 'Davies'.
[80] In the Manchester Conference, Jordan was replaced by T. Owens.

Castlebar,	2.	0.	0.
Athlone,	4.	0.	0.
Longford,	5.	0.	0.
Sligo,	1.	0.	0.
Ballyconnell,	1.	0.	0.
Clones,	7.	0.	0.
Lisbellaw and Enniskillen,	3.	0.	0.
Ballyshannon,	0.	10.	0.
Lisleen,	1.	0.	0.
Omagh,	1.	0.	0.
Charlemont,	2.	0.	0.
Londonderry,	1.	0.	0.
Coleraine,	3.	0.	0.
Belfast,	2.	10.	0.
Lisburn,	5.	0.	0.
Newry	2.	0.	0.
In all,	£84.	0s.	0d.

Q. 10. What numbers are in the societies?

A.
Dublin	1,137
Waterford,	320
Cork,	820
Limerick,	240
Castlebar,	351
Athlone,	356
Longford,	340
Sligo,	288
Ballyconnell,	700
Clones,	887
Enniskillen,	1,450
Charlemont,	680
Ballyshannon	800
Omagh,	413
Londonderry,	236
Coleraine,	446
Belfast,	425
Lisburn,	600
Newry,	824
In all,	11,313

Q. 11. What is the Kingswood collection?

A. £48. 14. 6.

Q. 12. What is contributed to the Preachers' Fund?

A. £59. 3. 0.

Q. 13. What is allowed out of it?

A. To John Bredin,

for one year	15.	0.	0.	5
John Mealy	12.	0.	0.	
Mary Penington	15.	0.	0.	
In all,	£42.	0*s*.	0*d*.	

Q. 14. What is contributed for the yearly expenses?

A. £79. 4. 6.

Q. 15. How was it expended?

A. In supplying the deficiencies of the preachers' salaries, and those of their wives and children.

Q. 16. What houses are to be built this year?

A. One at Tullamore, Carlow, Moate, and Tandragee, and the Waterford preaching-house to be altered.

Q. 17. Much dispute has been about a trifle; to prevent this for the future we would be glad to know how should we name the five English vowels?

A. You are to learn this in England. Now the English name them thus: *a* as in *face*, *e* as in *me*, *i* as in *high*. Concerning *o* and *u* there is no question.

Indeed the letter *a* has four sounds, as in *all*, *calf*, *name*, *can*. But the third is far the most common. Therefore we name the letter from this.

The letter *e* sounds either long as *me*, which is its proper sound, or short as in *men*. But in English it never sounds like *a*: that is a mere French corruption.

Q. 18. Can anything be done to preserve the freedom of debate in our Conference?

A. Those who divulge anything of importance mentioned in the Conference; if they be in full connection, let them be put back upon trial for four years; if they be on trial, let them be suspended for a year.

Q. 19. Are there any advices concerning smaller things which you would give us?

A. I advise the Assistants,

(1) To re-establish morning preaching in all large towns, at least.

(2) To exert themselves in restoring the bands;

(3) And the select societies.

(4) Change a general steward in every circuit, and a particular steward in every society, yearly.

I advise all the preachers,

(1) Always to conclude the service in about an hour.

(2) Never scream.

(3) Never lean upon or beat the Bible.

(4) Wherever you preach, meet the society.

(5) Do not, without the utmost necessity, go home at night.

(6) Never take part against the Assistant.

(7) Have love-feasts in more places.

(8) Introduce no new tunes. See that none sing too slow, and the women sing their parts. Exhort all to sing, and all to stand at singing, as well as to kneel at prayers.

(9) Let none repeat the last line unless the preacher does.

(10) Inform the leaders that every Assistant is to change both the stewards and leaders when he sees good; and that no leader has power to put any person either into or out of the society.

(11) Teach all the people to repeat the Lord's Prayer after the preacher.

(12) With all your might inculcate industry upon all;

(13) And cleanliness.

(14) Teach them to cure themselves and their children of the itch; and to prevent it by cold bathing.

(15) Avoid clownishness; therefore do not slouch your hats.

(16) Advise all our women to wear plain bonnets, or hats.

(17) Drink no brandy and water, but either malt-drink or toast and water.

(18) Discourage the drinking of whisky at wakes, and improve those meetings by solemn prayer; and preach the funeral sermon at another time.

(19) Diligently spread both the large and small hymn-books, the *Christian Pattern*, and the *Primitive Physic*.

(20) Sell none but our own books.

(21) Let a Book-Press be provided in every circuit.

(22) I will print the text of the New Testament alone.

Q. 20. When and where is the next Conference to be held?

A. At Dublin, on the first Friday in July, 1788.

FINIS

1788 *Minutes*[81]

Dublin, July 8th, 1788.

Q. 1. What preachers are *admitted* this year?

A. Benjamin Pearce.

Q. 2. Who *remain on trial?* 5

A. John Dinnen, Thomas Verner, Samuel Bates, Thomas Owens, David Gordon, Francis Frazier, Thomas Roberts, John Gillis, Samuel Moorhead, John Grace, Andrew Jefferys, John Black, William Johnson, John Darragh, Francis Armstrong, William McCornock, Jun., Thomas 10 Hewett, John Malcomson, Thomas Kerr, John West, Hugh Pue.

Q. 3. Who are *admitted on trial?*

A. John Stephens, James Lyons, James McMullen, Alex. Moore, Matthew Stewart, Thomas Elliott, Frederick 15 Hamilton, Andrew Hamilton, Robert Smith, Nebuchadnezzar Lee, John Stephenson, William Hamilton, Daniel Graham.

Q. 4. Who has *died* this year?

A. John Mealy, worn out in the service of his Master: he 20 suffered much in his last illness, and died triumphant in the Lord.

And *John Burnet*, a very pious, devoted, useful young man: he continued through a long illness in a very triumphant state of mind, and departed this life in extraor- 25 dinary triumph.

Q. 5. Are there any objections to any of our preachers?

A. They were examined one by one.

Q. 6. Who have desisted from travelling?

A. ———,[82] Robert Lindsay, James Jordan, Robert 30 Armstrong.

---

[81] The title runs, '*Minutes of some late Conversations, between the Rev. Thomas Coke, L.L.D. and others.* Dublin: Printed by B. Dugdale, No.150, Capel Street. 1788.' Once again in 1788, JW left Ireland to Coke, and Coke left America to Asbury. Coke followed JW's pattern, itinerating during the spring, and climaxing this trip with the Dublin Conference in early July, followed by leading a party over to England for the London Conference.

[82] Three opening dashes would seem to imply some unnamed preacher, but the CJ and the English *Minutes* offer no clue.

Q. 7. How are the preachers *stationed* this year?
A. As follows:

1. *Dublin*, A preacher from England,[83] William Myles.
2. *Wexford*, Hugh Moore, Thomas Verner.
3. *Waterford*, Richard Condy, Francis Frazier.
4. *Cork*, James Rogers, Thomas Roberts.
5. *Bandon*, John Kerr, Robert Bridge.
6. *Limerick*, Jonathan Brown, Andrew Jefferys.
7. *Birr*, Thomas Davis, Gustavus Armstrong.
8. *Castlebar*, James McDonald, Thomas Kerr.
9. *Athlone*, John Dinnen, William Wilson.
10. *Longford*, Thomas Barber, John Malcomson.
11. *Sligo*, David Gordon, Thomas Hewett.
12. *Ballyconnell*, George Brown, John Miller, Francis Armstrong; John Price, supernumerary.
13. *Clones*, Joseph Armstrong, Samuel Moorhead,[84] Alexander Moore.
14. *Brookeborough*, William McCornock, Jun., William Hamilton.
15. *Enniskillen*, John Black, Daniel Graham.
16. *Ballyshannon*, James Rennick, Andrew Hamilton.
17. *Killybeggs*, John Stephenson, Thomas Elliott.
18. *Lisleen*, Matthew Stewart, Nebuchadnezzar Lee.
19. *Omagh*, Samuel Bates, James McMullen.[85]
20. *Charlemont*, John Crook, David Barrowclough.
21. *Londonderry*, William West, John West.
22. *Coleraine*, Matthias Joyce, William Johnson, John Stephens; John Howe, supernumerary.
23. *Belfast*, Samuel Mitchell, John Darragh.
24. *Lisburn*, Thomas Hetherington, John Gillis, Frederick[86] Hamilton; Hugh Pue, supernumerary.
25. *Newry*, Walter Griffith, John Grace.
26. *Tandragee*, Nehemiah Price, James Lyons, Robert Smith.

Q. 8. How many wives are to be provided for?
A. Twelve.

---

[83] English *Minutes* supply Charles Boone.
[84] Orig., 'Moorehead', as in English *Minutes* (1788).
[85] Orig., 'McMullin'.
[86] Orig., 'Frederic', as in orig. English *Minutes* (1788).

Q. 9. How many of these are to be provided for by the
circuits?

A. Eight: namely, Sister Myles, West, Dinnen, (George)
Brown, Stewart, Rennick, Joyce, and Griffith.

Q. 10. In what proportion do the circuits provide for these? 5

A. As follows:

	English		
Dublin,	£24.	0s.	0d.
Wexford,	1.	10.	0.
Waterford,	2.	10.	0.
Cork,	12.	0.	0.	10
Bandon,	1.	0.	0.
Limerick,	4.	0.	0.
Birr,	1.	10.	0.
Castlebar,	2.	0.	0.
Athlone,	4.	10.	0.	15
Longford,	6.	0.	0.
Sligo,	1.	0.	0.
Ballyconnell,	1.	10.	0.
Clones,	7.	0.	0.
Brookeborough,	2.	0.	0.	20
Enniskillen,	3.	0.	0.
Ballyshannon,	1.	0.	0.
Lisleen,	1.	0.	0.
Omagh,	1.	0.	0.
Charlemont	3.	0.	0.	25
Londonderry,	1.	10.	0.
Coleraine,	3.	0.	0.
Belfast,	2.	10.	0.
Lisburn,	6.	0.	0.
Tandragee,	2.	10.	0.	30
Newry,	1.	0.	0.
In all,	£96.	0s.	0d.

Q. 11. How are the other four wives, namely, Sister Condy,
Crook, Price, and Hetherington, to be provided for? 35

A. From England.

Q. 12. What numbers are in the societies?

A. Dublin, 1,150

Waterford, 350

Cork, 550 40

Bandon,	280			
Limerick,	244			
Castlebar,	344			
Athlone,	396			
Longford,	331			
Sligo,	330			
Ballyconnell,	750			
Clones,	1,268			
Brookeborough,	648			
Enniskillen,	655			
Ballyshannon,	500			
Killybeggs,	300			
Lisleen,	327			
Omagh,	310			
Charlemont,	838			
Londonderry,	221			
Coleraine,	491			
Belfast,	373			
Lisburn,	611			
Newry,	946			
In all,	12,213			

Q. 13. What is the Kingswood collection?

A. £47. 11. 6.

Q. 14. What children are admitted this year?

A. Joseph Rogers, Edward Price.

Q. 15. What is contributed to the Preachers' Fund?

A. £59. 4. 6.

Q. 16. What is allowed out of it?

A. To John Price,   £12.   0 *s.*   0 *d.*

Mary Penington,   12.   0.   0.

For John Mealy's expenses

during his illness, and for his

funeral,   4.   17.   6.

Q. 17. What is contributed for the yearly expenses?

A. £78. 15. 0.

Q. 18. How was it expended?

A. In supplying the deficiencies of the preachers' salaries

and those of their wives and children.

Q. 19. What is contributed for the Foreign Missions?

A. £56. 13. 6.

Q. 20. What houses are to be built this year?

A. One at Wexford, Ross, Bandon, Ballinrobe, Richhill, and Brookeborough.

Q. 21. As some gross sinners have sprung up among us, whom we have expelled in the name of the Lord, what shall be done to prevent such evils in the future?

A. (1) We beg leave to humble ourselves under the hand of our gracious God for these evils which have sprung up among us, and to return him our fervent thanksgivings for the discovery he has made of the authors of them, and the strength he has given us to cut off those rotten members.

(2) We appoint the first Friday in next September as a day of fasting and humiliation throughout our societies, to deprecate the judgments we have deserved through these and other evils, and to pray the God of all grace to carry on the great revival he has begun among us.

(3) We do unanimously resolve, in the fear and presence of God, that we will in future set ourselves, unitedly and separately, to the utmost reach of our influence against all such persons and practices.

Q. 22. On strict examination we have found that many of the members of our society keep private stills, or sell spirituous liquors without a licence, and buy or sell uncustomed goods, particularly malt. What shall be done to extirpate these evils?

A. Let every Assistant be particularly diligent to enforce our rules against smuggling. Let them first warn the guilty persons, and if they do not repent and forsake their sins, let them be expelled, whether they be rich or poor. And let the Assistants look to this!

Q. 23. Can anything be done to lighten the great expenses of our society in Dublin, on account of our annual Conferences?

A. Let every Assistant raise in his circuit a sufficient sum to pay for the expense of his own and his Helpers' horses during their stay in Dublin.

Q. 24. Are any directions to be given the preachers concerning their attendance on their circuits?

A. Let no preacher be absent from his circuit at the Conference time above one Sunday; let him not leave his circuit till after the last Sunday before the Conference; and let him be in his appointed circuit on the first Sunday after the Conference, except on extraordinary occasions.

Q. 25. Are there not some circuits in this kingdom that are able fully to support their preachers, and do not?

A. There are; and let the members of our society in those circuits be informed that they shall have no more preachers in future than they will fully support.

Q. 26. What directions are to be given concerning the general collections?

A. Let the Assistants be diligent and faithful in making them according to the rules of Conference, and let their Helpers give them all possible assistance.

To be explicit. (1) Let a private and public collection be annually made in every circuit immediately after the Conference for the support of our most important missions among the heathens. (2) Let the yearly collection for the sending out preachers in these kingdoms, and for the making up of all the deficiencies in the salaries of the preachers' wives and children, and for the discharging of all the expenses incurred by preachers or their families through sickness, which cannot be other wise discharged—be made in all the societies in the month of March. (3) Let the private collection for the support of our superannuated preachers, and the distressed widows and orphans of preachers, be raised in the month of May. And, lastly, let the collection for the support of Kingswood School, where the sons of our married preachers are educated, boarded, and clothed, be made in all our congregations about midsummer.

Q. 27. When and where is the next Conference to be held?

A. At Dublin, on the first Friday in July, 1789.

FINIS

1789 *Minutes*[87]

Dublin, July 3d, 1789

Q. 1. What preachers are *admitted* this year?

A. Thomas Verner and John Dinnen.

Q. 2. Who *remain on trial?*[88]   5

A. Samuel Bates, David Gordon, Thomas Roberts, John
Gillis,[89] Samuel Moorhead, John Grace, Andrew Jefferys,
John Black, William Johnson, John Darragh, Francis
Armstrong, William McCornock, Thomas Hewett, John
Malcomson, Thomas Kerr, John West, James Lyons,   10
James McMullen, Alex. Moore, Matthew Stewart,
Thomas Elliott, Andrew Hamilton, Robert Smith,
Nebuchadnezzar Lee, William Hamilton, John
Stephenson, Daniel Graham, Michael Murphy, William
Wilson, and David Barrowclough.   15

Q. 3. Who are admitted on trial?

---

[87] The title runs, '*Minutes of some late Conversations, between the Rev. John Wesley,
M.A. and others.* Dublin: Printed by B. Dugdale, No. 150, Capel-Street, 1789.' This
year was JS's last biennial visit to Ireland. He arrived in Dublin on Sunday morning, Mar. 29, and left on Sunday, July 12, preaching and administering Communion
on both occasions. Again Coke had spent the spring and summer with the slightly
mollified Americans, leaving New York for the British Isles on June 5, after signing
with Asbury the Methodist Address to the new president of the United States,
George Washington. He landed in Liverpool on July 10, thus unable to attend the
Irish Conference, but in good time for that in Leeds, where he continued to act as
JW's secretary. JW's *Journal* reflections paid high tribute to the Irish preachers:
'Friday, July 3. Our little Conference began in Dublin and ended Tuesday 7. On
this I observe, (1) I never had between forty and fifty such preachers together
in Ireland before, all of them we had reason to hope, alive to God and earnestly
devoted to his service; (2) I never saw such a number of preachers before so
unanimous in all points, particularly as to leaving the church, which none of
them had the least thought of. It is no wonder that there had been this year so
large an increase of the Society. . . . I had much satisfaction in this Conference,
in which, conversing with between forty and fifty travelling preachers, I found
such a body of men as I hardly believed could have been found together in
Ireland; men of so sound experience, so deep piety, and so strong understanding, I am convinced they are no way inferior to the English Conference, except
it be in number.' (July 3, 1789, *Journal & Diaries*, 24:145–46 in this edn.)

[88] The English *Minutes* prefix to these thirty names those of John Stephens, John
Riles, and Mark Willis, who were not in Ireland, and duplicates of the names of
Lyons, McMullen, and Moore.

[89] Orig., 'Gilles', (2).

A. William Brandon, George Donovan, Samuel Wood,[90] Thomas Ridgeway,[91] James McQuigg, Thomas Patterson, Andrew Hamilton, Jun., James Irwin, Thomas Werrill,[92] and Robert McCay.

Q. 4. Who have died this year?

A. Hugh Pue, a zealous, pious young man, who suffered much in his illness, but died happy in God.

 Francis Frazier, a good young man, and a good preacher.

 And *John Stephens,* who being little more than a child in years, was a man both in knowledge and piety, and went hence in the full triumph of faith.

Q. 5. Are there any objections to any of our preachers?

A. They were examined one by one.

Q. 6. Who have desisted from travelling?

A. John Howe.

Q. 7. How are the preachers stationed this year?

A. As follows:

 1. *Dublin,* A preacher from England,[93] Charles Boone.

 2. *Wicklow,* John Gillis.

 3. *Wexford,* Thomas Kerr, Robert Smith.

 4. *Waterford,* Robert Bridge, John West.

 5. *Cork,* John Kerr, Thomas Roberts.

 6. *Bandon,* James Rogers, Gustavus Armstrong.

 7. *Limerick,* Richard Condy, Andrew Jefferys, J. McQuigg.

 8. *Birr,* William West, John Darragh.

 9. *Castlebar,* Hugh Moore, Thomas Verner.

 10. *Athlone,* John Dinnen, Tho. Davis.

 11. *Longford,* Thomas Barber, John Miller.

 12. *Sligo,* John Black, Michael Murphy.

 13. *Ballyconnell,* George Brown, Alexander Moore, John Stephenson; John Price, supernumerary.

 14. *Cavan,* Joseph Armstrong, James Irwin.

 15. *Clones,* Matthew Stewart, William Wilson, Tho. Ridgeway.

---

[90] Orig., 'Woods', (2), as in English *Minutes.*

[91] Orig., 'Ridgway', (2), as in English *Minutes.*

[92] Orig., 'Worrell', (2), as in English *Minutes.*

[93] The English *Minutes* add Thomas Rutherford.

16. *Brookeborough*, William McCornock, James Lyons, Andrew Hamilton, Sen.

17. *Enniskillen*, Tho. Hetherington, Robt. McCay.

18. *Ballyshannon*, Samuel Moorhead, William Hamilton, Francis Armstrong.

19. *Lisleen*, James Rennick, Thomas Elliot, Andrew Hamilton, Jun.

20. *Omagh*, Samuel Bates, Nebuchadnezzar Lee.

21. *Charlemont*, John Crook, Jas. McMullen.

22. *Londonderry*, John Grace, Tho. Werrill.

23. *Coleraine*, David Gordon, Tho. Patterson, Samuel Wood.

24. *Belfast*, Samuel Mitchell, Nehemiah Price, Wm. Brandon.

25. *Lisburn*, Matthias Joyce, William Johnson.

26. *Downpatrick*, John Malcomson, Daniel Graham.

27. *Tandragee*, David Barrowclough, Tho. Hewett, Geo. Donovan.

28. *Newry*, Walter Griffith, James McDonald.

Q. 8. How many wives are to be provided for?

A. Fifteen, and Sister Stephenson, £6.

Q. 9. How many of these are to be provided for by the circuits?

A. Nine: namely, a Sister from England, Boone, West, Dinnen, G. Brown, Stewart, Rennick, McDonald, Griffith, and £8 for a tenth.

Q. 10. In what proportion do the circuits provide for these?

A. As follows:

	English		
Dublin,	£24.	0s.	0d.
Wexford,	2.	0.	0.
Waterford,	3.	0.	0.
Cork,	16.	0.	0.
Bandon,	1.	10.	0.
Limerick,	5.	0.	0.
Birr,	1.	10.	0.
Castlebar,	2.	0.	0.
Athlone,	6.	0.	0.
Longford,	7.	0.	0.
Sligo,	1.	0.	0.
Ballyconnell,	2.	0.	0.
Clones,	6.	0.	0.

Cavan,	4.	0.	0.
Brookeborough,	2.	10.	0.
Enniskillen,	3.	0.	0.
Ballyshannon,	1.	10.	0.
Lisleen,	1.	10.	0.
Omagh,	1.	0.	0.
Charlemont,	4.	0.	0.
Londonderry,	2.	0.	0.
Coleraine,	4.	0.	0.
Belfast,	4.	0.	0.
Lisburn,	6.	0.	0.
Downpatrick,	1.	0.	0.
Tandragee,	3.	0.	0.
Newry,	1.	10.	0.
In all,	£116.	0*s*.	0*d*.[94]

Q. 11. How are the other six wives, namely, Sister Condy, Crook, Price, Hetherington, Joyce, J. Armstrong, to be provided for?

A. From England.

Q. 12. What numbers are in the societies?

A.

Dublin,	1,000
Wexford,	221
Waterford,	246
Cork,	600
Bandon,	220
Limerick,	350
Birr,	150
Castlebar,	200
Athlone,	540
Longford,	400
Sligo,	300
Ballyconnell,	880
Clones,	1,268
Brookeborough,	757
Enniskillen,	520
Ballyshannon,	570
Killybeggs,	480
Lisleen,	500
Omagh,	330

---

[94] Orig., '£115. 0. 0.'

Charlemont,	1,100
Londonderry,	288
Coleraine,	640
Belfast,	450
Lisburn,	800
Tandragee,	810
Newry,	390
	14,010

Q. 13. What is the Kingswood collection?

A. £48. 17. 6.

Q. 14. What is contributed to the Preachers' Fund?

A. £74. 12. 0.

Q. 15. What is allowed out of it?

A. To John Price   £12.   0*s.*   0*d.*
      John Bredin,   12   0.   0.
      Mary Penington,   12.   0.   0.

Q. 16. What is contributed for the yearly expenses?

A. £80. 4. 0.

Q. 17. How was it expended?

A. In supplying the deficiencies of the preachers' salaries, and those of their wives and children.

Q. 18. What is contributed for the foreign missions?

A. £62. 0. 0.

Q. 19. What houses are to be built this year?

A. One at Dunmanway, Newbliss, Brookeborough, Lisleen, Belfast, Bangor, and Ballybrack.[95]

Q. 20. Does it belong to the Conference to pay the little allowance for the wives and children of the travelling preachers, or the shoeing of their horses, letters on business, or other travelling expenses?

A. By no means, the Conference cannot do it, they have no fund for it; every circuit is to pay them at the Quarterly Meeting out of the first money that is brought, and each circuit may have two or more preachers, as they can afford. N.B. We don't engage to supply deficiencies.

The order of the stewards paying circuit expenses: wives, children, preachers carriage of luggage, letters on

---

[95] Orig., 'Ballyblack'.

business, shoeing horses, expenses to and from Conference, and also to give what is wanting to take the preachers who have[96] travelled with them to their new circuits.

Q. 21. Have the weekly and quarterly contributions been duly made in all our societies?

A. In many it has been shamefully neglected. To remedy this,

(1) Let every Assistant remind every society that this was our original rule, Every member contributes one penny weekly (unless he is in extreme poverty) and one shilling quarterly. Explain the reasonableness of this.

(2) Let every leader receive the weekly contributions from each person in his class.

(3) Let the Assistant ask every person, at changing their tickets, Can you afford to observe our rule? And receive what he is able to give.

Q. 22. The Scripture says, 'If any man that is called a brother be a fornicator, or covetous, with such an one, no, not to eat.'[97] And 'put away from among yourselves that wicked person.'[98] This is an express command, and it is of unspeakable importance. These 'money-lovers' are the pest of every Christian society. They have been the main cause of destroying every revival of religion. They will destroy *us* if we do not put them away. But how shall we know them, without the miraculous discernment of spirits?

A. (1) By their own confession. Tell anyone alone, with all tenderness: 'I am to give an account of your soul to God. Enable me to do it with joy. I am afraid you are covetous. Answer me a few questions, in order to remove that fear.'

(2) By their fruits. For instance. A man not worth a shilling enters our society. Yet he freely gives a penny a week. Five years after he is worth scores of pounds. He gives a penny a week still. I must think this man covetous, unless he assures me, he bestows his charity some other way. For everyone is covetous whose beneficence does not increase in the same proportion as his substance.

---

[96] Orig., 'has'.
[97] 1 Cor. 5:11.
[98] Cf. 1 Cor. 5:13.

Q. 23. Can anything be done with regard to the books?

A. (1) Sell no books on trust; if you do, you must pay for them yourself. (2) Make the circuit steward pay for the tickets which are used on the circuit, at the Christmas Quarterly Meeting. N.B. Mr. Wesley will not be account- 5 able for any loss.

Q. 24. A common report has run through Ireland, that the Methodists were resolved to separate from the Church! Is that report true?

A. Nothing can be more false. Although Mr. Wesley 10 believes it right to continue the Sunday Morning Service in Dublin, yet he never had any design of having it in any other part of the kingdom, not that he could be justly complained of if he did, seeing he is a regularly ordained minister. He thinks it needful to observe further, that the 15 Methodists never will separate from the Church till God calls him hence.

N.B. Except in extraordinary cases, every preacher is to go to bed before ten o'clock.

To our Societies in Ireland. 20

Fifty years ago, and for several years following, all our preachers were single men, when in process of time a few of them married. Those with whom they laboured maintained both them and
their wives, there being then no settled allowance either for the
one or the other. But above thirty years ago it was found most con- 25
venient to fix a stated allowance for both, and this was found by the
circuits where they were stationed, till one year some of the circuits
complained of poverty. Dr. Coke and I supplied what was wanting. The next year, the number of wives increasing, three or four
of them were supplied out of the Contingent Fund. This was a bad 30
precedent for more and more wives were thrown upon this fund,
till it was likely to be swallowed up thereby. We could think of no
way to prevent this but to consider the state of our societies in
England and Ireland, and to beg the members of each circuit to
give us that assistance, which they can easily do without hurting 35
their families.

Within these fifty years the substance of the Methodists is
increased in proportion to their numbers. Therefore if you are not
straitened in your own bowels, this will be no grievance, but you will

cheerfully give food and raiment to those who give up all their time, and strength, and labour to your service.

JOHN WESLEY
Dublin, July 3, 1789

5   *Q.* 25. When and where is the next Conference to be held?
A. At Dublin, on the first Friday in July, 1790.

FINIS

1790 *Minutes* [99]

Dublin, Friday, July 2, 1790
10   *Q.* 1. What preachers are *admitted* this year?
A. Samuel Bates, David Gordon, John Gillis, Samuel Moorhead, and John Grace.
Q. 2. Who *remain on trial*?
A. William Johnson, John Darragh, Francis Armstrong,
15   William McCornock, Thomas Hewett,[100] John Malcomson, Thomas Kerr, James Lyons, James McMullen, Alexander Moore, Matthew Stewart, Thomas Elliott, Andrew Hamilton, Robert Smith, William Hamilton, Daniel Graham, Michael Murphy, William
20   Wilson, David Barrowclough,[101] William Brandon, George Donovan, Samuel Wood, Thomas Ridgeway, James McQuigg, Thomas Patterson, Andrew Hamilton, Jun., James Irwin, Thomas Werrill, and John Stephenson.[102]

[99] The title runs, '*Minutes of some late Conversations between the Rev. Thomas Coke, L.L.D. and others.* Dublin: Printed by B. Dugdale, No. 150, Capel-Street. 1790.' This year, JW travelled around much of England, Scotland, and Wales, but left Ireland completely to Coke.

[100] Thomas Hewett is spelled 'Hewitt' here and in the English *Minutes* (twice each).

[101] Orig., 'Barraclough', (2), in the English *Minutes* (1790), the name is mentioned once only as 'Barraclough', and twice in 1791. The English *Minutes* (1789) have one each, but have 'Barraclough' for No. 98 Tandragee. The remainder use 'Barrowclough'.

[102] Strangely, the last fourteen names, from Graham to Stephenson, were not included in the list of those remaining on trial in the Conference Journal or the English *Minutes*.

Q. 3. Who are *admitted on trial*?

A. Archibald Murdock, Thomas Brown, John Graham, John Hurley, Charles Graham, Samuel Steel, William Smith, John Cross, James Lyons, and William Ferguson.[103]   5

Q. 4. Who has died this year?

A. *John Black*, a young man of an excellent spirit, clothed with humility and high in grace. His talents promised very extensive usefulness; but it pleased the Father of Mercies in his unsearchable providence to take him to his   10 great reward by an untimely death. As he was one day bathing in the sea he got unexpectedly beyond his depth and was drowned. 'How unsearchable are his judgments, and his ways past finding out!'[104]

Q. 5. Are there any objections to any of our preachers?   15

A. They were examined one by one.

Q. 6. Who have desisted from travelling?

A. ————.[105] Hugh Moore, Nehemiah Price, Robert Bridge, John West, Nebuchadnezzar Lee, Andrew Jefferys.   20

Q. 7. How are the preachers stationed this year?

A. As follows:

1. *Dublin*, Andrew Blair,[106] Thomas Rutherford.

2. *Wicklow*, Thomas Kerr, John Hurley.

3. *Carlow*, Thomas Barber, John Gillis.   25

4. *Waterford*, Walter Griffith, Thomas Werrill.[107]

5. *Cork*, John Kerr, William West.[108]

6. *Bandon*, Charles Boone, James Lyons, Jun., Andrew Hamilton, Jun.

7. *Limerick*, Matthias Joyce, Jas. McQuigg.   30

---

[103] These ten names are not included in the CJ or the English *Minutes*.

[104] This obituary was omitted from the English *Minutes*. The quotation is of Rom. 11:33.

[105] Again the insertion of dashes implies some missing information. The CJ shows that one of the Irish preachers, Nehemiah Price, was in fact 'expelled for too great familiarity with women'.

[106] The English *Minutes* replace Blair with Adam Clarke.

[107] The English *Minutes* replace Werrill (who was sent to the West Indies) with John Woodrow.

[108] Blair was moved from Dublin to be Assistant at Cork, with Kerr as his Helper; William West replaced Boone at Bandon.

8. *Kerry*, Charles Graham.
9. *Birr*, David Gordon, Thomas Patterson.[109]
10. *Castlebar*, John Darragh, James Lyons.
11. *Athlone*, Richard Condy, James Irwin.
12. *Longford*, Thomas Davis, John Miller.
13. *Sligo*, James Rennick, Daniel Graham.
14. *Ballyconnell*, Matthew Stewart, William Wilson, William Ferguson; John Price, supernumerary.
15. *Cavan*, Samuel Moorhead, William Hamilton, Thomas Ridgeway.
16. *Clones*, William McCornock, Thomas Hewett, William Brandon.
17. *Brookeborough*, William Johnson, Thomas Elliott, Thomas Brown; Andrew Hamilton, Sen., supernumerary.
18. *Enniskillen*, Joseph Armstrong, George Donovan.
19. *Ballyshannon*, Robert Smith, John Graham, Archibald Murdock.
20. *Lisleen*, George Brown, Alexander Moore.
21. *Omagh*, Michael Murphy, John Stephenson.
22. *Charlemont*, John Dinnen, John Malcomson; Samuel Bates, supernumerary.
23. *Londonderry*, David Barrowclough, William Smith.
24. *Coleraine*, John Grace, James McMullen.
25. *Belfast*, Thomas Hetherington, Thomas Verner.
26. *Lisburn*, Samuel Mitchell, Gustavus Armstrong.
27. *Downpatrick*, Francis Armstrong, Thomas Ryan.
28. *Tandragee*, John Crook, John Cross, Samuel Steel.
29. *Newry*, James McDonald, Samuel Wood.

Q. 8. How many wives are to be provided for?
A. Nineteen.

Q. 9. How many of these are to be provided for by the circuits?
A. Twelve; namely, Sister Blair, Rutherford, Boone, Griffith, West, Joyce, Graham, Dinnen, Condy, Rennick, Stewart; and Stephenson, £6.

Q. 10. In what proportion do the circuits provide for these?

---

[109] In the English *Minutes*, Patterson was replaced by James Hurley, while Patterson took the place of James Lyons (who was also sent to the West Indies) at Castlebar.

A. As follows:

	English.		
Dublin,	£30.	0s.	0d.
Carlow,	2.	10.	0.
Waterford,	3.	0.	0.
Cork,	16.	0.	0.
Bandon,	1.	10.	0.
Limerick,	5.	0.	0.
Birr,	3.	0.	0.
Castlebar,	2.	0.	0.
Athlone,	6.	10.	0.
Longford,	8.	0.	0.
Sligo,	1.	5.	0.
Ballyconnell,	2.	5.	0.
Clones,	6.	0.	0.
Cavan,	6.	0.	0.
Brookeborough,	3.	0.	0.
Enniskillen,	3.	0.	0.
Ballyshannon,	1.	10.	0.
Lisleen,	1.	10.	0.
Omagh,	1.	10.	0.
Charlemont,	5.	0.	0.
Londonderry,	3.	0.	0.
Coleraine,	5.	0.	0.
Belfast,	6.	0.	0.
Lisburn,	8.	0.	0.
Downpatrick,	1.	0.	0.
Tandragee,	4.	10.	0.
Newry,	2.	0.	0.
In all,	£138.	0s.	0d.

Q. 11. How are the other seven wives, namely, S. Price, Armstrong, Brown, Smith, Hetherington, Crook, and McDonald, to be provided for?

A. From England.

Q. 12. What numbers are in the societies?

A. Dublin,	1,040
Wicklow,	117
Wexford,	260
Waterford,	186
Cork,	660
Bandon,	250

Limerick,	330
Birr,	240
Castlebar,	155
Athlone,	560
Longford,	450
Sligo,	371
Ballyconnell,	875
Cavan,	580
Clones,	800
Brookeborough,	800
Enniskillen,	530
Ballyshannon,	838
Lisleen,	520
Omagh,	290
Charlemont,	1,023
Londonderry,	300
Coleraine,	440
Belfast,	560
Lisburn,	380
Downpatrick,	340
Tandragee,	856
Newry,	<u>355</u>
Total,	14,106

Q. 13. What is the Kingswood collection?

A. £57. 0. 0.

Q. 14. What is contributed to the Preachers' Fund?

A. £90. 1. 6.

Q. 15. What is allowed out of it?

A. To John Price,	£12	0*s.*	0*d.*
Samuel Bates,	12.	0.	0.
Mary Penington,	12.	0.	0.

Q. 16. What is contributed for the yearly expenses?

A. £100. 16. 0.

Q. 17. How was it expended?

A. In supplying the deficiencies of the preachers' salaries, and those of their wives and children.

Q. 18. What houses are to be built this year?

A. One at Rathdrum, Ballinrobe, Newtownbutler, Ballyhaise,[110] Brookeborough, Ballycastle, Dundalk, and Scotch Street.[111]

---

[110] Orig., 'Ballyhays'.

[111] In Armagh County.

N.B. If our friends in Dublin build a new preaching-house the ensuing year, let a private and public collection be made throughout the kingdom for their assistance, as a token of gratitude due to them by the whole Irish Connection, for the great expenses they have annually incurred for the support of our Conferences. 5

Q. 19. Are any directions to be given to the Assistants concerning the preachers who have been expelled for immorality?

A. Let none of them be employed, more or less, on any pretence, condition, or consideration whatsoever, till they have previously obtained permission from the Rev. Mr. Wesley or the Conference. And let none of them be received as private members of the society, unless the Assistant be fully satisfied of their real penitence. 10

 15

Q. 20. When and where is the next Conference to be held?

A. At Dublin, on the first Friday in July, 1791.[112]

FINIS

---

[112] On their biennial succession, it was JW's turn to conduct the Irish Conference in 1791. Coke had left for the West Indies in Oct. 1790, and from there went on to Charleston in South Carolina, travelling north to attend the various annual Conferences. On Apr. 29, he saw a Philadelphia newspaper announcing JW's death on Mar. 2, and took the speediest means possible to return to England, in order to attend the Irish Conference on July 1. His London friends warned him against attending, knowing the prejudice throughout the British Isles against what was felt to be his ambition to succeed JW in something like absolute power. When he arrived in Dublin, he discovered that the Irish preachers, with no delegate officially sent by JW, had elected John Crook as their chairman, 'in order to give Dr. Coke a plain intimation, once for all, that however highly they esteemed and loved him, they could not accept any minister as occupying the exalted position long sustained by the venerated Wesley'. Coke continued as a simple member of the Conference, somewhat prepared for the similar situation that would meet him when he attended the English Conference. Nothing was printed in Ireland but the Irish stations, all copies of which seem to have disappeared. Crookshank, *History of Methodism in Ireland*, 2:38. Confirmation of all actions was referred to the English Conference, meeting on July 26, whose *Minutes* remain our authority for the Irish Conference sessions of 1791.

INDEX
OF SCRIPTURAL REFERENCES

OLD TESTAMENT

APOCRYPHA

NEW TESTAMENT

GENERAL INDEX

The alphabetical arrangement of entries is on a word-by-word basis. Foreign words and phrases are listed under the appropriate language. Definite and indefinite articles are ignored in the titles of publications.

The abbreviation 'W' is used throughout for the surname 'Wesley', either alone when the reference is to John Wesley himself or following the Christian name of other members of the family. For John Wesley's publications and sermons, which are listed under his name, see under titles.

Footnote references are indicated by the addition of 'n' or 'nn' to the page numbers.

in Georgia, 16, 167n359, 202n563,
    261n863
handwriting of, 59, 104n388, 270n948
holiness and, 1–2, 33, 185
Moravians and, 136n143
old age of, 708n534
publications, see under titles:
    The Character of a Methodist
    Christian Library
    Collection of Moral and Sacred Poems
    *A Collection of Receipts for the Use of
        the Poor*
    *A Dialogue between an Antinomian and
        his Friend*
    *An Earnest Appeal to Men of Reason
        and Religion*
    *Explanatory Notes upon the New
        Testament*
    *Explanatory Notes upon the Old
        Testament*
    Extract of the Christian's Pattern
    *An Extract of the Life and Death of Mr.
        Thomas Haliburton*
    *Extract of the Life of the late Rev. Mr.
        David Brainerd, Missionary to the
        Indians*
    *A Farther Appeal to Men of Reason and
        Religion*
    Hymns and Sacred Poems
    *Hymns for those that seek and those that
        have Redemption*
    Hymns on the Lord's Supper
    Instructions for Children
    Memoirs
    Phaedri Fabulae Selectae
    A Plain Account of Christian Perfection
    *A Plain Account of the People Called
        Methodists*
    Primitive Physick
    *A Second Dialogue between an
        Antinomian and his Friend*
    Select Hymns with Tunes Annext
    Sermons on Several Occasions
    *A Short Account of the School in
        Kingswood, near Bristol*
    A Short History of Methodism
    *A Short History of the People Called
        Methodists*
    *A Short View of the Difference between
        the Moravian Brethren . . . and the
        Reverend Mr. John and Charles
        Wesley*
    Thoughts upon some Late Occurrences

use of power by, 68–74
Whitefield and, 10–11, 190n509,
    227n721, 261n864, 392n333
Wesley, Samuel, jun.
    Poems, 645n339
'Wesley and Money' (Heitzenrater),
    61n227
Wesley and the People Called Methodists
    (Heitzenrater), 11n24, 29n74,
    30n78, 36n94
Wesleyan Methodist Missionary Society,
    519n907
Wesley's Chapel, 461n649
West, Edward, 623, 628, 652, 673, 684, 719
West, John, 623, 644, 651, 713, 984, 985,
    995, 1003
West, William, 499, 519, 523, 531,
    607n217, 681, 751, 971, 1003
West Street Chapel, 59, 211n606, 508n873
Westell, Thomas, 159, 169, 328, 345n148,
    403n377, 446n582, 493, 504, 561,
    700, 900
Whatcoat, Richard, 95, 368, 380, 406, 521,
    587n159, 630, 686, 710, 743, 951
Wheatley, James, 147, 204, 237, 240n757,
    242n765, 246–47, 452n607, 786,
    822, 890
Wheeler, John, 184n483, 205, 827
Whiston, William
    *Astronomical Principles of Religion, natu-
        ral and revealed*, 164n336, 816
Whitaker, Mark, 568, 573, 596, 602, 622,
    629, 643, 720
Whitaker, William, 366, 368, 379, 417, 437,
    493, 527, 540, 561, 613, 700, 763
Whitby, Daniel
    *Brevissimum Compendium Metaphysicae
        sec Mentem Nominalium*, 222n696
    *Ethicis Compendium in usum Academicae
        juventutis*, 221n684
White, James, 567, 576, 595, 604, 622, 630,
    654, 677
White (bishop), 648n358
Whitefield, George, 6–8, 10, 124n29,
    147n252
    in America, 186n489, 226n721, 228n721
    as Book Steward, 38, 57–58
    George Whitefield's Journals, 8n17
    Moravians and, 16, 21, 187n495
    Tabernacle Society and, 161n317,
        223n701
    W and, 10–11, 190n509, 227n721,
        261n864, 392n333